A COMPLETE GUIDE
TO PASSING THE
EUROPEAN QUALIFYING EXAM

**AUSTRALIA**
Law Book Co.—Sydney

**CANADA** and **USA**
Carswell—Toronto

**HONG KONG**
Sweet & Maxwell Asia

**NEW ZEALAND**
Brookers—Wellington

**SINGAPORE** and **MALAYSIA**
Sweet & Maxwell Asia
Singapore and Kuala Lumpur

# A COMPLETE GUIDE TO PASSING THE EUROPEAN QUALIFYING EXAM

### and qualifying as a European Patent Attorney

**Simon Roberts**

*Chartered Patent Agent and European Patent Attorney*

**and**

**Andrew Rudge**

*Chartered Patent Agent and European Patent Attorney*

2007 Edition

LONDON
SWEET & MAXWELL
2007

Published in 2007 by
Sweet & Maxwell Limited of
100 Avenue Road, London, NW3 3PF
Typeset by Servis Filmsetting Ltd, Manchester
Printed in Great Britain by Antony Rowe Ltd, Chippenham, Wiltshire

No natural forests were destroyed to make this product,
only farmed timber was used and replanted

A CIP catalogue record for this book is available from the British Library

ISBN-10: 1847030068
ISBN-13: 9781847030061

All rights reserved. Crown copyright material is reproduced with the permission of the controller of HMSO and the Queen's Printer for Scotland.

No part of this publication may be reproduced or transmitted in any form or by any means, or stored in any retrieval system of any nature without prior written permission, except for permitted fair dealing under the Copyright, Designs and Patents Act 1988, or in accordance with the terms of a licence issued by the Copyright Licensing Agency in respect of photocopying and/or reprographic reproduction. Application for permission for other use of copyright material including permission to reproduce extracts in other published works shall be made to the publishers. Full acknowledgment of author, publisher and source must be given.

© Sweet and Maxwell 2007

*To Fernanda and Gabriel, with apologies for the many lost weekends and evenings, and with thanks for their understanding and support.*

**SR**

*To Wendy, Emma and Millie*
**AR**

# PREFACE

Each year hundreds of graduates, many with master's degrees or PhDs, seek to enter the patent profession in Europe. Prospective employers use rigorous selection processes to identify the best of those who put themselves forward. The selection processes typically assess—in addition to candidates' academic achievements—candidates' intellectual abilities, imagination, linguistic skills, common sense, commercial awareness and aptitude. Only the best of those candidates who appear to have the necessary skills to become competent patent attorneys are recruited.

Having been selected, new entrants to the profession are trained and their patent attorney skills developed over a period of at least three years prior to their sitting the European Qualifying Examinations (EQE). Within this period many will follow formal training courses arranged by their employers or external organisations. Most will also receive training specifically for the EQE as well as doing considerable self-study. It is shocking then to learn that the pass rate for those sitting the EQE for the first time in 2003 was only about 30 per cent, and the average pass rate for 2003–2005 was less than 36 per cent. Amazingly, those who re-sit the entire exam have a less than 1 per cent chance of passing the exam at that re-sitting. For many candidates failure in the EQE is their first ever exam failure and it consequently comes as a huge shock to them. For some the shock is so great that, despite having invested at least three years of their lives in the profession, they abandon the profession. This is a waste both in economic and human terms.

It is generally acknowledged that the fault for these problems cannot fairly be placed on those setting or marking the EQE. Unlike some national patents exams, the EQE is consistently well drafted, and set and marked fairly. It is also generally acknowledged that most of the candidates who fail do not do so because they are inherently incapable of doing the work of a patent attorney, although for a small proportion this may be the case. Rather it is thought that the problem lies with candidates' training and preparation for the EQE. The profession, notably FICPI, EPI and CIPA, and educational establishments such as CEIPI, are addressing these concerns by providing more training courses for those preparing for the EQE. Unfortunately, not all candidates are able to attend such courses and not every employer is able to provide appropriate in-house training. Also, many EQE candidates do not have supervisors or colleagues who have experience of preparing for and passing the EQE. Even those who are well provided with training opportunities will generally benefit from further self-study. There therefore exists a need for training material for candidates preparing themselves for the EQE.

This book is intended for those preparing for the EQE, whether or not they have access to formal training courses or other training material. It is not meant to be a substitute for serious study and revision, but as an aid and guide to study. In particular, the book gives guidance and advice on how to tackle the different exam papers. This should be especially valuable for those candidates who are unable to attend appropriate training courses or who do not have suitable mentors to guide them in their preparation. I believe that it is important for those preparing for the EQE to practise on past papers; eventually reaching the stage where they can complete a full answer to a paper under exam conditions and within the time set for the exam. While the EPO-provided compendia for the exams are very useful they do not attempt to show candidates how to approach the exams. I hope that this work will help candidates acquire the right approach.

I should also stress that this book is not intended as a substitute for the primary legal texts, such as the EPC, PCT or Paris Convention, nor for other important works such as the Guidelines or the Boards of Appeal Case Law book. It is important that candidates use and become familiar with all these sources. I was fortunate enough to work on many occasions with Dr Romuald Singer, one of the founding fathers of the EPC and long time Chairman of the Legal Board of Appeal. When faced with a question on European patent law, Dr Singer always made a point of consulting the primary legal text, such as the EPC, despite knowing the texts by heart. It always struck me that if Dr Singer felt it appropriate to adopt such an approach how much more appropriate for the ordinary practitioner or student.

I would like to thank my fellow author Andrew Rudge, the instigator and driving force behind this project, for his dedication and hard work as well as for the high quality of his contribution. Although he was my student on the London CEIPI course, I am not sure that I can claim much credit for his knowledge. Andrew and I would like to thank all of those users of the first and second editions who provided feedback. It was extremely gratifying to learn that those preparing for the EQE had found the book to be useful, in particular reporting that the book gave them insights which they had not found from other sources. For this third edition we have revised the section on Paper C, added a detailed section on priority, and provided some further worked examples, as well as updating the work generally to take account of changes in the law. We hope that users will find this new edition even more useful than the first, and that it contributes to greater success in the EQE. As before, Andrew and I would welcome feedback and any suggestions for improvements and additions for future editions.

The text is up to date to the end of July 2006.

**Simon Roberts**
July 2006

## Contents

|  | Page |
|---|---|
| *Preface* | vii |
| *Table of Cases* | xi |
| *References to Other Publications* | xvii |
| *Abbreviations* | xix |

### Part A—Guide to Preparing for and Passing Papers A to D

| | |
|---|---|
| Paper A (Chemistry) | 3 |
| Paper A (Electricity/Mechanics) | 51 |
| Paper B (Chemistry) | 107 |
| Paper B (Electricity/Mechanics) | 153 |
| Paper C | 201 |
| Paper D1 | 261 |
| Paper D2 | 293 |

### Part B—Guide to the Law under the European Patent Convention

| | |
|---|---|
| *Table of Articles and Rules of the European Patent Convention* | 345 |
| 1. Institutional Aspects | 353 |
| 2. Requirements of the Invention | 361 |
| 3. Filing a European Patent Application | 378 |
| 4. Requirements Relating to the Application as Filed | 382 |
| 5. Examination on Filing | 408 |
| 6. Drawing up the Search Report | 414 |
| 7. Publication of the Application and Search Report | 417 |
| 8. Substantive Examination | 419 |
| 9. The Grant Procedure | 423 |
| 10. Opposition | 427 |
| 11. Appeal | 442 |
| 12. National Phase Aspects | 454 |
| 13. The Calculation of Time Limits and Procedural Safeguards | 459 |
| 14. Amendment and Correction | 467 |
| 15. Inventorship, Ownership and Suspension of Proceedings | 472 |
| 16. Representation | 477 |
| 17. Languages | 482 |
| 18. Miscellaneous Common Provisions | 485 |
| 19. Information Made Available by the EPO | 505 |
| 20. Special Agreements under the EPC | 510 |
| 21. Rules Relating to Fees | 511 |

### Part C—Guide to the Law under the Patent Co-operation Treaty

| | |
|---|---|
| *Table of Articles and Rules of the Patent Co-operation Treaty* | 517 |
| *Table of Articles and Rules of the European Patent Convention* | 525 |
| 1. Institutional Aspects and Definitions | 528 |
| 2. Filing an International Patent Application | 530 |
| 3. Requirements Relating to the Application as Filed | 534 |
| 4. Procedure of the Receiving Office | 564 |
| 5. Drawing up the International Search Report | 573 |

| | |
|---|---|
| 6. Amendment of the Application under Article 19 | 582 |
| 7. Publication of the Application and the Search Report | 584 |
| 8. Communication to National/Regional Offices and Entry into the National Phase | 587 |
| 9. International Preliminary Examination | 601 |
| 10. National Phase Aspects | 623 |
| 11. The Calculation of Time Limits and Procedural Safeguards | 632 |
| 12. Correction | 638 |
| 13. Representation | 639 |
| 14. Miscellaneous Common Provisions | 642 |
| 15. Information Made Available by the International Authorities and Designated/Elected Offices | 648 |

*Index* 653

# TABLE OF CASES

(*References are to paragraph numbers*)

|  |  |
|---|---|
| G1/83 | 1–187 |
| G5/83 | 1–016, 1–187, 2–038, 2–049, 2–367 |
| G6/83 | 1–187 |
| G1/84 | 1–187, 2–202 |
| G1/86 | 1–168, 1–185, 1–187, 2–246, 2–249, 2–300 |
| G1/88 | 1–187, 2–232 |
| G2/88 | 1–016, 1–187, 2–047, 2–049, 2–050, 2–275, 2–319 |
| G4/88 | 1–153, 1–187, 2–241 |
| G5/88 | 1–187, 2–061, 2–201, 2–311, 2–368 |
| G6/88 | 1–016, 1–187, 2–050 |
| G7/88 | 1–187, 2–061, 2–311 |
| G8/88 | 1–187, 2–061, 2–311 |
| G1/89 | 1–187, 3–130 |
| G2/89 | 1–187, 3–130 |
| G3/89 | 1–093, 1–113, 1–128, 1–187, 1–207, 1–210, 2–316, 2–323, 2–324 |
| G1/90 | 1–187, 2–233, 2–410 |
| G2/90 | 1–187, 2–017 |
| G1/91 | 1–158, 1–187, 2–204, 2–232 |
| G2/91 | 1–187, 2–245 |
| G3/91 | 1–178, 1–180, 1–187, 2–125, 2–126, 2–170, 3–396, 3–398, 3–200, 3–211 |
| G4/91 | 1–187, 2–214, 2–409 |
| G5/91 | 1–187, 2–014, 2–015, 2–243 |
| G6/91 | 1–187, 2–121, 2–206, 2–250, 2–362 |
| G7/91 | 1–187, 2–214, 2–268 |
| G8/91 | 1–187, 2–268 |
| G9/91 | 1–187, 2–199, 2–202, 2–225, 2–242, 2–254 |
| G10/91 | 1–187, 2–199, 2–202, 2–214, 2–225, 2–254, 2–263 |
| G11/91 | 1–187, 2–323, 2–324 |
| G12/91 | 1–187, 2–214, 2–409 |
| G1/92 | 1–133, 1–187, 2–046, 2–221 |
| G2/92 | 1–187, 2–154 |
| G3/92 | 1–187, 1–193, 1–214, 2–339 |
| G4/92 | 1–187, 2–406, 2–419 |
| G5/92 | 1–181, 1–187, 2–170, 3–211 |
| G6/92 | 1–187, 2–170, 3–211 |
| G9/92 | 1–187, 2–242, 2–247, 2–256 |
| G10/92 | 1–187 |
| G1/93 | 1–187, 2–320 |
| G2/93 | 1–187, 2–090, 2–131 |
| G3/93 | 1–131, 1–187, 2–043, 2–106, 2–113 |
| G4/93 | 1–187 |
| G5/93 | 1–187, 2–311, 3–396, 3–200 |
| G7/93 | 1–187, 2–178, 2–192, 2–314 |
| G8/93 | 1–187, 2–223, 2–268 |
| G9/93 | 1–187, 2–202, 2–311 |
| G10/93 | 1–187, 2–255 |
| G1/94 | 1–187, 2–214 |
| G2/94 | 1–187, 2–258, 2–422 |
| G1/95 | 1–187, 2–204, 2–254 |
| G2/95 | 1–187, 1–210, 2–324 |
| G3/95 | 1–187 |
| G4/95 | 1–158, 1–187, 2–203, 2–258, 2–422 |
| G6/95 | 1–187, 2–021, 2–420 |
| G7/95 | 1–187, 2–254 |
| G8/95 | 1–187, 2–017 |
| G1/97 | 1–187, 2–243, 2–264 |
| G2/97 | 1–170, 1–187, 2–248, 2–311 |
| G3/97 | 1–187, 2–202 |
| G4/97 | 1–187, 2–202 |
| G1/98 | 1–187, 2–033, 2–034, 2–035 |
| G2/98 | 1–124, 1–131, 1–158, 1–187, 1–193, 1–207, 2–106, 2–109 |
| G3/98 | 1–178, 1–187, 2–051, 2–052, 2–125, 2–127 |
| G4/98 | 1–180, 1–187, 2–137, 2–145, 3–396, 3–398, 3–200 |
| G1/99 | 1–187, 2–256 |
| G2/99 | 1–187, 2–051, 2–125, 2–127 |
| G3/99 | 1–129, 1–187, 2–202, 2–245 |
| G1/02 | 1–187, 1–187, 2–209, 2–015 |
| G2/02 | 1–187, 2–110, 3–059 |
| G3/02 | 1–187, 2–102 |
| G1/03 | 1–088, 1–093, 1–098, 1–114, 1–187, 2–102, 2–317 |
| G2/03 | 1–088, 1–093, 1–098, 1–114, 1–128, 1–187, 2–041 |
| G3/03 | 1–187, 2–252, 2–267 |
| G1/04 | 1–187, 2–041 |
| G2/04 | 1–153, 1–187, 2–241, 2–245 |
| G3/04 | 1–187, 2–214, 2–268 |
| J1/80 | 2–144, 2–299, 2–322 |
| J3/80 | 2–299, 2–065 |
| J7/80 | 2–324, 2–360 |
| J8/80 | 2–322 |
| J11/80 | 2–374 |
| J12/80 | 2–324 |
| J15/80 | 2–106, 2–110 |
| J19/80 | 2–147 |
| J21/80 | 1–185, 2–248 |
| J5/81 | 2–044, 2–164 |
| J8/81 | 2–243, 2–408 |
| J1/82 | 2–147 |
| J2/82 | 2–301 |
| J4/82 | 2–324 |
| J7/82 | 2–302 |
| J8/82 | 2–115, 2–146, 2–330 |
| J12/82 | 1–181, 2–169, 2–173, 2–301 |
| J14/82 | 2–324 |
| J18/82 | 2–125, 2–126, 2–301 |
| J23/82 | 2–468 |
| J41/82 | 2–248 |
| J47/82 | 2–125 |
| J7/83 | 2–309 |
| J8/83 | 2–176, 3–200 |

| | | | |
|---|---|---|---|
| J12/83 | 2–193, 2–245 | J21/94 | 2–088, 2–324 |
| J12/84 | 2–383 | J28/94 | 2–244, 2–335 |
| J21/84 | 2–324 | J29/94 | 2–253 |
| J4/85 | 2–327 | J11/95 | 2–111 |
| J12/85 | 2–245 | J26/95 | 2–307 |
| J15/85 | 2–375 | J32/95 | 2–252 |
| J20/85 | 2–424 | J6/96 | 2–127 |
| J2/86 | 2–299 | J7/96 | 2–193, 2–326, 2–335 |
| J3/86 | 2–299 | J11/96 | 2–120 |
| J4/86 | 1–181, 2–137, 2–172 | J16/96 | 2–356 |
| J12/86 | 2–268 | J18/96 | 2–120 |
| J14/86 | 2–290 | J19/96 | 2–080 |
| J16/86 | 2–302 | J27/96 | 2–126, 2–325 |
| J18/86 | 2–134 | J4/97 | 2–374 |
| J22/86 | 2–249 | J37/97 | 2–243 |
| J25/86 | 2–134 | J5/98 | 2–126 |
| J33/86 | 2–012 | J8/98 | 2–244 |
| J2/87 | 1–170, 2–311 | J17/98 | 2–351 |
| J3/87 | 1–170, 2–311 | J21/98 | 2–175 |
| J4/87 | 2–134 | J79/99 | 2–418 |
| J6/87 | 3–027 | J14/00 | 2–081 |
| J10/87 | 2–324 | J2/01 | 2–070, 2–075, 2–132 |
| J11/87 | 2–374 | J8/01 | 3–027, 3–317 |
| J14/87 | 2–200 | J9/01 | 2–121 |
| J19/87 | 2–107 | J6/03 | 2–334 |
| J21/87 | 2–134 | J24/03 | 2–070, 2–299 |
| J26/87 | 3–155 | J28/03 | 2–193, 2–244 |
| J4/88 | 2–121 | T728/28 | 1–026 |
| J22/88 | 2–299 | T1/80 | 2–055 |
| J23/88 | 2–307 | T4/80 | 1–009, 1–114, 2–102 |
| J25/88 | 2–134 | T2/81 | 1–093, 2–057, 2–058 |
| J27/88 | 2–302 | T5/81 | 2–186, 2–267 |
| J1/89 | 2–383, 3–200 | T9/81 | 1–023 |
| J14/89 | 2–303 | T12/81 | 1–010, 2–047, 2–053 |
| J17/89 | 2–302 | T17/81 | 2–263 |
| J37/89 | 2–178 | T18/81 | 2–059 |
| J6/90 | 2–303 | T21/81 | 2–058 |
| J7/90 | 2–324 | T26/81 | 2–055 |
| J13/90 | 2–299 | T32/81 | 2–056 |
| J14/90 | 2–134 | T241/81 | 2–057 |
| J18/90 | 2–080, 2–134, 2–362 | T11/82 | 2–091, 2–183, 2–316 |
| J30/90 | 2–080 | T13/82 | 2–248 |
| J4/91 | 1–183, 1–188, 2–290, 2–383 | T22/82 | 1–020 |
| J5/91 | 1–180, 1–188, 2–126 | T32/82 | 1–061 |
| J6/91 | 2–324 | T37/82 | 2–055 |
| J9/91 | 2–324 | T39/82 | 2–058 |
| J14/91 | 2–418, 2–442 | T41/82 | 2–268 |
| J12/92 | 1–182, 1–186, 2–298 | T65/82 | 1–020 |
| J16/92 | 2–298 | T109/82 | 2–059 |
| J17/92 | 2–183 | T119/82 | 1–018, 1–090 |
| J19/92 | 2–268 | T128/82 | 1–016, 2–048 |
| J25/92 | 2–169 | T150/82 | 1–012, 2–099 |
| J29/92 | 2–243 | T181/82 | 1–008, 1–010, 2–053, 2–057, 2–058 |
| J42/92 | 2–326 | T184/82 | 2–055 |
| J47/92 | 2–125, 2–126, 2–173, 2–298 | T191/82 | 2–059, 2–302 |
| J2/93 | 2–243 | T192/82 | 1–136, 1–140, 2–055, 2–058 |
| J10/93 | 2–303 | T659/82 | 2–241 |
| J11/93 | 2–343 | T2/83 | 2–023, 2–057, 2–059 |
| J18/93 | 2–324, 2–333 | T14/83 | 2–090 |
| J20/94 | 2–134 | T20/83 | 1–093, 1–113, 2–316 |

Table of Cases    xiii

|  |  |
|------|-----------|
| T49/83 | 2–033 |
| T69/83 | 2–058 |
| T144/83 | 1–016, 2–030 |
| T201/83 | 1–093, 1–113, 2–316 |
| T204/83 | 2–047 |
| T205/83 | 1–012 |
| T206/83 | 2–046, 2–090 |
| T219/83 | 2–425 |
| T6/84 | 1–093, 1–113, 2–316 |
| T13/84 | 1–093, 1–113, 2–055, 2–096, 2–316 |
| T38/84 | 2–058 |
| T42/84 | 2–408 |
| T73/84 | 2–229, 2–380, 2–407 |
| T81/84 | 2–039 |
| T89/84 | 2–248 |
| T142/84 | 2–057 |
| T151/84 | 1–093, 1–113, 2–316 |
| T167/84 | 2–047 |
| T170/84 | 2–096 |
| T171/84 | 2–090 |
| T186/84 | 2–229 |
| T198/84 | 2–047 |
| T208/84 | 2–025, 2–030 |
| T265/84 | 2–057 |
| T271/84 | 2–059 |
| T273/84 | 2–263 |
| T22/85 | 2–023 |
| T25/85 | 2–210 |
| T26/85 | 1–010, 2–046 |
| T61/85 | 2–375 |
| T68/85 | 1–119 |
| T115/85 | 2–030 |
| T116/85 | 2–039 |
| T123/85 | 2–221, 2–375 |
| T149/85 | 2–121, 2–206, 2–250, 2–362 |
| T152/85 | 2–325 |
| T153/85 | 2–046, 2–314 |
| T163/85 | 2–023, 2–031 |
| T200/85 | 1–207 |
| T208/85 | 2–252, 2–267 |
| T213/85 | 2–249 |
| T222/85 | 2–210 |
| T226/85 | 2–090 |
| T229/85 | 1–090, 1–110, 2–055 |
| T260/85 | 1–210, 2–316 |
| T292/85 | 2–103 |
| T385/85 | 2–038 |
| T550/85 | 2–210 |
| T7/86 | 1–010, 2–053 |
| T16/86 | 1–093, 1–113, 2–316 |
| T19/86 | 2–039, 2–049 |
| T26/86 | 2–023 |
| T38/86 | 2–027 |
| T63/86 | 2–263 |
| T117/86 | 2–235, 2–268 |
| T219/86 | 2–324 |
| T234/86 | 2–407 |
| T237/86 | 2–229 |
| T246/86 | 2–316 |
| T254/86 | 2–055 |
| T290/86 | 2–039, 2–049 |
| T299/86 | 2–417 |
| T317/86 | 2–211 |
| T385/86 | 2–038 |
| T389/86 | 1–136, 1–140, 1–153, 2–246 |
| T390/86 | 2–246, 2–408, 2–409 |
| T406/86 | 2–221 |
| T51/87 | 2–056, 2–090, 2–316 |
| T56/87 | 2–046 |
| T58/87 | 2–039 |
| T77/87 | 2–046 |
| T81/87 | 2–109 |
| T89/87 | 2–046 |
| T105/87 | 2–249 |
| T118/87 | 2–131 |
| T139/87 | 2–252 |
| T141/87 | 2–056 |
| T170/87 | 1–009, 1–093, 1–114, 1–187 |
| T193/87 | 1–184, 2–138, 2–206, 2–362 |
| T243/87 | 2–411 |
| T245/87 | 2–039 |
| T295/87 | 2–220 |
| T296/87 | 1–008, 1–010, 2–053 |
| T301/87 | 2–046, 2–221 |
| T320/87 | 2–035 |
| T323/87 | 2–250 |
| T326/87 | 2–263 |
| T328/87 | 2–203, 2–208 |
| T331/87 | 1–089, 1–090, 1–109, 1–110, 1–121, 1–136, 1–139 |
| T361/87 | 2–131 |
| T381/87 | 2–045 |
| T407/87 | 2–091 |
| T438/87 | 2–200 |
| T73/88 | 2–245 |
| T92/88 | 2–380 |
| T119/88 | 2–026 |
| T140/88 | 2–249 |
| T145/88 | 2–249 |
| T158/88 | 2–030 |
| T169/88 | 1–090 |
| T194/88 | 2–224 |
| T197/88 | 2–223 |
| T198/88 | 1–129 |
| T212/88 | 2–235, 2–328, 2–409 |
| T227/88 | 2–221 |
| T251/88 | 2–015 |
| T329/88 | 2–224 |
| T426/88 | 2–056 |
| T432/88 | 2–249 |
| T459/88 | 2–249 |
| T461/88 | 2–046 |
| T522/88 | 2–303 |
| T536/88 | 2–225 |
| T550/88 | 2–044, 2–210 |
| T572/88 | 2–047 |
| T648/88 | 1–020 |
| T2/89 | 2–210 |
| T14/89 | 2–299 |
| T79/89 | 2–264 |

## Table of Cases

|  |  |
|---|---|
| T93/89 | 2–045, 2–203 |
| T150/89 | 2–199 |
| T173/89 | 2–199, 2–420 |
| T182/89 | 2–425 |
| T210/89 | 2–246, 2–300 |
| T268/89 | 2–057 |
| T275/89 | 2–220 |
| T279/89 | 1–008, 1–010, 1–090, 1–097, 1–098, 2–053 |
| T300/89 | 2–179 |
| T387/89 | 2–225 |
| T423/89 | 2–319 |
| T426/89 | 2–039 |
| T450/89 | 2–047 |
| T482/89 | 2–045, 2–425 |
| T516/89 | 2–443 |
| T563/89 | 2–241 |
| T606/89 | 2–055 |
| T641/89 | 2–055 |
| T666/89 | 1–010, 2–046, 2–047, 2–053 |
| T702/89 | 1–184, 2–200, 2–300 |
| T760/89 | 2–443 |
| T780/89 | 2–039 |
| T823/89 | 2–235 |
| T3/90 | 2–419 |
| T5/90 | 2–319 |
| T12/90 | 1–010, 1–012, 2–053 |
| T19/90 | 2–032, 2–034, 2–090 |
| T34/90 | 2–242, 2–363, 2–417 |
| T53/90 | 2–319 |
| T156/90 | 2–245 |
| T182/90 | 2–040 |
| T290/90 | 2–206, 2–226 |
| T324/90 | 2–303 |
| T338/90 | 2–419 |
| T376/90 | 2–210 |
| T424/90 | 2–056 |
| T595/90 | 1–090 |
| T611/90 | 2–245 |
| T629/90 | 2–268 |
| T666/90 | 2–408 |
| T669/90 | 2–220 |
| T689/90 | 1–090, 1–093, 1–110, 1–113, 2–316 |
| T958/90 | 2–050 |
| T17/91 | 2–416 |
| T24/91 | 2–039, 2–040 |
| T118/91 | 2–132 |
| T209/91 | 2–023 |
| T227/91 | 2–049 |
| T409/91 | 2–090 |
| T435/91 | 2–090, 2–103 |
| T438/91 | 2–039 |
| T453/91 | 2–027 |
| T473/91 | 2–303 |
| T495/91 | 2–055 |
| T677/91 | 2–046, 2–059 |
| T706/91 | 2–362 |
| T759/91 | 1–025, 1–065 |
| T842/91 | 2–045 |
| T925/91 | 2–208 |
| T1/92 | 2–191 |
| T95/92 | 2–252, 2–267 |
| T133/92 | 1–010, 2–053 |
| T219/92 | 2–252 |
| T371/92 | 2–247 |
| T441/92 | 2–132 |
| T472/92 | 2–045, 2–425 |
| T473/92 | 2–363 |
| T545/92 | 2–132 |
| T585/92 | 2–051 |
| T597/92 | 1–009, 1–093, 1–114, 1–187 |
| T659/92 | 2–241 |
| T703/92 | 1–164, 2–397 |
| T714/92 | 2–411 |
| T769/92 | 2–023, 2–029 |
| T804/92 | 2–199 |
| T820/92 | 2–039 |
| T930/92 | 2–235, 2–419 |
| T939/92 | 1–006, 1–091, 2–058 |
| T951/92 | 2–178 |
| T1002/92 | 2–029, 2–203 |
| T39/93 | 1–090, 1–110, 2–056 |
| T51/93 | 2–049 |
| T74/93 | 2–039 |
| T82/93 | 2–038, 2–319 |
| T167/93 | 1–128, 2–264 |
| T254/93 | 2–049 |
| T279/93 | 2–050 |
| T296/93 | 2–214 |
| T356/93 | 1–187, 2–032, 2–035 |
| T422/93 | 2–056 |
| T433/93 | 2–225 |
| T469/93 | 2–299 |
| T647/93 | 2–252, 2–267 |
| T798/93 | 2–424 |
| T926/93 | 2–263 |
| T1077/93 | 2–039 |
| T20/94 | 1–012, 2–319 |
| T97/94 | 2–425 |
| T291/94 | 2–252, 2–267 |
| T329/94 | 2–039 |
| T382/94 | 2–120 |
| T386/94 | 2–059 |
| T631/94 | 2–214 |
| T642/94 | 1–090 |
| T750/94 | 2–045 |
| T772/94 | 2–057 |
| T892/94 | 2–050, 2–406 |
| T26/95 | 2–299 |
| T241/95 | 2–049 |
| T274/95 | 2–254 |
| T337/95 | 1–026 |
| T446/95 | 2–214 |
| T460/95 | 2–247 |
| T555/95 | 2–192, 2–417 |
| T727/95 | 2–090 |
| T736/95 | 2–225 |
| T798/95 | 2–314 |
| T850/95 | 2–328 |
| T931/95 | 2–023, 2–029, 2–030 |
| T80/96 | 2–047 |

| | |
|---|---|
| T169/96 | 2–407 |
| T233/96 | 2–049 |
| T296/96 | 2–178 |
| T443/96 | 2–254 |
| T503/96 | 2–221 |
| T755/96 | 2–420 |
| T789/96 | 2–039 |
| T821/96 | 2–178 |
| T898/96 | 2–252 |
| T936/96 | 2–058 |
| T946/96 | 2–314 |
| T990/96 | 1–011 |
| T1028/96 | 2–022 |
| T1105/96 | 2–181 |
| T112/97 | 1–026 |
| T142/97 | 2–203 |
| T167/97 | 2–302 |
| T227/97 | 2–131 |
| T298/97 | 2–246, 2–249 |
| T425/97 | 2–408 |
| T443/97 | 2–204 |
| T450/97 | 2–316 |
| T517/97 | 1–188, 2–214, 2–268 |
| T631/97 | 2–154 |
| T838/97 | 2–045 |
| T951/97 | 2–420 |
| T1149/97 | 2–319, 2–375 |
| T1173/97 | 2–023, 2–030 |
| T1194/97 | 2–031, 2–375 |
| T4/98 | 2–049 |
| T92/88 | 2–380 |
| T97/98 | 2–251 |
| T201/98 | 2–178 |
| T226/98 | 1–026 |
| T428/98 | 2–302 |
| T587/98 | 2–132 |
| T656/98 | 2–245 |
| T685/98 | 2–178 |
| T862/98 | 2–411 |
| T1020/98 | 2–094 |
| T35/99 | 2–040 |
| T79/99 | 2–253 |
| T314/99 | 2–045 |
| T663/99 | 2–219 |
| T964/99 | 2–041 |
| T998/99 | 2–112A |
| T1022/99 | 2–045 |
| T1080/99 | 2–046 |
| T9/00 | 2–202 |
| T278/00 | 2–408 |
| T641/00 | 2–023, 2–029, 2–055 |
| T643/00 | 2–031 |
| T708/00 | 2–318 |
| T824/00 | 2–322 |
| T986/00 | 2–419 |
| T1173/00 | 2–090 |
| T15/01 | 2–112A |
| T131/01 | 2–254 |
| T295/01 | 1–187, 2–015, 2–209 |
| T694/01 | 2–214 |
| T1007/01 | 2–214 |
| T1158/01 | 2–070, 2–132 |
| T713/02 | 2–324, 2–409 |
| T858/02 | 2–031 |
| T890/02 | 2–056 |
| T914/02 | 2–027 |
| T1183/02 | 2–420 |
| T172/03 | 2–023, 2–029 |
| T258/03 | 2–023 |
| T309/03 | 2–322 |
| T315/03 | 2–032, 2–0324 |
| T383/03 | 2–040 |
| T49/04 | 2–031 |
| T125/04 | 2–031 |
| T474/04 | 2–425 |
| T1181/04 | 2–188 |
| T1255/04 | 2–188, 2–407 |
| W4/87 | 3–130 |
| W11/89 | 3–130 |

**UNITED KINGDOM**

Attorney General v Guardian Newspapers Ltd (No.2) [1990] 1 A.C. 109; [1988] 3 W.L.R. 776 ............... 1–158
Campbell v Mirror Group Newspapers Ltd [2004] UKHL 22; [2004] 2 A.C. 457 ........................... 1–158

# REFERENCES TO OTHER PUBLICATIONS

This book is intended to be used in conjunction with the European Patent Convention (12th ed., April 2006), Case law of the Boards of Appeal of the EPO (4th ed., 2001), Ancillary Regulations to the European Patent Convention (current ed.), Guidelines for Examination in the European Patent Office (June 2005 ed.), National Law Relating to the EPC (2003 ed.—see also updates at [2004] O.J. 290, [2004] O.J. 298, [2004] O.J. 344, [2004] O.J. 469, [2004] O.J. 521 and [2004] O.J. 531), the Patent Co-operation Treaty (2005 ed., incorporating amendments to the Regulations as in force from April 1, 2005), the PCT Applicant's Guide, the PCT Administrative Instructions, and the Paris Convention for the Protection of Industrial Property (1989 ed.).

EPO and WIPO material reproduced with kind permission of EPO and WIPO. EPO and WIPO are not responsible for any transformation of this material.

# ABBREVIATIONS

In Part A, the suffixes "EPC" and "PCT" have been used in order to distinguish between articles and rules of the European Patent Convention (EPC) and articles and rules of the Patent Co-operation Treaty (PCT). In Part B, articles and rules are taken to be those of the EPC unless otherwise explicitly indicated by the suffix "PCT". In Part C, articles and rules are taken to be those of the PCT if in normal typeface; articles and rules of the EPC are indicated in bold and italicised font and/or by use of the suffix "EPC".

The following abbreviations have been used in the text:

| | |
|---|---|
| AdminInst | The PCT Administrative Instructions |
| AnReg | Ancillary Regulations to the European Patent Convention |
| AppGuide | The PCT Applicant's Guide |
| CLBA | Case law of the Boards of Appeal of the EPO |
| EBA | Enlarged Board of Appeal |
| EPC | European Patent Convention |
| EPO | European Patent Office |
| Guidelines | Guidelines for Examination in the European Patent Office |
| IPEA | International Preliminary Examining Authority |
| NatLaw | National Law Relating to the EPC |
| O.J. | Official Journal of the European Patent Office |
| PC | Paris Convention |
| PCT | Patent Co-operation Treaty |
| PonC | Protocol on Centralisation |
| PonR | Protocol on Recognition |
| RRF | Rules Relating to Fees |
| RPBA | Rules of Procedure of the Boards of Appeal |
| USPTO | United States Patent and Trademark Office |
| WIPO | World Intellectual Property Organization |

# Part A

**Guide to Preparing for and Passing Papers A to D**

# PAPER A (CHEMISTRY)

## 1. General comments

1–001

In this paper the candidate is provided with a letter from a notional client describing his recent research work and any pertinent prior art he is aware of. The candidate must compare the results obtained by the client with the state of the art and establish what patentable inventions have been made. A patent application relating to the most important invention (or unified group of inventions) must then be drafted comprising a set of claims and a description (up to but excluding the specific embodiments). Any further non-unitary inventions may be mentioned in a letter to the examiner where appropriate. The client usually sets out his work in a single communication but occasionally (e.g. 2003) may provide late-breaking results in a second letter.

The claims drafted should give the client the broadest possible protection while also having a good chance of succeeding before the EPO without amendment. Particular attention should be given to novelty, inventive step and clarity. The claims must be novel over the prior art, since a lack of novelty gives rise to a large loss of marks. They must also be broad enough to obtain the maximum allowable protection for the client, since failure to protect something which could have been protected will also result in a loss of marks, the number of lost marks being linked to the extent of the failure. There should also be a good argument for inventive step across the whole claim breadth and this argument will be presented in the introduction to the description where the problem addressed by and the advantages provided by the invention are discussed. Claims which lack essential features or which are otherwise unsupported will also result in loss of marks. Because the subject matter is chemical there are likely to be a number of independent claim types. There should also be a reasonable number of dependent claims chosen as likely to survive in the event of failure of the main claim – *i.e.* to provide useful fall-back positions. An excessive number of dependent claims, however, will result in a loss of marks.

While Art.123(2) EPC is obviously not relevant, the candidate is expected to draft within the limited bounds of the information provided by the client, accepting all information at face value. No specialist knowledge that candidates may possess relating to the technology of the client's invention should be used. In the chemistry paper, there is no need to invent language — the answer to the question will already be present in the question. It is matter of dissecting information from parts of the paper and combining it to arrive at the right result. Very often, for instance, the expected main product claim will be a combination of the invention as set out in its broadest form by the client and one of the preferred features.

The paper is three and a half hours in length, and between one and a half and two of these hours should be devoted to analysing the paper and elucidating the answer, the remaining time being allocated to writing the answer. Typically, three-quarters of the available marks are awarded for the independent claims, so most effort should be spent on them. The balance of the available marks is allocated more or less evenly between the dependent claims and the introduction, the precise balance varying from year to year. The candidate is allowed to use sections of the examination paper in compiling the answer, so scissors, glue and transparent gummed tape should be brought into the exam to facilitate cutting out relevant paragraphs from the examination paper and fixing them into the answer. For the same reason, only pencil and yellow highlighter should be used to mark up important sections of the paper during the period of analysis; pencil can be easily erased and yellow highlighter does not cause problems when the answer is photocopied prior to marking. Using a cut and paste approach to creating the introduction can save a significant amount of time, as well as helping to ensure accuracy. It is important, however to practise the cut and paste technique under exam conditions before the exam — it is a skill not to be acquired during the exam itself. Other useful things to take into the exam are copies of Guidelines for Examination in the European Patent Office and Case Law of the Boards of Appeal of the European Patent Office — the extensive chemical case law relevant to selection inventions, in particular, is often relevant.

## 2. How to tackle the paper

*Understanding and annotating the paper*

1–002
Read through the entire paper, word by word, understanding each sentence thoroughly and appreciating its significance. Each word should be carefully read and considered, since it is easy to miss small but important facts later once the mind has started to make assumptions about the answer.

In general, a sentence relating to the client's invention will refer to either general instructions and advice from the client (e.g. "Please file a patent application"), technical information necessary for non-specialists to understand the technology of the invention, prior art and the problem to be solved by the invention in light of it, the invention according to the client in terms of its essential features, advantages associated with the invention, a preferred feature with some motivation (i.e. a specified further advantage), a preferred feature with no motivation (i.e. no specified extra advantage), general enablement of the invention, specific examples of the invention or data relating to specific examples.

The major task with this paper, in simplistic terms, is to subtract the totality of the prior art from the client's research in order to identify which subject matter is novel and to then establish which novel subject matter is associated with an inventive step. The patentable subject matter thus identified should then be claimed in one or more applications, as dictated by the requirement for unity. In order to carry out the first step in this sequence, it is therefore necessary to fully appreciate exactly what subject matter the client is presenting to you in order to correctly perform the subtraction. There are three main ways in which this can be accomplished: (1) the information can be held in your memory whilst considering the prior art and the subtraction can be performed mentally; (2) you can refer to the information as set out by the client in the paper and mark the prior art on the paper; or (3) you can make your own concise summary of the information presented by the client and mark the prior art disclosure on this summary. For all but the most exceptionally gifted individuals, the large amount of information presented in Paper A precludes the use of method (1). The choice for most people is therefore between methods (2) and (3). Method (2) has the advantage that no time is wasted in making a separate summary of the contents of the paper. On the other hand, it can be argued that such time is not "wasted" but, on the contrary, the mental discipline involved in making such a summary is the best way to ensure that you have considered all aspects of the clients work and classified them in a systematic way. Generally, reading and summarising technical subject matter leads to a greater level of understanding than just reading it. There is, in reality, no "best" way of tackling the paper. Whether method (2) or (3) works best will vary from paper to paper and from candidate to candidate. Those candidates who struggle with time may find method (2) works best for them. Equally, there will be papers where the subject matter is set out logically in the client's letter and/or large amount of the text of the client's letter are duplicated word for word in the prior art — method (2) will work well in these circumstances. Where, however, the client's invention is full of a multitude of branching embodiments, or where related aspects of the client's invention are set out in different parts of his letter, and where there is a more subtle correspondence between the prior art and the client's invention, method (3) will often work best. Worked examples applying methods (2) and (3) are set out in parts 7 and 8 of this Guide to Preparing for and Passing Paper A (Chemistry).

If you are using method (2), go through the client's letter and mark in the margin of the exam paper what each sentence signifies. Highlight in particular what categories of claim particular subject matter may form the basis for, essential features of the invention and preferred features with motivation.

If you are using method (3), summarise the various structural features of the client's disclosure on a separate sheet of paper, using annotated arrows between them to indicate any processes. Include specific embodiments and any information on which embodiments give surprising results.

The prior art should then be carefully read and annotated. The prior art will almost certainly be Art.54(2) art (though the client's own Art.54(3) art could in principle be included). Answer two questions in particular: (1) does what is described potentially fall within the description of the client's invention (relevant for novelty); and (2) is the prior art solving a similar, or the same, problem (relevant for inventive step)? Each piece of prior art should therefore be categorised as novelty only, inventive step only, novelty and inventive step or (rarely!) not relevant. Within each prior document, note those sections which are highly relevant to a particular claim type and those which may largely be ignored.

One further point to check is whether the prior art is enabling. For instance, if the prior art discloses a compound but no way of making it, it can be argued that the prior art is non-enabling and the compound is not comprised in the state of the art (T206/83).

*Establishing patentable subject matter* 1–003

Analyse which features of the invention as set out by the client are already described in the prior art and then mark this information on the paper, if using method (2), or on your summary, if using method (3). Any suitable means may be used, such as highlighter or hatching areas of text. However, only pencil or yellow highlighter should be used on the examination paper itself to facilitate later construction of the description. Pen may be used in the margins. It may be that large sections of the client's letter are duplicated in the prior art or, alternatively, the correspondence may be more subtle — this varies from year to year.

Through this process of subtraction, it should now start to become obvious where the client's invention or inventions lie. The client's broadest statement of invention, usually either a product or a process, may be novel in itself, either absolutely or by selection (for examples of novelty by selection, see 1995, 1996 and 1997), or may need to be made novel by introducing (1) a disclaimer, if the prior art is only relevant to novelty (e.g. 1992); (2) a preferred feature with some motivation (e.g. 2000); or (3) a change of claim category (e.g. product to use, 2002).

Before 1998, the A and B papers concerned the same subject matter, and it was more likely that the client's broadest statement of invention would be novel (since a later amendment in the B paper had to be allowed for). However, contemporary A and B papers concern different subject matter, and in the prior art now tends to be more relevant in Paper A, making some kind of amendment to the client's broadest statement of invention likely.

The novel claim must also be associated with some advantage which is unexpected enough in view of the state of the art to justify an inventive step. The argument for inventive step can be signposted in a number of ways. The client's invention will be associated with some advantageous property not achieved in the prior art. In some cases the prior art will be completely silent as to this property (e.g. 2002 where the client's components are herbicides), sometimes the client's invention will be quantitatively better and usually supported by data (e.g. 2001, more effective process) and other times the prior art will teach away from the invention (e.g. 2004, only coating agents known led to unstable suspensions).

Where the invention as described by the client is already novel and inventive it is likely that some significant effort will be required to frame the claim in respect of the correct essential technical features.

In Table 1 below some examples from recent EQE papers are given, showing how the invention as described by the client must be modified in order to obtain novel and inventive subject matter.

Table 1: Necessary steps to make the invention described by the client patentable

| Year | Invention according to client | D1 (relevance re novelty and inventive step) | D2 (relevance re novelty and inventive step) | Necessary action to make invention novel over prior art | Argument for inventive step |
|---|---|---|---|---|---|
| 2003 | Client thinks he's invented a new process: "We have succeeded in finding a way to manufacture 2,6-DMN by an economic and simple process ... on the following pages we have described our process in more detail." | Describes first step of process described by client but using a catalyst on an acidic support rather than a basic one. **Nov + inv step** | Describes second step of process as described by the client almost exactly. **Not relevant**. | Introduce preferred feature into description of the first step (basic catalyst): "The highest yields ... are obtained when the support is itself basic." | Greater selectivity is obtained — experimental results disclosed support this. |
| 2002 | Client thinks he's invented new compounds: "The novel compounds synthesised in our lab are those of formula (2)." | Describes the same compounds for a different use. **Nov only** | | Claim use rather than compounds *per se* (except for one remaining novel compound). | No expectation that prior art preservatives would have activity as herbicides. |
| 2000 | Client thinks he's invented a new filter device: "Our new filter device comprises ... ." | Same filter device as client but on a larger scale. **Nov and inv step**. | Same device as client and step of freezing it. **Nov and inv step**. | Introduce preferred feature "*In one preferred form of the filter device, the device is freeze-dried.*" | No hint in the prior art that device could be freeze dried and rapidly regenerated. |
| 1998 | Client describes new processes he's developed: "*In the course of our experiments we have made several observations, briefly summarised below, which we would like to patent as far as possible.*" | **Not relevant** (describes preparation of starting material for new processes). | **Not relevant** | Nothing required (but some care required in claiming the processes correctly). | No similar process known. |

## PART A

| | | | | |
|---|---|---|---|---|
| **1995** | Client thinks he's developed a process for making a new alloy: *"In order to achieve this, the alloy must be prepared by a special process which I shall now describe."* | Prior art process described by client. **Inv step only**. | Nothing required. | Alloy produced by modified process is now homogeneous. |
| **1992** | Client thinks he's developed new herbicides: *"The novel herbicides developed by us are compounds represented by the following formula . . ."* | Similar herbicidal compounds. **Inv step only**. | One of client's compounds for different use. **Nov only**. Use disclaimer to restore novelty. | Prior art herbicides either more toxic or not as potent. |

One favoured situation is to have two prior art documents. One of them is most relevant in structural terms, destroying the novelty of the client's broadest statement of his invention, and requiring a disclaimer or other amendment, but has no relevance to inventive step, solving a different problem. The other piece of prior art is relevant to inventive step but perhaps less structurally relevant — a different kind of amendment of the client's broadest statement is required so that the claimed matter is associated with some inventive advantage. See, for example, 2001 paper A where D1 is relevant to inventive step and both process and product claims need to be limited as a result and D2 is relevant to novelty, further limiting the product claim to one containing an aliphatic alcohol cosolvent.

However, many other situations are possible! Sometimes, there is only one prior art document (e.g. 2002) and other times both prior art documents are equally relevant to inventive step (e.g. 2004).

**1–004**  *Claiming the invention*

Having established what action needs to be taken in order to make the client's broadest statement of invention novel and inventive, the first independent claim can be drafted.

Include all essential features of the invention, especially those which underlie an effect associated with the inventive step (T32/82). If you omit an essential feature from a claim, you will lose a significant number of marks. Keywords that tend to flag an essential feature include: must, has to be, should be, is/are, provided that, is necessary, have, only, is required. Equally, avoid all features which are merely optional or preferred, as these would unnecessarily limit the claim. Again, if you include inessential features, you will lose marks. Keywords that tend to flag such features include: preferred, preferably, typically, usually, for example, normally, optimal, suitable, advantageous, good/better/best results, especially, particularly, special mention, may be.

If it seems that specific examples need to be excluded, think very hard before doing so, as this is very unusual.

Only use information that the client has provided; do not draft any more broadly than he suggests. In particular, if the client gives you clear instructions either not to protect something or that certain things or activities are not of interest, you should not claim them. The instructions to candidates tell you to accept the facts given in the paper and to limit yourself to those facts: if you do not do this, you will lose marks.

Write on every other line, to facilitate later changes.

Use the exact language and reference numerals that the client uses in order to make drafting the description easier.

In the majority of cases, the invention will concern a new product (though product claims are not always possible, e.g. 1998) and the first independent claim to be drafted will be in this category. Beware, however, the case where the client describes his invention in the context of a process or use and the product claim is disguised (e.g. 2003). In general, think very hard before submitting a set of claims without any product claim! Product inventions which can only be claimed in product-by-process format are always popular (e.g. 1997, 2001) and in this case claims to the product obtainable by the process and the process itself should be included. Apart from a product claim, independent process and use claims should be included where possible.

The new product on which the invention is usually based will most probably fall into one of three categories:

**Type A:** A substance (e.g. drug, agrochemical, emulsifier) which is applied to a target (e.g. human, animal, crop, liquid mixture) to achieve a beneficial effect (e.g. cure illness, prevent decay, achieve solution).

**Type B**: A substance (e.g. composition, catalyst, treatment solution) which is used to make a process work (e.g. oxidation of alkenes, tanning of hides, purification of petroleum).

**Type C**: A substance (e.g. a polymer, alloy, fat substitute) that can be processed into a useful article (e.g. contact lens, reaction vessel, food).

The main claim types to consider, bearing in mind this classification, are summarised in the following diagram:

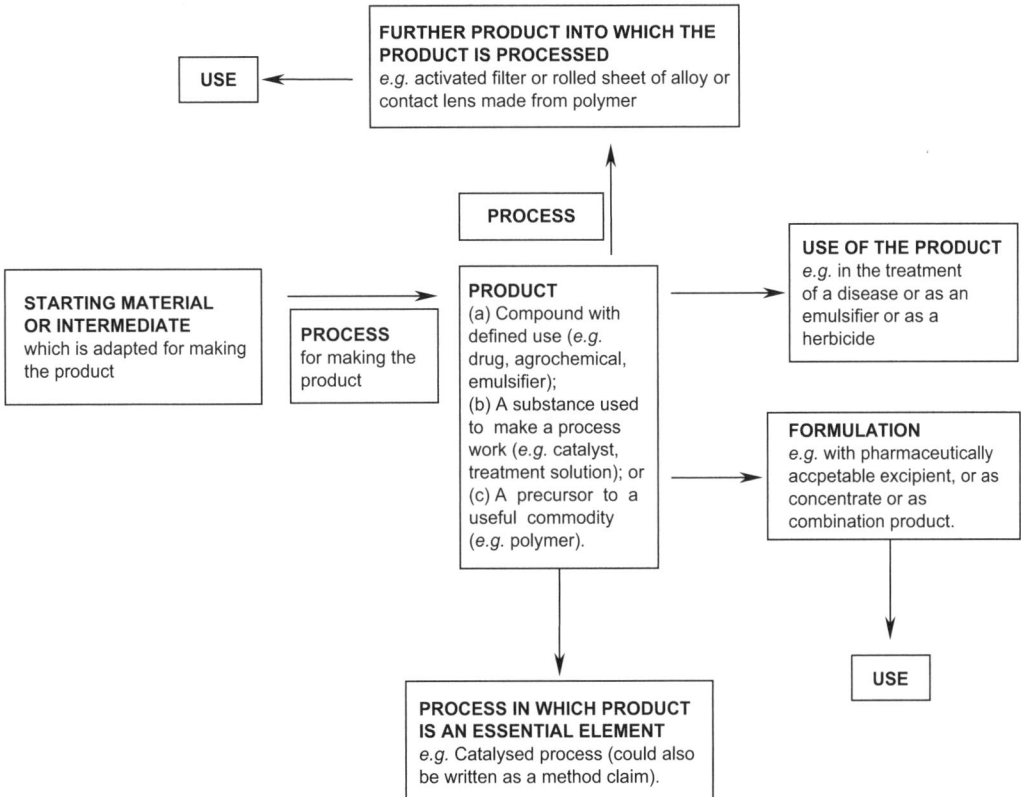

Some examples of main independent claim types from previous years are given below.

| Invention type | Year | Product | Process | Use |
|---|---|---|---|---|
| A | 2002 | Compound and composition. | For making compounds. | Of compounds as herbicides. |
| | 1997 | Compounds (product by process). | For making compounds. | Of compounds as emulsifiers in four fields. |
| | 1992 | Compounds and formulation. | For making compounds. | Of compounds as herbicides. |
| B | 2003 | Catalyst | For alkylating hydrocarbons using catalyst and for making catalyst. | In alkylation process. |
| | 2001 | Treatment solution and formulation. | For purifying petroleum using solution. | In purification of hydrocarbons. |
| | 2000 | Filter device (freeze-dried and activated). | For making device and using device to purify water. | Of device in purification of water. |
| C | 1996 | Polymer and contact lens comprising polymer. | For making polymer and contact lens. | In manufacture of contact lens. |
| | 1995 | Alloy (product by process), metal sheet comprising alloy and reactor comprising metal sheet. | For making alloy and metal sheet. | Of metal sheet in construction of reactor and reactor in manufacture of urea. |

For Type A inventions the compound may be defined by a different formula in the product, use and process claims where there is prior art which is relevant to novelty but not to inventive step. It may be more convenient when constructing the claim set to start with the claim type in which the compounds are defined most broadly. In particular, with a pharmaceutical question, consider different scopes for the compound claim, first medical use claim and second medical use claim. Also consider a cosmetic method of treatment claim.

Where one of the process or use claims is independently inventive in addition to the product claim and has a different scope of application there may well be a lack of unity and the filing of a divisional application should be suggested in a note to the examiner.

For Type C inventions the product is often converted more than once to increasingly valuable downstream products (e.g. 1994, Emulsifier→ Ground form of emulsifier→ Food or 1995, Alloy→ Sheet metal→ Reactor). Claims to each product should be included as well as claims to the processes for converting one product to another.

Consider what the client is making and selling and try to introduce claims that cover these commercial activities appropriately.

Having established the main categories of independent claim, draft dependent claims specifying further features that are associated with further advantages (preferred features with motivation). These will usually be signposted as "most preferred" or "particularly advantageous". Concentrate on those features which are structural rather than use-orientated. With compounds, any preferred sub-groups and specific examples are worth claiming. You should aim, in general, for a total of from 10 to 20 claims, preferably about 15 but the ideal number will vary from year to year. You will get no credit for dependent claims listing all alternative embodiments or relating to trivial items only. If you draft what the examiners deem to be an unreasonable number of dependent claims, you risk losing marks for contravening Art.84 and r.29(5) EPC. Consider whether preferred features are motivated by any data provided, e.g. showing that particular compounds are especially good in certain embodiments, such as providing a selective herbicidal effect when used with certain crops (2002).

**1–005**  *Drafting the description*

For the purposes of the exam, only a partial description needs to be drafted. The relevant part is the introduction, comprising that section of the description preceding the examples. It is sensible to follow the order suggested by r.27(1) EPC (a), (b) and (c). Use cutting and pasting of the exam paper as much as possible, remembering to delete any comments made during the analysis phase of the exam. Note, however, that the invention claimed is unlikely to be the same invention set out by the client in his letter and that marks will be lost if the description and claims are not consistent. You should therefore cut, paste and also *amend* appropriately!

Most time and effort should be devoted to describing the prior art and the problem to be solved in light of it and hence demonstrating an inventive step for the claimed subject matter. Most marks are likely to be available for drafting this part of the description since it involves the greatest amount of creativity and will have to be drafted from scratch.

First, specify the technical field to which the invention relates, consistent with the main independent claims. It is common to start with the general field ('The present invention relates to . . .') and then propose a more specific field ('More specifically, the invention relates to . . .') but a single statement may be sufficient. Foreshadow various independent claim types in this section (e.g. 'Further, the invention relates to the use of . . . in . . ., and a process for preparing . . .').

Next, describe that piece or those pieces of prior art which is/are relevant to inventive step. Summarise briefly the pertinent parts of the disclosure(s). Also mention what deficiencies and disadvantages the prior art suffers from, including where appropriate a mention of the key features it does not disclose, but only mention those disadvantages or missing features which are addressed by the claimed invention. If the prior art teaches away from your invention this teaching should also be summarised.

If one piece of prior art contains an accidental anticipation, which has been disclaimed in your main claim, then this prior art should also be summarised in this section. Prior art which has no relevance for inventive step and which has not led to a disclaimer can be summarised later.

The problem to be solved in relation to the closest prior art should then be set out. This problem should be as specific as is demanded by the facts of the question. Marks are lost if the problem is cast in too general terms (e.g. 'improved properties' or 'improved performance'). As usual, formulate the problem by considering the technical effect achieved by the novel feature of the claim vis-à-vis the closest prior art. The problem solved will be the provision of a product or process to achieve such an effect. And remember that the problem should be formulated so that it contains no features of the solution — failure to adhere to this rule loses marks.

For example, if the prior art describes coated particles which do not lead to stable suspensions and your client has invented particles with different coating agents which do provide stable suspensions, then summarise the coated particles of the prior art, making mention of the specific coating agents used, mention that the use of these coating agents do not provide coated particles that form a stable suspension and set out the technical problem as the provision of coated particles that lead to a stable suspension. Or, if the prior art describes a catalyst used with a particular support which, when used in a certain process provides the product contaminated with impurities which are hard to remove, and your client has provided a new support which makes the catalyst much more selective, then summarise the catalyst of the prior art, making mention of the specific support used, mention the fact that use of this supported catalyst leads to impurities in the product and set out the technical problem as the provision of a supported catalyst that catalyses the relevant process more selectively, leading to fewer impurities.

The solution provided by the invention in the form of the main independent claim should then be set out — you can save time here by simply referring to claim 1 rather than writing it out again ('The invention therefore provides coated particles as set out in claim 1'). The advantages provided by the invention can then be explained, bearing in mind the level of generality of the claim — i.e. do not suggest that the invention in its broadest definition provides an advantage which is in fact only achieved by only some of the preferred embodiments or examples. Always check, when drafting the introduction, that the problem and advantages which are set out actually match what is recited in the corresponding claim, paying particular attention to the need for each independent claim to recite all the essential technical features. If a feature is not in a claims, the description should not say it is essential in relation to the subject matter of that claim.

Basis should then be provided for the other main independent claim types, including a further problem/solution analysis if appropriate (beware that unity may well be a problem if different claims are solving different inventions!).

Any other art should then be discussed. Have a paragraph for each piece of art that is disclosed, no matter how irrelevant it is to novelty and inventive step.

Follow this by defining any integers in the claims and then list preferred features and their supplementary advantages (e.g. 'The X can be A, B or C. Preferably, the X is C since this provides the advantage that . . .'). This section will provide support for the dependent claims. Most of this information will come from cutting and pasting of the client's letter but remember, as mentioned above, to ensure consistency with the claims, which will probably have been limited in view of the prior art. The way certain things are expressed in a letter may also be unsuitable in the context of a patent application and relevant changes should be made.

**1-006**  *Notes to the Examiner*

The exam does not require or assume that you will write notes to the examiner: your answer should be complete and should speak for itself. But sometimes there is a justification for a brief note to the examiner. Consider whether any of the motivated preferred features lead to a separate, non-unitary invention (e.g. horizontal filter device in 2000). If so, either draft a claim to the further non-unitary invention, explaining why this extra invention does not have unity with the subject matter being claimed and that you would make it the subject of a separate application, or at least identify the extra invention in clear terms and again say that it would be made the subject of an extra application. If there is a lack of unity in the claim set which you propose, you will lose marks if you do not identify this fact (and how you would deal with it) in your answer. On the other hand, if you avoid a lack of unity by failing to claim something that could have been claimed, and you do not identify the relevant subject matter as potentially claimable in another application, you will again lose marks.

Extensive notes to the examiner should be avoided. Further things to consider pointing out to the examiner are: (1) assumptions made in light of ambiguities in the question; (2) reasons why you made any decision that was difficult to make (e.g. not claiming novel subject matter deemed to be obvious); and (3) instances where you have had to use claim language (on the basis of the client's instructions) which might not be allowable based on known case law (e.g. having to use "substituted phenyl" in a claim in light of T939/92 — AGREVO/Triazoles).

**1-007**  *Checking the answer*

It is always sensible to check the correctness of your claims, especially the independent claims, once you have drafted your sub-claims and introduction. Check for the absence of features essential to solve the problem which you have set out in the introduction; presence of inessential features; that all claimable examples are covered by the independent claims; that all patentable products have been claimed; and that the claims distinguish over the art. Unless you have made a big mistake, major changes to the answer are not recommended in the last 15 minutes and often lose more marks than they gain. If any time remains it is worth reading through the answer once, correcting typographical mistakes and ensuring that there is consistency between the description and the claims.

**1-008**  ## 3. Some important case law

*Case law relating to disclosure of the prior art*

The prior art is likely to disclose certain specific embodiments. It is important to remember, however, that the general disclosure may also disclose further specific embodiments. This is particularly true where the prior art discloses a range as part of the general disclosure, the ends of the range being additional specific embodiments. T181/82 is an important decision which makes this clear. In this decision it was held that the general disclosure of $C_1$-$C_4$ alkyl specifically discloses (1) methyl and (2) butyl as a group of 4 isomers. Such a term does not, of course, specifically disclose a value falling within the range, e.g. ethyl, or a value falling within $C_4$ such as tert-butyl — these could in principle still be seen as novel selections.

In the same way, where the prior art discloses a numerical range, the ends of the range are specifically disclosed embodiments. So, for example, a temperature range in a process $T = 2$–$10$ degrees discloses the specific temperatures $T = 2$ and $T = 10$ — these values are no longer novel. In the context of a selection invention, the range $T = 3$–$5$ may be novel (see T279/89 below) but the range $T = 2$–$4$ is anticipated. As an example, see 2005 paper B where the application disclosed a compound $HOOC(CH_2)mCOOH$ which showed particularly good results where $m = 2$ but the prior art disclosed $HOOC(CH_2)mCOOH$ where m was generally 'equal to or higher than 2' and specifically 5 or 6. The compound $HOOC(CH_2)_2COOH$ could not therefore be claimed, since it was not novel, even though it had ostensibly inventive properties.

*Allowability of disclaimers* 1–009

There is obviously no question of whether a disclaimer should be allowable under Article 123(2) EPC in paper A, as an application has not been filed yet. Disclaimers are therefore allowable in all circumstances where the subject matter cannot be described positively (T4/80).

However, a disclaimer cannot make a non-inventive teaching inventive (T170/87, T597/92). A disclaimer should therefore only be contemplated where the prior art being disclaimed is an accidental anticipation, i.e. is not relevant to the problem solved by invention embodied by the claim, or your claims will likely lack an inventive step.

*Selection inventions* 1–010

Selection inventions frequently arise in the EQE, particularly in papers A, B and C, and you should therefore be thoroughly familiar with the case law relating to them, which arises almost exclusively in the chemical field.

The general principle with selection inventions is that a general disclosure in the prior art does not take away the novelty of a later claim to a specific embodiment. Thus, where the disclosure in the prior art is to 'metal', a later claim to 'copper' will still be novel (the question of inventive step, of course, is a separate matter — the selection will have to be associated with some surprising effect). Specific chemical compounds are therefore novel unless there is a direct and unambiguous prior disclosure of the same compound in the form of a technical teaching (T181/82, T296/87). If the prior art discloses a generic formula covering many compounds is not a disclosure of all the specific compounds falling within the genus and a later claim to a specific compound will be novel (assuming it hasn't been also specifically disclosed in the prior art as an example). Further examples: if the prior art discloses heteroaryl, a later claim to pyridyl will be novel; if the prior art discloses halo, a later claim to fluoro will be novel; if the prior art discloses alkali metal, a later claim to potassium will be novel. In the extreme case, where the prior art discloses a racemate, a later claim to one of the two enantiomers making up the racemate is in principle also novel (T296/87).

The allowability of selecting from a generic disclosure of compounds a narrower generic group of compounds (as opposed to a single compound) is less clear. Practitioners will know that the EPO often allows such selections but the case law is somewhat ambiguous (T133/92 and T12/90). It is therefore unlikely that this situation will arise in the EQE — usually where the prior art destroys the novelty of a generic group of compounds only single compounds can subsequently be claimed.

See, for example, 2002 paper A, where the client has found that a generic group of compounds act as herbicides. Several specific examples of the genus are also specified. The prior art, however, discloses the same generic formula and all but one of the specific examples (as preservatives). The one remaining novel example can be claimed as a novel selection from the generic disclosure in the prior art.

Another important principle is the 'two list' selection invention derivable from T12/81 and made explicit in T7/86. According to this case law, if the prior art contains a general formula with at least two independently variable substituents, a later claim to a single compound which represents a selection of disclosed definitions from each list is novel. For example, if the prior art discloses substituted phenyl derivatives having para substituents $R^1$ and $R^2$, wherein $R^1$ is defined as methyl, ethyl or propyl and $R^2$ is defined as chloro, fluoro or bromo, a later claim to 1-methyl-4-fluorobenzene will be novel since a choice of structural information had to be made from at least two lists. This principle can be extrapolated to other situations where lists relating to structural features are involved.

An example arises in 2004 paper B where the application relates to a corrosion inhibitor comprising an alkanolamine and a metal nitrite. Lists of preferred alkanolamines and metal nitrites are given. The prior art, however, discloses the general concept of the combination and the lists of preferred examples. It is still possible, however, to claim a specific combination (calcium nitrite/triethanolamine) which shows superior properties since it is a novel selection from the prior art lists.

It must be emphasised that for the 'two list' principle to operate, each list must relate to structural information. Indeed, it is clear from T12/81 that where the prior art discloses a process, a list of starting materials and a list of potential process conditions, it implicitly discloses the product of any of the process conditions in combination with any of the starting materials. So, if the prior art discloses a certain process and lists three starting materials A, B and C along with three potential process conditions X, Y and Z, the inevitable product of carrying out the process with any one of the starting materials in combination with any one of the process conditions is made state of the art and cannot subsequently be claimed — here the selection is from one list encoding structural information and one list encoding process information. On the other hand, if the process requires two starting materials (e.g. the condensation of two amino acids), and individual lists of starting materials 1 ( = A, B or C) and 2 ( = X, Y or Z) were given, then the product resulting from the choice of a specific starting material from list 1 and a specific starting material from list 2 would still be novel over the disclosure — here the selection is from two lists both containing structural information.

Of course, this is a very simplistic analysis and the outcome may vary depending on the specific facts of the case. If, for example, starting material B is indicated as a preferred definition from list 1, then the product resulting from the choice of B with either X, Y or Z would no longer be novel since it would amount to a selection from one list in combination with a single individualised coupling partner B.

In the case of numerical ranges, there are two approaches to the later selection of a more specific range. A selected range from a broader prior art range is novel if it is (a) narrow, (b) removed from the preferred part of the prior art range and (c) is a purposive as opposed to an arbitrary selection (T279/89). On the other hand, an overlapping range is novel in the area of overlap where the skilled person would not seriously contemplate working in that area (T666/89 and T26/85) — note that the end of the prior art range, being a specific embodiment, would have to be disclaimed.

Since the assessment of the novelty of overlapping ranges under T666/89 is so subjective, it is unlikely to arise in the EQE. In contrast, the three-part test of T279/89 frequently arises. See, for example, 2000 paper B where the prior art describes a catalyst made by calcination at a temperature of greater than 250 degrees and exemplifies a specific temperature of 350 degrees. Data in the application shows that when the calcination is carried out at a temperature of between 500 and 600 degrees the resulting catalyst is surprisingly more selective when used to oxidise butanes. The selected range here is narrow (100 degree range selected from a theoretically infinite range in the prior art), removed from the preferred prior art range (150 degrees away from the prior art example) and purposive (the selected range leads to an advantageous effect not shared by the rest of the prior art range).

See Guidelines C/IV/7.7 for a further discussion of these principles.

1–011  *Novelty by purity*

A known compound is disclosed in all states of purity unless all conventional methods of purification have failed (T990/96). Consider the case in which a prior art process shows how to make a compound, but the product is inevitably contaminated by at least 5% of a byproduct which is difficult to remove, and the client has invented a new, improved process which provides the compound in 99% purity. A claim to the new process is clearly possible. However, in these circumstances, do not include a claim to the product 'in substantially pure form' or 'in at least 99% purity' unless the question clearly indicates that this level of purity was not obtainable by subjecting the prior art product to conventional purification techniques such as chromatography and recrystallisation.

## 4. Common claim types in chemistry

*Product claims* 1–012

In the chemical area a product claim is likely to be defined in terms of its structure. Compound claims, for instance, typically take the form of "A compound of the formula X", where formula X is a structural formula. In certain cases, however, a product may be defined in terms of the process used to make it. Such product by process claims are allowed only when there is difficulty defining the product in any other way. The product must be novel in itself (T150/82) since a product by process claim is construed as being directed to the product per se (T20/94) and a product is not novel just because it is produced by a novel process (T150/82). The "obtainable by" language should be used. Novelty must be demonstrated, e.g. with polymers, by showing a distinct difference in properties (T205/83) which implies a structural difference.

A product by process claim is quite common in the EQE and should be used where a new process leads to a product which displays an implicit or explicit structural difference over the prior art and which cannot be defined in structural terms. For instance, in 1995, a new alloy was homogeneous in structure by virtue of a new cooling process and this was a valid distinguishing feature.

*EQE examples* 1–013

1999 Sulphonated polycondensation products obtainable according to the process of any one of the preceding claims.

1993 Catalytic compositions defined by the general empirical formula $A_a D_b Sb_c Sn_d Te_e Y_f O_x$ wherein A represents one or more elements selected from copper, vanadium, molybdenum and/or tungsten; D represents one or more activator elements selected from cobalt and/or bismuth; Y is an alkali metal; a is 0.01 to 10; b is 0 to 10; c is 10; d is 0.1 to 10; e is 0.001 to 10; f is 0 to 0.01; $a + b + d + e \leq 11$; and x represents the number of oxygen atoms necessary to satisfy the valency requirements of the other elements present.

1992 Compound according to the general formula

wherein $R^1$ is a $C_3$–$C_4$ alkyl group, $R^2$ is a $C_1$–$C_4$ alkyl group, X is a methyl group and n is an integer from 0 to 3, other than the compound where $R^1$ is a propyl group, $R^2$ is an ethyl group and n is 0.

*Composition claims* 1–014

A composition claim is directed to a mixture of compounds, often a compound or product with useful properties that has already been claimed per se together with a carrier or diluent or other material.

Typically, in the case of bioactive compounds, a composition claim will read "A [pharmaceutical, veterinary, agricultural ...] composition comprising a compound of the formula X and ... Y" where Y is a carrier, diluent or other excipient.

Combination claims, which are also essentially composition claims, are described separately below.

*EQE examples* 1–015

1999 A pharmaceutical composition containing a compound according to claims 1–2 or 5–9 together with a pharmaceutically acceptable excipient and/or adjuvant (taken from Paper B).

16  Complete Guide to Passing the EQE

1994 A low calorie edible emulsion comprising at least 0.3% by weight of an ester according to any preceding claim and at least one edible ingredient.

1993 Catalytic compositions of claim 1 which are supported by an inert refractory material.

**1–016**  *Use/method of using claims*

A first medical use claim should be used where a compound or composition has never been used for a therapeutic purpose before — "Compound X/composition Y for use as a medicament" (Art.54(5), T128/82). The compound or composition may itself be novel or may, for instance, have been previously known as a dye or agrochemical.

A second medical use claim should be used where a new therapeutic application of a compound or composition is discovered — "The use of compound X/composition Y for the manufacture of a medicament for the treatment of disease Z" (G5/83). The compound or composition may be novel, previously known for a non-therapeutic use or previously known for a different therapeutic use.

A second non-medical use claim should be used where a compound or composition is found to have some new application which is associated with a new technical effect — "The use of compound X/composition Y as a friction-reducing additive" (G2/88, G6/88). The claim is novel even where the new application was inherently occurring in a prior art use as long as the new application was not appreciated. The compound or composition may be novel or known. These claims can also be written as method claims.

See, for instance, 1992 paper B, where the use of some compounds as herbicides was a novel claim (note: no Swiss style second medical use claim necessary since this is an agrochemical use and not a therapeutic use) despite the prior art disclosure of the compounds as agrochemical fungicides. The prior art had taught the application of the same compounds, in a similar formulation, for spraying crops to achieve a fungicidal effect and they must have inherently been achieving a herbicidal effect at the same time. However, because the knowledge of the herbicidal effect was not made available in the prior art, the second medical use claim relating to their herbicidal effect was novel.

A method of treatment claim should only be used for a cosmetic or other non-therapeutic use — e.g. T144/83 "A method of improving the bodily appearance of a non-opiate-addicted mammal which comprises orally administering to said mammal naltrexone or a pharmaceutically effective salt thereof in a dosage effective to reduce appetite, and repeating said dosage until a cosmetically beneficial loss of body weight has occurred."

**1–017**  *EQE examples*

2001 The use of 1,1,1,4,4,4-hexafluorobutane or 1,1,2,2-tetrafluorocyclobutane in cleaning fluid or as working fluid for heating pumps (taken from Paper B).

2000 Use of a catalyst as defined in claim 6 for oxidising hydrocarbons in the gas phase with oxygen or an oxygen containing gas (taken from Paper B).

1999 A compound of formula

$$RN-\underset{\underset{(CH_2)_n}{|}}{\overset{\overset{R^{III}}{|}}{C}}-N-(CH_2)_m-N-\underset{\underset{(CH_2)_n}{|}}{\overset{\overset{R^{III}}{|}}{C}}-NR$$

wherein m is an integer from 3 to 6; n is an integer from 3 to 6; R is a $C_1$–$C_5$ group; and $R^{III}$ is H, a $C_1$–$C_{12}$ alkyl group, an aryl group or an alkaryl group for use as a medicament (taken from Paper B).

1999B Use of a compound of the formula

$$RN-\underset{(CH_2)_n}{\underset{|}{\overset{R^{III}}{\overset{|}{C}}}}-\underset{H}{N}-(CH_2)_m-N-\underset{(CH_2)_n}{\underset{|}{\overset{R^{III}}{\overset{|}{C}}}}-NR$$

wherein m, n and R have the same meanings as in claim 11 and $R^{III}$ is H, a $C_1$–$C_{12}$ alkyl group, an aryl group or an alkaryl group for the manufacture of a medicament for the treatment of cancer or leukaemia (taken from Paper B).

## Process claims

Some processes are patentable in their own right, being novel and non-obvious. The inventive step will reside in an unexpected advantage such as increased yield or selectivity. An example of this claim type is: "A process for preparing methanol which comprises reacting carbon monoxide and hydrogen in the presence of catalyst X" where the choice of catalyst X is the novel feature associated with some unexpected advantage such as an increase in yield. In this case, the product of the process may be either known or new. A product by process claim will sometimes be appropriate where the product is new (see above).

Other processes, known as analogy processes, are allowed where the process is conventional but the product is novel and inventive (T119/82) — e.g. "A process for preparing a compound of the formula (I) which comprises reacting a compound of the formula (II) with a compound of the formula (III)".

Note that where an EQE paper discloses new compounds and includes two processes to make them, one being an analogy process and one being an inventive process, the two process claims may have a different scope in relation to the definition of the product. The analogy process will be limited to the preparation of those compounds which are novel and inventive (which may be limited in view of the prior art) whereas the inventive process, relying for patentability on a process feature, may be claimable in respect of a broader range of products. In this situation the two process claims will lack unity of invention.

## EQE examples

1999 A process for the manufacture of a compound according to claim 2 which comprises the step of condensing with formaldehyde a compound according to claim 1 (taken from Paper B — analogy process).

1998 A process for the introduction of vanadium into steel, characterised in that vanadium oxycarbide is added directly to molten steel in the absence of oxygen (inventive process).

1995 A process for the preparation of a homogeneous lead-antimony alloy consisting of 1–15% by weight of antimony, the balance being lead and usual impurities, the process comprising quenching the molten alloy to a temperature of less than 200 °C with a cooling agent (inventive process).

## Intermediate claims

Intermediates in an inventive process may be claimed if they are novel. Such claims are unusual in the EQE.

Inventive step conventionally follows by virtue of the "process effect" (T22/82, T648/88). However, in T65/82 it was suggested that intermediates in analogy processes must be independently inventive over any prior art close in structure to the intermediates themselves.

## Article incorporating or when treated with compound/composition (target)

These are further product claims. For example, "A plant treated with composition X".

1–022    *Apparatus for applying compound/composition*

Where a specially designed/adapted apparatus is necessary for applying a composition/compound to a target. Such claims are rare in the EQE.

1–023    *Combination claims*

Combination claims are essentially composition claims where the further ingredient is another active compound. If both the components are already known to be useful for the intended use of the combination then some synergy is usually necessary to support inventive step, i.e. if both components are merely carrying out their respective known functions together, rather than separately, there is no invention, but merely a collocation.

In the case of a pharmaceutical combination, a specially adapted product claim is possible: "A product containing X and Y as a combined preparation for simultaneous, separate or sequential use in the treatment of Z" (T9/81).

See 2002 paper A for an example of a combination claim.

1–024    *Omnibus claims*

These claims are generally not allowed (r.29(6)). Except where absolutely necessary, claims must not rely, in respect of technical features of the invention, on references to the description or drawings such as "as described in part . . . of the description" or "as illustrated in figure . . . of the drawings." Do not, therefore, include them in the EQE.

## 5. Notes on drafting the claims

1–025    *Claim language*

"For use as" means "suitable for use as" and does not provide any limitation (except for the first medical use).

"Comprising" is open and allows the presence of any further constituents.

"Consisting of" is closed and does not allow further constituents, so that if a product "consists of A, B and C", then A, B and C make up 100 per cent of it (T759/91).

"Consisting essentially of" allows some latitude in terms of impurities.

1–026    *Requirements of claims — form and content*

The claims must be clear and concise and be supported by the description (Art.84, CLBA pages 157 to 168). Relative terms such as "lower alkyl" which have no generally accepted meaning should not be used (T337/95), even if a definition is provided in the description (T1129/97). "Substantially pure" is not allowed (T728/28). "Pharmaceutical product" implying a particular grade of purity is unclear since there is no accepted definition of such purity level (T226/98).

The claims must define the matter for which protection is sought. Such definition must be in terms of the technical features of the invention (Art.84/r.29(1) EPC). Remember to include all those technical features which are necessary to obtain the technical effect on which an inventive step is based.

Two-part form is encouraged — r.29(1) EPC — such that wherever appropriate, claims must contain: (a) a statement indicating the designation of the subject matter of the invention and those technical features which are necessary for the definition of the claimed subject-matter but which, in combination, are part of the prior art; and (b) a characterising part — preceded by the expression "characterised in that" or "characterised by" — stating the technical features which, in combination with the features stated in (a), it is desired to protect. However, in the chemical field, the two part claim format is not usually advantageous and may largely be ignored. If it is used, it should be used properly as explained above.

The number of claims must be reasonable in consideration of the nature of the invention claimed (r.29(5) EPC). In particular (r.29(2) EPC), the inclusion of more than one independent claim in the same category (product, process, apparatus or use) is only allowed if the subject-matter of the application involves either: (a) a plurality of inter-related products, (b) different uses of a product or apparatus, or (c) alternative solutions to a particular problem, where it is not appropriate to cover these alternatives by a single claim.

Any claim stating the essential features of an invention may be followed by one or more claims containing particular embodiments of that invention. Dependent claims where possible must start with a reference to the other claim and then state the additional features which it is desired to protect. Such dependent claims are allowed even where the claim referred to is itself a dependent claim. All dependent claims must be grouped together in the most appropriate way (r.29(3)(4) EPC).

If there are several claims they must be numbered consecutively in arabic numerals (r.29(5) EPC).

Where drawings are included, the technical features in the claims should preferably be followed by reference signs relating to those features if the intelligibility of the claim can thereby be increased. Such reference signs should be placed in parentheses. Such reference signs may not be construed as limiting the claim (r.(29)7) EPC). Drawings are unusual in the chemistry paper, but occasionally arise (e.g. 2000 paper A — filter device).

### Unity of invention

1–027

A European patent application must relate to one invention only or to a group of inventions so linked as to form a single general inventive concept (A82).

Such a group of inventions is taken to be so linked when there is a technical relationship among the inventions involving one or more of the same or corresponding special technical features, i.e. those features which define a contribution which each of the claimed inventions considered as a whole makes over the prior art (R30(1)).

Unity of invention involves considering whether the claimed inventions are unified — it makes no differences whether the different inventions are in separate claims or are alternatives within a single claim (R30(2)). In most cases, however, in the EQE, the question of unity will arise in considering the relationship between the independent claims.

As indicated above, for two independent claims to have unity, the novel feature of each claim giving rise to an inventive step must be either (a) the same or (b) corresponding. In case (b) the key question in assessing whether the features are corresponding or not is whether the claims relate to inventions which both solve the same overall technical problem in a related way. This has to be to a certain extent a subjective assessment and the following notes give some guidance on which special technical features can be considered corresponding and which cannot. Unity of invention is not an issue as between an independent claim and dependent claim since the dependent claim must by definition share the special technical features of the independent claim.

If we divide independent claims into the three most common categories found in paper A (product, process for making a product and use of/method of using a product), we have six possible combinations to consider.

### Unity between two independent product claims

1–028

A claim defining a group of compounds by reference to a formula having several independently variable substituents is a good example of a single claim covering many product inventions. Each of the compounds covered by the general formula can be considered to be a separate invention. If all the compounds solve the same problem (e.g. by having the same inhibitory activity at a receptor or enzyme, or by all acting as surfactants) and have a common structural motif (i.e. solve the problem in a related way) then all the individual compounds covered by the claim will have unity. Sometimes it may be necessary to have such a group of compounds split between two independent claims and the same criteria apply. The same principle also applies to compositions and other product claims. See, for example, 2002 paper B, where three structurally related frits are novel and inventive. Because of the limited basis for amendment, only two of the frits fall under a claimable preferred genus of frits and the third frit must be claimed separately. The frits are all structurally related and give rise to the same inventive effect and the two claims therefore have unity.

As an example of two product claims not having unity, see 2000 paper A, the main invention of which concerned a freeze dried filter device. This invention solved the problem of being able to purify water in emergency situations since it was portable and could be activated quickly. The special technical feature here was 'freeze dried'. The application also disclosed an improved filter unit comprising several of the devices (whether freeze dried or not) vertically aligned. Such alignment was the special technical feature, leading to easy replacement of used devices. These special technical features were not corresponding since the two independent claims did not solve the same problem.

In 2001 paper B the invention related to a group of fluorinated hydrocarbons which were cleaning fluids. The prior art disclosed some of these compounds for the same use. One of the compounds was still novel and had advantageous properties (lower boiling point). The application further disclosed an azeotropic mixture of one of the known compounds with a lower alkanol which was also inventive (advantageous reduction in boiling point). These two inventions have different special technical features (specific structure vs combination with alkanol) which are not corresponding since, whilst they solve the same problem, they do not solve it in a related way.

**1–029** *Unity between two independent process claims*

Two process claims will clearly have unity if they are both analogy processes and the product is the same in each case, since the special technical feature of each claim is the novel and inventive product. Equally, if both processes are inventive by virtue of the same process feature (e.g. the choice of a particular catalyst) then they will also have unity. If two inventive processes have different inventive process features, however, an assessment of whether they are corresponding will have to be made. As with product claims, if the two processes solve the same objective technical problem in a related way (e.g. by using two different catalysts of an analogous structure) then the two process claims will have unity. If, on the other hand, they solve different problems, or solve the same problem in a different way, then the claims will lack unity.

In 2001 Paper A, the client had made various improvements to the known processes for extracting sulphur compounds from petroleum. One improvement related to removing olefins from the petroleum prior to extraction and the second to the use of an alcoholic co-solvent rather than a carboxylic acid. Both improvements were inventions in their own rights, giving a surprising increase in sulphur extraction but they solved the same problem in completely different ways and the special technical features were therefore not corresponding.

In 1998 paper A, the client had invented several new processes which could be divided into two main groups. On group of inventions involved the preparation of an alloy of vanadium with certain metals by adding vanadium oxycarbide to the relevant molten metal in the absence of oxygen. The second group of inventions involved the preparation of a pure group IV or V metal by heating the corresponding oxycarbide in the absence of oxygen. The common feature is the use of a group IV or V oxycarbide, with heat, in the absence of oxygen. However, these oxycarbides were known compounds. The processes have unity, however, since the absence of oxygen is a common special technical feature, as is the implicit thermal decomposition of the various oxycarbides.

In 1997 paper A, the client disclosed a new process for the preparation of emulsifiers. The process involved two process steps which were each individually known in different pieces of prior art. The client also described a process invention in which one of the known processes (a sulphonation) was improved by the use of sulphur trioxide instead of fuming sulphuric acid. The two processes did not have unity since the sulphonation step could be claimed more broadly in the first process and the two different process features (combination of steps vs use of specific sulphonating agent) did not solve the same problem.

### Unity between two independent use claims

1–030

If the two use claims relate to two different uses of the same novel and inventive product then they will have unity since the product itself will be the special technical feature in each case. Where, however, the product is known, and the special technical feature of each claim is the new use to which the product has been put, it is unlikely that the claims will have unity, since a product's use is so closely related to the problem solved. However, situations can be imagined where the new technical effect underlying the inventive step of these different uses is the same, e.g. where a known compound is found to have a previously unknown pharmacological activity at a receptor, such activity leading to two or three potential second medical uses. In this case there would be a good argument that the second medical use claims have unity.

### Unity between a product claim and a process claim

1–031

Where the claim set includes claims to a product and a process for making the product, the claims will necessarily have unity where the product is defined in exactly the same way in each claim — the product is the same special technical feature in each claim. The problems arise when the product is defined differently.

Consider the case where the product claim relates to compounds of formula X (or perhaps a single compound X), limited in relation to the client's broadest definition X' in view of the prior art, and the process claim is applicable to the broader range of compounds X'. If the process is an analogy process it must be limited to X to be patentable — no unity problem therefore exists. If, however, the process is also inventive in its own right by virtue of process step A, it can now be defined as a process for making compounds X'. The special technical feature of the product claim is X but the patentable feature of claim 2 is A (solves the different problem of providing a more efficient process). These will not usually be considered corresponding and the claims will lack unity.

For instance, in 2001 paper B, discussed above, there was actually a third invention! The application also disclosed a process for making the compounds which was novel and inventive over the known prior art process (fewer by-products). The corresponding special technical feature here, the process conditions, was not a corresponding one in relation to the specific compound or the combination of compounds since a completely different problem was solved.

### Unity between a product claim and a use claim

1–032

Often, the use set out in the use claim will correspond to the technical effect underlying the patentability of the product claim. Where the definition of the product (X) is the same in both claims, there is no unity problem. If the definition of the product is limited by an accidental anticipation (relevant to novelty only) in the prior art then the use claim may have a broader definition of the product, again relating to compounds X'. In this case the special technical features of the two claims are different but corresponding since the structural features X and X' both give rise to the same inventive use, i.e. solve the same technical problem.

If, on the other hand, the product claim has been limited by prior art relevant to inventive step, and the use claim is based on a different technical effect to that underlying the patentability of the product then there may a problem. Say, for instance, that X is a selection invention based on the surprisingly high activity of a few compounds in relation to a use known in the prior art and the client has found that the broader class X' also has a new inventive use. The claims will now lack unity since they solve different technical problems.

In general, where the product in the product claim is defined differently from the product in the use claim, the two will be held to have unity when the product is especially adapted for the use in question, as with the compound example above. Such 'special adaptation' generally means that the technical effect underlying the patentability of the product claim is demonstrated when the product is used in the claimed use.

For instance, in 2004 paper B, a certain composition was known for its preventative use in making reinforced concrete more corrosion-resistant. The application also disclosed a new inventive use of the known composition in restoring reinforced concrete structures by application to the surface of a corroded structure — this led to a patentable method of use claim. When a silane was added to the composition, experimental results showed that it was especially effective in the patentable use, giving a patentable composition claim. The claims had unity since the different special technical features (application to the exterior of a corroded structure and the addition of the silane) were corresponding in the sense that the new composition was adapted for use in the method, the technical effect supporting its patentability being demonstrated by its use in the method itself.

In 1997 paper B, the client described emulsifiers with four different uses: (1) in oil recovery, (2) in the production of polymer fibres, (3) as an additive in concrete and (4) in a polymerisation process. The emulsifiers were known in general terms in the prior art which also disclosed two of the uses (in the production of polymer fibres and as an additive in concrete). A selection of the emulsifiers could be claimed as a product-by-process claim, since they showed especially good stability. The two novel uses could also be claimed in relation to all the emulsifiers. These two claims lack unity since the corresponding special technical features (selected structures vs novel uses) solve different problems.

**1–033**  *Unity between a process claim and a use claim*

If there is no patentable product claim and the invention relates, for instance, to a new, inventive process for making compounds X and a new inventive use of compounds X then the process and use claims will lack unity since special technical features (process feature vs new use) are not solving the same overall problem.

An example of this may be seen in 2002 paper A where the client described a genus of compounds, an analogy process for making them, an inventive process for making them and their use as herbicides. The prior art, however, described the same compounds (except for one novel example) and their use as preservatives. The inventive process for making the compounds could still be claimed, as well as the use of the compounds as herbicides, but these two claims do not have unity.

**1–034**  *Further examples*

For further examples of unified and non-unified inventions, see Annex B of the Administrative Instructions under the Patent Cooperation Treaty (available from the WIPO website). The examples given are broadly in line with EPO practice and deal with other issues such as unity between intermediates and final products (not discussed here since it is not a common scenario in the EQE). The Guidelines also provide further guidance (see C/III/7).

## 7. Worked example using EQE 2002 Paper A

**1–035**  *Understanding and annotating the paper*

The following pages indicate how the 2002 A paper could be marked up on a first reading, using method (2), as described above.

Please note that some of the annotations are there merely to bring out the relevance of certain passages and are therefore not all indicative of the kind of annotation you would make when doing the exam!

# Paper A (Chemistry)

## CLIENT'S LETTER

From: Herb E. Syde & Co.                                    To: Candy Date

Dear Candy,

I know you are very busy. Nevertheless I would be grateful to you if you could work out a draft for a patent application on one of my inventions. This is very urgent, so please deal with this as soon as you can.

*Proceed to draft the application without further consultation.*

Our lab is currently working on the synthesis and use of 1,3-dioxane derivatives. 1,3-dioxane has a six-membered ring with oxygen atoms in positions 1 and 3. Its formula is depicted below.

$$\begin{array}{c} \mathbf{3} \quad \mathbf{4} \\ O - CH_2 \\ \mathbf{2}\ H_2C \qquad CH_2\ \mathbf{5} \\ O - CH_2 \\ \mathbf{1} \quad \mathbf{6} \end{array} \qquad (1)$$

where the numbers of the positions of the carbon and oxygen atoms are indicated in **bold** type.

*Background technical information to help non-specialists.*

1,3-Dioxane and many of its derivatives are known. For your convenience I enclose Document A which has been published recently.

*Scope of compound claim will be limited.*

The novel compounds synthesized in our lab are those of formula **(2)**:

$$\begin{array}{c} O - CH_2 \\ R^1 - CH \qquad CH - O - CH_2 - R^2 \\ O - CH_2 \end{array} \qquad (2)$$

where
**R¹**, i.e. the substituent in the 2-position on the ring, means alkyl, haloalkyl, alkoxyalkyl, aryl, heteroaryl or substituted aryl;
the group of the formula **-O-CH₂-R²** is situated at the 5-position;
and the radical **R²** is a phenyl radical which is optionally substituted with up to three radicals **X** selected form halogen, -CN, -CF₃, $C_1$-$C_4$-alkyl and $C_1$-$C_4$ alkoxy.

*Broadest possible scope of compound claim.*

Preferred compounds of formula **(2)** are those where **R¹** is phenyl, furyl or an alkyl or haloalkyl radical having from 1 to 4 carbon atoms.

**R²** is preferably phenyl, optionally substituted with a radical **X** in the 2-position (i.e. ortho). **R²** is more preferably phenyl, 2-chlorophenyl, 2-fluorophenyl or 2-methylphenyl.

*Possible dependent claims or main claim if broadest scope not patentable.*

You will have noted that the radicals **R¹** and **-O-CH₂-R²** in formula **(2)** are different. As a consequence of this, the compounds of formula **(2)** exist in two stereoisomeric forms.

In one isomer, the radicals **R¹** and **-O-CH₂-R²** are in a *cis* relationship, i.e. both radicals are above, or both radicals are below the 1,3-dioxane ring.

*Two different groups of compounds are encompassed by broad product claim with different properties and therefore potentially different patentability*

In the other isomer, the radicals **R¹** and **-O-CH₂-R²** are in a *trans* relationship, i.e. one of the radicals is above and the other below the 1,3-dioxane ring.

In the following, I will refer to these stereoisomers as the *cis* and the *trans* isomers. These somers can be easily separated and isolated since they have different physical properties, e.g. different melting and boiling points.

> Technical effect giving rise to inventive step. Will lead to use claims. Trans isomers are not inventive.

As you will recall, one of our major fields of interest is chemicals for use in agriculture. The *cis* isomers of formula (2) proved to be quite effective as herbicides. Herbicides are weed killers, i.e. compounds that control undesired plant growth. Said *cis* isomers are effective as herbicides when applied before the emergence of the weeds (i.e. as pre-emergence herbicides) or after the emergence of the weeds (i.e. as post-emergence herbicides). The *trans* isomers show no or only a negligible herbicidal effect.

The compounds of formula (2) may be prepared by

(1) first reacting an aldehyde of formula (3)

$R^1$-CHO          (3),

> Basis for process claim (could be analogy process or inventive in its own right).

with **glycerol** and then

(2) reacting the product of step (1) with a compound of the formula

$R^2$-CH$_2$-Y          (4),

Where $R^2$ has the same meaning as given above (see under formula (2)) and Y means a halogen atom.

> Claim to intermediate is not novel.

The products of step (1) are known from GB-A-1-001 001.

> Potential inventive step for process claim and potential further process.

As is evident, the aldehyde of formula (3) could also be reacted with a reaction product of glycerol with the compound of formula (4). However, such a process yields products of formula (2) where more than 50% is in the form of the *trans* isomer.

> General enablement.

This invention provides a new class of herbicidal materials, having both pre-emergence and post-emergence activity. The materials are highly suitable for the control and elimination of grassy plants, particularly annual grasses, in the presence of broad-leaved crops, such as cotton, sugar beets, peanuts, soya beans, snap beans, lima beans or tomatoes.

> Preferred features with motivation.

For use as a herbicide it is most economical to use materials of high *cis* content made by a process which reduces, or avoids, the formation of the *trans* isomer. The higher the *cis* content the greater is the herbicidal effect of the given mixture of *cis* and *trans* isomers. In the most preferred forms of the invention, the *cis* compound is present in an amount at least equal to that of the corresponding *trans* compound, preferably the *cis:trans* ratio is more than 1.5:1, more preferably over 2:1 and still more preferably at least 3:1.

> Further invention — basis for combination claims.

The products of formula (2) may be combined with other herbicides. The research department informed me yesterday that combinations of the *cis* isomers of formula (2) with the known herbicides bromoxynil and/or ioxynil show a synergetic effect against weeds whilst having a good crop tolerance. I will send you a summary of these experiments as soon as possible.

The preparation, properties, and herbicidal activities of representative compounds of this invention are illustrated further in the following Examples. Temperatures indicated are in °C, pressures in mm Hg unless indicated otherwise.

## Example 1

**5-benzyloxy-2-methyl-1,3-dioxane ($R^1$=methyl; $R^2$=phenyl in formula (2))**

> Specific example of the invention

A. Preparation of 5-hydroxy-2-methyl-1,3-dioxane
In a 500-ml three-necked flask equipped with a stirrer, a condenser and a Dean-Stark trap (for azeotropic removal of water), 44 g of **acetaldehyde** was slowly added to a

stirred mixture of 92 g of **glycerol** and 6 drops of concentrated sulphuric acid. The reaction mixture was heated at 100 °C for 3 hours, then cooled to room temperature and neutralised with potassium carbonate. The mixture was washed with 100 ml of petroleum ether and then distilled at 58–60 °C/100 Pa to give 68.4 g of **5-hydroxy-2-methyl-1, 3-dioxane**. The infrared spectrum of the product was consistent with the assigned structure.

**B.** Preparation of 5-benzyloxy-2-methyl-1,3-dioxane
1.6 g of sodium hydride in portions was added to a mixture of 4.8 g of **5-hydroxy-2-methyl-1,3-dioxane** and 100 ml of benzene.

This mixture was stirred at room temperature for 9 hours, after which 5.1 g of **benzyl chloride** ($C_6H_5$-$CH_2$-Cl, i.e. $R^2$=phenyl and Y=Cl in formula (**4**)) was added in portions over a 15 minute period. The reaction mixture was heated, with stirring, at 80 °C for 24 hours. The reaction mixture was washed with two 100-ml portions of water, and the organic layer was dried over magnesium sulphate. Solvent was removed under reduced pressure to give 7.5 g of oil, which was distilled to give 4.1 g of 5-benzyloxy-2-methyl-1,3-dioxane, boiling point: 111–112 °C/50 Pa. The IR and NMR spectra were consistent with the assigned structure.

Analysis: Calculated for $C_{12}H_{16}O_3$: C 69.21; H 7.69;
Found: C 68.97; H 7.73.

## Examples 2 to 6

*Further specific examples of the invention.*

In a completely analogous manner the following compounds were prepared:

(2) **5-benzyloxy-2-phenyl-1,3-dioxane** ($R^1$=phenyl; $R^2$ = phenyl):

melting point: 73–75 °C;

Analysis: Calculated for $C_{17}H_{18}O_3$: C 75.56; H 6.67;
Found: C 75.48; H 6.65.

NMR studies revealed the product to be 80–90% *cis* 5-benzyloxy-2-phenyl-1,3 dioxane.

*Data supporting inventive step of process claim.*

(3) **5-benzyloxy-2-(2-furly)-1,3-dioxane** ($R^1$=2-furyl; $R^2$=phenyl):

melting point: 50–52 °C;

Analysis: Calculated for $C_{15}H_{16}O_4$: C 69.21; H 6.20;
Found: C 69.44; H 6.00.

The NMR spectrum of the product indicated it to be a mixture of *cis* and *trans* isomers in a ratio of about 70:30. Separation of the isomers by fractional crystallization from hexane and benzene resulted in isolation of the pure *cis* compound, melting point 63–64 °C.

*Data supporting inventive step of process claim.*

(4) **5-benzyloxy-2-chloromethyl-1,3-dioxane** ($R^1$=chloromethyl; $R^2$=phenyl):

boiling point: 100–105 °C/0.025 mm Hg;

The NMR spectrum was consistent with the assigned structure and showed the *cis* isomer content to be 52%, the remainder being the *trans* isomer.

Analysis: Calculated for $C_{12}H_{16}ClO_3$: C 59.38; H 6.23;
Found: C 59.56; H 6.49.

The preparation was repeated and the isometric mixture separated by column chromatography. The pure *cis* isomer was a solid, melting point 38–39 °C, and the *trans* isomer was a liquid, $n_D^{22}$: 1.5200.

(5) **5-(2-methylbenzyloxy)2-chloromethyl-1,3-dioxane**

($R^1$=chloromethyl; $R^2$=2-methyl-phenyl):

The product was recrystallized twice from benzene and petroleum either yielding 2.2 g of 5-(2-methylbenzyloxy)-2-chloromethyl-1,3-dioxane, melting point: 62–63 °C, analysing 98% *cis* isomer by NMR spectroscopy.

Analysis:  Calculated for $C_{13}H_{17}ClO_3$:  C 60.82; H 6.82;
           Found:                              C 60.84; H 6.66.

(6) **5-(2-fluorobenzyloxy)-2-(methoxymethyl)-1,3 dioxane**

($R^1$=methoxymethyl; $R^2$=2-fluoro-phenyl):

The isomers were separated by passage through a silica gel column using mixtures of petroleum ether and ethyl acetate as eluting solvents.

The first fractions were combined and concentrated to give 3.0 g of *trans*-5-(2-fluoro-benzyloxy)-2-methoxymethyl)-1,3-dioxane, boiling point 151–152 °C/1.5 mm Hg. The later fractions were combined and concentrated to give 5.2 g of *cis*-5-(2-fluoro-benzyloxy)-2-(methoxymethyl)-1,3-dioxane, melting point: 31–32 °C. The IR and NMR spectra of the two products were consistent with the assigned structures.

Analysis:  Calculated for $C_{13}H_{17}FO_4$:  C 62.21; H 7.09;
           Found (*trans*-isomer):            C 62.44; H 6.85;
           Found (*cis*-isomer):              C 62.25; H 6.85.

# Example 7

**Pre-emergence and Post-emergence Herbicidal Activity**
The pre- and post-emergence herbicidal activity of substituted 5-benzyloxy-1,3-dioxanes was tested in the following manner:

Lima beans, corn, lettuce, cotton, crabgrass and barnyard grass were planted side by side in rows. The material to be tested was dissolved in an acetone-water mixture and was sprayed on the soil at a concentration of 4.48 or 6.72 kilograms per hectare for pre-emergence screening. In post-emergence screening, plants were sprayed with the same acetone-water mixture at a concentration of 4.48 or 6.72 kilograms of material to be tested per hectare approximately 2 weeks after planting. Two weeks after application, the effectiveness of the material was evaluated for both pre- and post-emergence tests. Untreated plants were maintained for comparison in both procedures. Pre-emergence results are presented in Table I and results of post-emergence tests are presented in Table II. Where no results are given in Tables I and II, measurements were not taken of the herbicidal activity.

For herbicidal applications, the active 1,3-dioxanes of formula (**2**) are formulated by admixture, with the adjuvants and carriers, normally employed for agricultural applications. Thus, these active herbicidal compounds may be formulated as granules, as powders, as emulsifiable concentrates, as solutions, or as any of several other known types of formulations, depending on the desired mode of application. Preferred formulations for both pre- and post-emergence herbicidal application are powders, emulsifiable concentrates, and granules. These formulations may contain as little as 0.5% to as much as 95% by weight of active ingredient.

## TABLE I

Pre-emergence herbicidal activity (in **percent kill at test concentration**) of substituted 1,3-dioxanes of formula **(2)**

| Compound of example | Test concentration kg/hectare | Test plant species ||||||  |
|---|---|---|---|---|---|---|---|---|
| | | crops |||| weeds ||  |
| | | A | B | C | D | E | F |  |
| | | per cent of killed plants at the test concentration ||||||  |
| 1 | 6.72* | 0 | 0 |   | 0 | 100 | 100 |  |
| 2 | 4.48 | 75 | 100 | 0 |   | 100 |   | *cis* isomer |
| 2 | 4.48 | 0 | 0 | 0 |   | 10 |   | *trans* isomer |
| 3 | 4.48 |   | 35 |   | 0 | 100 | 90 | *cis* isomer |
| 4 | 4.48 |   | 50 |   | 0 | 100 | 95 | *cis* isomer |
| 5 | 4.48* | 0 | 100 | 0 |   | 100 |   |  |

Test plants are:
- A - Lima beans
- B - Corn
- C - Lettuce
- D - Cotton
- E - Crabgrass
- F - Barnyard grass

\* Isomer mixture as obtained in the example; concentration is that of *cis* content applied.

## TABLE II

Post-emergence herbicidal activity of substituted 1,3-dioxanes of formula **(2)**

| Compound of example | Test concentration* kg/hectare | Test plant species (Percent kill at test concentration) ||||
|---|---|---|---|---|---|
| | | crops || weeds ||
| | | Corn | Cotton | Crabgrass | Barnyard grass |
| 1 | 4.48 | 100 | 0 | 100 | 100 |
| 2 | 4.48 | 0 |   | 20 | 80 |
| 3 | 4.48 | 100 | 0 | 100 | 100 |
| 4 | 6.72** |   | 0 | 60 | 20 |
| 5 | 6.72 | 0 |   | 80 | 70 |

\* Concentration is of the isomeric mixture as produced.
\*\* Concentration is that of *cis* content applied.

## 28  Complete Guide to Passing the EQE

*Novelty only — different activity associated with compounds.*

## DOCUMENT A

The present application relates to novel compounds of formula **(A)**:

$$R^1-CH\underset{O-CH_2}{\overset{O-CH_2}{\diagup\diagdown}}CH-O-CH_2-R^2 \quad (A)$$

where

*Relevant to novelty of compound claims.*

$R^1$, i.e. the substituent in 2-position on the ring, means alkyl, haloalkyl, alkoxyalkyl, heteroaryl or optionally substituted aryl;
the group of the formula **-O-CH$_2$-R$^2$** is situated at the 5-position;
the radical $R^2$ is a monovalent aromatic phenyl, furyl or thienyl radical which is optionally substituted with up to three radicals **X** selected from halogen, -CN, -CF$_3$, C$_1$-C$_4$-alkyl and C$_1$-C$_4$-alkoxy.

Preferred compounds of formula **(A)** are those where $R^1$ is phenyl, furyl or an alkyl or haloalkyl radical having from 1 to 4 carbon atoms.

$R^2$ preferably is phenyl, optionally substituted with a radical **X** in 2-position (i.e. ortho), especially phenyl, 2-chlorophenyl, 2-fluorophenyl or 2-methylphenyl.

*No relevance to inventive step.*

The compounds of formula **(A)** are useful as preservatives for aqueous compositions which normally spoil due to the action of bacteria and fungi. They are effective at low concentrations and non-toxic in the amounts employed.

*Cannot establish novelty by restricting to cis isomers.*

The compounds of formula **(A)** exist in two stereoisomeric forms. In one isomer, the radicals $R^1$ and **-O-CH$_2$-R$^2$** are in a *cis* relationship, in the other, they are in a *trans* relationship.

It is not worthwhile to separate or isolate these isomers as both are equally suitable for the given purpose.

*Irrelevant*

It is well known that many aqueous compositions are subject to a pronounced tendency to decompose and spoil through the action of bacteria and fungi. Examples of such compositions include emulsions such as cosmetic compositions, emulsion paints and cutting oils or products such as kerosene and fuel oil which acquire water due to condensation.

The products of the present invention may be produced by reacting an aldehyde of the formula **(B)**

$$R^1-CHO \quad (B)$$

with a compound of formula **(C)**

*Relevant to novelty of process claim.*

$$\underset{HO-CH_2}{\overset{HO-CH_2}{\diagdown\diagup}}CH-O-CH_2-R^2 \quad (C)$$

under standard condensation conditions.

Compounds **(C)** are obtained by the reaction of **glycerol** with a compound of formula **(D)**

$$R^2\text{-}CH_2\text{-}Y \qquad (D),$$

where **R²** has the same meaning as given above (see formula **(A)**) and **Y** means a halogen atom.

The invention is illustrated by the following examples:

## Example 1

(1) **5-benzyloxy-2-phenyl-1,3-dioxane**  (**R¹**=phenyl; **R²**=phenyl in formula **(A)**).

Relevant to novelty of compound claims.

A mixture of 5.0 g of 2-benzyloxy-1,3-propanediol (prepared by reacting glycerol with benzyl chloride), 3.3 g of benzaldehyde and 0.3 g of p-toluene-sulfonic acid in a three-necked, round-bottomed flask equipped with a stirrer, a thermometer and a condenser was heated in an oil bath until it reached 130 °C. The reaction mixture was cooled to room temperature and dissolved in ether. The ether solution was washed with 10% sodium-carbonate and then with water. After drying over anhydrous sodium sulphate, the ether was removed under reduced pressure. Distillation of the crude oil gave 3.3 g of 5-benzyloxy-2-phenyl-1,3 dioxane.

Analysis:  Calculated for $C_{17}H_{18}O_3$:  C 75.56; H 6.67;
Found:  C 75.49; H 6.64.

## Examples 2 to 5

Under analogous conditions the following compounds were prepared:

Relevant novelty of compound claims.

(2) **5-benzyloxy-2-(2-furyl)-1,3-dioxane**   (**R¹**=2-furyl; **R²**=phenyl):

Analysis:

Calculated for $C_{15}H_{16}O_4$:   C 69.21; H 6.20;
Found:   C 69.44; H 6.00.

(3) **5-benzyloxy-2-chloromethyl-1,3-dioxane**   (**R¹**=chloromethyl; **R²**=phenyl):

Analysis:

Calculated for $C_{12}H_{15}ClO_3$:   C 59.38; H 6.23;
Found:   C 59.56; H 6.49.

(4) **2-chloromethyl-5-(2-methylbenzyloxy)-1,3-dioxane**

(**R¹**=chloromethyl; **R²**=2-methyl-phenyl):

Analysis:

Calculated for $C_{13}H_{17}ClO_3$:   C 60.82; H 6.82;
Found:   C 60.84; H 6.66.

(5) **5-(2-fluorobenzyloxy)-2-(methoxymethyl)-1,3-dioxane**

(**R¹**=methoxymethyl; **R²**=2-fluoro-phenyl):

Analysis:

Calculated for $C_{13}H_{17}FO_4$:   C 62.21; H 7.09;
Found:   C 62.34; H 6.85.

## Example 6

To illustrate the effectiveness of **5-benzyloxy-2-phenyl-1,3-dioxane** as a preservative in a standard emulsion paint, formulations containing 0.1% **5-benzyloxy-2-phenyl-1,**

Irrelevant

**3-dioxane** (I) and 0.1% methyl p-hydroxybenzoate (II) were compared with paints containing no added preservative (III). Methyl p-hydroxybenzoate is a standard preservative.

The method employed to test the preserving properties of compositions under consideration is as follows:

Fifty gram samples were inoculated with 0.05 ml of a 24 hour broth culture of *Pseudomonas aeruginosa* which results in the samples having an initial bacterial count of approximately one million per gram. The inoculated samples were then held at 30 °C and bacterial counts made at 1, 24 and 72 hours after the inoculations.

The results are shown in the following table:

| Emulsion paint no. | Bacterial count after | | |
|---|---|---|---|
| | 1 h | 24 h | 72 h |
| I | $74 \times 10^4$ | $< 100$ | $< 100$ |
| II* | $100 \times 10^4$ | $240 \times 10^5$ | $520 \times 10^3$ |
| III* | $380 \times 10^4$ | $> 300 \times 10^5$ | $> 300 \times 10^5$ |

\* Comparative.

*Establishing novel subject matter* 1–036

The following pages indicate how the client's invention can be divided into novel features and features found in the prior art. A simple box has been used in the former case and a shaded box in the latter case. New comments have been added in bold.

*32    Complete Guide to Passing the EQE*

## CLIENT'S LETTER

From: Herb E. Syde & Co.                                        To: Candy Date

Dear Candy,

*Proceed to draft the application without further consulation.*

I know you are very busy. Nevertheless I would be grateful to you if you could work out a draft for a patent application on one of my inventions. This is very urgent, so please deal with this as soon as you can.

*Background technical information to help non-specialists.*

Our lab is currently working on the synthesis and use of 1,3-dioxane derivatives. 1,3-dioxane has a six-membered ring with oxygen atoms in positions 1 and 3. Its formula is depicted below.

$$\begin{array}{c} \phantom{2}\,\,\mathbf{3}\quad\mathbf{4}\\ \phantom{2}\,\,O-CH_2\\ \mathbf{2}\,\,H_2C\diagdown\quad\diagup CH_2\,\,\mathbf{5}\\ \phantom{2}\,\,O-CH_2\\ \phantom{2}\,\,\mathbf{1}\quad\mathbf{6} \end{array} \qquad (1)$$

where the numbers of the positions of the carbon and oxygen atoms are indicated in **bold** type.

*Scope of compound claim will be limited.*

1,3-dioxane and many of its derivatives are known. For your convenience I enclose Document A which has been published recently.

*No novel compounds here — disclosed in Document A.*

The novel compounds synthesized in our lab are those of formula **(2)**:

$$\begin{array}{c} O-CH_2\\ R^1-CH\diagdown\quad\diagup CH-O-CH_2-R^2\\ O-CH_2 \end{array} \qquad (2)$$

where
$R^1$, i.e. the substituent in the 2-position on the ring, means alkyl, haloalkyl, alkoxyalkyl, aryl, heteroaryl or substituted aryl;
the group of the formula **-O-CH$_2$-R$^2$** is situated at the 5-position;
and the radical $R^2$ is a phenyl radical which is optionally substituted with up to three radicals **X** selected from halogen, -CN, -CF$_3$, C$_1$-C$_4$-alkyl and C$_1$-C$_4$-alkoxy.

*Broadest possible scope of compound claim.*

*Possible dependent claims or main claim if broadest formulation not patentable.*

Preferred components of formula **(2)** are those where
$R^1$ is phenyl, furyl or an alkyl or haloalkyl radical having from 1 to 4 carbon atoms.

$R^2$ is preferably phenyl, optionally substituted with a radical **X** in the 2-position (i.e. ortho). $R^2$ is more preferably phenyl, 2-chlorophenyl, 2-fluorophenyl or 2-methylphenyl.

You will have noted that the radicals $R^1$ and -O-CH$_2$-R$^2$ in formula **(2)** are different. As a consequence of this, the compounds of formula **(2)** exist in two stereoisomeric forms.

*Two different groups of compounds are encompassed by broad product claim with different properties and therefore potentially different patentability*

In one isomer, the radicals $R^1$ and **-O-CH$_2$-R$^2$** are in a *cis* relationship, i.e. both radicals are above, or both radicals are below the 1,3-dioxane ring.

In the other isomer, the radicals $R^1$ and **-O-CH$_2$-R$^2$** are in a *trans* relationship, i.e. one of the radicals is above and the other below the 1,3-dioxane ring.

*Paper A (Chemistry)* 33

| | |
|---|---|
| In the following, I will refer to these stereoisomers as the *cis* and the *trans* isomers. These isomers can be easily separated and isolated since they have different physical properties, e.g. different melting and boiling points. | Known from Document A. |
| As you will recall, one of our major fields of interest is chemicals for use in agriculture. The *cis* isomers of formula (2) proved to be quite effective as herbicides. Herbicides are weed killers, i.e. compounds that control undesired plant growth. Said *cis* isomers are effective as herbicides when applied before the emergence of the weeds (i.e. as pre-emergence herbicides) or after the emergence of the weeds (i.e. as post-emergence herbicides). The *trans* isomers show no or only a negligible herbicidal effect. | Not known from Document A — new, inventive use. Technical effect giving rise to inventive step. Will lead to use claims. Trans isomers are not inventive. |
| The compounds of formula (2) may be prepared by<br>(1) first reacting an aldehyde of formula (3)<br>$$R^1\text{-CHO} \qquad (3),$$<br>with **glycerol** and then<br>(2) reacting the product of step (1) with a compound of the formula<br>$$R^2\text{-CH}_2\text{-Y} \qquad (4),$$<br>where $R^2$ has the same meaning as given above (see under formula (2)) and Y means a halogen atom. | Process novel over Document A since steps reversed.<br><br>Basis for process claim (could be analogy process or inventive in its own right). |
| The products of step (1) are known from GB-A-1-001 001. | Claim to intermediate is not novel. |
| As is evident, the aldehyde of formula (3) could also be reacted with a reaction product of glycerol with the compound of formula (4). However, such a process yields products of formula (2) where more than 50% is in the form of the *trans* isomer. | Potential inventive step for process claim and potential further process claim. |
| This invention provides a new class of herbicidal materials, having both pre-emergence and post-emergence activity. The materials are highly suitable for the control and elimination of grassy plants, particularly annual grasses, in the presence of broad-leaved crops, such as cotton, sugar beets, peanuts, soya beans, snap beans, lima beans or tomatoes. | Process known from Document A therefore could only use as an analogy process.<br><br>General enablement. |
| For use as a herbicide it is most economical to use materials of high *cis* content made by a process which reduces, or avoids, the formation of the *trans* isomer. The higher the *cis* content the greater is the herbicidal effect of the given mixture of *cis* and *trans* isomers. In the most preferred forms of the invention, the *cis* compound is present in an amount at least equal to that of the corresponding *trans* compound, preferably the *cis:trans* ratio is more than 1.5:1, more preferably over 2:1 and still more preferably at least 3:1. | Advantages of cis isomer not known from Document A.<br><br>Preferred features with motivation |
| The products of formula (2) may be combined with other herbicides. The research department informed me yesterday that combinations of the *cis* isomers of formula (2) with the known herbicides bromoxynil and/or ioxynil show a synergetic effect against weeds whilst having a good crop tolerance. I will send you a summary of these experiments as soon as possible. | This combination not disclosed in Document A<br><br>Further invention- basis for combination claims. |

The preparation, properties, and herbicidal activities of representative compounds of this invention are illustrated further in the following Examples. Temperatures indicated are in °C, pressures in mm Hg unless indicated otherwise.

# Example 1

| | |
|---|---|
| **5-benzyloxy-2-methyl-1,3-dioxane** ($R^1$=methyl; $R^2$=phenyl in formula (2)) | Novel compound |

| | |
|---|---|
| Specific example of the invention | **A.** Preparation of 5-hydroxy-2-methyl-1,3-dioxane<br>In a 500-ml three-necked flask equipped with a stirrer, a condenser and a Dean-Stark trap (for azeotropic removal of water), 44 g of **acetaldehyde** was slowly added to a stirred mixture of 92 g of **glycerol** and 6 drops of concentrated sulphuric acid. The reaction mixture was heated at 100 °C for 3 hours, then cooled to room temperature and neutralised with potassium carbonate. The mixture was washed with 100 ml of petroleum ether and then distilled at 58–60 °C/100 Pa to give 68.4 g of **5-hydroxy-2-methyl-1,3-dioxane**. The infrared spectrum of the product was consistent with the assigned structure. |
| Novel process. | |
| Novel process. | **B.** Preparation of 5-benzyloxy-2-methyl-1,3-dioxane<br>1.6 g of sodium hydride in portions was added to a mixture of 4.8 g of **5-hydroxy-2-methyl-1,3-dioxane** and 100 ml of benzene.<br><br>This mixture was stirred at room temperature for 9 hours, after which 5.1 g of **benzyl chloride** ($C_6H_5$-$CH_2$-Cl, i.e. $R^2$=phenyl and Y=Cl in formula (**4**)) was added in portions over a 15 minute period. The reaction mixture was heated, with stirring, at 80 °C for 24 hours. The reaction mixture was washed with two 100-ml portions of water, and the organic layer was dried over magnesium sulphate. Solvent was removed under reduced pressure to give 7.5 g of oil, which was distilled to give 4.1 g of 5-benzyloxy-2-methyl-1,3-dioxane, boiling point: 111–112 °C/50 Pa. The IR and NMR spectra were consistent with the assigned structure.<br><br>Analysis:   Calculated for $C_{12}H_{16}O_3$:   C 69.21; H 7.69;<br>               Found:                               C 68.97; H 7.73. |

## Examples 2 to 6

In a completely analogous manner the following compounds were prepared:

| | |
|---|---|
| Further specific examples of the invention. | (2) **5-benzyloxy-2-phenyl-1,3-dioxane**     ($R^1$=phenyl; $R^2$=phenyl):<br>melting point: 73–75 °C; |
| Compounds known from Document A. | Analysis:   Calculated for $C_{17}H_{18}O_3$:   C 75.56; H 6.67;<br>               Found:                               C 75.48; H 6.65. |
| Data supporting inventive step of process claim. | NMR studies revealed the product to be 80–90% *cis*-5-benzyloxy-2-phenyl-1,3 dioxane. |
| | (3) **5-benzyloxy-2-(2-furyl)-1,3-dioxane**     ($R^1$=2-furyl; $R^2$=phenyl):<br>melting point: 50–52 °C;<br><br>Analysis:   Calculated for $C_{15}H_{16}O_4$:   C 69.21; H 6.20;<br>               Found:                               C 69.44; H 6.00. |
| Data supporting inventive step of process claim. | The NMR spectrum of the product indicated it to be a mixture of *cis* and *trans* isomers in a ratio of about 70:30. Separation of the isomers by fractional crystallization from hexane and benzene resulted in isolation of the pure *cis* compound, melting point 63–64 °C. |
| | (4) **5-benzyloxy-2-chloromethyl-1,3-dioxane**     ($R^1$=chloromethyl; $R^2$=phenyl):<br>boiling point: 100–105 °C/0.025 mm Hg;<br><br>The NMR spectrum was consistent with the assigned structure and showed the *cis* isomer content to be 52%, the remainder being the *trans* isomer.<br><br>Analysis:   Calculated for $C_{12}H_{16}ClO_3$:   C 59.38; H 6.23;<br>               Found:                                 C 59.56; H 6.49. |

The preparation was repeated and the isomeric mixture separated by column chromatography. The pure *cis* isomer was a solid, melting point 38–39 °C, and the *trans* isomer was a liquid, $n_D^{22}$: 1.5200.

(5) **5-(2-methylbenzyloxy)-2-chloromethyl-1,3-dioxane**

($R^1$=chloromethyl; $R^2$=2-methyl-phenyl):

The product was recrystallized twice from benzene and petroleum either yielding 2.2 g of 5-(2-methylbenzyloxy)-2-chloromethyl-1,3-dioxane, melting point: 62–63 °C, analyzing 98% *cis*, isomer by NMR spectroscopy.

Analysis: Calculated for $C_{13}H_{17}ClO_3$: C 60.82; H 6.82;
Found: C 60.84; H 6.66.

(6) **5-(2-fluorobenzyloxy)-2-(methoxymethyl)-1,3 dioxane**

($R^1$=methoxymethyl; $R^2$=2-fluoro-phenyl):

The isomers were separated by passage through a silica gel column using mixtures of petroleum ether and ethyl acetate as eluting solvents.

The first fractions were combined and concentrated go give 3.0 g of *trans*-5-(2-fluoro-benzyloxy)-2-methoxymethyl-1,3-dioxane, boiling point 151–152 °C/1.5 mm Hg. The later fractions were combined and concentrated to give 5.2 g of *cis*-5-(2-fluoro-benzyloxy)-2-(methoxymethyl)-1,3-dioxane, melting point: 31–32 °C. The IR and NMR spectra of the two products were consistent with the assigned structures.

Analysis: Calculated for $C_{13}H_{17}FO_4$: C 62.21; H 7.09;
Found (*trans*-isomer): C 62.44; H 6.85;
Found (*cis*-isomer): C62.25; H 6.85.

*Compounds disclosed in Document A.*

*Data supporting inventive step of process claim.*

## Example 7

**Pre-emergence and Post-emergence Herbicidal Activity**
The pre- and post-emergence herbicidal activity of substituted 5-benzyloxy-1,3-dioxanes was tested in the following manner:

Lima beans, corn, lettuce, cotton, crabgrass and barnyard grass were planted side by side in rows. The material to be tested was dissolved in an acetone-water mixture and was sprayed on the soil at a concentration of 4.48 or 6.72 kilograms per hectare for pre-emergence screening. In post-emergence screening, plants were sprayed with the same acetone-water mixture at a concentration of 4.48 or 6.72 kilograms of material to be tested per hectare approximately 2 weeks after planting. Two weeks after application, the effectiveness of the material was evaluated for both pre- and post-emergence tests. Untreated plants were maintained for comparison in both procedures. Pre-emergence results are presented in Table I and results of post-emergence tests are presented in Table II. Where no results are given in Tables I and II, measurements were not taken of the herbicidal activity.

For herbicidal applications, the active 1,3-dioxanes of formula (**2**) are formulated by admixture, with the adjuvants and carriers, normally employed for agricultural applications. Thus, these active herbicidal compounds may be formulated as granules, as powders, as emulsifiable concentrates, as solutions, or as any of several other known types of formulations, depending on the desired mode of application. Preferred formulations for both pre- and post-emergence herbicidal application are powders, emulsifiable concentrates, and granules. These formulations may contain as little as 0.5% to as much as 95% by weight of active ingredient.

*General enablement and proof that technical effect exists.*

*Agricultural compositions are not described in the prior art though some accidental anticipation may need to be considered.*

## TABLE I

Pre-emergence herbicidal activity (in **percent kill at test concentration**) of substituted 1,3-dioxanes of formula **(2)**

| Compound of example | Test concentration kg/hectare | Test plant species | | | | | | |
|---|---|---|---|---|---|---|---|---|
| | | **crops** | | | | **weeds** | | |
| | | A | B | C | D | E | F | |
| | | percent of killed plants at the test concentration | | | | | | |
| 1 | 6.72* | 0 | 0 |  | 0 | 100 | 100 | |
| 2 | 4.48 | 75 | 100 | 0 |  | 100 |  | *cis* isomer |
| 2 | 4.48 | 0 | 0 | 0 |  | 10 |  | *trans* isomer |
| 3 | 4.48 |  | 35 |  | 0 | 100 | 90 | *cis* isomer |
| 4 | 4.48 |  | 50 |  | 0 | 100 | 95 | *cis* isomer |
| 5 | 4.48* | 0 | 100 | 0 |  | 100 |  | |

*Preferred feature with motivation (selectivity of Example 1).*

Test plants are:
- A - Lima beans
- B - Corn
- C - Lettuce
- D - Cotton
- E - Crabgrass
- F - Barnyard grass

\* Isomer mixture as obtained in the example; concentration is that of *cis* content applied.

## TABLE II

Post-emergence herbicidal activity of substituted 1,3-dioxanes of formula **(2)**

| Compound of example | Test concentration* kg/hectare | Test plant species (percent kill at test concentration) | | | |
|---|---|---|---|---|---|
| | | **crops** | | **weeds** | |
| | | Corn | Cotton | Crabgrass | Barnyard grass |
| 1 | 4.48 | 100 | 0 | 100 | 100 |
| 2 | 4.48 | 0 |  | 20 | 80 |
| 3 | 4.48 | 100 | 0 | 100 | 100 |
| 4 | 6.72** |  | 0 | 60 | 20 |
| 5 | 6.72 | 0 |  | 80 | 70 |

*Preferred features with motivation (Examples 1 and 3)*

\* Concentration is of the isomeric mixture as produced.
\*\* Concentration is that of *cis* content applied.

## Claiming the invention

The client's invention resides in the identification of compounds having herbicidal activity. Many possible categories of claims will therefore be possible in principle.

### Use claims

The client thinks he's invented the compounds described generically on 2002 Paper A, page 2 but these are already known *per se*, including the cis-and trans-isomers. These compounds may not therefore be claimed and a change of claim category is required to obtain a broad, novel claim.

In the prior art the compounds are only known to be preservatives, having an antibacterial and antifungal activity. Therefore, a second non-medical use claim to their herbicidal activity is possible.

The use claim is patentable since the herbicidal effect is a novel technical feature which was not predicable from the prior art.

It is arguable whether only the cis-isomers of the compounds should be claimed. Clearly, the herbicidal effect is an essential technical feature and only compounds possessing such activity should be claimed. However, some of the trans-isomers clearly show some effect, even if it is "negligible" (2002 Paper A, page 3, first paragraph) — see Table 1. For this reason, whichever choice is made, it warrants a note to the examiner so that it is clear you have considered the problem.

### Compound claims

Of the examples, only example 1 is not disclosed in the prior art. Example 1 may therefore be claimed.

The compound of example 1 is a novel selection since, whilst it falls within the general definition of the prior art, it is not specifically disclosed and is inventive by virtue of its herbicidal activity which is not predictable based on the prior art disclosure of antibacterial and antifungal activity.

### Composition claims

In the prior art, the only compositions described are aqueous compositions (2002 Paper A, page 1, line 23), cosmetic compositions, emulsion paints, cutting oils, kerosene and fuel oils (2002 Paper A, page 2, lines 6–8), and an ether solution (Example 1). No compositions specifically adapted for agricultural use are described though some of the above may be taken to be accidental anticipations and should be removed by disclaimer. The compounds can be defined broadly in this claim.

The composition claim is novel because no agricultural compositions are described in the prior art (and any accidental anticipations have been removed by disclaimer) and is inventive by virtue of the herbicidal effect of the compounds comprised in the composition which was not predictable from the prior art.

### Process claims

There are two processes described by the client on 2002 Paper A, page 3. In the first glycerol is reacted with aldehyde (3) and then alkylating agent (4) and in the second glycerol is reacted with alkylating agent (4) and then aldehyde (3). The first process is novel and the second is known from the prior art. Furthermore, there is information suggesting that the first process is inventive. Therefore, the first process may be claimed in its own right, as a way of making all the compounds described whilst the second process may only be claimed as an analogy process in respect of the one novel compound claimed.

The new process is novel since the order of the steps has been reversed with respect to the prior art process and inventive since it is selective for the more useful cis-isomers (see 2002 Paper A, page 3, paragraph 4 and Examples 2, 3 and 6).

The analogy process derives its novelty and inventive step from the fact that the product of the process is itself novel and inventive.

1–042 **Intermediate claims**

The intermediates of both the new process (see 2002 Paper A, page 3, third paragraph) and the analogy process are known so no intermediate claim is possible.

1–043 **Combination claims**

The combination of the compounds with bromoxynil and ioxynil is not described in the prior art. Such a combination may therefore be claimed without restricting the compound definition.

The combination is novel since it is not disclosed in the prior art and inventive by virtue of the herbicidal effect of the compounds which was not predictable from the prior art. In this case, the combination would have been inventive even if the herbicidal effect of the compounds was already known, by virtue of the synergistic effect of the combination.

1–044 **Unity**

There is a potential problem with unity in that the compounds themselves are known and as such the structure of the compounds can't serve as a special technical feature uniting the claims. For each class of claims, a different feature provides the novelty. It would be possible to argue that these different technical features are nevertheless "corresponding special technical features" linked as a common general inventive concept by the herbicidal activity of the compounds. This argument may fail in particular for the process claim which has a different inventive step. All this should be discussed in the note to the examiner. A sensible approach would be to suggest filing a separate application to the process claim.

1–045 **Claim order**

The claim order is not hugely important, but as noted above, it is usually easier to start with one of the claims where the compounds are defined most broadly. Here, the use claim would be a good choice.

1–046 **Dependent claims**

Dependent features that should be claimed include the preferred compounds as defined on 2002 Paper A, page 2, the preferred cis/trans ratios on 2002 Paper A, page 4 (unless only cis-isomers claimed) and the specific examples (particularly Examples 1 and 3 which look best from the data).

1–047 **Typical solution**

A typical claim set for the main application may therefore be:

(1) The use of a compound of the formula

$$R^1-CH \begin{matrix} O-CH_2 \\ \diagdown \diagup \\ \diagup \diagdown \\ O-CH_2 \end{matrix} CH-O-CH_2-R^2 \qquad (2)$$

wherein $R^1$ means alkyl, haloalkyl, alkoxyalkyl, aryl, heteroaryl or substituted aryl; $R^2$ is a phenyl radical which is optionally substituted with up to three radicals X selected from halogen, -CN, -CF$_3$, C$_1$–C$_4$-alkyl and C$_1$–C$_4$-alkoxy; and the R$^1$ and -O-CH$_2$-R$^2$ groups are in a cis relationship; as a herbicide.

(2) The use of claim 1 wherein R$^1$ is phenyl, furyl or an alkyl or haloalkyl radical having from 1 to 4 carbon atoms.

(3) The use of claim 1 or claim 2 wherein R$^2$ is phenyl, optionally substituted with a radical X at the 2-position.

(4) The use of claim 3 wherein R$^2$ is phenyl, 2-chlorophenyl, 2-fluorophenyl or 2-methylphenyl.

(5) The use of claim 1 wherein the compound is cis-5-benzyloxy-2-methyl-1,3-dioxane, cis-5-benzyloxy-2-phenyl-1,3-dioxane, cis-5-benzyloxy-2-(2-furyl)-1,3-dioxane, cis-5-benzyloxy-2-chloromethyl-1,3-dioxane, cis-5-(2-methylbenzyloxy)-2-chloromethyl-1,3-dioxane or cis-5-(2-fluorobenzyloxy)-2-(methoxymethyl)-1,3-dioxane, especially cis-5-benzyloxy-2-methyl-1,3-dioxane or cis-5-benzyloxy-2-(2-furyl)-1,3-dioxane.

(6) The compound cis-5-benzyloxy-2-methyl-1,3-dioxane.

(7) An agricultural composition comprising a compound of the formula (2), as defined in any one of claims 1 to 5 and an agriculturally acceptable adjuvant or carrier, excluding a composition consisting of a solution in water or ether.

(8) An agricultural composition comprising the compound of claim 6 and an agriculturally acceptable adjuvant or carrier.

(9) A process for preparing the compound of claim 6 comprising (a) first reacting a compound of the formula Ph-CH$_2$-Y with glycerol and then (b) reacting the product of step 1 with a compound of the formula CH$_3$CHO, wherein Y means a halogen atom.

(10) A combination of a compound of the formula (2), as defined in any one of claims 1 to 5, and bromoxynil or ioxynil.

A separate application would claim:

1. A process for preparing a compound of the formula (2), as defined in any one of claims 1 to 5 in the main claim set, comprising (1) first reacting an aldehyde of the formula R$^1$-CHO with glycerol and then (2) reacting the product of step 1 with a compound of the formula R$^2$-CH$_2$-Y, wherein R$^1$ and R$^2$ are as defined for the compound of the formula (2) and Y means a halogen atom.

*Drafting the introduction*

1–048

The following is an example of a suitable introduction drafted using the principles outlined above.

This invention relates to chemicals for use in agriculture. More specifically, it relates to the use of certain 1,3-dioxane derivatives as herbicides. The invention further relates to compositions and combinations comprising and to processes for making such compounds as well as to one novel compound itself.

Document A describes a class of 1,3-dioxane derivatives that are preservatives by virtue of their antibacterial and antifungal activity. A process for making the compounds is also disclosed which is selective for the trans-isomeric form.

The problem addressed by the present invention is the provision of new herbicidal compounds. It has been surprisingly found that certain of the compounds described in Document A, specifically compounds of the formula

$$R^1-CH\begin{smallmatrix}O-CH_2\\ \\O-CH_2\end{smallmatrix}CH-O-CH_2-R^2 \qquad(2)$$

wherein R¹ means alkyl, haloalkyl, alkoxyalkyl, aryl, heteroaryl or substituted aryl; R² is a phenyl radical which is optionally substituted with up to three radicals X selected from halogen, -CN, -CF₃, C₁-C₄-alkyl and C₁-C₄-alkoxy; and the R¹ and -O-CH₂-R² groups are in a cis relationship; have herbicidal activity.

Preferred compounds of the formula (2) are those where R¹ is phenyl, furyl or an alkyl or haloalkyl radical having from 1 to 4 carbon atoms.

R² is preferably phenyl, optionally substituted with a radical X at the 2-position. R² is more preferably phenyl, 2-chlorophenyl, 2-fluorophenyl or 2-methylphenyl.

These compounds are effective as herbicides when applied before the emergence of weeds (*i.e.* as pre-emergence herbicides) or after the emergence of weeds (*i.e.* as post-emergence herbicides). They are highly suitable for the control and elimination of grassy plants, particularly annual grasses, in the presence of broad-leaved crops such as cotton, sugar beets, peanuts, soya beans, snap beans, lima beans or tomatoes.

The compounds of the formula (2) may be prepared by (a) first reacting an aldehyde of the formula R¹-CHO (3) with glycerol and then (b) reacting the product of step a with a compound of the formula R²-CH₂-Y (4), wherein R¹ and R² are as defined above and Y means a halogen atom. This process is unexpectedly and advantageously selective for the desired cis-isomer.

The products of step (a) are known from GB-A-1001001.

The compounds of the formula (2) can also be prepared by reacting an aldehyde of the formula (3) with the reaction product of glycerol and a compound of the formula (4). However, such a process yields products of formula (2) where more than 50 per cent is in the undesired trans form.

The products of formula (2) may be combined with other herbicides. Combinations with bromoxynil and/or ioxynil show a synergistic effect against weeds whilst having a good crop tolerance.

For herbicidal applications, the compounds of formula (2) are formulated by admixture with the adjuvants and carriers normally employed for agricultural applications. Thus, these active herbicidal compounds may be formulated as granules, as powders, as emulsifiable concentrates, as solutions or as any of several other known types of formulations, depending on the desired mode of application. Preferred formulations for both pre- and post-emergence herbicidal application are powders, emulsifiable concentrates and granules. These formulations may contain as little as 0.5 per cent to as much as 95 per cent by weight of active ingredient.

*Notes to the examiner*

With this paper, the following notes would be useful.

(1) A discussion of unity, a proposal for a second application and an outline of the process to be claimed.

(2) A discussion of why the invention has, or has not, been limited to the cis-isomers.

(3) A note that the definitions in claim 1 are very broad and would most likely not be accepted by the EPO on the basis that not all the compounds would have herbicidal activity.

## 8. Partial worked example using EQE 2004 Paper A

*Understanding and annotating the paper*

The 2004 Paper A can be analysed in the following way, using method (3) (as described above). Noted below are those features which need to be transferred in schematic form to a summary sheet which is to be used in establishing novel subject matter. Comments on each paragraph are made in bold, words indicating an essential or preferred feature are underlined and italicised.

Dear Sirs

As you know, our company is interested in making compositions making use of gallium. For some time we have had a team working on the use of gallium and gallium alloys in particulate form as lubricants and now the results of this research are available. We ask you to file a European patent application covering this research based on the information provided in this letter. All matter worth patenting should be covered. In order to assist you in drafting the application(s), documents D1, D2 and D3, which in our opinion best illustrate the state of the art, are attached to this letter.

**Field of the invention: claims to some sort of gallium or gallium alloy particle, compositions containing such particles and their use as lubricants seem likely along with any possible process for making them.**

The melting point of gallium (29.8°C) and of certain gallium alloys is extremely low and unlike other metals or alloys, they cannot be made into particles at elevated temperatures.

**Possible problem to be solved by the invention: how to make particles of gallium and certain of its alloys.**

Use is made in the present invention of metallic gallium or alloys of gallium which have a melting point between 27 and 60°C. Such alloys typically contain at least one metal selected from the group consisting of zinc (Zn), indium (In), aluminium (Al) and tin (Sn). Examples of suitable gallium alloys are Ga-5Zn, Ga-15Zn, Ga-40In, Ga-5Al or Ga-15Al, wherein Ga-xM means an alloy consisting of 100 — x parts by weight (pbw) of gallium and x parts by weight (pbw) of metal M. For example Ga-5Zn defines an alloy consisting of 95 pbw of gallium and 5 pbw of zinc.

**Essential feature: *use is made* of gallium or a gallium alloy having a melting point between 27 and 60°C.**
**Preferred feature: alloys *typically* contain certain metals.**
**Specific embodiments of useful alloys.**
**Mark these features on summary.**

It has been observed that when a gallium alloy is used, the greater the content of gallium, the better are the gliding or lubricating properties of the composition containing particles of that alloy. The content of gallium in the alloy must be at least 50 wt% in order to ensure sufficient gliding and lubricating properties.

**Essential feature of the alloy: the content of gallium *must* be at least 50%. Mark on summary.**

We use a process with which metallic gallium or the above defined gallium alloys can be converted to fine particles of a diameter not larger than 500 μm and even to finer particles of a diameter not larger than 150 μm.

**Mark process on summary as an arrow and the particulate gallium or gallium alloy as the product. Not sure if diameter is an essential feature or not — depends if diameter is important for achieving a technical effect underlying inventive step.**

This process comprises the steps of:
    a) melting metallic gallium of a gallium alloy having a melting point between 27 and 60°C in an atmosphere of inert gas such as nitrogen at a temperature not higher than 100°C, preferably at a temperature in the range of 70–90°C and

    b) injecting the molten gallium or gallium alloy through a vibrating nozzle into a cooling medium. The cooling medium which may contain additives, is water or an aqueous solution. It is kept at a temperature not higher than 10°C, preferably not higher than 5°C, i.e. a temperature below the melting temperature of gallium or of the gallium alloys in order to ensure a rapid solidification of the droplets sprayed from the nozzle. The size of the particles is adjusted by varying the pressure applied for injecting the molten gallium or gallium alloy into the cooling medium.

The solidified gallium or gallium alloy particles settle to the bottom of the cooling medium and therefore can be easily separated from the cooling medium.

**Mark outline of process steps on summary.**
**Essential features of the process: melting gallium or alloy, use of inert gas, temperature 100°C or less, injecting through vibrating nozzle, aqueous cooling medium, temperature not higher than 10°C, separation of particles.**

The process so far described is known from document D1.

**No reason to doubt this but will need to be independently verified when analysing the prior art so don't mark summary at this stage.**

The surface of the gallium or gallium alloy particles can be optionally coated with any known coating agent. The amount of coating agent usually does not exceed 5 weight per cent (wt%) of the gallium or gallium alloy particles.

**Add coated particles to summary as a new facet of the invention.**
**Preferred feature: amount of coating agent _usually_ does not exceed 5 wt%.**

The gallium or gallium alloy particles can be coated after separation from the cooling medium using conventional coating methods. If the coating agent is a coupling agent or a surfactant (i.e. one of the coating agents we use for providing suspensions of gallium or gallium alloy particles in liquid media), it can be already present in the cooling medium as an additive, in which case gallium or gallium alloy particles coated with a coupling agent or a surfactant are directly obtained in step b) of the process described above.

**Two embodiments for the coating process exist so add two arrows to the summary; the first sounds conventional and the second possibly inventive.**
**Essential feature: in the case of the second embodiment of the coating process the coating agent _is_ (i.e. must be) a coupling agent or a surfactant. The implication is that in the first embodiment of the coating process the choice of coating agent is unrestricted.**

Use of the particles:

The gallium and gallium alloy particles may be either dispersed in polymeric resins or, subject to certain conditions explained further below, suspended in liquid media. If a polymeric resin is used, a material containing the gallium or gallium alloy particles results which can be used to make a gliding surface. If a liquid medium is used, a liquid composition, such as an engine oil or liquid ski wax, containing the gallium of gallium alloy particles results.

**Two new facets of the invention to mark on summary: compositions of the gallium or gallium alloy particles (coated or uncoated) which are polymeric resins or liquid suspensions. The liquid suspensions will be restricted by further essential features not shared by the polymeric resins. Also mark gliding surface as an example of the polymeric resin and engine oil/liquid ski wax as examples of the liquid suspension.**

The gallium or gallium alloy particles are preferably mixed in amounts of at least 0.05 parts (all parts to be designated hereinafter are based on weight) with 100 parts of the polymeric resin or liquid medium. The amount of gallium or gallium alloy particles to be used may vary depending upon their specific use, but is preferably not more than 5 parts of gallium or gallium alloy particles per 100 parts of resin or liquid medium in view of cost. It was established by experiment that using such small amounts of gallium or gallium alloy particles was sufficient to give good results. Moreover, the gallium or gallium alloy particles must be suspended in the liquid medium or uniformly dispersed in the resin composition to obtain sufficient lubricating and gliding properties.

**Preferred features: gallium/gallium alloy particles _preferably_ mixed in amounts of at least 0.05 parts per 100 parts of the polymeric resin/liquid medium; amount of gallium/gallium alloy particles _preferably_ not more than 5 parts per 100 parts of the resin/liquid medium.**
**Essential feature: in the resin embodiment the particles _must_ be uniformly dispersed. Add these features to the summary.**

*Dispersions in polymeric resins:*

As explained above the coated gallium or gallium alloy particles can be dispersed in polymeric resins, e.g. polystyrene, polyvinyl chloride, polyvinyl acetate, polyethylene or polypropylene using conventional techniques. When the gallium or gallium alloy particles are incorporated into polymeric resins, the coating agents in the amount indicated above do not affect the lubricating and gliding properties. The addition of uncoated gallium or gallium alloy particles to one of the above resins is also possible depending on the contemplated use of the resulting composition.

**Preferred feature: the polymeric resin is _e.g._ polystyrene, polyvinyl chloride, polyvinyl acetate, polyethylene or polypropylene. Add to the summary.**
**Also add 'conventional techniques' to the appropriate arrow on the summary.**
**Confirmation that the gallium/gallium alloy particles in the resin embodiment can be coated or uncoated.**

The resin compositions which contain the above gallium or gallium alloy particles exhibit high gliding properties on snow and water. They are therefore particularly suitable in the production of gliding surfaces for skis and motor boats.

**Add skis and motorboats to summary as preferred embodiments of the gliding surface.**

*Suspensions in liquid media:*

The gallium or gallium alloy particles are, as explained above, also useful for making suspensions, i.e. they can be suspended in a liquid medium (i.e. a medium which is liquid at 200°C) as illustrated by alcohols, oils, lubricants and aqueous solutions. This however requires a diameter of the gallium or gallium alloy particles of not greater than 150 μm, preferably not greater than 50 μm. This furthermore requires the use of a coating agent selected from the group consisting of paraffin waxes, surfactants and coupling agents. The use of other conventional coating agents such as low molecular weight ethylene oxide polymers and low molecular weight propylene oxide polymers does not lead to stable suspensions.

**Definition of 'suspension': will have to decide whether to incorporate into claims or not.**
**Preferred feature: suspensions are _illustrated by_ alcohols, oils, lubricants and aqueous solutions — add to summary.**
**Essential features: use in a suspension _requires_ a diameter of the gallium/gallium alloy particles of not greater than 150 mm; if a coating agent is used this _requires_ the selection of a paraffin wax, a surfactant or a coupling agent. Add to summary. These extra essential features were foreshadowed earlier in the text.**
**Preferred feature: diameter of the gallium/gallium alloy particles is _preferably_ not greater than 50 mm. Add to summary.**
**Negative teaching: conventional coating agents (low molecular weight ethylene and propylene oxide polymers) don't work in suspensions — negative teachings are unusual and therefore may be significant. Add to summary.**

A suitable paraffin wax is commercially available under the trade name Parawax. The surfactants used may be non-ionic, anionic, cationic or amphoteric. The surfactant is preferably a fluorochemical, for example, Fluorofact®. Coupling agents are compounds which have an organic functional group having affinity for organic materials and a hydrolysable group having affinity for inorganic materials and which are capable of chemically coupling organic and inorganic materials. Illustrative coupling agents are silane coupling agents such as those sold under the trade name Silacoupling,

**Preferred features: a _suitable_ paraffin wax is Parawax; the surfactant _may be_ non-ionic, anionic, cationic or amphoteric; the surfactant is _preferably_ a fluorochemical, _for example_ Fluorofact; _illustrative_ coupling agents are silane coupling agents such as Silacoupling. Mark on summary.**
**Definition of 'coupling agent': will have to decide whether to incorporate into claims or not.**

The suspensions usually will be prepared by incorporating the above described coated gallium or gallium alloy particles into the liquid medium, which is to be selected according to the intended use. Preferred liquid media are engine oils or the solvents conventionally used for making ski wax. The addition to a commercial engine oil of the above described coated gallium or gallium alloy coated particles reduced the consumption of gasoline, due to the lubricating effect of gallium. Liquid ski waxes obtained by using the coated gallium or gallium alloy particles have high performances on all types of snow.

**No new features. Advantages of the suspensions and ski wax are presented which may be important for inventive step.**

Which facets of the invention are covered by the four examples can also be added to the summary.

A typical example of a summary sheet established as a result of this process is shown overleaf.

46  Complete Guide to Passing the EQE

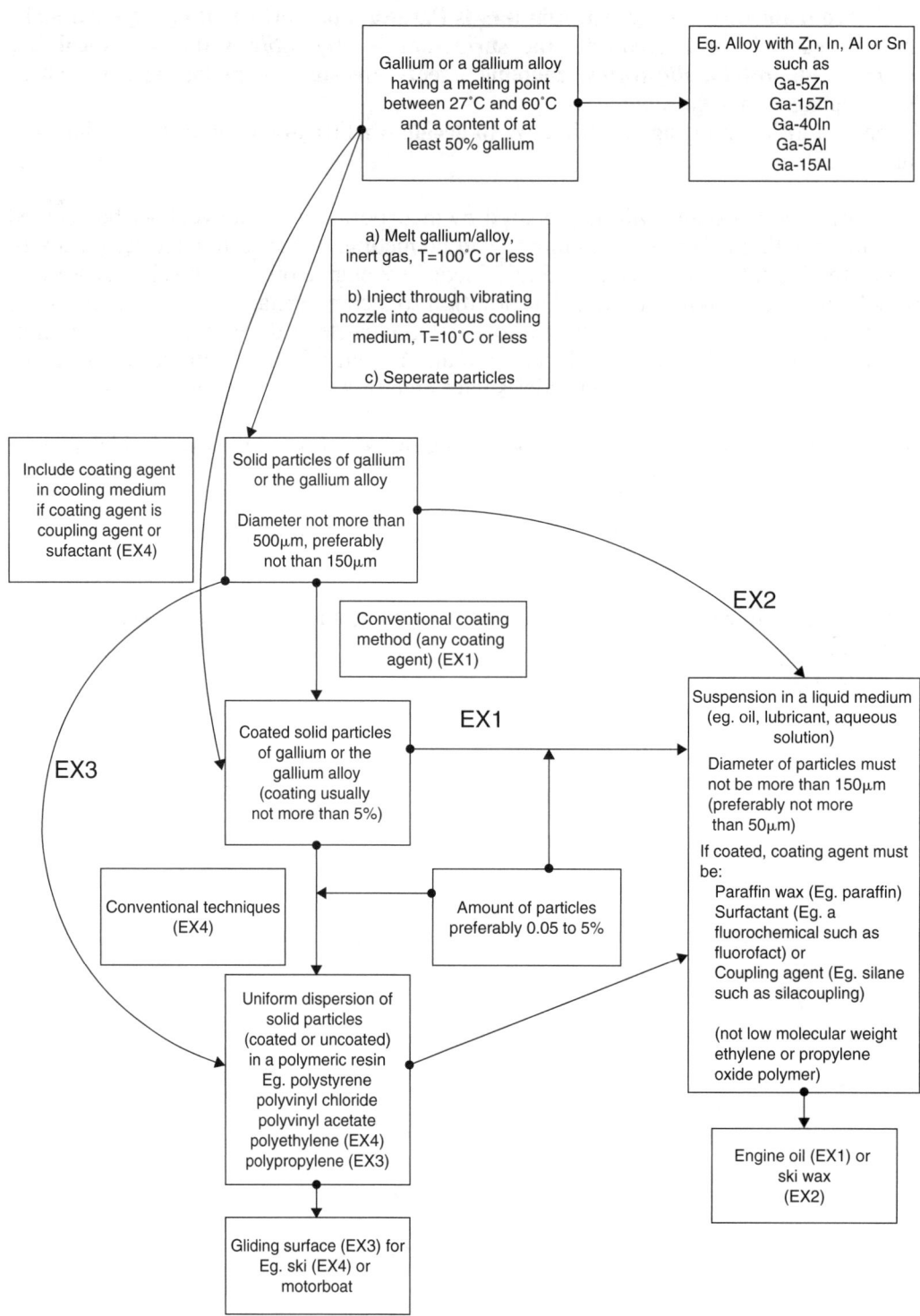

*Establishing patentable subject matter*

The summary document shows all the subject matter described by the client in diagrammatic form. The prior art must now be subtracted from this subject matter to establish how much is novel. That novel subject matter for which a surprising effect can be substantiated can then be claimed.

The three prior art documents should therefore be carefully considered and their content marked on the summary document. In the marked summary document overleaf the content of D1 has been indicated by the use of a bold typeface, the content of D2 has been indicated by the use of italicized typeface and the content of D3 has been indicated by the use of underlined typeface. In the exam, any suitable method may be used — the use of different coloured shading is perhaps the most visually striking.

The text left in normal font therefore represents novel subject matter.

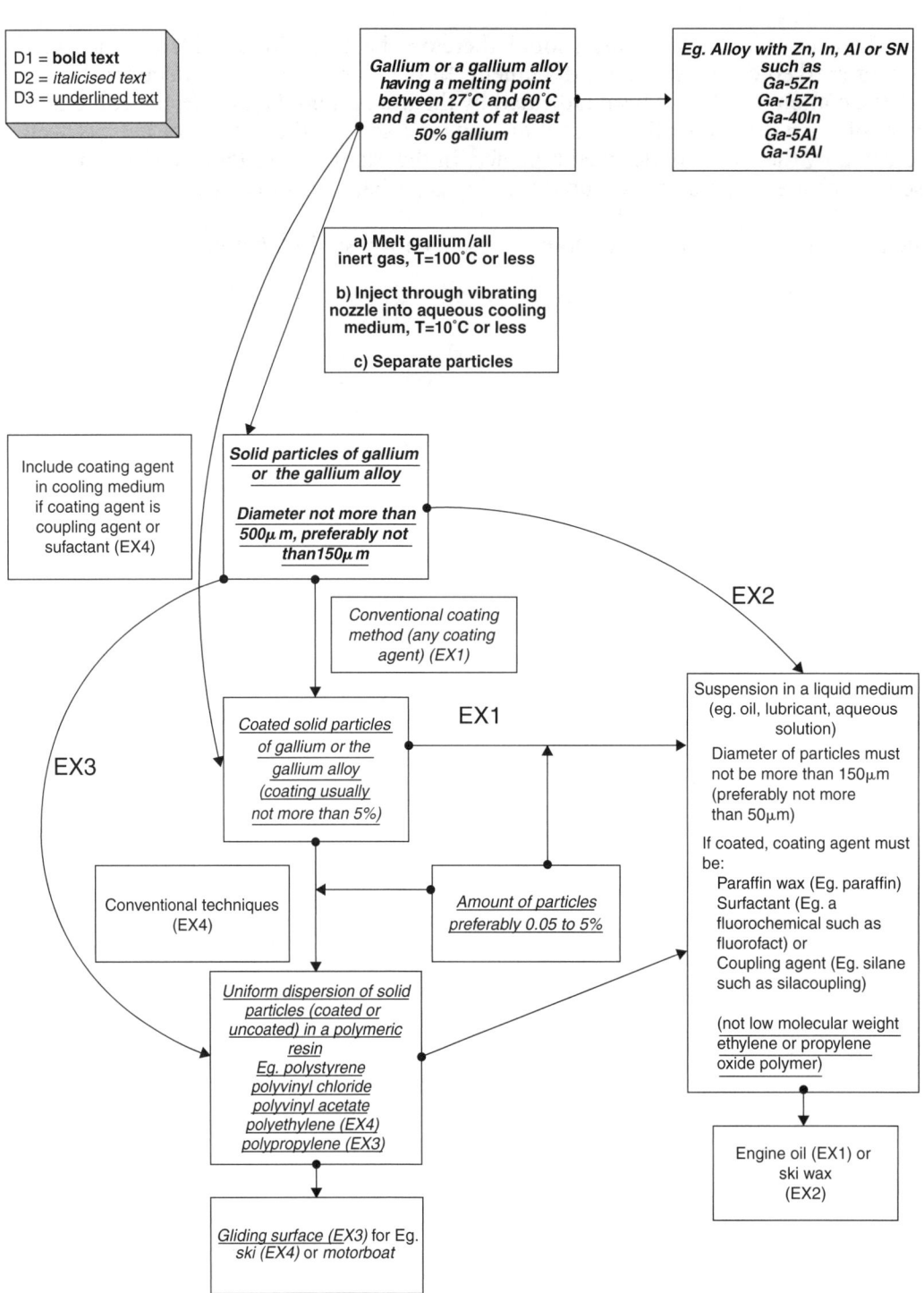

A brief analysis of the summary sheet marked up with the content of the prior art shows immediately that the two novel features are: (a) the modified process for coating particles by including a coating agent selected from a coupling agent and a surfactant in the cooling medium; and (b) liquid suspensions.

With regard to the new process for making coated particles, the closest prior art is known from the client's letter to be the use of the D1 process for making the particles themselves in combination with subsequent "conventional coating methods." The new process certainly has advantages over this known art and solves the problem of providing a more efficient method of providing coated particles of gallium or a gallium alloy where the coating agent is a coupling agent or a surfactant. Whether the solution of including the coupling agent in the cooling medium is inventive or not is not clear. However, on the basis of the limited information available, the answer is yes, in principle.

No liquid suspensions of gallium or gallium alloys, coated or not coated, are known in the prior art provided. However, in respect of the uncoated particles, it is not clear whether any technical barrier existed to their creation. In respect of uncoated particles, the invention solves the problem of providing liquid media suitable for use as lubricants. The solution is to suspend uncoated gallium particles in a liquid medium. Whether such a solution is obvious or not, given the known lubricating properties of uncoated gallium particles, is debatable and arguably weak in the absence of any technical prejudice against the formation of stable suspensions with uncoated gallium particles.

In the case of coated gallium particles, however, there is a cast-iron case for an inventive step since the only known prior art coating agents (low molecular weight ethylene and propylene oxide polymers) do not lead to stable suspensions in liquid media. In contrast, the invention provides specific coating agents which do lead to stable suspensions. The problem the invention solves is therefore how to provide a stable liquid suspension of coated gallium particles. The solution, to use a coating agent selected from a paraffin wax, a surfactant and a coating agent, is inherently surprising since known coating agents did not work, leading to the expectation that no coating agent would work.

Whilst in the real world you would probably claim all the novel subject matter discussed above, since there is at least an argument for inventive step in each case, in the EQE there is a solution which the examiners have hidden in the question and signposted with various clues. In this case the provision of stable suspensions with coated gallium and gallium alloy particles is clearly the answer that you are meant to find since a tailor-made inventive step argument has been provided. Moreover, the invention relates to a product rather than a process which is most common in the EQE. Therefore, your answer should relate to this subject matter and, if you have time, propose the filing of divisional applications relating to the other subject matter.

*Claiming the invention*

**Product claims**   1–052

Many candidates taking this paper would probably have included their main product claim as a suspension of coated gallium particles in a liquid medium, where the coating agent is a paraffin wax, a surfactant or a coupling agent (along with other essential features). However, this claim is too narrow and would have lost many marks. Although the coated particles are inventive by virtue of their ability to form stable suspensions in liquid media, they may be claimed per se since they are novel, just as a drug compound may be claimed *per se* (if novel) even though its inventive step may rest on its use in a particular kind of therapy. The prior art describes the concept of coated gallium and gallium alloy particles but not the specific coating agents provided by the invention, which are a novel selection.

When claiming the novel coated gallium and gallium alloy particles, several essential features, other than the specific coating agents, need to be included. The claim must be inventive across its whole breadth and thus must provide stable liquid suspensions across its whole breadth. We know, however, that only coated particles having a diameter of not more than 150 μm lead to stable suspensions; this feature must be included. Furthermore, we are told that the gallium alloy particles provided by the invention have a melting point between 27°C and 60°C and a content of at least 50% gallium; these features, deemed essential by the client, must be included.

Compositions comprising the inventive cooled particles (including oils and waxes) should also be claimed.

1–053   **Use claims**

The use of a suspension of the coated particles as an engine oil or a ski wax is clearly important. However, there is no reason why the use of a uniform dispersion of the coated particles in a polymeric resin as a gliding surface should not also be claimed. This is perhaps difficult to grasp since at first sight it may appear to contradict the principle that the claim must be inventive across its whole breadth. However, once you have established an inventive product claim, you may claim any use to which that product may be put, whether the use would have been inventive or not. Such a use claim is inventive across its scope since it relates to the use of a product which is inherently inventive.

1–054   **Process claims**

A process for making the inventive coated particles of the invention is available. This process has two embodiments. The first, which is clearly an analogy process, is to follow the instructions given by D1 and then use conventional coating methods. The second, which may be inventive in its own right, is to include the coating agent in the cooling medium described by D1. Do not forget to include all the process features which are described as essential features. Furthermore, do not forget to restrict the second embodiment of the process to a coating agent selected from a coupling agent or a surfactant — it will only work with these two coating agents according to the client. Since the size of the coated particles is now an essential feature of the product claim and depends on the pressure used in the process, some mention of appropriately adjusting the pressure should also be made.

1–055   **Dependent claims**

Possible features worth identifying in dependent claims include preferred structural features of the coated particles such as preferred metals for forming the alloys, the specific alloys used by the client and the preferred diameter of the coated particles, the preferred ratios in which the coated particles and liquid media should be mixed and preferred specific coating agents. None of them are particularly motivated in the text and so a reasonable selection should be made, focusing on novel structural features relating to the technical effect underlying inventive step.

1–056   **Claim language**

Since the claims must have a clear meaning on their own, without recourse to the description, some consideration must be given to whether "liquid medium" and "coupling agent", both of which are further defined in the text, can be used in the claims. We cannot know the answer since we are not specialists in the field and will therefore not know whether the definitions given by the client are the accepted definitions used by the skilled person or not. A choice must be made one way or the other and a note to the examiner would be appropriate.

1–057   **Drafting the introduction**

As usual, all three prior art documents should be discussed, summarizing briefly their contents in comparison with the invention. In particular, the particular coated particles disclosed by D2 and D3 should be highlighted. The problem can then be nicely set up and its unexpected solution subsequently unveiled. It may be worth noting that Examples 2 and 3 are no longer relevant, describing uncoated gallium and gallium alloy particles.

# PAPER A (ELECTRICITY/MECHANICS)

## 1. General comments

In this paper the candidate is provided with a letter from a notional client describing his recent research work and any pertinent prior art he is aware of. The candidate must compare the results obtained by the client with the state of the art and establish what patentable inventions have been made. A patent application relating to the most important invention (or unified group of inventions) must then be drafted comprising a set of claims and a description (up to but excluding the specific embodiments). Any further non-unitary inventions may be mentioned in a letter to the examiner where appropriate.

The claims drafted should give the client the broadest possible protection while also having a good chance of succeeding before the EPO without amendment. Particular attention should be given to novelty, inventive step and clarity. The claims must be novel over the prior art, since a lack of novelty gives rise to a large loss of marks. They must also be broad enough to obtain the maximum allowable protection for the client, since failure to protect something which could have been protected will also result in a loss of marks, the number of lost marks being linked to the extent of the failure. There should also be a good argument for inventive step across the whole claim breadth and this argument will be presented in the introduction to the description where the problem addressed by and the advantages provided by the invention are discussed. Claims which lack essential features or which are otherwise unsupported will also result in loss of marks. Often only a single independent claim is necessary, generally this will be a product claim rather than a method claim. Commonly in this paper there are several embodiments which must be protected. In this situation the examiners are virtually always looking for a solution which protects all the embodiments with a single claim. Such a solution will always garner more marks than alternative solutions which use several independent claims to protect all the embodiments. The 2005 paper, to which a solution is provided at the end of this chapter, is a clear example of such a situation. There should also be a reasonable number of dependent claims chosen as likely to survive in the event of failure of the main claim — i.e. to provide useful fall-back positions. Again, an excessive number of dependent claims will result in a loss of marks.

While Art.123(2) is obviously not relevant, the candidate is expected to draft within the limited bounds of the information provided by the client, accepting all information at face value. No specialist knowledge that candidates may possess relating to the technology of the client's invention should be used. There is generally no need to invent language — the answer to the question will already be present in the question, but often the claims should be written in functional rather than structural terms and this may require the use of language not expressly set out in the question.

The paper is three and a half hours in length, and between one and a half and two of these hours should be devoted to analysing the paper and elucidating the answer, the remaining time being allocated to writing the answer. Typically, half the available marks are awarded for the independent claims, so most effort should be spent on them. The bulk of the rest of the available marks is allocated to the dependent claims, with about 15 to 20 per cent of the marks allocated to the introduction, the precise balance varying from year to year. The candidate is encouraged to use sections of the examination paper in compiling the answer, so scissors, glue and transparent gummed tape should be brought into the exam to facilitate cutting out relevant paragraphs from the examination paper and fixing them into the answer. For the same reason, only pencil and yellow highlighter should be used to mark up important sections of the paper during the period of analysis; pencil can be easily erased and yellow highlighter does not cause problems when the answer is photocopied prior to marking. Using a cut and paste approach to creating the introduction can save a significant amount of time, as well as helping to ensure accuracy.

It is important, however to practise the cut and paste technique under exam conditions before the exam — it is a skill not to be acquired during the exam itself. Other useful things to take into the exam are copies of Guidelines for Examination in the European Patent Office and Case Law of the Boards of Appeal of the European Patent Office.

## 2. How to tackle the paper

**1–059**  *Understanding and annotating the paper*

Read through the entire paper, word by word, taking time to understand each sentence thoroughly and appreciate its significance. Consider each word carefully, since it is easy to miss small but important facts later once the mind has started to make assumptions about the answer. Assume that the information which you are given is correct. Do not use any specialist knowledge which you may have, although you can use common general knowledge.

In general, a sentence relating to the client's invention will concern: general instructions and advice from the client (e.g. "Please file a patent application"); technical information necessary for non-specialists to understand the technology of the invention; prior art and the problem to be solved by the invention in light of it; the invention according to the client in terms of its essential features; advantages associated with the invention; a preferred feature with a specified further advantage, a preferred feature with no specified extra advantage; general enablement of the invention; or specific examples of the invention.

Mark in the margin of the exam paper what each sentence signifies. Highlight in particular what categories of claim particular subject matter may form the basis for, potentially essential features of the invention and preferred features with further advantages.

When you get to the prior art, mark it up in a similar way: the problems that it addresses, the advantages, etc. Pay particular attention to alternatives. The prior art will almost certainly be Art.54(2) art (though the client's own Art.54(3) art could in principle be included). Answer two questions in particular: (1) does what is described potentially fall within the description of the client's invention (relevant for novelty); and (2) is the prior art solving a similar, or the same, problem (relevant for inventive step)? Each piece of prior art should therefore be categorised as novelty only, inventive step only, novelty and inventive step or (rarely!) not relevant. Read the prior art particularly attentively in those parts which seem close to what the client suggests is the invention. Within each prior document, note those sections which are highly relevant and those, if any, which may largely be ignored.

**1–060**  *Establishing patentable subject matter*

Analyse which features of the invention as set out by the client are already described in the prior art and then mark this information on the paper. Any suitable means may be used, such as highlighter or hatching areas of text. However, only pencil or yellow highlighter should be used on the text itself to facilitate later construction of the description. Pen may be used in the margins. It may be that large sections of the client's letter are duplicated in the prior art or, alternatively, the correspondence may be more subtle — this varies from year to year.

Through this process of subtraction, it should now start to become clear where the client's invention or inventions must lie.

You need to identify the problem or problems which the inventor has sought to solve — something which is normally flagged fairly clearly in the question. You then need to establish whether and how the prior art that has been provided is relevant to that problem. Then having decided what the objective problem is, you need to establish which feature(s) is (are) essential for solving that problem. At this stage you should consider carefully the extent to which you can generalise from the specific features which the inventor has disclosed while still solving the problem. A trivial example is where the client's device includes a spring to make it work. Before assuming that you must recite a spring, you need to establish why a spring is present. Is its resilience being used (to compensate for manufacturing tolerances, thermal expansion, or as a shock absorber)? Or is it simply biasing two or more parts together? Depending upon the answer to these questions you might recite a spring, resilient means, resilient biasing means, biasing means or can you say that the two or more parts are biased (towards or away from each other) but without expressly reciting the presence of biasing means? Is it enough to say that part A is biased towards part B (for example, could you use gravity, magnetism or gas pressure (positive or negative) to achieve the desired result?

The novel claim must also be associated with some advantage which is unexpected enough in view of the state of the art to justify an inventive step. Where the invention as described by the client is already novel and inventive it is likely that some significant effort will be required to frame the claim in respect of the correct essential technical features.

*Claiming the invention* 1–061

Another decision that needs to be made in the examination is what should be claimed. This is not a question of what the inventive features are, but rather what entity or activity should be claimed. Frequently this paper poses a problem where the invention concerns a component of a larger whole, so that candidates must decide whether to claim the element or component on its own or whether to claim the larger whole including the element or component.

For example, in the 2002 paper the invention concerned an arrangement to protect a disc drive against the effects of certain types of mechanical shocks. The disc drives were of the type to be fitted in portable computers and in such an application the incidence of the relevant mechanical shocks is high. Here one could claim a portable computer including a disc drive having the new features, or just the disc drive with the new features, or even the relevant parts of the disc drive, without reciting the presence of the other parts of the drive. The client was "a major manufacturer of hard disk drives". Some candidates did claim the computer, but they lost many marks by doing this. Other candidates claimed a disc drive and they only lost a few marks! The examiners wanted claims directed to a locking device for a disc drive.

In the 1999 paper the invention concerned a reader for reading mobile phone SIM cards. Such readers are part of mobile phones but do have other applications. Some candidates chose to claim a mobile phone including the reader, but the examiners wanted claims to the reader *per se*.

In the 1995 paper, the invention concerned an ink jet printer in which the print head produced ink droplets in a new way. The client was "a firm producing printers". Some candidates claimed only a printer including the new print head. Others claimed the print head *per se*. The former candidates lost many marks because the latter solution was the one the examiners wanted. In this paper, maximum marks were obtained by candidates who had an independent claim to the print head and an independent claim to a method of ejecting droplets, although the number of marks allocated to the method claim was small. One might have thought that claims to a method of printing using the new print head might have been sought — because Art.64(2) would extend protection to the printed matter produced using the method, but this does not appear to have occurred to the examiners.

So, the message is clear: if you can draft an allowable claim for the sub-component do so. It will generally be a good idea also to claim the greater assembly, but this may be through a sub-claim.

A further pointer to dealing with this issue is the nature of the client's business. Generally a client will want a patent which will be directly effective against competitors and not one which is of direct relevance only to customers. So, claims directed towards the client's products and services, and possibly their sub-systems or components are of most interest.

That is not to say that claims to customers' products which include the client's type of products should be avoided, but rather that such claims should not define the broadest protection sought for the client. The 2002 paper is one example of this. Another example is the 2005 paper, where the client was "a supplier of automotive components, in particular of lighting and electric components". The invention concerned a system of controlling the dipped headlight beam of a motorcycle whereby, as the motorcycle was banked to go round corners, the pattern of the dipped beam was adjusted to avoid dazzling the drivers of oncoming vehicles. The complete system involved sensors to monitor the degree of bank of the motorcycle, a new headlight assembly with a motor-driven shield to adjust the dipped headlight beam, and a processor to use the sensor output to control the position of the motor-driven shield. Motorcycles incorporating the new system were new and inventive and would certainly be worth claiming, but given the nature of the client's business and given that the new headlight assembly could be used to replace conventional headlights, it was essential to claim the new headlight assembly *per se*.

Having established what action needs to be taken in order to make the client's broadest statement of invention novel and inventive, the first independent claim can be drafted.

Include all essential features of the invention, especially those which underlie an effect associated with the inventive step (T32/82). If you omit an essential feature from a claim, you will lose a significant number of marks. Keywords that tend to flag an essential feature include: must, has to be, should be, is/are, provided that, is necessary, have, only, is required. Equally, avoid all features which are merely optional or preferred, as these would unnecessarily limit the claim. Again, if you include inessential features, you will lose marks. Keywords that tend to flag such features include: preferred, preferably, typically, usually, for example, normally, optimal, suitable, advantageous, good/better/best results, especially, particularly, special mention, may be.

The examiners have a particular dislike of claims which only state the problem of the invention or the result to be achieved. In extreme cases as much as three qurters of the marks available for the independent claim may be deducted for such a claim. With such a loss of marks it is most unlikely that the paper will be passed. In the 1999 paper, the SIM card reader had features which meant that it could read SIM cards of two different formats. Some candidates had independent claims which merely specified that the reader was suitable for reading modules of different formats without specifying any structural features which made this possible. Unsurprisingly they failed. Another example is the 2004 paper, for which a partially worked answer is provided later in this chapter. That paper mentioned that the client's objective had been to improve a known system for applying an impulse (having a direction and intensity) so that a desired effect could be produced "independently of the skill of the user, that is, automatically". Claims which were characterised only by "means for automatically controlling the direction and intensity of the impulse" only stated the result to be achieved. Such claims, so clearly lacking essential features, were heavily punished — being given about 15 of the 50 marks which were available for the independent claim. With such a claim it is therefore clearly very hard to pass the paper. So, when deciding how to characterise the invention, identify structural or functional features which are essential to achieving the desired effect and make sure that those features and the necessary interaction between them appear in your main claim. In particular, when you have drafted a nice broad claim, check to ensure that if it is directed towards a result to be achieved, it recites the features neccessary to achieve the result.

If it seems that specific embodiments need to be excluded, think very hard before doing so, as this is very unusual.

Remember that the examiners will generally be looking for a single independent product (or, more rarely, method) claim which protects all of the embodiments. Multiple independent claims protecting all the embodiments will always garner fewer marks that an equally competent single claim which protects all the embodiments. But if, in the tension of the exam, you cannot see one claim formulation that does cover all the embodiments, do draft independent claims to ensure that you do not leave any protectable embodiment unprotected. This will tend to be a better solution than either leaving embodiments unprotected or proposing a single independent claim which is deeply defective. Moreover, once you have drafted the different independent claims you may see how you can amend one or other of them to cover the other embodiments.

Only use information that the client has provided; do not draft any more broadly than he suggests — although, as already indicated, you can expect to need to make some generalisations and you may need to protect a sub-component as well as the whole. In particular, if the client gives you clear instructions either not to protect something or that certain things or activities are not of interest, you should not claim them. The instructions to candidates tell you to accept the facts given in the paper and to limit yourself to those facts: if you do not do this, you will lose marks.

Write on every other line, to facilitate later changes.

Use the exact language and reference numerals that the client uses in order to make drafting the description easier, unless you need to generalise a feature or introduce functional language.

In the majority of cases, the invention will concern a new product rather than a new activity and the first independent claim to be drafted will be in this category. Beware, however, the case where the client describes his invention in the context of a process or use and the product claim is disguised. In general, think very hard before submitting a set of claims without any product claim! If in real life (i.e. outside the exam) you would have a method claim in addition to any product claim, include one in your answer. This is despite the examiners' occasional disdain for method claims whose inclusion is sensible (such as in the 2001 paper, where the invention was a juicing machine: a claim to a method of extracting juice would, by virtue of Art.64(2) EPC have made the juice a patented product, but the examiners felt that an apparatus claim gave full protection). Provided you do not waste time that you'd be better spending on another aspect of your answer, you will not lose marks by including a method claim and you might well gain a few marks.

Consider what the client is making and selling and try to introduce claims that cover these commercial activities appropriately. As in real life, endeavour to draft claims which will cover directly the products which will be sold by the client, his competitors and his customers. If you have two or more separate parts that work together, e.g. a battery and a charger, a transmitter and a receiver, a key and a lock, a nut and bolt, do not rely on claims to the combination (system claims). Some candidates in this exam (and sadly some attorneys in real life) adopt this approach presumably with the expectation that the contributory infringement provisions will make everything all right. Until the CPC comes into force, if it ever does, national law relating to contributory infringement does not act to prevent sales or offers of sale of means relating to an essential element of the invention where those sales are for putting the invention into effect in another territory. So, if you have any possibility of claiming separately the component parts of a system, do so. By all means include a system claim too, but not as your only independent claim. Rule 29(2)(a) EPC permits multiple claims in the same category in such a situation, although you may have explain this fact in response to the first official communication under Art.96(2). In the unlikely event that you choose to submit such a claim set in the exam, provide a note to the examiner both explaining why the use of a single independent claim is not possible, and why the proposed claims comply with the requirements of r.29(2).

A particularly important situation in which independent claims in the same category should be prepared, even if they ultimately need to go into separate applications is where the invention involves one item consumed in or by another item — for example, ink cartridges for a pen or printer, glue refills for a glue gun, lubricant inserts for razors, etc. Often, as with ink-jet printers, the value of the market in refills is many orders of magnitude greater than the value of the market for the printers themselves. Consequently it is very important, if at all possible, to get independent protection for the consumable items and not just for the machine in which they are used.

Having established the main categories of independent claim, draft dependent claims specifying further features that are associated with further advantages. These will usually be signposted as "most preferred" or "particularly advantageous". You should aim, in general, for a total of from 10 to 20 claims, preferably about 15, but the ideal number will vary from year to year. You will get no credit for dependent claims listing all alternative embodiments or relating to trivial items only. If you draft what the examiners deem to be an unreasonable number of dependent claims, you risk losing marks for contravening Art.84 and r.29(5) EPC.

**1–062**    *Drafting the introduction*

The introduction should follow the order suggested by r.27 EPC.

Start with a statement of the technical field of the invention, consistent with the independent claims.

Describe the relevant background art useful to understand the invention. This should be the most relevant piece of art in the question; that is the one most relevant to assessing inventive step. The piece of art should be identified and the pertinent parts of its disclosure discussed. Marks are often lost through a failure properly to acknowledge and summarise the relevant piece of art. Only those disadvantages or deficiencies of the acknowledged art which are addressed by the invention should be mentioned. Also, these drawbacks should not be described in such a way as to give a pointer to the invention. You should also indicate in the introduction what piece of prior art has been used as the basis of the pre-characterising clause of the independent claim. An easy way to do this is to write "D3, on which preamble of claim 1 is based, provides . . .".

The problem to be solved with respect to the acknowledged art should be set out. This should be as specific as required by the question — marks are lost if the problem is cast in too general terms (e.g. "improved properties" or "improved performance"). The problem should be formulated in such a way that it contains no features of the solution: failure to adhere to this rule loses marks.

The solution according to the invention as specified in the first claim is then set out and this should be followed by, and linked to, the advantages which are inevitably achieved by the invention at the level of generality in which it is set out. That is, do not suggest that the invention in its broadest definition provides an advantage which is in fact achieved by only some of the forms or examples of the invention. Always check, when drafting your introduction, that the problem and advantages which are set out actually match what is recited in the corresponding claim, paying particular attention to the need for each independent claim to recite all the essential technical features.

This solution and advantage sequence should then be repeated for each of the other independent claims.

Generally, the exam does not require you to provide support for the dependent claims. If such support is needed, recite the relevant additional features and discuss the effect and / or advantage of the new combination of features.

Any further prior art may be briefly be discussed at this point — that is, after the invention has been discussed.

The introduction is where your cutting and pasting skills are put to the test. It is often possible to produce a good introduction by cutting and pasting the exam paper, with little of no additional writing being required. See the detailed section below for further guidance. Most time and effort should be devoted to describing the prior art and the problem to be solved in light of it and hence demonstrating an inventive step for the claimed subject matter. This will often require you to use your own wording — rather than a section cut out from the question paper. Always be alive to the need to write something slightly different from the language of the question: you may not need to write much, but always think carefully about what the introduction needs to say. Another important aspect is to ensure consistency between the claims and the introduction. You are only required to produce an introduction, not a specific description.

*Notes to the examiner* 1–063

The exam does not require or assume that you will write notes to the examiner: your answer should be complete and should speak for itself. But sometimes there is a justification for a brief note to the examiner. Consider whether any of the advantageous preferred features lead to a separate, non-unitary invention (e.g. in 1991 where the main invention was a hot-melt glue gun, there was an additional invention of a heater in cartridge form). If so, either draft a claim to the further non-unitary invention, explaining why this extra invention does not have unity with the subject matter being claimed and that you would make it the subject of a separate application, or at least identify the extra invention in clear terms and again say that it would be made the subject of an extra application. If there is a lack of unity in the claim set which you propose, you will lose marks if you do not identify this fact (and how you would deal with it) in your answer. On the other hand, if you avoid a lack of unity by failing to claim something that could have been claimed, and you do not identify the relevant subject matter as potentially claimable in another application, you will again lose marks.

Extensive notes to the examiner should be avoided. Further things to consider pointing out to the examiner are: (1) assumptions made in light of ambiguities in the question; (2) reasons why you made any decision that was difficult to make (e.g. not claiming novel subject matter deemed to be obvious); (3) the reason why you felt that having a method claim in addition to the main product claim was useful (e.g. because of the application of Art.64(2) to the direct product of the process), and the reasons why you presented multiple independent claims in the same category to protect alternative embodiments, rather than a single generic claim (but as noted above, this is generally not the optimum solution).

*Checking the answer* 1–064

It is always sensible to check the correctness of your claims, especially the independent claims, once you have drafted your sub-claims and introduction. Check for the absence of features essential to solve the problem which you have set out in the introduction; presence of inessential features; that all claimable examples are covered by the independent claims; that all patentable products have been claimed; and that the claims distinguish over the art. If any time remains, it is worth reading through the answer once, correcting typographical mistakes and ensuring that there is consistency between the description and the claims.

## 3. Notes on drafting the claims

*Claim language* 1–065

In this paper it is generally necessary to draft the claims functionally rather than purely structurally, if one is to achieve the maximum marks because functional claims generally give rise to broader claim formulation. See the Guidelines C.III.6.2 and 6.5. When you are drafting your claims, always ask yourself whether a particular structural feature is actually essential or whether in fact you could use a functional limitation to achieve greater breadth without a lack of clarity. The essential features need to be present and they should not only be present as a list of items — their inter-relationship needs to be made clear. See the Guidelines C.III.4.4 and 4.3(ii).

The Examiners have a particular dislike of claims which rely too heavily on the magic wand of "the arrangement being such that the invention achieves the desired result".

While it is permissible and often desirable to conclude a claim with a "so that it works" clause, if this merely follows a list of features whose inter-relationship is unclear, the claim will be unclear. See the Guidelines C.III.4.7. The 2004 paper's "means for automatically controlling" provides an example of this sort of trap for the unwary. Worst of all are claims which effectively recite the problem but do not disclose the features of the solution. It is surprisingly common to see such claims in candidates' answers to this paper, but the use of such claims is practically guaranteed to lead to failure. In this author's experience, the most common route to failure in this paper for UK-trained candidates is to draft claims which attempt to claim all solution to the problem but which do not recite the features necessary to solve the problem (an example of such a claim is that at the end of the worked example for the 2004 paper later in this chapter).

It is important that your claims cover the invention in its inoperative state (such as when packaged for sale) as well as when it is working. So, do not refer to a moving thing but to a movable thing, not rotating but rotatable, etc. Similarly, do not limit the claim to the thing when full or when empty, nor to the presence of its contents (e.g. do not claim the rechargeable glue gun only when charged with glue). Do not claim the thing only when connected to some other thing (the telephone network, a computer, the internet) if the invention can be defined without that feature. Do not claim a thing in a particular orientation. Where features move, refer to relative movement, rather than saying that A moves to B.

Claims should distinguish over prior art through positive rather than negative limitations. That is, say what the invention has, rather than what it does not have. Occasionally, in order to get reasonable claim scope, this rule needs to be broken, but this is unlikely to be the case in the EQE. Often there will be a way of using a positive limitation in place of a negative one. For example, in the 1998 Paper B, the invention concerned a smoke detector whose condition is monitored optically and which needs no electrical components. Rather than referring to an absence of electrical components, a negative limitation, this could be expressed positively as being electrically passive. A similar situation arose in the 2003 Paper A where the invention concerned a method of generating an alternating electric signal. A similar technique was known in the prior art but required the use of a battery. The invention simple used light. Once again, rather than saying that the device worked "without a separate source of energy", a negative limitation, it was preferable to recite the fact that optical radiation was directed onto a photovoltaic device whose output provided power to whatever needed to be activated. See the Guidelines C.III.4.12.

When drafting dependent claims, try to add only one feature per sub-claim, rather than several. Consider the usefulness of the feature of a sub-claim in providing a strong and useful fallback position. Ideally your early dependent claims should be for features which are not in the prior art (and hence likely to give a strong fallback position) and which apply to all or most of the embodiments (so that limiting to those sub-claims would not cause any of the embodiments to fall outside the amended claim).

"For use as" means "suitable for use as".

"Comprising" is open and allows the presence of any further constituents.

"Consisting of" is closed and does not allow further constituents, so that if a product "consists of A, B and C", then A, B and C make up 100 per cent of it (T759/91).

"Consisting essentially of" allows come latitude in terms of impurities.

**1-066**   *Requirements of claims — form and content*

The claims must be clear and concise and be supported by the description (Art.84, CLBA, pp.157–168).

The claims must define the matter for which protection is sought. Such definition must be in terms of the technical features of the invention (Art.84/r.29(1)).

Two-part form is encouraged — r.29(1) — such that wherever appropriate, claims must contain: (a) a statement indicating the designation of the subject matter of the invention and those technical features which are necessary for the definition of the claimed subject-matter but which, in combination, are part of the prior art; and (b) a characterising part — preceded by the expression "characterised in that" or "characterised by" — stating the technical features which, in combination with the features stated in (a), it is desired to protect. See the Guidelines C.III.2.2 to 2.3b. It is important that the pre-characterising clause is based on a single piece of prior art and not on a composite prior art which takes the known features from several prior art documents. Do not recite features of the prior art which are present in the invention but which are not essential for defining the invention. Do not use the terminology of the prior art in the pre-characterising clause if this terminology is not appropriate to the client's invention. Take particular care in this regard where your client has several embodiments — your main claim should cover them all and in order to do this you may need to draft the pre-characterising clause with more generic language than is used in the prior art.

The number of claims must be reasonable in consideration of the nature of the invention claimed (r.29(5)). In particular (r.29(2)), the inclusion of more than one independent claim in the same category (product, process, apparatus or use) is only allowed if the subject-matter of the application involves either: (a) a plurality of inter-related products, (b) different uses of a product or apparatus, or (c) alternative solutions to a particular problem, where it is not appropriate to cover these alternatives by a single claim. See the Guidelines C.III.3.2 and 5.

Any claim stating the essential features of an invention may be followed by one or more claims containing particular embodiments of that invention. Dependent claims where possible must start with a reference to the other claim and then state the additional features which it is desired to protect. Such dependent claims are allowed even where the claim referred to is itself a dependent claim. All dependent claims must be grouped together in the most appropriate way (r.29(3)(4)).

If there are several claims they must be numbered consecutively in arabic numerals (r.29(5)).

Where drawings are included, the technical features in the claims should preferably be followed by reference signs relating to those features if the intelligibility of the claim can thereby be increased. Such reference signs should be placed in parentheses. Such reference signs may not be construed as limiting the claim (r.29(7)). While this rule refers to signs, it is conventional to use reference numerals. The EPO considers that it is not clear whether words or acronyms placed in parentheses are intended to limit the claims, so their use is to be avoided. It is important in the exam to remember to use reference numerals in the claims. They should be used both in the pre-characterising and the characterising claims. Failure to use reference numerals will result in a loss of marks.

*Unity of invention* 1–067

The European patent application must relate to one invention only or to a group of inventions so linked as to form a single general inventive concept (Art.82).

Such a group of inventions is taken to be so linked when there is a technical relationship among the inventions involving one or more of the same or corresponding special technical features, i.e. those features which define a contribution which each of the claimed inventions considered as a whole makes over the prior art (r.30(1)).

It matters not, in determining whether a group of inventions is so linked, whether they are in separate claims or alternatives within a single claim (r.30(2)).

Remember that unity is seen to exist between the members of each of these groups:

(i) an independent claim for a given product, an independent claim for a process specially adapted for the manufacture of said product, and an independent claim for use of the product;

(ii) an independent claim for a given process, an independent claim for an apparatus or means specifically adapted for carrying out the process; and

(iii) an independent claim for a given product, an independent claim for a process specially adapted for the manufacture of said product, and an independent claim for an apparatus or means specifically adapted for carrying out the process.

See the Guidelines C.III.7.2.

See CLBA, pp.176–195.

**4. Notes on drafting the introduction**

For the purposes of the exam, only a partial description needs to be drafted. The following paragraphs follow the order suggested by r.27 EPC as desirable, though not mandatory.

First, specify the technical field to which the invention relates. It is common to start with the general field ("The present invention relates to . . .") and then propose a more specific field ("More specifically, the invention relates to . . ."). Foreshadow various independent claim types in this section (e.g. "Further, the invention relates to a method of . . ., and an apparatus for carrying out the method").

Next, indicate any background art and cite the most pertinent document(s) reflecting that art. Indicate what the closest prior art is, what it discloses and what it does NOT disclose, in what way it is deficient and hence the problem solved by the present invention. When doing this, care needs to be taken not to discuss the art's deficiencies in such a way that it leads the reader to the invention before it is described to him. State the advantages provided by the invention. "The problem that the present invention solves is the provision of . . . with . . . The solution is provided by . . . which has the advantage that . . .". You do not need to acknowledge each piece of art that is disclosed, no matter how irrelevant it is to novelty and inventive step. Often, however, there are only two pieces of prior art and there will be reasons to acknowledge both of them. If there is an item of prior art which has features in common with the invention, but which does not address the same problem or a related one, it is preferable that this not be discussed until after the invention has been introduced, i.e. until after the statement(s) of invention.

Then disclose the invention as claimed starting with the broadest statement of the invention corresponding to claim 1. Follow this by defining any integers of the broadest statement and then list preferred features and their advantages (e.g. "The X may be A, B or C. Preferably, the X is C since this provides the advantage that . . ."). Support for other claim types should also be included. Ensure consistency between the description and the claims, especially with regard to essential/non-essential features — if a feature is not in the claims, the description should not say it is essential.

You can save time in the exam by having statements of invention in the form: "In a first aspect the invention provides a method as in claim 1"; "In a second aspect the invention provides a catalyst as in claim 5"; etc., rather than reproducing the wording of the relevant claims.

## 5. Worked example using EQE 2002 Paper A

*Understanding and annotating the paper*

1–069

The following pages indicate how the 2002 A paper could be marked up on a first reading.

Please note that some of the annotations are there merely to bring out the relevance of certain passages and are therefore not all indicative of the kind of annotations you would make when doing the exam!

## CLIENT'S LETTER

*Consideration relevant to problems and advantages.*

We, Rifle incorporated, are a major manufacturer of hard disk drives. We have specialised in products designed for portable computers. <u>Power consumption and resistance to shocks are major concerns in this market segment</u>. We already have a successful patented product that addresses these concerns.

*Prior art provided both as technical background for non-experts and to explain the problem which the invention solves.*

Figures 1 and 2, taken from one of our published patents, are plan views from above of a disk drive 1 comprising a disk 2 with a data storage area 3 for storing information. A read/write head 4 is mounted on an actuator 5 which pivots about an axis 6. A magnet 7 and a coil 8 form a motor 9 for rotating the actuator 5 about the axis 6 so that the head 4 can be placed over selected positions of the data storage area 3 on the disk 2 for reading and/or writing information. The head 4 has a well-known aerodynamic design such that, when the disk is rotating, an air cushion forms under the head 4 to prevent it touching and scratching the surface of the data storage area 3. In the present example the disk 2 rotates counterclockwise in operation as represented by the arrow 16.

When the disk 1 is not in operation, the head 4 is parked in a parking zone 10 near the centre of the disk 2, outside the data storage area 3. In order to prevent the head 4 from leaving the parking zone 10, for example if the disk drive is subjected to external mechanical shocks, it is necessary to lock the actuator 5 so that the head 4 remains in the parking zone 10. To this end a lock 11 is provided. This lock operates without any electrical components, so that electrical power consumption is minimised.

Figure 1 shows a first state wherein the actuator 5 is locked and Figure 2 shows a second state wherein the actuator 5 is unlocked. The lock 11 is pivotally mounted about a pivot 14 and includes a first portion 12 in the form of an elongate wing and a second potion 13 having at its end an abutment 13a for contacting the actuator 5.

In the locked state, the abutment 13 a contacts the actuator 5, preventing the actuator 5 from rotating clockwise and thus preventing the head 4 from leaving the parking zone 10. The lock is biased in a counterclockwise direction about the pivot 14 by means of a spring 15 shown schematically in figures 1 and 2. In this position the lock 11 blocks clockwise movement of the actuator 5.

When the disk 2 is rotating, a counterclockwise airflow is generated above the disk 2 as illustrated by the arrow 16. When the disk 2 reaches a predetermined rotational speed (typically 5400 revolution per minute), the airflow acting on the first portion 12 of the lock 11 generates a force that exceeds the force exerted by the spring 15. As a result, the lock 11 rotates in a clockwise direction about the pivot 14 as represented by the arrow 30 in Figure 2. In this state the second portion 13 of the lock 11 is rotated away from the actuator 5 so that the actuator 5 is then able to pivot about its axis 6 for accessing the data storage area 3, as shown in Figure 2.

When the disk drive is switched off after use, the actuator 5 is driven to the parking zone 10 by the motor 9. The rotational speed of the disk 2 then diminishes, whereby the force exerted by the spring 15 rotates the lock 11 counterclockwise so that the second portion 13 moves back into the contact with the actuator 5.

The mass distribution of the lock 11 is balanced with respect to the pivot 14 such that the lock 11 maintains its position when the disk drive is subjected to the linear shocks. By a linear shock we mean a sudden and rapid linear (*i.e.* translational) movement of the disk drive.

*The problem with the prior art.*

However, we have found that in some instances, the disk drive can also be vulnerable to rotational shocks. By a rotational shock we mean a sudden and rapid rotational movement of the disk drive. When the disk drive is subjected to a counterclockwise rotational shock, the lock 11, due to its inertia, tends not to rotate with the remainder of the disk drive. The effect of this inertia can be significant enough to overcome the force of the spring 15, whereby the lock undergoes a relative clockwise rotation with respect to the remainder of the disk drive (which is rotating counterclockwise) such that the second portion 13 loses its contact with the actuator 5. The actuator 5 is then released, whereby a similar effect of inertia can cause the actuator 5 to undergo relative rotation about its axis 6. This causes the head 4 to skate over the data storage area 3 of the disk 2 with the risk of damaging the surface of the data storage area 3.

We have now improved our disk drive so that it may also resist rotational shocks. Figures 3 and 4 illustrate our new disk drive 20, Figure 3 illustrating the locked state and Figure 4 the unlocked state of the disk drive. Like components are given the same reference numerals as in Figures 1 and 2.     *The solution.*

In order to protect the disk drive against rotational shocks the disk drive of the invention includes a counter inertia member 17 rotatably mounted on a shaft 18 and modified lock 21. The counter inertia member 17 and the lock 21 each have a mass distribution balanced about their respective axes of rotation so that the protection against linear shocks is not compromised.     *The broad idea. Optimum solution protects both against linear and rotational shocks.*

The counter inertia member 17 has the form of gear wheel. The teeth of the gear wheel mesh with teeth of a corresponding gear segment 22 formed integrally with the lock 21. The configuration of the counter inertia member 17 is so chosen that the effect of the inertia of this member will balance the effect of the inertia of the lock 21 via the meshing gear teeth. This does not necessarily mean that the respective inertias of the counter inertia member 17 and the lock 21 have to be the same. However, the ratio of the inertias of the counter inertia member 17 and the lock 21 should be equal to the ratio of the radius of the gear wheel (counter inertia member 17) and of the radius of the gear segment 22 of the lock 21. The counter inertia member 17 moves with, and rotates in the opposite direction to the modified lock 21.     *The specific embodiment. The nub of the invention.*

The counter inertia member 17 does not play any active role in the unlocked state of the actuator 5 shown in Figure 4, *i.e.* the counter inertia member 17 does not have any negative influence on the normal operation of the disk drive.     *A desirable feature but not something easy to claim.*

While meshed gear are employed to couple the counter inertia member 17 and the lock 21 in the present example, other coupling arrangements may be employed, such as friction coupling.     *Alternatives to be mentioned in sub-claims; the broad claims must cover these and other approaches.*

We should also mention that the various rotational directions described relate to our specific embodiment. In other embodiments, for example, the disk 2 could be arranged to rotate clockwise. Also, some of our competitors make disk drives with the parking zone at the outer periphery of the disk 2 rather than near its centre.     *Alternatives which the claims must cover — hence not features to be recited in the main claims. Known features.*

For your information we attach the published document D1 which describes a locking device used in the current products of our major competitor, Dissdur.     *Prior art.*

## CLIENT'S DRAWINGS

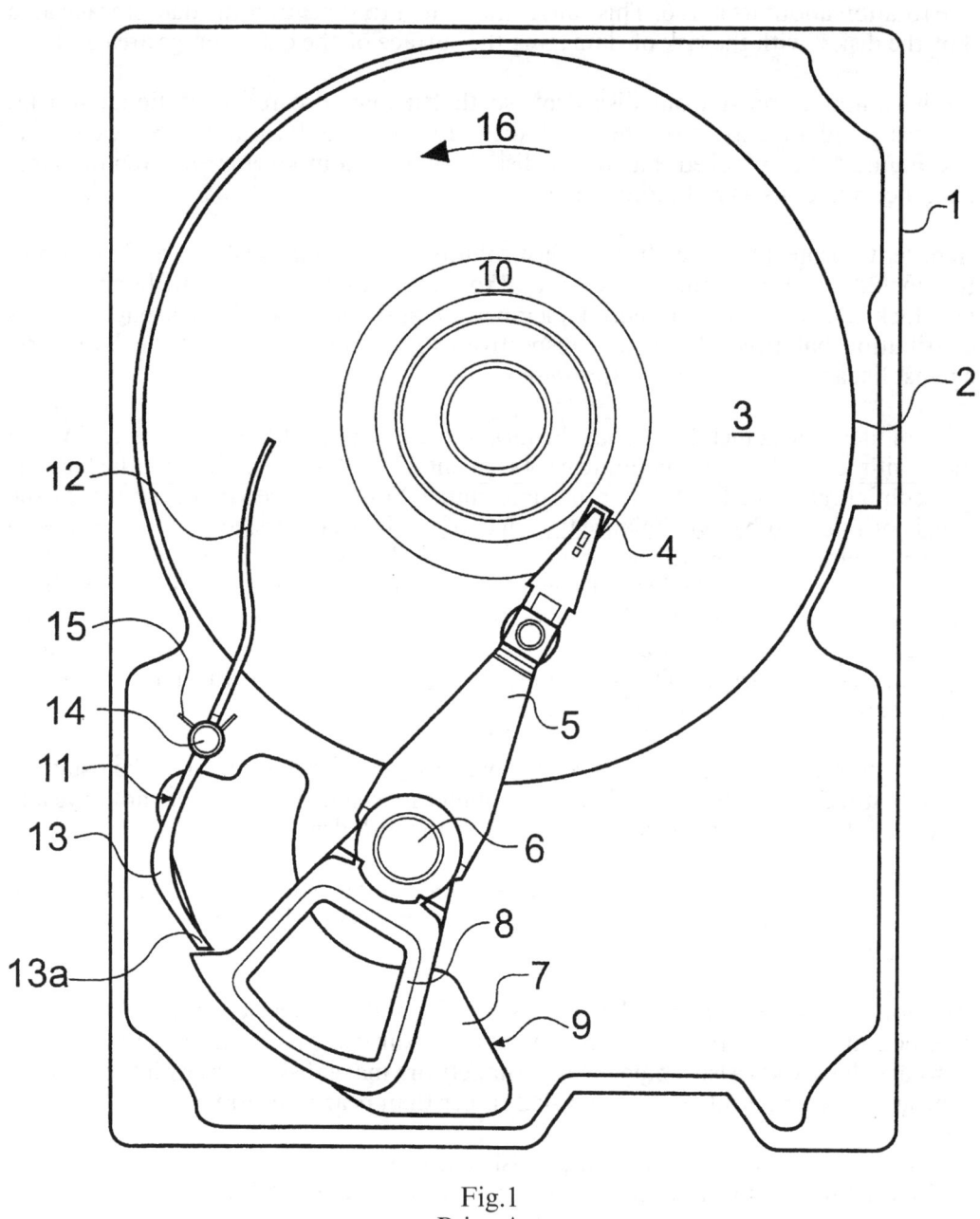

Fig.1
Prior Art

**CLIENT'S DRAWINGS**

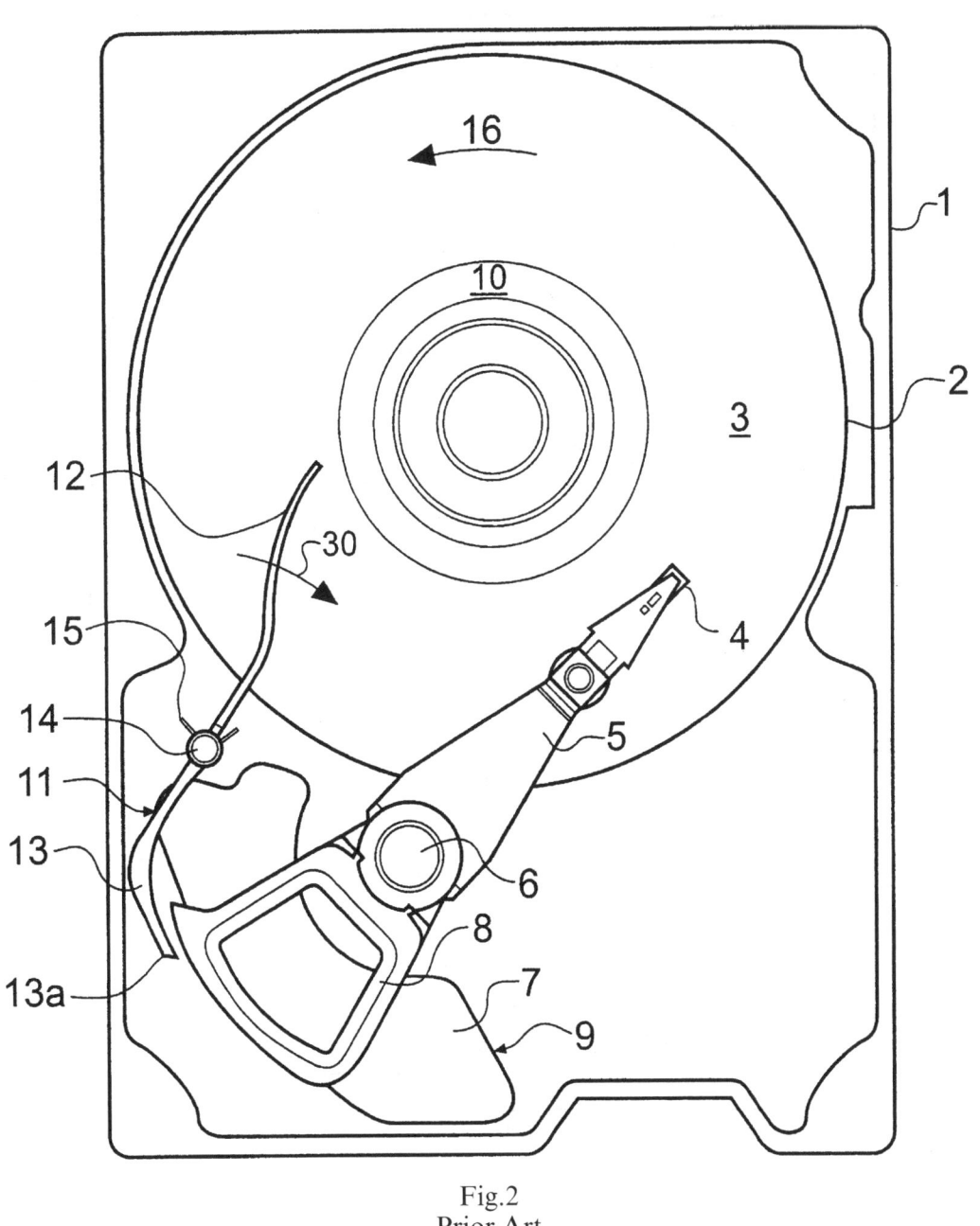

Fig.2
Prior Art

## CLIENT'S DRAWINGS

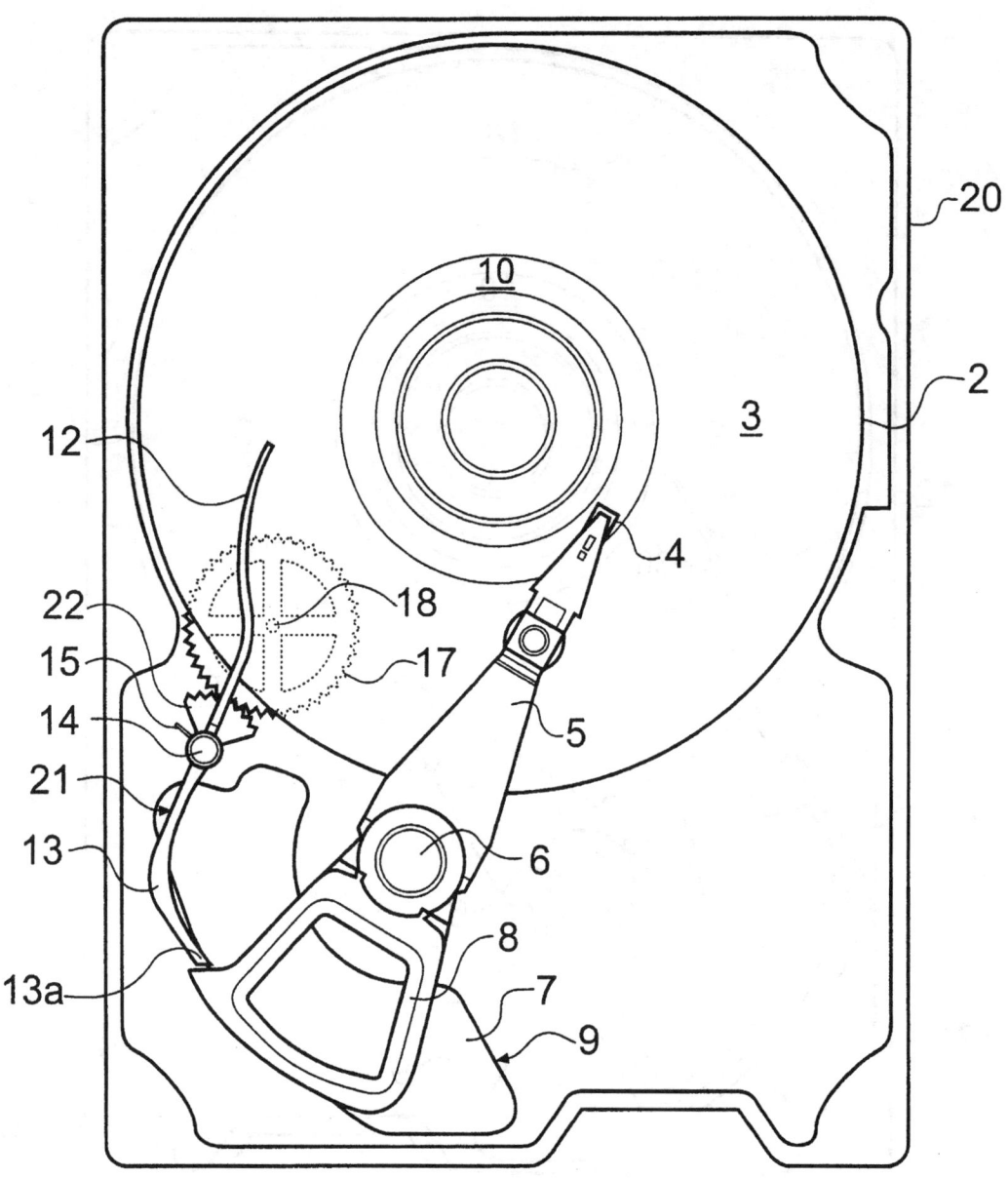

Fig.3

**CLIENT'S DRAWINGS**

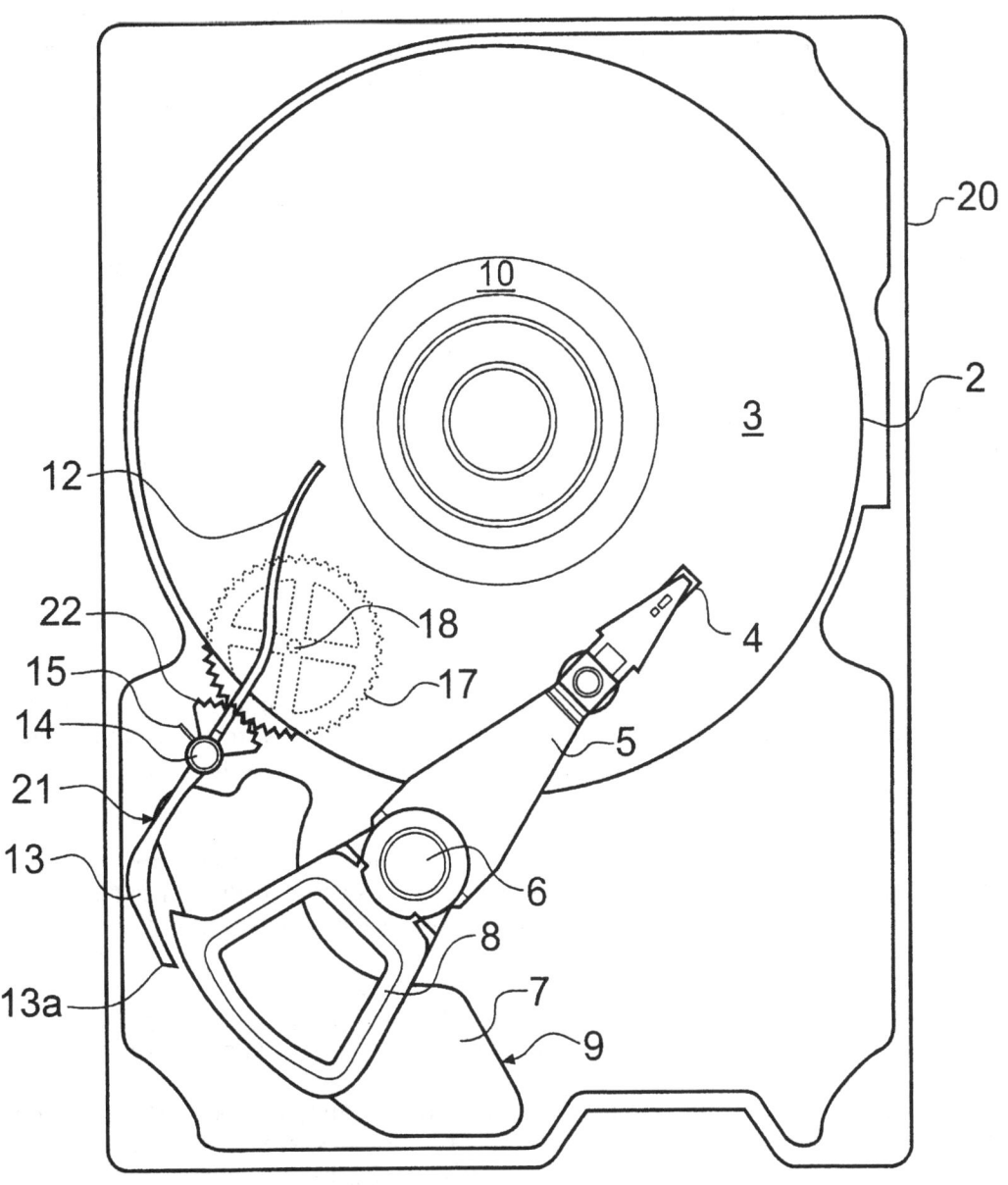

Fig.4

## DOCUMENT D1

*Background*

In computer systems, information is frequently stored in a magnetic film on the surface of a hard or flexible disk. The information is stored in concentric tracks in the magnetic film, and is written on or read from the film by means of a magnetic head mounted on the end of a rotary actuator. When writing or reading data, the magnetic head rides on a thin laminar layer of air over the rapidly rotating disk, thereby avoiding direct contact with the magnetic surface.

When the disk drive is not in operation, the head rests in a "park" position, that is, a position on a "non-data" zone of the disk which is reserved for landings and take-offs of the head. It is important that the head be held in its park position, as any physical contact between the head and the data zone of the disk may damage the magnetic film.

*The same generic problem.*

Rotary actuators are particularly vulnerable to rotational shocks and acceleration, which can cause the rotary actuator to swing about its axis out of the park position, thereby bringing the magnetic head in unwanted contact with the disk. A lock for reducing the chance of damage resulting from rotational shocks is described in the following.

*Same generic idea.*

Fig. 1 is a top view of a disk drive with an <u>inertial</u> lock.

Fig. 2 and 3 show a portion of a rotary actuator in the operational and locked states, respectively.

*Background*

The actuator 1 shown in Figure 1 is rotatably driven about an axis 2 by means of a motor constituted by a coil 3 and a magnet (not shown). The motor rotates the actuator 1 to position the magnetic head 4 over a desired location on the disk. An inertial lock 6 is positioned adjacent the actuator 1.

*Same generic idea.*

*How it works.*

Figure 2 shows the inertial lock 6 in an unlocked condition. An inertia member 8 is rotatably mounted about a shaft 7. A pin 9 is attached to the surface of the inertia member 8. In the operational state of the actuator 1 the inertial lock 6 is in its rest position which is determined by means of a helical spring 10 extending between a fixed pin 11 and a pin 12 located on the inertia member 8. A finger 13 protrudes from the actuator 1 and is <u>so arranged that, when the actuator 1 is in the park position, the locking pin 9 is</u> **able to** <u>engage the inner surface 14 of the finger 13 to block clockwise rotation of the actuator 1</u>.

*But it clearly does not rest there.*

*How it works.*

If the disk drive is submitted to a counterclockwise rotational shock, the actuator 1, due to its inertia, tends to maintain its absolute position in space or, in other words, the actuator 1 rotates in a clockwise direction relative to the disk drive. The inertial lock 6 overcomes the force of the spring 10 and also rotates in a clockwise direction relative to the disk drive. <u>The inertial lock 6, however, responds to the rotational shock much quicker than the actuator 1, whereby the inertial lock 6 rotates, before the actuator 1 has hardly moved</u>. Due to the rotation of the inertial lock 6, the pin 9 moves through an angle β as shown in Fig. 3 until it strikes the inner surface 14 of the finger 13. In this position, the pin 9 blocks any clockwise movement of the actuator 1 relative to the disk drive.

*So in the rest position the lock is always unlocked. It is only while subjected to a rotational shock that the lock works and even that does not happen instantly.*

Following the shock, the spring 10 urges the inertial lock 6 back to the unlocked position shown in Figure 2.

*Locks in response to shocks only in one direction. No balance is required between the inertia of the lock and that of the actuator: the lock just needs to respond more quickly to the shock.*

It can be seen therefore that the inertial lock 6 activates <u>in response to a counterclockwise</u> rotational shock. There is no need to provide a lock activated in case of a clockwise shock since in this case the head does not leave the non-data zone. Besides, in most of the known disk drives, the moment of the actuator from the park position towards the centre of the disk is limited by stop members (not shown). Stop members are also generally provided to prevent the head from moving outwardly beyond the disk outer circumference.

*So this is only a partial solution — unlike our embodiment.*

If desired, additional measures could be taken to protect against linear shocks.

## DRAWINGS DOCUMENT D1

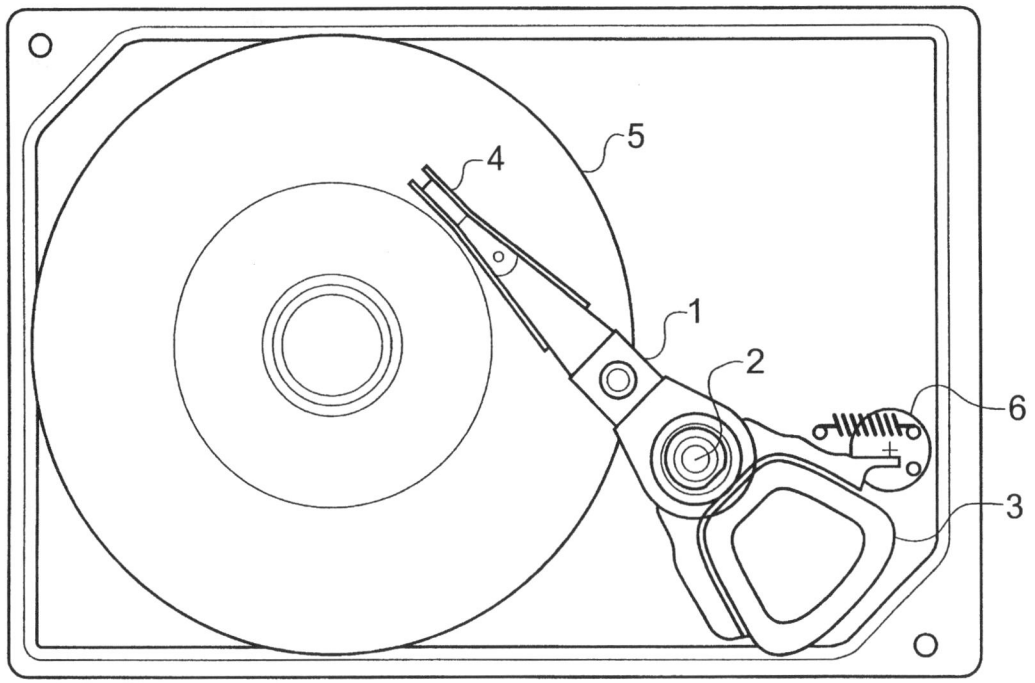

Fig.1

## DRAWINGS DOCUMENT D1

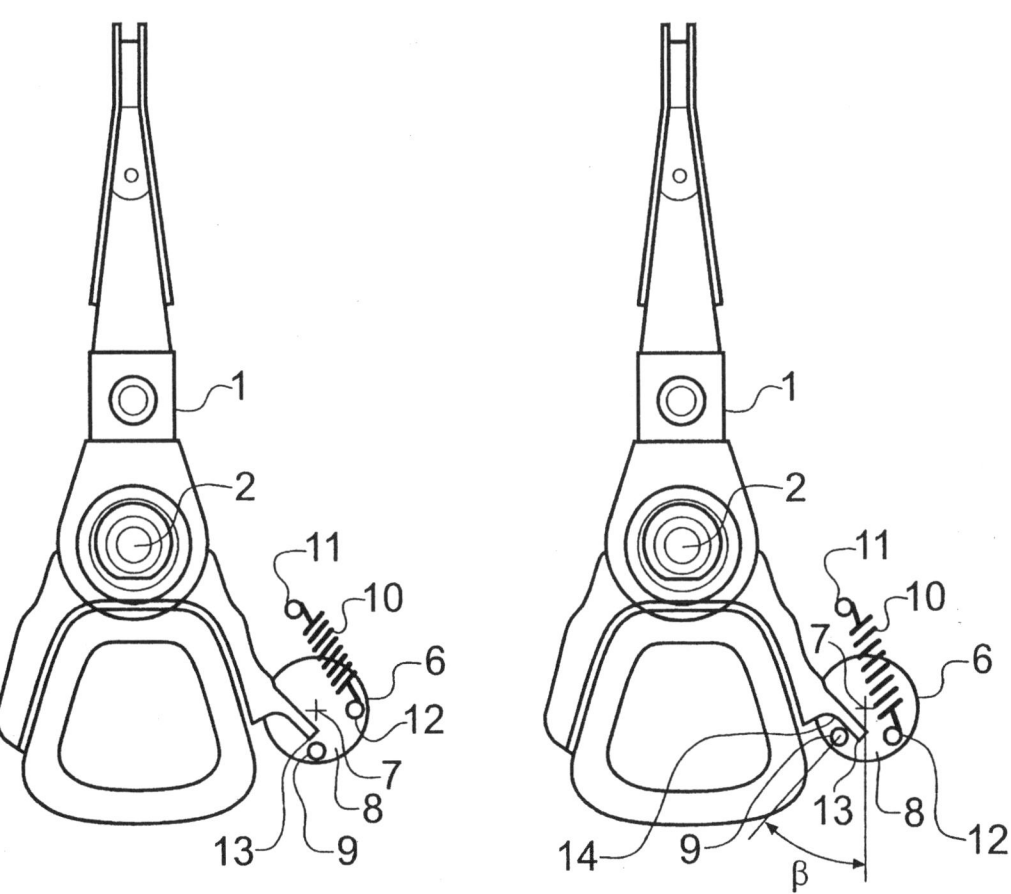

Fig.2        Fig. 3

**1–070**   *Establishing novel subject matter*

The following pages indicate how the client's invention can be divided into novel features and features found in the prior art. A simple box has been used in the former case and a shaded box in the latter case.

# CLIENT'S LETTER

We, Rifle incorporated, are a major manufacturer of hard disk drives. We have specialised in products designed for portable computers. Power consumption and resistance to shocks are major concerns in this market segment. We already have a successful patented product that addresses these concerns.

*Considerations relevant to problems and advantages.*

Figures 1 and 2, taken from one of our published patents, are plan views from above of a disk drive 1 comprising a disk 2 with a data storage area 3 for storing information. A read/write head 4 is mounted on an actuator 5 which pivots about an axis 6. A magnet 7 and a coil 8 form a motor 9 for rotating the actuator 5 about the axis 6 so that the head 4 can be placed over selected positions of the data storage area 3 on the disk 2 for reading and/or writing information. The head 4 has a well-known aerodynamic design such that, when the disk is rotating, an air cushion forms under the head 4 to prevent it touching and scratching the surface of the data storage are 3. In the present example the disk 2 rotates counterclockwise in operation as represented by the arrow 16.

*All Art.54(2) prior art.*

When the disk drive 1 is not in operation, the head 4 is parked in the parking zone 10 near the centre of the disk 2, outside the data storage area 3. In order to prevent the head 4 from leaving the parking zone 10, for example if the disk drive is subjected to external mechanical shocks, it is necessary to lock the actuator 5 so that the head 4 remains in the parking zone 10. To this end a lock 11 is provided. This lock operates without any electric components, so that electrical power consumption is minimised.

Figure 1 shows a first state wherein the actuator 5 is locked and Figure 2 shows a second state wherein the actuator 5 is unlocked. The lock 11 is pivotally mounted about a pivot 14 and includes a first portion 12 in the form of an elongate wing and a second portion 13 having at its end an abutment 13a for contacting the actuator 5.

In the locked state, the abutment 13a contacts the actuator 5, preventing the actuator 5 from rotating clockwise and thus preventing the head 4 from leaving the parking zone 10. The lock 11 is biased in a counterclockwise direction about the pivot 14 by means of a spring 15 shown schematically in Figures 1 and 2. In this position the lock 11 blocks clockwise movement of the actuator 5.

When the disk 2 is rotating, a counterclockwise airflow is generated above the disk 2 as illustrated by the arrow 16. When the disk 2 reaches a predetermined rotational speed (typically 5400 revolutions per minute), the airflow acting on the first portion 12 of the lock 11 generates a force that exceeds the force exerted by the spring 15. As a result, the lock 11 rotates in a clockwise direction about the pivot 14 as represented by the arrow 30 in Figure 2. In this state the second portion 13 of the lock 11 is rotated away from the actuator 5 so that the actuator 5 is then able to pivot about its axis 6 for accessing the data storage area 3, as shown in Figure 2.

When the disk drive is switched off after use, the actuator 5 is driven to the parking zone 10 by the motor 9. The rotational speed of the disk 2 then diminishes, whereby the force exerted on the first portion 12 of the lock 11 by the airflow is reduced. As a result, the force exerted by the spring 15 rotates the lock 11 counterclockwise so that the second portion 13 moves back into contact with the actuator 5.

The mass distribution of the lock 11 is balanced with the respect to the pivot 14 such that the lock 11 maintains its position when the disk drive is subjected to linear shocks. By a linear shock we mean a sudden and rapid linear (i.e. translational) movement of the disk drive.

| | |
|---|---|
| The problem with the prior art. **Problem** | However, we have found that in some instances, the disk drive can also be vulnerable to rotational shocks. By a rotational shock we mean a sudden and rapid rotational movement of the disk drive. When the disk drive is subjected to a counterclockwise rotational shock, the lock 11, due to its inertia, tends not to rotate with the remainder of the disk drive. The effect of this inertia can be significant enough to overcome the force of the spring 15, whereby the lock undergoes a relative clockwise rotation with respect to the remainder of the disk drive (which is rotating counterclockwise) such that the second portion 13 loses its contact with the actuator 5. The actuator is then released, whereby a similar effect of inertia can cause the actuator 5 to undergo relative rotation about its axis 6. This causes the head 4 to skate over the data storage area 3 of the disk 2 with the risk of damaging the surface of the data storage area 3. |
| The solution. | We have now improved our disk drive so that it may also resist rotational shocks. Figures 3 and 4 illustrate our new disk drive 20, Figure 3 illustrating the locked state and Figure 4 the unlocked state of the disk drive. Like components are given the same reference numerals as in Figures 1 and 2. |
| In Document 1 the Lock 6 and Actuator 1 rotate in the same sense. Document 1 shows this. Optimum solution protects both against linear and rotational shocks. Not in Document 1. All new. | In order to protect the disk drive against rotational shocks the disk drive of the invention includes a counter inertia member 17 rotatably mounted on a shaft 18 and modified lock 21. The counter inertia member 17 and the lock 21 each have a mass distribution balanced about their respective axes of rotation so that the protection against linear shocks is not compromised. |
| The nub of the invention. | The counter inertia member 17 has a form of gear wheel. The teeth of the gear wheel mesh with teeth of a corresponding gear segment 22 formed integrally with the lock 21. The configuration of the counter inertia member 17 is so chosen that the effect of the inertia of this member will balance the effect of the inertia of the lock 21 via the meshing gear teeth. This does not necessarily mean that the respective inertias of the counter inertia member 17 and the lock 21 have to be the same. However, the ratio of the inertias of the counter inertia member 17 and the lock 21 should be equal to the ratio of the radius of the gear wheel (counter inertia member 17) and of the radius of the gear segment 22 of the lock 21. The counter inertia member 17 moves with, and rotates in the opposite direction the modified lock 21. |
| A desirable feature but not something easy to claim. Not clearly true of D1. Alternatives to be mentioned in sub-claims; and broad claims must cover these and other approaches. New | The counter inertia member 17 does not play any active role in the unlocked state of the actuator 5 shown in Figure 4, i.e. the counter inertia member 17 does not have any negative influence on the normal operation of the desk drive.

While meshed gears are employed to couple the counter inertia member 17 and lock 21 in the present example, other coupling arrangements may be employed, such as friction coupling. |
| Alternatives which the claims must cover — hence not features to be recited in the main claims. Known features. | We should also mention that the various rotational directions described relate to our specific embodiment. In other embodiments, for example, the disk 2 could be arranged to rotate clockwise. Also, some of our competitors make disk drives with the parking zone at the outer periphery of the disk 2 rather than near its centre. |
| Prior art. | For your information we attach the published document D1 which describes a locking device used in the current products of our major competitor, Dissdur. |

*Claiming the invention* 1–071

The client's invention resides in the provision, in a locking device for a disk drive, of an inertia member the effect of whose inertia will balance the effect of the inertia of the locking member. The third sentence on page 3 of the client's letter gives us the form of words to use. Clearly, the use of meshing gear teeth is not an essential feature of the invention — the client tells us this, so we will save that feature for a sub-claim. D1 has shown that there may be a market for a lock which only protects against rotational shocks and not also linear shocks — so we should not limit our claims to locking devices which protect against both types of shock.

Arguably, it would not be too limiting to limit the claims to a disk drive, but on the other hand there seems to be no good reason to reduce the scope of protection in this way. It is conceivable that the actuator and its locking arrangement might be sold as a sub-assembly for incorporation into disk drives. On that basis, our main claim should be for a locking device but we should have sub-claims for the disc drive. It is a matter of personal preference whether or not one also includes a claim to a computer.

There seems to be nothing worth making the subject of a method claim.

**Unity** 1–072

No issue arises here.

**Dependent claims** 1–073

Clearly, one of the main strands for the dependent claims will concern the use of gears to couple the inertia member and the locking member. We are given quite a few features in the third and fourth paragraphs on page 3 which are claimable more or less independently: the use of gearing to link the inertia member and the locking member; the use of a segment and wheel and the ratio of their inertias to their radii; and the segment integral with the lock. There is also the use of friction coupling, mentioned on page 4. The opposite rotations of the inertia member and of the locking member (from the last line on page 3) is also worth claiming: it does not appear to be an essential feature.

Then there are the features which relate to the protection against linear shocks: the mass distribution of the locking member balanced about its axis of rotation; the mass distribution of the inertia member balanced about its axis of rotation; release means for releasing the actuator from the park position; airflow releasing the actuator; an abutment to contact; biasing means to bias the lock to block the actuator; biasing means is a spring.

**Typical solution** 1–074

A typical claim set may therefore be:

1. A locking device for locking an actuator (5) of a disk drive (1), comprising a rotatably mounted locking member (21), characterised in that the locking device further comprises a rotatably mounted inertia member (17) rotatably coupled with the locking member (21) and configured such that the effect of the inertia member (17) balances the effect of the inertia of the locking member (21).

2. A locking device as claimed in claim 1, wherein the locking member (21) and the inertia member are coupled via meshed gears.

3. A locking device as claimed in claim 2, wherein the locking member includes a gear segment (22) and the inertia member (17) has the form of a gear wheel, the teeth of the gear wheel meshing with teeth of the gear segment.

4. A locking device as claimed in claim 3, wherein the gear segment is formed integrally with the locking member (21).

5. A locking device as claimed in claim 3 or claim 4, wherein the ratio of the inertia of the locking member (17) to the inertia of the locking member (21) is equal to the ratio of the radius of the gear wheel to the radius of the gear segment (22).

6 A locking device as claimed in claim 1, wherein the locking member (21) and the inertia member are coupled via a friction coupling.

7 A locking device as claimed in any one of the preceding claims, configured so that in response to a rotational shock the inertia member (17) moves with, and rotates in the opposite direction to, the locking member (21).

8 A locking device as claimed in any one of the preceding claims, wherein the mass distribution of the locking member (21) and/or the inertia member is balanced with respect to its pivot axis.

9 A locking device as claimed in any one of the preceding claims, wherein the locking member (21) comprises an abutment (13a) for contacting the actuator (5) of the disk drive, to prevent the actuator from rotating.

10 A locking device as claimed in any one of the preceding claims, wherein the locking member (21) comprises a release means (12) for releasing the actuator (5) of the disk drive from a locked parking position.

11 A locking device as claimed in claim 10, wherein the release means comprises a portion (12) of the locking member (21) for generating a force in response to airflow generated by a disk (2) of the disk drive (1) to rotate the locking member (21) to an unlocked position.

12 A locking device as claimed in any one of the preceding claims, wherein biasing means (15) are provided to bias the locking member (21) towards a locking position about its pivot axis.

13 A locking device as claimed in claim 12, wherein the biasing means comprises a spring (15)

14 A disk drive (1) comprising an actuator (5) for mounting a read/write head (4) for reading and/or writing data on a data storage area (3) of a disk (2), wherein the actuator (5) is provided with a locking device according to any one of the preceding claims.

15 A disk drive as claimed in claim 14, having a disk (2) with a data storage area (3) for storing data.

16 A disk drive as claimed in claim 15, having a read/write head (4) mounted on the actuator (5).

17 A disk drive as claimed in claim 16, wherein the actuator (5) is arranged such that, when the disk drive (1) is not in operation, the read/write head (4) is parked in a parking zone either near the centre of the disk (2) or at the periphery of the disk (2).

**1–075**  *Drafting the introduction*

The following is an example of a suitable introduction drafted using the principles outlined above:

> This invention relates to a locking device for locking an actuator of a disk drive and also to a disk drive having such a locking device.
>
> A conventional disk drive comprises a disk with a data storage area for storing information. A read/write head is mounted on an actuator which pivots about an axis. Means are provided for rotating the actuator about the disk so that the head can be placed over selected positions of the data storage area on the disk for reading and/or writing information. Generally, the head has a well-known aerodynamic design such that, when the disk is rotating, an air cushion forms under the head to prevent it touching and scratching the surface of the data storage area.
>
> When the disk is not in operation, the head is parked in a parking zone outside the data storage area, either near the centre of the disk or near the periphery of the disk. In order to prevent the head from leaving the parking zone, for example if the disk drive is subjected to external mechanical shocks, it is necessary to lock the actuator so that the head remains in the parking zone. To this end a lock must be provided.

A locking device for locking an actuator of a disk drive is known in which a pivotally mounted lock has an abutment for contacting the actuator. The lock is spring biased to a locked position in which the abutment contacts the actuator with the head in the parked position. This prevents the head from leaving the parked position. When the disk drive becomes active, an airflow caused by rotation of the disk acts on a portion of the lock to generate a force that exceeds the spring bias causing the abutment to release the actuator. With the lock in this position, the actuator can be rotated to move the read/write head to the data storage area. When the disk drive is switched off, the actuator is driven to the parking zone. The rotational speed of the disk then diminishes, reducing the force exerted by the airflow on the lock. As a result, the force exerted by the spring bias rotates the lock so that the abutment portion once again contacts the actuator, locking it in place.

The mass distribution of this lock is balanced with respect to its pivot so that the lock maintains its position when the disk drive is subject to linear shocks. By a linear shock is meant a sudden and rapid linear (i.e. translational) movement of the disk drive. However, in some instances, the disk drive can also be vulnerable to rotational shocks. By a rotational shock is meant a sudden and rapid rotational movement of the disk drive. Such a rotational shock can release the actuator and cause the read/write head to skate over the data with the risk of damaging the surface of the data storage area.

Another example of a locking device for a disk drive is known from document D1. The locking device is suitable for reducing the likelihood of damage caused by rotational shocks. An inertial lock includes an inertia member rotationally mounted about a shaft. The inertia member has a locking pin to engage a finger on the actuator. The inertia member is spring biased into a position whereat the pin is not in contact with the finger, so that the actuator is free to rotate. When the disk drive is subjected to a rotational shock, the inertia member rotates to bring the pin into contact with the finger, locking the actuator. Following the shock, the spring bias urges the lock back to the unlocked position.

Although the lock described in D1 offers some protection against rotational shocks, it has some significant disadvantages. The lock does not react instantly to rotational shocks, but must itself first rotate to move into the locking position. For smaller shocks there is a risk that the spring bias will not be overcome, so that the actuator remains free to rotate. The lock also only works for rotational shocks in one direction. Finally, the lock is not effective to protect against linear shocks so that other means must be provided to protect the disk drive from such shocks.

It is therefore an object of the invention to provide a locking device with improved protection against rotational shocks. This object is achieved by the locking device according to claim 1.

In locking devices according to the invention the effect of the inertia member balances the effect of the inertia of the locking member in the event of a rotational shock. Thus the locked state of the actuator is not compromised by the rotational shock, unlike the operation of the locking device of D1.

*Notes to the Examiner* 1–076

With this paper, none appear to be needed.


## 6. Partial worked example using EQE 2004 Paper A

*Understanding and annotating the paper* 1–077

In the 2004 paper the technology was extremely simple and the difficulty lay more in drafting a single claim to cover the many embodiments than in understanding the invention. The presentation of the paper was quite different from that of 2002, with the entire prior art disclosure being in the client's letter and an accompanying drawing, rather than in separate documents. This simplified the process of marking up the paper.

The following pages indicate how the paper could be marked up on first reading.

## CLIENT'S LETTER

Dear Mr. Advoduck,

*General instructions.* — In the last few days I have invented a new type of egg shell breaker which is simple yet effective. Unfortunately I had a bad experience with my last invention being copied, and would therefore ask you to file a patent application as soon as possible.

*Art.54(2) prior art.* — Every Easter a traditional public competition takes place at the market square of Ducktown, where I live. The aim is to find the best way of opening a boiled egg. The many different egg openers developed by the participants are judged by a jury. The three best egg openers of last year's competition were published in the local press. I have cut out the pictures and annexed them to this letter as Fig. 1–3.

My entry for last year's competition is shown in Fig. 1. This is based on a set of old punches which I found at a flea market. Such punches are used by saddlers to stamp holes of different sizes in leather. Basically, these punches are solid bodies comprising a bottom recess 10a. The recess 10a results in a bottom opening of the punch 10 defined by a circular cutting edge 11. I had the idea to use one of these punches, of appropriate size, as an egg shell breaker. *[Definition likely to be useful for the claims.]* By "appropriate size" I mean that an end portion of an egg can be introduced into the bottom opening of the punch 10, in such a manner that the cutting edge 11 contacts the egg shell along a circumferential contact line.

*Technical information for understanding the invention.* — As illustrated in Fig. 1, I placed a boiled egg into an egg holder and held the punch 10 on top of this egg with one hand. In the other hand I held a light hammer. After a few trials I found that by hitting the flat upper surface 12 of the punch in the right manner, the impulse applied by the hammer to the punch 10 was transmitted to the egg, thus obtaining a really clean circular break of the egg shell along the contact line with the punch 10. To my surprise, most of the time I could do this without producing small fragments of egg shell and without damaging the contents of the egg. I *[Problem — need for skill.]* practised a lot in order to be able to hit the punch 10 with the hammer in a consistent way, so as to ensure a perfect demonstration of my egg shell breaker during the competition.

*Technical information for understanding the invention.* — However, my strongest competitor, Doughnut Duck, succeeded in spying on my work during this training phase. He copied my egg shell breaker and modified it slightly, as shown in Fig. 2. In his version he simply replaced my punch 10 with a sleeve-like hole drill 20, which also had the "appropriate size" as defined above. The serrated or saw-like cutting edge 21 of hole drill 20 achieved the same breaking effect as the continuous-contact cutting edge 11 of my punch 10. Nevertheless, Doughnut won first prize, whereas I had to be content with second place. I am sure that this was only because Doughnut's three nephews were on the jury.

*Problem.* — The third prize was awarded to Pierre McDucksbill. He cut off the end of an egg with his mini-guillotine, which he normally uses for cutting off the tips of his cigars (see Fig. 3). The result was, however, not very satisfactory, due to the fact that the yolk ran out. Moreover, the cut end of the egg rolled across the table and fell onto the trousers of a jury member.

In the end, both Pierre and I were furious; Pierre cannot stand losing and I felt cheated. For the next competition Pierre and I therefore decided to cooperate. As Pierre is very rich, he provided financial support, and tasked me with inventing a new egg shell breaker. True to character, Pierre himself wanted to present this new breaker to the jury.

*Object of the invention.* — I decided that the new egg shell breaker should be able to achieve the same fantastic clean circumferential break of the egg shell which had been produced by the punch 10 and the hole drill 20, and which had so much impressed the jury the previous year. At the same time it should be easier and more convenient to handle and operate, since

Pierre is, frankly, quite clumsy. Whenever Pierre tried my punch-hammer-system, he encountered problems in using the hammer. Unlike me, he was incapable of consistently reproducing the same impulse with the hammer, both in terms of the direction and the intensity of the impulse. In other words, he could not ensure that the hammer would hit the upper surface of the punch at the correct angle and with the appropriate force.

*Specific problem to be solved.*

I therefore tried to improve my punch-hammer-system with the aim of reproducing the impulse independently of the skill of the user, that is, "automatically".

*Object of the invention.*

I considered again Pierre's mini-guillotine (see Fig. 3). Despite the disadvantage that the end of the egg is completely cut off, I found it interesting that in this mechanism, the blade 30 applies the same impulse to the egg every time it is used, since the blade always falls from the same height and is guided in a frame 33.

*Art.54(2) prior art.*

Consequently I also tried to provide a guide to cooperate with the punch, as illustrated in Fig. 4. I bored an axial hole through the punch 40 and introduced a barbecue skewer 43 through this hole. I then poked the skewer 43 into the top of an egg, lifted the punch up to the eye 45 at the end of the skewer 43 and let it drop down towards the egg. In this way, the skewer 43 guides the punch 40 and thus determines the direction of the impulse imparted by the punch 40 to the egg. Furthermore, for a given weight of the punch 40, the maximum intensity of the impulse is determined by the length of the skewer 43.

*First embodiment novel combination.*

As an option, the weight of the punch 40 and/or the length of the skewer 43 could be reduced by providing a helical spring between the upper surface 42 of the punch 40 and the eye 45 of the skewer 43. In this case, the force of the compressed spring contributes to achieving the necessary intensity of the impulse.

*Second embodiment novel combination.*

However, I was still not satisfied. The egg shell breaker needed to be even easier for someone like Pierre to use. In particular, it was difficult to keep the skewer 43 in line with the axis of the egg. After further trials I finally developed two prototypes which I consider to be my best designs so far, as represented in Fig. 5 and 6–8, respectively.

*Secondary problem.*

As can be seen from Fig. 5, I selected a hollow cone-like body 50 which, as in the punch 10, comprises a circumferential cutting edge 51 defining an opening. A ball 57 is arranged in a sliding manner on a shaft 53 which is fixed to the top of the body 50 opposite the opening. When the ball 57 falls, gravity accelerates the ball, until it impacts the top of the body 50 in a direction determined by the shaft 53. Provided the ball 57 drops from a sufficient height, the impulse imparted to the egg is adequate to break the egg shell. An abutment 55 on the top of the shaft 53 limits the movement of the ball 57. As an amusing addition I made the abutment 55 in the form of the head of a hen.

*Third embodiment novel combination.*

*Technical explanation.*

*Non-technical feature.*

For the other prototype, I employed a spring in order to provide an adequate impulse. As can be seen in Fig. 6–8, this prototype also has a cone-like body 60, but this time with a flat upper impact surface 62. Fixed to this impact surface 62 are two guiding rails 63 between which a slider 64 runs. A helical spring 69 is interposed between the slider 64 and a crossbar 65 joining the two rails 63. A rod 66 is arranged inside the spring 69. This rod 66 is attached to the slider 64 near its free end 67, the free end 67 projecting from the slider 64 towards the impact surface 62. At its opposite end, the rod 66 passes freely through the crossbar 65 and is provided with a knob 68. The knob 68 is used to pull the rod 66, thereby retracting the slider 64 towards the crossbar 65 and compressing the helical spring 69 (see Fig. 8). Upon release of the knob 68, the spring 69 accelerates rod 66 and slider 64 in a direction determined by the rails 63, until the free end 67 of the rod 66 hits the impact surface 62, thereby imparting an impulse to the egg via the body 60. The intensity of the impulse is mainly determined by the characteristics of the helical spring 69. The contribution of gravity can be neglected in this prototype.

*Fourth embodiment novel combination.*

*Technical explanation.*

Fifth embodiment.
Sixth embodiment.

One could consider combining some aspects of both prototypes with each other, e.g. by providing a helical spring between the ball 57 and the abutment 55 in Fig. 5, or using a heavy ball fixed to the free end 67 of the rod 66 as an impact means in Figs 6–8. In both cases, the impulse transmitted by the body 50 or 60 to the egg would then result from gravity and the spring force in combination.

General instruction (to protect all embodiments).

I hope that I have provided you with all of the information that you need in order to draft a patent application covering all aspects of my invention, including the egg shell breaker of Fig. 4. Please send your invoice to Pierre McDucksbill.

Yours sincerely,

Toni Turbine
Inventor

Annex:  Newspaper cutting comprising 3 drawings
        5 drawings representing my invention

**NEWSPAPER CUTTINGS**

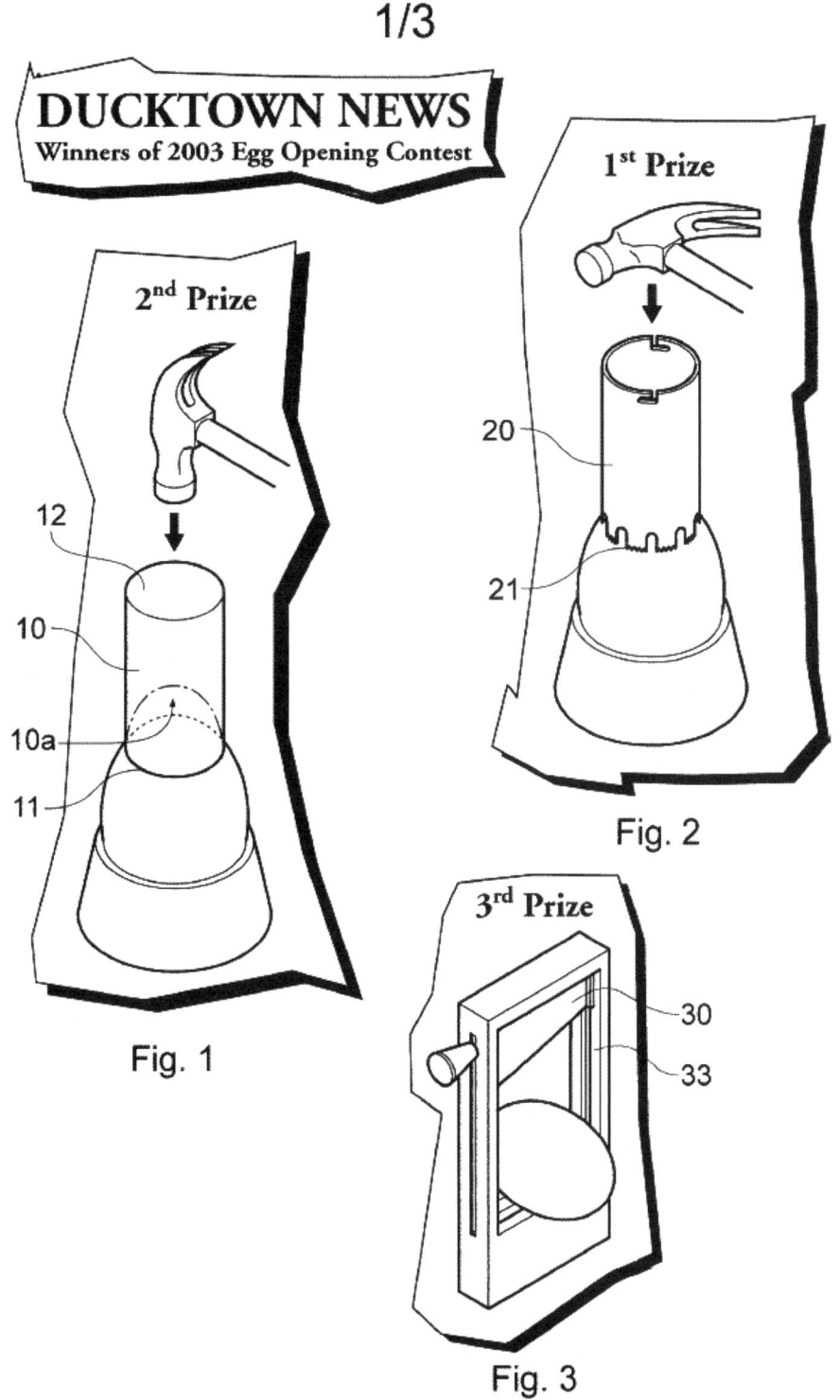

Fig. 1

Fig. 2

Fig. 3

**CLIENT'S DRAWINGS**

2/3

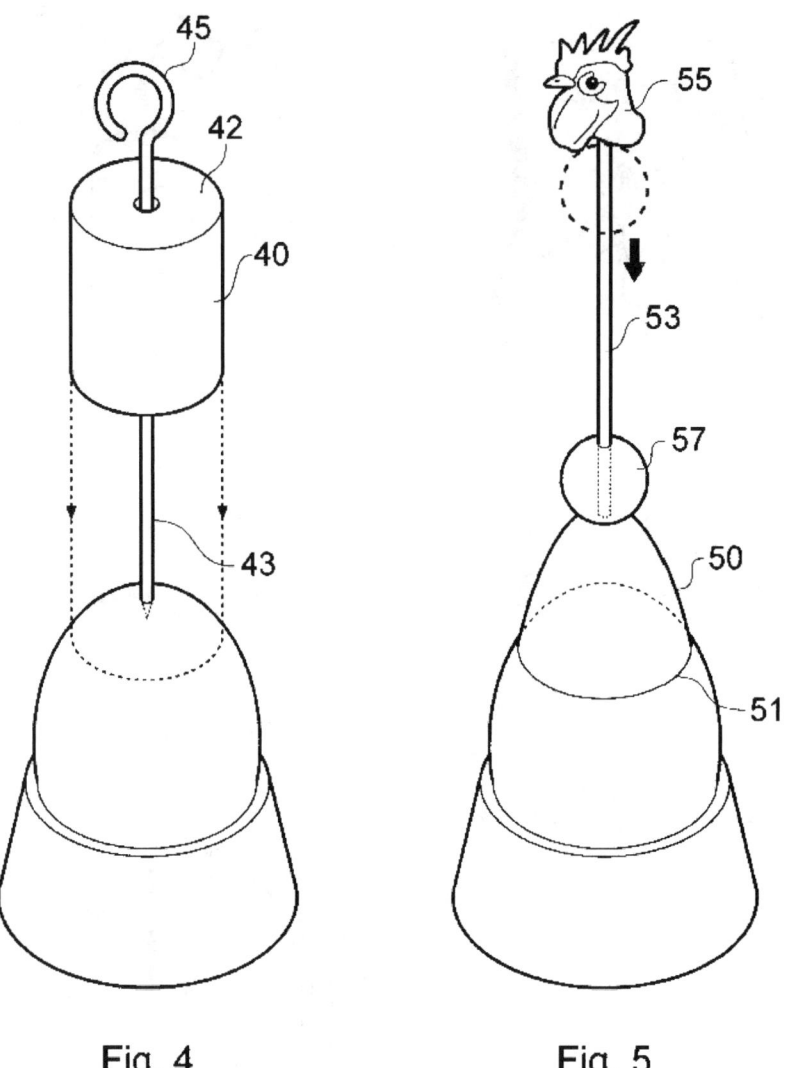

Fig. 4   Fig. 5

3/3

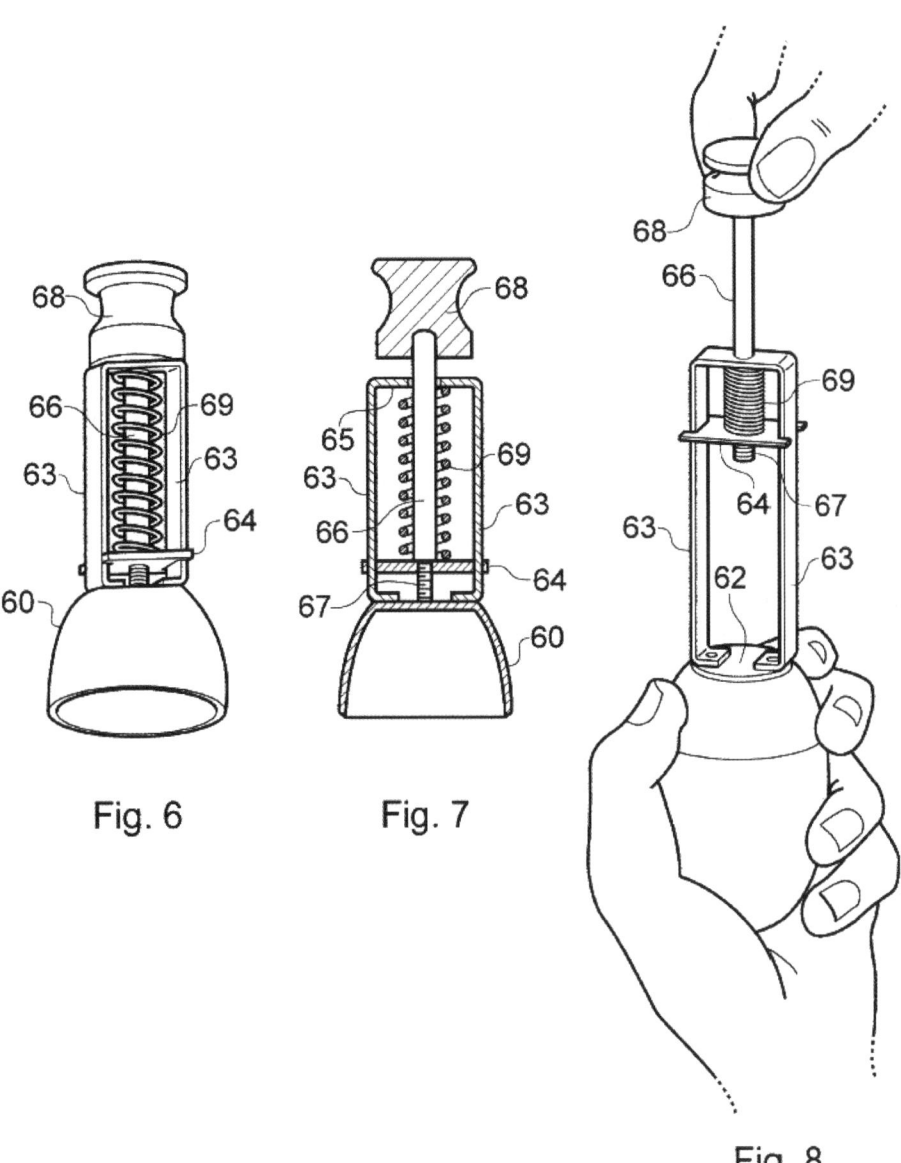

Fig. 6

Fig. 7

Fig. 8

**1–078**  *Identifying the invention*

It is clear that the problem with the guillotine prior art is that by slicing off the end of the egg it not only completely removes it but also permits the contents of the egg, if incompletely cooked, to leak out. The problem with the other two items of prior art is that achievement of a satisfactory result is dependent upon the skill of the user — in particular in terms of regulating the magnitude of the force used and its orientation.

The solution is to use the circumferential cutter form, of Figs 1 and 2, with control of the magnitude and direction of the applied impulse from Fig. 3. The invention is a device rather than a method. Care will clearly need to be taken to distinguish over the Fig. 3 prior art which has the guide and a controlled impulse and which includes an aperture into which the end of an egg can be inserted for cutting. To this end the language used to define "appropriate size", which appears in the third paragraph of the question looks likely to be extremely useful. As a general rule you should always pay attention to any such definition which you find in these questions.

An argument could be made for either prior art type to be the starting point, but in fact the client appears to have addressed his mind to improving the Figs 1 and 2 approach and a two-part claim based on this art looks easier to draft than one based on Fig. 3. It is evident that it is irrelevant whether or not the cutter provides a continuous cutting edge, as in Fig. 1, or a discontinuous one as in Fig. 2.

A difficulty with this question is that whereas the Figs 5 and 6–8 embodiments both use a cutter whose cutting edge bears on the shell of the egg before being struck by something which causes an impact on the cutter and thereby an impulse to the egg from the cutter, for which three main elements are required, in the Fig. 4 embodiment the momentum of the cutter body itself is applied directly to the egg, requiring only two main elements. So, in Figs 5 and 6 there are three main elements: the cutting body, having a cutting edge; an impacting element which is used to apply an impact to the cutting body and thence to the egg via the cutting edge; and a guide to control the direction of the applied impulse. Whereas in the Fig. 4 embodiment there are just two main elements: the guide; and the cutting body having a cutting edge.

The client tells us, in the last paragraph of the question, that he wants to protect all aspects of the invention. So we know that our claims must cover the Fig. 4 embodiment, plus the variants discussed in the twelfth paragraph of the question, as well as those of Figs 5 to 8 and their variants set out in the penultimate paragraph of the question.

**1–079**  *Claiming the invention*

The client tells us, in the first line of the question that he has invented a new type of "egg shell breaker", and that appears to be an appropriate name for the device.

What are the essential elements, common to all the embodiments? A circular cutting edge, as described in the last four lines of the third paragraph of the question — "the cutting edge having an opening into which an end portion of an egg can be introduced in such a manner that the cutting edge contacts the egg shell along a circumferential contact line — is common to all the embodiments. This feature also arguably distinguishes over the cutting arrangement of the Fig. 3 prior art (the cutting edge of the blade which does produce a circumferential cut, is on one side of the egg, the opposite side of the egg resting on something which does not in practice function as a cutting edge, the uprights of the frame also do not in practice function as a cutting edge). However, it is clearly not essential that the cutter has a circular cutting edge.

There must be something to impart an impulse to the egg via the cutting edge. There seems to be no suitably generic language for this feature in the question. The use of "impulse" suggests impact or strike and this leads us to "impact means", "striker" or "striking means".

Next we need a guide for guiding the impact means or striker and we should make it clear that the guide is relevant to the delivery of the impulse to the egg — which is after all its purpose. In the embodiments the guide acts to control the direction of the impulse. But in only some of the embodiments does the guide also limit the magnitude of the applied impulse. This suggests that we need to be careful about how we refer to the effects achieved by the combination of features.

To maximise our marks we should have a two-part claim. If we start from the Figs 1 and 2 prior art, the "characterised in that" transition would come between the striker means and the guide in the above list of features.

The following claim, drafted by Dr Diana Pisani in this way, garnered 45 of the 50 marks available for the independent claim in the exam.

> An egg shell breaker comprising: cutting means (40, 50, 60) including a cutting edge (51) and arranged to receive an end portion of an egg such that the cutting edge (51) contacts a shell of the egg along a circumferential contact line; and striking means (40, 57, 67) arranged to impart an impulse to the shell via said cutting edge (51); characterised by guiding means (43, 45, 53, 55, 63, 64) configured to guide said striking means (40, 57, 67) so as to limit the direction and intensity of the impulse imparted to the shell.

Conversely, the following claim, directed towards the result to be achieved, garnered only 15 of the 50 marks available for the independent claim.

> An egg shell breaker comprising a body (40, 50, 60) having a circumferential edge (51) for circumferentially breaking said egg shell; means for applying an impulse (40, 57, 67) via said body (40, 50, 60) to said egg shell adequate to circumferentially break said egg shell; characterised in that said egg shell breaker further comprises means for automatically controlling (40, 43, 53, 57, 63, 69) the direction and intensity of said impulse.

### 7. Partial worked example using EQE 2005 Paper A    1–080

The 2005 paper reverted to the usual format of a lengthy letter from the client, plus several separate prior art disclosures. The invention was in essence extremely simple, but there were three embodiments which differed quite significantly. The prior art was quite distant from the individual embodiments, but was close enough to make it hard to draft a single broad claim which covered all the embodiments.

*Understanding and annotating the paper*    1–081

The following pages indicate how the 2005 paper A could be marked up on first reading. The shaded passages in the client's letter are used to indicate what we can immediately recognise as prior art, even before we consider the separate prior art documents. Where text has been boxed it signifies that the text is of importance as indicating what the invention is or where it might lie.

# 84  Complete Guide to Passing the EQE

**CLIENT'S LETTER**

Dear Mr Hal Sangel,

*So client will want protection for automotive components and not just complete vehicles*

Our company is a supplier of automotive components, in particular of lighting and electric components.

Legislation requires that vehicle lighting includes a low beam and a high beam intended to illuminate the road ahead of the vehicle. The low beam is used when the vehicle meets or follows another vehicle, providing optimum road illumination and protecting other drivers from glare. The low beam is usually produced by providing a screen to cut-off the upper part of the light beam. For motorcycle lighting, a particular problem exists which will be explained in the following with reference to the Figs. 1 to 4.

In Fig. 1 a motorcycle 1 is travelling on a straight road (in a right-hand drive country), and its headlight illuminates the road ahead with a low beam as shown by the shaded portion. Fig. 2 shows the light distribution pattern of the low beam in the vertical plane A-A of Fig. 1. H-H represents a horizontal plane and V-V a vertical plane. The light distribution pattern of Fig. 2 comprises an upper edge, so defined as to prevent light from shining directly into the eyes of oncoming drivers.

*So the problem only exists with vehicles that are leant to negotiate corners.*

Fig. 3 shows the motorcycle 1 during turning. Turning a motorcycle, in particular at high speeds, is accomplished mainly by leaning rather than by steering with the front wheel. The rider leans the motorcycle towards the side to which he wishes to turn. The degree of leaning is proportional to both the speed of the motorcycle and the curvature of the turn. The headlight is fixed to the motorcycle and therefore also inclines, resulting in the light distribution pattern of Fig. 4. Consequently, an inadequate area of the road is illuminated, as illustrated by the shaded portion in Fig. 3. Thus, the motorcyclist may not see obstacles. Visibility becomes even more restricted as the radius of curvature of the road decreases. Moreover, during a turn to the right, as depicted, the beam of the headlight may blind oncoming drivers. This presents a serious safety hazard. In view of the above problems, our research team has been investigating possible improvements to motorcycle lighting. The following solutions have been developed.

*First Embodiment modifications (some must be inventive if we are to protect this embodiment).*

Fig. 5 shows a side view of one of our new headlights. This is based on a known type of headlight, which comprises a housing 10, a lamp 11 providing a light source, a parabolic reflector 12 and a cover-glass or lens 13 disposed at the front aperture of the housing 10. The axis of symmetry of the reflector 12 is the optical axis X-X of the headlight. In order to obtain a high beam and a low beam, a conventional, halogen lamp 11 with two filaments is used as shown in greater detail in Fig. 6. Such a lamp is inserted, without rotation, into a fitting where it is held by a spring clip (both not shown). Projections 21, 22, 23 ensure correct orientation of the lamp. The lamp 11 has a first filament 14 for producing a low beam and a second filament 15 for producing a high beam. As shown in Fig. 5, the first filament 14 is located in front of the reflector's focal point F, so that the light rays emitted upwards from this filament are reflected by the reflector 12 downwards onto the road as shown by the arrows. In order to cut-off the light rays that would otherwise be emitted upwards by the headlight, a screen 17 has to be provided within the lower half of the headlight. The screen 17 shields the first filament 14 from below, and has a shape so as to obtain a light distribution pattern with an upper edge as shown e.g. in Fig. 2.

*First embodiment – its known elements.*

In order to solve the aforementioned problem, the following modifications have been made. A gear wheel 20 has been provided which comprises an appropriate fitting (not shown) for receiving lamp 11. Lamp 11 is further supported by ball bearing 16. The gear wheel 20 meshes with the drive gear 19 of an electric motor 18. The rotation of the drive gear 19 causes a rotation of gear wheel 20, resulting in a rotation of the lamp 11, and therefore of the light distribution pattern. The axis of rotation of the lamp 11 corresponds to the optical axis X-X.

*By virtue of the rotation of the screen, which is an integral part of the lamp, with respect to the reflector.*

A different type of headlight is shown in Figs. 7 and 8. This type of headlight provides only a low beam. It comprises a housing portion 110 and an elliptic reflector 112. The axis of symmetry of the reflector 112 is the optical axis X-X of the headlight. A gas-discharge lamp 111 provides a light source positioned at the first focal point F1 of the reflector 112. Alternatively, a halogen lamp with a single filament may be used. Due to this geometrical arrangement, all the rays of light emitted by the lamp 111, and reflected by reflector 112, converge towards a second focal point F2. A screen 117 is arranged in the lower half of the headlight between lamp 111 and the second focal point F2 of the reflector 112. As apparent from Fig. 8, the screen 117 has a first edge 124 which is inclined by an angle of about 15° to a second edge 125. Referring again to Fig. 7, a lens 113 projects an inverted optical image of the screen 117, resulting in a light distribution pattern with an upper edge as shown e.g. in Fig. 2.

*Second embodiment – its known elements*

In our new headlight, screen 117 is rotatable about the axis X-X. During rotation, the screen 117 is guided by means of two pins 126 connected to the housing portion 110 and running in an arcuate groove of the screen. The screen 117 has a toothed portion 120. This meshes with a gear 119 which is driven by an electric motor 118 such that the screen 117, and therefore the light distribution pattern, is rotated about the axis X-X.

*Second embodiment – its new elements*

As for the first headlight configuration of Fig. 5, this configuration also allows the use of small-sized, lightweight drive components, all of which are mounted within a normal sized headlight housing. Consequently our new headlights can replace conventional headlights.

*So the client will want protection for what will be sold to motorcycle manufacturers – who may, for example, fit these headlights as "optional extras" to motorcycle ranges where otherwise a standard headlight is fitted.*

A third configuration would be to combine the lamp 11 and the rotating mechanism 18, 19, 20 of Fig. 5 with an elliptic reflector and a lens of the type shown in Fig. 7.

*Third embodiment*

In all configurations, rotation of the light distribution pattern by an appropriate angle compensates the effect of the inclination of the motorcycle, thus maintaining satisfactory illumination of the road whilst driving in a curve.

*– necessary to solve the problem*

In order to determine the appropriate angle of rotation of the light distribution pattern, it is necessary to detect the angle of inclination of the motorcycle. As shown in Fig. 9, an electronic distance sensor 31, 32 is fixed on each side of the motorcycle. A greater number of sensors may be mounted in order to improve precision and to provide redundancy. Each sensor comprises an infrared or ultrasonic transmitter, as well as a receiver for detecting the radiation reflected from the road surface. The sensors output electric signals which are proportional to the magnitude of the detected radiation. From these signals, the angle of inclination of the motorcycle can be calculated.

*– but this does not mean that we have to include this feature in our broadest claim to the headlight assembly.*

| | |
|---|---|
| This paragraph concerns examples of the type of features that motorcycle using the new lights will need to have, but they are not an essential part of the invention so that they need to be recited in the broadest claims. We will want to claim a headlight with a moveable screen (we need to review the prior art before we know how we will have to phrase this) | As shown in Fig. 10, the motorcycle further comprises an electronic control unit (ECU) 30 receiving the output from sensors 31, 32. A vehicle speed sensor 33 is also coupled to the ECU. The ECU 30 calculates the angle of inclination and registers the side to which the motorcycle is inclined. On the basis of this data, the ECU 30 then determines the appropriate angle of rotation of the light distribution pattern, and activates electric motor 18, 118 to compensate for the effect of the inclination of the motorcycle. This system is only activated when 1the vehicle speed is above a predetermined value such as 30 km/h. |
| Again not an essential part of the invention, but we will want to claim the new parts of this system as part of a lighting system for a motorcycle. | We have performed a search for similar headlight systems and enclose copies of documents D1, D2 and D3 which were published several years ago. We hope that the above description and these documents will prove helpful in drafting a European Patent application which covers all of our configurations.

Yours sincerely

E. C. Rider

R. Lee David & Son Ltd. |

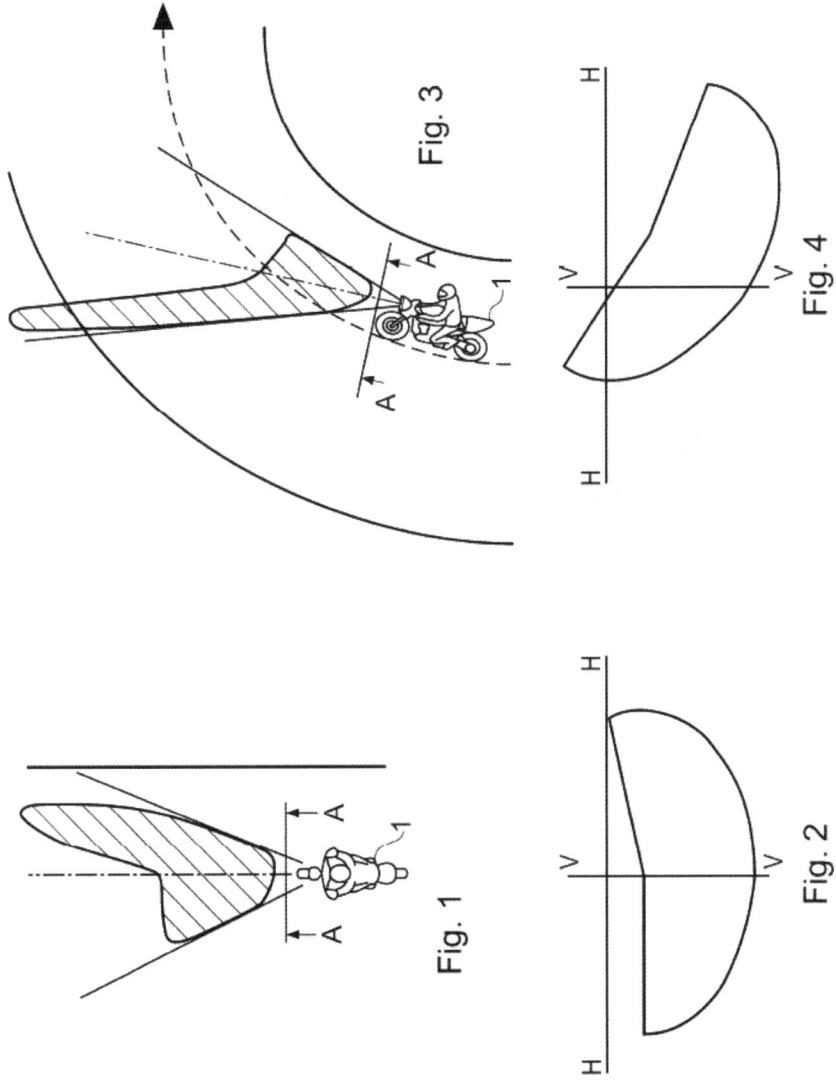

**CLIENT'S DRAWINGS**

2/4

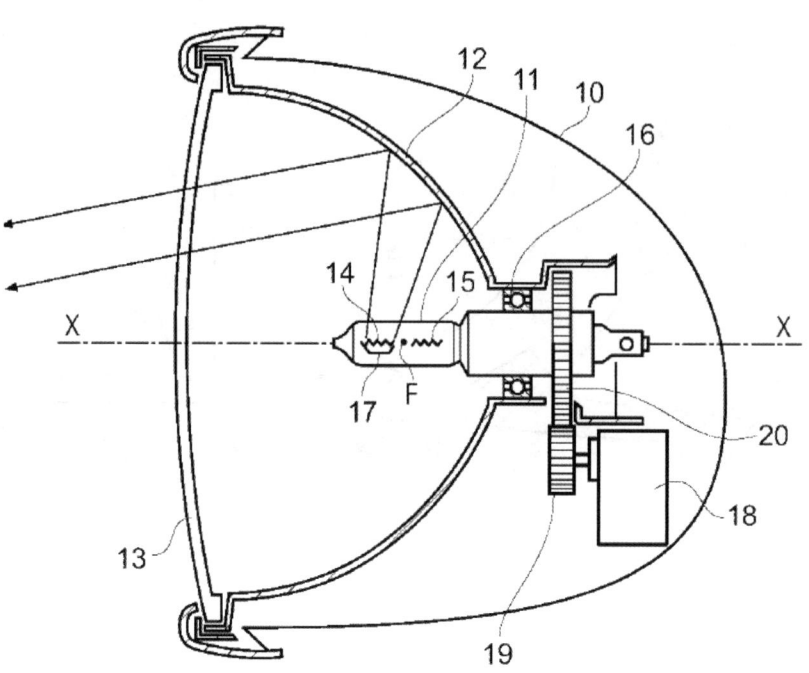

Fig. 5

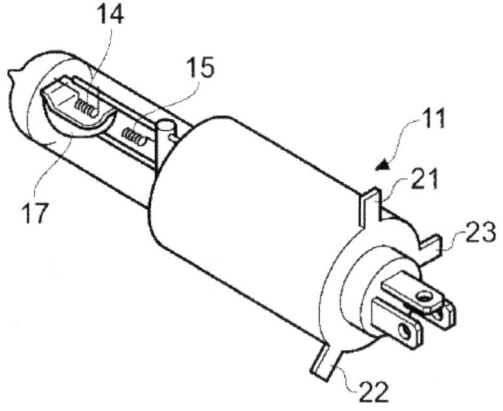

Fig. 6

3/4

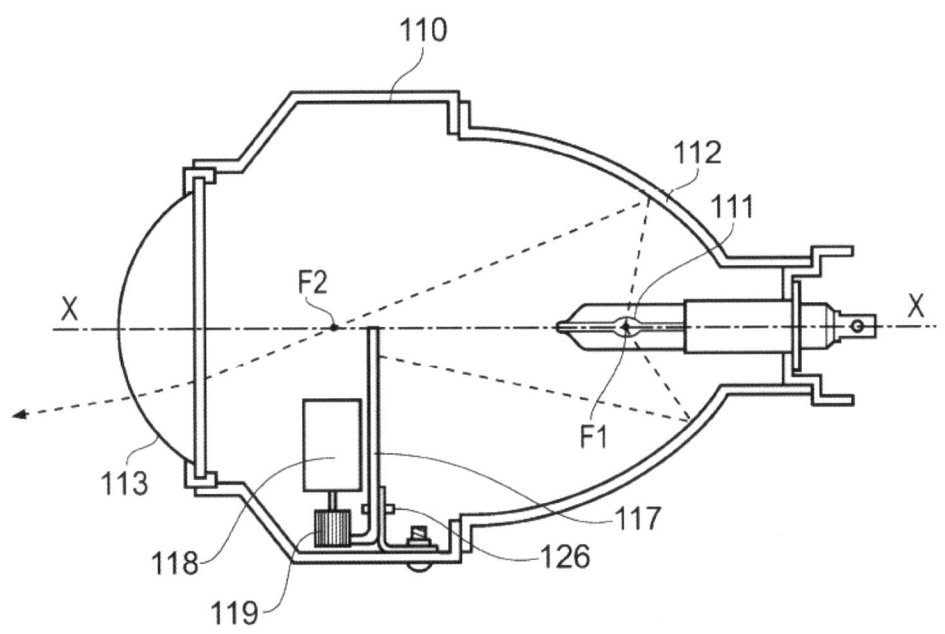

Fig. 7

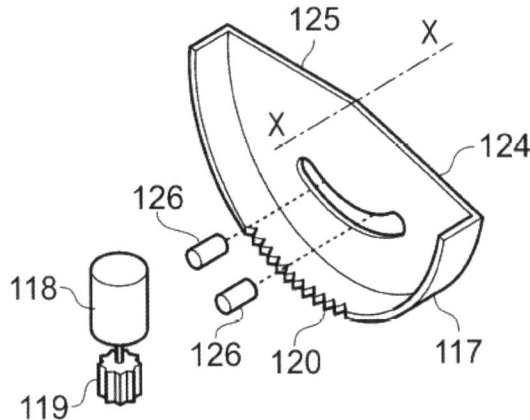

Fig. 8

4/4

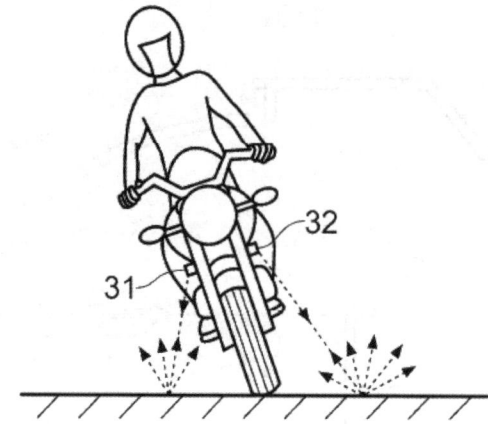

Fig. 9

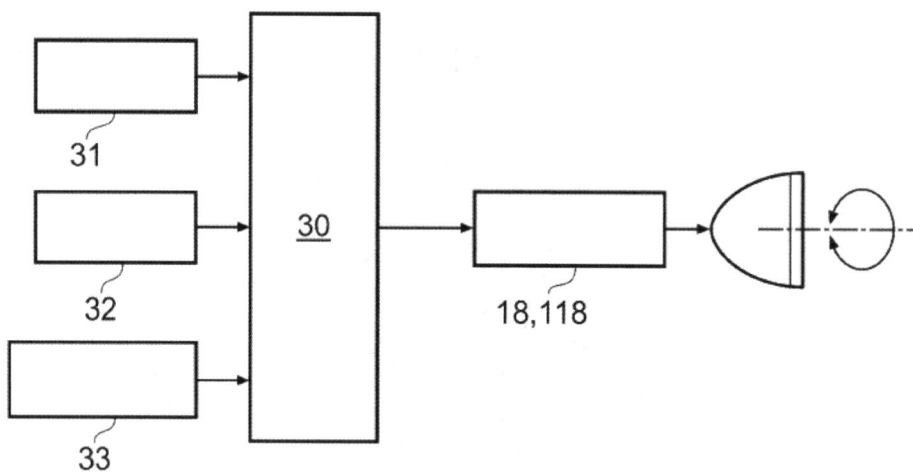

Fig. 10

## DOCUMENT D1 (MAGAZINE ARTICLE)

The auto industry is currently working on new technology to ensure adequate road illumination when turning. Some decades ago the Citroen DS already had pivoting headlights which were mechanically linked to the steering column via a control cable. However, the installation of cables or other mechanical linkage between the steering column and the headlights is complicated. Furthermore, a lot of space is necessary for mounting all of the parts.

Today, these problems can be overcome by replacing the previous mechanical systems by electric motors and sensors. Additionally, electrical components are more accurate and reliable, and allow the use of control algorithms that take into account other parameters such as the speed of the vehicle.

Teaches use of motors and electrical control to replace mechanical linkages.

Fig. 1 shows a vehicle turning. The light beam follows the direction of the turn. Fig. 2 is a simplified representation of the system used to produce this effect. For each headlight 43, this system comprises an electric motor 40, a worm gear 41, 44 and a rotary shaft 42, which is linked to the headlight 43. The headlight can be rotated about a vertical axis, as indicated by the arrows. The motor is controlled by a microprocessor, such that the headlight is rotated by an adequate angle to provide optimum illumination.

Headlight assembly as a whole is rotated about a vertical axis: for use in cars. Technique does not address the particular problems of motorcycles which must lean to turn.

## DOCUMENT D1

1/1

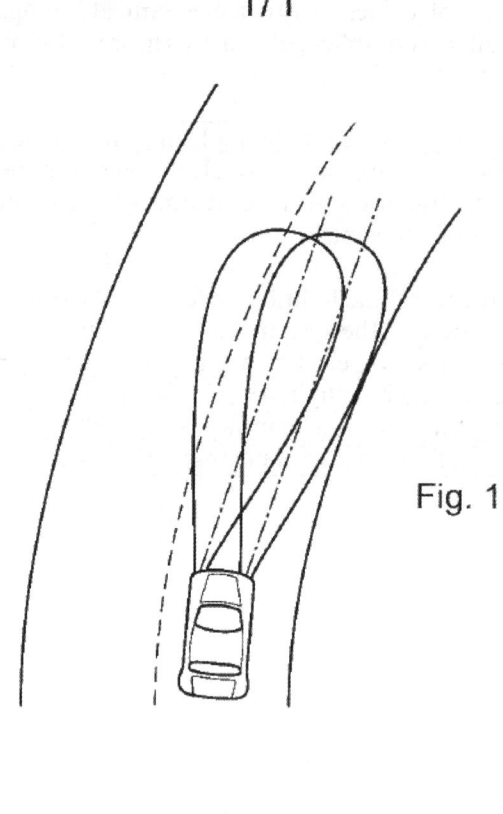

Fig. 1

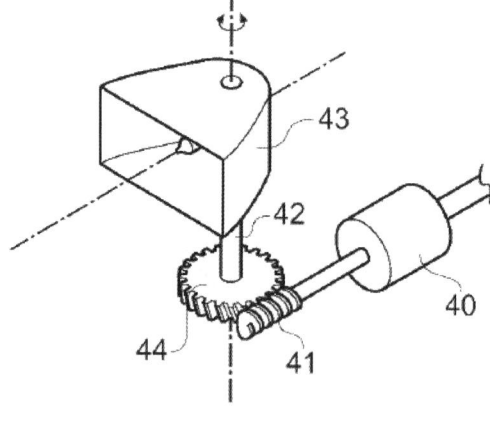

Fig. 2

## DOCUMENT D2 (PATENT SPECIFICATION)

The present invention relates to the field of motorcycle lighting. A known weakness of conventional motorcycle headlights is that when the motorcycle leans during turning, the light beam does not sufficiently illuminate the road. In the present invention, illumination during turning is improved through the use of a special headlight arrangement.

> Addresses the same general problem.

As shown in the appended drawing, the invention comprises three headlights: a central, main headlight 51 and two auxiliary headlights 52, 53. Each of the headlights 51, 52, 53 has a screen 57 for producing a low beam. The positions of the auxiliary headlights 52, 53 are determined by a theoretical rotation of the main headlight 51 around a common axis C, as shown in the drawing. As a result of this arrangement, when the motorcycle inclines by 25°, one of the auxiliary headlights 52, 53 provides substantially the same illumination as that provided by the central headlight 51 when the motorcycle is not inclined.

> Requires multiple headlights and does not accommodate extreme lean angles.

When the motorcycle is travelling on a straight road, only main headlight 51 is switched on. During turning, when the angle of inclination of the motorcycle exceeds a certain value, the auxiliary headlight on the opposite side to the direction of the turn is switched on and the main headlight 51 is switched off.

In order to detect the angle of inclination, an inclinometer with a gyroscope is used. However, ultrasonic distance-sensors could also be used. All output signals from these devices are sent to a microprocessor which is programmed to calculate the inclination angle of the motorcycle and control the switching of the headlights.

> Control technology is known; note alternative lean sensor which could be used in client's invention.

**DOCUMENT D2**

1/1

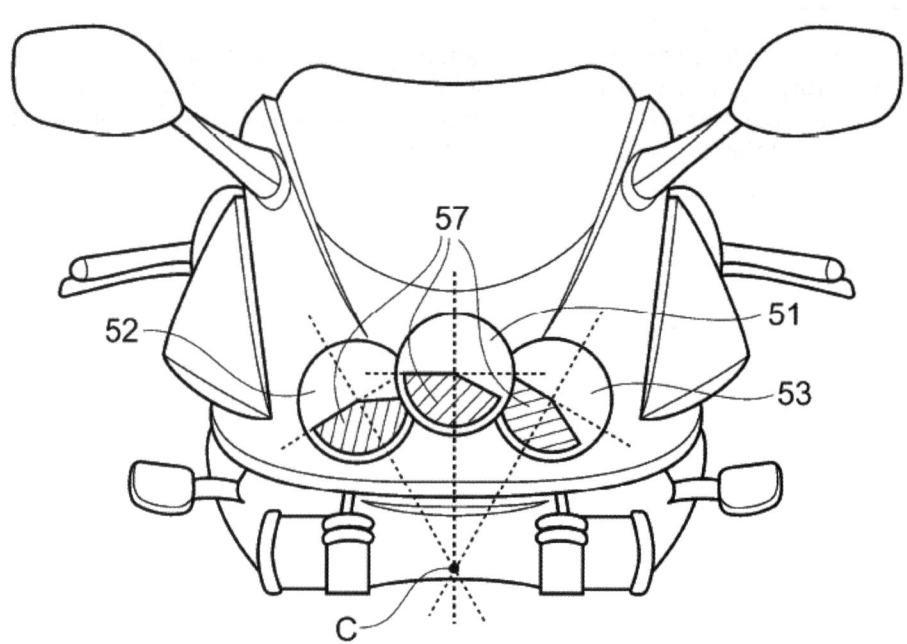

# DOCUMENT D3 (PATENT SPECIFICATION)

The present invention relates to a lighting system for a two-wheeled vehicle such as a motorcycle. In general, the lighting of such a vehicle deteriorates when the vehicle makes a turn. During turning, the vehicle is inclined. The headlight, and therefore also the projected light beam, follow the inclination of the vehicle.

The object of the invention is to provide means by which the headlight of the vehicle has its orientation corrected to an appropriate extent as the vehicle turns. [Addresses the same problem.]

As shown in the figure, a headlight comprises a reflector 61, a front lens 66 and a lamp with an integrated screen (not shown), for example a conventional halogen lamp with two filaments. The headlight is mounted in a bearing 62 for rotation about an axis Y-Y. The headlight is connected to first gear wheel 63 that cooperates with a second gear wheel 64. This second gear wheel 64 is freely rotatable about a parallel axis Y.-Y. and is provided at a radially outer portion with a weight 65.

When the vehicle starts to turn, the weight 65 causes rotation of the second gear wheel 64. As indicated by the arrows, this causes rotation of the first gear wheel 63 and 20 thus of the headlight in the required direction. Rotation of the whole headlamp assembly, including the bulb with its screen,

Due to its size, this arrangement will not fit into a conventional headlight housing. However, a specially-constructed housing may be provided to protect all of the above components from rain and snow. [So then whole headlight, including the screen, would rotate with respect to the special housing.]

**DOCUMENT D3**

1/1

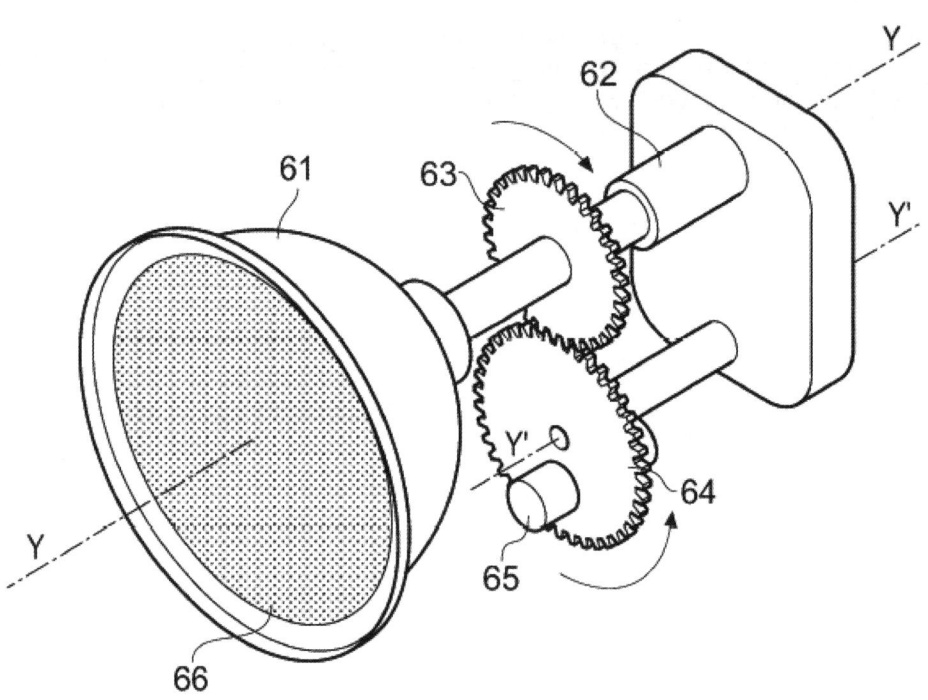

*Summary of the prior art* 1–082

D1 concerns headlights for vehicles such as cars, where the vehicle is steered and not leant to negotiate corners. The headlights are pivoted about a vertical axis, so that the headlights and their beams are swept laterally to "look around" corners. This has nothing to do with the problem addressed by the client's invention. What is of interest is the account of replacing mechanical systems (linkages etc.) with electric motors and sensors – which is relevant for an obviousness attack based on D3 (which has a mechanical/ gravitational operation). Rotation of a gear causes rotation of the headlight (and hence of the light source inside the headlight), but the rotation is around a vertical axis. The system is controlled by a microprocessor, and the control algorithm may take account of speed.

D2 is concerned with the same problem as the client's invention. In D2 multiple static headlights having screens for low beam are provided. There is a central main headlight and one auxiliary headlight on each side of the main headlight. The positions of the auxiliary headlights are determined by a theoretical rotation of the main headlight around a common axis. When the motorcycle is leant sufficiently, the appropriate auxiliary headlight is activated. Clearly the system only gives optimum illumination when the angle of lean matches that for which the auxiliary lights have been designed, or when the motorcycle is vertical. Also of course three headlights are required.

There is in effect a rotation of the headlight beam (albeit that the beam is switched between alternative headlights). A microprocessor can be fed with inclination information from ultrasonic distance-sensors or a gyroscope.

D3 is the closest prior art as it concerns the same problem and actively rotates a single headlight beam. The headlight has a reflector and a lamp with an integral screen, and these can rotate together around the optical axis of the reflector. A weighted gear wheel is used to rotate the headlight when the motorcycle is inclined. The effect of this arrangement is to provide the function of the client's invention: "rotation of the light distribution pattern by an appropriate angle compensates the effect of the inclination of the motorcycle". But in D3 this is achieved by rotating the complete headlight assembly from outside the assembly. D3 mentions the following disadvantage: "Due to its size, this arrangement will not fit into a conventional headlight housing.

However, a specially-constructed housing may be provided to protect all of the above components from rain and snow." The client's invention overcomes this disadvantage by rotating only a part of the headlight, rather than the whole assembly. This means that the new headlight can replace an existing headlight: "As for the first headlight configuration of Fig. 5, this configuration also allows the use of small-sized, lightweight drive components, all of which are mounted within a normal sized headlight housing. Consequently our new headlights can replace conventional headlights". `

*Establishing novel subject matter* 1–083

The following pages indicate how the client's invention can be divided into novel features and features found in the prior art. As before, shading is used to signify features found in the prior art, while un-shaded boxed text signifies

## CLIENT'S LETTER

Dear Mr Hal Sangel,

So client will want protection for automotive components and not just complete vehicles.

Our company is a supplier of automotive components, in particular of lighting and electric components.

Legislation requires that vehicle lighting includes a low beam and a high beam intended to illuminate the road ahead of the vehicle. The low beam is used when the vehicle meets or follows another vehicle, providing optimum road illumination and protecting other drivers from glare. The low beam is usually produced by providing a screen to cut-off the upper part of the light beam. For motorcycle lighting, a particular problem exists which will be explained in the following with reference to the Figs. 1 to 4.

In Fig. 1 a motorcycle 1 is travelling on a straight road (in a right-hand drive country), and its headlight illuminates the road ahead with a low beam as shown by the shaded portion. Fig. 2 shows the light distribution pattern of the low beam in the vertical plane A-A of Fig. 1. H-H represents a horizontal plane and V-V a vertical plane. The light distribution pattern of Fig. 2 comprises an upper edge, so defined as to prevent light from shining directly into the eyes of oncoming drivers.

So the problem only exists with vehicles that are leant to negotiate corners.

Fig. 3 shows the motorcycle 1 during turning. Turning a motorcycle, in particular at high speeds, is accomplished mainly by leaning rather than by steering with the front wheel. The rider leans the motorcycle towards the side to which he wishes to turn. The degree of leaning is proportional to both the speed of the motorcycle and the curvature of the turn. The headlight is fixed to the motorcycle and therefore also inclines, resulting in the light distribution pattern of Fig. 4. Consequently, an inadequate area of the road is illuminated, as illustrated by the shaded portion in Fig. 3. Thus, the motorcyclist may not see obstacles. Visibility becomes even more restricted as the radius of curvature of the road decreases. Moreover, during a turn to the right, as depicted, the beam of the headlight may blind oncoming drivers. This presents a serious safety hazard. In view of the above problems, our research team has been investigating possible improvements to motorcycle lighting. The following solutions have been developed.

First embodiment – its known elements

Fig. 5 shows a side view of one of our new headlights. This is based on a known type of headlight, which comprises a housing 10, a lamp 11 providing a light source, a parabolic reflector 12 and a cover-glass or lens 13 disposed at the front aperture of the housing 10. The axis of symmetry of the reflector 12 is the optical axis X-X of the headlight. In order to obtain a high beam and a low beam, a conventional, halogen lamp 11 with two filaments is used as shown in greater detail in Fig. 6. Such a lamp is inserted, without rotation, into a fitting where it is held by a spring clip (both not shown). Projections 21, 22, 23 ensure correct orientation of the lamp. The lamp 11 has a first filament 14 for producing a low beam and a second filament 15 for producing a high beam. As shown in Fig. 5, the first filament 14 is located in front of the reflector's focal point F, so that the light rays emitted upwards from this filament are reflected by the reflector 12 downwards onto the road as shown by the arrows. In order to cut-off the light rays that would otherwise be emitted upwards by the headlight, a screen 17 has to be provided within the lower half of the headlight. The screen 17 shields the first filament 14 from below, and has a shape so as to obtain a light distribution pattern with an upper edge as shown e.g. in Fig. 2.

Known from D3 – but there the whole headlight (reflector and bulb) rotates as one. This embodiment rotates the light pattern by virtue of the rotation of the screen, which is an integral part of the lamp, with respect to the

In order to solve the aforementioned problem, the following modifications have been made. A gear wheel 20 has been provided which comprises an appropriate fitting (not shown) for receiving lamp 11. Lamp 11 is further supported by ball bearing 16. The gear wheel 20 meshes with the drive gear 19 of an electric motor 18. The rotation of the drive gear 19 causes a rotation of gear wheel 20, resulting in a rotation of the lamp 11, and therefore of the light distribution pattern. The axis of rotation of the lamp 11 corresponds to the optical axis X-X.

| Paper A (Electricity/Mechanics) | 99 |

A different type of headlight is shown in Figs. 7 and 8. This type of headlight provides only a low beam. It comprises a housing portion 110 and an elliptic reflector 112. The axis of symmetry of the reflector 112 is the optical axis X-X of the headlight. A gas-discharge lamp 111 provides a light source positioned at the first focal point F1 of the reflector 112. Alternatively, a halogen lamp with a single filament may be used. Due to this geometrical arrangement, all the rays of light emitted by the lamp 111, and reflected by reflector 112, converge towards a second focal point F2. A screen 117 is arranged in the lower half of the headlight between lamp 111 and the second focal point F2 of the reflector 112. As apparent from Fig. 8, the screen 117 has a first edge 124 which is inclined by an angle of about 15° to a second edge 125. Referring again to Fig. 7, a lens 113 projects an inverted optical image of the screen 117, resulting in a light distribution pattern with an upper edge as shown e.g. in Fig. 2.

*reflector. There is no relative rotation between lamp and reflector in prior art.*

*Electric motor known from D1. D3 does not identify the lamp axis.*

In our new headlight, screen 117 is rotatable about the axis X-X. During rotation, the screen 117 is guided by means of two pins 126 connected to the housing portion 110 and running in an arcuate groove of the screen. The screen 117 has a toothed portion 120. This meshes with a gear 119 which is driven by an electric motor 118 such that the screen 117, and therefore the light distribution pattern, is rotated about the axis X-X.

*Probably also in D3 – but that is with a bulb having a screen, not a separate screen. Again, the whole headlight (reflector and bulb) rotates as one.*

*Probably that the lamp's screen rotates about this axis. The light distribution pattern does rotate about X-X. But this is with a bulb having a screen, not a separate screen.*

As for the first headlight configuration of Fig. 5, this configuration also allows the use of small-sized, lightweight drive components, all of which are mounted within a normal sized headlight housing. Consequently our new headlights can replace conventional headlights.

*So the client will want protection for what will be sold to motorcycle manufacturers – who may, for example, fit these headlights as "optional extras" to motorcycle ranges where otherwise a standard headlight is fitted.*

A third configuration would be to combine the lamp 11 and the rotating mechanism 18, 19, 20 of Fig. 5 with an elliptic reflector and a lens of the type shown in Fig. 7.

100   *Complete Guide to Passing the EQE*

| Margin notes | Main text |
|---|---|
| necessary to solve the problem, This is achieved in D3. | In all configurations, rotation of the light distribution pattern by an appropriate angle compensates the effect of the inclination of the motorcycle – thus maintaining satisfactory illumination of the road whilst driving in a curve. |
| but need not be included in broadest headlight assembly claim<br><br>Known from D2 – each side implicit..<br>Obvious over D2 | In order to determine the appropriate angle of rotation of the light distribution pattern, it is necessary to detect the angle of inclination of the motorcycle – As shown in Fig. 9, an electronic distance sensor 31, 32 is fixed on each side of the motorcycle. A greater number of sensors may be mounted in order to improve precision and to provide redundancy. Each sensor comprises an infrared or ultrasonic transmitter, as well as a receiver for detecting the radiation reflected from the road surface. The sensors output electric signals which are proportional to the magnitude of the detected radiation. From these signals, the angle of inclination of the motorcycle can be calculated. |
| The preceding paragraph concerns examples of the type of features that motorcycle using the new lights will need to have, but they are not an essential part of the invention so that they need to be recited in the broadest claims. He we will want to claim a headlight with a moveable screen (we need to review the prior art before we know how we will have to phrase this).<br><br>Again not an essential part of the invention, but we will want to claim the new parts of this system as part of a lighting system for a motorcycle. | As shown in Fig. 10, the motorcycle further comprises an electronic control unit (ECU) 30 receiving the output from sensors 31, 32. A vehicle speed sensor 33 is also coupled to the ECU. The ECU 30 calculates the angle of inclination and registers the side to which the motorcycle is inclined. On the basis of this data, the ECU 30 then determines the appropriate angle of rotation of the light distribution pattern, and activates electric motor 18, 118 to compensate for the effect of the inclination of the motorcycle. This system is only activated when the vehicle speed is above a predetermined value such as 30 km/h. |

We have performed a search for similar headlight systems and enclose copies of documents D1, D2 and D3 which were published several years ago. We hope that the above description and these documents will prove helpful in drafting a European Patent application which covers all of our configurations.

Yours sincerely

E. C. Rider

R. Lee David & Son Ltd.

**1–084**   *Claiming the invention*

The above analysis shows that the majority of the individual features of the embodiments are known, many of them in combination. But none of the items of prior art teaches relative movement between a screen (used to produce a low beam "a light distribution pattern with an upper edge") and a reflector. In the client's invention, that relative movement is used to cause rotation of the light distribution pattern by an appropriate angle to compensate for the effects of the inclination of the vehicle. D3 gives the same result, but because the whole of the headlight assembly has to be rotated, which requires extra components outside the main headlight, As D3 states: "Due to its size, this arrangement will not fit into a conventional headlight housing. However, a specially-constructed housing may be provided to protect all of the above components from rain and snow." In D2, the compensation for lean angle is only correct for the angle of lean for which the auxiliary headlights are set.

The broadest protection for the client is achieved by claiming the headlight on its own, rather than claiming the whole installation for a motorcycle, or the motorcycle including such an installation.

What are the elements of the headlight that must go into the claim?
All the embodiments include a reflector, and we have decided that the invention is based on the relative rotation of the screen (used to produce the special light distribution pattern) with respect to the reflector – so we have to recite the reflector. By the same token, we must recite the screen. What about the lens 13? It is certainly part of each of the three embodiments, but is it essential in the headlight as shipped? It plays no part in the rotation of the light pattern, but does serve to keep the reflector clean and would be a practical necessity in a real-world installation. But do you need it in the units that

you ship from the factory? The answer is probably not. A large proportion of motorcycles and scooters are fitted with fairings, to streamline the vehicle and to protect the rider of the vehicle from wind-blast. But such structures could easily include a transparent window section to replace the lens of the headlight, and this could take the place of the lens which might otherwise be included in the headlights shipped to the motorcycle manufacturers. Probably, therefore, we should not recite the lens. What about the mechanisms which cause the movement of the screen? How should we recite those? Is it essential to use an electric motor and gears? Clearly, gears are not essential – one could use toothed belts and pulleys instead, for example. Is an electric motor essential? No, an alternative would be to use a solenoid. Do we then need to recite anything to cause the movement of the screen? Certainly the examiner will mark down significantly any claims to the headlight that merely say that there is relative movement between the screen and the reflector – there must be something recited which gives rise to the relative movement. The broadest and easiest way is simply to recite "means to move the screen with respect to the reflector", or some such wording.

So, what do we have?
A headlight for a motorcycle . . . (but what of scooters and mopeds?)
A headlight for a two-wheeled vehicle . . . (although the invention solves a problem which only occurs with vehicles which lean to change direction - a not all two wheel vehicles do that, nor is leaning to change direction unique to two-wheel vehicles – there are three wheeled vehicles based on motorcycles which also lean around corners, but these exist in trivial numbers). . .
the headlight having a reflector
and a screen
the light output that we want to achieve this is termed a "low beam" (but this perhaps a rather vague term); the client refers to a "light distribution pattern" (at the foot of page 1), and at various places he refers to this "having an upper edge". We could use the first of these alone, or we could use them together. We need a term to refer to this pattern, since we will want our claim to make clear the consequence of the relative rotation between the screen and the reflector. – e.g. that this rotation causes a corresponding rotation of the light distribution pattern. We also need to introduce the idea that the angle by which the light distribution pattern is rotated is such as to compensate for the inclination of the vehicle, which the client's expresses as "rotation of the light distribution pattern by an appropriate angle compensates the effect of the inclination of the motorcycle", since that is what is involved in the solving the problem.

But before we can draft a sensible claim, there is something else that we need to consider. A problem arises with the first and third embodiments, which – unlike the second embodiment, both feature lamps which include the screen. The problem is that the lamp is a readily replaceable part (in general, the headlight will be configured so that the user can replace the lamp). But that ready replaceability means that motorcycle manufacturers could readily insert the lamp into the headlight when manufacturing motorcycles having such headlights, rather than buying headlights with the lamp already in place. Ideally we want to claim the headlight in the form that a competitor of the client might ship it, rather than only in the form that it might be in after installation into a motorcycle. That is because the client wants to be able to sue his competitors rather than his customers or potential customers, and the client wants to be able to sue for direct rather than contributory infringement (especially given that supply across the borders of contracting states can avoid liability for contributory infringement). For these reasons we would ideally not want to recite the lamp (or, more generically, light source) as a feature of the headlight. But in the first and third embodiments the lamp includes the screen – and the screen is an element of the inventive combination – or at least movement of that screen relative to the reflector is part of the invention. In order to avoid requiring the presence of a lamp in the first and third embodiments, we must not recite the presence of the screen, but if we fail to recite the presence of the screen, there is an evident risk of a significant lack of clarity. If we were to claim the second embodiment separately from the first and third embodiments, we could tailor the wording of the claims to fit more closely the relevant embodiments to void any lack of clarity, while keeping a claim scope which would give the client the ability to sue his competitors (rather than their customers) for direct infringement. This could be done without breaching r.29 (2) because the different embodiments constitute "alternative solutions to a particular problem based on the same inventive concept, where it is not appropriate to cover these alternatives by a single claim" as specified in r.29 (2) (c). But in paper A of the EQE there is a premium for providing a single independent claim which covers all the embodiments (at least without significant loss in scope compared to the use of multiple independent claims). So how do we resolve this? Let us look first at how potential claims might look.

If we claim the second embodiment separately from the first and third:
we could claim the second embodiment as follows:

A headlight for a two-wheeled vehicle, the headlight having a reflector (112) and a screen (117) for use in producing a desired light distribution pattern from the headlight, characterised in that the headlight includes means (118,119,120) to rotate the screen (117) with respect to the reflector (112) so that the desired light distribution pattern can be rotated to compensate for the effect of inclination of the vehicle.

The claim for the first and third embodiments would read as follows:
A headlight for a two-wheeled vehicle, the headlight having a reflector (12, 112) and including a fitting to receive a light source (11) having a screen (17), the screen (17) being for use in producing a desired light distribution pattern from the headlight, characterised in that the headlight includes means (18,19,20) to rotate the fitting, and hence the screen (17), with respect to the reflector(12,112) so that the desired light distribution pattern can be rotated to compensate for the effect of inclination of the vehicle.

Neither of these claims requires the presence of the light source. The second claim avoids the need to recite the screen as being present, by having instead the fitting to receive a light source (which seems in some form or other to be essential to these embodiments), so that we can refer to the presence of means to rotate that. But we have two independent claims, and that is non-optimum in this paper. Can we get to one claim covering all three embodiments and still leave out the light source?

A possible claim to cover all three embodiments, not reciting the presence of either the light source or the screen:

A headlight for a two-wheeled vehicle, the headlight having a reflector (12, 112) and being configured to produce a desired light distribution pattern by means of a screen (17,117), characterised in that the headlight includes means (18, 19, 20, 118, 119, 120) to rotate the screen (17,117) with respect to the reflector (12,112) so that the desired light distribution pattern can be rotated to compensate for the effect of inclination of the vehicle.

It could be argued that since the feature of the characterising clauses of these three claims "the desired light distribution pattern can be rotated to compensate for the effect of inclination of the vehicle" is also found in D3, it should be moved to the pre-characterising clause. There is a risk that this will make the claims somewhat less clear.

A headlight for a two-wheeled vehicle, the headlight having a reflector (12, 112) and being configured to produce a desired light distribution pattern by means of a screen (17,117), the headlight configuration being such that the desired light distribution pattern can be rotated to compensate for the effect of inclination of the vehicle , characterised in that the headlight includes means (18, 19, 20, 118, 119, 120) to rotate the screen (17,117) with respect to the reflector (12,112) to effect rotation of the desired light distribution pattern to compensate for the effect of inclination of the vehicle.

Dependent claims
Clearly we need to provide dependent claims for the different embodiments.
Where the screen is part of the light source:

having a fitting to receive the light source, the means to rotate acting on the fitting;
the gear wheel arrangement for the above;
Where the screen is separate from the light source:
the screen rotates with respect to the light source;
reflector with two focal points, screen between the light source and the second focal point;
screen with toothed portion (120) as part of the rotation means;
arcuate groove and guides (pins) within the groove;
Applicable to all embodiments:
electric motor to rotate the screen;
the motor is within a housing of the headlight.
lighting system claims with details of the inclination sensors and the controller;
a motorcycle including the lighting system.

A typical claim set based on this assessment may therefore be:

1. A headlight for a two-wheeled vehicle, the headlight having a reflector (12, 112) and being configured to produce a desired light distribution pattern by means of a screen (17,117), the headlight configuration being such that the desired light distribution pattern can be rotated to compensate for the effect of inclination of the vehicle , characterised in that the headlight includes means (18, 19, 20, 118, 119, 120) to rotate the screen (17,117) with respect to the reflector (12,112) to effect rotation of the desired light distribution pattern to compensate for the effect of inclination of the vehicle.

2. A headlight as claimed in claim 1, wherein the axis of rotation of the screen (17,117) is the optical axis of the reflector (12,112).

3. A headlight as claimed in claim 1 or claim 2, including a fitting to receive a light source (11) having the screen (17), and wherein the means to rotate the screen (18,19,20) act on the fitting, thereby to rotate the screen (17).

4. A headlight as claimed in claim 3, wherein the fitting is provided with a gear wheel (20) meshed with a drive gear (19).

5. A headlight as claimed in claim 1 or claim 2, wherein the reflector (17) is a parabolic reflector.

6. A headlight as claimed in claim 1 or claim 2, wherein the screen (117) is mounted for rotation with respect to a light source (111) of the headlight.

7. A headlight as claimed in claim 6, wherein an arcuate track is provided for guiding rotation of the screen (117).

8. A headlight as claimed in claim 7, wherein the arcuate track is formed as a groove in the screen (117).

9. A headlight as claimed in any one of claims 6 to 8, wherein the screen has a toothed portion (120) meshed with a drive gear (119) to effect rotation of the screen.

10. A headlight as claimed in any one of claims 6 to 9, wherein the screen has first edge (124) inclined to a second edges (125) to give the desired light distribution pattern.

11. A headlight as claimed in any one of claims 6 to 10, wherein the reflector is an elliptic reflector.

12. A headlight as claimed in claim 11, wherein an arrangement is provided to locate the light source (111) at a first focal point (F1) of the reflector (112).

13. A headlight as claimed in claim 12, wherein the screen (117) is located intermediate the first focal point (F1) and a second focal point (F2) of the reflector (117).

14. A headlight as claimed in any one of the preceding claims, including an electric motor (18,118) for driving rotation of the screen (17,117).

15. A lighting system including a headlight as claimed in any one of the preceding claims, and means (30, 31, 32) to detect the angle of inclination of the vehicle (1).

16 A lighting system as claimed in claim 15, wherein the means to detect the angle of inclination of the vehicle (1) includes at least one distance sensor (31,31)on each side of the vehicle (1).

17. A lighting system as claimed in claim 16, wherein the at least one distance sensor (31, 32) comprises a transmitter of infrared or ultrasonic radiation, and a receiver for detecting the radiation reflected from a surface over which the vehicle (1) travels.

18. A lighting system as claimed in claim 16, comprising an electronic control unit for receiving data from the at least one distance sensor (31, 32) , for calculating the angle of inclination and the side to which the vehicle is inclined, and for determining the appropriate angle of rotation of the light distribution pattern.

19. A lighting system as claimed in claim 18, wherein the electronic control unit is configured only to cause the rotation of the screen (17,117) with respect to the reflector (12, 112) above a predetermined speed of the vehicle.

20. A two-wheeled vehicle (1) comprising a lighting system according to any one of claims 15 to 19.

The Examiner's report for this paper stated that "the preferred independent claim comprises a combination of the following features, it being understood that the features might have been expressed using different wording:

(a) a headlight system for a two-wheeled vehicle comprising

(b) **a light source**

(c) a reflector

(d) a dimmer screen

(e) being configured to provide a light beam pattern

(f) which is rotatable so as to compensate for the effect of inclination of the vehicle

(g) the dimmer screen is rotatably mounted relative to the reflector."

The report also stated that "**candidates who drafted several independent claims of the same category or used alternatives within a single claim in order to cover the different embodiments lost points**." (The emphasis has been added in each of the quotes.)

It is instructive to see that the Examiners were happy with a relatively limited claim 1 – reciting the presence of the light source, but were unhappy with multiple independent claims in the same category and with the use of alternatives. This should come as no surprise – this is an examination, not real life. The examination is trying to see whether you can cover multiple embodiments with a single claim, without using alternatives within the claim. You should avoid unnecessary limitation, but if you have a choice between a broad single claim covering all embodiments or multiple broader claims each to cover one of the embodiments, you will almost certainly get higher marks for the single claim (all other things being equal). In the exam if you find yourself faced with this dilemma, the best option is to propose a single claim to cover all the embodiments. If it is narrower than you think you could draft individual claims to the different embodiments, explain the problem to the examiner in a note, preferably including your favoured claims to the embodiments. But it has to be said that the scale of mark loss for having separate independent claims (each of good scope) as compared with a solution having only a single independent claim is likely to be very small compared to the loss of marks involved in drafting a claim that lacks novelty, or which leaves one or more of the embodiments unprotected, or which only claims the solution and does not recite the features necessary to achieve the solution. The last of these and several others (depending upon the severity of the omission) will cost you a pass. The presence of several claims (in accordance with r.29(2)) should not in itself cause you to fail.

*Drafting the introduction*

**1–085**

The following is an example of an example of a suitable introduction drafted using the principles outlined above.

This invention relates to a headlight for a two-wheeled vehicle, the headlight having a reflector and being configured to produce a desired light distribution pattern by means of a screen, the headlight configuration being such that the desired light distribution pattern can be rotated to compensate for the effect of inclination of the vehicle. The invention also relates to a lighting system including such a headlight, and to a two-wheeled vehicle including such a lighting system.

A known problem with conventional motorcycle headlights is that, when the motorcycle negotiates a corner, the necessary inclination of the motorcycle causes the headlight beam also to incline, leading to an inadequate illumination of the road. Also, the low beam pattern which is meant to avoid dazzling drivers of oncoming vehicles ceases to be effective when the motorcycle takes a corner which involves the motorcycle leaning away from the oncoming traffic. Both of these problems give rise to dangers for road users.

One approach to solving these problems is set out in D2. A motorcycle is provided not only with a conventional headlight, but also with an auxiliary headlight to either side of the conventional one. The positions of the auxiliary headlights are determined by a theoretical rotation of the main headlight around a common axis. When the motorcycle is leant sufficiently, the appropriate auxiliary headlight is activated. Clearly the system only gives optimum illumination when the angle of lean matches that for which the auxiliary lights have been designed, or when the motorcycle is vertical. Also of course three headlights are required.

D3, upon which the preamble of claim 1 is based, provides an alternative approach in which there is provided a single headlight which is arranged to rotate to compensate for the angle of lean of the motorcycle. The headlight has a reflector and a lamp with an integral screen, and these can rotate together around the optical axis of the reflector. A weighted gear wheel is used to rotate the headlight when the motorcycle is inclined. Due to its size, this arrangement will not fit into a conventional headlight housing and requires a specially-constructed housing to protect all of the components from the elements.

The invention seeks to provide a headlight configured so that the desired light distribution pattern can be rotated to compensate for the effect of inclination of the vehicle, but which can be made more compact than the headlight provided by D3. The invention which is the subject of claim 1 achieves this goal.

With the invention according to claim 1 it is no longer necessary to rotate a complete headlight assembly, instead only the screen needs to be rotated with respect to the reflector. This arrangement permits a more compact construction which can enable a headlight according to the invention to fit inside a conventional housing. Headlights according to the invention may therefore be used to replace conventional headlights.

Note that in this introduction it is not necessary to mention D1, as this is unconnected with both the problem and the solution.

# PAPER B (CHEMISTRY)

## 1. General comments

In this paper the candidate is charged with representing his client before an examining division of the EPO and successfully prosecuting a filed patent application to grant while obtaining the broadest possible protection and meeting all the requirements of the Convention. The candidate is therefore presented with a copy of the application as filed, an Art.96(2) communication from the EPO and various items of prior art referred to in the communication. A letter providing specific instructions from the client on how the application should be prosecuted is also occasionally included (e.g. 2002).

The candidate is expected to file a complete response to the EPO communication and either argue for the patentability of the claims as filed if they are deemed patentable (extremely unlikely), or file an amended set of claims which are novel and inventive over the cited prior art and argue for the grant of a patent based on this amended claim set. Generally, half the available marks are available for amendment and half for argumentation. It is important that the amended claim set adequately protects the invention and is defensible over the art. If this is not the case you will lose marks for the claims and for the argumentation. As the task of the candidate is to secure the broadest allowable scope of protection for the client, amendments should not be more extensive than necessary. It is often necessary to explain and defend the unity of invention of the claim set proposed. If it is possible to secure maximum protection without dividing out any subject matter, more marks will be obtained by proposing such a response, with appropriate argumentation, than would be achieved by dividing out subject matter. If, in order to obtain maximum protection, it is necessary to divide out, you should clearly identify the features of the independent claim(s) of the divisional application(s), for example by referring to selected portions of the claims of the parent, or by drafting appropriate claims. Argument in support of novelty and inventive step should extend to the proposed subject matter of any proposed divisional(s). The amendment and response should address all actual or potential objections such that the next communication from the EPO will be under r.51(4) EPC. Arguments should be provided in support of the novelty and inventive step of the subject matter of all the independent claims. Basis for all the amendments must be specified and compliance with Art.123 (2) EPC must be justified. The requirements of clarity and conciseness must also be borne in mind. The submitted answer will thus consist of a letter to the EPO, and an annexed set of claims. The proposed treatment of divisional applications may be provided in the letter to the EPO, but will generally be provided in a note to the examiner. No amended description is required.

The paper is four hours in length and about half of this time should be spent analysing the question and elucidating the answer, the remaining time being allocated to writing the answer. As in Paper A, the candidate is allowed to use sections of the examination paper in compiling the amended claim set and scissors, glue and transparent gummed paper should be brought into the exam. Furthermore, only pencil and yellow highlighter should be used to mark up important sections of the paper during the period of analysis; pencil can be easily erased and yellow highlighter does not cause problems when the answer is photocopied prior to marking. Other useful things to take into the exam are copies of the Guidelines and EPO case law book — the extensive chemical case law relevant to selection inventions is often relevant.

Many of the notes provided for the purposes of Paper A will still be relevant for Paper B (e.g. case law, claim types, requirements of claims).

## 2. How to tackle the paper

**1-087**  *Understanding and annotating the paper*

Start by reading the client's patent application. Read through this in full, word by word, understanding each sentence thoroughly and appreciating its significance. Each word should be carefully read and considered since it is easy later to miss small but important facts once the mind has started to make assumptions about the answer. Reference is made to the corresponding notes for Paper A describing the kinds of information found in the client's letter — the same categorisation applies to the filed patent application in Paper B.

As with Paper A, you must first understand what subject matter is available, then establish what novel subject matter remains when the prior art has been considered and finally decide what novel subject matter is associated with an inventive step. A similar choice must therefore be made, when getting to grips with what subject matter the application contains, between marking up the examination paper with useful comments and producing a summary of its contents on a separate sheet of paper. Once again, the best choice depends on the way the examination paper has been drafted and the idiosyncratic approach of the individual candidate. Both approaches have been illustrated at the end of this chapter — the marked up paper approach using the 2002 Paper B and the separate summary approach using the 2004 Paper B.

If you have chosen not to prepare a separate summary, go through the application and mark in the margin of the exam paper what each sentence in the patent application signifies, particularly noting preferred features with motivation and, most particularly, noting those preferred features which are motivated by any data provided.

If you are preparing a separate summary, summarise the various structural features of the application on a separate sheet of paper, using annotated arrows between them to indicate any processes. Include specific embodiments and any information on which embodiments give surprising results.

See which claim types have been used, and identify any omissions. Be alive to the possibility that claimable subject matter has not been claimed. The claim set will usually be short.

Before you read the Art.96(2) communication, read through the cited prior art to understand it and see how it relates to the inventions described in the client's patent application. Mark up the prior art in a similar way to the application. Firstly, note whether each citation it is Art.54(2) or Art.54(3) prior art and the consequences. Then, bearing this in mind, answer two questions relating to its disclosure: (1) does what is described potentially fall within the description of the client's invention (relevant for novelty); and (2) is any Art.54(2) prior art solving a similar, or the same, problem (relevant for inventive step). Each piece of prior art should therefore be categorised as novelty only, inventive step only, novelty and inventive step or (rarely!) not relevant. Within each prior document note those sections which are particularly relevant to a particular claim type and those which may largely be ignored.

One further point to check is whether the prior art is enabling. For instance, if the prior art discloses a compound but no way of making it, it can be argued that the prior art is non-enabling and the compound is not comprised in the state of the art (T206/83).

Finally, read the Art.96(2) communication. This is likely to contain correct assertions of obviousness and/or lack of novelty. It is possible, however, for at least some of the assertions to be incorrect or too general. It is for this reason that it is preferable to defer the reading of the communication until after you have formed your own opinion on the relevance of the prior art.

*Establishing patentable subject matter* 1–088

Analyse which features of the invention disclosed in the application are already described in the prior art and then mark this information on the paper, or on your summary, as appropriate. Any suitable means may be used, such as highlighting or hatching areas of text. Don't be worried if very little seems to be left — often with Paper B, large parts of the text will be eliminated and sometimes all of the specific examples will be in the prior art!

It should now start to become obvious what amendments are necessary to make the claims novel and inventive. An amendment will take the form of a disclaimer, if the prior art is only relevant to novelty (e.g. 2002); the introduction of a preferred feature with some motivation (very common, e.g. 1996, 1997, 1998, 2000, 2002); or a change of claim category (e.g. product to use, e.g. 1992). The Enlarged Board of Appeal decisions G1/03 and G2/03 clarified when the introduction of a disclaimer does or does not contravene Art.123(2) EPC. Candidates are of course required to know all Decisions and Opinions of the Enlarged Board, but it would be foolish for candidates for Papers B, C and D not to be completely *au fait* with this pair of decisions.

Most commonly, one of the preferred, motivated features will provide an amendment that restores novel, inventive subject matter and in the vast majority of cases data supplied provide evidence of unexpected advantages which are also alluded to in the description. The relevant data will usually be in the description but are occasionally provided in a separate letter from the client (in 1996, relevant data were provided in both!). If the data are in a letter from the client they must naturally be annexed to the response. The relevant preferred feature will be associated with a further problem solved and indications that such a further problem exists should also be in the description.

The situation in which the new invention is a selection invention is particularly popular — see for example 2002 (frit for tile glaze), 2000 (catalyst for oxidising hydrocarbons), 1997 (emulsifiers), 1996 (copolymers for contact lenses), 1995 in part (alloy).

There may be more than one invention which remains, in which case there is usually a lack of unity (e.g. 2001 (three inventions left), 1995 (two inventions left), 1994 (two inventions left), 1993 (three inventions left), 1991 (three inventions left)).

Table 1 overleaf provides some examples of how the prior art commonly affects the novelty of the filed application in Paper B and how novelty and inventive step can be restored.

*Drafting an amended claim set* 1–089

The main independent claim types will usually already be present in the claims of the application as filed. However, this is not always the case and reference to the notes on Paper A should be made for the main independent claim types to include. Where several non-unitary inventions remain, restrict the application to the one which is most commercially significant based on a common sense reading of the information from the client. In your answer you need clearly to identify all the other inventions which have been excluded by the amendment (whether or not they were claimed previously). You do not need to write claims for these other inventions, though it would be a good idea to do so if you have time, but you need to make it clear to the examiner what else you consider to be patentable. To get maximum marks you need to provide arguments in support of the novelty and inventiveness of these other inventions. You should state what divisional applications will be filed. You will get no marks merely for including a statement such as "We reserve the right to file a divisional patent application for subject-matter deleted by these amendments".

When drafting the amended independent claims, use the language of the claims as filed as far as possible. It is very important not to add subject matter, either by deletion or addition of features — many marks are lost on this point. Do not broaden the teaching of examples without specific basis to do so. Special care needs to be taken when amendment derives from a referenced document (e.g. 1998). It is rare in the chemistry paper

**TABLE 1:** Necessary steps to make the claimed invention patentable

| Year | Main claims | D1 | D2 | Restoring novelty | Argument for inventive step |
|---|---|---|---|---|---|
| 2002 | 1. A frit for a tile glaze<br>2. Tile glaze consisting of ... frit ...<br>3. A method of producing wall tiles | **Art.54(3)**<br>Discloses a frit of claim number for different use but no tile.<br>**Nov only** | **Art.54(2)**<br>Discloses the frit and tile exactly as claimed and one of the frit examples.<br>**Nov + inv step** | Introduce preferred feature for frit: "Excellent results have been obtained when the frit contains ..." and a disclaimer *re* D1. Tile only needs preferred frit, no disclaimer. | Data are provided in a separate client letter showing that the tiles in the selected area are more wear and acid resistant. |
| 2000 | 1. Process for oxidising hydrocarbons<br>2. Catalyst | **Art.54(2)**<br>Describes the catalyst and its use in oxidising hydrocarbons.<br>**Nov and inv step** | **Art.54(2)**<br>Describes preferred process for preparing catalyst in detail (calcination temperature is >250 °C in general and 350 °C in the example).<br>**Nov and inv step** | Introduce preferred feature into process claim for preparing catalyst: *"The preferred calcination temperatures are ... most preferably from 500–600 °C"*. | Data in application show catalyst prepared at preferred calcinations temperature gives much greater selectivity in the oxidation of butanes. |
| 1999 | 1. Compounds of formula (I)<br>2. Composition<br>3. First medical use claim | **Art.54(2)**<br>Discloses compounds, general scope and several examples, with different non-medical use.<br>**Nov only** | **Art.54(2)**<br>Discloses compounds, general scope and several examples, with different medical use.<br>**Nov only** | Introduce preferred features:<br>(a) Three specific compounds are still novel.<br>(b) First medical use claim needs a restricted scope *re.* D2.<br>(c) Second medical use claim is OK with broad scope. | No change in argument — compounds of the invention have anticancer activity which was not disclosed or suggested in the prior art. |
| 1998 | 1. A process for manufacturing printed circuit boards | **Art.54(2)**<br>Discloses a process falling within the claims.<br>**Nov + inv step** | **Art.54(2)**<br>Discloses a process falling within the claims.<br>**Nov + inv step** | Introduce preferred feature:<br>*"A still further embodiment ..."* (treatment of oxidised copper layer with reducing agent at acid pH). | Data in the application show that an additional problem is solved by the amended process (elimination of haloing). |
| 1992 | 1. Herbicidal composition ...<br>2. Compound of formula ...<br>3. Process for preparing compound ...<br>4. Use of compound in the treatment of agricultural areas | **Art.54(2)**<br>Discloses same class of compounds as nematicides.<br>**Nov only** | **Art.54(2)**<br>Discloses two of the examples in the application and a method of making them (no activity).<br>**Nov only** | Change of main claim type (compound to use), claim one novel example and composition. | No change in argument since no extra art relevant to inventive step produced. |

for a claim as filed to contain an inessential limitation; if it does, and you want to delete it, do not make the deletion unless you comply with the T331/87 (Houdaille) test:

- the feature is not explained as essential in the disclosure;
- the feature is not indispensable for the function of the invention in light of the technical problem the invention seeks to solve; and
- the replacement or removal of the feature requires no real modification of other features to compensate for the change (Guidelines C/VI/ 5.3.10).

**Then, if you decide to make the deletion, ensure that you cite the basis for the broader combination in your letter to the EPO, explaining why the amendment passes the test.**

Ensure that all essential features relevant to the new problem solved have been incorporated and that the scope is limited to embodiments that solve the new problem. For instance, in 2001 a process invention should have been claimed limited to chlorine-containing starting materials, since only such starting materials could solve the new problem (greater selectivity). Equally, in 1998 the new problem solved related only to the use of copper metal (no haloing effect).

Also ensure that you have added no inessential limitations. The question assumes that the broadest allowable scope will require the use of arguments in support of, in particular, inventive step. Do not narrow to the point at which you feel no need to argue in support of the inventive step of the whole claim scope — it suggests that your claim scope is too narrow, and you will lose marks both for the claim and for the arguments to support the claim.

Unlike Paper A, the specific embodiments of the application are sometimes all found in the prior art. If, on the other hand, one of the examples is still novel but falls outside the scope of the claim as amended (due to the limited basis for amendment provided in the description) it may be possible to claim it separately (e.g. 2002), but always bear in mind the requirements of Art.82 for unity among the inventions claimed. In general, you argumentation should include an **explanation** of how/why the claimed inventions are linked by a single inventive concept. Remember the different categories of claim which are automatically permitted under r.30 (Guidelines C/III/7.2).

Attend to any necessary amendments for the purposes of clarity (e.g. 2001 where "lower alkanol" is not acceptable and 1991 where "lower aliphatic carboxylic acid" needs to be replaced).

Take into account any specific instructions provided by the client (e.g. a separate letter was provided in 1995 in which the client says claims to ternary alloys should be ignored).

Often, with a compound invention, different claim types will have a different scope with respect to the generic compound definition, since prior art only relevant to novelty will fall within one independent claim but not another. For instance, in 2002 a disclaimer to restore novelty over Art.54(3) art was relevant to a frit claim but not a tile claim. In 1999, Art.54(2) prior art having only a novelty effect was relevant to a first medical use claim but not a second medical use claim.

Where the invention as amended resides in a new process, always consider a product-by-process claim. A common trick is that a restricted process claim can give rise to a valid product-by-process claim whereas the broader process claim as filed could not (e.g. 1998, printed circuit board is now novel; 1991, stronger film and semi-permeable membrane are now novel).

A secondary independent claim type sometimes needs amending by introduction of a new essential feature (e.g. 2002 where the tiles have to be fired at a particular temperature range to obtain the advantages of the new frit and the process claim needs amending accordingly).

Draft dependent claims that are associated with further advantages. There are not usually many in Paper B and typically a total of 10 claims will be about right though sometimes fewer will be required. Do not delete subclaims where the added feature has not been shown to be known in the art. Only add claims to those features associated with further inventive step arguments and "most preferred" or "particularly advantageous" features. Also concentrate on those features which are structural rather than use-orientated. Always claim preferred/specific embodiments that are novel, unless this means that you will have a very large number of claims. Consider also preferred features motivated by any data provided.

**1–090** *Writing a response to the Art.96(2) communication*

When writing the response, number paragraphs for ease of reference. Generally, no marks are awarded for standard paragraphs reserving the right to oral proceedings and the like – concentrate on providing clear basis for amendments, demonstrating that the claims are novel and arguing for inventive step. When arguing for inventive step use the problem and solution approach rigidly.

The following notes give guidance on the content and style of the response in the form of a standard template for use in the exam. Sentences in normal typeface are suggestions for phrases to adapt when writing the answer, and sentences in italics provide further useful comments.

Please remember that you are not allowed to write your answer on a pre-prepared template — you must not prepare standard sections of text in advance of the exam and paste them into your answer on the day.

This letter is in response to the communication pursuant to Art.96(2) EPC.

**1. Amendment**

1.1 In response to the objections raised, I attach new claims pages to replace the corresponding existing pages which are now cancelled, without prejudice to the later filing of a divisional application directed to any aspect of the subject matter thereof. These amendments are believed to render moot all those of the examiner's objections which are not otherwise dealt with below.

1.2 Claim 1 has been amended by . . . Support for this amendment is to be found on page x, line y . . . which discloses . . . .

*Explain carefully the basis for the amendments made, explaining why the new features of the claim are disclosed in combination in the description and why any linguistic differences are justified. If there is explicit basis in the application as filed, specify the page and line number. If you rely on an implicit reference, again specify the location of the relevant disclosure **and** provide argument for why the amendment is allowable. Where a feature is removed from a claim as filed, explain how you meet the requirements of T331/87. In the case of incorporation by reference, explain in some detail why the requirements of T689/90 are met (see below). With a disclaimer, the basis will naturally be in the prior art. In addition to explaining where the basis for the new features can be found, explain why the new combination of features in the amended claim is based on the application as filed and not a novel combination, e.g. because new feature x is identified in the description as a preferred aspect of originally claimed subject matter y.*

1.3 Claim 2. . .etc

1.4 Since all the features of the amended claims are directly and unambiguously derivable from the application as filed, it is submitted that there is no contravention of Art.123(2) EPC.

## 2. Novelty

2.1 D1 discloses ... D1 does not disclose the features of the invention of claim 1 that ... and ... In particular, the phrase ... does not explicitly disclose ... Claim 1 is therefore novel over D1.

*List all the distinguishing features. In the case of a novel selection, explain why the three requirements of T279/89 are met (see above under notes relating to Paper A).*

2.2 Since claims 2 to x are dependent on claim 1 and include all its features they are therefore also novel over D1.

*Reference the Guidelines C/IV/9.12 which explain that where an independent claim is new and non-obvious over a piece of prior art there is no need to investigate the novelty or non-obviousness of a dependent claim in light of that prior art.*

2.3 Claim y is novel over D1 because ... etc.

2.4 D2 discloses ... etc.

## 3. Inventive step

3.1 D1 may be taken to be the closest prior art since ...

*Do not simply select the document that has the greatest number of features in common with the claimed invention. Choose the prior art document that is most relevant to new problem solved and which has the most technical features in common. The closest prior art in the case of an inventive process to make a known compound is the most similar prior art process to make the same compound. In appropriate cases, and if time permits, consider arguing inventive step from more than one starting point.*

**Do not use an Art.54(3) citation as the closest prior art!**

3.2 The differences between D1 and the invention of claim 1 are ...

*Inventive step arguments can only be based on mandatory, as opposed to optional, features of the claim that make the claim novel with respect to the relevant art (D1).*

3.3 This difference leads to ... (unexpected property). The objective problem solved by the present invention is therefore ...

*Consider the technical effects or results achieved by the claimed invention when compared to the closest prior art when formulating the problem — no part of the solution should be in the problem (T229/85).*

3.4 Indicate where necessary the basis for the problem in the application where the problem has changed in light of the cited prior art (T39/93).

3.5 The invention of claim 1 solves this problem by providing ... Evidence that the problem is solved is provided by ...

*Point out the advantages of the invention, emphasising why they are important and surprising.*

3.6 There is no suggestion in D1 that xxx could be replaced by yyy since ...(e.g. no pointer, teaching away, prejudice in the art). There is not the slightest incentive for the skilled man to choose ... with a reasonable expectation of achieving ...

The prior art does not give any indication that selection of ... would have an impact on [property X]. Therefore, the dramatic improvements observed on selection of ... must be surprising for the skilled person.

*Emphasise the drawbacks of the closest prior art. For a product by process claim, emphasise that there was no previous way of making a product with such desirable characteristics and hence the new inventive process makes the product itself inventive (T595/90).*

3.7 Starting from D1 and faced with this problem, the skilled person would not look to D2 to find the solution to the problem because. . . . (*e.g.* in different fields, solve different problems, unlikely to be read together by the skilled man (*e.g.* very different dates)). Even if the skilled person starting from D1 and faced with this problem were to try to combine D1 and D2, he would not arrive at the claimed subject matter because (incompatible teaching, structural incompatibility, missing feature. . .).

**Do not consider an Art.54(3) citation in combination with the closest prior art!**

3.8 The invention of claim 1 is therefore not obvious over any of the prior art documents, either taken alone or in combination.

3.9 Dependent claims

*Reference the Guidelines C/IV/9.12 which explain that where an independent claim is new and non-obvious over a piece of prior art there is no need to investigate the novelty or non-obviousness of a dependent claim in light of that prior art.*

3.10 Other independent claims

*Where appropriate reference the Guidelines C/IV/9.12 which explain that where a claim to a product is patentable, claims to a process which results in that product (T169/88) and to a use of the product (T642/94) are also patentable (the only exception being where claims have different effective dates). For an analogy process claim, T119/82 may also be referenced.*

## 4. Unity

The independent claims are believed to meet the requirements for unity of invention (Art.82 EPC). The common special technical feature, required by r.30, is provided by Q, which is present in independent claims 1, A and B, a corresponding special technical feature Q', being found in the remaining independent claims. Q and Q' are clearly corresponding special technical features because. . .

*According to r.30 EPC, unity exists between a group of inventions when there is a technical relationship among the inventions involving one or more of the same or corresponding special technical features, i.e. those features which define a contribution which each of the claimed inventions considered as a whole makes over the prior art. This is explained in the Guidelines C/III/7.2 and in the notes given above in relation to Paper A.*

## 5. Number of independent claims — rule 29(2)

5.1 The presence of more than one claim independent claim in one category, that is product claims 1, X and Y, is believed to comply with the requirements of Rule 29(2) because there are a plurality of inter-related products (meeting the requirement of sub-paragraph (a) of Rule 29(2)).

*Rule 29(2) applies to all European patent applications for which no r.51(4) communication was issued by January 2, 2002. It states that only one independent claim in the same category (product, process, apparatus or use) is allowed, unless the subject matter of the application involves one of:*

  (a) *a plurality of inter-related products;*
  (b) *different uses of a product or apparatus;*
  (c) *alternate solutions to a particular problem, where it is not appropriate to cover these alternatives by a single claim.*

*The EPO is increasingly raising objections under this rule, and it is not unthinkable that Paper B might involve this issue. The Guidelines C/III/3.2 give as examples of cases where multiple independent claims would be allowable under this rule:*

  (a) *gene — gene construct — host — protein — medicament;*
  (b) *second or further medical uses in the claim format of a "second medical use" — type claim;*

(c) *a group of chemical compounds; two or more processes for the manufacture of such compounds.*

*The wording of the rule suggests that if the subject-matter of a patent application satisfies the requirement of at least one of tests (a), (b), or (c), no restraint on the number or category of the independent claims is then imposed by the rule. Certainly one is not limited to either all product claims or all use or method claims. Of course, the Art.84 requirements of clarity and conciseness always apply.*

**6. Objections in the communication**

6.1 In point x.x of the Communication, the examiner objects to . . . This is not the case since . . .

*Go through the communication and respond to all the specific points made by the examiner, even if only by referring to a previous paragraph, unless the objection has been rendered moot by amendments you have made and you have mentioned this under 1.1 above.*

Attached:   New claims

(Anything else — e.g. data supplied in a letter from the client?)

*Notes to the examiner*

The exam does not require or assume that you will write notes to the examiner: your answer should be complete and should speak for itself. But sometimes there is a justification for a brief note to the examiner. Extensive notes to the examiner should be avoided. Things to consider pointing out to the examiner are: (1) assumptions made in light of ambiguities in the question; (2) reasons why you made any decision that was difficult to make (e.g. not claiming novel subject matter deemed to be obvious); and (3) instances where you have had to use claim language (on the basis of the client's instructions) which might not be allowable based on known case law (e.g. having to use "substituted phenyl" in a claim in light of T939/92 — AGREVO/Triazoles).

*Checking answer*

It is always sensible to check the correctness of your claims, especially that the independent claims are clearly novel over the cited art. Is every feature that you have added in fact essential? Check for the absence of features essential to solve the problem which you are now claiming to have solved in light of the new prior art. Have you claimed everything that you intended to claim? Do your arguments in support of novelty and inventive step actually fit the claims that you are proposing? Have you clearly identified anything that should be the subject of a divisional application? Unless you have made a big mistake, major changes to the answer are not recommended in the last 15 minutes and often lose more marks than they gain. If any time remains it is worth reading through the answer once, correcting typographical mistakes and ensuring that there is consistency between the description and the claims.

**3. Notes on amendment**

*Added matter*

A European patent application or a European patent may not be amended in such a way that it contains subject-matter which extends beyond the content of the application as filed (A123(2)). The basic test is whether the subject matter can be directly and unambiguously derived from the application as filed (T20/83) and hence whether 'new information' is provided by the amendment.

Both the explicit and implicit content of the application as filed may be used as basis (T151/84, T201/83). The content of the application as filed is the description, claims and drawings (G3/89) but does not include the abstract, nor the priority document, even if this is filed with the application. Cross-referenced documents are prima facie not part of the application as filed (T689/90) but can sometimes be used under strict conditions (T689/90, T6/84). The conditions are that the description as filed leaves no doubt to a skilled reader: (1) that protection is, or may be sought for such features; (2) that such features contribute to solving the technical problem underlying the invention; (3) that such features at least implicitly clearly belong to the description of the invention contained in the application as filed and thus to the content of the application as filed; and (4) that such features are precisely defined and identifiable within the disclosure of the reference document. Usually, it is only legitimate to incorporate the <u>general</u> teaching of the referenced document, not features in specific examples. See Guidelines C/VI/5.3.8.

Amendments to the claim preamble in view of the closest prior art changing (T13/84) or changing the position of a feature from the preamble to the characterising portion (T16/86) are both allowed.

In most cases in paper B, it will be necessary to make an amendment which is based on a combination of one of the claims as filed and a part or parts of the description. The basis is likely to be explicit. Occasionally (see the 1998 paper described below) some features may need to be taken from a cross-referenced document. As compared to the relevant claim as filed, the claim as amended will contain <u>a new combination of features.</u> Whether the amendment adds subject matter will be a matter of whether this combination is derivable from the application as filed, in particular whether the description anticipates this new combination of features. Typically, for example, the description will identify the added feature as a preferred aspect of the subject matter of the unamended claim.

The most important traps to avoid are (1) making an intermediate generalisation, (2) combining features from separate embodiments and (3) introducing one preferred feature A to make a claim patentable without also introducing a feature B which is an essential counterpart to feature A. In all of these cases, you will end up with a claim which violates the fundamental rule, i.e. contains a combination of features which were not disclosed in combination in the application as filed.

An intermediate generalisation is most often created when you limit a general disclosure having several variable features with only one of the specific features of a disclosed embodiment. For instance, a disclosure may refer to a group of compounds defined by reference to a general formula having variable groups $R^1$ and $R^2$, wherein $R^1$ can be $C_1$-$C_6$ alkyl or halo and $R^2$ can be aryl or heteroaryl and may include a specific embodiment wherein $R^1$ is methyl and $R^2$ is phenyl. If a claim to the compounds of the general formula needs to be limited then it would be possible to limit $R^1$ to methyl and $R^2$ to phenyl (i.e. to claim the specific example) but it would not be permissible to limit $R^1$ to methyl and maintain $R^2$ as aryl or heteroaryl, nor would it be permissible to limit $R^2$ to phenyl and maintain $R^1$ as $C_1$-$C_6$ alkyl or halo. This is because the latter two combinations were not disclosed in the application as filed – methyl has only been disclosed in combination with phenyl and to combine it with aryl/heteroaryl instead is an impermissible generalisation. Of course, if the description indicated that methyl was a preferred definition for $R^1$ then the limitation of $R^1$ to methyl while maintaining the original definition for $R^2$ would be allowable.

Combining features from different embodiments is another trap. It will almost certainly add subject matter unless the description clearly states that features of the different embodiments are interchangeable. An embodiment, after all, is a specific combination of features and, as seen above, you cannot take one of these features alone and use it out of that context. If, for example, in the case quoted above there had been a second embodiment where $R^1$ was ethyl and $R^2$ was pyridyl then to claim the combination of $R^1$ = methyl and $R^2$ = pyridyl would represent added matter. This is not a combination of features which can be derived from the application as filed since methyl has only be disclosed in the narrow context of phenyl.

The other common mistake involves limiting a claim but missing another feature which becomes an essential feature due to the limitation made. For instance, a disclosure may describe a process in which hydrocarbons can be oxidised using a transition metal catalyst. The description may say that the oxidation of ethane works particularly well when palladium is chosen as the catalyst. If the claim is now limited to the use of palladium in the process, in order to make the claim patentable, it is also necessary to limit the starting material to ethane since the superior results of palladium are only demonstrated in the context of using ethane as a starting material.

The 1998 paper B describes three improved methods for preparing a printed circuit board comprising a metal layer and a polymeric support. The first two methods are applicable to circuit boards comprising any metal but both turn out to be unpatentable. In relation to the third method, the description states: 'A still further embodiment of the invention can be used when the metal is copper. In this embodiment, the metal oxide treatment of the copper surface, as described above, is followed by a chemical treatment wherein the copper surface is chemically oxidised in accordance with Document 1 with aqueous alkaline solutions of sodium chlorite to give an oxidised copper surface.' Document 1 contains the following disclosure: 'According to the present invention, there is provided a method of manufacturing a multi-layer printed circuit board from individual boards which bear a printed copper circuit on a dielectric polymeric support, the process comprising the steps of (a) oxidising the copper circuit with a first alkaline oxidising solution, (b) etching the first oxidised circuit thus obtained with a diluted acidic solution thereby removing at least part of the CuO contained in the surface of this layer, (c) oxidising the said first oxidiused and etched circuit with a second alkaline oxidising solution having a higher alkalinity, and (d) laminating a plurality of said oxidised boards with an insulating layer interposed there between. As in the past, sodium chlorite can be used as oxidising agent.' A specific example is also provided.

This paper was full of added matter traps. Firstly, when limiting the process claim as filed to the third embodiment, it is necessary to limit the metal to copper, since the third embodiment is only described in this limited context. Secondly, although the description says that 'the copper surface is chemically oxidised in accordance with Document 1' and Document 1 merely refers to an 'oxidising solution' the oxidant used must be limited to sodium chlorite since the description specifies the use of 'aqueous alkaline solutions of sodium chlorite' when the Document 1 process is used. Thirdly, the amendment must be carefully based on the disclosure of referenced Document 1. It would have been impermissible to have simply referred to Document 1 in the claims since the claims must be self-contained and understandable without reference to other documents (or, for example, the description and drawings — Rule 29(6) EPC). Lastly, it would have been impermissible to have combined the features of two of the embodiments to arrive an novel subject matter since the embodiments were all described individually and without cross-reference.

The impermissibility of combining features from different embodiments is also clearly demonstrated by the 2001 paper B, which described a group of fluorinated hydrocarbons, defined by a general formula, and cited several specific examples falling within the scope of the formula. It also disclosed that one of these specific examples could be advantageously combined with a lower alkanol. One of the claimable inventions was directed to this combination of the specific compound and a lower alkanol. However, it is clear from the examiner's comments that some candidates made the mistake of claiming a combination of any one of fluorinated hydrocarbons, as defined by the general formula, and an alkanol. This is a clear case of adding subject matter since the paper does not contain any disclosure of this combination of features — the description of the combination is clearly limited to the single example. The amendment provides new information since the skilled addressee would only have a contemplated the narrow combination on the basis of the application as filed but is now presented with a broader teaching.

The case law (T02/81) has legitimised the use of one particular manner of combining the features of different numerical ranges which is perhaps rather surprising given the general principles discussed above. When the application discloses a range for a certain parameter A to B and also discloses a preferred range X to Y, falling within the broader range, the two different ranges can be combined to produce a composite range including one of the outer values A or B and one of the inner values X or Y. For example, in 1997 the description stated: 'The subject matter of the invention is new emulsifiers which can be produced by reacting a para-alkyl phenol having the formula p-R-$C_6H_4$-OH, wherein R is a $C_6$- to $C_{24}$-alkyl group, in two consecutive and separate reaction steps.' and 'The alkyl groups R of the starting materials have 6 to 24 carbon atoms. Outside this range the desired well-balanced properties cannot be achieved since the hydrophobic portion of the compound is either too small or too large. Linear alkyl groups having 8 to 16 carbon atoms have proved to be especially advantageous.' Certain embodiments including smaller alkyl groups showed unexpectedly improved properties and it was expected that candidates would draft a claim including a definition of R as a $C_6$- to $C_{16}$-alkyl group, a combination of the lower limit of the broader range and the upper limit of the preferred range.

Where matter cannot be added to the application it may still be added to the file wrapper and used as evidence to support the patentability of an invention. For example, additional examples may justify the scope claimed or evidence of a new effect may justify an inventive step. Where an inventive step is based on data supplied in a letter from the client, for example, it should be included in the response (see 2002 paper B).

One kind of amendment that is often allowed, even though there is no direct basis in the application as filed, is the introduction of a disclaimer. The allowability of such a disclaimer under Article 123(2) EPC has now been definitively decided by the Enlarged Board of Appeal (G1/03 and G2/03). Disclaimers are always allowable when they restore novelty over a 54(3) document. In the case of a 54(2) document a disclaimer is only allowed where the anticipation is accidental, i.e. the prior art reference is so remote and unrelated to the subject matter of the invention that it would never have been taken into account by the skilled person in making the invention. Disclaimers are also allowable to exclude subject matter which is classed as non-patentable for non-technical, policy-related reasons (particularly under A52(4), A53(a) and A57 EPC) where the claim covers some embodiments which fall under the relevant exclusion and some which don't. In all cases, no more than the novelty-destroying part of the prior art or the non-patentable embodiments may be removed from the claim. The rationale is that, in line with previous case law (e.g. T170/87, T597/92) a disclaimer cannot make a non-inventive teaching inventive. A disclaimer may therefore only be used when inventive step is not an issue. How the new definition of 'accidental' will be applied in practice is yet to be seen. The EPO seem to taking a 'business as usual' attitude but the definition could be interpreted to be quite narrow.

Disclaimers, like selection inventions, are most common in the chemical field. The typical case in which a disclaimer should be applied is where a broad, generic claim to a group of compounds is anticipated by the disclosure of a single compound in a 54(2) prior art document and the prior art discloses no use for the compound (e.g. being a disclosure of pure synthetic chemistry) or a completely different use (e.g. the claimed compounds are pharmaceutical compounds and the anticipation is a compound used in photographic emulsions). In these cases, an amendment can be introduced to disclaim the specific compound (. . . 'with the proviso that the compound is not compound X'). A good example can be seen in the 1992 paper A where the client has invented a group of herbicidal compounds but a claim to these compounds is anticipated by the prior art disclosure of a compound which is an additive in resins and oils. In other cases, it may be necessary to remove a broader disclosure by disclaimer – see for instance the 2002 paper B where a prior art frit defined by several ranges anticipated the frit claim as filed. The prior art in this case was A54(3).

As confirmed in G1/03, the disclaimer should be drafted so as to exclude the prior art anticipation and no more broadly. If it is broader than necessary to fulfil its novelty-restoring function then it will add subject matter. Drafting a disclaimer as narrowly as possible also makes sense from the point of view of securing the maximum protection for the client. Some care and skill is therefore necessary when drafting a disclaimer. It seems that quite a few marks were available in 2005 paper B for such careful drafting. In this paper, the main claim as filed related to a detergent composition comprising, amongst other things, sodium percarbonate and one of a group of alkali metal salts of carboxylic acids. The carboxylic acid salt, which was the novel feature of the invention, improved the stability of the sodium percarbonate, particularly when coated on the sodium percarbonate particles as opposed to simply added to the mixture. One of the prior art documents (D1) was clearly relevant to inventive step, describing the use of some of the carboxylic acid salts in detergents to increase the solubility of sodium percarbonate, by coating or simple admixture. This prior art resulted in a restriction of the claim to only some of the originally claimed carboxylic acid salts, which were not expected to be active based on the teaching of D1. The other prior art document (D2), however, was not relevant to inventive step, describing the use of one of the salts, sodium citrate, as a detergent additive for the purpose of reducing fabric incrustation. This required a disclaimer relating to sodium citrate, but only in the context of an admixture of the compound — the disclaimer should not have also encompassed the 'coated' embodiment which was not disclosed in D2. In fact, in this paper, basis for the disclaimer could be derived from the application as filed, and Art.123(2) EPC was not an issue. It does, however, nicely illustrate the principles involved, and introducing the narrowest possible disclaimer would have attracted more marks in view of the broader protection obtained for the client.

*Amended claims not to relate to unsearched subject matter not having unity*       **1–094**

Amended claims may not relate to unsearched subject matter which does not combine with the originally claimed invention or group of inventions to form a single general inventive concept (R86(4) EPC). A divisional application must be filed for such subject matter. This provision relates to matter not present in the claims during search rather than, for instance, matter which was not completely searched. The restrictions imposed by R86(4) EPC have never been an issue in the EQE, to this author's knowledge, but should be borne in mind.

## 4. Worked example using EQE 2002 Paper B

*Understanding and annotating the paper*       **1–095**

The following pages indicate how the 2002 B paper could be marked up on a first reading. No separate summary has been used in this worked example.

## Annex 1 (the application)

## DESCRIPTION OF THE APPLICATION

*Field of the invention — claims to tiles and glazes.*

Our invention relates to wall tiles and in particular to a glaze for such tiles. Tile glazes are made by mixing a powdered pre-melted precursor (a frit) with powdered minerals and if required a pigment. This mixture is applied to the tile surface and fired to give the desired surface finish. We have developed a new frit for tile glazing, which is particularly useful for interior wall tiles. Using our frit an interior wall tile can be produced using a single firing step. The tile glazes enable us to produce tiles which combine an attractive appearance with good wear resistance and acid resistance.

*Prior art.*

It has been common practice to produce interior wall tiles by a double firing process. This conventional process includes the steps of forming a green tile (i.e. a raw, unfired tile), a first firing (biscuit firing), cooling, glazing, and a secondary firing (gloss firing).

*Part of problem to be overcome by invention — prior art methods for wall tiles involve double firing to produce high quality finish.*

Interior wall tiles are produced by double firing because they require a thick glaze. Gases are generated when green tiles are fired as the result of the thermal decomposition of carbonate minerals and the combustion of organic substances. The presence of a molten or partially molten thick glazed layer will prevent the free passage of these gases, giving rise to bubbles in the glaze layer and an unacceptable appearance of the final tile.

The gas generation depends on the firing conditions. If the green tile is heated slowly so that a thermal equilibrium exists between the green tile and the furnace atmosphere, gases will cease to be generated at the furnace temperature of between 700 and 800 °C. The typical commercial furnaces (e.g. a roller hearth kiln), however raise the temperature rapidly and in this case a thermal gradient exists in the green tile. In a roller hearth kiln gases are still generated at furnace temperatures in excess of the initial softening and melting point of a standard glaze (ca. 1000 °C). thus the presence of a thick glaze during the firing of a green tile leads to bubbles being present in the final glaze.

*As above.*

This drawback is absent in the double firing system, because the body to which the glaze is applied is in a form which can release no gases. Hence even a very thick glaze layer is free of bubbles. Thus it is possible to produce interior wall tiles with a high quality smooth glazed surface. Obviously, however, the requirement to fire the tiles twice is associated with considerable cost.

*Further potential problem to overcome.*

The tile glazes must also be wear and acid resistant since otherwise they will rapidly become damaged during routine household cleaning.

According to one aspect of the present invention, a frit for a tile glaze has the following components:

*New frit provided by the invention.*

| | |
|---|---|
| $SiO_2$: | 55 to 65 wt% |
| $Al_2O_3$: | 10 to 18 wt% |
| CaO: | 18 to 25 wt% |
| Alkali metal oxides: | 0.5 to 4 wt% |
| $ZrO_2$: | 0 to 10 wt% |
| $B_2O_3$: | 0 to 2 wt% |
| MgO, BaO, SrO, and ZnO: | 0 to 10 wt% in total |
| Other oxides, chlorides or sulfates: | up to 3 wt% |

According to another aspect of the present invention, a tile glaze is composed of 100 parts by weight of the following components (a) to (i) and 0 to 15 parts by weight of pigment.

(a) 50 to 90 parts by weight of a frit of the following composition:

*New tile provided by the invention and comprising the frit.*

| | |
|---|---|
| $SiO_2$ | 55 to 65 wt% |
| $Al_2O_3$ | 10 to 18 wt% |
| CaO | 18 to 25 wt% |
| Alkali metal oxides | 0.5 to 4 wt% |

| | |
|---|---|
| $ZrO_2$ | 0 to 10 wt% |
| $B_2O_3$ | 0 to 2 wt% |
| MgO, BaO, SrO, and ZnO | 0 to 10 wt% in total |
| Other oxides, chlorides or sulfates | up to 3 wt% |
| (b) Feldspar: | 8 to 25 parts by weight |
| (c) Clay: | 0.5 to 10 parts by weight |
| (d) Zirconium silicate: | 0 to 20 parts by weight |
| (e) Quartz: | 0 to 10 parts by weight |
| (f) Alumina: | 0 to 5 parts by weight |
| (g) Titania: | 0 to 10 parts by weight |
| (h) Barium carbonate: | 0 to 10 parts by weight |
| (i) Zinc Oxide: | 0 to 5 parts by weight |

[Further components of the tile.]

According to a further aspect of the present invention, a method for producing interior wall tiles comprises applying to a green tile a glaze composed of 100 parts by weight of said components (a) to (i) and 0 to 15 parts by weight of a pigment, drying and firing the glazed body.

[Process involving single firing step made possible by new frit.]

Embodiments of the present invention will now be described by way of example only:

The frit of the present invention contains less alkali metal oxides and $B_2O_3$ than frits used to make conventional glazed tiles; therefore, it decreases in viscosity very slowly when heated above its softening point. A tile glaze made using this frit consequently does not flow to cover the entire surface of the tile until it is heated to far above its softening point. This means that gases released from a green tile body can pass through a glaze based on the present frit without causing bubbles to remain in the final glazed tile.

[How the invention works. New composition leads to greater viscosity and delays spreading until all gases released.]

The following is a detailed description of each component and preferred embodiments of the frit of the present invention.

The frit of the present invention contains $SiO_2$ and $Al_2O_3$ as its major constituents. These components are primarily responsible for the high softening point of the frit. They form a network of aluminosilicate glass in the final glaze.

[Further essential frit components for obtaining single firing process.]

The frit contains alkaki metal oxides (abbreviated as $R_2O$ hereinafter) and CaO which promote vitrification.

[Important components for "vitrification".]

According to the present invention, the frit comprises 55 to 65 wt% of $SiO_2$, 10 to 18 wt% of $Al_2O_3$, 18 to 25 wt% of CaO, and 0.5 to 4 wt% of $R_2O$. These ranges ensure that the frit has softening properties which avoid bubbles in the glaze but which at the same time ensure that the glaze completely melts to cover the tile.

[As above.]

<u>Excellent results have been obtained when the frit contains 60 to 64 wt% $SiO_2$, 12 to 16 wt% $Al_2O_3$, 19 to 23 wt% CaO, and 1 to 3 wt% $R_2O$.</u>

[Preferred feature! Motivation?]

The frit may optionally contain as one of the alkali metal oxides $Li_2O$. The presence of $Li_2O$ ensures that the glaze has a very smooth surface. <u>The content of $Li_2O$ should preferably be 0.5 to 1.5 wt%</u>. With less than 0.5 wt%, it does not contribute to the smoothness of the glazed surface; and with more than 1.5 wt%, it can result in pinholes in the glazed surface.

[Preferred feature with motivation.]

The frit of the present invention may contain $B_2O_3$, MgO, ZnO, SrO, and BaO, according to need. These oxides however lower the softening point of the frit, and if present at a concentration which is too high bubbles may form. Thus $B_2O_3$ must be present at less than 2 wt%, <u>especially less than 1 wt%</u>. MgO, BaO, SrO, and ZnO are each preferably present at less that 5 wt%, <u>especially less than 3 wt%</u>. The total amount of MgO, BaO, SrO, and ZnO must be 10 wt% or less.

[Explanation of further frit components.]

[$B_2O_3$ <1% = preferred feature. Motivation? (Same for other oxides <3%).]

The frit of the present invention may optionally contain 10 wt% or less of $ZrO_2$ to impart a hiding power to the glaze (i.e. to ensure that the glaze is opaque and covers up the colour and roughness of the tile).

[Explanation of feature of frit.]

| | |
|---|---|
| 1% = preferred feature. Motivation? | The frit of the present invention may further contain other oxides (*e.g.*, BaO), chlorides, and sulfates. The total amount of these compounds must be less than 3 wt%, <u>preferably less than 1 wt%</u>. |
| General enablement. | The frit at the present invention can be produced by mixing standard frit raw materials, melting them, followed by cooling and crushing the resulting mixture. For example, the production process may include crushing the raw materials, melting the powder at 1300–1500 °C for 1 to 1.5 hours, followed by quenching and crushing, typically in a ball mill. |
| Restatement. | The tile glaze of the present invention is composed of 100 parts by weight of components (a) (the frit) to (i) mentioned above, and 0 to 15 parts by weight of pigment. |
| Function of tile components. Preferred features but no motivation yet. | Feldspar (b) and clay (c) raise the melting point of the glaze. For the glaze of the present invention to have an adequate melting point, the content of feldspar should be 8 to 25 parts by weight, preferably 15 to 21 parts by weight, and the content of clay (*e.g.*, kaolin) should be 0.5 to 10 parts by weight <u>preferably 2 to 4 parts by weight</u>. |
| | Zirconium silicate (d) imparts a hiding power to the glaze. The content of zirconium silicate should be 0 to 20 parts by weight, <u>preferably 10 to 15 parts by weight</u>. |
| Function of further tile components. | Quartz (e), alumina (f), titania (g), barium carbonate (h), and zinc oxide (i) control the melting point of the glaze and the gloss of the glazed surface. Their content should be 0 to 10 parts by weight for quartz, 0 to 5 parts by weight for alumina, 0 to 10 parts by weight for titania, 0 to 10 parts by weight for barium carbonate, and 0 to 5 parts by weight for zinc oxide. |
| Function of the pigment. | The pigment is added, if necessary, to improve the appearance of the glazed surface of tile. Any pigment used for tiles is acceptable for this purpose. The amount of the pigment is 0 to 15 parts by weight per 100 parts by weight of the total amount of components (a) to (i). |
| General enablement. | The tile glaze of the present invention is prepared by suspending the components (a) to (i) and the pigment in water or alcohol. A suspending agent is usually used in this step. The tile glaze is made by adding all the solid components, 30 to 45 parts by weight of water and 0.05 to 0.50 parts by weight of suspending agent for 100 parts by weight of the component mixture to a ball mill and ball milling the mixture. The resulting tile glaze suspension is the tile glaze slip. |
| General enablement and three preferred process features (one motivated in general terms). | The tile glaze slip is subsequently applied to pre-formed green tiles in such an amount that the glaze thickness after drying will be 0.1 to 2 mm, <u>preferably 0.3 to 1mm</u>. The application of the glaze may be performed in any manner. Once the tile glaze slip has been applied to the green tile bodies, the tile bodies are dried and then fired. The firing should <u>preferably be performed by means of a roller hearth kiln</u>. <u>The best quality tiles are obtained when the firing temperature is 1170 to 1220 °C</u>. The fired tile is removed from the roller hearth kiln and is ready for shipment after packaging. |
| | The invention will be described in more detail with reference to the following examples and comparative examples, in which experiments were carried out with green tile bodies measuring 10 x 10 x 0.5 cm which were produced from a ball-milled mixture composed of 45 parts by weight of agalmatolite, 40 parts by weight of clay, 10 parts by weight of limestone, and 5 parts by weight of chamotte. The firing in all the examples was performed in a 25 metre long roller hearth kiln through which the tiles were conveyed at a speed of 1.0 m/min. The maximum temperature in the firing zone was kept at 1190 °C. |

### Example 1

| | |
|---|---|
| Specific embodiment. | A frit was prepared. The chemical composition of the frit is shown in table 1. |
| | Seventy parts by weight of this frit was mixed with 15 parts by weight of feldspar (b), 2 parts by weight clay (c), and 13 parts by weight of zirconium silicate (d), no pigment |

was used. The resulting mixture was ball-milled together with 33 parts by weight of water and 0.20 parts by weight of suspending agent. Thus there was obtained a glaze slip. This glaze slip was applied to the above-mentioned green tile bodies in such an amount that the glaze thickness after drying was 0.6 mm. After drying, the glazed bodies were fired.

Thus there were obtained interior wall tiles of high quality having a smooth, thick, glossy glaze layer free of bubbles. The tile glaze was also wear and acid resistant.

## Examples 2 to 8

Frits having the compositions as detailed in table 1 were prepared in the same manner as in example 1, except that the amounts of raw materials were changed and additional raw materials (boron oxide, magnesia, and zinc oxide) were used. The frit was made into a glaze slip and the glaze slip was applied to the green bodies, followed by drying and firing, in the same manner as in example 1.

The interior wall tiles obtained had the same excellent surface appearance and properties as those produced in example 1.

## Comparative Examples 1 to 3

The procedure as in example 1 was repeated except that the composition was changed as shown in table 1. All of the resulting tiles suffered from bubbles in the glaze layer.

### TABLE 1

Composition of the frits (all the figures are parts by weight of the frit):

| Example | $SiO_2$ | $Al_2O_3$ | CaO | Alkali Metal Oxides $R_2O$ | $ZrO_2$ | $B_2O_3$ | Sum of MgO, SrO, ZnO, and BaO | Bubbles Formed |
|---|---|---|---|---|---|---|---|---|
| 1 | 61.4 | 15.1 | 23.0 | 0.5 | – | – | – | No |
| 2 | 61.4 | 14.0 | 22.6 | 1.0 | – | – | 1.0 | No |
| 3 | 63.4 | 12.0 | 19.6 | 2.0 | – | 1.0 | 2.0 | No |
| 4 | 57.5 | 12.2 | 19.6 | 1.7 | 8.5 | – | – | No |
| 5 | 60.0 | 16.0 | 18.5 | 2.0 | – | 1.5 | 1.0 | No |
| 6 | 58.0 | 14.0 | 24.0 | 3.0 | – | – | 1.0 | No |
| 7 | 61.0 | 14.0 | 20.0 | 3.0 | – | – | 2.0 | No |
| 8 | 59.8 | 12.6 | 21.6 | 2.0 | – | – | 4.0 | No |
| Comp. 1 | 60.0 | 12.0 | 20.0 | 7.0 | – | 1.0 | – | Yes |
| Comp. 2 | 53.0 | 19.0 | 18.0 | 3.0 | – | 2.0 | 3.0 | Yes |
| Comp. 3 | 68.0 | 6.0 | 23.0 | 2.0 | – | 1.0 | – | Yes |

## Examples 9 to 14 and Comparative Examples 4 to 6

Glazes were prepared in the same manner as example 1. The frit of example 2 was combined with feldspar, clay, pigment and the other components as shown in Table 2. Pigment was used at 5 parts per 100 parts of the tile glaze. The pigment was a standard commercially available manganese and cobalt based mixture which produces tiles with a wine red coloured glaze. The glazes were applied to green tiles, followed by drying and firing.

In examples 9 to 14, there were obtained interior wall tiles of high quality having a smooth, thick, glossy glaze layer free of bubbles and with a good wear and acid resistance. In contrast, in comparative examples 4 to 6, bubbles were generated in the glaze during firing.

## TABLE 2

**Composition of the tile glaze (all figures are parts by weight of the glaze)**

| Example | Frit | Feldspar | Clay | Zirconium silicate | Quartz | Alumina or Titania | Barium Carbonate | Zinc Oxide |
|---|---|---|---|---|---|---|---|---|
| 9 | 68 | 17 | 2 | 13 | – | – | – | – |
| 10 | 60 | 21 | 2 | 13 | – | – | – | 4 |
| 11 | 55 | 20 | 2 | 13 | 10 | 3 (alumina) | – | – |
| 12 | 80 | 15 | 5 | – | – | – | – | – |
| 13 | 60 | 20 | 2 | 10 | – | 8 (titania) | – | – |
| 14 | 55 | 20 | 2 | 10 | 4 | 2 (alumina) | 7 | – |
| Comp. 4 | 95 | 3 | 2 | – | – | – | – | – |
| Comp. 5 | 70 | – | 5 | 10 | 15 | – | – | – |
| Comp. 6 | 70 | – | 5 | – | – | 15 | – | 5 |

## Claims

*Product claims to the frit and a tile glaze incorporating the frit and a method claim.*

1. A frit for a tile glaze consisting of:

    SiO$_2$: 55 to 65 wt%
    Al$_2$O$_3$: 10 to 18 wt%
    CaO: 18 to 25 wt%
    Alkali metal oxides: 0.5 to 4 wt%
    ZrO$_2$: 0 to 10 wt%
    B$_2$O$_3$: 0 to 2 wt%
    MgO, BaO, SrO, and ZnO: 0 to 10 wt% in total
    Other oxides, chlorides or sulfates: up to 3 wt%

2. Tile glaze consisting of 100 parts by weight of the following components (a) to (i) and 0 to 15 parts by weight of pigment.

    (a) Frit as defined in claim 1: 50 to 90 parts by weight
    (b) Feldspar: 8 to 25 parts by weight
    (c) Clay: 0.5 to 10 parts by weight
    (d) Zirconium silicate: 0 to 20 parts by weight
    (e) Quartz: 0 to 10 parts by weight
    (f) Alumina: 0 to 5 parts by weight
    (g) Titania: 0 to 10 parts by weight
    (h) Barium carbonate: 0 to 10 parts by weight
    (i) Zinc oxide: 0 to 5 parts by weight

3. A method for producing wall tiles comprises applying to a green tile a glaze composed as defined in claim 2, drying and firing the glazed tile.

## Annex 2 (COMMUNICATION)

1) Document 1, which represents prior art in the sense of Article 54(3) and (4) EPC for all the contracting states, discloses a frit which is novelty destroying for claim 1 (see paragraph 4 and claim 1).

*Note Document 1 is novelty only and only refers to frits, not tiles.*

1.1) Document 2 discloses frits, title glazes and methods which are novelty destroying for the subject-matter of claims 1–3 (Articles 52(1), 54(1) and 54(2) EPC) (see claim 1, example).

*Document 2 is relevant to novelty and inventive step and all claims.*

2) If the applicant wishes to maintain the application, new claims should be filed which take the above objections into account. Care should be taken to ensure that the new claims comply with the requirements of the EPC in respect of novelty, inventive step, clarity and if necessary unit (Articles 54, 56, 84 and 82 EPC). The applicant should also ensure that any amendments do not introduce subject-matter which extends beyond the content of the application as originally filed (Article 123(2) EPC).

*Reminder of main EPC provisions that must be taken into account.*

3) In the letter of reply, the difference between the new claims and the state of the art as well as its significance should be identified. In addition the invention should be presented in such a way that the technical problem being solved in view of the state of the art, the solution proposed to this problem, as well as the position of the applicant in respect of inventive step (Rule 27(1)(c) EPC and Guidelines C-IV, 9.5) can be clearly understood.

*Reminder to set out arguments for novelty and inventive step properly in answer.*

4) An independent claim must specify all the technical features necessary to define the invention (Guidelines C-III, 4.4). Thus each independent claim must contain all the technical features essential to the solution of the problem on which the invention is based.

*Must include in claim all features underlying the inventive advantage.*

5) In order to facilitate the examination as to whether the new claims contain subject-matter which extends beyond the content of the application as filed, the applicant is requested to indicate precisely where in the application documents any amendments proposed find a basis (Article 123(2) EPC, Guidelines E-II, and C-VI, 5,4).

*Reminder to set out basis for amended claims in answer.*

6) It is suggested that the adaptation of the description to any new claims be postponed until the Examining Division indicates that a set of claims is allowable.

*Reminder that an amended description is not required for Paper B.*

## Annex 3 (DOCUMENT 1, prior art in the sense of Articles 54(3) and (4) for all the contracting states)

*Novelty only.*

This invention relates to a glazed alumina ceramic and to a frit suitable for making the glaze.

*Different field but irrelevant since document is novelty only.*

Ceramics are being increasingly used in electronic applications. It has recently been determined that the thermal properties of alumina ceramics make them ideal candidates for the thermal head for a printer or a fax receiver. Thermal heads are however required to have one very smooth surface and it is not economically viable to polish an alumina ceramic to the degree of smoothness now required.

*As above.*

The problem addressed by the present invention is thus to provide an alumina ceramic with a very smooth surface by an economical method. The solution proposed to this problem is to glaze a surface of the alumina ceramic using the frit composition defined below. It has surprisingly been found that by using this frit it is possible to produce a glazed surface having the required smoothness without degrading the thermal properties of the alumina ceramic.

The frit used has the following composition:

*Relevant to novelty of frit claim.*

| | |
|---|---|
| $SiO_2$: | from 63 to 65 wt% |
| $Al_2O_3$: | from 12 to 14 wt% |
| $ZrO_2$: | from 1 to 5 wt% |
| CaO: | from 15% to 20 wt% |
| Alkali metal oxides: | 0,5 to 4 wt% |
| ZnO: | up to 5 wt% |
| $B_2O_3$: | up to 5 wt% |

Additional oxides may be present at up to 5wt%

### Example

100 parts by weight of a granulated frit having the following composition: $SiO_2$: 64 wt%; $Al_2O_3$: 12 wt%; $ZrO_2$: 2 wt%; CaO: 19.5 wt%, $Li_2O$: 1 wt% and $B_2O_3$: 1.5 wt% was placed in a ball mill. 33 parts by weight of water and 1.5 parts by weight ethyl cellulose were added and the mixture was milled until it formed a flowable paste.

*Specific embodiment relevant to novelty of frit claim and enablement.*

The glass frit paste was applied by screen printing to a surface of a pre-fired alumina ceramic to give a uniform coating. The past layer was dried at 120 °C and then fired at 1400 °C so as to ensure that the glaze melted and covered the surface of the alumina. The resulting alumina plate was covered with a very uniform glaze layer 0.1 mm thick. The thermal properties of the glazed alumina and the smoothness of the glazed surface were tested. The thermal properties and the smoothness were found to be excellent and thus the product was ideally suited for use as a thermal head for a fax receiver or a printer.

### Claims

1. A frit having the following composition:

| | |
|---|---|
| $SiO_2$: | from 63 to 65 wt% |
| $Al_2O_3$: | from 12 to 14 wt% |
| $ZrO_2$: | from 1 to 5 wt% |
| CaO: | from 15% to 20 wt% |
| Alkali metal oxides: | 0,5 to 4 wt% |
| ZnO: | up to 5 wt% |
| $B_2O_3$: | up to 5 wt% |
| Additional oxides: | up to 5 wt% |

2. An alumina ceramic body characterised in that, at least one surface of the body is glazed with a frit of composition of claim 1.

3. The use of the alumina ceramic body of claim 2 as a thermal head for a fax receiver.

| Margin note | Main text |
|---|---|
| Novelty and inventive step. | **Annex 4 (DOCUMENT 2 illustrative of the state of the art)** |

Our invention relates a glaze for interior wall tiles. Tile glazes are made by mixing a powered pre-melted precursor (a frit) with powdered minerals and if required a pigment. This mixture is applied to the tile surface and fired to give an attractive tile with a surface which is hand wearing and resistant to acidic household cleaning agents. We have developed a tile glaze which fulfills all of these requirements. The tile glaze can be produced using a single firing step.

<small>Solves same problem as our application (single firing that gives attractive surface).</small>

Glazed tiles which are produced using a single firing step (ie the firing of the green tile occurs simultaneously with the melting of the glaze) often either suffer from a poor appearance of the glaze due to the presence due to the presence of bubbles or are not sufficiently wear and acid resistant. We have developed a title glaze for a single firing process able to combine an attractive appearance with good a wear resistance and acid resistance.

The title glaze of the present invention has the following composition:

100 parts by weight of the following components (a) to (i) and 0 to 15 parts by weight of pigment.

(a) 50 to 90 parts by weight of a frit of the following composition:

<small>Relevant to novelty and inventive step of tile and glaze claims.</small>

| | |
|---|---|
| $SiO_2$ | 55 to 65 wt% |
| $Al_2O_3$ | 10 to 18 wt% |
| CaO | 18 to 25 wt% |
| Alkali metal oxides | 0.5 to 4 wt% |
| $ZrO_2$ | 0 to 10 wt% |
| $B_2O_3$ | 0 to 2 wt% |
| MgO, BaO, SrO, and ZnO | 0 to 10 wt% in total |
| (b) Fedspar: | 8 to 25 parts by weight |
| (c) Clay: | 0.5 to 10 parts by weight |
| (d) Zironium Silicate: | 0 to 20 parts by weight |
| (e) Quartz: | 0 to 10 parts by weight |
| (f) Alumina: | 0 to 5 parts by weight |
| (g) Titania: | 0 to 10 parts by weight |
| (h) Barium carbonate: | 0 to 10 parts by weight |
| (i) Zinc oxide: | 0 to 5 parts by weight |

The tile glaze of the present invention has the following features. It is composed of 100 parts by weights of component (a) (the frit) and components (b) to (i) mentioned above, and 0 to 15 parts by weight of pigment.

<small>General enablement and relevant to the novelty of some of the preferred features in the application.</small>

According to the present invention, the frit (a) comprises 55 to 65 wt% of $SiO_2$, 10 to 18 wt% of $Al_2O_3$, 18 to 25 wt% of CaO, and 0.5 to 4 wt% of $R_2O$ (alkali metal oxides) optionally along with other oxides. These ranges ensure that the frit has softening properties which avoid bubbles in the glaze but which at the same time ensure that the glaze completely melts to cover the title.

The frit may optionally contain as one of the alkali metal oxides $Li_2O$. The presence of $Li_2O$ ensures that the glaze has a very smooth surface. The content of $Li_2O$ should preferably be 0.5 to 1.5 wt%. With less than 0.5 wt%, it does not contribute to the smoothness of the glazed surface; and with more than 1.5 wt%, it can result in pinholes in the glazed surface. The frit of the present invention may contain $B_2O_3$, MgO, ZnO, SrO, and BaO, according to need. These oxides however lower the softening point of the frit and if present at a concentration which is too high bubbles may form. Thus $B_2O_3$ must be present at less than 2 wt%, especially less than 1 wt%.

<small>As above.</small>

MgO, BaO, SrO, and ZnO are each preferably present at less than 5 wt%, especially less than 3 wt%. The total amount of MgO, BaO, SrO, and ZnO must be 10 wt% or less.

The frit of the present invention may optionally contain 10 wt% or less of $ZrO_2$ to impart a hiding power to the glaze.

The components (b) to (i) when present at concentrations inside the ranges indicated ensure that the glaze is sufficiently hard wearing and acid resistant as well as contributing to the attractive appearance of the glaze.

The title glaze of the present invention is prepared by suspending the components (a) to (i) and if required the pigment in water or alcohol. A suspending agent is usually used in this step. The title glaze is made by adding all the solid components, 30 to 45 parts by weight of water and 0.05 to 0.50 parts by weight of suspending agent for 100 parts by weight of the component mixture to a ball mill and ball milling the mixture. The resulting tile glaze suspension is the tile glaze slip.

The tile glaze slip is subsequently applied to pre-formed green title bodies in such an amount that the glaze thickness after drying will be 0.1 to 2 mm, preferably 0.3 to 1 mm. The application of the glaze may be performed in any manner. Once the title glaze slip has been applied to the green title bodies, the title bodies are dried and then fired. The firing should preferably be performed by means of a roller hearth kiln. The fired title is removed from the roller hearth kiln and is ready for shipment after packaging.

The invention will be described in more detail with reference to the following examples and comparative examples, in which experiments were carried out with green title bodies measuring 10 x 10 x 0.5 cm which were produced from a ball-milled mixture composed of 45 parts by weight of agalmatolite, 40 parts by weight of clay, 10 parts by weight of limestone, and 5 parts by weight of chamotte. The firing in all the examples was performed in a 25 metre long roller hearth kiln through which the tiles were conveyed at a speed of 1.0 m/min. The temperature in the firing zone was kept at 1190 °C

## Example

Seventy parts by weight of a frit having the following composition (57.5 wt% of $SiO_2$, 12.2 wt% of $Al_2O_3$, 19.6 wt% of CaO, 1.7 wt% of $R_2O$ and 8.5 wt% $ZrO_2$) was mixed with 15 parts by weight of feldspar, 2 parts by weight clay, and 13 parts by weight of zirconium silicate. The resulting mixture was ball-milled, together with 33 parts of weight of water and 0.20 parts by weight of suspending agent. Thus there was obtained a glaze slip. This glaze slip was applied to the above-mentioned green tiles in such an amount that the glaze thickness after drying was 0.6 mm. After drying, the glazed tiles were fired. Thus there were obtained interior wall tiles of high quality having a smooth, thick, glossy glaze layer free of bubbles. The wear resistance and the acid resistance of the tile were measured in accordance with the Standard DIN xxxyyy and were determined to have a rating of 5 or above (good).

## Claim

1. Tile glaze consisting of 100 parts by weight of the following components (a) to (i) and 0 to 15 parts of weight of pigment.

(a) 50 to 90 parts by weight of a frit of the following composition:

| | |
|---|---|
| $SiO_2$ | 55 to 65 wt% |
| $Al_2O_3$ | 10 to 18 wt% |
| CaO | 18 to 25 wt% |
| Alkali metal oxides | 0.5 to 4 wt% |
| $ZrO_2$ | 0 to 10 wt% |
| $B_2O_3$ | 0 to 2 wt% |
| MgO, BaO, SrO, and ZnO | 0 to 10 wt% in total |

(b) Feldspar: 8 to 25 parts by weight
(c) Clay: 0.5 to 10 parts by weight
(d) Zironium silicate: 0 to 20 parts by weight
(e) Quartz: 0 to 10 parts by weight
(f) Alumina: 0 to 5 parts by weight
(g) Titania: 0 to 10 parts by weight
(h) Barium carbonate: 0 to 10 parts by weight
(i) Zinc oxide: 0 to 5 parts by weight

## Annex 5 (letter from the applicant)

Dear sir,

We have carefully studied the communication and the most relevant document 2. We decided to perform some further experiments in order to compare the title glaze exemplified in document 2 with that made in examples of our application. The tiles of our examples 1–3 and the tile made in accordance with the example in document 2 were manufactured exactly as indicated in our application and document 2 respectively. The wear resistance and the acid resistance of these tiles were measured in accordance with the standard No. DIN xxxyyy. The wear resistance and acid residence were each rated from 1–10 in accordance with this standard. A value of 5 or above is considered to be good. A value of 8 or above is excellent.

*Comparative data showing advantages over closest prior art and new problem solved — will justify inventive step for appropriate claim amendment.*

| Example | Firing Temperature | Wear Resistance | Acid Resistance | Bubbles Observed |
|---|---|---|---|---|
| 1 | 1190 °C | 8 | 8 | No |
| 2 | 1190 °C | 9 | 7 | No |
| 3 | 1190 °C | 7 | 9 | No |
| Example of Document 2 | 1190 °C | 5 | 6 | No |

The excellent results shown above are however only obtained when the tiles are fired at a temperature between 1170 °C and 1220 °C.

*Essential feature relevant to new problem solved.*

We hope that these results are of use when drafting a response to the communication.

Yours faithfully

Mr. T Layer
BathFitz Inc

**1–096** *Establishing patentable subject matter*

The following pages indicate how the client's application can be divided into novel features and features found in the prior art. A shaded box has been used to indicate a lack of novelty. New comments have been added in bold.

## Annex 1 (the application)
## DESCRIPTION OF THE APPLICATION

Our invention relates to wall tiles and in particular to a glaze for such tiles. The glazes are made by mixing a powdered pre-melted precursor (a frit) with powdered minerals and if required a pigment. This mixture is applied to the tile surface and fired to give the desired surface finish. We have developed a new frit for tile glazing, which is particularly useful for interior wall tiles. Using our frit an interior wall tile can be produced using a single firing step. The tile glazes enable us to produce tiles which combine an attractive appearance with good wear resistance and acid resistance.

Field of the invention — claims to tiles and glazes.

It has been common practice to produce interior wall tiles by a double fring process. This conventional process includes the steps of forming a green tile (i.e. a raw, unfired tile), a first firing (biscuit firing), cooling glazing, and a secondary firing (gloss firing).

Prior art.

Interior wall tiles are produced by double firing because they require a thick glaze. Gasses are generated when green tiles are fired as the result of the thermal decomposition of carbonate minerals and the combustion of organic substances. The presence of a molten a partially molten thick glazed layer will prevent the free passage of these gases, giving rise to bubbles in the glaze layer and an unacceptable appearance of the final tile.

Part of problem to be overcome by invention — prior art methods for wall tiles involve double firing to produce high quality finish.

The gas generation depends on the firing conditions. If the green tile is heated slowly so that a thermal equilibrium exists between the green tile and the furnace atmosphere, gases will cease to be generated at a furnace temperature of between 700 and 800 °C. The typical commercial furnaces (e.g. a roller hearth kiln), however raise then temperature rapidly and in this case a thermal gradient exists in the green tile. In a roller hearth kiln gases are still generated at furnace temperatures in excess of the initial softening and melting point of a standard glaze (ca. 1000 °C) Thus the presence of a thick glaze during the firing of a green tile to the bubbles being present in the final glaze.

This drawback is absent in the double firing system, because the body to which the glaze is applied is in a form which can release no gases. Hence even very thick glaze layer is free of bubbles. Thus it is possible to produce interior wall tiles with a high quality smooth glazed surface. Obviously, however, the requirement to the fire the tiles twice is associated with considerable cost.

As above.

The tile glazes must also be wear and acid resistant since otherwise they will rapidly become damaged during routine household cleaning.

**New problem solved by amended claim and supported by comparative data.**

According to one aspect of the present invention, a frit for a tile glaze has the following components.

**Disclosed exactly in Document 2 and partly in Document 1.**

| | |
|---|---|
| $SiO_2$: | 55 to 65 wt% |
| $Al_2O_3$: | 10 to 18 wt% |
| CaO: | 18 to 25 wt% |
| Alkali metal oxides: | 0.5 to 4 wt% |
| $ZrO_2$: | 0 to 10 wt% |
| $B_2O$: | 0 to 2 wt% |
| MgO, BaO, SrO, and ZnO: | 0 to 10 wt% in total. |
| Other oxides, chlorides or sulfates: | up to 3 wt% |

New frit provided by the invention.

According to another aspect of the present invention, a tile glaze composed of 100 parts by weight of the following components (a) to (i) and 0 to 15 parts by weight of pigment

(a) 50 to 90 parts by weight of a frit of the following composition:

| | |
|---|---|
| $SiO_2$ | 55 to 65 wt% |
| $Al_2O_3$ | 10 to 18 wt% |

New tile provided by the invention and comprising the frit.

| | | |
|---|---|---|
| Disclosed exactly in Document 2. | CaO<br>Alkali metal oxides<br>$ZrO_2$<br>$B_2O_3$<br>MgO, BaO, SrO and ZnO | 18 to 25 wt%<br>0.5 to 4 wt%<br>0 to 10 wt%<br>0 to 2 wt%<br>0 to 10 wt% in total |
| | Other oxides, chlorides or sulfates: | up to 3 wt% |
| All disclosed in Document 2.<br><br>Further components of the tile. | (b) Feldspar:<br>(c) Clay:<br>(d) Zirconium silicate:<br>(e) Quartz:<br>(f) Alumina:<br>(g) Titania:<br>(h) Barium carbonate:<br>(i) Zinc oxide: | 8 to 25 parts by weight<br>0.5 to 10 parts by weight<br>0 to 20 parts by weight<br>0 to 5 parts by weight<br>0 to 10 parts by weight<br>0 to 10 parts by weight<br>0 to 10 parts by weight<br>0 to 5 parts by weight |
| Process involving single firing step made possible by new frit. | According to a further aspect of the present invention, a method for producing interior wall tiles comprises applying to green tile a glaze composed of 100 parts by weight of said components (a) to (i) and 0 to 15 parts by weight of a pigment, drying and firing the glazed body. | |
| | Embodiments of the present invention will now be described by wall of example only: | |
| How the invention works. New composition leads to greater viscosity and delays in spreading until all gases released. | The frit of the present invention contains less alkali metal oxide and $B_2O_3$ then frits used to make conventional glazed tiles; therefore, it decreases in viscosity very slowly when heated above its softening point. A tile glaze made using this frit consequently does not flow to cover the entire surface of the tile until it is heated to far above its softening point. This means that gases released from a green tile body can pass through a glaze based on the present frit without causing bubbles to remain in the final glazed tile. | |
| | The following is a detailed description of each component and preferred embodiments of the frit of the present invention. | |
| Further essential frit components for obtaining single firing process. | The frit of the present invention contains $SiO_2$ and $Al_2O_3$ as its major constituents. These components are primarily responsible for the high softening point of the frit. They form a network of aluminosilicate glass in a final glaze. | |
| Important component for "vitrification". | The frit contains alkali metal oxides (abbreviated as $R_2O$ hereinafter) and CaO which promote vitrification. | |
| Disclosed in Document 2.<br><br>As above. | According to the present invention, the frit comprises 55 to 65 wt% of $SiO_2$ 10 to 18 wt% of $Al_2O_3$ 18 to 25 of CaO, and 0.5 to 4 wt% of $R_2O$. These ranges ensure that the frit has softening properties which avoid bubbles in the glaze but which at the same time ensure that the glaze completely melts to cover the tile. | |
| Preferred feature! Motivation? Yes! See comparative data. | <u>Excellent results have been obtained when the frit contains 60 to 64 wt% $SiO_2$ 12 to 16 wt% $Al_2O_3$ 19 to 23 wt% CaO, and 1 to 3 wt% $R_2O$.</u> | |
| Disclosed in Document 2.<br><br>Preferred feature with motivation.<br><br>Explanation of further frit components.<br><br>$B_2O_3$ <1% = preferred feature. Motivation? (Same for other oxides <3%). | The frit may optionally contain as one of the alkali metal oxides $Li_2O$. The presence of $Li_2O$ ensures that the glaze has a very smooth surface. <u>The content of $Li_2O$ preferably be 0.5 to 1.5 wt%</u>. With less then 0.5wt% it does not contribute to the smoothness of the glazed surface; and with more than 1.5 wt%, it can result in pinholes in the glazed surface. The frit of the present invention may contain $B_2O_3$, MgO, ZnO, SrO, and BaO, according to need. These oxides however lower the softening point of the frit, and if present at a concentration which is to high bubbles may form. Thus $B_2O_3$ must be present at less than 2 wt%, <u>especially less than 1 wt%</u>. MgO, BaO, SrO, and ZnO are each preferably present at less than 5 wt%, <u>especially less than 3 wt%</u>. The total amount of MgO, BaO, and ZnO must be 10 wt% or less. | |

The frit of the present invention may optionally contain 10 wt% or less of $ZnO_2$ to impart a hiding power to glaze (ie to ensure that the glaze is opaque and covers up the colour and roughness of the tile).

*Explanation of feature of frit.*

The frit of the present invention may further contain other oxides (e.g., BaO), chlorides and sulfates. The total amount of these compounds must be less than 3 wt%, preferably less than 1 wt%.

*1% = preferred feature. Motivation?*

The frit of the present invention can be produced by mixing standard frit raw materials, melting them, followed by cooling and crushing the resulting mixture. For example, the production process may include crushing the raw materials, melting the powder at 1300–1500 °C for 1 to 1.5 hours, followed by quenching and crushing, typically in a ball mill.

*General enablement.*

The tile glaze of the present invention is composed of 100 parts by weight of components (a) (the frit) to (i) mentioned above, and 0 to 15 parts by weight of pigment.

*Restatement.*

Feldspar (b) and clay (c) raise the melting point of the glaze. For the glaze of the present invention to have an adequate melting point, the content of the feldspar should be 8 to 25 parts of weight, preferably 15 to 21 parts of weight, and the content of clay (e.g., Kaolin) should be 0.5 to 10 parts by weigh, preferably 2 to 4 parts of weight.

*Function of tile components. Preferred features but no motivation yet.*

Zirconium silicate (d) imparts a hiding power of the glaze. The content of the Zirconium silicate should be 0 to 20 parts by weight, preferably 10 to 15 parts of weight.

Quartz (e) alumina (f), titania (g), barium carbonate (h), and zinc oxide (i) control the melting point of the glaze and the gloss of the glazed surface. Their content should be 0 to 10 parts by weight for quartz, 0 to 5 parts by weight for alumina, 0 to 10 parts by weight for titania, 0 to 10 parts by weight for barium carbonate, and 0 to 5 parts of weight for zinc oxide.

*Function of further tile components.*

The pigment is added, if necessary, to improve the appearance of the glazed surface of tile. Any pigment used for tiles is acceptable for this purpose. The amount of the pigment is 0 to 15 parts of weight per 100 parts by weight of the total amount of components (a) to (i).

*Function of the pigment.*

The tile glaze of the present invention is prepared by suspending the components (a) to (i) and the pigment in water or alcohol. A suspending agent is usually used in this step. The tile glaze is made by adding all the solid components, 30 to 45 parts by weight of water and 0.05 to 0.50 parts by weight of suspending agent for 100 parts by weight of the component mixture to a ball mill and ball milling the mixture. The resulting tile glaze suspension is the tile glaze slip.

*Exactly as in Document 2.*

*General enablement.*

The tile glaze slip is subsequently applied to pre-formed green tiles in such an amount that the glaze thickness after drying will be 0.1 to 2 mm, preferably 0.3 to 1 mm. The application of the glaze may be performed in any manner. Once the tile glaze slip has been applied to the green tile bodies, the tile bodies are dried and then fired. The firing should preferably be performed by means of a roller hearth kiln. The best quality tiles are obtained when the ifring temperature is 1170 to 1220°c The fired tile is removed from the roller hearth kiln and is ready for shipment after packaging.

*Exactly as in Document 2.*

*General enablement and three preferred process features (one motivated in general terms).*

*Temperative range motivated by corporative data.*

The invention will be described in more detail with reference to the following examples and comparative examples, in which experiments were carried out with green tile bodies measuring 10 x 10 x 0.5 cm which were produced from a ball-milled mixture composed of 45 parts by weight of agalmatolite, 40 parts by weight of clay, 10 parts of weight limestone, and 5 parts of weight of chamotte. The firing in all the examples was performed in a 25 metre long roller hearth kiln through which the tiles were coveyed at a speed of 1.0 m/min. The maximum temperature in the firing zone was kept at 1190 °C.

*Exactly as in Document 2.*

### Example 1

*Specific embodiment.*

A frit was prepared. The chemical composition of the frit is shown in table 1. Seventy parts by weight of the frit was mixed with 15 parts by weight of feldspar (b), 2 parts by the weight clay (c), and 13 parts by weight of zirconium silicate (d), no pigment was used. The resulting mixture was ball-milled together with 33 parts by weight of water and 0.20 parts by weight of suspending agent. Thus there was obtained a glaze slip. The glaze slip was applied to the above-mentioned green tile bodies in such an amount that the glaze thickness after drying was 0.6mm. After drying, the glazed bodies were fired.

Thus there were obtained interior wall tiles of high quality a smooth, thick, glossy glaze layer free of bubbles. The tile glaze was also wear and acid resistant.

### Example 2 to 8

*Further specific examples.*

Frits having the compositions as detailed in table 1 were prepared in the same manner as in example 1, except that the amounts of raw materials were changed and additional raw materials (boron oxide, magnesia, and zinc oxide) were used. The frit was made into a glaze slip and the glaze slip was applied to the green bodies, followed by the drying and firing, in the same manner as in example 1.

The interior wall tiles obtained had the same excellent surface appearance and properties as those produced in example 1.

### Comparative Examples 1 to 3

*Proof that problem existed in prior art.*

The procedure as in example 1 was repeated except that the composition was changed as shown in table 1. All of the resulting tiles suffered from bubbles in the glaze layer.

### TABLE 1

Composition of the frits (all the figures are parts by weight of the frit):

*Novel compositions except for Example 4 which is disclosed in D1.*

| Example | $SiO_2$ | $Al_2O_3$ | CaO | Alkali Metal Oxides $R_2O$ | $ZrO_2$ | $B_2O_3$ | Sum of MgO, SrO, ZnO, and BaO | Bubbles Formed |
|---|---|---|---|---|---|---|---|---|
| 1 | 61.4 | 15.1 | 23.0 | 0.5 | – | – | – | No |
| 2 | 61.4 | 14.0 | 22.6 | 1.0 | – | – | 1.0 | No |
| 3 | 63.4 | 12.0 | 19.6 | 2.0 | – | 1.0 | 2.0 | No |
| 4 | 57.5 | 12.2 | 19.6 | 1.7 | 8.5 | – | – | No |
| 5 | 60.0 | 16.0 | 18.5 | 2.0 | – | 1.5 | 1.0 | No |
| 6 | 58.0 | 14.0 | 24.0 | 3.0 | – | – | 1.0 | No |
| 7 | 61.0 | 14.0 | 20.0 | 3.0 | – | – | 2.0 | No |
| 8 | 59.8 | 12.6 | 21.6 | 2.0 | – | – | 4.0 | No |
| Comp. 1 | 60.0 | 12.0 | 20.0 | 7.0 | – | 1.0 | – | Yes |
| Comp. 2 | 53.0 | 19.0 | 18.0 | 3.0 | – | 2.0 | 3.0 | Yes |
| Comp. 3 | 68.0 | 6.0 | 23.0 | 2.0 | – | 1.0 | – | Yes |
| D2 | 57.5 | 12.2 | 19.6 | 1.7 | 8.5 | – | – | No |
| D1 | 64 | 12 | 19.5 | 1 | 2 | 1.5 | – | N/A |

### Example 9 to 14 and comparative examples 4 to 6

Glazes were prepared in the same manner as in example 1. The frit of example 2 was combined with feldspar, clay, pigment and the other components as shown in Table 2. Pigment was used at 5 parts per 100 parts of the tile glaze. The pigment was a standard commercially available manganese and cobalt based mixture which produces tiles with a wine red coloured glaze. The glazes were applied to green tiles, followed by drying and firing.

*Further specific embodiments including pigment.*

In examples 9 to 14, there were obtained interior wall tiles of high quality having a smooth, thick, glossy glaze layer free of bubbles and with a good wear and acid residence. In contrast, in comparative examples 4 to 6, bubbles were generated in the glaze during firing.

### TABLE 2

Composition of the tile glaze (all figures are parts by weight of the glaze)

| Example | Frit | Feldspar | Clay | Zirconium silicate | Quartz | Alumina or Titania | Barium Carbonate | Zinc Oxide |
|---|---|---|---|---|---|---|---|---|
| 9 | 68 | 17 | 2 | 13 | – | – | – | – |
| 10 | 60 | 21 | 2 | 13 | – | – | – | 4 |
| 11 | 55 | 20 | 2 | 13 | 10 | 3 (alumina) | – | – |
| 12 | 80 | 15 | 5 | – | – | – | – | – |
| 13 | 60 | 20 | 2 | 10 | – | 8 (titania) | – | – |
| 14 | 55 | 20 | 2 | 10 | 4 | 2 (alumina) | 7 | – |
| Comp. 4 | 95 | 3 | 2 | – | – | – | – | – |
| Comp. 5 | 70 | – | 5 | 10 | 15 | – | – | – |
| Comp. 6 | 70 | – | 5 | - | – | 15 | – | 5 |

### Claims

1. A frit for a tile glaze consisting of:

   | | |
   |---|---|
   | $SiO_2$: | 55 to 65 wt% |
   | $Al_2O_3$: | 10 to 18 wt% |
   | CaO: | 18 to 25 wt% |
   | Alkali metal oxides: | 0.5 to 4 wt% |
   | $ZnO_2$: | 0 to 10 wt% |
   | $B_2O_3$: | 0 to 2 wt% |
   | MgO, BaO, SrO, and ZnO: | 0 to 10 wt% in total, |

   other oxides, chlorides or sulfates: up to 3 wt%.

   *Not novel over Document 1 (part of scope) and Document 2 (entire scope).*

2. Tile glaze consisting of 100 parts by weight of the following components (a) to (i) and 0 to 15 parts by weight of pigment.

   | | |
   |---|---|
   | (a) Frit as defined in claim 1: | 50 to 90 parts by weight |
   | (b) Feldspar: | 8 to 25 parts by weight |
   | (c) Clay: | 0.5 to 10 parts by weight |
   | (d) Zirconium silicate: | 0 to 20 parts by weight |
   | (e) Quartz: | 0 to 10 parts by weight |
   | (f) Alumina: | 0 to 5 parts by weight |
   | (g) Titania: | 0 to 10 parts by weight |
   | (h) Barium carbonate: | 0 to 10 parts by weight |
   | (i) Zinc oxide: | 0 to 5 parts by weight |

   *Product claims to the frit and a tile glaze incorporating the frit and a method claim.*

   *Not novel over Document 2 (entire scope).*

3. A method for producing wall tiles comprises applying to a green tile a glaze composed as defined in claim 2 drying and firing the glazed tile.

   *Not novel over Document 2.*

**1–097** *Drafting an amended claim set*

Since all the frits and tiles described in the application fall within the disclosure of prior art document D2, and since D2 is in the same field, the only possible invention that remains is a selection invention, i.e. a small, non-individualised part of the prior art that provides unexpected advantages.

In the present case, the only unexpected advantage that can be derived from the examination paper resides in the comparative data in the client's letter demonstrating that three of the exemplified frits lead to tiles with increased wear and acid resistance. It is therefore possible to claim each of these frits, tiles comprising them and a method of making tiles comprising them.

It is then necessary to look for basis in the application for claiming a small scope including these three examples. Only two novel features are left when the prior art has been subtracted from the description, both on 2002 Paper B, page 4:

- "60–64% $SiO_2$, 12–16% $Al_2O_3$, 19–23% CaO, 1–3% $R_2O$"; and
- "less than 3%, preferably less than 1% other oxides, chlorides, sulfates".

The second feature does not distinguish Examples 1–3 from the D2 example and hence is not helpful in this respect. However, the first feature does include Examples 2 and 3 and excludes the Example of D2 which has a lower silica content. Furthermore, the description maintains that frits within this small range give excellent results. Even though these results are not specified as increased wear and acid resistance, the general need for such resistance is identified in the application (2002 Paper B, page 1, line 7) and hence the new problem solved is disclosed in the application as filed.

Claim 1 as amended to incorporate these narrow ranges can therefore be argued to be a novel and inventive selection from the disclosure of D2 bearing in mind the requirements set out in T279/89. Example 1 must be separately claimed.

Unfortunately, the specific example of D1 still falls within the narrow selected range, and the general disclosure of D1 overlaps with it. Since D1 is only relevant to novelty, it is legitimate to exclude the area of overlap using a disclaimer, the basis for which is in the prior art. The exact wording of the prior art should be used if possible in order to avoid any allegation that Art.123(2) has been contravened by excluding any more than the area of overlap.

Claim 2 is novel and inventive over D2 by virtue of the amended frit it incorporates. However, no disclaimer is necessary in light of D1 since D1 does not disclose a tile glaze.

Claim 3 is novel and inventive over D1 and D2 for the same reasons as Claim 2 but does need to be amended since inventive results are only obtained within the range of temperatures disclosed in the client's letter. Fortunately, there is direct basis for this amendment in 2002 Paper B, page 6, lines 5–6.

Since it is the tiles which will be sold, it would be useful to have a claim to the tiles incorporating the inventive frit. This is easily established by introducing a product-by-process claim to the tiles obtainable by Claim 3. These tiles are clearly novel *per se* since they have different properties to the prior art tiles (greater acid and wear resistance) that indicate a structural difference.

The only preferred feature which is motivated is the composition of the specific inventive Examples 1–3. No other inventions seem to remain so no divisional application is necessary.

*Writing a response to the Art.96(2) communication*  1–098

This letter is in response to the Communication pursuant to Art.96(2) EPC.

**1. Amendment**

1.1 In response to the objections raised, I attach new claims pages to replace the corresponding existing pages which are now cancelled, without prejudice to the later filing of a divisional application directed to any aspect of the subject matter thereof.

1.2 New claim 1 is based on previous claim 1 in combination with the preferred ranges specified on 2002 Paper B, page 4, lines 11–12 of the description. The proviso has been introduced in order to distinguish the subject matter of claim 1 from the disclosure of D1. This is permissible since D1 is an Art.54(3) document which is novelty-destroying to claim 1 (see G1/03 and G2/03). The disclaimer is based precisely on the language of D1, only the necessary overlap being removed. New claims 2, 3 and 4 are based on Examples 2, 3 and 1 respectively. New claim 5 is based on claim 2 as filed. New claim 6 is based on claim 2 as filed and Examples 1, 2 and 3 of the application as filed. New claim 7 is based on claim 3 as filed with the addition of the preferred firing temperature disclosed on 2002 Paper B, page 6, lines 5 to 6. New claim 8 is based on claim 3 as filed.

1.3 It is therefore submitted that the new claims are in conformity with Article 123(2) EPC.

**2. Novelty**

2.1 Claim 1 is novel over D1 by virtue of the disclaimer which removes the area of overlap. Claim 1 further represents a novel selection from the disclosure of D2 within the 3-part test of T279/89: (1) only a small portion of the scope disclosed by D2 has been selected; (2) the selected scope is some distance from the specific example of D2; and (3) the selection is purposive in the sense that frits falling within the selected range have an unexpectedly improved acid and wear resistance as compared with the frit disclosed in D2 (see below).

2.2 Claims 2 to 3 are novel by virtue of being dependent on claim 1 (see Guidelines C/IV/9.12).

2.3 The frit of claim 4 falls outside the scope of D1 and is therefore novel over D1 (see, for instance the $SiO_2$ range). In the same way as the frits of claim 1, the frit of claim 4 is a novel selection from the disclosure of D2, fulfilling the same criteria outlined above in paragraph 2.1.

2.4 Claim 5 is novel over D1 which does not disclose a tile glaze and novel over D2 by virtue of the frit it comprises (see paragraphs 2.1 to 2.3 above).

2.5 Claim 6 is novel by virtue of being dependent on claim 5 (see Guidelines C/IV/9.12).

2.6 Claim 7 is novel over D1 which does not disclose any process for making a wall tile. Claim 7 is also novel over D2 since the process incorporates as an essential technical feature the glaze of claim 5 or claim 6 both of which are themselves novel (see paragraphs 2.4 and 2.5).

2.7 Claim 8 is novel over D1 which does not disclose any wall tiles. Claim 8 is also novel over D2 since the tiles obtained by the method of claim 7 have unique properties (acid and wear resistance) that distinguish them from all known tiles, being a function of the particular frit composition used (see below). This difference in properties is indicative of a structural difference.

**3. Inventive step**

3.1 The closest prior art for the assessment of inventive step is D2 since it is the only known art relevant to inventive step. D2 discloses a frit defined very broadly by reference to its composition, a tile glaze incorporating such a frit and a process for making a tile using the tile glaze. One specific example is given.

3.2 The difference between the frit of D2 and the frit of claim 1 of the present application is the choice of a specific composition for the frit of claim 1. The technical effect associated with this selection of a specific composition is an unexpected increase in acid and wear resistance. Glazed tiles have been made according to the example of D2 and according to Examples 1–3 of the present application. In each case the tiles were fired at a temperature between 1170 and 1220 °C. The wear and acid resistance of the four tiles made were measured in accordance with the Standard No. DIN xxxyyy and rated from 1–10. The results are shown in the attached table (annex 1) from which it can be seen, as stated above, that the tiles of Examples 2 and 3 (falling within the scope of claim 1) and Example 1 (claimed in claim 4) have an unexpectedly greater acid and wear resistance than the tile of D2.

3.3 The objective problem solved in light of the closest prior art is therefore the provision of frits that, when incorporated into a standard tile glaze, lead to improved acid and wear resistance. This problem is disclosed in the application as filed (see 2002 Paper B, page 1, lines 6–7 and page 2, lines 7–8). The problem is solved by the frits of claim 1 and claim 4, as demonstrated above.

3.4 The prior art does not give any indication that selection of a frit with a specific composition would have an impact on acid and wear resistance. Therefore, the dramatic improvements observed on selection of the frits of claims 1 and 4 must be surprising for the skilled person. The skilled person would therefore not be led in a routine way to the frits of claims 1 and 4 by the prior art. Rather, inventive skill is necessary to appreciate the dramatically improved properties offered by the frits of the present invention. An inventive step must therefore be acknowledged in respect of claims 1 and 4.

3.5 Claims 2 and 3 are inventive by virtue of their dependency on claim 1 (see Guidelines C/IV/9.12). Furthermore, since the glaze of claim 5 incorporates the inventive frits of claims 1–4 and since the glaze of claim 5 is an essential feature of the method of claim 6, an inventive step must also be acknowledged for claims 5 and 6. The inventive step of the wall tiles of claim 7 is derived from the improved properties of the tiles obtainable from the method of claim 6.

## 4. Unity

Pursuant to Art.82 EPC, a European patent application must relate to one invention or to a group of inventions so linked as to form a single general inventive concept. According to r.30 EPC, such a group of inventions is taken to be so linked when there is a technical relationship among the inventions involving one or more of the same or corresponding special technical features, i.e. those features which define a contribution which each of the claimed inventions considered as a whole makes over the prior art. In the present case, such corresponding special technical features are represented by the specific compositions of the frits of claims 1 and 4 which lead to superior properties. The frits of claim 1 and claim 4 both solve the same problem in the same way by virtue of their unique frit compositions. These compositions are therefore corresponding technical features.

## 5. Communication

Turning specifically to the numbered paragraphs in the communication:

(1) Novelty is restored by the amendments made (see sections 1 and 2).

(2) New claims have been filed (see section 1) which are novel (see section 2), are inventive (see section 3) have unity (see section 4) and do not contravene Art.123(2) EPC (see section 1). The new claims are also clear.

(3) See sections 2 and 3.

(4) See in particular section 1 and the amendment to claim 7. This range of firing temperatures is necessary to obtain the improved acid and wear resistance.

(5) See section 1.

(6) Amendments to the description will be undertaken when the claims have been agreed.

Attached:  New claims
Annex 1 (Table)

## CLAIMS

1. A frit for a tile glaze consisting of:

| | |
|---|---|
| $SiO_2$ | 60–64 wt%; |
| $Al_2O_3$ | 12–16 wt%; |
| CaO | 19–23 wt%; |
| Alkali metal oxides | 1–3 wt%; |
| $ZrO_2$ | 0–10 wt%; |
| $B_2O_3$ | 0–2 wt%; |
| MgO, BaO, SrO and ZnO | 0–10 wt%; |
| other oxides, chlorides or sulphates | up to 3 wt%; |

with the proviso that the frit may not have a composition in the range:

| | |
|---|---|
| $SiO_2$ | 63–65 wt%; |
| $Al_2O_3$ | 12–14 wt%; |
| CaO | 15–20 wt%; |
| Alkali metal oxides | 0.5–4 wt%; |
| $ZrO_2$ | 1-5 wt%; |
| $B_2O_3$ | up to 5 wt%; |
| ZnO | up to 5 wt%; |
| Additional oxides | up to 5 wt%. |

2. A frit as claimed in claim 1 consisting of:

| | |
|---|---|
| $SiO_2$ | 61.4 wt%; |
| $Al_2O_3$ | 14 wt%; |
| CaO | 22.6 wt%; |
| Alkali metal oxides | 1 wt%; and |
| MgO, BaO, SrO and ZnO | 1 wt%. |

3. A frit as claimed in claim 1 consisting of:

| | |
|---|---|
| $SiO_2$ | 63.4 wt%; |
| $Al_2O_3$ | 12 wt%; |
| CaO | 19.6 wt%; |
| Alkali metal oxides | 2 wt%; |
| $B_2O_3$ | 1 wt%; and |
| MgO, BaO, SrO and ZnO | 2 wt%. |

4. A frit for a tile glaze consisting of:

| | |
|---|---|
| $SiO_2$ | 61.4 wt%; |
| $Al_2O_3$ | 15.1 wt%; |
| CaO | 23 wt%; and |
| Alkali metal oxides | 0.5 wt%. |

5. Tile glaze consisting of 100 parts by weight of the following components (a) to (i) and 0 to 15 parts by weight of pigment:

| | |
|---|---|
| (a) a frit for a tile glaze | 50–90 parts by weight; |
| (b) feldspar | 8 to 25 parts by weight; |
| (c) clay | 0.5 to 10 parts by weight; |
| (d) zirconium silicate | 0 to 20 parts by weight; |
| (e) quartz | 0 to 10 parts by weight; |

|                  |                       |
|------------------|-----------------------|
| (f) alumina      | 0 to 5 parts by weight; |
| (g) titania      | 0 to 10 parts by weight; |
| (h) barium carbonate | 0 to 10 parts by weight; and |
| (i) zinc oxide   | 0 to 5 parts by weight; |

said frit having the composition:

| | |
|---|---|
| $SiO_2$ | 60–64 wt%; |
| $Al_2O_3$ | 12–16 wt%; |
| CaO | 19–23 wt%; |
| Alkali metal oxides | 1–3 wt%; |
| $ZrO_2$ | 0–10 wt%; |
| $B_2O_3$ | 0–2 wt%; |
| MgO, BaO, SrO and ZnO | 0–10 wt%. |

6. A tile glaze as claimed in claim 5 wherein the frit has the composition specified in any one of claims 2 to 4.

7. A method for producing wall tiles comprises applying to a green tile a glaze composed as defined in claim 5 or claim 6, drying and firing the glazed tile wherein the firing temperature is 1170 to 1220 °C.

8. A wall tile obtainable by the method of claim 7.

**Annex 1 — Table**

Experiments have been conducted in order to compare the tile glaze exemplified in D2 with that made in examples of the application. The tiles of our Examples 1–3 and the tile made in accordance with the example in D2 were manufactured exactly as indicated in our application and document D2 respectively. The wear resistance and the acid resistance of these tiles were measured in accordance with the Standard No. DIN xxxyyy. The wear resistance and acid resistance were each rated from 1–10 in accordance with this standard. A value of 5 or above is considered to be good. A value of 8 or above is excellent.

| Example | Firing temperature | Wear resistance | Acid resistance | Bubbles observed |
|---------|--------------------|-----------------|-----------------|------------------|
| 1 | 1190 °C | 8 | 8 | No |
| 2 | 1190 °C | 9 | 7 | No |
| 3 | 1190 °C | 7 | 9 | No |
| Examples of D2 | 1190 °C | 5 | 6 | No |

## 5. Partial worked example using EQE 2004 Paper B

*Understanding and annotating the paper*

The 2004 Paper B can be analysed in the following way, noting which features need to be transferred in schematic form to a summary sheet which is to be used in establishing novel subject matter. Comments on each paragraph are made in bold, words indicating an essential or preferred feature are underlined and italicised.

## Annex 1 (Patent Application)

### Corrosion inhibitor for protecting steel reinforcement in concrete

The present invention is related to the inhibition of corrosion of reinforcing steel embedded in a concrete structure. In particular, this invention provides corrosion inhibitors for the protective corrosion inhibition of steel reinforcements embedded in a concrete structure when the structure is exposed to aggressive chloride-containing environments. The corrosion inhibitors are also useful for restoring a concrete structure by the reduction of the corrosion rate of already corroding steel reinforcements embedded in a concrete structure exposed to an aggressive chloride-containing environment.

**Field of the invention: claims to a corrosion inhibitor, its use in preventing the corrosion of embedded steel reinforcements and its use in the restoration of corroded steel reinforcements can be expected.**

### Background of the invention

Durability limitations of steel reinforced concrete are well documented. Chloride-containing corrosive environments can quickly cause corrosion of the reinforcing steel. Chloride ions in concrete can originate from the ingress of de-icing salts or seawater diffusing to the reinforcement through the pore network of the concrete.

Normally, reinforcing steel embedded in concrete is protected because the concrete cover acts as a barrier and the high pH value of liquid in the pore-network of the concrete ensures that no significant corrosion occurs. The presence of chloride ions at concentrations above a given threshold level, however results in corrosion rates that markedly decrease the expected service lives of reinforced concrete structures. Thousands of bridges and other structures made of reinforced concrete need to be repaired worldwide as a consequence of corrosion of the steel reinforcement.

**Possible problem solved by the invention: the provision of a corrosion inhibitor.**

The present invention relates to corrosion inhibitors for the precautionary, protective corrosion inhibition of reinforcing steel exposed to chloride-containing corrosive environments as well as for application to restore corroded reinforcing steel embedded in hardened concrete.

Corrosion inhibitors are compounds or compositions that, when used in small concentrations in a corrosive environment, decrease the corrosion rate. The use of corrosion inhibitors is widespread and well established. The most commonly used corrosion inhibitor for reinforcing steel in concrete is calcium nitrite. Cyclic amines such as dicyclohexylamine have also been used. These inhibitors are typically applied preventatively and are mixed into the slurry from which the concrete is obtained.

**Prior art: calcium nitrite and cyclic amines are both known individually as corrosion inhibitors in reinforced concrete.**

The problem addressed by the present invention is to find improved corrosion inhibitors for reinforcing steel in concrete, which provide an effective protection against corrosion to reinforcing steel. In addition the inhibitors must be useful for the preventative treatment of reinforcing steel in new concrete structures and for the treatment of existing concrete structures during their repair to minimise further corrosion.

**Confirmation of problem solved and three anticipated claim types.**

### Summary of the invention

The corrosion inhibitor of the present invention consists of two components:

The first component is an alkanolamine of the formula:

$$\underset{\overset{|}{R1-N-R3{}''OH}}{R2} \quad \text{or} \quad \underset{\overset{|}{HO{}''R4-N-R3{}''OH}}{R2} \quad \text{or} \quad \underset{\overset{|}{HO{}''R4-N-R3{}''OH}}{R5{}''-OH}$$

in which R1 and R2 are, independently, hydrogen, C1-C6 alkyl or C4-C6 cycloalkyl, and wherein R3, R4 and R5 are, independently, C2-C5 alkylene or C4-C6 cycloalkylene.

The second component is an alkaline metal nitrite or an alkaline earth metal nitrite.

**Broadest statement of invention: the new corrosion inhibitors are a combination of a metal nitrite (one of which, calcium nitrite, is known from the prior art) and an alkanolamine, a class of compounds which has not previously been used as corrosion inhibitors. Mark on the summary. Since this is an amendment paper, this combination is likely to lack novelty and/or inventive step.**

The present corrosion inhibitor can be used in methods for inhibiting the corrosion of steel reinforcements in concrete, which include adding the above corrosion inhibitor to the slurry from which the concrete is formed, incorporating the inhibitor into a protective polymer coating on the steel reinforcement or applying a composition containing the corrosion inhibitor to an existing concrete structure.

**The corrosion inhibitor of the invention can be used to inhibit corrosion in three distinct embodiments: (a) by addition to a concrete slurry; (b) by incorporation into a polymer coating around the steel; and (c) by application to an existing concrete structure. Add these to the summary.**

## Detailed description of the invention

The present invention thus provides a corrosion inhibitor for inhibiting the corrosion of steel reinforcement members present in a concrete structure.

The alkanolamine and the nitrite are preferably used in a weight ratio varying between 5:1 and 1:5. The corrosion inhibitor of the present invention is a mixture of an alkanolamine of the formula:

$$\underset{\overset{|}{R1-N-R3{}''OH}}{R2} \quad \text{or} \quad \underset{\overset{|}{HO{}''R4-N-R3{}''OH}}{R2} \quad \text{or} \quad \underset{\overset{|}{HO{}''R4-N-R3{}''OH}}{R5{}''-OH}$$

(in which R1 and R2 are, independently, hydrogen, C1-C6 alkyl or C4-C6 cycloalkyl, and wherein R3, R4, and R5 are, independently, C2-C6 alkylene or C4-C6 cycloalkylene) with an alkaline metal nitrite or an alkaline earth metal nitrite.

**Preferred feature: ratio of alkanolamine to nitrite is *preferably* from 5:1 to 1:5. Add to summary. No motivation for this feature yet.**

Excellent results have been obtained when the alkanolamine is selected from 3-amino-1-propanol, 2-aminoethanol, 2-(dimethylamino)ethanol, 2-(ethylamino)ethanol, 2-(butylamino)ethanol, 2-[(1,1-dimethylethyl)amino]ethanol, 2-(cyclohexylamino)ethanol and triethanolamine. The nitrite is preferably selected from sodium and calcium nitrite.

**Preferred feature: specific embodiments of the alkanolamine component of the combination. Add to summary. No motivation for any of them yet.**
**Preferred feature: the nitrite is *preferably* sodium or calcium nitrite. Add to summary. No motivation for this feature yet.**

The present corrosion inhibitors have been found to be highly effective when used in any of the standard methods for the preventative protection of reinforcing steel and are also useful for restoring concrete structures by reducing the corrosion rate of reinforcing steel in existing concrete structures.

Two standard methods are known which employ corrosion inhibitors for the preventative protection of steel reinforcements from corrosion.

The first method comprises incorporating the corrosion inhibitor into the concrete slurry from which the structure is to be formed.

**No new information in these paragraphs.**

The amount of the corrosion inhibitor, which is incorporated into the concrete slurry, is normally within the range of from 0.01 to 1% by weight, based on the weight of the concrete slurry. The corrosion inhibitor when used in this method is dissolved in a minimum quantity of water and then mixed into the slurry.

**Preferred feature: amount of the inhibitor is normally from 0.01 to 1%. Add to summary.**

The second standard preventative method for inhibiting the corrosion of steel reinforcements in concrete involves coating the steel reinforcements with a polymeric resin and then incorporating the coated steel into the concrete. The polymeric coating serves to restrict the access of the aggressive chloride ions to the metal. The corrosion rate of the metal can be further reduced if a corrosion inhibitor is also included in the coating.

The coating composition is preferably based on an alkyd resin. An alkyd resin is a synthetic resin made from a dicarboxylic acid and a diol or a triol. A particularly good protection against corrosion has been obtained when a composition containing 10–15 wt% alkyd resin, 10–20 wt% butyl glycol, and 4–9 wt% corrosion inhibitor of the present invention in deionised water is used. This composition preferably also contains up to 1 wt% of surfactant to improve its coating properties.

**Preferred feature: the coating composition preferably comprises an alkyd resin.**
**Specific embodiment: a composition containing 10–15 wt% alkyd resin, 10–20 wt% butyl glycol, and 4–9 wt% corrosion inhibitor. Motivated by particularly good protection obtained.**
**Preferred feature: the coating composition preferably also contains up to 1% of a surfactant. Motivated by improved coating properties.**
**Add these features to the summary.**

A further method in which the present corrosion inhibitor can be used is a method for the restoration of concrete structures. This method involves impregnating the surface of a hardened concrete structure with an aqueous composition containing the present corrosion inhibitor. It has surprisingly been found that the present corrosion inhibitor is able to penetrate into the concrete material to reach the steel reinforcements and reduce the corrosion rate of the steel reinforcements to an acceptable level.

**Motivation for the restorative method, which has surprisingly been found to be able to penetrate concrete — possible indication of inventive step. Mark on summary.**

This method is economically very beneficial as compared to previous standard methods for the restoration of concrete structures. The standard restoration methods always involve the removal of the surface portion of the concrete structure so as to expose the steel reinforcement closest to the surface, which is always the most severely corroded. The steel reinforcement is then cleaned or replaced and fresh concrete slurry is applied to replace the concrete removed. The present restoration method is very economical as compared to these standard methods as it requires no concrete to be removed.

**An indication of the advantages of the restorative method compared to the prior art and its commercial value to the client.**

The aqueous corrosion-inhibiting composition used in the restoration method is preferably applied on the concrete surface by brush, by paint roller or by a spraying device. The composition is typically used in a total amount of 200–2000 g/m$^2$, preferably 300–1000 g/m$^2$. This composition preferably contains as a further component an alkylalkoxysilane of the following formula:

$$R6\text{-}Si(OR7)_3,$$

in which R6 is C6 to C16 alkyl and R7 is C1 to C3 alkyl.

**Preferred feature: the restorative composition is typically used at a level of 200–2000 g/m$^2$, preferably 300–1000 g/m$^2$.**
**Preferred feature: the restorative composition preferably also contains an alkylalkoxysilane.**
**Add these features to the summary — neither motivated as yet.**

These alkylalkoxysilanes are commercially available and, as is well known in the art, produce a hydrophobic layer on the exterior of concrete structures. This hydrophobic layer when it contains the present corrosion inhibitor, has surprisingly been found to reduce the ingress of aggressive chloride ions into the concrete structure and improves the corrosion protection. The composition may also contain a surfactant, which when used in combination with the alkylalkoxysilane and the present corrosion inhibitor further improves the corrosion protection.

**Motivation for the alkylalkoxysilane embodiment — surprisingly reduces the ingress of chloride ions.**
**Preferred feature: the restorative composition *may* further comprise a surfactant — motivated by extra corrosion protection.**
**Add these features to the summary.**

A preferred composition for use in a restoration method comprises 10–20 wt% of the present corrosion inhibitor, 15–25 wt% of the alkylalkoxysilane, 1–5% of surfactant, remainder water.

**A specific embodiment of the restorative method. Add to the summary. No motivation as yet.**

Example 1

**This example demonstrates an inventive step (surprising increase in the inhibition of corrosion) for the broadest statement of invention (nitrite + alkanolamine). A combination of calcium nitrite and triethanolamine seems particularly good.**

Example 2

**Further demonstration of inventive step for the broadest statement of invention when used preventatively in a concrete slurry (surprisingly better results than calcium nitrite alone) and demonstration that the inhibitors work preventatively in a polymeric sheath. A combination of calcium nitrite and triethanolamine seems particularly good.**

Example 3

**Proof that the inhibitors of the invention work to restore steel reinforcements by penetrating concrete. A combination of calcium nitrite and triethanolamine seems particularly good once again. Further data justifies separate inventive steps for the three way**

**combination of nitrite+alkanolamine+alkylalkoxysilane and the four way combination of nitrite+alkanolamine+alkylalkoxysilane+surfactant.**

The information gleaned from the examples should also be added to the summary.

A typical example of a summary sheet established as a result of this process is shown overleaf.

# 148 Complete Guide to Passing the EQE

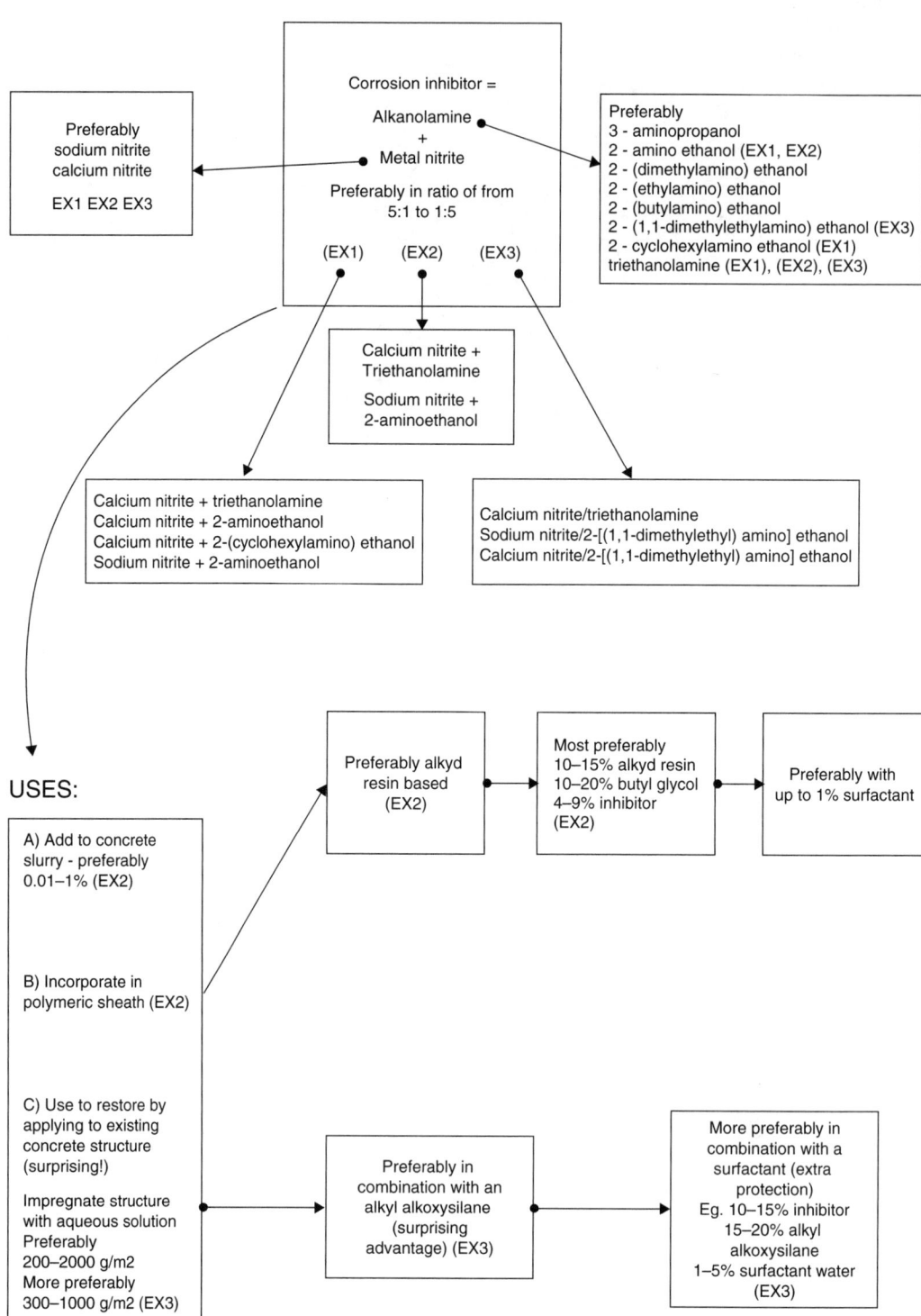

*Establishing patentable subject matter*

The summary document shows all the subject matter described by the client in diagrammatic form. The prior art must now be subtracted from this subject matter to establish how much is novel. That novel subject matter for which a surprising effect can be substantiated can then be claimed.

The two prior art documents should therefore be carefully considered and their content marked on the summary document. In the marked summary document overleaf the content of D1 has been indicated by the use of a bold typeface and the content of D2 has been indicated by the use of italicized typeface. In the exam, any suitable method may be used — the use of different coloured shading is perhaps the most visually striking.

The text left in normal font therefore represents novel subject matter.

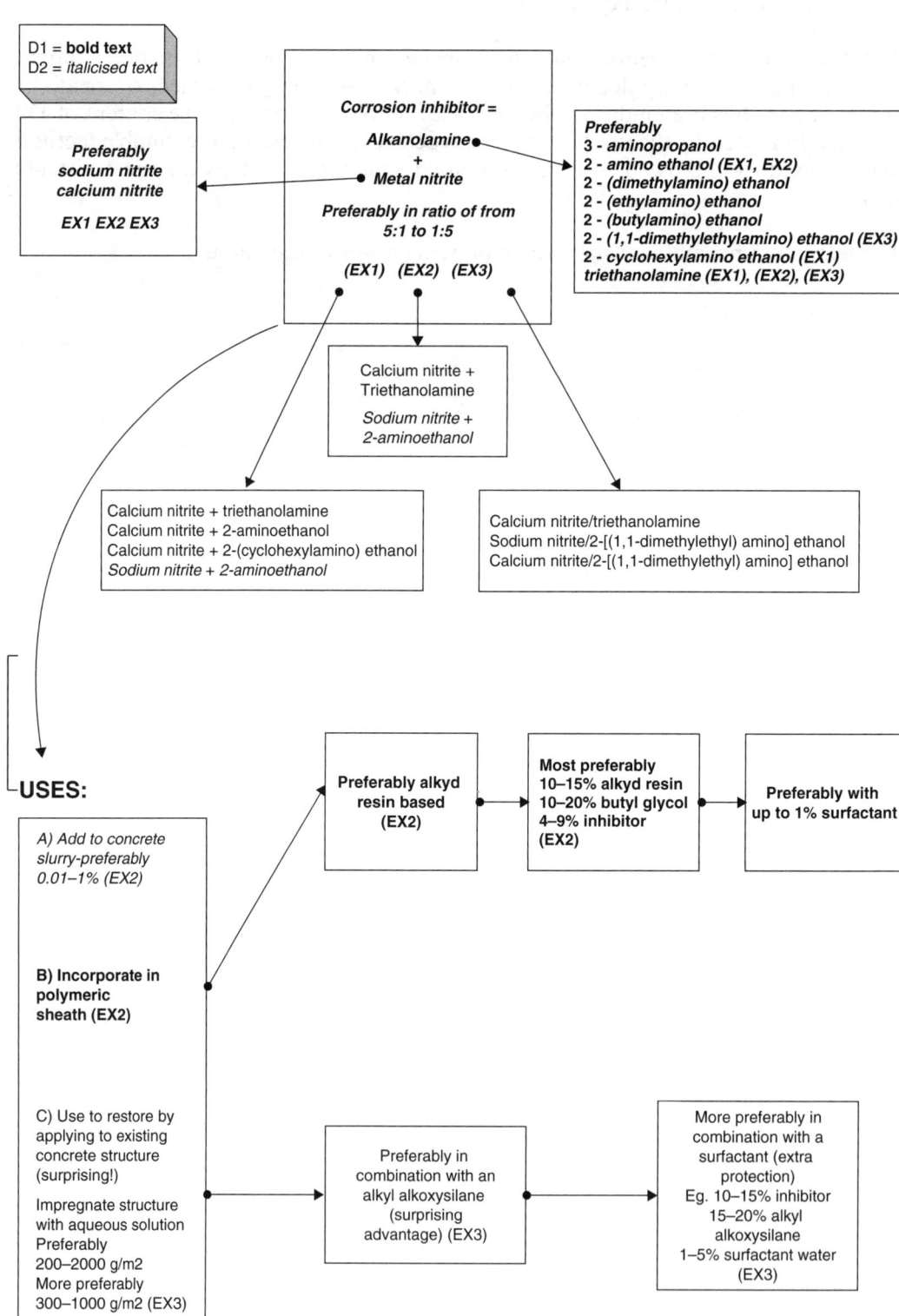

A brief analysis of the summary sheet marked up with the content of the prior art shows immediately that the novel features are: (a) the use of the corrosion inhibitor (alkanolamine + metal nitrite) to restore a reinforced concrete structure by impregnating the surface; (b) a composition containing an alkanolamine, a metal nitrite and an alkylalkoxysilane (and preferably a surfactant); and (c) several specific combinations of metal nitrite and alkanolamine.

There is clearly a good argument for inventive step in respect of the use of the corrosion inhibitor (alkanolamine + metal nitrite) to restore a reinforced concrete structure by impregnating the surface. We are told that it is surprising and highly advantageous that this method works since prior art methods (e.g. D1) involve removing the concrete prior to treatment of the steel reinforcements. The objective problem in light of D1 is thus how to provide an improved method for restoring corroded reinforcements in concrete structures. The solution is to impregnate the surface with an aqueous solution comprising a metal nitrite and an alkanolamine.

There is also a good argument for inventive step with respect to a claim to a three-way combination of a metal nitrite, an alkanolamine and a alkylalkoxysilane. We are told that such a combination surprisingly reduces the ingress of chloride ions into the concrete and makes the restorative method more effective. The data in Example 3 supports this contention since the rate of corrosion subsequent to treatment is considerably reduced in the presence of the alkylalkoxysilane. The objective problem in the light of the prior art is thus how to provide a more efficient corrosion inhibitor. The solution is to provide a corrosion inhibitor comprising both a metal nitrite and alkanolamine and an alkylalkoxysilane.

With respect to the specific combinations in the examples, only one of them is known — sodium nitrite/2-aminoethanol. To be patentable as a selection invention, the other examples will have to demonstrate some surprising advantage in comparison with this combination. This appears to be the case for calcium nitrite/triethanolamine from the data presented in Examples 1 and 2 where a surprising increase in activity is seen. The objective problem in light of D2 is thus how to provide a more effective specific corrosion inhibitor. The solution is to use a combination of calcium nitrite and triethanolamine.

*Claiming the invention*

### Unity of invention 1–101

There is unity of invention between: (a) the method of restoring a concrete structure using an aqueous composition comprising an alkanolamine (as defined) and an alkaline metal nitrite or an alkaline earth metal nitrite; and (b) the aqueous composition comprising an alkanolamine (as defined), an alkaline metal nitrite or an alkaline earth metal nitrite and an alkylalkoxysilane (as defined) since the composition is specifically designed for use in the method (see Guidelines C/III/7.2) and hence the composition and the use both contribute to the solution of the same underlying problem (how to restore corroded, reinforced concrete structures without removing the concrete).

There is however, no unity of invention between the aqueous composition as defined above and the specific combination of calcium nitrite and triethanolamine since the specific combination solves a different problem (improved anti-corrosion properties when incorporated into concrete slurries). A divisional application is therefore required for the specific combination of calcium nitrite and triethanolamine.

### Product claims 1–102

The main product claim will thus be to an aqueous corrosion-inhibiting composition (2004 Paper B, page 4, lines 26–29) comprising: (a) alkanolamine as defined in claim 1 as filed; (b) an alkaline metal nitrite or an alkaline earth metal nitrite; and (c) an alkylalkoxysilane of the formula R6-Si-(OR7)3 wherein R6 is C6-C16 alkyl and R7 is C1-C3 alkyl.

In a divisional application, a main product claim to a corrosion inhibitor for steel reinforcements in concrete comprising calcium nitrite and triethanolamine may be filed.

## 1–103 Method/use claims

The method of restoring a steel-reinforced concrete structure using an aqueous composition comprising an alkanolamine (as defined) and an alkaline metal nitrite or an alkaline earth metal nitrite is the main claim in this category. The claim needs to include the feature of impregnating the surface of the structure with the composition since this is the novel feature.

## 1–104 Process claims

No process claims of any value are available in this paper.

## 1–105 Dependent claims

Possible features worth identifying in dependent method claims include the use of specific alkanolamines, the use of sodium nitrite/calcium nitrite, the use of a composition further comprising an alkylalkoxysilane, the use of a composition further comprising a surfactant and the use of the specific compositions of the examples. Possible features worth identifying in dependent product claims include the use of specific alkanolamines, the use of sodium nitrite/calcium nitrite, the inclusion of a surfactant and the specific compositions of the examples.

# PAPER B (ELECTRICITY/MECHANICS)

## 1. General comments

In this paper the candidate is charged with representing a client before an examining division of the EPO and successfully prosecuting a filed patent application to grant while obtaining the broadest possible protection and meeting all the requirements of the Convention. The candidate is therefore presented with a copy of the application as filed, an Art.96(2) communication from the EPO and various items of prior art referred to in the communication. A letter providing specific instructions from the client on how the application should be prosecuted is also occasionally included.

The candidate is expected to file a complete response to the EPO communication and either argue for the patentability of the claims as filed if they are deemed patentable (extremely unlikely) or file an amended set of claims which are novel and inventive over the cited prior art and argue for the grant of a patent based on this amended claim set. Generally, half the available marks are available for amendment and half for argumentation. It is important that the amended claim set adequately protects the invention and is defensible over the art. If this is not the case you will lose marks for the claims and for the argumentation. As the task of the candidate is to secure the broadest allowable scope of protection for the client, amendments should not be more extensive than necessary. It is sometimes necessary to explain and defend the unity of invention of the claim set proposed. If it is possible to secure maximum protection without dividing out any subject matter, more marks will be obtained by proposing such a response, with appropriate argumentation, than would be achieved by dividing out subject matter. If, in order to obtain maximum protection, it is necessary to divide out, you should clearly identify the features of the independent claim(s) of the divisional application(s), for example by referring to selected portions of the claims of the parent, or by drafting appropriate claims. Argument in support of novelty and inventive step should extend to the proposed subject matter of any proposed divisional(s). It is, however, relatively uncommon for division to be required in this Electricity/Mechanics paper. The amendment and response should address all actual or potential objections such that the next communication from the EPO will be under r.51(4) EPC. Arguments should be provided in support of the novelty and inventive step of the subject matter of all the independent claims. Basis for all the amendments must be specified and the reasons given why Art.123(2) EPC is not contravened. The requirements of clarity and conciseness must also be borne in mind. The submitted answer will thus consist of a letter to the EPO, and an annexed set of claims. The proposed treatment of any divisional applications may be provided in the letter to the EPO, but will generally be provided in a note to the examiner. No amended description is required.

The paper is four hours in length and about half of this time should be spent analysing the question and elucidating the answer, the remaining time being allocated to writing the answer. As in Paper A, the candidate is allowed to use sections of the examination paper in compiling the amended claim set and scissors, glue and transparent gummed tape should be brought into the exam. Furthermore, only pencil and yellow highlighter should be used to mark up important sections of the paper during the period of analysis; pencil can be easily erased and yellow highlighter does not cause problems when the answer is photocopied prior to marking. Other useful things to take into the exam are copies of the Guidelines and the EPO case law book.

## 2. How to tackle the paper

**1–107**  *Understanding and annotating the paper*

Start by reading the client's patent application. Read through this in full, word by word, understanding each sentence thoroughly and appreciating its significance. Each word should be carefully read and considered since it is easy later to miss small but important facts once the mind has started to make assumptions about the answer.

Mark in the margin of the exam paper what each sentence in the patent application signifies, particularly noting preferred features which are linked to advantages.

Consider what has been claimed and identify any omissions. Be alive to the possibility that claimable subject matter has not been claimed. The claim set will usually be short.

Before you read the Art.96(2) communication, read through the cited prior art to understand it and see how it relates to the inventions described in the client's patent application. Pay particular attention to any alternatives or variants which are disclosed. Often these will not be shown in the drawings and hence there is a risk that they may later be overlooked. Then read the client's letter as it may have relevant things to say about the prior art. Mark up the prior art in a similar way to the application. Firstly, note whether each citation is Art.54(2) or Art.54(3) prior art and the consequences. It is very unusual in the Electricity/Mechanics paper for Art.54(3) prior art to arise, but in principle it could. Then, answer two questions relating to its disclosure: (1) does what is described potentially fall within the description of the client's invention (relevant for novelty); and (2) is any Art.54(2) prior art solving a similar, or the same, problem (relevant for inventive step). Each piece of prior art should therefore be categorised as novelty only, inventive step only, novelty and inventive step or (rarely!) not relevant. Within each prior document, mark those sections which are particularly relevant to the claims and those which may largely be ignored.

Finally, read the Art.96(2) communication. This is likely to contain correct assertions of obviousness and/or lack of novelty. It is usual, however, for at least some of the assertions to be incorrect or too general. It is for this reason that it is preferable to defer the reading of the communication until after you have formed your own opinion on the relevance of the prior art. It is very easy to be misled by the examiner's arguments with the result that the art seems more damning than it really is. Given that the object of the exercise is to secure the best protection for the client's subject matter, overlooking potentially patentable subject matter will lose you marks, even when — especially when! — you have been misled by the Art.96(2) communication.

**1–108**  *Establishing patentable subject matter*

Assess the relevance of the prior art to the claims of the application. Often all the claims will be unsustainable for obviousness or lack of novelty, but you need to make you own assessment of this. You may well see a claim which is anticipated because it has been drafted carelessly, but which could be saved with a minor amendment. So do not always assume that wholesale amendment is required. In addition, you need to analyse which features of the invention disclosed in the application are already described in the prior art and then mark this information on the paper. Any suitable means may be used, such as highlighting or hatching areas of text. Don't be worried if very little seems to be left — often with Paper B, large parts of the text will be eliminated.

You may find that one or more of the dependent claims in the application relate to subject-matter which is novel and inventive over all the prior art. It is extremely unlikely that the best amendment will be based on those claims. Securing maximum protection will generally involve the addition to the main claim of some feature from the description, perhaps with the addition of a feature from an indefensible sub-claim.

You will now be able to see what possible distinctions there are over the prior art cited. Always follow any instructions of the client regarding what is to be protected. If you can, choose distinctions that protect more rather than fewer embodiments. An amendment could take the form of a disclaimer, if the prior art is only relevant to novelty (i.e. Art.54(3)), but this is unlikely in this paper. The Enlarged Board of Appeal decisions G1/03 and G2/03, which clarified when the introduction of a disclaimer does or does not contravene Art.123(2) EPC, date from after the 2004 EQE. Candidates are of course required to know all Decisions and Opinions of the Enlarged Board, but it would be foolish for candidates for Papers B, C and D not to be completely *au fait* with this pair of decisions.

Most commonly, one of the preferred, advantageous features will provide an amendment that restores novel, inventive subject matter. The relevant preferred feature will be associated with a further problem solved and indications that such a further problem exists should also be in the description.

Sometimes, optimum protection will require that a feature introduced from the description be expressed in a generalised, functional way rather than in a structural way. For example, in the 1995 paper, a flexible membrane was disclosed for separating ink from a working fluid: the examiners thought this too narrow, preferring means for separating. Argument should be provided to show that such a generalisation does not contravene Art.123(2).

*Drafting an amended claim set* 1–109

It is rare in this paper for the Examiners to be looking for the addition of extra claim types, e.g. the addition of method claims, but you should always consider whether such additions are appropriate. In the 2002 paper a claim to an apparatus could usefully be added to the existing product and method claims and this earnt a few marks. Since 1991 there has been no paper where the filing of a divisional application was appropriate, but any future question could of course raise this as an issue. Where there is a lack of unity, restrict the application to the invention which is most commercially significant — generally the letter from the client will give you some clue as to which this is. In your answer you need clearly to identify all the other inventions which have been excluded by the amendment (whether or not they were claimed previously). You do not need to write claims for these other inventions, but you need to make it clear to the examiner what else you consider to be patentable. To get maximum marks you need to provide arguments in support of the novelty and inventiveness of these other inventions. You should state what divisional applications will be filed. You will get no marks merely for including a statement such as "we reserve the right to file a divisional patent application for subject-matter deleted by these amendments".

When drafting the amended independent claims, use the language of the claims as filed as far as possible. It is very important not to add subject matter, either by deletion or addition of features — many marks are lost on this point. Do not broaden the teaching of examples without specific basis to do so. If you decide that a claim as filed contains an inessential limitation which you want to delete, do not make the deletion unless you comply with the T331/87 (Houdaille) test:

> the feature is not explained as essential in the disclosure;
>
> the feature is not indispensable for the function of the invention in light of the technical problem the invention seeks to solve; and
>
> the replacement or removal of the feature requires no real modification of other features to compensate for the change (Guidelines C.VI. 5.3.10).

**Then, if you decide to make the deletion, ensure that you cite the basis for the broader combination in your letter to the EPO, explaining why the amendment passes the test.**

In the year 2000 paper the client's letter referred to new embodiments which were to be protected and which were not covered by the main claim as filed. The main claim as filed referred to a cylindrical wall and a helical mixing rib, whereas the new embodiments had a frusto-conical shape and staggered mixing ribs/recesses. Deletion or broadening of the features of the claim as filed clearly raised the issue of added matter, but the Examiners wanted candidates to appreciate that both amendments could be made but both would need argument in support. While this was a fairly extreme example — which is worth studying — it is not uncommon for the optimum solution to need some generalisation.

A less extreme example occurred in the 2005 paper. Here claim 1 needed limitations found in claim 3 and claim 5, but as filed these claims included the limitations "**flat base**" and "adapted to secured by **gluing**". Neither of the features in bold was related to the solution of the problem either before or after amendment. There was no basis for the amendment, and the client had not requested the amendment (he had asked for a different broadening amendment of claim 1, for which there was support and which also needed to be made), but the deletion of the two terms did pass the Houdaille test.

While the examiners do not want to see any added matter, they penalise most heavily amendments which add matter and which, if present on grant, could not be removed post grant without contravening Art.123(3). That is, the addition of a feature for which there is no basis in the application as filed is likely to be more heavily punished than the addition of subject matter by the deletion of a feature.

Ensure that all essential features relevant to the new problem solved have been incorporated and that the scope is limited to embodiments that solve the new problem.

Also ensure that you have added no inessential limitations. The question assumes that the broadest allowable scope will require the use of arguments in support to justify, in particular, inventive step. Do not narrow to the point at which you feel no need to argue in support of the inventive step of the whole claim scope — it suggests that your claim scope is too narrow, and you will lose marks both for the claim and for the missing arguments to support the claim.

In general, where you have more than one independent claim, your argumentation should include an **explanation** of how/why the claimed inventions are linked by a single inventive concept. Remember the different categories of claim which are automatically permitted under r.30 (Guidelines C/III.7/2).

Attend to any necessary amendments for the purposes of clarity.

Take into account any specific instructions provided by the client (e.g. the client's request in the year 2000 exam for later-developed embodiments to be protected; in 1998 protection sought for the optical rather than the electrical embodiments, in 1995 protection for the Figure 8 and 9 embodiments rather than that of Figure 1).

Draft dependent claims that are associated with further advantages. There are not usually many in Paper B and typically a total of 10 to 15 claims will be about right though sometimes substantially fewer will be required. Do not delete subclaims where the added feature has not been shown to be known in the art. Only add claims to those features associated with further inventive step arguments and "most preferred" or "particularly advantageous" features.

1–110   *Writing a response to the Art.96(2) communication*

When writing the response, number paragraphs for ease of reference. Generally, no marks are awarded for standard paragraphs reserving the right to oral proceedings and the like — concentrate on providing clear basis for amendments, demonstrating that the claims are novel and arguing for inventive step. When arguing for inventive step use the problem and solution approach rigidly.

The following notes give guidance on the content and style of the response. Sentences in normal typeface are suggestions for phrases to adapt when writing the answer and sentence in italics provide further useful comments. Remember that you are not allowed to write any part of your answer on a pre-prepared template. You must not prepare sections of text in advance of the exam and paste them into your answer on the day.

This letter is in response to the communication pursuant to Art.96(2) EPC.

## 1. Amendment

1.1 In response to the objections raised, the validity of which is not conceded, I attach new claims pages to replace the corresponding existing pages which are now cancelled, without prejudice to the later filing of a divisional application directed to any aspect of the subject matter thereof. These amendments are believed to render moot all those of the examiner's objections which are not otherwise dealt with below.

1.2 Claim 1 has been amended by . . . . Support for this amendment is to be found on page x, line y . . . which discloses . . . .

*Explain carefully the basis for the amendments made, explaining why the new features of the claim are disclosed in combination in the description and why any linguistic differences are justified. If there is explicit basis in the application as filed, specify the page and line number, If you rely on an implicit reference, again specify the location of the relevant disclosure **and** provide argument for why the amendment is allowable. Where a feature is removed from a claim as filed, explain how you meet the requirements of T331/87. In the case of incorporation by reference, explain in some detail why the requirements of T689/90 are met (see below). With a disclaimer, the basis will naturally be in the prior art.*

1.3 Claim 2. . .etc

1.4 Since all the features of the amended claims are directly and unambiguously derivable from the application as filed, it is submitted that there is no contravention of Article 123(2) EPC.

## 2. Novelty

2.1 D1 discloses . . . . D1 does not disclose the features of the invention of claim 1 that . . . . and . . . . In particular, the phrase . . . does not explicitly disclose . . . Claim 1 is therefore novel over D1.

*A good argument with respect to novelty of the subject-matter claimed should establish that the claim contains at least one feature of distinction from each of the prior art documents available. It is not necessary that the same feature distinguishes over each of the prior art documents. It is not sufficient merely to state that none of the documents discloses the combination of features claimed.*

2.2 Since claims 2 to x are dependent on claim 1 and include all its features they are therefore also novel over D1.

*Reference the Guidelines C/IV/9.12 which explain that where an independent claim is new and non-obvious over a piece of prior art there is no need to investigate the novelty or non-obviousness of a dependent claim in light of that prior art.*

2.3 Claim y is novel over D1 because . . . etc.

2.4 D2 discloses . . . etc.

### 3. Inventive step

3.1 D1 may be taken to be the closest prior art since . . .

*Do not simply select the document that has the greatest number of features in common with the claimed invention. Choose the prior art document that is most relevant to the problem solved and which has the most technical features in common. In appropriate cases, and if time permits, consider arguing inventive step from more than one starting point.*

**Do not use an Art.54(3) citation as the closest prior art!**

3.2 The differences between D1 and the invention of claim 1 are . . .

*Inventive step arguments can only be based on mandatory, as opposed to optional, features of the claim that make the claim novel with respect to the relevant art (D1).*

3.3 This difference leads to . . . (unexpected property or advantage). The objective problem solved by the present invention is therefore . . .

*Consider the technical effects or results achieved by the claimed invention when compared to the closest prior art when formulating the problem — no part of the solution should be in the problem (T229/85).*

3.4 *Indicate where necessary the basis for the problem in the application where the problem has changed in light of the cited prior art (T39/93).*

3.5 The invention of claim 1 solves this problem by providing . . . . Evidence that the problem is solved is provided by . . .

*Point out the advantages of the invention, emphasising why they are important and surprising.*

3.6 There is no suggestion in D1 that xxx could be replaced by yyy since . . . (e.g. *no pointer, teaching away, prejudice in the art*). There is not the slightest incentive for the skilled man to choose . . . with a reasonable expectation of achieving . . . .

The prior art does not give any indication that selection of . . . would have an impact on [property X]. Therefore, the dramatic improvements observed on selection of . . . must be surprising for the skilled person.

*Emphasise the drawbacks of the closest prior art.*

3.7 Starting from D1 and faced with this problem, the skilled person would not look to D2 to find the solution to the problem because . . . Even if the skilled person were to consider D2, he would not combine this with D1 because. . . . . . . . . . . . Even if the skilled person starting from D1 and faced with this problem were to try to combine D1 and D2, he would not arrive at the claimed subject matter because . . . (e.g. *in different fields, solve different problems, unlikely to be read together by the skilled man* (e.g. *very different dates*), *incompatible teaching*).

**Do not consider an Art.54(3) citation in combination with the closest prior art!**

3.8 The invention of claim 1 is therefore not obvious over any of the prior art documents, either taken alone or in combination.

3.9 Dependent claims

*Reference the Guidelines C/IV/9.12 which explain that where an independent claim is new and non-obvious over a piece of prior art there is no need to investigate the novelty or non-obviousness of a dependent claim in light of that prior art.*

3.10 Other independent claims

*Repeat the process with each of the independent claims.*

## 4. Unity

The independent claims are believed to meet the requirements for unity of invention (Art.82 EPC). The common special technical feature, required by r.30, is provided by Q, which is present in independent claims 1, A and B, a corresponding special technical feature Q', being found in the remaining independent claims. Q and Q' are clearly corresponding special technical features because................

*According to r.30 EPC, unity exists between a group of inventions when there is a technical relationship among the inventions involving one or more of the same or corresponding special technical features, i.e. those features which define a contribution which each of the claimed inventions considered as a whole makes over the prior art. This is explained in the Guidelines C/III/7.2 It is quite common for the optimum answer to this paper to include only a single independent claim. As such, no discussion of unity is generally required, but this does not mean that the issue may not arise in future.*

## 5. Number of independent Claims — rule 29(2)

5.1 The presence of more than one independent claim in one category, that is product claims 1, X and Y, is believed to comply with the requirements of rule 29(2) because there are a plurality of inter-related products (meeting the requirement of sub-paragraph (a) of rule 29(2)).

*Again, past papers have not given rise to this issue, but it could arise. Rule 29(2) applies to all European patent applications for which no rule 51(4) communication was issued by January 2, 2002. It states that only one independent claim in the same category (product, process, apparatus or use) is allowed, unless the subject matter of the application involves one of:*

(a) *a plurality of inter-related products;*
(b) *different uses of a product or apparatus;*
(c) *alternate solutions to a particular problem, where it is not appropriate to cover these alternatives by a single claim.*

*The EPO is increasingly raising objections under this rule, and it is not unthinkable that Paper B might involve this issue. The Guidelines C/III/3.2 give as examples of cases where multiple independent claims would be allowable under this rule:*

(a) *plug and socket; or transmitter-receiver;*
(b) *second or further medical uses in the claim format of a "second medical use" — type claim;*
(c) *a group of chemical compounds; two or more processes for the manufacture of such compounds.*

*The wording of the rule suggests that if the subject-matter of a patent application satisfies the requirement of at least one of tests (a), (b), or (c), no restraint on the number or category of the independent claims is then imposed by the rule. Certainly one is not limited to either all product claims or all use or method claims. Of course, the Art.84 requirements of clarity and conciseness always apply.*

## 6. Objections in the communication

6.1 In point x.x of the Communication, the examiner objects to . . . This is not the case since . . .

*Go through the communication and respond to all the specific points made by the examiner, even if only by referring to a previous paragraph, unless the objection has been rendered moot by amendments you have made and you have mentioned this as under 1.1 above.*

Attached:   New claims

**1–111**  *Notes to the examiner*

The exam does not require or assume that you will write notes to the examiner: your answer should be complete and should speak for itself. But sometimes there is a justification for a brief note to the examiner. Extensive notes to the examiner should be avoided. Things to consider pointing out to the examiner are: (1) assumptions made in light of ambiguities in the question; and (2) reasons why you made any decision that was difficult to make (e.g. not making an amendment which the client wanted you to make, because of concerns over added matter).

**1–112**  *Checking the answer*

It is always sensible to check the correctness of your claims, especially that the independent claims are clearly novel over the cited art. Is every feature that you have added in fact essential? Check for the absence of features essential to solve the problem which you are now claiming to have solved in light of the new prior art. Have you claimed everything that you intended to claim? Do your arguments in support of novelty and inventive step actually fit the claims that you are proposing? Have you clearly identified anything that should be the subject of a divisional application? Unless you have made a big mistake, major changes to the answer are not recommended in the last 15 minutes and often lose more marks than they gain. If any time remains it is worth reading through the answer once, correcting typographical mistakes and ensuring that there is consistency between the description and the claims.

### 3. Notes on amendment

**1–113**  *Added matter*

A European patent application or a European patent may not be amended in such a way that it contains subject-matter which extends beyond the content of the application as filed (Art.123(2)). The basic test is whether the subject matter can be directly and unambiguously derived from the application as filed (T20/83) and hence whether "new information" is provided by the amendment. Both the explicit and implicit content of the application as filed may be used as basis (T151/84, T201/83). The content of the application as filed is the description, claims and drawings, but does not include the abstract, nor priority documents even if these are filed with the application (G3/89).

Cross-referenced documents are prima facie not part of the application as filed (T689/90) but can sometimes be used under strict conditions (T689/90, T6/84). The conditions are that the description as filed leaves no doubt to a skilled reader: (1) that protection is, or may be sought for such features; (2) that such features contribute to solving the technical problem underlying the invention; (3) that such features at least implicitly clearly belong to the description of the invention contained in the application as filed and thus to the content of the application as filed; and (4) that such features are precisely defined and identifiable within the disclosure of the referenced document. Usually, it is only legitimate to incorporate the general teaching of the referenced document, not features in specific examples. See Guidelines C/VI/5.3.8.

Amendments to the claim preamble in view of the closest prior art changing (T13/84) or changing the position of a feature from the preamble to the characterising portion (T16/86) are both allowed.

Where matter cannot be added to the application it may still be added to the file wrapper and used as evidence to support the patentability of an invention. For example, additional examples may justify the scope claimed or evidence of a new effect may justify an inventive step.

*Disclaimers*  1–114

Disclaimers are allowed where the subject matter cannot be described positively (T4/80). The allowability of a disclaimer that has no basis in the application as filed has now been definitively decided by the Enlarged Board of Appeal (G1/03 and G2/03). Disclaimers are always allowable when the prior art is an Art.54(3) document as long as no more than the novelty-destroying part of the prior art is removed from the claim. In the case of an Art.54(2) document a disclaimer is only allowed where the anticipation is accidental, i.e. the prior art reference is so remote and unrelated to the subject matter of the invention that it would never have been taken into account by the skilled person in making the invention. Again, no more than the novelty-destroying part of the prior art may be removed from the claim. The rationale is that, in line with previous case law (e.g. T170/87, T597/92) a disclaimer cannot make a non-inventive teaching inventive. A disclaimer may therefore only be used when inventive step is not an issue. How the new definition of "accidental" will be applied by the EPO in practice is yet to be seen but the definition is very narrow and henceforth only Art.54(2) art in a very remote field is likely to be successfully disclaimed.

*Amended claims not to relate to unsearched subject matter not having unity*  1–115

Amended claims may not relate to unsearched subject matter which does not combine with the originally claimed invention or group of inventions to form a single general inventive concept (r.86(4)). A divisional application needs to be filed for such subject matter if it is to be protected. This provision relates to matter not present in the claims during search rather than, for instance, matter which was not completely searched.

## 4. Worked example using EQE 2002 Paper B

*Understanding and annotating the paper*  1–116

The following pages indicate how the 2002 B paper could be marked up on a first reading.

# APPLICATION

Description

*Prior art.*

Simple and robust pressure sensors in which two electrodes are kept apart by a compressible medium such as a spring or a block of foam are known. On compression of the medium, when a specific pressure has been reached or exceeded, the electrodes make contact, which is detected by an electrical circuit. Such a sensor, by itself, cannot be used to measure a plurality of pressures. State of the art sensors for measuring a plurality of pressures or forces, such as those based on piezo-resistance or silicium membranes, are susceptible to damage. They thus require complicated protective means, and are expensive to manufacture.

*Problem to be overcome.*

*Problem to be overcome.*

There is therefore a need for an improved pressure sensor capable of measuring a plurality of pressures. The present invention, according to the independent claims, results in a cheap, simple and robust solution to this problem.

*New sensors.*

Fig. 1 shows the sensor of the invention in its most simple form, with two electrodes.

Fig. 2 shows an embodiment of the invention, using an array of electrodes.

Fig. 3 shows one arrangement for producing conductive polymeric foam according to the invention.

*New apparatus/method new foam.*

Fig. 4 shows a cross-section through a layer of foam according to the invention.

*New sensors.*

In its most simple form as shown in Fig. 1, the sensor of the invention comprises an electrically non-conducting substrate 2 on which are provided, at a distance from each other, two electrodes 1. The substrate may be rigid or flexible. Above and in contact with the electrodes is a layer of polymeric foam 6. The foam contains graphite particles which, upon compression of the foam, are brought into contact with each other, and thus form an electrically conducting path through the foam. As the foam is subjected to increasing pressure, it is further compressed and more graphite particles contact each other. The electrical resistance of the foam is thus reduced. The electrical signal measured across the electrodes may be fed to a processor or computer and converted by means of a suitable algorithm into a signal for giving a corresponding pressure reading.

*How the sensors works.*

*Optional construction features.*

The electrodes may be discrete elements, or may be etched on a printed circuit board. In the latter case, the printed circuit board also fulfils the function of the substrate. Fig. 2 shows a sensor arrangement using a plurality of circular electrodes 1' provided on substrate 2' and in contact with foam layer 6'. The electrodes may be placed anywhere on the various surfaces of the foam, e.g on a two dimensional surface or a three dimensional object, which allows precise measurement of the pressures in different areas of the foam.

*Advantageous affects.*

*Possible applications.*

The sensor can be used as an electrical switch. With a suitable mass provided on the foam layer, it can be used as a vibration detector. It could also be used as part of a robot hand.

*Production process and apparatus — prior art.*

The foam may be made from any suitable polymer such as polyurethane, and is produced as a continuous web. Fig. 3 shows an apparatus capable of producing the foam of the invention, in which the details of the right side of the drawing are shown in magnified view. Polymeric materials is firstly extruded through an extruder 30 and then shaped by a die 31. Shortly after the material 5 leaves the die 31, it enters expansion and curing chamber 32, where it transforms into foam. At this stage the foam thus obtained is supported by conveyor belt 34. Inside chamber 32 heaters 35 circulate hot air to accelerate the foaming and curing process. Graphite particles are applied to the curing foam by spraying through spray heads 36 onto its upper surface.

*Process features.*

The particles sink under gravity into the foam, until they are trapped in a certain position as the foam is sufficiently cured. The penetration depth of the graphite particles into the foam is regulated principally by control of the curing temperature inside the chamber 32. As the fully expanded web of foam 6″ exits the chamber 32 it undergoes a final shaping step by rollers 33 for ensuring accurate dimensions. The apparatus of Fig. 3 is well known, apart from the presence of the plurality of spray heads 36. A spray head may be any device suitably adapted for the even distribution of particles across the width of the foam. Such spray heads are commercially available and normally take the form of slits or nozzles. The apparatus also comprises a computerised control system, enabling the automatic regulation of all process parameters.

Fig. 4 shows a cross-section through a layer of foam 6″ thus produced. The cross-section shows visible bands 61, 62, 63 and 64 of graphite particles, each band being laid down by a different spray head. In each band, the concentration of graphite particles is slightly more dense towards the centre of the band (i.e. it appears darker), and slightly less dense at the edges of the band (i.e. it appears lighter). This is a result of the movement of the particles during the foaming process. The particles at the edges of adjacent bands are intermingled. The particle distribution within each band, and the thickness of the band itself, may be very finely regulated by careful control of process parameters such as the curing-rate of the foam, the speed of the foam passing through the apparatus, the weight and size of the particles, and the spraying velocity and density. These process parameters are regulated so that each band has a substantially identical thickness and a substantially identical particle distribution.

The electrical resistance characteristics of the foam layer are a function of the particle size and particle distribution within the bands, the thickness of the bands, and the total number of bands in the foam layer. These can be regulated by adjustment of appropriate process parameters and by the number, position and design of the spray heads so as to produce a foam layer having an even, predetermined electrical change in resistance per unit change of pressure. It has been found that particle distribution in a band is difficult to regulate if the band is too thick. It is therefore desirable that the thickness of each band is limited, in order to ensure a predictable particle distribution. For instance, for a layer of polyurethane foam having a thickness of 15 mm, 12 bands or more are necessary to ensure predictable particle distribution. The process of the invention allows greater reproducibility of identical foam layers, and hence identical sensors. Using such sensors, highly accurate measurements may be achieved, whilst at the same time guaranteeing consistent and reproducible performance.

To produce the sensor, firstly the substrate is provided with electrodes. This may be by etching electrodes on a printed circuit board. Alternatively, electrodes may be attached at specific intervals to a suitable substrate by means of e.g. adhesive. The substrate with electrodes is then joined to the foam layer by any suitable means (such as application of adhesive near the edges of the substrate), such that electrical contact between the electrodes and foam is not impeded.

## Claims

1. Polymeric foam (6, 6′, 6″) comprising graphite particles.

2. A sensor for the measurement of pressure comprising:

an electrically non-conducting substrate (2, 2′), and

a plurality of electrodes (1, 1′) provided at a distance from each other on a first side of the substrate, and

a layer of foam (6, 6′, 6″) according to claim 1 provided on the first side of the substrate and in electrical contact with the electrodes.

3. The sensor of claim 2, comprising more than two electrodes (1, 1′) provided on the substrate (2, 2′).

*164    Complete Guide to Passing the EQE*

**Dependent claim to sensor.**

4. A device for measuring pressure comprising the sensor of claim 2 or 3 and a processor or electrical circuit capable of converting the electrical resistance between the electrodes into a signal for giving corresponding pressure reading.

**Dependent claim to sensor.**

5. A switch comprising a sensor according to claim 2 or 3.

6. A method of making polymeric foam comprising graphite particles, whereby the foam is produced continuously, and the graphite particles are sprayed onto the foam before the foam has fully cured.

[For "Drawings of the Application" see pp.166 and 167, below.]

## Communication under Article 96(2) and Rule 51(2) EPC

The examination is being carried out on the application documents as originally filed.

**Both docs apparently citable under A54(2).**

1. The following pre-published documents are mentioned in the communication:

Document D1 and Document D2

2. The present application does not meet the requirements of Article 52(1) and 54(1)(2) EPC, because the subject-matter of claims 1–6 is not new.

3. A polymeric foam comprising graphite particles is known from both D1 (reference 5 of Fig. 1) and D2 (reference 1 of Fig. 1). The subject-matter of claim 1 therefore lacks novelty with respect of these documents.

**D2 not applied against claims 2–5, despite being cited against the two independent claims.**

4. D1 furthermore teaches a sensor for the measurement of pressure comprising an electrically non-conducting substrate 3, and more than two electrodes 4 provided at a distance from each other on a first side of the substrate, and a polymeric foam layer 5 comprising graphite particles provided on the first side of the substrate and in electrical contact with the electrodes. Moreover it discloses a cavity 7 with an electrical circuit capable of converting the electrical resistance between the electrodes 4 into a signal for the activation of the warning lamp 8, this signal being also suitable for giving a corresponding pressure reading. The sensor arrangement of D1, Fig. 1 is also a switch, which activates a light.

**D1 not applied against claim 6.**

The subject-matter of claims 2–5 therefore also lacks novelty with respect to D1.

5. D2 teaches a method for making polymeric foam comprising graphite particles, whereby the foam is produced by spraying it on the surface or a roller. The roller is rotated and the uncured foam is further sprayed with graphite particles from a stationary nozzle before the foam has fully cured. D2 states that this outer layer of foam may, alternatively, be produced separately as a continuous polymeric foam web which is later cut to length and fixed around the roller. Clearly, producing this web in a continuous process leads to the subject-matter of claim 6, which is therefore not new.

**Reminder to argue novelty and step inventive step.**

6. It is not at present apparent which part of the application could serve as a basis for a new, allowable claim. Should the applicant nevertheless regard some particular matter as patentable, an independent claim including such matter should be filed. The applicant should indicate and justify in the letter of reply, on the one hand, the difference of the subject-matter of the new claim vis-à-vis the state of the art and, on the other hand, the inventive significance thereof.

**A clear flag that marks have been allocated to this aspect: must be addressed in the answer**

7. Should the applicant submit an amended set of claims with a plurality of independent claims, convincing arguments justifying the unity of invention are expected.

## DOCUMENT D1 [citable for novelty and inventive step.]

Milking cups for milking machines comprise a rubber sleeve that surrounds and squeezes the teat to produce milk flow. It is vital that this sleeve exerts the correct pressure, as excessive pressure can lead to inefficient milking and even infection of the teat. This invention provides a test apparatus that can be inserted into the milking cup in place of a teat, in order to verify that the rubber sleeve is not exerting excessive pressure and therefore not defective.

*Excessive pressure with respect to a threshold.*

*No teaching re multiple pressures.*

*Not concerned with measuring plurality of pressures.*

Fig. 1 shows a cross-section through the test apparatus.

Fig. 2 shows a perspective view of the test apparatus.

The apparatus comprises a probe 1 and a head portion 2. The probe 1 has a solid central core 3 on which are provided a series of gold-plated electrical contacts 4. Around and in contact with these contacts is a sleeve of electrically conductive foam 5. The foam is protected by an elastomeric outer layer 6. The head portion 2 contains a cavity 7 with an electrical circuit (not shown) and an aperture for a warning lamp 8 comprising a red lens 9. As the conductive foam is compressed by the rubber sleeve of the milking cup, the electrical resistance of the foam decreases. This resistance is detected by a resistance measuring circuit connected to the contacts. Once the resistance drops below a preset level, this is detected by the circuit which illuminates the warning lamp, indicating that the milking cup is defective.

*Single, preset threshold. Relevant to claims 4 and 5.*

To produce the probe, an electrically non-conducting solid core 3 is injection moulded from polypropylene. A series of gold-plated metallic strips 4 are glued along the core to provide the electrical contacts. Wires (not shown) are connected to each contact for connection to the measuring circuitry. The core and contacts are placed into a mould and a polymeric resin pre-mixed with graphite particles is then introduced into the mould. The resin expands and cures to form electrically conductive foam layer 5, and the thus formed probe is then extracted from the mould. A thin elastomeric tube is placed over the foam to protect it. The probe and connecting wires are connected to the head portion, which carries the resistance measuring circuit and warning lamp. The simple and robust apparatus is subsequently calibrated and sold as a sealed i.e. tamper-proof unit.

*Electrically non-conducting substrate. Plurality of electrodes relevant to claims 2 and 3.*

*Anticipates claim 1*

*Relevant to claims 4 and 5.*

*Individual calibration required (to set threshold).*

[For "Drawings of Document D1" see p.168, below.]

## DOCUMENT D2 (STATE OF THE ART) [citable for novelty and inventive step.]

Conveyor belt systems are prone to generate static electricity, the discharge of which poses a potential fire risk. In the prior art this problem is overcome by supporting the conveyor belt on rollers which have an electrically conducting surface. When the roller is installed, this surface is electrically earthed via contact brushes. The build up of a static charge is thereby avoided.

*Different technical field, different and un-related problem.*

Prior art rollers are manufactured by attaching a layer of electrically conductive foam to the periphery of the roller. This conductive layer is made in a continuous process from foam which has been pre-mixed with graphite particles. However, poor mixing leads to particle agglomeration and voids, and a generally non-homogenous particle distribution. This result is unpredictable effects and an irregular conductivity of the coating, with potentially serious consequences for the earthing of the conveyor belt.

*Same foam as in D1.*

*Anticipates claim 1.*

*Disadvantage of non-homogenous particle distribution.*

*Specific problem unrelated to ours.*

Fig. 1 shows a cross-section of the roller of the invention.

Fig. 2 shows a perspective view of the roller of the invention.

Fig. 3a shows an open mould and the central axle.

Fig. 3b shows the second foam layer being sprayed on the insulating layer.

## DRAWINGS OF THE APPLICATION

1/2

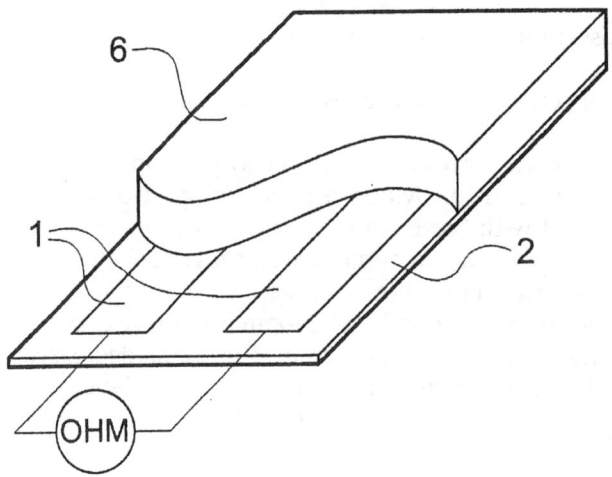

Fig. 1

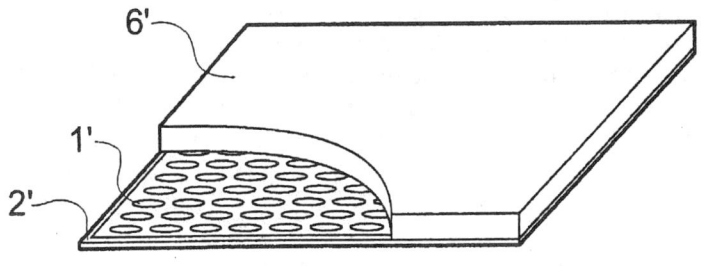

Fig. 2

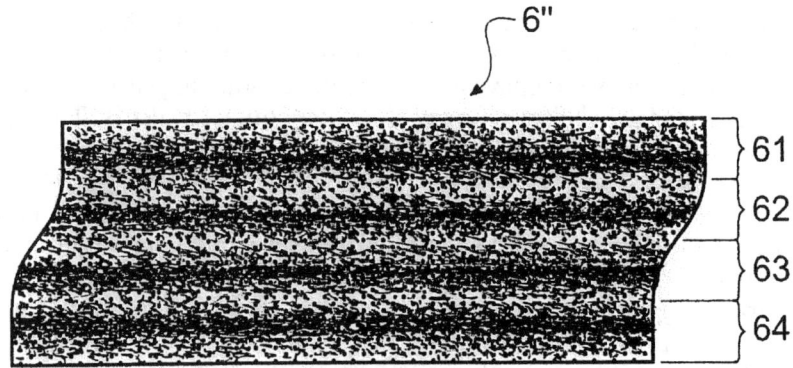

Fig. 4

## DRAWINGS OF THE APPLICATION

2/2

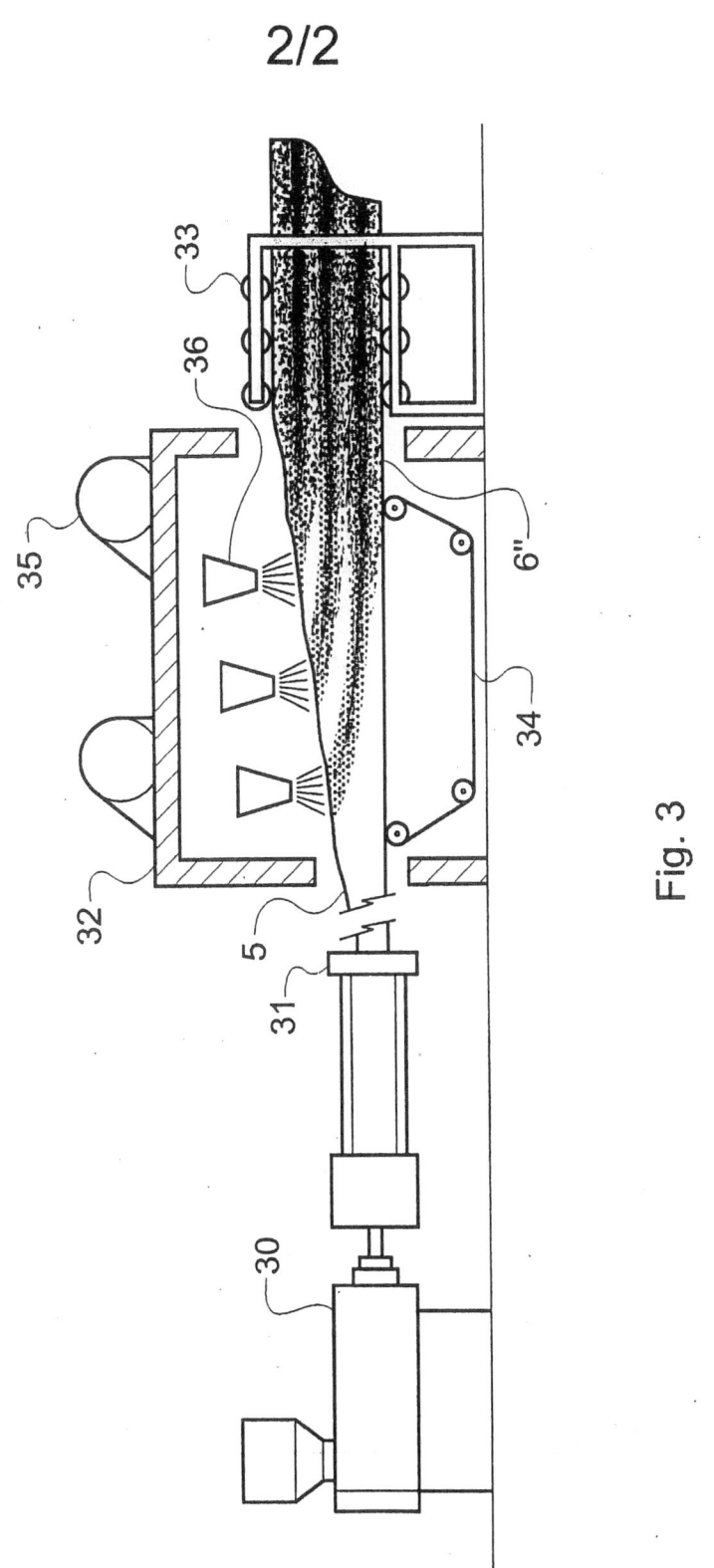

Fig. 3

## DRAWINGS OF DOCUMENT D1

1/1

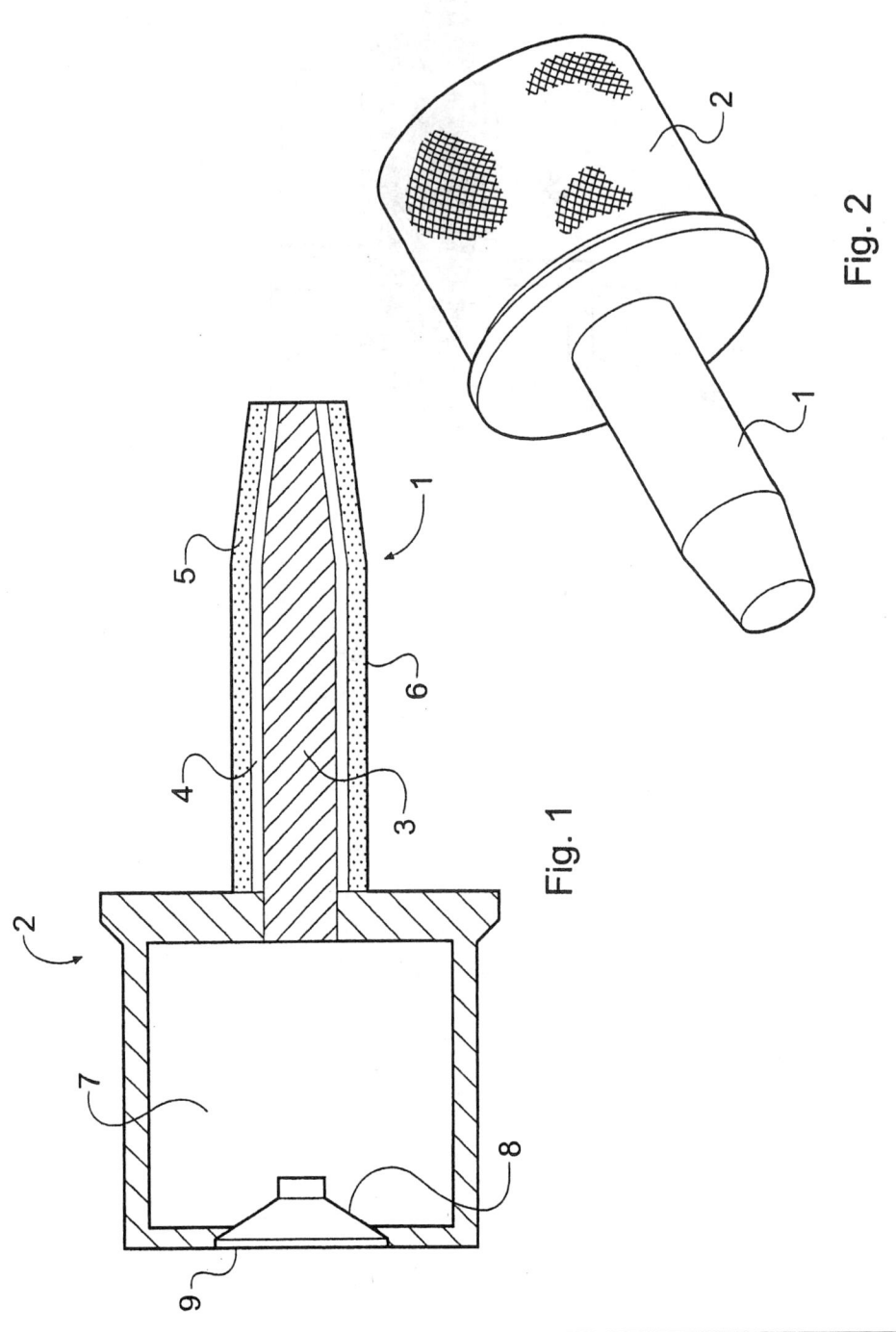

Fig. 1

Fig. 2

Fig. 3c shows the second foam layer being sprayed with graphite particles.  *Relevant to claim 6.*

The rollers used in the present invention comprise a central axle 2, an electrically non-conducting layer 3, and a peripheral electrically conductive covering 1. The central axle 2 has end pieces 4 which are insulated from the electrically conductive covering 1 by the non-conducting layer 3. The roller comprises two different layers of foam. The foam is preferably polyurethane.  *The only foam matrix identified in application.*

To manufacture the conducting roller, the central axle 2 is first placed in a mould 10. An insulating layer 3 of polymeric foam is then moulded directly onto the central axle 2. Once this foam is fully cured, the axle 2 with its electrically non-conducting first foam layer 3, is removed from the mould 10. The axle 2 and first foam layer 3 are then rotated and sprayed from a first spray nozzle 20 with a thin layer of a second foam 5. Before the second foam layer cures, it is sprayed with graphite particles 6 whilst rotating in front of a second spray nozzle 30. Particles 6 build up and contact each other both within and on the surface of the foam 5, so as to form, together with the foam 5, the conductive covering 1. Alternatively, the conductive foam layer can be manufactured separately in a continuous process similar to that used for the prior art, but applying the graphite particles by spraying rather than by pre-mixing. The resultant foam web is then cut to length and attached around the roller.

*Discontinuous otherwise as claim 6.*

*Not clearly novelty — destroying for claim 6 but obviousness an issue.*

*Continuous but is foam then uncured?*

[For "Drawings of Document D2", see p.170, below.]

## CLIENT'S LETTER

Wim Sickle Engineering Solutions

Sir Lee Gyt, Frank Lee Te Deus and Partners
Patent Agents
Normandy House
Teddington
Bertshire

Dear Mr. Te Deus,

Thank you for the copy of the examiner's communication. Since filing the application I have had more time to compare the pressure-sensor of my invention to similar products on the market, and that of D1 in particular. Whilst pressure-sensors based on conductive foam are known, mine appears to give more accurate and consistent results.  *Advantage to be argued.*

I ask you to obtain the broadest possible protection for my invention.  *Claim whatever can be claimed.*

Yours sincerely,

Wim Sickle

## DRAWINGS OF DOCUMENT D2

1/1

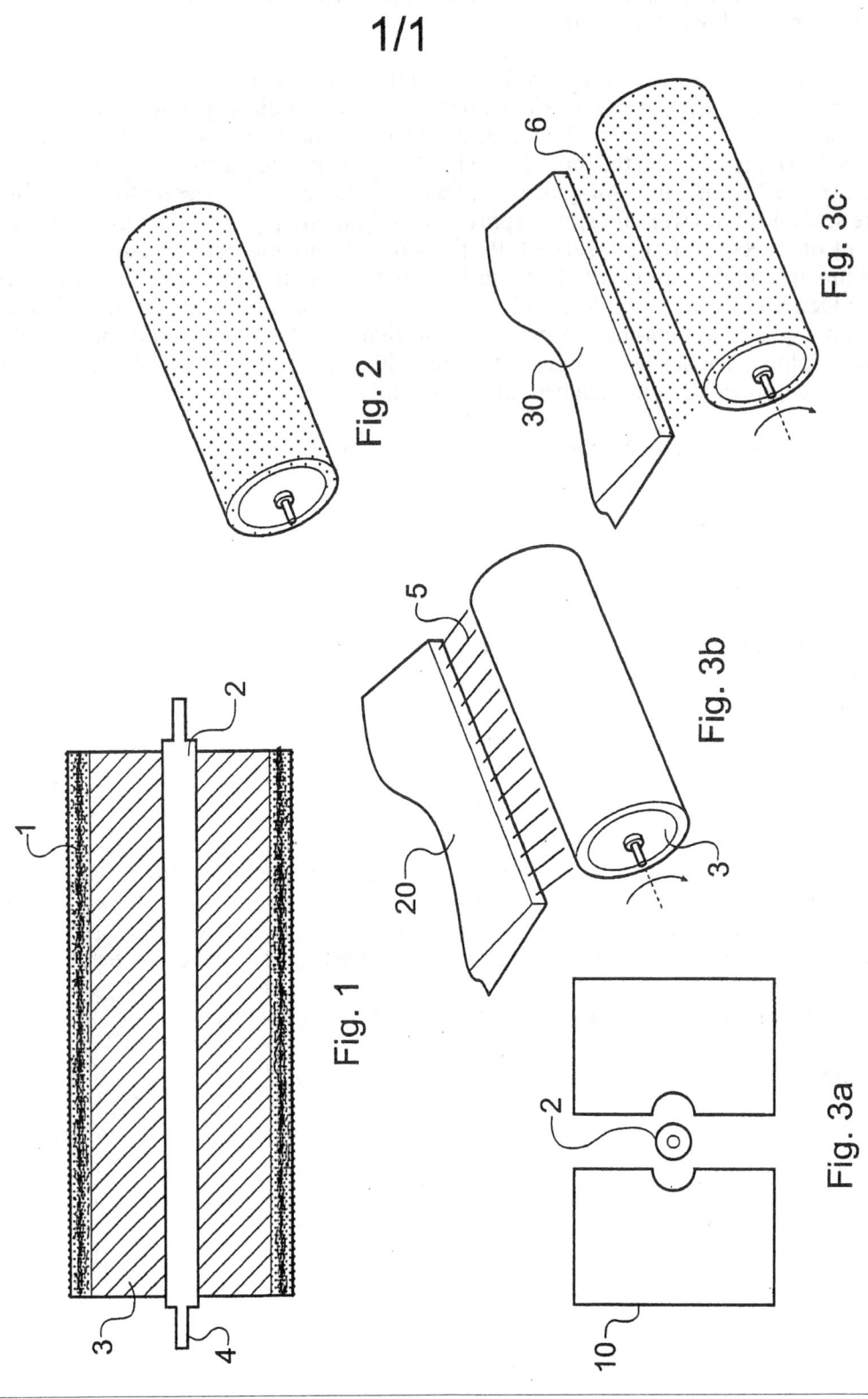

*Establishing patentable subject matter* **1–117**

The following pages indicate how the client's application can be divided into novel features and features found in the prior art. A shaded box has been used to indicate a lack of novelty.

## APPLICATION

### Description

| | |
|---|---|
| Prior art. | Simple and robust pressure sensors in which two electrodes are kept apart by a compressible medium such as a spring or a block of foam are known. On compression of the medium, when a specific pressure has been reached or exceeded, the electrodes make contact, which is detected by an electrical circuit. Such a sensor, by itself, cannot be used to measure a plurality of pressures. State of the art sensors for measuring a plurality of pressures or forces, such as those based on piezo-resistance or silicium membranes, are susceptible to damage. They thus require complicated protective means, and are expensive to manufacture. |
| Problem to be overcome. | |
| Problem to be overcome. | There is therefore a need for an improved pressure sensor capable of measuring a plurality of pressures. The present invention, according to the independent claims, results in a cheap, simple and robust solution to this problem. |
| Shown in D1. | Fig. 1 shows the sensor of the invention in its most simple form, with two electrodes. |
| | Fig. 2 shows an embodiment of the invention, using an array of electrodes. |
| New apparatus / method new foaM. | Fig. 3 shows one arrangement for producing conductive polymeric foam according to the invention. |
| Not shown in prior art | Fig. 4 shows a cross-section through a layer of foam according to the invention. |
| Shown in D1. | In its most simple form as shown in Fig. 1, the senor of the invention comprises an electrically non-conducting substrate 2 on which are provided, at a distance from each other, two electrodes 1. The substrate may be rigid or flexible. Above and in contact with the electrodes is a layer of polymeric foam 6. The foam contains graphite particles which, upon compression of the foam, are brought into contact with each other, and thus form an electronically conducting path through the foam. As the foam is subjected to increasing pressure, it is further compressed and more graphite particles contact each other. The electrical resistance of the foam is thus reduced. The electrical signal measured across the electrodes may be fed to a processor or computer and converted by means of a suitable algorithm into a signal for giving a correspondence pressure reading. |
| Computer not taught in D1. | |
| Shown in D1. | The electrodes may be discrete elements, or may be etched on a printed circuit board. In the latter case the printed circuit board also fulfils the function of the substrate. Fig. 2 shows a sensor arrangement using a plurality of circular electrodes 1' provided on substrate 2' and in contact with foam layer 6'. The electrodes may be placed anywhere on the various surfaces of the foam, e.g. on a two dimensional surface or a three dimensional object, which allows precise measurement of the pressures in different areas of |
| Not taught in D1. | |
| D1 shows 3-D substrate. Advantageous effect. | |
| Shown in D1. Not known. | The sensor can be used as an electrical switch. With a suitable mass provided on the foam layer, it can be used as a vibration detector. It could also be used as a part of a robot hand. |
| Known from D2. | The foam may be made from any suitable polymer such as polyurethane and is produced as a continuous web. Fig. 3 shows an apparatus capable producing the foam of the invention, in which the details of the right side of the drawing are shown in magnified view. Polymeric material is firstly extruded through an extruder 30 and then shaped by a die 31. Shortly after the material 5 leaves the die 31, it enters expansion and curing chamber 32, where it transforms into foam. At this stage the foam thus obtained is supported by conveyor belt 34. Inside chamber 32 heaters 35 circulate hot air to accelerate the foaming and curing process. Graphite particles are applied to the curing foam by spraying through spray heads 36 onto its upper surface. |
| Known from D2. | |

The particles sink under gravity into the foam, until they are trapped in a certain position as the foam is sufficiently cured. The penetration depth of the graphite particles into the foam is regulated principally by the control of the curing temperature inside the chamber 32. As the fully expanded web of foam 6″ exists the chamber 32 it undergoes a final shaping step by rollers 33 for ensuring accurate dimensions. The apparatus of Fig. 3 is well known, apart from the presence of the plurality of spray heads 36. A spray head may be any device suitably adapted for the even distribution of particles across the width of the foam. Such spray heads are commercially available and normally take the form of slits or nozzles. The apparatus also comprises a computerised control system, enabling the automatic regulation of all process parameters.

*Process features.*

*Prior art.*

Fig. 4 shows a cross-section through a layer of foam 6′ thus produced. The cross-section shows visible bands 61, 62, 63 and 64 of graphite particles, each band being laid down by a different spray head. In each band, the concentration of graphite particles is slightly more dense towards the centre of the band (i.e. it appears darker), and slightly less dense at the edges of the band (i.e. it appears lighter). This is a result of the movement of the particles during the foaming process. The particles at the edges of adjacent bands are intermingled. The particle distribution within each band, and the thickness of the band itself, may be very finely regulated by careful control of process parameters such as the curing-rate of the foam, the speed of the foam passing through the apparatus, the weight and the size of the particles, and the spraying velocity and density. These process parameters are regulated so that each band has a substantially identical thickness and a substantially identical particle distribution.

*Characteristics of the foam.*

*Process parameters.*

The electrical resistance characteristics of the foam layer are a function of the particle size and particle distribution within the bands, the thickness of the bands, and the total number of bands in the foam layer. These can be regulated by adjustment of appropriate process parameters and by the number, position and design of the spray heads so as to produce a foam layer having an even, predetermined electrical change in resistance per unit change of pressure. It has been found that particle distribution in a band is difficult to regulate if the band is too thick. It is therefore desirable that the thickness of each band is limited, in order to ensure a predictable particle distribution. For instance, for a layer of polyurethane foam having a thickness of 15 mm, 12 bands or more are necessary to ensure predictable particle distribution. The process of the invention allows greater reproducibility of identical foam layers, and hence identical sensors. Using such sensors, highly accurate measurements may be achieved, whilst at the same time guaranteeing consistent and reproducible performance.

*Foam properties.*

*Advantage of foam.*

*Example*
*Advantage of foam and sensors.*

To produce the sensor, firstly the substrate is provided with electrodes. This may be by etching electrodes on a printed circuit board. Alternatively, electrodes may be attached at specific intervals to a suitable substrate by means of e.g. adhesive. The substrate with electrodes is then joined to the foam layer by any suitable means (such as application of adhesive near the edges of the substrate), such that electrical contact between the electrodes and foam is not impeded.

*Known from D1.*
*Etched electrodes on pcbs not known.*
*Not expressly disclosed.*

## Claims

1. Polymeric foam (6, 6′, 6″) comprising graphite particles.

*Known from D1 and D2.*

2. A sensor for the measurement of pressure comprising:

*Known from D1.*

an electrically non-conducting substrate (2, 2′)

a plurality of electrodes (1, 1′) provided at a distance from each other on a first side of the substrate, and

a layer of foam (6, 6′, 6″) according to claim 1 provided on the first side of the substrate and in electrical contact with the electrodes.

| | |
|---|---|
| Known from D2. | 3. The sensor of claim 2, comprising more than two electrodes (1, 1') provided on the substrate (2, 2'). |
| | 4. A device for measuring pressure comprising the sensor of claim 2 or 3 and a processor of electrical circuit capable of converting the electrical resistance between the electrodes into a signal for giving a corresponding pressure reading. |
| | 5. A switch comprising a sensor according to claim 2 or 3. |
| Known from D2. Probably obvious over D2. | 6. A method for making polymeric foam comprising graphite particles, whereby the foam <u>is produced continuously and the graphite particles are sprayed onto the foam before the foam has fully cured</u>. |

## Drafting an amended claim set

1–118

The prior art discloses polymeric foams including graphite particles, as well as sensors and a switch using such foams. What stands out from the application, once we have excluded all that is known, is the presence of graphite particles in bands throughout the foam. The advantages of this distribution of graphite is that an even, predetermined electrical change in resistance per unit change of pressure (presumably compressive pressure applied to the foam) is achieved. Through an appropriate regulation of the process parameters, giving the predictable particle distribution, it is possible to get great reproducibility of identical foam layers and hence identical sensors. With such sensors, highly accurate measurements may be achieved, whilst at the same time guaranteeing consistent and reproducible performance. These advantages are clearly not provided by either of the prior art documents and at the same time they are clearly desirable advantages.

The layered graphite distribution is a consequence of the production process and the production process is made possible through the design of the apparatus. This suggests that there should be no problem with unity of invention. It also suggests that, in view of our client's desire for "the broadest possible protection for my invention", we should add a claim to the apparatus. With the new graphite layered foam recited in claim 1 the original sensor and switch claims would be sustainable.

In the claims of the application as examined there was only one claim to the foam *per se*. However over and above the presence of the graphite particles in the form of a plurality of bands in the foam, there are other characteristics or properties which might usefully be made the subject of sub-claims for the foam. Whilst we do not know an advantage which results from it, we are told that in each band the concentration of graphite particles is denser towards the centre of the band and less dense at the edges of the band. This is clearly a consequence of the particular fabrication technique used. Even without an associated advantage such a claim could provide a useful fall back position to distinguish over as yet unidentified prior art. By the same token, the fact that the particles at the edges of adjacent bands are intermingled may have an advantage, although we do not know what it is, but this too is a consequence of the production process.

We are not given concrete details of exactly how to control the process parameters to achieve the desired goal of having a foam layer which has an even, predetermined electrical change in resistance per unit change of pressure applied to compress it. But we can still have a claim to a foam in which the particle size, the particle distribution within the bands, the thickness of the bands and the total number of bands are selected so that the foam has an even, predetermined change in electrical resistance per unit change of pressure upon compression of the foam.

Finally, there is the specific example of a layer of polyurethane foam having a thickness of 15 mm with 12 or more bands of graphite particles. While this may seem overly specific and narrow, it is the only numerical example that we have and as such it may be worth claiming.

Claims 2 through 5 can be retained as they were, but with the dependencies adjusted to take account of the fact that we now have five claims to the foam rather than merely one.

The method claim, old claim 6 needs to be amended to reflect that fact that we produce a foam in which the graphite particle are arranged in a plurality of bands. The desirable result is achieved through the use of a plurality of spray heads. Claim 6 is limited to a continuous production process, although clearly a continuous production process is not the only way that a layered foam according to the invention could be made. However, there is no basis for removing the continuous process limitation from old claim 6 and given that we have broad claims to the foam *per se*, it would not be worth risking the application to try to broaden the claim in this respect. However, although the process shown in Fig. 3 and described in the application is one in which the spray heads are stationary, there seems to be no good reason for limiting the claims to such an arrangement. In addition, the nozzles are shown in Fig. 3 as being spaced apart along the path of travel of the curing foam. However it is conceivable that the nozzles could be arranged side by side, the spray which they produce being directed to different, spaced-apart locations, along the travelling foam. But if the method claim is not going to be recite the relative movement between the spray heads and the foam, nor the fact that the spray heads are spaced apart along the path of travel of the foam, it will be necessary to refer instead to the fact that the foam produced using the method has particular properties. Of course, claiming a result to be achieved is something of which the Guidelines (Part C, Chapter III, 4.7) disapprove. However, this section of the Guidelines does say that such claims "may be allowed if the invention can only be defined in such terms or cannot otherwise be defined more precisely without unduly restricting the scope of claims and if the result is one which can be directly and positively verified by tests or procedures adequately specified in the description or known to the person skilled in the art and which do not require undue experimentation (see T68/85, O.J. 6 [1987]228)". In the present case one could argue that it would unduly restrict the scope of the claims if we had to recite that the nozzles were spaced apart or if we had to talk about the path of movement of the foam, when arguably no path of movement need exist. This thought rather goes to the meaning of the word continuous. Does the foam really have to move or could you move the chamber 32 with its multiple heads 36? If we are to use this formulation it would be worth explaining why it is appropriate to adopt this formulation and how the requirements of para.4.7 of the Guidelines have been met. A similar consideration arises with respect to the independent apparatus claim in which a result to be achieved is also recited.

1–119     *Writing a response to the Art.96(2) communication*

European Patent Office
D – 80298 München
GERMANY

Dear Sirs

This letter is filed in response to the communication under Article 96(2).

**1. Amendment**

**1.1** Enclosed with this letter is a new set of claims to replace the claims currently on file.

**1.2** Claim 1 is based on originally filed claim 1, with the characterising clause taken from the second sentence of the fifth paragraph on page 2 of the application as filed. This feature is also illustrated in Figures 3 and 4, where, respectively, three and four bands of particles are shown.

**1.3** Independent claim 11 is based on old claim 6 the characterising clause again drawn from the second sentence of the fifth paragraph on page 2 of the application as filed. The feature is also shown in Figure 3, where three spray heads produce three bands of graphite particles.

**1.4** New independent claim 13 is based on Figure 3 and the corresponding disclosure in the fourth and fifth paragraphs on page 5 of the application as filed.

**1.5** Therefore, the subject-matter of new independent claims 1, 11 and 13 satisfies the requirements of Article 123(2) EPC.

**1.6** The features of dependent claims 2 to 10, 12 and 14 are disclosed as follows:

Claim 2: the third sentence of the fifth paragraph of page 2;
Claim 3: fifth sentence in the fifth paragraph on page 2;
Claim 4: sixth sentence in the fifth paragraph on page 2;
Claim 5: fifth sentence in the last paragraph on page 2;
Claim 6: corresponds to old claim 2;

Claim 7: corresponds to old claim 3;
Claim 8: based on the second sentence on page 3;
Claim 9: corresponds to old claim 4;
Claim 10: corresponds to old claim 5;
Claim 12: this is based on the second sentence of the sixth paragraph on page 2; and
Claim 14: based on the last sentence of the fourth paragraph on page 2.

**1.7** Therefore, the subject matter of the dependent claims satisfies the requirements of Article 123(2) EPC.

## 2. Novelty (Article 54 EPC)

**2.1** Independent claim 1 now requires there to be a plurality of bands of graphite particles. In D1 the graphite particles are pre-mixed with the resin. The pre-mixed resin is expanded and cured to form the electrically conductive foam layer 5. Clearly there will be no bands or layers of graphite particles in such a foam. In D2, either a thin layer of a second foam 5, applied about a first foam layer 3, is sprayed with graphite particles whilst rotating in front of a spray nozzle; or a conductive foam layer can be manufactured separately in a continuous process in which graphite particles are sprayed rather than pre-mixed. Again, in each case there will only be a single layer of graphite particles.

**2.2** Independent claim 11 requires that the graphite particles are sprayed onto the foam before the foam has fully cured and that a plurality of spray heads are used to produce a plurality of bands of graphite particles in the foam, each band being laid down by a different spray head. In document D1 the graphite particles are pre-mixed with the polymeric resin. No spray heads are used. In document D2 there is no teaching that, in the continuous process, the graphite particles are sprayed onto an uncured foam — as distinct from the situation where graphite particles are sprayed on to the second foam layer which lies on top of the first foam layer. Moreover, in both the continuous process and the batch process there is no disclosure to use anything more than a single spray nozzle. Nor is there any teaching to use a method which will produce foam having a plurality of bands of graphite particles.

**2.3** Independent claim 13 requires that an apparatus for making a polymeric foam containing graphite particles includes an expansion and curing chamber and a plurality of spray head for spraying graphite particles onto incompletely cured foam in the curing chamber. Document D1 does not teach an apparatus in which spray heads are used. Document D2 does not expressly disclose an apparatus including an expansion and curing chamber, nor does it disclose the use of a plurality of spray heads for spraying graphite particles on to incompletely cured foam.

**2.4** Thus, none of the products, apparatus or methods disclosed in D1 or D2 shows all the features claimed in the independent claims 1, 11 or 13. Therefore, the subject-matter of these claims is novel in the sense of Article 54 EPC.

## 3. Inventive Step (Article 56 EPC)

### Claim 1

**3.1** Polymeric foams including graphite particles are known from both D1 and D2. In D2 the electrically conductive foams are used to facilitate the discharge of static electricity from conveyor belts. In D1 the electricity conductive foam is used in a pressure sensor. As such, D1 is clearly the closest prior art for the assessment of inventive step.

**3.2** The subject matter of claim 1 differs from the disclosure of D1 in that the graphite particles are present in the form of a plurality of bands. The technical effect which is provided by this difference is the greater reproducibility of identical foam layers, and hence identical sensors (page 2, sixth paragraph, last sentence).

- **3.3** Starting from D1, the objective technical problem is to modify the conductive polymeric foam of D1 to achieve this effect. The solution to this problem — the distribution of the graphite particles in a plurality of bands, is set out in claim 1.

- **3.4** This solution is not obvious. D1 itself does not hint at or suggest this solution. In D1 the probes are only intended to detect an excess of pressure with respect of a single threshold. Individual probes are calibrated after production and it is not clear that lack of reproducibility was identified as a problem. D2 is not concerned with changes in conductivity. What is required in D2 is that the conductive foams used in the control of static electricity have regular and predictable conductivity. Problems in this regard are attributed to poor mixing of the graphite particles in the resin prior to foaming. D2 proposes as a solution to this problem the spraying of graphite particles on to the surface of a foam layer. As previously indicated, this approach results in only a single layer or band of graphite particles. As such, D2 does not lead the skilled person to the claimed solution. Moreover, it is to be noted that D2 expressly teaches away from the use of an inhomogeneous particle distribution — since such a distribution gives rise to unpredictable effects and regular conductivity — the very things which D2 seeks to avoid.

- **3.5** Thus, starting from D1, the skilled person would not arrive at the combination of features set out in claim 1.

**Claim 11**

- **3.6** D1 teaches a method of making a polymeric foam, but it is not a continuous process and the graphite particles are pre-mixed with the resin prior to foaming. There is no spraying of graphite particles. In contrast, D2 does teach the production of a polymeric foam comprising graphite particles in a continuous process and the graphite particles are introduced into the foam by spraying. Thus, D2 is the relevant prior art for considering the inventiveness of the subject matter of claim 11. Note that while D2 makes it clear that in the Figure 3 embodiment the graphite particles are sprayed onto the foam layer before it cures, D2 is silent as to the state of cure of the foam at the time when the graphite particles are sprayed on in the continuous process. The preamble for claim 1 is based on D2.

- **3.7** The subject matter of claim 11 differs from that of D1 in that the graphite particles are sprayed from a plurality of spray heads before the foam is fully cured, to produce a plurality of bands of graphite particles in the foam, each band being laid down by a different spray head. The technical effect of these differences is that this method gives rise to a more predictable distribution of graphite particles in the resultant foam, allowing a more reproducible production of identical foam layers. This permits the production of identical sensors. The objective technical problem can be seen to be how to adjust the process of D2 to achieve this technical effect. The problem has been solved, as specified in claim 11, by the plurality of spray heads to spray graphite particles so that they form a plurality of bands of graphite particles, each band being laid down by a different spray head. The solution is not obvious over the cited art. D1 provides no pointer to the use of spray heads, let alone multiple spray heads. D2 while teaching the use of a spray nozzle does not teach the use of multiple spray heads. Moreover, D2 itself is seeking to solve the problem of non-homogeneous particle distribution. Thus, absent any teaching to use multiple spray heads, and given the fact that the use for multiple spray heads gives rise to a non-homogeneous particle distribution, it cannot sensibly be argued that the skilled person would be led to the solution set out in claim 11 following the teaching of D2.

**Claim 13**

- **3.8** D1 teaches the use of a mould in which a resin pre-mixed with the graphite particles is expanded and cured to form an electrically conductive foam and layer. D2 does not explicitly teach the presence of an expansion and curing chamber, although it does teach the use of a single spray nozzle for the application of graphite particles to a layer of foam. The preamble of claim 13 is based on D1. The subject matter of claim 13 differs from the teaching of D1 in that the apparatus includes a plurality of spray heads for spraying graphite particles onto incompletely cured foam in the curing chamber, the spray heads being arranged within the apparatus to produce a plurality of bands of graphite particles within the foam, each spray head producing one of the plurality of bands. The technical effect of these differences is that the apparatus permits the production of electrically conductive foam with more predictable properties and greater reproducibility of identical foam layers. The objective technical problem can thus be seen to be the adaptation of the apparatus of D1 to achieve this technical effect. The problem is solved using the construction specified in claim 13. This solution is not obvious. D1 itself provides no teaching to spray graphite particles. There is such teaching in D2. However in D2 there is no teaching to use a plurality of spray heads nor to produce a plurality of bands of graphite particles within the foam. As already indicated, D2 expressly teaches against non-homogeneous particle distribution. The skilled person, starting from D1, trying to apply the teaching of D2, would not be led to produce an apparatus as claimed in claim 13.

3.9 If D2 is taken as the appropriate starting point for the assessment of inventive step, the differences between the claimed subject matter and D2 is the presence of a plurality of spray heads arranged within the apparatus to produce a plurality of bands of graphite particles within the foam, each spray head producing one of the plurality of bands, the spraying being onto incompletely cured foam. The technical effects of these differences are as set out in the preceding paragraphs. The objective technical problem can therefore be seen to be how to modify the apparatus of D2 to achieve these desirable effects. Claim 13 provides a solution to this problem. This solution is not obvious. As already indicated, D2 provides not only no teaching towards the use of multiple spray heads, but teaches against the use of non-homogeneous particle distribution. Starting from D2, the skilled person would clearly not arrive at an apparatus as claimed in claim 13 without the exercise of inventive ingenuity.

3.10 It can therefore be seen that the subject matter of each of the independent claims is inventive over the cited art and hence the requirements of Article 56 EPC have been met.

3.11 The dependent claims, depending from allowable independent claims must also be considered to be allowable.

## 4. Unity of Invention (Article 82 EPC)

4.1 New claim 13 to an apparatus for making a polymeric foam has been introduced to give the Applicant the fuller protection to which he is entitled. As is clear from the Guidelines, C.III.7.2(iii), rule 30 EPC permits "in addition to an independent claim for a given product, an independent claim for a process specially adapted for the manufacture of the said product and an independent claim for an apparatus or means specifically designed for carrying out the said process". It is believed that claims 1, 11 and 13 meet this requirement.

4.2 As required by rule 30 EPC, the three independent claims share the same special technical feature — the presence of a plurality of bands of graphite particles in a polymeric foam. Claim 1 claims such a foam *per se*. Claim 11 is a claim to a process specially adapted for the manufacture of such a foam. Claim 11 specifies that the foam produced by the method has a plurality of bands of graphite particles. Claim 13 claims an apparatus specially designed for carrying out the process of claim 11. This apparatus claim also refers to the presence of a plurality of bands of graphite particles in the foam. The method and apparatus claims 11 and 13 both refer to the use/presence of a plurality of spray heads, each spray head producing one of the plurality of bands.

**4.3** Both claim 11 and claim 13 refer to a result to be achieved — the production of a plurality of bands of graphite particles in the foam made using the method/apparatus. Nevertheless, it is believed that the requirements of Guidelines C.III.4.7 are met. Certainly the skilled person can readily verify, using very simple physical tests and inspections, the presence of such bands of graphite particles in any foam produced using the method/apparatus. No undue experimentation would be required. The alternative to referring to the result to be achieved would be to specify precisely the relationship between the various spray heads and the foam during manufacture. However many possible arrangements can be envisaged and not all of these could readily be covered in a single clear and concise claim. For example, the spray heads could be arranged side by side but with the sprays which they produce directed at spaced-apart locations on the foam. The heads could move and the foam could be stationary, etc.

Annex:   New Claims 1 to 14.

**CLAIMS**

1. A polymeric foam (6, 6′, 6″) comprising graphite particles, characterised in that the graphite particles are dispersed within the foam in the form of a plurality of bands (61, 62, 63, 64).

2. A foam according to claim 1, wherein in each band the concentration of graphite particles is denser towards the centre of the band and less dense at the edges of the band.

3. A foam according to claim 2, wherein the graphite particles at the edges of adjacent bands are intermingled.

4. A foam as claimed in any one of claims 1 to 3, wherein the particle size, the particle distribution within the bands, the thickness of the bands and the total number of bands are selected so that the foam has an even, predetermined change in electrical resistance per unit change of pressure upon compression of the foam.

5. A foam according to any one of claims 1 to 4, wherein the foam is a polyurethane foam, the foam being 15 mm thick and having at least twelve bands of graphite particles.

6. A sensor for the measurement of pressure, comprising an electrically non-conductive substrate (2, 2′), and a plurality of electrodes (1, 1′) provided at a distance from each other on a first side of the substrate and a layer of foam (6, 6′, 6″) according to any one of claims 1 to 5 provided on the first side of the substrate and in electrical contact with the electrodes.

7. A sensor as claimed in claim 6, comprising more than two electrodes (1, 1′) provided on the substrate (2, 2′).

8. A sensor as claimed in claim 7, wherein the substrate is a printed circuit board on which the electrodes have been formed by etching.

9. A device for measuring pressure, comprising the sensor of any one of claims 6 to 8 and a processor or electrical circuit capable of converting the electrical resistance between the electrodes into a signal for giving a corresponding pressure reading.

10. A switch comprising a sensor according to any one of claims 6 to 8.

11. A method of making polymeric foam comprising graphite particles, the method being performed in a continuous process in which graphite particles are sprayed on to the foam, characterised in that the graphite particles are sprayed from a plurality of spray heads on to the foam before the foam has fully cured, to produce a plurality of bands of graphite particles in the foam, each band being laid down by a different spray head.

12. A method as claimed in claim 11, wherein the number, position and design of the spray heads are such that, after adjustment of the appropriate process parameters, there is produced a foam layer having an even, predetermined change in resistance per unit change of pressure upon compression of the foam.

13. An apparatus for making a polymeric foam containing graphite particles, the apparatus including an expansion and curing chamber (32) for curing the foam, characterised in that the apparatus includes a plurality of spray heads (36) for spraying graphite particles on to incompletely cured foam in the curing chamber, the spray heads being arranged within the apparatus to produce a plurality of bands of graphite particles within the foam, each spray head producing one of the plurality of bands.

14. An apparatus as in claim 13 having a computerised control system for regulating the process parameters.

## 5. Worked example using EQE 2005 Paper B

*Understanding and annotating the paper*

The following pages indicate how the 2005 B paper could be marked up on a first reading. Shading is used to indicate parts of the paper which relate to prior art.

**Description of the Application**

The invention relates to a wind indicator for indicating whether a sail of a sailing vessel is optimally orientated with respect to the wind direction. An optimal orientation of the sail maximises the speed of the vessel.

As shown in Fig. 1, a known wind indicator 1, attached to a sail 2 of a sailing vessel 3, indicates to the sailor, whether the sail 2 has the optimum orientation relative to the wind direction W. The wind indicator 1 comprises a piece of light-weight, flexible material, one end of which is fixed to the sail 2, whereas the other end is free and can be moved by the wind. The piece of light-weight, flexible material can be a yarn or a ribbon.

At least one such wind indicator 1 is attached to each side of the sail 2 so that, when sailing, at least one ribbon is on the so-called windward side of the sail (facing the wind) and at least one ribbon is on the so-called leeward side of the sail (facing away from the wind).

Figs. 2A to 2C illustrate how the wind indicator 1 may be used to distinguish between an optimal and a less advantageous orientation of the sail 2 with respect to the wind direction W. The wind indicator on the windward side of the sail 2 is shown as a solid line and the one on the leeward side of the sail 2 is shown in dotted lines. If the free end of a ribbon on either the windward or leeward side of the sail 2 is fluttering (Fig. 2A and 2B respectively), due to turbulent airflow, then the sail 2 is not optimally orientated with respect to the wind. Only when the free ends of the ribbons on both the windward and the leeward sides of the sail 2 trail back in a substantially straight manner (as shown in Fig. 2C), i.e. the airflow is laminar, is the orientation of the sail 2 optimal with respect to the wind direction W.

A problem may arise when a ribbon is wet. The free end of a wet ribbon may stick to the sail and can then no longer be moved by the wind. It is difficult for a sailor to manually free a wet ribbon which has become stuck to the sail. The strength of the wind flow along the sail is often not sufficient to free the ribbon from the sail. The same problem may occur when using a yarn, instead of a ribbon.

It is therefore an object of the invention to provide a wind indicator whose free end does not remain stuck to the sail.

This object is achieved by a wind indicator according to appended claim 1.

A spacing member is positioned between the sail and the fixed end of the ribbon such that a distance is maintained between them. The wind is therefore able to flow between the sail and the ribbon. This helps to detach a ribbon that has become stuck to the sail.

Further advantageous embodiments of the invention are the subject of the dependent claims.

The drawings will be briefly described as follows:

Fig. 1 shows a sailing vessel fitted with known wind indicators.

Figs. 2A to 2C show the known wind indicators under different sailing conditions.

Fig. 3 shows a wind indicator according to the present invention.

Fig. 4A shows the wind flow in the region of the wind indicator of Fig. 3.

Figs. 4B and 4C show the wind flow in the region of further wind indicators according to the present invention.

Referring to Fig. 3, a wind indicator 1 comprises a ribbon 6 and a spacing member in the form of an arm 5. The ribbon 6 comprises a fixed end 6a, fixed to the arm 5 and a free end 6b. When the arm 5 is tubular, the fixed end 6a of the ribbon 6 can be pushed into the arm 5 and fastened therein by any suitable manner, such as by gluing. The ribbon 6 is an example of a piece of light-weight, flexible material suitable for wind indicators. A suitable length of the ribbon is between 5 and 20 cm.

The arm 5 is attached to a sail by a wedge shaped attachment member 4. The attachment member 4 is provided with a flat lower surface 7 having a waterproof adhesive layer, which is protected by a removable protective layer 8, so that the attachment member 4 can easily be attached to the sail. The attachment member 4 and the arm 5 may be formed as a single part or as two separate parts. In the latter case the arm 5 may be glued into an opening in the inclined surface 9 of the attachment member 4.

The arm 5 keeps the fixed end 6a of the ribbon 6 at a distance from the sail so that the wind can flow between the underside of the ribbon 6 and the sail. The underside of the ribbon 6 is the side of the ribbon 6 facing the sail, when in normal use.

As shown in Figs. 4A, 4B and 4C, the wedge shape of the attachment member 4 contributes to the separation of a wet ribbon 6 from the sail 2. The wedge shaped attachment member 4 is arranged such that, in normal use, the wind flows over the inclined surface 9 as indicated by the arrows. In other words, the thin end of the wedge shaped attachment member 4 is directed towards the front edge of the sail 2. The angle of inclination of the surface 9 relative to the flat lower surface 7 is in the range of 10°-20° to minimise disturbance of the airflow along the sail 2. The inclined surface 9 can be planar or concavely curved.

1/2

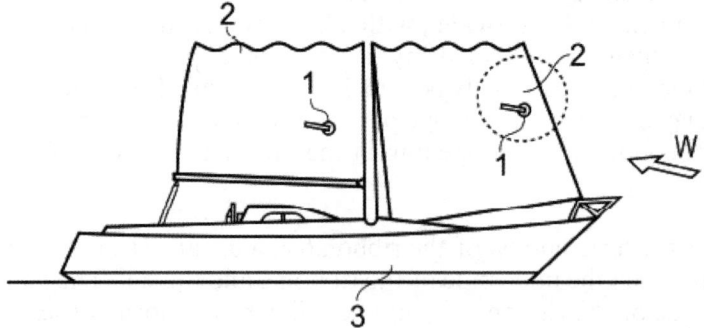

Fig. 1 PRIOR ART

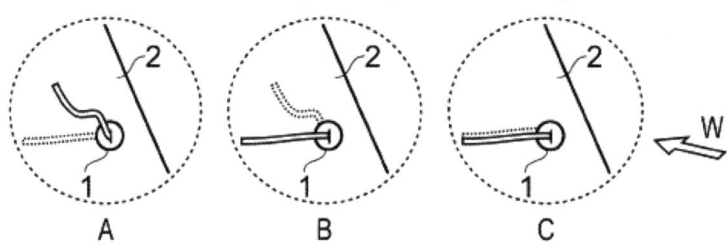

Fig. 2 PRIOR ART

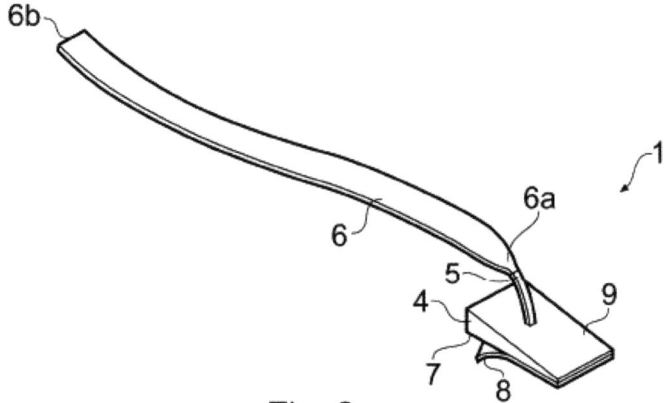

Fig. 3

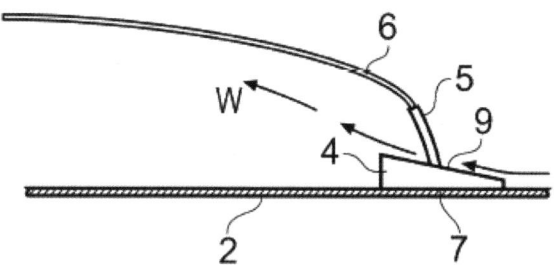

Fig. 4A

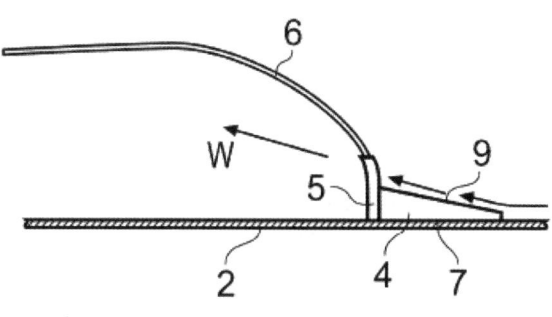

Fig. 4B

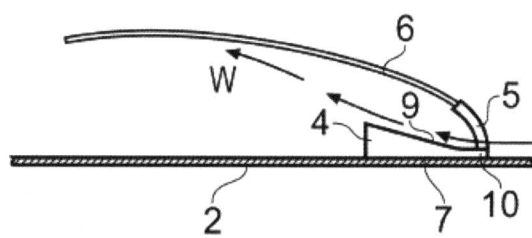

Fig. 4C

As shown in Fig. 4A, a portion of the wind, which flows along the sail 2 and approaches the wind indicator 1, is redirected by the inclined surface 9 of the attachment member 4 towards the underside of the ribbon 6. The redirected wind portion applies a force to the underside of the ribbon 6 which keeps the ribbon away from the sail 2. The width of the inclined surface 9 is greater than the width of the arm 5 and greater than the width of the ribbon 6, so that the redirected wind portion engages with the full width of the underside of the ribbon 6. In order to achieve the same effect of redirecting the wind, other forms for the attachment member 4 may be used, provided that they include a suitably inclined surface.

The same effect of redirecting the wind towards the underside of the ribbon 6 may be achieved by other locations of the arm 5 relative to the attachment member 4. For example, as shown in Fig. 4B, the arm 5 is attached at the thick end of the wedge-shaped attachment member 4. The arm 5 extends beyond the height of the thick end of the wedge shaped attachment member 4. In Fig. 4C, the arm 5 is attached at the thin end of the wedge shaped attachment member 4. The arm 5 is fixed on an extension 10 of the attachment member 4.

## Claims

1. Wind indicator (1) for a sail (2) comprising a wind indicating ribbon (6), the ribbon (6) having a fixed end (6a) and a free end (6b) characterised in that the wind indicator (1) further comprises a spacing member (5) to which the fixed end (6a) of the ribbon (6) is fixed, such that, when the wind indicator (1) is attached to the sail (2), the spacing member (5) keeps the ribbon (6) spaced from the sail (2).

2. Wind indicator (1) according to claim 1 wherein the spacing member (5) is an arm.

3. Wind indicator (1) according to claim 1 or 2 further comprising an attachment member (4) having a flat lower surface (7) which is adapted to be glued on to the sail (2).

4. Wind indicator (1) according to claim 3 wherein the spacing member (5) and the attachment member (4) are formed as one piece.

5. Wind indicator (1) according to claim 3 or 4, whereby the attachment member (4) comprises a surface (9) which is inclined with respect to the flat lower surface (7).

6. Wind indicator (1) according to claim 5 wherein attachment member (4) is wedge-shaped.

## Communication

1. D1 and D2, which were both published before the priority date of the present application, are referred to in this communication.

2. Claim 1 is not allowable under Art. 52(1) EPC, since its subject-matter is not new with respect to D1 in the sense of Art. 54(1) and (2) EPC.

   D1 discloses a wind indicator (100) for a sail comprising a wind indicating ribbon (20), the ribbon (20) having a fixed end (21) and a free end (22), whereby the wind indicator (100) further comprises a spacing member (50) to which the fixed end (21) of the ribbon (20) is fixed, such that, when the wind indicator (100) is attached to the sail, the spacing member (50) keeps the ribbon (20) spaced from the sail.

   Furthermore, the wind indicator of claim 1 is also not new with respect to the document D2 (see for example Figs. 1 and 2 and the last paragraph).

3. The subject-matter of claims 2 to 6 does not meet the requirements of Art. 52(1) EPC, since it is not new in the sense of Art. 54(1) and (2) EPC, for the following reasons:

   The arm of claim 2 is known from document D2 (see reference 12).

   The attachment member according to claim 3 is known from D1 (see reference 50) and from D2 (see references 11 in Fig. 1 and 15 in Fig. 2).

   From D1 it is also known to form the attachment member and spacing member as one piece (see reference 50) as defined in claim 4.

   The inclined surface according to claim 5 is disclosed in D1 (see Fig. 2) and also in D2 (see Fig. 2).

   The wedge shape according to claim 6 is known from Fig. 2 of D1 and from Fig. 2 of D2.

4. It would also appear that the embodiment shown in Fig. 3 of the application could be obtained by replacing the attachment member 11 of D2 (see Fig. 1) with the wedge shaped attachment member 50 of D1 (see Fig. 2).

5. The applicant is invited to submit an amended set of claims, which takes account of the above objections.

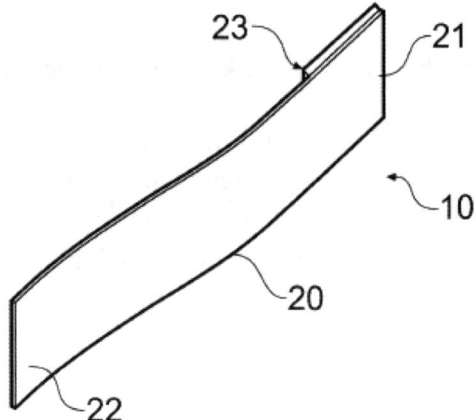

Fig. 1

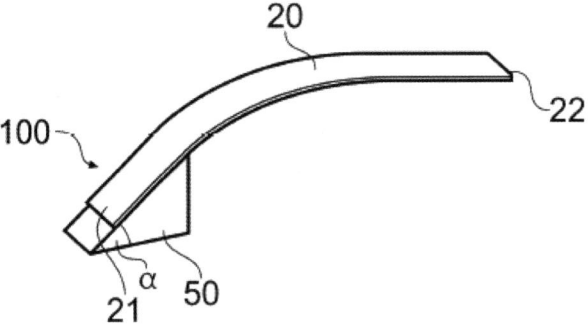

Fig. 2

## DOCUMENT D1 (STATE OF THE ART)

The invention relates to a wind indicator for indicating the correct adjustment of a sail of a sailing vessel with respect to the direction of the wind.

Fig. 1 illustrates a conventional wind indicator 10. The wind indicator 10 comprises a ribbon 20. One end 21 of the ribbon 20 is fixed to a sail, e.g. via an adhesive layer 23. The other end 22 of the ribbon 20 is moved by the wind.

Long ribbons, especially when they are wet, tend to stick to the surface of the sail. The invention solves this problem.

Fig. 2 illustrates a wind indicator 100 in accordance with the present invention. A rigid base 50, on which the ribbon 20 is attached, has a thickness which increases in the direction of the end 22 of the ribbon 20. This creates a wide gap between the ribbon 20 and the sail, thereby reducing the risk that the ribbon 20 sticks to the sail.

To minimize disturbance of the airflow by the base 50, the inclination angle < of the base 50 should not exceed 45°.

The wind indicator 100 may be glued to the sail. The base 50 may comprise an adhesive layer protected by a thin detachable layer.

1/1

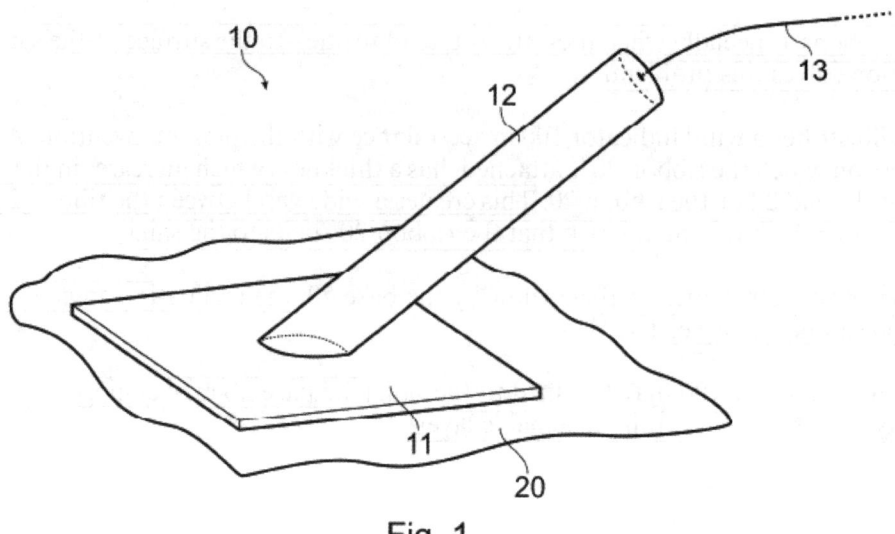

Fig. 1

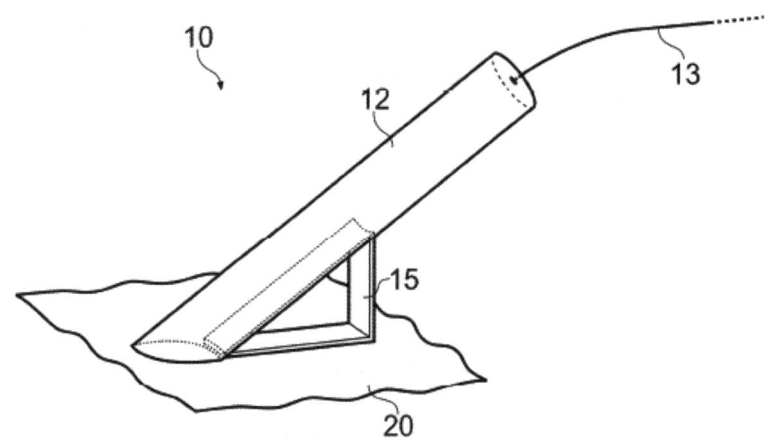

Fig. 2

## DOCUMENT D2 (STATE OF THE ART)

The invention relates to a device that indicates whether the airflow on a sail is laminar or turbulent.

For this purpose, a piece of flexible, light-weight material, such as a yarn, is attached to the sail. If the airflow along the sail is laminar, the yarn trails in a straight manner. If the airflow is turbulent, the yarn flutters irregularly.

A disadvantage of a yarn is that, when it is wet, it sticks to the sail. The invention overcomes this disadvantage.

The airflow indicator 10 of the present invention, as shown in Fig. 1, comprises a cylindrical element 12 and a yarn 13. The yarn 13 is fixed at one end of the element 12, for example with glue. The element 12 is inclined relative to the sail 20, so that the disturbance to the airflow along the sail 20 is minimised. The element 12 is attached to a base 11. The underside of the base 11 has an adhesive layer for attaching the airflow indicator 10 to the sail 20.

The airflow indicator 10 may alternatively comprise a triangular support 15 instead of base 11, as shown in Fig. 2. This support 15 is attached to the element 12 and to the sail 20. The support 15 reduces the risk of the element 12 breaking or being ripped off the sail 20 in strong winds. The width of the support 15 is less than the diameter of the cylindrical element 12 so that, in use, disturbance to the airflow due to the support 15 is minimal.

The surface of the triangular support 15 which is directly in contact with the element 12 has a concave form adapted to receive the element 12. The triangular support 15 shown in Fig. 2 has a frame-like structure, but alternatively may be solid.

It is noted that the airflow indicators described above may have a ribbon instead of the yarn 13.

## CLIENT'S LETTER

Dear Ms Carrie Cannon,

In reply to your letter we confirm that we are still interested in achieving patent protection for our wind indicator, despite the communication of the European Patent Office.

Our wind indicator offers a quicker detachment of a wet ribbon that has stuck to the sail, and prevents it from sticking again, even in light winds. This has been successfully tested in wind tunnels. We are of the opinion that both cited documents fail to suggest a wind indicator with such an advantageous effect.

I would like to point out that the claims as filed define a ribbon as the flexible part moved by the wind. Please make sure that other alternatives such as a yarn, which is also part of our product line, are not excluded from the scope of the claims.

Please take all the necessary steps to achieve the broadest possible protection for our invention, taking account of the above comments.

Yours sincerely,

I. Ayesir

Brig, Privateer & Co.

**1–120** *Establishing patentable subject matter*

The following pages indicate how the client's application can be divided into novel features and features found in the prior art. As before, shading has been used to indicate a lack of novelty.

### Description of the Application

The invention relates to a wind indicator for indicating whether a sail of a sailing vessel is optimally orientated with respect to the wind direction. An optimal orientation of the sail maximises the speed of the vessel.

As shown in Fig. 1, a known wind indicator 1, attached to a sail 2 of a sailing vessel 3, indicates to the sailor, whether the sail 2 has the optimum orientation relative to the wind direction W. The wind indicator 1 comprises a piece of light-weight, flexible material, one end of which is fixed to the sail 2, whereas the other end is free and can be moved by the wind. The piece of light-weight, flexible material can be a yarn or a ribbon.

At least one such wind indicator 1 is attached to each side of the sail 2 so that, when sailing, at least one ribbon is on the so-called windward side of the sail (facing the wind) and at least one ribbon is on the so-called leeward side of the sail (facing away from the wind).

Figs. 2A to 2C illustrate how the wind indicator 1 may be used to distinguish between an optimal and a less advantageous orientation of the sail 2 with respect to the wind direction W. The wind indicator on the windward side of the sail 2 is shown as a solid line and the one on the leeward side of the sail 2 is shown in dotted lines. If the free end of a ribbon on either the windward or leeward side of the sail 2 is fluttering (Fig. 2A and 2B respectively), due to turbulent airflow, then the sail 2 is not optimally orientated with respect to the wind. Only when the free ends of the ribbons on both the windward and the leeward sides of the sail 2 trail back in a substantially straight manner (as shown in Fig. 2C), i.e. the airflow is laminar, is the orientation of the sail 2 optimal with respect to the wind direction W.

A problem may arise when a ribbon is wet. The free end of a wet ribbon may stick to the sail and can then no longer be moved by the wind. It is difficult for a sailor to manually free a wet ribbon which has become stuck to the sail. The strength of the wind flow along the sail is often not sufficient to free the ribbon from the sail. The same problem may occur when using a yarn, instead of a ribbon.

It is therefore an object of the invention to provide a wind indicator whose free end does not remain stuck to the sail.

This object is achieved by a wind indicator according to appended claim 1.

A spacing member is positioned between the sail and the fixed end of the ribbon such that a distance is maintained between them. The wind is therefore able to flow between the sail and the ribbon. This helps to detach a ribbon that has become stuck to the sail.

Further advantageous embodiments of the invention are the subject of the dependent claims.

The drawings will be briefly described as follows:

Fig. 1 shows a sailing vessel fitted with known wind indicators.

Figs. 2A to 2C show the known wind indicators under different sailing conditions.

Fig. 3 shows a wind indicator according to the present invention.

Fig. 4A shows the wind flow in the region of the wind indicator of Fig. 3.

Figs. 4B and 4C show the wind flow in the region of further wind indicators according to the present invention.

Referring to Fig. 3, a wind indicator 1 comprises a ribbon 6 and a spacing member in the form of an arm 5. The ribbon 6 comprises a fixed end 6a, fixed to the arm 5 and a free end 6b. When the arm 5 is tubular, the fixed end 6a of the ribbon 6 can be pushed into the arm 5 and fastened therein by any suitable manner, such as by gluing. The ribbon 6 is an example of a piece of light-weight, flexible material suitable for wind indicators. A suitable length of the ribbon is between 5 and 20 cm.

The arm 5 is attached to a sail by a wedge shaped attachment member 4. The attachment member 4 is provided with a flat lower surface 7 having a waterproof adhesive layer, which is protected by a removable protective layer 8, so that the attachment member 4 can easily be attached to the sail. The attachment member 4 and the arm 5 may be formed as a single part or as two separate parts. In the latter case the arm 5 may be glued into an opening in the inclined surface 9 of the attachment member 4.

The arm 5 keeps the fixed end 6a of the ribbon 6 at a distance from the sail so that the wind can flow between the underside of the ribbon 6 and the sail. The underside of the ribbon 6 is the side of the ribbon 6 facing the sail, when in normal use.

As shown in Figs. 4A, 4B and 4C, the wedge shape of the attachment member 4 contributes to the separation of a wet ribbon 6 from the sail 2. The wedge shaped attachment member 4 is arranged such that, in normal use, the wind flows over the inclined surface 9 as indicated by the arrows. In other words, the thin end of the wedge shaped attachment member 4 is directed towards the front edge of the sail 2. The angle of inclination of the surface 9 relative to the flat lower surface 7 is in the range of 10°-20° to minimise disturbance of the airflow along the sail 2. The inclined surface 9 can be planar or concavely curved.

As shown in Fig. 4A, a portion of the wind, which flows along the sail 2 and approaches the wind indicator 1, is redirected by the inclined surface 9 of the attach-

194  Complete Guide to Passing the EQE

ment member 4 towards the underside of the ribbon 6. The redirected wind portion applies a force to the underside of the ribbon 6 which keeps the ribbon away from the sail 2. The width of the inclined surface 9 is greater than the width of the arm 5 and greater than the width of the ribbon 6, so that the redirected wind portion engages with the full width of the underside of the ribbon 6. In order to achieve the same effect of redirecting the wind, other forms for the attachment member 4 may be used, provided that they include a suitably inclined surface.

The same effect of redirecting the wind towards the underside of the ribbon 6 may be achieved by other locations of the arm 5 relative to the attachment member 4. For example, as shown in Fig. 4B, the arm 5 is attached at the thick end of the wedge-shaped attachment member 4. The arm 5 extends beyond the height of the thick end of the wedge shaped attachment member 4. In Fig. 4C, the arm 5 is attached at the thin end of the wedge shaped attachment member 4. The arm 5 is fixed on an extension 10 of the attachment member 4.

**Claims**

1. Wind indicator (1) for a sail (2) comprising a wind indicating ribbon (6), the ribbon (6) having a fixed end (6a) and a free end (6b) characterised in that the wind indicator (1) further comprises a spacing member (5) to which the fixed end (6a) of the ribbon (6) is fixed, such that, when the wind indicator (1) is attached to the sail (2), the spacing member (5) keeps the ribbon (6) spaced from the sail (2).

2. Wind indicator (1) according to claim 1 wherein the spacing member (5) is an arm.

3. Wind indicator (1) according to claim 1 or 2 further comprising an attachment member (4) having a flat lower surface (7) which is adapted to be glued on to the sail (2).

4. Wind indicator (1) according to claim 3 wherein the spacing member (5) and the attachment member (4) are formed as one piece.

5. Wind indicator (1) according to claim 3 or 4, whereby the attachment member (4) comprises a surface (9) which is inclined with respect to the flat lower surface (7).

6. Wind indicator (1) according to claim 5 wherein attachment member (4) is wedge-shaped.

**1–121**  *Drafting an amended claim set*

The prior art discloses wind indicators including a spacing member that keeps the ribbon spaced from the sail. What stands out from the application, once we have excluded all that is known, is the function of the inclined surface of the attachment member to direct wind towards the underside of the ribbon (that is the side of the ribbon which faces the sail in normal use). This function contributes to the separation of a wet ribbon that has stuck to a sail. The difficulty of freeing a stuck ribbon is mentioned in the third sentence on page 2 of the application. Moreover, the object of the invention is to provide a wind indication whose free end does not <u>remain</u> stuck to the sail. In lines 13 and 14 of page 2 there is mention of wind flow between the sail and the ribbon helping "to detach a ribbon that has become stuck to the sail". The inventive solution is mentioned in the first sentence of the fourth paragraph on page 3 of the specification, and explained more fully in the first paragraph on page 4. This is also the sole distinction referred to (in the second paragraph) in the client's letter.

The problem of detaching the stuck ribbon is not mentioned in either of the prior art documents and neither of them addresses this problem.

Moreover, nothing in either of the two documents when they are taken separately teaches or suggests the construction of the wind indicator which would direct wind towards the underside of the ribbon. If the two documents are taken together is there anything that might lead the skilled person to construct a wind indicator in which wind would be directed to the underside of the ribbon? In paragraph four of the communication, the Examiner implicitly suggests that there is: "the embodiment shown in Figure 3 could be obtained by replacing the attachment member 11 of D2 (see Figure 1) with a wedge shaped attachment 50 of D1 (see Figure 2)".

In D1 the wedge–shaped base 50 acts as a support for the ribbon 20, providing both an attachment surface for the ribbon and a stand off to distance the free end of the ribbon from the sail. No other function is ascribed to the wedge shape of the base, but in the fifth paragraph of D1 we are taught to minimise the disturbance of the air flow by the base. In D2 there is also positive teaching to minimise the disturbance to the air flow due to the support. In the Figure 1 embodiment the support is flat and not ramped. In the Figure 2 embodiment there is a sloping support, but it is in the wind shadow of the cylindrical element 12. Moreover the width of the support (15) is made less than the diameter of the cylindrical element 12 which supports the yarn — "so that, in use, disturbance to the airflow due to the support 15 is minimal".

There is nothing in D1 or D2 pointing towards the combination suggested by the examiner. Such an arrangement appears more likely to create a disturbance of the air flow than, for example, the Figure 2 embodiment of D2. Given that the common teaching of the prior art is to avoid disturbing the air flow, the skilled person following the teaching of the prior art would not make such a combination.

So the invention that we want to claim appears non obvious.

Once we have restricted the independent claim to direct wind to the underside of the ribbon, which will involve using features from examined claims 3 and 5, we are not left with any particularly strong dependent claims which would provide a good full-back position. Replacement dependant claims should be directed towards:
The width of the inclined surface being greater than the width of the spacing member and the ribbon;
The angle between the inclined surface and the attachment surface with the attachment member;
The embodiment of figures 4A to 4C;
The inclined surface being either planar or concavely curved.

The novel and inventive feature which we need to add to claim 1 is the use of an inclined surface to direct wind on to the underside of the ribbon (a term which the client wants us to broaden). The inclined surface is provided by an attachment member. Without some reference, the use of the word "inclined" is unclear. In the application the reference with respect to which the inclination is determined is that surface of the attachment means which is to be glued to the sail - which is termed the lower surface. These features are recited in the combination of claims 3 and 5, but neither of these includes the wind-directing feature. However these claims do contain two limitations which stand out as undesirably narrow -

    (i) That the lower surface is flat;
    (ii) That the lower surface is adapted to be glued to the sail.

Clearly the wind indicator could be secured to a sail in some other way than by gluing, such as magnetically, by stitching, riveting, or by use of some other mechanical fastener. Equally clearly, the base of the wind indicator does not need to be flat - it could be concave or convex (perhaps to form a matching pair of indicators that mate with each other), it could have a serrated or otherwise roughened surface, etc. Can we omit these two features without contravening article 123(2)? If we can, we should omit them because otherwise we will lose marks for having an independent claim which is narrower than it need be. We would also lose the marks which we could earn for arguing why these changes are permissible. But if we cannot make these amendments without contravening Article 123(2) we should not make them - as we would be docked points for such contravention of Article 123(2).

We need to apply the Houdaille test (T331/87) which is discussed in the Guidelines (C.VI.5.3.10) and which is mentioned earlier in this chapter. We can make each amendment if

  i) The relevant feature is not explained as essential in the disclosure;
  ii) The relevant feature is not indispensable for the function of the invention in light of the technical problem the invention seeks to solve;
  iii) The replacement or removal of the feature requires no real modification of other features to compensate for the change.

These requirements <u>are</u> all met for both the flatness of the base and the adaptation for fastening with glue — but we will need to explain this in our response to the communication.

Another amendment which we want to make is that requested by the client — the broadening of claim 1 to cover the use both of ribbon and yarn as the indicator element. Of course extending the protection conferred, by broadening an independent claim, pre-grant does not contravene Article 123(3). Pre-grant, the only issue is Article 123(2) — does the amendment add subject matter?

In the discussion of the prior art on page 1 of the application we are told that a known wind indicator "comprises a piece of light-weight, flexible material"... which "can be a yarn or a ribbon". Also, when the problem of the indictor element sticking to the sail is discussed, in the first paragraph of page 2 of the application, we are told that "the same problem may occur when using a yarn, instead of a ribbon". Finally, in the discussion of figure 3 (which on page 2, line 23, we are told "shows a wind indictor according to the present invention") we are told that "the ribbon 6 is an <u>example</u> of a <u>piece of light-weight, flexible material</u> suitable for wind indicators" (emphasis added). Thus we are told that ribbon is an example of the class of "light-weight, flexible material suitable for wind indicators". We are also told that yarn is another example from the class of suitable materials. Hence, we will not be adding matter by substituting "piece of light-weight, flexible material" for "ribbon" in the claims.

Finally, the client has (as usual in paper B) asked that we get the broadest possible protection for the invention. Given this slight encouragement one might consider adding a claim directed to a sail including wind indicators (we are told that they are used on both sides of the sail), and even a claim to a sailing vessel including such a sail. There is scant express basis for such claims, but the description of the operation of the invention refers to the presence of the sail — since the wind indicators according to the invention are only ever used when mounted on a sail. And the sails which are mentioned are only ever used on sailing vessels. So it is not unreasonable to suggest that there is sufficient basis for the addition of such claims. It is unlikely that the addition of such claims would attract more than a few marks, but in the real world such claims can have value in licensing and other commercial discussions. They may sometimes have value in litigation.

**1–122**    *Writing a response to the article 96(2) communication*

EPO

Munich

Dear Sirs,
This letter is filed in response to the communication under article 96(2).

 1. Amendment

 1.1 Enclosed with this letter is a new set of claims to replace the claims currently on file.

1.2 Claim 1 is based on originally claims 1,3 and 5, with the characterising clause based on page 4, first paragraph last sentence; and page 3, second paragraph, first sentence.

1.3 The term "ribbon", which was used in claim 1 as filed, has been replaced with "piece of light-weight, flexible material". Basis for this amendment can be found at lines four and five of page 3. It is also noted that, as mentioned in line four and five on page 2, the problem of the indicator element sticking to the sail is common to ribbons and yarns.

1.4 In incorporating into claim 1 features of claim 3 and 5, two features of claim 3 have been omitted: Namely, that the lower surface is flat and that the surface is adapted to be glued on. Applying the test from the Guidelines C.VI.5.3.10, it can be seen that "neither feature is explained as essential in the disclosure; neither feature is related to the function of the invention (the features are not indispensable for the function of the invention in light of the technical problem invention seeks to solve); and the replacement or removal of the feature requires no real modification of other features to compensate for the change."

1.5 The expression "the spacing member and the attachment member are located with a respect to each other so that" is used so that all the disclosed embodiments are covered by a single independent claim. In particular, the examiner's attention is drawn to the first sentence of the last paragraph of the description of the application, which explains that the relative location of the spacing member (termed "arm" in the passage of interest) and the attachment means should be chosen – along with the form of the attachment means (see last line of the penultimate paragraph of the description) to achieve the same effect of redirecting the wind towards the underside of the ribbon.

1.6 The way in which the wind indicator is attached to a sail is connected with neither the overall function of the wind indicator (detection of laminar or turbulent flow) nor with solving the problem of how to unstick an indicator element which has become stuck to a sail.

1.7 Thus, it is believed that none of the amendments to claim 1 contravenes article 123(2).

1.8 Dependant claims. The features of the dependant claims are disclosed as follows:

Claim 2 is based on line 25 of page 3.

Claim 3 is based on line 27 of page 3.

Claim 4 is based on lines 4 to 7 on page 4. Although the spacing member is here referred to as being an arm, it is clearly not essential that the spacing member have this form for the redirected wind portion to engage with the full width of the underside of the ribbon.

Claim 5 is based on Figure 4C and page 4, lines 15 to 16.

Claim 6 is based on Figure 4B, and page 4, lines 12 to 14.

Claim 7 is based on Figures 3 and 4A.

Claim 8 is based on page 3, lines 12 to 14.

It is clearly not essential that the spacing member be glued into the opening as it could as easily be wedged, threaded into place or welded in place.

Claim 9 is old claim 4.

Claim 10 is old claim 6.

Claim 11 is a new dependent claim for a sail, and is based on Figures 3 and 4, the passage from the second paragraph on page three to the end of the first paragraph on page four of the application, and the four paragraphs from page one of the application.

Claim 12 is a new dependent claim for a sailing vessel, and is based on the first paragraph of page 1.

It is therefore submitted that none of the amendments to the claims contravenes A123(2) EPC.

Novelty (Article 54 EPC)

Claim 1 requires that the spacing number and the attachment number are located with respect with each other such that, in use, the inclined surface redirects a portion of wind towards the side of the piece of light-weight, flexible material that is arranged to face the sail in normal use. This feature is absent from both D1 and D2.

In D1 the base, 50, has an inclined surface, but this is not arranged to redirect wind towards the underside of the ribbon. Rather, redirected wind will tend to impinge on the upper surface of the ribbon (i.e. the side of the ribbon opposite to that specified in the claim).

In D2, the support 15 (Figure 2) has an inclined surface, but this is completely obscured by the cylindrical element 12 and is incapable of directing wind to the underside of the yarn 13. Even if one considered the free end of the cylindrical element 12 to be the spacing member and the sail end (the foot) of that element to be the attachment member, so that the uppermost surface of the foot of the cylinder became the inclined surface, that inclined surface does not act to redirect a portion of the wind towards the underside of the yarn or ribbon.

Thus, claim1 is novel over both D1 and D2.

Inventive step

Neither D1 nor D2 addresses the problem of unsticking or releasing an indicator element which has become stuck to a sail. The two documents are only concerned with spacing the indicator element (the yarn or the ribbon) from the sail. Thus in terms of identifying the closest prior art for determining inventive step it seems appropriate to consider structural similarity.

In D1, a wind indicator is provided in which a wedge-shaped spacing member is used both to space a ribbon from, and attach it to, the surface of a sail. The ribbon is directly attached to the sloping surface of the spacing member. The thicker end of the wedge, from which the free length of the ribbon extends, is intended to keep the ribbon spaced from the sail.

In the Figure 1 embodiment of D2 there is a planar base to which is attached a cylindrical element to which the yarn is attached. Apart from the cylindrical element, there is no inclined surface. In the Figure 2 embodiment of D2 there is an inclined attachment member which supports a cylindrical spacing member. These two elements are structurally similar to the elements of the embodiments illustrated in the present application, albeit that their arrangement is different. Nevertheless, this embodiment of D2 would appear to be the most relevant for assessing inventive step.

The subject matter of claim 1 differs from the disclosure of D2 in that the inclined surface of the attachment number redirects a portion of wind towards the side of the piece of light-weight, flexible material that is arranged to face the sail in normal use.

The technical effect which is provided by this difference is that the redirected wind can detach the indicator piece should it have become stuck to the sail. In this way, manual intervention is not required to free a stuck indicator piece. Starting from D2, the objective technical problem is to configure the wind indicator such that an indicator element which has become stuck to the sail can be freed without manual intervention. The solution to the problem is to locate the spacing member and the attachment member with respect to each other such that, in use, the inclined surface of the attachment member redirects a portion of the wind towards the underside of the indicator piece – as set out in claim 1.

This solution is not obvious over D2. D2 teaches, in lines 23 to 25, that the width of the support 15 (the attachment member of claim 1) should be less than the diameter of the cylindrical element (the support member of claim 1) "so that, in use, disturbance to the air flow due to the support is minimal". This clearly teaches away from the inventive solution. Moreover, in D2's Figure 2 arrangement, the support 15 is entirely in the wind shadow of the cylindrical element 12. D1 provides no contrary teaching to cause the skilled person to disregard this teaching in D2.

It is noted that in both D1 and D2 the approach to the problem of sticking indicator elements is to space them from the sail surface so that they are less likely to become stuck – i.e. in D1, at lines 15 to 16 "this creates a wide gap between the ribbon 20 and the sail, thereby reducing the risk that the ribbon sticks to the sail". Neither document provides any clue as to how one could free an indicator, without manual intervention, in the event the indicator does stick to the sail.

The Examiner's assertion, in paragraph 4 of the communication, ignores the express teaching of D2 itself that the support of the cylindrical element 12 should be arranged to produce minimal disturbance to the air flow. Moreover, the Figure 2 embodiment of D2 uses the support 15 to reduce "the risk of the element 12 breaking or being ripped off the sail 20 in strong winds" – this benefit would seem to be lost if one merely replaced the planar base of D2 with the wedge-shaped body of D1. Finally, a clear purpose of having a wedge-shaped support of D1 is both to provide a large surface area for the attachment of the ribbon, and simultaneously to provide a stand-off to space the free part of the ribbon from the sail. Yet these two functions are already provided in D2 by the cylindrical element 12. The Examiner's assertion can therefore be seen to be based on ex-post facto analysis rather than a proper analysis of what the skilled person faced with the problem would do if given D1 and D2.

In the hopefully unlikely event that the Examiner is minded to reject the application, the applicants request Oral Proceedings in accordance with Article 116EPC.

Yours faithfully,

Carrie Cannon

Authorised Representative

## Claims

1. Wind indicator (1) for a sail (2) comprising a wind indicating piece of light-weight, flexible material (6), the piece of light-weight, flexible material (6) having a fixed end (6a) and a free end (6b), a spacing member (5) to which the fixed end (6a) of the piece of light-weight, flexible material (6) is fixed, such that, when the wind indicator (1) is attached to the sail (2), the spacing member (5) keeps the piece of light-weight, flexible material (6) spaced from the sail (2), and an attachment member (4) having a lower surface (7) which is adapted to be attached to the sail (2) and a surface (9) which is inclined with respect to the lower surface (7), characterised in that the spacing member (5) and the attachment member (4) are located with respect to each other such that, in use, the inclined surface (9) redirects a portion of wind towards the side of the piece of light-weight, flexible material (6) that is arranged to face the sail in normal use.

2. Wind indicator (1) according to claim 1 wherein the angle of inclination of the inclined surface (9) relative to the lower surface (7) is in the range 10° - 20°.

3. Wind indicator (1) according to claim 2, wherein the inclined surface (9) is planar or concavely curved.

4. Wind indicator (1) according to any one of the preceding claims, wherein the width of the inclined surface (9) is greater than the width of the spacing member (5) and greater than the width of the piece of light-weight, flexible material (6).

5. Wind indicator (1) according to any one of the preceding claims, wherein the spacing member (5) and the attachment member (4) are attached at what, in use, is the windward end of the attachment member(4).

6. Wind indicator (1) according to any one of claims 1 to 4, wherein the spacing member (5) and the attachment member (4) are attached at what, in use, is the leeward end of the attachment member(4).

7. Wind indicator (1) according to any one of claims 1 to 4, wherein the spacing member (5) and the attachment member (4) are attached at a point which is, in use, intermediate the windward and leeward ends of the attachment member(4).

8. Wind indicator (1) according to claim 7, wherein the spacing member (5) is mounted in an opening on the inclined surface (9).

9. Wind indicator (1) according to any one of the preceding claims wherein the spacing member (5) and the attachment member (4) are formed as one piece.

10. Wind indicator (1) according to any one of the preceding claims, wherein the attachment member (4) is wedge shaped.

11. A sail (2) for a sailing vessel (3), at least one wind indicator (1) according to any of the preceding claims being attached to each side of the sail (2).

12. A sailing vessel (3) having a sail (2) as claimed in claim 11.

# Paper C

## 1. General comments

*Overview*

In this paper the candidate must file an admissible opposition to a granted European patent, acting on the instructions of a client. A copy of the European Patent to be opposed, a letter from the client and various documents that the client considers to be relevant prior art are therefore provided. The candidate must assess the relevance of the prior art documents to the claims and either draft both a notice of opposition and either a letter to the client or a note on the legal issues raised by the client. The notice of opposition must be constructed solely on the basis of the information available — no further contact with the client is to be presumed.

However, the paper is not merely a test of whether a candidate can prepare a valid opposition. Much more than that is required. Rule 55(c) EPC states that the notice of opposition should contain an *indication* of the facts, evidence and arguments presented in support of the asserted grounds of opposition. This is a very modest requirement. In particular, only an indication of the arguments needs be provided: arguments do not need to be fully reasoned. Also, reasons why features in the opposed claims correspond to differently named features in the prior art need not be supplied.

Conversely, in this paper about half the available marks are allocated for argumentation. The importance of good argumentation cannot be over-emphasised. Unfortunately, in day to day practice, most candidates are not required to argue in favour of obviousness or lack of novelty. This can be true even where there is a good deal of opposition practice since, as noted above, to be admissible an opposition does not require reasoned arguments. Candidates are often quite used to arguing *against* novelty and obviousness arguments from patent office examiners. Unfortunately, with the pressure of work which patent office examiners now face, particularly in the EPO, it is often the case that such attacks are not well argued. In this paper, candidates who model their own novelty and obviousness attacks on those they have seen coming from patent offices are likely to fail.

After argumentation, the bulk of the rest of the marks are allocated to use of information; that is the extent to which a candidate finds the various available attacks, how well they have analysed the prior art, etc. The remaining marks are allocated to legal points, such as priority issues, added matter, authorisation, etc. which are generally strongly flagged in the client's letter. Up to 20 per cent of the available marks are allocated for legal issues, but generally fewer marks than this are available — in 2002 the figure was 12 per cent. The legal points, once they have been identified, generally can and should be dealt with quickly and concisely.

In the notice of opposition all the granted claim embodiments should be opposed where possible. All attacks that have a reasonable chance of success should be included. Attacks based on a lack of novelty or lack of inventive step should be constructed using only the prior art provided. Any information in the client's letter relating to amendments made during the prosecution of the granted patent should be used, where appropriate, to construct attacks based on added subject matter. No attacks based on insufficiency, however, should be considered.

Although six hours are now available for answering the paper, candidates often fail to deal with all the points at issue. In particular, it is not uncommon for later claims to remain un-attacked. This is a serious failure, because attacks on any individual dependent claim can be worth at least as much as an attack on one of the independent claims or as much as all the legal points.

Because it is important to attack all the claims against which sensible attacks can be made, it is important to argue all the potentially valid attacks against the independent claims. This is because the strongest attack on a dependent claim may be based on one of the weaker attacks against the independent claim from which the dependent claim depends.

In the letter to the client, which should be in note form, the candidate should answer any questions arising from the client's instructing letter. Various legal points will need to be addressed, any misunderstandings expressed by the client will need to be rectified and the reasons for any difficult decisions explained. Where it is not possible, for legal reasons, to carry out the wishes of the client, an explanation should also be given.

The available time should be divided almost equally between elucidating and writing the answer. The bias however should be towards finding the answer: it should not take more than two hours to write down the answer. In this paper it is certainly worth leaving time to check that you have: written what you meant to write; read the claim dependencies correctly; attacked all the claims and all variants, dealt with all the legal points raised; and provided sufficient legal basis.

The prior art documents are presented in such a way that two of the EPO official languages are always needed in assessing the relevance of the prior art. So in addition to the EPO language in which the question paper will be read, candidates need to be able to read and understand one or more prior art documents in a second EPO language. It is <u>not</u> necessary to make a complete translation of such documents: if your skills in your favoured second language are good enough you can obviously just highlight or otherwise mark the pertinent passages. Even if you skills are not so strong, you should resist the temptation to make a full translation. It is very easy to waste a huge amount of time and become very stressed because some part of a document is a bit obscure, even though it is evident that the obscure part has no relevance to the invention. It may be prudent, however, to capture your understanding of any obscure or key words when you first read the document: under the stress of the exam it is possible to forget such crucial pieces of information.

If your language skills in the second EPO language are not good enough for you to read all or most of the prior art documents without using a dictionary, start work now on improving those skills. It is important that when you sit the exam you have a sufficiently practical grasp of the language to be able to read and generally understand the texts even if you do not know the meaning of all the words. The diverse subjects which occur in opposition papers mean that almost any vocabulary that you learn in your second EPO language can be useful. But it is important to get plenty of exposure to simple patent specifications and other simple technical literature. Past opposition papers are one obvious source, but short patent specifications on simple mechanical inventions are also a good choice — and freely available via the internet. Ideally, form a study group and get some professional help, at least initially, working on the standard phrases and constructions which are used in patents. Working one or two hours each week on this for six to twelve months or so can reap enormous benefits in terms of confidence (and results) in the exam.

Useful things to take into the exam include the Guidelines and EPO case law book — case law relevant to selection inventions and the making available of information to the public (e.g. prior use) is frequently relevant. The notice of opposition must be complete and the use of Form 2300, which is provided in the exam documentation, is recommended (though not obligatory). A filled-out example of Form 2300, is therefore also useful in the exam. A hole-punch and a tabbed file may be useful for arranging the examination paper (see below), although others may prefer to use a stapler and staples, and different coloured highlighters are useful for marking up the patent and prior art documents.

While the following advice may seem obvious, this author every year meets candidates who admit to never having sat a paper under anything like exam conditions before they sit down on the day of the exam. So, dear reader (assuming that you still have to achieve a pass in paper C in order to qualify as an EPA): **it is absolutely vital to practice past exam papers, under exam conditions, well before the paper is to be sat in the examination hall**. It is much too easy for those who are going to sit the exam to give themselves a false sense of security by dabbling with past papers. Typically this involves a candidate either sitting down for a few hours, looking at a past paper (which may not be completely new to the candidate) to see whether they can "spot the main points" — which they may or may not record in writing, before turning to the examiners' comments and answer in the compendium. The candidate then mentally ticks off all the points that seem to match the points found in the few hours of study — those that are missed being noted with a smile because "I would have spotted that when I wrote an answer, especially if I gave the paper the full 6 hours". Dear reader, if you recognise yourself in this portrayal, please, please, set aside 6 hours and attempt a past paper (which must be completely unknown to you), under exam conditions. (So no music, no intermission while you read the paper or prepare a meal, no getting up for a chat part way through, no fortifying hot meals, cold beer, coffee, tea or other stimulants). Ideally, you should attempt the papers (for there should be more than one of these attempts) under conditions as similar as to the real conditions as possible. This means you should be in your office rather than in the comfort of your home. Ideally this also means starting at the hour at which you will sit the real exam, rather than in the afternoon when you may well feel more awake.

You must aim to finish every one of the papers that you attempt — and you must set aside the whole 6 hours, in one lump. The next day, or later, go through the Examiners' comments and attempt to mark your paper (unless your boss or some other noble character will mark the paper for you using the Examiners' comments as the reference) rigorously according to the solution proposed by the Examiners. Identify the points that you missed — why did you miss them? The hardest part of your own paper to mark is the argumentation — which is unfortunate, as argumentation is often where the paper is failed. But with rigorous self assessment and practice your chances of passing the exam will rise considerably. Ideally, you should also try out the two approaches which are exemplified here. These suit different temperaments — see which suits you.

Finally, because this is a six-hour examination, it is sensible to bring food (preferably protein and complex carbohydrate, rather than simply sugary snacks) and drink (again avoiding high sugar content). Obviously, this should be chosen and packaged in such a way that its consumption does not disturb your fellow candidates.

*The fundamental tasks* 1–124

One of the fundamental tasks facing candidates is the identification of the distinct variants or combinations specified by the claims of the patent to be opposed. If this task is not done correctly, many marks will be lost because if a variant is not identified no clear case can be made out against it. Often, a candidate's failure to tackle this task properly will result in the candidate failing the exam.

Once all the variants have been identified, it is necessary to determine the effective date of each of them. This requires an understanding of how priority works. It is important to know and to understand the EBA Decision G2/98. In every Paper C, candidates should expect there to be some variants or combinations which are only entitled to the filing date, while others are entitled to a claimed priority date. Clearly it is vital to be able to allocate the different dates correctly. However, while loss of priority for some variants is very common in this paper, there is no rule that says that such a situation must arise in every Paper C. If there is in fact no evidence in the paper that this is an issue, candidates should not invent such a problem.

The third fundamental task is to determine the effective date of the other annexes, that is the potential prior art, to see which of the annexes is citable under Art.54(2) (and hence available for novelty and obviousness), which are citable under Art.54(3) and (4) — (only for novelty), and which, if any, are not available for use under Art.54(2) or (3).

Once these three tasks have been achieved, the next task is to apply to each of the identified variants only those annexes with an effective date earlier than the effective date of the relevant variant. The object here is to decide what, if any, novelty attacks can be made against the different variants, and what obviousness attacks can be made. It is very important to distinguish between novelty and obviousness attacks. In arguing obviousness attacks, the use of the EPO's problem and solution approach should be used.

**2. How to tackle the paper**

1–125

*Organising the paper*

Although it is a six-hour paper, good time management and good organisation are very important. There are numerous annexes, each available in at least two languages, and a great many pages. Some way is needed of dealing efficiently with these. Certainly the first step is to remove the staple that secures the exam paper bundle! Then for each annex the version in the favoured language is selected, and either the pages of each annex stapled or hole-punched and located in a pre-tabbed binder as set out below. In general, a candidate only needs each annex in just one language — so the other language version(s) can be put to one side (they may later be useful when an annex needs translating).

The choice of approach to organising the paper is a personal one. The ring binder approach has the advantage that each annex is always readily locatable. With the stapled loose annexes, comparison between annexes is much easier and quicker.

If using the ring binder approach, hole-punch the pages and split them into the following sections in a pre-tabbed ring binder: (a) client's letter; (b) patent to be opposed; (c)–(x) each piece of prior art in the language you intend to use it. Any unnecessary documents in other languages can then be put aside.

1–126

*Analysing the client's letter*

The client's letter is your starting point for the paper. It contains not only the identity and address of the opponent, which you will need in order to be able to file the opposition, but also information about the patent to be opposed, notably about priority and amendments, and legal issues and questions which you need to address. Generally the issues raised by the client's letter account for about 15 to 20% of the available marks. This means that you have to devote sufficient time to the consideration of these issues and to the recording of the relevant conclusions. In general, everything mentioned in the client's letter needs to be taken into account and addressed in some way in your answer. The client's misconceptions and questions need to be addressed and answered in a letter to the client. Those matters which are important to the opposition should however appear in your opposition statement and not simply be addressed in a letter to the client.

It is usual for the client's letter to address issues of priority, namely either telling you that the priority claim of the opposed patent is good, e.g. "from a file inspection we have determined that the description and claims of the priority application are identical to those of the application as filed", or identifying differences between the priority application and the application as filed. In either case, you are to accept the information as given. Where the priority claim is good, that is the end of the matter. But where you are told about differences between the application as filed and the priority application, you need to work out the effects of the differences, i.e. which claims or claim variants are entitled to what date, and practical consequences of this. Any analysis and conclusions on priority should generally appear in the opposition grounds, e.g. "claim 3 is not entitled to the claimed priority date, as the feature X was not present in the priority application". In such a case you do not need to repeat these facts in a letter to the client.

Some examples of these kinds of issues from past papers are presented in the next three sections. This is not done in the expectation that these precise issues will arise again, but rather because seeing these examples will give you a feel for what to expect and what to prepare for.

*Issues of priority*  1–127

In the 1990 paper one of the background documents, a PCT application published on the priority date of the patent to be opposed, had the same inventor as the patent to be opposed. The PCT application, which designated the EPO, was not effective under Art.54(3) because it did not enter the regional phase. Moreover, the subject matter of claim 1 of the patent to be opposed was disclosed in the PCT application. The client reported that the contents of the PCT application and its priority document were identical. Thus the subject matter of claim 1 of the patent to be opposed was not entitled to the claimed priority date and could therefore be attacked under Art.54(2) based on the publication of the PCT application.

In the 1991 paper the patent to be opposed claimed two priorities. The client had marked the patent with the subject matter which was in the first priority document. The second priority document was Annex 2. The patent to be opposed had some subject matter, and a claim, which had not been marked by the client and which was not in Annex 2: this subject matter, and the related claim, had an effective date of the filing date.

In the 1992 paper the client provided a copy of an examination report for the patent to be opposed which provided information about a first earlier priority-claiming application having the same applicant as the patent to be opposed. The exam report observed that the earlier application was entitled to its claimed priority date. The report also stated that claims 4 to 6 of the patent to be opposed were not entitled to the claimed priority date. A further application from the same applicant included a discussion of the earlier application which showed that the subject matter of claims 1 and 2 of the patent to be opposed was disclosed in the earlier application. Thus claims 1 and 2 were not entitled to their claimed priority date as the priority claim was based on an application which was not the first for the relevant subject matter.

In the 1998 paper the client reported that the priority number of Annex 1, the patent to be opposed, "was corrected from GB956162 to GB946162 during examination". There was thus a query as to whether the priority claim was valid. The filing date of Annex 1 was March 21, 1995 and the priority date was March 22, 1994. The correction of a priority claim after publication, under r.88 requires there to be an obvious error. The client only states the priority number to have been corrected, not the priority date. The priority number usually reflects the year of filing. The priority date could not have been March 22, 1995 as this was after the filing date. Thus it suggests the year component of the priority number should have been 1994 rather than 1995. On this basis there is no reason to believe that the priority claim is invalid.

*Issues of added matter*  1–128

In the 1992 paper a copy of an examination report for the patent to be opposed was provided. This included some amendments proposed by the examiner, from which one could see the text of claims 4 to 6 as filed. Claim 4 as granted lacked two features which had been present in the claim as filed ("stepwise" and "during the stand-still periods of the chain"). However the description of the patent, which the client told us had never been amended, stated that "Essential for obtaining the advantages of the invention, ... is the provision of means for driving the rollers step-wise, as this allows the frames to be adhered during the stand still periods of the chain". From this it was clear that claim 4 as granted contained added matter and could be attacked under Art.123(2). The fact that the description had not been amended also meant that it could be seen that mention of "plastic strips" in claim 6 was also added matter. Neither of these infractions of Art.123(2) was mentioned in the client's letter.

Conversely, in the 1995 paper the client's letter reported that from a file inspection it had been determined that a limitation (at least 60% of the particles were in the rear half of the structure) present in one of the claims of the granted patent had no basis in the application as filed. The only indication of the distribution of particles was that most of the particles were situated in the back half of the structure. The client reported that the applicant had argued that one of the figures provided support for this feature. Candidates could readily determine that the drawing revealed no basis for this amendment. The client also reported that the priority document had been used to justify a correction of the term polyethylene to read polypropylene. Of course the priority document is not part of the application as filed, even if filed with it, and cannot be used either as a basis for amendment nor as a justification for a correction (G3/89).

In the 1996 paper the client reported that the content of the application as filed was identical to the priority document. The only difference between the application and the patent as granted is that claim 6 was not in the application as filed. The client opines "I do not believe that this information is very useful for the opposition, since the process according to claim 6 is, in my opinion, implicitly contained in claim 5". Claim 5 was to a fireplace and claim 6 to a method for cleaning the fireplace of claim 5 in which ashes were removed in a particular way. Inspection of the description revealed a clear statement that removal of ashes was achieved in a different way. The added claim therefore contradicted a clear statement in the application as filed and hence was added matter.

In the 2001 paper the client reported that the sole drawing of the patent was not in the original documents filed at the EPO on December 23, 1994, but that it had been filed by fax on January 2, 1995, with a confirmation copy filed three weeks later. Inspection of the cover page of the patent revealed a filing date of January 2, 1995 and a priority date of January 6, 1994. The application had therefore been re-dated to the date of filing the missing drawing (under r.43). There was therefore no issue of added matter. Candidates were expected to notice and comment on the fact that the new filing date was still within the priority year, so that any priority entitlement had not been lost. The client also reported that the only amendment made during prosecution was the addition of a passage underlined in the patent. This passage had been filed in response to an objection of lack of support for one of the claims. The amendment had been objected to, under Art.84, by the Examining Division and an appeal argued. The text as granted was that approved by the Board of Appeal. Study of the wording of the new passage and of the claim from which it had notionally been drawn revealed added matter. That the text had been approved by a Board of Appeal did not change that fact, nor did it mean that the Opposition Division would automatically follow the earlier decision, as that decision bound only the department responsible for the decision appealed (T167/93).

In the 2003 paper the only question potentially on added matter concerned the presence of a disclaimer in one of the claims. The client confirmed that the disclaimer had been present on filing. Candidates were meant to realise that there is no bar to the use of disclaimers (although the EPO would rather that claim features were defined positively) and that the possibility of adding matter by an amendment which introduces a disclaimer (see G2/03) were not relevant (and therefore should not even have been discussed). All that was required was a simple statement to the effect that, as the disclaimer had been present on filing there was no issue of added matter.

In the 2004 paper the client reported that the only amendments during prosecution had been the addition of two claims, 4 and 5. These were based on a single paragraph of the application which concerned an embodiment which used a wiper blade having a leading edge made of a high surface adhesion material and a trailing edge of a low surface adhesion material. Claim 4 merely required the use of a wiper blade having a surface exhibiting a low surface adhesion. Claim 5, which depended from claim 4, required the presence of all the relevant features of the supporting paragraph. Applicants were meant to spot that claim 4 added matter by omitting an essential feature (it had taken only one of two features which had only been presented in combination). Candidates were supposed to realise that claim 5 was not objectionable under Art.123(2) EPC, despite depending from a claim which was objectionable, because it re-introduced the feature whose omission gave rise to the Art.123(2) EPC objection.

*Legal issues*

In the 1990 paper the client manufactured a product in Portugal, for the European market, according to the method of one of the independent claims. The patent did not designate Portugal, and the client suggested that the relevant claim need not be attacked since he did not use the method in a territory covered by the patent. Candidates were meant to appreciate that the opposition needed to cover the independent method claim because, by virtue of Art.64(2) EPC the direct product of a patented process is also protected. Hence products manufactured in Portugal but sold in states covered by the patent would constitute infringements.

In the 1991 paper there were several minor legal issues. Is prior art cited in an opposed patent automatically taken into account in the opposition or do they need to be specifically cited in the opposition? T198/88 confirmed that they are not automatically included and should be cited in the opposition if they are to be taken into account. The patent was published with claims 1 to 8, yet the grant decision had been made on the basis of 9 claims. A correction was published in the patents bulletin. Does the reinstatement of claim 9 constitute added matter? Does the date of the notice of correction extend the opposition period for claim 9 or for all the claims? The answer to these three questions is of course no: the authentic text of the patent is that on the basis of which the grant decision was made. The opposition period runs from the publication of the mention of grant even if there are errors in the published text of the patent. There was also a question of whether an internal, unpublished document was citable as prior art — no; as well as a question about seeking an award of costs based on the non-entitlement of the patentee (beyond the competence of the Opposition Division according to Art.104 EPC).

In the 2000 paper the client provided a letter as evidence that climbing shoes according to the patent had been used on a climbing trip, during which other climbers were present, before the priority date of the patent. The wearer of the shoes was bound by a confidentiality agreement with the patentee and disclosed no information when questioned about the shoes by the other climbers. Had the shoes been made available to the public? The other climbers were not bound by any confidentiality agreement and anything which they could see of the external structure of the shoe had been made available to the public. The wearer of the shoes and the other climbers could be offered as witnesses in support of an allegation of prior public use.

In the 2004 paper the client explained that another company was interested in filing an opposition but were in financial difficulties, and asked whether in principle two companies could file a single opposition to save money. G3/99 is legal basis for saying that this is acceptable. The names of the multiple opponents need to be disclosed before the end of the opposition period and, in order to safeguard the procedural rights of the patentee and for procedural efficiency, it has to be clear throughout the procedure who belongs to the group of common opponents or common appellants.

*Working with the client's letter*

When considering the client's letter, read it carefully and make margin notes as you go along. As you will be reading this letter at the start of the exam you brain will be at its freshest and you are likely to see solutions and points to be raised in your answer that you may well have forgotten or not see by the time you come to write up your answer. For this reason it is sensible to make fairly full notes in the margin rather than anything too brief. You can fill in the first page of form 2300 at this stage, ticking the box for the voucher of payments for fees or costs, as well as signing the last page of the form in the name of the fictional representative. These formal matters are worth about four marks and are easy to overlook at the end of the examination.

On a notepad, note any information on added matter obtained from the prosecution history of the patent to be opposed. If you are told about any amendments that have been made by the proprietor during prosecution it is likely that the question requires you to consider whether Art.123(2) EPC has been contravened. Bear in mind that Art.123(2) applies not only to the claims but also to the description and drawings. Note any information on the priority dates of various claims. Note any information concerning the availability to the public of any of the prior art documents and any prior uses. Note specific points of law that need to be addressed. Note any false assumptions that the client has made that need to be dispelled. All these points should be noted on one page of your notepad, so that you can use it subsequently as a reminder to deal with these points in your answer or in preparing a novelty matrix if you are going to use one. You can also use the list when you check your answer towards the end of the examination. Many candidates find it useful also to highlight these points where they arise in the exam paper. A pencilled note of the point's significance is also often useful, as later in the exam you may have forgotten how you wanted to tackle the issue that you saw.

**1–131** *Identifying claim variants and their effective dates*

Your first task with the patent, best tackled before you look at the other annexes, is to identify all the distinct variants or combinations specified by the claims. From the examiners' comments on Paper C, it is clear that many candidates fail to do this satisfactorily in the exam.

The 1991 paper is a good example of a claim set with traps for the unwary. The claims read as follows:

(1) A liquid crystal display device of the transmission type for indicating alphanumeric signs and symbols in automobiles and which is provided with a heating device, in which display device at least one glass plate (1,2;9) is arranged on both sides of the liquid crystal (3), characterised in that one of the glass plates (2,9) is a composite structure in which a resistance heating means (10) is arranged between two glass layers (2a,2b;9a,9b).

(2) Device according to claim 1, characterised in that the glass layer (2a,9a) closer to the liquid crystal is thinner than the more remote glass layer (2b,9b).

(3) Device according to claim 1 or claim 2, characterised in that the composite structure (2a,10,2b) is located adjacent the liquid crystal (3).

(4) Device according to claim 1 or claim 2, characterised in that on one side of the liquid crystal (3) two superposed glass plates (2,9) are arranged the outer glass plate being the composite structure (9a, 10, 9b).

(5) Device according to any of claims 1 to 4, characterised in that the resistance heating means (10) is a meshed or wave-shaped heating conductor (11).

(6) A device according to claim 4, characterised in that the resistance heating means (10) is formed from a transparent film which is substantially co-extensive with the adjacent glass layers.

(7) Device in particular according to claim 6, characterised in that it comprises a constant voltage source for the supply of current to a heating device provided with a heating means made of resistance material whose electrical resistance increases strongly with increasing temperature.

(8) Device according to claim 7, characterised in that the resistance material consists of metal oxides of indium, gallium and tin.

Claim 1 is an independent claim with no alternatives or optional features, so this will have only one date.

Claim 2 depends from claim 1. It is unclear, but there are again no alternatives or optional features. Again there will only be one date.

Claim 3 depends in the alternative from claim 1 or claim 2. There are no optional features or other alternatives in the claim. When dependent only on claim 1 it protects the combination of claim 1 with the additional features of claim 3 — the composite structure is located adjacent the liquid crystal. When dependent on claim 2 its scope is further limited to devices having the features added by claim 2. These two variants may have different effective dates.

Claim 4 depends in the alternative from claim 1 or claim 2. There are no optional features or other alternatives in the claim. The alternate dependency gives rise to two variants: one being the combination of the features added by claim 4 with the features of claim 1; the other being the combination of the features of claims 4, 2 and 1. Again, these two variants may have different effective dates.

Claim 5 is dependent on any one of claims 1 to 4, and this coupled with the alternate dependencies of claims 3 and 4 gives rise to many variants. However, before considering what the variants are, it is important to notice that claim 5 includes two alternate features:

(i) the resistance heating means is a meshed heating conductor; or

(ii) the resistance heating means is a wave-shaped conductor.

So, for every possible dependency path, claim 5 provides two alternative constructions.

The dependency paths of claim 5 are:

(a) 1+5

(b) 1+2+5

(c) 1+2+3+5

(d) 1+2+4+5

(e) 1+3+5

(f) 1+4+5

So, in total, claim 5 embraces 12 variants:

(a)–(f) with option (i); and

(a)–(f) with option (ii).

These different variants may again have different dates.

Claim 6 is dependent just from claim 4 and contains no other variants or optional features. But claim 4 contained two alternatives — one with the features of claim 2 and one without. So, claim 6 likewise contains the same two alternatives.

Claim 7 is a nice example of an examiner's trap. At first sight, claim 7 seems to depend from claim 6. Indeed, in one guise it does. But the presence of "in particular" means that claim 7 is also an independent claim not limited to the features of claim 6 or indeed any other claim. As dependent on claim 6, claim 7 provides two variants because claim 6 contained two variants — that with the features of claim 2 and that without those features. There are no other alternatives or variants set out in the claim. So, overall, claim 7 provides three variants.

Claim 8 depends only from claim 7 and contains no other alternatives or variants. Because claim 7 contained three variants, claim 8 also contains three variants.

Another nice trick with the 1991 paper is that the client's letter mentions that "the grant of the patent was decided on the basis of claims 1 to 9", yet only claims 1 to 8 appear in the printed patent. The text of claim 9, which appeared in the European patent bulletin, is "Apparatus according to claim 1, modified in that the glass plates are replaced by plates of another transparent material." While this looks like a dependent claim, in fact it is independent. This is because although it makes reference to claim 1, it contains only some and not all the limitations of claim 1.

For each claim embodiment identified, note the date at which validity is to be assessed. This date will be the filing date of the granted application unless the granted application validly claims priority from an earlier application disclosing the same subject matter, in which case it will be the filing date of that earlier application. Any priority claim should be assumed to be fully valid unless information to the contrary is provided. Do not annoy the examiner and waste time by stating that you would check the priority claim. It is important that you understand how priority works. Read and understand the EBA Decisions G3/93 and G2/98. The effective date of a claim, when determining the novelty and inventiveness of its subject matter, is always either a claimed priority date or the filing date. A claim amendment made after filing, in contravention of Art.123(2) EPC, does not change that fact. A claim including such an amendment should first of all be attacked under Art.100(c) EPC, and for such an attack there is no concept of "effective date". An auxiliary attack should then be made for lack of novelty and/or inventive step, as appropriate, based on the assumption that the Art.123(2) EPC attack is found to be incorrect. For such an attack the determination of the effective date of the claim is required. This date will either be the priority date or the filing date. If you are told that the contents of the application as filed were identical to the priority document, the effective date will be the priority date. Otherwise, it is likely that the effective date will be the filing date (subject to anything said to the contrary in the question paper).

Consider carefully whether any priority claim is valid. Has the priority claim been lost during prosecution (information in the letter from the client)? Only the priority applicant or his successor in title can validly claim priority in respect of the granted patent. If the priority claiming application is filed by someone who only subsequently becomes the successor in title, the priority claim is bad. Is the priority document the first filing of the subject matter it discloses (e.g. 1992)? Sometimes the priority document will be a US continuation application and therefore clearly not a first filing (e.g. 2000). One of the annexes may be relevant to this question: in particular, always check the applicant, inventor, and priority details of the various annexes to see whether you have the information to show that a priority claimed in the opposed patent is not from the first filing for the relevant subject matter.

When you have worked out the effective date of each variant, record the dates on a separate sheet of paper as well as, preferably, against the relevant claim of the patent to be opposed. Obviously if each claim has only one effective date, this is easy. However, if a claim has many variants, such as claim 5 of the 1991 paper, it may not be possible to show clearly on the patent the correspondence between the different variants and their dates. In that case your separate sheet of paper becomes a table or chart showing, as simply as possible, the variants and their effective dates: this may be used as the basis of your novelty matrix if you are going to use one.

1–132       *Determining the effective dates of the prior art documents*

Next capture the effective date of each of the other annexes. This may simply be the publication date, as it will be for documents published before the earliest claimed priority date. Remember that to be prior art, the publication must have occurred **before** the relevant date — publication on the day of filing or on the priority date (whichever applies) does not count as prior art. Or it may be the filing or priority date for earlier-filed but later published European or international patent applications (if they designate the EPO and enter the regional phase) provided there is an overlap of states for which designation fees have been paid. Note the priority, filing and publication dates of all patent applications and patents. Remember that earlier-filed but later published national applications are not citable under Art.54(3) EPC.

Identify any annexes which are only citable under Art.54(3) EPC for claims which are not entitled to any claimed priority date (i.e. against claims which are only entitled to the filing date) and note the countries of overlap. Mark the annex(es) prominently with a warning such as: NOVELTY ONLY! ONLY USEABLE AGAINST CLAIMS 1–3. FOR STATES XYZ. Also make a note of these facts on the cover of the opposed patent and/or on your notes page.

This process needs to be repeated for all other annexes which are, at least for some claims, only citable under Art.54(3) EPC. Again, it is important to label each annex prominently and clearly with an appropriate warning.

Annexes, which are in whole or in part citable under Art.54(2) EPC and hence useable in an obviousness attack, should also be labelled appropriately, e.g.: CITABLE AGAINST ALL CLAIMS FOR NOVELTY AND OBVIOUSNESS.

Consider whether any disclosure was made in confidence or is covered by the provisions of Art.55 EPC. Also watch out for the situation where an application is withdrawn before publication but published anyway (no Art.54(3) EPC effect, see 2003). The candidate should be familiar with the extensive case law on prior use and oral disclosure.

*Assessing the relevance of the prior art* 1–133

It is necessary to develop a systematic method for comparing the disclosure of each piece of prior art with the identified claim embodiments against which that prior art can be cited in order to establish which novelty and inventive step attacks are available. Several methods are commonly used and, of these, the use of a novelty matrix is perhaps the most popular (see below, particularly the 2002 worked example).

As an alternative to a full novelty matrix, you can write a very simple table and label either the prior art annex or the relevant claim (or more preferably both) with details of any issues — e.g. features only arguably present, features that are present but for which an explanation of the correspondence between the prior art feature and the claim feature is required. The table, constructed on the first page of the patent or elsewhere, should have a row for each claim (or for each claim variant) and columns for lack of novelty under Art.54(3) EPC, lack of novelty under Art.54(2) EPC and obviousness.

If you are going to use a formal novelty matrix, split up the integers of the claims into individual features or manageable groups of features. Look at the example provided later in this chapter, based on the 2002 paper, to see how to lay out the matrix. Knowing where to split the claim is a skill that can only be learnt with practice — each feature that could distinguish the claim from the prior art should in principle be a separate integer but sometimes it is more convenient to bundle related features together since a larger number of integers will take a longer time to analyse. Number the integers, e.g. 1.1, 1.2, 1.3 . . . 1.x for claim 1. Include preferred features within claims as separate integers, e.g. 1.2pref. Where elements will need to be added/subtracted from a claim due to added matter, include modified features separately, e.g. 1.3new. In the left hand margin of the grid, note the date at which the validity of the claims is to be assessed. Add notes where necessary on any points of interpretation that need to be taken into account (e.g. XX for YY means XX suitable for YY). Clearly mark the grid according to whether each piece of prior art is citeable under novelty and/or inventive step for each claim embodiment by crossing out areas (not citeable at all), highlighting areas (only citeable for novelty) or leaving areas blank (citeable for novelty and inventive step).

When you are assessing the relevance of the annexes it is sensible to deal first with those which are only citeable under Art.54(3) EPC. This approach helps to ensure that you only apply such annexes in novelty attacks. The first Art.54(3) EPC annex is thus used to determine the novelty of the claims for which it is prior art. Clearly, this process begins with the independent claims. Go through the citation carefully, understanding exactly what is disclosed (and carefully translating if in a foreign language). Where translation is difficult, the French/German version of the opposed patent may provide the meaning of useful words. Abstracts are not part of the disclosure under

Art.54(3) EPC (Art.85 EPC) and are to be disregarded under Art.54(2) EPC where there is conflict with the main text. They may, however, contain useful evidentiary information relevant to another annex. Note any information in the annexes which suggests they could be combined with other annexes (e.g. cross-references, identical IPC codes, search report citations). For an alleged prior use, consider exactly what was made available, including what could have been ascertained from analysis (G1/92) in the case that samples were distributed.

If a lack of novelty is found, this can be recorded in the simple chart (if this method is preferred) and, preferably, by the relevant claim. The cover of the prior art annex should also be annotated to record the fact that the annex anticipates claim X, and any issues of interpretation or other matters to be discussed are briefly noted on the front page. While comparing an annex with a claim, many people like to highlight or otherwise indicate the passages of relevance — flagging them with the claim number. This process is repeated for the other Art.54(3) EPC annexes. It is then repeated with the Art.54(2) EPC annexes, starting with the most likely anticipations. Identify any novelty attacks first. These are used to populate the second column of the table and are again identified and captured on the front page of the relevant annex and the pertinent pieces of disclosure marked up. While studying these Art.54(2) EPC annexes also note on them and indicate in the table any relevance that they may have for potential obviousness attacks, both against the independent claims and against the dependent claims. Again, also capture the salient points on the front page of the relevant annex, indicating any features which will require explanation. Repeat this process for the remaining annexes and with a view to completing any obviousness attacks. Once you have completed an obviousness attack, indicate the relevant combination in your table (e.g. A4+A6), and repeat this for all the other complete attacks.

If using a formal novelty matrix, fill in each box corresponding to a claim integer with a tick (feature disclosed), a cross (feature not disclosed) or a question mark (feature possibly disclosed depending on interpretation), a page and line reference and any necessary explanatory comments. Also, summarise the problem the annex addresses. Where there are two or more distinct embodiments in an annex, these should be analysed separately. Consider whether any extra art acknowledged in one of the annexes should be given a separate column of its own or represents common general knowledge.

**1–134**  *Formulating an attack strategy*

When all the prior art has been analysed, an attack plan can be formulated, setting out which attacks are to be made in the notice of opposition. Using the novelty grid or simple table, consider in respect of each claim embodiment identified, which attacks are possible under excluded subject matter (unusual), added matter, novelty and inventive step. There will probably be some embodiments which have no attacks available, or just a novelty attack.

Consider novelty and inventive step attacks that are almost possible in more detail, examining whether a missing feature is actually disclosed on a fair reading. Analyse the claim wording carefully to see whether you may be missing a different possible interpretation. Consider too whether you can stretch an interpretation of a term in the claim or in a prior art annex. Ask yourself what you are missing. Are you reading "for" too narrowly? Irrespective of the application of a feature or combination in the prior art, is the feature or combination in fact suitable for the use recited in the claim? Are you reading what you feel to be the intent behind the claim, rather than what the claim actually says? In the exam it is possible there is no valid attack for one or more of the claims. This is unusual though. What is common is for some valid attacks to rely on some subtlety which is easy to overlook in the exam. Clearly, marks will have been allocated for any such attacks and these marks will be lost if the attack is not made out in the candidate's opposition. Another annex may be relevant, proving that the feature is inherently there (novelty) or providing information as to why the missing feature is an obvious equivalent (inventive step, e.g. 1999). Include all attacks that have a reasonable chance of success, including both ways of combining two documents relevant to inventive step.

Don't try and argue a feature is implicit when there is doubt as to whether it is there or not (e.g. 2000, A3 climbing shoe could have been laced or unlaced). However, it is permissible to stretch the meaning of words where there is room for argument to cover prior art (e.g. 2000, a "cut-out" which was very large in the patent was taken to cover the small "openings" of A2 and the "small blind holes" of A3).

Make sure, again, that you have not used a document citeable only under novelty for an inventive step attack! Furthermore, don't use the same document for a novelty attack and an inventive step attack unless you make it clear that the inventive step attack is based on a particular alternative interpretation the opposition division might take.

Remember that a prior use can be used to attack inventive step as well as novelty.

If you have not used one of the annexes at all, think again (though this does, very rarely, happen).

*Writing the notice of opposition*

1–135

First of all, fill out Form 2300 using the appropriate information from the client's letter and the published patent. You will be given sufficient information to enable you to file an admissible opposition, even if there are gaps which prevent your completing the form. Where any information is incomplete (e.g. an address) this will need to be highlighted in the notes for the client asking for this information. Do not forget to pay the opposition fee, preferably by ticking the appropriate box on the form. Also, sign the form in the guise of the representative identified in the question.

Next, write the statement of grounds. The following notes give guidance on content and style. Sentences in normal typeface are suggestions for phrases to adapt when writing the answer and sentences in italics provide further useful comments. In some instances (e.g. inventive step), several different examples of useful language are suggested and they should be used selectively according to the circumstances.

Note that in Paper C, as in the other papers, no pre-prepared materials may be handed in as part of your answer — you will get no marks for the content of such materials if you do. The complete answers must be written during the exam on the answer sheets provided.

### Statement of grounds

1–136

The patent is opposed in its English text and is referred to herein as Annex 1.

### 1. Priority date of claims

1–137

*For each claim embodiment, explain which date is relevant for the assessment of novelty and inventive step.*

    1.1 The subject matter of claims x–y was first disclosed in priority application z, having a filing date of xx.yy.zz. Since the priority claim is valid the validity of these claims is to be assessed at xx.yy.zz.

    1.2 The subject matter of claim y–z was first disclosed in European patent application z, having a filing date of xx.yy.zz. The validity of these claims is therefore to be assessed at xx.yy.zz.

### 2. Prior art

1–138

*For each piece of prior art used in the attack plan, say which language version you have used and then explain why it is part of the state of the art.*

    2.1 References to Annex z are to the English/French/German translation.

*In the case of an earlier European patent application:*

    2.2 Annex z is citeable against claims x–y under Article 54(3)–(4) and rule 23a EPC for all common, validly designated contracting states (i.e. a . . . z) because Annex z is a European patent application published after but having a priority date/filing date earlier than the priority date to which these claims are entitled. It is therefore only relevant to the novelty of these claims.

*In the case of an earlier International patent application:*

    2.3 Annex z is citeable against claims x–y under Article 54(3)–(4), Article 158(1) and rule 23a EPC for all common, validly designated contracting states (i.e. a . . . z) because Annex z is an International Patent Application, published after but having a priority date/filing date earlier than the priority date to which these claims are entitled. Furthermore, annex z validly designated EP and validly entered the European regional phase. It is therefore relevant to the novelty of these claims.

*In the case of an earlier publication:*

    2.4 Annex y is citeable against claims y–z under Article 54(2) EPC since it has a publication date prior to the priority date/filing date to which these claims are entitled. It is therefore relevant to the novelty and inventive step of these claims.

*In the case of a prior use:*

    2.5 Annex v is not a prior art document but is evidence of a prior use of [invention]. Mr x is offered as a witness in order to testify to the alleged prior use. Further, x/y/z will also be offered as witnesses and their names will be supplied at a later date. The prior use took place on . . . at . . . and took the form of . . . . The public were represented by . . . The information that became available to the public was . . .

*In some cases there will be no annex to prove a prior use, only the client's letter. In which case use the paragraph above, duly completed, but without the first sentence.*

1–139

### 3. Claim 1

*Attack the patent, taking each claim embodiment separately and considering non-patentable subject matter, added matter, novelty and inventive step. In particular, deal fully with each claim for novelty and inventive step, before moving on to the next claim. This is preferable to dealing first with the novelty of all claims, then the inventiveness of all claims.*

Non-patentable subject matter

    3.1 . . . *This is rarely a useful ground of attack.*

Added matter

    3.2 The feature "xx" of claim x/on page z, line y of the description was not explicitly disclosed in the application as filed. Furthermore, there is no implicit disclosure of this feature in the application as filed since . . . which the applicant relied on as basis does not . . . . The amendment that introduced feature "xx" therefore introduced subject-matter which extends beyond the content of the application as filed and should not have been allowed pursuant to Article 123(2) EPC. The patent is consequently opposed pursuant to Article 100(c) EPC.

  or

    3.3 The features of claim x were not disclosed in combination in the application as filed, either explicitly or implicitly, since in the application as filed they were only disclosed in combination with additional feature "xx". Furthermore, feature "xx" is said to be an essential feature. Claim x of the patent as granted therefore represents an impermissible generalisation of the claim as disclosed in the application as filed. The amendment that deleted feature "xx" therefore introduced subject-matter which extends beyond the content of the application as filed and should not have been allowed pursuant to Article 123(2) EPC. The patent is consequently opposed pursuant to Article 100(c) EPC.

*The removal of a feature from a claim is only allowed if (a) the feature was not explained to be essential in the disclosure, (b) the feature is not, in fact, indispensable for the function of the invention and (c) removal requires no modification of other features (T331/87).*

*Point out where any further amendment to take out added matter is likely to extend the protection as granted and hence is unallowable under Art.123(3) EPC.*

**Novelty**

*Go through the integers of the claim, demonstrating that they are all disclosed in combination in one prior art document. Use the language of the claim and add references and explanations. Beware the potential trap of a piece of prior art which discloses multiple embodiments with different elements of the claimed invention being in different embodiments. If there is no clear teaching to combine the relevant parts of the different embodiments, the attack is one of obviousness rather than novelty, albeit that it is based on only one document. For example, in Annex 3 of the 1991 paper there are two embodiments, one operating in transmission, the other in reflection, and these could not be combined in a novelty attack.*

    3.4  Annex y describes a [*language of the claim*], specifically a . . . [*feature and reference*] . . .

*Some short comments concerning interpretation may be necessary. Equally, some comments to rebuff a selection argument may be useful.*

*Where information from another annex is used to interpret a feature of the prior art (e.g. that it inherently has a certain property) then say it was available before the effective date of the claim where appropriate.*

    3.5  Consequently, since all the features of claim z are disclosed in combination by Annex y, claim z lacks novelty pursuant to Article 54(2)/Article 54(3)–(4) EPC and is opposed pursuant to Article 100(a) EPC.

Inventive step

*Use the problem and solution approach to demonstrate in a systematic way why the skilled man would have been led routinely to combine the relevant disclosures and arrive without invention at the relevant claim embodiment.*

    3.6  Annex y is determined to be the closest prior art for the assessment of inventive step since it is concerned with the same problem as Annex 1, namely. . . or it is concerned with the related problem of . . . and has more technical features in common with the invention of claim x than any of the other cited prior art (or, is in the same technical field and has more technical features in common with the invention of claim x than any of the other cited prior art ).

    3.7  Annex y discloses . . . (same as novelty analysis for all common features).

    3.8  The step that lies between Annex y and the invention of claim x is . . .

    3.9  The objective problem that the invention of claim x solves is therefore merely . . . since the provision of . . . is not associated with any disclosed technical effect (*consider the technical effect associated with the additional feature(s) when formulating the objective problem — do not include any pointer to the solution*).

    3.10  Annex z teaches that this problem may be solved by . . . feature zz.

*Where two extra features are present in relation to the closest prior art but they have no interrelationship, each feature solves a partial problem which can be considered separately and solved by reference to a different prior art document:*

The two partial problems solved have no interrelationship and can be considered separately (T389/86).

*Reasons why the teaching of two prior art documents would have been naturally combined by the skilled person:*

Annexes y and z both lie within precisely the same technical field which is . . . /the neighbouring technical fields of . . . (reference) and would consequently have both been well known to the skilled person. In particular, the devices of Annex y/z are stated to have been in circulation (reference).

Furthermore, both Annexes y and z were published contemporaneously and would have been associated with each other in the mind of the skilled person. It would therefore have been natural for the skilled person to consider combining their disclosures if such combination was straightforward and offered advantages.

Annexes y and z are both concerned with solving the same problem, namely . . ., and the skilled person would therefore naturally consider combining their teachings.

*The invention may consist of choosing a means to perform a particular function, the suitability of the chosen means for that function being fully appreciated in the prior art (e.g. choosing copper where a metallic conductor is required):*

When seeking to solve the problem of . . . the skilled person would have looked for a feature that has the necessary function/property. Feature zz, disclosed in annex z, is said to (necessary function/property) and is therefore precisely the kind of feature that will solve the objective technical problem established above, since it performs exactly the same function in precisely the same way in each case. It is thus clear that the problem addressed by claim x had already been appreciated and solved in the art in a complementary context (analogous substitution — T192/82 — incorporation of a known feature, having a known effect, into a known article is obvious in view of the predictability of the advantageous effect).

The invention therefore resides merely in the new use of a well known material employing the known properties of that material.

Indeed, feature zz is a well-known, commercially available item, as demonstrated by . . . (e.g. common general knowledge from within the exam paper).

*No technical difficulties are encountered in combining the teachings of the two annexes and no surprising effects are produced by the combination:*

Furthermore, feature zz is entirely compatible with the other features of claim x, as disclosed in Annex y. No modification or rearrangement of features is necessary to introduce new feature zz since . . . . Hence, feature xx is easily and routinely incorporated in to the teaching of Annex y.

Since the teachings of Annex y and Annex z are complementary it would therefore have been no more than a matter of routine variation for the skilled person to replace the . . . of annex y with the . . . of annex z and arrive at the present invention of claim x.

The skilled person, wishing to improve the . . . of Annex y, would therefore have . . . since this is the routine solution suggested to him by Annex z.

No surprising effect is observed on the combination of the relevant features since they are all simply performing the functions that are respectively known from Annexes y and z, and have no special interaction or synergy.

The use of xx as opposed to yy is no more than the use of a well-known equivalent which can involve no invention.

*Where the extra feature over the prior art is not explicitly disclosed in any other document but involves, for instance, an arbitrary selection from a range in the closest prior art document which does not lead to any surprising effect:*

The skilled person, motivated by ... to seek the optimum ... would have come to the solution to the problem by a process of routine trial and error, by testing various possible values and selecting the most advantageous values according to the results.

The solution to the objective technical problem therefore involves nothing more than choosing from a number of equally likely alternatives, no unexpected effect being associated with the particular selection made.

*Final sentence to conclude inventive step attack:*

Claim x can therefore be seen to lack an inventive step pursuant to Article 56 EPC as it represents an obvious modification of Annex y in light of the teaching of Annex z and is consequently opposed pursuant to Article 100(a) EPC.

### 4. Further claim embodiments

*Repeat for every further claim embodiment. Avoid repetition and refer back to previous paragraphs where possible in order to save time. For instance, where an independent claim lacks novelty over Annex y and a dependent claim lacks inventive step in light of Annex y as the closest prior art, a reference to the novelty attack is enough to demonstrate that the only new feature of the dependent claim over Annex y is the feature that that claim discloses.*

### 5. Description

*Do not forget to include in your opposition an attack in respect of any added matter in the description.*

*Letter to the client — legal questions*

Write notes for a letter to the client (in effect, a note to the examiner). Answer the legal questions set and clarify any false assumptions made by the client. As with answers in Paper D, quote the full basis for your legal opinion.

If a document has not been used (unlikely), explain why. Equally, if an embodiment has not been attacked (unlikely), explain why. Point out any attacks which you consider weak and explain why they are weak. If there is a chance that a weak attack might succeed, it is better to include it in the opposition and explain its weakness in the letter to the client/examiner than not to include it or only include it in the letter to the client/examiner.

Ask for any extra information needed to complete the notice of opposition (e.g. full address of opponent) and point out any evidence which may be required (e.g. to support a prior use allegation) and the timeframe for submitting it.

Point out any assumptions which you have had to make. For international 54(3) documents, explain you will have to check the register to confirm that the regional phase was entered.

Consider pointing out that a fee reduction is possible if the client is able to use a non-official language but point out that the overall costs would be greater due to translation fees. Consider pointing out that proceedings can be accelerated where infringement actions are ongoing/likely.

### 3. Worked example using EQE 2002 Paper C

*Analysing the client's letter*

General: all the necessary information regarding the name and address of the opponent and representative is present.

Paragraph 1: a legal point arises with respect to the differences between authorisation and appointment which must be addressed in the answer.

Paragraph 2: the information suggests a possible added matter attack against claim 1.

Paragraph 3: information is provided on which claims are entitled to the priority date and which claims are entitled only to the filing date.

Paragraph 4: a legal point with regard to transfer of an opposition from one party to another arises and must be addressed in the answer.

**1–145**  *Identifying claim variants and their effective dates*

Eight embodiments can be identified from the six claims due to the multiple dependency of claim 6 and the presence of added matter. No preferred features are hidden in the claims. Claims 4–6 are entitled to the priority date and claims 1–3 take the filing date.

| Embodiment | Date for validity assessment |
|---|---|
| Claim 1 | July 25, 1997 |
| Claim 1 minus added matter | July 25, 1997 |
| Claim 2 dependent on claim 1 | July 25, 1997 |
| Claim 3 dependent on claim 2 | July 25, 1997 |
| Claim 4 | July 26, 1996 |
| Claim 5 dependent on claim 4 | July 26, 1996 |
| Claim 6 dependent on claim 4 | July 26, 1996 |
| Claim 6 dependent on claim 5 | July 26, 1996 |

See below for a proposed distribution of claim integers in the novelty matrix.

**1–146**  *Determining the effective dates of the prior art documents*

Annex 2: International patent application, European regional designation (all states). Made available by publication on October 15, 1998.
Art.54(3) effect, for the states designated in common, from April 8, 1997 if entered regional phase.
Relevant to claims 1, 2 and 3 for novelty only.

Annex 3: European patent application designates all the states designated in Annex 1. Made available by publication on October 29, 1997.
Art.54(3) effect from April 26, 1996.
Relevant to all claims for all countries, for novelty only.

Annex 4: Made available by publication on September 15, 1988.
Relevant to all claims for novelty and inventive step.

Annex 5: Made available by publication sometime in August 1995.
Relevant to all claims for novelty and inventive step.

Annex 6: Made available by publication on March 14, 1996.
Relevant to all claims for novelty and inventive step.

**1–147**  *Assessing the relevance of the prior art*

See overleaf for novelty matrix.

| Claim integer | | Annex 2 | Annex 3 | Annex 4 | Annex 5 | Annex 6 | |
|---|---|---|---|---|---|---|---|
| | | | | | | Fig 1 embodiment | Fig 2 embodiment |
| | Problem addressed by the invention is how to improve the strength of mechanical fasteners (solution = having mechanical and adhesive elements). | Not relevant for inventive step. | Not relevant for inventive step. | Problem solved = how to control the stiffness of a mechanical fastening means. | Problem solved = how to make nappy tabs easier to grip and allow easier opening of nappies. | Problem solved = how to provide a better fastening means (solution = having mechanical and adhesive elements). | |
| 1.1 | A fastener suitable for engagement with a fastener of the same type, | ✓ Page 1, lines 1–2, "interengaging". | ✓ Since adhesive is used. | ✓ See claim 1, "engaging with itself". | ✗ | ✓ Fig 1 and page 1, lines 5–7. | ✓ Fig 2 and page 1, lines 10–12. |
| 1.2 | comprising a plurality of engaging heads (3) on stems(2) | ✓ Page 1, line 5, "bulbous elements". Stalk 30 and head 40 in Fig 1/2. | ✓ See hook 61 in Fig 1. | ✓ Page 2, line 4, "headed stems" and Fig 2. | ✗ | ✓ Fig 1 and page 1, lines 15–16 | ✓ Fig 2 and page 2, lines 1–3. |
| 1.3 | projecting from a first surface (12) of a base (1) | ✓ Page 1, lines 5–6, "backing web" 10 and "top surface". | ✓ Top surface of support fabric 85. | ✓ Page 2, line 4, top surface of base "B". | ✗ | ✓ Top surface of base 82. | ✓ Top surface of base 82. |
| 1.4 | wherein said base (1), stems (2) and engaging heads (3) are integrally moulded from a thermoplastic material, | ✓ Moulded from polyPPPC or polyBLE (see Annex 4, page 2, line 9). | ✗ | ? Unclear whether the base is integral with the headed stems. | ✗ | ✓ Page 3, lines 1–2. | |
| 1.5 | characterised by: a pressure sensitive adhesive (4) is applied on an upper surface of the engaging heads (3) | ✓ Page 2, lines 9–10, and 12–13 and Fig 2. | ✓? See Fig 1 — only part of the hook is covered. | ✗ | ✗ | ✓ Page 1, lines 15–16, "adhesif . . . sur la tete". | ✗ |

| Claim integer | | Annex 2 | Annex 3 | Annex 4 | Annex 5 | Annex 6 | |
|---|---|---|---|---|---|---|---|
| | | | | | | Fig 1 embodiment | Fig 2 embodiment |
| 1.6 | and in that said adhesive (4) is also applied to the base between the stems (2) and | ✓ Page 2, lines 9–10, and 12–13 and Fig 2. | ✓ See 71 in Fig 1. | ✗ | ✗ | ✓ Page 2, lines 18–19, small quantity drips down. | ✓ |
| 1.7 | in that a second surface (13) of the base (1) opposite the first surface (12) is provided with adhesive (4). | ✓ Page 2, lines 19–20, adhesive applied to bottom surface 60. | ✓ See page 2, lines 10–11. | ✗ | ✗ | ✓ Page 3, lines 4–5. | |
| 1 added matter | Upper surface of the engaging heads is flat | ? Not completely flat but flat enough to keep glue on it | ✗ | ✗ | ✗ | ✓ Page 1, line 16. | |
| 2.1 | As 1, wherein adhesive (4) has a viscosity of between 6,000 and 16,000 mPas when measured at the application temperature. | ✓ Page 2, lines 16–17, 10,000–20,000. | ✗ Reference is silent. | ✗ | ✗ | ✗ Silent as to viscosity. | |
| 3.1 | As 2, wherein engaging head (3) is of the mushroom type having a cylindrical stem (2) | ✓ See Fig 1, stem is substantially cylindrical. | ✗ | ✓ See Fig 1. | ✗ | ✓? Page 1, line 15, mushroom shaped — but are the stems cylindrical? Possibly implicit. | |
| 3.2 | and an undercut (10) having an angle α of between 25° and 50°. | ✗ No undercut disclosed. | ✗ | ✓ Page 2, lines 18–20, 60° disclosed. | ✗ | ✗ | ✗ |

| | | | | | |
|---|---|---|---|---|---|
| 4.1 | Closure tab for a sanitary article wherein | | ✓ Page 2, line 13, "closure tab for diaper". | ✓ Line 2, "diaper", "tab fastener". | ✓? Implicit from disclosure of sanitary article on page 1, line 2? |
| 4.2 | the tab is provided with a fastening region (6) and a non-fastening region | | ✓ Page 2, line 15, "central part... free of hooks and adhesive". | ✓ See second para | ✗ |
| 4.3 | and wherein the fastening region (6) is provided with a dual fastening means comprising | | ✓ | ✗ Silent as to nature of fastening means. | ✓ |
| 4.4 | (a) mechanical fastening elements for engaging with further mechanical fastening elements on a surface to which the tab is to be attached | | ✓ Page 1, lines 4–6, hooks and loops. | ✗ Silent as to nature of fastening means. | ✓ |
| 4.5 | and (b) an adhesive on the fastening elements for attaching to a surface of the sanitary article. | | ✓ Page 1, lines 16–17, adhesive on hooks. | ✗ Silent as to nature of fastening means. | ✓ |
| 5.1 | As 4, wherein the non-fastening region (5) is an outer region of the tab thereby enabling easy handling of the tab. | | ✗ Here, central part is non-fastening region. | ✓ Second para, "end of tab". | ✗ |
| 6.1 | As 4 or 5, wherein the tab is elastic. | | ✓ See Page 2, line 13. | ✓ Last line, "elastic tab". | ✗ |

| KEY | |
|---|---|
| ▓ (dark) | Prior art not citeable |
| ▒ (light) | Prior art relevant to novelty only |
| ☐ | Prior art relevant to novelty and inventive step |
| ✓ | Feature present |
| ✗ | Feature not present |
| ? | Some doubt exists as to whether feature present |

**1–151** *Formulating an attack strategy*

The following attacks are deemed worth making.

| Embodiment | Added matter | Novelty | Inventive step |
|---|---|---|---|
| Claim 1 | Yes | A2. A6 | X |
| Claim 1$^{AM}$ | X | A2. A6 | X |
| Claim 2$^1$ | Yes | A2 | A6 (CPA) |
| Claim 3$^2$ | Yes | X | A6 (CPA) + A4 |
| Claim 4 | X | A3 | A6 (CPA) + A5 |
| | | | A5 (CPA) + A6 |
| Claim 5$^4$ | X | X | A6 (CPA) + A5 |
| | | | A5 (CPA) + A6 |
| Claim 6$^4$ | X | A3 | A6 (CPA) + A5 |
| | | | A5 (CPA) + A6 |
| Claim 6$^5$ | X | X | A6 (CPA) + A5 |
| | | | A5 (CPA) + A6 |

Key

Claim x$^y$ = claim x dependent on claim y
AM = with added matter removed
CPA = closest prior art
X = no reasonable attack available

**1–152** *Writing the notice of opposition*

See overleaf for a filled-out Form 2300.

# Notice of Opposition to a European Patent

To the European Patent Office

## I. Patent opposed

| | |
|---|---|
| Opp. No. | OPPO (1) |
| Patent No. | EP-0845965 B1 |
| Application No. | 97 245 876.1 |
| Date of mention of the grant in the European Patent Bulletin (Art. 97(4), 99(1) EPC) | 27 June 2001 |

Title of the invention:
Surface fastener for sanitary products

## II. Proprietor of the Patent

Burretape A/S

first named in the patent specification

Opponent's or representative's reference (max. 15 spaces)     OREF

## III. Opponent

OPPO (2)

**Name:** Fastenall

**Address:** 1002 Sun Drive
Colorado Springs
Colorado 80906
USA

**State of residence or of principal place of business:** USA

**Telephone/Telex/Fax:**

**Multiple opponents:** [ ] further opponents see additional sheet

## IV. Authorisation

### 1. Representative
(Name only one representative to whom notification is to be made)

OPPO (9)

**Name:** Whitcomb Judson

**Address of place of business:** 18 High Street
Stratford-Upon-Avon
Warwickshire CV3 7XJ
United Kingdom

**Telephone/Telex/Fax:**

**Additional representative(s):** [ ] (on additional sheet/see authorisation)    OPPO (5)

### 2. Employee(s) of the opponent authorised for these opposition proceedings under Art. 133(3) EPC

Name(s):

**Authorisation(s):**
[ ] not considered necessary
[X] has/have been registered under No.   xxxxxx
[ ] is/are enclosed

To 1./2.

EPO Form 2300.1 04.93 (int. ad. 12/97)

## V. Opposition is filed against

— the patent as a whole  ☒

— claim(s) No(s).

## VI. Grounds for opposition:

**Opposition is based on the following grounds:**

(a) the subject-matter of the European patent opposed is not patentable (Art. 100(a) EPC) because:

— it is not new (Art. 52(1); 54 EPC)  ☒

— it does not involve an inventive step (Art. 52(1); 56 EPC)  ☒

— patentability is excluded on other grounds, i. e.  Art.  ☐

(b) the patent opposed does not disclose the invention in a manner sufficiently clear and complete for it to be carried out by a person skilled in the art (Art. 100(b) EPC; see Art. 83 EPC).  ☐

(c) the subject-matter of the patent opposed extends beyond the content of the application/ of the earlier application as filed (Art. 100(c) EPC, see Art. 123(2) EPC).  ☒

## VII. Facts and arguments
(Rule 55(c) EPC)
presented in support of the opposition are submitted herewith on a separate sheet (annex 1)  ☒

## VIII. Other requests:

Oral proceedings are requested in the case that the Opposition Division decides not to revoke the patent completely.

EPO Form 2300.2 04.93 (int. ad. 12/97)

## IX. Evidence presented

Enclosed =
will be filed at a later date =

### A. Publications:

Publication date

1

Particular relevance (page, column, line, fig.):

2

Particular relevance (page, column, line, fig.):

3

Particular relevance (page, column, line, fig.):

4

Particular relevance (page, column, line, fig.):

5

Particular relevance (page, column, line, fig.):

6

Particular relevance (page, column, line, fig.):

7

Particular relevance (page, column, line, fig.):

Continued on additional sheet

### B. Other evidence

Continued on additional sheet

EPO Form 2300.3 04.93 (int. ad. 12/97)

| | | for EPO use only |
|---|---|---|
| **X.** **Payment of the opposition fee is made** | | |
| ☒ as indicated in the enclosed voucher for payment of fees and costs (EPO Form 1010) | | |
| ☐ | | |

**XI. List of documents**

| Enclosure No. | | | No. of copies | |
|---|---|---|---|---|
| 0 | ☒ | Form for notice of opposition | 2 | (min. 2) |
| 1 | ☒ | Facts and arguments (see VII.) | 2 | (min. 2) |
| 2 | | Copies of documents presented as evidence (see IX.) | | |
| 2a | ☒ | — Publications | 2 | (min. 2 of each) |
| 2b | ☐ | — Other documents | | (min. 2 of each) |
| 3 | ☐ | Signed authorisation(s) (see IV.) | | |
| 4 | ☒ | Voucher for payment of fees and costs (see X.) | 1 | |
| 5 | ☐ | Cheque | | |
| 6 | ☐ | Additional sheet(s) | | (min. 2 of each) |
| 7 | ☐ | Other (please specify here): | | |

**XII. Signature**
**of opponent or representative**

*[signature]*

Place   Stratford

Date    xx.yy.200z

Please type name under signature. In the case of legal persons, the position which the person signing holds within the company should also be typed.

EPO Form 2300.4 04.93 (int. ad. 12/97)

## Statement of grounds

The patent is opposed in its English text and is referred to herein as Annex 1.

### 1. Priority date of claims

1.1 The subject matter of claims 1 to 3 was first disclosed in European patent application No. 97 245 876.1 as filed. The validity of these claims is therefore to be assessed at the filing date, 25 July 1997.

1.2 The subject matter of claims 4 to 6 was first disclosed in priority application DK-0159/96, having a filing date of 26 July 1996. Since the priority claim is assumed to be valid, and by virtue of Articles 87(1) and 89 EPC, the validity of these claims is to be assessed at 26 July 1996.

### 2. Prior art

2.1 Annex 2 (which has been read in its English translation), is citable against claims 1–3 under Article 54(3)–(4), Article 158(1) and rule 23a EPC for all common, validly designated states (i.e., AT, CH, DE, DK, ES, FR, GB, IT, LI, NL, SE) because it is an international patent application, published after, but having a priority date earlier than, the priority date to which these claims are entitled. Furthermore, Annex 2 validly designated EP, validly entered the European regional phase for the above-mentioned states and validly claims priority.

Annex 2 is therefore citable, under Article 54(3) against claims 1–3, for novelty purposes only.

2.2 Annex 3 (which has been read in its English translation) is citable against claims 1–6 under Article 54(3)–(4) and rule 23a EPC for all common, validly designated states (i.e., AT, CH, DE, DK, ES, FR, GB, IT, LI, NL, SE) because it is a European patent application, published after, but having a priority date earlier than, the priority date to which these claims are entitled. Furthermore, Annex 3 validly claims priority.

Annex 3 is therefore citable, under Article 54(3) against claims 1–6, for novelty purposes only.

2.3 Annex 4 (which has been read in its English translation) is citable against claims 1–6 under Article 54(2) EPC since it has a publication date prior to the priority date to which these claims are entitled.

Annex 4 is therefore potentially relevant to the novelty and inventive step of claims 1–6.

2.4 Annex 5 (which has been read in its English translation) is citable against claims 1–6 under Article 54(2) EPC since it has a publication date prior to the priority date to which these claims are entitled.

Annex 5 is therefore potentially relevant to the novelty and inventive step of claims 1–6.

2.5 Annex 6 (which has been read in its French translation) is citable against claims 1–6 under Article 54(2) EPC since it has a publication date prior to the priority date to which these claims are entitled.

Annex 6 is therefore potentially relevant to the novelty and inventive step of claims 1–6.

### 3. Added Matter

3.1 The characterising features of claim 1 were present in the application as filed only in combination with the additional feature that the upper surface of the engaging heads is flat. There was no basis in the application as filed for the combination of the characterising clause without the flat upper surface. The disclosure of the application as filed presented the flat upper surface as an essential feature of the invention (see paragraph15, last sentence). The deletion of this feature from the combination in which it was originally disclosed resulted in the subject matter of the application being extended, contrary to the requirements of Article 123(2) EPC. This added matter is present not only in claim 1, but also in the statement of invention of paragraph 5, as this refers to the characterising clause of claim 1. The patent is consequently opposed under Article 100(c) EPC.

### 4. Claim 1

4.1 Annex 2 discloses, in the language of claim 1, a fastener suitable for engagement with a fastener of the same type ("fastener having . . . means for inter-engaging", page 1, lines 1–2) comprising a plurality of engaging heads on stems (= bulbous elements 20 each comprising a stalk 30, page 2, lines 1–2) projecting from a first surface of a base ("backing web having bulbous elements protruding from its top surface", page 1, lines 5–6), the base, stems and engaging heads being integrally moulded from a material ("the web and bulbous elements are moulded from a suitable material such as Poly PPPC or Poly BLE", page 2, lines 3–4) a pressure sensitive adhesive is applied on an upper surface of the engaging heads (see page 2, lines 9–10 in combination with lines 12–13), to the base between the stems (see page 2, lines 12–14 and layer 50 in Fig.2) and a second surface of the base opposite to the first surface is provided with said adhesive (page 2, lines 19–20). Thus the only feature of claim 1 which is not expressly disclosed is that the base, stems and engaging heads are moulded from a thermoplastic. However, as is clear from Annex 4, the polymers Poly PPPC and Poly BLE are in fact thermoplastics. Annex 4 was published well before 25 July 1997, the effective date of claim 1. Consequently, since all the features of claim 1 are disclosed in combination in Annex 2, claim 1 lacks novelty pursuant to Article 54(3)–(4) EPC and is opposed pursuant to Article 100(a) EPC.

4.2 Annex 6 discloses, in the language of claim 1, a fastener suitable for engagement with a fastener of the same type (page 2, lines 5–7 and 10–12 — "auto-accrochant") comprising a plurality of engaging heads on stems ("éléments de fermetures ayant la forme de champignon", page 1, line 15 and Fig 1) projecting from a first surface of a base (= top surface of the "élément porteur" 82 in Fig 1) wherein said base, stems and engaging heads are integrally moulded from a thermoplastic material (page 3, lines 1–2), a pressure sensitive adhesive is applied on an upper surface of the engaging heads ("avec un adhésif sensible à la pression 12 sure leur tête 11" page 1, lines 15–16) the adhesive 4 also being applied to the base between the stems ("une quantité minimale d'adhésif goutte des têtes sur l'élément porteur", page 2, lines 18–19) and to a second surface of the base opposite to the first surface (page 3, lines 4–5). Consequently, since all the features of claim 1 are disclosed in combination by the Fig 1 embodiment of Annex 6, claim 1 lacks novelty pursuant to Article 54(2) EPC and is opposed pursuant to Article 100(a) EPC.

### 5. Claim 1 as amended to remove added matter

When claim 1 has been amended to add back the "flat" feature it will still lack novelty in view of Annexes 2 and 6. Regarding Annex 6, it is clear from page 1, line 16 that the heads of the "éléments de fermeture 10" are preferably flat. In Annex 2, the bulbous elements 40 have a slightly curved upper surface. However, this must be taken to fall within the meaning of "flat" when Annex 1 is properly construed since the heads must only be flat to the extent necessary to ensure that adhesive stays on the upper surface of the heads during application (see Annex 1, page 3, lines 8–10). It is clear in Annex 2 that the adhesive "does not flow preferentially into the spaces between the bulbous heads" (page 2, lines 13–14). Furthermore, claim 3, which is dependent on claim 1 indirectly, demands an engaging head of the "mushroom type", which would generally be construed to have a gently sloping upper surface.

## 6. Claim 2

6.1 Claim 2 is dependent on claim 1 and includes the same added matter. It therefore cannot be maintained in its present form and is opposed pursuant to Article 100(c) EPC.

6.2 As is the case with claim 1, claim 2 lacks novelty over Annex 2 since the additional feature "a pressure-sensitive adhesive has a viscosity of between 6000 and 16000 MPa.s when measured at the application temperature" is also disclosed in Annex 2 (page 2, lines 16–17). The value of 10,000, clearly disclosed in Annex 2 as the lower limit of the range, falls within the range defined by claim 2. Since all the other features of claim 2 are disclosed in Annex 2 (see paragraph 3.2), claim 2 lacks novelty and is opposed pursuant to Article 100(a) EPC.

6.3 As shown in paragraph 4.2, all the features of claim 1 are present in Annex 6. The extra feature of claim 2 is, however, not expressly recited. Annex 6, like Annex 1, is concerned with providing a surface fastener with a combination of mechanical and adhesive fastening. Annex 6 therefore represents the closest prior art for the assessment of inventive step, being in the same field (fastening means for sanitary articles) and having the most technical features in common.

The technical effect of the additional features of claim 2, the viscosity range, is that this "ensures that part of the adhesive stays on the (flat) heads and part of the adhesive flows off the heads and fills the spaces between the stems" (paragraph 15, second and third sentence of Annex 1).

Thus, the objective technical problem is how to find the viscosity at which the adhesive should be applied to achieve this desired adhesive distribution.

Annex 6 teaches that by an appropriate choice of viscosity it is possible to make a fastener in which some adhesive adheres to the heads of the fastening elements and some spreads between them (3rd and 5th paragraphs on page 2 of A6). As indicated above, in the context of claim 1, A6 teaches that in the Figure 1 embodiment some flow of adhesive between the fastening elements is expected (3rd para, page 2). The paragraph goes on to say that the viscosity should be sufficiently high that only a limited quantity drops from the heads otherwise one would have a fastening system too strong for some applications (but, by implication, not too strong for other applications). Thus, depending upon the strength of attachment that the skilled person requires, he chooses a more or less viscous adhesive. The selection of the appropriate viscosity is nothing more than simple trial and error. A6 already tells the skilled person to choose a viscosity at which there is adhesive both on the heads and between the fastening elements. No advantage accrues from the choice of this range of viscosities. As acknowledged in Guidelines C/IV/Annex/3.1(ii), there is no invention in such a trial and error selection of parameters from a limited range of possibilities.

Claim 2 therefore lacks inventive step over Annex 6 pursuant to Article 56 EPC and is opposed pursuant to Article 100(a) EPC.

## 7. Claim 3

7.1 Claim 3 is dependent on claim 1 via claim 2 and includes the same added matter. It therefore cannot be maintained in its present form and is opposed pursuant to Article 100(c) EPC.

7.2 Compared to claim 3, Annex 6 (embodiment of Fig 1) lacks the following features: (a) adhesive viscosity = 6000–16000; (b) heads have an undercut of between 25° and 50°. This is clear from paragraph 3.3 and the fact that Annex 6 clearly discloses mushroom-type heads ("ayant la forme de champignon", page 1, line 15) having a cylindrical stem (see Fig 1 in combination with what is implicit in the term "mushroom-shaped").

For the reasons given in paragraph 6.3, A6 is the closest prior art for the assessment of inventive step in relation to claim 3.

The objective problem to be solved by claim 3 in the light of Annex 6 is therefore how to (a) choose a suitable viscosity for the adhesive to ensure that it stays on the heads and (b) how to improve the mechanical engagement of the heads (see page 3, lines 12–14 of Annex 1).

The two partial problems solved have no interrelationship and can be considered separately (T389/86).

It has already been shown in paragraph 6.3 that the solution to part (a) of the objective problem is not inventive in light of the teaching of Annex 6. Furthermore, Annex 4 teaches that part (b) of the problem may be solved by the incorporation of an undercut in the heads having an angle of between 20 and 60° (see page 2, lines 18–20). The range 25° to 50° cannot be seen as a novel selection from 20° to 60° since it is neither small nor purposive and hence this feature is disclosed in Annex 4. Annex 6 and Annex 4 both lie within the same technical field (fasteners which can be repeatedly re-closed) and would consequently both have been well known to the skilled person at the priority date of claim 3. Furthermore, they were published within a few years of each other and would have been associated with each other in the mind of the skilled person, both addressing the problem of improving the properties of mechanical fasteners. It would therefore have been natural for the skilled person to have considered combining their disclosures if such a combination was straightforward and offered advantages.

When seeking to solve part (b) of the problem, the skilled person would therefore have looked for a disclosure teaching a means of improving mechanical fasteners and would have found that the disclosure of Annex 4 was entirely suitable, since the undercut of Annex 4 will perform exactly the same function, in exactly the same way when incorporated into Annex 6.

Furthermore, the undercut feature of Annex 4 is entirely compatible with the features of Annex 6 and no modification or rearrangement of features is necessary when combining the two.

In summary, the skilled person, wishing to improve the mechanical fastening of Annex 6, Fig 1 embodiment, would have incorporated the teaching of Annex 4 since this is the routine solution suggested by Annex 4. Claim 3 therefore lacks an inventive step pursuant to Article 56 EPC since it represents an obvious modification of Annex 6 in light of Annex 4 and is consequently opposed pursuant to Article 100(a) EPC.

### 8. Claim 4

8.1 Annex 3 discloses, in the words of claim 4, a closure tab for a sanitary article ("closure tab for diaper", page 2, line 13) wherein the tab is provided with a fastening region and a non-fastening region ("a central part of the tab is free of hooks and adhesive", page 2, line 15) and wherein the fastening region is provided with a dual fastening means comprising (a) mechanical fastening elements for engaging with further mechanical fastening elements on a surface to which the tab is to be attached (page 1, lines 1–6) and (b) an adhesive on the fastening elements for attaching to a surface of the sanitary article (page 1, lines 16–17). Consequently, since all the features of claim 4 are disclosed in combination by Annex 3, claim 4 lacks novelty pursuant to Article 54(3)–(4) and is opposed pursuant to Article 100(a) EPC.

8.2 Annex 5 may be taken to be the closest prior art for the assessment of inventive step in respect of claim 4 since it is concerned with the provision of a closure tab for sanitary articles (A4, line 2), the closure tab having both a fastening region and a non-fastening region (2nd paragraph, first sentence).

However, Annex 5 is silent as to what kind of fastening means should be used for the fastening region.

The objective problem solved by the invention of claim 4 in light of Annex 5 is hence how to provide a suitable fastening means for the fastening region of the tab.

Annex 6 teaches that this problem may be solved by providing a fastening region having a dual fastening means comprising mechanical and adhesive elements (see page 1, lines 11–12).

Annexes 5 and 6 lie within precisely the same technical field (fastening means for sanitary articles) and would consequently have been well known to the skilled person. Furthermore, both Annexes 5 and 6 were published within a few months of each other and would have been associated in the mind of the skilled person since they both provide improvements in the manufacture of sanitary articles such as diapers. It would therefore have been natural for the skilled person to have considered combining their disclosures if such combination was straightforward and offered advantages.

Annex 6 specifically teaches that the fastening means it provides is suitable for use in a sanitary article (page 1, lines 1–2) and the skilled person is therefore motivated to select this disclosure in solving the problem set out above. Furthermore, the fastening means of A6 performs exactly the same function in exactly the same way when incorporated into the tab of Annex 5 and is entirely compatible with the tab of Annex 5, no modification or rearrangement of features being necessary.

The skilled person, faced with the problem of providing a suitable fastening means for the tab of Annex 5 would therefore have incorporated the fastening means of Annex 6 since this is the routine solution suggested to him by Annex 6.

Claim 4 can therefore be seen to lack an inventive step pursuant to Article 56 EPC as the invention it embodies represents an obvious modification of Annex 5 in the light of Annex 6 and is consequently opposed pursuant to Article 100(a) EPC.

8.3 Furthermore, if Annex 6 is chosen as the closest prior art, claim 4 also lacks an inventive step.

Annex 6 discloses all the features of claim 4 except for the provision of fastening and non-fastening regions.

The objective problem solved by the invention of claim 4 in light of Annex 6 is therefore how to make a sanitary article easier to open and re-close.

The solution to this problem is taught by Annex 5, paragraph 2, where a tab bearing a section free of any fastening means is suggested.

The compatibility of the teaching of Annexes 5 and 6 has been discussed in paragraph 8.2 above. No surprising effect is observed on combination of the relevant features since they are simply performing the functions that are respectively known from Annexes 5 and 6 independently and have no special interaction or synergy.

Claim 4 can therefore be seen to lack an inventive step pursuant to Article 56 EPC as it represents an obvious modification of Annex 5 in light of the teaching of Annex 6 and is consequently opposed pursuant to Article 100(a) EPC.

## 9. Claim 5

9.1 The extra feature of claim 5, wherein the non-fastening region is an outer region of the tab is disclosed in Annex 5 ("the end of the tab is free from any fastening means", line 6 — see also the drawing).

Therefore, taking Annex 5 as the closest prior art for the assessment of inventive step, the objective problem solved by the invention of claim 5 is the same as that described in paragraph 8.2 above. The solution to this problem has already been shown to be obvious, taking into account Annex 6.

Claim 5 can therefore be seen to lack an inventive step pursuant to Article 56 EPC as it represents an obvious modification of Annex 5 in light of the teaching of Annex 6 and is consequently opposed pursuant to Article 100(a) EPC.

9.2 Furthermore, if Annex 6 is taken to be the closest prior art, claim 5 equally lacks an inventive step since, as described in paragraph 8.3, it would be obvious to incorporate the teaching of Annex 5 to solve the technical problem posed in paragraph 8.3 and in doing so the skilled person would inevitably also introduce the non-fastening region at the end of the tab since this is the only arrangement that is taught by Annex 5.

### 10. Claim 6 dependent on claim 4

10.1 The extra feature of claim 6 relative to claim 4 is the use of an elastic tab. This feature is present in the tab of Annex 3 (page 2, line 13). Since all the features of claim 4 are also present in Annex 3 in combination (see paragraph 7.1), claim 6, when dependent on claim 4, lacks novelty under Article 54(3) over Annex 3 and is opposed pursuant to Article 100(a) EPC.

10.2 The elastic tab feature of claim 6 is also taught by Annex 5 (see the last paragraph). Therefore, taking Annex 5 as the closest prior art for the assessment of inventive step, the objective problem to be solved is the same as that described in paragraph 8.2 above. The solution to this problem was shown to be obvious in paragraph 8.2. Claim 6, as dependent on claim 4, can therefore be seen to lack an inventive step pursuant to Article 56 EPC as it represents an obvious modification of Annex 5 in light of the teaching of Annex 6 and is consequently opposed pursuant to Article 100(a) EPC.

10.3 Furthermore, if Annex 6 is taken to be the closest prior art, claim 6, when dependent on claim 4, equally lacks an inventive step for the reasons given in paragraph 9.2 above, *mutatis mutandis*.

### 11. Claim 6 dependent on claim 5

11.1 The extra feature of claim 6 relative to claim 5 is the use of an elastic tab. This feature is also taught by Annex 5 (see paragraph 10.1). Therefore, by virtue of the same reasoning given in paras 9.1 and 9.2, claim 6, as dependent on claim 5, lacks an inventive step pursuant to Article 56 EPC since it represents an obvious modification of Annex 5 in light of the teaching of Annex 6 and, equally, an obvious modification of Annex 6 in light of the teaching of Annex 5. It is consequently opposed pursuant to Article 100(a) EPC.

### Notes for letter to client

A European patent attorney does not need to submit an authorisation when new proceedings are commenced with the EPO. An authorisation may be needed when there is a change of representative during the course of proceedings (Decision of the President of the EPO dated July 19, 1991). There is no change of representative in this case since the opposition has not yet been filed — and hence proceedings have not begun. The fact that Mr Pitt has a general authorisation does not mean that he has been **appointed** as representative on any new proceedings between Fastenall and the EPO, and hence that there is a change of representative if another is used instead of him. However, it would be good practice to have a valid authorisation on file. The client can give a general authorisation for me (Judson) to work on any application/opposition owned by Fastenall or a specific authorisation to represent Fastenall in this specific opposition. The managing director can sign on behalf of the company.

An opposition cannot be assigned to another party (G4/88, G2/04). However, an opposition may be transferred from one party to another along with business assets if the business assets in respect of which the opposition was filed are being transferred.

You refer to "at least partly transferring ownership" of Fastenall. Unless all the relevant assets were transferred, it would not be possible to transfer the opposition. It would therefore be prudent for Pooter and Grovel to file their own opposition before the opposition period ends.

It will be necessary to check the European patent register to see whether Annex 2 entered the regional phase and hence whether it is Art.54(3) prior art or not.

## 4. Worked example using EQE 2005 paper C.

This example is given to contrast with the example of using a novelty matrix, based on the 2002 paper C, which precedes it. Of course both approaches are trying to achieve the same result — a good pass mark in the paper C exam that you sit for real. The approaches differ in the extent to which the candidate must write material which will not form part of the answer which the Examiners will mark. The novelty matrix approach has lots to commend it, and many people pass the exam using this approach. The matrix approach lends itself to the full analysis of subtle points, and allows the main parts of the answer to be gathered together ready to be deployed as soon as the formal answer is to be written up. But it can involve a great deal of writing and a lot of time can be wasted producing a superb novelty matrix which in itself will gather no marks — it is merely a pre-cursor to the writing of an answer proper. The Examiner's comments for the 2005 exam contained a reminder that "feature charts prepared during the examination by candidates as an aid to analysis of the prior art will be disregarded".

Conversely, the simple approach dispenses with the preparation of a formal novelty matrix, potentially reducing significantly the amount of writing and preparation involved as work prior to the writing of the exam answer. But rather than try further to explain the differences between the two approaches, we will move straight into the example of this alternative approach.

### *Organising the paper*                                                                 1–154

This approach to the paper generally involves more direct cross comparison of the papers — particularly of the claims and the prior art. You may find that simply stapling together the individual sheets of each of the pieces of prior art, and of the patent in suit, is therefore preferable to gathering the papers together in a ring binder, but the merit of the ring binder is that you should waste less time hunting for the right Annex. Find out which approach you prefer before you sit the exam.

### *Analysing the client's letter*                                                        1–155

General: All the necessary information regarding the name and address of the opponent and representative is present.

Paragraph 2:
There is clearly no added matter objection to be made, but the change to the wording of claim 3 between the priority filing and the European filing suggests that claim 3 as directly dependant upon claim1 may only be entitled to the filing date rather than to the claimed priority date. If we have any prior art which was published in the interval between the priority and filing dates, we will need to decide the issue of the date of claim 3 as directly dependant on claim 1.

Paragraph 3:
The information suggests that we have a document that may have been published in October 1998 by disclosure to Claus Sandler (the author of the letter from the client) and to colleagues. If we find that we want to rely on this disclosure, it may be necessary to include in the opposition an undertaking to supply a declaration (or sworn state-

ment) from at least Claus Sandler. Sandler and his colleagues could also be summoned as witnesses. We do not have the original of letter, but the copy of the letter that we supply will be evidence of the content of the original letter. There is also an issue concerning the name of the author of the letter — which clearly needs to be addressed, at least in a letter to the client or in the section of our answer that deals with legal points. We should note the express question seeking our advice regarding this document.

Paragraph 4:
There is a false assumption from the client concerning a territorially-limited opposition. Again we have an express question which we need to answer.

Paragraph 5:
This raises the issue of non-unity as a potential ground of opposition — which of course it is not. Again, we need to explain to the client why the mooted attack is not possible.

Paragraph 6:
This should ring some bells concerning case law of the Enlarged Board of Appeal. Note the wording of the question — "could he make submissions on our behalf?" — Not "could he represent us?"

**1-156** *Identify claim variants and their effective dates*

In the priority filing, claim 3 (horseshoe-like cross-section) depended from claim 2 only (shape memory effect film). The amendment (made pre-filing) to make claim 3 depend in the alternative from claim 1 links the horseshoe shape to a shape modification process which has no apparent link to the shape memory effect. The description provides no basis for such a combination. Thus the new combination provided by the amendment to claim 3 gives rise to subject matter which is not clearly and unambiguously derivable from the priority document. Hence claim 3 as dependant on claim 1 is not entitled to the claimed priority date, but must be judged as at the filing date.

For claim 3 as directly dependant on claim 1 the effective date for assessing novelty and inventive step in the 26th November 1999.

For all the other claims, including claim 3 as dependant on claim 2, the date for assessment is the priority date, the 27th November 1998.

The set of claims are deceptively simple. The simplicity of claims 4, 5 and 6 stands out, but so should the deception.

Claim 4 is extremely broad. It is not limited to size in any way — there is no limitation to sewer pipe (unlike claims 1 to 3). More trickily, while the claim requires a thermally recoverable shape, it does not have to be of the type suggested by claims 1 to 3. In particular, the claim covers tubular films which shrink widthways when re-heated, not just those that expand widthways on heating.

Claim 5 is also notable. It is a product by process claim that appears to be limited to the use of the method of claim 2. But "produced using" should be read as though it were "produceable using" (as is clear from the Guidelines, C.III.4.7b). The claim does not in fact require that the sewer pipe was lined in a process which used the shape memory effect — although it does not extend to sewer pipes lined with a film which cannot be made to exhibit such an effect. It is unlikely to be possible to distinguish pipes lined using the claim 2 method from those using a similar method in which step iii is performed without blowing hot air. Thus the claim will cover such indistinguishable pipes.

Claim 6 is also a challenge. It is not immediately clear what the claim covers. At first sight it might be thought to relate solely to the use of the film for making something which will subsequently be implanted. But on closer inspection, it appears that the claim actually covers the use of a film in an implanting process. Providing an implant in the arteries or veins of a patient (human or animal) would clearly require a surgical process — even it were only the opening of the artery or vein that was to be repaired. Such a repair would obviously constitute a method of surgical treatment which, by virtue of Article 52(4), is not to be regarded as an invention susceptible of industrial application. Article 52(4) is embraced in the grounds of opposition of Article 100(a). Consequently we do not need find prior art for this claim in order to attack it.

| Embodiment | Date for Validity Assessment |
|---|---|
| Claim 1 | November 27th, 1998 |
| Claim 2 | November 27th, 1998 |
| Claim 3 as dependant on Claim 2 | November 27th, 1998 |
| Claim 3 as dependant on Claim 1 | November 26th, 1999 |
| Claim 4 | November 27th, 1998 |
| Claim 5 | November 27th, 1998 |
| Claim 6 | November 27th, 1998 |

*Determining the effective dates of the prior art documents*

Annex 2: Extract from handbook of plastics, made available by publication in April 1998. The title of the book, and the content of the extract, suggest that the disclosure constitutes common general knowledge (in the field of plastics).
Annex 2 is therefore relevant to all claims for novelty and inventive step.

Annex 3: European patent application designating all states designated in Annex 1. Made available by publication on November 10th, 1999; filing date May 6th 1998. This citation is relevant, for novelty only, against all claims (other than claim 3 as directly dependant on claim 1) in respect of those commonly designated states for which designation fees were correctly paid. The citation is relevant to claim 3 as directly dependant on claim 1 for novelty and inventive step (all states).

Annex 4: British patent application made available by publication on April 14th, 1993: relevant to all claims for novelty and inventive step.

Annex 5: If the letter and its content were not governed by confidentiality, then the disclosure to Mr Sandler and his two colleagues on the journey to the trade fair in October 1998 would clearly constitute publication. Even if that disclosure were deemed to be the consequence of an evident abuse against USE Kunststofftechnik, it took place more than 6 months before the filing date of the Annex 1 and hence is not caught by Article 55.

So, if no confidentiality applies, the citation is citable for novelty and obviousness against all claims.

The issue of confidentiality is explored in the "Notes for letter to client" section below. The conclusion there is that although the letter and its disclosure are probably not citable, there is nothing to be lost by using this Annex in the opposition.

Conclusion: treat as citable for novelty and obviousness against all claims.

Annex 6: Journal extract published in June 19th, 1995: relevant to all claims for novelty and obviousness.

*Assessing the relevance of the prior art*

The prior art Annexes are here marked up as they might be during the examination to show the passages and features relevant to the claims. The passages and comments which have been added are shaded and written in bold capitals. Particularly relevant or useful parts of the text have been enclosed in boxes.

**CITABLE ALL CLAIMS NOVELTY AND OBVIOUSNESS**
**COMMON GENERAL KNOWLEDGE**
**TEACHES ALL CLAIM 2 FEATURES <u>EXCEPT</u> BLOWING HOT AIR THROUGH TUBES**
**ANTICIPATES CLAIM 4**

**Annexe 2**

**Extrait de "Handbuch der Kunststoffe", publié au mois d'avril 1988**
**Eléments plastiques à mémoire de formes**

Il est possible de donner à certaines matières plastiques, notamment des polymères tels que les polyéthylènes ou les polyamides, la capacité de modifier leur forme puis de la reprendre sous l'action de la chaleur. Pour obtenir cette propriété, appelée 'mémoire de forme', la matière doit posséder une structure interne particulière et être soumise à un traitement spécial pendant sa fabrication. Pour modifier la forme de la matière, ce traitement spécial nécessite de chauffer la matière dans sa forme originale à une température supérieure à celle dite température d'activation et de lui donner à cette température une autre forme désirée, généralement par étirage. Si la matière déformée est ensuite rapidement refroidie au-dessous de la température d'activation, elle conserve cet état de déformation. La matière ne reprend sa forme initiale, en raison de

sa structure interne spéciale, que si elle est chauffée ultérieurement au-dessus de sa température d'activation. Lorsqu'elle reprend sa forme initiale, les mouvements directionnels qu'elle a subis pendant sa fabrication s'inversent, par exemple les mouvements d'étirage deviennent des contractions. Ainsi, la forme d'un objet, par exemple un tube, fabriqué dans une matière à mémoire de forme peut être modifiée par application de chaleur.

Les gaines rétractables servant à recouvrir des câbles ou des canalisations sont un produit typique fait d'une matière plastique reprenant sa forme initiale sous l'action de la chaleur. Les gaines rétractables, autrement dit des gaines fabriquées dans une matière à mémoire de formes, qui ont été élargies par application de chaleur pendant leur fabrication, sont facilement tirées sur le câble ou la canalisation à température ambiante, puis sont de nouveau chauffées à leur température d'activation ou au-dessus, ce qui provoque leur contraction et leur rétraction sur le câble ou la canalisation. Dans ce but, il est possible d'utiliser toute source de chaleur appropriée, par exemple un radiateur à rayons infrarouges, un courant d'air chaud ou de la vapeur surchauffée, tous ces moyens produisant le même effet.

**A54(3) NOVELTY ONLY ALL CLAIMS
[EXCEPT 3 ON 1 (FOR WHICH A54(2)]
ANTICIPATES CLAIMS 1,5 - A54(3)
ANTICIPATES CLAIM 3 ON 1 A54(2)
ARGUE "FILM"**

Annex 3

EP 0 962 399 A1

| | |
|---|---|
| Date of publication: | 10.11.1999 Bulletin 1999/45 |
| Int. Cl.⁶: | F16L 58/10 |
| Application number: | 98109221.4 |
| Date of filing: | 06.05.1998 |
| Designated Contracting States: | AT BE CH CY DE DK ES FI FR GB GR IE IT |
| **DESIGNATION FEES PAID (FOR 54(3) EFFECT?** | LI LU MC NL PT SE |
| Applicant: | Rohrfrei GmbH |
| | 60311 Frankfurt (DE) |
| Inventor: | Stein, Frank N. |
| | 60599 Frankfurt (DE) |
| Representative: | Dr. A. Kula |
| | Waldstr. |
| | 785316 Hohentann(DE) |

**Method of lining pipes**

[001] The present invention relates to a method for lining pipes, for example pipes made of concrete, which have been laid in the ground.

[002] Throughout the world there is a very large number of pipes, which need repair or restoration. For example, the wall of an underground sewer pipe made of concrete may become brittle and crack so that sewage leaks into the surrounding soil.

[003] It is therefore the object of the present invention to provide a simple and effective method of repairing a pipe to make it leak-proof.

[004] This object is achieved by a method as defined in the claim.

[005] A preferred embodiment of the invention will now be described, by way of example, with reference to the accompanying cross-sectional drawings.

[006] Figure 1 shows a pipe 31, e. g. a sewer pipe, which is to be lined with an elastic liner tube 32 having a diameter D1 corresponding to the inner diameter of the pipe 31. The liner tube 32 is made from a plastics material such as polyethylene.

**< HERE PRE-AMBLE CLAIM 1
BELOW IS STEP (i) OF CLAIM 1**

[007] In order to facilitate the insertion of the liner tube 32 into the pipe 31, the outer diameter of the liner tube 32 is reduced. This is achieved by elastically deforming the liner tube 32 from its original circular cross-section into a liner tube 32' of horseshoe-shaped cross-section having a considerably reduced diameter D2. Preferably, D2 is 20 to 35% smaller than D1. The liner tube 32' is held in the deformed condition by a thin plastics film, which is wrapped around the deformed liner tube 32' to form a sleeve 33. The plastics film may be made of polymeric material such as polyvinyl chloride, polyamide or polyethylene. The sleeve 33 contains a heating wire 34, which extends along the length of the sleeve. This is shown in Figure 2.

**BELOW IS STEP (ii) OF CLAIM 1**

[008] The deformed liner tube 32' wrapped in the sleeve 33 is then inserted into the pipe 31 that is to be lined, see Figure 3. The insertion may be done by means of a pulling rope fixed at the front end of the liner tube (not shown).

**BELOW IS STEP (iii) OF CLAIM 1**

[009] When the liner tube 32' is at the desired position in the pipe 31, the wire 34 is heated to melt and rupture the sleeve 33. When the sleeve 33 is ruptured, the deformed liner tube 32', due to its elasticity, springs back to its original circular cross section and into a position lining the interior of the pipe 31. Figure 4 shows the liner tube 32 in this position (the ruptured sleeve 33 has been omitted for the sake of clarity). Applying air pressure inside the liner tube 32 can accelerate its return to the circular shape. **INDISTINGUISHABLE FROM CLAIM 2 RESULT? SO ANTICIPATES CLAIM 5?**

**Claim**

Method for lining a pipe (31), comprising elastically deforming a liner tube (32) having an outer diameter (D1) substantially equal to the inner diameter of the pipe (31) to be lined into a horseshoe-shaped cross-section of a smaller diameter (D2), holding the deformed shape of the liner tube by wrapping a sleeve (33) around the deformed liner tube (32'), inserting the deformed liner tube (32') into the pipe (31) and allowing the deformed liner tube (32') to return to its circular shape by rupturing the sleeve (33).

**THIS CLAIM ANTICIPATES CLAIM 1 EXCEPT <u>HERE</u> NOT EXPRESSLY A SEWER PIPE (ALBEIT THAT FIGURE 1, WHICH PROVIDES THE REFERENCE NUMERALS IS SAID TO SHOW SUCH A PIPE), AND NEED TO ARGUE "FILM".**

**Annex 3**

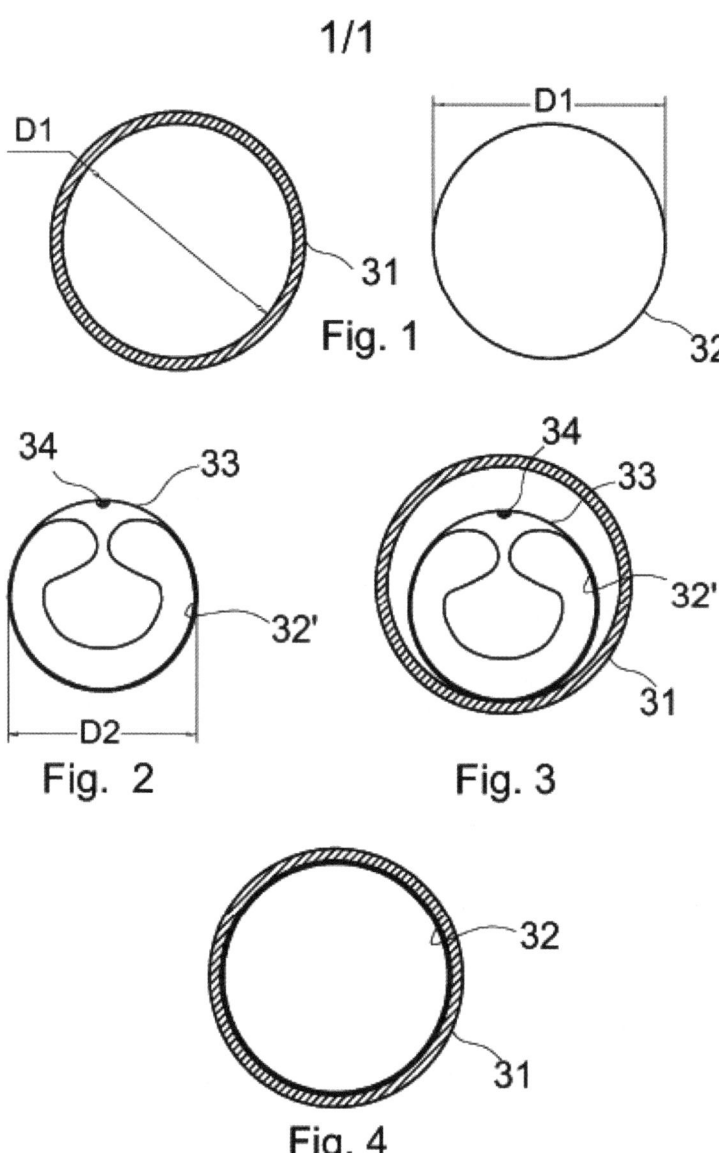

**CITABLE ALL CLAIMS NOVELTY AND OBVIOUSNESS**
**ANTICIPATES CLAIMS 1,4,5 (ARGUE "FILM" - ALSO FOR CLAIM 2 BELOW)**
**WITH A2 RENDERS CLAIM 2 OBVIOUS — ARGUE ASPECT RATIO = SHAPE**

Annex 4

Patent Application GB-A-2 263 023
Date of Filing: 11.10.1991
Date of Publication: 14.04.1993
Applicant: CLEANPIPE Ltd.
Inventor: Jones, Davey
Representative: William C. Borington, et al.
c/o Borington, Drew, Barrimore
25 Chelsea Road
London WC4 2UC

### Lining pipes

[001] When sewer pipes laid below ground begin to leak, an alternative to replacement is to insert a liner. The liner must be inserted along relatively long pipe lengths and so must have enough clearance during insertion to avoid friction. On the other hand, the liner bore must correspond as much as possible to the pipe bore, in order to minimise the reduction in capacity caused by the liner.

[002] Since pipe diameters vary along their length owing to tolerances and deformations, one cannot select a liner of a single diameter that will be ideal for the whole length of pipe to be lined. Therefore, there will be areas in which the liner is too small, resulting in an unused gap between the liner and the pipe, and areas in which the liner is too large, resulting in deformations in the circumference. Neither is acceptable for the requirement of close fit and optimum flow cross-section.

[003] The above-mentioned deficiencies are overcome by the method according to the present invention as defined in the claim.

[004] The method according to the present invention makes use of the properties of known shape memory materials to return to their original shape from a transitional shape that they have been given, by the application of heat.

**ABOVE PARA. LINKS TO ANNEX 2?**

[005] An example of the invention will now be described with reference to the accompanying figures 1 to 4.

**NEXT PARA. ANTICIPATES CLAIM 4**

[006] Figure 1 shows a cross-section of a sewer pipe 41 having a crack 42 in its wall. Figure 2 shows a liner tube 43 for lining the pipe 41. The liner tube 43 consists of a thermally recoverable plastics material, preferably a thermally recoverable polyolefin. In its original shape, the liner tube 43 has an outer diameter corresponding to the maximum inner diameter of the pipe 41.

**PARAS 7–9 ANTICIPATE CLAIM 1 AND TEACH CLAIM 2 FEATURES (NOT HOT AIR- BUT THAT FOUND IN ANNEX 20)**

[007] The liner tube is heated to a temperature above the activation temperature of the plastics material, for example between 100 and 140 °C. At this temperature, the diameter of the liner tube 43 is reduced as indicated with arrows 44, by stretching it in its axial direction, i.e. lengthwise. This stretching results in a reduction in diameter of the liner tube, indicated by dashed line 43'. Typically, the diameter is reduced by about 10%, which in most cases is sufficient to allow insertion of the liner tube into the pipe.

[008] After reduction of its diameter by stretching, the liner tube is cooled to a temperature well below the activation temperature. Thereby the diameter-reduced

shape is fixed ("frozen"). In this state, the liner tube is inserted into the pipe 41. Figure 3 shows the liner tube 43' inserted in the pipe 41.

**Annex 4**

[009] When the liner tube 43' is in place, it is heated to a temperature above the activation temperature of the plastics material to activate its memory. Heating is

preferably effected by an infrared lamp, which is pulled through the liner tube 43.. Owing to its shape memory, the liner tube 43, with reduced diameter expands radially, and at the same time contracts axially to its original length, and thus returns to its original shape, corresponding to the inner diameter of the pipe 41 (figure 4). **ABOVE ANTICIPATES CLAIM 5**

[010] A diameter reduction of more than 10% can in principle be obtained by stretching the liner tube. However, with greater reductions, the liner tube contracts significantly in the axial direction when it reverts to its original shape. This can cause damage of the liner tube due to the frictional contact with the pipe wall.

**Claim**

A method for lining a pipe with a liner tube having an outer diameter corresponding to the maximum inner diameter of the pipe, the method comprising reducing in cross-section a liner tube of thermally recoverable plastics material, inserting the reduced liner tube into the pipe to be lined and heating the liner tube above its activation temperature to return it to its original cross-sectional dimension.

**Annex 4**

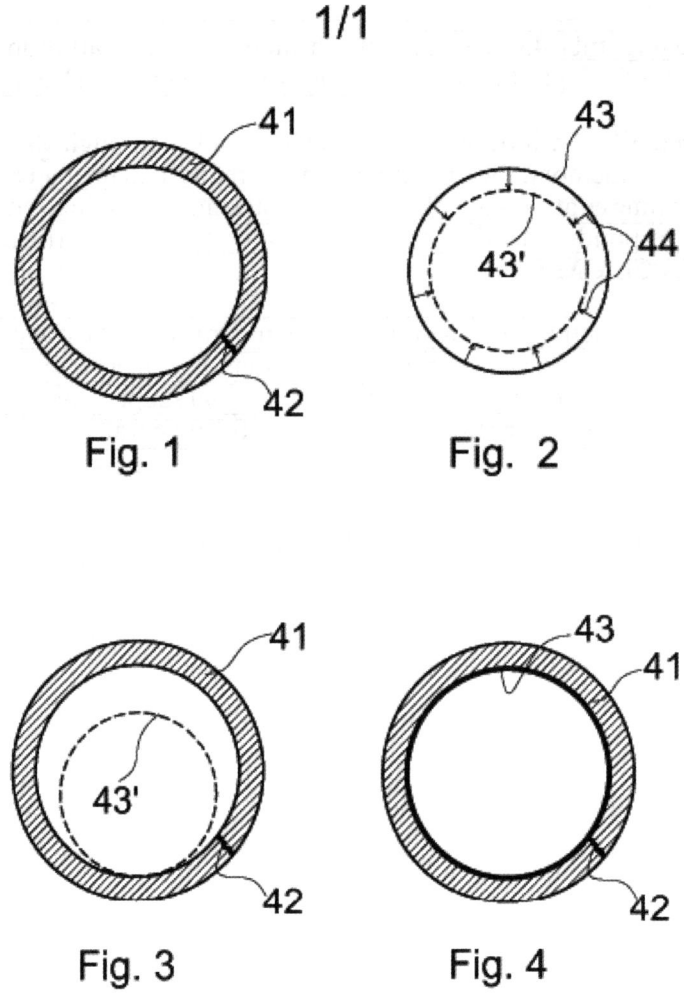

> **ARGUABLY MADE AVAILABLE TO THE PUBLIC NOT LATER THAN 14.10.98 (NOT UNDER ENGLISH LAW!) NEED TO RESOLVE! IF PUBLISHED, WAS MORE THAN 6 MONTHS BEFORE FILING DATE, SO NOT CAUGHT BY A55. IF CITABLE, CAN BE APPLIED AGAINST ALL CLAIMS NOVELTY AND OBVIOUSNESS. TEACHES CLAIM 3 FEATURES, AND ANTICIPATES CLAIM 4**

**Annex 5**

XXXXXXXXX  
XXXXXXXXXXX

Monday, 5 October 1998

Mr W. Hansen  
HAKU-Werke GmbH & Co. KG  
Hollandiastrasse 63-65  
D – 28197 Bremen

Dear Mr Hansen,

Here is the information about the new tubing, as discussed over the phone. Made of shape-memory polyethylene, it recovers its form in response to heat, and should be of interest to your company. I played a key role in developing this tubing at USF Kunststofftechnik GmbH, but my work was, regrettably, not recognised sufficiently.

The interesting thing about this tubing is that its cross-section has been changed from round to roughly U-shaped with relatively small outer dimensions in order to facilitate transportation and storage. When heated to above its activation temperature, it will return to its round cross-section without any change in its length, thus enabling its outer dimensions to be varied greatly.

Even though the company is still treating the invention as confidential, I have decided, in view of my situation, to share this information with you. You are at liberty to discuss it with other interested parties, but please if possible do not disclose my name.

Yours sincerely,

XXXXXXXXXXXXXXXXXX

CITABLE FOR NOVELTY AND OBVIOUSNESS AGAINST ALL CLAIMS
NOT RELEVANT — IGNORE

**Annex 6**

**Extract from "Medical Review" No. 25/95, published 19 June 1995**

BIOSHRINKTM, developed by MEDITEC Inc., USA, is a new film sheet that is *biocompatible*, meaning that it can be safely used with human tissue. Heat restores this shape-memory film to its original shape. Although it has long been known that several plastics have this property, the newly developed material has the advantage that it changes its shape at the relatively low activation temperature of around 30 °C. This means that BIOSHRINKTM can be used directly as a wound dressing on human tissue and activated by body heat.

During the analysis of the prior art Annexes and the comparison with Annex 1, Annex 1 itself can usefully be marked up to show which claim features are known from which prior art Annexes.

# Annex 1

(19)  Europäisches Patentamt
European Patent Office
Office européen des brevets

(11) **EP 1 011 743 B1**

(12) **EUROPEAN PATENT SPECIFICATION**

(45) Date of publication and mention
of the grant of the patent:

16.06.2004 Bulletin 2004/25

(51) Int. Cl.$^7$: **F16L55/16, A61M25/04**

(21) Application number: 99123321.4

(22) Date of filing: 26.11.1999

(54) Liner and lining method

Auskleidung und Verfahren zur Auskleidung

Revêtement et procédé de revêtement

(84) Designated Contracting States:
AT BE DE DK ES FR GB IT LU NL SE

(30) Priority: 27.11.1998 DE 19841974

(43) Date of publication of application:
31.05.2000 Bulletin 2000/22

(73) Proprietor:
USE Kunststofftechnik GmbH
20024 Hamburg (DE)

(72) Inventors:
Reibach, Paul
20095 Hamburg (DE)
Redlich, Georg
20174 Hamburg (DE)

(74) Representative:
Herrlich, Christoph
Baumstraße 124
22175 Hamburg (DE)

Note: Within nine months from the publication of the mention of the grant of the European patent, any person may give notice to the European Patent Office of opposition to the European patent granted. Notice of opposition shall be filed in a written reasoned statement. It shall not be deemed to have been filed until the opposition fee has been paid (Art. 99(1) European Patent Convention).

[001] The present invention primarily relates to a method for lining pipes, particularly sewer pipes, a tubular film well-suited to this method and the use thereof.

[002] In pipes, such as concrete sewer pipes that are prone to corrosion or stress, cracks develop in the walls over time, resulting in leaks.

**AS DISTINCT FROM THE USE OF A FILM?**

[003] An established method of lining pipes involves the introduction of a relatively rigid liner into the pipe. However, as a result of damage or deviations from the ideal cross-section, the cross-section of the pipe's inner wall is often narrower in places than the nominal value. Thus, the liner's outer diameter can be no wider than the pipe's cross-section at its narrowest point. This method therefore has the disadvantage that, after lining, the effective usable pipe cross-section is significantly diminished, often by 50 to 60%. A further disadvantage is that friction between the inner surface of the pipe and the outer surface of the liner means that only relatively short lengths of liner can be introduced at a time.

[004] The problem addressed by the present invention is to overcome these disadvantages.

[005] This is achieved by the features cited in the claims.

[006] The invention also comprises a tubular film for use with the claimed method and a section of lined sewer pipe.

[007] An embodiment of the invention will now be described with reference to the accompanying figures 1 to 5.

[008] Figure 1 is a cross-section through a pipe 1, damaged by a crack 2. Figure 2 shows a cross-section of a tubular film 3 for lining the pipe. The tubular film 3 is made of a polyolefin, e. g. polyethylene. In order for the film to be deformed in the manner set out below, it must be manufactured in such a way that its original shape is thermally recoverable. Materials having thermally recoverable properties, also known as shape memory materials, are commercially available.

[009] The tubular film, which originally has an outer diameter d1 equal to the inner diameter of the pipe 1, is first heated to a temperature, typically 130 °C, which is above the activation temperature for achieving shape memory properties of the polyolefin. At this temperature, the circular tubular film is deformed into a cross-section 3' that is horseshoe-like in shape (see Figure 3), for example, by guiding it over appropriately positioned rollers (not shown). This reduces its maximum outer dimension d2 by around 20–30%. The deformed tubular film is then quenched to a temperature below its activation temperature, e. g. to 10 °C. This fixes or .freezes. its deformed shape.

[010] The tubular film deformed as described above is drawn into the pipe 1 to produce the configuration shown in Figure 4. Once the deformed tubular film is in place, it is reheated to above its activation temperature, again typically to 130 °C for polyolefin, preferably by blowing hot air through it. Because of its shape memory properties, the tubular film recovers its original shape having a circular cross-section of diameter d1 (Figure 5). During this recovery step, the tubular film only moves radially, so that there is no axial movement relative to the pipe inner wall that could damage the tubular film.

[011] While the present invention was being developed, it was surprisingly found that tubular film made from a material that recovers its shape at an activation temperature close to body temperature is ideally suited for implanting into damaged arteries or veins during an operation with a technique similar to the method according to claim 1. Such a material is marketed under the name BIOSHRINKTM by MEDITEC Inc., USA.

## Claims

**MUST ARGUE "FILM"**
**ALL FEATURES IN ANNEX 3 A54(3) (ARGUE ASPECT RATIO = SHAPE) & ANNEX 4 A54(2)**

1. A method of lining a sewer pipe (1) with a tubular film (3) having an outer diameter (d1) substantially matching the inner diameter of the sewer pipe (1), comprising the following steps: (i) modifying the shape of the tubular film (3) to allow it to be introduced into the sewer pipe (1), (ii) introducing the tubular film with the modified shape (3') into the sewer pipe (1) to be lined, and (iii) restoring the original shape of the tubular film (3).

**OBVIOUS OVER A4 + CGK (A2)**

2. A method according to claim 1, wherein the tubular film (3) is made of a material having a thermally recoverable shape, step (i) takes place above the material's activation temperature, and the modified shape (3') of the tubular film is fixed by cooling it to a temperature below the material's activation temperature, and **ALL ABOVE TAUGHT IN A2 (?FILM?)**

   step (iii) is carried out by heating the tubular film to above the activation temperature of the material by blowing hot air through the tubular film.

**LAST SECTION OF A2 VERY GOOD FOR OBVIOUSNESS OF THIS LAST FEATURE**

3. A method according to claim 1 or 2, wherein the shape of the tubular film (3) is modified by giving the tubular film (3) a horseshoe-like cross-section.

**CLAIM 3 ON 1 LACKS NOVELTY A54(2) OVER A3.**

**IF A5 USEABLE, OBVIOUSNESS OF 3 ON 2, WITH A4, A2, A5.**

4. Tubular film (3) for lining a pipe, wherein the tubular film (3) comprises a polyolefin material having a thermally recoverable shape.

**ANTICIPATED BY A4, A2, (A5 IF CITEABLE)**

5. Sewer pipe (1) lined with a tubular film (3), produced using the method according to claim 2. **VERY BROAD "PRODUCEABLE BY"**

**ABOVE ANTICIPATED BY A3 - A54(3); ARGUABLY ALSO A4 (A54(2))**

6. Use of a tubular film made of a material having a thermally recoverable shape for implanting into damaged arteries or veins in a patient.

**SURGICAL METHOD OF TREATMENT — A52(4) REQUIRES INCISION**

**Annex 1**

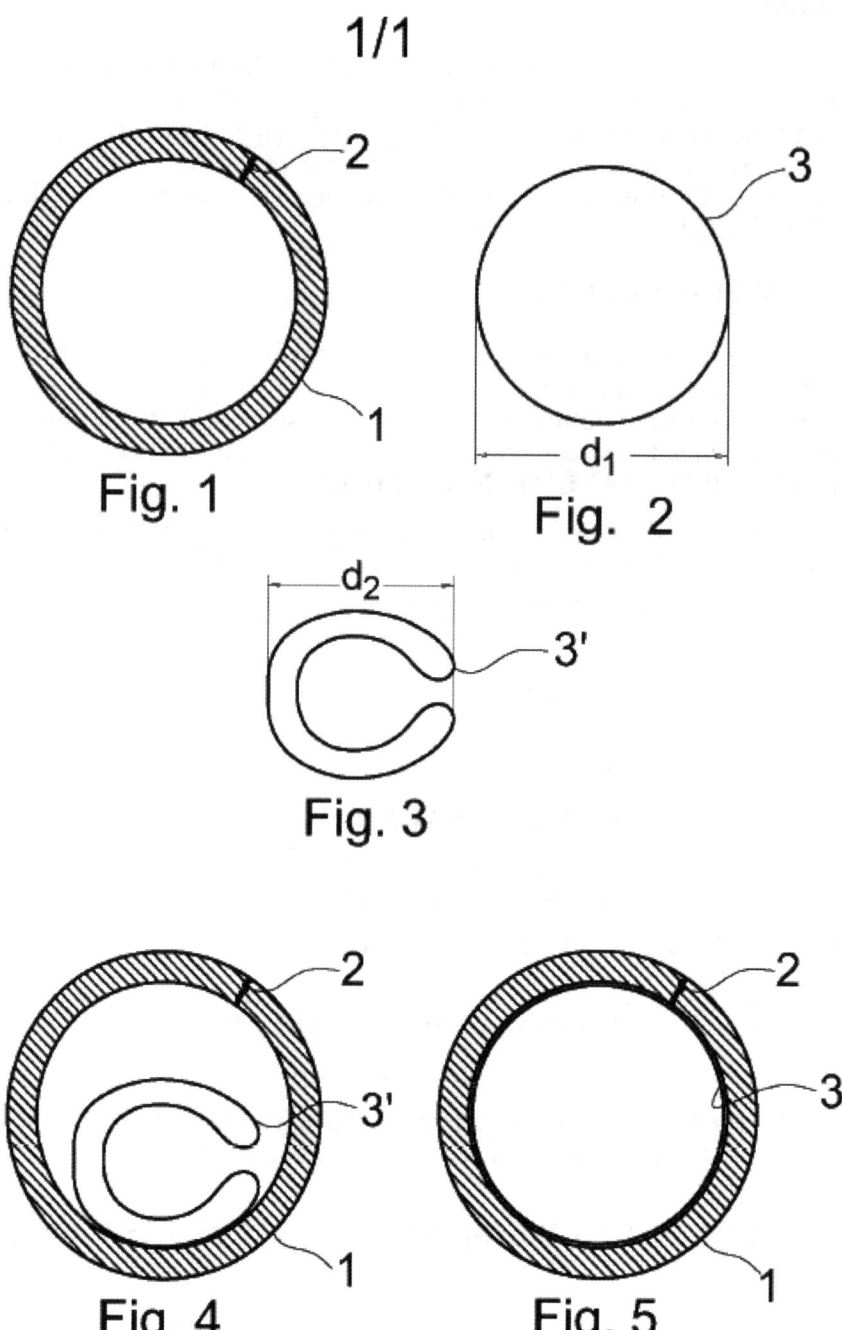

*Formulating an attack strategy*

The following attacks are deemed worth making

| Embodiment | Novelty | Inventive step | Article 52(4) |
|---|---|---|---|
| Claim 1 | A3 (A54(3)), A4 (A54(2)) | X | X |
| Claim 2 | X | A4 (CPA) + CGK (A2) | X |
| Claim 3 [1] | A3 (A54(2)) | A4 (CPA) + A5 | X |
| Claim 3 [2] | X | A4 (CPA) + CGK (A2) + A5 | X |
| Claim 4 | A2, A4, A5 | X | X |
| Claim 5 | A3 (A54(3)), A4 | X | X |
| Claim 6 | X | X | ✓ |

Key

Claim $X^y$ = Claim X dependant on Claim Y.
CPA = Closest Prior Art.
CGK = Common General Knowledge
X = No reasonable attack available.
✓ = Attack possible

*Writing the notice of opposition*

See overleaf for a filled-out form 2300.

## Notice of Opposition to a European Patent

To the European Patent Office

**I. Patent opposed**

Opp. No. / OPPO (1)

Patent No.: EP1011743B1

Application No.: 99123321.4

Date of mention of the grant in the European Patent Bulletin (Art. 97(4), 99(1) EPC): 16.06.2004

Title of the invention: Liner and lining method

**II. Proprietor of the Patent** (first named in the patent specification): USE Kunststifftechnik GmbH

Opponent's or representative's reference (max. 15 spaces) — OREF

**III. Opponent** — OPPO (2)

Name / Address:
Allplast GmbH
Am Alsterwasser 1
D-20149
Hamburg

State of residence or of principal place of business: Germany

Telephone/Telex/Fax:

Multiple opponents: further opponents see additional sheet

**IV. Authorisation**

1. Representative (Name only one representative to whom notification is to be made) — OPPO (9)

Name / Address of place of business:
Dr R Ambo
Hauerstrasse 47
D-81547
Munich

Telephone/Telex/Fax:

Additional representative(s): (on additional sheet/see authorisation) — OPPO (5)

2. Employee(s) of the opponent authorised for these opposition proceedings under Art. 133(3) EPC

Name(s):

Authorisation(s) To 1./2.:
[X] not considered necessary
[ ] has/have been registered under No.
[ ] is/are enclosed

EPO Form 2300.1 04.93 (int. ad. 12/97)

## V. Opposition is filed against

— the patent as a whole ☒

— claim(s) No(s).

## VI. Grounds for opposition:

Opposition is based on the following grounds:

(a) the subject-matter of the European patent opposed is not patentable (Art. 100(a) EPC) because:

— it is not new (Art. 52(1); 54 EPC) ☒

— it does not involve an inventive step (Art. 52(1); 56 EPC) ☒

— patentability is excluded on other grounds, i.e. Art. 52(4) ☒

(b) the patent opposed does not disclose the invention in a manner sufficiently clear and complete for it to be carried out by a person skilled in the art (Art. 100(b) EPC; see Art. 83 EPC). ☐

(c) the subject-matter of the patent opposed extends beyond the content of the application/ of the earlier application as filed (Art. 100(c) EPC, see Art. 123(2) EPC). ☐

## VII. Facts and arguments
(Rule 55(c) EPC)
presented in support of the opposition are submitted herewith on a separate sheet (annex 1) ☒

## VIII. Other requests:

Oral Proceedings are requested in accordance with Article 116 EPC in the event that the patent is not revoked by the Opposition Division as requested.

| | | for EPO use only |
|---|---|---|
| **IX. Evidence presented** Enclosed = [X]  will be filed at a later date = [ ] | | |
| A. **Publications:** | | Publication date |
| 1 Handbuch der Kunststoffe published April 1988 | | |
| Particular relevance (page, column, line, fig.): extract enclosed - entire text | | |
| 2 EP-0962399A1 filed May 6th, 1998, published 10 November 1999 | | |
| Particular relevance (page, column, line, fig.): Page 2, and Figures | | |
| 3 GB-A-2263023 filed 11 October 1991, published 14 April 1993 | | |
| Particular relevance (page, column, line, fig.): Pages 2 and 3. | | |
| 4 | | |
| Particular relevance (page, column, line, fig.): | | |
| 5 | | |
| Particular relevance (page, column, line, fig.): | | |
| 6 | | |
| Particular relevance (page, column, line, fig.): | | |
| 7 | | |
| Particular relevance (page, column, line, fig.): | | |
| Continued on additional sheet [ ] | | |
| B. **Other evidence** Letter dated October 5th, addressed to Mr W Hansen, published no later than 14 October 1998. | | |
| Continued on additional sheet [ ] | | |

EPO Form 2300.3 04.93 (int. ad. 12/97)

## X. Payment of the opposition fee is made

[X] as indicated in the enclosed voucher for payment of fees and costs (EPO Form 1010)

[ ]

## XI. List of documents

| Enclosure No. | | Description | No. of copies | |
|---|---|---|---|---|
| 0 | [X] | Form for notice of opposition | 2 | (min. 2) |
| 1 | [X] | Facts and arguments (see VII.) | 2 | (min. 2) |
| 2 | | Copies of documents presented as evidence (see IX.) | | |
| 2a | [ ] | — Publications | 2 | (min. 2 of each) |
| 2b | [ ] | — Other documents | 2 | (min. 2 of each) |
| 3 | [ ] | Signed authorisation(s) (see IV.) | | |
| 4 | [ ] | Voucher for payment of fees and costs (see X.) | 1 | |
| 5 | [ ] | Cheque | | |
| 6 | [ ] | Additional sheet(s) | | (min. 2 of each) |
| 7 | [X] | Other (please specify here): acknowledgement of receipt form | 1 | |

## XII. Signature of opponent or representative

Place    Munich

Date    10 March 2005

Zzzzzzzzzzzz

Dr R Ambo

1–158  **Statement of grounds**

The patent is opposed in its English text and is referred to herein as Annex 1.

**1. Priority date of claims**

1.1 In the priority document a horseshoe-shaped liner is only mentioned in the context of use of a shape memory material. This feature is essential for achieving the required shape recovery. Consequently, the combination of the features of claim1 and claim3 without the limitation of claim 2 cannot be derived directly and unambiguously from the priority application. As such, claim 3 as directly dependant on claim 1 is not entitled to the claimed priority date (Article 87(1) and G2/98): Its effective date is the filing date (26$^{th}$ November 1999). All the other claims have basis in the priority application and, as such, they are entitled to the claimed priority date of the 27$^{th}$ November 1998.

**2. Prior art**

2.1 Annex 2 (which has been read in its French translation) is an extract from a handbook of plastics published in 1998. As such, the reference is citable under Article 54(2) against all claims. It is submitted that as a handbook, published 10 years before the priority date, this reference represents material which may be considered to be common general knowledge of those working in the field of plastics.

2.2 Annex 3 (which has been read in its English translation) is citable against all the claims (other than claim 3 as directly dependant on claim 1), under Article 54(3) — (4) for all common validly designated states because it is a European patent application, published after, but having a filing date earlier than the priority date of these claims.

Annex 3 was published before the filing date of Annex 1 and is therefore citable under Article 54(2) for novelty and obviousness against claim 3 as directly dependant on claim 1.

2.3 Annex 4 (which has been read in its English translation) is citable against all claims for both novelty and obviousness.

2.4 Annex 5 (which has been read in its English translation) is a copy of a letter received by Mr Hansen who was not bound by confidentiality. He showed the letter to Mr Sandler and two colleagues, employees of the opponent, on or before October 14$^{th,}$ 1988, during a train journey to Amsterdam. Mr Sandler and his colleagues were not bound to confidentiality. The disclosure of the letter in this way clearly constitutes publication of the letter's content in accordance with A54(2).The copy of the letter is submitted as evidence of the content of the original letter. Affidavits from one or more of these persons will be provided in due course, and of course these individuals may be summoned as witnesses.

**3. Initial observations regarding use of the term "film" in the claims**

The specification contains no dimensions and says nothing about the thickness of the material which is used as the film. The specification makes no mention of any special motivation for using any particular thickness of liner. However, it obviously makes economic sense to use a material layer as thin as makes practical sense — thereby reducing the cost of the material used. Such a motivation applies equally in the prior art documents which is cited in the following grounds, which is similarly silent concerning the thickness of the lining which is appliant. As such, it is observed that the word "film" fails to distinguish the subject matter from that of the prior art Annexes.

## 4. Claim 1.

4.1 Annex 3 discloses, in the language of claim 1, a method of lining a sewer pipe having an outer diameter substantially matching the inner diameter of the pipe (paragraph 6, first sentence), comprising the steps of

(i) Modifying the shape of the tubular film to allow it to be introduced into the sewer pipe (paragraph 7, first 2 sentences),

(ii) Introducing the tubular film with the modified shape into the sewer pipe to be lined (paragraph 8, first sentence), and

(iii) Restoring the original shape of the tubular film (paragraph 9, second sentence).

Thus, all the features of claim 1 are present in combination in Annex 3. Claim 1 therefore lacks novelty under Article 54(3). [This attack is of course based on the assumption that the designation fees for all the Annex 1 contracting states were paid — a fact to be established before filing the opposition].

It is also noted that in Annex 1 the liner tube is elastically deformed from its original circular cross-section into a horseshoe shaped cross-section and is then held in this shape using a thin plastics film. That it is possible to elastically deform the liner tube in this way is suggestive of its being made of a thin material. It is also made of polyethylene (paragraph 6, second sentence) the same basic material as is used in Annex 1. Furthermore, the fact that the elastic deformation can be maintained simply be wrapping the sleeve in a thin film suggests that there is not much stored energy to be overcome — again suggestive of a thin construction. Also, as noted in the discussion of the term film above, the apparent motive in Annex 1 for use of a film (in so far as the term has meaning) is to save on the use of material, for sensible economic reasons. Just the same motive applies in Annex 3. Thus, it is clear that claim 1 lacks novelty over Annex 3 under Article 54(3).

3.2 Annex 4 discloses, in the language of claim 1, a method of lining a sewer pipe with a tubular film having an outer diameter substantially matching the inner diameter of the sewer pipe (paragraph 6, first and third sentences), comprising the steps of

(i) Modifying the shape of the tubular film to allow it to be introduced into the sewer pipe (paragraph 7, third and forth sentences, the tube is elongated and its diameter is reduced. In other words, its aspect ratio of length to diameter is changed significantly — clearly this is a modification of the shape, to allow the tube to be introduced into the sewer pipe).

(ii) Introducing the tubular film with the modified shape into the sewer pipe to be lined (paragraph 8, third and forth sentences),

(iii) Restoring the original shape of the tubular film (paragraph 9, first and third sentences).

As argued above, in so far as the word film has technical meaning, it is implicit that a film is also used in Annex 4. Thus all the features of claim 1 are known in combination from Annex 4. Claim 1 therefore lacks novelty by virtue of Article 54(2).

## 5. Claim 2, dependant on claim 1.

Claim 2 lacks an inventive step over Annex 4 and common general knowledge (as exemplified by Annex 2). Annex 4 is the closest prior art since it alone discloses a method according to claim 1 based on the use of a shape memory effect material.

In the words of claim 2, Annex 4 adds to the features of claim1, that the tubular film is made of a material having a thermally recoverable shape (paragraph 6; line 3 of the claim), step (i) takes place above the material's activation temperature (paragraph 7, first sentence), and the modified shape of the tubular film is fixed by cooling it to a temperature below the material's activation temperature (paragraph 8, first sentence), and step (iii) is carried out by heating the tubular film to above the activation temperature of the material (paragraph 9, first sentence).

Claim 2 is distinguished from the disclosure of Annex 4 in that the heating is achieved by blowing hot air through the tubular film. This distinguishing feature does not lead to a different effect when compared to the use of a heating lamp as in Annex 4. A further effect of the different heating techniques is that the use of hot air may avoid the need to pull a heat source through the pipe.

The objective technical problem is either to find an alternative heating method to the use of an infrared heat lamp, or to find an alternative heating technique which avoids the need to pull the heat source through sewer liner.

Annex 2, which represents common general knowledge, teaches that when heat treating shape memory materials to cause them to regain their original shape it is possible to use any appropriate source of heat — for example a source of infrared radiation, a current of hot air, or super heated steam, and that these heat sources produce the same effect (see the last sentence). Replacing the infrared lamp with one of the other heat sources solves either of the problems identified above. Moreover, hot air can readily be blown along within the tubular film. Therefore the subject-matter of claim 2 is obvious by the combination of Annex 4 and common general knowledge (in the form of Annex 2).

**6. Claim 3 as dependant on claim 1.**

As explained above the effective date of this claim is the filing date (26$^{th}$ November 1999). Annex 3 discloses all the features of claim 1. Claim 3 adds to claim 1 the feature that the modified shape is a horseshoe-like cross-section. This feature is also taught by Annex 3 — see paragraph 7, second sentence and figures 2 and 3. The subject matter of claim 3 therefore lacks novelty over Annex 3 by virtue of Article 54(2).

Annex 4 anticipates claim 1. For the determination of obviousness of claim 3, Annex 4 can be considered to be the closest prior art to claim 3 as it relates to the method of claim 1 and is concerned with modifying the shape of a tubular film in order to reduce its diameter so that it can be introduced into a sewer to be lined.

Claim 3 is distinguished from the disclosure of Annex 4 by the modification of shape giving a horseshoe-like cross-section, rather than a simple axial stretch (Annex 4 paragraph 7, second sentence). This has the effect that during recovery the film moves only radially, so that there is no axial movement of the pipe relative to the pipe inner wall that could damage the film (Annex 1, paragraph 10, last sentence), and consequently allows a greater diameter reduction (20-30%, Annex 1, paragraph 9, 3$^{rd}$ sentence, compared with about 10% in Annex 4, paragraph 7, last sentence).

The objective technical problem is therefore to allow a diameter reduction of more than 10% while preventing damage to the liner during recovery (Annex 4, paragraph 10).

The solution to this problem is rendered obvious by the teaching of Annex 5. Annex 5 discloses tubing made of a polyethylene shape-memory (thermally recoverable) material (Annex 5, first paragraph, second sentence). Thermally recoverable polyolefins are preferred materials for the Annex 4 method (paragraph 6, second sentence). Polyethylene is a polyolefin (Annex 1, paragraph 8, second sentence). The tubing is deformed to give a roughly U-shaped (= horseshoe shape) cross-section which gives it relatively small outer dimensions. When heated above its activation temperature it regains its round cross-section without any change in length — "thus enabling its outer dimensions to be varied greatly" (all in the second paragraph of Annex 5). Thus Annex 5 provides the solution to the above-identified problem. Thus, using the tubing from Annex 5 in the method of Annex 4 leads immediately to the subject-matter of claim 3 as directly dependent on claim 1.

## 7. Claim 3 as dependant on claim 2.

Annex 4 is the closest prior art document for the assessment of inventive step, for the reasons given above in relation to claim 2. The claim is distinguished from the teaching of Annex 4 by two features:

   a) heating being performed with hot air blown through the film; and

   b) modifying the tubular film to give a horseshoe shape rather than the use of axial stretching.

   There is no interaction between these two features and they produce no synergistic effect. As such they solve two separate partial problems and can be treated individually.

   The problem and solution concerning feature a) are discussed above in the context of claim 2. The problem and solution concerning feature b) are discussed above in the context of claim 3 as directly dependant on claim 1.

   The method of claim 3 as dependant on claim 2 is therefore rendered obvious by the application of common general knowledge (Annex 2) and the teaching of Annex 5 to the method of Annex 4.

## 8. Claim 4 independent

Tubular film for — means "tubular film suitable for" see Guidelines, C-III, 4.8 or C.IV.7.6. Annex 4 teaches a liner tube (tubular film as argued above) of polyolefin having a thermally recoverable shape for lining a pipe (paragraph 6, third sentence, and paragraph 8, third sentence). Claim 4 therefore lacks novelty over Annex 4.

Annex 2 teaches the use of tubing (last sentence of the first paragraph, and first sentence of the second paragraph) made of a polymer such as polyethylene (which Annex 1 identifies (paragraph 8, third sentence) as a polyolefin), which is thermally recoverable (first paragraph, first sentence). The heat shrinkable sleeving used to cover cables (first sentence of second paragraph) will be made of a thin material (for reasons of economy and speed of reaction to heat) and as such constitutes a tubular film. Such tubing could be used as a liner of a pipe. The claim does not require that the shape recovers to a larger diameter, nor that the liner holds itself in place in the lined pipe. Thus claim 4 also lacks novelty over Annex 2.

Annex 5 discloses tubing made of a shape-memory (thermally recoverable) polyethylene (a polyolefin). The heat recoverable tubing would naturally be made of a thin material (for reasons of economy and speed of reaction to heat) and as such constitutes a tubular film. Thus, claim 4 lacks novelty over Annex 5.

## 9 Claim 5 Independent.

(See Guidelines C-III.4.7b)

Annex 4 teaches the method of claim 2 apart from the use of hot air in the final step of the method. This difference in the method will not be discernable in the resulting lined sewer pipe. As such, the product of the Annex 4 method and the product of claim 2 method will be indistinguishable. This argument is supported by the last sentence of Annex 2. Hence the product defined by claim 5 lacks novelty over the teaching of Annex 4.

It can also be argued that the product of the method of Annex 3 is indistinguishable from that of the claim 2 method. Annex 3 teaches the use of a polyethylene liner which is introduced in a deformed form to a sewer pipe. Once in the pipe, the liner is allowed to expand, to recover to its original diameter matching the inner diameter of the pipe (paragraph 6). This recovery may also be assisted by applying air pressure (paragraph 9, last sentence). Once the shape memory material used in claim 2 has recovered its original form it is no longer further recoverable. As such, it would appear to be indistinguishable from the polyethylene tube of Annex 3 once that has been installed. While it might be argued that the remains of the plastics film (33) and the heating wire (34) would show that the Annex 3 method had been used, that does not distinguish over the method of claim 2. Claim 2 does not exclude the use or presence of a further thin film and a wire about the thermally recoverable material. The addition of such features to the recited features of claim 2 would not avoid infringement. In the same way, their presence does not show that a lined sewer pipe having such extra features <u>could not</u> have been made using the claim 2 method. As such, claim 5 also lacks novelty of Annex 3 by virtue Article 54(3)."

### 10. Claim 6 Independent

"Use… for implanting into damaged arteries or veins" is construed as a method of treatment excluded under Article 52(4). See the Guidelines C.IV.4.2, forth paragraph. The method is practiced on a patient (a live human or animal) and must include at least one surgical step — the making of an incision to gain access to the interior of an artery or vein. As such the claimed subject matter clearly falls under the exclusion of Article 52(4) and is not industrially applicable.

**Notes for letter to client**

Annex 5

It is clear from the wording of Annex 5 that:
the technical information which it contains is still being treated as confidential by USE Kunststofftechnik (USEK);
the author was involved in the generation/development of that technical information; and that therefore USEK must consider the author of the letter to be under an obligation of confidentiality — which he would be if he were an employee or ex-employee, and which he would also be if he were an external consultant or contractor;
the author has not been given permission by USEK to disclose the technical information; and that the letter was written for the author's personal motives.

Against this background, no-one reading the letter or being read the letter could reasonably claim that they did not know that the information which it contained should be treated as confidential and that the author of the letter was not entitled to waive that confidentiality. As such, Mr Sandler and his colleagues on the train, as well as Mr Hansen, were also caught by the obligation to keep the information confidential. They knew that they should keep the information confidential — despite the author's encouragement to share the information with other interested parties. Consequently, neither the delivery of the letter to Mr Hansen, nor the showing of the letter on the train constituted publication.

This is certainly the situation in England ["In this country this development was recognised clearly in the judgment of Lord Goff of Chieveley in *Attorney-General v Guardian Newspapers Ltd (No 2)* [1990] 1 AC 109, 281. Now the law imposes a 'duty of confidence' whenever a person receives information he knows or ought to know is fairly and reasonably to be regarded as confidential." *Campbell v MGN* [2004] UKHL 22], but is believed to hold more generally.

Nevertheless, it might be possible to persuade an Opposition Division (or a Board of Appeal) that disclosure of the letter was not covered by any form of confidentiality and that therefore Annex 5 constitutes prior art. As such, it would be sensible to include the Annex in the opposition (since it might not be possible to introduce it into the proceedings after the end of the opposition period). The technical information which the Annex contains has now been made available to the public through publication of Annex 1 and is thus no longer confidential. Hence Dr Ambo, the representative, would not be breaching any restriction of confidentiality by including the Annex in the opposition.

If Annex 5 were published by disclosure to Mr Sandler and his colleagues on the train journey to the trade fair in October 1998 (no later than October 14$^{th}$), that publication occurred more than 6 months before the filing of Annex 1 and is hence not excusable based on Article 55(EPC) (G2/99).

Territorially-limited opposition
Article 99(2) states that "the opposition shall apply to the European patent in all the contracting states in which the patent has effect". So it is not possible to restrict the opposition to Spain, Germany and Italy.

Claim 6 for a different invention
While unity of invention is a requirement of the EPC (Article 82) which applies to European patent applications pre-grant, there is no such requirement post grant (G1/91). Nor is lack of unity a ground of opposition (Article 100).

US Attorney to make submissions
The qualification of US Patent Attorney does not entitle a person to represent parties before the EPO. I am an authorised representative and I am entitled to represent you before the EPO. However, in Oral Proceedings in opposition, so-called "accompanying persons" can make oral submissions on specific legal or technical issues with the discretion of the relevant EPO instance. Enlarged Board of Appeal decision G4/95 sets criteria which must be met if such submissions are to be made by an accompanying person: that the person's name, their qualifications, and the subject-matter on which the person is to speak, need to be submitted to the EPO (and the other parties) well in advance of the oral proceedings. In addition it must be clear that the oral submissions by the accompanying person are made under the continuing responsibility and control of the professional representative.

# Paper D1

## 1. General comments

In Paper D1 the candidate must answer a series of short questions relating to aspects of substantive and procedural law under the EPC and PCT. The balance between EPC and PCT questions varies from year to year but at least two thirds of the marks are usually given for answering questions relating to the EPC. In general, the examiners are looking for answers which demonstrate that a candidate knows how to apply the law, not merely which show that a candidate knows what the law says. Moreover, the examiners want candidates to demonstrate their legal reasoning rather than merely providing a bare answer.

A thorough knowledge of the EPC and PCT (as in force at the end of the year previous to the year of the exam) is therefore required. In terms of the EPC, the candidate must be particularly familiar with Arts 1 to 25 and 52 to 158 and all the Rules. Knowledge of the Protocols, the Rules Relating to Fees, important case law, the ancillary regulations and the guidelines for examination is also required. Important case law can be considered to be any case referred to in the most recent edition of the white case law book and any later case published in the Official Journal. Decisions of the Enlarged Board of Appeal are clearly of paramount importance. In terms of the PCT, the candidate must be particularly familiar with Arts 1 to 49 and rr.1 to 96. Knowledge of the main provisions of the Paris Convention is also required. The syllabus extends also to knowledge of the most significant provisions of Japanese and US patent law. Time is short in the exam and the opportunity to search for answers is therefore limited. To ensure success the candidate must be thoroughly familiar with the materials described above and know instantly where to locate the relevant information.

Apart from the guides to the EPC and PCT included in this publication (see below) and the other publications they reference (EPC, PCT, Guidelines for Examination in the European Patent Office, Ancillary Regulations, Case Law of the Boards of Appeal of the EPO) several other reference works are useful in the exam. These include the PCT applicants guide, a list of countries that are members of the EPC, PCT, Paris Convention and WTO (available from the WIPO website), a pre-marked EPO calendar showing closed days for the year of the exam and the previous year and a copy of the EPO publication relating to aspects of national law. The EPO calendars showing closed days are supplied in the exam but time can be saved by obtaining copies in advance and marking closed days with a highlighter.

## 2. How to tackle the paper

*Use of time*

The paper is three hours long and there are 40 marks to be gained. This equates to four and a half minutes per mark, but it is more prudent to work on the basis of three minutes per mark, so that you have a little time in hand for the trickier questions as well as for reviewing your answer before the end of the exam. Since the number of marks available for each question is clearly indicated it is possible to work out how much time should be allocated to each question. Stick to this time limit and move on as soon as you have reached it since, in any given question, the first 50 per cent of the marks will be much easier to obtain than the second 50 per cent. It is better, therefore, to have half answered all the questions rather than fully answered half the questions. It is important to answer the question that has been asked, rather than merely addressing the topic on which the question is based. Many candidates waste a lot of time by failing to adhere to this basic point. In general, most of the questions can be answered succinctly, reducing the amount of time spent writing, if some thought is given to what the question is actually asking.

As all the questions have to be answered, there is little point reading through the paper before you attempt to answer your first question. Unless it is too daunting, start with question 1. If it is too daunting, move on to question 2, and return to question 1 later. To facilitate this approach, start each new question on a new sheet of paper. It is also sensible to write on every other line and leave space between paragraphs to facilitate later corrections and additions. But beware the risk of writing too much and off the point simply because a question's topic is one about which you know a lot. As a very rough guide, for every point that is allocated to a question, there will be a separate part–answer. Use this knowledge to judge what and how much the examiner wants by way of answer. To learn how this works in practice, take a couple of past papers, consider each question individually to see whether you can spot the elements of the answer which are required. Then look at the relevant answer in the model solution to identify the elements of the given answer. With practice you will become better at seeing what is likely to be needed in the answers to these questions.

**1–160**    *Finding the answer*

In order to find the answer to a question, use the guides to the EPC and PCT included in this publication. Become very familiar with the layout of these guides so that relevant sections can be rapidly located. They have been designed to be used during revision prior to taking the exam and in the exam itself. They have not, however, been designed as a substitute for revision: you still need to study and revise before you sit the exams. Both guides have been arranged in a logical order to make access to specific information rapid, even for a relative newcomer to European and PCT law. The order follows the sequence in which an applicant for a patent will encounter the stages of the European and PCT procedure. Thus, common sections relate to where to file an application, what to file, formalities examination, search, publication, substantive examination, national phase consequences and common provisions. The EPC guide also has sections relating to patentability, grant/refusal, opposition and appeal while the PCT guide has sections relating to Art.19 amendment and national/regional phase entry. Sections of the EPC and PCT not considered very relevant to the EQE have been omitted to avoid diluting the important sections. Beware though that the EQE examiners always like to ask something new, so that the exams do not become stale or predictable! So, do not think that you can ignore any part of the EPC or PCT.

It is hoped, nevertheless, that most answers to typical Paper D1 questions should be derivable from the attached guides. The guide to the EPC is to be used in conjunction with current copies of the white case law book (Case Law of the Boards of Appeal of the EPO), the guidelines (Guidelines for Examination in the European Patent Office) and the ancillary regulations: references to these important works are included in the text (as CLBA, Guidelines and AnReg respectively). All articles and rules in the EPC relating to aspects of PCT procedure have been consolidated in the PCT section.

**1–161**    *Writing the answer*

Before starting to write an answer, re-read the question to ensure that you are addressing the actual question set and providing the answer required. If a question appears too unclear, decide what the most likely meaning is and state your assumption in the preamble to your answer. If you have time, and if it makes sense, capture also the less likely meaning and give the appropriate answer to that too.

Set out the answer by first writing down, briefly, what the relevant law says, secondly applying that law to the facts of the question and thirdly setting out the legal consequences. The second of these steps is probably the most important and the most often overlooked. The third part is important but must be accompanied by the other two parts. The law will be primarily an article and/or rule, as interpreted by any relevant case law or, in rare cases, the guidelines. Always think through this hierarchy in the order given above. You need to know and remember, however, that many important procedural rules find their source in the Decisions of the President and other official notices, and these will all be found in the ancillary regulations book. Examples of important topics for which this applies are: the agreements relating to extension states; the President's decisions on the filing of authorisations, fax filing, arrangements for deposit accounts, etc. If you have cited the article(s) you do not need to cite the guidelines or decisions unless they change the answer. Sometimes the basis will only be the guidelines, but this is rare. All basis relied on should be clearly stated in the answer, not forgetting to distinguish clearly between EPC articles and rules and PCT articles and rules.

The length of the answer should roughly correlate with the number of marks to be gained. Where many marks are available and you have not dealt with many points in your answer, reconsider the question and consider other aspects that require comment.

If there is time, check for relevant case law even where none seems necessary — often the answer to a question is directly addressed by a decided case. Decisions of the Enlarged Board of Appeal are particularly important and often provide the basis for questions in Paper D1. It is therefore very important to know all these decisions in some detail — often they establish an interpretation of the EPC that is very different to the direct meaning of the Articles and Rules! Remember that the official EPC publication includes footnotes relating EBA Decisions to the relevant article. Nevertheless, you should not use this as your sole source of knowledge: you should ideally read all the EBA Decisions to ensure that you understand the reasoning behind the Decisions.

### 3. Preserving the rights of an applicant, proprietor or opponent which have apparently been lost under the EPC  1–162

In the world of the EQE things are always going wrong. Due dates are frequently missed and the candidate is often given the task of recommending appropriate remedial action to claw back the rights that the client has apparently lost. In such a situation, the following remedies should be considered.

*Was notification sent to the correct address?*  1–163

Where a representative has been appointed, notification must be sent to the representative and not the applicant (r.81(1) EPC). Where the EPO has notified the wrong party then notification only takes effect when the correct party has been notified (T703/92). If the EPO has properly been informed of a change of representative, subsequent communications are not notified until they are delivered to the newly appointed representative.

*Can the time limit be extended?*  1–164

Most time limits determined by the EPO can be extended on request, under r.84 EPC, provided that the total period does not exceed six months. If the total period as extended would exceed six months, an extension will generally only be given if convincing reasons are provided to show that a reply in the period previously laid down will not be possible (Notice of Vice President of DG2 ([1989] O.J. 180) — Guidelines E/VIII/1.6. The request for an extension must be made before the expiry of the time limit. The exceptions to this freedom to extend are time limits where the EPC sets an upper time limit, such as with r.46(1). Here it is possible to obtain an extension up to the maximum period specified by the EPC, but extension beyond that period is not possible.

Remember that r.78(2) EPC provides that, where notification is effected by registered letter, delivery is deemed to have taken place 10 days following the date of posting (taken to be date marked on the communication). The period for response is counted from that date of deemed notification and not from the date of the communication. In other words, 10 days are added to the date of the letter and then the correct number of months are added. If the resultant date is a day when one of the EPO offices is not open for receipt of documents, the period extends to the next day when all the offices are open (by virtue of r.85(1) EPC). Beware, however, that if this communication is one that is relevant under Art.122(2) EPC as removing the cause of non-compliance (i.e. it tells you that you have failed to do something the consequence of which was withdrawal, etc.), it is the actual date of receipt of that communication by the relevant person (generally the authorised representative) which starts the two-month period for applying for *restitutio*. Remember that the 10-day rule of r.78(2) does not apply to communications from the EPO when it is acting as one of the organs of the PCT — the relevant rule is then r.80.6 PCT, which operates quite differently. Time limits specified in Article or Rules of the EPC may be extended under certain circumstances: where there is a general interruption in the mail service in a contracting state (r.85(2) EPC), where a war, revolution or similar event affects the applicant or his representative (Art.85(5) EPC) and where the EPO is not functioning properly (r.85(4) EPC).

1–165 *Is a grace period available?*

Grace periods are provided by the EPC in respect of the time limits for paying the filing and search fees (r.85a(1) EPC), the examination fee (r.85b EPC), and the designation fees (r.85a(1) EPC (notified) and r.85a(2) EPC (not notified)).

1–166 *Further processing*

Further processing (Art.121 EPC) is only available to the applicant (and therefore only available pre-grant) and only in respect of time limits determined by the EPO (i.e. not specified in the EPC). It must be requested within two months of notification of the loss of rights, and within this time the fee must be paid and the omitted act performed.

1–167 *Restitutio*

*Restitutio* (Art.122 EPC) is available to the applicant pre-grant and the proprietor during opposition proceedings. It is also available, for the filing of the grounds of appeal, to an unsuccessful opponent who has validly filed an appeal (G1/86). It is available in respect of all time limits other than those specifically excluded by Art.122(5) EPC (importantly, time limits for which a grace period is available are excluded, as are the relevant grace periods even though these are not specified in Art.122(5) EPC). However, there is a necessity to show that the loss of rights occurred despite all due care having been taken by the relevant party. An application for *restitutio* must be made, and the relevant fee paid, within two months of removal of the cause of missing the time limit and, in any case, within 12 months of the expiry of the time limit. *Restitutio* of the period for requesting further processing is not excluded, and this can save what otherwise seem to be extinct applications, but it is important of course to complete the requirements for getting further processing.

1–168 *Can proceedings be interrupted?*

Proceedings can be interrupted in the event of the death or legal incapacity or bankruptcy of the applicant or proprietor or his representative (r.90(1) EPC).

1–169 *Can the good faith principle be invoked?*

Under certain circumstances (see G2/97) the EPO is under an obligation to warn the applicant, proprietor or opponent of any loss of rights if such a warning can be expected in all good faith. Equally, the applicant, proprietor or opponent must not suffer a disadvantage as a result of having relied on erroneous information received from the EPO (e.g. J2/87) or on a misleading communication (e.g. J3/87).

*File an appeal*

1–170

Any party adversely affected by a decision of the Receiving Section, an Examining Division, an Opposition Division or the Legal Division (but not a Search Division) may file an appeal (Art.106, 107 EPC). In the event of a loss of rights, an appealable decision may be requested under r.69(2) EPC. If good grounds for the appeal are presented, the appeal will succeed and proceedings will resume. Even if there are no good grounds for an appeal filed by the applicant, its suspensive effect means that the proceedings are still ongoing and the application may be re-filed as a divisional application. Note, however, that this only generally applies when the contested decision is a refusal of the application. It does not apply when the decision is taken pursuant to R69(2) EPC and in the case where a decision to grant is appealed the outcome of the appeal is decisive (J28/03)

*Conversion*

1–171

If a European patent is no longer obtainable (e.g. following a decision to refuse an application on appeal) consider whether any national rights could be salvaged through conversion (Art.135 EPC). The possibilities available vary from country to country — for details see Table VII in the EPO publication National Law relating to the EPC.

*Can the failure to pay a fee on time be excused?*

1–172

Under certain circumstances, where an effort to pay a necessary fee was made before the expiry of the relevant deadline but the money was not received by the EPO until after the deadline, the late payment can be excused (RRF8(3)–(4)).

*A document arrived late at the EPO*

1–173

If a document sent to the EPO was posted, or delivered to a recognised delivery service, five days or more before expiry of the relevant time limit, it can be deemed to have been received in due time provided that it arrived within three months of the expiry of the time limit. The relevant provision is r.84a EPC. To qualify, posting from outside Europe has to be by airmail. Within Europe, registered post has to be used. Accepted delivery services are Chronopost, Deutsche Post Express, DHL, Federal Express, LTA, TNT, Skynet and UPS. Within Europe means that it was despatched in one of the states belonging to the European Conference on Postal and Telecommunications Administrations (CEPT) or in a state which is generally understood to be part of Europe. A list on non-contracting states belonging to CEPT can be found in the Guidelines E/VIII/1.7. This rule even applies to the filing of a priority-claiming European patent application being filed by post. If the relevant conditions are met, the application will be deemed to have been filed by the due date (anniversary of the first convention date or as extended under r.85(1) EPC), with the priority claim intact — rather than on the date on which it actually did arrive. Note, however, that for a non priority-claiming application there is no time limit to be met and hence the rule does not apply. This is true even if the applicant had intended the application to be filed before some planned public disclosure of the invention and the application arrived after that date.

### 4. Preserving rights apparently lost in the international phase

*Extension of time limits*

1–174

A time limit can be extended pursuant to r.80.6 PCT where notification is received more than seven days from date of sending, though the burden of proof is on applicant. A time limit is also extended where the applicant can show that the relevant communication was mailed by an international authority on a date later than the date marked (r.80.6 PCT).

In certain circumstances a missed time limit can be excused due to a loss or delay in the postal system or when a document is sent by certain delivery services (r.82.1 PCT analogous to r.84a EPC). Amongst other requirements, the letter must have been sent by the applicant five days or more prior to the expiration of the time limit. Time limits can also be extended in the case of interruption to the postal service on account of war, revolution, civil disorder, strike and natural calamity (r.82.2 PCT).

1–175 *Grace periods*

Grace periods are available to the applicant in respect of paying the transmittal, international filing and search fees (r.16*bis* PCT) and the fees due for international preliminary examination (r.58*bis* PCT). Late payments are accepted anyway if received before the relevant international authority deems the application withdrawn.

1–176 *Enter the regional phase and argue before each national/regional authority*

Where an international patent application is not accorded a filing date or an international application is deemed withdrawn (*in toto* or in respect of any designation), the IB can be requested (within two months of the loss of rights) to send copies of documents in the file to relevant designated states (Art.25 and r.51 PCT). The applicant can then enter the national phase in these states and argue that the loss of rights was not justified. If the relevant authority in any designated state agrees with the applicant then the application will be restored in respect of that state. In any case, the applicant's rights may be restored if the relevant authority so wishes (Art.24(2) PCT).

Under Art.48(2) PCT, a state must excuse, for reasons admitted under its national law, and may excuse, for any other reason, any delay in meeting a time limit set pursuant to the PCT. Such reasons relevant to the EPC include further processing and *restitutio*.

Mistakes in respect of the filing date and lost priority claims can also be rectified in the national/regional phase (r.82*ter* PCT).

1–177 ## 5. Fees

One of the most important procedural aspects of securing a European patent application is the payment of fees. A thorough knowledge of when they are due, the amount that needs to be paid and the remedies available when payment is overlooked is necessary in order to answer many D1 questions. The following notes summarise such important information in relation to the main fees encountered during European grant and opposition proceedings.

1–178 *Filing fee and search fee*

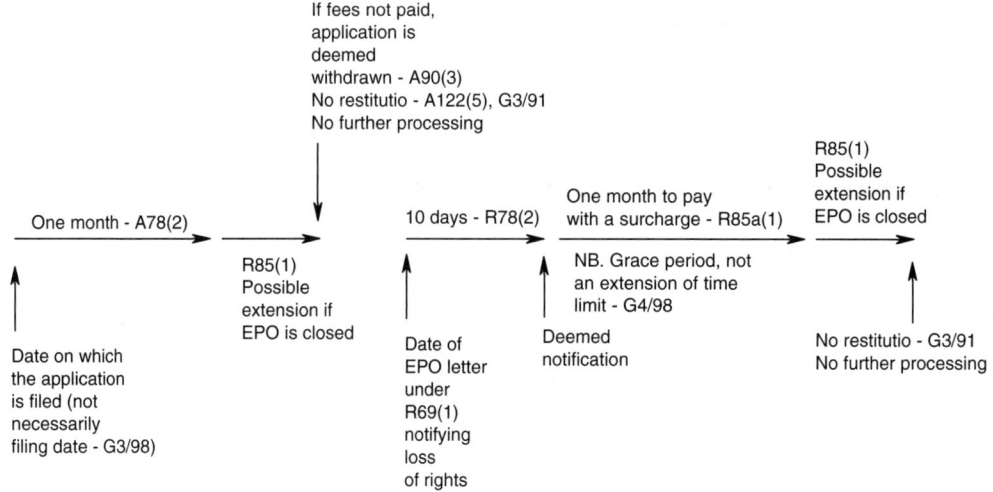

Filing fee:

| Amount | Reduction | Refund |
|---|---|---|
| 95 Euros for online filing, 170 Euros otherwise. RRF2(1) | 20% when using official language of a contracting state. R6(3), RRF12(1) | In full if application not forwarded to EPO by national office. A77(5). |

Search fee:

| Amount | Reduction | Refund |
|---|---|---|
| 1000 Euros for applications filed on or after 1.7.05 and 720 euros for applications filed before this date. RRF2(2) | None | In full if application not forwarded to EPO by national office A77(5). In full if application withdrawn or refused prior to start of search RRF10(1). In part if based on a previous EPO search RRF10(2). In part for a Euro-PCT application where the international search was carried out by the patent office of US, Japan, China, Australia, Russia or Korea (A157(3)(b)). |

*Claims fees*

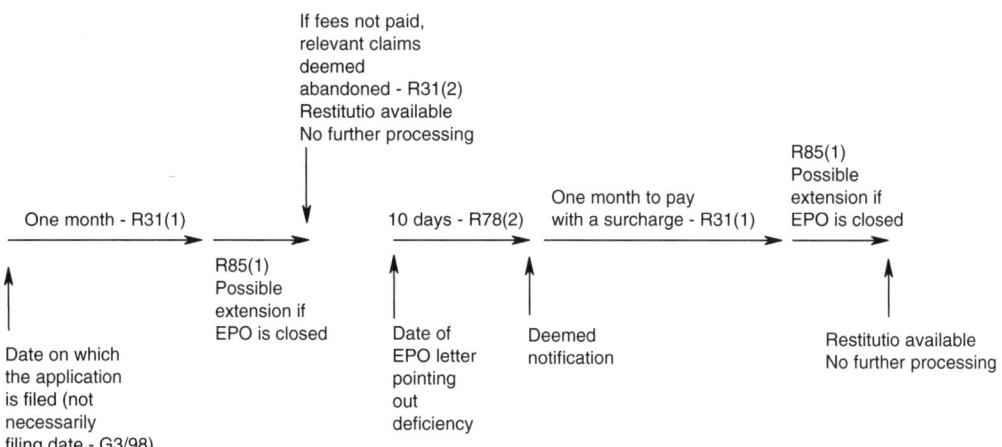

NB. Claims fees are also due on grant if number of claims has increased (R51(7)). They need to be paid within the R51(4) time limit for paying the grant and printing fees (see below) and the consequence of non-payment, as well as the potential remedy, is the same.

| Amount | Reduction | Refund |
|---|---|---|
| 45 Euros per claim over 10. RRF2(15) | None | In full if application not forwarded to EPO by national office A77(5) and R31(2). |

1–180    *Designation fees*

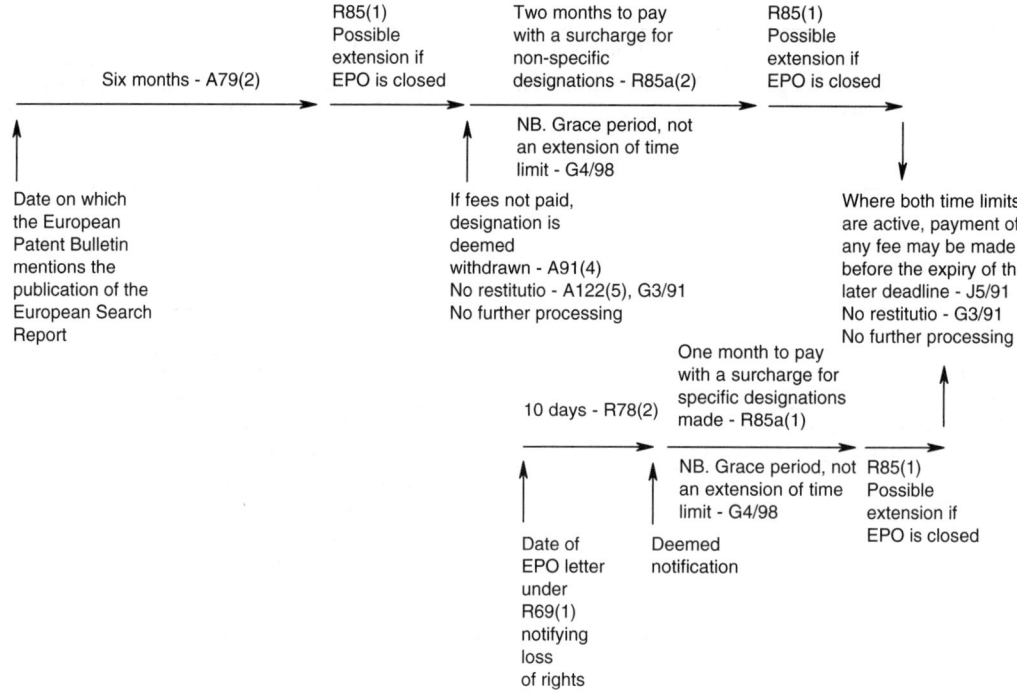

| Amount | Reduction | Refund |
|---|---|---|
| 80 Euros per designation (RRF2(3)), joint CH/LI designation the same (RRF2(3a)) but a maximum of 7 fees are needed to designate all states (RRF2(3)) | None | In full if application not forwarded to EPO by national office — A77(5). No refund in the case the application is withdrawn — A79(3). |

1–181    *Examination fee*

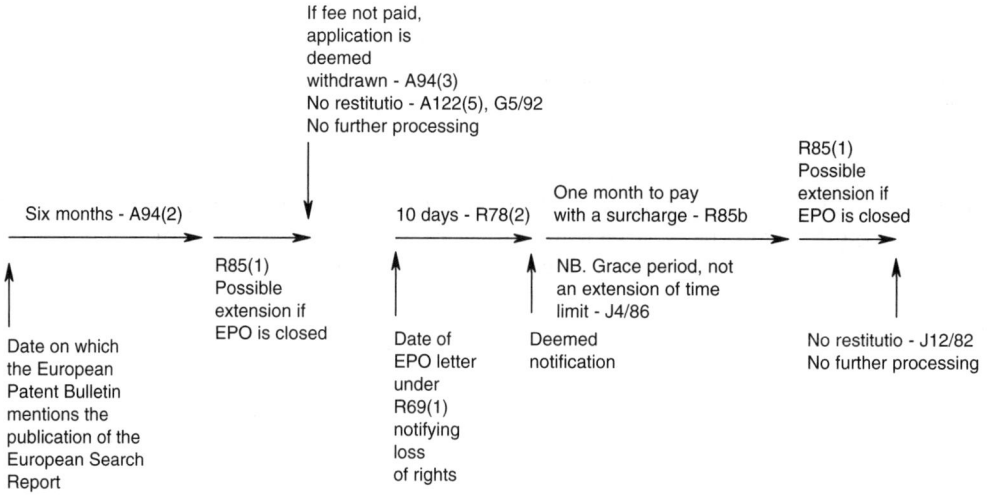

| Amount | Reduction | Refund |
|---|---|---|
| 1335 Euros for European application filed on or after 1.7.05<br>1490 Euros for a European application filed before 1.7.05 and Euro-PCT application where no supplementary search is necessary.<br>RRF2(6) | 20% when using official language of a contracting state — R6(3), RRF12(1)<br>50% reduction for Euro-PCT application where the EPO carried out a detailed international preliminary examination | In full if application withdrawn or refused before examining division has resumed responsibility or 75% where examining division has assumed responsibility but not yet begun the examination — RRF10b |

## Grant and printing fees

1–182

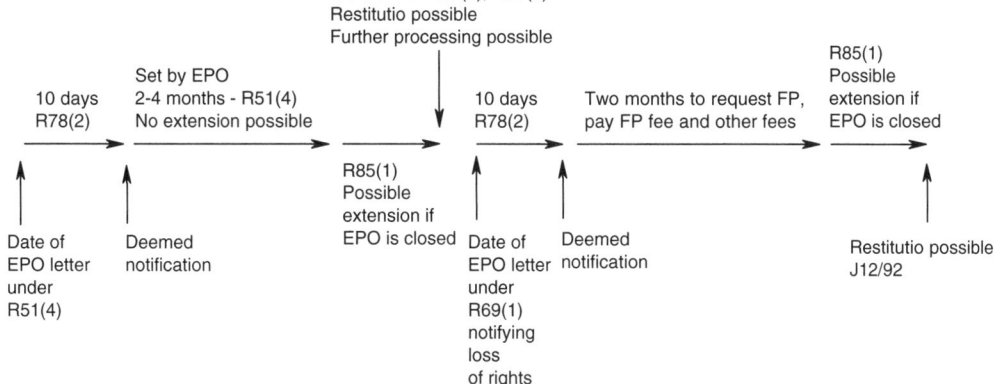

| Amount | Reduction | Refund |
|---|---|---|
| 750 Euros for the first 35 pages and 11 Euros for every subsequent page. RRF2(8) | None | In full if the application is refused or withdrawn before a decision to grant is communicated — R51(6). |

## Renewal fees

1–183

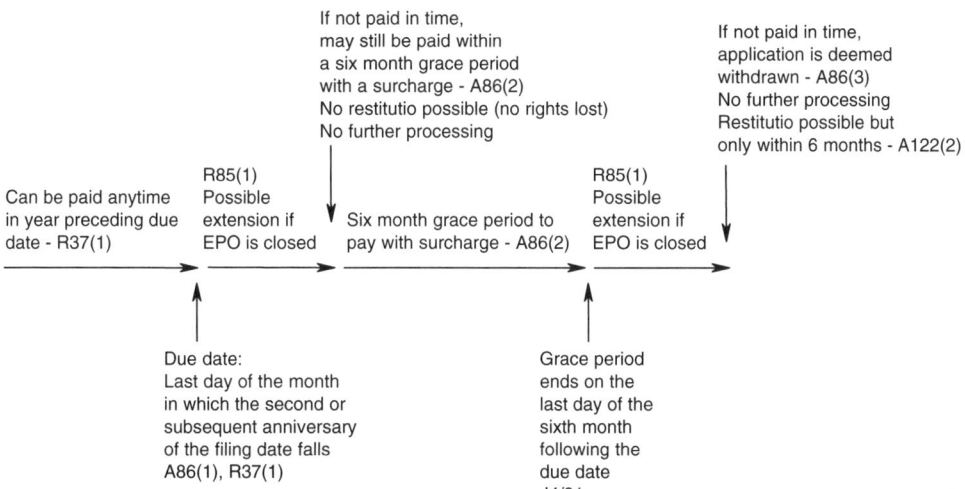

NB. The due date for the first renewal fee in the case of an international application entering the national phase more than 24 months from the international filing date is 31 months from the priority date (R107(1)(g)), not the end of the month in which the 31 month date falls.

| Amount | Reduction | Refund |
|---|---|---|
| Varies from 400 Euros for the third year to 1065 Euros for the tenth and subsequent years. RRF2(4) | None | In full if application is withdrawn before the due date (GL A/XI/10.1.1). |

**1–184** *Opposition fee*

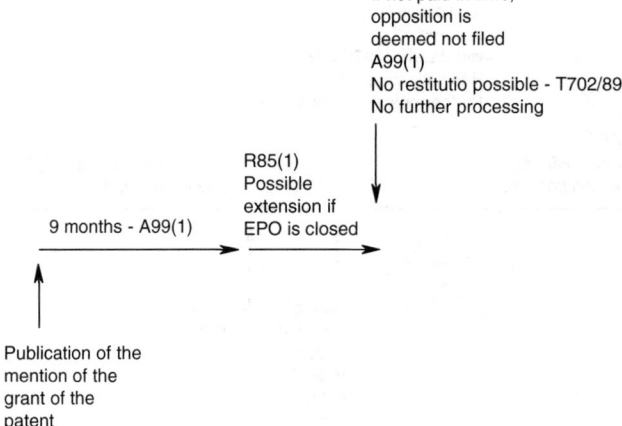

| Amount | Reduction | Refund |
|---|---|---|
| 635 Euros — RRF2(10) | 20% when using official language of a contracting state — R6(3), RRF12(1) | In full if opposition deemed not filed (e.g. no translation filed where one is necessary, T193/87) but not if it is withdrawn or inadmissible. |

**1–185** *Appeal fee*

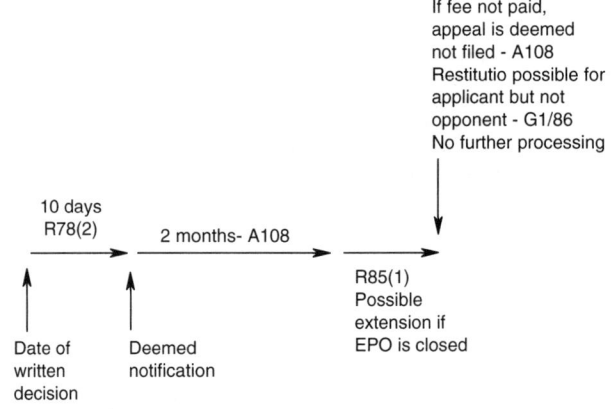

| Amount | Reduction | Refund |
|---|---|---|
| 1065 Euros RRF2(11) | 20% when using official language of a contracting state — R6(3), RRF12(1). | In full if appeal is deemed on filed (J21/80) but not where it is withdrawn or inadmissible. |

**1–186** *Further processing fee*

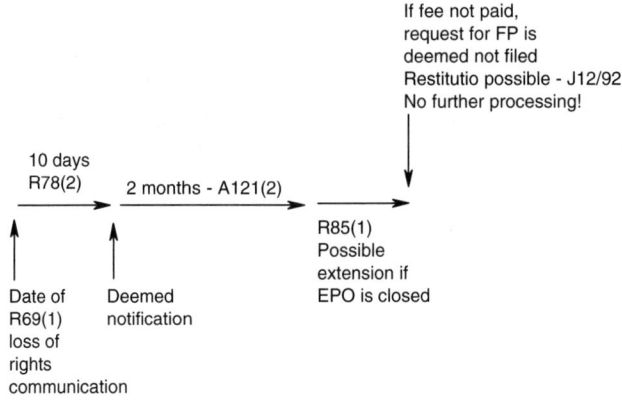

| Amount | Reduction | Refund |
|---|---|---|
| 210 Euros — RRF2(12) | None | None |

*Fee for restitutio*

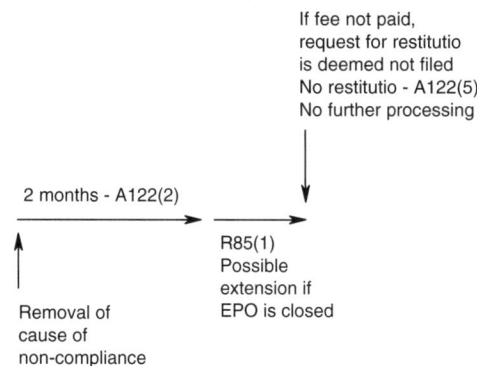

| Amount | Reduction | Refund |
|---|---|---|
| 365 Euros — RRF2(13) | None | None |

## 6. Enlarged Board Decisions

Decisions of the Enlarged Board of Appeal of the EPO are of fundamental importance, as discussed above. For ease of reference, headnotes and brief comments have been compiled in this section.

*G5/83 — Second medical indication/EISAI (see also G1/83 and G 6/83)*

Headnote (1): 'A European patent with claims directed to the use may not be granted for the use of a substance or composition for the treatment of the human or animal body by therapy.'

Headnote (2): 'A European patent may be granted with claims directed to the use of a substance or composition for the manufacture of a medicament for a specified new and inventive therapeutic application.'

The Enlarged Board felt that there was no substantive difference, for the purposes of the EPC, between a use claim and a method claim and thus that a claim to the use of a substance or composition for treatment lacked industrial applicability under A52(4) EPC in the same way as a method of treatment claim. However, it was decided that since, under A54(5) EPC, a use-limited product claim was novel by virtue of the use feature, so a use-limited process claim (i.e. use of a substance/composition for the manufacture of a medicament for treatment of a disease) could be seen to be novel by virtue of the use feature. Swiss style second medical use claims are therefore allowable and their novelty is recognised even if the process for manufacturing a medicament was already known.

*G1/86 — Re-establishment of rights of opponent/VOEST ALPINE*

Headnote: 'Article 122 EPC is not to be interpreted as being applicable only to the applicant and patent proprietor. An appellant as opponent may have his rights re-established under Article 122 EPC if he has failed to observe the time limit for filing the statement of grounds of appeal.'

An opponent may not apply for restitutio under A122 EPC for missing the time limit for filing an appeal since the proprietor is seen to need some legal certainty as to whether an opposition decision is to be contested and the travaux preparatoire address this point. This is also in conformity with national laws. However, since the appeal procedure is essentially judicial and judicial procedures demand that parties be accorded equal rights, it was seen as appropriate that once an appeal was pending (notice of appeal and appeal fee filed) the opponent should also be able to take advantage of A122 EPC in subsequent proceedings. This is a good example of an Enlarged Board decision establishing a purposive interpretation of the EPC very different from the simple meaning of the words used.

### G1/88 — Opponent's silence/HOECHST

Headnote: 'The fact that an opponent has failed, within the time allowed, to make any observations on the text in which it is intended to maintain the European patent after being invited to do so under R58(4) EPC does not render his appeal inadmissible.'

It had become practice that, in the event the opponent made no comment when invited to do so pursuant to Rule 58(4) EPC, his silence was interpreted as tacit approval of the decision of the Opposition Division from which it was inferred that he was not 'adversely effected' by the decision and could not appeal. The practice was reversed by this decision. Rule 58(4) EPC was seen not as a mandatory procedure but one option for obtaining the proprietor's approval of the text (A113(2)) and giving the opponent a chance to comment (A113(1)). These objects can also be achieved, for instance, at oral proceedings. The right to comment on the proposed text under Rule 58(4) EPC was therefore seen as supplementary to the right to appeal the decision to uphold the patent in amended form.

### G2/88 — Friction reducing additive/MOBIL OIL III

Headnote (1): 'A change of category of granted claims in opposition proceedings is not open to objection under A123(3) EPC, if it does not result in extension of the protection conferred by the claims as a whole, when they are interpreted in accordance with A69 EPC and its protocol. In this context, the national laws of the Contracting States relating to infringement should not be considered.'

Headnote (2): 'An amendment of granted claims directed to a compound and to a composition including such compound, so that the amended claims are directed to the use of that compound in a composition for a particular purpose is not open to objection under A123(3) EPC.'

Headnote (3): 'A claim to the use of a known compound for a particular purpose, which is based on a technical effect which is described in the patent, should be interpreted as including that technical effect as a functional technical feature, and is accordingly not open to objection under A54(1) EPC provided that such technical feature has not previously been made available to the public.'

Regarding A123(3) EPC, the Enlarged Board reasoned that the protection conferred by the claims is to be decided under the EPC whereas the rights conferred (infringing acts etc) are a matter for national law. Here, the compound/composition claims conferred absolute protection in respect of all uses and hence the change to a use claim necessarily narrowed the extent of protection. The new use was the use of a known compound, used in the same way to achieve a different purpose (reducing friction — previous purpose was rust inhibition). The Enlarged Board reasoned that the claim should be construed to include the functional feature of attaining the new technical effect. This technical feature was inherent in the prior art but not made available, by inevitable result or description. Second non-medical use claims are therefore allowable, even if the new use was inherent (but secret) in a prior art use.

### G4/88 — Transfer of opposition/MAN

Headnote: 'An opposition pending before the EPO may be transferred or assigned to a third party as part of the opponent's business assets together with the assets in the interests of which the opposition was filed.'

The Enlarged Board considered that an opposition could not be transferred or assigned per se. However, since an opposition gives the opponent legal rights as a party to the proceedings and constitutes as inseparable part of that party's business's assets it may be transferred with those assets if they are sold. See also G2/04 in which this question was considered again.

*G5/88 — Administrative agreement/MEDTRONIC (consolidated with G7/88 and G8/88)*

Headnote (1): 'The capacity of the President of the EPO to represent the European Patent Organisation by virtue of A5(3) EPC is one of his functions but is not one of his powers. The extent of the President's power is governed by the EPC, but not by A5(3) EPC'

Headnote (2): 'To the extent that the Administrative Agreement dated 29.6.1981 between the President of the EPO and the President of the German Patent Office contains terms regulating the treatment of documents intended for the EPO and received by the German Patent Office in Berlin, the President of the EPO did not himself have the power to enter into such an agreement on behalf of the EPO, at any time before the opening of the Filing Office for the EPO in Berlin on 1.7.1989.'

Headnote (3): 'In application of the principle of good faith and the protection of the legitimate expectations of users of the EPO, if a person has at any time since publication of the agreement in the OJ and before 1.7.1989, filed documents intended for the EPO at the German Patent Office in Berlin (otherwise than by hand), the EPO was then bound to treat such documents as if it had received them on the date of receipt at the German Patent Office in Berlin.'

The Enlarged Board took the view that A10(2)(a), which gives the President the power to 'take all necessary steps . . . to ensure the functioning of the EPO' entitled him to set up the agreement in respect of the Munich office but not the Berlin office since in Berlin there was no EPO filing office and no risk of confusion. In fact, Berlin was inserted into the agreement by the German Patent Office for political reasons. When the EPO filing office in Berlin came into being, however, the whole agreement was justified. In any case, those people who had relied on the unjustified part of the agreement should not be retrospectively penalised in order to protect their legitimate expectations. The agreement has since been terminated.

*G6/88 — Plant growth regulating agent/BAYER*

Headnote: 'A claim to the use of a known compound for a particular purpose, which is based on a technical effect which is described in the patent, should be interpreted as including that technical effect as a functional technical feature, and is accordingly not open to objection under Article 54(1) EPC provided that such technical feature has not previously been made available to the public.'

The decision given by the Enlarged Board in this case was essentially the same as the decision in G2/88 and the headnotes therefore correspond. In this case the known use was the use of a compound for influencing plant growth whereas the new use was the use of the same compound, applied in the same way, for controlling fungi. A second non-medical use claim in theses circumstance was seen as allowable in principle.

*G1/89 — Polysuccinate esters*

Headnote: 'The agreement between the EPO and WIPO dated 7.10.87, including the obligation under its Article 2 for the EPO to be guided by the PCT guidelines for international search, is binding on the EPO when acting as an International Searching Authority and upon the Boards of Appeal of the EPO when deciding on protests against the charging of additional search fees under the provisions of Article 17(3)(a) PCT. Consequently, as foreseen in these guidelines, an international application may, under Article 17(3)(a) PCT, be considered not to comply with the requirement of unity of invention, not only 'a priori' but also 'a posteriori', i.e. after taking prior art into consideration. However, such consideration has only the procedural effect of initiating the special procedure laid down in Article 17 and Rule 40 PCT and is, therefore, not a 'substantive examination' in the normal sense of the term.'

### G2/89 — Non-unity a posteriori

Headnote: 'The EPO in its function as an International Searching Authority may, pursuant to Article 17(3)(a) PCT, request a further search fee where the international application is considered to lack unity 'a posteriori'.

### G3/89 — Correction under Rule 88, second sentence, EPC

Headnote (1): 'The parts of a European patent application or of a European patent relating to the disclosure (the description, claims and drawings) may be corrected under R88, second sentence, EPC only within the limits of what a skilled person would derive directly and unambiguously, using common general knowledge, and seen objectively and relative to the date of filing, from the whole of these documents as filed. Such a correction is of a strictly declaratory nature and thus does not infringe the prohibition of extension under A123(2) EPC.'

Headnote (2): 'Evidence of what was common general knowledge on the date of filing may be furnished in connection with an admissible request for correction in any suitable form.'

The Enlarged Board considered that A123(2) EPC applies equally to amendments which are and which are not corrections. Further, the requirements of R88 EPC imply that the skilled person is able to recognise that certain information in the disclosure is incorrect as well as what the correct version should be. Hence, the correction is declaratory in the sense of the corrected version merely expressing what the skilled person would already understand. The only relevant evidence is that contained in documents shedding light on the common general knowledge of the skilled man at the filing date. These proceedings were joined with G11/91.

### G1/90 — Revocation of the patent

Headnote: 'The revocation of a patent under A102(4) and (5) EPC requires a decision.'

There was confusion as to whether, in the event of A102(4) or (5) being activated (patent revoked following a decision in opposition proceedings to maintain the patent in amended form and necessary fees or translations not filed in time), there was a deemed revocation of the patent leading to a loss of rights communication under R69(1) or whether the opposition decision needed to take a decision under R69(2). The Enlarged Board considered that whereas grant proceedings can be terminated by a loss of rights or a decision, the EPC provides for opposition proceedings being terminated only by a decision and that this literal interpretation of the EPC was in accord with the travaux preparatoire, procedural convenience and legal certainty.

### G2/90 — Responsibility of the Legal Board of Appeal/KOLBENSCHMIDT

Headnote (1): 'Under A21(3)(c) EPC, the Legal Board of Appeal is competent only to hear appeals against decisions taken by an Examining Division consisting of fewer than four members when the decision does not concern the refusal of a European patent application or the grant of a European patent. In all other cases, i.e. those covered by A21(3)(a), 3(b) and (4) EPC, the Technical Board of Appeal is competent.

Headnote (2): 'The provisions relating to competence in A21(3) and (4) EPC are not affected by R9(3) EPC.'

The Enlarged Board decided that since only duties involving no legal difficulties could be entrusted to a formalities officer under R9(3) EPC, an appeal from such a decision should rightly be entrusted to the Technical Board of Appeal and no special considerations applied to change the normal operation of A21(3) and (4) concerning which appeals are allocated to which Board.

## G1/91 — Unity/SIEMENS

Headnote: 'Unity of invention (A82) does not come under the requirements which a European patent and the invention to which it relates must meet under A102(3) EPC when the patent is maintained in amended form. It is consequently irrelevant in opposition proceedings that the European patent as granted or as amended does not meet the requirement of unity.'

Hence, unity of invention is only of concern in pre-grant proceedings.

## G2/91 — Appeal fees/KROHNE

Headnote (1): 'A person who is entitled to appeal but does no do so and instead confines himself to being a party to the appeal proceedings under A107 second sentence has no independent right to continue the proceedings if the appellant withdraws the appeal.'

Headnote (2): 'Appeal fees cannot be reimbursed simply because several parties to proceedings before the EPO have validly filed an appeal against the same decision.'

Only the appellant or appellants can decide the fate of the appeal (aside from the EPO's own right to continue proceedings in certain circumstances). Other parties to the proceedings have no such right.

## G3/91 — Re-establishment of rights/FABRITIUS II

Headnote: 'Article 122(5) EPC is applicable both to the time limits provided for in Articles 78(2) and 79(2) EPC and to those provided for in Rule 104b(1)(b) and (c) EPC in conjunction with Articles 157(2)(b) and 158(2) EPC.'

This decision confirmed that A122(5) EPC, restricting the application of restitutio in integrum, applies to the A78(2) EPC time limit (for paying the search and filing fees) and the A79(2) EPC time limit (for paying the designation fees), including the grace periods under R85a EPC. By analogy, it was decided that A122(5) EPC also applies to the corresponding time limits for Euro-PCT applications entering the national phase. In these circumstances the national basic fee equates to the filing fee. Note that the reference to Rule 104b in the headnote no longer makes sense due to amendment made to the Regulations. The relevant rule is now Rule 107 EPC.

## G4/91 — Intervention/DOLEZYCH II

Headnote (1): 'It is a prerequisite for intervention in opposition proceedings by an assumed infringer pursuant to Article 105 EPC that there are opposition proceedings in existence at the point in time when a notice of intervention is filed.'

Headnote (2): 'A decision by an Opposition Division which decides upon the issues raised by the opposition is a final decision in the sense that thereafter the Opposition Division has no power to change its decision.'

Headnote (3): 'Proceedings before an Opposition Division are terminated upon issue of such a final decision, regardless of when such decision takes legal effect.'

Headnote (4): 'In a case where, after issue of a final decision by an Opposition Division, no appeal is filed by a party to the proceedings before the Opposition

Division, a notice of intervention which is filed during the two-month period for appeal provided by Article 108 EPC has no legal effect.

The Enlarged Board decided that an intervention can only be filed if opposition proceedings are in existence. This is not so where a decision of the Opposition Division has been issued, such a decision being final in the sense that the Opposition Division has no power to change it. Such a decision therefore terminates the opposition proceedings regardless of the fact that it finally takes legal effect only after the period for appeal has expired. For intervention in appeal proceedings, see G1/94 and G3/04.

### G5/91 — Appealable decision/DISCOVISION

Headnote (1): 'Although A24 EPC applies only to members of the Boards of Appeal and of the Enlarged Board of Appeal, the requirement of impartiality applies in principle also to employees of the departments of first instance of the EPO taking part in decision making activities affecting the rights of any party.'

Headnote (2): 'There is no legal basis under the EPC for any separate appeal against an order of a director of a department of the first instance such as an Opposition Division rejecting an objection to a member of the division on the ground of suspected partiality. However, the composition of the Opposition Division may be challenged on such a ground of appeal against the final decision of the division or against an interlocutory decision under Article 106(3) EPC allowing separate appeal.'

The Enlarged Board concluded that the decision of an Examining Division or an Opposition Division may be appealed on the basis of impartiality. Article 125 provides the legal basis. The Director of the department concerned decides on any request for a change in composition — there is no separate appeal from the decision but it may be challenged as part of the appeal on substantive matters. If upheld on appeal, a substantial procedural violation has occurred and the decision at first instance is void.

### G6/91 — Fee reduction/ASULAB

Headnote (1): 'The persons referred to in A14(2) EPC are entitled to the fee reduction under R6(3) EPC if they file the essential item of the first act in filing, examination or appeal proceedings in an official language of the state concerned other than English, French or German, and supply the necessary translation no earlier than simultaneously.

Headnote (2): 'The essential item of the first act in appeal proceedings is the notice of appeal, so to secure entitlement to the reduction in the appeal fee it suffices that said document be filed in a Contracting State official language which is not an official language of the EPO and translated into one of the latter languages, even if subsequent items such as the statement of grounds of appeal are filed only in an EPO official language.'

### G7/91 — Withdrawal of appeal/BASF (consolidated with G8/91)

Headnote: 'In so far as the substantive issues settled by the contested decision at first instance are concerned, a Board of Appeal may not continue opposition appeal proceedings after the sole appellant, who was the opponent in the first instance, has withdrawn his appeal.'

This is to be contrasted with opposition proceedings, where under R60(2) EPC the examination of an opposition by the opposition division can be continued even if the opposition is withdrawn, and is a reflection of the fact that the Boards of Appeal consider themselves to be essentially judicial in nature rather than administrative. The reasoning of the Enlarged Board was based on the principle of party disposition whereby a court cannot continue proceedings if the procedural act giving rise to the proceedings has been retracted.

## G8/91 — Withdrawal of appeal/BELL (consolidated with G7/91)

Headnote: 'In so far as the substantive issues settled by the contested decision at first instance are concerned, appeal proceedings are terminated, in ex parte and inter partes proceedings alike, when the sole appellant withdraws the appeal.'

## G9/91 — Power to examine/ROHM AND HAAS

Headnote: 'The power of an Opposition Division or a Board of Appeal to examine and decide on the maintenance of a European patent under Articles 101 and 102 EPC depends upon the extent to which the patent is opposed in the notice of opposition pursuant to Rule 55(c) EPC. However, subject-matters of claims depending on an independent claim, which falls in opposition or appeal proceedings, may be examined as to their patentability even if they have not been explicitly opposed, provided their validity is prima facie in doubt on the basis of already available information.'

Rule 55(c) was interpreted by the Enlarged Board as governing the legal and factual framework within which substantive examination of an opposition must in principle be conducted. Therefore, if the extent of the opposition is only partial (i.e. not all the independent claims are opposed) the Opposition Division has no competence to examine those claims, which are not subject to any 'opposition' at all. In contrast, where an independent claim is opposed, the Opposition Division may also examine any claims dependent on the opposed independent claim provided that their validity is prima facie in doubt on the basis of the available information.

## G10/91 — Examination of oppositions/appeals

Headnote (1): 'An Opposition Division or a Board of Appeal is not obliged to consider all the grounds for opposition referred to in Article 100 EPC, going beyond the grounds covered by the statement under Rule 55(c) EPC.'

Headnote (2): 'In principle, the Opposition Division shall examine only such grounds for opposition which have been properly submitted and substantiated in accordance with Article 99(1) in conjunction with Rule 55(c) EPC. Exceptionally, the Opposition Division may in application of Article 114(1) EPC consider other grounds for opposition which, prima facie, in whole or in part would seem to prejudice the maintenance of the European patent.'

Headnote (3): 'Fresh grounds for opposition may be considered in appeal proceedings only with the approval of the patentee.'

## G11/91 — Glu-Gln/CELTRIX

See above under G3/89. The headnotes and reasoning are identical.

## G12/91 — Final decision/NOVATOME II

Headnote: 'The decision-making process following written proceedings is completed on the date the decision to be notified is handed over to the EPO postal service by the decision-taking department's formalities section.'

On this date the Examining or Opposition Division no longer have the power to change their minds. It corresponds to the moment in oral proceedings where debate is closed and the parties may no longer submit anything further. Further amendments or comments will therefore not be taken into account after this date.

## G1/92 — Availability to the public

Headnote (1): 'The chemical composition of a product is state of the art when the product as such is available to the public and can be analysed and reproduced by the skilled person, irrespective of whether or not particular reasons can be identified for analysing the composition.'

Headnote (2): 'The same principle applies mutatis mutandis to any other product.'

Availability of a product to the public thus frequently makes available its composition and structure but not any properties that depend on further action being taken (e.g. a particular use).

### G2/92 — Non-payment of further search fees

Headnote: 'An applicant who fails to pay the further search fees for a non-unitary application when requested to do so by the Search Division under R46(1) EPC cannot pursue that application for the subject matter in respect of which no search fees have been paid. Such an applicant must file a divisional application in respect of such subject matter if he wishes to seek protection for it.'

The Enlarged Board felt that only one examination fee is payable and so only one invention may be examined and that this invention must have been one searched by the Search Division. The applicant who pays the extra fees may not only argue for unity subsequently before the Examining Division but may also select which of the inventions is examined if unsuccessful in this argument. These fees are not lost since the search fees payable on any divisional application which must be filed are reduced to the extent the first search can be used.

### G3/92 — Unlawful applicant/LATCHWAYS

Headnote: 'When it has been adjudged by a final decision of a national court that a person other than the applicant is entitled to the grant of a European patent, and that person, in compliance with the specific requirements of A61(1) EPC, files a new European patent application in respect of the same invention under A61(1)(b) EPC, it is not a pre-condition for the application to be accepted that the earlier original usurping application is still pending before the EPO at the time the new application is filed.'

This case split the Enlarged Board of Appeal. The majority decided, as stated in the headnote, that the potential risk to legal certainty in respect of parties commencing commercial activities on the basis that the application was dead were outweighed by the damaging consequences of parties stealing an invention and withdrawing their application shortly after publication (they felt that national courts could take into account particular circumstances of this kind with regard to third parties). Nothing in the language of the EPC was seen to prevent this interpretation and, in particular, the provision governing divisional applications, that a pending parent application must be in existence, was seen not to apply. The reference in A61(3) to the Implementing Regulations was deemed to be to R15 and R16 and not to R25. The Board felt that exercise of the remedies provided by A61(1)(a) and (c) did require a pending application.

### G4/92 — Basis of decisions

Headnote (1): 'A decision against a party who has been duly summoned but who fails to appear at oral proceedings may not be based on facts put forward for the first time during those oral proceedings.'

Headnote (2): 'Similarly, new evidence may not be considered unless it has been previously notified and it merely supports the assertions of the party who submits it, whereas new arguments may in principle be used to support the reasons for the decision.'

### G5/92 — Re-establishment/HOUPT (consolidated with G6/92)

Headnote: 'The time limit under A94(2) EPC is excluded from restitutio in integrum by the provisions of paragraph 5 of A122 EPC.'

These consolidated proceedings provided confirmation of the obvious and augmented G3/91 which had confirmed the same in respect of the filing and search fees.

## G6/92 — Re-establishment/DURIRON (consolidated with G5/92)

See under G5/92 above.

## G9/92 — Non-appealing party/BMW (consolidated with G4/93)

Headnote (1): 'If the patent proprietor is the sole appellant against an interlocutory decision maintaining a patent in amended form, neither the Board of Appeal nor the non-appealing opponent as a party to the proceedings as of right under A107(2) EPC may challenge the maintenance of the patent as amended in accordance with the interlocutory decision.'

Headnote (2): 'If the opponent is the sole appellant against an interlocutory decision maintaining a patent in amended form, the patent proprietor is primarily restricted during appeal proceedings to defending the patent in the form in which it was maintained by the Opposition Division in its interlocutory decision. Amendments proposed by the patent proprietor as a party to the proceedings as of right under A107(2) may be rejected as inadmissible by the Board of Appeal if they are neither appropriate nor necessary.'

This case examines the situation where a patent is maintained in amended form during opposition proceedings and only one of the parties appeals. The principle of reformatio in pieus applies such that the non-appealing party may not make requests more favourable to itself then the decision of the Opposition Division. The Enlarged Board (by majority) felt that the subject matter of proceedings is the appeal itself and not a general re-examination. Further, it would be unfair if one party did not comply with the time limit for appeal but was still allowed, effectively, to appeal the decision. The subject matter of Headnote (2) was further elucidated in G1/99.

## G10/92 — Divisional application

Headnote: 'Under the amended version of Rule 25 EPC in force since 1 October 1988 an applicant may only file a divisional application on the pending earlier European patent application up to the approval in accordance with Rule 51(4) EPC.'

This decision is no longer relevant. A divisional application may now be filed up until (but not including) the date of mention of grant in the Bulletin.

## G1/93 — Limiting feature/ADVANCED SEMICONDUCTOR PRODUCTS

Headnote (1): 'If a European patent as granted contains subject matter which extends beyond the content of the application as filed within the meaning of A123(2) EPC and which also limits the scope of protection conferred by the patent, such a patent cannot be maintained in opposition proceedings unamended, because the ground for opposition under A100(c) EPC prejudices the maintenance of the patent. Nor can it be amended by deleting such limiting subject-matter from the claims, because such amendment would extend the protection conferred, which is prohibited by A123(3) EPC. Such a patent can, therefore, only be maintained if there is a basis in the application as filed for replacing such subject-matter without violating A123(3) EPC.

Headnote (2): 'A feature which has not been disclosed in the application as filed but which has been added to the application during examination and which, without providing a technical contribution to the subject-matter of the claimed invention, merely limits the protection conferred by the patent as granted by excluding protection for part of the subject-matter of the claimed invention as covered by the application as filed, is not to be considered as subject-matter which extends beyond the content of the application as filed within the meaning of Article 123(2) EPC. The ground for opposition under Article 100(c) EPC therefore does not prejudice the maintenance of a European patent which includes such a feature.'

This decision confirmed that an inescapable trap lurks for the unwary applicant who makes a limiting amendment during examination which amounts to added subject matter. Such an offending amendment would likely have to be replaced with an even more limiting amendment for which there was clear basis. The applicability of Headnote 2 must be considered somewhat narrow in view of later decisions such as G2/98 — but it could certainly apply to a disclaimer which was allowable according to the criteria set out in G1/03.

### G2/93 — Hepatitis A virus/UNITED STATES OF AMERICA II

Headnote: 'The information concerning the file number of a culture deposit according to Rule 28(1)(c) EPC may not be submitted after expiry of the time limit set out in Rule 28(2)(a) EPC.'

An application must be sufficient at its filing date: any deficiency cannot be later remedied. Thus, if the sufficiency of a disclosure depends on access to a culture, the relevant deposit must be made on or before the filing date (R28(1)(a) EPC) and information identifying the deposit must be supplied (R28(1)(c) EPC) in time for inclusion in the publication of the application (R28(2) EPC).

### G3/93 — Priority interval

Headnote (1): 'A document published during the priority interval, the technical contents of which correspond to that of the priority document, constitutes prior art citable under A54(2) EPC against a European patent application claiming that priority, to the extent such priority is not validly claimed.'

Headnote (2): 'This also applies if a claim to priority is invalid due to the fact that the priority document and the subsequent European patent application do not concern the same invention because the European application claims subject matter not disclosed in the priority document.'

The A89 effect on A54, whereby the patentability of a claim is to be judged as of the priority date, thus only applies where priority is validly claimed in respect of 'the same invention' (A87(1) EPC). See G2/98, where the concept of 'the same invention' was fully considered. Publication of the contents of a priority application during the priority year can, therefore, have unfortunate consequences for any claims based on subject matter added at the filing date — such claims must be inventive over the priority disclosure.

### G4/93 (consolidated with G9/92)

See above under G9/92.

### G5/93 — Re-establishment/NELLCOR

Headnote: 'The provisions of Article 122(5) EPC apply to the time limits provided for in Rule 104b(1)(b)(i) and (ii) EPC in conjunction with Articles 157(2)(b) and 158(2) EPC. This notwithstanding, Euro-PCT applications may be re-established in the time limit for paying the national fee provided for in Rule 104b EPC in all cases where re-establishment of rights was applied for before decision G3/91 was made available to the public.

See G3/91 above in which A122(5) EPC was seen to apply to payment of the national fee for entering the EPO regional phase since it is the equivalent of the filing and designation fees which are both explicitly mentioned in A122(5) EPC. No restitutio is therefore possible if these fees are not paid in time. This decision is a good example of the application of the 'good faith' principle whereby nobody should suffer a disadvantage when relying on the established practice of the EPO when such practice changes.

## G7/93 — Late amendments/WHITBY II

Headnote (1): 'An approval of the text submitted by an applicant pursuant to R51(4) EPC does not become binding once a communication in accordance with R51(6) has been issued. Following issue of such a communication under R51(6) EPC and until issue of a decision to grant the patent, the Examining Division has a discretion under R86(3), second sentence, EPC, whether or not to allow amendment of the application.'

Headnote (2): 'When exercising such discretion following issue of a communication under Rule 51(6) EPC, an Examining Division must consider all relevant factors. In particular it must consider and balance the applicant's interest in obtaining a patent which is legally valid in all of the designated States, and the EPO's interest in bringing the examination procedure to a close by the issue of a decision to grant the patent. Having regard to the object underlying the issue of a communication under Rule 51(6) EPC, which is to conclude the granting procedure on the basis of the previously approved text, the allowance of a request for amendment at that late stage in the granting procedure will be an exception rather than the rule.'

Headnote (3): 'Reservations under Article 167(2) EPC do not constitute requirements of the EPC which have to be met according to Article 96(2) EPC.'

This decision was taken under the old law where R51(6) had a different meaning from present R51(6). However, the principles established are still important. The Enlarged Board decided that A113(2) (EPO to decide only on text approved by applicant) did not give the applicant a right to amend. Any amendment under R86(3) had to be made with the consent of the Examining Division. Equally, the Examining Division is not bound in any way by the text as approved and can authorise amendments prior to the issue of a decision to grant. Discretion will only be exercised in favour of the applicant as an exception rather than a rule at such a late stage of the grant procedure. The Examining Division must balance the applicant's interest in obtaining a valid patent against the EPO's interest in bringing grant proceedings to a close. Typically, amendments should be allowed which do not involve re-opening of substantive examination, e.g. amendments establishing a separate set of claims in respect of states who have made reservations under A167(2) EPC.

## G8/93 — Withdrawal of opposition/SERWANE II

Headnote: 'The filing by an opponent, who is sole appellant, of a statement withdrawing his opposition immediately and automatically terminates the appeal proceedings, irrespective of whether the patent proprietor agrees to termination of those proceedings and even if in the Board of Appeal's view the requirements under the EPC for maintaining the patent are not satisfied.'

It was the opinion of the Enlarged Board that withdrawal of the opposition by the opponent and sole appellant could only mean he wished to withdraw the appeal which was examining whether any ground of opposition might prejudice maintenance of the patent. The rest follows from G7/91 and G8/91 (see above).

## G9/93 — Opposition by patent proprietor/PEUGEOT AND CITROEN

Headnote: 'A European patent cannot be opposed by its own proprietor.'

The Enlarged Board overruled G1/84, holding that 'any person' must be interpreted in the context of the EPC as a whole to exclude the patentee and, as determined in G9/91 and G10/91, opposition proceedings are essentially contentious proceedings involving two opposed parties. In the interests of equity and good faith the decision did not apply to pending self-oppositions.

## G10/93 — Scope of examination in ex parte appeal/SIEMENS

Headnote: 'In an appeal from a decision of an Examining Division in which a European patent application was refused, the Board of Appeal has the power to examine whether the application or the invention to which it relates meets the requirements of the EPC. The same is true for requirements which the Examining Division did not take into consideration in the examination proceedings or which it regarded as having been met. If there is reason to believe that such a requirement has not been met, the board shall include this ground in the proceedings.'

The Enlarged Board contrasted ex parte examination appeals where the grounds for refusal under A97(1) EPC are comprehensive and the appeal can only improve the position of the applicant whose application has been refused with inter partes opposition appeals where the grounds for opposition are limited and in the event of the patent being upheld in amended form the applicant could have his position improved or made worse. Whether an additional matter should be ruled on by the board or remitted to the first instance for examination was a matter of judgement depending on the facts of each case.

## G1/94 — Intervention/ALLIED COLLOIDS

Headnote: 'Intervention of the assumed infringer under A105 EPC is admissible during pending appeal proceedings and may be based on any ground for opposition under A100 EPC.'

The convenience of having centralised revocation being balanced by the complication and delay to the appeal proceedings, the Enlarged Board was most swayed by the travaux preparatoires which indicated that intervention was contemplated during the appeal stage. The Board further considered that the intervener should be given the unfettered right to raise any ground of opposition. However, in view of G10/91, if a fresh ground is raised then the case should be remitted to the first instance unless there are special reasons to decide otherwise, such as the agreement of the patentee. The decision does not address the question of whether the intervener should be allowed to attack any independent claim not opposed in the original notice of opposition. Later decision G3/04 adds to this decision, confirming that the intervener does not obtain appellant status.

## G2/94 — Representation/HAUTAU II

Headnote (1): 'A Board of Appeal has a discretion to allow an accompanying person (who is not entitled under A134(1) or (7) EPC to represent parties in proceedings before the EPO) to make submissions during oral proceedings in ex parte proceedings, in addition to the complete presentation of a party's case by the professional representative.

Headnote (2): '(a) In ex parte proceedings a professional representative should request permission for the making of such oral submissions in advance of the day appointed for oral proceedings. The request should state the name and qualifications of the person for whom permission is requested, and should specify the subject matter of the proposed oral submissions. The Board of Appeal should exercise its discretion in accordance with the circumstances of each individual case. The main criterion to be considered is that the Board should be fully informed of all relevant matters before deciding the case. The Board should be satisfied that the oral submissions are made by the accompanying person under the continuing responsibility and control of the professional representative. (b) During either ex parte or inter partes proceedings, a Board of Appeal should refuse permission for a former member of the boards of appeal to make oral submissions during oral proceedings before it, unless it is completely satisfied that a sufficient period of time has elapsed following termination of such former member's appointment to the boards of appeal, so that the Board of Appeal could not reasonably be suspected of partiality in deciding the case if it allowed such oral submissions to be made. A Board of Appeal should normally refuse permission for a former member of the Boards of Appeal to make oral submissions during oral proceedings before it, until at least three years have elapsed following termination of the former member's appointment to the boards of appeal. After three years have elapsed, permission should be granted except in very special circumstances.'

## G1/95 — Fresh grounds for opposition/DE LA RUE (consolidated with G7/95)

Headnote: 'In a case where a patent has been opposed on the grounds set out in A100(a) EPC, but the opposition has only been substantiated on the grounds of lack of novelty and lack of inventive step, the grounds of unpatentable subject matter based on A52(1) and (2) EPC (i.e. non-invention) is a fresh ground for opposition and accordingly may not be introduced into the appeal proceedings without the agreement of the patentee.'

The Enlarged Board decided that a ground is an individual legal basis and A100(a) describes a collection of individual grounds rather than one single ground with different aspects. See also below under G7/95. See G10/91 for the criteria to be considered in assessing whether a new ground may be raised in opposition or opposition appeal proceedings.

## G2/95 — Replacement of application documents/ATOTECH

Headnote: 'The complete documents forming a European patent application, that is the description, claims and drawings, cannot be replaced by way of a correction under R88 EPC by other documents which the applicants had intended to file with their request for grant.'

This decision follows very straightforwardly from G3/89 and G11/91 in that the subject matter that may not be extended under A123(2) is that contained in the claims, description and drawings accorded a filing date under A80.

## G3/95 — Inadmissible referral

Headnote (1): 'In decision T 356/93 (OJ EPO 1995, 545) it was held that a claim defining genetically modified plants having a distinct, stable, herbicide-resistance genetic characteristic was not allowable under Article 53(b) EPC because the claimed genetic modification itself made the modified or transformed plant a "plant variety" within the meaning of Article 53(b) EPC.'

Headnote (2): 'This finding is not in conflict with the findings in either of decisions T 49/83 (OJ EPO 1984, 112) or T 19/90 (OJ EPO 1990, 476).

Headnote (3): 'Consequently, the referral of the question: "Does a claim which relates to plants or animals but wherein specific plant or animal varieties are not individually claimed contravene the prohibition on patenting in Article 53(b) EPC if it embraces plant or animal varieties?" to the Enlarged Board of Appeal by the President of the EPO is inadmissible under Article 112(1)(b) EPC.

The question as to the extent of the exclusion under A52(b) EPC was finally addressed in G1/98 — see below.

## G4/95 — Representation/BOGASKY

Headnote (1): 'During oral proceedings under A116 EPC in the context of opposition or opposition appeal proceedings, a person accompanying the professional representative of a party may be allowed to make oral submissions on specific legal or technical issues (including facts, evidence or argument) on behalf of that party, otherwise than under A117 EPC, in addition to the complete presentation of the party's case by the professional representative.'

Headnote (2): '(a) Such oral submissions cannot be made as a matter of right, but only with the permission of and under the discretion of the EPO. (b) The following main criteria should be considered by the EPO when exercising its discretion to allow the making of oral submissions by an accompanying person in opposition or opposition appeal proceedings: (i) The professional representative should request permission for such oral submissions to be made. The request should state the name and qualifications of the accompanying person, and should specify the subject-matter of the proposed oral submissions. (ii) The request should be made sufficiently in advance of the oral proceedings so that all opposing parties are able properly to prepare themselves in relation to the proposed oral submissions. (iii) A request which is made shortly before or at the oral proceedings should in the absence of exceptional circumstances be refused, unless each opposing party agrees to the making of the oral submissions requested. (iv) The EPO should be satisfied that oral submissions by an accompanying person are made under the continuing responsibility and control of the professional representative. (c) No special criteria apply to the making of oral submissions by qualified patent lawyers of countries which are not Contracting States to the EPC.

### G6/95 — Interpretation of Rule 71a(1) EPC vis-à-vis the Boards of Appeal

Headnote: 'R71a(1) EPC does not apply to the Boards of Appeal.'

The rules of procedure of the Boards of Appeal make the communication provided for in R71a(1) optional, depending on the facts of the case (A11(2) RPBA). Such rules of procedure were adopted by the Presidium under A23(4) and approved by the Administrative Council. The Enlarged Board decided that the Administrative Council must be presumed to know the limits of its own power and that it therefore did not intend to amend R71 EPC so as to conflict with the RPBA (A164(2) makes the provisions of the EPC superior to the provisions of the Implementing Regulations).

### G7/95 — Fresh grounds for opposition/ETHICON (consolidated with G1/95)

Headnote: 'In a case where a patent has been opposed under A100(a) EPC, on the ground that the claims lack an inventive step in view of documents cited in the notice of opposition, the ground of lack of novelty based on A52(1) and A54 EPC is a fresh ground for opposition and accordingly may not be introduced into the appeal proceedings without the agreement of the patentee. However, the allegation that the claims lack novelty in view of the closest prior art document (i.e. only this document which is an integral part of the inventive step determination may be used) may be considered in the context of deciding upon the ground of lack of inventive step.'

In consolidated cases G1/95 and G7/95 'grounds for opposition' under A100(a) were interpreted as individual legal bases for objection, i.e. 'invention', 'novelty', 'inventive step' and 'industrial application'. In the context of G10/91, a fresh ground was seen as one which was neither raised and substantiated in the notice of opposition nor introduced into the proceedings by the Opposition Division under A114(1). It had been held in G10/91 that a new ground may not be introduced at the appeal stage without the agreement of the patentee. So, if lack of inventive step was the only ground substantiated during opposition then lack of novelty may not, in principle, be argued during appeal. However, it was seen that determining whether the claimed invention had any novel features over the closest prior art document was an inherent part of determining inventive step. Thus, the novelty of the claim over the closest prior art document (NB. not any other document) could be considered in appeal proceedings and if there was a lack of novelty the claim must inherently lack inventive step and thus would be rejected for lack of inventive step (NB. not lack of novelty).

### G8/95 — Correction of decision to grant/US GYPSUM II

Headnote: 'An appeal from a decision of an Examining Division refusing a request under R89 EPC for correction of the decision to grant is to be decided by a technical Board of Appeal.'

Article 21(3) EPC determines that an appeal from a decision of an examining division will be heard by a technical board of appeal when the decision concerns the refusal or grant of a European patent (as opposed to a legal board of appeal). An appeal against a decision to refuse correction of a decision to grant was seen to 'concern the grant of the patent' in contrast, for instance, to a decision to refuse a correction of a designation under R88 EPC. Whether or not the decision terminates proceedings was seen to be key.

## G1/97 — Request with a view to revision/ETA

Headnote (1): 'In the context of the EPC, the jurisdictional measure to be taken in response to requests based on the alleged violation of a fundamental procedural principle and aimed at the revision of a final decision of a Board of Appeal having the force of res judicata should be the refusal of the requests as inadmissible.'

Headnote (2): 'The decision on admissibility is to be issued by the Board of Appeal which took the decision forming the subject of the request for revision. The decision may be issued immediately and without further procedural formalities.'

Headnote (3): 'This jurisdictional measure applies only to requests directed against a decision of a Board of Appeal bearing a date after that of the present decision.'

Headnote (4): 'If the Legal Division of the EPO is asked to decide on the entry in the Register of European Patents of a request directed against a decision of a Board of Appeal, it must refrain from ordering that the entry be made if the request, in whatever form, is based on the alleged violation of a fundamental procedural principle and aimed at the revision of a final decision of a Board of Appeal.'

The Enlarged Board considered that there was no mechanism under the EPC for the review of a decision of a Board of Appeal, even where a procedural violation had occurred. Nevertheless the Enlarged Board urged the legislator to create such a mechanism (see EPC 2000). Previously, instead of such a request for review being deemed inadmissible (see headnotes 2 and 3) an administrative rejection had been issued to the same effect.

## G2/97 — Good faith/UNILEVER

Headnote: 'The principle of good faith does not impose any obligations on the Boards of Appeal to notify an applicant that an appeal fee is missing when the notice of appeal is filed so early that the appellant could react and pay the fee in time, if there is no indication — either in the notice of appeal or in any other document filed in relation to the appeal — from which it could be inferred that the appellant would, without such notification, inadvertently miss the time limit for payment of the appeal fee.'

The EPO does not have any duty to warn a party that it has not paid a fee when it is not possible for the EPO to know whether the client has made a mistake or is merely waiting to pay the fee at a later date.

## G3/97 — Opposition on behalf of a third party/INDUPACK (consolidated with G4/97)

Headnote (1): '(a) An opposition is not inadmissible purely because the person named as opponent according to R55(a) EPC is acting on behalf of a third party (i.e. as a strawman). (b) Such an opposition is, however, inadmissible if the involvement of the opponent is to be regarded as circumventing the law by abuse of process. (c) Such a circumvention of the law arises, in particular, if: (i) the opponent is acting on behalf of the patent proprietor; (ii) the opponent is acting on behalf of a client in the context of activities which, taken as a whole, are typically associated with professional representatives, without possessing the relevant qualifications required by A134 EPC. (d) However, a circumvention of the law by abuse of process does not arise purely because

(i) a professional representative is acting in his own name on behalf of a client; (ii) an opponent with either a residence or principle place of business in one of the EPC Contracting States is acting on behalf of a third party who does not meet this requirement.'

Headnote (2): 'In determining whether the law has been circumvented by abuse of process, the principle of the free evaluation of evidence is to be applied (i.e. on case by case basis, no special rules to be applied). The burden of proof is to be borne by the person alleging that the opposition is inadmissible. The deciding body has to be satisfied on the basis of clear and convincing evidence that the law has been circumvented by abuse of process (i.e. more than on balance of probabilities).

See below under G4/97 for comment.

### G4/97 — Opposition on behalf of a third party/GENENTECH (consolidated with G3/97)

Headnotes (1) and (2): Identical to G3/97 (see above).

Headnote (3): 'The admissibility of an opposition on grounds relating to the identity of an opponent may be challenged during the course of the appeal, even if no such challenge has been raised before the Opposition Division.'

The Enlarged Board decided that in principle it was allowable for a strawman to file an opposition on behalf of another party. Such a procedure would only be unallowable if a further provision of the EPC was being circumvented (e.g. a strawman cannot act on behalf of the proprietor as this would amount to self-opposition — see G9/93). No special interest is necessary to act as an opponent since every member of the public has an interest to the extent that the ability to carry out certain acts is restricted by the patent. The Enlarged Board also decided that the decision should be applied to all pending proceedings since there was no valid legitimate expectation to protect on the basis of past case law.

### G1/98 — Transgenic plant/NOVARTIS II

Headnote (1): 'A claim wherein specific plant varieties are not individually claimed is not excluded from patentability under A53(b) EPC even though it may embrace plant varieties.'

Headnote (2): 'When a claim to a process for the production of a plant variety is examined, A64(2) EPC is not to be taken into consideration.'

Headnote (3): 'The exception to patentability in A53(b), first half-sentence, EPC applies to plant varieties irrespective of the way in which they were produced. Therefore, plant varieties containing genes introduced into an ancestral plant by recombinant gene technology are excluded from patentability.'

The Enlarged Board held that A53(b) excluded plant varieties rather than plants and existed to exclude double protection via a patent and a plant breeders right. Therefore, anything that could not be protected under UPOV should be patentable, including the claim in dispute, directed to a genetically modified plant, which neither expressly or implicitly defined a plant variety according to UPOV.

### G2/98 — Requirement for claiming priority of the 'same invention'

Headnote: 'The requirement for claiming priority of 'the same invention', referred to in A87(1) EPC means that priority of a previous application in respect of a claim in a European patent application in accordance with A88 EPC is to be acknowledged only if the skilled person can derive the subject matter of the claim directly and unambiguously, using common general knowledge, from the previous application as a whole.'

The alternative (i.e. allowing priority where a feature not disclosed in the priority application has been inserted which merely limits scope and is not related to function and effect) was seen to be dangerously subjective and changeable during prosecution in the light of fresh prior art. The strict approach was seen to be consistent with the Paris Convention and A87–89 EPC.

### G3/98 — Six-month period/UNIVERSITY PATENTS (consolidated with G2/99)

Headnote: 'For the calculation of the six-month period referred to in A55(1) EPC, the relevant date is the date of the actual filing of the European patent application; the date of priority is not to be taken account of in calculating this period.'

The Enlarged Board differentiated the terms 'filing of the application' which is the date that the applicant files the documents and used in A75, A76(1), A133(2) and A78(2), determining the time limit for paying fees, and 'date of filing' which is the date given to the application after examination under A90(1) and, for instance, determines the term of the patent under A63.

### G4/98 — Designation fees

Headnote (1): 'Without prejudice to A67(4) EPC, the designation of a Contracting State party to the EPC in a European patent application does not retroactively lose its legal effect and is not deemed never to have taken place if the relevant designation fee has not been paid within the applicable time limit.'

Headnote (2): 'The deemed withdrawal of the designation of a Contracting State provided for in A91(4) EPC takes effect upon expiry of the time limits mentioned in A79(2), R15(2), R25(2) and R107(1) EPC, as applicable, and not upon expiry of the period of grace provided for by R85a EPC

### G1/99 — Reformatio in peius/3M

Headnote: 'In principle, an amended claim, which would put the opponent and sole appellant in a worse situation than if it had not appealed, must be rejected. However, an exception to this principle may be made in order to meet an objection put forward by the opponent/appellant or the Board during the appeal proceedings, in circumstances where the patent as maintained in amended form would otherwise have to be revoked as a direct consequence of an inadmissible amendment held allowable by the Opposition Division in its interlocutory decision. In such circumstances, in order to overcome the deficiency, the patent proprietor/respondent may be allowed to file requests, as follows: (i) in the first place, for an amendment introducing one or more originally disclosed features which limit the scope of the patent as maintained; (ii) if such a limitation is not possible, for an amendment introducing one or more originally disclosed features which extend the scope of the patent as maintained, but within the limits of A123(3) EPC; (iii) finally, if such amendments are not possible, for deletion of the inadmissible amendment but within the limits of A123(3) EPC.'

This decision considered in more detail the position in Headnote (2) of G9/92 where the opponent is sole appellant and in particular the meaning of 'appropriate nor necessary' in relation to amendments. In the view of the Enlarged Board, equity demands that the proprietor should not lose his patent where he has not appealed against a decision by the Opposition Division to maintain a patent in a form considered by the Board of Appeal to be invalid, the invalidity only being curable by increasing the scope of protection viz a viz the interlocutory decision. In particular, the opponent always has another chance to contest validity at the national level.

### G2/99 — Six-month period/DEWERT (consolidated with G3/98)

See above under G3/98.

### G3/99 — Admissibility of joint opposition or joint appeal/HOWARD FLOREY

Headnote (1): 'An opposition filed in common by two or more persons, which otherwise meets the requirements of A99 EPC and R1 and R55 EPC is admissible on payment of only one opposition fee.'

Headnote (2): 'If the opposing party consists of a plurality of persons, an appeal must be filed by the common representative under Rule 100 EPC. Where the appeal is filed by a non-entitled person, the Board of Appeal shall consider it not to be duly signed and consequently invite the common representative to sign it within a given time limit. The non-entitled person who filed the appeal shall be informed of this invitation. If the previous common representative is no longer participating in the proceedings, a new common representative shall be determined pursuant to Rule 100 EPC.'

Headnote (3): 'In order to safeguard the rights of the patent proprietor and in the interests of procedural efficiency, it has to be clear throughout the procedure who belongs to the group of common opponents or common appellants. If either a common opponent or appellant (including the common representative) intends to withdraw from the proceedings, the EPO shall be notified accordingly by the common representative or by a new common representative determined under R100(1) EPC in order for the withdrawal to take effect.'

The situation where several natural or legal persons file an opposition in common is anticipated by R100(1).

### G1/02 — Formalities officers' powers

Headnote: 'Points 4 and 6 of the Notice from the Vice-President Directorate-General 2 dated 28 April 1999 (OJ, 1999 506) do not conflict with provisions of a higher level.'

This decision overruled T295/01, which had suggested that formalities officers could never decide on the admissibility of an opposition, only the Opposition Division being competent. A formalities officer can decide on admissibility where there are no technical or legal difficulties.

### G2/02 — Priorities from India/ASTRAZENECA (consolidated with G3/02)

Headnote: 'The TRIPs Agreement does not entitle the applicant for a European patent application to claim priority from a first filing in a State which was not at the relevant date a member of the Paris Convention but was a member of the WTO/TRIPs Agreement.'

The legal board of appeal had referred a question asking whether a Euro-PCT application which claimed the priority of an earlier application filed in a WTO country not party to the Paris Convention was entitled to that priority claim in the regional phase. The priority right should not in principle be recognised since A87(1) EPC only refers to Paris Convention countries (note A87(1) of EPC 2000 has been extended to WTO countries as well). The Enlarged Board confirmed that TRIPS was not applicable to the EPC, Article 87(1) was determinative, and such a priority claim would not therefore be recognised.

### G3/02 — Priorities from India/ASTRAZENECA (consolidated with G2/02)

See above under G2/02.

### G1/03 — Disclaimer/PPG (consolidated with G2/03)

Headnote (1): 'An amendment to a claim by the introduction of a disclaimer may not be refused under Article 123(2) EPC for the sole reason that neither the disclaimer nor the subject-matter excluded by it from the scope of the claim have a basis in the application as filed.'

Headnote (2): 'The following criteria are to be applied for assessing the allowability of a disclaimer which is not disclosed in the application as filed:

2.1 A disclaimer may be allowable in order to:
 – restore novelty by delimiting a claim against state of the art under Article 54(3) and (4) EPC;
 – restore novelty by delimiting a claim against an accidental anticipation under Article 54(2) EPC; an anticipation is accidental if it is so unrelated to and remote from the claimed invention that the person skilled in the art would never have taken it into consideration when making the invention; and
 – disclaim subject-matter which, under Articles 52 to 57 EPC, is excluded from patentability for non-technical reasons.
2.2 A disclaimer should not remove more than is necessary either to restore novelty or to disclaim subject-matter excluded from patentability for non-technical reasons.
2.3 A disclaimer which is or becomes relevant for the assessment of inventive step or sufficiency of disclosure adds subject-matter contrary to Article 123(2) EPC.
2.4 A claim containing a disclaimer must meet the requirements of clarity and conciseness of Article 84 EPC.'

This case concerned the extent to which a disclaimer, having no basis in the application as filed, may be introduced during prosecution in order to distinguish over novelty-destroying prior art. Disclaimers are always allowable when they restore novelty over a 54(3) document. In the case of a 54(2) document a disclaimer is only allowed where the anticipation is accidental, i.e. the prior art reference is so remote and unrelated to the subject matter of the invention that it would never have been taken into account by the skilled person in making the invention. Disclaimers are also allowable to exclude subject matter which is classed as non-patentable for non-technical, policy-related reasons (particularly under A52(4), A53(a) and A57 EPC) where the claim covers some embodiments which fall under the relevant exclusion and some which don't. In all cases, no more than the novelty-destroying part of the prior art or the non-patentable embodiments may be removed from the claim. The rationale is that, in line with previous case law (e.g. T170/87, T597/92), a disclaimer cannot make a non-inventive teaching inventive. A disclaimer may therefore only be used when inventive step is not an issue. How the new definition of 'accidental' will be applied in practice is yet to be seen. The EPO seems to be taking a 'business as usual' attitude but the definition could be interpreted to be quite narrow.

*G2/03 — Disclaimer/GENETIC SYSTEMS (consolidated with G1/03)*

See above under G1/03.

*G3/03 — Reimbursement of the appeal fee/HIGHLAND*

Headnote (1): 'In the event of interlocutory revision under Article 109(1) EPC, the department of the first instance whose decision has been appealed is not competent to refuse a request of the appellant for reimbursement of the appeal fee.'

Headnote (2): 'The board of appeal which would have been competent under Article 21 EPC to deal with the substantive issues of the appeal if no interlocutory revision had been granted is competent to decide on the request.'

The first instance division that reviews a request for interlocutory revision must therefore decide if they think a request for reimbursement of the appeal fee is valid. If they decide it is then they have the power to order reimbursement. However, if they think it isn't then they must remit the case to a board of appeal who will make the final decision on reimbursement.

*G1/04 — Diagnostic methods*

Headnote (1): 'In order that the subject-matter of a claim relating to a diagnostic method practised on the human or animal body falls under the prohibition of Article

52(4) EPC, the claim is to include the features relating to: (i) the diagnosis for curative purposes stricto sensu representing the deductive medical or veterinary decision phase as a purely intellectual exercise, (ii) the preceding steps which are constitutive for making that diagnosis, and (iii) the specific interactions with the human or animal body which occur when carrying those out among these preceding steps which are of a technical nature.'

Headnote (2): 'Whether or not a method is a diagnostic method within the meaning of Article 52(4) EPC may neither depend on the participation of a medical or veterinary practitioner, by being present or by bearing the responsibility, nor on the fact that all method steps can also, or only, be practised by medical or technical support staff, the patient himself or herself or an automated system. Moreover, no distinction is to be made in this context between essential method steps having diagnostic character and non-essential method steps lacking it.'

Headnote (3): 'In a diagnostic method under Article 52(4) EPC, the method steps of a technical nature belonging to the preceding steps which are constitutive for making the diagnosis for curative purposes stricto sensu must satisfy the criterion "practised on the human or animal body".'

Headnote (4): 'Article 52(4) EPC does not require a specific type and intensity of interaction with the human or animal body; a preceding step of a technical nature thus satisfies the criterion "practised on the human or animal body" if its performance implies any interaction with the human or animal body, necessitating the presence of the latter.'

The Enlarged Board have given the diagnostic methods exclusion a narrow interpretation in line with its purpose. The only diagnostic methods excluded are those that include both a data collection step and a step in which a course of therapy is proposed on the basis of that data. Moreover, each of the data collection steps must be practiced on the human or animal body, in the sense that they must require its presence. The case for broadening the exclusion, made in T964/99, was thus rejected and the old status quo, whereby a method of generating interim results for use in diagnosis was regarded as patentable, has been re-established.

### G2/04 — Transfer of opposition/HOFFMAN-LA ROCHE

Headnote (1): '(a) The status as an opponent cannot be freely transferred. (b) A legal person who was a subsidiary of the opponent when the opposition was filed and who carries on the business to which the opposed patent relates cannot acquire the status as opponent if all its shares are assigned to another company.'

Headnote (2): 'If, when filing an appeal, there is a justifiable legal uncertainty as to how the law is to be interpreted in respect of the question of who the correct party to the proceedings is, it is legitimate that the appeal is filed in the name of the person whom the person acting considers, according to his interpretation, to be the correct party, and at the same time, as an auxiliary request, in the name of a different person who might, according to another possible interpretation, also be considered the correct party to the proceedings.'

This decision confirmed that an opposition cannot be freely assigned but may be transferred as a result of universal succession (e.g. from a deceased opponent to his/her heir (R60(2) EPC) or in the takeover of a company, or the relevant assets of a company, by another legal entity (G4/88)). Where, however, company A, which has a legally independent subsidiary B, files an opposition relating to a business area in which company B operates, the opposition may not be transferred from A to a company which buys subsidiary B. The opposition would have been transferable if: (a) it had been filed in the name of subsidiary company B; or (b) B had not had its own legal status but had merely been a department of company A. Where a holding company files an opposition on behalf of a legally distinct subsidiary it is thus safer to file the opposition jointly in both names.

The decision also established that if, when filing an appeal, there is justifiable legal uncertainty as to who the correct party to the proceedings is, it is legitimate for the appeal to be filed in the name of the person whom the person acting considers to be the correct party, and at the same time, as an auxiliary request, in the name of a different person who might, according to another possible interpretation, also be considered the correct party to the proceedings.

*G3/04 — Intervention/EOS*

Headnote: 'After withdrawal of the sole appeal, the proceedings may not be continued with a third party who intervened during the appeal proceedings.'

The Enlarged Board had previously decided that intervention during opposition appeal proceedings was possible (G1/94) but there was some doubt about the intervener's procedural status in this situation. This decision has made it clear that the intervener attains the status of an opponent under A105(2) EPC and is a party to the appeal proceedings of right under A107 EPC. The intervener does not, however, have the status of an appellant since he was not adversely affected by the decision taken. No appeal fee therefore needs to be paid. It also follows, from decision G7/91, that withdrawal of a sole appeal will terminate the proceedings, the consent of the intervener not being required.

## 7. Common errors

1–188

One common reason for losing marks in Paper D1 is the miscalculation of time limits following notification by the EPO. Remember to calculate the deemed date of notification by adding 10 days to the date of the EPO letter (r.78(2) EPC) before adding the relevant number of months. Then remember to extend the deadline calculated if it falls on a day when any of the EPO sites is shut (r.85(1) EPC). In contrast, under the PCT a time limit runs from the date of the relevant communication (subject to r.80.6 PCT).

Renewal fees are easy to forget about since they are usually associated with post-grant proceedings. However, under the EPC renewal fees are due at the end of the month in which the second anniversary of the filing date falls (Art.86(1) EPC) and annually thereafter until grant. But bear in mind the ruling in J4/91 which provides that the period for paying a missed renewal fee and the necessary additional fees, lasts until the last day of the later month even if there are more days in the later month than there were in the month when the renewal fee was originally due. This is a very important decision and must be understood perfectly. Always bear renewal fees in mind when advising a client what steps need to be taken to keep a European application pending. Another important case on time limits, which like J4/91 interprets the EPC in a way that seems at variance with its wording, is J5/91 which concerns payment of designation fees. Again, this must be completely understood by candidates for Paper D. This decision is dealt with in Legal Advice No.5/93 rev.

For EPO proceedings, only a European patent application may be filed at a national office and be accorded as a filing date the date of receipt at the national office. All other documents take the date of receipt at the EPO. The exception to this used to be documents which were intended for the EPO but which were sent to the German patent office, in Berlin or Munich. These were treated as having been received by the EPO on their date of receipt at the German patent office: see the administrative agreement between the Presidents of the GPO and the EPO, dated June 29, 1981, but revised on October 13, 1989. Documents posted through the night letter box of the German patent office were included in this agreement, but documents which are brought by hand to a filing office of the GPO were not accepted. However, this agreement has been terminated as of September 1, 2005 and documents handed to the German patent office will only be given the date they actually arrived at the EPO. When a document arrives at the EPO on the same day as the occurrence of another important event (e.g. the filing of an intervention on the day a sole opposition is withdrawn) and the exact point in time a document arrives can be established, this exact point of receipt is determinative (T517/97). Remember that certain things, including priority documents and authorisations, cannot be filed by fax (see the Decision of the President of May 26, 1992, regarding r.24(1) EPC).

Marks will be lost, even though the correct answer is appreciated by the candidate, if an insufficient amount of detail is given in the answer. It is generally said that if you provide no legal basis in an answer, the answer will get no marks. Where a question asks whether something can be done and the answer is yes, always say what steps would be taken, what time limit applies, what fees would be due, and do not forget to include the answer to the question — say "yes". Consider in any given situation whether either *restitutio* or further processing is applicable and state the expected outcome.

When acting for a new client, always consider the need for authorisation and appointment (see the Decision of the President of July 19, 1991, regarding r.101(1)).

1–189 ### 8. Worked example using EQE 2005 Paper D1

The Examiner's comments are very good for Paper D1 and include model answers which make any further comment regarding the 2005 paper unnecessary. However, when tackling past papers, particularly those in the earlier published compendia, be aware that the law has changed rapidly over the last decade and the answers given may be quite wrong in relation to the EPC and PCT as in force in 2007.

# PAPER D2

## 1. General comments

In this paper the candidate is expected to provide comprehensive advice to a client who finds himself in the midst of a complicated legal situation. The client will usually have certain patent applications and/or patents of his own and advice on how best to prosecute these applications or use these patents will often be necessary. The client may also have made certain inventions for which no application has been filed and advice on patentability as well as which filing strategy to pursue will need to be given. The client will also usually have competitors with their own patent applications and patents and will need to be advised how to best pursue his business without infringing any valid third party rights. Other complicating factors may include the theft of one of the client's inventions and the consequent filing of a patent application by someone not entitled to its grant.

The examiners have found, from long experience, that candidates can be relied upon not to understand priority rights. Given the importance of priority rights in the real world practice of intellectual property law, it is unsurprising that almost every D2 paper involves some sort of priority question. You should not expect to pass the exam if you do not understand how a priority right arises, who can use it, for what, and how it can be lost.

As indicated above, this paper is intended to test whether or not candidates can give appropriate practical advice to their clients. Unlike the drafting and amendment papers, this paper does not come in two variants to cater for chemists and electrical/mechanical disciplines. Consequently, legal questions more appropriate to one or other discipline can be expected and need to be answered by all candidates. Thus the electrical/mechanical specialist needs to know about selection inventions, first and second medical use claims, diagnostic methods, medical treatments, cosmetic treatments, genetically modified organisms, etc. Likewise, the chemist or biotechnologist needs to know about the patenting of computer related inventions, computer program product claims, business methods, signals, etc. These matters may seem strange and irrelevant in your day to day practice, but knowing about these matters which are strange to you can make the difference between passing and failing the European Qualifying Examination. So, learn these things now, before you face such a topic in your qualifying exam.

The same materials useful for answering the D1 questions will also be useful in the D2 paper. Legal basis should once again be quoted wherever possible. However, in general, Paper D2 is less about finding the right answer to a narrowly-framed question and more about analysing a complicated set of facts and providing sensible advice that the typical client could understand and act on. The advice given should be pragmatic and attuned to commercial reality rather than dogmatic and overly legalistic, and the financial implications for the client of any recommended action should be borne in mind. The possibility of negotiation should also be considered. Where possible, different alternatives should be presented to the client, along with an assessment of their strengths and weaknesses: but you should always aim to recommend a course of action, not just sit on the fence.

The format of the paper varies somewhat from year to year, being either in the form of one long question or two or more shorter and more or less independent questions. The approach laid out below is framed primarily with the former situation in mind but can be adapted to either situation.

The paper is four hours long and, as with previous papers, about half this time should be spent analysing the question and elucidating the answer, the other half being devoted to writing the answer.

## 2. How to tackle the paper

**1-191**    *Preparing a timeline*

First of all, read through the question once and gain general understanding of the facts. It is sensible to highlight or flag any dates, as well as any issues which spring to mind, while you read the paper for the first time. You will be reading and re-reading the paper, but sometimes things occur to you when your mind is still fresh which have faded by the time you re-read the paper.

Then, read through the question a second time, noting all dates in a list on a separate sheet of paper. From this list you can see which dates you have to deal with and it is then easier to produce a chronological list or timeline at your first attempt. The timeline is not just a list of dates, because with each date you need to record the relevant facts (what was filed or disclosed, etc. on this date). Check whether any dates (including dates in the future for carrying out important acts) fall on an EPO closed day. The timeline should include the dates of all significant events including those relating to filed patent applications (priority dates, filing dates, publication dates, grant dates, renewal fee dates, dates by which a response is due, regional phase entry dates etc) and disclosures (whether by publication, prior use or oral disclosure). In the case of patent applications, you should calculate and capture dates such as publication dates, ends of convention years, opposition periods, etc., which you are not given directly in the question, whether these are in the past or in the future. Where the question can be split into two or more separate parts that do not overlap, two or more corresponding timelines may be required. See the worked example below for a typical timeline.

**1-192**    *Analysing the paper*

In this paper the examiners go to considerable trouble to build in lots of useful information which should either prompt a good candidate to see issues to be dealt with which are not directly recited, or which should enable the good candidate to answer the questions which were expressly asked. Many candidates struggle with this paper because they do not see or do not pay attention to such information. If you want to pass this paper, you need to train to ensure that you can spot the clues and hints that the examiner provides. Once you can see what the examiner is telling you, you need to work out why you have been told and hence what you should do with the information. Examples of how this problem can be approached are given below in the worked examples.

One of the aspects that always needs to be addressed is to identify what inventions have been made (including those for which applications have been filed and those for which applications have not yet been filed). Such inventions may have been made by the client or one of his competitors, or they may be joint. The results of this analysis, when summarised in a table (see worked example below), will show who owns or can obtain valid patent rights in relevant countries in respect of each invention and hence what commercial options are available.

The first question to be asked, in respect of each identified invention, is whether an application has been filed or not.

**1-193**    **Where an application has been filed for an invention**

The theft of inventions is commonplace in the unprincipled world of the EQE. Consider firstly, therefore, whether the applicant (usually one of the client's competitors) has the right to be granted a patent as the inventor or his successor in title. If the answer is no then several steps can be taken. Firstly, an application could be made to the court of a contracting state for an entitlement decision (the Protocol on Recognition, part of the EPC, determines which contracting state must be used). Consider whether the known evidence is persuasive.

Once such an application has been made, proceedings before the EPO can be suspended using r.13 EPC, but only after publication of the European patent application.

Action must be taken prior to grant (but can be made no earlier than entry into the regional phase in the case of a PCT application). During the period of suspension a check should be made to see if renewal fees have been paid. Anybody can validly pay a due renewal fee and thus keep the application pending.

Following a positive final decision on entitlement from the national court, the wronged party can choose under Art.61 EPC to prosecute the application itself or file a new application in its place (it does not matter if application has lapsed, G3/92). Alternatively, the entitled person can request that the application be refused — worth considering if the application is worth little (e.g. if the client has his own application with a similar content and an earlier date).

If negotiation is possible then a straight assignment of the application containing the stolen material would be more straightforward for everybody. Care should be taken in alerting the third party if they are likely to be hostile since they may accelerate the grant procedure. For any material that the client is not entitled to, the filing of a divisional application may be best (but only possible on a pending application, obviously), or a free license could be granted to the competitor. In general, joint ownership of patents is likely to cause problems (in the real world and hence also in the world of the EQEs) and is not to be recommended. In any case, consideration should be given to filing an application immediately on behalf of the client since the prior application may not, pursuant to Art.55 EPC, be valid prior art.

Having addressed the issue of entitlement, consider the status of the application and what steps need to be taken to keep it alive. Timelines showing the main procedural steps to be taken in respect of European and PCT applications are provided below. Often an application will have been filed in an inappropriate language or necessary fees will not have been paid (e.g. a renewal fee). Sometimes a priority document (or a translation thereof) will not have been filed. In the unusual circumstance that an application cannot be rescued, consider the filing of another application claiming its priority if there is any priority right from which to benefit.

Having established the legal status of the application, and assuming that it is not irrevocably flawed, assess what subject matter is disclosed in the application and could be claimed.

Then, determine the effective date for the assessment of patentability. This will be the filing date or a priority date where priority has been validly claimed. The validity of a priority claim is a useful source of examination material.

A priority claim is not valid where: (1) the claimed invention is not clearly and unambiguously derivable from the priority document (G2/98); (2) priority is claimed from an application which is not the first qualifying application for that subject matter (Art.87 EPC); (3) a declaration of priority was not filed in due time or the request was not corrected before publication; (4) the applicant is not the applicant of the priority application or his successor in title; (5) the application was filed outside the priority year (only excusable using r.84a EPC (posted/sent in time) or r.85 EPC (closed days); (6) the previous application was not an application for an invention in the sense of Art.87 EPC; (7) the priority application was not filed in an appropriate country; (8) a copy of the priority application was not filed within the appropriate time limit; or (9) a translation (where necessary) of the priority document was not filed.

Having established the effective date of the subject matter in the application, assess novelty and inventive step in respect of this subject matter on the basis of any known disclosures and hence establish what valid claims might be granted.

Consider all the events described in the question before the effective date of the application and consider whether any of them rank as a publication, an oral public disclosure or a prior use. Consider all co-pending EP and PCT applications as potential 54(3) art. Consider whether any disclosure should be discounted on the basis of the Art.55 six-month period (or 12-month US grace period for US applications) or on the basis that it was covered by any express or implied term of confidence. In the case of an oral disclosure or prior use, consider if there is enough proof available (note that these disclosures do not form part of International Preliminary Examination).

Consider possible amendments that would be necessary and allowable in view of the prior art.

Assess patentability on other grounds such as sufficiency. Where an application is insufficient *per se*, consider whether any other disclosure prior to the filing date could be considered to make it sufficient or whether a further application claiming priority from the insufficient application should be filed with additional information included to improve the situation.

Finally, summarise which granted claims might be obtained and in respect of which states such patent rights would be obtained. Where a national patent application has been used as a priority basis for a European patent application don't forget to consider the possibility of the national application being prosecuted to grant.

Where a designation has been lost, consider filing a national application in that state if not too late (e.g. because before publication).

1–194   **Where an application has not been filed**

Consider how much of the material is patentable and formulate a filing strategy for the patentable material. If possible, the answer should include a description of what claims will be allowable — which is where your knowledge of what can be claimed in any technology comes into play.

In some cases the new matter may be associated with another invention for which an application has already been filed and the new application could include the contents of the filed application, claiming its priority (or be filed as a continuation in part application in the US). Consider who the applicant should be. Where it is too late to obtain assignments of the priority right, file in joint names and assign later.

Take into account the six month non-prejudicial disclosure period under the EPC and the US (12 months) and Japanese (six months under limited circumstances) grace periods if necessary.

Make sure that the inventor is the applicant for any US or PCT(US) application (later transfer of rights, if appropriate, takes place in the national phase).

For broadest coverage, file via the PCT and file national patents in non-PCT countries. A PCT application will be particularly useful where the commercial importance of the case will not be known for some time.

Consider incorporating features disclosed in competitor applications, provided that you have not acquired this information in confidence, but applied to your own novel subject matter.

Consider what the language of filing should be in respect of the fee reductions available to applicants from EPC contracting states that have an official language other than French, English and German.

Where an inventor is not available for signing documents, use the usual PCT procedure of r.4.15(b) PCT or, in the case of a European patent application, consider adding this inventor later on when he has been located.

1–195   **What national rights are therefore obtainable by the client and might be used to keep competitors off the market?**

Based on your analysis of any inventions made by the client for which patent applications have been filed (who owns them, what claims are likely to be granted in which states) and for which patent applications have not been filed (what granted patents a sensible filing strategy might lead to) it should now be possible to assess what rights the client has or may expect to obtain in countries of commercial importance and advise him how to get these rights and what he can do with them. The question will generally tell you, directly or indirectly, which are the countries of commercial significance — that is countries where your client tells you he wants patents and also, probably, the countries where competitors and/or suppliers are based. The advice will include sections on how to get back stolen patent rights, how to rescue applications and prosecute them to grant, how to amend invalid claims and what further applications need to be filed. The balance will vary markedly from year to year, depending on the facts presented in the paper. However, as indicated earlier, it is very unusual for issues of priority not to be material. If you have not spotted any priority issues, look again.

Where a granted patent is needed to take action against an infringer, and a relevant application exists, consider accelerating proceedings. In order for the client to claim damages back to publication, analyse the search report and suggest the filing of amendments, if necessary, so that the claims of the published application are patentable. Translations of published claims should be filed where necessary and a copy of the application served on any infringer. Consider amending to a narrow claim covering the infringement which will be granted straightforwardly and filing a divisional application to other material.

**What national rights are therefore obtainable by any competitor which might limit your client's commercial freedom?**

1–196

Based on your analysis of any patentable inventions made by third parties you should also be in a position to assess, in important countries (i.e. the ones that the client says are important to him), what rights exist, or could be obtained, which could be used against your client.

Where relevant European patents exist, consider filing an opposition if the opposition period has not yet expired or intervening in any ongoing opposition where infringement proceedings have been initiated against the client. National revocation actions are also possible.

Where relevant European patent applications exist, a file watch should be set up to monitor their progress to grant. An opposition can be filed on grant. It is often worthwhile filing observations (Art.115 EPC) if a novelty-destroying reference is available which has not been cited in the search report. However, filing observations is not as effective where inventive step or sufficiency is concerned since the party filing the observations is not a party to the proceedings and cannot assert its case properly. There is no mechanism in the PCT for handling third party observations.

If a competitor and the client both hold relevant rights that could be used against each other, advise your client about the possibility of cross-licensing, explaining what claims/rights would be licensed by each party.

*Answering the paper*

1–197

If the paper asks specific questions then set out your response in reply to those questions, but also ensure that you identify and answer any questions which are implicit in the paper. Otherwise, structure your answer as described above in respect of each invention, grouping together related inventions in a sensible way.

Remember that your answer is primarily addressed to a notional client and should include concrete advice on how to proceed in respect of obtaining patent rights relevant to his commercial activities and/or dealing with a third party patent right relevant to his commercial activities. The advice should preferably be tailored to the nature of the commercial activities in which the client is engaged (i.e. what he is making or selling and where his main markets are) — it may help to summarise the client's commercial objectives in the answer.

Make sure you specifically correct any false assumptions made by the client in his instructing letter.

As with Paper D1, set out individual points in the answer by first writing down briefly what the relevant law says, secondly applying that law to the facts of the question and thirdly setting out the legal consequences. Then advise the client on the basis of those consequences. Cite basis where possible.

1–198

## 3. Relevant timelines for European and EuroPCT applications

### A. Regular European patent application

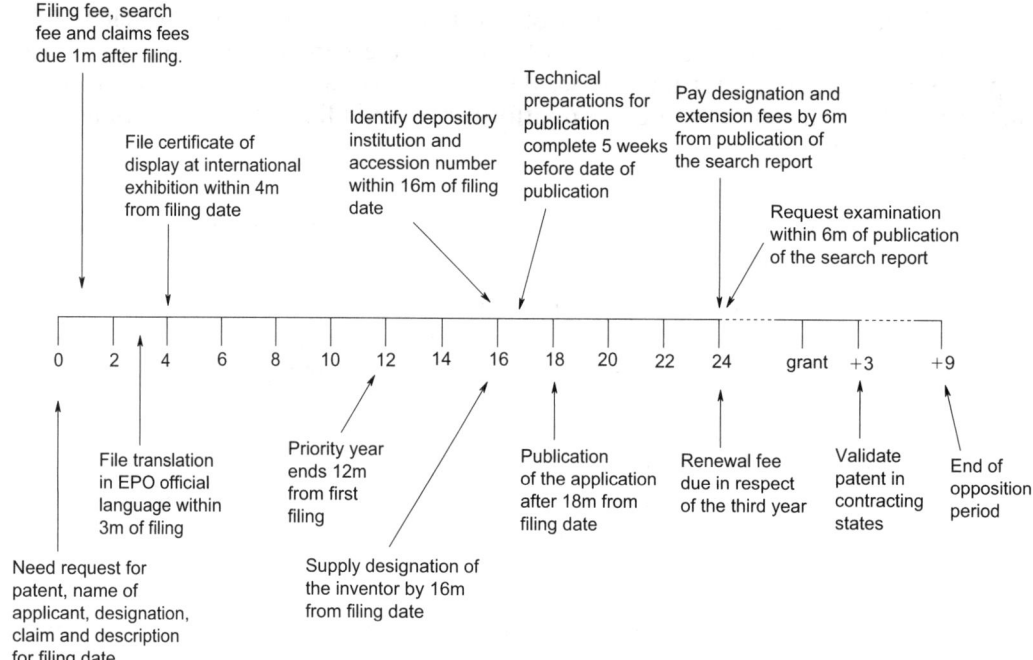

There is a period of grace for paying the filing fee, the search fee or a designation fee (r.85a EPC); the request for examination, the examination fee (r.85b EPC); claims fees (r.31.2 EPC); of one month from notification of the deficiency. The translation referred to in Art.14(2) EPC must be filed no later than 13 months from priority. If the designation of inventor is not filed by 16 months from the priority date, it may still validly be filed within two months of a notification of the deficiency. If the designation of inventor is filed but is defective, the deficiency may be remedied within the 16 months or within the period set in the notification of the deficiency (two months for major deficiencies, at least two months for minor deficiencies). If the copy of the priority document is not filed within 16 months of priority it may still be validly filed within the period set for response in the notification of the error (at least two months).

### B. European patent application filed via the PCT

For PCT patent applications filed before January 1, 2004 a basic fee (r.15.1 PCT), a transmittal fee (r.14.1 PCT) and a search fee (r.16 PCT) were all due within one month of filing. Designations fees were payable within one year from the priority date, or one month from the date of receipt of the international application if that one-month period expired later than one year from the priority date (r.15.4.b PCT). In the event that no fees are paid, or if the amount paid is insufficient, the receiving office invites the applicant (under r.16*bis*.1.a or b) to pay the missing amount, together with a surcharge (r.16*bis*.2 PCT), within one month from the date of the invitation.

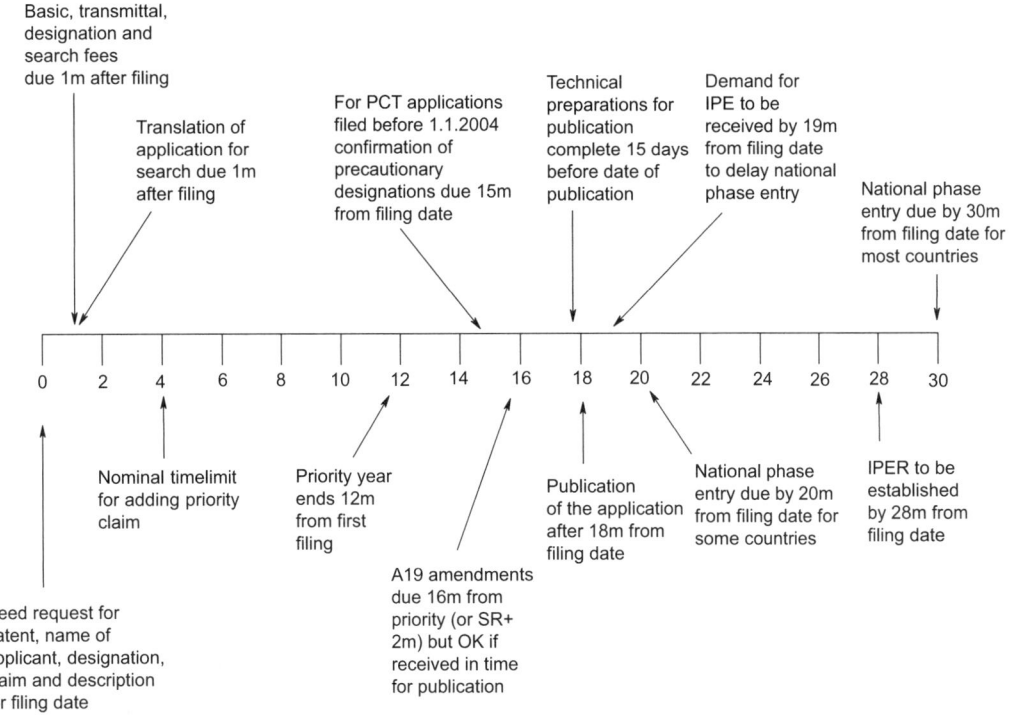

For PCT patent applications filed on or after January 1, 2004 the basic fee and the designation fees have been combined in the form of an international filing fee (r.15.1 of the 2004 PCT regulations). This fee is payable within one month of filing. The requirement for a transmittal fee, search fee, and the provision for late payment within a month of notification of the deficiency, remain the same as under the previous regulations.

## 4. Aspects of US and Japanese patent law

According to the examination syllabus for the EQE, candidates are expected to have a general knowledge of US and Japanese patent law. This knowledge is most frequently tested in Paper D2 where a client may have commercial interests which stretch across the globe. The following paragraphs highlight some of the main differences between the patent laws of Japan and the US as compared with European patent law. In general, Japanese and European law are quite similar.

Whereas in Europe and Japan the right to a patent for an invention belongs to the entitled person who first files a patent application describing the invention, in the US the right to a patent belongs to the person who first conceives the invention and diligently reduces it to practice. There is therefore no provision similar to Art.54(3) in the US. Instead, where two parties have co-pending applications directed to the same subject matter, ownership is decided in complicated legal proceedings called interference proceedings where evidence is presented as to which party made the invention first.

Whereas in Europe and Japan the applicant should be the inventor or his legal successor, in the US the applicant must always be the inventor. Subsequent assignment of the application to the legal owner occurs during prosecution of the application. A PCT application designating the US should therefore always include the inventors as applicants for the US designation.

In the US a person is entitled to a patent even if there was a public disclosure of the invention within the 12 months preceding the filing of the application in the US, whether or not that disclosure originated from the inventor of that application (35 USC 102(b)). This is known as the grace period. However, the inventor for the patent application must have made the invention before the relevant publication. If the invention was known or used by others in the US, or patented or described in a printed publication in the US or a foreign country, before the invention thereof by the applicant for the patent, the applicant is not entitled to a patent (35 USC 102(a)). Offer for sale of the invention in the US more than one year before the US filing date is also a bar to getting a valid patent (35 USC 102(b)). In Japan there is a universal novelty requirement and no general grace period. However if a novelty or obviousness bar arises, this will not bar the grant of a patent by reason of the fact that the person having the right to obtain a patent has conducted an experiment, has made a presentation in a printed publication, has made a presentation through telecommunication lines (i.e. posted something on a website) or has made a presentation in writing at a study meeting held by a scientific body designated by the Commissioner of the JPO, provided that the patent application is filed within six months of the relevant disclosure, and a written statement of the facts is provided within 30 days of filing the application. There is also a provision equivalent to Art.55(a) and (b) EPC which provides protection from abusive disclosures or disclosures at qualifying exhibitions occurring no more than six months before the filing of the Japanese patent application.

In Europe there is no grace period, just the limited provisions of Art.55 EPC.

In the US there is no restriction on the filing of patent applications in respect of computer-implemented inventions, business methods, or methods of medical treatment. In Japan the situation is not quite so liberal, but computer implemented business methods may be patentable, and methods of medical treatment of non-human animals are patentable. In Europe there is a need to show that the invention has technical character, that is that it addresses a technical problem, and this requirement is effective to prevent the grant of patents for business methods and non-technical computer-related inventions. In Europe, only some cosmetic medical treatments are patentable.

In the US, infringement is judged by the doctrine of equivalents whereby the scope of a granted patent includes all obvious equivalents of claim features (except where a means plus function formulation is used — in which case the equivalents are only those of the features disclosed in the description). This doctrine is limited by prosecution history estoppel. This means that any limiting amendment to a claim made by an applicant during prosecution may, in certain circumstances, be seen to bar the application of the doctrine of equivalents to the limited features.

In the US it is possible to file a continuation in part (CIP) application whereby a pending application is refiled with additional subject matter included. The patentability of the new matter is judged as of the date of filing of the CIP application. It is also possible, under certain circumstances and within two years of grant, to have a granted US patent reissued with broadened claims.

A US application must disclose the best mode, that is to say the best way of carrying out the invention known to the inventor at the time of filing the application. There is also a duty of candour in the US which means that any relevant prior art known to the inventor must be disclosed to the US Patent and Trademark Office. Failure to comply with these requirements can render a US patent unenforceable.

### 5. Notes on claiming priority

1–200

*Relevance of the Paris Convention to European and Euro-PCT applications*

For international applications, the Paris Convention is directly applicable by virtue of Art.8 PCT. The Patent Co-operation Treaty, however, also contains its own supplementary set of provisions which extend the minimum provisions set by the Paris Convention and allow, for instance, priority claims to be added after the filing date (r.26*bis*) as well as recognising priority rights originating in WTO member countries which are not members of the Paris Convention (r.4.10).

In contrast, the European Patent Convention does not apply the Paris Convention but instead contains its own priority code in Arts 87–89. However, these provisions have been written to be consistent with the Paris Convention (note the preamble to the EPC which states that the EPC is a special agreement within the meaning of Art.19 of the Paris Convention) which can therefore be used in interpreting the meaning of Arts 87–89 EPC.

For a Euro-PCT application the situation is therefore somewhat complicated. During the international phase the Paris Convention supplemented by the provisions of the PCT applies. During the regional phase, the provisions of the Paris Convention are still relevant to the extent they are duplicated by Arts 87–89 EPC, and some PCT provisions still apply, imposing certain obligations on contracting states during the national/regional phase, such as the need to give the applicant a chance to produce a priority document not furnished in the international phase (r.17.1 PCT). Although during the regional phase the provisions of the PCT override the provisions on the EPC in cases of conflict (Art.150(2) EPC), priority is one of the substantive provisions relating to patentability in which national law is unfettered by the provisions of the PCT (Art.27(5) PCT). Thus, for instance, until the coming into force of EPC 2000, a priority claim originating in a WTO member state not a party to the Paris Convention will be valid during the international phase but subsequently invalid in the European regional phase (see G2/02).

*The importance of the "first filing" under the European Patent Convention*   **1–201**

A priority right comes into being when an application disclosing certain subject matter is allocated a filing date in a Paris Convention country (Art.87(1) EPC; Art.4A(2) Paris Convention), whatever the subsequent fate of the application (Art.87(2) EPC; Art.4A(3) Paris Convention), i.e. whether it is withdrawn or refused, before or after publication.

The filing of an application for certain subject matter in a Paris Convention country is thus a very important event since it determines the period (12 months from the filing date) during which further applications may be filed validly claiming priority in respect of that subject matter. In principle (subject to the narrow exception outlined below) **no subsequent application disclosing the same subject matter may be used to claim priority in respect of that subject matter**. The Paris Convention (Art.4C(2)) and the European Patent Convention (Art.87(1)) both dictate that **priority may only be claimed from the first filing of any particular subject matter**.

*The limited circumstances in which priority may be claimed from a second or*   **1–202**
*subsequent filing*

Priority may validly be claimed from the second filing of certain subject matter only if: (a) the first and second applications were made in or in respect of the same state; (b) at the date of filing the second application the first application had already been withdrawn, abandoned or refused, without being open to public inspection and without leaving any rights outstanding (including the right to claim priority); and (c) at the date of filing the second application the priority of the first application had not already been claimed (Art.87(4) EPC; Art.4C(4) Paris Convention). If one or more of these criteria are not met then priority for the subject matter in question may only be claimed from the first application; a claim to priority for this subject matter from the second application will be invalid. If all these criteria are met, then priority for the subject matter in question may only be claimed from the second application; a claim to priority from the first application will be invalid. **At any given time, only one application can exist for a given subject matter from which priority may validly be claimed.**

*Illustrative examples of how priority works*   **1–203**

A. Application P1 is filed in a Paris Convention country (e.g. Germany) containing subject matter X. European application E1, claiming subject matter X, is filed within 12 months claiming priority from P1.

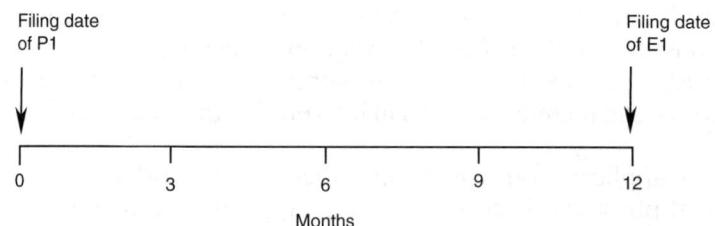

The priority claim is valid (at least in principle; there are many formal requirements which must also be satisfied).

B. Application P1 is filed in a Paris Convention country (e.g. Germany) containing subject matter X. An identical application P2 is filed three months later in another Paris Convention country (e.g. France), while P1 is still pending. European application E1 is filed within 12 months of P2 claiming its priority.

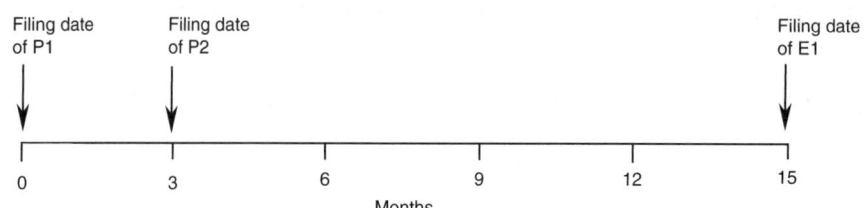

The priority claim is not valid since P2 was not the first filing and the conditions of Art.87(4) EPC have not been complied with. In the exam, P2 could be referred to as a US continuation application which therefore cannot be the first filing.

C. Application P1 is filed in a Paris Convention country (e.g. Germany) containing subject matter X. An application P2 is filed three months later in another Paris Convention country (e.g. France), while P1 is still pending, containing subject matters X and Y. European application E1 is filed within 12 months of P2 claiming its priority.

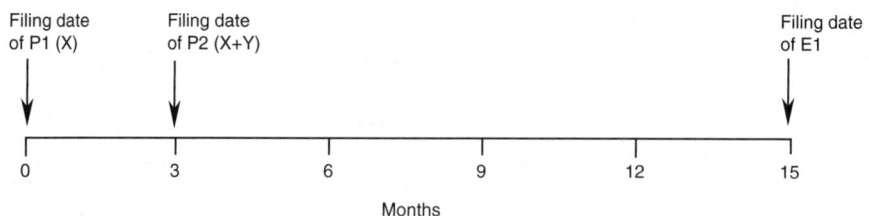

The priority claim is valid in respect of subject matter Y but not valid in respect of subject matter X for which P2 is not the first filing. In the exam P2 could be a US continuation-in-part of earlier US application P1 and only the extra subject matter would be entitled to the priority date.

D. Application P1 is filed in a Paris Convention country (e.g. Germany) containing subject matter X. The application is withdrawn leaving no rights outstanding and an identical application P2 is filed immediately after the withdrawal of P1 in the same Paris Convention country. European application E1 is filed within 12 months of P2, claiming its priority.

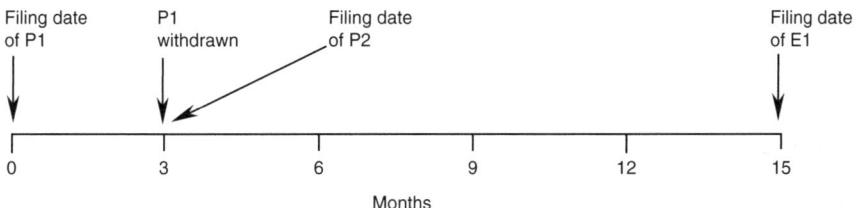

The priority claim is valid since under Art.87(4) P2 replaces P1 as the application from which priority is to be claimed.

E. Application P1 is filed in a Paris Convention country (e.g. Germany) containing subject matter X. The application is withdrawn leaving no rights outstanding and an identical application P2 is filed immediately after the withdrawal of P1 in a different Paris Convention country (e.g. France). European application E1 is filed within 12 months of P2, claiming its priority.

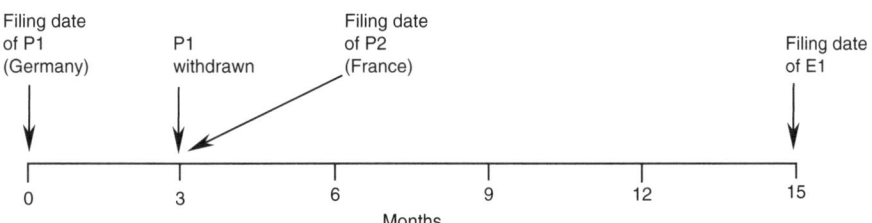

The priority claim is not valid since P2 was not re-filed in the same country as P1.

F. Application P1 is filed in a Paris Convention country (e.g. Germany) containing subject matter X. The application is withdrawn leaving no rights outstanding and an identical application P2 is filed the next day in the same Paris Convention country. European application E1 is filed within 12 months of P1, claiming its priority.

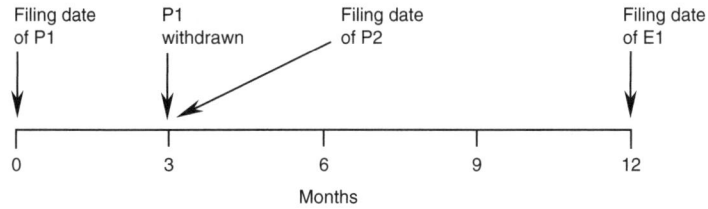

The priority claim is not valid since under Art.87(4) P2 replaces P1 as the application from which priority is to be claimed. This may seem surprising — since Art.87 (3) concludes with "whatever be the outcome of the application" (which is very similar to the corresponding wording of Art. 4A (3) of the Paris Convention) which suggests that you can still claim priority from an application which has been withdrawn — and of course you can. But the question specified "leaving no rights outstanding" (wording taken from Art.87 (4) EPC and Art. 4C4 PC). Art. 87(4) specifies the conditions under which a subsequent application can serve as a priority basis by taking the place of a first application. But the "leaving no rights outstanding" is also a requirement that prior to filing the subsequent patent application the right to priority also be withdrawn! Where you file a subsequent application for the same subject matter as a first application, you can never validly be in a position where you have a choice of application from which to claim priority.

If no rights are outstanding from the withdrawn application, there is no longer a priority right to claim from it. There is an important lesson here. If you want to withdraw a first application so that you can file a subsequent application as a replacement, with a view to that subsequent application later serving as the priority basis for matter common to the two applications, the withdrawal of the first application must expressly withdraw or abandon the right to claim priority from that application.

G. Application P1 is filed in a Paris Convention country (e.g. Germany) containing subject matter X. Three months later an identical application P2 is filed in the same Paris Convention country. Application P1 is then withdrawn, leaving no rights outstanding. European application E1 is filed within 12 months of P2, claiming its priority.

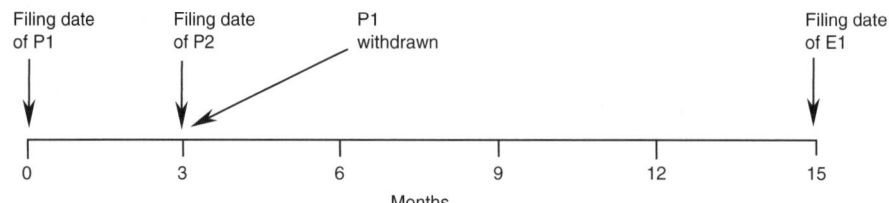

The priority claim is not valid since under P1 should have been withdrawn before the filing of P2 according to Art.87(4) EPC.

H. Application P1 is filed in a Paris Convention country (e.g. Germany) containing subject matter X and is published early at the applicant's request after 6 months. Four months later application P1 is withdrawn, leaving no rights outstanding. An identical application P2 is then filed in the same Paris Convention country. European application E1 is filed within 12 months of P2, claiming its priority.

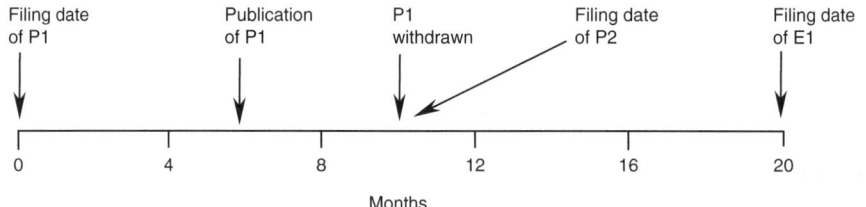

The priority claim is not valid since P1 was published and therefore open to public inspection.

I. Application P1 is filed in a Paris Convention country (e.g. Germany) containing subject matter X. Four months later application P2 is filed in the same country claiming priority from P1 and disclosing subject matters X and Y. Six months later applications P1 and P2 are withdrawn, leaving no rights outstanding. An application P3, identical to P2 is then filed in the same Paris Convention country. European application E1 is filed within 12 months of P3, claiming its priority.

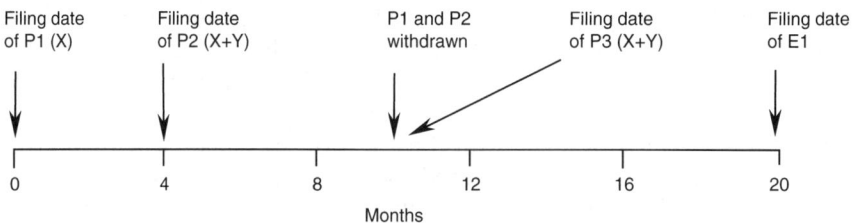

The priority claim is not valid for subject matter X since P3 is not the first application for this subject matter and P1 has already served as a basis for a priority claim before it was withdrawn. The priority claim is valid in respect of subject matter Y.

*Examples of questions relating to priority rights in the EQE*  1–204

**Paper D2, 2001**

A competitor of the client (Niffy Shoe liners Ltd) has filed a European application NF-EU1 on 01 June 1999 claiming the priority of Irish application NF-IE1 filed on 15 October 1998. Both applications are identical and describe (i) product A, (ii) a new class of polymers having moisture-absorbent properties, (iii) a process for making the polymers as fibres, (iv) use of the fibres as a shoe liner. However, Niffy have already filed a previous European application NF-EU2 on 30 September 1998 claiming the priority of Irish application NF-IE2 filed on 01 October 1997. Both of these applications are also identical and disclose (i) product A, (ii) the new class of polymers, (iii) the process for making the polymers as fibres, (iv) use of fibres of product A as a shoe liner.

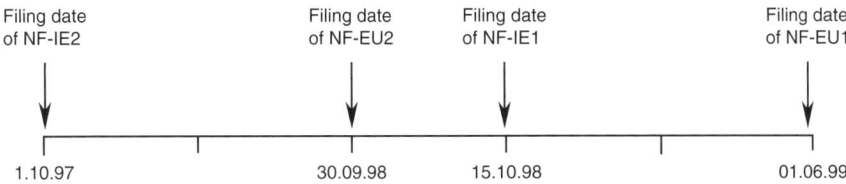

Therefore, the NF-EU1 is not entitled to claim the priority of NF-IE1 to the extent that it claims any subject matter already disclosed in NF-IE2 and NF-EU2 since NF-IE1 is not the first filing of this subject matter in a Paris Convention country. So, the patentability of product A, the new class of polymers and the new process, in so far as they are claimed in NF-EU1, will be judged at the filing date of NF-EU1, 01 June 1999.

**Paper C, 2000**

The patent being opposed (EP-0712647) was filed as an application on 20 February 1995 and claims the priority of a US application (US163946) filed on 10 March 1994. In his letter, the client reveals that the priority application is in fact a continuation of an earlier US application filed on 07 September 1989, which has been withdrawn.

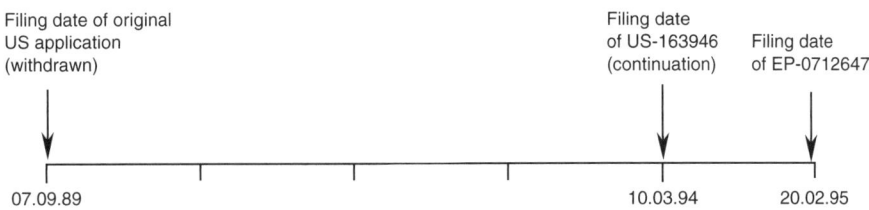

The priority claim from US-163946 is completely invalid and the patentability of all the claims of EP-0712647 must be assessed as of its filing date 20.02.95. This is because a continuation application has the same text as its parent application and the parent application must be pending at the time the continuation application is filed. Therefore, US-163946 is not the first filing of the subject matter it contains and Art.87(4) does not apply since the original US application was not withdrawn at the time the continuation application was filed.

### 6. Worked example using EQE 2002 Paper D2

*Preparing a timeline*  1–205

A first reading of the paper establishes that the client has filed some patent applications, some of which have prosecution problems, has some new inventions for which applications need to be filed and has some potential infringement issues with respect to third parties, one of whom has filed an application containing subject matter for which he is not entitled to be granted a patent.

Having collated the important dates, a task which is dealt with at greater length below, a typical time-line can be constructed as follows:

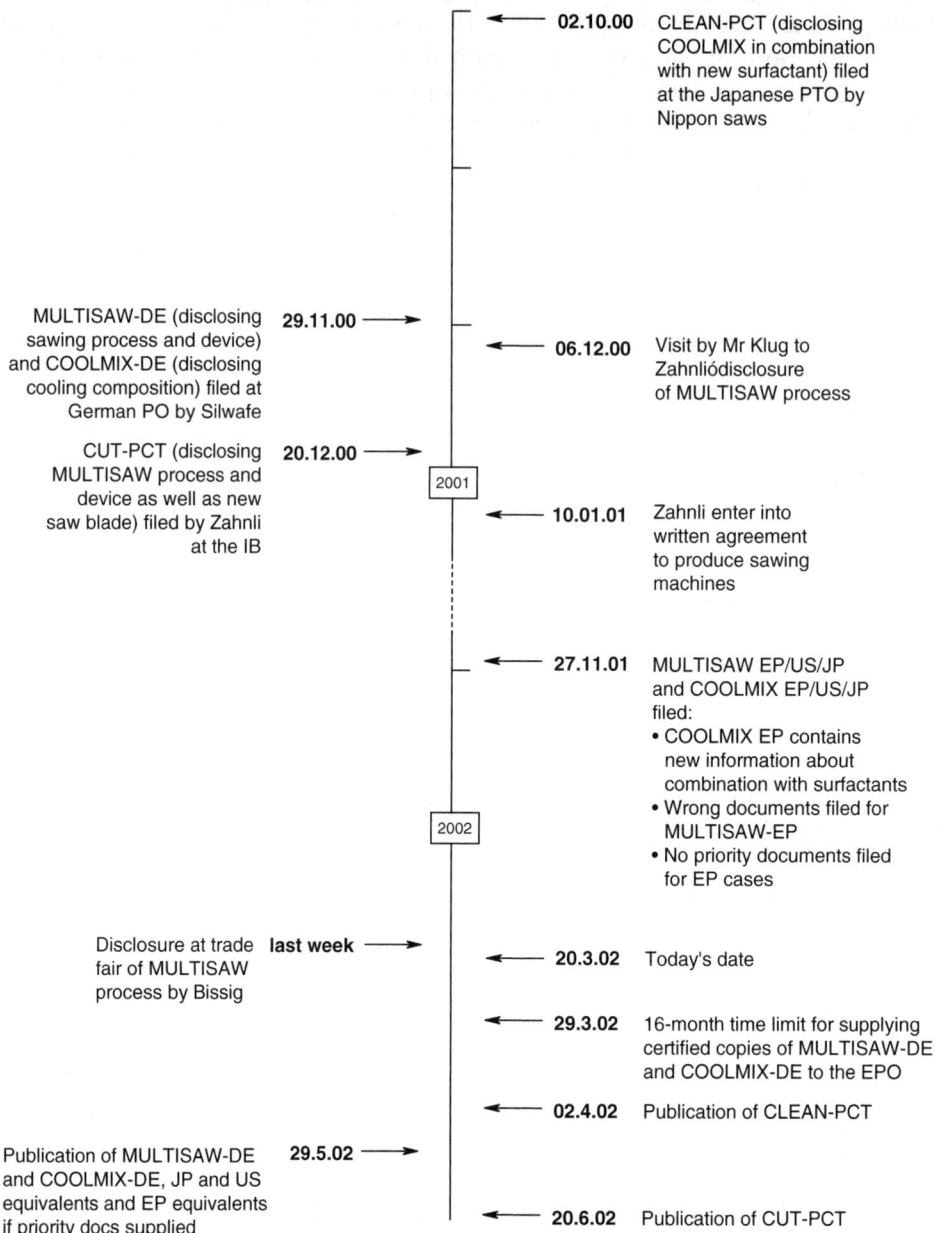

**1–206**  *Analysing the paper*

Here is an example of the level of attention with which you might approach analysing a D2 paper. The points which have been flagged are not the only ones which have some meaning in the exam. Nor do you need to do something with all of the information which you derive from such an analysis. But you need to be tuned to spot details, most of which have some part to play in the formulation of a good answer. Certainly no one expects you to make notes of the volume or length that appear in the section below which follows the exam question. But you need to be able to recognise these kinds of points in a question and then know which items of information to use and which ones to discard. If you are not used to seeing so much in a D2 paper, try to develop your skills by repeating this sort of analysis on another D2 paper. In essence, every item of information in the D2 paper is provided for some purpose — either to confirm that an issue does not arise, or to hint at something that needs to be addressed.

## The 2002 Paper D2

*You are a European patent attorney and have today[1] had a meeting with Dr Wichtig, managing director[2] of your new client SILWAFE AG, Munich, DE[3], which you validly represent in proceedings before the EPO. Dr Wichtig has informed you about the following facts:*

"SILWAFE AG is a supplier of[4] silicon wafers to the electronic industry. These wafers are thin discs of about 0.5 mm thickness and 15 or 20 cm diameter. In our factory,[5] they are produced by sawing from monocrystalline silicon rods. My company's R&D department[6] is in charge of developing and improving the sawing process we use; however, we do not ourselves manufacture the sawing devices for use in production,[7] but have them made by external engineering companies.[8]

The patent affairs of my company have, in the past, been entrusted to our employee[9] Dr Zornig. At the end of last month,[10] I informed him that his job was to be taken over by an external patent attorney from 2003 on, for reasons of rationalisation. Dr Zornig was furious. He immediately left his workplace and will no longer be available to do any work for the company.[11] Since Dr Zornig left us, all we have been able to do is to carry out a stock-taking of the present situation, with the following result.

During the last few years, our R&D department has been developing a new sawing process[12] MULTISAW, in which the silicon rods are not cut by a single saw blade as in the state-of-the-art processes, but simultaneously with a plurality of parallel saw blades.[13] Thus we obtain, instead of only one wafer per sawing step, several wafers at the same time. This process will revolutionise the sawing technology[14] in the field of wafer sawing and will, as we hope, give us a considerable advantage over our competitors.[15] We have also developed a new cooling composition[16] COOLMIX which turned out to be especially suitable for this process.[17] This composition is sprayed into the sawing gap during the sawing,[18] for removal of heat and abraded material.[19]

Dr Zornig had on 29 November 2000[20] and in the name of SILWAFE AG[21] filed an application MULTISAW-DE *claiming and describing the sawing process and the device for carrying out the process*,[22] and an application COOLMIX-DE *claiming and describing the cooling composition*,[23] at the German Patent and Trademark Office.[24] Both applications are still pending.[25] On 27 November 2001[26] and each claiming the corresponding priority,[27] the following applications were filed: applications MULTISAW-EP and COOLMIX-EP at the EPO, both designating all contracting states[28]; applications MULTISAW-US and COOLMIX-US in the US and applications MULTISAW-JP and COOLMIX-JP in Japan. Dr Zornig had intended[29] the content of these MULTISAW applications to be the same as that of the respective priority application. Only *in the case of application COOLMIX-EP further embodiments were described wherein COOLMIX was mixed with several types of surfactants*.[30] It should be noted that no reference to the MULTISAW process is made in the COOLMIX applications.[31] We have also found no indication in our files that an official communication or a search report was issued on any of the above mentioned applications.[32]

While checking our internal files we noted that Dr Zornig made a mistake when MULTISAW-EP and COOLMIX-EP were filed.[33] In both cases, the application documents contained a request for grant of a patent which was correctly filled in. In the case of COOLMIX-EP, the correct claims, description and drawings were filed.[34] Unfortunately, the claims, description and drawings pertaining to COOLMIX-EP were erroneously also filed in the case of MULTISAW-EP[35] instead of the correct claims, description and drawings. The respective priority data were correctly filled in, in both cases,[36] but apparently no priority documents were filed at the filing stage, since the certified copies of MULTISAW-DE and COOLMIX-DE are still in our internal files.[37] We hope that, having the correct priority documents for MULTISAW-EP in our hands,[38] we will be able to prove that what we had in fact intended[39] to file, so that we can continue the case as intended.[40] Contrary to the EP cases, the correct application documents and the certified copies of MULTISAW-DE and COOLMIX-DE were duly filed in the corresponding US and JP cases.[41]

Some of our conventional sawing devices are manufactured by the Japanese[42] company NIPPON SAWS KK. They have recently informed us that they have filed, on 2 October 2000,[43] an international patent application CLEAN-PCT as a first filing[44] in Japanese[45] at the Japanese Patent Office,[46] designating all contracting states.[47] This application concerns the cleaning of the used saw blades.[48] *It discloses, amongst others, a mixture of a composition identical to COOLMIX with a surfactant which was not described in our COOLMIX-EP.*[49] We are now worried since we have recently[50] realised that mixtures of COOLMIX with any[51] surfactant are not only very efficient[52] in cooling, but also have excellent[53] properties in subsequently cleaning the sawn wafers.[54] Therefore, we believe that *mixtures of COOLMIX with any surfactant*[55] should be protected by us.[56] We are highly interested in such protection,[57] but in EPC contracting states only.[58]

Mr Klug from our R&D department informed me earlier today that he and a colleague have been developing, since the beginning of this year,[59] an improved[60] MULTISAW-process. In this embodiment BLOWSAW, a computer[61] control unit *compares the actual saw blade positions during sawing with the desired, ideal positions, and regulates the intensity of a stream of air laterally blown towards the saw blades by a system of nozzles, to compensate for deviations from the desired cutting line.*[62] The BLOWSAW technique has given surprising good results in our tests.[63] By the way, the *computer program controlling the process*[64] was developed by a student[65] during a period of practical training in Mr Klug's group in our company. *The student had signed an employment agreement which gives us all the rights for the inventions developed during the course of the employment.*[66] He has meanwhile left our company and the university for a job in a Silicon Valley computer company,[67] and has moved to the United States[68] with unknown address.[69]

On 6 December 2000,[70] shortly after the filing of[71] MULTISAW-DE and COOLMIX-DE, Mr Klug, the inventor, had been visiting the Swiss[72] engineering company[73] Zähnli AG. *We have a long and successful working relationship with this company*[74]; they have for instance fabricated a number of the sawing machines we presently use in our production process.[75] In the meeting, Mr Klug presented the MULTISAW-process, but did not mention the COOLMIX composition.[76] He handed over documents marked "confidential"[77] including a description of the process[78] and sketches of the sawing machines.[79] He asked Ing. Listig, head of the development of Zähnli AG, whether Zähnli AG would be able to produce such a machine.[80] Ing. Listig replied that this task was highly interesting for his company in view of the possibilities of worldwide commercialisation of the sawing machines.[81] Mr Klug stated that such a worldwide commercialisation would only benefit our competitors and was not in the interest[82] of Silwafe AG. On 10 January 2001[83] Zähnli AG had given their written agreement for producing the machines for us and since January this year[84] we have been testing[85] three of the new sawing machines produced by them and we intend *to start commercial use of the new process in October.*[86]

Last week[87] I met Dr Bissig, the managing director[88] of Zähnli AG at the semiconductor fair Semitec 2002, where he told that one of his employees, Ing. Listig,[89] had invented a new sawing process. Zähnli AG had filed an international patent application CUT-PCT[90] for this process as a first filing[91] with the International Bureau on 20 December 2000[92] for EP, JP and US[93]. Dr Bissig provided me[94] with a copy of the text to the application since he believed the process — which is still a trade secret[95] — might be of interest to our company. The text has meanwhile been carefully reviewed by Mr Klug. The process according to CUT-PCT appeared to him to be very similar to our MULTISAW-process.[96] When we checked our files, we noted that part of the description of CUT-PCT is almost a word-for-word copy[97] of the documents we had handed over at the first meeting. Some of the drawings, too, are only fair copies of the sketches we had handed over.[98] There are claims to a multiple blade sawing process[99] and to multiple blade sawing machines[100] which are drafted in such a general way that they cover our MULTISAW-process and device.[101] However, CUT-PCT *also contains a description and claims for a special type of saw blade unknown to us*,[102] for use in a multiple blade sawing process.[103]

In my opinion, the way *Ing. Listig of Zähnli AG*[104] has acted is very annoying, when you consider *the long and good business relations between our companies*.[105]

Therefore, I have arranged a meeting with Dr Bissig on Wednesday next week[106] *in order to clarify the situation.*[107] Personally, I would strive to maintain good business relations.[108] However, I do not know if this is achievable and therefore want to *be prepared for all possibilities.*[109]

**In preparation of this meeting,[110] I would like you to report in writing and as soon as possible on:**

(1) your assessment of the patent situation[111] concerning the above applications[112];

(2) what option do we have[113], and how we should proceed[114] with Zähnli AG[115] concerning our MULTISAW- invention; and

*(3) what steps you would take*[116] in order to protect our interests.[117]"

**Points that arise**

(1) Today is March 20, 2002. It is good practice in the exam to note, prominently, on the paper, the date of the exam. It is essential to show today's date on your timeline.

(2) As Managing Director, Wichtig can clearly act for the company and his position suggests that you can trust him — albeit that he may not know much, if anything, about patents. The views that he later expresses about the importance of good working relationships with suppliers also carry weight because of his position.

(3) Silwafe are based on Germany. This is relevant as it:

- removes issues which might otherwise have arisen under Art.14(2);
- indicates a country of importance as far as the threat from third party rights arises;
- could be relevant to entitlement proceedings, under the Protocol on Recognition (in this question it is not).

(4) Silwafe are in the business of supplying silicon wafers. Their competitors will be other companies who also sell such wafers. Protection for the product will be important to Silwafe, and third party rights to such wafers would be a threat.

(5) Silwafe produce the wafers in their own factory. Thus third party process protection could be a serious threat. However, the in-house production suggests that we do not have to worry about the actions/threats/or liabilities of a supplier.

(6) Silwafe has its own R&D Department reducing (but not removing) risk of third party rights to Silwafe inventions. It also means that we have no reason not to trust what our researchers say – whereas if they were employed by a third party, and a conflict arose with a further third party, we would not know who to trust.

(7) Silwafe develop and improve the sawing process but do not manufacture sawing machines. This suggests that Silwafe make prototypes sawing machines themselves. It is clear that Silwafe must be reliant on a third party to manufacture their machines. This means that Silwafe's production of wafers is likely to be dependent on ongoing support (maintenance, servicing, repair, spare parts, consumables) from the machine manufacturer. Do Silwafe license the manufacturers to sell the machines to Silwafe's competitors? That could be attractive to the manufacturers and would reduce the effective cost of the machines to Silwafe. But it would mean that Silwafe's competitors would benefit from the Silwafe developments — something unlikely to be in Silwafe's interests, given the nature of their business.

(8) "External engineering companies" — as distinct from some sort of manufacturing company (e.g. machine tool company) suggests small-scale supply. So probably the risk of conflict with the supplier of the machines is less likely to be a problem.

(9) We are not told that this employee was a patent attorney. This passage in the question suggests that he was not and hence there is an increased risk of mistakes and errors having occurred.

(10) Not long ago, but long enough for time-related actions to have been missed.

(11) So, we will get no help from Zornig! Zornig's actions and behaviour give support for the view that Zornig was only an employee representative, rather than an employed professional representative. So you must expect some mistakes.

(12) A new sawing process is important because it is the technology at the centre of Silwafe's business. Will the new process give rise to new, patentable products (product-by-process formulation or product *per se*)?

(13) The first identified invention in the paper — a simple idea, likely to improve efficiency and perhaps hence reduce costs. From the description of the invention it seems likely that there would have been problems to overcome — how to deal with the multiple wafers which are created simultaneously, at the end of the sawing process? No obvious patentability issues spring to mind.

(14) The Managing Director's use of "revolutionise" tells us that this is an important invention. We must do our best to get protection for this.

(15) A considerable advantage over our competitors — re-emphasises the importance of the invention *and* of proper patent protection. Clearly, Silwafe's competitors must be prevented from gaining access to the new process — or must be made to pay Silwafe a lot to use the process. These aims are only likely to be achievable if we get good patent protection in the relevant territories.

(16) The second invention — this time a composition, which suggests a claim to the composition and its use. Note that Coolmix is a composition rather than a compound.

(17) Now we know the purpose of the new composition. We now think of claiming not only the new machine, new process (and new wafers — we hope), and the composition, but also the use of the new composition and the method of making wafers by the new process, coolmix being used during the sawing process.

(18) This confirms our initial thoughts about the combination of the sawing process and coolmix as patentable subject matter.

(19) Information to be noted as to the purpose/use of coolmix.

(20) Apart from today's date, this is the first "concrete" date. Two points which you must observe are that it is more than 12 months ago, so we are too late to claim priority, but less than 18 months ago — so the application is likely still to be unpublished.

(21) Zornig seems to have identified the correct applicant: the invention arose in Silwafe's own R&D Department, where workers are presumably employees paid to invent, hence the invention is likely to belong to Silwafe rather than to the inventors (depending of course upon national law). The identity of the applicant for this first filing is of course important for purposes of priority.

(22) At this point we need to note what has been disclosed in the patent application and what protection has been sought. In particular, we need to check to see whether all the claim categories and subject matter which we have already identified are in fact present.

(23) As with point 22, we need to note what has been done, as well as checking to see that all appropriate subject matter and claims have been included.

(24) German national patent applications are hinted at by the suffix DE (*cf* the use of EP for European applications). Filed in German, so no translation of the priority document will be needed for a subsequent priority-claiming EP application. Also relevant is the fact that, in any question, the first filing may still be alive or restorable and hence potentially secure patent protection can be obtained in that state — without having to worry about priority claims, etc.

(25) That is handy! You should have the feeling that these applications may be prove to be valuable. Being told this, we do not have to speculate about it. If we were

not told of their status, our answer would have to deal with the consequences of the two possible statuses.

(26) Another date, plus data, for our timeline. This date is less than a year after the first date mentioned — which is a good start.

(27) So, Zornig remembered to do that. Note also that Multi-saw DE and Coolmix DE have both now served as bases for priority claims and hence no application filed after these can serve as the basis of priority for subject matter disclosed in them.

(28) All states designated — but we are not told that the designation fees have been paid. Remember that they will need to be. Note on your timeline the corresponding US and Japanese filings on the same day as the EP applications — again within the convention year.

(29) "Had intended" should alert you to trouble ahead.

(30) Note that it seems that Coolmix EP, but apparently not the corresponding US and Japanese applications, includes new matter. Such a situation always raises two new issues. The first is that this new filing gives rise to a new priority right for the new matter. Here this is the combination of coolmix with various surfactants. So your timeline should include the date of the end of the convention year from this filing. The second is that claims directed to the new matter or broadened to cover the new matter may not be entitled to right of priority from the relevant first application. We need to think about the consequences of applying G2/98 here. Here, and in all equivalent situations, your answer needs to address this issue — and come to a decision as to the likely position.

(31) This clear flagging of a problem should trigger you forcibly to see that you must propose a solution to deal with it — if any solution can be found. Always consider in such a situation — could I validly file a further new application now? Has the combination been disclosed so that the disclosure is relevant under Art.54 (2)? Is there any Art.54 (3) prior art which actually discloses this combination? Your answer must address these questions and propose an appropriate course of action.

(32) This suggests that the applications were thought by the EPO to be formally correct. The non-receipt of search reports by this stage is of course not uncommon. Consider requesting accelerated prosecution "PACE", if the question hints that search results/early grant would be useful.

(33) This picks up on the problem foreseen by point 29.

(34) So the new subject-matter in this application has been filed and, so far, our priority claim for this case looks sound.

(35) This rather reduces the value of this filing. It is a duplicate of Coolmix EP and there is nothing that we can do now to introduce the subject matter of Multi-saw EP while keeping the filing date.

(36) The date of filing and the state of filing of both Multisaw DE and Coolmix DE were the same. If we wanted to correct the priority details on Multi-saw EP, we would only have to correct the file number, which we can probably do up to 16 months from priority. But here there is no point "correcting" the priority because we would only end up with two applications for Coolmix EP. Of course if we did not correct the priority, then Coolmix EP would be a complete anticipation under Art.54 (3) for Multisaw EP. However, given that we have no search results on Multisaw EP we should withdraw it now to get a complete refund of the search fee and a complete refund of the examination fee if this has been paid.

(37) The priority documents need to be at the EPO within 16 months of priority, that is by March 29, 2002, subject to any excluded days. That is still in the future. If we miss that date, we should receive an invitation from the receiving section to rectify the deficiency within a period set by them — under r.41 (1). Rule 84 says that the minimum period should be not less than two months.

(38) An expectation which you will have to deal with in your answer. It would be worth mentioning the fact that even had the priority documents been filed with the applications, this would have made no difference — G3/89, T200/85.

(39) Again, to be dealt with, expressly, in your answer. The applicant's intention is not relevant to this issue.

(40) No! It is of no value.

(41) That is good news. It would be prudent to check this though by checking with the foreign associates today. If there has been a lapse, we may still be able to correct it. Your client is not an IP professional and neither was Zornig.

(42) So we have to think about the patent situation in Japan.

(43) Another date for the time line. Sadly it is earlier than our client's earliest priority date. So this application may become relevant as prior art. Again, this date is between 12 and 18 months ago. There has probably been no Patent Office publication yet, but the 18 months will soon end — put that date on your timeline.

(44) So no priority claim — the 18 month date at point 43 is still relevant.

(45) Japanese is a PCT publication language. Translation into an EPO language is needed on regional entry before the European Patent Office. Generally no Art.67 effect in Europe unless local-language translation is filed.

(46) The Japanese Patent Office obviously accepts Japanese language applications.

(47) So there is an EPO regional designation. All our client's countries of interest are covered.

(48) Cleaning of used saw blades — strongly suggests cleaned after use as opposed to during use. This sounds like a new activity — at least it is not quite the same as what is mentioned at points 18 and 19. Has the client seen a translation of the whole application – or did Nippon just describe the application to Wichtig? We are probably meant to accept this description of the disclosure of Clean-PCT but if there is uncertainty about what is disclosed/claimed in an earlier application always address the various possibilities (at least to a reasonable extent) in your answer.

(49) Is there a disclosure of the coolmix composition *per se* — or only as part of a mixture with the surfactant? The wording suggests the latter. We are told that coolmix is a composition, we are not told that it is a compound. Is only one surfactant disclosed – the one not disclosed in Coolmix EP? Is the surfactant referred to a specific example of one of the types (class) referred to at point 30 or is it a different type (class)? Such considerations are of course relevant to the question of claim scope available to Nippon and the prior art effect, if any, which the EP part of Clean PCT may have on our client's applications.

(50) That is, something not contemplated in Coolmix EP.

(51) So our thoughts under point 49 as to precisely what Clean PCT discloses and claims were relevant. "Any surfactant" clearly embraces the particular surfactant disclosed in Clean PCT.

(52) An advantage – to be noted in respect of obviousness.

(53) Excellence is also a good thing to note.

(54) Compare this with Nippon's cleaning of used saw blades. They are similar uses, but not identical. The broad claims to use of the Coolmix-surfactant mixture as a cleaner or to a method of cleaning with such a mixture could cover the cleaning of wafers.

(55) The disclosure in Clean PCT pre-dates our client's first disclosure of coolmix plus a surfactant. If the EP part of Clean PCT validly enters the region of phase before the EPO, it will be prior art under Art.54 (3).

(56) Could potentially disclaim the Nippon combination — filing a new application with the disclaimer before Clean PCT publishes. The excellence and efficiency

(57) of mixtures of Coolmix with any surfactant, if evidenced with a sufficient diversity of surfactants and with impressive comparative tests, could support a broad claim to the generic mixture and its use for either purpose (cleaning or cooling).

(57) So the filing of a further application, now, as soon as possible, before Clean PCT publishes, is worth doing.

(58) It would be worth suggesting going for cover in Japan to give Silwafe a lever to use against Nippon to get a licence, should that be needed, under the patents coming from Clean PCT.

(59) Another new invention, not foreshadowed in the existing filings.

(60) The multi-saw process was said to revolutionary and to offer Silwafe considerable advantage over their competitors. So an improved process must be a good thing. We must protect this well.

(61) What will be patentable? What, if anything, will be unpatentable under Art.52 (2) EPC? Will the situation be different in the US or Japan?

(62) This is certainly technical enough, addressing a real technical problem, to be patentable before the EPO. Protection for the method, the machine, potentially the program *per se*. Are the wafers made using this technique distinguishable in any way from those produced using conventional techniques? If so, claim them *per se*, if possible, or using a product by process "obtainable by" formulation. Does the blowsaw work and offer any advantages with a single-saw system? If so, consider providing an example and claiming to this breadth. It would be worth filing the blowsaw application before multisaw publishes.

(63) Surprisingly good results suggest inventiveness and further confirm the commercial significance of this invention.

(64) This suggests that the process is dependent on the computer program. For the US at least we will need, for best mode purposes, to disclose the algorithm(s) used in the computer control. A computer-controlled manufacturing process should always be expected to be sufficiently technical to escape the Art.52(2) exclusion. In Europe we should even be able to get a claim granted for the program *per se*, as well as claims for the process and the equipment.

(65) Alarm bells should ring when we see this! Anyone identified as a student must be expected not to have the status of employee and will often not have a contract of employment. Hence a student's contribution may not belong to the company for whom work is being done. This gives rise to problems of ownership of inventions, etc.

(66) That takes care of the potential problem caused by the student's status.

(67) A computer company rather than a competitor to Silwafe or a manufacturer of machine tools, so, happily, no direct conflict seems likely between the interests of Silwafe and those of the new employer.

(68) The remoteness suggests that we cannot expect to quiz the student before we file a patent application. Also, the US is a country where the value and importance of patents are highly rated — especially in silicon valley. If Silwafe did not own the student's contribution this might suggest a potential problem.

(69) This will be a particular issue if we want to file a US patent application or a PCT patent application designating the US, since we need the student's signature. This suggests that, rather than doing this now, we file a priority application to give us at least a year in which to track down the student so that we can have his signature when we eventually file a priority claiming application.

(70) This is after our earliest priority date — but still add the date to your time line.

(71) Confirmation of an important point.

(72) Potentially relevant to protocol on recognition issues.

(73) Suggestive of someone who might be able to commercialise Silwafe's machine technology.

(74) Remember, these words are coming from the managing director of your client company. These words are significant — as noted at point 2.

(75) As noted above, Silwafe must, to some extent, be reliant on the goodwill and co-operation of the companies who supply their production equipment. This also suggests some mutual dependence — Silwafe being a customer of Zähnli.

(76) So no possible disclosure of Coolmix.

(77) Obviously this confidential marking is important with regard to whether this disclosure made the multisaw public or not.

(78) Description of the process would obviously be relevant to a discussion of the technique and the machine with a potential manufacturer.

(79) Similar observation to 78.

(80) Again, consistent with the past relationship between these two companies and not suggestive of publication.

(81) So the potential conflict existing between the manufacturer of machines and a user who wants to stop others using the machines is now clear.

(82) This point emphasises the confidential nature of the disclosure, from Silwafe's point of view.

(83) Another date for your time line, before our filing date but after our priority date – although we know we have a problem with the multisaw priority date. The agreement may provide further confirmation of the confidential nature of the relationship – it would be worth looking at to see exactly what restrictions there are in terms of disclosure or sale of the machines or technology. Obviously this should be done before the proposed meeting between the two managing directors.

(84) Only a couple of months ago, and as we see later in this sentence, not yet used in production.

(85) Confirmation of the experimental nature — so that if wafers produced using this new technique are new compared to conventional wafers, they may not have been disclosed to the public.

(86) Again relevant to the issue raised under point 85. This is another date for your time line — you will see it relevance shortly.

(87) Another date for your time line. The fact that it is recent suggests that the situation is unlikely to have changed significantly since then.

(88) It is important that Bissig is more senior than Listig. There is a possibility that he has been misled by Listig, rather than being involved with him.

(89) When you see the name of an exhibition or fair, it always worth checking to see whether it is one caught by Art.55b — a list of such exhibitions is published periodically by the EPO, although they are very rare. Again, Bissig may be thought to be recounting a story that he believes to be true.

(90) Another patent application to work into your time line and also to consider because of the inventions and patent applications about which you already know.

(91) So publication will probably not be for 18 months after the first filing date. Note that this date is also after the original Multi-saw DE application. Do not forget to add this publication date, and all the other future publication dates to your timeline.

(92) Another date for the time line. Notice that it is before the signing of the agreement by Zähnli — which is consistent with Bissig's view of the situation — if he really felt that the invention had been made by his employee, he would not have wanted to sign the contract until after the patent application was filed.

(93) Again, territorial coverage for everywhere of interest to our client.

(94) Note that Bissig gave the text of the application directly to Wichtig — Wichtig did not get the paper from some display or exhibit.

(95) Despite the age of the Zähnli patent application, the information is still being considered a trade secret. This is relevant to our client's desire to secure patent protection for multisaw in Europe, where a new application will need to be filed.

(96) This is hardly a surprise.

(97) The fact that there is an almost a word-for-word copy is useful, both in terms of persuading Bissig of the theft and also for any entitlement action. The rest of the sentence suggest that our client still has a copy of what was handed over at the meeting in December 2000. There is also the certified copy of the multisaw priority document which will clearly show that it was filed two weeks before Zähnli's patent application was filed and which will presumably be similar in content to the material that was handed over.

(98) Yet more evidence of the underhand behaviour of Listig.

(99) These claims, if granted, will pose a severe threat to Silwafe. Under Art.64(2) (EPC) such claims would cover the direct product of the sawing process – the wafers.

(100) Even these claims would be a threat to Silwafe.

(101) Further emphasising the threat that this patent application represents.

(102) Something that our client did not invent, mixed in with what they did invent. This suggest that our client is not fully entitled to this application, although see point 103 below. This suggests that perhaps division of the application when it enters the regional phase and the national phase might be appropriate.

(103) It seems likely that the idea of a multiple blade sawing process came from our client. What is the significance of this when it comes to Zähnli's invention, within a few days of being exposed to the multi-saw idea, of a saw blade for use in such a process?

(104) Wichtig is, helpfully, focussing his displeasure on Listig rather than on the company. This is perhaps of small importance in the question. It suggests that in your answer you should not complain about the behaviour of the company. Rather you should focus on giving your client information and arguments to be used with Bissig, to show Bissig that there is no antagonism between the companies. The arguments and evidence should show Bissig that there has been unacceptable behaviour from an employee, albeit a fairly senior one — Listig being the head of development.

(105) Again this emphasis on the long and good business relations should encourage you to propose negotiated solutions rather than simply the commencement of entitlement actions, etc.

(106) We have a week to take care of problems as well as to advise Wichtig for the meeting.

(107) Again, our client is interested in sorting things out, rather than going to war.

(108) As if this point needed any further emphasis!

(109) But, you have to tell your client about entitlement proceedings etc, not just the solution which requires both sides to act reasonably.

(110) This is the purpose of your answer — your client needs to know from you all the things that he is going to need in that meeting.

(111) So, as usual, in this exam you need to explain to your client how the various inventions can best be protected and the impact and effect of the various third-party patent rights.

(112) Here is a small reminder of the fact that not only does your client want to know about his own inventions, but also the threats posed by the patent applications of third parties.

(113) This should have said what option**s** do we have? — the emphasis here being on what could be done, that is **all** the options.

(114) Here, in contrast to point 113, the examiner wants to see what you would recommend and he wants you to make the recommendation.

(115) So, points 113 and 114 apply only to the Zähnli situation.

(116) Again, here you are expected to set out your recommendations – this is what you are going to do. The examiner likes it if you explain why you propose doing what you are proposing to do. They do not like to think that you have made an arbitrary choice!

(117) Again, do not forget that the examiner is looking to see whether you can provide sensible, pragmatic, *commercially focused* advice in the face of a complex legal situation. The question has told you a lot about the client's commercial interests and activities and, by implication, those of his competitors, as well as explaining the rather different situation of the two other companies whose patent applications feature in this question. Demonstrate that you understand this commercial environment by providing appropriate, clear and sensible advice.

The different inventions which can be identified include: new sawing process MULTI-SAW and device for carrying it out (applications filed by Silwafe and Zähnli); new cooling composition COOLMIX (applications filed by Silwafe); mixture of COOLMIX and a surfactant (applications filed by Silwafe and Nippon); improved sawing process BLOWSAW (no application filed yet); new type of saw blade (application filed by Zähnli). Analysis of these inventions and the applications filed in respect of them leads to the following table.

# PART A

| Invention/patent application | Entitlement issues | Prosecution issues | Subject matter disclosed/claimed | Relevant prior art | Patentability of subject matter disclosed/claimed | Likely patent rights that will be obtained |
|---|---|---|---|---|---|---|
| APPLICATIONS ALREADY FILED | | | | | | |
| MULTISAW-DE | None | Application pending — check all necessary pre-publication steps have been taken. | Sawing process MULTISAW and device. | None | Yes | Claims in DE for sawing process and device. |
| MULTISAW-EP | None | Wrong specification filed — application worthless. | Sawing process MULTISAW and device. | N/A | N/A | None |
| MULTISAW-US | None | Check all necessary documents filed. | Sawing process MULTISAW and device. | None | Yes | Claims in US for sawing process and device. |
| MULTISAW-JP | None | Check all necessary pre-publication steps have been taken | Sawing process MULTISAW and device. | None | Yes | Claims in JP for sawing process and device. |
| CUT-PCT | Yes, in respect of MULTISAW process and device. | None | Sawing process MULTISAW, device and new saw blade. | MULTISAW-DE/JP/US and 06.12.00 disclosure by Mr Klug (probably in confidence). | Yes, except for process and device in DE/JP/US | Only really entitled to claims to new saw blade worldwide but could get claims to sawing process and device (except DE/JP/US) if no entitlement action taken. Interference proceedings possible in US. |
| COOLMIX-DE | None | Application pending — check all necessary pre-publication steps have been taken. | Cooling composition COOLMIX. | CLEAN-PCT (if enters DE national phase or EP regional phase designating DE) — relevant to novelty only. | Will lack novelty if COOLMIX is disclosed *per se* in the PCT application and it becomes prior art. | None (probably) |
| COOLMIX-EP | None | Need to file priority document before P+16m (29.3.2001). | Cooling composition COOLMIX and combination with several surfactants. | CLEAN-PCT (if enters EP regional phase) — relevant to novelty only. | COOLMIX itself may lack novelty but claim combination with specified surfactants will be OK. | Claims in EP to combination of COOLMIX and specified surfactants. |

| Invention/patent application | Entitlement issues | Prosecution issues | Subject matter disclosed/claimed | Relevant prior art | Patentability of subject matter disclosed/claimed | Likely patent rights that will be obtained |
|---|---|---|---|---|---|---|
| COOLMIX-US | None | Check all necessary documents filed. | Cooling composition COOLMIX. | CLEAN-PCT (if enters US national phase) – could lead to interference proceedings. Depends whether coolmix per se disclosed. Relevant for novelty and obviousness. | If coolmix per se not disclosed in CLEAN-PCT, Silwafe's claim to that should survive. If coolmix disclosed: the position is uncertain — first to invent and reduce to practice will own patent rights | Unknown outcome |
| COOLMIX-JP | None | Check all necessary pre-publication steps have been taken. | Cooling composition COOLMIX. | CLEAN-PCT (if enters JP national phase) – relevant to novelty only. | Will lack novelty if COOLMIX is disclosed *per se* in the PCT application and it becomes prior art. | None (probably) |
| CLEAN-PCT | None | None – should publish soon. | COOLMIX with specific surfactant — possibly COOLMIX per se. Probably the use of the mixture (or Coolmix) for cleaning saw blades, maybe as broad as cleaning articles (would cover wafers). | None | Yes | Claims worldwide to specific combination — and possibly to COOLMIX *per se*. Method of cleaning saw blades (maybe as general as articles) |

PART A

| Invention/patent application | Entitlement issues | Prosecution issues | Subject matter disclosed/claimed | Relevant prior art | Patentability of subject matter disclosed/claimed | Likely patent rights that will be obtained |
|---|---|---|---|---|---|---|
| POSSIBLE FUTURE FILINGS | | | | | | |
| BLOWSAW | No | Will need to establish inventor details. | Claims possible to process, apparatus and computer program, maybe wafers cut using the process (if novel). | Multisaw DE,JP, US, and CUT-PCT closest, relevant for obviousness only. | Yes | Worldwide claims to process, apparatus and program possible: consider wafer claims. |
| MULTISAW-EP refiling | None | None | Claims to process, device, and use of COOLMIX in process. | MULTISAW-DE, disclosure by Klug (probably in confidence); CUT-PCT – novelty only unless we delay filing; and if we delay filing MULTISAW-JP and; MULTISAW-US, disclosure at trade fair (probably in confidence). | Nothing yet published., Novelty over CUT-PCT is the only problem: saved by Art.55(1)(a). | Claims in EP countries (clash in DE for multisaw alone, not for use with coolmix) for process, device and use of COOLMIX in process. |
| COOLMIX & any Surfactant | None | None | Claims to the combination and its various uses. | CUT-PCT (if it enters regional/national phases. | Should be able to disclaim specific anticipation. | Worldwide claims to the combination and its uses (with one specific surfactant disclaimed). |

1–208    *Answering the paper*

There are many ways of setting out the answer, but most of the information in the table needs to be discussed and, in addition, the question demands that several options should be proposed in relation to Zähnli. A possible answer is set out below.

1–209    **Client's commercial objectives**

Silwafe makes and sells silicon wafers and therefore needs freedom to carry out the new process (in Germany?) and sell the wafers (presumably in Europe, Japan and US mainly).

Silwafe needs a reliable supplier of the new machines with which to carry out the new process — a good relationship with Zähnli could be important.

Silwafe would like to stop all competitors worldwide using the new sawing process as it will give them a competitive advantage.

Silwafe would like to be able to use a mixture of COOLMIX and any surfactant to clean their wafers after manufacture and would like to stop others doing the same, but only in Europe.

**Maximising the client's patent protection**

1–210    *(a) MULTISAW process and device*

The applications MULTISAW-US and MULTISAW-JP appear to have been validly filed. The files should be checked (best via foreign associates, rather than relying on Zornig's files) to ensure that there are no outstanding actions that need to be taken, especially since publication is due in a little over a month (ensure inventorship details etc. have been filed). Since these applications validly claim priority there is no relevant prior art and granted patents in the US and Japan should be obtained with claims to the MULTISAW process and the device for carrying it out. Ask associates if product by process protection is available. In USA, if a process is patented, no automatic protection akin to Art.64(2)EPC available for the product of a process unless the product is imported into the US after manufacture using the process outside the US.

MULTISAW-DE is pending — a file check should be made to ensure all pre-publication procedural steps have been taken. There is no relevant prior art and so a granted patent in Germany should be obtained with claims to the MULTISAW process and the device for carrying it out.

However, MULTISAW-EP will not lead to any granted claims covering the MULTISAW process since it is not possible under r.88 EPC to replace a description, claims and drawings which have been erroneously filed (G2/95). Even if the priority document had been filed with the application, this does not form part of the application as filed and could not have been used to replace the incorrect documents (G3/89 and T260/85) without contravening Art.123(2) EPC. Therefore, MULTISAW-EP is no more than a duplicate of COOLMIX-EP and should be withdrawn so that some of the fees (if paid) can be recouped (i.e. the search fee – no search yet reported, and the examination fee, if that has been paid: designation fees, if paid, not currently refundable).

Therefore, in order to obtain protection for the MULTISAW process in Europe, it will be necessary to file a new European patent application as soon as possible, before MULTISAW US and JP publish, and ideally before CUT-PCT publishes. This should be done in spite of possible attempts to obtain ownership of subject matter in CUT-PCT (see below) since such entitlement proceedings are lengthy and inherently uncertain. Such a new application will not be able to claim priority from MULTISAW-DE since the priority year expired on November 29, 2001 but should still be valid anyway. Mr Klug's disclosure on December 6, 2000 was clearly in confidence (nature of business relationship between the companies, documents marked "confidential") and so does not form part of the state of the art. The filing of CUT-PCT (unpublished) was an evident abuse in relation to Silwafe since Zähnli had clearly not invented the process or device and had been given the information under confidence and for the limited purpose of evaluating whether they could make devices for Silwafe. The six-month period applies to the publication of CUT-PCT rather than its filing date . The contents of CUT-PCT will therefore not form part of the state of the art by virtue of Art.55(1)(a) EPC. MULTISAW-JP and MULTISAW-US have not published yet and have no effect as prior applications in Europe. The disclosure by Dr Bissig at the trade fair last week was clearly in confidence (nature of business relationship) and we know that Zähnli have kept the process a trade secret. Therefore, the new application should be filed immediately, before the publication of MULTISAW-JP. A further section should be added to the original description of MULTISAW-EP describing COOLMIX and its application in the process.

In the US, a continuation-in-part application based on MULTISAW-US could be filed with the additional information relating to the use of COOLMIX in the process.

In Japan, if Silwafe want protection for a method of sawing using a multisaw while using coolmix, a new application could be filed before the publication of MULTISAW-JP and COOLMIX-JP. Japanese law on the effect of earlier filed co-pending applications is similar to that in Europe, hence Silwafe's earlier applications would be relevant for novelty only.

These measures should ensure that Silwafe have full patent protection in EP, US and JP for the MULTISAW process and device.

*(b) COOLMIX compositions*  1–211

In Europe, the priority document for COOLMIX-EP should be filed as soon as possible. It should be filed by 16 months from the priority date (=March 29, 2002, extended under r.85(1) until April 2, 2003) under r.38(3).If it is not filed by April 2, the EPO will issue a reminder under Art.91(1)(d), Art.91(2) and r.41(1) EPC, with a two-month deadline (r.84EPC).

A check of the COOLMIX-US, COOLMIX-JP and COOLMIX-DE files should also be undertaken to ensure that no formal steps need to be taken to keep these applications pending.

Whether any granted, patentable claims can be obtained from the COOLMIX-DE, COOLMIX-EP and COOLMIX-JP applications depends on the specific contents of CLEAN-PCT and whether it enters the national phase or not in these countries. To become A54(3) prior art the conditions of A158(2) must be fulfilled: a translation into an EPC official language must be filed and the national fee must be paid.

To determine the position on patentability, a copy of CLEAN-PCT should be obtained from Nippon if possible, or a copy of the published application should be obtained in April and translated from Japanese. If COOLMIX is disclosed per se then COOLMIX-JP and COOLMIX-DE will lack novelty if CLEAN-PCT enters the national phase. If however, COOLMIX is disclosed solely as an inherent component of the mixture with the surfactant then novel claims to COOLMIX in its substantially pure state may still be possible. Entry into the national phases should be monitored.

The same situation pertains to COOLMIX-EP but here there is at least the guarantee that claims to a combination of COOLMIX with the specific surfactants listed in COOLMIX-EP will be patentable and possibly a general claim to COOLMIX with any surfactant if there is basis for such a claim. In this event, the specific combination of CLEAN-PCT could be removed from the claim by a proviso.

Silwafe's realisation that mixtures of coolmix with ANY surfactant (as opposed to merely those specified in COOLMIX-EP) are not only very efficient in cooling, but also have excellent properties in subsequently cleaning the sawn wafers, suggests that a further application should be filed. This should disclose the invention set out in the preceding sentence – that is coolmix surfactant mixtures and their use for cleaning wafers (are these mixtures useful/relevant only to silicon or to other materials/ semiconductors too, and only in the form of wafers, or more generally?) or possibly more generally for cleaning items (depending upon the nature of cleaning for which such a mixture is actually useful). If the claim is directed at cleaning wafers rather than being more general, there would be no need to limit it further to distinguish over CLEAN-PCT's disclosure: obviously the new application should be filed before CLEAN-PCT publishes. Otherwise, with broader claims, a disclaimer to the use of a mixture of Coolmix with the specific surfactant disclosed in CLEAN-PCT should be included (on filing). Such a disclaimer could also be used to distinguish generic product claims to the mixture of Coolmix with a surfactant over the CLEAN-PCT disclosure. Wichtig has said that he is only interested in protecting this invention in EPC contracting states. But the fact that Nippon has an earlier priority application disclosing Coolmix in some form, plus probably disclosure of cleaning, means that Silwafe would benefit from having a bargaining counter to use in negotiations with Nippon. A patent application as just described could potentially be used to secure a licence under the Nippon patent: Nippon being given a limited licence under the new Silwafe patent application. To this end, it would make sense to file the new application as a PCT application, designating at least EPO, JP, US and claiming priority from COOLMIX-EP.

In the US, should CLEAN-PCT enter the national phase, the eventual fate of COOLMIX-US would be decided by interference proceedings, i.e. the rights to COOLMIX would be awarded to the party that first conceived of the invention and reduced it diligently to practice. Lengthy and expensive proceedings would probably be necessary.

1–212

*(c) BLOWSAW*

New applications should be filed to protect the BLOWSAW invention. A single priority application could be filed followed by a PCT application at the end of the priority year or individual applications could be filed in Europe, Japan, US and other countries of interest. Alternatively, a PCT or national applications could be filed now without taking advantage of the priority year. The former strategy effectively gains an extra year of patent life. It seems clear, by virtue of the student's employment contract, that Silwafe own all the rights to the invention. However, the student will have to be named as an inventor since his program is a key aspect of the invention and his address will therefore be important. Indeed, for the US application, he will have to be the applicant. The need to disclose the best mode in a US patent application means that it would not be possible to omit his contribution from the patent application. It would therefore seem prudent to file a national (DE) or European patent application covering the invention and use this application as a basis for claiming priority. This gives time for locating the student and obtaining his address and necessary assignments/power of attorney. Claims will be possible to the process, apparatus and computer program.

**Client's freedom to operate in respect of third party rights**

1–213

*(a) CLEAN-PCT*

There is no relevant prior art known which may prejudice the validity of CLEAN-PCT. It will therefore become obvious from the discussion above that Nippon could potentially obtain protection in all PCT contracting states for the specific combination of COOLMIX and the surfactant disclosed in their application and possibly for COOLMIX itself. It will therefore be necessary to monitor the progress of CLEAN-PCT carefully to see (1) which national/regional phases are entered and (2) which claims are granted in those countries.

If any relevant claims are granted in a country where the client is interested in using COOLMIX or a COOLMIX/surfactant combination, client has the possibility of (1) designing round the granted claim(s) — should be relatively easy in respect of the combination since the CLEAN-PCT surfactant is not one of the client's preferred surfactants, (2) taking a licence from Nippon, which should be possible in view of their good working relationship and lack of direct competition or (3) try and revoke the patent — a full prior art search could be undertaken in order to assess validity.

In the US, any claim to COOLMIX itself may be granted to Silwafe in interference proceedings if they can show an earlier date of conception and diligent reduction to practice.

*(b) CUT-PCT*

In Germany, any granted claims to the MULTISAW process and device resulting from CUT-PCT will be invalid due to the prior art effect of MULTISAW-DE under the German equivalent of Art.54(3) EPC, assuming that MULTISAW-DE is published (need to make sure application is in good order as stated above). Client therefore has no infringement problem in Germany.

In Japan, would need to seek advice on the provisions of local law, but the situation is probably the same as in Germany since MULTISAW-JP validly claims priority. There is therefore unlikely to be an infringement problem in Japan.

In the US, interference proceedings would have to be established to decide on patent ownership. Since it is clear that the invention was made by Silwafe, there should be little problem in winning. There is therefore unlikely to be an infringement problem in the US.

However, in the rest of Europe apart from Germany, Zähnli is likely to obtain granted claims to the MULTISAW process and device by virtue of their EP designation if no action on entitlement is taken (see below). This would be a problem since infringement under most national laws applies to the direct product of a claimed process — hence the sale of the wafers would be an infringement if made using the patented process.

One possible course of action for Silwafe would therefore be to contest entitlement of the EP application when CUT-PCT enters the regional phase (and similar action in JP and US). Silwafe is likely to win such proceedings if it can produce enough evidence and is entitled to the parts of CUT-PCT referring to the process and device. Zähnli will retain their rights in the part of CUT-PCT relating to the new saw blade.

Under the Protocol on Recognition, Silwafe should apply to the Swiss courts for a declaration that they are entitled to the grant of the process and device parts of CUT-PCT(EP). They can then suspend proceedings before the EPO (r.13(1) EPC). They should then ensure that renewal fees are paid during the period of suspension. No withdrawal of the application would be possible once proceedings have been suspended (r.14 EPC). When a final favourable decision is obtained from the Swiss courts, Silwafe would have several options under Art.61(1) and r.16 EPC in respect of the subject matter it owns — to prosecute the application itself, file a new application or request refusal of the application.

(Swiss national law may also provide that an entitlement action may be brought in respect of an international patent application before it enters the national/regional phase. Rule 13(1) EPC is not applicable before the application enters the regional phase before the EPO, but even if Zähnli abandoned the case before regional phase entry (thereby eliminating the Art.54(3) effect), Silwafe could, if successful in the entitlement action, use the provisions of A61(EPC) to file a new application before the EPO directed to the multisaw part of CUT-PCT, following G3/92.)

However, given the fact that Silwafe want to maintain good relations with Zähnli, it may be possible to negotiate a mutually satisfactory agreement rather than taking legal action. For instance, Zähnli could assign CUT-PCT to Silwafe, who in return could grant Zähnli a royalty-free licence in respect of the new blades. Alternatively, Zähnli could formally agree to split CUT-PCT on entry into the national and regional phases into patent application directed to the saw blades which they would keep and divisional applications directed to the process and device which they would assign to Silwafe. Lastly, and less satisfactorily, Zähnli could grant Silwafe a worldwide, royalty-free, exclusive licence in respect of the process and device.

## 6. Worked example using EQE 2005 Paper D2

**1–215** *Preparing a timeline*

A first reading of the paper establishes that the client has filed a patent application, a friend has filed two patent applications, and an enemy has filed further patent applications, all relating generally to products which the client manufactures, or would like to manufacture, and sells. So the usual questions arise of who has what rights to what inventions, which patents dominate, and what can be done by the client or the enemy to improve their respective positions.

Having collated the important dates, a task which is dealt with at greater length below, a typical time-line can be constructed as shown below.

| | |
|---|---|
| 29.04.2002 | Vinge EP1 filed: foamed-core, hard shell windmill wing and process, **also discloses content of EP2 – wing with adjustable flaps** |
| 29.04.2002 | **DATE LOST** Vinge EP2 filed: windmill wing with adjustable flaps |
| 15.05.2002 | **Confidential** disclosure of EP1 and EP2 Vinge to Möller |
| 25.05.2002 | Re-dated filing Vinge EP2: windmill wing with adjustable flaps |
| 04.07.2002 | Wedding: "accidental" **disclosure of wing with flaps** |
| 04.07.2002 | disclosure of wings with dimples to reduce noise (Möller invention) |
| 04.07.02 19h00 | Möller EP3 filed disclosure of wings with dimples to reduce noise |
| 04.07.02 after 19h00 | Möller discusses wings with dimples to reduce noise with Cervantes and others. |
| 04.07.02 23h00 | Cervantes EP4 wing with dimples to reduce noise, wing with knobs to reduce noise. |
| 04.07.2002 late | Vinge disclosure to Cervantes of wings with foamed plastics core – not provable? |
| 15.07.2002 | Cervantes PCT1, wing and process, foamed recycled plastic core |
| 25.07.2002 | EN translation of EP1 (DK) filed |
| 25.07.2002 | EN translation of EP2 (DK) filed |
| Autumn 03 | Vinge EP2 published windmill wing with adjustable flaps |
| Autumn 03 | Vinge EP1 published foamed-core, hard shell wing & process |
| January 04 | Möller EP3 published wings with dimples to reduce noise |
| January 04 | Cervantes EP4 published wing with dimples/knobs to reduce noise. |
| January 04 | Cervantes PCT1 published wing foamed, recycled plastics core, and process. |
| February 04 | Möller: Delivery in Germany, wing with foamed, recycled plastics core. |
| February 04 | Möller: accidental disclosure of foamed recycled plastics core when wing broke in Germany. |
| 2 August 04 | GRANT Vinge EP2 windmill wing with adjustable flaps |
| February 2005 | Cervantes US GRANT (ex-PCT1) wing foamed, recycled plastics core, and process. |
| **8 March 05** | **TODAY** |
| 10/11 March 05 | Vinge deadline for Möller to purchase EP1, EP2. |
| End March 05 | Divisional filings still possible on Vinge EP1 |
| Early April 05 | Vinge EP1 WILL GRANT |
| 16.04.05 | Möller Cervantes meeting |
| 30.04.05 | Tender deadline Californian windmill park |

## Analysing the paper

1-216

Here is a further example of the level of detail in which you need to be analysing the D2 paper. As with the 2002 example given above, the points chosen for comment are not the only ones which are of relevance, but they do include the main issues. Again, the notes which appear in the marked-up question paper are not intended to show you what or how much to write in the exam. Rather, they are meant to trigger your thoughts so that you see **why** you have been given this information. Many of the items are there to tell you NOT to worry about (and hence not address) certain issues which otherwise you might have felt the need to raise. Yet other items of information are hooks which should link up with other items of information later in the question, often to give you an important topic to address. For example, the emphasis surrounding the needless addition of drawings to, and hence the re-dating of, EP2, which links with the information about the textual basis of EP2 also having been in EP1 as filed – completely eliminating any need to address sufficiency/enablement, and showing you both that EP2 is utterly worthless and that EP1 is the master card which your client must hold if he is to prevail over Cervantes. The lesson to be learnt here is that, as you slowly read through the paper, you must continually ask yourself why you are being given the different "atoms" of information: which ones are eliminating concerns, which ones are flagging concerns, and which ones interact and must be dealt with together.

**The 2005 Paper D2**                                                        Today is March 8th, 2005[0]

You are a qualified European Patent Attorney and today you received the following letter from the Danish Company Möller Wind Enterprises (MÖWE), for whom you hold a general authorization[1] before the EPO. MÖWE sells[2] windmills and has all its development and manufacturing[3] facilities situated in Denmark[4].

Dear Madam/Sir,

Earlier today, I had a meeting with Mr Vinge, an inventor and close friend[5], who for many years[6] has been active in the field of windmill technology. During this meeting, I became aware of certain facts and problems[7], which I believe need immediate[8] attention.

On 29.04.2002[9], Mr Vinge filed in Danish[10] a European application, EP1, designating all contracting states[11]. Mr Vinge is applicant[12] and named as inventor[13]. EP1 describes a process[14] for manufacturing a windmill wing having a core made of a foamed plastic material fully encapsulated by a smooth, hard shell[15]. In this way a lighter and less expensive wing is obtainable as compared to prior art wings[16]. The claims are directed to both the process and to the wing[17]. The application includes no drawings[18]. A translation into English was filed on 25.07.2002[19]. EP1 was published in autumn 2003[20] and the search report cited no relevant documents[21]. Mr Vinge has been informed by the EPO that publication of the grant[22] of the European patent will take place in early April 2005[23]. The patent will be granted with the same text as the published application[24].

Also on 29.04.2002 Mr Vinge filed another European application, EP2[25], in Danish and designating all contracting states. Again, Mr Vinge is applicant and is named as inventor[26]. EP2 describes and claims a windmill wing with adjustable flaps[27]. By means of such flaps a wing can be adjusted to almost any wind condition[28]. Shortly after filing, Mr Vinge realized that the drawings were missing[29] from the application.

Although the claims of EP2 are fully supported[30] by the description and the invention is fully understandable based on the seven pages of description alone[31], he filed the missing drawings[32] on 25.05.2002. When asked by the EPO, Mr Vinge requested that the application be re-dated[33] to the date on which the drawings were filed. These drawings contain no further technical information[34]. An English translation was filed on 25.07.2002[35].

EP2 was published in autumn 2003[36] and again the search report cited no relevant documents[37]. Publication of the grant of the European patent took place[38] on 02.08.2004[39] and the patent has been duly validated in all designated states[40].

In order to enable testing and evaluation, Mr Vinge informed me fully and in all detail about EP1 and EP2 on the 15.05.2002[41] under a written secrecy agreement[42].

On 04.07.2002[43] we celebrated the wedding between Mr Vinge's daughter[44] and my son.

The wedding party took place in my house[45] and garden and some 200 invited guests, including important business associates[46] and contacts of Mr Vinge and myself, participated. Much to my surprise and immediate concern, I realized that my wife had arranged for a large five tons prototype wing to be placed in the garden for decorative purposes, on the day of the wedding[47]. The wing included flaps according to EP2[48], a foamed non-visible core[49] according to EP1 and a plurality of small dimples[50]. Dimples are small surface indentations, which are known to be noise reducing[51]. However, I found out that when the dimples are placed exclusively in a very specific[52] region near the wing tip (as in the prototype[53]), they are surprisingly[54] efficient in reducing noise generation[55]. Later the same evening[56], around 19h00[57], I managed to put together and file by fax[58] a European patent application, EP3, in English language[59] describing and claiming[60] a wing with this dimple-arrangement and describing the surprising effect[61] of this arrangement. I am applicant and named as inventor[62]. EP3 was published in January 2004[63] with a search report citing no relevant documents[64]. The application is validly pending in the examination phase before the EPO and all relevant fees have been paid[65].

Present at the party was also Mr Cervantes, who owns our main competitor[66], the Spanish[67] company Don Quichotte Wind Enterprises (DQWE). Mr Cervantes, who had been invited by Mr Vinge, is known to run his business in a rather aggressive[68] manner.

Shortly after filing[69] EP3, I discussed with Mr Cervantes[70] and some other guests[71] from the windmill industry[72] my new dimple-based noise-reduction technology[73].

Later I learned that on the very evening of the wedding[74], around 23h00[75], Mr Cervantes filed also by fax[76] a European application, EP4. He is applicant and named as inventor[77].

EP4 describes and claims[78] a wing with the very same arrangement of dimples as shown by the prototype[79]. EP4 also claims[80] an alternative in the form of a wing with small knobs, i.e. protrusions[81], in the same region near the wing tip. The dimples and the knobs are, as is commonly known[82] and as also acknowledged in the description[83] of EP4, equivalents[84] in that they serve substantially the same purpose and obtain substantially the same effect[85]. From the description of EP4, it is clear that the inventive contribution is seen solely[86] in the new and surprising noise reduction[87] resulting from the specific location of the dimples/knobs near the wing tip. EP4 was published in January 2004[88] with a search report citing no relevant documents[89]. The application is validly pending in the examination phase[90] before the EPO and all relevant fees have been paid[91].

In their current sales catalogues, both[92] MÖWE and DQWE show wings with dimples[93]. DQWE additionally shows the equivalent knobs[94]. No sales have yet been made[95] by either company. However, the technology is believed to be commercially important[96], since low noise windmills can be placed closer to residential areas[97].

Another possible conflict[98] with DQWE may arise due to a PCT application[99], PCT1, filed in English[100] at the EPO[101] on 15.07.2002[102] by Mr Cervantes. He is applicant and named as inventor[103]. PCT1 describes a process for manufacturing[104] a windmill wing having a core made from foamed[105], recycled[106] plastics. The foamed core is fully encapsulated by a smooth, hard shell[107] making the core as such non-visible[108]. In PCT1, the essence of the invention is seen in the use of recycled plastic[109], which is a very cheap[110] material in comparison with virgin plastic. Recycled plastic is easily distinguishable[111] from virgin plastic in that it is multicoloured. The claims of PCT1 are directed to the process and to the resulting wing[112]. PCT1 was published in January 2004[113] with a search report citing no relevant documents[114]. PCT1 was validly regionalized[115] and is pending in the examination phase before the EPO[116]. A corresponding US application was granted[117] in un-amended form in February 2005[118].

To me[119] it appears obvious[120] that Mr Cervantes somehow[121] had gained knowledge of the foamed core technology of EP1[122] and based PCT1 on this knowledge[123]. Mr Vinge, being the only other person[124] apart from me knowing about the interior of the displayed wing, vaguely[125] remembers a late-night[126] discussion at the wedding[127] with Mr Cervantes about the wing. However, this was shortly before he had to be brought home by[128] Mrs Vinge and he cannot[129] - or will not[130] - recall the conversation in any detail[131].

The use of recycled plastic for the foam core is not really new to me[132], since I have myself considered this obvious choice[133] of material after having learned in May 2002[134] about the foam core structure of EP1. In fact, the wing shown at the wedding[135] also included a foam core made from recycled plastic material[136]. At that time, I decided to try to keep the use of recycled plastic secret[137], since the interior of a wing would not be visible[138]. No delivery was made before February 2004[139], when I delivered some wings with a core of foamed, recycled plastic to a customer in Germany[140]. However, during installation, an accident happened and one of the wings dropped to the ground and broke. With a letter of last week[141], Mr Cervantes indicated having recently[142] gained knowledge of this incident, and thus of our use of recycled plastics[143] for foamed wing cores. Consequently, he has invited us to a meeting on 16.04.2005[144].

We know that DQWE, whose manufacturing facilities all are located in Spain[145], already has made extensive sales of wings according to the technology disclosed[146] in PCT1 in Europe[147] and in the USA[148].

Another aspect of commercial importance[149] is a tender[150] for a large[151] contract for supplying wings to a major[152] Californian windmill park where we are competing against[153] DQWE. The deadline for submitting offers is 30.04.05[154]. Strong interest[155] has been expressed by the Californian company[156] in the recently patented flap technology[157] of EP2 and we are convinced[158] that being able to deliver wings with this technology would be vital[159] to securing the order[160]. If getting the order, we would of course prefer[161] to make use of the less expensive recycled[162] plastic material for the foamed cores.

During the meeting earlier today[163], Mr Vinge informed me that he would like to retire and give up all business activities[164]. He offered to assign to me all rights resulting from EP1 for the price of EUR 2 million[165]. He also offered EP2[166] and all national patents resulting from EP2 to me for the price of EUR 5 million[167]. Further, he informed me that the same offer had been made to DQWE[168]. However, for family reasons, Mr Vinge has given me two days to consider these offers[169] before resuming talks with DQWE. Mr. Vinge also informed me that Mr Cervantes has deposited a binding agreement[170] to purchase any rights that MÖWE does not purchase[171].

To assist me in making my decision, Mr Vinge handed over a copy of his complete files[172] regarding both EP1 and EP2. I noticed that EP1 as originally filed[173] additionally contains the seven pages of text identical[174] to the description of EP2[175], but that the technical content of these pages appear nowhere in the application as later published[176]. When asked about this, Mr Vinge explained, that erroneously[177] these pages were omitted when filing the English translation[178] of EP1. All relevant fees for EP1 and EP2 have been duly paid[179].

I consider the flap technology of vital[180] importance and I am thus inclined to accept buying EP2[181] for the stated price. As regards EP1, I consider this technology alone[182] as being less important for MÖWE[183], and as such not worth the asking price[184] of EUR 2 million. In my belief, the foamed core technology is only truly interesting in economical terms[185] when used in combination with the recycled plastics[186] as disclosed by PCT1.

**Please advice me urgently in the above matters, in particular on:**

1. **What is the patent situation[187] regarding:**
   **- the foamed core technology, and**
   **- the use of recycled plastic material?**

What should be my strategy[188] and can my position be improved[189] before[190] the upcoming meeting with Mr Cervantes?

2. **What is the patent situation regarding the adjustable flap technology[191] and can I take any actions to improve my position [192]?**

3. **What is the patent situation regarding the dimples and the equivalent knobs[193] and can I take any actions[194] to improve my position?**

4. **If hostile actions against DQWE become unavoidable, I would prefer to remain anonymous[195] to not further deteriorate the business climate. What are the options[196]?**

Yours faithfully,

Möller.

**Points that arise**

(0) Capture the date of the exam, somewhere on your exam paper and in your time line. Not because you might forget the date (although that has been known to happen), but because you can too easily overlook the consequences that stem from today's date (e.g. whether a priority year has ended, or whether restitutio is still available).

(1) This suggests that Möller (MOWE) already has some experience of patents. Of course, as a qualified European patent attorney you do not require an authorisation.

(2) The fact that the company sells windmills means that there is a potential patent infringement risk – something which would not arise if they merely designed windmills.

(3) The location of manufacturing facilities is obviously relevant to the question of infringement. The location of the development facilities at first sight appears irrelevant, but it could be relevant to some right of prior use, particularly to "serious and effective preparations" to perform an invention. The existence of any such right in Denmark is irrelevant to the question, although had it been Germany, then it would have had potential relevance.

(4) Obviously we need to consider the existence of third-party patent rights in Denmark. The client's market, as we see later in the question, extends to other European countries and, as such, third-party patent rights elsewhere in Europe can also be of significance.

(5) The fact that Vinge is a close friend suggests that, on the one hand, our client probably feels he can trust him, and on the other that the client is unlikely to want to get tough with Mr Vinge.

(6) This suggests that Vinge is knowledgeable about windmills.

(7) These facts and problems are what we must address in answering the question. Despite the assumption that the client has some knowledge of patents, we should expect that he may not have appreciated all the problems inherent in the facts.

(8) Obviously we need to address the problems that need immediate attention, but we should also propose courses of action which avoid or overcome longer term problems.

(9) This is the second date for our time line. We note that the date is more than 12 months ago, so we are beyond the priority year. As the date is more than 18 months ago, we can expect the publication will have occurred. Even if a PCT application were filed based on this date, then the 31 month term would have passed.

(10) We're not told that Mr Vinge is a Danish national or a resident in Denmark, but one or other of these conditions needed to have been satisfied for the filing in Danish to be legitimate. The eventual fate of the patent application suggests that Mr Vinge is a compatriot of our client.

(11) It is worth having a list of contracting states and the date of their accession, so that you can check, should it be necessary, to see whether a particular state would have been caught by an "all states" application filed on a particular date. As we see later in the question, a major country of interest is Spain, but Spain was a contracting state long before April 2002.

(12) The question gives no details of any company belonging to Vinge. Under such circumstances, being told that Vinge is the applicant means that we should not concern ourselves with possible complications about ownership.

(13) Again, this information removes some possible doubts. With Vinge named as applicant and inventor, and no suggestion of a company or third party involvement, we know that our client can deal with Vinge in respect of EP1.

(14) It is important to spot the different technologies and claimable inventions as they are introduced throughout the question. Your time line needs to capture not only the fact that EP1 was filed on the 29th April 2002, but also what it disclosed, what it claimed, and what it could have claimed based on the disclosure. Also bear in mind the fact that under the European patent convention the protection conferred by a claim to a process extends to the direct product of that process (Art.64(2)).

(15) This description of the technology will no doubt become important later in the question.

(16) A lighter and less expensive wing compared to the prior art (about which Mr Vinge can be expected to be knowledgeable) is obviously likely to be of commercial significance.

(17) It appears that we do not have to worry about unclaimed subject matter.

(18) Now, why are we told this? It is an unusual fact and its presence should make us stop and think.

(19) This date is within 3 months of the filing date (priority not being an issue) and hence the rule 6(1) requirement was met.

(20) Another date for the time line. The fact that we do not have a specific date suggests that nothing rides on the precise date of publication. And note that publication would have been in English and that now, of course, the subject matter of EP1 is public.

(21) This tells us that we do not have to worry about earlier third party rights and also know we can expect EP1 to mature to a patent.

(22) The EPO has indeed accepted the patentability of the claimed invention.

(23) Another date for the timeline and this one is in the future. Early April logically means the first half of April. When in these questions you see that a patent is shortly to be granted you need always to be considering whether there is any need to file a divisional application, because of course to be validly filed as a divisional application the filing needs to be made not later than the day before the publication of the mention of grant of the patent. At this point we cannot see any reason to file a divisional application, but do not discount the possibility of needing to file a divisional application. After all, we are only on the first page of the question. Indeed, at this stage of writing a time line I would recommend adding to the "EP1 to be granted" a flag "file a divisional?".

(24) This sentence tells us a few things immediately but at first sight it is an odd thing to tell us. The fact that it is odd should make you register this fact for later use. Among the things it tells us immediately are that there can be no added matter objection and that there has been no limitation of the claims.

(25) Another date for the timeline.

(26) Again, this confirms that we don't need to worry about ownership (subject to any complication that appears later in the question).

(27) More technology to be captured on the time line. You also need to keep track of the different technologies that are introduced because you can be sure that you will need to deal with each of them when you finally come to answer the question.

(28) This adjustability for wind condition sounds like a good idea with a practical application.

(29) Missing drawings should always set alarm bells ringing.

(30) You should ask yourself "why am I being told this?".

(31) Again "why am I being told this?". At this stage in the question it is not clear why, but you need to carry that question with you as you read on through the text so that you can find the complement to this fact which shows you why it is important.

(32) Oh dear, a loss of filing date. You need to show on your time line that the original filing date for EP2 is no longer correct and that it is now the 25$^{th}$ May 2002. We can be certain that consequences will follow from this.

(33) Confirmation of the fears that arose when we read point 29.

(34) At first sight this seems like an odd statement – why are we told this? When you ask yourself that question you realise that the content of EP2 is still exactly the same as it was before. But why do you want to know that? Again, you have to carry that question with you through the rest of the paper until you come to the answer. You must look for the complement to this odd fact.

(35) It is interesting to see that the rule 6 time limit based on the original filing date was met. As this is a date, it should go on your time line, although it doesn't appear to have profound significance.

(36) To the content of EP2 was made public in autumn 2003. This is another date for your time line.

(37) So again the prospects for getting a patent appear good.

(38) Vinge has his patent already.

(39) When you see a date of grant you should always calculate the date on which the opposition period would end. In the present case, a moment's reflection will tell you that the opposition period doesn't end until the 2$^{nd}$ May 2005 (subject to

(40) We do not yet know which states, other than Denmark, are likely to be of significance, but we can be certain that there will be some.

(41) This date should go on our time line and we note that it is between the filing date of EP1 and the revised filing date of EP2. Could that be significant?

(42) The written secrecy agreement means that this disclosure is not relevant to the patentability to EP2. Moreover, our earliest known publication of the content of EP1 and EP2 remains autumn 2003.

(43) Another date for the time line.

(44) The marriage between Vinge's daughter and Möller's son gives us extra reason for Möller not to be too aggressive with Vinge.

(45) At first sight this is an odd piece of information to be given. But the fact that it was Möller's house, which he can be presumed to control, rather than a property belonging to a third party or a public space, may have significance.

(46) Vinge's long activity in the field of windmill technology suggests that his business associates are likely to have some familiarity with windmill technology. As such, they may be able to appreciate rather more than an ordinary person when it comes to windmills.

(47) To be placed on the day of the wedding, suggests that any accidental disclosure was not before that date.

(48) Possibly the functionality of the flaps would have been evident to the business associates.

(49) As the core was non-visible the business associates could not have become aware of the EP1 invention by inspection.

(50) A new technology to be noted.

(51) The technical function for the dimples where which shows that the general function is known.

(52) "Exclusively in a very specific" is already starting to suggest a non-obvious invention.

(53) The location could have been seen by the business associates.

(54) The "surprisingly" is a clear flag to inventiveness.

(55) The problem of noise generation is clearly one of practical and commercial significance in the field of windmills. Altogether this passage should be telling us that the dimples are likely to constitute a patentable and commercially worthwhile invention.

(56) Another date for the time line – that is, it should be clear that what follows also took place on the 4th July.

(57) Why are we told this? Does the hour of which a patent application was filed matter? There is obviously going to be an issue to be discussed.

(58) Filing by fax suggests that the filing actually took place on the 4th July.

(59) This tells us that there is no need for a translation and it may also be relevant to the question of provisional protection.

(60) Again our time line should capture this information.

(61) So our client does know something about patents! The inclusion of this information strengthens the patent application.

(62) Mr Möller is the inventor removes doubt as to inventor ship.

(63) Another date for the time line, with full disclosure of content of EP3.

(64) This is again a flag to say that EP3 is likely to mature into a patent.

(65) This is telling you that you don't need to worry about anything to do with status of the application, so do not waste time debating or considering any issues on this point.

(66) Not only do we have a name, but we are told that this person is the main competitor.

(67) So our client will be interested in getting patents in Spain.

(68) The unprincipled shark is a common feature of paper D2.

(69) At first we might think that this was on some later date, but it becomes clear that it was later the same day.

(70) We should expect something bad to come from this disclosure.

(71) Potential witnesses?

(72) Who might then be expected to understand more about the technology of windmills than would the average person from the street.

(73) The audience would be expected to understand what they were told. In any event there is no suggestion that this was in any sense a confidential disclosure. The venue and the situation do not suggest or imply condition of confidentiality. So this material must be taken to have been published by this disclosure. This should be marked on the timeline.

(74) Confirmation that the disclosure that we just learnt about also took place on July 4$^{th.}$

(75) Again, you have to ask yourself why are we told the time. As we soon see, at issue is the question of events happening on the same date but at known, different times. What can we do with this information? We have to address whatever issue exists or is implied.

(76) Two faxed events on the same day: that should sound familiar, but what were the circumstances in the decided case where this arose?

(77) Again, this is a simplification. In particular there is no complication from an alleged further inventor.

(78) More data for the timeline.

(79) Which Cervantes saw and was told about earlier on July 4$^{th}$, and corresponding to EP3.

(80) So EP4 has something extra: more data for the timeline.

(81) Something not shown on the prototype, and presumably not disclosed by Möller.

(82) No special insight required.

(83) What is the effect of including this statement in the application? Is it of potential significance to scope of protection?

(84) Unlikely therefore to be any invention in substituting one for the other.

(85) This should remind you of the commonly used mantra derived from US law on infringement by equivalents (the Graver tank Test). Consider why you are being told this.

(86) Cervantes would appear to have added nothing at all inventive to the invention of Möller.

(87) This is the same understanding that underpins the invention in EP3.

(88) A date for the time line.

(89) No prior art unless one or more of EP3 or the prototype or the wedding disclosure constitute a citable disclosure.

(90) At the same stage as EP3 and also not yet granted.

(91) Again this removes issues, so you do not need to discuss them.

(92) They both want to sell the product.

(93) They both have pending patent applications for this subject matter. An evident conflict emerges.

(94) These are, at first sight not covered by EP3.

(95) No revenue at stake, and no customer liabilities to take on, yet.

(96) In this exam, if the client tells you that something is commercially important, it is. Moreover, you have to pay special attention to the protection of the subject matter, as well as being concerned to minimise the threat posed by third party rights.

(97) This is an explanation of value which is understandable even to those ignorant of windmill technology. Now we know why this is said to be commercially important.

(98) A clear signpost to another issue which we will almost certainly need to resolve.

(99) A PCT application should make us think of the 30 and 31 month time limits, the requirements for regional phase entry, and the introduction of countries outside Europe.

(100) So no translation needed for European regional phase entry. Also relevant to the countries where provisional protection arises without further translation.

(101) Of significance perhaps to the assumed quality of the search, and the expectation that no further art will be found in the European regional phase?

(102) After the wedding, but before publication of EP1 and EP2. Another date for the timeline.

(103) Again, the elimination of issues which might have distracted us.

(104) A necessary thing for the purpose of sufficiency? Likely to be of interest to Möller.

(105) Reminiscent of EP1.

(106) Something new – another invention for our timeline.

(107) It sounds very similar to EP1.

(108) The similarity to EP1 continues.

(109) Not rocket science one would think, but new compared to EP1. Probably economically attractive?

(110) So commercially very attractive.

(111) Good for policeability of the patent.

(112) Claim types of great potential relevance to Möller.

(113) Another date for the time line.

(114) This raises the spectre of PCT1 giving rise to enforceable rights.

(115) Again the removal of complications and distractions. Do not question such a statement in this exam.

(116) At least it is not granted yet.

(117) That sounds like potential bad news- expect the client to want to do something in the US now.

(118) We can perhaps expect the same in the EPO. Note the extra date in the timeline.

(119) Möller may be more likely to see foul play than a dispassionate observer, but that does not make him wrong.

(120) Which suggests that Möller has no hard evidence to back up his suspicions.

(121) Confirmation of the last point.

(122) EP1 is clearly very close to PCT1, but of course EP1 was not published until after PCT1 was filed.

(123) A plausible assumption, but where is the evidence?

(124) This confirms what we have been told so far.

(125) That is we cannot rely on what Mr Vinge says about this.

(126) This explains why he is vague, perhaps?

(127) Vinge's imperfect recollection is understandable.

(128) As above.

(129) Understandable

(130) It does not really matter which it is- he would not make a persuasive witness.

(131) So by now you should have given up on the idea of being able to prove to a court or the patent office that Cervantes got the invention from Vinge.

(132) Not useable as prior art in an attack on PCT1.

(133) Such an "obvious" change to EP1 is of no help in mounting an attack based on EP1 – which would only be citable under Art 54(3).

(134) Which was the secret disclosure and hence not usable in an attack on PCT1.

(135) The wing was public, but the construction of the core was not visible and again cannot be used in an attack on PCT1.

(136) But still not prior art.

(137) No corroboration and presumably no publication to be relied upon.

(138) Further confirmation of this fact.

(139) Delivery makes the content/structure of the core public, even without an incentive to analyse. Mark this on the time line. Note that this date is after the publication of PCT1. PCT1 provisional protection at issue?

(140) PCT1 was published in English. German provisional protection requires German translation. When was the wing made? Danish provisional protection? Possible DK prior use rights? Unlikely perhaps.

(141) Early March 2005.

(142) No EP enforceable rights yet, so no risk of rapid injunction?

(143) A technology covered by Cervantes' PCT1.

(144) More than a month away. After the due date for grant of EP1. Why?

(145) Manufacturing facilities in Spain so validation in Spain of EP1, quickly, is important.

(146) The technology of PCT1 is covered by EP1.

(147) EP1 should be validated outside ES, although we do not yet know where.

(148) EP1 has no US equivalent, but manufacture in ES for equipment sold in the US makes the ES part of EP1 very valuable, and relevant to DQWE's activities in the US.

(149) Again, if we are told that this is of commercial importance, that is how we should treat it.

(150) An invitation to submit bids for the supply of products or services against some statement of requirements.

(151) Emphasising the commercial importance.

(152) Again emphasising the commercial importance.

(153) So the patent issues here are of great significance, and we need to give our client advice on how to get the best commercial position as against DQWE prior to and at the meeting proposed for the end of April.

(154) After the proposed meeting with DQWE.

(155) Not to be ignored

(156) The company over whose business DQWE and MOWE are competing.

(157) In which neither DQWE nor MOWE yet has rights.

(158) This makes EP2 seem attractive.

(159) No more positive signal could be given of the importance of the flap technology.

(160) Which we know to be very important. The fact that a particular technology is said to be vital in this paper does not mean that the client will control or get access to the technology, but it does mean that you have to look harder if you cannot at least see a way or forcing a cross licence from the relevant patent proprietor.

(161) A much lower level wish, but still a wish.

(162) The subject of PCT1 which is in Cervantes's hands.

(163) 8 March 2005

(164) We are primed for some news about the various Vinge patents.

(165) Not too expensive for a patent that dominates PCT1 in Europe.

(166) Which we should not buy at any price. See below.

(167) No thank you.

(168) It would be very bad news for MOWE if DQWE bought EP1.

(169) Another date for our time line, lest we forget it. We already know how to advise our client on this.

(170) Unusual.

(171) So we want to get MOWE to make the right decision: there can be no turning back.

(172) A usual feature of the D2 paper.

(173) In Danish, on 29 April 2002 – the earliest patent application in the paper.

(174) The use of the word "identical" is very significant.

(175) And now we remember that we were told that the text of EP2 was fully understandable based on the description alone. Now we should know why.

(176) In English, the authentic text, but not the text against which added matter is determined.

(177) Does that fact matter or is this a red herring?

(178) Which can still be corrected to bring it into agreement with the text originally submitted (Danish), without recourse to Rule 88.

(179) Again, the removal of issues which could distract you.

(180) Re-emphasised yet again. We really can be in no doubt as to the significance of that technology.

(181) By now we should have realised that this is the last thing that Möller should do: EP2 is worthless.

(182) Does he mean "without rights to use recycled plastics" or "without the flap technology"?

(183) Yet EP1, we now know, contains the basis for protection of both the flap and foamed core technologies.

(184) EUR 2 million for both these technologies must be better value than flap technology alone for EUR 5 million.

(185) But EP1 dominates PCT1 in Europe.

(186) With EP1 Möller has a basis for negotiating a cross licence under PCT1 if he really wants one.

(187) This requires an analysis of the interplay between EP1 and PCT1.

(188) This obviously goes beyond the bare facts about the patents.

(189) What tools can we give Möller, which he does not already have, to help him with his negotiation?

(190) This should trigger you to consider what can be changed or what must be changed before the meeting towards the end of April. Your time line should help you with this question.

(191) The situation with EP2 and, of course, EP1.

(192) Buy EP1, don't buy EP2.

(193) The interplay between EP3 and EP4

(194) An entitlement action perhaps? Negotiate a cross licence between EP3 and EP4?

(195) Opposition against EP2 using a man of straw?

(196) No anonymity in entitlement proceedings.

*Table of inventions, patent rights, ownership*

| Technology | Europe | USA | Elsewhere | Möller | Cervantes |
|---|---|---|---|---|---|
| Windmill wing with foamed plastic core, and process for making. | EP1 Vinge, allowed | No known patent | No known patent | Should buy EP1 for use against Cervantes. | Subject to EP1. If Möller buys it and validates it in Spain, Cervantes cannot make the wings in his current base (which serves Europe and the US). |
| Windmill wing with foamed core of recycled plastic, and process for making. | EP(PCT1) pending | US(PCT1) granted | No known patent | Can be prevented from manufacturing or selling in Europe and in US by PCT1. | Owns PCT1 and can use it to stop Möller, but this technology is also covered by EP1. If Möller buys that, there is basis to negotiate a cross licence. |
| Windmill wing with adjustable flaps. | Apparently covered by EP2 Vinge, but that is incurably invalid. EP1 provides basis for divisional to replace EP2 (same content and scope). | No known patent | No known patent | Should not buy EP2. Should buy EP1 before it is granted and file divisional with EP2 content and claims before EP1 is granted. Should oppose grant of EP2. | Contractually obliged to buy EP2 if MOWE does not. If Möller files EP1 DIV it could be used to prevent Cervantes making wings with flaps ES manufacture for US also caught) and selling. |
| Windmill wing with dimples for noise reduction. | Möller's EP3<br><br>Cervantes' EP4 | No known patent | No known patent | Can use EP3, when granted, to stop manufacture and sale of dimpled wings. Can be prevented from manufacture and sale of dimpled wings by EP4. But should seek entitlement of his part of EP4 (witnesses available from the wedding party of Möller's disclosure to Cervantes prior to filing (hour) of EP4. Seek insertion of disclaimer to dimples in amended EP4 to prevent subsequent cover of dimples "by equivalence" to knobs. | Subject to EP3, (after grants), can be prevented from manufacture and sale of dimpled wings.<br><br>Own patent rights to dimples subject to challenge by Möller. |

PART A

1-217 *Answering the paper*

The question puts you in the position of a European Patent Attorney who has received the letter from Möller who has asked you to advise him urgently. In such a situation it makes sense to address your answer to Möller. An alternative would be to write notes for a meeting with Möller, which some candidates might find less constraining. We have several direct questions to answer and at least as important is the need to give advice on how to secure the best position vis-à-vis Cervantes. A possible answer is set out below.

Dear Mr Möller,

in reply to your recent letter, I give the following advice.

1-218 **1(a) The patent situation regarding the foamed core technology**

The Vinge patent application EP1 is the first patent filing, with a filing date of 29 April 2002, for windmill wings having foamed plastics cores with a smooth, hard shell, and a process for making these. No prior art has been cited and the European patent will grant early in April (although to become effective in the designated contracting states, such a Spain, the formal procedure of validation needs to be undertaken within each state, within three months of grant). Although the patent application does not mention the use of recycled plastics, wings with foamed cores made from recycled plastics and their manufacture (in one of the states covered by EP1) will infringe EP1.

You should note that the proprietor of EP1 (Mr Vinge or whoever he sells it to) could potentially seek compensation from you for your manufacture in Denmark and supply of the foamed wings of recycled plastics to Germany in February 2004. But such compensation is conditional, in Denmark on a Danish translation having been filed appropriately before the manufacture took place, and in Germany on the appropriate filing of a German translation prior to importation or supply. The installation in Germany also becomes an actionable infringement once an appropriate German translation of the granted patent is appropriately filed.

1-219 **1(b) The patent situation for foamed core technology using recycled plastics**

Cervantes' PCT1 was the first patent application filed for this technology. No pertinent prior art has been found. EP1 was not published until after the filing of PCT1 and hence cannot be cited under Art. 54(2). EP1 does not mention recycled plastics and hence is not effective prior art under Art.54(3) — which concerns novelty only. The disclosure by Vinge to you of the details about EP1 in May 2002 was under a written secrecy agreement and hence does not constitute publication. The fact that the wing, which was on display at your son's wedding, had a foamed core was not discernible to observers.

While you clearly suspect that Cervantes learnt about the foamed core technology at your son's wedding following some indiscretion of Mr Vinge, you tell me that Mr Vinge cannot or will not admit to this. With Mr Vinge's testimony (if it could be relied upon – as he was not in a fit state to take himself home on the night of the wedding) it might have been possible to show that the subject matter of PCT1 was obvious. But without it, there is no evidence on which to base such an attack. Thus it seems that Cervantes' PCT1 will survive. Once the European part of PCT1 is granted, Cervantes will be able to stop you making or selling windmill wings having foamed cores of recycled plastics, and that is true even if you buy EP1. The granted US patent means that you would be unwise even to tender for the Californian contract until you have settled matters with Mr Cervantes.

The situation concerning the wing of foamed recycled plastic in Germany, that I mention above, took place after the publication of PCT1 (at least the delivery did, it is unclear from your letter when manufacture took place) and hence there is again risk of a liability because of the provisional protection conferred by PCT1. But as with EP1, appropriate translations needed to be in place and there is a good chance that they were not.

Because your development and manufacturing facilities are in Denmark rather than Germany, I do not believe that you could rely upon rights of continued use (prior use rights) since these are strictly national. It is possible that you could rely on these in Denmark but you need to have been using or making serious and effective preparations to use the technology from before the filing of PCT1 in July 2002 – the precise details vary from country to country and so we need to check the situation for Denmark as well as checking what you actually did and when you did it. We need to discuss this when we meet.

It does not appear that there is any reasonable chance to knock out the US patent corresponding to PCT1. In the US patents are awarded to the "first and true inventor" rather than to the first person to file a patent application for a particular invention. While we are suspicious that Cervantes clearly got the idea for PCT1 from Vinge, we cannot prove it. Moreover, the invention protected in PCT1 is based on the application of recycled plastics – something which was unknown to Vinge as far as we know (I understand that you kept your use of recycled plastics secret from Vinge). Certainly if you were unlucky enough to be sued under US(PCT1), it would be worth arguing that Cervantes got the idea from Vinge, but this is not a sound policy to pursue if you have a choice (as I believe you do).

DQWE is a Spanish business all of whose manufacturing facilities are located in Spain. You say that DQWE has already made extensive sales of wings according to PCT1 in the US and Europe. All of these wings will have been manufactured in Spain. DQWE will be infringing EP1 (albeit that is has yet to grant) by manufacturing wings with foamed cores of recycled plastics. For this reason I recommend strongly that you buy EP1 (as you will see below, you should not buy EP2 but by buying EP1 you will also get rights to the flaps technology of EP2). You need to do that immediately – I suggest at your imminently forthcoming meeting with Vinge. There are various actions which we should perform in relation to EP1, and among these is the urgent validation of the patent in Spain and such other countries as represent attractive markets for DQWE or any of your competitors. Because EP1 is to grant early in April, before the planned meeting with Cervantes, buying EP1 gives us time to validate the patent in Spain before that meeting. As proprietor of that patent you will be in a position to threaten DQWE over their use of your foamed core technology (using recycled plastics) – and demand a licence under US(PCT1) and EP(PCT1) as the price of not suing DQWE under EP1.

## 2. The patent situation on the adjustable flap technology

While EP2 was the first patent application filed for this technology, on 29 April 2002, that filing date was lost when the application was re-dated following filing of the drawings. The revised filing date is now 25 May 2002. The disclosure to you by Vinge of the details of EP2 on May 15 2002 was under conditions of secrecy and hence is not prior art. Similarly, the disclosure of the prototype at your son's wedding is not prior art because it took place after the filing of EP2. But, the whole contents of EP2 were also included in EP1 when it was filed, in Danish, also on April 29, 2002. EP1 is citable under Art.54(3) EPC because it was filed before and published later than the filing date of EP2. This is true even though the text of the published patent application, in English, did not include the EP2 matter. This is because the authentic text of EP1 is the text in the language of filing (here Danish). EP2 was granted less than 9 months ago and can still be opposed (until May 2$^{nd}$ 2005) on the basis that it lacks novelty over EP1. For this reason, you should not buy EP2 – it is worthless.

But protection is still available for the flap technology in Europe. Although the EP2 material was not in the published application of EP1, it was still part of the application as filed. As such, it can be made the subject of a divisional application based on EP1, provided that it is filed before the date of grant of EP1 – which is scheduled for early April 2005 (a few weeks' time). This is the second reason why you should buy EP1 rather than EP2!

You should obtain an assignment from Vinge immediately (which I can draft for you) which at least he needs to sign. We then register that at the EPO to make you (MOWE or Mr Möller) the proprietor of EP1. Once that important formality is completed, you can file the divisional application in the name of the new proprietor

These actions can be completed before your scheduled meeting with Cervantes (EP1 will grant before the date of your meeting). You will then command the patent rights for this flap technology. This again gives you a psychological edge for your meeting. You can explain to Cervantes that you now own the patent rights in Europe to the flap technology. (He will no doubt be upset and shocked to learn that he has paid EUR5 Million for EP2 only to find that it is only so much waste paper!) In the event that things do not go according to plan with Cervantes, we will file a Spanish translation to get provisional protection in Spain as soon as the divisional is published.

As it is too late to file a US patent application corresponding to EP1 (for the EP2 subject matter), no patent rights exist (as far as we know) for the flap technology in the US. DQWE and MOWE are therefore both free to exploit this technology in the US.

1–221

### 3. What is the situation concerning the dimples and the equivalent knobs?

Both EP3 and EP4 are entitled to the filing date of July 4$^{th}$ 2002. EP3 is not prior art to EP4, despite having been filed some hours earlier. Even though it is possible to know that EP3 was filed before EP4, it is still not prior art. Because EP3 and EP4 have the same date of filing, neither one is prior art to the other under Art.54 (3).

Prior art is what exists the day before the filing date (or priority date if claimed). Any disclosure on the day of filing is not prior art. Hence the disclosure at the wedding, also on July 4$^{th}$, is not prior art. Thus, given that no other relevant citations have been found, it is likely that both EP3 and EP4 could lead to granted patents for the dimple technology.

However, from your letter, it seems clear that in fact Cervantes got the idea for "his" dimples invention from your disclosure to him at the wedding. If that is the situation, then Cervantes is not entitled to be granted a patent to that invention. In order to achieve this result it will be necessary to bring what is called an entitlement action before a Spanish Court. You could rely on testimony or possibly a statement from any of the other guests who were with you and Cervantes when you explained the dimple technology if they can remember the incident.

As for the protrusions part of EP4, it depends upon the view of the Court hearing the entitlement action as to whether or not they consider that to be the same invention as the dimples. If they find in your favour for the dimples but not for the knobs, it would be worth trying to get the EPO to require a disclaimer to dimples in the claims to the wings with knobs. Such a request might not succeed – as it is without a precedent as far as I know, but it would be worth trying. The reason for seeking such a limitation is that the equivalence between knobs and dimples may mean that a court might find that a wing with dimples infringes a claim to a wing with knobs. In other words, there is a potential risk that EP4 even if limited to the use of knobs could be used to prevent your selling wings with dimples. But on the same basis, there is a chance (and rather stronger given Cervantes' bad behaviour) that EP3 could be used in some European jurisdictions to prevent DQWE from making or selling wings with knobs. As you probably appreciate, the uncertainties here provide a reason to at least consider tying to agree a cross licence covering EP3 and EP4.

**4. If hostile actions become unavoidable, I would prefer to remain anonymous: what are the options?**

If DQWE do buy EP2 you would be well advised to oppose the grant of EP2. While this cannot be done anonymously, it does not have to be done in your name. I could file such an opposition in my own name at your expense.

If you were to seek entitlement in respect of EP4, you would have to disclose your name and involvement at the outset of proceedings.

# PART B

## Guide to the Law under the European Patent Convention

## Table of Articles and Rules of the European Patent Convention

*(References are to paragraph numbers in Part B only)*

### Articles
**1970 European Patent Convention**

| | |
|---|---|
| Art.1 | 2–001 |
| Arts.2–6 | 2–334 |
| Art.2(1) | 2–001 |
| Art.2(2) | 2–272 |
| Art.3 | 2–080, 2–081 |
| Art.4(1) | 2–002 |
| Art.4(2) | 2–003 |
| Art.4(3) | 2–004 |
| Art.5(1) | 2–004 |
| Art.5(3) | 2–004, 2–061 |
| Art.6 | 2–201 |
| Art.6(1) | 2–005 |
| Art.7 | 2–005 |
| Art.10 | 2–081 |
| Art.10(1) | 2–006 |
| Art.10(2) | 2–006, 2–061, 2–201, 2–450 |
| Art.10(2)(a) | 2–006, 2–061 |
| Art.10(3) | 2–006, 2–450 |
| Art.11 | 2–006 |
| Art.11(1) | 2–007 |
| Art.11(2) | 2–007 |
| Art.11(3) | 2–007 |
| Art.11(4) | 2–007 |
| Art.12 | 2–008 |
| Art.13(1) | 2–009 |
| Art.13(2) | 2–009 |
| Art.14(1) | 2–120, 2–134, 2–358, 2–359 |
| Art.14(2) | 2–044, 2–117, 2–121, 2–123, 2–134, 2–138, 2–206, 2–316, 2–359, 2–360, 2–362, 2–434 |
| Art.14(3) | 2–360, 2–361, 2–441 |
| Art.14(4) | 2–175, 2–206, 2–213, 2–250, 2–362, 2–394 |
| Art.14(5) | 2–206, 2–213, 2–250, 2–362 |
| Art.14(6) | 2–165, 2–365 |
| Art.14(7) | 2–195, 2–365 |
| Art.14(8) | 2–365, 2–446, 2–447 |
| Art.14(9) | 2–365 |
| Art.15 | 2–010 |
| Art.16 | 2–012 |
| Art.17 | 2–013 |
| Art.18 | 2–014 |
| Art.18(1) | 2–014 |
| Art.18(2) | 2–014 |
| Art.19(1) | 2–015 |
| Art.19(2) | 2–015 |
| Art.20 | 2–300, 2–341 |
| Art.20(1) | 2–016 |
| Art.20(2) | 2–016 |
| Art.21(1) | 2–017 |
| Art.21(2) | 2–017 |
| Art.21(3) | 2–017 |
| Art.21(3)(a) | 2–017 |
| Art.21(3)(b) | 2–017 |
| Art.21(3)(c) | 2–017 |
| Art.21(4) | 2–017 |
| Art.22(1) | 2–019, 2–269 |
| Art.22(2) | 2–019 |
| Art.23(1) | 2–020 |
| Art.23(2) | 2–020 |
| Art.23(3) | 2–020 |
| Art.23(4) | 2–021, 2–420 |
| Art.24 | 2–014, 2–015 |
| Art.24(1) | 2–022 |
| Art.24(2) | 2–022 |
| Art.24(3) | 2–022 |
| Art.24(4) | 2–022 |
| Art.25 | 2–288 |
| Art.31 | 2–367 |
| Art.31(1) | 2–366 |
| Art.31(2) | 2–366 |
| Art.32 | 2–367 |
| Art.33 | 2–131 |
| Art.33(1) | 2–177 |
| Art.33(2)(d) | 2–456 |
| Art.33(3) | 2–014 |
| Art.36(3) | 2–203 |
| Art.36(5) | 2–203 |
| Art.39(2) | 2–453 |
| Art.39(4) | 2–453 |
| Art.41 | 2–453 |
| Art.47 | 2–453 |
| Art.51 | 2–457 |
| Arts.52–57 | 2–282, 2–317 |
| Art.52 | 2–023 |
| Art.52(1) | 2–023, 2–036, 2–254 |
| Art.52(2)–(3) | 2–024, 2–025, 2–026, 2–027, 2–028, 2–029, 2–030, 2–031, 2–038 |
| Art.52(2) | 2–023, 2–254 |
| Art.52(2)(c) | 2–023 |
| Art.52(4) | 2–038, 2–041, 2–048, 2–320 |
| Art.53(a) | 2–032 |
| Art.53(b) | 2–033, 2–034, 2–035 |
| Art.54 | 2–023, 2–051, 2–052, 2–254 |
| Art.54(1)–(4) | 2–048 |
| Art.54(1) | 2–023, 2–042, 2–050 |
| Art.54(2) | 2–043, 2–051, 2–113, 2–317 |
| Art.54(3) | 2–044, 2–051, 2–054, 2–096, 2–104, 2–113, 2–180, 2–317, 2–435 |
| Art.54(4) | 2–044, 2–317 |
| Art.54(5) | 2–048, 2–049 |
| Art.55(1) | 2–051 |
| Art.55(1)(a) | 2–051 |
| Art.55(1)(b) | 2–052 |

| | |
|---|---|
| Art.55(2) | 2–052 |
| Art.55(c) | 2–206 |
| Art.56 | 2–023, 2–054 |
| Art.57 | 2–023, 2–037 |
| Art.58 | 2–060, 3–343 |
| Art.59 | 2–060 |
| Art.60(1) | 2–282, 2–333, 2–334, 2–238 |
| Art.60(2) | 2–113, 2–333 |
| Art.60(3) | 2–333 |
| Art.61 | 2–070, 2–075, 2–132, 2–204, 2–282, 2–300, 2–339, 2–340 |
| Art.61(1) | 2–136, 2–339, 2–442 |
| Art.61(1)(a) | 2–339 |
| Art.61(1)(b) | 2–063, 2–083, 2–111, 2–121, 2–335, 2–339, 2–386, 2–438 |
| Art.61(1)(c) | 2–339 |
| Art.61(2) | 2–136, 2–339 |
| Art.61(3) | 2–301, 2–339 |
| Art.62 | 2–331 |
| Art.63 | 2–051 |
| Art.63(1) | 2–276 |
| Art.63(2) | 2–276 |
| Art.63(2)(b) | 2–276 |
| Art.63(3) | 2–276, 2–464 |
| Art.63(4) | 2–276 |
| Art.64 | 2–271, 2–274, 2–374 |
| Art.64(1) | 2–272 |
| Art.64(2) | 2–033, 2–272, 2–275 |
| Art.64(3) | 2–272 |
| Art.65(1) | 2–188, 2–232, 2–273 |
| Art.65(2) | 2–273, 2–434 |
| Art.65(3) | 2–273 |
| Art.66 | 2–269, 2–278, 2–279, 2–286 |
| Art.67 | 2–271, 2–274 |
| Art.67(1) | 2–271 |
| Art.67(2) | 2–271 |
| Art.67(3) | 2–271, 2–434 |
| Art.67(4) | 2–145, 2–271, 2–374 |
| Art.68 | 2–274 |
| Art.69 | 2–177, 2–275, 2–319, 2–367 |
| Art.69(1) | 2–275 |
| Art.69(2) | 2–233, 2–275, 2–417 |
| Art.70 | 2–287 |
| Art.70(1) | 2–360, 2–434 |
| Art.70(2) | 2–121, 2–316, 2–434 |
| Art.70(3) | 2–434 |
| Art.70(4) | 2–434 |
| Art.71 | 2–388 |
| Art.72 | 2–389 |
| Art.72(1) | 2–051 |
| Art.73 | 2–390 |
| Art.74 | 2–391, 2–454 |
| Art.75 | 2–051, 2–066, 2–157, 2–184, 2–194 |
| Art.75(1) | 2–006, 2–061, 2–064, 2–073, 2–201 |
| Art.75(1)(a) | 2–005, 2–294 |
| Art.75(1)(b) | 2–133, 2–293, 2–294, 2–295 |
| Art.75(2) | 2–064, 2–201, 2–448 |
| Art.75(2)(b) | 2–293, 2–294, 2–295 |
| Art.75(3) | 2–062, 2–464 |
| Art.76 | 2–125 |
| Art.76(1) | 2–051, 2–062, 2–070, 2–123, 2–132, 2–136, 2–339 |
| Art.76(2) | 2–080 |
| Art.76(3) | 2–070, 2–123, 2–128, 2–301 |
| Art.77(1) | 2–065 |
| Art.77(2) | 2–065 |
| Art.77(3) | 2–065, 2–299, 2–339 |
| Art.77(4) | 2–065 |
| Art.77(5) | 2–065, 2–125, 2–127, 2–277, 2–279, 2–295, 2–339 |
| Art.78(1)(a) | 2–072 |
| Art.78(1)(b) | 2–089 |
| Art.78(1)(c) | 2–093 |
| Art.78(1)(d) | 2–105, 2–147 |
| Art.78(1)(e) | 2–104 |
| Art.78(2) | 2–051, 2–125, 2–301, 2–302 |
| Art.78(3) | 2–071 |
| Art.79 | 2–081 |
| Art.79(1) | 2–080 |
| Art.79(2) | 2–044, 2–080, 2–126, 2–134, 2–145, 2–301 |
| Art.79(3) | 2–080, 2–126, 2–374, 2–376 |
| Art.80 | 2–120, 2–134, 2–324 |
| Art.80(d) | 2–134 |
| Art.81 | 2–077, 2–115, 2–145 |
| Art.82 | 2–101, 2–232 |
| Art.83 | 2–090, 2–091, 2–128 |
| Art.84 | 2–094, 2–095, 2–221, 2–317 |
| Art.85 | 2–044, 2–104 |
| Art.86(1) | 2–128, 2–381, 2–382 |
| Art.86(2) | 2–290, 2–302, 2–383, 2–385 |
| Art.86(3) | 2–253, 2–384 |
| Art.86(4) | 2–285, 2–318, 2–381 |
| Arts 87–89 | 2–109 |
| Art.87(1)–(4) | 2–110, 2–301 |
| Art.87(1) | 2–107, 2–108, 2–109, 2–110 |
| Art.87(2) | 2–110 |
| Art.87(3) | 2–110 |
| Art.87(4) | 2–110 |
| Art.87(5) | 2–110 |
| Art.88 | 2–109 |
| Art.88(1) | 2–111 |
| Art.88(2) | 2–112 |
| Art.88(3) | 2–109 |
| Art.88(4) | 2–109 |
| Art.89 | 2–043, 2–044, 2–113, 2–333 |
| Art.90(1) | 2–051, 2–125, 2–127 |
| Art.90(1)(a) | 2–134 |
| Art.90(1)(b) | 2–137 |
| Art.90(1)(c) | 2–138 |
| Art.90(2) | 2–135 |
| Art.90(3) | 2–121, 2–137, 2–138, 2–139, 2–150 |
| Art.91(1) | 2–139 |
| Art.91(1)(a) | 2–140 |
| Art.91(1)(b) | 2–141 |
| Art.91(1)(c) | 2–142 |
| Art.91(1)(d) | 2–143, 2–144, 2–299 |
| Art.91(1)(e) | 2–145 |
| Art.91(1)(f) | 2–115, 2–146 |
| Art.91(1)(g) | 2–147 |
| Art.91(2) | 2–140, 2–141, 2–142, 2–143, 2–144, 2–145, |

|  |  |
|---|---|
| | 2–146, 2–147 |
| Art.91(3) | 2–067, 2–140, 2–141, 2–142, 2–143, 2–144, 2–189, 2–417 |
| Art.91(4) | 2–145 |
| Art.91(5) | 2–146 |
| Art.91(6) | 2–147 |
| Art.92(1) | 2–150, 2–152 |
| Art.92(2) | 2–161 |
| Art.93 | 2–044, 2–166, 2–271, 2–275, 2–333, 2–438, 2–447, 2–458 |
| Art.93(1) | 2–163 |
| Art.93(2) | 2–166 |
| Art.93(4) | 2–195 |
| Art.94 | 2–177 |
| Art.94(1) | 2–169 |
| Art.94(2) | 2–168, 2–170, 2–171, 2–301 |
| Art.94(3) | 2–168, 2–172 |
| Art.95 | 2–177 |
| Art.95(1) | 2–177 |
| Art.95(2) | 2–177 |
| Art.95(3) | 2–177 |
| Art.95(4) | 2–177 |
| Art.96(1) | 2–012, 2–160, 2–176 |
| Art.96(2) | 2–178, 2–298, 2–406 |
| Art.96(3) | 2–176, 2–178 |
| Art.97(1) | 2–186, 2–191, 2–255 |
| Art.97(2) | 2–187, 2–193, 2–194 |
| Art.97(2)(b) | 2–194 |
| Art.97(3) | 2–189 |
| Art.97(4) | 2–194 |
| Art.97(5) | 2–187, 2–189, 2–194 |
| Art.97(6) | 2–194 |
| Art.98 | 2–195, 2–458 |
| Art.99 | 2–199, 2–202, 2–225 |
| Art.99(1) | 2–200, 2–201, 2–202, 2–203, 2–205, 2–210, 2–213 |
| Art.99(2) | 2–215 |
| Art.99(3) | 2–207 |
| Art.99(4) | 2–216 |
| Art.99(5) | 2–217, 2–228, 2–340, 2–435 |
| Art.100 | 2–204, 2–214, 2–220, 2–221, 2–225, 2–230, 2–231, 2–254 |
| Art.100a | 2–204, 2–254 |
| Art.100c | 2–254, 2–320 |
| Art.101(1) | 2–208, 2–220 |
| Art.101(2) | 2–220 |
| Art.102(1) | 2–230 |
| Art.102(2) | 2–231 |
| Art.102(3) | 2–221, 2–232, 2–233, 2–234 |
| Art.102(4) | 2–233 |
| Art.102(5) | 2–233 |
| Art.103 | 2–234, 2–458 |
| Art.104(1) | 2–235 |
| Art.104(2) | 2–015, 2–236, 2–237 |
| Art.104(3) | 2–238 |
| Art.105 | 2–214 |
| Art.105(1) | 2–213 |
| Art.105(2) | 2–214 |
| Arts.106–108 | 2–251, 2–408 |
| Art.106 | 2–256 |
| Art.106(1) | 2–154, 2–243, 2–244 |
| Art.106(2) | 2–243 |
| Art.106(3) | 2–232, 2–243, 2–414 |
| Art.106(4) | 2–239, 2–243 |
| Art.106(5) | 2–239, 2–243 |
| Art.107 | 2–214, 2–245 |
| Art.107(2) | 2–256 |
| Art.108 | 2–214, 2–245, 2–246, 2–248, 2–249, 2–251 |
| Art.109(1) | 2–252 |
| Art.109(2) | 2–252 |
| Art.110(1) | 2–251, 2–253 |
| Art.110(2) | 2–253 |
| Art.110(3) | 2–253 |
| Art.111(2) | 2–264 |
| Art.112 | 2–019, 2–269 |
| Art.112(1) | 2–269 |
| Art.112(1)(a) | 2–269 |
| Art.112(2) | 2–269 |
| Art.112(3) | 2–269 |
| Art.113(1) | 2–178, 2–220, 2–232, 2–252, 2–267, 2–314, 2–406 |
| Art.113(2) | 2–181, 2–192, 2–232, 2–252, 2–267, 2–322, 2–407, 2–419 |
| Art.114(1) | 2–225, 2–254, 2–394, 2–415 |
| Art.114(2) | 2–203, 2–416, 2–420 |
| Art.115(1) | 2–202, 2–394 |
| Art.115(2) | 2–394 |
| Art.116 | 2–363, 2–418, 2–422 |
| Art.116(1) | 2–417 |
| Art.116(2) | 2–417 |
| Art.116(3) | 2–421 |
| Art.116(4) | 2–421 |
| Art.117 | 2–422 |
| Art.117(1) | 2–424 |
| Art.117(2) | 2–429 |
| Art.117(3) | 2–426 |
| Art.117(4) | 2–427, 2–428 |
| Art.117(5) | 2–427, 2–428 |
| Art.117(6) | 2–428 |
| Art.118 | 2–044, 2–217, 2–284, 2–421, 2–435 |
| Art.119 | 2–395, 2–402, 2–404, 2–412 |
| Art.120 | 2–290, 2–291, 2–292, 2–294, 2–295, 2–296 |
| Art.121 | 2–176, 2–178, 2–189, 2–253, 2–264, 2–464 |
| Art.121(1) | 2–298 |
| Art.121(2) | 2–298 |
| Art.122 | 2–127, 2–176, 2–178, 2–189, 2–246, 2–249, 2–253, 2–264, 2–301, 2–306, 2–464 |
| Art.122(1) | 2–299, 2–300, 2–305 |
| Art.122(2) | 2–301, 2–302 |
| Art.122(3) | 2–303 |
| Art.122(4) | 2–303 |
| Art.122(5) | 2–108, 2–125, 2–126, 2–128, 2–170, 2–301, 2–339 |
| Art.122(6) | 2–305 |
| Art.122(7) | 2–306 |
| Art.123(1) | 2–162, 2–178, 2–312, 2–313, 2–314 |
| Art.123(2) | 2–120, 2–254, 2–316, 2–317, 2–320, 2–323, 2–324 |
| Art.123(3) | 2–221, 2–256, 2–319 |

| | |
|---|---|
| Art.124 | 2–286 |
| Art.124(1) | 2–185, 2–266 |
| Art.124(2) | 2–185, 2–266 |
| Art.125 | 2–014, 2–436 |
| Art.126(1) | 2–437 |
| Art.126(2) | 2–437 |
| Art.126(3) | 2–437 |
| Art.127 | 2–392, 2–438, 2–439, 2–440 |
| Art.128 | 2–444, 2–448 |
| Art.128(1) | 2–442 |
| Art.128(2) | 2–442 |
| Art.128(3) | 2–442 |
| Art.128(4) | 2–443 |
| Art.128(5) | 2–115, 2–442 |
| Art.129 | 2–446, 2–447, 2–458 |
| Art.129(a) | 2–374 |
| Art.130(1) | 2–448 |
| Art.130(2) | 2–448 |
| Art.130(2)(a) | 2–448 |
| Art.130(2)(b) | 2–448 |
| Art.130(2)(c) | 2–448 |
| Art.130(3) | 2–448 |
| Art.131(1) | 2–448 |
| Art.131(2) | 2–426, 2–427, 2–428, 2–448 |
| Art.132(1) | 2–448 |
| Art.132(2) | 2–051, 2–448 |
| Art.133(1) | 2–342 |
| Art.133(2) | 2–140, 2–308, 2–342, 2–343 |
| Art.133(3) | 2–342 |
| Art.133(4) | 2–343 |
| Art.134 | 2–202, 2–307, 2–438 |
| Art.134(1) | 2–342, 2–343, 2–345, 2–422 |
| Art.134(2) | 2–346 |
| Art.134(2)(a) | 2–346 |
| Art.134(3) | 2–346 |
| Art.134(4) | 2–342, 2–343, 2–345 |
| Art.134(5) | 2–345 |
| Art.134(6) | 2–346, 2–349 |
| Art.134(7) | 2–342, 2–343, 2–345, 2–346, 2–422 |
| Art.134(8)>2–347, 2–348 | |
| Art.134(8)(c) | 2–017, 2–346, 2–349 |
| Arts.135–137 | 2–286 |
| Art.135 | 2–065, 2–438 |
| Art.135(1) | 2–277 |
| Art.135(1)(b) | 2–277 |
| Art.135(2) | 2–278 |
| Art.136 | 2–280, 2–281 |
| Art.136(1) | 2–279, 2–464 |
| Art.136(2) | 2–279 |
| Art.137(1) | 2–280 |
| Art.137(2) | 2–280 |
| Art.138(1) | 2–282 |
| Art.138(2) | 2–283 |
| Art.139 | 2–282, 2–286 |
| Art.139(1) | 2–284 |
| Art.139(2) | 2–284, 2–435 |
| Art.139(3) | 2–284 |
| Art.140 | 2–184, 2–270, 2–277, 2–284, 2–286, 2–464 |
| Art.141(1) | 2–285 |
| Art.141(2) | 2–285 |
| Arts.142–149 | 2–449 |
| Art.142 | 2–276, 2–449 |
| Art.142(1) | 2–449 |
| Art.142(2) | 2–449 |
| Art.143 | 2–453 |
| Art.143(1) | 2–450 |
| Art.143(2) | 2–450, 2–451, 2–452 |
| Art.144 | 2–451 |
| Art.145(1) | 2–452 |
| Art.145(2) | 2–452 |
| Art.146 | 2–453 |
| Art.148(1) | 2–454 |
| Art.148(2) | 2–454 |
| Art.149 | 2–455 |
| Art.149(1) | 2–080, 2–455 |
| Art.149(2) | 2–455 |
| Art.153(1) | –455 |
| Art.158 | 2–044 |
| Art.160(2) | 2–019 |
| Art.162(4) | 2–277 |
| Art.163(1) | 2–349 |
| Art.163(1)(b) | 2–346 |
| Art.163(7) | 2–346, 2–348 |
| Art.164(1) | 2–275, 2–367 |
| Art.164(2) | 2–020, 2–367, 2–420 |
| Art.167(2) | 2–178, 2–192 |
| Art.177(1) | 2–357 |
| Art.177(2) | 2–357 |

**Rules**

| | |
|---|---|
| r.1(1) | 2–121, 2–206, 2–210, 2–250, 2–251, 2–362, 2–393 |
| r.1(3) | 2–362 |
| r.2(1) | 2–363 |
| r.2(2) | 2–363 |
| r.2(3) | 2–363 |
| r.2(4) | 2–363 |
| r.2(5) | 2–363 |
| r.2(6) | 2–363 |
| r.4 | 2–123 |
| r.5 | 2–364 |
| r.6(1) | 2–121 |
| r.6(2) | 2–362 |
| r.6(3) | 2–121, 2–125, 2–175, 2–206, 2–250, 2–362 |
| r.7 | 2–121 |
| r.8 | 2–010 |
| r.8(1) | 2–156 |
| r.8(2) | 2–156 |
| r.9(1) | 2–010 |
| r.9(2) | 2–012, 2–013, 2–014, 2–015, 2–016 |
| r.9(3) | 2–014, 2–015, 2–017 |
| r.9(4) | 2–015, 2–236 |
| r.10 | 3–246 |
| r.10(1) | 2–018 |
| r.10(2)–(5) | 2–018 |
| r.10(3) | 2–017, 21 |
| r.10(6) | 2–017 |
| r.11(1)–(3) | 3–246 |
| r.11(1) | 2–019 |

## Table of Articles and Rules of the European Patent Convention 349

|  |  |
|---|---|
| r.11(2) | 2–019, 2–021 |
| r.11(3) | 2–019 |
| r.12(1) | 2–011 |
| r.12(2) | 2–011 |
| r.12(3) | 2–011 |
| r.13 | 2–438 |
| r.13(1) | 2–335, 2–235 |
| r.13(2) | 2–335, 2–336 |
| r.13(3) | 2–335, 2–336 |
| r.13(4) | 2–217, 2–336 |
| r.13(5) | 2–337 |
| r.14 | 2–141, 2–338, 2–374, 2–376 |
| r.14(2) | 2–250 |
| r.15 | 2–125, 2–329, 2–339, 2–340 |
| r.15(1) | 2–339, 2–340 |
| r.15(2) | 2–145, 2–339 |
| r.15(3) | 2–065, 2–339 |
| r.16 | 2–339 |
| r.16(1) | 2–340 |
| r.16(2) | 2–340, 2–435 |
| r.16(3) | 2–225, 2–340, 2–435 |
| r.17 | 2–146, 2–330 |
| r.17(1) | 2–077, 2–115 |
| r.17(2) | 2–115 |
| r.17(3) | 2–115 |
| r.17(4) | 2–115 |
| r.18(1) | 2–166, 2–195, 2–332, 2–438, 2–443 |
| r.18(2) | 2–166, 2–195, 2–332 |
| r.19 | 2–301 |
| r.19(1) | 2–330 |
| r.19(2) | 2–330 |
| r.19(3) | 2–330 |
| r.20 | 2–075, 2–240, 2–245, 2–393 |
| r.20(1) | 2–392 |
| r.20(2) | 2–392 |
| r.20(3) | 2–070, 2–132, 2–392 |
| r.21(1) | 2–393 |
| r.21(2) | 2–393 |
| r.22(1) | 2–393 |
| r.22(2) | 2–393 |
| r.23 | 2–052 |
| r.23a | 2–044 |
| r.23b(4) | 2–033 |
| r.23b(5) | 2–035 |
| r.23b(6) | 2–035 |
| r.23c(a) | 2–024 |
| r.23c(b) | 2–033, 2–034 |
| r.23d | 2–032 |
| r.23e(1) | 2–024 |
| r.23e(2) | 2–024 |
| r.23e(3) | 2–091 |
| r.24(1) | 2–061, 2–066, 2–067, 2–068, 2–111, 2–213, 2–351, 2–368, 2–369 |
| r.24(2) | 2–133 |
| r.24(3) | 2–133 |
| r.24(4) | 2–133 |
| r.25 | 2–339 |
| r.25(1) | 2–070, 2–299 |
| r.25(2) | 2–128, 2–145 |
| rr.26–36 | 2–203, 2–222 |
| r.26(1) | 2–073 |
| r.26(2) | 2–143 |
| r.26(2)(a) | 2–074 |
| r.26(2)(b) | 2–078, 2–148 |
| r.26(2)(c) | 2–075, 2–203, 2–247, 2–432 |
| r.26(2)(d) | 2–076 |
| r.26(2)(e) | 2–082 |
| r.26(2)(f) | 2–083 |
| r.26(2)(g) | 2–079, 2–111 |
| r.26(2)(h) | 2–080 |
| r.26(2)(i) | 2–086 |
| r.26(2)(j) | 2–087 |
| r.26(2)(k) | 2–077, 2–115 |
| r.26(3) | 2–076 |
| r.27 | 2–371 |
| r.27a | 2–091, 2–130 |
| r.27a(1)–(3) | 2–141 |
| r.27(1) | 2–023, 2–091, 2–092 |
| r.27(1)(b) | 2–091 |
| r.27(1)(d) | 2–055 |
| r.27(1)(e) | 2–091 |
| r.27(2) | 2–092 |
| r.28 | 2–090, 2–131 |
| r.28a | 2–131 |
| r.28(1)(c) | 2–131 |
| r.28(2)(a) | 2–131 |
| r.29 | 2–371 |
| r.29(1) | 2–023, 2–096 |
| r.29(2) | 2–097 |
| r.29(2)(a) | 2–097 |
| r.29(2)(b) | 2–097 |
| r.29(2)(c) | 2–097 |
| r.29(3) | 2–097 |
| r.29(4) | 2–097 |
| r.29(5) | 2–097, 2–098 |
| r.29(6) | 2–099 |
| r.29(7) | 2–100 |
| r.30(1) | 2–023, 2–101 |
| r.30(2) | 2–101 |
| r.31(1) | 2–127, 2–128 |
| r.31(1)(a) | 2–149 |
| r.31(2) | 2–127 |
| r.32 | 2–105, 2–371 |
| r.32(1)–(2) | 2–141 |
| r.32j | 2–120 |
| r.33 | 2–371 |
| r.33(1) | 2–104 |
| r.33(2) | 2–104 |
| r.33(3) | 2–104 |
| r.33(4) | 2–084, 2–104, 2–166 |
| r.33(5) | 2–104 |
| r.34 | 2–371 |
| r.34(1) | 2–116 |
| r.34(1)(a) | 2–167 |
| r.34(1)(b) | 2–167 |
| r.34(2) | 2–116, 2–167 |
| r.34(3) | 2–167 |
| r.35 | 2–371 |
| r.35(1) | 2–117, 2–121 |
| r.35(2)–(11) | 2–141 |

| | |
|---|---|
| r.35(2)–(14) | 2–371 |
| r.35(2) | 2–118 |
| r.35(3)–(14) | 2–119 |
| r.36(1) | 2–371 |
| r.36(2) | 2–141, 2–369, 2–371 |
| r.36(3) | 2–213, 2–369, 2–372 |
| r.36(4) | 2–141, 2–369, 2–373 |
| r.36(5) | 2–213, 2–369 |
| r.37(1) | 2–285, 2–382 |
| r.37(2) | 2–383 |
| r.37(3) | 2–385 |
| r.37(4) | 2–339, 2–386 |
| r.38a | 2–111 |
| r.38(1) | 2–111 |
| r.38(2) | 2–111 |
| r.38(3) | 2–111, 2–299 |
| r.38(4) | 2–111 |
| r.38(5) | 2–111, 2–158, 2–188 |
| r.38(6) | 2–111, 2–166, 2–195 |
| r.39 | 2–135 |
| r.40 | 2–141 |
| r.41(1) | 2–086, 2–140, 2–141, 2–142, 2–143, 2–144, 2–146 |
| r.41(2) | 2–144 |
| r.41(3) | 2–144 |
| r.42 | 2–146 |
| r.43 | 2–147 |
| r.43(1) | 2–147 |
| r.43(2) | 2–147 |
| r.43(3) | 2–147 |
| r.44 | 2–158 |
| r.44a(1) | 2–160 |
| r.44a(2) | 2–160, 2–166 |
| r.44(1) | 2–151, 2–158 |
| r.44(2) | 2–158 |
| r.44(3) | 2–158 |
| r.44(4) | 2–158 |
| r.44(5) | 2–159 |
| r.44(6) | 2–158 |
| r.45(1) | 2–153 |
| r.46 | 2–154 |
| r.46(1) | 2–154, 2–318 |
| r.47(1) | 2–155 |
| r.47(2) | 2–161 |
| r.48 | 2–164, 2–195 |
| r.48(1) | 2–164, 2–195 |
| r.48(2) | 2–164, 2–195 |
| r.49 | 2–195 |
| r.49(1) | 2–165, 2–166, 2–234 |
| r.49(2) | 2–165, 2–234 |
| r.49(3) | 2–165 |
| r.50(1) | 2–126, 2–168, 2–170 |
| r.50(2) | 2–126, 2–168, 2–170 |
| r.51 | 2–371 |
| r.51(1) | 2–176, 2–178 |
| r.51(2) | 2–160, 2–178 |
| r.51(3) | 2–178 |
| r.51(4) | 2–111, 2–160, 2–188, 2–188, 2–189, 2–190, 2–191, 2–192, 2–193, 2–194, 2–197, 2–328, 2–407, 2–438 |
| r.51(5) | 2–190, 2–191 |
| r.51(6) | 2–191, 2–191 |
| r.51(7) | 2–188 |
| r.51(8) | 2–189 |
| r.51(8)(a) | 2–193 |
| r.51(9) | 2–193 |
| r.51(10) | 2–188 |
| r.51(11) | 2–193 |
| r.52 | 2–196 |
| r.53 | 2–195 |
| r.54 | 2–197, 2–234 |
| r.55 | 2–202, 2–203 |
| r.55(a) | 2–202 |
| r.55(c) | 2–203, 2–209, 2–210, 2–225, 2–254 |
| r.56(1) | 2–210, 2–211 |
| r.56(2) | 2–211 |
| r.56(3) | 2–212 |
| r.57(1) | 2–219, 2–220, 2–221 |
| r.57(2) | 2–219 |
| r.57(3) | 2–219 |
| r.57a | 2–221, 2–321 |
| r.58 | 2–232 |
| r.58(1) | 2–220 |
| r.58(2) | 2–220, 2–221 |
| r.58(3) | 2–220 |
| r.58(4) | 2–223, 2–232, 2–233 |
| r.58(5) | 2–197, 2–232, 2–233 |
| r.58(6) | 2–197, 2–233 |
| r.58(7) | 2–233 |
| r.58(8) | 2–232 |
| r.59 | 2–222 |
| r.60(1) | 2–224 |
| r.60(2) | 2–223, 2–241, 2–268 |
| r.61 | 2–240, 2–392 |
| r.61a | 2–203, 2–222 |
| r.62 | 2–234 |
| r.62a | 2–234 |
| r.63(1) | 2–235 |
| r.63(2) | 2–236 |
| r.63(3) | 2–237 |
| r.63(4) | 2–237 |
| r.64 | 2–247 |
| r.64a | 2–251 |
| r.64b | 2–251 |
| r.65(1) | 2–251 |
| r.65(2) | 2–251 |
| r.66(1) | 2–253, 2–256 |
| r.66(2) | 2–265, 2–408 |
| r.67 | 2–252, 2–267 |
| r.68(1) | 2–264, 2–407 |
| r.68(2) | 2–408 |
| r.69(1) | 2–070, 2–233, 2–403, 2–410 |
| r.69(2) | 2–410 |
| r.70(1) | 2–405, 2–411 |
| r.70(2) | 2–405, 2–411 |
| r.71 | 2–418, 2–420, 2–420 |
| r.71(1) | 2–418 |
| r.71a | 2–420 |
| r.71a(1) | 2–416, 2–420 |
| r.71a(2) | 2–416, 2–420 |

| | | | |
|---|---|---|---|
| r.71(2) | 2–418, 2–419 | r.85(4) | 2–297 |
| r.72 | 2–235 | r.85(5) | 2–296 |
| r.72(1) | 2–426 | r.86(1) | 2–312 |
| r.72(2) | 2–427 | r.86(2) | 2–162, 2–166, 2–313 |
| r.72(3) | 2–427, 2–428 | r.86(3) | 2–181, 2–191, 2–192, 2–314 |
| r.72(4) | 2–427 | r.86(4) | 2–204, 2–318 |
| r.73(1) | 2–430 | r.87 | 2–044, 2–220, 2–284, 2–435 |
| r.73(2) | 2–430 | r.88 | 2–017, 2–081, 2–114, 2–126, 2–134, 2–166, 2–322, 2–323, 2–324, 2–325, 2–326, 2–374 |
| r.73(3) | 2–430 | | |
| r.73(4) | 2–430 | r.89 | 2–017, 2–193, 2–326, 2–328, 2–409, 2–413 |
| r.74(1) | 2–431 | r.90 | 2–302, 2–438 |
| r.74(2)–(4) | 2–427, 2–431 | r.90(1) | 2–307 |
| r.74(2) | 2–431 | r.90(1)(a) | 2–308 |
| r.74(3) | 2–431 | r.90(1)(b) | 2–308 |
| r.74(4) | 2–431 | r.90(1)(c) | 2–308 |
| r.75(1) | 2–432 | r.90(2) | 2–308 |
| r.75(2) | 2–432 | r.90(3) | 2–308 |
| r.75(3) | 2–432 | r.90(4) | 2–309 |
| r.75(4) | 2–432 | r.91 | 2–437 |
| r.76(1) | 2–423, 2–433 | r.92(1) | 2–438 |
| r.76(2) | 2–423, 2–433 | r.92(2) | 2–438, 2–438 |
| r.76(3) | 2–423, 2–433 | r.92(3) | 2–440 |
| r.76(4) | 2–423, 2–433 | r.92(m) | 2–374 |
| r.77(1) | 2–396 | r.93 | 2–443, 2–444 |
| r.77(2)(a) | 2–398 | r.93a | 2–022 |
| r.77(2)(b) | 2–399 | r.93d | 2–443 |
| r.77(2)(c) | 2–400 | r.94 | 2–444 |
| r.77(2)(d) | 2–401 | r.94(1) | 2–444 |
| r.77(3) | 2–402 | r.94(2) | 2–444 |
| r.78 | 2–397 | r.95 | 2–444 |
| r.78(1) | 2–398, 2–400 | r.95a | 2–445 |
| r.78(2) | 2–290, 2–398 | r.95a(1) | 2–445 |
| r.78(3) | 2–398 | r.96(1) | 2–442 |
| r.78(4) | 2–398 | r.96(2) | 2–166, 2–447 |
| r.79 | 2–399 | r.97 | 2–4498 |
| r.80 | 2–400 | r.98(1) | 2–444 |
| r.80(1) | 2–400 | r.98(2) | 2–448 |
| r.80(2) | 2–400 | r.98(3) | 2–448 |
| r.81(1) | 2–397 | r.99 | 2–426, 2–427, 2–428, 2–448 |
| r.81(2) | 2–397 | r.100 | 2–245 |
| r.81(3) | 2–397 | r.100(1) | 2–202, 2–213, 2–245, 2–343, 2–344 |
| r.80 | 2–403 | r.100(1) | 2–344 |
| r.83(1) | 2–289 | r.100(4) | 2–202 |
| r.83(2) | 2–290, 2–291 | r.101(1) | 2–351, 2–354 |
| r.83(3) | 2–291 | r.101(2) | 2–352, 2–354 |
| r.83(4) | 2–291 | r.101(3) | 2–352 |
| r.84 | 2–140, 2–141, 2–142, 2–143, 2–144, 2–146, 2–178, 2–292, 2–420 | r.101(4) | 2–353 |
| | | r.101(5) | 2–354 |
| r.84a | 2–108, 2–134, 2–293 | r.101(6) | 2–354 |
| r.84a(1) | 2–293 | r.101(7) | 2–354 |
| r.84a(2) | 2–293 | r.101(8) | 2–355 |
| r.85 | 2–108 | r.101(9) | 2–356, 2–438 |
| r.85a | 2–137, 2–145 | r.102(1) | 2–349 |
| r.85a(1) | 2–125, 2–126, 2–128, 2–339 | r.102(2) | 2–349 |
| r.85a(2) | 2–061, 2–081, 2–126 | r.102(3) | 2–350 |
| r.85b | 2–173, 2–295 | r.103 | 2–281 |
| r.85(1) | 2–061, 2–064, 2–294 | r.107(1) | 2–145 |
| r.85(2) | 2–061, 2–294, 2–295 | r.108 | 2–245 |
| r.85(3) | 2–061, 2–064, 2–294, 2–295 | | |

# 1. Institutional aspects

## Aims of the Contracting States in drafting the European Patent Convention
2–001

The Contracting States, *Preamble*
DESIRING to strengthen co-operation between the States of Europe in respect of the protection of inventions,
DESIRING that such protection may be obtained in those States by a single procedure for the grant of patents and by the establishment of certain standard rules governing patents so granted,
DESIRING, for this purpose, to conclude a Convention which establishes a European Patent Organisation and which constitutes a special agreement within the meaning of Article 19 of the Convention for the Protection of Industrial Property, signed in Paris on 20 March 1883 and last revised on 14 July 1967, and a regional patent treaty within the meaning of Article 45, paragraph 1, of the Patent Cooperation Treaty of 19 June 1970,
HAVE AGREED on the following provisions.

The countries of the Union (as established by the Paris Convention) have the right to make separately between themselves special agreements for the protection of industrial property, as long as these agreements do not contravene the provisions of the Paris Convention. *PCArt.19*

Any treaty providing for the grant of regional patents ("regional patent treaty"), and giving to all persons who, according to Article 9, are entitled to file international applications the right to file applications for such patents, may provide that international applications designating or electing a party to both the regional patent treaty and the present Treaty may be filed as applications for such patents. *PCTArt.45(1)*

The EPC establishes a system of law, common to the Contracting States, for the grant of patents for invention. *Art.1*

Patents granted by virtue of the EPC are called European Patents. *Art.2(1)*

## The European Patent Organisation

### *Formation of the Organisation*
2–002

The EPC establishes a European Patent Organisation, referred to in the EPC as the Organisation. It has administrative and financial autonomy. *Art.4(1)*

### *Structure of the Organisation*
2–003

The organs of the Organisation are: *Art.4(2)*

(a) a European Patent Office;

(b) an Administrative Council.

### *Purpose of the Organisation*
2–004

The task of the Organisation is to grant European Patents. This is carried out by the European Patent Office supervised by the Administrative Council. *Art.4(3)*

| | |
|---|---|
| Art.5(1)(3) | The Organisation has legal personality and is represented by the President of the European Patent Office. |
| Art.6(1) | The Organisation has its seat in Munich. |

**The European Patent Office and its employees**

2–005 *Location of the European patent office and its sub-offices*

| | |
|---|---|
| Art.6(2) | The European Patent Office is based in Munich and has a branch at The Hague. |
| Art.7 | By decision of the Administrative Council, sub-offices of the European Patent Office may be created if need be, for the purpose of information and liaison, in the Contracting States and with inter-governmental organisations in the field of intellectual property, subject to the approval of the Contracting State or organisation concerned. |
| PonC3(a)(b) | A sub-office of the EPO, under the direction of the Hague, is located in Berlin, its duties being determined by the Administrative Council. |
| AnReg | The Berlin sub-office is a filing office within the meaning of Art.75(1)(a) EPC (see AnReg under Art.10(2) – [1989] O.J. 218). |
| AnReg | A sub-office in Vienna was set up in 1991 (see AnReg under Art.7 – [1990] O.J. 492). This is not a filing office within the meaning of Art.75(1)(a) (see An Reg under Art.75 [1992] OJ 183). |

2–006 *President of the European Patent Office and his duties*

| | |
|---|---|
| Art.10(1) | The European Patent Office is directed by the President who is responsible for its activities to the Administrative Council. |
| Art.10(2) | To this end, the President has in particular the following functions and powers: |

    (a) he must take all necessary steps, including the adoption of internal administrative instructions and the publication of guidance for the public, to ensure the functioning of the European Patent Office;

    (b) in so far as the EPC contains no provisions in this respect, he will prescribe which transactions are to be carried out at the European Patent Office at Munich and its branch at The Hague respectively;

    (c) he may place before the Administrative Council any proposal for amending the EPC and any proposal for general regulations or decisions which come within the competence of the Administrative Council;

    (d) he will prepare and implement the budget and any amending or supplementary budget;

    (e) he will submit a management report to the Administrative Council each year;

    (f) he will exercise supervisory authority over the personnel;

    (g) subject to the provisions of Art.11, he will appoint and promote the employees;

    (h) he will exercise disciplinary authority over the employees other than those referred to in Art.11, and may propose disciplinary action to the Administrative Council with regard to employees referred to in Art.11, paras 2 and 3; and

    (i) he may delegate his functions and powers.

The Guidelines for Examination in the EPO and the agreement with the German Patent Office re. forwarding for mail (see AnReg under Art.75(1) – [1991] O.J. 187) are examples of the President exercising his power under the authority of Art.10(2)(a).

The President is assisted by a number of Vice-Presidents. If the President is absent or indisposed, one of the Vice-Presidents takes his place in accordance with the procedure laid down by the Administrative Council.

Art.10(3)

### *Appointment of senior EPO employees*

**2–007**

The President of the European Patent Office is appointed by decision of the Administrative Council.

Art.11(1)

The Vice-Presidents are appointed by decision of the Administrative Council after the President has been consulted.

Art.11(2)

The members, including the Chairmen, of the Boards of Appeal and of the Enlarged Board of Appeal are appointed by decision of the Administrative Council, taken on a proposal from the President of the European Patent Office. They may be re-appointed by decision of the Administrative Council after the President of the European Patent Office has been consulted.

Art.11(3)

The Administrative Council exercises disciplinary authority over the employees referred to in Art.11(1) to (3).

Art.11(4)

### *Employees not to disclose or make use of confidential information*

**2–008**

The employees of the European Patent Office are bound, even after the termination of their employment, neither to disclose nor to make use of information which by its nature is a professional secret.

Art.12

### *Disputes between the Organisation and the employees of the European Patent Office*

**2–009**

Employees and former employees of the European Patent Office or their successors in title may apply to the Administrative Tribunal of the International Labour Organisation in the case of disputes with the European Patent Organisation in accordance with the Statute of the Tribunal and within the limits and subject to the conditions laid down in the Service Regulations for permanent employees or the Pension Scheme Regulations or arising from the conditions of employment of other employees.

Art.13(1)

An appeal is only admissible if the person concerned has exhausted such other means of appeal as are available to him under the Service Regulations, the Pension Scheme Regulations or the conditions of employment, as the case may be.

Art.13(2)

### The departments of the European Patent Office

### *The departments charged with procedure*

**2–010**

For implementing the procedures laid down in the EPC, there are set up within the European Patent Office:

Art.15

(a) a Receiving Section;

(b) Search Divisions;

(c) Examining Divisions;

(d) Opposition Divisions;

(e) a Legal Division;

(f) Boards of Appeal;

(g) an Enlarged Board of Appeal.

| | |
|---|---|
| r.9(1) | The President of the EPO determines the number of Search Divisions, Examining Divisions and Opposition Divisions. He allocates duties to these departments by reference to the international classification (see r.8) and decides where necessary on the classification of a European patent application or a European patent in accordance with that classification. |

## 2–011    *Administrative structure of the EPO*

| | |
|---|---|
| r.12(1) | The Examining Divisions and the Opposition Divisions are grouped together administratively so as to form Directorates, the number of which are laid down by the President of the EPO. |
| r.12(2) | The Directorates, the Legal Division, the Boards of Appeal and the Enlarged Board of Appeal, and the administrative services of the EPO are grouped together administratively so as to form Directorates-General. The Receiving Section and the Search Divisions are grouped together administratively so as to form a Directorate-General. |
| r.12(3) | Each Directorate-General is directed by a Vice-President. The appointment of a Vice-President to a Directorate-General is decided upon by the Administrative Council, after the President of the EPO has been consulted. |

## 2–012    **The Receiving Section**

| | |
|---|---|
| Art.16 | The Receiving Section is responsible for the examination on filing and the examination as to formal requirements of European patent applications. |
| | This Art.16 replaced the previous Art.16 with provisional effect as of November 29, 2000. |
| J33/86 | Under Art.16 in its previous form, the Receiving Section was responsible for the application until a request for examination was filed or, where such a request was filed prior to receipt of the search report, until the applicant indicated under Art.96(1) that he wished to proceed further. |
| r.9(2) | The President of the EPO may also allocate further duties to the Receiving Section. |

## 2–013    **The Search Divisions**

| | |
|---|---|
| Art.17 | The Search Divisions are responsible for drawing up European search reports. |
| | This Art.17 replaced the previous Art.17 with provisional effect as of November 29, 2000. |
| r.9(2) | The President of the EPO may also allocate further duties to the Search Divisions. |
| | The Search Divisions and Receiving Section are organised administratively as Directorate General 1. |

## 2–014    **The Examining Divisions**

| | |
|---|---|
| Art.18(1) | An Examining Division is responsible for the examination of European patent applications. |
| Art.18(2) | An Examining Division consists of three technically qualified examiners. However, before a decision is taken on a European patent application, its examination is, as a general rule, entrusted to one member of the Examining Division. Oral proceedings are |

before the Examining Division itself. If the Examining Division considers that the nature of the decision so requires, it is enlarged by the addition of a legally qualified examiner. In the event of parity of votes, the vote of the Chairman of the Division is decisive.

This Art.18 replaced the previous Art.18 with provisional effect as of November 29, 2000.

The Administrative Council is competent to decide that one examiner is enough in certain cases.     Art.33(3)

Headnote (1): "Although Art.24 EPC applies only to members of the Boards of Appeal and of the Enlarged Board of Appeal, the requirement of impartiality applies in principle also to employees of the departments of first instance of the EPO taking part in decision making activities affecting the rights of any party."     G5/91

So, the decision of an Examining Division can be appealed on the basis of lack of impartiality. Article 125, which requires that the EPO take into account the principles of procedural law generally recognised in the Contracting States, provides a legal basis for this decision. The Director of the department concerned decides on any request for a change in composition—there is no separate appeal from the decision but it may be challenged as part of the appeal on substantive matters. If upheld on appeal, a substantial procedural violation has occurred and the decision at first instance is void.

See CLBA, pp.376–381 for case law relating to changes in examination division composition and partiality.     CLBA

The President of the EPO may also allocate further duties to the Examining Divisions.     r.9(2)

The President of the EPO may entrust to employees who are not technically or legally qualified examiners the execution of individual duties falling to the Examining Divisions and involving no technical or legal difficulties.     r.9(3)

See under r.9(3) for a list of these duties ([1999] O.J. 504).     AnReg

The Examining Divisions are organised under Directorate General 2.

## The Opposition Divisions     2–015

An Opposition Division is responsible for the examination of oppositions against any European patent.     Art.19(1)

An Opposition Division consists of three technical examiners, at least two of whom must not have taken part in the proceedings for grant of the patent to which the opposition relates. An examiner who has taken part in the proceedings for the grant of the European patent cannot be the chairman. Prior to the taking of a final decision on the opposition, the Opposition Division may entrust the examination of the opposition to one of its members. Oral proceedings are before the Opposition Division itself. If the Opposition Division considers that the nature of the decision so requires, it is enlarged by the addition of a legally qualified examiner who must not have taken part in the proceedings for grant of the patent. In the event of parity of votes, the vote of the Chairman of the Division is decisive.     Art.19(2)

Headnote (1): "Although Art.24 EPC applies only to members of the Boards of Appeal and of the Enlarged Board of Appeal, the requirement of impartiality applies in principle also to employees of the departments of first instance of the EPO taking part in decision making activities affecting the rights of any party."     G5/91

| | |
|---|---|
| | See above under "The Examining Divisions" for comment. |
| CLBA | See CLBA, pp.376–381 for case law relating to changes in Opposition Division composition and partiality. Where the composition is wrong, any decision taken is void ab initio and a substantial procedural violation has occurred (T251/88). |
| r.9(2) | The President of the EPO may also allocate further duties to the Opposition Divisions. |
| r.9(3) | The President of the EPO may entrust to employees who are not technically or legally qualified examiners the execution of individual duties falling to the Opposition Divisions and involving no technical or legal difficulties. |
| AnReg | See under r.9(3) for a list of these duties ([1999] O.J. 504). |
| G1/02 | Headnote: "Points 4 and 6 of the Notice from the Vice-President Directorate-General 2 dated April 28, 1999 ([1999] O.J. 506) do not conflict with provisions of a higher level." |
| | This decision overruled T295/01, which had suggested that formalities officers could never decide on the admissibility of an opposition, only the Opposition Division being competent. |
| r.9(4) | The President of the EPO may grant exclusive responsibilities to one of the registries of the Opposition Divisions for fixing the amount of costs as provided for in Art.104(2). |
| | The Opposition Divisions are organised under DG2. |

## 2–016  The Legal Division

| | |
|---|---|
| Art.20(1) | The Legal Division is responsible for decisions in respect of entries in the Register of European Patents and in respect of registration on, and deletion from, the list of professional representatives. |
| Art.20(2) | Decisions of the Legal Division are taken by one legally qualified member. |
| r.9(2) | The President of the EPO may also allocate further duties to the Legal Division. |
| AnReg | See under Art.20. The legal division has sole responsibility for various entries and deletions in the Register of Patents and the Register of Representatives ([1989] O.J. 177). |

### The Boards of Appeal and the Enlarged Board of Appeal

## 2–017  *Composition of the Board of Appeal*

| | |
|---|---|
| Art.21(1) | The Boards of Appeal are responsible for the examination of appeals from the decisions of the Receiving Section, Examining Divisions, Opposition Divisions and of the Legal Division. (Note, not the Search Division.) |
| Art.21(2) | For appeals from a decision of the Receiving Section or the Legal Division, a Board of Appeal consists of three legally qualified members. |
| Art.21(3) | For appeals from a decision of an Examining Division, a Board of Appeal consists of: |

> (a) two technically qualified members and one legally qualified member, when the decision concerns the refusal of a European patent application or the grant of a European patent and was taken by an Examining Division consisting of less than four members;

(b) three technically qualified members and two legally qualified members, when the decision was taken by an Examining Division consisting of four members or when the Board of Appeal considers that the nature of the appeal so requires*; or

(c) three legally qualified members in all other cases.

(a) and (b) are known as Technical Boards of Appeal whereas (c) is known as the legal Board of Appeal.

For appeals from a decision of an Opposition Division, a Board of Appeal consists of:     Art.21(4)

(a) two technically qualified members and one legally qualified member, when the decision was taken by an Opposition Division consisting of three members;

(b) three technically qualified members and two legally qualified members, when the decision was taken by an Opposition Division consisting of four members or when the Board of Appeal considers that the nature of the appeal so requires*.

Such a situation may, for instance, arise where there are mixed technologies or difficult legal or technical issues.     *

Headnote (1): "Under Art.21(3)(c) EPC, the Legal Board of Appeal is competent only to hear appeals against decisions taken by an Examining Division consisting of fewer than four members when the decision does not concern the refusal of a European patent application or the grant of a European patent. In all other cases, i.e. those covered by Art.21(3)(a), 3(b) and (4) EPC, the Technical Board of Appeal is competent."     G2/90

Headnote (2): "The provisions relating to competence in Art.21(3) and (4) EPC are not affected by r.9(3) EPC (i.e. whether the decision is delegated to a formalities officer or not)."

The Enlarged Board felt that since only duties involving no legal difficulties could be entrusted to a formalities officer, an appeal from such a decision should rightly be entrusted to the Technical Board of Appeal and no special considerations applied to change the normal operation of Art.21(3) and (4) concerning which appeals are allocated to which Board.

Headnote: "An appeal from a decision of an Examining Division refusing a request under r.89 EPC for correction of the decision to grant is to be decided by a Technical Board of Appeal."     G8/95

An appeal against a decision to refuse correction of a decision to grant was seen to "concern the grant of the patent" in contrast, for instance, to a decision to refuse a correction of a designation under r.88. Whether or not the decision terminates proceedings was seen to be key.

See CLBA, pp.378–381.     CLBA

The Administrative Council may allocate duties under Art.134(8)(c) to the Boards of Appeal (concerning discipline of professional representatives).     r.10(6)

The Boards of Appeal are organised as Directorate General 3.

### Presidium of the Boards of Appeal     2–018

The autonomous authority within the organizational unit comprising the Boards of Appeal (the "Presidium of the Boards of Appeal") consists of the Vice-President in     r.10(1)

|  |  |
|---|---|
|  | charge of the Boards of Appeal, who acts as chairman, and twelve members of the Boards of Appeal, six being chairmen and six being other members. |
| r.10(2)–(5) | Further rules for the functioning of the Presidium are specified. |

## 2–019 *Enlarged Board of Appeal*

|  |  |
|---|---|
| Art.22(1) | The Enlarged Board of Appeal is responsible for:<br><br>(a) deciding points of law referred to it by Boards of Appeal;<br>(b) giving opinions on points of law referred to it by the President of the European Patent Office under the conditions laid down in Art.112. |
| Art.22(2) | For giving decisions or opinions, the Enlarged Board of Appeal consists of five legally qualified members and two technically qualified members. One of the legally qualified members is the Chairman. |
| r.11(1) | Before the beginning of each working year, the members of the Enlarged Board of Appeal who have not been appointed under Art.160(2) (legally qualified people from Contracting States during transitional period) designate the regular and alternate members of the Enlarged Board of Appeal. |
| r.11(2) | The members of the Enlarged Board of Appeal who have not been appointed under Art.160(2) adopt the rules of procedure of the Enlarged Board of Appeal. |
| r.11(3) | Decisions on matters mentioned in r.11(1) and r.11(2) may only be taken if at least five members are present, including the Chairman of the Enlarged Board of Appeal or his deputy; in the event of parity of votes the Chairman or his deputy has the casting vote. Abstentions are not considered as votes. |

## 2–020 *Independence and exclusion of Board of Appeal members*

|  |  |
|---|---|
| Art.23(1) | The members of the Enlarged Board of Appeal and of the Boards of Appeal are appointed for a term of five years and may not be removed from office during this term, except if there are serious grounds for such removal and if the Administrative Council, on a proposal from the Enlarged Board of Appeal, takes a decision to this effect. |
| Art.23(2) | The members of the Boards may not be members of the Receiving Section, Examining Divisions, Opposition Divisions or of the Legal Division. |
| Art.23(3) | In their decisions the members of the Boards are not bound by any instructions and comply only with the provisions of the Convention (which in this sense does not include the Implementing Regulations (as in Art.164(2)). |

## 2–021 *Adoption of Rules of Procedure by the Boards of Appeal and the Enlarged Board*

|  |  |
|---|---|
| Art.23(4) | The Rules of Procedure of the Boards of Appeal and the Enlarged Board of Appeal are adopted in accordance with the provisions of the Implementing Regulations. They are subject to the approval of the Administrative Council. |
| r.11(2) | This rule specifies which members of the Enlarged Board adopt the Rules of Procedure. |
| r.10(3) | The Presidium adopts the Rules of Procedure of the Boards of Appeal. |
| AnReg | See under Art.23(4). The Rules of Procedure of the Enlarged Board of Appeal were adopted on December 10, 1982 and approved on December 10, 1982. ([1983] |

O.J. 3). Subsequent amendments have been made ([1989] O.J. 362; [1994] O.J. 443; [2003] O.J. 58). The Rules of Procedure of the Boards of Appeal were adopted on June 4, 1980 and approved on June 6, 1980 ([1980] O.J. 171). Subsequent amendments have been made ([1989] O.J. 361; [2000] O.J. 316; [2003] O.J. 61 [2004] O.J. 541). Various functions of the Boards of Appeal have been delegated to the Registrar under the authority of r.23(4) ([1985] O.J. 249, amended [2002] O.J. 590).

The Rules of procedure of the Boards of Appeal have higher status than the Implementing Regulations.   G6/95

### Exclusion and objection   2–022

Members of the Boards of Appeal or of the Enlarged Board of Appeal may not take part in any appeal if they have any personal interest therein, if they have previously been involved as representatives of one of the parties or if they have participated in the decision under appeal.   Art.24(1)

If, for one of the reasons mentioned in Art.24(1), or for any other reason, a member of a Board of Appeal or of the Enlarged Board of Appeal considers that he should not take part in any appeal, he must inform the Board accordingly.   Art.24(2)

Members of a Board of Appeal or of the Enlarged Board of Appeal may be objected to by any party for one of the reasons mentioned in Art.24(1), or if suspected of partiality. An objection is not admissible if, while being aware of a reason for objection, the party has taken a procedural step. No objection may be based upon the nationality of members.   Art.24(3)

If a member of the Board of Appeal in a particular case has already given a decision in that same case on substantially the same issue, that member's impartiality may be challenged (e.g. in opposition appeal where the same issue was the subject of appeal during examination).   T1028/96

Another member of the Board may also object to a fellow member.   RPBArt.3

The Boards of Appeal and the Enlarged Board of Appeal decide as to the action to be taken in the cases specified in Art.24(2) and (3) without the participation of the member concerned. For the purposes of taking this decision the member objected to is replaced by his alternate.   Art.24(4)

A decision on admissibility under the terms of Art.24(3) is taken with the Board as originally assembled. If the objection is admissible then the Board will decide on its substantive merits with the alternate member replacing the objected member.

See CLBA, pp.378–381.   CLBA

Documents relating to exclusion or objection are not part of the public file.   r.93a

## 2. REQUIREMENTS OF THE INVENTION

### What is not an invention for the purposes of the EPC?

#### Requirement for technical subject matter   2–023

The description must, inter alia, specify the technical field to which the invention relates and disclose the invention, as claimed, in such terms that the technical problem and its solution can be understood.   r.27(1)

| | |
|---|---|
| r.29(1) | The claims must define the matter for which protection is sought in terms of the technical features of the invention. |
| r.30(1) | A single general inventive concept exists between a group of inventions when there is a technical relationship among the inventions involving one or more of the same or corresponding special technical features. |
| Case law | From the above, an implicit requirement for an invention to have a technical character has been derived by the Boards of Appeal (e.g. T22/85, T931/95). Examples of subject matter not having a technical character are given in A52(2) and (3) but these examples do not represent an exhaustive list (T163/85). |

The required technical character may be provided by a technical effect achieved by the invention (e.g. T1173/97) or by the fact that technical considerations were necessary to carry out the invention (T769/92). In assessing technical character a claim must be judged as a whole (T26/86, T931/95). A mix of technical and non-technical features is therefore allowable in a claim (T26/86, T209/91). However, the mere dressing-up of a claim with technical features does not make it patentable (T22/85).

In T931/95 (Pension Benefits System), the Appeal Board 3.5.1. concluded that "a computer system suitably programmed for use in a particular field, even if that is the field of business and economy, has the character of a concrete apparatus in the sense of a physical entity, man-made for a utilitarian purpose and is thus an invention within the meaning of Article 52(1) EPC". The Board also stated that "there is no basis in the EPC for distinguishing between "new features" of an invention and features of that invention which are known from the prior art when examining whether the invention concerned may be considered to be an invention within the meaning of Article 52(1) EPC. Thus there is no basis in the EPC for applying this so-called contribution approach for this purpose."

The Board's conclusion makes any programmed computer a patentable invention — a significant weakening of the scope of Art.52(2). However, this is compensated by their approach to the assessment of inventive step of inventions which now escape the trap of Art.52(2). The new approach is discussed at length below.

The Board stated that a distinction with regard to patentability between "a method for doing business and an apparatus suited to perform such a method is justified in the light of the wording of Article 52(2) (c) EPC, according to which "schemes, rules and methods" are non-patentable categories in the field of economy and business, but the category of "apparatus" in the sense of "physical entity" or "product" is not mentioned in Article 52(2) EPC. This means that, if a claim is directed to such an entity, the formal category of such a claim does in fact imply physical features of the claimed subject-matter which may qualify as technical features of the invention concerned and thus be relevant for its patentability". This distinction was subsequently removed by the same board, in a different composition, in T258/03 (Hitachi auction method) which is discussed below.

Having decided in T931/95 that the apparatus claim could not be excluded under Art.52 (2), the Board considered obviousness. The decision under appeal had found that "no technical problem or contribution" could be ascribed to the claimed subject-matter. The Board found that "the improvement envisaged by the invention according to the application is an essentially economic one i.e. lies in the field of economy, which, therefore, <u>cannot contribute to inventive step</u>" (emphasis added).

A surprising part of the Board's reasoning was their conclusion that "assessment of inventive step has thus to be carried out from the point of view of a software developer or application programmer, as the appropriate person skilled in the art, <u>having the knowledge of the concept and structure of the improved pension benefits system</u>

and of the underlying schemes of information processing as set out for example in the present method claims" (emphasis added). In other words no patentable invention would have been found if the new apparatus had included technical features which were inventive over the known state of the art but which were obvious once you knew about the new method. It is interesting to compare this situation with that which applies for so-called "problem inventions" where identification of a problem constitutes an invention – the obvious solutions to which can be patented, provided that the problem was real and previously unidentified (see Guidelines C.IV.9.6 (i), and T2/83).

This approach to obviousness was followed in T172/03 (Ricoh, order management system), but revised by the same Board (in a different composition) in T641/00 (Comvik). There it was held that "an invention consisting of a mixture of technical and non-technical features and having technical character as a whole is to be assessed with respect to the requirement of inventive step by taking account of all those features which contribute to said technical character whereas features making no such contribution cannot support the presence of inventive step. Although the technical problem to be solved should not be formulated to contain pointers to the solution or partially anticipate it, merely because some feature appears in the claim does not automatically exclude it from appearing in the formulation of the problem. In particular where the claim refers to an aim to be achieved in a non-technical field, this aim may legitimately appear in the formulation of the problem as part of the framework of the technical problem that is to be solved, in particular as a constraint that has to be met".

A further development in the handling of cases in this area occurred on T258/03 (Hitachi auction method) — another 3.5.1 case. Consideration of Art. 52, 54, 56, and 57 led the Board to conclude that "the verification that claimed subject-matter is an invention within the meaning of Article 52(1) EPC is in principle a prerequisite for the examination with respect to novelty, inventive step and industrial application since these latter requirements are defined only for inventions (cf. Articles 54(1), 56, and 57 EPC). The structure of the EPC therefore suggests that it should be possible to determine whether subject-matter is excluded under Article 52(2) EPC without any knowledge of the state of the art (including common general knowledge)". Also, "Therefore, taking into account both that a mix of technical and non-technical features may be regarded as an invention within the meaning of Article 52(1) EPC and that prior art should not be considered when deciding whether claimed subject-matter is such an invention, a compelling reason for not refusing under Article 52(2) EPC subject-matter consisting of technical and non-technical features is simply that the technical features may in themselves turn out to fulfil all requirements of Article 52(1) EPC". Since this rationale was independent of claim category, it followed that method claims for activities listed in Art.52(2) are not excluded from protection provided that the claims include technical features.

See CLBA, pp.1 and 15–16. CLBA

See C/IV/1.2–2.2 Guidelines

### *Discoveries* 2–024

To the extent that a European patent application relates to a discovery as such, it is not regarded as containing patentable subject matter. Art.52(2)(3)

Thus, in the field of biotechnology, the human body, at the various stages of its formation and development, and the simple discovery of one of its elements, including the sequence or partial sequence of a gene, cannot constitute patentable inventions. r.23e(1)

However, biotechnological inventions are patentable if they concern biological material which is isolated from its natural environment or produced by means of a technical process even if it previously occurred in nature. r.23c(a)

| | |
|---|---|
| r.23e(2) | Thus, an element isolated from the human body or otherwise produced by means of a technical process, including the sequence or partial sequence of a gene, may constitute a patentable invention, even if the structure of that element is identical to that of a natural element.

Finding a substance in nature is a discovery but if that substance is isolated for the first time the process will be patentable and if the substance can be properly characterised then it will be patentable itself (Opposition Division in Howard Florey/Relaxin). |
| Guidelines | See C/IV/2.3.1 |

## 2–025 Scientific theories and mathematical methods

| | |
|---|---|
| Art.52(2)(3) | To the extent that a European patent application relates to a scientific theory or a mathematical method as such, it is not regarded as containing patentable subject matter. |
| Case law | For mathematical methods see T208/84 (VICOM). A mathematical method as such was seen to be a method practiced on numbers and having a numerical outcome whereas a mathematical method used in a technical process carried out on a physical entity and resulting in a change to that entity is not a mathematical method as such. |
| Guidelines | See C/IV/2.3.2–2.3.3 |

## 2–026 Aesthetic creations

| | |
|---|---|
| Art.52(2)(3) | To the extent that a European patent application relates to an aesthetic creation as such, it is not regarded as containing patentable subject matter. |
| T119/88 | A disc sleeve of a particular colour was said to have the technical benefit of reducing fingerprints. However, this effect was not directly related to the colour specified in the claim and was essentially aesthetic in character. The application was therefore refused. |
| CLBA | See CLBA, pp. 14–15. |
| Guidelines | C/IV/2.3.4 |

## 2–027 Scheme, rule or method for performing a mental act

| | |
|---|---|
| Art.52(2)(3) | To the extent that a European patent application relates to a scheme, rule or method for performing a mental act as such, it is not regarded as containing patentable subject matter. |
| T914/02 | The involvement of technical considerations is not sufficient to ensure patentability of a method which may be carried out mentally. But technical character may be provided through technical implementation of the method, resulting in the method providing a tangible technical effect, such as the provision of a physical entity as the resulting product or a non-abstract activity, such as through use of technical means. Here a claim to a method for designing a core loading arrangement for loading nuclear fuel bundles into a reactor core, which only concerned steps which could all be performed mentally, was refused. Surprisingly, the Board did not require the claim to be limited to the physical activity of loading a reactor core, but allowed the claim once it had been limited to: "A method **using a suitably programmed computer** . . ." with the remainder of the claim unchanged. This contrasts with the much earlier T453/91 in which claims to a method of designing a semiconductor chip were held unallowable, even though a step of the claimed method was specified as being carried |

out on a computer. In that case to be allowable the claims had to be limited to a method of manufacturing a real physical object (and not just, for example a pictorial design for a chip).

See under 'word processing', pages 6 to 8, in particular, T38/86. The automation of a mental act does not make it patentable. CLBA

See C/IV/2.3.5 Guidelines

### Scheme, rule or method for playing games 2–028

To the extent that a European patent application relates to a scheme, rule or method for playing games as such, it is not regarded as containing patentable subject matter. Art.52(2)(3)

See C/IV/2.3.5 Guidelines

### Scheme, rule or method for doing business 2–029

To the extent that a European patent application relates to a scheme, rule or method for doing business as such, it is not regarded as containing patentable subject matter. Art.52(2)(3)

If a method for doing business has technical character then it is not a method of doing business as such (T931/95). A computer system set up to carry out a method generally in the category of 'doing business' is allowable where technical considerations are necessary for its implementation (T769/92 — improved screen display). An apparatus constituting a physical entity would not be excluded even if the method it was set up to run was excluded (T931/95, T1002/92) (although, since all the non-technical elements of the claim are ignored when assessing inventive step, it may well be obvious (T931/95, T641/00, T172/03). See section 2-023. Case law

See CLBA, pp. 11–14. CLBA

See C/IV/2.3.5 Guidelines

### Computer program 2–030

To the extent that a European patent application relates to a program for a computer as such, it is not regarded as containing patentable subject matter. Art.52(2)(3)

Computer-related inventions must have technical character (T931/95), which may be provided by a further technical effect (i.e. other than the usual physical interactions between any software and the computer running it) achieved by the invention (e.g. T1173/97). A claim to a technical process carried out under the control of a program or a claim to a computer set up to operate in accordance with a program for controlling that technical process is allowable (T208/84). Furthermore, where a program produces a further technical effect, it may in principle be claimed in the form of a record on a carrier or as a program per se (T1173/97). Case law

See CLBA, pp.2–8 for further cases. CLBA

See C/IV/2.3.6 Guidelines

### Presentation of information 2–031

To the extent that a European patent application relates to a presentation of information as such, it is not regarded as containing patentable subject matter. Art.52(2)(3)

| | |
|---|---|
| T49/04 | The presentation of natural language on a display in a manner which improves readability, enabling the user to perform their task more efficiently, relates to how, i.e. by what physical arrangement of the text, cognitive content is conveyed to the reader and can thus be considered as contributing to a technical solution to a technical problem. This very well-reasoned decision, from Board 3.4.3, followed T643/00 rather than T125/04. |
| CLBA | See CLBA, pp. 8–11 for cases. |
| T163/85 | A TV signal characterised by certain physical parameters was not seen to be a presentation of information as such whereas if it had been characterised by its informational content it would have been. |
| T1194/97 | A claim to a record carrier bearing functional data is not objectionable as a presentation of information. |
| T858/02 | An electronic message is not automatically excluded from patentability as a presentation of information. This will depend on whether the message is defined by its structure or its content. |
| Guidelines | See C/IV/2.3.7 |

**What inventions are barred from patentability?**

### 2–032 *Morality exemption*

| | |
|---|---|
| Art.53(a) | European patents cannot be granted in respect of inventions the publication or exploitation of which would be contrary to "ordre public" or morality, provided that the exploitation is not deemed to be so contrary merely because it is prohibited by law or regulation in some or all of the Contracting States. |
| r.23d | Under Art.53(a), a European patent will not be granted in respect of biotechnological inventions which, in particular, concern the following: (a) processes for cloning human beings, (b) processes for modifying the germ line genetic identity of human beings, (c) uses of human embryos for industrial or commercial purposes, (d) processes for modifying the genetic identity of animals which are likely to cause them suffering without any substantial medical benefit to man or animal, and also animals resulting from such processes. |
| G2/06 | The Enlarged Board has been asked to consider whether r.23d(c) applies to applications filed before its coming into force and also to clarify the extent of the exclusion, particularly with reference to whether human embryos are destroyed or not. |
| T315/03 | The exclusions in r.23d represent specific instances of the general exclusion of Art.53(a). The exclusions are to be judged at the filing/priority date though relevant evidence may have been published later. |
| Case law | Whether an invention is contrary to ordre public or morality is a matter of balancing the advantages and disadvantages—benefit to mankind versus any cruelty to animals or risk to the environment (Examining Division in Oncomouse case ([1992] O.J. 588) and T19/90). Ordre public includes public security and a consideration of possible environmental hazards but such hazards must be properly substantiated to be persuasive (T356/93). The morality question is to be judged on the basis of conventionally accepted standards of European culture (T356/93). For a case to be excluded under morality there must be an overwhelming consensus that the exploitation or publication of the invention would be immoral (Opposition Division in Howard Florey/relaxin). If carrying out the invention is sanctioned by statutory law then it is probably allowable under Art.53(a) (Opposition Division in Oncomouse case—[2003] O.J. 473). |

| | |
|---|---|
| See CLBA, pp.32–34. | CLBA |
| See C/IV/3.1–3.3b. | Guidelines |

### *Plant varieties* 2–033

| | |
|---|---|
| European patents cannot be granted in respect of plant varieties. | Art.53(b) |
| Plant variety means any plant grouping within a single botanical taxon of the lowest known rank, which grouping, irrespective of whether the conditions for the grant of a plant variety right are fully met, can be: (a) defined by the expression of the characteristics that results from a given genotype or combination of genotypes; (b) distinguished from any other plant grouping by the expression of at least one of the said characteristics; and (c) considered as a unit with regard to its suitability for being propagated unchanged (this corresponds to the UPOV definition). | r.23b(4) |
| Biotechnological inventions are patentable if they concern plants if the technical feasibility of the invention is not confined to a particular plant variety. | r.23c(b) |
| The exclusion does not relate to plants in general but plant varieties. | T49/83 |
| Headnote (1): "A claim wherein specific plant varieties are not individually claimed is not excluded from patentability under Art.53(b) EPC even though it may embrace plant varieties." | G1/98 |

Headnote (2): "When a claim to a process for the production of a plant variety is examined, Art.64(2) EPC is not to be taken into consideration."

Headnote (3): "The exception to patentability in Art.53(b), first half-sentence, EPC applies to plant varieties irrespective of the way in which they were produced. Therefore, plant varieties containing genes introduced into an ancestral plant by recombinant gene technology are excluded from patentability."

The Enlarged Board held that Art.53(b) excluded plant varieties rather than plants and existed to exclude double protection via a patent and a plant breeders right. Therefore, anything that could not be protected under UPOV should be patentable, including the claim in dispute, which was directed to a genetically modified plant which neither expressly or implicitly defined a plant variety according to UPOV.

| | |
|---|---|
| See CLBA, pp.34–38. | CLBA |
| See C/IV/3.4.1. | Guidelines |

### *Animal varieties* 2–034

| | |
|---|---|
| European patents cannot be granted in respect of animal varieties. | Art.53(b) |
| Biotechnological inventions are also patentable if they concern animals if the technical feasibility of the invention is not confined to a particular animal variety. | r.23c(b) |
| The exclusion applies to certain categories of animals but not to animals as such (T19/90). The Examining Division in the Oncomouse case ([1992] O.J. 588) decided that no accepted definition of animal variety exists. However, neither "rodent" nor "mammal" were felt to be specific enough to amount to an animal variety. The Opposition Division in the *Oncomouse* case ([2003] O.J. 473) also felt that "mouse" did not amount to an animal variety, indicating that a particular "strain" of mice might. The Board of Appeal (T315/03) decided that G1/98 (see above under Plant varieties) should be applied as far as possible. Thus, a claim can be granted if it embraces many varieties as long as it is not directed at a single animal variety. | Case law |
| See CLBA, pp.34–38. | CLBA |

| | |
|---|---|
| **2–035** | ***Essentially biological processes*** |
| Art.53(b) | European patents cannot be granted in respect of essentially biological processes for the production of plants or animals; this provision does not apply to microbiological processes or the products thereof. |
| r.23b(5) | A process for the production of plants and animals is essentially biological if it consists entirely of natural phenomena such as crossing or selection. |
| Case law | Whether a process is "essentially" biological is to be judged on the basis of the totality of human intervention and its effect on the final result (T320/87). A process involving the essential technical step of transforming plant cells with recombinant DNA was not essentially biological since human intervention was necessary and had a decisive impact on the result (T356/93). |
| r.23b(6) | "Microbiological process" means any process involving or performed upon or resulting in microbiological material. |
| Case law | "Microbiological" refers to generally unicellular organisms too small to be seen with the eye, including bacteria, yeasts, fungi, algae, protozoa, human cells, animal cells and plant cells. The products of microbiolgial processes include new microorganisms as well as chemical products (T356/93). However, the processes of genetic engineering are not identical to microbiological processes (G1/98). |
| CLBA | See CLBA, pp.34–38. |
| Guidelines | See C/IV/3.5. |

| | |
|---|---|
| **2–036** | **What is a patentable invention?** |
| Art.52(1) | European patents are granted for any inventions which are susceptible of industrial application, which are new and which involve an inventive step. |

**Which inventions are susceptible of industrial application?**

| | |
|---|---|
| **2–037** | ***General definition of industrial application*** |
| Art.57 | An invention is considered as susceptible of industrial application if it can be made or used in any kind of industry, including agriculture. |
| CLBA | See CLBA, pp.141–144. See the decision of the Examining Division reported at [2002] O.J. 293 for gene sequence—not industrially applicable without a credible function. |
| Guidelines | See C/IV/4.1 and 4.4. |
| **2–038** | ***Method of treatment or diagnosis exclusion—general points*** |
| Art.52(4) | Methods for treatment of the human or animal body by surgery or therapy and diagnostic methods practised on the human or animal body are not regarded as inventions which are susceptible of industrial application. However, this exclusion does not apply to products, in particular substances or compositions, for use in any of these methods. |
| G5/83 | Headnote (1): "A European patent with claims directed to the use may not be granted for the use of a substance or composition for the treatment of the human or animal body by therapy." |

The Enlarged Board felt that there was no substantive difference, for the purposes of the EPC, between a use claim and a method claim and thus that a claim to the use of a substance or composition for treatment were excluded in the same way as a method claim as lacking industrial applicability (see below for allowable second medical use format).

The purpose of these exclusions is to prevent non-commercial and non-industrial medical and veterinary activities from being restrained by patent rights (G5/83) and they should be construed narrowly according to this purpose (T385/86). A claim which contains any element excluded by Art.52(4) is excluded from patentability. Whether the feature is technical or not is irrelevant (T82/93) (*cf.* claims excluded under Art.52(2)(3)).

Case law

See CLBA, pp.16–32.

CLBA

See C/IV/4.1–4.3.

Guidelines

## *Method of treatment of the human or animal body by therapy*

2–039

"Treatment" is "the application of medicines, surgery, psychotherapy etc. to a patient or to a disease or symptom" (*Collins English Dictionary*).

"Therapy" is "the treatment of physical, mental or social disorders or disease" (*Collins English Dictionary*).

Therapy is any non-surgical treatment designed to cure, alleviate, remove or lessen the symptoms of, or prevent or reduce the possibility of contracting, any malfunction of the body.

T58/87

Therapy includes both curative and prophylactic treatment (e.g. immunisation) (T19/86, T290/86) and all methods of alleviating pain (T144/83, T81/84). Whether the treatment is performed by a medical practitioner or vet is not conclusive but can be indicative (T24/91, T329/94). For instance, it makes no difference if the therapeutic treatment is applied by a farmer as opposed to a vet (T116/85). If therapy occurs during a treatment, that treatment is excluded even though therapy might not be the main purpose of the treatment (e.g. T780/89—immunisation increases meat production; T438/91—prevention of scours increases animal weight; T290/86—eliminating plaque prevented caries and other dental disease). Therapy includes internal and external treatment, e.g. of ectoparasites (T116/85).

Case law

Cosmetic treatments are not excluded (T144/83) as long as therapy is not inherently also taking place (T290/86, T1077/93). The claim must be worded so as to exclude any therapeutic treatment. Methods of contraception are also allowable in principle since pregnancy is not an illness and its prevention is not therapy (T820/92) though acts performed in the personal sphere may not be considered capable of industrial application in the ordinary sense (T74/93).

Method claims are allowed where there is no functional relationship between the effect of the method on a therapeutic apparatus and the therapeutic effect produced by the apparatus (e.g. pacemaker cases T426/89 and T789/96 and T245/87 Seimens/Flow measurement). Equally, an allowable method can interact with the human body (e.g. facilitating the flow of blood to an extraction point) as long as no therapeutic purpose exists (T329/94).

Prevention of accidents and possible harm or death (e.g. a mother pig smothering her piglets) is not therapy (T58/87).

See CLBA, pp.141–144.

CLBA

See C/IV/4.2.

Guidelines

**2–040**   ***Method of treatment of the human or animal body by surgery***

"Surgery" is "the branch of medicine concerned with treating disease, injuries etc by means of manual or operative procedures, especially by incision into the body" (*Collins English Dictionary*).

Case law

Surgery is not defined by the purpose of the treatment but by the nature of the treatment so that the exclusion covers surgical methods that are for cosmetic purposes or fertility treatment (T35/99). However, a recent decision (T383/03) has suggested that if a surgical method does not maintain or restore health it is not excluded (here, a cosmetic method for removing unwanted hair by manipulating the skin with heat). Any method incorporating even one surgical step is excluded from patentability; however, where a treatment results in an animal inevitably dying, the fact that the treatment includes a surgical step does not exclude it (T182/90). An act performed on an implant which has become part of the human body is a surgical treatment (T24/91). However, acts performed on prostheses are not excluded.

CLBA

See CLBA, pp.141–144.

Guidelines

See C/IV/4.2.

**2–041**   ***Diagnostic method practiced on the human or animal body***

"Diagnosis" is "the identification of diseases from the examination of symptoms" which are "sensations or changes in bodily function experienced by a patient that are associated with a disease" (*Collins English Dictionary*).

G1/04

Diagnostic methods

Headnote (1): 'In order that the subject-matter of a claim relating to a diagnostic method practised on the human or animal body falls under the prohibition of Article 52 (4) EPC, the claim is to include the features relating to: (i) the diagnosis for curative purposes stricto sensu representing the deductive medical or veterinary decision phase as a purely intellectual exercise, (ii) the preceding steps which are constitutive for making that diagnosis, and (iii) the specific interactions with the human or animal body which occur when carrying those out among these preceding steps which are of a technical nature.'

Headnote (2): 'Whether or not a method is a diagnostic method within the meaning of Article 52(4) EPC may neither depend on the participation of a medical or veterinary practitioner, by being present or by bearing the responsibility, nor on the fact that all method steps can also, or only, be practised by medical or technical support staff, the patient himself or herself or an automated system. Moreover, no distinction is to be made in this context between essential method steps having diagnostic character and non-essential method steps lacking it.'

Headnote (3): 'In a diagnostic method under Article 52(4) EPC, the method steps of a technical nature belonging to the preceding steps which are constitutive for making the diagnosis for curative purposes stricto sensu must satisfy the criterion "practised on the human or animal body'.

Headnote (4): 'Article 52 (4) EPC does not require a specific type and intensity of interaction with the human or animal body; a preceding step of a technical nature thus satisfies the criterion "practised on the human or animal body" if its performance implies any interaction with the human or animal body, necessitating the presence of the latter'.

The Enlarged Board have given the diagnostic methods exclusion a narrow interpretation in line with its purpose. The only diagnostic methods excluded are those that include both a data collection step and a step in which a course of therapy is proposed on the basis of those data. Moreover, each of the data collection steps must be practiced on the human or animal body, in the sense that they must require its presence. The case for broadening the exclusion, made in T964/99, was thus rejected and the old status quo, whereby a method of generating interim results for use in diagnosis was regarded as patentable, has been re-established.

See CLBA, pp.141–144. CLBA

See C/IV/4.2. Guidelines

## Which inventions are new?

### *Definition of novelty*     2–042

An invention is considered to be new if it does not form part of the state of the art. Art.54(1)

### *The state of the art includes earlier publications*     2–043

The state of the art is held to comprise everything made available to the public by means of a written or oral description, by use, or in any other way, before the date of filing (or priority date—Art.89) of the European patent application of interest. Art.54(2)

The Art.89 effect only applies where priority is validly claimed in respect of "the same invention".

Headnote (1): "A document published during the priority interval, the technical contents of which correspond to that of the priority document, constitutes prior art citable under Art.54(2) EPC against a European patent application claiming that priority, to the extent such priority is not validly claimed." G3/93

Headnote (2): "This also applies if a claim to priority is invalid due to the fact that the priority document and the subsequent European patent application do not concern the same invention because the European application claims subject matter not disclosed in the priority document."

See CLBA, pp.39–85. CLBA

See C/IV/5.1. Guidelines

### *The state of the art includes the contents of earlier European patent applications*     2–044

The state of the art also comprises the (whole) content of European patent applications as filed, the dates of filing (or priority—Art.89) of which are prior to the date of filing (or priority—Art.89) of the European patent application of interest and which were published under Art.93 on or after that date. Art.54(3)

However, such matter is only taken to be prior art in so far as a Contracting State designated in respect of the later application, was also designated in respect of the earlier application as published and to the extent that designation fees pursuant to Art.79(2) have been paid. The final effect of an Art.54(3) citation is not therefore known for some time after its publication. Art.54(4)/r.23a

An international application only becomes Art.54(3) art if it validly enters the European regional phase. Art.158

Where an Art.54(3) document exists in respect of only some designated states, the application and corresponding patent may have different claims and, if the EPO agrees, a different description and drawings for different states, as an exception to the unity requirement of Art.118. r.87

The content of the abstract is to be disregarded when applying Art.54(3). Art.85

Where an application has been withdrawn before publication but published anyway (e.g. because technical preparations were complete) it does NOT form part of the state J5/81 of the art under Art.54(3) (as withdrawal of an application is equivalent to the withdrawal of all designations, so no effect arises under Art.54(4)).

CLBA
See CLBA, pp.39–85. National rights are not citeable under Art.54(3)—T550/88.

Guidelines
See C/IV/6.1–6a. Changes after publication (e.g. withdrawal of priority claim) do not affect the Art.54(3) effect of the application. Applications of the same date are allowed to co-exist unless from the same applicant, in which case only one is allowed to progress to grant.

Where the A54 (3) prior art application is filed in an official language of a contracting state under A14(2) EPC, the text in this language is determinative in deciding its prior art effect — any mistakes or omissions in the translation in an EPO official language do not have any effect.

**2–045**  *Under what circumstances is something "made available to the public"?*

Case law
Information is made available when any member of the public can access it and is not under any duty of confidentiality (T482/89). However, disclosure under confidence does not make information available, even if in the form of a lecture (T838/97).

The fact of availability is enough—there is no requirement for a document to have been consulted by a member of the public as long as the possibility was there. In T381/87 the presence of a book on a library shelf made its contents available and in T750/94 the fact that a document was known to be available on demand from a publisher was enough. However, T314/99 suggests that in some cases a publication must be catalogued to make it truly available. Likewise, a single sale of an article makes it part of the state of the art (T1022/99). However, posting a document before the filing date is not enough—it must be received before that date (T381/87). Equally, giving permission to publish is not enough (T842/91).

In cases of prior use, there is a considerable burden of proof to be discharged by an opponent (T472/92—up to the hilt) and full details along the lines of when/what/how/where/whom must be provided (T93/89 and T472/92).

CLBA
See CLBA, pp.39–85.

Guidelines
See C/IV/5.1.

**2–046**  *Judging the content of what has been made available*

G1/92
Headnote (1): "The chemical composition of a product is state of the art when the product as such is available to the public and can be analysed and reproduced by the skilled person, irrespective of whether or not particular reasons can be identified for analysing the composition."

Headnote (2): "The same principle applies *mutatis mutandis* to any other product."

Case law
Availability of a product thus frequently makes available its composition and structure but not any properties that depend on further action being taken (e.g. a particular use). However, the principle of G1/92 may not apply where the information is hidden or deeply buried in the product made available. For example, in T301/87 a gene sequence was not made available since it only existed as part of a very large library and in T461/88 information on a microchip in a printing machine would have required complex reverse-engineering to obtain.

In the case of a publication, the document must be considered in its entirety and particular passages must be read in context (T56/87, T89/87). Where a disclosure (e.g. an abstract) is clearly erroneous (e.g. ascertainable by reference to a fuller disclosure) its teaching must be discounted (T77/87, T1080/99). The content of a document should be interpreted as of its date of publication (T677/91).

The inevitable result of carrying out instructions in the prior art is also part of its disclosure (T666/89). For instance, where a disclosure refers to a chemical compound and proposes that it may be used as a starting material in a particular process, the inevitable product of using that process in combination with the identified starting material is also disclosed.

Normally, documents may not be combined when assessing novelty. However, where a further document is clearly referred to, the contents of the further document specifically identified can be incorporated if it was available at the publication date of the first document (T153/85). Where one document refers to separate embodiments, these may not be combined without any relevant cross-reference.

The disclosure of something as part of a negative teaching (e.g. disclosure of X in the context "don't use X") does not make it available (T26/85).

The disclosure in the prior art must be enabling to destroy novelty (T206/83), i.e. the skilled man must be able to carry out its technical teaching with no more than his common general knowledge. For instance, a chemical compound is not disclosed in an enabling way if it cannot be made on the basis of the teaching or disclosure combined with common general knowledge.

See CLBA, pp.39–85. — CLBA

See C/IV/7.1–7.6. — Guidelines

### Judging whether the content of what has been made available is prejudicial to novelty
2–047

To destroy novelty, there must be a 'clear and unmistakeable' disclosure (T450/89) of all the features of the invention as claimed in combination (G2/88). Put another way, the invention must be directly and unambiguously derivable from the prior art (T204/83). Novelty is a matter of substance rather than form and the use of different wording is not enough to establish novelty (T12/81, T198/84). — Case law

What is implicit in the prior art is taken into account (T666/89) but not what is obvious from the prior art (T572/88) or what is an equivalent (T167/84). For instance, where a compound is known to be water-soluble, describing it as a solution does not impart novelty (T80/96).

See CLBA, pp.39–85. — CLBA

See C/IV/7.1–7.6. — Guidelines

### First medical use
2–048

The provisions of Art.54(1) to (4) do not exclude the patentability of any substance or composition, comprised in the state of the art, for use in a method referred to in Art.52(4), provided that its use for any method referred to in that paragraph is not comprised in the state of the art. — Art.54(5)

A first medical use claim does not have to be restricted to the newly discovered therapeutic use but can claim all therapeutic uses. The format "Compound/composition X for use as a medicament" is usually used. — T128/82

See CLBA, pp.85–87. — CLBA

See C/IV/4.2. — Guidelines

## 2–049 *Second medical use*

**G5/83**

Headnote (2): "A European patent may be granted with claims directed to the use of a substance or composition for the manufacture of a medicament for a specified new and inventive therapeutic application."

The Enlarged Board decided that since under Art.54(5), a use-limited product claim was novel by virtue of the use feature, so a use-limited process claim (i.e. use of a substance/composition for the manufacture of a medicament for treatment) could be seen to be novel by virtue of the use feature and hence Swiss-style claims would be novel even if the process described was already known.

**Case law**

Normally the new medical use will concern a newly identified disease state. See T4/98 for a discussion of the features necessary in a second medical use claim (information *re* the disease, substance and subject to be treated). According to T241/95, a defined condition must be included in the claim, the selective occupancy of a receptor not being a second medical use in itself. However, a claim directed to the use of a substance in the treatment of a different population of the same animals is an allowable second medical use (T19/86, T233/96) and a claim directed to the use of a known drug for a known indication but utilising a different route of administration (here subcutaneous versus intra-muscular administration) is also allowable as a new second medical use (T51/93).

Where there is a new technical effect underlying the new use, a second medical use claim is allowable even if the means of realisation are known—here removal of dental plaque versus inhibiting tooth decay by reducing enamel solubility (T290/86—same reasoning as Mobil, G2/88). However, when only new information about the old use has been discovered, e.g. an explanation of how it works, this cannot be a further technical effect supporting a further second medical use claim (T254/93).

It is not possible to use the second medical use claim format in relation to an apparatus (e.g. an instrument) as the apparatus is not consumed during treatment but can be used repeatedly (T227/91).

**CLBA**

See CLBA, pp.88–94.

**Guidelines**

See C/IV/4.2.

## 2–050 *Second non-medical use*

**G2/88**

Headnote (3): "A claim to the use of a known compound for a particular purpose, which is based on a technical effect which is described in the patent, should be interpreted as including that technical effect as a functional technical feature, and is accordingly not open to objection under Art.54(1) EPC provided that such technical feature has not previously been made available to the public."

Here, the new use was the use of a known compound, used in the same way to achieve a different purpose (reducing friction—previous purpose was rust inhibition). The Enlarged Board reasoned that the claim should be construed to include the functional feature of attaining the new technical effect. This technical feature was inherent in the prior art but not made available, by inevitable result or description. Second non-medical use claims are therefore allowable, even if the new use was inherent (but secret) in a prior art use.

**G6/88**

Essentially the same decision was given in this case where the known use was the use of a compound for influencing plant growth whereas the new use was the use of the same compound for controlling fungi.

**Case law**

For a valid second non-medical use claim there must be a new technical effect underlying the new use that has not been previously made available. An increase in activity resulting from the known technical effect or an explanation of how a known technical effect is caused is not sufficient. In T958/90 the applicant had discovered that the known technical effect (use of compounds as sequestering agents) was merely present to a hitherto unknown extent and there was no new invention. Similarly, in T279/93 the applicant had merely shown that the known technical effect (use of a compound in a process) had the advantage of leading to fewer impurities. In T892/94 an explanation of the mechanism underlying the known technical effect was the contribution made by the new invention (that it was the esterase activity of the compounds that led to their deodorising activity) and this was not sufficient to make the claim novel.

See CLBA, pp.95–101. CLBA

### *Abusive disclosure exemption* 2–051

For the application of Art.54 a disclosure of the invention is not taken into consideration if it occurred no earlier than six months preceding the filing of the European patent application and if it was due to, or in consequence of an evident abuse in relation to the applicant or his legal predecessor. Art.55(1)(a)

The "no earlier than" language was chosen carefully so as to include the publication of Art.54(3) documents after the filing date of the application in question. Thus, Art.55(1)(a) applies to Art.54(2) and Art.54(3) documents, the "disclosure" of the invention being in each case its publication.

Headnote: "For the calculation of the six-month period referred to in Art.55(1) EPC, the relevant date is the date of the actual filing of the European patent application; the date of priority is not to be taken account of in calculating this period." G3/98/G2/99

The Enlarged Board differentiated the terms "filing of the application" which is the date that the applicant files the documents and used in Art.75, Art.76(1), Art.133(2) and Art.78(2) determining the time limit for fees and "date of filing" which is the date given to the application after examination under Art.90(1) and, for instance, determines the term of the patent under Art.63.

There is no evident abuse when a government department accidentally publishes a patent application early since the term implies some intent to cause harm or reasonable expectation that harm would ensue. T585/92

See C/IV/8.1–8.3. Guidelines

### *Exhibition exemption* 2–052

For the application of Art.54 a disclosure of the invention is not taken into consideration if it occurred no earlier than six months preceding the filing of the European patent application and if it was due to, or in consequence of the fact that the applicant or his legal predecessor has displayed the invention at an official, or officially recognised, international exhibition falling within the terms of the Convention on international exhibitions signed at Paris on November 22, 1928 and last revised on November 30, 1972. Art.55(1)(b)

In the case of Art.55(1)(b), the exemption only applies if the applicant states, when filing the European patent application, that the invention has been so displayed and files a supporting certificate within the period and under the conditions laid down in the Implementing Regulations. Art.55(2)

There is no remedy if the statement is not made on the filing date except perhaps to file another application if still within the six-month period.

The period for filing the certificate is four months from the filing date. The certificate must also state the opening date of the exhibition and, where the first disclosure of the r.23

invention did not coincide with the opening date of the exhibition, the date of the first disclosure. The certificate must be accompanied by an identification of the invention, duly authenticated by the above-mentioned authority.

*Restitutio* is possible if the 4 month time limit is missed.

G3/98     See comments above under "abusive disclosure exemption".

AnReg     See under Art.55(1)(b) for a list of exhibitions which qualify as relevant international exhibitions ([1979] O.J. 159 and annual updates).

Guidelines     See C/IV/8.4.

## 2–053    *Novelty of selection inventions*

Guidelines     The disclosure in the prior art of a general term does not, in principle, destroy the novelty of a subsequent claim to a specific embodiment falling within the general term but described at a lower order of generality (see Guidelines C/IV/7.4—the disclosure of "metal" would not destroy the novelty of a later claim to "copper"). The subsequent claim embodies a selection invention.

Case law     Selection inventions are most common in the chemical field. The lead case is T12/81. Here it was decided that the disclosure of a list of starting materials in combination with a list of potential processes made available the product of each process when carried out in respect of each starting material. However, it was acknowledged that when two starting materials had to be chosen from lists of some length, any particular product would be new. This concept was extended analogously in T7/86 to a prior art generic formula with multiple substituents where selection of any particular compound by choosing a substituent from each of at least two lists represents a novel selection.

Specific chemical compounds are thus novel unless there is a direct and unambiguous prior disclosure of the same compound in the form of a technical teaching (T181/82, T296/87), the same applying to enantiomers where only the racemate is known (T296/87). However, with overlapping generic formulae the situation is less clear (T133/92, T12/90).

In the case of ranges, there are two approaches. A sub-range selected from a broader range disclosed in the prior art is novel if it is: (a) narrow; (b) removed from the preferred part of the prior art range; and (c) is a purposive as opposed to an arbitrary selection, i.e. has some new property associated with it (T279/89). A claimed range that overlaps with a prior art range (assuming the end point of the prior art range is disclaimed) is novel where the skilled person would not seriously contemplate working in the area of overlap (T666/89).

Guidelines     See C/IV/7.7.

### Which inventions involve an inventive step?

## 2–054    *Definition of inventive step*

Art.56     An invention is considered to involve an inventive step if, having regard to the state of the art, it is not obvious to a person skilled in the art. However, for this purpose the state of the art does not include documents within the meaning of Art.54(3).

CLBA     See in general CLBA, pp.101–141.

Guidelines     See C/IV/9.1–9.13.

## 2. Requirements of the Invention

### Problem-solution approach

2–055

The problem-solution approach is derived from r.27(1)(d) which states that the description must, inter alia, specify the technical field to which the invention relates and disclose the invention, as claimed, in such terms that the technical problem and its solution can be understood. This is a mandatory requirement of the description (T26/81). The problem-solution approach is used by the EPO universally in assessing inventive step and should be used by the candidate throughout the EQE, particularly in Papers B and C.

Case law

The first step in applying the problem-solution approach is to identify the closest prior art. This is the piece of prior art that, in retrospect, represents the most promising springboard for making the invention (T254/86) and is usually the piece of art aimed at solving the same problem as the invention which requires the minimum structural modification (T606/89). Where the invention is a new process for making a known compound, the closest prior art will be a known process for making the compound (T641/89).

The second step is to assess the technical results achieved by the invention in relation to the closest prior art and hence derive the objective problem that the invention has solved, i.e. (1) what is the difference between the prior art and the claim, (2) what technical effect is associated with the difference and (3) the problem will be providing means delivering such an effect. Only those features which contribute to the solution (T37/82) and which distinguish over the prior art (T192/82) can contribute to an inventive improvement and be used in deriving the objective technical problem. Furthermore, only features which contribute to the technical character of the invention can be taken into account (T641/00).

The objective technical problem will often be the problem disclosed in the application (T495/91) but may be different where the closest prior art has changed (T13/84). It is possible to provide data during prosecution showing that a more challenging problem has been solved (T1/80, T184/82) as long as the new problem is consistent with the application as a whole and the skilled person would recognise the new problem as implied by or related to the original problem (T184/82). The formulated problem should include no pointer to the solution (T229/85), although a non-technical feature of a claim (e.g. an aim to be achieved in a non-technical field) may form part of the problem (T641/00).

The third step in the problem-solution approach is to assess whether the solution to the objective problem proposed by the invention would have been obvious to the skilled person at the filing/priority date on the basis of his common general knowledge or on the basis of a further piece of prior art that can be legitimately combined with the closest prior art (see below).

See C/IV/9.8.

Guidelines

### The skilled person and common general knowledge

2–056

The skilled person can be a person or a team (e.g. T141/87, T424/90) but has no inventive capacity (T39/93). The skilled person usually works in the same field as that in which the problem is formulated (T422/93) but if the problem prompts the skilled man to seek a solution in another technical field then the skilled person is in the latter field (T32/81).

Case law

Common general knowledge includes handbooks and textbooks in any language (T426/88) and may even include patents/publications in very new fields (T51/87).

In general, which sources are classed as common general knowledge is a unique assessment to be made for each technical area based on the practice of skilled people and, for example, included generally available databases in the field of gene technology (T890/02)

### Considerations when asking whether invention obvious

2–057

Inventive step is to be assessed at the priority date of the application (T241/81, T268/89, T772/94). Hindsight is to be avoided (hence the absence of any pointer to the solution when formulating the objective technical problem) and the invention is to be

Case law

judged from the closest prior art looking forwards, not from the invention looking backwards (T181/82).

When assessing obviousness it is not a question of whether the skilled man could have made the invention but whether he would have done so in the expectation of some improvement or advantage (T2/83, T265/84).

Documents may only be combined if it would have been obvious to the skilled man to do so (e.g. T142/84) and as long as there is no conflict between them (T2/81, T39/82).

Guidelines  C/IV/9.8.3–9.9.

## 2–058 *Inventive step based on an unexpected advantage*

Case law  Unforseeable advantages achieved by a new invention may indicate an inventive step (T2/81, T39/82) and even a small increase in yield (e.g. 0.5 per cent) can be taken into account if commercially significant (T38/84). Where comparative tests are necessary to substantiate such an advantage, the closest structural prior art must be chosen for data generation (T181/82). Where inventive step relies on an unexpected technical effect, this property must extend to everything embraced by the claim scope (T939/92).

However, where there is an obvious advantage to combining features, further unexpected advantages are merely a bonus and cannot be used to justify inventive step (T21/81, T936/96). Equally, if only one way forward exists for the skilled man (one way street) a resulting advantage is irrelevant (T192/82, T69/83).

Guidelines  See C/IV/9.10.2–9.11.

## 2–059 *Further indicators of inventive step*

Case law  An inventive step is present where there is no reasonable expectation of success (T386/94). Secondary indications of inventive step include a long-felt want (T109/82, T271/84), overcoming a prejudice (T18/81) and commercial success (T191/82, T677/91). Sometimes, the discovery of an unrecognised problem can be non-obvious in itself, even where the solution is immediately apparent when the problem is recognised (T2/83) but not if the problem could have been posed by one of ordinary skill in the art, particularly if arising during routine use of a known object (T109/82).

## 3. FILING A EUROPEAN PATENT APPLICATION

### 2–060 Who is entitled to file a European patent application?

Art.58  A European patent application may be filed by any natural or legal person, or any body equivalent to a legal person by virtue of the law governing it.

Art.59  A European patent application may also be filed either by joint applicants or by two or more applicants designating different Contracting States.

In contrast to the PCT, anybody of any nationality can file a European patent application.

### Where may a European patent application be filed?

## 2–061 *Where to file a regular European patent application*

Art.75(1)  A European patent application may be filed:

(a) at the European Patent Office at Munich or its branch at The Hague, or

(b) if the law of a Contracting State so permits, at the central industrial property office or other competent authority of that State. An application filed in this way has the same effect as if it had been filed on the same date at the European Patent Office.

Applications may also be filed with the Berlin sub-office of the EPO (see under Art.10(2)—[1989] O.J. 218). However, the Vienna sub-office is not a filing office (see under Art.75 — [1992] O.J. 183). Applications may be filed in Munich at the EPO Pschorrhofe building or at the Erhardstrasse building (see under Art.10(2)—[1991] O.J. 223). Documents filed with the German patent office (except when delivered by hand), in Berlin or Munich, used to be considered as received on behalf of the EPO and forwarded directly. Payments by post fell within this safeguard but not payments to a German Patent Office account which were refunded (see under Art.75 — [1991] O.J. 187). However, this agreement has been cancelled as at September 1, 2005 and applications will now receive the date that they actually arrive at the EPO ([2005] O.J. 445). See under r.24(1) for the opening hours of the filing offices ([1994] O.J. 954) and information on the correct addressing of mail ([2002] O.J. 374).

AnReg

Headnote (1): "The capacity of the President of the EPO to represent the European Patent Organisation by virtue of Art.5(3) EPC is one of his functions but is not one of his powers. The extent of the President's power is governed by the EPC, but not by Art.5(3) EPC."

G5/88

Headnote (2): "To the extent that the Administrative Agreement dated June 29, 1981 between the President of the EPO and the President of the German Patent Office contains terms regulating the treatment of documents intended for the EPO and received by the German Patent Office in Berlin, the President of the EPO did not himself have the power to enter into such an agreement on behalf of the EPO, at any time before the opening of the Filing Office for the EPO in Berlin on July 1, 1989."

Headnote (3): "In application of the principle of good faith and the protection of the legitimate expectations of users of the EPO, if a person has at any time since publication of the agreement in the O.J. and before July 1, 1989, filed documents intended for the EPO at the German Patent Office in Berlin (otherwise than by hand), the EPO was then bound to treat such documents as if it had received them on the date of receipt at the German Patent Office in Berlin."

The Enlarged Board took the view that Art.10(2)(a), which gives the President the power to "take all necessary steps ... to ensure the functioning of the EPO" entitled him to set up the agreement in respect of the Munich office but not the Berlin office since in Berlin there was no EPO filing office and no risk of confusion. In fact, Berlin was inserted into the agreement by the German Patent Office for political reasons. When the EPO filing office in Berlin came into being, however, the whole agreement was justified. Those people who had relied on the unjustified part of the agreement, however, should not be disadvantaged in order to protect their legitimate expectations. The case was joined with G7/88 and G8/88.

See CLBA, p.591.

CLBA

See A/II/1.

Guidelines

See Table II for information on whether a particular country allows the filing of European applications with its national authority and, if so, what languages are accepted.

NatLaw

The extension of time-limits in the case of shut-days and mail interruptions (r.85(1) and (2)) applies to national offices as it applies to the EPO.

r.85(3)

### *Where to file a divisional application*

2–062

A European divisional application must be filed directly with the European Patent Office at Munich or its branch at The Hague or in Berlin.

Art.76(1)

| | |
|---|---|
| Art.75(3) | No Contracting State can therefore provide for or allow the filing of a divisional application at a competent authority in that state. |
| Guidelines | See A/IV/1.3.1. |

### 2–063 Where to file a replacement application under Art.61(1)(b)

| | |
|---|---|
| Guidelines | A national office may be used in addition to the EPO (see A/IV/2.7). |

### 2–064 Restrictions on the filing of European patent applications under national law

| | |
|---|---|
| Art.75(2) | In spite of Art.75(1), national law may contain legislative or regulatory provisions which, in any Contracting State: |

    (a) govern inventions which, owing to the nature of their subject-matter, may not be communicated abroad without the prior authorisation of the competent authorities of that State, or

    (b) prescribe that each application is to be filed initially with a national authority or make direct filing with another authority subject to prior authorisation.

| | |
|---|---|
| NatLaw | See Table II for such restrictions imposed by national law. |
| r.85(3) | The extension of time-limits in the case of shut-days and mail interruptions (r.85(1) and (2)) applies to national offices as it applies to the EPO. |

### 2–065 Procedure where the application is filed with a national office — time limit for forwarding to the EPO

| | |
|---|---|
| Art.77(1) | The central industrial property office of a Contracting State is obliged to forward to the European Patent Office, in the shortest time compatible with the application of national law concerning the secrecy of inventions in the interests of the State, any European patent applications which have been filed with that office or with other competent authorities in that State. |
| Art.77(2) | Contracting States must take all appropriate steps to ensure that European patent applications, the subject of which is obviously not liable to secrecy by virtue of the law referred to Art.77(1), are forwarded to the European Patent Office within six weeks after filing. |
| Art.77(3) | European patent applications which require further examination as to their liability to secrecy must be forwarded in such manner as to reach the European Patent Office within four months after filing, or, where priority has been claimed, fourteen months after the date of priority. |
| Art.77(4) | A European patent application, the subject of which has been made secret, is not forwarded to the European Patent Office. |
| Art.77(5) | European patent applications which do not reach the European Patent Office before the end of the fourteenth month after filing or, if priority has been claimed, after the date of priority, are deemed to be withdrawn. The filing, search and designation fees are refunded. |
| J3/80 | No *restitutio* is available where the time limit for forwarding is missed since the applicant is not responsible for complying with the time limit. |
| | No further processing is available either. However, conversion is possible (Art.135). |
| r.15(3) | In the case of a replacement application the time limit for forwarding by a national office is four months. |

## Manner of filing the application

### *Filing in writing by post or by hand* — 2–066

The application may be filed in writing with any of the Art.75 authorities, either directly or by post. r.24(1)

See A/II/1.1. Guidelines

### *Filing by fax* — 2–067

In addition to filing in writing, the President of the EPO may permit applications to be filed by other means of communication and may lay down conditions governing their use. He may, in particular, require that within such period as the EPO specifies, written confirmation be supplied, reproducing the contents of applications so filed in response to an invitation and complying with the requirements of the Implementing Regulations. r.24(1)

See under r.24(1). Applications may also be filed with the EPO (and those national offices which so allow) by fax. The applicant may be invited to file a confirmation copy within a non-extensible period of one month but this is no longer routinely required ([2005] O.J. 41—see also CLBA, p.405). If the confirmation is not filed in response to an invitation, the application is refused under Art.91(3). AnReg

See A/II/1.2. Guidelines

### *Filing electronically* — 2–068

See above under filing by fax. r.24(1)

See under Art.24(1). Applications may also be filed with the EPO (and those national offices which so allow) electronically, either on-line or on CD-ROM ([2002] O.J. 543). AnReg

See [2004] O.J. 270 for details relating to electronic filing of a European patent application at the German Patent Office. O.J.

See A/II/1.3 Guidelines

### *Filing by other means* — 2–069

No other means of filing (e.g. telex, email) are allowed (see [2005] O.J. 44 and A/II/1.4). If filed by such means, an application will not be treated as such and no date of filing will be accorded. Guidelines

## Under what circumstances can a divisional application be filed? — 2–070

All details relating to the filing of divisional applications are to be found in the Implementing Regulations. Art.76(3)

The applicant may file a divisional application relating to any pending earlier European patent application. r.25(1)

"Pending" means up to but not including the date of the mention of grant (see A/IV/1.1.1 and [2002] O.J. 112). Guidelines

Where the time limit under r.25(1) for filing a divisional application has been missed, *restitutio* cannot be applied. J24/03

Where the earlier application is not pending at the time of filing the divisional application, the EPO sends a r.69(1) communication saying that it can't be treated as a divisional application and refunds fees.

| | |
|---|---|
| T1158/01 | The "earlier" European patent application may itself be a divisional application as long as it complied with Art.76(1) (subject matter not to be extended). |
| J2/01 | Where the earlier application has been filed jointly by two or more applicants and the requirements of Art.61 or r.20(3) have not been met, the right to file a divisional application is only available to these joint applicants and not to one alone or to fewer than all of them. |

An important series of cases concerning divisional applications have been referred to the Enlarged Board of Appeal and are currently (September 2006) pending. The first of these, which is pending as G1/05 posed the following questions for the Enlarged Board of Appeal:

(1) Can a divisional application which does not meet the requirements of Article 76(1) EPC because, at its actual filing date, it extends beyond the content of the earlier application, be amended later in order to make it a valid divisional application?

(2) If the answer to question (1) is yes, is this still possible when the earlier application is no longer pending?

(3) If the answer to question (2) is yes, are there any further limitations of substance to this possibility beyond those imposed by Articles 76(1) and 123(2) EPC? Can the corrected divisional application in particular be directed to aspects of the earlier application not encompassed by those to which the divisional as filed had been directed?

In the second case, G1/06, the following questions were referred: (1) In the case of a sequence of applications consisting of a root (originating) application followed by divisional applications, each divided from its predecessor, is it a necessary and sufficient condition for a divisional application of that sequence to comply with Article 76(1) EPC, second sentence, that anything disclosed in that divisional application be directly, unambiguously and separately derivable from what is disclosed in each of the preceding applications as filed?

(2) If the above condition is not sufficient, does said sentence impose the additional requirement (a) that the subject-matter of the claims of said divisional be nested within the subject-matter of the claims of its divisional predecessors? or (b) that all the divisional predecessors of said divisional comply with Article 76(1) EPC?

In the third case, G3/06, the following questions were referred: Can a patent which has been granted on a divisional application which did not meet the requirements of Article 76(1) EPC because at its actual date of filing it extended beyond the content of the earlier application, be amended during opposition proceedings in order to overcome the ground of opposition under Article 100(c) EPC and thereby fulfill said requirements?

| | |
|---|---|
| 2–071 | **4. REQUIREMENTS RELATING TO THE APPLICATION AS FILED** |
| Art.78(3) | A European patent application must satisfy the conditions laid down in the Implementing Regulations. |
| 2–072 | **Requirements relating to the request** |
| Art.78(1)(a) | A European patent application must contain a request for grant. |
| 2–073 | *Use of a specified form* |
| r.26(1) | A form drawn up by the EPO must be used. It is available free of charge from Art.75(1) authorities (EPO Hague, Munich and Berlin and national patent offices). |

### Petition for grant
2–074

The request must contain a petition for the grant of a European patent.  r.26(2)(a)

### Details of the applicant
2–075

The request must state the name, address and nationality of the applicant and the State in which his residence or principal place of business is located.  r.26(2)(c)

Names of natural persons must be indicated by the person's family name and given name(s), the family name being indicated before the given name(s). Names of legal entities, such as companies considered to be legal entities by reason of the legislation to which they are subject, must be indicated by their official designations.

Addresses must be indicated in such a way as to satisfy the customary requirements for the prompt postal delivery at the indicated address. They must in any case comprise all the relevant administrative units, including the house number, if any. It is recommended that the telegraphic and telex address and telephone number be indicated.

For a divisional application the applicant(s) must be the registered applicant(s) for the parent application, unless the requirements of Art.61 or r.20 have been met (this cannot be remedied after filing the notional divisional application).  J2/01

### Details of any representative
2–076

Where there is more than one applicant, the request should preferably contain the appointment of one applicant or representative as common representative.  r.26(3)

If a representative has been appointed, his name and the address of his place of business must be specified using the same format specified for the applicant details.  r.26(2)(d)

### Designation of the inventor
2–077

A European patent application must designate the inventor.  Art.81

The designation of the inventor must be filed in the request (as confirmed by r.26(2)(k)) when the applicant and the inventor are the same. In the alternative, the designation of the inventor must be filed in a separate document.  r.17(1)

See separate section below for further details.

### Title of the invention
2–078

The request must contain the title of the invention which must clearly and concisely state the technical designation of the invention and must exclude all "fancy names".  r.26(2)(b)

The title will be changed by the EPO if it does not conform to this standard (see under r.26(2)(b)—[1991] O.J. 224).  AnReg

See A/III/7.  Guidelines

### Priority claim
2–079

Where applicable, the request must contain a declaration claiming the priority of an earlier application and indicating the date on which and the country in or for which the earlier application was filed.  r.26(2)(g)

See separate section below for further details.

# Antrag auf Erteilung eines europäischen Patents / Request for grant of a European patent / Requête en délivrance d'un brevet européen

☐ Bestätigung einer bereits durch Telefax eingereichten Anmeldung/
Confirmation of an application already filed by fax/
Confirmation d'une demande déjà déposée par télécopie     am / on / le _____ bei / with / auprès de _____

| Nur für amtlichen Gebrauch / For official use only / Cadre réservé à l'administration | | | |
|---|---|---|---|
| Anmeldenummer / Application No. / N° de la demande | MKEY | 1 | |
| Tag des Eingangs (Regel 24 (2)) / Date of receipt (Rule 24(2)) / Date de réception (règle 24(2)) | DREC | 2 | |
| Tag des Eingangs beim EPA (Regel 24 (4)) / Date of receipt at EPO (Rule 24(4)) / Date de réception à l'OEB (règle 24(4)) | RENA | 3 | |
| Anmeldetag / Date of filing / Date de dépôt | | 4 | |

Es wird die Erteilung eines europäischen Patents und gemäß Artikel 94 die Prüfung der Anmeldung beantragt / Grant of a European patent, and examination of the application under Article 94, are hereby requested / Il est demandé la délivrance d'un brevet européen et, conformément à l'article 94, l'examen de la demande     EXAM 4     5

*Prüfungsantrag in einer zugelassenen Nichtamtssprache (siehe Merkblatt II, 5): / Request for examination in an admissible non-EPO language (see Notes II,5): / Requête en examen dans une langue non officielle autorisée (voir notice II,5):* ☒

Auf die Aufforderung nach Artikel 96 (1), zu erklären, ob die Anmeldung aufrechterhalten wird, wird verzichtet / The applicant waives his right to indicate whether he wishes to proceed further with the application (Art. 96(1)) / Le demandeur renonce à l'invitation selon l'article 96(1) à déclarer si la demande est maintenue     MEPA     5a

Zeichen des Anmelders oder Vertreters (max. 15 Positionen) / Applicant's or representative's reference (maximum 15 spaces) / Référence du demandeur ou du mandataire (max. 15 caractères ou espaces)     AREF     6

**Anmelder / Applicant / Demandeur**
Name / Nom     7

Anschrift / Address / Adresse     8

APPR 01 #
# DEST #

Zustellanschrift / Address for correspondence / Adresse pour la correspondance     9

PADR

Staat des Wohnsitzes oder Sitzes / State of residence or of principal place of business / Etat du domicile ou du siège     10

Staatsangehörigkeit / Nationality / Nationalité     11

Telefon / Telephone / Téléphone     12

Telefax / Fax / Télécopie     13

Weitere(r) Anmelder auf Zusatzblatt / Additional applicant(s) on additional sheet / Autre(s) demandeur(s) sur feuille supplémentaire     14

**Vertreter / Representative / Mandataire**
Name / Nom     15
(**Nur einen** Vertreter angeben, der in das europäische Patentregister einzutragen ist und an den zugestellt wird) / (Name **only one** representative, who is to be listed in the Register of European Patents and to whom notification is to be made) / (N'indiquer qu'**un seul** mandataire, qui sera inscrit au Registre européen des brevets et auquel signification sera faite)

FREP 01     #     # #

Geschäftsanschrift / Address of place of business / Adresse professionnelle     16

Telefon / Telephone / Téléphone     17

Telefax / Fax / Télécopie     18

Weitere(r) Vertreter auf Zusatzblatt / Additional representative(s) on additional sheet / Autre(s) mandataire(s) sur feuille supplémentaire     19

TRAN     FILL

EPA/EPO/OEB Form 1001.1 07.05

Raum für Zeichen des Anmelders /
Space for applicant's reference /
Espace réservé à la référence du demandeur _____

## 4. Requirements Relating to the Application as Filed

| | | |
|---|---|---|
| **Vollmacht / Authorisation / Pouvoir** | | |
| ist beigefügt / is enclosed / joint | 20 | |
| Allgemeine Vollmacht ist registriert unter Nummer / General authorisation has been registered under No. / Un pouvoir général a été enregistré sous le numéro    GENA | 21 | Nummer / Number / Numéro |
| **Erfinder / Inventor / Inventeur**    INVT 20 #   # | | |
| Anmelder ist (sind) alleinige(r) Erfinder / The applicant(s) is (are) the sole inventor(s) / Le(s) demandeur(s) est (sont) le (les) seul(s) inventeur(s) | 22 | |
| Erfindernennung in gesondertem Schriftstück / Designation of inventor attached / Voir la désignation de l'inventeur ci-jointe | 23 | |
| **Bezeichnung der Erfindung / Title of invention / Titre de l'invention**    TIDE   TIEN   TIFR | 24 | |
| **Prioritätserklärung / Declaration of priority / Déclaration de priorité**    PRIO | 25 | Staat/State/Etat   Anmeldetag / Date of filing / Date de dépôt   Aktenzeichen / File No. / N° de dépôt |
| 01 # . . # . . . . . . . . # . . . . . . . . . . . . . # | | 1 |
| 02 # . . # . . . . . . . . # . . . . . . . . . . . . . # | | 2 |
| 03 # . . # . . . . . . . . # . . . . . . . . . . . . . # | | 3 |
| 04 # . . # . . . . . . . . # . . . . . . . . . . . . . # | | 4 |
| Weitere Prioritätserklärung(en) auf Zusatzblatt / Additional declaration(s) of priority on additional sheet / Autre(s) déclaration(s) de priorité sur feuille supplémentaire | | |
| Es wird hiermit erklärt, dass die Anmeldung eine vollständige Übersetzung der früheren Anmeldung ist (Regel 38 (5)) / The applicant hereby declares that the application is a complete translation of the previous application (Rule 38(5)) / Il est déclaré par la présente que la demande est une traduction intégrale de la demande antérieure (règle 38(5))    PRIO 6 | 25a | |
| **Biologisches Material**    **Biological material** | 26 | **Matière biologique** |
| Die Erfindung bezieht sich auf bzw. verwendet biologisches Material, das nach Regel 28 hinterlegt worden ist. Die Angaben nach Regel 28 (1) c) (falls noch nicht bekannt, die Hinterlegungsstelle und das (die) Bezugszeichen [Nummer, Symbole usw.] des Hinterlegers) sind in den technischen Anmeldungsunterlagen enthalten auf    BIOM 1 | | The invention relates to and/or uses biological material deposited under Rule 28. The particulars referred to in Rule 28(1)c) (if not yet known, the depositary institution and the identification reference(s) [number, symbols, etc.] of the depositor) are given in the technical documents in the application on    L'invention concerne et/ou utilise de la matière biologique, déposée conformément à la règle 28. Les indications visées à la règle 28(1)c) (si elles ne sont pas encore connues, l'autorité de dépôt et la (les) référence(s) d'identification [numéro ou symboles, etc.] du déposant) figurent dans les pièces techniques de la demande à la/aux |
| | 27 | Seite(n) / page(s)    Zeile(n) / line(s) / ligne(s) |
| werden später mitgeteilt / will be submitted later / seront communiquées ultérieurement | 27a | |
| Die Empfangsbescheinigung(en) der Hinterlegungsstelle ist (sind) beigefügt / The receipt(s) of deposit issued by the depositary institution is (are) enclosed / Le(s) récépissé(s) de dépôt délivré(s) par l'autorité de dépôt est (sont) joint(s) | 27b | |
| wird (werden) nachgereicht / will be filed later / sera (seront) produit(s) ultérieurement | 27c | |

EPA/EPO/OEB Form 1001.2 07.05

Raum für Zeichen des Anmelders / Space for applicant's reference / Espace réservé à la référence du demandeur

## 2-080 Designations

Art.3 — The grant of a European patent may be requested for one or more of the Contracting States.

Art.79(1) — The request for the grant of a European patent must contain the designation of the Contracting State or States in which protection for the invention is desired (see also r.26(2)(h)).

Current Contracting States are:

| State | Entry into force | State | Entry into force |
| --- | --- | --- | --- |
| Austria (AT) | 1.5.79 | Liechtenstein (LI) | 1.4.80 |
| Belgium (BE) | 7.10.77 | Lithuania (LT) | 1.12.2004 |
| Bulgaria (BG) | 1.7.2002 | Luxembourg (LU) | 7.10.77 |
| Cyprus (CY) | 1.4.98 | Monaco (MC) | 1.12.91 |
| Czech Republic (CZ) | 1.7.2002 | Netherlands (NL) | 7.10.77 |
| Denmark (DK) | 1.1.90 | Poland (PL) | 1.3.2004 |
| Estonia (EE) | 1.7.2002 | Portugal (PT) | 1.1.92 |
| Finland (FI) | 1.3.96 | Romania (RO) | 1.3.2003 |
| France (FR) | 7.10.77 | Slovakia (SK) | 1.7.2002 |
| Germany (DE) | 7.10.77 | Slovenia (SI) | 1.12.2002 |
| Greece (GR) | 1.10.86 | Spain (ES) | 1.10.86 |
| Hungary (HU) | 1.1.2003 | Sweden (SE) | 1.5.78 |
| Iceland (IS) | 1.11.2004 | Switzerland (CH) | 7.10.77 |
| Ireland (IE) | 1.8.92 | Turkey (TR) | 1.11.2000 |
| Italy (IT) | 1.12.78 | United Kingdom (GB) | 7.10.77 |
| Latvia (LV) | 1.7.2005 | | |

Art.79(2) — Designations are subject to a fee—see below under fees.

Art.79(3) — Later withdrawal of a designation is possible—see the section on common provisions under withdrawal.

Art.76(2) — In the case of a European divisional application only Contracting States that were designated in the earlier application, and whose designation is still current at the time of filing of the divisional, may be designated in the divisional (see J19/96—CLBA, p.413).

CLBA — See CLBA, pp.408–410.

J30/90 — The EPC must be in force in a Contracting State on the filing date of the application for that State to be designated, whether the application is initiated under the EPC or PCT.

J18/90 — Where a designation is made for a State which is not yet eligible, the EPO will write and ask if the applicant wishes to post-date the application's filing date to make the designation effective.

Art.149(1) — A group of Contracting States may decide that they may only be designated jointly. This is the case with Switzerland and Lichtenstein.

Guidelines — See A/III/12.

## 4. Requirements Relating to the Application as Filed 387

| | | |
|---|---|---|
| Falls das biologische Material nicht vom Anmelder, sondern von einem Dritten hinterlegt wurde: / Where the biological material has been deposited by a person other than the applicant: / Lorsque la matière biologique a été déposée par une personne autre que le demandeur : | 28 | Name und Anschrift des Hinterlegers / Name and address of depositor / Nom et adresse du déposant : |
| Ermächtigung nach Regel 28 (1) d) / Authorisation under Rule 28(1)(d) / L'autorisation en vertu de la règle 28(1)d) | | |
| ist beigefügt / is enclosed / est jointe | 28a | ☐ |
| wird nachgereicht / will be filed later / sera produite ultérieurement | 28b | ☐ |
| Verzicht auf die Verpflichtung des Antragstellers nach Regel 28 (3) in gesondertem Schriftstück / Waiver of the right to an undertaking from the requester pursuant to Rule 28(3) attached | 29 | ☐ Renonciation, sur document distinct, à l'engagement du requérant au titre de la règle 28(3) |
| Gemäß Regel 28 (4) wird hiermit mitgeteilt, dass der Zugang zu dem in den Feldern 26 und 27 genannten biologischen Material nur durch Herausgabe einer Probe an einen Sachverständigen hergestellt wird / The applicant hereby declares under Rule 28(4) that the availability of the biological material referred to in Sections 26 and 27 shall be effected only by the issue of a sample to an expert    BIOM 3 | 30 | ☐ Conformément à la règle 28(4), il est déclaré par la présente que l'accessibilité à la matière biologique mentionnée aux rubriques 26 et 27 ne peut être réalisée que par la remise d'un échantillon à un expert |

### Nucleotid- und Aminosäuresequenzen / Nucleotide and amino acid sequences / Séquences de nucléotides et d'acides aminés    SEQL 1

31

Die Beschreibung enthält ein Sequenzprotokoll nach Regel 27a (1) / The description contains a sequence listing in accordance with Rule 27a(1)

☐ La description contient une liste de séquences selon la règle 27bis(1)

Der vorgeschriebene Datenträger ist beigefügt / The prescribed data carrier is enclosed

☐ Le support de données prescrit est joint

Es wird hiermit erklärt, dass die auf dem Datenträger gespeicherte Information mit dem schriftlichen Sequenzprotokoll übereinstimmt (Regel 27a (2)) / The applicant hereby states that the information recorded on the data carrier is identical to the written sequence listing (Rule 27a(2))

☐ Il est déclaré par la présente que l'information figurant sur le support de données est identique à celle que contient la liste de séquences écrite (règle 27bis(2))

### Benennung der Vertragsstaaten und Erklärungen hierzu / Designation of contracting states and associated declarations    DEST / Désignation d'Etats contractants et déclarations à ce propos

32

1. Hiermit werden sämtliche Vertragsstaaten des EPÜ benannt, die diesem bei Einreichung dieser Anmeldung angehören*.

1. All states which are contracting states to the EPC at the filing of this application are hereby designated*.

☒ 1. Sont désignés tous les Etats qui sont des Etats parties à la CBE à la date du dépôt de la présente demande*.

2a. Es ist derzeit beabsichtigt, den **siebenfachen** Betrag einer Benennungsgebühr zu entrichten. Damit gelten die Benennungsgebühren für alle Vertragsstaaten als entrichtet (Art. 2 Nr. 3 GebO).

2a. It is currently intended to pay **seven times** the amount of the designation fee. The designation fees for all the contracting states are thereby deemed to have been paid (Art. 2, No. 3, RFees).

☒ 2a. Il est actuellement envisagé de payer un montant correspondant à **sept fois** la taxe de désignation. Les taxes de désignation sont ainsi réputées payées pour tous les Etats contractants (art. 2, point 3 du RRT).

2b. Abweichend von der Erklärung in Nr. 2a ist derzeit beabsichtigt, **weniger als sieben** Benennungsgebühren für folgende Vertragsstaaten zu entrichten (bitte Ländercodes und Vertragsstaaten angeben*):

2b. The declaration in No. 2a does not apply. Instead, it is currently intended to pay **fewer than seven** designation fees for the following contracting states (please indicate country codes and contracting states*):

☐ 2b. Contrairement à ce qui est indiqué au n° 2a, il est actuellement envisagé de payer **moins de sept** taxes de désignation pour les Etats contractants suivants (prière d'indiquer codes de pays et Etats contractants*) :

(1) ☐ _____
(2) ☐ _____
(3) ☐ _____
(4) ☐ _____
(5) ☐ _____
(6) ☐ _____

Es wird beantragt, für die unter Nr. 2b nicht aufgeführten Vertragsstaaten von der Zustellung von Mitteilungen nach Regel 85a (1) und Regel 69 (1) abzusehen.

No communications under Rules 85a(1) or 69(1) need be notified in respect of the contracting states not indicated under No. 2b.

Prière de ne pas procéder à la signification des notifications prévues par les règles 85bis(1) et 69(1) pour les Etats contractants n'ayant pas été mentionnés au n° 2b.

---

\* Stand bei Drucklegung: 31 Vertragsstaaten, und zwar: / Status when this form was printed: 31 contracting states, namely / Situation à la date d'impression : 31 Etats contractants, à savoir : **AT** Österreich / Austria / Autriche, **BE** Belgien / Belgium / Belgique, **BG** Bulgarien / Bulgaria / Bulgarie, **CH/LI** Schweiz und Liechtenstein / Switzerland and Liechtenstein / Suisse et Liechtenstein, **CY** Zypern / Cyprus / Chypre, **CZ** Tschechische Republik / Czech Republic / République tchèque, **DE** Deutschland / Germany / Allemagne, **DK** Dänemark / Denmark / Danemark, **EE** Estland / Estonia / Estonie, **ES** Spanien / Spain / Espagne, **FI** Finnland / Finland / Finlande, **FR** Frankreich / France / France, **GB** Vereinigtes Königreich / United Kingdom / Royaume-Uni, **GR** Griechenland / Greece / Grèce, **HU** Ungarn / Hungary / Hongrie, **IE** Irland / Ireland / Irlande, **IS** Island / Iceland / Islande, **IT** Italien / Italy / Italie, **LT** Litauen / Lithuania / Lituanie, **LU** Luxemburg / Luxembourg / Luxembourg, **LV** Lettland / Latvia / Lettonie, **MC** Monaco / Monaco / Monaco, **NL** Niederlande / Netherlands / Pays-Bas, **PL** Polen / Poland / Pologne, **PT** Portugal / Portugal / Portugal, **RO** Rumänien / Romania / Roumanie, **SE** Schweden / Sweden / Suède, **SI** Slowenien / Slovenia / Slovénie, **SK** Slowakische Republik / Slovak Republic / République slovaque, **TR** Türkei / Turkey / Turquie

EPA/EPO/OEB Form 1001.3 07.05

| | |
|---|---|
| 2–081 | ***Extension and registration of a European patent*** |
| AnReg | See under Art.79. A European patent can currently be extended to Albania ([1995] O.J. 803 and [1996] O.J. 82), Bosnia and Herzegovina ([2004] O.J. 619), Croatia ([2004] O.J. 117), the former Yugoslav Republic of Macedonia ([1997] O.J. 345 and [1997] O.J. 538) and Serbia and Montenegro ([2004] O.J. 563). |
| | Extension agreements with Latvia ([1994] O.J. 201 and [1995] O.J. 345), Lithuania ([1994] O.J. 201 and [1994] O.J. 527), Slovenia ([1994] O.J. 75 and [1999] O.J. 183) and Romania ([1994] O.J. 746 and [1996] O.J. 601) terminated when the EPC came into force for these states. |
| | Under the extension agreements, extension is deemed requested on filing. |
| | The extension fees must be paid within the same time limit as the designation fees. See section in the Guidelines for further details. |
| J14/00 | Under the extension agreements, r.85a(2) applies (Art.3). However, no other EPC provisions apply (Art.10) and so, for instance, r.88 may not be used to make corrections. |

| Extension state | Effective date of agreement | Date agreement terminated |
|---|---|---|
| Albania (AL) | 1.2.1996 | — |
| Bosnia and Herzegovina (BA) | 1.12.2004 | — |
| Croatia (HR) | 1.4.2004 | — |
| Latvia (LT) | 1.5.1995 | 1.07.2005 |
| Lithuania (LT) | 5.7.1994 | 1.12.2004 |
| Macedonia (MK) | 1.11.1997 | — |
| Romania (RO) | 15.10.1996 | 1.3.2003 |
| Serbia and Montenegro (YU) | 1.11.2004 | — |
| Slovenia (SI) | 1.3.1994 | 1.12.2002 |

| | |
|---|---|
| Guidelines | See A/III/13. |
| AnReg | See under Art.79. A European patent (UK) may be registered in Hong Kong—a request must be filed within six months of publication of the application ([1997] O.J. 429). A European patent (UK) may also be registered in several overseas territories after grant ([2004] O.J. 179). |
| 2–082 | ***Indication of divisional status*** |
| r.26(2)(e) | Where appropriate, the request must state that the application is a divisional application and indicate the number of the earlier European patent application. |
| 2–083 | ***Indication that application is a replacement application*** |
| r.26(2)(f) | In all cases covered by Art.61(1)(b) (new application filed because applicant had no right to the original application) the request must state the number of the original application. |
| 2–084 | ***Figure of the drawings to be published with the abstract*** |
| r.33(4) | Where the application contains drawings, the applicant should indicate the figure, or exceptionally figures, which should accompany the abstract when it is published. |

## 4. Requirements Relating to the Application as Filed

**33** Verschiedene Anmelder für verschiedene Vertragsstaaten / Different applicants for different contracting states / Différents demandeurs pour différents Etats contractants

APPR 02 # | | | | | | | # | | | | | | | | | | |

Name(n) des (der) Anmelder(s) und benannte Vertragsstaaten / Name(s) of applicant(s) and designated contracting states / Nom(s) du (des) demandeur(s) et des Etats contractants désignés

**34**

**Erstreckung des europäischen Patents**

Diese Anmeldung gilt als Antrag, die europäische Patentanmeldung und das darauf erteilte europäische Patent auf alle Nicht-Vertragsstaaten des EPÜ zu erstrecken, mit denen am Tag ihrer Einreichung „Erstreckungsabkommen" bestehen. Die Erstreckung wird jedoch nur wirksam, wenn die vorgeschriebene Erstreckungsgebühr entrichtet wird.

**Extension of the European patent**

This application is deemed to be a request to extend the European patent application and the European patent granted in respect of it to all non-contracting states to the EPC with which "extension agreements" exist on the date on which the application is filed. However, the extension only takes effect if the prescribed extension fee is paid.

EXPT

**Extension des effets du brevet européen**

[X] La présente demande est réputée constituer une requête en extension des effets de la demande de brevet européen et du brevet européen délivré sur la base de cette demande à tous les Etats non parties à la CBE avec lesquels il existe un «accord d'extension» à la date du dépôt de la demande. Toutefois, l'extension ne produit ses effets que si la taxe d'extension prescrite est acquittée.

Es ist derzeit beabsichtigt, die Erstreckungsgebühr für die nachfolgend angekreuzten Staaten zu entrichten: / It is currently intended to pay the extension fee for the states marked below with a cross: / Il est actuellement envisagé de payer la taxe d'extension pour les Etats dont le nom est coché ci-après :

Albanien / Albania / Albanie — AL

Bosnien und Herzegowina / Bosnia and Herzegovina / Bosnie-Herzégovine — BA

Kroatien / Croatia / Croatie — HR

Ehemalige jugoslawische Republik Mazedonien / Former Yugoslav Republic of Macedonia / Ex-République yougoslave de Macédoine — MK

Serbien und Montenegro / Serbia and Montenegro / Serbie-et-Monténégro — YU

(Platz für Staaten, mit denen nach Drucklegung dieses Formblatts „Erstreckungsabkommen" in Kraft treten) / (Space for states with which "extension agreements" enter into force after this form has been printed) / (Espace prévu pour des Etats à l'égard desquels des «accords d'extension» entreront en vigueur après l'impression du présent formulaire)

Die Anmeldung ist eine Teilanmeldung / The application is a divisional application / La présente demande constitue une demande divisionnaire

DFIL 9 | | | | | | | | #
PANR | | | | | | | | | #

**35** Nummer der früheren Anmeldung: Number of earlier application: Numéro de la demande initiale :

Es handelt sich um eine Anmeldung nach Artikel 61 (1) b) / The application is an Article 61(1)(b) application / La présente demande constitue une demande selon l'article 61(1)b)

DFIL 9 | | | | | | | | #
EANR | | | | | | | | | #

**36** Nummer der früheren Anmeldung: Number of earlier application: Numéro de la demande initiale :

**Patentansprüche / Claims / Revendications**   CLMS

**37** Zahl der Patentansprüche Number of claims Nombre de revendications

Zur Veröffentlichung mit der Zusammenfassung wird vorgeschlagen die Abbildung Nr. / It is proposed that the abstract be published together with figure No. / Il est proposé de publier avec l'abrégé la figure n°   DRAW 2

**39** Nummer / Number / Numéro

EPA/EPO/OEB Form 1001.4 07.05

Raum für Zeichen des Anmelders / Space for applicant's reference / Espace réservé à la référence du demandeur

PART B

| | |
|---|---|
| **2–085** | ***Additional copies of citations*** |
| RRF3(1) | The amount of the administrative fee is fixed by the President of the EPO. |
| AnReg | See under RRF. The amount is 25 euros ([2006] O.J. 257). |
| **2–086** | ***Signature*** |
| r.26(2)(i) | The request must contain the signature of the applicant or his representative (a failure to sign is correctable following an invitation under r.41(1)) . |
| Guidelines | Where there is more than one applicant, each (or the representative of each) must sign (A/III/4.2.2). |

| | |
|---|---|
| Zusätzliche Abschrift(en) der im europäischen Recherchenbericht angeführten Schriftstücke wird (werden) beantragt / Additional copy (copies) of the documents cited in the European search report is (are) requested / Prière de fournir une (des) copie(s) supplémentaire(s) des documents cités dans le rapport de recherche européenne   ASOC | 40   Anzahl der **zusätzlichen** Sätze von Abschriften / Number of **additional** sets of copies / Nombre de jeux **supplémentaires** de copies |
| Es wird die Rückerstattung der Recherchengebühr gemäß Artikel 10 Gebührenordnung beantragt / Refund of the search fee is requested pursuant to Article 10 of the Rules relating to Fees / Le remboursement de la taxe de recherche est demandé en vertu de l'article 10 du règlement relatif aux taxes | 41 |
| Eine Kopie des Recherchenberichts ist beigefügt / A copy of the search report is attached / Une copie du rapport de recherche est jointe | 42 |

**Automatischer Abbuchungsauftrag** (nur möglich für Inhaber von beim EPA geführten laufenden Konten)

**Automatic debit order** (for EPO deposit account holders only)

43 **Ordre de prélèvement automatique** (possibilité offerte uniquement aux titulaires de comptes courants ouverts auprès de l'OEB)

Das EPA wird hiermit beauftragt, fällig werdende Gebühren und Auslagen nach Maßgabe der Vorschriften über das automatische Abbuchungsverfahren vom nebenstehenden laufenden Konto abzubuchen.

The EPO is hereby authorised, under the Arrangements for the automatic debiting procedure, to debit from the deposit account opposite any fees and costs falling due.

Par la présente, il est demandé à l'OEB de prélever du compte courant ci-dessous les taxes et frais venant à échéance, conformément à la réglementation relative à la procédure de prélèvement automatique.

**Für automatischen Abbuchungsauftrag: For automatic debit order: Pour l'ordre de prélèvement automatique :**   DECA

Nummer des laufenden Kontos / Deposit account number / Numéro du compte courant

Name des Kontoinhabers / Account holder's name / Nom du titulaire du compte

Eventuelle **Rückzahlungen** auf das nebenstehende beim EPA geführte laufende Konto / Any **reimbursement** to EPO deposit account opposite / **Remboursements** éventuels à effectuer sur le compte courant ci-contre ouvert auprès de l'OEB   DEPA

44  Nummer des laufenden Kontos / Deposit account number / Numéro du compte courant

Name des Kontoinhabers / Account holder's name / Nom du titulaire du compte

| | |
|---|---|
| Die vorgeschriebene Liste über die diesem Antrag beigefügten Unterlagen ergibt sich aus der vorbereiteten Empfangsbescheinigung (Seite 6 dieses Antrags) | The prescribed list of documents enclosed with this request is shown on the prepared receipt (page 6 of this request) | 45 [X] La liste prescrite des documents joints à cette requête figure sur le récépissé préétabli (page 6 de la présente requête) |

46  Für Angestellte nach Artikel 133(3) Satz 1 mit allgemeiner Vollmacht / For employees under Article 133(3), first sentence, having a general authorisation / Pour les employés mentionnés à l'article 133(3), 1ère phrase, munis d'un pouvoir général

Nr. / No. / n° :

Unterschrift(en) des (der) Anmelder(s) oder Vertreter(s) / Signature(s) of applicant(s) or representative(s) / Signature(s) du (des) demandeur(s) ou du (des) mandataire(s)

Ort / Place / Lieu

Datum / Date

Name des (der) Unterzeichneten bitte in Druckschrift wiederholen. Bei juristischen Personen bitte die Stellung des (der) Unterzeichneten innerhalb der Gesellschaft in Druckschrift angeben. / Please print name under signature. In the case of legal persons, the position of the signatory within the company should also be printed. / Le ou les noms des signataires doivent être indiqués en caractères d'imprimerie. S'il s'agit d'une personne morale, la position occupée au sein de celle-ci par le ou les signataires doit être indiquée en caractères d'imprimerie.

EPA/EPO/OEB Form 1001.5 07.05

Raum für Zeichen des Anmelders / Space for applicant's reference / Espace réservé à la référence du demandeur

**2-087**  *List of documents accompanying the request*

r.26(2)(j)  The request must include a list of accompanying documents which also indicates the number of sheets of the description, claims, drawings and abstract filed with the request.

**2-088**  *Correction of the request*

J21/94  Correction of the request is possible when the wrong request is filed with an application (CLBA, p.404).

## 4. Requirements Relating to the Application as Filed

### Empfangsbescheinigung
(Liste der diesem Antrag beigefügten Unterlagen)
Hiermit wird der Empfang der unten bezeichneten Dokumente bescheinigt.
Wird im Falle der Einreichung der europäischen Patentanmeldung bei einer nationalen Behörde diese Empfangsbescheinigung vom Europäischen Patentamt übersandt, so ist sie als Mitteilung gemäß Regel 24 (4) anzusehen (siehe Feld RENA).

### Receipt for documents
(Checklist of enclosed documents)
Receipt of the documents indicated below is hereby acknowledged.
If this receipt is issued by the European Patent Office and the European patent application was filed with a national authority, it serves as a communication under Rule 24(4) (see Section RENA).

### Récépissé de documents  6
(Liste des documents annexés à la présente requête)
Nous attestons le dépôt des documents désignés ci-dessous.
Si, en cas de dépôt de la demande de brevet européen auprès d'un service national, l'Office européen des brevets délivre le présent récépissé de documents, ce récépissé est réputé être la notification visée à la règle 24(4) (cf. rubrique RENA).

*Nur für amtlichen Gebrauch / For official use only / Cadre réservé à l'administration*

*Amtsstempel / Official stamp / Cachet officiel*

Tag des Eingangs (Regel 24 (2)) / Date of receipt (Rule 24(2)) / Date de réception (règle 24(2)) — DREC

Anmeldenummer für den Schriftverkehr mit dem EPA; *Aktenzeichen für Prioritätserklärungen* / Application No. to be used in correspondence with the EPO; *File No. to be used for priority declarations* / N° de la demande à utiliser dans la correspondance avec l'OEB; *N° de dépôt à utiliser pour la déclaration de priorité*

Tag des Eingangs beim EPA (Regel 24 (4)) / Date of receipt at EPO (Rule 24(4)) / Date de réception à l'OEB (règle 24(4)) — RENA

**A. Anmeldungsunterlagen und Prioritätsbeleg(e) / Application documents and priority document(s) / Pièces de la demande et document(s) de priorité** — 47

1. Beschreibung (ohne Sequenzprotokollteil) / Description (excluding sequence listing part) / Description (sauf partie réservée au listage des séquences)
2. Patentansprüche / Claim(s) / Revendication(s)
3. Zeichnung(en) / Drawing(s) / Dessin(s) — DRAW 1 #
4. Sequenzprotokollteil der Beschreibung / Sequence listing part of description / Partie de la description réservée au listage des séquences
5. Zusammenfassung / Abstract / Abrégé
6. Übersetzung der Anmeldungsunterlagen / Translation of the application documents / Traduction des pièces de la demande
7. Prioritätsbeleg(e) / Priority document(s) / Document(s) de priorité
8. Übersetzung des (der) Prioritätsbelegs(belege) / Translation of priority document(s) / Traduction du (des) document(s) de priorité

Blattzahl* / Number of sheets* / Nombre de feuilles*

Gesamtzahl der Abbildungen* / Total number of figures* / Nombre total de figures*

* Die Richtigkeit der Angabe der Blattzahl und der Gesamtzahl der Abbildungen wurde bei Eingang nicht geprüft / No check was made on receipt that the number of sheets and the total number of figures indicated were correct / L'exactitude du nombre de feuilles et du nombre total de figures n'a pas été contrôlée lors du dépôt

**B. Der Anmeldung in der eingereichten Fassung liegen folgende Unterlagen bei: / This application as filed is accompanied by the items below: / Les pièces ci-après sont annexées à la présente demande :** — 48

1. Vollmacht / Authorisation / Pouvoir
2. Allgemeine Vollmacht / General authorisation / Pouvoir général
3. Erfindernennung / Designation of inventor / Désignation de l'inventeur
4. Früherer Recherchenbericht / Earlier search report / Rapport de recherche antérieure
5. Gebührenzahlungsvordruck (EPA Form 1010) / Voucher for the settlement of fees (EPO Form 1010) / Bordereau de règlement de taxes (OEB Form 1010)
6. Scheck *(nicht bei Einreichung bei den nationalen Behörden)* / Cheque *(not when filing with national authorities)* / Chèque *(pas de chèque en cas de dépôt auprès des services nationaux)*
7. Datenträger für Sequenzprotokoll / Data carrier for sequence listing / Support de données pour listage des séquences — SEQL 4
8. Zusatzblatt / Additional sheet / Feuille supplémentaire
9. Sonstige Unterlagen (bitte hier spezifizieren) / Other documents (please specify here) / Autres documents (veuillez préciser)

Zeichen des Anmelders: / Applicant's reference: / Référence du demandeur : — AREF

Betrag / Amount / Montant
(Ausfüllung freigestellt / optional / facultatif)
EUR

**C. Exemplare dieser Empfangsbescheinigung /** (bitte zutreffende Zahl ankreuzen)
**Copies of this receipt for documents /** (please mark appropriate number with a cross)
**Exemplaires du présent récépissé de documents** (veuillez cocher le chiffre correspondant) — 49

3 — Einreichung beim EPA direkt / Direct filing with the EPO / Dépôt direct auprès de l'OEB

4 — Einreichung bei einer nationalen Behörde / Filing with a national authority / Dépôt auprès d'un service national

EPA/EPO/OEB Form 1001.6 07.05

Raum für Zeichen des Anmelders /
Space for applicant's reference /
Espace réservé à la référence du demandeur

PART B

## 2–089 Requirements relating to the description

Art.78(1)(b)     A European patent application must contain a description.

## 2–090 *Need for a sufficient disclosure*

Art.83     A European patent application must disclose an invention in a manner sufficiently clear and complete for it to be carried out by a person skilled in the art.

G2/93     Sufficiency must be complied with at the filing date.

CLBA     See CLBA, pp.145–156. The disclosure is sufficient if the invention can be carried out without undue burden (T435/91). A reasonable amount of trial and error (T226/85) and the occasional lack of success (T14/83) are not fatal but the skilled man must not be expected to rely on chance events (T727/95). Common general knowledge may be used to supplement the disclosure of an application (T171/84, T51/87) and this includes the contents of textbooks (T206/83) but not usually patent applications (T206/83) unless special circumstances, e.g. a new field of technology, prevail (T51/87). However, a comprehensive search should not be necessary (T206/83). It should be possible to perform the invention over the entire area of the claims (T409/91) and in this respect the disclosure of a single example may (e.g. oncomouse, T19/90) or may not be enough (T409/91). It may (T206/83) or may not (T51/87) be a requirement to show how to make starting materials.

T1173/00     The decisive issue is whether the invention is sufficiently disclosed such that an average person skilled in the art, with knowledge of the patent and on the basis of that person's common general knowledge, could have carried it out.

r.28     Where a sample of biological material is necessary to practice the invention a deposit must be made before the filing date and certain information must be supplied in time for publication in order for the application to be sufficient (see under biotech section below).

Guidelines     See C/II/4.9.

## 2–091 *Content of the description*

r.27(1)     The description must:

       (a) specify the technical field to which the invention relates;

       (b) indicate the background art which, as far as known to the applicant, can be regarded as useful for understanding the invention, for drawing up the European search report and for the examination, and, preferably, cite the documents reflecting such art;

       (c) disclose the invention, as claimed, in such terms that the technical problem (even if not expressly stated as such) and its solution can be understood, and state any advantageous effects of the invention with reference to the background art;

       (d) briefly describe the figures in the drawings, if any;

       (e) describe in detail at least one way of carrying out the invention claimed using examples where appropriate and referring to the drawings, if any; and

       (f) indicate explicitly, when it is not obvious from the description or nature of the invention, the way in which the invention is capable of exploitation in industry.

T11/82     Pursuant to r.27(1)(b), prior art references must be added later where they are not in the application as filed.

T407/87     The requirement under r.27(1)(e) is part of the more general requirement under Art.83 for a sufficient disclosure. The lack of a detailed specific example is not necessarily fatal.

| | |
|---|---|
| The industrial application of a sequence or partial sequence of a gene must be disclosed in the patent application. | r.23e(3) |
| The description must include a sequence listing in certain circumstances. | r.27a |
| See C/II/4. | Guidelines |

### *Order of presentation of the content of the description* — 2–092

| | |
|---|---|
| The description must be presented in the manner and order specified in r.27(1) unless because of the nature of the invention, a different manner or a different order would afford a better understanding and a more economic presentation. | r.27(2) |
| See C/II/4.13. | Guidelines |

## Requirements relating to the claims — 2–093

| | |
|---|---|
| A European patent application must contain one or more claims. | Art.78(1)(c) |

### *Requirement for clarity, conciseness and support* — 2–094

| | |
|---|---|
| The claims must be clear and concise and be supported by the description. | Art.84 |
| Clarity should not be confused with simplicity. A claim may be complex but clear. In particular, a Markush formula is the most concise way of defining a group of chemical compounds. | T1020/98 |
| See CLBA, pp.157–168. | CLBA |
| See C/III/4–6. | Guidelines |

### *Claims to define matter the applicant seeks to protect* — 2–095

| | |
|---|---|
| The claims must define the matter for which protection is sought. Such definition must be in terms of the technical features of the invention. | Art.84/r.29(1) |

### *Situations in which two-part form is required* — 2–096

Wherever appropriate, claims must contain:   r.29(1)

(a) a statement indicating the designation of the subject matter of the invention and those technical features which are necessary for the definition of the claimed subject-matter but which, in combination, are part of the prior art; and

(b) a characterising part—preceded by the expression "characterised in that" or "characterised by"—stating the technical features which, in combination with the features stated in (a), it is desired to protect.

| | |
|---|---|
| The pre-characterising portion is normally based on the structurally closest prior art rather than the closest prior art for determining inventive step. | T13/84 |
| The two-part form is not always appropriate. This is particularly true in the field of chemistry. | T170/84 |
| Where the only relevant prior art is an Art.54(3) citation, the two-part form should not be used. The relevant art should however be clearly acknowledged in the description. | |
| See C/III/2.2–2.3b. | Guidelines |

| | |
|---|---|
| **2–097** | ***Number and type of claims allowed*** |
| r.29(5) | The number of claims must be reasonable in consideration of the nature of the invention claimed. |
| r.29(2) | In particular, the inclusion of more than one independent claim in the same category (product, process, apparatus or use) is only allowed if the subject-matter of the application involves either: |
| | (a) a plurality of inter-related products; |
| | (b) different uses of a product or apparatus; or |
| | (c) alternative solutions to a particular problem, where it is not appropriate to cover these alternatives by a single claim. |
| O.J. | See [2002] O.J. 113 for further explanation. Note in particular that it is incumbent on the applicant to justify the presence of multiple claims in the same category, even where the requirements of r.29(2) (a), (b), or (c) are met. |
| r.29(3) | Any claim stating the essential features of an invention may be followed by one or more claims containing particular embodiments of that invention. |
| r.29(4) | A dependent claim must, where possible, start with a reference to the claim from which it depends and then state the additional features which it is desired to protect. Such dependent claims are allowed even where the claim referred to is itself a dependent claim. All dependent claims must be grouped together in the most appropriate way. |
| Guidelines | See C/III/3. |
| **2–098** | ***Numbering of the claims*** |
| r.29(5) | If there are several claims they must be numbered consecutively in Arabic numerals. |
| **2–099** | ***Omnibus claims generally not allowed*** |
| r.29(6) | Except where absolutely necessary, claims may not rely, in respect of technical features of the invention, on references to the description or drawings such as "as described in part . . . of the description" or "as illustrated in figure . . . of the drawings." |
| T150/82 | The onus is on the applicant to demonstrate that an exceptional situation justifying the use of an omnibus claim prevails. |
| Guidelines | See C/III/4.10. |
| **2–100** | ***References in claims to reference signs in figures*** |
| r.29(7) | Where drawings are included, the technical features in the claims should preferably be followed by reference signs relating to those features if the intelligibility of the claim can thereby be increased. Such reference signs should be placed in parentheses. Such reference signs may not be construed as limiting the claim. |
| Guidelines | See C/III/4.11. |
| **2–101** | ***Unity of invention*** |
| Art.82 | A European patent application must relate to one invention only or to a group of inventions so linked as to form a single general inventive concept. |
| r.30(1) | Such a group of inventions is taken to be so linked when there is a technical relationship among the inventions involving one or more of the same or corresponding special |

technical features, i.e. those features which define a contribution which each of the claimed inventions considered as a whole makes over the prior art.

It matters not, in determining whether a group of inventions is so linked, whether they are in separate claims or alternatives within a single claim.  r.30(2)

See CLBA, pp.176–195.  CLBA

See C/III/7.  Guidelines

### *Allowability of disclaimers*  2–102

Disclaimers are allowed where the subject matter cannot be described positively. Subject to this requirement, disclaimers present on the filing of an application are not subject to the restrictions imposed by the Enlarged Board of Appeal Decisions G1/03 and G2/03.  T4/80

See below under amendment for the rules governing the introduction of an undisclosed disclaimer during prosecution.

### *Functional features*  2–103

Functional features are allowed where appropriate in order to obtain fair protection. The functional language can cover known or future variants (T292/85) and, as long as some suitable variants are known, some of the variants covered may be unsuitable or unavailable (T292/85). However, they are not allowed where the functional feature defines a technical effect central to inventive step (T435/91).  Case law

### **Requirements relating to the abstract**  2–104

A European patent application must contain an abstract.  Art.78(1)(e)

The abstract serves for use as technical information; it may not be taken into account for any other purpose, in particular not for the purpose of interpreting the scope of the protection sought nor for the purpose of applying Art.54, para.3.  Art.85

It should therefore be drafted so that it constitutes an efficient instrument for the purposes of searching in the particular technical field. In particular, it should enable the searcher to assess whether there is any need to consult the European patent application itself.  r.33(5)

The abstract must indicate the title of the invention.  r.33(1)

The abstract must contain a concise summary of the disclosure as contained in the description, the claims and any drawings; the summary must indicate the technical field to which the invention pertains and must be drafted in a way which allows the clear understanding of the technical problem, the gist of the solution of that problem through the invention and the principal use or uses of the invention. The abstract must, where applicable, contain the chemical formula which, among those contained in the application, best characterises the invention. It must not contain statements on the alleged merits or value of the invention or on its speculative application.  r.33(2)

The abstract should not be more than 150 words in length.  r.33(3)

Where the application contains drawings, the applicant should indicate the figure, or exceptionally figures, which should accompany the abstract when it is published. However, the EPO may decide to publish a different figure if of the view that it better characterises the invention.  r.33(4)

All features in the abstract illustrated by a drawing should be followed by a reference sign in parentheses.  r.33(4)

See C/II/2.  Guidelines

| | |
|---|---|
| 2–105 | **Requirements relating to the drawings** |
| Art.78(1)(d) | A European patent application must contain any drawings referred to in the description or claims. |
| r.32 | The formal requirements for drawings are set out in r.32. |
| AnReg | See under r.32. Drawings must be on pliable paper, not card ([1994] O.J. 74). |
| Guidelines | See C/II/5. |

**Requirements relating to a priority claim**

| | |
|---|---|
| 2–106 | *Relevance of the Paris Convention* |
| Case law | Unlike the PCT, which specifically applies it, the Paris Convention is not applicable to the EPC in the sense of being part of the law since the EPC contains its own complete priority code. However, this code should be consistent with the Paris Convention which can therefore be used to interpret it (see EPC preamble, J15/80, G 3/93, G2/98). |
| 2–107 | *Who may make a claim to priority?* |
| Art.87(1) | The priority right is enjoyed by a person who has duly filed in or for any State party to the Paris Convention for the Protection of Industrial Property (or other recognised state, see below), a certain kind of application (see below) and his successors in title. |
| J19/87 | National law applies to determine a valid successor in title. |
| 2–108 | *Time limit for making a claim to priority* |
| Art.87(1) | A right of priority exists during a period of 12 months from the date of filing of the first application. |
| Art.122(5) | *Restitutio* is not allowed in respect of the priority year time limit. |
| Guidelines | However, the priority year may be validly "extended" under r.84a (document posted in time) or r.85 (office not open)—see A/III/6.6. |
| 2–109 | *Valid priority claim to be in respect of the same invention* |
| Art.87(1) | The claims of the subsequent application that claims priority must be in respect of the same invention as disclosed in the earlier application. |
| Art.88(3) | If one or more priorities are claimed in respect of a European patent application, the right of priority covers only those elements of the European patent application which are included in the application or applications whose priority is claimed. |
| Art.88(4) | If certain elements of the invention for which priority is claimed do not appear among the claims formulated in the previous application, priority may nonetheless be granted, provided that the documents of the previous application as a whole specifically disclose such elements. |
| G2/98 | Headnote: "The requirement for claiming priority of 'the same invention', referred to in Art.87(1) EPC means that priority of a previous application in respect of a claim in a European patent application in accordance with Art.88 EPC is to be acknowledged only if the skilled person can derive the subject matter of the claim directly and unambiguously, using common general knowledge, from the previous application as a whole." |
| | The alternative (i.e. allowing priority where a feature not disclosed in the priority application has been inserted which merely limits scope and is not related to function and |

effect) was seen to be dangerously subjective and changeable during prosecution in the light of fresh prior art. The strict approach was seen to be consistent with the Paris Convention and Arts 87–89 EPC.

The priority document must also be an enabling disclosure of the invention for a priority claim to be valid.    T81/87

See CLBA, pp.236–248.    CLBA

See C/V/2.2.    Guidelines

### *What kind of application may be used as a basis for claiming priority?*    2–110

The priority application must be an application for a patent or for the registration of a utility model or for a utility certificate or for an inventor's certificate in or for any state party to the Paris Convention for the Protection of Industrial Property; but . . .    Art.87(1)

. . . if the first filing has been made in a state which is not a party to the Paris Convention for the Protection of Industrial Property, Art.87(1)–(4) apply only in so far as that state, according to a notification published by the Administrative Council, and by virtue of bilateral or multilateral agreements, grants on the basis of a first filing made in or for any Contracting State and subject to conditions equivalent to those laid down in the Paris Convention, a right of priority having equivalent effect.    Art.87(5)

No use has been made of Art.87(5) yet. In particular, since Monaco is not a WTO country, new r.4.10 PCT recognising priority applications filed in WTO countries has not been recognised.

Headnote: The TRIPS agreement does not entitle the applicant for a European patent application to claim priority from a first filing in a state which was not at the relevant dates a member of the Paris Convention but was a member of the WTO/TRIPS agreement (joined with G3/02).    G2/02

A design application such as a German Geschmacksmuster does not give rise to a priority right under the terms of Art.87(1).    J15/80

The EPO recognises a US provisional application as being a valid earlier application for claiming priority from (see under Art.87(1)—[1996] O.J. 81).    AnReg

Every filing that is equivalent to a regular national filing under the national law of the state where it was made or under bilateral or multilateral agreements, including the EPC, is recognised as giving rise to a right of priority.    Art.87(2)

By a regular national filing is meant any filing that is sufficient to establish the date on which the application was filed, whatever may be the outcome of the application.    Art.87(3)

Priority may normally ony be claimed from the first filing of any particular subject matter but a subsequent application for the same subject-matter as a previous first application and filed in or in respect of the same state is considered as the first application for the purposes of determining priority, provided that, at the date of filing the subsequent application, the previous application has been withdrawn, abandoned or refused, without being open to public inspection and without leaving any rights outstanding, and has not served as a basis for claiming a right of priority. The previous application may not thereafter serve as a basis for claiming a right of priority.    Art.87(4)

### *Procedure for claiming priority—what to file*    2–111

An applicant for a European patent desiring to take advantage of the priority of a previous application must file a declaration of priority.    Art.88(1)

| | |
|---|---|
| r.38(1)(2) | This declaration must indicate the date on which and the country in or for which the earlier application was filed and its file number. The date and country must be stated on filing. The file number must be indicated by the expiry of 16 months from the priority date. |
| r.26(2)(g) | The declaration must be included in the request (see above). |
| Art.88(1) | An applicant for a European patent desiring to take advantage of the priority of a previous application must also file a copy of the previous application. |
| r.38(3)(4) | The copy must be filed before the expiry of 16 months from the priority date, must be certified as an exact copy of the previous application by the authority which received the previous application and must be accompanied by a certificate issued by that authority stating the date of filing of the previous application. The copy will be deemed filed if a copy of the previous application is available to the EPO and the applicant requests a copy be included in the new file under the conditions laid down by the President of the EPO. |
| AnReg | See under r.38(3)(4) where these conditions are laid out ([1999] O.J. 80). The previous application must be a European patent application, an international patent application for which the EPO was receiving office or a Japanese patent or utility model application or an international patent application filed with the JPO as receiving office. When the EPO has included a copy of the previous application in the file, it informs the applicant ([2000] O.J. 227). Where the application claiming priority is a divisional application or a replacement application under Art.61(1)(b), there is no need to file the copy of the priority application if it was filed during prosecution of the parent application ([1979] O.J. 290). See also [1992] O.J. 299 under r.24(1). Priority documents are one of the few documents which cannot be filed by fax. |
| [2004] O.J. 562 AnReg | Priority documents issued by the USPTO in electronic form are now accepted by the EPO. See under r.38(3)(4) where the details are set out. |
| J11/95 | The priority document must be sent to the correct file to have been received in time (CLBA, p.396). |
| r.38a | Where the previous application is a European patent application, a certified copy can be obtained from the EPO. |
| RRF3(1) | The amount of the administrative fee for providing a certified copy is fixed by the President of the EPO and is currently 35 euros (see AnReg under RRF, [2006] O.J. 255). |
| RRF4(1)(2) | Where a due date is not specified for the payment of a fee, either in the EPC or the PCT, or their regulations, it falls due on the date of receipt of the request for the service incurring the fee concerned. However, the President of the EPO may decide that such services may be carried out without advance payment. |
| Art.88(1) | An applicant for a European patent desiring to take advantage of the priority of a previous application must, if the copy of the previous application is not one of the official languages of the European Patent Office, file a translation of it in one of those official languages. |
| r.38(5) | Alternatively, a declaration may be submitted to the effect that the European patent application is a complete translation of the previous application. |
| r.38(4)(5) | The translation must be filed within a time limit set by the EPO but at the latest within the r.51(4) time limit. The translation will be deemed filed if a copy of it is available to the EPO and the applicant requests a copy be included in the new file under the conditions laid down by the President of the EPO (see [1999] O.J. 80). |
| AnReg | See under r.38(3)(4), as described above, for the conditions under which a copy of an application available to the EPO will be included in the file ([1999] O.J. 80). Legal advice (19/99) is available concerning the translation or declaration ([1999] O.J. 296). Where the application claiming priority is a divisional application or a replacement application under Art.61(1)(b), there is no need to file the translation of the priority application if it was filed during prosecution of the parent application ([1979] O.J. 290). |

The particulars in the declaration of priority are published with the application. r.38(6)

See C/V/3. Guidelines

## Can one application claim more than one priority? 2–112

Multiple priorities may be claimed in respect of a European patent application, notwithstanding the fact that they originated in different countries. Where appropriate, multiple priorities may be claimed for any one claim. Where multiple priorities are claimed, time limits which run from the date of priority run from the earliest date of priority. Art.88(2)

## Can one priority be claimed in more than one application? 2–112A

This decision seemed to indicate that in respect of any particular subject matter and any particular state, the priority right is exhausted when once claimed. However, this has not been followed by the EPO and was disapproved in later decision T15/01. Thus once a priority right has been generated, it may be validly claimed in one or more later European applications filed in the Convention year. T998/99

## Effect of priority right 2–113

The right of priority has the effect that the date of priority counts as the date of filing of the European patent application for the purposes of Art.54(2), Art.54(3) (state of the art) and Art.60(2) (right to a European patent). Art.89

See under novelty for discussion. This effect only applies when the claim in the application concerns the same invention disclosed in the priority document. Where this is not the case, a document published by the applicant in the priority year and having the same content as the priority document will be citeable against the later claim. G3/93

## Correction of a priority claim 2–114

See under Chapter 5 for the chance to remedy deficiencies that the Receiving Section must give the applicant.

See CLBA, pp.413–416—correction of the request under r.88 is allowed up to publication but is much harder to obtain thereafter. See chapter 14 for further details. CLBA

### Requirements relating to designation of the inventor 2–115

A European patent application must designate the inventor. If the applicant is not the inventor or is not the sole inventor, the designation must contain a statement indicating the origin of or the right to the European patent. Art.81

The designation of the inventor must be filed in the request (as confirmed by r.26(2)(k)) when the applicant and the inventor are the same. In the alternative, the designation of the inventor must be filed in a separate document—the designation must state the family name, given names and full address of the inventor and the statement referred to in Art.81 (see above) and must bear the signature of the applicant or his representative. r.17(1)

The EPO does not verify the accuracy of the designation of the inventor. r.17(2)

If the applicant and the inventor are not the same, the EPO will inform the designated inventor of the data in the document designating him and the further data mentioned in Art.128(5) (things the EPO can communicate prior to publication). However, the applicant or the inventor may invoke neither the omission of this notification nor any errors in it. r.17(3)(4)

See under r.17(3). The inventor may renounce his right to be notified by supplying to the EPO the information the EPO must notify to him ([1991] O.J. 266). This should be filed with the designation of the inventor. AnReg

| | |
|---|---|
| J8/82 | A designation of the inventor may also be corrected if the correction is appropriately authorised. |
| Guidelines | See A/III/5. |
| Art.91(1)(f) | Where the designation of the inventor is not filed or is incorrect the Receiving Section will take appropriate action (see below). |

**General and physical requirements of the application**

### 2–116 *Prohibited matter*

r.34(1)     A European patent application may not contain:

         (a) statements or other matter contrary to "ordre public" or morality;

         (b) statements disparaging the products or processes of any particular person other than the applicant, or the merits or validity of applications or patents of any such person. Mere comparisons with the prior art are not considered disparaging *per se*;

         (c) any statement or other matter obviously irrelevant or unnecessary under the circumstances.

r.34(2)     See below under publication and examination of formal requirements for the consequences of including prohibited matter.

Guidelines     See A/III/8 and C/II/4.4–4.5.

### 2–117 *Definition of application documents includes translations*

r.35(1)     Translations submitted under Art.14(2) are included within the meaning of "documents making up the European patent application."

### 2–118 *Number of copies to be filed*

r.35(2)     Three copies of documents making up a European patent application are required unless the President of the EPO decides otherwise.

AnReg     See under r.35(2). The President has decided ([2001] O.J. 563) that only one copy is necessary.

### 2–119 *Physical requirements*

r.35(3)–(14)     Detailed physical requirements are laid down in detail in r.35(3)–(14).

**Language requirements of the application**

### 2–120 *Use of an EPO official language*

Art.14(1)     The official languages of the European Patent Office are English, French and German. European patent applications must be filed in one of these languages.

J18/96     The whole application must be filed in one chosen official language of the EPO under Art.80 and so a description in English accompanied by a claim in German is not acceptable and a filing date cannot be accorded (CLBA, p.403).

T382/94     However, where an application is in a single language (here German) apart from text matter in the drawings which is in another official language (here English) the text matter can be translated into German as an allowable amendment under Art.123(2) EPC (CLBA, p.404). Text matter in drawings is in any case limited by r.32(j). It is debatable whether the situation would have been different if the text matter had been in a non-official EPO language. The matter of whether the language of the proceedings can be determined may be the crucial factor.

See A/VIII/1.1 and 3.1. Guidelines

### *Use of an official language of a Contracting State* — 2–121

Natural or legal persons having their residence or principal place of business within the territory of a Contracting State having a language other than English, French or German as an official language, and nationals of that State who are resident abroad, may file European patent applications in an official language of that State. Nevertheless, a translation in one of the official languages of the European Patent Office must be filed within the time limit prescribed in the Implementing Regulations; throughout the proceedings before the European Patent Office, such translation may be brought into conformity with the original text of the application. Art.14(2)

NB. The word "principal" qualifying "place of business" is not present in the French and German texts and may not be meaningful.

If an application is filed in one of the languages specified by Art.14(2) by an applicant who does not possess the relevant residence/nationality a date of filing cannot be accorded. J9/01

See A/VIII.3.1. Guidelines

The translation must be filed within three months after the filing of the application but no later than 13 months after the date of priority. In the case of a divisional application or a replacement application under Art.61(1)(b) the translation may in any case be filed within one month of the filing of such application. r.6(1)

The translation may be in any official language. r.1(1)

If the translation is not received then the application is deemed withdrawn. *Restitutio* and conversion are possible. Art.90(3)

A reduction in the filing fee is available to an applicant, proprietor or opponent who avails himself of the Art.14(2) option. The reduction is fixed in the RRF at a percentage of the total of the fees. This is a reduction, not a refund and so only the fee as reduced needs to be paid. r.6(3)

The nationality/residency of the applicant is determinative, not that of the representative. T149/85

The fee reduction is allowed where the "essential item" of the first act in filing is in an official non-EPO language and the necessary translation is filed no earlier than simultaneously. G6/91

Here, the essential item is the description and claims. J4/88

The reduction is 20 per cent. RRF12(1)

Translations submitted under Art.14(2) are included within the meaning of "documents making up the European patent application." r.35(1)

In the case referred to in Art.14(2), the original text constitutes, in proceedings before the European Patent Office, the basis for determining whether the subject matter of the application or patent extends beyond the content of the application as filed. Art.70(2)

However, saving proof to the contrary, the EPO may, for the purposes of determining whether the subject matter of a European patent application or European patent extends beyond the content of the European patent application as filed, assume that the translation referred to in Art.14(2) is in conformity with the original text of the application. r.7

| | |
|---|---|
| Guidelines | See A/VIII/1.1. |
| NatLaw | See Table II for the official languages of the Contracting States. |

**2–122** *Filing the application at a national office*

| | |
|---|---|
| NatLaw | Some national offices demand that the application as filed be accompanied by a translation where it is not in certain specified languages (see book on national law, Table II). |

**2–123** *Language of divisional application or replacement application*

| | |
|---|---|
| r.4 | In the case of a divisional application, the application as filed or the Art.14(2) translation must be in the language of the proceedings for the earlier patent application. |
| Guidelines | See A/VIII/1.3. The Guidelines indicate that the same non-official language must also be used but there is no basis for this. |
| | In the case of a replacement application, no specific provision exists. It is debatable whether the provision relating to divisional applications applies since only Art.76(1) applies to replacement applications, not Art.76(3). |

**2–124** **Fees**

For the manner in which fees may be paid, see the later section under Rules Relating to Fees.

**2–125** *Filing fee and search fee*

| | |
|---|---|
| Art.78(2) | A European patent application is subject to the payment of the filing fee and the search fee within one month after the filing of the application. |
| G3/98 | The "filing of the application" is the date the applicant lodges documents rather than the filing date accorded under Art.90(1) (also G2/99). |
| RRFA4(1) | The filing and search fee can be paid from the day the application is filed (the due date). |
| RRF2(1) | The filing fee is 95 euros where the European patent application is filed online, and 170 euros where it is not filed online. This split fee system applies to European applications filed on or after January 1, 2005 and to international applications entering the regional phase on or after that date. If within six months of January 1, 2005 the new fee is not paid in due time but only in the amount due before that date (125 euros), it will be deemed to have been validly paid if the defect is made good within two months of an invitation to that effect from the EPO. |
| RRF2(2) | The search fee is 1000 euros (for applications filed after July 1, 2005). For applications filed before July 1, 2005 the fee is 720 euros. |
| Art.122(5) | *Restitutio* is not available in respect of the Art.78(2) time limit. |
| G3/91 | This decision confirmed that Art.122(5) applies validly to the Art.78(2) time limit, including the grace period under r.85a(1) (see below). See also J18/82. |
| r.85a(1) | If the filing fee or search fee is not paid within the Art.78(2) time limit, it may still be validly paid within a period of grace of one month from notification of a communication pointing out the failure to observe the time limit, provided that within this period a surcharge is paid. |
| RRF2(3b) | The surcharge is 50 per cent of the relevant fee or fees but is capped at 680 euros. |
| J47/92 | By analogy with this decision on requesting examination, further processing is not possible for the grace period since the time limit is not set by the EPO. |

| | |
|---|---|
| The search and filing fees are refunded where the application is not forwarded by a national office. | Art.77(5) |
| The filing fee is reduced where an official language of a Contracting State is used (see above under languages). | r.6(3) |
| The search fee paid for a European or supplementary European search will be fully refunded if the European patent application is withdrawn or refused or deemed to be withdrawn at a time when the office has not yet begun to draw up the search report (amended as at July 1, 2005). | RRF10(1) |
| Where the European search report is based on an earlier search report prepared by the EPO or an application whose priority is claimed or an earlier application within the meaning of Art.76 or an original application within the meaning of r.15 the EPO will refund the applicant, in accordance with a decision of the president, an amount which depends on the type of the earlier search and the extent to which the EPO benefits from the earlier search report when carrying out the subsequent search (amended as at February 17, 2006 (2006, OJ, 189)). | RRF10(2) |
| For the legal consequences of not paying the filing and search fees on time, see below under procedure of the Receiving Section. | |
| See A/II/4.2.1. | Guidelines |

## *Designation fees*

2–126

| | |
|---|---|
| The designation of a Contracting State is subject to the payment of the designation fee. The designation fees must be paid within six months of the date on which the European Patent Bulletin mentions the publication of the European search report. | Art.79(2) |
| The applicant is informed by the Receiving Section of the date on which the mention of the publication of the search report was made- see below under publication. Even if this date is not correct, the applicant may rely on it in certain circumstances- see A/V1/2.1 | R50(1)(2) |
| The designation fees can be paid from the day the application is filed (the due date). | RRFA4(1) |
| Each designation costs 80 euros but payment of seven fees is enough to designate all Contracting States. | RRF2(3) |
| The joint designation of Switzerland and Liechtenstein is 80 euros. | RRF2(3a) |
| *Restitutio* is not allowed in respect of the Art.79(2) time limit. | Art.122(5) |
| This decision confirmed that Art.122(5) applies to the Art.79(2) time limit, including the grace periods under r.85a(1) and (2) (see below). See also J18/82. | G3/91 |
| If a designation fee is not paid within the Art.79(2) time limit, it may still be validly paid within a period of grace of one month from notification of a communication pointing out the failure to observe the time limit, provided that within this period a surcharge is paid. | r.85a(1) |
| In the Request for Grant form as currently configured, the applicant forgoes any notification under r.85a(1) unless specific designations are made. | |
| The surcharge is 50 per cent of the relevant fee or fees but is capped at 680 euros. | RRF2(3b) |
| By analogy with this decision on requesting examination, further processing is not possible for the grace period since the time limit is not set by the EPO. | J47/92 |
| Designation fees in respect of which the applicant has dispensed with notification under r.85a(1) may still be validly paid within a period of grace of two months of | r.85a(2) |

| | |
|---|---|
| | expiry of the normal time limits referred to in r.85a(1), provided that within this period a surcharge is paid. |
| RRF2(3b) | The surcharge is 50 per cent of the relevant fee or fees but is capped at 680 euros. |
| AnReg | See legal advice 5/93 on the calculation of aggregate time limits ([1993] O.J. 229). Both first and second periods are extended if the time limit falls on a day where the EPO is shut. |
| J5/91 | If the period under r.85a(2)—two months without notification for precautionary designations—ends on a different date to the period under r.85a(1)—one month with notification—then all the designation fees can be validly paid at the later date (CLBA, p.286). This happens where specific designations are made in combination with the usual precautionary designation of all states in the request. |
| J5/98 | The r.85a(2) grace period is not extended if a national holiday in a Contracting State falls on the last day of the period (CLBA, p.286). |
| RRF7(2) | Where designation fees are insufficient, the EPO asks the applicant which states the fees paid are in respect of. |
| RRF9(2) | Where there is no response to the RRF7(2) invitation a specific procedure for allocating the fees paid operates (see also CLBA, p.337). |
| J27/96 | Failure to pay a designation fee in time can't be remedied under r.88 (CLBA, p.410). |
| Art.79(3) | No refund of designation fees is made where the application is withdrawn. |
| | For the legal consequences of not paying the designation fees on time, see below under procedure of the Receiving Section. |
| Guidelines | See A/III/12.2. |
| AnReg | See the extension agreements for provisions relating to the payment of extension fees. The deadline is the same as that for paying designation fees and extension is deemed requested on filing. Rule 85a(2) EPC applies if the deadline is missed. |

## 2–127 Claims fees

| | |
|---|---|
| r.31(1) | For the 11th and each subsequent claim in the application as filed, a claims fee is due, payable within one month of the filing of the application. |
| G3/98 | The "filing of the application" is the date the applicant lodges documents rather than the filing date accorded under Art.90(1) (also G2/99). |
| RRFA4(1) | The claims fees can be paid from the day the application is filed (the due date). |
| RRF2(15) | The fee is 45 euros per claim. |
| r.31(1) | If overdue, the EPO will send a communication to the applicant pointing out the deficiency and they may still be validly paid within one month of notification of this communication. |
| r.31(2) | If claims fees are not paid in time, the relevant claims are deemed to be abandoned. |
| r.31(2) | Claims fees will only be refunded where an application does not reach the EPO within 14 months after the filing/priority date (e.g. because it has been delayed for national security reasons) (Art.77(5)). |
| Art.122 | *Restitutio* is available for missing the time limit for paying claims fees. |
| AnReg | See legal advice 3/85 for detailed comments on several aspects of the payment of claims fees ([1985] O.J. 347). |

## 4. Requirements Relating to the Application as Filed

The number of claims fees due is to be calculated at the end of the normal period for payment. — J6/96

See CLBA, p.350—it is unsettled as to what extent an applicant may maintain the subject matter of claims for which no fee has been paid where that matter is not repeated in the description. — CLBA

See A/III/9. — Guidelines

### Fees for divisional applications    2–128

The time limit for paying the filing, search and designation fees in respect of a divisional application are laid down in the Implementing Regulations. — Art.76(3)

The filing fee and search fee must be paid within one month of the filing date of the divisional application. — r.25(2)

The designation fees must be paid within six months of the mention of the publication of the search report relating to the divisional application in the Bulletin. — r.25(2)

*Restitutio* is not possible in respect of the Art.76(3) time limits. — Art.122(5)

If the filing fee, search fee or a designation fee is not paid within the r.25(2) time limit, it may still be validly paid within a period of grace of one month from notification of a communication pointing out the failure to observe the time limit, provided that within this period a surcharge is paid. — r.85a(1)

Claims fees are payable in the normal way (see above). — r.31(1)

Renewal fees in respect of previous years may be payable—see section on renewal fees under common provisions. — Art.86(1)

### Fees for replacement applications    2–129

See the section on inventorship/ownership.

## Requirements relating to biotechnological inventions

### Sequence listings    2–130

There are specific requirements relating to sequence listings for nucleotide and amino acid sequences. — r.27a

See under r.27a. Further details are provided ([1998] O.J. supplement 2; [1992] O.J. 312). — AnReg

### Deposit of biological material    2–131

There are specific requirements relating to the deposit of biological material.

Rule 28 is only important where the written description is not in itself sufficient (T361/87). This being the case, a deposit is necessary at the filing date (corresponding to the filing of the written description) and the culture must be available at the publication date (corresponding to the publication of the description). Certain information regarding the deposit must therefore be supplied in time for publication. An "expert option" may be used to restrict the availability of the deposit before grant of the application. — r.28/r.28a

Usually, the applicant and depositor must be the same (T118/87). If this is not the case then suitable measures need to be taken to ensure the sample is freely available (T118/87). — Case law

See under r.28 and r.28a. These pages contain advice on the application of the Budapest Treaty and other related matters ([1980] O.J. 380; [1981] O.J. 359; [1986] O.J. 269; [1991] — AnReg

G2/93 — Headnote: "The information concerning the file number of a culture deposit according to r.28(1)(c) EPC may not be submitted after expiry of the time limit set out in r.28(2)(a) EPC."

O.J. 461; [1996] O.J. 596; [1981] O.J. 358. See also under Art.33 where amendments made to r.28 and r.28a in 1996 are explained ([1996] O.J. 596).

G2/93

Headnote: "The information concerning the file number of a culture deposit according to r.28(1)(c) EPC may not be submitted after expiry of the time limit set out in r.28(2)(a) EPC."

The Enlarged Board decided that Art.83 (sufficiency of disclosure) must be complied with at the filing date. The later provision of the file number must be able to be linked to information in the application as filed showing the deposit has been made. The indication of the file number is instrumental in enabling a person to carry out the invention and must be provided by the time limit set by the legislator to ensure it is included in the application as published. Following this case,

T227/97

*Restitutio* is possible for the r.28(2)(a) time limit.

Guidelines

See A/IV/4–5.

## 2–132 Special requirements for divisional applications

Art.76(1)

To be awarded the filing date of its parent application, a divisional application must not contain subject matter extending beyond the content of the parent application as filed.

T587/98

A divisional application may include a claim with all the features of a claim in the parent application except one.

T1158/01

A divisional application may be filed from an earlier divisional application, but if the earlier divisional was an improper divisional application (e.g. contains added matter) and never compiled with Art.76(1), the second generation divisional application will also be invalid. Following this case, directions have now been put to the Enlarged Board of Appeal (G1/05, G1/06 and G3/06, consolidated) in order to clarify the extent to which a divisional must comply with A76(i) and at which point it must do so.

T587/98

There is nothing to prevent a parent and divisional application having overlapping claims.

T441/92

A description identical to the patent may be filed for the divisional.

T118/91

There is no question of the subject matter of the divisional application becoming abandoned in respect of the parent application.

T545/92

Where the divisional is directed to only part of the original application, that matter must be clearly derivable as a separate entity.

J2/01

The applicant(s) for a divisional application must be the same as for the parent application unless a transfer of rights has been registered (r.20(3)) or an entitlement dispute has been successfully prosecuted (Art.61).

CLBA

See CLBA, pp.444–445. After filing, the applications become quite separate.

## 5. EXAMINATION ON FILING

## 2–133 Procedure on receipt of a new application

r.24(2)

The authority with which the application is filed (i.e. the EPO or national authority) marks the documents making up the application with the date of receipt and issues, without delay, a receipt to the applicant which states at least the application number, the nature and number of the documents and the date of their receipt.

*5. Examination on Filing* 409

If the application is filed with an Art.75(1)(b) authority (a central industrial property office of a Contracting State), that authority will, without delay, inform the EPO of the receipt of documents making up the application, the nature and date of receipt of the documents, the application number and any priority date claimed. — r.24(3)

When the EPO has received a new application which has been forwarded by the IP office of a Contracting State, it informs the applicant accordingly, indicating the date of receipt at the EPO. — r.24(4)

See A/II/3. — Guidelines

## Examination as to whether a filing date can be accorded

### *Requirements for a filing date* — 2–134

The Receiving Section examines whether a filing date can be accorded to the application. — Art.90(1)(a)

The filing date is the date on which documents are actually received, either at a national office (J18/86) or directly at the EPO (J4/87). No discretion exists to excuse postal delays (except where r.84a EPC can be applied for a priority-claiming application). A filing date later than the date of receipt, *e.g.* to allow for the designation of new Contracting States, can be given but only if this is made clear at the time of filing (J14/90, J18/90). — CLBA

The date of filing of a European patent application is the date on which documents filed by the applicant contain: — Art.80

(a) an indication that a European patent is sought;

(b) the designation of at least one Contracting State;

(c) information identifying the applicant; and

(d) a description and one or more claims in one of the official languages referred to in Art.14(1)–(2), even though the description and the claims do not comply with the other requirements of the EPC.

Where Form 1001 has not been used this decision suggests that the absence of a specific designation is to be interpreted as a precautionary designation of all states (see CLBA, p.409—decided under old Art.79(2)). — J25/88

The information identifying the applicant must make it possible to establish beyond reasonable doubt the identity of the applicant (CLBA, p.407). Here the applicant was sufficiently identified though his first name was wrong. — J25/86

The information identifying the applicant can be corrected later under r.88 but must in any case be specified in some form for a filing date. — J21/87

It has not yet been decided if a part of the description "defining matter for which protection is sought" can be regarded as a claim for the purpose of obtaining a filing date or whether a separate formulation of the same material as a "claim" is necessary. — J20/94

See under language requirements of the application above for case law relating to the requirements of Art.80(d). — Case law

See A/II/4.1. — Guidelines

### *Procedure where a filing date cannot be accorded* — 2–135

If a date of filing cannot be accorded, the Receiving Section gives the applicant an opportunity to correct the deficiencies. — Art.90(2)

| | |
|---|---|
| r.39 | In its communication to the applicant, the Receiving Section must state the deficiencies they have found and inform him that the application will not be dealt with as a European application unless he remedies those deficiencies within one month. |
| r.39 | If the applicant remedies the deficiencies he is informed of the filing date. |
| Art.90(2) | If the deficiencies are not remedied in due time, the application is not dealt with as a European patent application. |
| | *Restitutio* is not possible since no application exists to restore. |
| | See under the section on fees above for refunds. |
| Guidelines | See A/II/4.1.4. |

## 2–136 Filing date in the case of a divisional or application or replacement application

| | |
|---|---|
| Art.76(1) | In so far as a divisional application only contains subject-matter which does not extend beyond the content of the earlier application as filed, it will be deemed to have been filed on the date of filing of the earlier application and will have the benefit of any right to priority. |
| Art.61(2) | The provisions of Art.76(1) apply *mutatis mutandis* to a new application filed under Art.61(1). |

## 2–137 Determination as to whether fees have been paid

| | |
|---|---|
| Art.90(1)(b) | The Receiving Section next examines whether the filing fee and the search fee have been paid in due time. |
| Art.90(3) | If the filing fee and the search fee have not been paid in due time the application is deemed withdrawn. |
| G4/98 | By analogy with this decision concerning designation fees, deemed withdrawal according to Art.90(3) occurs at the end of the normal period, not the end of the r.85a grace period. See also J4/86. |
| Guidelines | See A/II/4.2. |

## 2–138 Determination as to whether any necessary translation has been filed

| | |
|---|---|
| Art.90(1)(c) | The Receiving Section also examines whether any translation necessary under Art.14(2) has been filed (translation of an application filed in official language of a Contracting State which is not an EPO official language). |
| Art.90(3) | If a necessary translation of the application in the language of the proceedings has not been filed in due time, the application is deemed withdrawn. |
| T193/87 | Any fees paid are refunded. |
| Guidelines | See A/II/4.2. |

## 2–139 Examination of formal requirements

| | |
|---|---|
| Art.91(1) | If a European patent application has been accorded a date of filing, and is not deemed to be withdrawn by virtue of Art.90(3) (search and filing fees paid and any necessary translation filed) the Receiving Section examines certain formal requirements as set out below. |

## 2–140 *Representation*

| | |
|---|---|
| Art.91(1)(a) | The Receiving Section examines whether the requirements of Art.133(2) (representation), have been satisfied. |

Where the Receiving Section notes that a deficiency exists which may be corrected, it will inform the applicant accordingly and invite him to remedy the deficiency. Art.91(2)

The deficiency must be remedied within a time limit set by the Receiving Section. r.41(1)

The time limit is from two to four months. r.84

If any deficiency is not corrected, the application will be refused. Art.91(3)

See A/III/2 and 14. Guidelines

## *Physical requirements*     2–141

The Receiving Section examines whether the application meets the following physical requirements: Art.91(1)(b)

| | |
|---|---|
| r.27a(1)–(3) | Requirements for sequence listing |
| r.32(1)–(2) | Form of drawings |
| r.35(2)–(11) and 14 | General provisions for application |
| r.36(2) and (4) | Documents filed subsequently |

r.40

Where the Receiving Section notes that a deficiency exists which may be corrected, it will inform the applicant accordingly and invite him to remedy the deficiency. Art.91(2)

The deficiency must be remedied within a time limit set by the Receiving Section. Amendments to the description, claims and drawings offered in response may not go beyond what is necessary to remedy the deficiencies. r.41(1)

The time limit is from two to four months. r.84

If any deficiency is not corrected, the application will be refused. Art.91(3)

See A/III/3 and 14. Guidelines

## *Filing of an abstract*     2–142

The Receiving Section examines whether an abstract has been filed. Art.91(1)(c)

Where the Receiving Section notes that a deficiency exists which may be corrected, it will inform the applicant accordingly and invite him to remedy the deficiency. Art.91(2)

The deficiency must be remedied within a time limit set by the Receiving Section. r.41(1)

The time limit is from two to four months. r.84

If any deficiency is not corrected, the application will be refused. Art.91(3)

See A/III/11 and 14. Guidelines

## *Content of the request*     2–143

The Receiving Section examines whether the request for the grant of a European patent satisfies the mandatory provisions of the Implementing Regulations concerning its content (see r.26(2)). Art.91(1)(d)

Where the Receiving Section notes that a deficiency exists which may be corrected, it will inform the applicant accordingly and invite him to remedy the deficiency. Art.91(2)

The deficiency must be remedied within a time limit set by the Receiving Section. r.41(1)

The time limit is from two to four months. r.84

| | |
|---|---|
| Art.91(3) | If any deficiency is not corrected, the application will be refused. |
| Guidelines | See A/III/4 and 14. |

**2–144**     *Priority claim*

| | |
|---|---|
| Art.91(1)(d) | The Receiving Section examines, where appropriate, whether the requirements of the EPC concerning the claim to priority have been satisfied. |
| Art.91(2) | Where the Receiving Section notes that a deficiency exists which may be corrected, it will inform the applicant accordingly and invite him to remedy the deficiency. |
| r.41(1) | The deficiency must be remedied within a time limit set by the Receiving Section. |
| r.84 | The time limit is from two to four months. |
| r.41(2) | However, no invitation is sent where the applicant has omitted to indicate on filing the date or state of first filing. |
| r.41(3) | Furthermore, no invitation is sent when the date of the priority application precedes the filing of date of the application by more than a year. In this latter case the Receiving Section will inform the applicant that there will be no right of priority for the application unless, within one month, the applicant indicates a corrected date, lying within the priority year. |
| J1/80 | In respect of the filing of the certified copy of the priority document, a deficiency only exists after the 16 month period has elapsed. At this point, the EPO must give the applicant a chance to correct and a loss of rights only occurs if this invitation is ignored. No restitutio can be applied for until such loss of rights occurs. |
| Art.91(3) | If any deficiency is not corrected, the right to priority is lost for the application. |
| Guidelines | See A/III/6 and 14. |

**2–145**     *Designation fees*

| | |
|---|---|
| Art.91(1)(e) | The Receiving Section examines whether the designation fees have been paid (see above under fees for the time limit and grace period). |
| Art.91(4) | Where the designation fee has not been paid in due time in respect of any designated state, the designation of that state will be deemed to be withdrawn. |
| G4/98 | Headnote (1): "Without prejudice to Art.67(4) EPC, the designation of a Contracting State party to the EPC in a European patent application does not retroactively lose its legal effect and is not deemed never to have taken place if the relevant designation fee has not been paid within the applicable time limit." |
| | Headnote (2): "The deemed withdrawal of the designation of a Contracting State provided for in Art.91(4) EPC takes effect upon expiry of the time limits mentioned in Art.79(2), r.15(2), r.25(2) and r.107(1) EPC, as applicable, and not upon expiry of the period of grace provided for by r.85a EPC." |
| Guidelines | See A/III/12. |

**2–146**     *Designation of the inventor*

| | |
|---|---|
| Art.91(1)(f) | The Receiving Section examines whether the designation of the inventor has been made in accordance with Art.81. |
| Art.91(2) | Where the Receiving Section notes that a deficiency exists which may be corrected, it will inform the applicant accordingly and invite him to remedy the deficiency. |

## 5. Examination on Filing

The deficiency must be remedied within a time limit set by the Receiving Section. r.41(1)

The time limit is from two to four months. r.84

Where the Receiving Section notes that the inventor has not been identified in accordance with r.17, the Receiving Section will inform the applicant that the application will be deemed to be withdrawn unless this deficiency is remedied within the Art.91(5) time limit (see below), except that in the case of a divisional or replacement application the time limit may not expire earlier than two months after this communication which will state the appropriate deadline. r.42

Where the omission of the designation of the inventor is not, in accordance with the Implementing Regulations and subject to the exceptions laid down therein, corrected within 16 months after the date of filing of a European patent application or, if priority is claimed, after the date of priority, the application is deemed to be withdrawn — but see the next paragraph to see what actually happens. Art.91(5)

See A/III/5.5. EPO procedure departs somewhat from the provisions set out in the EPC in that the applicant is asked to remedy the lack of a designation of the inventor, or a major defect in such a designation, within the Art.91(5) time limit or within two months from notification, whichever period is longer, whether the application is a regular application or a divisional or replacement application. *Restitutio* is available. Minor deficiencies are notified under Art.91(2) and corrections are to be submitted within a time limit set by the EPO (R.84). *Restitutio* and further processing are both available in this case. Guidelines

A designation of the inventor may also be corrected later if the correction is appropriately authorised. J8/82

### Late filed drawings

2–147

The Receiving Section examines whether the drawings referred to in Art.78(1)(d), were filed on the date of filing of the application. Art.91(1)(g)

Where the drawings were not filed on the date of filing of the application and no steps have been taken to correct the deficiency, either the application is re-dated to the date of filing of the drawings or any reference to the drawings in the application is deemed to be deleted, according to the choice exercised by the applicant. Art.91(6)

The Receiving Section, on noting that a deficiency exists which may be corrected, therefore informs the applicant accordingly and invites him to remedy the deficiency. Art.91(2)

The Receiving Section will inform the applicant that the drawings and references to them in the description will be deemed to be deleted unless, within one month, the applicant requests that the application be re-dated to the date on which the drawings were filed. r.43(1)

Where no drawings have been filed, the Receiving Section will invite the applicant to file them within one month and explain that the application will be re-dated to the date on which that are filed, or, if they are not filed that references to them in the description will be deemed to be deleted. r.43(2)

The applicant is informed of any new filing date. r.43(3)

See CLBA, p.406. If part of a drawing is missing the only option is to attempt correction under r.88 (J19/80) whereas if one complete figure of the drawings is missing redating under r.43 is still an option (J1/82). CLBA

See A/III/10. Guidelines

| | |
|---|---|
| 2–148 | **Title of the invention** |
| Guidelines | See A/III/7. The Receiving Section also checks that the title is reasonable and takes action if necessary. |
| AnReg | See under r.26(2)(b). The title will be changed by the EPO if it does not conform to the required standard ([1991] O.J. 224). |
| 2–149 | **Check for prohibited matter prior to publication** |
| Guidelines | See A/III/8. The Receiving Section must also check for prohibited matter as defined by r.31(1)(a) to ensure that such matter is not published (see below under publication and above under requirements of the application). |

## 6. DRAWING UP THE SEARCH REPORT

### Procedure for conducting the search

| | |
|---|---|
| 2–150 | *When does the search begin?* |
| Art.92(1) | If a European patent application has been accorded a date of filing and is not deemed to be withdrawn by virtue of Art.90(3) (filing and search fees paid, any necessary translation filed), the Search Division will draw up a European search report. |
| 2–151 | *What is the purpose and scope of the search?* |
| r.44(1) | The purpose of the search is to identify those documents, available to the EPO at the time of drawing up the report, which should be taken into consideration in deciding whether the invention to which the European patent application relates is new and involves an inventive step. |
| Guidelines | See B/VI/5.1. As a general rule, the basic reference date for the purpose of drawing up the search report is the date of filing rather than the priority date. This is not though the case for the search opinion of the Extended European Search Report (EESR) (B.XII.4). |
| 2–152 | *What is the basis of the search?* |
| Art.92(1) | The search report is drawn up on the basis of the claims, with due regard to the description and any drawings. |
| 2–153 | *Procedure where a complete search cannot be established* |
| r.45 | If an application does not comply with the provisions of the EPC to such an extent that it is not possible to carry out a meaningful search for one or more claims, the Search Division will either declare that a search is not possible or drawn up a partial search report, so far as is practicable. For the purposes of further proceedings, the declaration or partial search report will be considered as the European search report. |
| 2–154 | *Procedure where the application lacks unity* |
| r.46 | Where the Search Division decides that the application does not comply with the requirement for unity it will draw up a partial search report relating to the invention, or unified group of inventions, first mentioned in the claims. The applicant will then be informed that if the search report is to cover further inventions or sets of unified inventions, a further search fee must be paid for each one within a period set by the Search Division which may not be shorter than two weeks or longer than six weeks. |
| RRF2(2) | The search fee is 1000 euros for applications filed on or after July 1, 2005. For applications filed before July 1, 2005 the fee is 720 euros. |

It is not possible to appeal the request for further fees (no appeal is possible from a decision of the Search Division). Art.106(1)

The Search Division will draw up a search report for those inventions or groups of unified inventions for which search fees have been paid. r.46

Any additional fees paid will be refunded if, during examination by the Examining Division, the applicant requests a refund and the Examining Division (or Board of Appeal) finds the demand for extra fees was not justified. r.46

Headnote: "An applicant who fails to pay the further search fees for a non-unitary application when requested to do so by the Search Division under r.46(1) EPC cannot pursue that application for the subject matter in respect of which no search fees have been paid. Such an applicant must file a divisional application in respect of such subject matter if he wishes to seek protection for it." G2/92

The Enlarged Board felt that only one examination fee is payable and so only one invention may be examined and that this invention must have been one searched by the Search Division. The applicant who pays the extra fees may not only argue for unity subsequently before the Examining Division but may also select which of the inventions is examined if they are unsuccessful in this argument. These fees are not lost since the search fees payable on any divisional application which must be filed are reduced to the extent the first search can be used.

Whether additional fees are paid or not, the applicant has the same right to argue against the non-unity finding before the Examining Division. The only advantage of paying the extra fees is being able to choose which invention to prosecute in the parent application if such arguments are unsuccessful. T631/97

See B/VII. Guidelines

## *Establishing of the definitive content of the abstract*     2–155

While drawing up the search report, the Search Division also determines the definitive content of the abstract. r.47(1)

See B/XI. Guidelines

## *Patent classification used by the EPO*     2–156

The EPO will use: r.8(1)

(a) the classification referred to in Art.1 of the European Convention on the International Classification of Patents for Invention of December 19, 1954 until the entry into force of the Strasbourg Agreement concerning the International Patent Classification of March 24, 1971;

(b) the classification referred to in Art.1 of the aforementioned Strasbourg Agreement after its entry into force.

This classification (under r.8(1)) is referred to in the EPC as the international classification. r.8(2)

## *Accelerated procedure*     2–157

See under Art.75. A seven-point plan for accelerating search, examination and grant, known as "PACE", is described ([2001] O.J. 459). AnReg

## The European search report

**2–158** *Content of the search report*

r.44(1) — The search report mentions those documents, available to the EPO at the time of drawing up the report, which may be taken into consideration in deciding whether the invention to which the European patent application relates is new and involves an inventive step.

r.44(2) — The claims to which each citation relates will be noted, if necessary specifying the relevant parts of the citation, *e.g.* by indicating the relevant pages, columns, lines or diagrams.

r.44(3) — The search report distinguishes between citations published before the claimed priority date, between the claimed priority date and the filing date and on or after the filing date.

r.44(4) — Documents referring to any disclosure before the filing date (e.g. an oral disclosure or prior use) are mentioned in the search report together with an indication of the publication date, if any, of the document and the date of the non-written disclosure.

r.44(6) — The search report also contains the classification of the subject matter of the application in accordance with the international classification (see r.8 above).

AnReg — From 1982 onwards, search reports have also included, in an annex, information on the patent families of cited applications or patents (see under r.38(5) [1982] O.J. 448). From 1999, the annex has also listed "family members" and their publication dates (see under r.44[1999] O.J. 90).

**2–159** *Language of the search report*

r.44(5) — The search report is drawn up in the language of the proceedings.

**2–160 The extended European search report**

r.44a(1) — For all European and Euro PCT patent applications filed on or after July 1, 2005, the European search report will be accompanied by an opinion as to whether the application and the invention to which it relates seem to meet the requirements of the EPC, unless a communication under r.51(2) or r.51(4) can be issued (examination requested and Art. 96(1) communication waived). See the Notice from the EPO dated July 1, 2005 ([2005] O.J. 435). An extended search report is also drawn up for divisional applications filed on or after July 1, 2005, even if the parent has an earlier filing date.

Guidelines — See also B.XII.

r.44a(2) — The opinion is not published with the search report (but will of course be made available to the public as part of the application file once the application is published).

No extended European search report is provided for PCT applications filed before July 1, 2005, even if they enter the European regional phase after that date ([2006 O.J. 194).

**2–161 Transmittal of the search report and definitive content of the abstract**

Art.92(2) — Immediately after it has been drawn up, the European search report is transmitted to the applicant together with copies of any cited documents.

r.47(2) — The definitive content of the abstract is also submitted to the applicant along with the search report.

**2–162 Chance to amend after receipt of the search report**

Art.123(1) — The conditions under which amendment is possible are laid down in the Regulations.

r.86(2) — After receiving the European search report and before receipt of the first communication from the Examining Division, the applicant may, of his own volition, amend the description, claims and drawings.

# 7. PUBLICATION OF THE APPLICATION AND SEARCH REPORT

**Timing of publication** 2–163

A European patent application is published as soon as possible after the expiry of a period of 18 months from the date of filing or, if priority has been claimed, as from the date of priority. — Art.93(1)

Nevertheless, at the request of the applicant the application may be published before the expiry of the period referred to above.

It is published simultaneously with the publication of the specification of the European patent when the grant of the patent has become effective before the expiry of the period referred to above.

The publication will be delayed if the priority claim is withdrawn before the technical preparations are completed (see C/V/3.5). — Guidelines

At present, publication is every Wednesday.

**No publication to take place when the application is withdrawn or refused** 2–164

The application will not be published if it has been finally refused or withdrawn or deemed to be withdrawn before the termination of the technical preparation for publication. — r.48(2)

Such technical preparations are deemed to be complete at a time specified by the President of the EPO. The most recent Decision of the president was dated April 25, 2006 and entered into force on May 1, 2006. — r.48(1)

See under r.48. The date is five weeks before the 18-month mark (decision of the President dated April 25, 2006, [2006] O.J. 405). — AnReg

The EPO can prevent publication, at its own discretion, even after the technical preparations are complete (CLBA, p.417). Indeed, the EPO will do its best to prevent publication where a request is received after the technical preparations are complete (see AnReg under r.48—Notice dated April 25, 2006 [2006] O.J. 405). — J5/81

See legal advice 8/80 ([1981] O.J. 6), which states that where the application is withdrawn, such withdrawal is binding on the applicant. See also under r.48. This notice summarises whether publication will occur or not in the situation where a loss of rights has not yet become final and publication is due ([1990] O.J. 455). — AnReg

See A/VI/1.2. Withdrawal may be made conditional on publication being avoided. — Guidelines

See also below under common provisions for further details relating to the withdrawal of an application.

**Language and form of the publication** 2–165

European patent applications are published in the language of the proceedings. — Art.14(6)

The President of the EPO determines the form of the publication. — r.49(1)

The publication is in electronic form by means of a publication server from which the application and search report can be downloaded (as from April 1, 2005). — [2005] O.J.124

| | | |
|---|---|---|
| **2–166** | | **Contents of the publication** |
| Art.93(2) | | The publication contains the description, the claims and any drawings as filed and, in an annex, the European search report and the abstract, in so far as the latter are available before the termination of the technical preparations for publication. If the European search report and the abstract are not published at the same time as the application, they are published separately. |
| r.44a(2) | | The opinion as to whether the invention and application meet the requirements of the EPC is not part of the publication (but can be inspected as part of the contents of the application file once the application has been published). |
| r.49(1) | | In either case, the President of the EPO prescribes the form of the publication and the data to be included. He may also lay down special conditions for the publication of the abstract. |
| r.33(4) | | Where the application contains drawings, the applicant should indicate the figure, or exceptionally figures, which should accompany the abstract when it is published. However, the EPO may decide to publish a different figure if it is of the view that it better characterises the invention. |
| r.49(2) | | The designated Contracting States are specified in the publication. |
| AnReg | | See under Art.93. All states designated in the application as filed are now shown in the publication since designation fees are not due until later. Those states for which designation fees have been paid can be ascertained by inspecting the Register ([2001] O.J. 117). |
| r.38(6) | | The particulars in the declaration of priority are published with the application. |
| r.49(3) | | If the claims have been amended under r.86(2) before the technical preparations for publication are terminated, both claims as filed and claims as amended are included in the publication. |
| r.96(2) | | The President of the EPO decides whether amended claims received after this time limit are published and, if so, the form of such a publication. |
| r.18(1) | | The person designated as the inventor is mentioned as such in the published European patent application, unless the said person informs the EPO in writing that he waives his right to be thus mentioned. |
| r.18(2) | | In the event of a third party filing with the EPO a final decision whereby the applicant for or proprietor of a patent is required to designate him as the inventor, the provisions of r.18(1) apply. |
| Guidelines | | See A/VI/1.3. Where an application for correction under r.88 is pending, or has been granted, this fact is included in the publication. |
| AnReg | | A list of any art cited by the applicant in the description pursuant to Rule 27(i)(b) is now listed separately at the end of the published application ([2006] O.J. 428). |
| **2–167** | | **Matter excluded from the publication** |
| r.34(2) | | If a European patent application contains prohibited matter within the meaning of r.34(1)(a) (statements contrary to ordre public or morality) the EPO will omit it when publishing the application but will indicate the place and number of words or drawings omitted. |
| r.34(3) | | Further, if a European patent application contains prohibited matter within the meaning of r.34(1)(b) (disparaging statements) the EPO may omit it when publishing the application but will indicate the place and number of words omitted and will furnish, on request, a copy of omitted passages. |

## Communication to the applicant relating to publication of the search report and the request for examination

2–168

The EPO tells the applicant the date on which the Bulletin mentions the publication of the search report and draw his attention to the provisions of Art.94(2) and (3) (time limit for filing the request for examination and paying the examination fee; consequences of not doing so).

r.50(1)

However, the applicant may not invoke the omission of this communication.

r.50(2)

See A/VI/2.1. If the communication specifies a date later than the actual date of mention in the Bulletin this later date will be decisive for calculating the time limit for filing a request for examination unless the mistake is apparent (i.e. obvious, such as where the year is wrong).

Guidelines

## 8. SUBSTANTIVE EXAMINATION

### Examination must be requested

#### *Requesting examination*

2–169

The European Patent Office will examine, on written request, whether a European patent application and the invention to which it relates meet the requirements of the EPC.

Art.94(1)

Paying the fee is not enough, a request must also be filed. Such a request is now built into Form 1001.1 (CLBA, p.417) so that paying the fee is the determinative factor (J25/92).

J12/82

#### *Time limit for requesting examination—request cannot be withdrawn*

2–170

A request for examination may be filed by the applicant up to the end of six months after the date on which the European Patent Bulletin mentions the publication of the European Search Report. The request may not be withdrawn.

Art.94(2)

The applicant is informed by the Receiving Section of the date on which the mention of the publication of the search report was made—see above under publication. Even if this date is not correct, the applicant may still rely on it in certain circumstances—see A/VI/2.1.

r.50(1)(2)

*Restitutio* is not available in respect of the Art.94(2) time limit.

Art.122(5)

Headnote: "The time limit under Art.94(2) EPC is excluded from *restitutio in integrum* by the provisions of paragraph 5 of Art.122 EPC." See also G6/92.

G5/92

These consolidated proceedings provided confirmation of the obvious and augmented G3/91 which had confirmed the same in respect of the filing and search fees.

#### *Payment of an examination fee*

2–171

The request for examination is not deemed to be filed until after the examination fee has been paid.

Art.94(2)

For applications filed before July 1, 2005, the examination fee is 1,490 euros, but for applications filed on or after July 1, 2005 the fee is 1,335 euros. For international patent applications filed on or after July 1, 2005, for which no supplementary search is drawn up the fee is 1490 euros.

RRF2(6)

The fee is reduced by 50 per cent in the case of a Euro-PCT application where the EPO was International Preliminary Examining Authority provided that for international applications filed before January 1, 2004 the EPO as IPEA has carried out a detailed preliminary examination.

RRF12(2)

| | |
|---|---|
| **2–172** | ***Consequences of not requesting examination*** |
| Art.94(3) | If no request for examination has been filed by the end of the period for requesting examination, the application will be deemed to be withdrawn. |
| J4/86 | Deemed withdrawal takes effect on the expiry of the basic six-month period, not the end of the grace period (see below)—CLBA, p.418. |
| **2–173** | ***Grace period for requesting examination*** |
| r.85b | The request for examination may still be filed within a grace period of one month from notification of a communication pointing out the failure to observe the time limit provided that a surcharge is also paid within this period. |
| RRF2(7) | The surcharge is 50 per cent of the examination fee. |
| J47/92 | Further processing not possible for the grace period since the time limit is not set by the EPO. |
| J12/82 | Equally, *restitutio* is not available in respect of the grace period. |
| Guidelines | See A/VI/2.3. |
| **2–174** | ***Refund of the examination fee*** |
| RRF10b | The examination fee is refunded:<br><br>(a) in full where the application is refused, withdrawn or deemed withdrawn before the Examining Divisions have assumed responsibility;<br><br>(b) at a rate of 75 per cent if the application is refused, withdrawn or deemed withdrawn after the Examining Divisions have assumed responsibility but before substantive examination has begun. |
| Guidelines | See A/VI/2.5. |
| **2–175** | ***Language of the request for examination—fee reduction*** |
| r.6(3) | A reduction in examination fee (NB. reduction, not refund) is available to an applicant who avails himself of the Art.14(4) option. The reduction is fixed in the RRF at a percentage of the total of the fees. |
| RRF12(1) | The reduction available is 20 per cent. |
| J21/98 | This decision provides clarification. See CLBA, p.395 and other cases cited in that section. Examination is only requested when the fee is paid so the applicant can still benefit from an available fee reduction when using the request form with a pre-checked request for examination unless the fee is paid on filing.<br><br>Further, the language of filing is irrelevant—the status of the applicant at the time of requesting examination is determinative of whether a reduction is possible or not. |
| **2–176** | **A request for examination filed before transmittal of the search report must be confirmed** |
| Art.96(1) | If the applicant for a European patent has filed a request for examination before the European search report has been transmitted to him, the European Patent Office will invite him after the transmission of the report to indicate, within a period to be determined, whether he desires to proceed further with the European patent application. |

*8. Substantive Examination*

In the communication, the EPO will give the applicant an opportunity to comment on the search report and to amend, where appropriate, the description, claims and drawings. — r.51(1)

The time limit set is six months from publication of the search report (A/VI/2.3). — Guidelines

If the applicant fails to reply in due time to this invitation the application will be deemed to be withdrawn. — Art.96(3)

Further processing and *restitutio* are available. — Art.121/Art.122

This provision also applies to international applications in respect of which a supplementary search has been carried out (CLBA, p.418). — J8/83

The need to confirm examination can be avoided by a categorical statement before the search requesting examination whatever the outcome of the search (see C/VI/1.1.2). This can now be achieved by crossing box 5a on the Request form. — Guidelines

### Extension of the period for requesting examination
**2–177**

The Administrative Council is competent to amend the time limits laid down in the EPC; this applies to the time limit laid down in Art.94 (request for examination) only in the conditions laid down in Art.95. — Art.33(1)

The Administrative Council may extend the period within which requests for examination may be filed if it is established that European patent applications cannot be examined in due time. — Art.95(1)

If the Administrative Council extends the period, it may decide that third parties will be entitled to make requests for examination. In such cases, it will determine the appropriate rules in the Implementing Regulations. — Art.95(2)

Any decision of the Administrative Council to extend the period will apply only in respect of applications filed after the publication of such decision in the Official Journal of the European Patent Office. — Art.95(3)

If the Administrative Council extends the period, it must lay down measures with a view to restoring the original period as soon as possible. — Art.95(4)

### Examination procedure

#### *Formal written procedure*
**2–178**

If the examination of a European patent application reveals that the application or the invention to which it relates does not meet the requirements of the EPC, the Examining Division will invite the applicant in accordance with the Implementing Regulations and as often as necessary, to file his observations within a period to be fixed by the Examining Division. — Art.96(2)

The Examining Division has a discretionary power to refuse an application after a single Art.96(2) communication as long as the applicant has had the chance to comment on the grounds, even if the applicant makes a bona fide response (see also T296/96, T821/96 and CLBA, p.262). — T201/98

However, the view of other Boards has been different. See CLBA, pp.420–421. See also CLBA, pp.426–428 for comment on the situations in which Art.113(1) (chance for applicant to comment on grounds or evidence) justifies another examination report being issued. — CLBA

The communication will contain a reasoned statement covering, where appropriate, all the grounds against the grant of the European patent. In the communication, the EPO — r.51(2)(3)

| | will, where appropriate, invite the applicant to correct the deficiencies noted and amend the description, claims and abstract. |
|---|---|
| CLBA | See CLBA, pp.421–422. The applicant should be notified of each requirement of the EPC that has not been met and, in each case, of the legal and factual reasons (T951/92). |
| r.84 | The time limit set for reply is from two to four months, usually four months. This can be extended as of right up to six months and further in exceptional circumstances. See Guidelines E/VIII/1.6. |
| J37/89 | This decision explains how to proceed where a valid request for extension of the time limit is not granted—request further processing and refund of the further processing fee. |
| Art.96(3) | If the applicant fails to reply in due time to an invitation pursuant to Art.96(2) EPC the application will be deemed to be withdrawn. |
| CLBA | See CLBA, pp.430–431. A letter which does not waive or exercise the right to present comments pursuant to Art.113(1) does not count as a reply and in these circumstances no refusal of the application is possible, the application must be deemed withdrawn (T685/98). |
| Art.121/Art.122 | Further processing and restitutio are both possible. |
| Art.123(1)/r.86 | The applicant has one chance to submit voluntary amendments—see the section under amendment and correction. |
| G7/93 | Headnote (2): "The EPO is not obliged to consider reservations under Art.167(2) as constituting requirements of the EPC which have to be met according to Art.96(2)." |

## 2–179 Informal communications by telephone or interview

| Guidelines | See C/VI/4.3 and 6.2. Minor matters of disagreement and misunderstandings are often best dealt with in this way. |
|---|---|
| CLBA | See CLBA, pp.428–430. All such contacts are entirely at the discretion of the Examiner (T300/89). |

## 2–180 Further searches

| Guidelines | See C/VI/8. The Examining Division may carry out an additional European search where one is required. In any case, a search for Art.54(3) documents will be performed. |
|---|---|

## 2–181 Auxiliary requests

| Art.113(2) | It is possible to make auxiliary requests in addition to the main request in examination proceedings (T1105/96). See under basis of decisions below. Each auxiliary request is a request for amendment and may be refused under r.86(3). See Legal Advice 15/05 (rev.2). |
|---|---|

## 2–182 Double patenting

| Guidelines | Where grant would lead to the same applicant being granted two patents for the same subject matter, the Examining Division will demand amendment. See C/IV/6.4. |
|---|---|

## 2–183 Consolidation of proceedings

| CLBA | See CLBA, p.444 where the principle of consolidating proceedings for grant of two applications is approved. |
|---|---|

A Euro and Euro-PCT can be consolidated where they have the same priority and filing dates provided that their description, claims and drawings are identical (see also legal advice 10/92).

J17/92

## *Accelerated procedure*

2–184

See under Art.75. A seven-point plan for accelerating search, examination and grant, known as "PACE", is described ([2001] O.J. 459).

AnReg

## *Request for information concerning national patent applications*

2–185

The Examining Division may invite the applicant to indicate, within a period to be determined by it, the States in which he has made applications for national patents for the whole or part of the invention to which the European patent application relates, and to give the reference numbers of the said applications.

Art.124(1)

If the applicant fails to reply in due time to an invitation under Art.124(1), the European patent application is deemed to be withdrawn.

Art.124(2)

Such an invitation may also relate, where appropriate, to utility models, utility certificates and applications for the same.

Art.140

## Refusal of the application

2–186

The Examining Division will refuse a European patent application if it is of the opinion that such application or the invention to which it relates does not meet the requirements of the EPC, except where a different sanction is provided for in the EPC.

Art.97(1)

See CLBA, pp.432–433. An application must be refused in its entirety if even one claim does not meet the requirements of the EPC (T5/81), including the Implementing Regulations (T11/82).

CLBA

## 9. THE GRANT PROCEDURE

### Circumstances in which a patent is granted

2–187

If the Examining Division is of the opinion that the application and the invention to which it relates meet the requirements of the EPC, it will decide to grant a patent provided that the applicant approves the text for grant, pays the fees for grant and printing and pays any renewal fees (including any additional fees) that are due.

Art.97(2)

Provision may also be made in the Regulations for the filing of translations of the approved claims into the two other official languages of the EPC (see below).

Art.97(5)

### Approval of the text for grant, payment of fees and the filing of claim translations

#### *Communication from the Examining Division under r.51(4)*

2–188

Before deciding to grant a patent, the Examining Division:

r.51(4)(7)(10)

  (a) informs the applicant of the text which it intends to grant;

  (b) indicates the designated Contracting States which require a translation pursuant to Art.65(1);

and invites the applicant to:

  (c) pay the fees for grant and printing;

(d) file translations of the claims into the two official languages of the EPO other than the language of proceedings; and

(e) pay claims fees for any claim over 10 for which a fee has not already been paid;

within a non-extensible period to be specified which may not be less than two months or more than four months (NB. for r.51(4) communications dispatched before April 1, 2005 a two month extension was available). Currently the period usually set is four months.

RRF2(8) — The fee for grant, including the fee for printing, is 750 euros for the first 35 pages and an extra 11 euros for every subsequent page.

RRF2(15) — The claims fee is 45 euros per claim.

r.38(5) — Any necessary translation of a priority document must be filed at the latest within the r.51(4) time limit. The communication under r.51(4) will raise this matter where appropriate.

T1255/04 — If during examination proceedings a main and a subsidiary request have been filed and one of the subsidiary requests is allowable, the communication pursuant to r.51(4) is to be issued on the basis of the (first) allowable request and must be accompanied by an explanation of the reasons why the higher-ranking requests are not allowable and must expressly mention the applicant's right to maintain the main request and thus obtain an appealable decision (see below). See also, T1181/04. See Legal Advice 15/05 (rev.2) ([2005] O.J. 357).

Guidelines — See C/VI/2.5 and 15.1.

## 2–189 Consequences of not responding fully to the r.51(4) communication

Art.97(5) — If the translations of the claims are not filed in due time, the application is deemed to be withdrawn (as echoed by r.51(8)).

Art.97(3) — If the fees for grant and printing are not paid in due time, the application is deemed to be withdrawn (as echoed by r.51(8)).

r.51(8) — If any due claims fees are not paid in due time, the application is deemed to be withdrawn.

Art.91(3) — If the translation of the priority document is not filed in due time the right to priority is lost for the application.

Art.121/Art.122 — Further processing and *restitutio* are both available.

## 2–190 Implicit approval of the text by payment of fees and filing of translations

r.51(4) — If the applicant pays the fees due and files the translations within the period set then he will be deemed to have approved the text intended for grant.

## 2–191 Procedure where the proposed text is not acceptable to the applicant

r.51(5) — If the applicant requests amendments under r.86(3) or corrections under r.88 within the r.51(4) time limit he must, where the claims are amended or corrected, file a translation of the claims as amended or corrected. If the applicant pays the fees due and files translations within the time limit he is deemed to have approved the grant of the patent as amended or corrected.

r.86(3) — The EPO has a discretion to refuse any amendments proposed by the applicant unless the r.51(4) communication is the first communication from the Examining Division.

r.51(6) — Where the Examining Division does not consent to an amendment or correction it must, before taking a decision, give the applicant an opportunity to submit, within a period to be specified, his observations and any amendments considered necessary by the Examining

Division and, where the claims are amended, a translation of the claims as amended. If the applicant submits such amendments, he is deemed to have approved the text as amended.

There are exceptions to the requirement of r.51(5) concerning the filing of translations and payment of fees in three situations, in which the changes to the applicant's requests do not represent amendments within the meaning of r.86(3): (i) if the r.51(4) communication was based on a subsidiary request, and the applicant replies by maintaining one or more higher requests which do not meet the requirements of the EPC (see also Legal Advice 15/05 (rev.02), ([2005] O.J. 357)); (ii) if the r.51(4) communication included amendments to the claims carried out by the examining division, and the applicant states his non-approval of these amendments and maintains his request as on file when the communication under Rule 51(4) was issued; or (iii) if, due to an error on the part of the EPO, the r.51(4) communication was based on the wrong documents, and the applicant replies by pointing out or correcting that error.

In case (i) or (ii) if the text of the application as maintained by the applicant is unallowable, a reasoned refusal under Art.97(1) is issued, preceded where necessary by a communication setting out the reasons why the request is not allowable. However, if agreement is reached on an allowable text, where necessary following further communication from the examining division and response from the applicant, a second communication under r.51(4) is issued. In case (iii) no new r.51(4) communication is required if the applicant's reply to the original r.51(4) communications included the correct documents together with the translations and fees: the application proceeds directly to grant.

See C.VI.15.4a. Guidelines

It is possible to approve the text and then disapprove it within the time limit, the latest request filed within a time limit being the one that validly expresses the position of the party concerned. T1/92

See C/VI/15.4. Guidelines

### Amendments and oral proceedings after approval of the text 2–192

Headnote (1): "An approval of the text submitted by an applicant pursuant to r.51(4) EPC does not become binding once a communication in accordance with r.51(6) has been issued. Following issue of such a communication under r.51(6) EPC and until issue of a decision to grant the patent, the Examining Division has a discretion under r.86(3), second sentence, EPC, whether or not to allow amendment of the application." G7/93

This decision was taken under the old law where r.51(6) had a different meaning from present r.51(6). However, the principles established are still important. The Enlarged Board decided that Art.113(2) (EPO to decide only on text approved by applicant) did not give the applicant a right to amend. Any amendment under r.86(3) had to be made with the consent of the Examining Division. Equally, the Examining Division is not bound in any way by the text as approved and can authorise amendments prior to the issue of a decision to grant. Discretion will only be exercised in favour of the applicant as an exception rather than a rule at such a late stage of the grant procedure. The Examining Division must balance the applicant's interest in obtaining a valid patent against the EPO's interest in bringing grant proceedings to a close. Typically, amendments should be allowed which do not involve re-opening of substantive examination, *e.g.* separate sets of claims in respect of states who have made reservations under Art.167(2).

A request for oral proceedings must be honoured at any time while proceedings are pending, *i.e.* up to the decision to grant or refuse (CLBA, p.443). T555/95

### Decision to grant 2–193

When the text has been duly approved, translations duly filed and grant, printing and claims fees duly paid, as outlined above, the Examining Division will consider whether any renewal fees and any additional fees are due before taking a decision to grant a patent. Art.97(2)

| | |
|---|---|
| r.51(8a)(9) | The mention of the grant will therefore not be published until |

    (a) the designation fees have been paid where they have become due after the r.51(4) communication has been notified; and

    (b) any renewal fee has been paid where it becomes due after the r.51(4) communication has been notified and before the next possible date for publication of the mention of grant.

In either case, the applicant will be informed accordingly.

| | |
|---|---|
| r.51(11) | The decision to grant will state which text of the European patent application forms the basis for the grant of the European patent. |
| J7/96 | Between the decision to grant and the grant taking effect there are only certain things that may be done in relation to the application. Linguistic errors, errors or transcription and obvious mistakes may be corrected under r.89, the application may be withdrawn or transferred or a designation may be withdrawn (CLBA, p.445). |
| J12/83 | Where a patent is granted with a text not approved by the applicant there is a right of appeal since the applicant is adversely affected by the decision. |
| J28/03 | A divisional application can only be validly filed following the appeal of a decision to grant if the appeal is upheld — the suspensive effect on its own is not enough in this case (unlike the appeal of a decision to refuse). |
| Guidelines | See C/VI/15.2. |

## 2–194    Date that grant takes effect—minimum period after the r.51(4) communication

| | |
|---|---|
| Art.97(4) | The decision to grant a European patent will not take effect until the date on which the European Patent Bulletin mentions the grant. |
| CLBA | See CLBA, p.446 for correction of details in the mention of grant. |
| Art.97(4)(5) | This mention is published at least two months after the start of the time limit referred to in Art.97(2)(b) (time limit for payment of grant and printing fees). Where translation of the claims must be filed (as is currently the case) this period is at least three months. |
| Art.97(6) | However, at the request of the applicant, mention of grant of the European patent will be published before the expiry of the time limit under Art.97(4) or (5). Such request may only be made if the requirements pursuant to Art.97(2) and (5) are met (fees for grant/printing and renewal fees paid, text approved and claim translations filed). |
| AnReg | See under Art.97(6) where the procedure for obtaining an early grant is explained ([1995] O.J. 841). See also under Art.75. A seven-point plan for accelerating search, examination and grant, known as "PACE", is described ([2001] O.J. 459). |

## 2–195    Publication of the granted patent

| | |
|---|---|
| Art.98 | At the same time as it publishes the mention of the grant of the European patent, the European Patent Office publishes a specification of the European patent containing the description, the claims and any drawings. |
| Art.14(7) | The specifications of European patents are published in the language of the proceedings; they include a translation of the claims in the two other official languages of the European Patent Office. |
| r.38(6) | The particulars in the declaration of priority are published with the granted patent. |
| r.53 | The published specification also contains an indication of the time limit for opposing the European patent. |

Rules 48 and 49(1)–(2) apply to the publication of the granted patent as they apply to the publication of the application (not published if withdrawn before technical preparations complete, designated offices specified, President to prescribe form). See under publication of the application. r.53

The European patent as granted or amended is published in electronic form by means of a publication server from which it may be downloaded (as at April 1, 2005). [2005] O.J. 124

The person designated as the inventor will be mentioned as such in the published European patent unless the said person informs the EPO in writing that he waives his right to be thus mentioned. r.18(1)

In the event of a third party filing with the EPO a final decision whereby the applicant for or proprietor of a patent is required to designate him as the inventor, the provisions of r.18(1) apply. r.18(2)

See under Art.93. Additional copies of the patent may be ordered ([1987] O.J. 242). See also under r.49. Where technical information has been included in the file wrapper during prosecution, the granted patent will contain a reference to such material ([1981] O.J. 74). See also under r.53. The title of the invention is now only shown on the title page and not as a heading to the description ([1984] O.J. 88). See also legal advice 17/90. The published specification is not legally authentic (the text agreed for grant is) and any mistakes in it may readily be corrected ([1990] O.J. 260—see also CLBA, p.390—T150/89). AnReg

### Grant to different applicants 2–196

Where there are different applicants for different states the Examining Division will grant the European patent for each Contracting State to the applicant or applicants registered in respect of that state. r.52

### Issue of a certificate 2–197

As soon as the patent is published the EPO issues to the proprietor of the patent a certificate. The President of the EPO prescribes the content, form and means of communication of the certificate and the circumstances in which an administrative fee is due (amended as at April 1, 2005). r.54

The certificate is supplied in paper form to each proprietor. Any proprietor may ask for a copy of the granted patent to be sent at the same time, free of charge, but the request must be received within the period prescribed be r.51(4) or r.58(5) or (6). The supply of any additional copies of the certificate and patent are subject to an administrative fee. The certificate must state the patent number and certify that a patent has been granted, to the persons named in the certificate, for the invention described and the states designated in the patent specification, or has been maintained in amended form. [2005] O.J. 122

The amount of the administrative fee is fixed by the President of the EPO. RRF3(1)

See under RRF. The amount is 35 euros ([2006] O.J. 255). AnReg

### Validation in designated states 2–198

See below under national phase aspects.

# 10. Opposition

### General considerations 2–199

Opposition proceedings are by nature essentially contentious and not administrative. The EPO must therefore be impartial and not suggest how either side might improve its position (also G9/91, G10/91, T804/92). T173/89

| | |
|---|---|
| AnReg | See under Art.99. A guide to opposition procedure has been published by the EPO ([2001] O.J. 148). |

**Filing an opposition**

**2–200** *Time limit for filing a notice of opposition*

| | |
|---|---|
| Art.99(1) | Notice of opposition to a granted European patent must be given to the EPO within nine months from the publication of the mention of the grant of the European Patent. |
| T438/87 | Any delay in the publication of the patent specification does not affect the opposition period since the publication of the mention of grant is decisive (CLBA, p.465). However, see J14/87 where it was left undecided whether an error in the publication of the mention of grant might have an effect on the opposition period. |
| T702/89 | A would-be opponent is not entitled to *restitutio* in respect of the missed nine-month time limit (CLBA, p.296). |

**2–201** *Where should the opposition be filed?*

| | |
|---|---|
| Art.99(1) | The opposition must be filed at the EPO. |
| | In this context, the relevant filing offices are Munich and the Hague (Art.6) and Berlin (see AnReg under Art.10(2)—[1989] O.J. 218). See also AnReg under r.24(1) ([2005] O.J. 44) for information on filing documents other than applications in general. |
| | An opposition cannot be filed with the Vienna sub-office (see AnReg under Art.75(2)—[1992] O.J. 183) or the national authority of a Contracting State. In these cases they will receive the date they are given in Munich when forwarded. |
| | Documents filed with the German patent office (except by hand), in Berlin or Munich, used to be considered as received on behalf of the EPO and were forwarded directly (see AnReg under Art.75(1)—[1991] O.J. 187). However, the relevant agreement terminated as of September 1, 2005 and an opposition will now only be accorded the date it actually arrives at the EPO. |
| G5/88 | In this case a notice of opposition was filed at the German Patent Office in Berlin on the last day of the opposition period but was accepted as filed in time at the EPO. |

**2–202** *Who may file a notice of opposition*

| | |
|---|---|
| Art.99(1) | Any person may give notice to the European Patent Office of opposition to a granted European patent. |
| G1/84 | In this early decision of the Enlarged Board, "any person" was given its natural meaning of anybody, including the proprietor of the patent. The reasoning was mainly that the proprietor should have some means of amending the European patent when relevant art becomes known just before or after grant, the purpose of the EPC being to grant patents for novel and non-obvious inventions. Furthermore, opposition proceedings were not seen as essentially contentious but investigative. It was also noted that in Art.115(1) EPC the term "any person" meant any third party in the French and German texts, whereas it meant any person in Art.99(1), suggesting that it was not meant to exclude the proprietor in Art.99(1). Headnote: "A notice of opposition against a European patent is not inadmissible merely because it has been filed by the proprietor of that patent." |
| G9/93 | Headnote: "A European patent cannot be opposed by its own proprietor." |
| | The Enlarged Board overruled G1/84, holding that "any person" must be interpreted in the context of the EPC as a whole and, as determined in G9/91 and G10/91, opposition proceedings are essentially contentious proceedings. In the interests of equity and good faith the decision did not apply to pending self-oppositions. |

Headnote (1): "(a) An opposition is not inadmissible purely because the person named as opponent according to r.55(a) EPC is acting on behalf of a third party (*i.e.* as a strawman). (b) Such an opposition is, however, inadmissible if the involvement of the opponent is to be regarded as circumventing the law by abuse of process. (c) Such a circumvention of the law arises, in particular, if: (i) the opponent is acting on behalf of the patent proprietor; (ii) the opponent is acting on behalf of a client in the context of activities which, taken as a whole, are typically associated with professional representatives, without possessing the relevant qualifications required by Art.134 EPC. (d) However, a circumvention of the law by abuse of process does not arise purely because (i) a professional representative is acting in his own name on behalf of a client; (ii) an opponent with either a residence or principal place of business in one of the EPC Contracting States is acting on behalf of a third party who does not meet this requirement."

G3/97

Headnote (2): "In determining whether the law has been circumvented by abuse of process, the principle of the free evaluation of evidence is to be applied (i.e. on case by case basis, no special rules to be applied). The burden of proof is to be borne by the person alleging that the opposition is inadmissible. The deciding body has to be satisfied on the basis of clear and convincing evidence that the law has been circumvented by abuse of process (i.e. more than on balance of probabilities)."

Headnotes (1) and (2): Identical to G3/97 (1)(2).

G4/97

Headnote (3): "The admissibility of an opposition on grounds relating to the identity of an opponent may be challenged during the course of the appeal, even if no such challenge has been raised before the Opposition Division."

The Enlarged Board also decided that the decision should be applied to all pending proceedings since there was no valid legitimate expectation to protect on the basis of past case law.

In both these cases the Enlarged Board felt that it was allowable for a strawman to file an opposition as long as the "principal" he was acting for would have had the legal right to do so. No special interest is necessary since every member of the public has an interest to the extent that the ability to carry out certain acts is restricted by the patent.

Headnote (1): "An opposition filed in common by two or more persons, which otherwise meets the requirements of Art.99 EPC and r.1 and r.55 EPC is admissible on payment of only one opposition fee."

G3/99

The situation where several natural or legal persons file an opposition in common is anticipated by r.100(1).

Headnote (3): "In order to safeguard the rights of the patent proprietor and in the interests of procedural efficiency, it has to be clear throughout the procedure who belongs to the group of common opponents or common appellants. If either a common opponent or appellant (including the common representative) intends to withdraw from the proceedings, the EPO shall be notified accordingly by the common representative or by a new common representative determined under r.100(1) EPC in order for the withdrawal to take effect."

One legal or natural entity may only file one opposition to a given patent—second opposition filed will be deemed inadmissible for lack of legitimate interest.

T9/00

See CLBA, pp.466–468. An exclusive licensee is not barred from opposing the patent under which he is licensed (Decision of Opposition Division, [1992] O.J. 747).

CLBA

### Content of the notice of opposition

2–203

Notice of opposition must be filed in a written reasoned statement. It must contain:

Art.99(1)/r.55

(a) the name and address of the opponent and the state in which his residence or principal place of business is located, complying with r.26(2)(c) (requirement for the request);

(b) the number of the European patent which is opposed, the name of the proprietor and the title of the invention;

(c) a statement of the extent to which the patent is opposed (e.g. which claims), the grounds on which the opposition is based and an indication of the facts, evidence and arguments presented in support of these grounds; and

(d) the name, address and place of business of any representative appointed by the opponent, complying with r.26(2)(c).

CLBA

See CLBA, pp.468–474 for "substantiation of the opposition" under r.55(c). Only an "indication" is necessary so that further facts and evidence can in principle be filed later (T328/87), though subject to the inherent discretion of the EPO to refuse late filed facts and evidence under Art.114(2). There is a distinction between "facts and evidence" and "arguments", the latter being admissible at any stage of the proceedings (G4/95). In any case, new facts and evidence will be admitted at any stage if there are clear reasons to think that they prejudice the maintenance of the patent (T1002/92) and their relevance must therefore always be considered (T142/97). Where they are late filed, the remedy of awarding costs may be used. In the case of a prior use, the substantiation should include specific details of what was made available, where, when and by whom (T93/89). See pages CLBA 482 to 483 for a discussion of the circumstances in which one opponent may use another opponent's evidence.

r.61a

Rules 26 to 36 (provisions governing the application) apply to documents filed during opposition proceedings—see Guidelines D/III/3. In particular, the opposition must be signed (Art.36(3)) and filed in the correct manner (Art.36(5), i.e. by post or facsimile) —see under common provisions.

Guidelines

See D/III/6.

### 2–204    *Grounds for opposition*

Art.100

Opposition may only be filed on the grounds that:

(a) the subject-matter of the European patent is not patentable within the terms of Arts.52 to 57;

(b) the European patent does not disclose the invention in a manner sufficiently clear and complete for it to be carried out by a person skilled in the art;

(c) the subject matter of the European patent extends beyond the content of the application as filed, or, if the patent was granted on a divisional application or on a new application filed in accordance with Art.61, beyond the content of the earlier application as filed.

G1/91

Lack of unity is not a ground of opposition and may not even be raised against a patent which has been amended in opposition proceedings.

T443/97

Equally, the provisions of r.86(4) (amendment not to relate to unsearched subject matter) is seen as a pre-grant issue only (CLBA, p.425).

G1/95

A ground is an individual legal basis and Art.100(a) describes a collection of individual grounds.

Guidelines

See D/III/5 and D/V/3–5.

### 2–205    *Payment of the opposition fee*

Art.99(1)

The notice of opposition is not deemed to have been filed until the opposition fee has been paid.

RRF2(10)

The opposition fee is 635 euros.

### Language of the notice of opposition—fee reduction 2–206

The notice of opposition must be filed in an official language of the EPO. r.1(1)

Nevertheless, natural or legal persons having their residence or principal place of business within the territory of a Contracting State having a language other than English, French or German as an official language, and nationals of that state who are resident abroad may file an opposition in an official language of that state and file a translation into an official language later. See general section on languages below. Art.14(4)(2)

A reduction (NB. reduction, not refund) in the opposition fee is available to an opponent who avails himself of the Art.14(4) option. The reduction is fixed in the RRF at a percentage of the total of the fees. r.6(3)

The reduction is 20 per cent. RRF12(1)

For the 20 per cent reduction in the opposition fee, the matter prescribed by Art.55(c) (notice and grounds) must be filed in an official language of a Contracting State (see CLBA, 394 and G6/91). T290/90

As with the filing of the application a person who files an opposition in an official language of a Contracting State must possess the necessary nationality/residence demanded by Art.14(2) (CLBA, p.394). T149/85

The nationality/residency of the opponent is determinative, not that of the representative. T149/85

If any document, other than those making up the European patent application, is not filed in the language prescribed by the EPC, or if any translation required by virtue of the EPC is not filed in due time, the document is deemed not to have been received. Any fees paid are refunded (T193/87). Art.14(5)

### Opposition may be filed even where a patent is surrendered or has lapsed 2–207

An opposition may be filed even if a European patent has been surrendered or has lapsed for all the designated states. Art.99(3)

An opposition may also be continued in similar circumstances (see below).

## Examination of the opposition for admissibility and circumstances in which it is deemed not filed

### An opposition must be admissible to be examined 2–208

The opposition must be admissible before it will be fully examined by the Opposition Division (see T328/87). Art.101(1)

No comment is made on the substantive issues if the opposition is deemed inadmissible. T925/91

See CLBA, pp.462–463. Admissibility may be re-examined at any time during opposition or opposition appeal proceedings. A decision that an opposition is inadmissible is appealable. CLBA

### A formalities officer can decide on admissibility in certain circumstances 2–209

Headnote: "Points 4 and 6 of the Notice from the Vice-President Directorate-General 2 dated 28 April 1999 ([1999] O.J. 506) do not conflict with provisions of a higher level." G1/02

This decision overruled T295/01, which had suggested that formalities officers could never decide on the admissibility of an opposition, only the Opposition Division being competent. A formalities officer can decide on admissibility where there are no technical or legal difficulties.

CLBA  See CLBA, p.466. A formalities officer cannot decide on admissibility under r.55(c) (T295/01) due to the complicated legal and technical matters involved.

## 2–210 *Deficiencies that must be corrected before the opposition period expires*

r.56(1)  If the notice of opposition does not comply with:

(a) Art.99(1) (within nine-month period, written reasoned statement, opposition fee paid);

(b) r.1(1) (language); or

(c) r.55(c) (extent opposed, grounds of opposition, facts/evidence/argument); or

(d) does not sufficiently identify the opposed patent;

the Opposition Division will reject it as inadmissible unless the deficiencies are remedied before the expiry of the opposition period.

T25/85  If the identity of the opponent is not established in the nine-month period, the opposition is inadmissible—does not comply with Art.99(1) (CLBA, p.465).

T376/90  If there is serious doubt about the extent of the opposition, it must be rejected as inadmissible.

T222/85  Admissibility has nothing to do with the strength of the case—an opposition that would have succeeded can be rejected as inadmissible whilst an opposition doomed to failure might be properly substantiated (see also T2/89).

T222/85  Substantiation by way of just citing certain documents to support the alleged grounds is not enough. The legal and factual reasons (T550/85) must also be stated in order to allow the opponent's case to be understood on an objective basis (T222/85, T2/89).

T550/88  If the facts and evidence supplied cannot support the grounds of opposition as a matter of law then the opposition is inadmissible (e.g. using prior national rights against novelty).

Guidelines  See D/IV/1.2.2.1. The EPO should inform an opponent of any such deficiency in good time for him to correct it where this is possible. However, such a communication cannot be expected as of right (Guidelines D/IV/1.3.3).

## 2–211 *Deficiencies that may be corrected after the opposition period expires*

r.56(2)  Where the Opposition Division notices that the notice of opposition does not comply with any requirement other than those listed in r.56(1) it will point the deficiency out to the opponent and invite the filing of a correction within a period it will specify. If the notice of opposition is not corrected in good time the Opposition Division will reject it as inadmissible.

CLBA  See CLBA, pp.464–465. Where the title of the invention was not supplied within the r.56(2) period the opposition was declared admissible anyway since the identity of the opposed patent was not in any doubt (T317/86).

Guidelines  See D/IV/1.2.2.2.

## 2–212 *Decision that opposition is inadmissible is to be communicated to the proprietor*

r.56(3)  Any decision to reject an opposition as inadmissible is communicated to the proprietor of the patent, together with a copy of the notice.

## Circumstances in which the opposition is deemed not to have been filed

2–213

Where no opposition fee is paid before the end of opposition period, the opposition is deemed not to have been filed. — Art.99(1)

The opposition must be signed. Where such a defect is not remedied following an invitation from the EPO the opposition is deemed not to have been received. — r.36(3)

If the opposition is filed by facsimile, written confirmation must be supplied if asked for by the EPO (see AnReg under r.24(1)—[1992] O.J. 299). If this is not provided within the time limit the opposition is deemed not to have been received. — r.36(5)

Where the opposition is filed by a representative, and an authorisation is for some reason requested (see AnReg under r.101(1)—[1991] O.J. 489) if the authorisation is not filed in due time, the procedural step of filing the opposition is deemed not to have been taken. — r.101(1)(4)

Where the opposition is filed in the official language of a Contracting State and the translation required by Art.14(4) is not filed in due time, the opposition is deemed not to have been received. — Art.14(5)

## Intervening in an opposition

2–214

In the event of an opposition to a European patent being filed, any third party who proves that proceedings for infringement of the same patent have been instituted against him (action letter not enough—proceedings must have started—this is a matter of national law) may, after the opposition period has expired, intervene in the opposition proceedings, if he gives notice of intervention within three months of the date on which the infringement proceedings were instituted. The same applies in respect of any third party who proves both that the proprietor of the patent has requested that he cease alleged infringement of the patent and that he has instituted proceedings for a court ruling that he is not infringing the patent. — Art.105(1)

The three-month period starts from the first relevant proceedings (e.g. in the case where the proprietor has sued for infringement and the "infringer" has later applied for a declaration of non-infringement, the date of institution of the first action). — T296/93

Headnote: "In a case where, after issue of a final decision by an Opposition Division (=date decision handed to internal EPO postal system in the case of written proceedings—T631/94 as *per* G12/91), no appeal is filed by a party to the proceedings before the Opposition Division, a notice of intervention which is filed during the two-month period for appeal provided by Art.108 EPC has no legal effect." — G4/91

The Enlarged Board decided that an intervention can only be filed if opposition proceedings are in existence. This is not so where a decision of the Opposition Division has been issued, such a decision being final in the sense that the Opposition Division has no power to change it. Such a decision therefore terminates the opposition proceedings regardless of the fact that it takes legal effect only after the period for appeal has expired.

Where it can be shown that a sole appeal was withdrawn before an intervention was received, even if the two events occurred on the same day, the intervention is not admissible. — T517/97

See CLBA, pp.458–459. It is not possible to intervene based on proceedings initiated in respect of a national patent, even if the opposed European patent claims the priority of the national patent (T446/95). — CLBA

Headnote: "Intervention of the assumed infringer under Art.105 EPC is admissible during pending appeal proceedings and may be based on any ground for opposition under Art.100 EPC." — G1/94

The convenience of having centralised revocation being balanced by the complication and delay to the appeal proceedings, the Enlarged Board was most swayed by the travaux préparatoires which indicated that intervention was contemplated during the appeal stage. The Board further considered that the intervener should be given the unfettered right to raise any ground of opposition. However, in view of G10/91, if a fresh ground is raised then the case should be remitted to the first instance unless there are special reasons to decide otherwise, such as the agreement of the patentee. It is not yet clear, however, whether an interveners could attack claims which were not attacked in the original opposition.

T694/01

An intervention is dependent on the degree to which opposition/appeal proceedings are still pending. Thus, where the intervention occurs after a Board of Appeal has already decided on the allowable claims, in subsequent appeal proceedings concerning the adaptation of those claims to the description, the allowed claims may not be challenged.

G3/04

Headnote: 'After withdrawal of the sole appeal, the proceedings may not be continued with a third party who intervened during the appeal proceedings.'

The Enlarged Board had previously decided that intervention during opposition appeal proceedings was possible (G1/94) but there was some doubt about the intervener's procedural status in this situation. This decision has made it clear that the intervener attains the status of an opponent under A105(2) EPC and is a party to the appeal proceedings of right under A107 EPC. The intervener does not, however, have the status of an appellant since he was not adversely affected by the decision taken. No appeal fee therefore needs to be paid. It also follows, from decision G7/91, that withdrawal of a sole appeal will terminate the proceedings, the consent of the intervener not being required.

Art.105(2)

Notice of intervention must be filed in a written reasoned statement. It is not deemed to have been filed until the opposition fee has been paid. Thereafter the intervention is, subject to any exceptions laid down in the Implementing Regulations, treated as an opposition.

RRF2(10)

The opposition fee is 635 euros.

The notice of intervention must satisfy the same admissibility requirements as a notice of opposition.

Guidelines

See D/I/5 and D/VII/7.

## 2–215 Opposition to apply to all designated states

Art.99(2)

An opposition applies to the European patent in all the Contracting States in which that patent has effect.

Guidelines

See D/I/3. If the opposition is filed in respect of some of the states, it is treated as if it were in respect of all the states.

### Parties to the opposition

2–216 *The opponent is a party to the proceedings*

Art.99(4)

An opponent is a party to the opposition proceedings as well as the proprietor of the patent.

2–217 *Change of proprietor through entitlement proceedings*

Art.99(5)

Where a person provides evidence that in a Contracting State, following a final decision, he has been entered in the patent register of such state instead of the previous proprietor, such person will, at his request, replace the previous proprietor in respect of such state. By derogation from Art.118, the previous proprietor and the person making the request will not be deemed to be joint proprietors unless both so request.

Suspension of proceedings does apply during opposition proceedings but the Protocol on Recognition does not operate. r.13(4)

See D/VII/5. Guidelines

## Procedure for examination of the opposition

### *Nature of the proceedings* — 2–218

See CLBA, pp.447–451. Opposition proceedings are contentious proceedings between two parties and the Opposition Division must take an impartial stance. The principle of party disposition applies (the initial request determines the extent of the proceedings). CLBA

### *Steps taken prior to examination* — 2–219

The following communications and invitations are made by the Opposition Division prior to examination of an opposition. However, they may be dispensed with in the case of an intervention. r.57(4)

The Opposition Division communicates the contents of the opposition to the proprietor and invites him to file his observations and, where appropriate, any amendments to the description, claims and drawings, within a period that the Opposition Division sets. At the same time, where several notices of opposition have been filed, the Opposition Division will communicate them to the other opponents. r.57(1)(2)

The proprietor can, for instance, contest the admissibility of the opposition at this stage and such is decided in inter partes proceedings by the Opposition Division.

The proprietor's right to be heard is violated if the Opposition Division hands a revocation decision to the internal postal service before this time limit for filing observations has expired. T663/99

Any observations and/or amendments filed are communicated to the other parties concerned who are themselves invited, if the Opposition Division considers it expedient, to file observations within a set period. r.57(3)

See D/IV/5.2 and 5.4. Guidelines

### *Examination as to whether the grounds of opposition prejudice the patent* — 2–220

The Opposition Division will examine whether the grounds for opposition laid down in Art.100 prejudice the maintenance of the European patent. Art.101(1)

In the examination of the opposition, the Opposition Division will invite the parties, as often as necessary, to file observations, within a period to be fixed by the Opposition Division, on communications from another party or issued by itself. Art.101(2)

See CLBA, pp.451–456. The Opposition Division has discretion whether or not to treat observations (other than those under r.57(1)) as admissible (T295/87) and in certain circumstances no Art.101(2) invitation will be necessary (e.g. T275/89). However, Art.113(1) must be respected (e.g. T669/90). CLBA

All such communications, and the replies thereto, are communicated to all parties. r.58(1)

Any such communication to the proprietor will, where necessary, contain a reasoned statement which will, where appropriate, cover all the grounds against the maintenance of the patent. The proprietor will, in addition, be invited to file, where necessary, amendments to the description, claims and drawings. r.58(2)(3)

See D/VI/3–4. Guidelines

| | |
|---|---|
| **2–221** | **Permissible amendments of the patent during opposition** |
| r.57a | Without prejudice to r.87 (different claims for different states due to prior national rights), the description, claims and drawings may be amended provided that the amendments are occasioned by one of the grounds for opposition stated in Art.100, even if the relevant ground has not been invoked by an opponent. |
| r.57(1)/r.58(2) | Amendments must be "appropriate" and "necessary". |
| CLBA | See CLBA, pp.483–488. Amendments for the sake of clarity are generally not allowed. |
| Art.102(3) | Amendments made must meet all the requirements of the EPC. In particular, the protection should not be extended (Art.123(3)). |
| CLBA | See CLBA, pp.488–489. There is a wide power to consider all the requirements of the EPC (T227/88) except unity (G1/92) but only to the extent that objections (*e.g.* under Art.84) arise from the amendments themselves (T301/87). |
| T503/96 | Sometimes, amendments made will require an additional search (CLBA, p.489). |
| T406/86 | Amendments filed late in the proceedings may be ignored. |
| T123/85 | Where claims are limited during opposition proceedings, this does not imply any surrender of the subject matter of the claims as granted and deleted claims may be reinstated during appeal proceedings. |
| **2–222** | **Requirements relating to documents filed during opposition proceedings** |
| r.61a | Rule 26 to r.36 (provisions governing the application) apply to documents filed during opposition proceedings. |
| r.59 | If any party refers to a document during opposition proceedings it must file two copies of it with the notice of opposition or the relevant written submission. Where such a document is neither enclosed nor filed in due time upon invitation by the EPO, the EPO may decide not to take into account any arguments based on it. |
| **2–223** | **Continuation of the opposition by the EPO of its own motion in the event of the withdrawal of an opposition or the death of an opponent** |
| r.60(2) | Where an opposition is withdrawn or in the event of the death or legal incapacity of an opponent, the opposition proceedings may be continued by the EPO of its own motion, even without the participation of heirs or legal representatives. |
| CLBA | See CLBA, pp.460–461. The opposition should be continued if it has reached the stage where a limitation or revocation is likely without further assistance from the opponent, *e.g.* in T197/88 where a r.58(4) communication had issued, the granted form not being maintained. If the Opposition Division does not continue the proceedings, it takes a decision to reject the opposition. |
| Guidelines | See D/VII/6.2 and 6.3. |
| G8/93 | This provision is not applicable during appeal proceedings (see under appeal). |
| **2–224** | **Continuation of the opposition where the patent has been surrendered or has lapsed** |
| r.60(1) | Even if the European patent has been surrendered or has lapsed for all the designated states, opposition proceedings may be continued where the opponent so requests within two months of a notification by the EPO of the surrender or lapse. |
| T329/88 | The EPO must terminate the opposition if no reply is received from the opponent. |

See CLBA, pp.461–462. See CLBA, p.541 for equivalent during appeal. The EPO is not obliged to ascertain the legal status of an opposed patent. Confirmation should be received from all designated states (T194/88).   CLBA

See D/VII/6.1.   Guidelines

### Extent to which the Opposition Division may examine the patent beyond the stated extent of and grounds for the opposition   2–225

Rule 55(c) was interpreted by the Enlarged Board as governing the legal and factual framework within which substantive examination of an opposition must in principle be conducted. Therefore, if the extent of the opposition is only partial (*i.e.* not all the independent claims are opposed) the Opposition Division has no competence to examine those claims which are not subject to any "opposition" at all. In contrast, where an independent claim is opposed, the Opposition Division may also examine any dependent claims provided that their validity is prima facie in doubt on the basis of the available information.   G9/91

The situation is slightly different as regards grounds of opposition. In this case, an Opposition Division is not obliged to consider all the grounds for opposition referred to in Art.100. However, it may raise a ground not covered by the opposition statement pursuant to r.55(c), using its power under Art.114(1), but only where, prima facie, there are clear reasons to believe that such a ground is relevant and would in whole or in part prejudice the maintenance of the European patent.   G10/91

The Opposition Division is obliged to at least consider whether any new ground should be admitted.   T736/95

See CLBA, pp.475–482. Where an Opposition Division introduces a new ground it must inform the proprietor of the legal and factual bases supporting the new ground and give him a proper opportunity to comment (T433/93). In terms of citing new documents, the Opposition Division may introduce a document from the Search Report if it has strong reasons to consider it relevant (T387/89) or a document cited in the patent as important prior art related to the problem solved (T536/88).   CLBA

See D/V/2.1 and 2.2.   Guidelines

### Acceleration of proceedings   2–226

Opposition proceedings are accelerated at the request of the proprietor who has commenced infringement proceedings (CLBA, p.458).   T290/90

See under Art.99 ([1998] O.J. 361).   AnReg

See D/VII/1.2.   Guidelines

### Further searches   2–227

See D/VI/5. The Opposition Division may request the Search Division to carry out an additional European search where one is required.   Guidelines

### Different claims for different states when two proprietors are defending the patent   2–228

Where a third party has, in accordance with Art.99(5), replaced the previous proprietor for one or some of the designated Contracting States, the patent as maintained in opposition proceedings may contain for these states claims, a description and drawings which are different from those for the other designated Contracting States.   r.16(3)

| | |
|---|---|
| **2–229** | ***Revocation where no text is approved*** |
| Guidelines | See D/VIII/1.2.5. The patent will be revoked where the proprietor no longer approves the text as granted and does not propose another text, asks for revocation or "surrenders" the application. See T73/84, T186/84 and T237/86. |
| **2–230** | **Procedure if the opposition succeeds** |
| Art.102(1) | If the Opposition Division is of the opinion that the grounds for opposition mentioned in Art.100 prejudice the maintenance of the European patent, it will revoke the patent. |
| **2–231** | **Procedure if the opposition fails** |
| Art.102(2) | If the Opposition Division is of the opinion that the grounds for opposition mentioned in Art.100 do not prejudice the maintenance of the patent unamended, it will reject the opposition. |

**Procedure if the opposition is partly successful**

| | |
|---|---|
| **2–232** | ***Notification of text which the Opposition Division proposes to maintain*** |
| Art.102(3) | If the Opposition Division is of the opinion that, taking into consideration the amendments made by the proprietor of the patent during the opposition proceedings, the patent and the invention to which it relates meet the requirements of the EPC, it will decide to maintain the patent as amended, provided that it is established that the proprietor of the patent approves the text in which the Opposition Division intends to maintain the patent. |
| G1/91 | Headnote: "Unity of invention (Art.82) does not come under the requirements which a European patent and the invention to which it relates must meet under Art.102(3) EPC when the patent is maintained in amended form. It is consequently irrelevant in opposition proceedings that the European patent as granted or as amended does not meet the requirement of unity." |
| | An interlocutory decision is issued which can be appealed to avoid the proprietor having to pay translation and printing fees several times. Such an interlocutory decision is provided for in principle by Art.106(3)—one that does not terminate proceedings with respect to one of the parties—and was recognised by G1/88. |
| CLBA | See CLBA, pp.490–492. |
| r.58(8) | The decision to maintain the patent as amended will state which text forms the basis for the maintenance thereof. |
| r.58(4) | In order to obtain the proprietor's approval of the text, the Opposition Division will inform the parties that it intends to maintain the patent as amended and invite them to state their observations within a period of two months if they disapprove of the text in which it is intended to maintain the patent. |
| AnReg | See under r.58. The communication under r.58(4) is rarely used now following G1/88 since the parties will usually be asked to comment on the proposed text during oral proceedings and this suffices for an interlocutory decision to be issued ([1989] O.J. 393). |
| G1/88 | Headnote: "The fact that an opponent has failed, within the time allowed, to make any observations on the text in which it is intended to maintain the European patent after being invited to do so under r.58(4) EPC does not render his appeal inadmissible." It had become practice that in the event the opponent made no comment his silence was |

interpreted as tacit approval and hence he was not 'adversely effected' and could not appeal. This practice was reversed. Rule 58(4) is seen not as a mandatory procedure but one option for obtaining the proprietor's approval of the text (Art.113(2)) and giving the opponent a chance to comment (Art.113(1)). These objects can also be achieved at oral proceedings.

See CLBA, p.456. CLBA

If the proposed text is disapproved, examination of the opposition may be continued. r.58(5)

See D/VI/7.2. Guidelines

### Need for payment of printing fee / filing of claim translations  2–233

Where the patent is to be maintained in amended form a fee for printing the new specification must be paid. Art.102(3)

Translations of the new claims in the two other official languages of the EPC must also be filed, as anticipated by Art.102(5). r.58(5)

The Opposition Division requests the proprietor to pay the fee and file the translations on expiry of any two-month period for filing observations set pursuant to r.58(4), and sets a three-month period for doing so. This communication will also indicate the Contracting States which require a translation pursuant to Art.65(1). r.58(5)(7)

Note that no provision exists for the payment of any claims fees if the number of claims has increased.

If these acts are not carried out in due time they may still be validly performed within two months of notification of a communication pointing out the failure to observe the time limit, provided that within this two month period a surcharge equal to twice the printing fee is paid. r.58(6)

The printing fee is 55 euros. RRF2(9)

If the fee for the printing of a new specification is not paid in due time, the patent will be revoked. Art.102(4)

If the translations are not filed in due time the patent will be revoked. Art.102(5)

Headnote: "The revocation of a patent under Art.102(4) and (5) EPC requires a decision." G1/90

There was confusion as to whether, in the event of Art.102(4) or (5) being activated, there was a deemed revocation of the patent leading to a loss of rights communication under r.69(1) or whether the opposition decision needed to take a decision under Art.69(2). The Enlarged Board considered that whereas grant proceedings can be terminated by a loss of rights or a decision, the EPC provides for opposition proceedings being terminated only by a decision and this literal interpretation of the EPC is in accord with the travaux préparatoires, procedural convenience and legal certainty.

See CLBA, p.489. CLBA

See D/VI/7.2.3 and D/VIII/1.2.2. Guidelines

### Publication of a new specification where the patent is amended— new patent certificate  2–234

If a European patent is amended under Art.102(3), the EPO will, at the same time as it publishes the mention of the decision of the opposition decision, publish a new Art.103

440    Complete Guide to Passing the EQE

|  |  |
|---|---|
| | specification of the European patent containing the description, the claims and any drawings, in the amended form. |
| r.62 | Rule 49(1)–(2) applies to the new specification (designated Contracting States identified, President to decide form). |
| r.62a | A new certificate will be sent to the proprietor after the new specification is published. Rule 54 applies (see under grant procedure for details). |
| Guidelines | See D/VII/8. |

**Costs**

**2–235**     *Rules for the apportionment of costs*

| | |
|---|---|
| Art.104(1) | Each party to the proceedings must meet the costs he has incurred unless a decision of an Opposition Division or Board of Appeal, for reasons of equity, orders, in accordance with the Implementing Regulations, a different apportionment of costs incurred during taking of evidence or in oral proceedings. |
| T117/86 | Such taking of evidence relates to the taking of evidence in general throughout the proceedings and is not, for instance, restricted to the r.72 procedure (T823/89). |
| Case law | Equity may demand a different apportionment where evidence has been late filed (e.g. T117/86) or a party has not attended oral proceedings (e.g. T930/92). |
| r.63(1) | Apportionment of costs will be dealt with in the decision on the opposition. Such apportionment will only take into consideration the expenses necessary to assure proper protection of the rights involved. The costs will include the renumeration of the representatives of the parties. |
| T212/88 | A request for a decision on costs must be made before the final decision is taken. |
| CLBA | See CLBA, pp.492–504 and CLBA, p.272 for some guidance. See also CLBA, p.336 for the effect of late filed documents on subsequent costs. |
| Guidelines | See D/IX and E/IV/1.9. |

**2–236**     *Registry to fix amount of costs to be paid*

| | |
|---|---|
| Art.104(2) | On request, the registry of the Opposition Division will fix the amount of the costs to be paid under a decision apportioning them. |
| r.9(4) | The President of the EPO may grant exclusive responsibilities to one of the registries of the Opposition Divisions for fixing the amount of costs as provided for in Art.104(2). |
| r.63(2) | A bill of costs, with supporting evidence, must be attached to the request for the fixing of costs. The request will only be admissible if the decision in respect of which the fixing of costs is required has become final. Costs may be fixed once their credibility is established. |

**2–237**     *Review of costs fixed by the registry*

| | |
|---|---|
| Art.104(2) | The fixing of the costs by the registry may be reviewed by a decision of the Opposition Division on a request filed within the period laid down in the Implementing Regulations. |

Such a request for a decision must be filed in writing to the EPO within one month after the date of notification of the awarding of costs and must state the reasons on which it is based. It will not be deemed to have been filed until the fee for the awarding of costs has been paid. r.63(3)

The fee for the awarding of costs is 55 euros. RRF2(16)

The Opposition Division will take a decision on the request referred to in r.63(3) without oral proceedings. r.63(4)

### Enforcement of decisions on costs in Contracting States  2–238

Any final decision of the European Patent Office fixing the amount of costs must be dealt with, for the purpose of enforcement in the Contracting States, in the same way as a final decision given by a civil court of the State in the territory of which enforcement is to be carried out. Verification of such decision must be limited to its authenticity. Art.104(3)

### No appeal solely on costs  2–239

The apportionment of costs of opposition proceedings may not be the sole subject of an appeal. Art.106(4)

A decision fixing the amount of costs of opposition proceedings cannot be appealed unless the amount is in excess of that laid down in the rules relating to fees. Art.106(5)

The amount must be in excess of the fee for appeal. RRF11

### Transfer of the patent during opposition  2–240

The transfer of a patent may be recorded at the EPO during the opposition period or during any opposition proceedings. Rule 20 applies. r.61

The transfer must also be recorded in many designated states (see Table IX). NatLaw

### Transfer of the opposition to another party  2–241

This rule (see above) seems to imply that an heir to a deceased opponent may continue the opposition. r.60(2)

Headnote: "An opposition pending before the EPO may be transferred or assigned to a third party as part of the opponent's business assets together with the assets in the interests of which the opposition was filed." G4/88

The Enlarged Board considered that an opposition, giving rise to legal rights as a party, constitutes as inseparable part of a business's assets and may therefore be transferred with those assets.

Headnote (1): '(a) The status as an opponent cannot be freely transferred. (b) A legal person who was a subsidiary of the opponent when the opposition was filed and who carries on the business to which the opposed patent relates cannot acquire the status as opponent if all its shares are assigned to another company.' G2/04

Headnote (2): 'If, when filing an appeal, there is a justifiable legal uncertainty as to how the law is to be interpreted in respect of the question of who the correct party to the proceedings is, it is legitimate that the appeal is filed in the name of the person whom the person acting considers, according to his interpretation, to be the correct party, and at the same time, as an auxiliary request, in the name of a different person who might, according to another possible interpretation, also be considered the correct party to the proceedings'.

This decision confirmed that an opposition cannot be freely assigned but may be transferred as a result of universal succession (e.g. from a deceased opponent to his/her heir (R60(2) EPC) or in the takeover of a company, or the relevant assets of a company, by another legal entity (G4/88)). Where, however, company A, which has a legally independent subsidiary B, files an opposition relating to a business area in which company B operates, the opposition may not be transferred from A to a company which buys subsidiary B. The opposition would have been transferable if: (a) it had been filed in the name of the subsidiary company; or (b) B had not had its own legal status but had merely been a department of company A. Where a holding company files an opposition on behalf of a legally distinct subsidiary it is thus safer to file the opposition jointly in both names.

The decision also established that if, when filing an appeal, there is justifiable legal uncertainty as to who the correct party to the proceedings is, it is legitimate for the appeal to be filed in the name of the person whom the person acting considers to be the correct party, and at the same time, as an auxiliary request, in the name of a different person who might, according to another possible interpretation, also be considered the correct party to the proceedings.

CLBA    See CLBA, pp.459–460 and 507–508 (transfer during appeal proceedings). The right to appeal against maintenance of the patent may be transferred in the same way (T563/89) as may an appeal once initiated (T659/92).

## 11. Appeal

**2–242**    **The nature of appeal proceedings**

G9/91    Appeal is a judicial procedure and the boards of appeal act as courts.

T34/90    An appeal is a review of the decision under appeal on its merits and not a re-examination (T34/90).

G9/92    The initial request on appeal determines the extent of the proceedings in accordance with the principle of party disposition.

CLBA    See CLBA, pp.504–505 on the general character of an appeal. See CLBA, p.519 for the extent to which Appeal Board should review decisions taken under the discretion of the first instance department.

**2–243**    **Decisions which can be appealed**

Art.106(1)    An appeal lies from decisions of the Receiving Section, Examining Divisions, Opposition Divisions and the Legal Division (NB. not the Search Division).

J8/81, J2/93    A decision decides one or more issues and should be distinguished from a notification (of some event) and a communication (which usually requires a reply). Whether a document issued is a decision is a matter of substance, not a matter of form.

J29/92    Where no decision has been issued, an appeal is inadmissible. However, the appeal fee is not refunded (J37/97).

Art.106(2)    An appeal may be filed against the decision of the Opposition Division even if the European patent has been surrendered or has lapsed for all the designated states.

Art.106(3)    A decision which does not terminate proceedings as regards one of the parties can only be appealed together with the final decision, unless the decision allows separate appeal (interlocutory decision).

The apportionment of costs of opposition proceedings cannot be the sole subject of an appeal. — Art.106(4)

See CLBA, pp.503–504 and 519–521. — CLBA

A decision fixing the amount of costs of opposition proceedings cannot be appealed unless the amount is in excess of that laid down in the Rules relating to Fees. — Art.106(5)

The amount must be in excess of the fee for appeal. — RRF11

Headnote (2): "There is no legal basis under the EPC for any separate appeal against an order of a director of a department of the first instance such as an Opposition Division rejecting an objection to a member of the division on the ground of suspected partiality. However, the composition of the Opposition Division may be challenged on such a ground of appeal against the final decision of the division or against an interlocutory decision under Art.106(3) EPC allowing separate appeal." — G5/91

Here it was seen that Examining and Opposition Divisions have a duty to be impartial even though the EPC does not expressly provide for objections to their composition.

Headnote (1): "In the context of the EPC, the jurisdictional measure to be taken in response to requests based on the alleged violation of a fundamental procedural principle and aimed at the revision of a final decision of a Board of Appeal having the force of res judicata should be the refusal of the requests as inadmissible." — G1/97

Headnote (2): "The decision on admissibility is to be issued by the Board of Appeal which took the decision forming the subject of the request for revision. The decision may be issued immediately and without further procedural formalities."

Headnote (3): "This jurisdictional measure applies only to requests directed against a decision of a Board of Appeal bearing a date after that of the present decision." Previously, an administrative rejection was issued to the same effect.

Headnote (4): "If the Legal Division of the EPO is asked to decide on the entry in the Register of European Patents of a request directed against a decision of a Board of Appeal, it must refrain from ordering that the entry be made if the request, in whatever form, is based on the alleged violation of a fundamental procedural principle and aimed at the revision of a final decision of a Board of Appeal."

Nevertheless the Enlarged Board urged the legislator to create a mechanism for reviewing Board of Appeal decisions in the event of a substantial procedural violation (see EPC 2000).

## Suspensive effect of an appeal on the decision appealed — 2–244

An appeal has suspensive effect. — Art.106(1)

See CLBA, p.505. The suspensive effect deprives the contested decision of all legal effect until the appeal is decided (J28/94). Such suspensive effect does not depend on the admissibility of the appeal (J8/98). However, the suspensive effect does not cancel the decision, it merely 'freezes' the usual consequences of the decision until the appeal had been decided (J28/03). In this decision of the legal board of appeal it was decided that a divisional application could validly be filed following the appeal of a decision to refuse but where a decision to grant was appealed a subsequently filed divisional would only be validly filed if the appeal was upheld. — CLBA

See E/XI/1. — Guidelines

## 2–245 Who may appeal and who is a party to the appeal

**Art.107** — Any party to proceedings adversely affected by a decision may appeal. Any other parties to the proceedings are parties to the Appeal proceedings as of right.

**J12/85** — A party is adversely affected when what is decided is contrary to what was requested, e.g. if a patent is granted with a text not approved by the applicant (J12/83). In contrast, if an opponent has indicated that he would not object to a patent amended in a certain way, he cannot be adversely affected by a decision maintaining the patent in that form (T156/90).

**T611/90** — There is no right of appeal when a party is only adversely affected to the extent that it disagrees with the reasoning or the grounds of a decision in its favour (see also T73/88).

**G2/91** — Headnote (1): "A person who is entitled to appeal but does no do so and instead confines himself to being a party to the appeal proceedings under Art.107 second sentence has no independent right to continue the proceedings if the appellant withdraws the appeal."

Headnote (2): "Appeal fees cannot be reimbursed simply because several parties to proceedings before the EPO have validly filed an appeal against the same decision."

This decision is based on the view that only the appellant can decide the fate of the appeal (aside from the EPO's own right to continue proceedings in certain circumstances). Parties to the proceedings have no such right.

**G3/99** — This case concerns the filing of an appeal by several opponents acting in common.

Headnote (2): "If the opposing party consists of a plurality of persons, an appeal must be filed by the common representative under r.100 EPC. Where the appeal is filed by a non-entitled person, the Board of Appeal will consider it not to be duly signed and consequently invite the common representative to sign it within a given time limit. The non-entitled person who filed the appeal will be informed of this invitation. If the previous common representative is no longer participating in the proceedings, a new common representative will be determined pursuant to r.100 EPC."

Headnote (3): "In order to safeguard the rights of the patent proprietor and in the interests of procedural efficiency, it has to be clear throughout the procedure who belongs to the group of common opponents or common appellants. If either a common opponent or appellant (including the common representative) intends to withdraw from the proceedings, the EPO shall be notified accordingly by the common representative or by a new common representative determined under r.100(1) EPC in order for the withdrawal to take effect."

**T656/98** — The party that appeals must be the same party that was adversely affected. If the company name has changed in the meantime, the transfer must be recorded at the EPO pursuant to r.20 before the expiry of the period for appeal under Art.108. Later recordal does not retroactively validate the appeal.

**G2/04** — Headnote (2): "If, when filing an appeal, there is a justifiable legal uncertainty as to how the law is to be interpreted in respect of the question of who the correct party to the proceedings is, it is legitimate that the appeal is filed in the name of the person whom the person acting considers, according to his interpretation, to be the correct party, and at the same time, as an auxiliary request, in the name of a different person who might, according to another possible interpretation, also be considered to be the correct party to the proceedings."

The questions answered by this decision at the Enlarged Board arose in opposition proceedings where the opposition had been filed by a holding company on behalf of its subsidiary which had been sold during the opposition proceedings. It was not clear whether the holding company or the new owner of the subsidiary was the correct appellant—in fact it was the holding company.

**CLBA** — See CLBA, pp.506–507 and 522–525.

## Filing an appeal

### Time limit for filing a notice of appeal 2–246

A notice of appeal must be filed in writing at the EPO within two months of the date of notification of the decision appealed from. | Art.108

The notice must be filed by the adversely affected party. | T298/97

The appeal period starts from notification in writing (CLBA, p.383) even if the decision has been announced orally after oral proceedings. | T390/86

A notice of appeal may nevertheless be validly filed between oral pronouncement of a decision and written notification (CLBA, p.527). | T389/86

An opponent may not apply for *restitutio* under Art.122 for missing the time limit for appeal since the proprietor is seen to need some legal certainty as to whether an opposition decision is to be contested and the travaux préparatoires address this point. This is also in conformity with national laws. See also T210/89 (CLBA, p.295). | G1/86

However, the proprietor or applicant can apply for *restitutio* in this situation.

### Content of the notice of appeal 2–247

The notice of appeal must contain: | r.64

(a) the name and address of the appellant in accordance with r.26(2)(c) (requirements of the request); and

(b) a statement identifying the decision which is impugned and the extent to which amendment or cancellation of the decision is requested.

See CLBA, pp.519 and 525–527. Simply filing the appeal fee is not sufficient; the notice must contain an unequivocal statement of definite intent to contest the decision (T460/95) so that e.g. an appeal as a subsidiary request is not good enough (T371/92). | CLBA

The initial request defines the legal framework of the appeal proceedings according to the principle of party disposition (*ne ultra petita*). | G9/92

### Appeal fee 2–248

The notice of appeal is not deemed to have been filed until after the appeal fee has been paid. | Art.108

The appeal fee is 1,065 euros. | RRF2(11)

Headnote: "The principle of good faith does not impose any obligations on the Boards of Appeal to notify an applicant that an appeal fee is missing when the notice of appeal is filed so early that the appellant could react and pay the fee in time, if there is no indication—either in the notice of appeal or in any other document filed in relation to the appeal—from which it could be inferred that the appellant would, without such notification, inadvertently miss the time limit for payment of the appeal fee." | G2/97

If the appeal fee is filed too late or if the fee is filed in time but a notice of appeal is not filed then it is refunded since no appeal exists (CLBA, p.552). However, it is not refunded when an appeal is withdrawn (J41/82) or the statement of grounds is not filed (T13/82, T89/84). | J21/80

### Filing of grounds of appeal 2–249

Within four months after the date of notification of the decision, a written statement setting out the grounds of appeal must be filed. | Art.108

| | |
|---|---|
| T298/97 | The grounds must be filed by the adversely affected party. |
| G1/86 | It was decided that an opponent who files a notice of appeal but misses the time limit for filing the grounds can take advantage of the *restitutio* provisions of Art.122. This point had not been addressed in the travaux préparatoires and was justified on the basis that a Board of Appeal was akin to a court and that the Contracting States all recognised the principle that parties before a court must be accorded the same procedural rights. Thus, once an appeal was started, by filing a notice of appeal, the parties must be given equal procedural rights. |
| | Headnote: "Art.122 is not to be interpreted as being applicable only to the applicant and patent proprietor. An appellant as opponent may have his rights re-established under Art.122 if he has failed to observe the time limit for filing the statement of grounds of appeal." |
| CLBA | See CLBA, pp.527–532. The statement of grounds must include a concise statement of the reasons why the appeal should be allowed and the contested decision set aside (J22/86, T145/88). Mere reference to arguments made at first instance, e.g. in a notice of opposition or at oral proceedings is sometimes accepted as sufficient (e.g. T140/88) but not always (e.g. T432/88). The notice must address the actual grounds of the decision and not just add new material (T213/85) unless the situation has changed, e.g. new claims have been filed (T105/87) or the patentee has requested revocation in the meantime (T459/88). It is a legitimate ground for appeal that an opposition was itself inadmissible. |

## 2–250    *Language of the notice of appeal—fee reduction*

| | |
|---|---|
| r.1(1) | Any official language of the EPO may be used. |
| Art.14(4) | An official language of one of the Contracting States may also be used in certain circumstances (see section below under languages). |
| r.6(3) | A reduction (NB. reduction, not refund) in the appeal fee is available to an applicant, proprietor or opponent who avails himself of the Art.14(4) option. The reduction is fixed in the RRF at a percentage of the total of the fees. See CLBA, page 394. |
| RRF12(1) | The reduction is 20 per cent. |
| G6/91 | Headnote (1): "The persons referred to in Art.14(2) EPC are entitled to the fee reduction under r.6(3) EPC if they file the essential item of the first act in filing, examination or appeal proceedings in an official language of the state concerned other than English, French or German, and supply the necessary translation no earlier than simultaneously. |
| | Headnote (2): "The essential item of the first act in appeal proceedings is the notice of appeal, so to secure entitlement to the reduction in the appeal fee it suffices that said document be filed in a Contracting State official language which is not an official language of the EPO and translated into one of the latter languages, even if subsequent items such as the statement of grounds of appeal are filed only in an EPO official language." |
| T149/85 | It is the residence/nationality of the applicant, proprietor or opponent that is important, not that of the representative. |
| Art.14(5) | Where the translation is not filed in time the appeal will be deemed not to have been filed (see CLBA, p.519, T323/87). |

## 2–251    Examination of the appeal for admissibility

| | |
|---|---|
| Art.110(1) | The appeal must be admissible for it to be examined. |
| r.65(1) | If the appeal does not comply with Art.106 to Art.108 (appealable decision, person entitled to appeal, time limit and form of appeal), r.1(1) (language) or r.64(b) (identify |

decision appealed and extent of appeal) the Board of Appeal will reject it as inadmissible unless each deficiency has been rectified before the two or four month time limit of Art.108 (whichever is relevant).

If the Board of Appeal notes that the appeal does not comply with r.64(a) (name and address of appellant) it will invite the appellant to remedy the deficiency within a period it will specify. If the appeal is not rectified in good time it will be rejected as inadmissible.  r.65(2)

The name of the appellant can be corrected later by substituting a new name if there was always the intention to file in the new name and indications on the file make it probable that this was the intention.  T97/98

## Interlocutory revision  2–252

If the department whose decision is contested considers the appeal to be admissible and well founded, it will rectify its decision. This does not apply where the appellant is opposed by another party to the proceedings (i.e. it is possible only during examination proceedings or where all opponents have withdrawn their appeals).  Art.109(1)

An appeal is "well founded" where the first instance changes its mind or where amendments submitted meet the objection on which the decision was based, even where other objections still exist.  T139/87

Where an application is refused because no text for grant has been approved and the applicant files an appeal, approving the previously proposed text, interlocutory revision should be allowed but the appeal fee should not be refunded.  T898/96

Where amendments are proposed that meet the objections in the decision but raise new issues not yet discussed, interlocutory revision must be allowed since the applicant is entitled to consideration by two instances.  T219/92

Reimbursement of the appeal fee is possible in the case of a substantial procedural violation and is ordered by the department whose decision is impugned or in other cases by the Board of Appeal (Guidelines E/XI/7.3).  r.67

The first instance can decide to refund the appeal fee but do not have the power to decide not to refund it. In the case where the first instance believe that interlocutory revision is possible but the appeal fee should not be refunded it rectifies its decision and remits the request for reimbursement to the Board of Appeal.  J32/95

This Enlarged Board decision confirmed that the department of first instance is not competent to refuse reimbursement of the appeal fee when allowing interlocutory revision. The competent body is the board of appeal which would have heard the appeal if interlocutory revision need not take place.  G3/03

If the appeal is not allowed within three months after receipt of the statement of grounds, it must be remitted to the Board of Appeal without delay, and without comment as to its merit.  Art.109(2)

See CLBA, pp.541–543 in general and CLBA, pp.552–564 regarding substantial procedural violations. Examples of substantial procedural violations include denying the right to be heard under Art.113(1) (T95/92), deciding on text not agreed by applicant/proprietor under Art.113(2) (T647/93), failure to apply interlocutory revision (T208/85), not providing proper reasons for a decision (T291/94) and ignoring a request for oral proceedings.  CLBA

See E/XI/7–8.  Guidelines

**Examination of the appeal**

2–253  *General procedure to be used*

Art.110(1)  If the appeal is admissible, the Board of Appeal will examine whether the appeal is allowable.

Art.110(2)  In the examination of the appeal, which is conducted in accordance with the provisions of the Implementing Regulations, the Board of Appeal invites the parties, as often as necessary, to file observations, within a period to be fixed by the Board of Appeal, on communications from another party or issued by itself.

T79/99  Requests for extensions of time will only be granted if properly reasoned (CLBA, p.287).

Art.110(3)  In pre-grant appeal proceedings, if the applicant fails to reply in due time to an invitation under Art.110(2), the European patent application is deemed to be withdrawn, unless the decision under appeal was taken by the Legal Division. See CLBA, p.417—J29/94.

Art.121/Art.122  Further processing and *restitutio* are possible.

r.66(1)  Unless otherwise provided, the provisions relating to proceedings before the department which has made the decision from which the appeal is brought are applicable to appeal proceedings mutatis mutandis.

CLBA  See CLBA, pp.433–434 for situations in which the Board will exercise the discretion of the Examining Division under Art.86(3) in allowing an amendment.

2–254  *Extent to which the appeal board in opposition proceedings may introduce new grounds or examine new claims*

G9/91  This case, along with G10/91, concerns the extent to which an Opposition Division or Appeal Board is allowed to or obliged to examine a patent beyond the stated extent of and grounds for an opposition.

Rule 55(c) was interpreted by the Enlarged Board as governing the legal and factual framework within which substantive examination of an opposition must in principle be conducted. Therefore, if the extent of the opposition is only partial (i.e. not all the independent claims are opposed) the Appeal Board has no competence to examine non-opposed claims, such claims not being subject to any "opposition" at all. In contrast, where an independent claim is opposed, the Appeal Board may also examine any dependent claims provided that their validity is prima facie in doubt on the basis of the available information.

G10/91  As regards grounds of opposition, an Appeal Board is not obliged to consider all grounds of opposition referred to in Art.100 and indeed may in principle not introduce new grounds of opposition at the appeal stage. The only exception is where the patentee consents to the introduction of such grounds. This more restricted approach (as compared with the Opposition Division) is justified by the less administrative, more judicial nature of appeal proceedings.

G1/95  Headnote: "In a case where a patent has been opposed on the grounds set out in Art.100(a) EPC, but the opposition has only been substantiated on the grounds of lack of novelty and lack of inventive step, the grounds of unpatentable subject matter based on Art.52(1) and (2) EPC (i.e. non-invention) is a fresh ground for opposition and accordingly may not be introduced into the appeal proceedings without the agreement of the patentee."

G7/95  Headnote: "In a case where a patent has been opposed under Art.100(a) EPC, on the ground that the claims lack an inventive step in view of documents cited in the notice of opposition, the ground of lack of novelty based on Art.52(1) and Art.54 EPC is a fresh ground for opposition and accordingly may not be introduced into the appeal proceedings without the agreement of the patentee. However, the allegation that the claims lack novelty in view of the closest prior art document (i.e. only this document which is an integral part of the inventive step determination may be used) may be considered in the context of deciding upon the ground of lack of inventive step."

In consolidated cases G1/95 and G7/95 "grounds for opposition" under Art.100(a) were interpreted as individual legal bases for objection, i.e. "invention", "novelty", "inventive step" and "industrial application". In the context of G10/91, a fresh ground was seen as one which was neither raised and substantiated in the notice of opposition nor introduced into the proceedings by the Opposition Division under Art.114(1).

Similarly, a ground of added matter under Art.123(2)/Art.100(c) cannot be raised during appeal proceedings if not raised during the opposition.

T443/96

Where a notice of opposition has raised the grounds of lack of novelty and lack of inventive step over a particular document but only the lack of novelty has been substantiated, it would be inconsistent to argue for lack of inventive step at the same time (there being no "step" between the prior art and the invention). In these circumstances, the Board of Appeal may consider a lack of inventive step attack without the permission of the patentee.

T131/01

It is possible to introduce a ground substantiated in the notice of opposition even if it is not part of the decision appealed and was not relied on by the opponent before the first instance.

T274/95

See CLBA, pp.513–516. New arguments are always possible (p. 518).

CLBA

### Extent to which the appeal board in examination proceedings may introduce new grounds or examine new claims

2–255

Headnote: "In an appeal from a decision of an Examining Division in which a European patent application was refused, the Board of Appeal has the power to examine whether the application or the invention to which it relates meets the requirements of the EPC. The same is true for requirements which the Examining Division did not take into consideration in the examination proceedings or which it regarded as having been met. If there is reason to believe that such a requirement has not been met, the board shall include this ground in the proceedings."

G10/93

The Enlarged Board contrasted ex parte examination appeals where the grounds for refusal under Art.97(1) are comprehensive and the appeal can only improve the position of the applicant whose application has been refused with inter partes opposition appeals where the grounds for opposition are limited and in the event of the patent being upheld in amended form the applicant could have his position improved or made worse. Whether an additional matter should be ruled on by the board or remitted to the first instance for examination was a matter of judgement depending on the facts of each case.

See CLBA, pp.516–517.

CLBA

### Reformatio in peius

2–256

"Reformatio in peius" refers to the principle that when somebody appeals a legal decision, they should not end up in a worse position that if they had not appealed if they are the sole appelant.

This case examines the situation where a patent is maintained in amended form during opposition proceedings and only one of the parties appeals. The principle of reformatio in peius applies such that the non-appealing party may not make requests more favourable to itself then the decision of the Opposition Division.

G9/92

Headnote (1): "If the patent proprietor is the sole appellant against an interlocutory decision maintaining a patent in amended form, neither the Board of Appeal or the non-appealing opponent as a party to the proceedings as of right under Art.107(2) EPC may challenge the maintenance of the patent as amended in accordance with the interlocutory decision."

Headnote (2): "If the opponent is the sole appellant against an interlocutory decision maintaining a patent in amended form, the patent proprietor is primarily restricted during appeal proceedings to defending the patent in the form in which it was maintained by the Opposition Division in its interlocutory decision. Amendments proposed by the patent proprietor as a party to the proceedings as of right under Art.107(2) may be rejected as inadmissible by the Board of Appeal if they are neither appropriate nor necessary."

The Enlarged Board (by majority) felt that the subject matter of proceedings is the appeal itself and not a general re-examination. Further, it would be unfair if one party did not comply with the time limit for appeal but was still allowed, effectively, to appeal the decision.

G1/99

This decision considered in more detail the position in Headnote (2) of G9/92 where the opponent is sole appellant and in particular the meaning of "appropriate nor necessary."

Headnote: "In principle, an amended claim, which would put the opponent and sole appellant in a worse situation than if it had not appealed, must be rejected. However, an exception to this principle may be made in order to meet an objection put forward by the opponent/appellant or the Board during the appeal proceedings, in circumstances where the patent as maintained in amended form would otherwise have to be revoked as a direct consequence of an inadmissible amendment held allowable by the Opposition Division in its interlocutory decision. In such circumstances, in order to overcome the deficiency, the patent proprietor/respondent may be allowed to file requests, as follows: (i) in the first place, for an amendment introducing one or more originally disclosed features which limit the scope of the patent as maintained; (ii) if such a limitation is not possible, for an amendment introducing one or more originally disclosed features which extend the scope of the patent as maintained, but within the limits of Art.123(3) EPC; (iii) finally, if such amendments are not possible, for deletion of the inadmissible amendment but within the limits of Art.123(3) EPC."

In the view of the Enlarged Board, equity demands that the proprietor should not lose his patent where he has not appealed against a decision by the Opposition Division to maintain a patent in a form considered by the Board of Appeal to be invalid, the invalidity only being curable by increasing the scope of protection *vis à vis* the interlocutory decision. In particular, the opponent always has another chance to contest validity at the national level.

CLBA

See CLBA, pp.511–513.

## 2–257 *Intervention of an assumed infringer is possible in appeal proceedings*

See section on intervention under opposition.

## 2–258 *Discretion to hear accompanying persons*

See under "oral proceedings", in particular G4/95 and G2/94.

## 2–259 *Impartiality of the Board of Appeal*

CLBA

Due to the judicial nature of proceedings, the Board must maintain strict impartiality and treat all parties the same (see CLBA, p.508).

## 2–260 *Request for revocation of the patent by the proprietor*

CLBA

See CLBA, pp.540–541. Where no text is approved by the proprietor, the patent must be revoked.

*Amendment during appeal proceedings* — 2–261

No special provisions exist—r.66(1) applies the same procedure as before the first instance. See CLBA, pp.545–552. — CLBA

*Accelerated procedure* — 2–262

See under Art.106. Appeal proceedings may be accelerated where a legitimate interest exists ([1998] O.J. 362). — AnReg

## Decision on the appeal

*Taking a decision—discretion of the board to remit proceedings to the first instance* — 2–263

Following the examination as to the allowability of the appeal, the Board of Appeal decides on the appeal. The Board of Appeal may either exercise any power within the competence of the department which was responsible for the decision appealed or remit the case to that department for further prosecution. — Art.111(1)

See CLBA, pp.532–535 for closure of debate and the taking of a decision. The overriding reason for remitting to the first instance is to allow examination of all issues by two instances. Remittal is more likely: where major amendments are proposed (T63/86), unless the amendments are submitted at a late stage in the proceedings (T926/93); the appeal is allowed (e.g. on an added matter rejection) but other grounds (e.g. novelty) are yet to be examined; the Enlarged Board has dramatically clarified the law (T17/81); a fresh ground of opposition is raised (G10/91); new facts or evidence are admitted (T273/84, T326/87); or the description needs to be adapted to agreed claims and substantial amendment is necessary. — CLBA

*The binding effect of a decision on remittal* — 2–264

If the Board of Appeal remits the case for further prosecution to the department whose decision was appealed, that department is bound by the ratio decidendi of the Board of Appeal, in so far as the facts are the same. If the decision which was appealed emanated from the Receiving Section, the Examining Division is similarly bound by the ratio decidendi of the Board of Appeal (see Guidelines E/X/7). — Art.111(2)

The decision is final once taken and can not be challenged even if there has been a substantial procedural violation. — G1/97

The decision is either issued in writing or orally, at the end of oral proceedings, with written confirmation. — r.68(1)

See CLBA, pp.536–538. Decisions of the Boards of Appeal are final and cannot be contested even by another Board of Appeal in subsequent proceedings after remission to the first instance (T79/89). However, a decision on appeal before the Examining Division has no binding effect on either instance during opposition (T167/93). — CLBA

*Form and content of the decision* — 2–265

The decision must be authenticated by the Chairman of the Board of Appeal and by the competent employee of the registry of the Board of Appeal, either by their signature or by any other appropriate means.
The decision must contain: — r.66(2)

(a) a statement that it is delivered by the Board of Appeal;
(b) the date when the decision was taken;

(c) the names of the chairman and of the other members of the Board of Appeal taking part;

(d) the names of the parties and their representatives;

(e) a statement of the issues to be decided;

(f) a summary of the facts;

(g) the reasons; and

(h) the order of the Board of Appeal, including, where appropriate, a decision on costs.

## 2–266 Request for information concerning national patent applications

Art.124(1) The Board of Appeal may invite the applicant to indicate, within a period to be determined by it, the States in which he has made applications for national patents for the whole or part of the invention to which the European patent application relates, and to give the reference numbers of the said applications.

Art.124(2) If the applicant fails to reply in due time to an invitation under Art.124(1), the European patent application will be deemed to be withdrawn.

Art.121/Art.122 Further processing and *restitutio* are available.

## 2–267 Reimbursement of the appeal fee

r.67 The reimbursement of the appeal fee is ordered where the Board of Appeal deems an appeal to be allowable, if such reimbursement is equitable by reason of a substantial procedural violation. In the event of interlocutory revision, reimbursement is ordered by the department whose decision has been impugned and, in other cases, by the Board of Appeal.

G3/03 The first instance can decide to refund the appeal fee but do not have the power to decide not to refund it—that decision lies with a board of appeal.

T5/81 If the violation does not affect the *ratio decidendi* then it cannot be substantial.

CLBA See CLBA, pp.552–564. Examples of substantial procedural violations include denying the right to be heard under Art.113(1) (T95/92), deciding on text not agreed by applicant/proprietor under Art.113(2) (T647/93), failure to apply interlocutory revision (T208/85), not providing proper reasons for a decision (T291/94) and ignoring a request for oral proceedings.

## 2–268 Withdrawal of the appeal

G7/91 Headnote: "In so far as the substantive issues settled by the contested decision at first instance are concerned, a Board of Appeal may not continue opposition appeal proceedings after the sole appellant, who was the opponent in the first instance, has withdrawn his appeal." See also G8/91.

This is to be contrasted with opposition proceedings where under r.60(2) an opposition can be continued. The reasoning of the Enlarged Board was that current, unquestioned practice should not be abandoned without very good reasons which were lacking in this case and that such practice was in accordance with party disposition whereby a court could not continue proceedings if the procedural act giving rise to the proceedings has been retracted.

Headnote: "The filing by an opponent, who is sole appellant, of a statement withdrawing his opposition immediately and automatically terminates the appeal proceedings, irrespective of whether the patent proprietor agrees to termination of those proceedings and even if in the Board of Appeal's view the requirements under the EPC for maintaining the patent are not satisfied." — G8/93

It was the opinion of the Enlarged Board that withdrawal of the opposition by the opponent and sole appellant could only mean he wished to withdraw the appeal which was examining whether any ground of opposition might prejudice maintenance of the patent. The rest follows from G7/91 and G8/91 (see above).

When the sole appellant withdraws, the appeal may not even be continued for an intervener who intervened at the appeal stage. — G3/04

Withdrawal is effective from the precise time that receipt of the withdrawal can be established—later procedural steps, even if on the same day, e.g. intervention, are not admissible. — T517/97

Where the patentee has appealed against revocation by the Opposition Division and the opponent withdraws his opposition, the proceedings continue. — T629/90

See CLBA, pp.538–540. Once an appeal is withdrawn it cannot be reinstated. The suspensive effect finishes immediately and the decision of the first instance becomes final. The consent of the Board is not necessary for the withdrawal to take effect (J19/92). Where there are multiple appellants the withdrawing party remains a party to the proceedings and the extent of the appeal is limited to the initial requests of the remaining parties. Auxiliary procedural issues can still be decided after withdrawal, including apportionment of costs (T117/86) and refund of the appeal fee (J12/86), though T41/82 suggests that the appeal fee may not be refunded where an appeal has been withdrawn. — CLBA

## The Enlarged Board of Appeal  2–269

The Enlarged Board of Appeal is responsible for: — Art.22(1)

(a) deciding points of law referred to it by Boards of Appeal;
(b) giving opinions on points of law referred to it by the President of the EPO under the conditions laid down in Art.112.

In order to ensure uniform application of the law, or if an important point of law arises the Board of Appeal will, during proceedings on a case and either of its own motion or following a request from a party to the appeal, refer any question to the Enlarged Board of Appeal if it considers that a decision is required for the above purposes. If the Board of Appeal rejects the request, it must give the reasons in its final decision. — Art.112(1)

The President of the EPO may also refer a point of law to the Enlarged Board of Appeal where two Boards of Appeal have given different decisions on that question. — Art.112(1)

In the cases covered by Art.112(1)(a) the parties to the appeal proceedings are parties to the proceedings before the Enlarged Board of Appeal. — Art.112(2)

The decision of the Enlarged Board of Appeal referred to in Art.112(1)(a) is binding on the Board of Appeal in respect of the appeal in question. — Art.112(3)

Furthermore, where a board wishes to depart from a previous decision of the Enlarged Board it must refer the question back to the Enlarged Board. — RPBArt.16

See CLBA, pp.543–545. A referral must be made by a Board of Appeal before it has decided the issues to be referred. The referral is by means of a written decision — CLBA

(RPBArt.17) setting out the background and the questions. Appeal proceedings are stayed pending the outcome of the referral.

## 12. NATIONAL PHASE ASPECTS

2–270 **The effect of a European patent application having a filing date**

Art.66  A European patent application which has been accorded a date of filing is, in the designated Contracting States, equivalent to a regular national filing, where appropriate with the priority claimed for the European patent application.

Art.140  The European application is also, where appropriate, equivalent to a national application in respect of a utility model or utility certificate.

2–271 **The effect of a published European patent application**

Art.67(1)  A European patent application provisionally confers upon the applicant, from the date of its publication under Art.93, such protection as is conferred by Art.64 (rights conferred by a European Patent), in the Contracting States designated in the application as published.

Art.67(2)  Any Contracting State may prescribe that a European patent application will not confer such protection as is conferred by Art.64. However, the protection attached to the publication of a European patent application may not be less than that which the law of the State concerned attaches to the compulsory publication of unexamined national patent applications. In any event, every State must ensure at least that, from the date of publication of a European patent application, the applicant can claim compensation reasonable in the circumstances from any person who has used the invention in the said State in circumstances where that person would be liable under national law for infringement of a national patent.

Art.67(3)  Any Contracting State which does not have as an official language the language of the proceedings, may prescribe that provisional protection in accordance with Art.67(1) and (2) will not be effective until such time as a translation of the claims in one of its official languages at the option of the applicant or, where that State has prescribed the use of one specific official language, in that language:

(a) has been made available to the public in the manner prescribed by national law, or

(b) has been communicated to the person using the invention in the said State.

Art.67(4)  A European patent application will be deemed never to have had the effects set out in Art.67(1) and (2) above if it is withdrawn, deemed to be withdrawn or finally refused. The same applies in respect of the effects of a European patent application in a Contracting State the designation of which is withdrawn or deemed to be withdrawn.

NatLaw  See Table III for national provisions relating to provisional protection under Art.67.

2–272 **The effect of a granted European patent**

Art.2(2)  The European patent will, in each of the Contracting States for which it is granted, have the effect of and be subject to the same conditions as a national patent granted by that State, unless otherwise provided for by the EPC.

Art.64(1)  A European patent confers on its proprietor, from the date of publication of the mention of grant, in each Contracting State in respect of which it is granted, the same rights as would be conferred by a national patent granted in that State (except that Art.64(2) stipulates the direct product of a process will in any case be protected).

Any infringement of a European patent is to be dealt with by national law.   Art.64(3)

### Effect of a granted European patent may be dependent on the filing of a translation   2–273

Any Contracting State may prescribe that if the text, in which the EPO intends to grant a European patent or maintain a European patent as amended for that State, is not drawn up in one of its official languages, the applicant for or proprietor of the patent must supply to its central industrial property office a translation of this text in one of its official languages at his option or, where that State has prescribed the use of one specific official language, in that language.   Art.65(1)

The period for supplying the translation ends three months after the date on which the mention of the grant of the European patent or of the maintenance of the European patent as amended is published in the European Patent Bulletin, unless the State concerned prescribes a longer period.

Any Contracting State which has adopted provisions pursuant to Art.65(1) may prescribe that the applicant for or proprietor of the patent must pay all or part of the costs of publication of such translation within a period laid down by that State.   Art.65(2)

Any Contracting State may prescribe that in the event of failure to observe the provisions adopted in accordance with Art.65(1) and (2), the European patent will be deemed to be void *ab initio* in that State.   Art.65(3)

See Table IV for national requirements relating to the filing of a translation, the payment of a fee, requirements for representation and other related matters.   NatLaw

### Effect of revocation during opposition on rights pre- and post-grant   2–274

A European patent application and the resulting patent will be deemed not to have had, as from the outset, the effects specified in Art.64 and Art.67, to the extent that the patent is revoked in opposition proceedings.   Art.68

### Extent of protection of a European application or patent   2–275

The extent of the protection conferred by a European patent or a European patent application is to be determined by the terms of the claims. Nevertheless, the description and drawings are to be used to interpret the claims   Art.69(1)

The Protocol on the Interpretation of Art.69 is an integral part of the EPC.   Art.164(1)

Art.69 should not be interpreted in the sense that the extent of the protection conferred by a European patent is to be understood as that defined by the strict, literal meaning of the wording used in the claims, the description and drawings being employed only for the purpose of resolving an ambiguity found in the claims. Neither should it be interpreted in the sense that the claims serve only as a guideline and that the actual protection conferred may extend to what, from a consideration of the description and drawings by a person skilled in the art, the patentee has contemplated. On the contrary, it is to be interpreted as defining a position between these extremes which combines a fair protection for the patentee with a reasonable degree of certainty for third parties.   Protocol

See CLBA, pp.168–172.   CLBA

| | |
|---|---|
| Art.69(2) | For the period up to grant of a European patent, the extent of the protection conferred by a European patent application is determined by the latest filed claims contained in the publication under Art.93. However, the European patent as granted or as amended in opposition proceedings determines retroactively the protection conferred by a European patent application, in so far as such protection is not thereby extended. |
| Art.64(2) | If the subject-matter of the European patent is a process, the protection conferred by the patent extends to the products directly obtained by such a process. |
| G2/88 | Art.64(2) relates to processes for the manufacture of a product and does not relate to processes to achieve an effect (i.e. use claims). |

## 2–276 The term of a European patent

| | |
|---|---|
| Art.63(1) | The term of a European patent is 20 years as from the date of filing of the application. |
| Art.63(2) | However, this does not limit the right of a Contracting State to extend the term of a European patent, or to grant corresponding protection which follows immediately on expiry of the term of the patent, under the same conditions as those applying to national patents: |

    (a) in order to take account of a state of war or similar emergency conditions affecting that State;

    (b) if the subject-matter of the European patent is a product or process of manufacturing a product or a use of a product which has to undergo an administrative authorisation procedure required by law before it can be put on the market in that State.

| | |
|---|---|
| Art.63(3) | Article 63(2) applies *mutatis mutandis* to European patents granted jointly for a group of Contracting States in accordance with Art.142. |
| Art.63(4) | A Contracting State which makes provision for extension of the term or corresponding protection under Art.63(2)(b) may, in accordance with an agreement concluded with the Organisation, entrust to the EPO tasks associated with implementation of the relevant provisions. |

### Conversion of a European patent application into a national patent application

## 2–277 *Circumstances in which conversion is possible*

| | |
|---|---|
| Art.135(1) | The central industrial property office of a designated Contracting State will apply the procedure for the grant of a national patent only at the request of the applicant for or proprietor of a European patent, and in the following circumstances: |

    (a) when the European patent application is deemed to be withdrawn pursuant to Art.77(5) or Art.162(4);

    (b) in such other cases as are provided for by the national law in which the European patent application is refused or withdrawn or deemed to be withdrawn, or the European patent is revoked under the EPC.

| | |
|---|---|
| Art.77(5) | European patent applications which do not reach the EPO before the end of the fourteenth month after filing or, if priority has been claimed, after the date of priority, are deemed to be withdrawn. |
| Art.162(4) | When the EPO first opened, the EPC provided for initial restrictions on the kind of applications that could be processed. |

See Table VII for national laws relating to Art.135(1)(b). — NatLaw

See A/IV/6. — Guidelines

A European patent application can, where appropriate, be converted into a national application for a utility model or utility certificate. — Art.140

## Time limit for requesting conversion — 2–278

The request for conversion must be filed within three months after the European patent application has been withdrawn or after notification has been made that the application is deemed to be withdrawn, or after a decision has been notified refusing the application or revoking the European patent. The effect referred to in Art.66 (that a European patent application is equivalent to a national filing) lapses if the request is not filed in due time. — Art.135(2)

## Submission and transmission of the request — 2–279

A request for conversion must be filed with the EPO and must specify the Contracting States in which application of the procedure for the grant of a national patent is desired. The request will not be deemed to be filed until the conversion fee has been paid. The EPO will transmit the request to the central industrial property offices of the Contracting States specified therein, accompanied by a copy of the files relating to the European patent application or the European patent. — Art.136(1)

The conversion fee is 55 euros. — RRF2(14)

However, if the applicant is notified that the European patent application has been deemed to be withdrawn pursuant to Art.77(5) (not forwarded for national security reasons), the request must be filed with the central industrial property office with which the application was filed. That office will, subject to the provisions of national security, transmit the request, together with a copy of the European patent application, directly to the central industrial property offices of the Contracting States specified by the applicant in the request. The effect referred to in Art.66 (that a European patent application is equivalent to a national filing) will lapse if such transmission is not made within 20 months after the date of filing or, if a priority has been claimed, after the date of priority. — Art.136(2)

## Formal requirements that may be imposed — 2–280

A European patent application transmitted in accordance with Art.136 cannot be subjected to formal requirements of national law which are different from or additional to those provided for in the EPC. — Art.137(1)

Any central industrial property office to which the application is transmitted may require that the applicant, within not less than two months: — Art.137(2)

(a) pays the national fee; and
(b) files a translation (in one of the official languages of the State in question) of the original text of the European patent application and, where appropriate, of the text, as amended during proceedings before the EPO, which the applicant wishes to submit to the national procedure.

## Information available to the public in the event of conversion — 2–281

The documents which, in accordance with Art.136, accompany the request for conversion, will be communicated to the public by the relevant central industrial property office under the same conditions and to the same extent as documents relating to national proceedings. — r.103

The printed specifications of any national patent resulting from the conversion of a European patent application must mention that application.

**Revocation of a European patent in Contracting States**

2–282 *Grounds for revocation*

Art.138(1)  Subject to the provisions of Art.139 (collision with national applications and patents), a European patent may only be revoked under the law of a Contracting State, with effect for its territory, on the following grounds:

(a) if the subject-matter of the European patent is not patentable within the terms of Art.52 to Art.57;

(b) if the European patent does not disclose the invention in a manner sufficiently clear and complete for it to be carried out by a person skilled in the art;

(c) if the subject-matter of the European patent extends beyond the content of the application as filed or, if the patent was granted on a divisional application or on a new application filed in accordance with Art.61, beyond the content of the earlier application as filed;

(d) if the protection conferred by the European patent has been extended; or

(e) if the proprietor of the European patent is not entitled under Art.60(1).

2–283 *Partial revocation*

Art.138(2)  If the grounds for revocation only affect the European patent in part, revocation must be pronounced in the form of a corresponding limitation of the said patent. If the national law so allows, the limitation may be effected in the form of an amendment to the claims, the description or the drawings.

2–284 **Collision of European and national patents**

Art.139(1)  In any designated Contracting State a European patent application and a European patent have with regard to a national patent application and a national patent the same prior right effect as a national patent application and a national patent.

Art.139(2)  A national patent application and a national patent in a Contracting State have with regard to a European patent in which that Contracting State is designated the same prior art effect as they have with regard to a national patent.

r.87  Where an earlier national right exists in respect of only some designated states, a European patent application and corresponding patent may have different claims and, if the EPO agrees, a different description and drawings for different states, as an exception to the unity requirement of Art.118.

Art.139(3)  Any Contracting State may prescribe whether and on what terms an invention disclosed in both a European patent application or patent and a national application or patent having the same date of filing or, where priority is claimed, the same date of priority, may be protected simultaneously by both applications or patents.

Guidelines  See C/IV/6a.

NatLaw  See Table X for national provisions relating to Art.139(3).

Art.140  These provisions also apply, where appropriate, to granted utility models and utility certificates and applications for the same.

## National renewal fees for European patents     2–285

Renewal fees in respect of a European patent may only be imposed for the years which follow that referred to in Art.86(4) (year in which the mention of grant is published).   Art.141(1)

Any renewal fees falling due within two months after the publication of the mention of the grant of the European patent are deemed to have been validly paid if they are paid within that period. Any additional fee provided for under national law cannot be charged.   Art.141(2)

See under r.37(1). Guidance is given as to when EPO and national renewal fees are due ([1980] O.J. 101; [1984] O.J. 272).   AnReg

See Table VI for national provisions relating to the payment of renewal fees.   NatLaw

## Effect of European patents and applications on national utility models and utility certificates     2–286

Art.66 (equivalence of European filing and national filing), Art.124 (supply of information by applicant/proprietor regarding national applications), Art.135 to Art.137 (conversion) and Art.139 (collision of European and national rights) apply to utility models and utility certificates and to applications for utility models and utility certificates registered or deposited in the Contracting States whose laws make provision for such models or certificates.   Art.140

## Authentic text in national proceedings     2–287

See under common provisions.   Art.70

## Request by a national court for a technical opinion from an Examining Division     2–288

At the request of the competent national court trying an infringement or revocation action, the EPO is obliged, against payment of an appropriate fee, to give a technical opinion concerning the European patent which is the subject of the action. The Examining Division is responsible for the issue of such an opinion.   Art.25

The fee for a technical opinion is 3,185 euros.   RRF2(20)

However, 75 per cent of the fee will be refunded where the request is withdrawn at a time when the EPO has not yet begun to draw up the technical opinion.   RRF10a

The due date is the date of receipt of the request. However, the President of the EPO may decide that such services may be carried out without advance payment.   RRF4(1)(2)

See E/XII.   Guidelines

# 13. THE CALCULATION OF TIME LIMITS AND PROCEDURAL SAFEGUARDS

## Computation of time limits

### *Units of time used*     2–289

Periods are laid down in terms of full years, months, weeks or days.   Art.120/r.83(1)

| | |
|---|---|
| **2–290** | ***Day on which computation of time limit is to start*** |
| Art.120/r.83(2) | Computation starts on the day following the day on which the relevant event occurred, the event being either a procedural step or the expiry of another period. Where the procedural step is a notification, the event considered is the receipt of the document notified, unless otherwise provided. |
| J14/86 | This does NOT mean that a day must be added to time limits fixed in years, months of weeks. |
| r.78(2) | Where the relevant event is notification by post, the applicant will be deemed to have received the notification on the tenth day following its posting, unless the letter has failed to reach the addressee or has reached him at a later date. In the case of a dispute, the EPO bears the burden of proving that the letter reached its destination or establishing the date on which the letter was delivered to the addressee, as the case may be. |
| AnReg | Where the relevant event is the expiry of another time limit, see legal advice 5/93 on the calculation of aggregate time limits ([1993] O.J. 229). Note that this does not apply to the six-month additional period of Art.86(2)—since the six-month additional period starts on the last day of the month containing the anniversary of the filing date—and that start date does not change even if the EPO is closed for the receipt of documents on that day. Moreover, the six-month additional period expires on the last day of the sixth month, not on the day having the same number as that of the last day of the start month. In other words, for applications filed in February, the six-month additional period always expires no earlier than August 31. If August 31 is an excluded day, the additional period extends to the next regular working day. See J4/91. |
| **2–291** | ***Expiry of time limits—years, months and weeks*** |
| Art.120/r.83(3) | A period expressed as one or more years will expire in the relevant subsequent year, in the month having the same name and on the day having the same number as the month and the day on which the said event occurred (see r.83(2)—procedural step or expiry of other period), provided that if the relevant subsequent month has no day with the same number, the period will expire on the last day of that month. |
| Art.120/r.83(4) | A period expressed as one or more months will expire in the relevant subsequent month on the day having the same number as the day on which the said event occurred (see r.83(2)—procedural step or expiry of other period), provided that if the relevant subsequent month has no day with the same number, the period will expire on the last day of that month. |
| Art.120/r.83(5) | A period expressed as one or more weeks will expire in the relevant subsequent week on the day having the same name as the day on which the said event occurred (see r.83(2)—procedural step or expiry of other period). |
| **2–292** | **Duration of time limits that are to be determined by the EPO** |
| Art.120/r.84 | Where the EPC or Implementing Regulations specify a period to be determined by the EPO, such period must be not less than two months and not more than four months, except in certain special circumstances when it may be up to six months. In certain special cases the period may be extended upon request, presented before the expiry of such period. |
| AnReg | See under r.84. The President has specified a uniform practice for the setting of such periods ([1979] O.J. 289; [1980] O.J. 68; [1989] O.J. 180). An automatic extension is available where the total time limit does not exceed six months. Further extensions are difficult to obtain. |
| Guidelines | See E/VIII/1.2 and 1.6. |

### Circumstances in which a missed time limit is excused where a document is sent in good time

2–293

Where a document (does not apply to fees—see RRF8(3) for the complementary provision) is received late at the EPO it will be nevertheless deemed to have been received in good time if it was posted, or delivered to a recognised delivery service, in due time before the expiry of the time limit in accordance with the conditions laid down by the President of the EPO and it was not received later than three months after expiry of the time limit.

r.84a(1)

This provision also applies to the time limits provided for in the EPC where transactions are carried out with the competent authority in accordance with Art.75(1)(b) or Art.75(2)(b) (application filed with the competent central industrial property office of a Contracting State).

r.84a(2)

See under r.84a. The President has decided that the document must have been posted or handed over to a specified delivery service at least five days prior to the expiry of the time limit. The specified delivery services are Chronopost, Deutsche Post Express, DHL, Express Post, Federal Express, LTA, TNT, Skynet and UPS. Furthermore, the document, if posted, must have been sent by registered letter (or in a form of consignment corresponding to registration) and, if posted outside Europe, sent by airmail ([2003] O.J. 283).

AnReg

Rule 84a can be used to "extend" the priority year. The filing date allocated remains the date on which the date on which the application documents were actually received by the EPO. It should also be noted that r.84a applies to time limits, which must have a duration, so that single points in time cannot be extended.

See E/VIII/1.7. For a list of non-European states which are "European" for r.84a.

Guidelines

### Extension of time limits where the EPO is not open for business

2–294

If a time limit expires on a day on which one of the filing offices of the EPO as defined by Art.75(1)(a) (i.e. Munich, the Hague or Berlin) is not open for receipt of documents or on which, for reasons other than those referred to in r.85(2) (general interruption etc.), ordinary mail is not delivered there, the time limit will extend until the first day thereafter on which all the filing offices are open for the receipt of documents and on which ordinary mail is delivered.

Art.120/r.85(1)

These provisions apply equally to time limits provided for in the EPC in the case of transactions carried out with the competent authority in accordance with Art.75(1)(b) and Art.75(2)(b) (application filed with the central industrial property office of a Contracting State).

r.85(3)

See under r.85(1) for information on EPO closed days in the years 1995–2002. See [2003] O.J. 507 for the extension of any deadline falling on September 1, 2003 until September 2, 2003, due to faxing problems.

AnReg

### Extension of time limits where there is a general interruption in mail delivery in a Contracting State

2–295

If a time limit expires on a day on which there is a general interruption or subsequent dislocation in the delivery of mail in a Contracting State or between a Contracting State and the EPO, the time limit will extend to the first day following the end of the period of interruption or dislocation for parties resident in the state concerned or who have appointed a representative with a place of business in that State.

Art.120/r.85(2)

This safeguard applies equally to the time limit referred to in Art.77(5) (14 month period for forwarding of applications by the central industrial property office of a Contracting State).

In the case where the state concerned is a state in which the EPO is located, this provision applies to all parties.

The duration of the period of interruption or dislocation is decided by the President of the EPO.

r.85(3)   These provisions apply equally to time limits provided for in the EPC in the case of transactions carried out with the competent authority in accordance with Art.75(1)(b) and Art.75(2)(b) (filing of an application with the central industrial property offices of a Contracting State).

AnReg   See under r.85(2) for all interruptions declared between 1990 and 2001.

O.J.   See [2003] O.J. 581 for the interruption in the UK from September 1, 2003 to November 21, 2003.

CLBA   See CLBA, p.293—loss of a single postbag is not enough; an area of some magnitude must be affected for the interruption to be "general".

## 2–296  Extension of time limits where there is a war, revolution or similar event affecting the applicant or his representative

Art.120/r.85(5)   Where evidence is offered that on any of the ten days preceding the day of expiration of a time limit, the mail service was interrupted or subsequently dislocated on account of war, revolution, civil disorder, strike, natural calamity or other like reason, in the locality where a party or his representative resides or has his place of business or is staying and such circumstances are proven to the satisfaction of the EPO, a document received late will be deemed to have been received in due time providing that the mailing has been effected within five days after the mail service was resumed. As an example of this see the Notice of the President of August 1, 2005 concerning the events of July 7, 2005 in London.

## 2–297  Extension of time limits where the EPO ceases to function properly

r.85(4)   Where an exceptional occurrence, such as a natural disaster or strike, interrupts or dislocates the proper functioning of the EPO so that any communication from the EPO to parties concerning the expiry of a time limit is delayed, acts to be completed within such a time limit may still be validly be completed within one month after the notification of the delayed communication. The date of commencement and the end of any such interruption or dislocation will be decided by the President of the EPO.

## 2–298  Further processing

Art.121(1)   If a European patent application is to be refused or is refused or deemed to be withdrawn following failure to reply within a time limit set by the EPO, the legal consequence provided for will not ensue or, if it has already ensued, will be retracted if the applicant requests further processing of the application.

Therefore, further processing does not apply after grant (relating only to an application) or where the time limit is specified in the EPC or the Regulations.

J47/92   The duration of a time limit must be set by the EPO for further processing to apply so that the r.85b grace period (where the start is determined by the EPO) does not count (CLBA, p.288).

Art.121(2)   The request must be filed in writing within two months of the date on which either the decision to refuse the application or the communication that the application is deemed to be withdrawn is notified. The omitted act must be completed within this time limit. The request is not deemed to have been filed until the fee for further processing has been paid.

RRF2(12)   The fee for further processing is 210 euros.

Where the omitted act is a response to an Art.96(2) communication, it is not completed by asking for an extension of the original time limit (CLBA, p.288). J16/92

*Restitutio* is possible in respect of the Art.121(2) time limit (CLBA, p.303). J12/92

See legal advice 13/82. The request for further processing can be filed before the communication from the EPO of loss of rights ([1982] O.J. 196). AnReg

## *Restitutio in integrum*

### *Conditions necessary for restitutio* 2–299

The applicant for or proprietor of a European patent who, in spite of all due care required by the circumstances having been taken, was unable to observe a time limit *vis-à-vis* the EPO will, upon application, have his rights re-established if the non-observance in question has the direct consequence, by virtue of the EPC, of causing the refusal of the European patent application, or of a request, or the deeming of the European patent application to have been withdrawn, or the revocation of the European patent, or the loss of any other right or means of redress. Art.122(1)

*Restitutio* is therefore possible before and after grant and in respect of time limits set in the EPC and Regulations.

The time limit must be one that the applicant has to observe and therefore the Art.77(3) time limit regarding forwarding of an application to the EPO by a national patent office does not count. J3/80

Where the time limit under r.25(1) for filing a divisional application has been missed, *restitutio* cannot be applied. J24/03

Where several time limits have been missed a separate application and fee is necessary in respect of each of them. T26/95

Where a mistake can be corrected (e.g. the r.38(3) time limit for filing certified copy of priority document is correctable under Art.91(1)(d)) no restitutio is possible since no rights have been lost. J1/80

See CLBA, pp.294–296 and, for "due care", CLBA, pp.306–321. Usually, the mistake must be shown to be an isolated mistake in an otherwise satisfactory system (J2/86, J3/86) or else exceptional circumstances must apply. Such exceptional circumstances include a complex transfer of company ownership (T469/93), an unexpected breakdown in takeover negotiations (J13/90) and internal reorganisation (T14/89). Financial difficulties can also justify *restitutio* (J22/88) where all due care has been taken in attempting to gain financial support. CLBA

See E/VIII/2.2.1–2.2.3. Guidelines

### *Who can file an application for restitutio?* 2–300

An applicant or a proprietor is entitled to apply for *restitutio*. Art.122(1)

An opponent who has filed a notice of appeal but missed the time limit for filing the grounds of appeal may also apply for *restitutio* (see under Appeal). G1/86

However, an opponent is not entitled to *restitutio* for missing the time limit for appeal (CLBA, p.295). T210/89

Neither is a would-be opponent entitled to file for *restitutio* having missed the nine-month time limit for filing an opposition. T702/89

| | |
|---|---|
| G1/86 | *Restitutio* is probably also available to a professional representative in Art.20 proceedings, an inventor under r.19 proceedings and a person entitled to a patent under Art.61 proceedings. |

## 2–301  *Exclusion of certain time limits from restitutio*

| | |
|---|---|
| Art.122(5) | The provisions of Art.122 are not applicable to the time limits referred to in Art.122(2) (time limit for *restitutio*), Art.61, para.3 (time limit for paying filing, search and examination fees on replacement application), Art.76, para.3 (time limit for paying filing, search and examination fees on divisional), Art.78, para.2 (payment of filing fee and search fee), Art.79, para.2 (payment of designation fees), Art.87, para.1 (priority year) and Art.94, para.2 (filing a request for examination). |
| J12/82 | Any grace periods that apply to these time limits are equally excluded (see also J18/82). |
| CLBA | See CLBA, pp.303–305. |
| Guidelines | See E/VIII/2.2.4. |

## 2–302  *Procedure for applying for restitutio—time limits*

| | |
|---|---|
| Art.122(2) | The application must be filed in writing within two months from the removal of the cause of non-compliance with the time limit. The omitted act must be completed within this period. The application is only admissible within the year immediately following the expiry of the unobserved time limit. In the case of non-payment of a renewal fee, the period specified in Art.86(2), must be deducted from the period of one year (i.e. must file for *restitutio* within six months of due date for the payment of a renewal fee with an additional fee). |
| Case law | The cause of non-compliance is removed, for example, on the actual date of receipt by the responsible person (the person responsible to take decision on applying for restitution, such as the applicant or agent, T191/82, J27/88) of notification from the EPO that a loss of rights has occurred (J7/82) or the date on which the responsible person otherwise realises the mistake (J17/89). |
| T428/98 | Where the removal of the cause for compliance is an EPO notification, there is no 10-day deemed notification period. That is, the removal of the cause of non-compliance is the actual date on which the notification was received by the relevant person and not the date deemed to be the date of notification under r.78(2). |
| T167/97 | The completed omitted act must meet the requirements of the EPC, e.g. be admissible. |
| J16/86 | The two-month and one-year time limits can be interrupted under r.90 but are otherwise absolute in the interests of legal certainty. |
| CLBA | See CLBA, pp.298–301. |
| Guidelines | See E/VIII/2.2.5. |

## 2–303  *Grounds must be filed and fee paid*

| | |
|---|---|
| Art.122(3) | The application must state the grounds on which it is based, and must set out the facts on which it relies. It is not deemed to be filed until after the fee for re-establishment of rights has been paid. |
| RRF2(13) | The fee for re-establishment is 365 euros. |
| J6/90 | Where the request is filed in due time, the grounds may be filed after the one year time limit. |

Evidence may be supplied later than the two-month time limit. T324/90

Where an appeal is mistakenly filed instead of an application for *restitutio*, it can be accepted as the latter where the contents are sufficient to cover the grounds that must be filed and sufficient funds to cover the fee have been paid (see also T522/88). In this case there is a duty on the EPO to request the fee if sufficient time remains. J14/89

See CLBA, pp.301–302. CLBA

### *Department qualified to decide on the application for restitutio* — 2–304

The department competent to decide on the omitted act decides on the application. Art.122(4)

See CLBA, pp.296–297. Where a non-competent department decides, the decision is void (J10/93). Where the two-month and four-month periods for filing an appeal are concerned, the Board of Appeal takes the decision (T473/91). CLBA

See E/VIII/2.2.7. Guidelines

### *Third party rights may be awarded* — 2–305

Any person who, in a designated Contracting State, in good faith has used or made effective and serious preparations for using an invention which is the subject of a published European patent application or a European patent in the course of the period between the loss of rights referred to in Art.122(1) and publication of the mention of re-establishment of those rights, may without payment continue such use in the course of his business or for the needs thereof. Art.122(6)

See CLBA, pp.321–322. CLBA

### *Contracting States may grant restitutio for the EPC time limits that they have to administer* — 2–306

Nothing in Art.122 limits the right of a Contracting State to grant *restitutio* in integrum in respect of time limits provided for in the EPC and to be observed *vis-à-vis* the authorities of such State. Art.122(7)

## Interruption of proceedings

### *Circumstances under which proceedings may be interrupted* — 2–307

Proceedings before the EPO are interrupted: r.90(1)

(a) in the event of the death or legal incapacity of the applicant for or proprietor of a European patent or of the person authorised by national law to act on his behalf. To the extent that the above events do not affect the authorisation of a representative appointed under Art.134, proceedings are interrupted only on application by such a representative;

(b) in the event of the applicant for or proprietor of a European patent, as the result of some action taken against his property, being prevented by legal reasons from continuing the proceedings before the EPO; or

(c) in the event of the death or legal incapacity of the representative of an applicant for or proprietor of a European patent or of his being prevented for legal reasons resulting from action taken against his property from continuing the proceedings before the EPO.

A "person authorised" under (a) does not apply to a non-European patent attorney except when filing an application. J23/88

| | |
|---|---|
| J26/95 | The crucial question under (b) is whether the action taken makes it impossible for the applicant to continue the proceedings. |
| CLBA | See CLBA, pp.288–293. In particular, the EPO must apply this rule of its own motion. Legal incapacity is defined by reference to national law for the applicant and proprietor but according to a uniform standard for representatives (unnumbered J decision). |
| Guidelines | See E/VII. |

## 2–308 Resumption of the proceedings

**r.90(2)** Where proceedings have been interrupted under r.90(1)(a) or (b) and the EPO has been informed of the identity of the person authorised to continue the proceedings before the EPO, the EPO will communicate to such person and any interested third party that the proceedings will be resumed as from a date to be fixed by the EPO.

**r.90(3)** Where proceedings have been interrupted under r.90(1)(c), the proceedings will be resumed when the EPO has been informed of the appointment of a new representative of the applicant or when the EPO has notified to the other parties the communication of the appointment of a new representative of the proprietor of the patent.

However, where three months have elapsed since the proceedings were interrupted and the EPO have not yet been informed of the appointment of a new representative, it will communicate to the applicant for or proprietor of the patent:

(a) where Art.133(2) is applicable (natural or legal persons not having residence/principal place of business within a Contracting State), that the application will be deemed withdrawn or the patent revoked if the information is not submitted within two months of the notification of the communication; or

(b) where Art.133(2) does not apply, that the proceedings will be resumed with the applicant for or proprietor of the patent as from the date on which the communication is notified.

## 2–309 Time limits on resumption

**r.90(4)** Time limits, other than the time limits for requesting examination and paying renewal fees, in force as regards the applicant for or proprietor of the patent at the date of interruption of the proceedings, begin again as from the day on which the proceedings are resumed. If the date on which proceedings are resumed is less than two months before the end of the period within which the request for examination must be filed, such a request may be filed up to the end of two months after such date.

Thus, on resumption, all time limits start again for their full term except for the period for requesting examination where only the remaining time resumes, subject to a minimum of two months (J7/83) and the period for paying renewal fees. Where the due date for a renewal fee has fallen due during the period of incapacity it becomes due on the date of resumption (J ../87 [1988] O.J. 323).

## 2–310 Department responsible for questions concerning interruption

Guidelines See E/VII/1.3. The Legal Division has responsibility.

## 2–311 Principle of good faith—protection of legitimate expectations

Case law This is a doctrine which has no direct basis in the EPC but is a principle generally recognised in the Contracting States to the EPC which has been applied by the Boards of Appeal consistently and by the Enlarged Board in, e.g. G5/88, G7/88 and G8/88 (*re* President's agreement with German Patent Office).

The protection of the legitimate expectations of users of the European patent system requires that such a user must not suffer a disadvantage as a result of having relied on erroneous information received from the EPO (e.g. J2/87) or on a misleading communication (e.g. J3/87). The protection of legitimate expectations also requires the EPO to warn the applicant of any loss of rights if such a warning can be expected in all good faith. This presupposes that the deficiency can be readily identified by the EPO within the framework of the normal handling of the case at the relevant stage of the proceedings and that the user is in a position to correct it within the time limit.  G2/97

When the law changes fundamentally as a result of a new interpretation established by The Engaged Board of Appeal, the principle of protecting legitimate expectations acts to protect those who have relied on the law as it was. See for instance G9/93 where proprietors who have already opposed their patents were allowed to continue and G5/93 where applicants for restitution following a failure to pay the national fee for regional phase entry were allowed to continue under A122.

See CLBA, pp.251–261.  CLBA

## 14. AMENDMENT AND CORRECTION

### Circumstances in which amendment is allowed

#### *Amendment before receipt of the search report*  2–312

The conditions under which amendment is possible are laid down in the Regulations.  Art.123(1)

Before receiving the European search report, the applicant may not amend the description, claims or drawings of a European patent application, except where otherwise provided.  r.86(1)

#### *Amendment after receipt of the search report and before receipt of the first examination report*  2–313

The conditions under which amendment is possible are laid down in the Regulations.  Art.123(1)

After receiving the European search report and before receipt of the first communication from the Examining Division, the applicant may, of his own volition, amend the description, claims and drawings.  r.86(2)

See CLBA, p.419.  CLBA

See C/VI/3.1–3.2.  Guidelines

#### *Amendment after receipt of the first examination report*  2–314

The conditions under which amendment is possible are laid down in the Regulations.  Art.123(1)

After receipt of the first communication from the Examining Division the applicant may, of his own volition, amend once the description, claims and drawings, provided that the amendment is filed at the same time as the reply to the communication. No further amendment may be made without the consent of the Examining Division.  r.86(3)

See CLBA, pp.422–424. See also CLBA, pp.433–434 for situations in which a Board of Appeal will exercise discretion on behalf of the Examining Division (if late filed, must be clearly allowable, T153/85). See CLBA, pp.437–439 and 441–443 for amendments proposed during grant proceedings where discretion is exercised less generously.  CLBA

| | |
|---|---|
| T946/96 | If the Examining Division is not going to allow such a discretionary amendment then it must communicate its decision in a reasoned way to the applicant to satisfy Art.113(1) (applicant has the chance to comment) prior to refusal (CLBA, p.427). |
| T798/95 | The handing over to the EPO postal service of the decision to grant is the point at which no further amendment under r.86(3) is possible (CLBA, p.443). See also G7/93. |
| Guidelines | See C/VI/4.7–4.10. |

### 2–315  Form of amendments

| | |
|---|---|
| Guidelines | See E/II. Replacement pages are preferred but handwritten amendments on copied pages are also allowed. |

### 2–316  Amendment must not add subject matter

#### General principles

| | |
|---|---|
| Art.123(2) | A European patent application or a European patent may not be amended in such a way that it contains subject-matter which extends beyond the content of the application as filed. |
| Art.70(2) | In the case referred to in Art.14(2), the original text (and not the translation) constitutes, in proceedings before the EPO, the basis for determining whether the subject matter of the application or patent extends beyond the content of the application as filed. |
| r.7 | However, saving proof to the contrary, the EPO may, for the purposes of determining whether the subject matter of a European patent application or European patent extends beyond the content of the European patent application as filed, assume that the translation referred to in Art.14(2) is in conformity with the original text of the application. |
| Case law | The basic test for assessing whether an amendment adds subject matter or not is whether the amended text can be directly and unambiguously derived from the application as filed (T20/83). Both the explicit and implicit content of the application as filed may be used as basis (T151/84, T201/83). The content of the application as filed is the description, claims and drawings (G3/89) but not the abstract (T246/86) or the priority document (T260/85). Cross-referenced documents are prima facie not part of the application as filed (T689/90) but can sometimes be used under strict conditions (T689/90, T6/84). An addition of a reference to the prior art does not contravene Art.123(2) (T11/82, T51/87, T450/97). Equally, amendments to the claim preamble in view of the closest prior art changing (T13/84) or changing the position of a feature from the preamble to the characterising portion (T16/86) are both allowed. |
| CLBA | See CLBA, pp.197–221. |
| Guidelines | See C/VI/5.3. |

### 2–317  Disclaimers

| | |
|---|---|
| G1/03 | Headnote (1): "An amendment to a claim by the introduction of a disclaimer may not be refused under Art.123(2) EPC for the sole reason that neither the disclaimer nor the subject-matter excluded by it from the scope of the claim have a basis in the application as filed." |
| | Headnote (2): "The following criteria are to be applied for assessing the allowability of a disclaimer which is not disclosed in the application as filed: |
| | 2.1 A disclaimer may be allowable in order to: |

— restore novelty by delimiting a claim against state of the art under Art.54(3) and (4) EPC;

— restore novelty by delimiting a claim against an accidental anticipation under Art.54(2) EPC; an anticipation is accidental if it is so unrelated to and remote from the claimed invention that the person skilled in the art would never have taken it into consideration when making the invention; and

— disclaim subject-matter which, under Arts 52 to 57 EPC, is excluded from patentability for non-technical reasons.

2.2 A disclaimer should not remove more than is necessary either to restore novelty or to disclaim subject-matter excluded from patentability for non-technical reasons.

2.3 A disclaimer which is or becomes relevant for the assessment of inventive step or sufficiency of disclosure adds subject-matter contrary to Art.123(2) EPC.

2.4 A claim containing a disclaimer must meet the requirements of clarity and conciseness of Art.84 EPC."

See C/VI/5.3.11. — Guidelines

## Amended claims not to relate to unsearched subject matter not having unity — 2–318

Amended claims may not relate to unsearched subject matter which does not combine with the originally claimed invention or group of inventions to form a single general inventive concept. — r.86(4)

Amended claims may only be refused on the basis of Art.86(4) if the subject matter of the claims filed originally and that of the amended claims is such that, had all the claims originally been filed together, a further search fee would have been payable in respect of the amended claims, these claims relating to a different invention within the meaning of r.46(1). — T708/00

See CLBA, pp.424–426. If such subject-matter is to be protected, a divisional application must be filed. This provision relates to matter not present in the claims during search rather than, for instance, matter which was not completely searched. — CLBA

See C/VI/5.2(ii). — Guidelines

## Amendment must not extend the protection conferred by a patent

### General principles — 2–319

The claims of the European patent may not be amended during opposition proceedings in such a way as to extend the protection conferred. — Art.123(3)

Headnote (1): "A change of category of granted claims in opposition proceedings is not open to objection under Art.123(3) EPC, if it does not result in extension of the protection conferred by the claims as a whole, when they are interpreted in accordance with Art.69 EPC and its protocol. In this context, the national laws of the Contracting States relating to infringement should not be considered. — G2/88

Headnote (2): "An amendment of granted claims directed to a compound and to a composition including such compound, so that the amended claims are directed to the use of that compound in a composition for a particular purpose is not open to objection under Art.123(3) EPC."

The reasoning is that the protection conferred is to be decided under the EPC whereas the rights conferred (infringing acts etc.) are a matter for national law.

Here, the compound/composition claims conferred absolute protection in respect of all uses and hence the change to a use claims necessarily narrowed the extent of protection.

T5/90  A product claim may be amended to a process claim (see also T53/90).

T423/89  A product-by-process claim may be amended to a process claim.

T20/94  A process claim may not be amended to a product-by-process claim since the latter claim is construed as relating to the product *per se*.

T1149/97  It is possible for Art.123(3) to be contravened by amendments to the description.

CLBA  See CLBA, pp.221–229. That which doesn't infringe the patent as granted should not infringe it as amended (T1149/97). It is occasionally permissible to broaden the wording of a claim to include an embodiment in the description if the amendment amounts to no more than clarification of an unclear term which the skilled man would have used the description to clarify in any case.

Guidelines  See D/V/6.

## 2–320  *The inescapable trap*

G1/93  This decision confirmed that an inescapable trap lurks for the unwary applicant who makes a limiting amendment during examination which amounts to added subject matter.

Headnote (1): "If a European patent as granted contains subject matter which extends beyond the content of the application as filed within the meaning of Art.123(2) EPC and which also limits the scope of protection conferred by the patent, such a patent cannot be maintained in opposition proceedings unamended, because the ground for opposition under Art.100(c) EPC prejudices the maintenance of the patent. Nor can it be amended by deleting such limiting subject-matter from the claims, because such amendment would extend the protection conferred, which is prohibited by Art.123(3) EPC. Such a patent can, therefore, only be maintained if there is a basis in the application as filed for replacing such subject-matter without violating Art.123(3) EPC."

T82/93  Where a claim includes method steps not allowable pursuant to Art.52(4) EPC, the claim cannot be maintained since to take out these features would extend the protection.

## 2–321  Restrictions on amendment during opposition proceedings

r.57a  See under opposition.

## 2–322  Correction of errors in documents

### What corrections are allowable?

r.88  Linguistic errors, errors of transcription and mistakes in any document filed with the EPO may be corrected on request.

However, where the error is in the description, claims or drawings, the correction must be obvious in the sense that it is immediately evident that nothing else would have been intended other than what is offered as the correction.

J8/80  A mistake in this sense is something which does not truly express the intention of the person filing the document and correction of such can involve putting right an incorrect statement or adding wrongly omitted matter. It is not possible to make a correction under r.88 where there has simply been a change of mind (J1/80).

A correction under r.88 is not normally allowable if the result of the correction would be to breach a principle relating to the fundamental value of legal procedural certainty. Such principles include the ability of the EPO to take a decision under Art.113(2) based on the final requests of the parties and that a party is not adversely affected by and hence cannot appeal a decision which grants his final request. A party statement relied on in a formal juridical act cannot therefore be corrected under r.88. T824/00

Rule 88 cannot be used to correct a document in which an appeal has been filed such that no appeal is subsequently deemed to have been filed when a representative has filed the appeal against the wishes of his client. T309/03

See A/V/3 and C/VI/5.4. Guidelines

## Corrections to the description, claims and drawings are governed by Art.123(2) EPC

2–323

Headnote (1): "The parts of a European patent application or of a European patent relating to the disclosure (the description, claims and drawings) may be corrected under r.88, second sentence, EPC only within the limits of what a skilled person would derive directly and unambiguously, using common general knowledge, and seen objectively and relative to the date of filing, from the whole of these documents (therefore not including priority document/abstract) as filed. Such a correction is of a strictly declaratory nature and thus does not infringe the prohibition of extension under Art.123(2) EPC." G3/89

Headnote (2): "Evidence of what was common general knowledge on the date of filing may be furnished in connection with an admissible request for correction in any suitable form."

The Enlarged Board considered that Art.123(2) applies equally to amendments which are and which are not corrections. Further, the requirements of r.88 imply that the skilled person is able to recognise that certain information in the disclosure is incorrect as well as what the correct version should be. Hence, the correction is declaratory in the sense of the corrected version merely expressing what the skilled person would already understand. The only relevant evidence is that contained in documents shedding light on the common general knowledge of the skilled man at the filing date. These proceedings were joined with G11/91.

## Examples of allowable and non-allowable corrections

2–324

Headnote: "The complete documents forming a European patent application, that is the description, claims and drawings, cannot be replaced by way of a correction under r.88 EPC by other documents which the applicants had intended to file with their request for grant." G2/95

This decision follows very straightforwardly from G3/89 and G11/91 in that the subject matter that may not be extended under Art.123(2) is that contained in the claims, description and drawings accorded a filing date under Art.80.

However, correction of the request is possible when the wrong request is filed with an application (CLBA, pp.404, 406–407). J21/94

See CLBA, pp.229–233 (general), 407 (correction of the name of the applicant) and 413 to 416 (correction of a priority claim). CLBA

It is possible to correct the name of the applicant (J18/93, J7/80) or the name of the opponent (T219/86). Many corrections are contingent on the public not being adversely affected or misled. Correction of an omitted designation (J21/84, J7/90), Case law correction of the withdrawal of a designation (J10/87) and correction of the withdrawal of an application (J10/87) fall into this category. An inaccurate or missing priority claim may be corrected (e.g. J4/82, J14/82, J9/91) but only if received in time for a warning to be included in the publication of the application (as recalculated if necessary) or otherwise in exceptional circumstances (e.g. J12/80, EPO partly to blame; J6/91, correction of an obvious discrepancy).

A decision to correct a priority claim does not become final until the decision terminating the grant procedure is taken (T713/02).

| | |
|---|---|
| **2–325** | ***Non-payment of fees cannot be corrected under r.88*** |
| J27/96 | Failure to pay a designation fee in time can't be remedied under r.88 (CLBA, p.410) since r.88 is concerned with mistakes in documents. |
| T152/85 | Equally, lack of payment of the opposition fee may not be corrected. |
| **2–326** | ***Correction is only possible where proceedings are pending*** |
| J42/92 | Corrections under r.88 are only possible where application or opposition proceedings are pending. Thus, after the mention of grant in the Bulletin, corrections are only possible if opposition proceedings are opened (CLBA, 393). |
| J7/96 | This decision suggests that between a decision to grant and the grant taking effect, errors may only be corrected under r.89. |
| **2–327** | ***Competent body to decide on correction*** |
| J4/85 | A request for correction of the description, claims or drawings must be decided by the Examining Division. |
| **2–328** | **Correction of errors in decisions** |
| r.89 | In decisions of the EPO, only linguistic errors, errors of transcription and obvious mistakes may be corrected. |
| T212/88 | The correction has retrospective effect to the date of the decision. |
| CLBA | See CLBA, pp.388–391. The text approved under r.51(4) is an integral part of the decision to grant and can potentially be corrected if not in a form corresponding to the intention of the deciding instance (T850/95). |
| Guidelines | See E/X/10. |

## 15. INVENTORSHIP, OWNERSHIP AND SUSPENSION OF PROCEEDINGS

**Right of the inventor to be mentioned**

| | |
|---|---|
| **2–329** | ***Designation of the inventor*** |
| r.15 | See under contents of the application. |
| **2–330** | ***Rectification of the designation of the inventor*** |
| r.19(1) | An incorrect designation of an inventor may not be rectified save on request, accompanied by the consent of the wrongly designated person and, in the event of such request not being |

filed by the applicant for or proprietor of the European patent, by the consent of that party. The provisions of r.17 (publication of mention of the inventor) apply *mutatis mutandis*.

In the event of an incorrect mention of the inventor having been entered in the Register of European patents or published in the European patent bulletin such entry or publication will be corrected. r.19(2)

Rule 19(2) applies *mutatis mutandis* to the cancellation of an incorrect designation of the inventor. r.19(3)

Designation of an additional inventor does not require the permission of the existing inventors. J8/82

## Right to be mentioned 2–331

The inventor has the right, *vis-à-vis* the applicant for or proprietor of a European patent, to be mentioned as such before the EPO. Art.62

## Publication of mention of the inventor 2–332

The person designated as the inventor will be mentioned as such in the published European patent application and the European patent specification, unless the said person informs the EPO in writing that he waives his right to be thus mentioned. r.18(1)

In the event of a third party filing with the EPO a final decision whereby the applicant for or proprietor of a patent is required to designate him as the inventor, the provisions of r.18(1) apply. r.18(2)

## Right to a European Patent 2–333

The right to a European patent belongs to the inventor or his successor in title. If the inventor is an employee the right to the European patent is determined in accordance with the law of the state in which the employee is mainly employed; if the state in which the employee is mainly employed cannot be determined, the law to be applied is that of the state in which the employer has his place of business to which the employee is attached. Art.60(1)

If two or more persons have made an invention independently of each other, the right to the European patent belongs to the person whose European patent application has the earliest date of filing; however, this provision applies only if this application has been published under Art.93 and only has effect in respect of the Contracting States designated in that application as published. Art.60(2)

The right of priority has the effect that the date of priority counts as the date of filing of a European patent application for the purposes of Art.60, para.2. Art.89

For the purposes of proceedings before the EPO, the applicant is deemed to be entitled to exercise the right to the European patent. Art.60(3)

The EPO does not need to investigate the existence of entitlement. J18/93

## Procedure where the applicant does not have the right to a European patent

### Jurisdiction of the Contracting States 2–334

The courts of the Contracting States have, in accordance with Art.2 to Art.6 jurisdiction to decide claims, against the applicant, to the right to the grant of a European patent in respect of one or more of the Contracting States designated in the European patent application. PonR.1(1)

| | |
|---|---|
| | The Protocol on Recognition only applies pre-grant. |
| PonR.5 | If the parties agree on the courts of a particular EPC state, that court applies, as long as, in the case of an employee/employer dispute, the agreement conforms to national law governing the contract of employment. |
| PonR.4 | If the parties don't have an agreement and the invention has been made by an employee and the right to be granted a patent is determined by the law of a contracting state pursuant to Art.60(1) second sentence, the court of that contracting states applies. |
| PonR.2 | Where neither PonR.4 nor PonR.5 applies, the court of the EPC state where the applicant has his residence or principle place of business should be chosen. |
| PonR.3 | Where neither PonR.4 nor PonR.5 applies, and the applicant does not have his residence or principle place of business in an EPC state, the court of the EPC state in which the person raising the entitlement question has his residence or principle place of business should be chosen. |
| PonR.6 | The default court is the German court. |
| J6/03 | The legal board of appeal confirmed that decisions of a non-EPC state court (here Canada) could not be used to suspend proceedings before the EPO. |

## 2–335 Suspension and resumption of proceedings during examination

| | |
|---|---|
| r.13(1) | If a third party provides proof to the EPO that he has opened proceedings against the applicant for the purpose of seeking a judgement that he is entitled to the grant of the European patent (e.g. in the UK, a copy of Form 21/77 initiating proceedings before the Comptroller), the EPO will, provided that the application has been published, stay the proceedings for grant (i.e. only applies up until mention of grant in Bulletin, not possible if application refused or withdrawn) unless the third party consents to the continuation of such proceedings. Such consent must be communicated in writing to the EPO; it is irrevocable. |
| r.13(2) | Where proof is provided to the EPO that a decision which has become final has been given in the proceedings concerning entitlement to the grant of the European patent, the EPO will communicate to the applicant and any other party that the proceedings for grant will be resumed as from the date stated in the communication unless a new European patent application pursuant to Art.61(1)(b) has been filed for all the states designated in the contested application. If the decision is in favour of the third party, the proceedings may only be resumed after a period of three months of that decision becoming final unless the third party requests the resumption of the proceedings for grant. |
| r.13(3) | When giving a decision on the suspension of proceedings or thereafter, the EPO may set a date on which it intends to continue the proceedings pending before it regardless of the stage reached in the proceedings referred to in r.13(1) opened against the applicant. The date is communicated to the third party, the applicant and any other party. If no proof has been provided by that date that a declaration which has become final has been given, the EPO may continue proceedings. |
| CLBA | See CLBA, pp.397–398 and 506–507. The legal division decides on suspension and can grant a stay without consulting the applicant. If the stay is refused, the third party can appeal. If granted, the applicant can challenge the decision and then appeal if the stay is maintained. If the stay is removed after challenge from the applicant the third party can appeal. The applicant is party to any appeal proceedings initiated by the third party (J28/94). An appeal by a third party has suspensive effect so that the application cannot proceed to grant (J7/96, J28/94). If necessary, the EPO must publish a cancellation of the mention of grant. |
| Guidelines | See A/IV/2.2–2.3 |

## Suspension of proceedings during opposition 2–336

If a third party provides proof to the EPO during opposition proceedings or during the opposition period that he has opened proceedings against the proprietor of the European patent for the purpose of seeking a judgment that he is entitled to the European patent, the EPO will stay the opposition proceedings unless the third party consents to the continuation of such proceedings. Such consent must be communicated in writing to the EPO; it is irrevocable. However, the suspension of the proceedings may not be ordered until the Opposition Division has deemed the opposition admissible. Rule 13(2) and (3) apply *mutatis mutandis* (see above).

r.13(4)

See D/VII/5.

Guidelines

## Calculation of time limits when proceedings are resumed 2–337

The time limits in force at the date of suspension, other than the time limit for payment of a renewal fee, are interrupted by such suspension. The time which has not yet elapsed begins to run as from the date on which proceedings are resumed; however, the time still to run after the resumption of the proceedings is a minimum of two months.

r.13(5)

Therefore, the rightful owner of the invention needs to monitor renewal fee payments and pay them himself if necessary.

See A/IV/2.4.

Guidelines

## No withdrawal during suspension 2–338

As from the time when a third party proves to the EPO that he has initiated proceedings concerning entitlement and up to the date on which the EPO resumes the proceedings for grant, neither the European patent application nor the designation of any Contracting State may be withdrawn.

r.14

## Remedies following a final decision 2–339

If by a final decision it is adjudged that a person referred to in Art.60, para.1, other than the applicant, is entitled to the grant of a European patent, that person may, within a period of three months after the decision has become final, provided that the European patent has not yet been granted, in respect of those Contracting States designated in the European patent application in which the decision has been taken or recognised, or has to be recognised on the basis of the Protocol on Recognition annexed to the EPC:

Art.61(1)

(a) prosecute the application as his own application in place of the applicant,

(b) file a new European patent application in respect of the same invention, or

(c) request that the application be refused.

This case split the Enlarged Board of Appeal. The majority decided that "When it has been adjudged by a final decision of a national court that a person other than the applicant is entitled to the grant of a European patent, and that person, in compliance with the specific requirements of Art.61(1) EPC, files a new European patent application in respect of the same invention under Art.61(1)(b) EPC, it is not a pre-condition for the application to be accepted that the earlier original usurping application is still pending before the EPO at the time the new application is filed."

G3/92

The Enlarged Board felt that the potential risk to legal certainty in respect of parties commencing commercial activities on the basis that the application was dead were outweighed by the damaging consequences of parties stealing an invention and withdrawing their application shortly after publication (they felt that national courts could take into account particular circumstances of this kind). Nothing in the language of the EPC was seen to prevent this interpretation and in particular the provision governing divisional applications that a pending parent application must be in existence

| | |
|---|---|
| | was seen not to apply. The reference in Art.61(3) to the Implementing Regulations was deemed to be to r.15 and r.16 and not to r.25. The Board felt that exercise of the remedies provided by Art.61(1)(a) and (c) did require a pending application. |
| CLBA | See CLBA, p.249. |
| Art.61(2) | The provisions of Art.76, para.1, apply *mutatis mutandis* to a new application filed under Art.61(1). An exception is that such new applications can also be filed with the competent authorities of a Contracting State, if the national law of the state so provides. |
| Art.76(1) | A replacement application can therefore be filed only in respect of subject matter which does not extend beyond the content of the earlier application as filed; in so far as this provision is complied with, the replacement application will be deemed to have been filed on the date of filing of the earlier application and will have the benefit of any right to priority. |
| Art.61(3) | The procedure to be followed in carrying out the provisions of Art.61(1), the special conditions applying to a new application filed under Art.61(1) and the time limit for paying the filing, search and designation fees on it are laid down in the Implementing Regulations. |
| r.15(1) | Where the person adjudged by a final decision to be entitled to the grant of the European patent files a new European patent application pursuant to Art.61(1)(b), the original European patent application will be deemed to be withdrawn on the date of filing of the new application for the Contracting States designated therein in which the decision has been taken or recognised. |
| r.15(2) | The filing fee and search fee must be paid in respect of the new European patent application within one month after the filing thereof. The designation fees must be paid within six months of the date on which the European Patent Bulletin mentions the publication of the European search report drawn up in respect of the new European patent application. |
| r.85a(1) | If the filing fee, search fee or a designation fee is not paid within the r.15(2) time limit, it may still be validly paid within a period of grace of one month from notification of a communication pointing out the failure to observe the time limit, provided that within this period a surcharge is paid. |
| Art.122(5) | *Restitutio* is not available for the time limits referred to in Art.61(3). |
| r.15(3) | The time limits for forwarding European patent applications provided for in Art.77(3) and (5) (when filed with national office) are, for the new patent application, four months from the actual date of filing of that application. |
| r.37(4) | No renewal fees are payable in respect of the year of filing of the replacement application and in respect of past years. |
| Guidelines | See C/VI/9.2. |

## 2–340 *Partial transfer of right by virtue of a final decision*

| | |
|---|---|
| r.16(1) | If by a final decision it is adjudged that a third party is entitled to the grant of a European patent in respect of only part of the matter disclosed in the European patent application, Art.61 and r.15 apply *mutatis mutandis* to such part. |
| r.16(2) | Where appropriate, the original European patent application may contain, for the designated Contracting States in which the decision was taken or recognised, claims, a description and drawings which are different from those for the other designated Contracting States. |
| r.16(3) | Where a third party has, in accordance with Art.99(5), replaced the previous proprietor for one or some of the designated Contracting States, the patent as maintained in opposition proceedings may contain for these states claims, a description and drawings which are different from those for the other designated Contracting States. |

See C/III/8.2 and C/VI/5.5. — Guidelines

### *EPO division responsible*  2–341

The legal division is responsible for decisions relating to the suspension and resumption of proceedings (Guidelines D/VII/5.4). — Art.20

## 16. REPRESENTATION

### Kinds of representation available

#### *Choice of representation for a person having a residence or principal place of business within a Contracting State*  2–342

A natural or legal person having either a residence or principal place of business within the territory of a Contracting State is not compelled to be represented by a professional representative and may therefore represent him or herself. — Art.133(1)(2)

A legal person may represent itself through an officer of a corporation or a director.

The word "principal" is missing from the DE and FR texts and may be unimportant.

Natural or legal persons having their residence or principal place of business within the territory of one of the Contracting States may also be represented in proceedings established by the EPC by an employee, who need not be a professional representative but who must be authorised in accordance with the Implementing Regulations. The Implementing Regulations may provide whether and under what conditions an employee of such a legal person may also represent other legal persons which have their principal place of business within the territory of one of the Contracting States and which have economic connections with the first legal person. — Art.133(3)

No such provision has been made in the Regulations.

Natural or legal persons having their residence or principal place of business within the territory of one of the Contracting States may also be represented professionally, either by a professional representative on the EPO list or by a qualified legal practitioner (see below). — Art.134(1)(4)(7)

See A/IX/1.1–1.2 — Guidelines

#### *Choice of representation for a person not having a residence or principal place of business within a Contracting State*  2–343

Any natural or legal person not having either a residence or principal place of business within the territory of a Contracting State must be represented by a professional representative and act through him in all proceedings established by the EPC, other than in filing a European patent application (in view of Art.58—see also J11/93); the Implementing Regulations may permit other exceptions. — Art.133(2)

It is also possible for any person to pay a fee. See legal advice 6/91 ([1991] O.J. 573). — AnReg

Such professional representation may be provided by either a professional representative on the EPO list or by a qualified legal practitioner (see below). — Art.134(1)(4)(7)

Where professional representation is necessary, the same period will be specified for the notification of the appointment of a representative and for the filing of an authorisation. — r.101(1)

| | |
|---|---|
| CLBA | See CLBA, p.367 for the validity of acts performed by a non-entitled person. Such acts, apart from the filing of a European patent application, are normally invalid. |
| Guidelines | See A/IX/1.1-1.2. |

**2–344** *Representation of parties acting in common*

Art.133(4) — The Implementing Regulations may prescribe special provisions concerning the common representation of parties acting in common.

r.100(1) — Where there is more than one applicant, the following rules apply:

(a) if the request names a common representative then that person will be the common representative; if not then

(b) if the first named applicant has appointed a professional representative then that person will be the common representative; if not, then

(c) if one of the applicants is obliged to appoint a representative then that person will be considered to be the common representative; if not then

(d) the applicant first named in the request will be considered to be the common representative.

The same rules apply to *mutatis mutandis* to third parties acting in common to file a notice of opposition or intervention and to joint proprietors of a European patent.

r.100(2) — Where, in the course of proceedings, transfer is made to more than one person, and such persons have not appointed a common representative, the above rules will apply. If it is not possible to apply these rules then the EPO will require the person to appoint a common representative within two months. If such a request is not complied with then the EPO will appoint the common representative.

Guidelines — See A/IX/1.3.

**Professional representation**

**2–345** *Who can act as a professional representative—right to set up in business*

Art.134(1)(4)(7) — Professional representation of natural or legal persons in proceedings established by the EPC may only be undertaken by:

(a) professional representatives whose names appear on a list maintained for this purpose by the EPO; or

(b) any legal practitioner qualified in one of the Contracting States and having his place of business within such State, to the extent that he is entitled, within the said State, to act as a professional representative in patent matters.

Whilst legal practitioners can "act as" professional representatives they do not become professional representatives.

CLBA — See CLBA, pp.365–367 regarding the definition of "legal practitioner"—patent attorneys don't count.

Art.134(5) — In either case, for the purposes of acting as a professional representative, any such person (on the list or legal practitioner) is entitled to establish a place of business in any Contracting State in which proceedings established by the EPC may be conducted (probably means Germany or Holland), having regard to the Protocol on Centralisation annexed to the EPC. The authorities of such State may remove that entitlement in individual cases only in the application of legal provisions adopted for the purpose of protecting public security and law and order. Before such action is taken, the President of the EPO must be consulted.

See A/IX/1.4. Guidelines

### *Procedure for being entered on the list of professional representatives*   2–346

Any natural person who fulfils the following conditions may be entered on the list of professional representatives: Art.134(2)

(a) he must be a national of one of the Contracting States;

(b) he must have his place of business or employment within the territory of one of the Contracting States;

(c) he must have passed the European qualifying examination.

See under Art.134(2). The Administrative Council has issued guidance as to what titles a person on the list may use ([1979] O.J. 452). AnReg

Entry is effected upon request, accompanied by certificates which must indicate that the conditions laid down in Art.134(2) are fulfilled. Art.134(3)

The President of the EPO may, in special circumstances, grant exemption from the requirement of Art.134(2)(a). Art.134(6)

After the expiry of the transitional period (which ended on October 7, 1981), any person whose name was entered on the list of professional representatives during that period will, without prejudice to any disciplinary measures taken under Art.134(8)(c), remain thereon or, on request, be restored thereto, provided that he then fulfils the requirement of Art.163(1)(b) (i.e. has his place of business or employment within the territory of one of the Contracting States). Art.163(7)

### *The European qualifying exam*   2–347

The Administrative Council may adopt provisions governing the qualifications and training required of a person for admission to the European qualifying examination and the conduct of such examination. Art.134(8)

See under Art.134(8). A regulation on the EQE for professional representatives has been drawn up by the Administrative Council ([1994] O.J. 7; [2004] O.J. Suppl. to O.J. 12/2004). Further, Implementing Regulations for this regulation have been drawn up by the Examination Board ([1998] O.J. 364; [2004] O.J. Suppl. to O.J. 14). Relevant qualifications for enrolment for the EQE have been published ([1994] O.J. 599; [1996] O.J. 357; [1999] O.J. 92; [2004] O.J. Supplement to O.J. 12/2004, 17). Instructions for candidates and invigilators have also been published by the Examination Board ([1995] O.J. 145; O.J. [2004] Suppl. to O.J. 12/2004 21, 25, 31). AnReg

For case law on appeals to the disciplinary Board of Appeal relating to the EQE, see CLBA, pp.565–569. CLBA

### *The European Patent Institute*   2–348

The Administrative Council may adopt provisions governing the establishment or recognition of an institute constituted by the persons entitled to act as professional representatives by virtue of either the European qualifying examination or the provisions of Art.163, para.7. Art.134(8)

See under Art.134(8). The Administrative Council has indeed set up an institute of professional representatives called the European Patent Institute (EPI) ([1997] O.J. 350; [1997] O.J. 130; [2002] O.J. 429). A code of conduct for EPI members has been drawn up ([1999] O.J. 537). AnReg

| | |
|---|---|
| Art.134(8) | The Administrative Council may adopt provisions governing any disciplinary power to be exercised by that institute (i.e. the European Patent Institute) or the EPO on such persons (i.e. professional representatives). |
| AnReg | See under Art.134(8). A code of conduct has been drawn up by the Administrative Council ([1978] O.J. 91). Under this code a disciplinary committee of EPI is set up with its own rules of procedure ([1980] O.J. 177). Further, the code also allows for a disciplinary board of the EPO which has its own rules of procedure ([1980] O.J. 183). Further, the code also allows for a disciplinary Board of Appeal which has its own rules of procedure ([1980] O.J. 188). See CLBA, pp.569–571 for important decisions. Decisions of this Appeal Board are now available to the public ([1998] O.J. 211). |

## 2–349 *Circumstances in which a representative may be deleted from the list*

| | |
|---|---|
| r.102(1) | The entry of a professional representative on the list of professional representatives may be deleted if he so requests or if, despite repeated reminders, he fails to pay the annual subscription to the Institute of Professional Representatives before the EPO before the end of the year for which the subscription is due. |
| r.102(2) | Furthermore, after the expiry of the transitional period provided for in Art.163(1), and without prejudice to any disciplinary measures taken under Art.134(8)(c), the entry of any professional representative may be deleted automatically in the following cases only: |

    (a) in the event of the death or legal incapacity of the professional representative;

    (b) in the event of the professional representative no longer being a national of one of the Contracting States, unless he was entered on the list during the transitional period or was granted exemption by the President of the EPO under Art.134(6); or

    (c) in the event of the professional representative no longer having his place of business or employment within the territory of one of the Contracting States.

## 2–350 *Re-entry on the list following deletion*

| | |
|---|---|
| r.102(3) | A person whose entry has been deleted will, upon request, be re-entered in the list of professional representatives if the conditions for deletion no longer exist. |

**Authorisation**

## 2–351 *Requirement to file an authorisation*

Authorisation is giving an agent the power to act as opposed to appointment, which is a matter of telling the EPO who the representative is going to be. If authorised, it is possible for a professional representative to appoint himself. According to J17/98, filing a general authorisation does not on its own imply appointment with respect to any specific case.

| | |
|---|---|
| r.101(1) | Representatives acting before the EPO must, on request, file a signed authorisation within a period to be specified by the EPO. The President of the EPO decides under which circumstances such an authorisation must be filed. The authorisation may cover one or more European patent applications or patents and must be filed in the corresponding number of copies. Where professional representation is necessary, the same period will be specified for the notification of the appointment of a representative and for the filing of the authorisation. |
| AnReg | See under r.101(1). The President has decided that professional representatives appearing on the list only need to present a signed authorisation when there is a change of representation and the previous representative does not terminate his representation or |

in specific cases where there is some doubt about the representative's entitlement to act. Legal practitioners and employee representatives, however, always need to file a signed authorisation ([1991] O.J. 489). See also [2005] O.J. 41 under r.24(1). Authorisations are one of the few documents which cannot be filed by fax.

## *Form and content of an authorisation* — 2–352

The President of the EPO may determine and publish in the O.J. the form and content of an authorisation in so far as it relates to the representation of persons as defined in Art.133(2). — r.101(3)

A general authorisation enabling a representative to act in respect of all the patent transactions of the party making the authorisation may be filed. A single copy is sufficient. — r.101(2)

The President of the EPO may determine and publish in the O.J. the form and content of a general authorisation. — r.101(3)

See under r.101(3). Form 1004.1 is recommended for general authorisation ([1985] O.J. 42; [1986] O.J. 327). — AnReg

Where there are several authorisers, a general authorization can also be used when only one or more of them are to be represented. If one of several authorisers cancels a general authorization, it remains valid for the other authorisers under the old number.

See CLBA, pp.368–371. — CLBA

## *Consequences of not filing an authorisation when requested* — 2–353

If an authorisation is not filed in due time, any procedural steps taken by the representative, other than the filing of the application, will, without prejudice to any other legal consequences provided for in the EPC, be deemed not to have been taken. — r.101(4)

## *Withdrawal/termination of an authorisation* — 2–354

Rule 101(1) and r.101(2) apply *mutatis mutandis* to a document withdrawing an authorisation. — r.101(5)

Until the termination of an authorisation has been communicated to the EPO, a representative who has ceased to be authorised will continue to be regarded as the representative. — r.101(6)

Subject to any provisions to the contrary contained therein, an authorisation will not terminate *vis-à-vis* the EPO upon the death of the person who gave it. — r.101(7)

## Where several representatives are appointed — 2–355

If several representatives are appointed by a party, they may, notwithstanding any provision to the contrary in the notification of their appointment or in the authorisation, act either jointly or singly. — r.101(8)

## The authorisation of an association — 2–356

The authorisation of an association of representatives will be deemed to be authorisation of any representative who can establish that he practises within that association. — r.101(9)

It is not necessary to be in private practice to be an "association". — J16/96

See under r.101(9) for the meaning of an "association" ([1979] O.J. 92). — AnReg

## 17. LANGUAGES

**2–357** **Languages of the EPC—authentic text**

Art.177(1)     The EPC, drawn up in a single original, in the English, French and German languages, is deposited in the archives of the Government of the Federal Republic of Germany, the three texts being equally authentic.

Art.177(2)     The texts of the EPC drawn up in official languages of Contracting States other than those referred to in Art.177(1) will, if they have been approved by the Administrative Council, be considered as official texts. In the event of conflict on the interpretation of the various texts, the texts referred to in Art.177(1) are authentic.

**2–358** **Official languages of the EPO**

Art.14(1)     The official languages of the EPO are English, French and German.

**2–359** **Language of filing the application**

Art.14(1)(2)     An official language of the EPO or, in certain circumstances, a Contracting State may be used. In the latter case a translation is necessary. See above under content of the application.

**2–360** **Language of filing determines the language of proceedings**

Art.14(3)     The official language of the EPO in which a European patent application is filed or, in the case referred to in Art.14(2), that of the translation, is the language of the proceedings.

J7/80     The language of the description and claims is determinative.

Art.70(1)     The text of the application and corresponding patent in the language of the proceedings is the authentic text in all proceedings before the EPO and in the national phase.

Guidelines     See A/VIII/1.2.

**2–361** **Language of the proceedings to be used in all proceedings except where exceptions are provided for**

Art.14(3)     The language of the proceedings must be used in all proceedings before the EPO concerning the application or the resulting patent, unless otherwise provided in the Implementing Regulations.

**2–362** **Language to be used in written procedures - exceptions to the use of the language of the proceedings**

r.1(1)     In written proceedings before the EPO, any party may use any official language of the EPO.

T706/91     References to the application during opposition proceedings must be in the language of proceedings even if the opposition is drawn up in another official language (CLBA, p.506).

J18/90     The EPO may also use any official language in proceedings and decisions as long as the parties agree (CLBA, p.506). In reality the EPO uses the language of the proceedings.

Art.14(4)     The persons referred to in Art.14(2) may also file documents which have to be filed within a time limit in an official language of the Contracting State concerned. They must however, file a translation in the language of the proceedings within the time limit prescribed in the Implementing Regulations; in the cases provided for in the Implementing Regulations, they may file a translation in a different official language of the EPO.

Such a translation may be filed in any official language, except for amendments which must be in the language of the proceedings. r.1(1)

The translation must be filed within one month of the filing of the document. Where the document is a notice of opposition or an appeal this period is extended where appropriate to the end of the opposition period or appeal period, respectively. r.6(2)

A reduction (NB. reduction, not refund) in the examination fee, opposition fee or appeal fee is available to an applicant, proprietor or opponent who avails himself of the Art.14(4) option. The reduction is fixed in the RRF at a percentage of the total of the fees. r.6(3)

The reduction is 20 per cent. RRF12(1)

Headnote (1): "The persons referred to in Art.14(2) EPC are entitled to the fee reduction under r.6(3) EPC if they file the essential item of the first act in filing, examination or appeal proceedings in an official language of the state concerned other than English, French or German, and supply the necessary translation no earlier than simultaneously." See also CLBA, p.394. G6/91

Headnote (2): "The essential item of the first act in appeal proceedings is the notice of appeal, so to secure entitlement to the reduction in the appeal fee it suffices that said document be filed in a Contracting State official language which is not an official language of the EPO and translated into one of the latter languages, even if subsequent items such as the statement of grounds of appeal are filed only in an EPO official language."

The nationality/residency of the applicant is determinative, not that of the representative. T149/85

If any document, other than those making up a European patent application, is not filed in the language prescribed by the EPC, or if any translation required by virtue of the EPC is not filed in due time, the document is deemed not to have been received. Any fees paid are refunded (T193/87). Art.14(5)

Documents that are to be used for the purposes of evidence before the EPO, particularly publications, may be filed in any language. However, the EPO may require that a translation be filed, within a given time limit of not less than one month, in one of its official languages. r.1(3)

See A/VIII/2. Guidelines

### Language to be used in oral procedings—exceptions to the use of the language of the proceedings

2–363

If the parties and the EPO agree, any language may be used in oral proceedings. r.2(4)

Any party to oral proceedings before the EPO may, in lieu of the language of the proceedings, use one of the other official languages of the EPO, on condition either that such party gives notice to the EPO at least one month before the date laid down for such oral proceedings or makes provision for interpreting into the language of the proceedings. r.2(1)

A party asking for translation three days before the proceedings was made to pay for that translation. T473/92

Any party may likewise use one of the official languages of the Contracting States, on condition that he makes provision for interpretation into the language of the proceedings. The EPO may permit derogations from the provisions of this paragraph. r.2(1)

| | |
|---|---|
| AnReg | See under r.2(1) and Art.116. Parties are discouraged from making requests for interpretation in oral proceedings where possible ([1994] O.J. 583). A separate request must be made before an appeal hearing where a request has already been made before first instance proceedings ([1995] O.J. 489). See also CLBA, p.506 (T34/90). |
| r.2(2) | In the course of oral proceedings, the employees of the EPO may, in lieu of the language of the proceedings, use one of the other official languages of the EPO. |
| r.2(3) | In the case of taking evidence, any party to be heard, witness or expert, who is unable to express himself adequately in one of the official languages of the EPO or the Contracting States may use another language. Should the taking of evidence be decided upon following a request by a party to the proceedings then parties to be heard, witnesses or experts who express themselves in a language other than the official languages of the EPO may be heard only if the party who made the request makes provision for interpretation into the language of the proceedings; the EPO may, however, authorise interpretation into one of its other official languages. |
| r.2(5) | The EPO will, if necessary, make provision at its own expense for interpretation into the language of the proceedings, or, where appropriate, into its other official languages, unless this interpretation is the responsibility of one of the parties to the proceedings. |
| r.2(6) | Statements made by employees of the EPO, by parties to the proceedings and by witnesses and experts, made in one of the official languages of the EPO during oral proceedings will be entered in the minutes in the language employed. Statements made in any other language are entered in the official language into which they are translated. Amendments to the text of the description or claims of a European patent application or European patent will be entered in the minutes in the language of the proceedings. |
| Guidelines | See E/V/1–6. |

## 2–364 Certification of translated documents

| | |
|---|---|
| r.5 | Where a translation of any document must be filed, the EPO may require the filing of a certificate that the translation corresponds to the original text within a period to be determined by it. Failure to file such a certificate in due time will lead to the document being deemed not to have been received unless the EPC provides otherwise. |
| Guidelines | See A/VIII/6. |

## 2–365 Language of publication of applications, patents, the Bulletin, the Official Journal and entries in the Register

| | |
|---|---|
| Art.14(6) | European patent applications are published in the language of the proceedings. |
| Art.14(7) | The specifications of European patents are published in the language of the proceedings; they include a translation of the claims in the two other official languages of the EPO. |
| Art.14(8) | There are published in the three official languages of the EPO:<br><br>(a) the European Patent Bulletin;<br>(b) the Official Journal of the EPO. |
| Art.14(9) | Entries in the Register of European Patents are made in the three official languages of the EPO. In cases of doubt, the entry in the language of the proceedings is authentic. |

## Languages of the Administrative Council

2–366

The languages used in the deliberations of the Administrative Council are English, French and German.

Art.31(1)

Documents submitted to the Administrative Council, and the minutes of its deliberations, are drawn up in the three languages mentioned in Art.31(1).

Art.31(2)

## 18. MISCELLANEOUS COMMON PROVISIONS

### Principles of interpretation relevant to the EPC

2–367

The Enlarged Board has indicated that the Vienna Convention should be used to help interpret the EPC even though it did not apply when the EPC was concluded. The relevant principles of Arts 31 and 32 of the Vienna Convention are:

G5/83

(a) the EPC should be interpreted in good faith;

(b) unless it is established that the Contracting States intended a particular meaning should be given to a term, the terms of the EPC should be given their ordinary meaning in their context and in light of the object and purpose of the EPC;

(c) that context is the text of the EPC (including preamble, regulations and Protocols);

(d) also to be taken into account are any subsequent agreement between the parties regarding the interpretation or application of the provisions, any subsequent practice which establishes the agreement of the parties regarding interpretation and any relevant rules of public international law;

(e) the preparatory documents and the circumstances of the conclusion of the EPC may be taken into consideration in order to confirm the meaning resulting from the application of the previous rules or to determine the meaning when applying those rules either leaves the meaning ambiguous/obscure or leads to a manifestly absurd or unreasonable result.

The Implementing Regulations, the Protocol on Recognition, the Protocol on Privileges and Immunities, the Protocol on Centralisation and the Protocol on Interpretation of Art.69 are integral parts of the EPC.

Art.164(1)

In the case of conflict between the provisions of the EPC and those of the Implementing Regulations, the provisions of the EPC prevail.

Art.164(2)

See pages 399 to 401.

CLBA

### Rules relating to documents filed subsequently to the filing of the application

#### *Where to file subsequent documents*

2–368

See under r.24(1). The EPO notice published at [2005] O.J. 44 provides general guidance on the filing of applications and subsequent documentation. All subsequent documents must be filed at one of the EPO filing offices (Munich, the Hague and Berlin). Documents filed with the German patent office (except by hand), in Berlin or Munich, used to be considered as received on behalf of the EPO and forwarded directly. Payments by post fell within this safeguard but not payments to a GPO account which were refunded. Notices of opposition, even filed by fax, were also included. See [1991] O.J. 187. However, the agreement has been terminated as of September 1, 2005 and now any subsequent document is only given the date it actually arrives at the EPO.

AnReg

| | |
|---|---|
| G5/88 | See under section on filing of application for this case where a notice of opposition was filed at the German Patent Office in Berlin on the last day of the opposition period but was accepted as filed in time at the EPO. |

## 2–369 *Means of communication*

| | |
|---|---|
| r.36(5) | The President of the EPO may allow other means of communication in spite of the provisions of r.36(2) to (4) and provide regulations for their use. In particular, he may require written communication within a time limit or the documents will be deemed not to have been received. |
| AnReg | See under r.24(1). The notice published at [2005] O.J. 41 allows the filing of subsequent documents by facsimile, except for authorisations and priority documents which must be filed in writing, by post or by hand. Subsequent documents may no longer be filed by telegram or telex. The applicant may be invited to file a confirmation copy but this is not routinely required. E-mail should not be used as it has no legal force ([1999] O.J. 509; [2000] O.J. 458). From December 3, 2003, all documents other than priority documents may also be filed electronically in grant proceedings. This does not apply to opposition or appeal proceedings. See [2003] O.J. 609. |
| Guidelines | See A/IX/2.5. |

## 2–370 *Language of subsequent documents*

See under the section on languages above.

## 2–371 *Rules relating to content and form*

| | |
|---|---|
| r.36(1) | As far as documents replacing documents making up a European patent application are concerned, the following rules apply: |

    r.27 Content of the description

    r.29 Form and content of claims

    r.32 Form of drawings

    r.33 Form and content of the abstract

    r.34 Prohibited matter

    r.35 General provisions concerning presentation.

As far as the translations of the claims referred to in r.51 are concerned, the provisions of r.35(2) to (14) apply.

| | |
|---|---|
| r.36(2) | All documents must normally be type-written or printed. A margin of about 2.5 cm must be left on the left-hand side of the page. |

## 2–372 *Need for a signature*

| | |
|---|---|
| r.36(3) | All documents, with the exception of annexed documents, filed after the filing of a European patent application must be signed. If a document has not been signed, the EPO will invite the party concerned to do so within a time limit specified by the EPO. If signed in due time, the document will retain its original date of receipt; otherwise, it will be deemed not to have been received. |
| CLBA | See CLBA, p.341. |
| Guidelines | See A/IX/3. |

## 2–373 *Number of copies*

| | |
|---|---|
| r.36(4) | Such documents as must be communicated to other persons or as relate to two or more European patent applications or European patents must be filed in a sufficient number |

of copies. If the party concerned does not comply with this obligation in spite of a request from the EPO, the missing copies will be provided by the EPO at the expense of the party concerned.

See A/IX/2.4.    Guidelines

## Withdrawal of applications, patents, designations, priority claims, oppositions and appeals

### *Withdrawal of an application*    2–374

An application may be withdrawn any time before grant but the withdrawal must be unambiguous and unqualified (J11/87, J11/80). The withdrawal is binding in the interests of legal certainty and no further processing or retraction is possible (see AnReg, legal advice 8/80, [1981] O.J. 6) though a withdrawal, if mistaken, may be corrected under r.88 in certain circumstances (see J4/97). Generally speaking, once the withdrawal has been notified to the public, through publication in the European Patent Bulletin or via the Register of European patents, correction is no longer possible (J4/97, J25/03).    Case law

See also under publication.    CLBA

See CLBA, pp.344–350.    r.92(m)

Withdrawal is recorded in the Register and published in the Bulletin under Art.129(a).    Art.67(4)

When an application is withdrawn it is deemed that no protection existed under Art.64.    Art.79(3)

Withdrawal of the designation of all the Contracting States is deemed to be a withdrawal of the European patent application.

Applications may not, however, be withdrawn during a period of suspension following entitlement proceedings.    r.14

### *Withdrawal of part of the subject matter of an application*    2–375

Claims may be seen to be irrevocably abandoned if they are deleted and no phrase such as "without prejudice to the filing of a divisional application" is used (J15/85). This applies to any subject matter abandoned (T61/85), e.g. by deletion before grant (T1149/97). However, according to T123/85, when a request is made in opposition proceedings to maintain the patent in amended form, this does not represent abandonment of any of the subject matter of the claims as granted.    Case law

### *Withdrawal of a designation*    2–376

The designation of a Contracting State may be withdrawn at any time up to the grant of the European patent.    Art.79(3)

Withdrawal of the designation of all the Contracting States is deemed to be a withdrawal of the European patent application.    Art.79(3)

Designations may not, however, be withdrawn during a period of suspension following entitlement proceedings.    r.14

### *Withdrawal of a priority claim*    2–377

See C/V/3.5. Priority claims may be withdrawn at any time and publication will be delayed in appropriate circumstances.    Guidelines

### *Withdrawal of an opposition*    2–378

See under opposition section.

| | |
|---|---|
| 2–379 | ***Withdrawal of an appeal*** |
| | See under appeal section. |
| 2–380 | ***Withdrawal of a patent*** |
| | A patent will be revoked if no text is approved in opposition proceedings (e.g. T73/84). Alternatively, the proprietor can simply request revocation (T92/88). |

**Renewal fees**

| | |
|---|---|
| 2–381 | ***Years in respect of which renewal fees are due*** |
| Art.86(1) | Renewal fees are due in respect of the third year and each subsequent year, calculated from the date of filing of the application. |
| RRF2(4) | Renewal fees are 400 euros for the third year, 425 euros for the fourth year, 450 euros for the fifth year, 745 euros for the sixth year, 770 euros for the seventh year, 800 euros for the eighth year, 1010 euros for the ninth year and 1065 euros for the tenth and each subsequent year. |
| Art.86(4) | The obligation to pay renewal fees terminates with the payment of the renewal fee due in respect of the year in which the mention of the grant of the European patent is published. |
| 2–382 | ***Due date and period for payment of renewal fees*** |
| Art.86(1) | Renewal fees are paid in accordance with the Implementing Regulations. |
| r.37(1) | Renewal fees in respect of the coming year are due on the last day of the month containing the anniversary of the filing date of a European patent application. They may not be validly paid more than one year before they fall due. |
| AnReg | See under r.37(1). Guidance is given as to when EPO and national renewal fees are due ([1980] O.J. 101; [1984] O.J. 272). |
| Guidelines | See A/XI/4.2.4. |
| 2–383 | ***Grace period for late payment*** |
| Art.86(2) | When a renewal fee has not been paid on or before the due date, the fee may be validly paid within six months of the said date, provided that an additional fee is paid at the same time. |
| RRF2(5) | The additional fee is 10 per cent of the belated renewal fee. |
| r.37(2) | As long as the additional fee is paid within the six-month period it will be deemed paid "at the same time". |
| AnReg | See legal advice 5/93 on the calculation of aggregate time limits ([1993] O.J. 229). This advice followed J4/91 in which it was decided that the six-month period ended on the last day of the sixth month from the month in which the renewal fee fell due. |
| J12/84 | The applicant is informed of the period for later payment but may not invoke the lack of such a communication (see also J1/89). |
| 2–384 | ***Consequences of non-payment*** |
| Art.86(3) | If the renewal fee (accompanied by any additional fee where necessary) is not paid in due time the European patent application is deemed withdrawn. The EPO alone is competent to decide this. |

## Provisions in respect of divisional applications   2–385

Renewal fees already due in respect of an earlier application up to the date on which a divisional application is filed must also be paid for the divisional application and fall due when the divisional application is filed. These fees and any renewal fee falling due within a period of four months from the filing date of the divisional application may be paid without an additional fee within that period (the one-year *restitutio* period will be from the end of the four-month period). If payment is not made in due time, the renewal fees may still be validly paid within six months of the due date, provided that the additional fee under Art.86(2) is paid at the same time.   r.37(3)

See legal advice 5/93 on the calculation of aggregate time limits ([1993] O.J. 229).   AnReg

See A/IV/1.4.3.   Guidelines

## Provisions in respect of replacement applications   2–386

Renewal fees are not due for a new application filed pursuant to Art.61(1)(b) in respect of the year in which it was actually filed and any preceding year.   r.37(4)

## Refund of a renewal fee   2–387

A renewal fee will be refunded if the application is withdrawn before the due date (see Guidelines A/XI/10.1.1).   Guidelines

### Assignment, licensing and other property transactions

## Transfer and constitution of rights   2–388

A European patent application may be transferred or give rise to rights for one or more of the designated Contracting States.   Art.71

See E/XIII.   Guidelines

## Assignment   2–389

An assignment of a European patent application must be made in writing and requires the signatures of the parties to the contract.   Art.72

## Contractual licensing   2–390

A European patent application may be licensed in whole or in part for the whole or part of the territories of the designated Contracting States.   Art.73

## Law applicable   2–391

Unless otherwise specified in the EPC, a European patent application as an object of property is, in each designated Contracting State and with effect for such State, subject to the law applicable in that State to national patent applications.   Art.74

## Registration of a transfer of an application or a patent   2–392

A transfer of a European patent application (or patent during opposition proceedings or the opposition period—see r.61) will be recorded in the Register of European patents at the request of an interested party and on production of documents satisfying the EPO that the transfer has taken place.   r.20(1)

No entry is made in the register prior to publication of the application.   Art.127

| | |
|---|---|
| r.20(2) | The request will not be deemed to have been filed until such time as an administrative fee has been paid. It may be rejected only in the event of failure to comply with the conditions laid down in r.20(1). |
| RRF3(1) | The amount of the administrative fee is fixed by the President of the EPO. |
| AnReg | See under RRF. The amount is 80 Euros ([2006] O.J. 255). |
| r.20(3) | A transfer has effect *vis-à-vis* the EPO only when and to the extent that the documents referred to in r.20(1) have been produced. |

**2–393** **Registration of the grant or transfer of a licence and other transactions relating to a patent application**

| | |
|---|---|
| r.21(1) | The provisions of r.20 (registration of a transfer) apply equally to the grant or transfer of a licence, the establishment or transfer of a right *in rem* (e.g. a security right) in respect of a European patent application and any legal means of execution of such an application. Rule 61 only applies to the transfer of a patent so this provision (r.21(1)) does not apply to patents, only applications. |
| r.21(2) | In respect of the rights recorded under r.21(1), the registration may be cancelled upon request, which will not be deemed to be filed until an administrative fee has been paid. Such request must be supported either by documents establishing that the right has lapsed, or by a declaration whereby the proprietor of the right consents to the cancellation of the registration; it may be rejected only if these conditions are not fulfilled. |
| RRF3(1) | The amount of the administrative fee is fixed by the President of the EPO. |
| AnReg | See under RRF. The amount is 80 euros ([2006] O.J. 255). |
| r.22(1) | A licence in respect of a European patent application will be recorded in the Register as an exclusive licence if the applicant and the licensee so require. |
| r.22(2) | A licence in respect of a European patent application will be recorded in the Register as a sub-licence where it is granted by a licensee whose licence is recorded in the said Register. |
| CLBA | See CLBA, pp.396–397. |

**2–394** **Observations by third parties**

| | |
|---|---|
| Art.115(1) | Following the publication of a European patent application, any person may present observations concerning the patentability of the invention in respect of which the application has been filed. Such observations must be filed in writing and must include a statement of the grounds on which they are based. That person does not become a party to the proceedings before the EPO. |
| Art.115(2) | The observations referred to in Art.115(1) are communicated to the applicant for or proprietor of the patent who may comment on them. |
| r.1(1) | Third party observations must be filed in an EPO official language since Art.14(4) does not apply—they are not a document to be filed within a time limit. |
| CLBA | See CLBA, p.510—such a person is not party to the proceedings. Observations may be filed in examination or opposition proceedings and are considered by the EPO under Art.114(1) as a matter of discretion. |
| Guidelines | See E/VI/3. |

## Notification by the EPO

### *Subject matter of notifications* 2–395

The EPO must, as a matter of course, notify those concerned of decisions and summonses, and of any notice or other communication from which a time limit is reckoned, or of which those concerned must be notified under other provisions of the EPC, or of which notification has been ordered by the President of the EPO.

Art.119

### *Form of notification* 2–396

In proceedings before the EPO, notification must be in the form of either:

r.77(1)

(a) the original document;

(b) a copy of the original document certified by or bearing the seal of the EPO; or

(c) a computer print-out bearing the seal of the EPO.

Copies of documents emanating from the parties themselves do not require such certification.

### *Person to whom notification is made* 2–397

See under r.78. Where no representative is appointed, the notification will be made to the applicant who may specify an address for service different from the address recorded in the register and the published application ([1980] O.J. 397).

AnReg

If a representative has been appointed, notification will be addressed to him.

r.81(1)

Thus, where a representative has been appointed and notification is made to the applicant, notification only occurs when the representative receives the relevant document.

T703/92

If several such representatives have been appointed for a single interested party, notification may be made to any of them.

r.81(2)

If several interested parties have a common representative, notification of a single document to the common representative will be sufficient.

r.81(3)

See CLBA, p.398.

CLBA

See E/I/2.4.

Guidelines

### *Notification by post—deemed notification on the 10th day following posting* 2–398

Notification may be made by post.

r.77(2)(a)

Decisions incurring a time limit for appeal, summonses and other documents specified by the President of the EPO must be notified by registered letter with advice of delivery.

r.78(1)

All other notifications by post must be by registered letter.

r.78(1)

Where notification is by registered letter (with or without advice of delivery) the addressee will be deemed to have received the notification on the tenth day following its posting, unless the letter has failed to reach the addressee or has reached him at a later date. In the case of a dispute, the EPO bears the burden of proving that the letter reached its destination or to establish the date on which the letter was delivered to the addressee, as the case may be.

r.78(2)

Notification by registered letter (with or without advice of delivery) will be deemed to have been effected even if acceptance of the letter has been refused.

r.78(3)

| | |
|---|---|
| r.78(4) | To the extent that notification by post is not covered by these provisions (r.78(1) to (3)) the law of the state on the territory of which the notification is made will apply. |
| CLBA | See CLBA, p.398. |
| Guidelines | See E/I/2.3. |

### 2–399 Notification by delivery by hand

| | |
|---|---|
| r.77(2)(b) | Notification may be made by delivery on the premises of the EPO. |
| r.79 | Such notification is by delivery by hand of the document to the addressee who must acknowledge receipt on delivery. Notification will be deemed to have taken place even if the addressee refuses to accept the document or acknowledge receipt of it. |

### 2–400 Notification by public notice

| | |
|---|---|
| r.77(2)(c) | Notification may be made by public notice. |
| r.80(1) | However, such notification may only be made where the address of the addressee cannot be established or if notification by post in accordance with r.78(1) has proved to be impossible, even after a second attempt by the EPO. |
| r.80(2) | The President of the EPO determines how the public notice is to be given and the beginning of the period of one month on the expiry of which the document will be deemed to have been notified. |
| AnReg | See under r.80. The President has decided that public notification should occur via the Bulletin ([1980] O.J. 36). |

### 2–401 Notification by technical means

| | |
|---|---|
| r.77(2)(d) | Notification may be made by technical means of communication as determined by the President of the EPO and under the conditions laid down by him governing their use. |

### 2–402 Notification through the central industrial property office of a Contracting State

| | |
|---|---|
| Art.119 | Notifications may, where exceptional circumstances so require, be given through the intermediary of the central industrial property offices of the Contracting States. |
| r.77(3) | Such notification must be made in accordance with the provisions that apply to that office in national proceedings. |

### 2–403 Irregularities in notifications

| | |
|---|---|
| r.82 | Where a document has reached the addressee, if the EPO is unable to prove that it has been duly notified, or if provisions relating to its notification have not been observed, the document will be deemed to have been notified on the date established by the EPO as the date of receipt. |
| Guidelines | See E/I/2.5. |

### 2–404 Notification of loss of rights

| | |
|---|---|
| r.69(1) | If the EPO notes that the loss of any right results from the EPC, without any decision concerning the refusal of the European patent application or the grant, revocation or maintenance of the European patent, or the taking of evidence, it will communicate this to the person concerned in accordance with Art.119. |
| CLBA | See CLBA, p.375. |

See E/VIII/1.9. Guidelines

## *Communications and notices to be signed and identify author*   2–405

Any decision, communication and notice from the EPO is to be signed by and to state the name of the employee responsible. r.70(1)

Where such documents are produced by the employee responsible using a computer, a seal may replace the signature. Where the documents are produced automatically by a computer, the employee's name may also be dispensed with. The same applies to pre-printed notices and communications. r.70(2)

See E/I/1.3. Guidelines

## Decisions

### *Decisions only to be based on grounds/evidence on which the parties have had an opportunity to comment*   2–406

The decisions of the EPO may only be based on grounds or evidence on which the parties concerned have had an opportunity to present their comments. Art.113(1)

Headnote (1): "A decision against a party who has been duly summoned but who fails to appear at oral proceedings may not be based on facts put forward for the first time during those oral proceedings." G4/92

Headnote (2): "Similarly, new evidence may not be considered unless it has been previously notified and it merely supports the assertions of the party who submits it, whereas new arguments may in principle be used to support the reasons for the decision."

By deciding to take no further part in proceedings a party forfeits his right under Art.113(1). T892/94

See CLBA, pp.216–270 for general comment and CLBA, pp.268–270 on the application of G4/92 in practice. See also CLBA, pp.426–428 for the effect of Art.113(1) on the need for a further examination report under Art.96(2). See CLBA, pp.450–458 for application of Art.113(1) in opposition proceedings. CLBA

See E/X/I. Guidelines

### *Applicant or proprietor to agree text decided on—auxiliary requests*   2–407

The EPO can consider and decide upon a European patent application or a European patent only in the text submitted to it, or agreed, by the applicant for or proprietor of the patent. Art.113(2)

See legal advice 11/82. Where a proprietor withdraws his approval of the text the patent will be revoked ([1982] O.J. 57). See also T73/84 and Guidelines D/VI/2. See also legal advice 15/05 (rev.2) [2005] O.J. 357. Auxiliary requests are possible in examination and opposition. AnReg

See CLBA, pp.270–271 *re* decisions. See CLBA, pp.342–343 *re* auxiliary requests. An auxiliary request is a request for amendment contingent on a main or preceding request being held unallowable (T169/96). The EPO is bound by auxiliary requests and their order such that when granting an auxiliary request, reasons must be given for the rejection of all preceding requests (T234/86). This applies equally where an auxiliary request forms the basis for a r.51(4) communication. The communication must give reasons for the non-allowance of the main and any earlier auxiliary request (T1255/04). CLBA

| | |
|---|---|
| Guidelines | See E/X/3 and D/VI/15. |

## 2–408 Form of decisions

| | |
|---|---|
| r.68(1) | Where oral proceedings are held before the EPO, the decision may be given orally. Subsequently the decision in writing will be notified to the parties. |
| T390/86 | The appeal period starts from the notification in writing (CLBA, p.383). |
| T666/90 | A disparity between the oral and written decision represents a substantial procedural violation (CLBA, p.384). See also T425/97. |
| RPBA Art.7(1) | Where the composition of the Board of Appeal is changed after oral proceedings any party may request fresh oral proceedings. |
| r.68(2) | Decisions of the EPO which are open to appeal must be reasoned and accompanied by a written communication of the possibility of appeal. The communication must also draw the attention of the parties to the provisions laid down in Art.106 to Art.108, the text of which must be attached. However, the parties may not invoke the omission of the communication (i.e. omission does not on its own invalidate the decision). |
| | Decisions pronounced orally do not have to be reasoned but the written confirmation must be. |
| J8/81 | Whether a document is a decision or a communication is a matter of substance rather than form (CLBA, p.383). See also T42/84. |
| T278/00 | A lack of proper reasoning in a decision, which is, for instance, inconsistent, amounts to a substantial procedural violation. |
| CLBA | See CLBA, pp.384–387 for cases contesting whether a decision was "reasoned" or not. A reasoned decision must be given in respect of both main and auxiliary requests. |
| r.66(2) | See also under appeal for the requirements for a decision of a Board of Appeal. |
| Guidelines | See E/III/9 and E/X/4. |

## 2–409 The finality of a decision

| | |
|---|---|
| T390/86 | Once a decision is taken it is final and binding and can only be changed by the filing of an appeal or correction under r.89 (see also G4/91 and T212/88). |
| G12/91 | Headnote: "The decision-making process following written proceedings is completed on the date the decision to be notified is handed over to the EPO postal service by the decision-taking department's formalities section." |
| | On this date the Examining or Opposition Division no longer have the power to change their minds. It corresponds to the moment in oral proceedings where debate is closed and the parties may no longer submit anything further. Further amendments or comments will therefore not be taken into account after this date. |
| T713/02 | A decision during the grant procedure which does not terminate it (e.g. a decision to allow the correction of a priority claim) does not become final until the final decision to grant or refuse is taken. |

## 2–410 Obtaining a decision after the EPO has notified a loss of rights

| | |
|---|---|
| r.69(2) | Where the EPO has communicated a loss of rights to the EPO under Art.69(1), and the person concerned considers that the finding of the EPO is inaccurate, he may, within two months after notification of the Art.69(1) communication, apply for a decision on the matter by the EPO. Such decision will be given only if the EPO does not |

share the opinion of the person requesting it; otherwise the EPO will inform the person requesting the decision.

The loss of rights becomes final if the time limit is missed. G1/90

See legal advice 16/85 for information on the loss of rights and the request for a decision ([1985] O.J. 141). AnReg

See CLBA, pp.375 and 393 (*re* formalities officer). CLBA

See E/VIII/1.9.3. Guidelines

### *Decisions to be signed and identify author* — 2–411

Any decision, communication and notice from the EPO must be signed by and state the name of the employee responsible. r.70(1)

Where such documents are produced by the employee responsible using a computer, a seal may replace the signature. Where the documents are produced automatically by a computer, the employee's name may also be dispensed with. The same applies to pre-printed notices and communications. r.70(2)

Where the composition of an Opposition Division changes after oral proceedings, so that the decision cannot be signed by the original members of the division, new oral proceedings should generally be appointed. See also, CLBA, pp.376–378. T862/98

A decision was set aside as nul and void where it was not clear from the public part of the file that a member of the Examining Division had signed or at least approved the decision before leaving the board (CLBA, p.376). T714/92

However, if, following oral proceedings, a member of a division is prevented from signing the written decision by incapacity, another member can sign on his behalf. T243/87

See CLBA, pp.387–388. CLBA

See E/X/4.1. Guidelines

### *Notification of decisions* — 2–412

The EPO must, as a matter of course, notify those concerned of decisions. Art.119

### *Correction of errors in decisions* — 2–413

See section on amendment and correction. r.89

### *Interlocutory decisions* — 2–414

See under sections on opposition and appeal. Art.106(3)

### **Examination by the EPO of its own motion** — 2–415

In proceedings before it, the EPO examines the facts of its own motion; it is not be restricted in this examination to the facts, evidence and arguments provided by the parties and the relief sought. Art.114(1)

See CLBA, p.474 for prior use allegations. See CLBA, pp.517–518 *re* appeal proceedings where this provision is somewhat restricted. CLBA

See E/VI/1. Guidelines

| | |
|---|---|
| **2–416** | **Facts and evidence submitted late may be ignored** |
| Art.114(2) | The EPO may disregard facts or evidence which are not submitted in due time by the parties concerned. |
| CLBA | See CLBA, pp.324–337. In general, late filed submissions may only be rejected if they do not have a decisive impact on the proceedings or, regardless of their relevance, they are an abuse of procedure (e.g. T17/91). |
| r.71a(1) | This specific provision in oral proceedings is also relevant—see section below. |
| Guidelines | See E/VI/2. |

**Oral proceedings**

| | |
|---|---|
| **2–417** | ***Extent of the right to oral proceedings*** |
| Art.116(1) | Oral proceedings will take place either at the instance of the EPO if it considers this to be expedient or at the request of any party to the proceedings. However, the EPO may reject a request for further oral proceedings before the same department where the parties and the subject of the proceedings are the same. |
| Art.116(2) | Nevertheless, oral proceedings will take place before the Receiving Section at the request of the applicant only where the Receiving Section considers this to be expedient or where it envisages refusing the European patent application (the refusal must be pursuant to Art.91(3), a decision under Art.69(2) following the loss of rights not counting ([1985] O.J. 159)). |
| CLBA | See CLBA, pp.271–285. |
| T299/86 | A request for oral proceedings must be unambiguous (CLBA, p.272). Reserving the right to oral proceedings is not sufficient. |
| T555/95 | A request for oral proceedings must be honoured at any time while proceedings are pending, i.e. up to the decision to grant or refuse (CLBA, p.443). |
| T34/90 | A fresh request is necessary in all new proceedings, e.g. at the appeal stage. |
| Guidelines | See E/III/2–4. |
| **2–418** | ***Summons to oral proceedings*** |
| r.71(1) | Parties are summoned to oral proceedings and their attention is drawn to r.71(2) (proceedings may be conducted in the absence of a summoned party who does not turn up). Unless the parties agree to a shorter period, at least two months notice of the oral proceedings must be given (though some exceptions to the two-month minimum exist, e.g. J14/91, where the subject of the oral proceedings would have been irrelevant after publication). |
| AnReg | See under Art.116. A single date is selected which may be changed only in exceptional circumstances ([2000] O.J. 456). See also J79/99 (CLBA, p.287) and Guidelines E/III/7. See also under r.71. The summons is by registered letter and contains a white acknowledgement card which recipients are encouraged to use ([1991] O.J. 577). |
| Guidelines | See D/VI/3.2 (*re* opposition) and E/III/6. |
| **2–419** | ***Consequence of summoned party not turning up*** |
| r.71(2) | Oral proceedings may continue in the absence of a party who has been summoned but does not appear. |

Where a party says that they will not turn up this is interpreted as a withdrawal of a request for oral proceedings. — T3/90

A late decision not to attend may lead to an award of costs in opposition proceedings (see also T338/90). — T930/92

Headnote (1): "A decision against a party who has been duly summoned but who fails to appear at oral proceedings may not be based on facts put forward for the first time during those oral proceedings." — G4/92

Headnote (2): "Similarly, new evidence may not be considered unless it has been previously notified and it merely supports the assertions of the party who submits it, whereas new arguments may in principle be used to support the reasons for the decision."

A proprietor who chooses not to be present at oral proceedings should ensure that he has filed all amendments that he wishes to be considered. Here, the main request was seen to lack inventive step and all auxiliary requests to lack clarity. In the absence of the proprietor to agree an acceptable text under Art.113(2) EPC the patent was revoked. — T986/00

See E/III/8.3. — Guidelines

## *Preparation for oral proceedings by the parties* — 2–420

When issuing the summons to oral proceedings, the EPO will draw attention to the points which in its opinion need to be discussed for the purposes of the decision to be taken. — r.71a(1)

At the same time, a final date for making written submissions in preparation for the oral proceedings will be fixed. Rule 84 does not apply (i.e. there is no two-month minimum, nor four-month maximum and the date cannot be extended). New facts and evidence presented after that date need not be considered, unless admitted on the grounds that the subject of the proceedings has changed.

Headnote: "Rule 71a(1) EPC does not apply to the Boards of Appeal." — G6/95

The rules of procedure of the Boards of Appeal make the communication provided for in r.71a(1) optional, depending on the facts of the case (Art.11(2) RPBA). Such rules of procedure were adopted by the Presidium under Art.23(4) and approved by the Administrative Council. The Enlarged Board decided that the Administrative Council must be presumed to know the limits of its own power and that it therefore did not intend to amend r.71 EPC so as to conflict with the RPBA (Art.164(2) makes the provisions of the EPC superior to the provisions of the Implementing Regulations).

Where a response is filed to the summons to oral proceedings including good faith responsive amendments and arguments, the summons is not suspended and the oral proceedings will, in principle, go ahead. The Examining Division is not under a duty to confirm that the summons remains valid. — T1183/02

See CLBA, p.592. In *inter partes* proceedings, any communication must be impartial (T173/89). — CLBA

If the applicant or proprietor has been notified of the grounds prejudicing the grant or maintenance of the patent, he may be invited to submit, by the date for making written submissions, documents which meet the requirements of the EPC. Rule 84 does not apply (sets limits on what EPO may set as a time limit). New documents presented after that date need not be considered, unless admitted on the grounds that the subject of the proceedings has changed. — r.71a(2)

Clearly allowable amendments overcoming the outstanding objections should always be admitted. The subject of the proceedings may change e.g. where the Examining Division has introduced a new document during oral proceedings. — T951/97

| | |
|---|---|
| T755/96 | If amended claims are not admitted then reasons must be given. |
| CLBA | See CLBA, pp.280–283. In particular, the EPO may still reject documents filed within the r.71a time limit if they are regarded as not submitted in due time (as required by Art.114(2)). There is more chance of admission in *ex parte* proceedings where no other party exists who might be taken by surprise. See also pages 324 to 337 on late submissions in general. |
| Guidelines | See D/VI/3.2 and E/III/6. |

## 2–421  *Extent to which oral proceedings are open to the public*

| | |
|---|---|
| Art.116(3) | Oral proceedings before the Receiving Section, the Examining Divisions and the Legal Division are not public. |
| Art.116(4) | Oral proceedings, including delivery of the decision, are public as regards the Boards of Appeal and the Enlarged Board of Appeal, after publication of the European patent application, and also before the Opposition Divisions, in so far as the department before which the proceedings are taking place does not decide otherwise in cases where the admission of the public could have serious and unjustified disadvantages, in particular for a party to the proceedings. |
| Guidelines | See E/III/8.1. |

## 2–422  *Procedure in oral proceedings*

| | |
|---|---|
| AnReg | See under Art.116. Recording devices are not allowed ([1986] O.J. 63). In oral proceedings before the Examining Division, a videoconference may be requested ([1997] O.J. 572). |
| G4/95 | Headnote (1): "During oral proceedings under Art.116 EPC in the context of opposition or opposition appeal proceedings, a person accompanying the professional representative of a party may be allowed to make oral submissions on specific legal or technical issues (including facts, evidence or argument) on behalf of that party, otherwise than under Art.117 EPC, in addition to the complete presentation of the party's case by the professional representative." |
| | Headnote (2): "(a) Such oral submissions cannot be made as a matter of right, but only with the permission of and under the discretion of the EPO. (b) The following main criteria should be considered by the EPO when exercising its discretion to allow the making of oral submissions by an accompanying person in opposition or opposition appeal proceedings: (i) The professional representative should request permission for such oral submissions to be made. The request should state the name and qualifications of the accompanying person, and should specify the subject-matter of the proposed oral submissions. (ii) The request should be made sufficiently in advance of the oral proceedings so that all opposing parties are able properly to prepare themselves in relation to the proposed oral submissions. (iii) A request which is made shortly before or at the oral proceedings should in the absence of exceptional circumstances be refused, unless each opposing party agrees to the making of the oral submissions requested. (iv) The EPO should be satisfied that oral submissions by an accompanying person are made under the continuing responsibility and control of the professional representative. (c) No special criteria apply to the making of oral submissions by qualified patent lawyers of countries which are not Contracting States to the EPC." |
| G2/94 | Headnote (1): "A Board of Appeal has a discretion to allow an accompanying person (who is not entitled under Art.134(1) or (7) EPC to represent parties in proceedings before the EPO) to make submissions during oral proceedings in ex parte proceedings, in addition to the complete presentation of a party's case by the professional representative." |

Headnote (2): "(a) In *ex parte* proceedings a professional representative should request permission for the making of such oral submissions in advance of the day appointed for oral proceedings. The request should state the name and qualifications of the person for whom permission is requested, and should specify the subject matter of the proposed oral submissions. The Board of Appeal should exercise its discretion in accordance with the circumstances of each individual case. The main criterion to be considered is that the Board should be fully informed of all relevant matters before deciding the case. The Board should be satisfied that the oral submissions are made by the accompanying person under the continuing responsibility and control of the professional representative. (b) During either *ex parte* or *inter partes* proceedings, a Board of Appeal should refuse permission for a former member of the boards of appeal to make oral submissions during oral proceedings before it, unless it is completely satisfied that a sufficient period of time has elapsed following termination of such former member's appointment to the boards of appeal, so that the Board of Appeal could not reasonably be suspected of partiality in deciding the case if it allowed such oral submissions to be made. A Board of Appeal should normally refuse permission for a former member of the Boards of Appeal to make oral submissions during oral proceedings before it, until at least three years have elapsed following termination of the former member's appointment to the boards of appeal. After three years have elapsed, permission should be granted except in very special circumstances."

At the end of oral proceedings a decision is usually announced before the Board of Appeal. — RPBA Art.11(3)

See E/III/8 and 9. — Guidelines

### *Minutes of oral proceedings*

2–423

The minutes of oral proceedings are drawn up containing the essentials of the oral proceedings, the relevant statements made by the parties, the testimony of the parties, witnesses or experts and the result of any inspection. — r.76(1)

The minutes of the testimony of a witness, expert or party must be read out or submitted to him so that he may examine them. It is noted in the minutes that this formality has been carried out and that the person who gave the testimony approved the minutes. If his approval is not given, his objections are noted. — r.76(2)

The minutes are authenticated by the employee who drew them up and by the employee who conducted the oral proceedings, either by their signature or by any other appropriate means. — r.76(3)

The parties are provided with a copy of the minutes. — r.76(4)

See CLBA, pp.283–284. — CLBA

See E/III/10. — Guidelines

## Taking of evidence

### *Forms of evidence available to the EPO*

2–424

In any proceedings before an Examining Division, an Opposition Division, the Legal Division or a Board of Appeal the means of giving or obtaining evidence include the following: — Art.117(1)

(a) hearing the parties;

(b) requests for information;

(c) the production of documents;

(d) hearing the witnesses;

(e) opinions by experts;

(f) inspection;

(g) sworn statements in writing.

J20/85     The Receiving Section may also take evidence (CLBA, p.353).

T798/93     All these means of gathering evidence are entirely at the discretion of the EPO and cannot be ordered by a party to proceedings (CLBA, p.354).

Guidelines     See E/IV/1.2.

### 2–425     *Principles to be applied when evaluating evidence*

T482/89     Unfettered evaluation of evidence applies to the department taking a decision (CLBA, p.354).

T182/89     The standard of proof to be applied in most cases, with notable exceptions (e.g. the allegation of public use by an opponent—T472/92, T97/94), is the balance of probabilities (CLBA, p.357).

T219/83     The burden of proof is always on the party asserting a particular fact. In opposition proceedings where there are contrary assertions and the truth can't easily be established by the EPO, the proprietor has the benefit of the doubt.

T474/04     If assertions made in an unsworn witness declaration remain contested, as a rule a request from a party to hear the witness must be granted before these assertions are made the basis of a decision against the contesting party.

Guidelines     See E/IV/4 for general comments on the evaluation of evidence.

### 2–426     *Decision to take oral evidence—choice of taking evidence before the EPO or a competent court*

r.72(1)     When the EPO decides it needs to hear oral evidence (either from parties, witnesses or experts) or to carry out an inspection, it will take a decision to that end, setting out the investigation which it intends to carry out, relevant facts to be proved and the date, time and place of the investigation.

r.72(1)     Where a party has requested the oral evidence of a witness or expert be heard, the decision of the EPO will determine the period of time within which the party making the request must make known to the EPO the names and addresses of the witnesses and experts whom it wishes to be heard.

Art.117(3)     If the EPO considers it necessary for a party, witness or expert to give evidence orally, it will either:

(a) issue a summons to the person concerned to appear before it, or

(b) request, in accordance with the provisions of Art.131(2) (submission of letters rogatory—see r.99), the competent court in the country of residence of the person concerned to take such evidence.

Guidelines     See D/VI/1 (*re* opposition) and E/IV/1.4.

### 2–427     *Procedure where oral evidence is to be heard before the EPO*

r.72(2)     Where a summons is issued at least two months notice to attend will be given unless the party, witness or expert agrees to a shorter period. The summons must contain:

(a) an extract from the decision indicating in particular the date, time and place of the investigation ordered and stating the facts regarding which parties, witnesses and experts are to be heard;

(b) the names of the parties to the proceedings and particulars of the rights which the witnesses or experts may invoke under the provisions of r.74(2) to (4) (reimbursement of expenses); and

(c) an indication that the party, witness or expert may request to be heard by the competent court of his country of residence and a requirement that he inform the EPO within a time limit to be fixed by the EPO whether he is prepared to appear before it.

A party, witness or expert who is summoned before the EPO may request the latter to allow his evidence to be heard by a competent court in his country of residence. On receipt of such a request, or if there has been no reply to the summons by the expiry of a period fixed by the EPO in the summons, the EPO may, in accordance with the provisions of Art.131(2) (submission of letters rogatory—see r.99), request the competent court to hear the person concerned. Art.117(4)

Before being heard, a party must be reminded that a request may be made by the EPO for the evidence to be re-heard under oath or in an equally binding form. r.72(3)

If a party, witness or expert gives evidence before the EPO, the latter may, if it considers it advisable for the evidence to be given on oath or in an equally binding form, request the competent court in the country of residence of the person concerned to re-examine his evidence under such conditions. Art.117(5)

The parties may attend an investigation and put relevant questions to the testifying parties, witnesses and experts. r.72(4)

See E/IV/1.5–1.6. Guidelines

## *Procedure where oral evidence is to be heard before a competent court* 2–428

Upon receipt of letters rogatory from the EPO, the courts or other competent authorities of Contracting States must undertake, on behalf of that Office and within the limits of their jurisdiction, any necessary enquiries or other legal measures. Art.131(2)

When the EPO requests a competent court to take evidence, it may request the court to take the evidence on oath or in an equally binding form and to permit a member of the department concerned to attend the hearing and question the party, witness or expert either through the intermediary of the court or directly. Art.117(6)

Special provisions apply to the sending of letters rogatory by the EPO. r.99

See also Art.117(4), r.72(3) and Art.117(5) above.

See E/IV/3. Guidelines

## *Commissioning of one member of the Examining/Opposition Division or Board of Appeal to examine evidence adduced* 2–429

The Examining Division, Opposition Division or Board of Appeal may commission one of its members to examine the evidence adduced. Art.117(2)

## *The opinion of experts* 2–430

When it appoints an expert the EPO decides what form of report should be used. r.73(1)

The terms of reference of the expert must include: r.73(2)

502    Complete Guide to Passing the EQE

> (a) a precise description of his task;
>
> (b) the time limit laid down for the submission of the expert report;
>
> (c) the names of the parties to the proceedings; and
>
> (d) particulars of the rights which he may invoke under the provisions of r.74(2) to (4) (reimbursement of expenses).

r.73(3) — A copy of the written report is submitted to the parties.

r.73(4) — The parties may object to an expert. The department of the EPO concerned will decide on any objection.

Guidelines — See E/IV/1.8.

## 2–431 Costs of taking evidence

r.74(1) — The taking of evidence by the EPO may be made conditional upon deposit with the EPO, by the party requesting that the evidence be taken, of a sum the amount of which will be fixed by reference to an estimate of the costs.

r.74(2) — Witnesses and experts who are summoned by and appear before the EPO are entitled to appropriate reimbursement of expenses for travel and subsistence. An advance for these expenses may be granted to them.

r.74(2) — Witnesses and experts who appear before the EPO without being summoned by it and are heard as witnesses and experts are also entitled to appropriate reimbursement of expenses for travel and subsistence.

r.74(3) — All such witnesses entitled to reimbursement are also entitled to appropriate compensation for loss of earnings and all such experts entitled to reimbursement are also entitled to fees for their work. These payments are made after the witness or expert has fulfilled his duty or task.

r.74(4) — The details governing the implementation of Art.74(2) and Art.74(3) are laid down by the Administrative Council. Payments of amounts due are made by the EPO.

AnReg — See under r.74(4). The decision of the Administrative Council is given and discussed ([1983] O.J. 100).

Guidelines — See E/IV/1.9–1.10.

## 2–432 Conservation of evidence

r.75(1) — On request, the EPO may, without delay, hear oral evidence or conduct inspections, with a view to conserving evidence of facts liable to affect a decision which it may be called upon to take with regard to an existing European patent application or a European patent, where there is reason to fear that it might subsequently become more difficult or even impossible to take evidence. The date on which the measures are to be taken will be communicated to the applicant for or proprietor of the patent in sufficient time to allow him to attend. He may ask relevant questions.

r.75(2) — The request must contain:

> (a) the name and address of the person filing the request and the state in which his residence or principal place of business is located, in accordance with r.26(2)(c) (as for the request);
>
> (b) sufficient identification of the European patent application or European patent in question;

(c) the designation of the facts in respect of which evidence is to be taken;

(d) particulars of the way in which evidence is to be taken; and

(e) a statement establishing a prima facie case for fearing that it might subsequently become more difficult or impossible to take evidence.

The request will not be deemed to have been filed until the fee for conservation of evidence has been paid. r.75(3)

The fee for the conservation of evidence is 55 euros. RRF2(17)

The decision on the request and any resulting taking of evidence will be incumbent on the department of the EPO required to take the decision liable to be affected by the facts to be established. The provisions of the EPC with regard to the taking of evidence in proceedings before the EPO will be applicable. r.75(4)

See E/IV/2. Guidelines

## *Minutes of taking of evidence/inspection*     2–433

The minutes of the taking of evidence must be drawn up containing the essentials of the taking of evidence, the relevant statements made by the parties, the testimony of the parties, witnesses or experts and the result of any inspection. r.76(1)

The minutes of the testimony of a witness, expert or party must be read out or submitted to him so that he may examine them. It will be noted in the minutes that this formality has been carried out and that the person who gave the testimony approved the minutes. If his approval is not given, his objections will be noted. r.76(2)

The minutes must be authenticated by the employee who drew them up and by the employee who conducted the taking of evidence, either by their signature or by any other appropriate means. r.76(3)

The parties will be provided with a copy of the minutes. r.76(4)

See E/IV/1.7. Guidelines

## **Authentic text of a European patent or application**     2–434

The text of a European patent application or a European patent in the language of the proceedings is the authentic text in any proceedings before the EPO and in any Contracting State. Art.70(1)

However, in the case referred to in Art.14(2), the original text constitutes, in proceedings before the EPO, the basis for determining whether the subject matter of the application or patent extends beyond the content of the application as filed. Art.70(2)

Any Contracting State may provide that a translation, as provided for in the EPC, in an official language of that State, will in that State be regarded as authentic, except for revocation proceedings, in the event of the application or patent in the language of the translation conferring protection which is narrower than that conferred by it in the language of the proceedings. Art.70(3)

Any Contracting State which adopts a provision under Art.70(3): Art.70(4)

(a) must allow the applicant for or proprietor of the patent to file a corrected translation of the European patent application or European patent. Such corrected translation does not have any legal effect until any conditions established by the Contracting State under Art.65(2), and Art.67(3), have been complied with *mutatis mutandis*;

(b) may prescribe that any person who, in that State in good faith is using or has made effective and serious preparations for using an invention the use of which would not constitute infringement of the application or patent in the original translation may, after the corrected translation takes effect, continue such use in the course of his business or for the needs thereof without payment.

Guidelines        See A/VIII/5.

NatLaw            See Table V for national provisions relating to the authentic text.

## 2–435    Unity of a European patent application or European Patent

Art.118           Where the applicants for or proprietors of a European patent are not the same in respect of different designated Contracting States, they are regarded as joint applicants or proprietors for the purposes of proceedings before the EPO. The unity of the application or patent in these proceedings is not affected; in particular the text of the application or patent must be uniform for all designated Contracting States unless otherwise provided for in the EPC.

r.87              A European patent or patent application may contain different claims for different Contracting States and, where the EPO fells it is necessary, different descriptions and drawings as well, when:

(a) there is an earlier European patent application which is relevant under Art.54(3) to some of the Contracting States; or

(b) there is an earlier national prior right under Art.139(2).

r.16(2)           Where appropriate, a European patent application may contain, for the designated Contracting States in which a decision that the applicant is not entitled to be granted a patent has been taken or recognised, claims, a description and drawings which are different from those for the other designated Contracting States.

r.16(3)           Where a third party has, in accordance with Art.99(5), replaced the previous proprietor for one or some of the designated Contracting States, the patent as maintained in opposition proceedings may contain for these states claims, a description and drawings which are different from those for the other designated Contracting States.

CLBA              See CLBA, p.399—where the owner in respect of some states appeals an opposition decision successfully, the patent is maintained for all states.

Guidelines        See C/III/8.1 and 8.4 and D/VII/3.

## 2–436    Reference to the procedural law of the Contracting States

Art.125           In the absence of procedural provisions in the EPC, the EPO takes into account the principles of procedural law generally recognised in the Contracting States.

## 2–437    Termination of financial obligations

Art.126(1)        Rights of the Organisation to the payment of a fee to the EPO are extinguished after four years from the end of the calendar year in which the fee fell due.

r.91              The President of the EPO may waive action for the enforced recovery of any sum due if the sum to be recovered is minimal or if such recovery is too uncertain.

Rights against the Organisation for the refunding by the EPO of fees or sums of money paid in excess of a fee are extinguished after four years from the end of the calendar year in which the right arose.

Art.126(2)

The period laid down in Art.126(1) and (2) is interrupted in the case covered by Art.126(1) by a request for payment of the fee and in the case covered by Art.126(2) by a reasoned claim in writing. On interruption it begins again immediately and ends at the latest six years after the end of the year in which it originally began, unless, in the meantime, judicial proceedings to enforce the right have begun; in this case the period ends at the earliest one year after the judgement enters into force.

Art.126(3)

## 19. INFORMATION MADE AVAILABLE BY THE EPO

### The register of European patents

#### *Content of the register*

2–438

The EPO keeps a register, known as the Register of European Patents.

Art.127

The register has the following entries:

r.92(1)(2)

(a) the application number;

(b) the publication date of the application and, if appropriate, the later publication date of the search report;

(c) the publication date of the mention of the grant of the European patent;

(d) the filing date of the application;

(e) any priority data (date, state and file number of the previous application);

(f) the classification code assigned to the application;

(g) the Contracting States designated;

(h) the title of the invention;

(i) the family names, given names and address of the applicant(s) for or proprietor(s) of the European patent and the state(s) in which his/their residence or principal place of business is located, and if there are different applicants/ proprieters for different contracting states, the state(s) for which each is applicant/proprietor;

(j) the family names, given names and address of the inventor designated by the applicant for or the proprietor of the European patent, unless he has waived his right to be mentioned under r.18(1) EPC;

(k) the family name, given names and address of the place of business of the representative of the applicant for or proprietor of the patent referred to in Art.134; in the case where several representatives are appointed, this applies to the first named representative only and the words "and others" will be additionally entered; in the case of an association referred to in r.101(9), only the name and address of the association will be entered;

(l) the filing date of the request for examination;

(m) in the event of a division of an application, the numbers of the divisional applications;

(n) in the case of divisional applications and replacement applications filed under Art.61(1)(b), the number, filing date and priority data for the earlier application;

(o) the date on which the application is refused, withdrawn or deemed to be withdrawn;

(p) the date of lapse of the European patent in a Contracting State during the opposition period and, where appropriate, pending a final decision on opposition;

(q) the filing date of any opposition;

(r) the date and purport of a decision on an opposition;

(s) dates of suspension and resumption of proceedings in the cases referred to in r.13;

(t) dates of interruption and resumption of proceedings in the case referred to in r.90;

(u) any date of re-establishment of rights provided that an entry has been made in accordance with (o) or (r);

(v) the filing of a request to the EPO under Art.135 (conversion to national application);

(w) rights and transfer of rights over a European patent application or patent where these are recorded pursuant to the regulations;

(x) any other entry that the President of the EPO decided should be made. Currently this means the dates of dispatch of examination reports, the dates of any reply, the date of dispatch of the r.51(4) communication and the date of payment of the grant and printing fees, details of renewal fees due and when paid, details of any related divisional applications, identities of documents cited in the search report.

AnReg

See under Art.93. The register is updated promptly after the dates for paying designation fees and the grace period have expired ([1997] O.J. 479). Details of extension states are also included ([1997] O.J. 115). See also under r.92(2). An entry has been made since 1984 "no opposition filed" when the opposition period has expired with no notice of opposition filed and an entry has been made since 1984 "patent specification rectified on (date)" when errors have been rectified ([1983] O.J. 458).

2–439      *No entry in the register prior to publication of the application*

Art.127    No entry is made in the Register prior to the publication of a European patent application.

2–440      *Register to be open to the public*

Art.127    The Register is open to public inspection.

r.92(3)    Extracts of the register are available on payment of an administrative fee.

RRF3(1)    The amount of the administrative fee fixed by the President of the EPO.

AnReg      See under RRF. The amount is 25 euros ([2006] O.J. 255). See also under Art.127. The register may now be inspected via the internet ([2001] O.J. 249; [1995] O.J. 235). Holders of deposit accounts can get information on the balance from on-line inspection of the register ([1997] O.J. 576).

2–441      *Language of the register*

Art.14(3)  Entries are made in all three EPO official languages.

### Inspection of files relating to applications

2–442      *No inspection of files relating to unpublished application except where rights have been invoked*

Art.128(1) The files relating to European patent applications, which have not yet been published, are not available for inspection without the consent of the applicant.

Any person who can prove that the applicant for a European patent has invoked the rights under the application against him may obtain inspection of the files prior to the publication of that application and without the consent of the applicant. Art.128(2)

Inspection will be allowed where the European application has been invoked against somebody or a national application has been invoked and the European application has been mentioned. J14/91

See CLBA, p.395. CLBA

Where a European divisional application or a new European patent application filed under Art.61(1), is published, any person may obtain inspection of the files of the earlier application prior to the publication of that application and without the consent of the relevant applicant. Art.128(3)

Even prior to the publication of a European patent application, the EPO may communicate the following bibliographic data to third parties or publish them: Art.128(5)

(a) the number of the European patent application;

(b) the date of filing of the European patent application and, where the priority of a previous application is claimed, the date, State and file number of the previous application;

(c) the name of the applicant;

(d) the title of the invention;

(e) the Contracting States designated.

The President of the EPO decides on the details of when and how this provision (Art.128(5)) is carried out. r.96(1)

See A/XII. Guidelines

### *Inspection of files after publication of the application* — 2–443

Subsequent to the publication of a European patent application, the files relating to such application and the resulting European patent may be inspected on request, subject to the restrictions laid down in the Implementing Regulations. Art.128(4)

The parts that may not be inspected are: r.93

(a) the documents relating to the exclusion of or objections to members of the Boards of Appeal or of the Enlarged Board of Appeal;

(b) draft decisions and opinions, and all other documents, used for the preparation of decisions and opinions, which are not sent to the parties;

(c) the designation of the inventor, if he has waived the right to be mentioned under r.18(1); and

(d) any other document excluded from inspection by the President of the EPO on the ground that such inspection would not serve the purpose of informing the public about the European patent application or the resulting patent.

A party can ask for evidence submitted to be confidential and a decision is taken by the President. If the answer is no then the evidence is returned unexamined. T516/89

Documents filed in breach of confidentiality may also be returned. T760/89

See under r.93(d). The President has specified those documents that will be excluded under r.93(d) ([2001] O.J. 458). These include medical certificates, documents relating AnReg

| | to the issue of priority documents, file-inspection proceedings or the communication of information from the files, requests for exclusion from inspection and requests for accelerated procedure (PACE). |
|---|---|
| CLBA | See CLBA, p.396. |

## 2–444 Procedure for the inspection of files

| | |
|---|---|
| r.94(1) | The file may be inspected either in its original form, in the form of a copy or by technical means, if the files are stored in such a way. |
| r.94(2) | The President of the EPO determines all file inspection arrangements, including the circumstances in which a fee is payable. |
| r.95 | Any information in a file that may be freely communicated (see Art.128 and r.93) may be communicated by the EPO on request subject to the payment of an administrative fee. However, the EPO may require that the file be inspected instead, should this be appropriate in view of the amount of information requested. |
| RRF3(1) | The amount of the administrative fee is fixed by the President of the EPO. |
| AnReg | See under r. 94. Various charges apply depending on the exact request made ([2003] O.J. 371). Files are now available for inspection online (free), by personal inspection at the EPO (in respect of parts that are not scannable) and by the provision of copies (providing a fee is paid) ([2003] O.J. 370 and 373). |
| RRF4(1)(2) | The fee is due on the date of the request for inspection. |
| r.98(1) | Rule 94 does not apply to inspection by courts or other authorities in the Contracting States—originals or copies are inspected in these cases. |
| Guidelines | See A/XII/2. |

## 2–445 Maintenance of the files

| | |
|---|---|
| r.95a | See r.95a for the requirements the EPO must conform to in the keeping of files relating to applications and patents. |
| AnReg | See under r.95a(1). This rule has been supplemented by decisions of the President ([1990] O.J. 365; [1998] O.J. 360). |

## 2–446 The Official Journal

| | |
|---|---|
| Art.129 | The EPO periodically publishes an Official Journal of the EPO, containing notices and information of a general character issued by the President of the EPO, as well as any other information relevant to the EPC or its implementation. |
| Art.14(8) | The Official Journal is published in all three official EPO languages. |

## 2–447 The Bulletin

| | |
|---|---|
| Art.129 | The EPO periodically publishes a European Patent Bulletin containing entries made in the Register of European Patents, as well as other particulars the publication of which is prescribed by the EPC. |
| AnReg | See under Art.93. Details of designation fees paid are published in the Bulletin ([1997] O.J. 479). Details of extension of a European patent to other states are also published in the Bulletin ([1997] O.J. 115). See also under Art.129 for modifications made to the content of the Bulletin ([1983] O.J. 459; [1986] O.J. 63; [1988] O.J. 37). |

The President of the EPO will decide what entry should be made in the Bulletin of particulars concerning amended claims submitted too late for inclusion in the published application.     r.96(2)

The Bulletin is published in all three official EPO languages.     Art.14(8)

### Exchanges of information between the EPO and national authorities/courts     2–448

The EPO and, subject to the application of the legislative or regulatory provisions referred to in Art.75(2) (national security provisions), the central industrial property office of any Contracting State, on request, communicate to each other useful information regarding the filing of European or national patent applications and regarding any proceedings concerning such applications and the resulting patents.     Art.130(1)

The provisions of Art.130(1) apply to the communication of information by virtue of working agreements between the EPO and:     Art.130(2)

(a) the central industrial property office of any State which is not a party to the EPC;

(b) any inter-governmental organisation entrusted with the task of granting patents;

(c) any other organisation.

The communications under Art.130(1) and Art.130(2)(a) and (b) are not subject to the restrictions laid down in Art.128. The Administrative Council may decide that communications under Art.130(2)(c) are not be subject to such restrictions, provided that the organisation concerned treats the information communicated as confidential until the European patent application has been published.     Art.130(3)

The EPO communicates directly with central industrial property offices but has the option of communicating with courts indirectly via such offices. Expenditure is charged to the authority making the communication and the communication is exempt from fees.     r.97

Unless otherwise provided in the EPC or in national laws, the EPO and the courts or authorities of Contracting States must on request give assistance to each other by communicating information or opening files for inspection. Where the EPO lays files open to inspection by courts, Public Prosecutors' Offices or central industrial property offices, the inspection is not subject to the restrictions laid down in Art.128.     Art.131(1)

Information regarding files transmitted by the EPO to courts or public prosecutors offices in the Contracting States may be communicated to third parties; Art.128 applies and the EPO indicates the relevant restrictions.     r.98(2)(3)

Upon receipt of letters rogatory from the EPO, the courts or other competent authorities of Contracting States must undertake, on behalf of the EPO and within the limits of their jurisdiction, any necessary enquiries or other legal measures.     Art.131(2)

Special provisions apply to the sending of letters rogatory by the EPO.     r.99

The EPO and the central industrial property offices of the Contracting States despatch to each other on request and for their own use one or more copies of their respective publications free of charge.     Art.132(1)

The EPO may conclude agreements relating to the exchange or supply of publications.     Art.132(2)

## 20. Special agreements under the EPC

**2–449 Unitary patents**

Art.142(1) Any group of Contracting States, which has provided by a special agreement that a European patent granted for those States has a unitary character throughout their territories, may provide that a European patent may only be granted jointly in respect of all those States.

Art.142(2) Where any group of Contracting States has availed itself of the authorisation given in Art.142(1), the provisions of this Part apply (Art.142–149).

AnReg See under Art.142. Some guidance is given relating to the Community Patent Convention, should it ever come into force ([1991] O.J. 623).

**2–450 Special departments of the EPO**

Art.143(1) The group of Contracting States may give additional tasks to the EPO.

Art.143(2) Special departments common to the Contracting States in the group may be set up within the EPO in order to carry out the additional tasks. The President of the EPO will direct such special departments; Art.10, para.2 and 3 apply *mutatis mutandis* (President's powers and functions).

**2–451 Representation before special departments**

Art.144 The group of Contracting States may lay down special provisions to govern representation of the parties before the departments referred to in Art.143, para.2.

**2–452 Select committee of the Administrative Council**

Art.145(1) The group of Contracting States may set up a select committee of the Administrative Council for the purpose of supervising the activities of the special departments set up under Art.143, para.2; the EPO will place at its disposal such staff, premises and equipment as may be necessary for the performance of its duties. The President of the EPO will be responsible for the activities of the special departments to the select committee of the Administrative Council.

Art.145(2) The composition, powers and functions of the select committee are determined by the group of Contracting States.

**2–453 Cover for expenditure for carrying out special tasks**

Art.146 Where additional tasks have been given to the EPO under Art.143, the group of Contracting States bears the expenses incurred by the Organisation in carrying out these tasks. Where special departments have been set up in the EPO to carry out these additional tasks, the group must bear the expenditure on staff, premises and equipment chargeable in respect of these departments. Art.39, para.2 and 4, Art.41 and Art.47 apply *mutatis mutandis*.

**2–454 The European patent application as an object of property**

Art.148(1) Art.74 applies unless the group of Contracting States has specified otherwise (law applicable to an object of property).

Art.148(2) The group of Contracting States may provide that a European patent application for which these Contracting States are designated may only be transferred, mortgaged or subjected to any legal means of execution in respect of all the Contracting States of the group and in accordance with the provisions of the special agreement.

### Joint designation 2–455

The group of Contracting States may provide that these States may only be designated jointly, and that the designation of one or some only of such States will be deemed to constitute the designation of all the States in the group.     Art.149(1)

Where the EPO acts as a designated office under Art.153, para.1, Art.149(1) applies if the applicant has indicated in the international application that he wishes to obtain a European patent for one or more of the designated States of the group. The same applies if the applicant designates in the international application one of the Contracting States in the group, whose national law provides that the designation of that State has the effect of the application being for a European patent.     Art.149(2)

See under Art.149. Such an agreement has been drawn up between Switzerland and Liechtenstein ([1980] O.J. 407).     AnReg

## 21. RULES RELATING TO FEES

### The Administrative Council adopts the rules relating to fees 2–456

The Administrative Council is competent to adopt the rules relating to fees.     Art.33(2)(d)

See under RRF where the up-to-date consolidated text of the RRF is provided ([2002] O.J. 58).     AnReg

### Purpose of the rules relating to fees 2–457

The rules relating to fees determine the amount of the fees and the way in which they are paid.     Art.51

The rules relating to fees provide for the fees due to the EPO under the EPC and regulations, the fees and costs which the President of the EPO lays down under RRF(3)(1) and fees and costs pursuant to the PCT that are fixed by the EPO.     RRF1

### Fees, costs and prices are laid down by the President 2–458

The President lays down the amount of the administrative fees provided for in the Regulations and, where appropriate, the amount of the fees and costs for any services rendered by the EPO other than those specified in RRF2.     RRF3(1)

The President also lays down the prices of the publications referred to in Art.93, Art.98, Art.103 and Art.129.     RRF3(2)

### Amounts of fees to be published in the Journal 2–459

The amounts of the fees laid down in RRF2 and under RRF3(1) are published in the O.J. (See OJ, 2006 255 for the latest rates.)     RRF3(3)

### Due date for fees where not specified 2–460

Where a due date is not specified for the payment of a fee, either in the EPC or the PCT, or their regulations, it falls due on the date of receipt of the request for the service     RRF4(1)(2)

incurring the fee concerned. However, the President of the EPO may decide that such services may be carried out without advance payment.

## 2–461 Currency to be used

RRF5    All fees must be paid in euros.

## 2–462 Payment or transfer to an EPO bank account or Giro account

RRF5(1)(a)(b)    Payments may be made by payment or transfer to a bank account or Giro account held by the EPO.

RRF8(1)(a)    Payment will be considered to have been made on the date on which the amount of the payment or of the transfer is actually entered in a bank account or a Giro account held by the EPO.

Guidelines    See A/XI/2 and 3.1.

## 2–463 Payment by cheque

RRF5(1)(c)    Payment may be made by the delivery or remittance of cheques made payable to the EPO.

RRF8(1)(b)    Payment will be considered to have been made on the date of receipt of the cheque by the EPO, provided that the cheque is met.

Guidelines    See A/XI/2 and 3.2.

## 2–464 Payment by other methods — deposit accounts

RRF5(2)    Payment may be made by any other method allowed by the President of the EPO.

RRF8(2)    In these cases the President decides when payments are considered to have been made.

AnReg    Payment may be made by means of a deposit account (see OJ, 2005, supplement 2 to issue 1 for full details).

A deposit account may be set up by any natural or legal person. The account is kept in Euros and is replenished by payment into an EPO account. Debiting is carried out most frequently by means of a debit order which may be filed by post, fax or online (in the latter case via epoline or diskette). The other option is automatic direct debiting of the account by the EPO.

Where a debit order is used, the date of payment is the date that the debit order is received by the EPO, assuming there are sufficient funds in the deposit account. If there are insufficient funds then the date may still be maintained by replenishing the account within a period set by the EPO and paying an administrative fee. If the debit order is received late then RRF8(3)(4) may be applicable.

The automatic debiting procedure may be applied to any European application. It is then the EPO's responsibility to debit from the deposit account most fees which fall due. The fee is debited on the last possible day on which it can be paid where a time limit is involved. If there are insufficient funds on that day then the payment is still deemed made in time if the account is replenished within a period set by the EPO and an administrative fee is paid. Some points to note include: (1) only applicants and proprietors can use automatic debiting — it does not apply to other parties such as opponents; (2) for a Euro-PCT application, direct debiting only applies on entry to the regional phase and thereafter — it does not apply to payments made in the international phase to the EPO acting as an international authority; (3) most fees are covered — exceptions include the conversion fee (A136(1), A140 EPC), the fee for the awarding of costs (R63(3) EPC), the fee for the conservation of evidence (R75(3) EPC) and the fee for a technical opinion; (4) whilst the fees for further processing and restitutio are covered by automatic debiting, any unpaid fee which resulted in the relevant loss of rights will not be automatically paid when the request under A121 or A122 EPC is made; (5) a fee can still be paid by other means — in this case the automatic debit is not made; and (6) care must be taken when the EPO finds a lack of unity and requests additional search fees — such fees will automatically be debited unless the applicant specifically says they shouldn't and if there is a multiple lack of unity this can quickly exhaust a deposit account.

See page 337 for cases involving incorrect debit orders. CLBA

See A/XI/2 and 3.3 Guidelines

### Safeguard in cases where payment is deemed not to have been made in time    2–465

Where a payment is deemed not to have been made in time pursuant to RRF8(1) and (2), it will be considered to have been made in time if evidence is provided to the EPO that the person who made the payment: RRF8(3)

(a) fulfilled one of the following conditions in a Contracting State within the period in which the fee should have been paid:

    (i) he effected the payment through a banking establishment or a post office;
    (ii) he duly gave an order to a banking establishment or a post office to transfer the amount of the payment; or
    (iii) he dispatched at a post office a letter bearing the address of the EPO and containing a cheque within the meaning of RRF5(1)(c), said cheque being met; and

(b) paid a surcharge of 10 per cent on the relevant fee or fees, but not exceeding 150 euros; no surcharge is payable if a condition under (a) above has been fulfilled not later than ten days before the expiry of the period for payment.

The EPO may request the person who made the payment to produce evidence as to the date on which a condition under (a) was fulfilled and, where appropriate, pay the surcharge referred to under (b), within a period specified by the EPO. If no evidence is submitted, the evidence is insufficient or the surcharge is not paid in time, the period for payment will be considered not to have been observed. RRF8(4)

See A/XI/6.2. Guidelines

### The EPO must be able to establish what a payment is for    2–466

A payment must indicate the name of person making the payment and must contain enough information to allow the EPO to establish the purpose of the payment immediately. RRF7(1)

See under RRF. Use of Form 1010 is recommended but the EPO also allow the use of a diskette ([1996] O.J. 553). AnReg

Where the purpose of the payment cannot be immediately established, the EPO will require the person making the payment to notify it in writing of this purpose within a person specified by the EPO. If such a request is not complied with in due time, the payment will be considered not to have been made. RRF7(2)

See A/XI/7. Guidelines

| | |
|---|---|
| 2–467 | **Who may make payments? To whom will refunds be paid?** |
| AnReg | See legal advice (6/91) which explains that fees may validly be paid by anyone and that refunds are made to the party or to a representative authorised to receive payments ([1991] O.J. 573). |
| 2–468 | **Procedure where the amount paid is insufficient** |
| RRF9(1) | In principle, a time limit for payment is only complied with if the full amount due is paid in time and where the full amount is not received in time, the EPO will refund the amount paid after the expiry of the time limit.<br><br>However, the EPO may:<br><br>(a) give the person making the payment the opportunity to pay the amount lacking, in so far as it is possible within the time remaining before the expiry of the period; or<br><br>(b) overlook any small amounts lacking, where it is considered justified and without prejudice to the rights of the person making the payment. |
| CLBA | See CLBA, p.339. Even 20 per cent has been seen in some cases as small. |
| RRF9(2) | In the case of designation fees, the amount received will be applied according to the specifications made by the applicant at the time of payment. In the absence of such specifications, the fees will be deemed to be paid only for as many designations as are covered by the amount paid and in the order in which the Contracting States are designated in the request. |
| CLBA | However, where designation fees are insufficient a communication pursuant to RRF7(2) will first be sent to obtain clarification before the RRF9(2) procedure is applied (see CLBA, p.337, J23/82). |
| 2–469 | **Refund of insignificant amounts** |
| RRF10c | Where too large a sum is paid to cover a fee, the excess will not be refunded if the amount is insignificant and the party concerned has not expressly requested a refund.<br><br>The President of the EPO decides what constitutes an insignificant amount. |
| AnReg | See under RRF10c. In this notice the President decided what an insignificant amount is and how this impacts on arrangements for deposit accounts ([1999] O.J. 42). |

# PART C

## Guide to the Law under the Patent Co-operation Treaty

# TABLE OF ARTICLES AND RULES OF THE PATENT CO-OPERATION TREATY

(*References are to paragraph numbers in Part C only*)

## Articles
1970 Patent Cooperation Treaty
Art.1 .................................................. 3–001, 3–007
Art.2 ................................ 3–007, 3–058, 3–062, 3–130
Art.2(ii) ................................................ 3–028, 3–133
Art.2(vi) ...................................................... 3–029
Art.3(2) ....... 3–017, 3–038, 3–042, 3–052, 3–053, 3–101
Art.3(3) ............................................................ 3–052
Art.3(4)(i) ........................................................ 3–069
Art.3(4)(ii) ....................................................... 3–068
Art.3(4)(iii) ...................................................... 3–051
Art.3(4)(iv) ............................................ 3–075, 3–108
Art.4 ......................................................... 3–007, 3–128
Art.4(1)(i) ......................................................... 3–019
Art.4(1)(ii) ........................................................ 3–026
Art.4(1)(iii) ........................................... 3–021, 3–023
Art.4(1)(iv) ....................................................... 3–020
Art.4(1)(v) ........................................................ 3–022
Art.4(2) ........................................................... 3–108
Art.4(3) ........................................................... 3–028
Art.4(4) ........................................................... 3–022
Art.5 ......................................................... 3–039, 3–128
Art.6 .............................................. 3–043, 3–044, 3–128
Art.7 ......................................................... 3–053, 3–128
Art.7(2) ........................................................... 3–286
Art.8   3–007, 3–026, 3–029, 3–058, 3–060, 3–062, 3–064
Art.8(1) ........................................................... 3–343
Art.9 .................................... 3–026, 3–085, 3–330
Art.9(1) ........................................................... 3–008
Art.9(2) ................................ 3–008, 3–009, 3–213
Art.9(3) ........................................................... 3–008
Art.10 .............................................................. 3–009
Art.11(1) ..... 3–078, 3–080, 3–085, 3–092, 3–274, 3–312
Art.11(1)(1)(i)–(iii) ................................. 3–098, 3–113
Art.11(2) .......................................................... 3–087
Art.11(2)(a) ............................................ 3–084, 3–087
Art.11(2)(b) ..................................................... 3–087
Art.11(3) .... 3–186, 3–189, 3–192, 3–274, 3–275, 3–276,
3–314, 3–319
Art.11(4) .......................................................... 3–274
Art.12(1) ................ 3–090, 3–091, 3–092, 3–096, 3–348
Art.12(2) ................................................ 3–086, 3–092
Art.12(3) ........................... 3–093, 3–275, 3–312, 3–313
Art.13 .................................................... 3–175, 3–348
Art.13(1) .......................................................... 3–175
Art.13(2) .......................................................... 3–175
Art.14(1)(a) ..................................................... 3–104
Art.14(1)(a)(i) ......................................... 3–099, 3–112
Art.14(1)(a)(ii) ........................................ 3–100, 3–112
Art.14(1)(a)(iii) ....................................... 3–101, 3–125
Art.14(1)(a)(iv) ....................................... 3–101, 3–125
Art.14(1)(a)(v) ........................................ 3–102, 3–112

Art.14(1)(b)  3–099, 3–100, 3–101, 3–102, 3–104, 3–112,
3–113, 3–275
Art.14(2) ................................................ 3–084, 3–106
Art.14(3) ................................................ 3–081, 3–108
Art.14(3)(a) ............................................ 3–113, 3–275
Art.14(3)(b) ............................................ 3–275, 3–312
Art.14(4) ....................... 3–098, 3–112, 3–113, 3–275
Art.15(1) .......................................................... 3–119
Art.15(2) ................................................ 3–119, 3–121
Art.15(3) .......................................................... 3–120
Art.15(4) .......................................................... 3–119
Art.15(5) ............................... 3–009, 3–031, 3–124
Art.15(5)(a) ..................................................... 3–124
Art.15(5)(b) ..................................................... 3–124
Art.15(5)(c) ..................................................... 3–124
Art.16 .............................................................. 3–124
Art.16(1) .......................................................... 3–114
Art.16(2) .......................................................... 3–117
Art.16(3) .......................................................... 3–214
Art.16(3)(a) ..................................................... 3–116
Art.16(3)(b) ............ 3–080, 3–116, 3–131, 3–139, 3–356
Art.16(3)(c) ..................................................... 3–115
Art.16(3)(d) ..................................................... 3–116
Art.16(3)(e) ..................................................... 3–116
Art.17 ................................................... 3–130, 3–169
Art.17(1) .......................................................... 3–125
Art.17(2) .......................................................... 3–128
Art.17(2)(a)  3–132, 3–133, 3–135, 3–137, 3–152, 3–155,
3–159, 3–177, 3–190, 3–217, 3–242, 3–299
Art.17(2)(b) ............................... 3–046, 3–128, 3–133
Art.17(3)(a) ....................... 3–129, 3–130, 3–133, 3–285
Art.17(3)(b) ............................................ 3–129, 3–284
Art.18 .............................................................. 3–299
Art.18(1) ................................................ 3–132, 3–133
Art.18(2) ................................................ 3–133, 3–135
Art.18(3) .......................................................... 3–137
Art.19 ........ 3–142, 3–146, 3–157, 3–168, 3–169, 3–180,
3–183, 3–193, 3–213, 3–228, 3–237, 3–242, 3–245, 3–268
Art.19(1) .... 3–140, 3–144, 3–157, 3–159, 3–169, 3–179,
3–183
Art.19(2) .......................................................... 3–145
Art.19(3) .......................................................... 3–145
Art.20 ........ 3–167, 3–168, 3–169, 3–172, 3–173, 3–175,
3–179, 3–191, 3–236, 3–281, 3–301, 3–324, 3–348
Art.20(1)(a) ..................................................... 3–167
Art.20(3) ................................................ 3–139, 3–356
Art.21 ......... 3–198, 3–200, 3–202, 3–205, 3–278, 3–299
Art.21(1) .......................................................... 3–147
Art.21(2)(a) ............................................ 3–148, 3–343
Art.21(2)(b) ............................... 3–063, 3–148, 3–159
Art.21(4) .......................................................... 3–153
Art.21(5) .......................................................... 3–149

Art.21(6) .................................................. 3–065, 3–159
Art.22 ......... 3–006, 3–050, 3–051, 3–093, 3–129, 3–176,
   3–177, 3–178, 3–179, 3–180, 3–183, 3–184, 3–186,
   3–187, 3–188, 3–189, 3–190, 3–191, 3–193, 3–205,
   3–211, 3–275, 3–280, 3–281, 3–286, 3–288, 3–290,
   3–291, 3–294, 3–297, 3–319, 3–327, 3–344, 3–348
Art.22(1) .... 3–172, 3–177, 3–179, 3–180, 3–181, 3–182,
3–197, 3–198
Art.22(3) .................................................. 3–177, 3–178
Art.23 .................................................................. 3–280
Art.23(2) .... 3–138, 3–168, 3–195, 3–289, 3–341, 3–342,
   3–343, 3–344
Art.24(1) ............................................................. 3–275
Art.24(1)(iii) ................................................ 3–189, 3–319
Art.24(2) ...................... 3–186, 3–193, 3–275, 3–314
Art.25 .......... 3–093, 3–098, 3–104, 3–108, 3–113, 3–275
Art.25(1) ................................. 3–087, 3–312, 3–313
Art.25(2) ............................................................. 3–314
Art.25(2)(a) ......................................... 3–313, 3–315
Art.25(2)(b) ....................................................... 3–313
Art.26 ................................................... 3–027, 3–317
Art.27 .................................................................. 3–290
Art.27(1) ............................................................. 3–286
Art.27(2) .................................................. 3–286, 3–287
Art.27(2)(i)(a) ..................................................... 3–287
Art.27(2)(ii)(b) ................................... 3–287Art.27(1)
Art.27(3) .................................................. 3–008, 3–292
Art.27(4) ............................................................. 3–286
Art.27(5) ............................................................. 3–291
Art.27(6) ............................................................. 3–291
Art.27(7) ........................... 3–011, 3–294, 3–326, 3–327
Art.27(8) .......................... 3–009, 3–089, 3–293
Art.28 .................................................................. 3–281
Art.28(1) ............................................................. 3–281
Art.28(2) ............................................................. 3–281
Art.28(3) ............................................................. 3–281
Art.28(4) ............................................................. 3–281
Art.29 .................................................................. 3–278
Art.30 .................................................................. 3–280
Art.30(1) ............................................................. 3–348
Art.30(2) ............................................................. 3–348
Art.30(3) ............................................................. 3–348
Art.30(4) .................................................. 3–348, 3–350
Art.31 .................................................................. 3–222
Art.31(a) ............................................................. 3–225
Art.31(b) ............................................................. 3–225
Art.31(2) ............................................................. 3–213
Art.31(2)(b) ......................................................... 3–214
Art.31(3) ............................................................. 3–216
Art.31(4)(a) ........................................................ 3–213
Art.31(4)(b) ........................................................ 3–213
Art.31(3) ............................................................. 3–216
Art.31(6)(a) ........................................................ 3–219
Art.31(6)(b) ........................................................ 3–230
Art.31(7) ............................................................. 3–236
Art.32 .................................................... 3–214, 3–219
Art.32(2) .................................................. 3–273, 3–357
Art.32(3) ............................................................. 3–214
Art.33 .................................................................. 3–264
Art.33(1) .................................................. 3–238, 3–248

Art.33(2) .................................... 3–134, 3–239, 3–240
Art.33(3) .................................... 3–134, 3–239, 3–240
Art.33(4) .................................... 3–134, 3–239
Art.33(6) .................................... 3–134, 3–241
Art.34 ......... 3–082, 3–213, 3–228, 3–233, 3–242, 3–245,
   3–246, 3–268
Art.34(1) ............................................................. 3–243
Art.34(2)(a) ........................................................ 3–244
Art.34(2)(b) ............................................... 3–127, 3–246
Art.34(2)(c) ........................................................ 3–248
Art.34(2)(c)(i)–(iii) ............................................... 3–134
Art.34(2)(d) ........................................................ 3–248
Art.34(3) .................................................. 3–252, 3–263
Art.34(3)(a) .............................................. 3–253, 3–263
Art.34(3)(b) ........................................................ 3–284
Art.34(3)(c) ........................................ 3–252, 3–263, 3–284
Art.34(4) ............................................................. 3–248
Art.34(4)(a) ........................................................ 3–262
Art.34(4)(a)(i) ..................................................... 3–247
Art.34(4)(a)(ii) .................................................... 3–247
Art.34(4)(b) .............................................. 3–247, 3–262
Art.34(4)(a)(ii) .................................................... 3–247
Art.34(4)(b) ........................................................ 3–252
Art.35(1) .................................................. 3–255, 3–256
Art.35(2) ................ 3–134, 3–248, 3–262, 3–264, 3–264
Art.35(3) .................................................. 3–134, 3–262
Art.36(1) .................................... 3–269, 3–282, 3–350
Art.36(2) .................................................. 3–270, 3–272
Art.36(3) .................................................. 3–271, 3–350
Art.36(3)(a) ........................................................ 3–270
Art.36(3)(b) ........................................................ 3–272
Art.36(4) .................................................. 3–273, 3–357
Art.37(1) ............................................................. 3–344
Art.37(2) ............................................................. 3–344
Art.37(3)(a) ........................................................ 3–344
Art.37(3)(b) .............................................. 3–344, 3–350
Art.37(4) ............................................................. 3–344
Art.38 .................................................... 3–280, 3–352
Art.38(1) ............................................................. 3–350
Art.38(2) ............................................................. 3–350
Art.39 ......... 3–006, 3–190, 3–191, 3–192, 3–193, 3–194,
   3–200, 3–205, 3–211, 3–272, 3–280, 3–297
Art.39(1) .... 3–190, 3–193, 3–197, 3–198, 3–272, 3–319,
   3–341, 3–342, 3–343
Art.39(1)(a) .............................................. 3–190, 3–282
Art.39(1)(b) ........................................................ 3–191
Art.39(2) ............................................................. 3–192
Art.39(3) .................................................. 3–192, 3–193
Art.40 .................................................................. 3–280
Art.40(2) .... 3–168, 3–195, 3–270, 3–341, 3–342, 3–343,
   3–344
Art.41 .................................................................. 3–282
Art.41(1) ............................................................. 3–282
Art.41(2) ............................................................. 3–282
Art.41(3) ............................................................. 3–282
Art.41(4) ............................................................. 3–282
Art.42 .................................................................. 3–298
Art.43 .................................................... 3–026, 3–188
Art.44 .................................................... 3–026, 3–188
Art.45 .................................................................. 3–026

| | | | |
|---|---|---|---|
| Art.45(1) | 3–026 | r.4.9 | 3–026, 3–028, 3–035 |
| Art.45(2) | 3–026 | r.4.10 | 3–029, 3–058, 3–060, 3–109, 3–354 |
| Art.46 | 3–303 | r.4.10(a) | 3–035 |
| Art.48(1) | 3–308, 3–309 | r.4.10(b) | 3–035 |
| Art.48(2) | 3–313, 3–316 | r.4.10(d) | 3–059 |
| Art.49 | 3–328 | r.4.11 | 3–031, 3–035, 3–131 |
| Art.53(1) | 3–002 | r.4.11(a) | 3–035 |
| Art.55(1)–(3) | 3–003 | r.4.11(b) | 3–035 |
| Art.55(4) | 3–006 | r.4.14*bis* | 3–030 |
| Art.56 | 3–116 | r.4.15 | 3–034, 3–099 |
| Art.58(1) | 3–004 | r.4.15(b) | 3–222, 3–341 |
| Art.58(4) | 3–005 | r.4.16 | 3–037, 3–222 |
| Art.58(5) | 3–004 | r.4.17 | 3–032, 3–110, 3–155 |
| Art.64(1) | 3–190, 3–212, 3–280 | r.4.17(i) | 3–032, 3–287 |
| Art.64(2)(a)(i) | 3–190 | r.4.17(ii) | 3–032, 3–287 |
| Art.64(2)(a)(ii) | 3–280 | r.4.17(iii) | 3–032, 3–287 |
| Art.64(3) | 3–109, 3–149, 3–324 | r.4.17(iv) | 3–032, 3–110, 3–287 |
| Art.64(3)(c)(i) | 3–148, 3–159 | r.4.17(v) | 3–032, 3–163 |
| Art.64(4) | 3–274, 3–276 | r.4.18 | 3–036 |
| | | r.5.1 | 3–041 |
| **Rules** | | r.5(1(a) | 3–040 |
| | | r.5(1(b) | 3–041 |
| r.1 | 3–007 | r.5(1(c) | 3–041 |
| r.2 | 3–007 | r.5.2 | 3–082, 3–296 |
| r.2.3 | 3–034, 3–222 | r.5.2(a) | 3–069, 3–127 |
| r.3 | 3–107, 3–180 | r.5.2(b) | 3–127, 3–180 |
| r.3.1 | 3–018 | rr.6.1–6.4 | 3–050 |
| r.3.2 | 3–018 | r.6.1 | 3–046, 3–047, 3–297 |
| r.3.3 | 3–033 | r.6.2 | 3–295, 3–297 |
| r.3.3(a)(ii) | 3–066 | r.6.2(a) | 3–048 |
| r.3.3(a)(iii) | 3–052 | r.6.2(b) | 3–049 |
| r.3.4 | 3–018 | r.6.3 | 3–044, 3–045, 3–297 |
| rr.4.1–4.17 | 3–036 | r.6.4 | 3–297 |
| r.4 | 3–180 | r.6.4(a) | 3–046, 3–247, 3–248 |
| r.4.1(a)(i) | 3–019 | r.6.4(b) | 3–046 |
| r.4.1(a)(ii) | 3–020, 3–101 | r.6.4(c) | 3–046 |
| r.4.1(a)(iii) | 3–021, 3–022 | r.6.5 | 3–050, 3–297 |
| r.4.1(a)(iv) | 3–022 | r.7.1 | 3–053 |
| r.4.1(b)(i) | 3–029 | r.7.2 | 3–053 |
| r.4.1(b)(ii) | 3–031 | r.8 | 3–101, 3–126 |
| r.4.1(b)(iii) | 3–035 | r.8.1(a) | 3–052 |
| r.4.1(b)(iv) | 3–030 | r.8.1(b)–(d) | 3–052 |
| r.4.1(c) | 3–022 | r.8.2 | 3–052, 3–126, 3–155 |
| r.4.1(c)(ii) | 3–060 | r.8.2(b) | 3–155 |
| r.4.1(c)(iii) | 3–032 | r.8.3 | 3–052 |
| r.4.1(d) | 3–034 | r.9.1 | 3–065 |
| r.4.2 | 3–019 | r.9.1(iii) | 3–164 |
| r.4.3 | 3–020, 3–126, 3–180 | r.9.2 | 3–065 |
| r.4.4 | 3–021, 3–022, 3–023, 3–037, 3–100, 3–222, 3–332, 3–333 | r.9.3 | 3–065 |
| | | r.10 | 3–067 |
| r.4.4(d) | 3–025 | r.11 | 3–015, 3–031, 3–102, 3–104, 3–183, 3–339 |
| r.4.5 | , 3–100, 3–222 | r.11.1–11.13 | 3–338 |
| r.4.5(a)–(e) | 3–021 | r.11.1 | 3–066, 3–089 |
| r.4.5(a)(ii) | 3–100, 3–232 | r.11.2–11.13 | 3–068 |
| r.4.5(a)(iii) | 3–100 | r.11.13 | 3–053 |
| r.4.5(d) | 3–008 | r.11.14 | 3–246, 3–338, 3–339 |
| r.4.6 | 3–287 | r.12.1 | 3–010, 3–069 |
| r.4.6(a)–(c) | 3–022 | r.12.1(a) | 3–085 |
| r.4.7 | 3–023, 3–222 | r.12.1(b) | 3–070 |
| r.4.8 | 3–024 | r.12.1(d) | 3–180 |

| | |
|---|---|
| r.12.2 | 3–142 |
| r.12.2(b) | 3–325 |
| r.12.2(c) | 3–104, 3–107, 3–227 |
| r.12.3 | 3–095, 3–102, 3–104, 3–151 |
| r.12.3(a) | 3–071, 3–096, 3–107, 3–325 |
| r.12.3(b) | 3–071 |
| r.12.3(a) | 3–072 |
| r.12.3(c)(i) | 3–071 |
| r.12.3(c)(ii) | 3–071 |
| r.12.3(d) | 3–071, 3–113 |
| r.12.3(e) | 3–071 |
| r.12.4 | 3–095, 3–102, 3–151 |
| r.12.4(a) | 3–072, 3–325 |
| r.12.4(b) | 3–072 |
| r.12.4(c) | 3–072 |
| r.12.4(d) | 3–072 |
| r.12.4(e) | 3–072 |
| r.13 | 3–252 |
| r.13.1 | 3–051, 3–297 |
| r.13.2 | 3–051, 3–297 |
| r.13.3 | 3–051, 3–297 |
| r.13.4 | 3–046, 3–297 |
| r.13.5 | 3–051, 3–297 |
| r.13*bis* | 3–083, 3–061 |
| r.13*bis*2 | 3–083 |
| r.13*bis*3(a) | 3–083 |
| r.13*bis*3(b) | 3–083 |
| r.13*bis*4 | 3–180 |
| r.13*bis*4(b) | 3–180 |
| r.13*ter* | 3–082 |
| r.13.*ter*1 | 3–254 |
| r.13.*ter*1(a) | 3–127 |
| r.13.*ter*1(b) | 3–127 |
| r.13.*ter*1(c) | 3–127 |
| r.13.*ter*1(d) | 3–127 |
| r.13.*ter*1(e) | 3–127 |
| r.13.*ter*1(f) | 3–082, 3–127 |
| r.13.*ter*3 | 3–193, 3–296 |
| r.14 | 3–010, 3–108 |
| r.14.1(a) | 3–076 |
| r.14.1(b) | 3–076 |
| r.14.1(c) | 3–010, 3–074, 3–076 |
| r.14.4*bis.* | 3–030 |
| r.15 | 3–347 |
| r.15.1 | 3–078, 3–108 |
| r.15.2 | 3–078 |
| r.15.2(b) | 3–225 |
| r.15.4 | 3–074, 3–078, 3–079 |
| r.15.4(a)–(c) | 3–010 |
| r.15.6 | 3–078 |
| r.16 | 3–108 |
| r.16.1(a) | 3–080 |
| r.16.1(b)–(e) | 3–080 |
| r.16.1(b) | 3–080 |
| r.16.1(f) | 3–010, 3–074, 3–080 |
| r.16.2 | 3–080 |
| r.16.3 | 3–080 |
| r.16*bis*1(a) | 3–081 |
| r.16*bis*1(c) | 3–081 |
| r.16*bis*1(d) | 3–081 |
| r.16*bis*1(e) | 3–081 |
| r.16*bis*2 | 3–081 |
| r.17 | 3–060 |
| r.17.1 | 3–251 |
| r.17.1(a) | 3–060, 3–289 |
| r.17.1(b) | 3–060, 3–289 |
| r.17.1(b–*bis.*) | 3–060, 3–289 |
| r.17.1(c) | 3–060, 3–289 |
| r.17.1(d) | 3–060 |
| r.17.2 | 3–289 |
| r.17.2(a) | 3–290 |
| r.17.2(b) | 3–354 |
| r.17.2(c) | 3–354 |
| r.18.1 | 3–008 |
| r.18.1(a) | 3–213 |
| r.18.1(b) | 3–213 |
| r.18.1(c) | 3–008 |
| r.18.3 | 3–008 |
| r.18.4 | 3–008 |
| r.19.1 | 3–010, 3–100, 3–124, 3–124 |
| r.19.1(a) | 3–009 |
| r.19.1(a)(i) | 3–117, 3–214 |
| r.19.1(a)(ii) | 3–117, 3–214 |
| r.19.1(a)(iii) | 3–010, 3–328 |
| r.19.1(b) | 3–009, 3–117, 3–214 |
| r.19.1(c) | 3–009, 3–117, 3–214 |
| r.19.2 | 3–009, 3–010 |
| r.19.2(i) | 3–117, 3–214 |
| r.19.3 | 3–009 |
| r.19.4 | 3–010 |
| r.19.4(a) | 3–085, 3–087 |
| r.19.4(a)(i) | 3–085, 3–087 |
| r.19.4(a)(ii) | 3–074, 3–085, 3–087 |
| r.19.4(c) | 3–075, 3–078, 3–080 |
| r.20.1 | 3–084 |
| r.20.2(a) | 3–084 |
| r.20.2(a)(iii) | 3–106 |
| r.20.2(b) | 3–084 |
| r.20.3 | 3–087 |
| r.20.4 | 3–085 |
| r.20.4(d) | 3–085 |
| r.20.5 | 3–087 |
| r.20.5(a) | 3–086 |
| r.20.5(b) | 3–086, 3–090 |
| r.20.5(c) | 3–071, 3–086, 3–093 |
| r.20.6 | 3–084, 3–087 |
| r.20.7 | 3–087 |
| r.20.7(i) | 3–312 |
| r.20.8 | 3–087 |
| r.20.9 | 3–088 |
| r.21 | 3–066 |
| r.21.1(a) | 3–090 |
| r.21.1(b) | 3–090 |
| r.21.1(c) | 3–090 |
| r.22.1 | 3–089 |
| r.22.1(a) | 3–086, 3–092 |
| r.22.1(b) | 3–093 |
| r.22.1(c) | 3–093 |
| r.22.1(d) | 3–093 |
| r.22.1(g) | 3–093, 3–187, 3–193 |

| | |
|---|---|
| r.22.1(h) ............................................. 3–095 | r.35.2 ............................................. 3–117 |
| r.22.3 ................................... 3–093, 3–312 | r.35.3 ............................................. 3–117 |
| r.23 ................................................. 3–113 | r.36 ............................................... 3–115 |
| r.23(1)(a) ......................................... 3–096 | r.37 ............................................... 3–133 |
| r.23(1)(b) ............... 3–096, 3–126, 3–133, 3–227, 3–337 | r.37.1 ................................... 3–125, 3–201 |
| r.23(1)(c) ......................................... 3–096 | r.37.2 ................................... 3–125, 3–180 |
| r.24.2 .............................................. 3–094 | r.38 ............................................... 3–133 |
| r.24.2(c) ................................. 3–093, 3–312 | r.38.1 ............................................. 3–125 |
| r.25 ................................................. 3–097 | r.38.2 ............................................. 3–125 |
| r.25.4 .............................................. 3–127 | r.38.2(b) ......................................... 3–125 |
| r.26 ................................ 3–104, 3–112, 3–227 | r.39 ............................................... 3–128 |
| r.26(3) ............................................. 3–339 | r.40 ............................................... 3–128 |
| r.26.4 .............................................. 3–323 | r.40.1 ............................................. 3–129 |
| r.26*bis*1(c) ...................................... 3–177 | r.40.1(iii) ........................................ 3–129 |
| r.26*bis*2 .......................................... 3–109 | r.40.2 ............................................. 3–129 |
| r.26*bis*2(b) ............................ 3–162, 3–355 | r.40.2(c) ......................................... 3–129 |
| r.26*bis*2(c) .................................... 3–162 | r.40.2(d) ......................................... 3–129 |
| r.26.1 .............................................. 3–104 | r.40.2(e) ................................. 3–129, 3–130 |
| r.26.1(a) ................................. 3–073, 3–107 | r.41 ............................................... 3–131 |
| r.26.2 ....................... 3–073, 3–104, 3–107 | r.41.1 ............................................. 3–080 |
| r.26.2*bis*(a) .................................... 3–099 | r.41*bis*.1(a) .................................... 3–287 |
| r.26.2*bis*(b) .................................... 3–100 | r.41*bis*.1(g) .................................... 3–287 |
| r.26.2*ter*2 ....................................... 3–110 | r.41*bis*.1(h) .................................... 3–287 |
| r.26.3 ....................... 3–015, 3–104, 3–107 | r.43.1 ............................................. 3–133 |
| r.26.3(a) ......................................... 3–102 | r.43.2 ............................................. 3–133 |
| r.26.3(b) ......................................... 3–102 | r.43.3 ............................................. 3–133 |
| r.26.3*bis* ............................... 3–104, 3–107 | r.43.4 ................................... 3–133, 3–134 |
| r.26.3*ter*(a) .................................... 3–107 | r.43.5 ............................................. 3–133 |
| r.26.3*ter*(b) .................................... 3–107 | r.43.6 ............................................. 3–133 |
| r.26.3*ter*(c) ................... 3–104, 3–107, 3–325 | r.43.7 ............................................. 3–133 |
| r.26.3*ter*(d) .................................... 3–107 | r.43.8 ............................................. 3–133 |
| r.26.4 .............................................. 3–105 | r.43.9 ............................................. 3–133 |
| r.26.5 ....................... 3–073, 3–104, 3–107 | r.43.10 ............................................ 3–133 |
| r.26.6(a) ......................................... 3–106 | r.43*bis*1 ....... 3–134, 3–136, 3–217, 3–237, 3–242, 3–249, 3–271 |
| r.26.6(b) ......................................... 3–106 | r.43*bis*1(a) .................................... 3–134 |
| r.26*bis*.1 ........................................ 3–028 | r.43*bis*1(b) .................................... 3–134 |
| r.26*bis*.1(a) ............................ 3–063, 3–109 | r.43*bis*1(c) .................................... 3–134 |
| r.26*bis*.1(b) .................................... 3–063 | r.44.1 ............................................. 3–135 |
| r.26*bis*.1(c) ............................ 3–063, 3–148 | r.43*bis*2 ........................................ 3–190 |
| r.26*bis*.2 ........................................ 3–109 | r.44. ................................... 3–139, 3–356 |
| r.26*ter*.1 ................................ 3–032, 3–155 | r.44*bis* .......................................... 3–136 |
| r.26.3*ter*(c) .................................... 3–073 | r.44*bis*1 ....................... 3–136, 3–138, 3–349 |
| r.27 ................................................. 3–108 | r.44*bis*2 ........................................ 3–138 |
| r.27.1(a) ......................................... 3–113 | r.44*bis*2(b) .................................... 3–138 |
| r.28 ................................................. 3–112 | r.44*bis*3(a) .................................... 3–138 |
| r.29 ..................................... 3–081, 3–113 | r.44*bis*3(b) ............................ 3–138, 3–349 |
| r.29.1 ....................... 3–073, 3–107, 3–312 | r.44*bis*3(c) .................................... 3–138 |
| r.29.1(a)(ii) .............................. 3–166, 3–312 | r.44*bis*3(d) ............................ 3–138, 3–349 |
| r.29.3 .............................................. 3–112 | r.44*bis*4 ................................ 3–138, 3–349 |
| r.29.4 .............................................. 3–098 | r.44*ter*1 ........................................ 3–352 |
| r.31.1 .............................................. 3–175 | r.44*ter*1(a) .................................... 3–349 |
| r.31.2 .............................................. 3–175 | r.44*ter*1(b) .................................... 3–349 |
| r.33.1(a) ......................................... 3–121 | r.44.2 ............................................. 3–133 |
| r.33.1(b) ................................. 3–121, 3–133 | r.45 ..................................... 3–133, 3–137 |
| r.33.1(c) ................................. 3–121, 3–133 | r.45.1 ............................................. 3–169 |
| r.33.2(a)–(c) ..................................... 3–122 | r.46.1 ....................... 3–140, 3–222, 3–242 |
| r.33.1(d) ......................................... 3–122 | r.46.2 ............................................. 3–141 |
| r.33.3 .............................................. 3–120 | r.46.3 ............................................. 3–142 |
| r.34 ................... 3–115, 3–122, 3–133, 3–214 | r.46.4 ................................... 3–144, 3–157 |
| r.35.1 .............................................. 3–117 | |

| | | | |
|---|---|---|---|
| r.46.5 | 3–143 | r.49.6(d) | 3–319 |
| r.47.1 | 3–168, 3–173, 3–179, 3–193 | r.49.6(e) | 3–319 |
| r.47.1(a) | 3–168, 3–193 | r.49.6(f) | 3–319 |
| r.47.1(b) | 3–168 | r.49*bis* | 3–193 |
| r.47.1(c) | 3–172, 3–173 | r.49*bis*.1(a) | 3–035, 3–188 |
| r.47.1(e) | 3–179 | r.49*bis*.1(b) | 3–035, 3–188 |
| r.47.1(a-*bis*) | 3–174 | r.49*bis*.1(d) | 3–035, 3–188 |
| r.47.1(c-*bis*) | 3–173, 3–179 | r.49*bis*.1(e) | 3–035, 3–188 |
| r.47.2 | 3–170 | r.49*bis*.2(a) | 3–188 |
| r.47.3 | 3–171 | r.49*bis*.2(b) | 3–188 |
| r.47.4 | 3–168, 3–193 | r.50.1 | 3–178 |
| r.48.1 | 3–153 | r.51.1 | 3–093, 3–098, 3–104, 3–108, 3–113, 3–312 |
| r.48.1(a)(vi) | 3–157 | r.51.2 | 3–312 |
| r.48.2 | 3–154 | r.51.3 | 3–313 |
| r.48.2(a)(v) | 3–152, 3–159 | r.51*bis*. | 3–193, 3–286, 3–287, 3–288, 3–290, 3–291, 3–294, 3–327 |
| r.48.2(a)(vi) | 3–144 | r.51*bis*.1(a) | 3–287 |
| r.48.2(a)(vii) | 3–160 | r.51*bis*.1(a)(i) | 3–032, 3–287 |
| r.48.2(a)(viii) | 3–161 | r.51*bis*.1(a)(ii) | 3–032, 3–287 |
| r.48.2(a)(ix) | 3–162 | r.51*bis*.1(a)(iii) | 3–032, 3–287 |
| r.48.2(a)(x) | 3–163 | r.51*bis*.1(a)(iv) | 3–032, 3–287 |
| r.48.2(b) | 3–155 | r.51*bis*.1(a)(v) | 3–032 |
| r.48.2(c) | 3–155 | r.51*bis*.1(b) | 3–294, 3–327 |
| r.48.2(d) | 3–155 | r.51*bis*.1(c) | 3–286, 3–287 |
| r.48.2(e) | 3–155 | r.51*bis*.1(d) | 3–180, 3–287, 3–288 |
| r.48.2(f) | 3–157 | r.51*bis*.1(e) | 3–287, 3–290 |
| r.48.2(g) | 3–158 | r.51*bis*.1(f) | 3–287, 3–290 |
| r.48.2(h) | 3–157 | r.51*bis*.2(a) | 3–287 |
| r.48.2(i) | 3–157 | r.51*bis*.2(a)(i) | 3–287 |
| r.48.3 | 3–069 | r.51*bis*.2(a)(ii) | 3–287 |
| r.48.3(a) | 3–150 | r.51*bis*.2(a)(iii) | 3–287 |
| r.48.3(b) | 3–150 | r.51*bis*.2(b) | 3–287 |
| r.48.3(c) | 3–152, 3–155 | r.51*bis*.2(c) | 3–287 |
| r.48.3(e) | 3–152 | r.51*bis*.3(a) | 3–286, 3–287, 3–288, 3–290 |
| r.48.4(a) | 3–048 | r.51*bis*.3(b) | 3–290, 3–294, 3–327 |
| r.48.4(b) | 3–048 | r.51*bis*.3(c) | 3–286, 3–287, 3–288, 3–290 |
| r.48.5 | 3–149 | r.52 | 3–281 |
| r.48.6(a) | 3–166, 3–177 | r.52.1(a) | 3–281 |
| r.48.6(c) | 3–166 | r.52.1(b) | 3–281 |
| r.49 | 3–193 | r.53.1 | 3–221, 3–232 |
| r.49.1 | 3–181 | r.53.2 | 3–222 |
| r.49.1(a) | 3–180 | r.53.2(a) | 3–232 |
| r.49.1(c) | 3–185, 3–193 | r.53.2(b) | 3–232 |
| r.49.1(a-*bis*.) | 3–179 | r.53.3 | 3–222, 3–232 |
| r.49.1(a-*ter*) | 3–186 | r.53.4 | 3–222, 3–232 |
| r.49.2 | 3–180 | r.53.5 | 3–222, 3–232 |
| r.49.3 | 3–179, 3–180 | r.53.6 | 3–222, 3–232 |
| r.49.4 | 3–184 | r.53.7 | 3–223, 3–230 |
| r.49.5(a) | 3–180 | r.53.8 | 3–222, 3–232 |
| r.49.5(c) | 3–183 | r.53.8(b) | 3–344 |
| r.49.5(e) | 3–183 | r.53.9 | 3–222, 3–227 |
| r.49.5(g) | 3–183 | r.53.9(a)(i) | 3–242 |
| r.49.5(h) | 3–183 | r.53.9(b) | 3–242 |
| r.49.5(j) | 3–180 | r.54 | 3–213 |
| r.49.5(k) | 3–180 | r.54.1(a) | 3–213 |
| r.49.5(l) | 3–180, 3–183 | r.54.1(b) | 3–213 |
| r.49.5(c-*bis*) | 3–183 | r.54.2 | 3–213, 3–230, 3–232 |
| r.49.6 | 3–189, 3–319 | r.54.3 | 3–213 |
| r.49.6(a) | 3–319 | r.54.4 | 3–213, 3–225, 3–231, 3–235 |
| r.49.6(b) | 3–319 | r.54*bis*. | 3–190, 3–282 |
| r.49.6(c) | 3–319 | | |

| | |
|---|---|
| r.54*bis*. 1(a) ................... 3–134, 3–220, 3–242 | r.66 ........................................................... 3–222 |
| r.54*bis*.(a) ................................................ 3–217 | r.66.1 ........................................................ 3–233 |
| r.54*bis*.(b) ................................................ 3–218 | r.66.1(a)–(d) ............................................. 3–245 |
| r.55.1 ...................................... 3–226, 3–232, 3–337 | r.66.1(b) ................................................... 3–246 |
| r.55.2  3–226, 3–227, 3–242, 3–246, 3–255, 3–257, 3–337 | r.66.1(c) ................................................... 3–227 |
| r.55.2(a) ........................................ 3–227, 3–325 | r.66.1(e) .......................... 3–134, 3–245, 3–247, 3–252 |
| r.55.2(b) ................................................... 3–227 | r.66.1*bis* ................................................. 3–222 |
| r.55.2(c) ................................................... 3–227 | r.66.1*bis*(a) ................................... 3–134, 3–249 |
| r.55.2(d) ........................................ 3–227, 3–235 | r.66.1*bis*(b) ................................... 3–134, 3–249 |
| r.55.3 ........................................................ 3–246 | r.66.1*bis*(c) ............................................ 3–249 |
| r.55.3(a) ................................................... 3–227 | r.66.1*bis*(d) ............................................ 3–249 |
| r.55.3(b) ................................................... 3–227 | r.66.2 ................................................ 3–247, 3–248 |
| r.55.3(c) ................................................... 3–227 | r.66.2(a) ........................... 3–134, 3–248, 3–249 |
| r.57 ........................................................... 3–347 | r.66.2(a)(i) ................................................ 3–247 |
| r.57.1 ........................................................ 3–225 | r.66.2(a)(iii) .............................................. 3–266 |
| r.57.2 ........................................................ 3–225 | r.66.2(a)(v) ............................................... 3–267 |
| r.57.3 ........................................................ 3–225 | r.66.2(a)(vi) .............................................. 3–247 |
| r.57.3(d) ................................................... 3–225 | r.66.2(a)(vii) ............................................. 3–254 |
| r.57.6 ........................................................ 3–225 | r.66.2(b) ................................................... 3–248 |
| r.58.1 ........................................................ 3–225 | r.66.2(c) ................................................... 3–248 |
| r.58.3 ........................................................ 3–225 | r.66.2(d) ................................................... 3–248 |
| r.58.*bis*1 ................................................. 3–225 | r.66.3 ........................................................ 3–248 |
| r.58.*bis*.1(b) ........................................... 3–235 | r.66.4 ........................................................ 3–248 |
| r.58.*bis*2 ................................................. 3–225 | r.66.4*bis* .......................... 3–245, 3–246, 3–250 |
| r.59.1 ........................................................ 3–214 | r.66.5 ........................................................ 3–246 |
| r.59.2 ........................................................ 3–214 | r.66.6 ........................................................ 3–244 |
| r.59.3 ........................................................ 3–225 | r.66.7 ................................................ 3–134, 3–247 |
| r.59.3(a) ................................................... 3–220 | r.66.7(a) ........................................ 3–251, 3–261 |
| r.59.3(b) ................................................... 3–220 | r.66.7(b) ........................................ 3–251, 3–261 |
| r.59.3(c) ........................................ 3–220, 3–233 | r.66.8 ................................................ 3–246, 3–268 |
| r.59.3(d) ................................................... 3–220 | r.66.8(a) ................................................... 3–268 |
| r.59.3(e) ................................................... 3–220 | r.66.8(b) ................................................... 3–268 |
| r.59.3(f) ................................................... 3–220 | r.66.9 ........................................................ 3–337 |
| r.60.1 ........................................................ 3–232 | r.66.9(a) ................................................... 3–246 |
| r.60.1(a) ................................................... 3–234 | r.66.9(b) ................................................... 3–246 |
| r.60.1(b) ................................ 3–232, 3–234, 3–235 | r.66.9(c) ................................................... 3–246 |
| r.60.1(c) ................................ 3–232, 3–234, 3–235 | r.66.9(d) ................................................... 3–246 |
| r.60.1(e) ................................................... 3–234 | r.67 ........................................................... 3–134 |
| r.60.1(f) ................................................... 3–233 | r.68.1 ............................................ 3–252, 3–263 |
| r.60.1(g) ........................................ 3–233, 3–242 | r.68.2 ........................................................ 3–252 |
| r.60.1(a-*bis*) .......................................... 3–232 | r.68.2(v) ................................................... 3–252 |
| r.60.1(a-*ter*) .......................................... 3–232 | r.68.3(a)–(b) ............................................. 3–252 |
| r.61.1(a) ................................................... 3–235 | r.68.3(c)–(e) ............................................. 3–252 |
| r.61.1(b) ........................................ 3–231, 3–235 | r.68.3(e) ................................................... 3–253 |
| r.61.2 ........................................................ 3–236 | r.68.4 ........................................................ 3–252 |
| r.61.2(b) ................................................... 3–236 | r.68.5 ........................................................ 3–252 |
| r.61.2(c) ................................................... 3–236 | r.69.1 ................................................ 3–242, 3–255 |
| r.61.2(d) ........................................ 3–168, 3–193 | r.69.1(a) ........................................ 3–233, 3–242 |
| r.61.3 ........................................................ 3–236 | r.69.1(b) ..................... 3–222, 3–225, 3–233, 3–242 |
| r.61.4 ........................................................ 3–236 | r.69.1(d) ................................................... 3–222 |
| r.62.1 ............................................ 3–146, 3–237 | r.69.1(e) ................................................... 3–233 |
| r.62.2 ............................................ 3–146, 3–237 | r.69.1(*b-bis*) .......................................... 3–134 |
| r.62*bis* ................................................... 3–138 | r.69.2 ................................................ 3–242, 3–255 |
| r.63 ........................................................... 3–214 | r.70.2 ........................................................ 3–258 |
| r.64 ........................................................... 3–134 | r.70.2(b) ........................................ 3–134, 3–261 |
| r.64.1 ............................................ 3–239, 3–240 | r.70.2(c) .......................... 3–246, 3–260, 3–268 |
| r.64.1(b) ................................................... 3–240 | r.70.2(d) .......................... 3–134, 3–247, 3–262 |
| r.64.2 ................................ 3–239, 3–240, 3–265 | r.70.3 ................................................ 3–134, 3–259 |
| r.64.3 ........................................................ 3–265 | r.70.4 ........................................................ 3–259 |
| r.65 ................................................ 3–134, 3–239 | r.70.4(ii) ................................................... 3–134 |

| | | | |
|---|---|---|---|
| r.70.5 | 3–259 | r.82*bis*.2 | 3–316 |
| r.70.5(a) | 3–134 | r.82*ter* | 3–087, 3–318 |
| r.70.6 | 3–134 | r.83.1 | 3–328 |
| r.70.6(a) | 3–264 | r.83.1*bis* | 3–328 |
| r.70.6(b) | 3–264 | r.83.2 | 3–328 |
| r.70.7 | 3–264 | r.86 | 3–006 |
| r.70.8 | 3– | r.86.1(a)(i) | 3–165 |
| r.70.9 | 3–240, 3–265 | r.89 | 3–005 |
| r.70.10 | 3–134, 3–240, 3–265 | r.89*bis*.1(a) | 3–014, 3–016 |
| r.70.11 | 3–260 | r.89*bis*.1(b) | 3–016 |
| r.70.12 | 3–134 | r.89*bis*.1(c) | 3–016 |
| r.70.12(i) | 3–266 | r.89*bis*.1(d) | 3–016 |
| r.70.12(ii) | 3–267 | r.89*bis*.1(e) | 3–016 |
| r.70.12(iii) | 3–247, 3–262 | r.89*bis*.2 | 3–340 |
| r.70.12(iv) | 3–254, 3–262 | r.89*bis*.3 | 3–340 |
| r.70.13 | 3–263 | r.89*ter*. | 3–014, 3–340 |
| r.70.14 | 3–134, 3–134259 | r.90.1 | 3–007 |
| r.70.15(a) | 3–134, 3–256 | r.90.1(a) | 3–329, 3–330, 3–333 |
| r.70.15(b) | 3–259 | r.90.1(b) | 3–329, 3–332, 3–333 |
| r.70.16 | 3–272 | r.90.1(c) | 3–329, 3–332, 3–333 |
| r.70.16(a) | 3–268 | r.90.1(d) | 3–329, 3–333 |
| r.70.16(b) | 3–268 | r.90.1(d)(ii) | 3–332, 3–333 |
| r.70.17 | 3–257 | r.90.2 | 3–007, 3–330 |
| r.71.1 | 3–269 | r.90.2(b) | 3–341, 3–344 |
| r.71.2 | 3–273, 3–357 | r.90.3 | 3–034, 3–331 |
| r.72.1 | 3–270 | r.90.4 | 3–332, 3–341, 3–342, 3–343, 3–344 |
| r.72.2 | 3–270 | r.90.4(a) | 3–332 |
| r.72.2*bis* | 3–271 | r.90.4(b) | 3–332 |
| r.72.3 | 3–270 | r.90.4(c) | 3–332 |
| r.73.1 | 3–270 | r.90.4(d) | 3–332 |
| r.73.2(a) | 3–270 | r.90.4(e) | 3–332 |
| r.73.2(b) | 3–270 | r.90.5 | 3–332, 3–341, 3–342, 3–343, 3–344 |
| r.73.2(b)(ii) | 3–271 | r.90.5(a) | 3–332 |
| r.73.2(c) | 3–270 | r.90.5(a)(ii) | 3–332 |
| r.74.1 | 3–272 | r.90.5(b) | 3–332 |
| r.74.1(a) | 3–272 | r.90.5(c) | 3–332 |
| r.76.1 | 3–168, 3–188 | r.90.5(d) | 3–332 |
| r.76.4 | 3–193 | r.90.6(a) | 3–333 |
| r.76.5 | 3–093, 3–193, 3–286, 3–287, 3–288, 3–290, 3–291, 3–294, 3–296, 3–327 | r.90.6(b) | 3–333 |
| | | r.90.6(c) | 3–333 |
| r.77 | 3–191 | r.90.6(d) | 3–333 |
| r.78.1(a) | 3–282 | r.90.6(e) | 3–333 |
| r.78.1(b) | 3–282 | r.90*bis* | 3–166 |
| r.78.3 | 3–290 | r.90*bis*1 | 3–172, 3–174, 3–332, 3–341, 3–342, 3–343, 3–344 |
| r.79 | 3–304 | | |
| r.80.1 | 3–305 | r.90*bis*1(a) | 3–341 |
| r.80.2 | 3–305 | r.90*bis*1(b) | 3–341 |
| r.80.3 | 3–305 | r.90*bis*1(c) | 3–341 |
| r.80.4 | 3–305 | r.90*bis* 2 | 3–332, 3–341, 3–342, 3–343, 3–344 |
| r.80.5 | 3–306, 3–307 | r.90*bis* 2(a) | 3–342, 3–342 |
| r.80.6 | 3–310, 3–311 | r.90*bis* 2(b) | 3–342 |
| r.80.7 | 3–305 | r.90*bis* 2(b) | 3–342 |
| r.82.1(a) | 3–308 | r.90*bis* 2(d) | 3–342 |
| r.82.1(b) | 3–308 | r.90*bis* 2(e) | 3–155, 3–342 |
| r.82.1(c) | 3–308 | r.90*bis* 3 | 3–332, 3–341, 3–342, 3–343, 3–344 |
| r.82.1(d) | 3–308 | r.90*bis* 3(a) | 3–343 |
| r.82.1(e) | 3–308 | r.90*bis* 3(b) | 3–343 |
| r.82.2(a) | 3–309 | r.90*bis* 3(c) | 3–343 |
| r.82.2(b) | 3–308 | r.90*bis* 3(d) | 3–148, 3–343 |
| r.82*bis*.1 | 3–316 | r.90*bis* 3(e) | 3–148, 3–343 |

| | |
|---|---|
| r.90*bis* 4 .................. 3–332, 3–341, 3–342, 3–343, 3–344 | r.92.1(c) ............................................................................ 3–336 |
| r.90*bis* 4(a) ...................................................................... 3–344 | r.92.2(a) ............................................................................ 3–337 |
| r.90*bis* 4(b) ...................................................................... 3–344 | r.92.2(b) ............................................................................ 3–337 |
| r.90*bis* 4(c) ...................................................................... 3–344 | r.92.2(d) ............................................................................ 3–337 |
| r.90*bis* 5 .............................. 3–341, 3–342, 3–343, 3–344 | r.92.2(e) ............................................................................ 3–337 |
| r.90*bis* 5(a) ...................................................................... 3–331 | r.92.3 .................................................................................. 3–346 |
| r.90*bis* 6(a) ........................ 3–341, 3–342, 3–343, 3–344 | r.92.4(a) ............................................................ 3–015, 3–339 |
| r.90*bis* 6(b) ...................................................................... 3–341 | r.92.4(b) ................................................ 3–015, 3–034, 3–339 |
| r.90*bis* 6(c) ...................................................................... 3–344 | r.92.4(c) ............................................................ 3–015, 3–339 |
| r.90*bis* 7 .......................................................................... 3–344 | r.92.4(d)–(e) .................................................... 3–015, 3–339 |
| r.91.1(a) ............................................................................ 3–320 | r.92.4(e) ............................................................ 3–015, 3–339 |
| r.91.1(b) ............................................................................ 3–320 | r.92.4(f) ............................................................. 3–015, 3–339 |
| r.91.1(c) ............................................................................ 3–321 | r.92.4(g) ................................................ 3–015, 3–113, 3–339 |
| r.91.1(d) ............................................................ 3–322, 3–323 | r.92.4(h) ............................................................ 3–015, 3–339 |
| r.91.1(e) ............................................................................ 3–324 | r.92.4(i) .............................................................................. 3–113 |
| r.91.1(e)(i) ........................................................................ 3–325 | r.92*bis* ............................................................................. 3–345 |
| r.91.1(e)(ii) ....................................................................... 3–325 | r.93.1 .................................................................................. 3–350 |
| r.91.1(e)(iii) ..................................................... 3–268, 3–325 | r.93.1 .................................................................................. 3–087 |
| r.91.1(f) .............................................................. 3–060, 3–324 | r.93.*bis*1 ........................... 3–138, 3–167, 3–168, 3–270 |
| r.91.1(g-*bis*) ................................................................... 3–324 | r.94 ...................................................................... 3–352, 3–353 |
| r.91.1(g-*quat*) ................................................................. 3–324 | r.95 ...................................................................................... 3–355 |
| r.91.1(g-*ter*) ................................................................... 3–324 | r.96 ...................................................................................... 3–345 |
| r.92.1(a) ............................................................ 3–336, 3–339 | r.104.(3) ............................................................................ 3–013 |
| r.92.1(b) ............................................................................ 3–336 | |

# TABLE OF ARTICLES AND RULES OF THE EUROPEAN PATENT CONVENTION

(*References are to paragraph numbers in Part C only*)

## Articles

1970 European Patent Convention

| | |
|---|---|
| Art.14(1) ............................................................ 3–196, 3–211 | Art.106(a) ......................................................................... 3–197 |
| Art.54(3) ............................................................................ 3–302 | Art.106(b) ......................................................................... 3–198 |
| Art.55(1) ............................................................................ 3–211 | Art.107(1)(a) .................................................................... 3–196 |
| Art.55(2) ............................................................ 3–206, 3–211 | Art.107(1)(b) .................................................................... 3–204 |
| Art.67(1) ............................................................................ 3–279 | Art.107(1)(c) .................................................................... 3–197 |
| Art.67(2) ............................................................................ 3–279 | Art.107(1)(d) .................................................................... 3–198 |
| Art.67(23 ........................................................................... 3–279 | Art.107(1)(e) .................................................................... 3–200 |
| Art.75(2) ............................................................................ 3–013 | Art.107(1)(f) ....................................................... 3–202, 3–205 |
| Art.78(2) ............................................................................ 3–197 | Art.107(1)(g) .................................................................... 3–201 |
| Art.79(2) ............................................................ 3–198, 3–211 | Art.107(1)(h) .................................................................... 3–206 |
| Art.81 ................................................................................. 3–211 | Art.107(2) ......................................................................... 3–202 |
| Art.86(1) ............................................................ 3–200, 3–211 | Art.108(1) ............... 3–196, 3–198, 3–200, 3–205, 3–207 |
| Art.86(2) ............................................................ 3–202, 3–211 | Art.108(2) ......................................................... 3–199, 3–207 |
| Art.86(3) ............................................................................ 3–211 | Art.108(2) ......................................................... 3–207, 3–207 |
| Art.88(1) ............................................................ 3–209, 3–211 | Art.109 ............................................................................... 3–300 |
| Art.90(2) ............................................................................ 3–211 | Art.110(1) ......................................................................... 3–203 |
| Art.91(1)(f) ....................................................................... 3–211 | Art.110(2) ......................................................................... 3–203 |
| Art.91(3) ............................................................................ 3–211 | Art.110(3) ......................................................................... 3–203 |
| Art.91(5) ............................................................ 3–209, 3–211 | Art.110(4) ......................................................................... 3–203 |
| Art.94(2) ...................................... 3–202, 3–205, 3–211 | Art.122(5) ......................................................................... 3–211 |
| Art.96(1) ............................................................................ 3–200 | Art.133 ................................................................ 3–011, 3–326 |
| Art.104(1) .......................................................................... 3–066 | Art.133(2) ......................................................................... 3–210 |
| Art.104(2) .......................................................................... 3–066 | Art.134 ................................................................ 3–011, 3–326 |
| Art.105(1) ............................................................ 3–066, 3–130 | Art.149(2) ......................................................................... 3–224 |
| Art.105(2) .......................................................................... 3–253 | Art.150 ....... 3–116, 3–118, 3–124, 3–128, 3–131, 3–215, |
| Art.105(3) .......................................................................... 3–130 | 3–225, 3–352 |
| | Art.150(1) ......................................................................... 3–334 |
| | Art.150(2) ............................................................ 3–205, 3–334 |

| | |
|---|---|
| Art.150(3) | 3–277 |
| Art.150(4) | 3–334 |
| Art.151 | 3–012, 3–081, 3–225 |
| Art.152(1) | 3–013 |
| Art.152(2) | 3–013 |
| Art.152(3) | 3–077 |
| Art.153(1) | 3–027, 3–224 |
| Art.153(2) | 3–315 |
| Art.154 | 3–130, 3–253 |
| Art.154(1) | 3–118 |
| Art.154(2) | 3–118 |
| Art.154(3) | 3–130 |
| Art.155(1) | 3–215 |
| Art.155(2) | 3–215 |
| Art.155(3) | 3–253 |
| Art.156 | 3–224 |
| Art.157(1) | 3–198, 3–202, 3–207, 3–211, 3–299 |
| Art.157(2) | 3–200, 3–211, 3–300 |
| Art.157(2)(b) | 3–200, 3–211 |
| Art.157(3) | 3–080, 3–200 |
| Art.157(4) | 3–200 |
| Art.158(1) | 3–279, 3–301, 3–302 |
| Art.158(2) | 3–179, 3–196, 3–197, 3–198, 3–211, 3–301, 3–302 |
| Art.158(3) | 3–179, 3–301 |

**Rules**

| | |
|---|---|
| r.17(1) | 3–208, 3–211 |
| r.23 | 3–206, 3–211 |
| r.24(1) | 3–016 |
| r.37(1) | 3–211 |
| r.38(1)–(3) | 3–209, 3–211 |
| r.38(3) | 3–209 |
| r.38(4) | 3–209 |
| r.46(2) | 3–285 |
| r.69(2) | 3–207 |
| r.84a | 3–308 |
| r.86(2)–(4) | 3–283 |
| r.88 | 3–027, 3–317 |
| r.104(1) | 3–069 |
| r.104(3) | 3–013 |
| r.106(a) | 3–013, 3–197, 3–211 |
| r.106(b) | 3–198, 3–211 |
| r.107(1) | 3–211 |
| r.107(1)(a) | 3–196, 3–211 |
| r.107(1)(c) | 3–197, 3–211 |
| r.107(1)(d) | 3–198, 3–211 |
| r.107(1)(e) | 3–211 |
| r.107(1)(f) | 3–211 |
| r.107(1)(g) | 3–211 |
| r.107(1)(h) | , 3–211 |
| r.108(1) | 3–196, 3–198, 3–211 |
| r.108(1)(a) | 3–196 |
| r.108(3) | 3–207, 3–211 |
| r.108(4) | 3–207 |
| r.109 | 3–283 |
| r.110(1) | 3–211 |
| r.110(2) | 3–211 |
| r.110(4) | 3–211 |
| r.111(1) | 3–208, 3–211 |
| r.111(2) | 3–209, 3–211, 3–289 |
| r.111(3) | 3–296 |
| r.112 | 3–285 |

# Guide to the Law under the Patent Co-operation Treaty

# 1. Institutional aspects and definitions

| | |
|---|---|
| 3–001 | **Establishment of a Union** |
| Art.1 | The states party to the PCT constitute a union for co-operation in the filing, searching and examination of applications for the protection of inventions and for rendering special technical services. The union is known as the International Patent Cooperation Union. |
| | **Parts of the Union** |
| 3–002 | *The Assembly* |
| Art.53(1) | The Assembly consists essentially of the Contracting States, each government being represented by one delegate. |
| 3–003 | *The International Bureau* |
| Art.55(1)–(3) | The International Bureau performs the administrative tasks of the Union and provides the secretariat of the various organs of the Union, the chief executive of which is the Director General. |
| | **Regulations and Administrative Instructions** |
| 3–004 | *Regulations under the PCT* |
| Art.58(1) | Regulations are annexed to the PCT and provide rules concerning: |

(a) matters in respect of which the PCT expressly refers to the Regulations or provides that they are or will be prescribed;

(b) any administrative requirements, matters or procedures; and

(c) any details useful in the implementation of the provisions of the PCT.

| | |
|---|---|
| Art.58(5) | In the case of conflict between the provisions of the PCT and those of the Regulations, the provisions of the PCT prevail. |
| 3–005 | *Administrative Instructions* |
| Art.58(4) | The Regulations provide for the establishment, under the control of the Assembly, of Administrative Instructions by the Director General. |
| r.89 | The Administrative Instructions contain provisions concerning: |

(a) matters in respect of which the Regulations expressly refer; and

(b) any details in respect of the application of the Regulations.

| | |
|---|---|
| 3–006 | **The Gazette** |
| Art.55(4) | The International Bureau publishes a Gazette (now only available in electronic form). |

The Gazette contains: r.86

(a) for each published application, data as specified in the Administrative Instructions taken from the front page of the publication, any drawing on the front page and the abstract;

(b) the schedule of all fees payable to the Receiving Offices, the International Bureau and the International Preliminary Examining and Searching Authorities;

(c) notices the publication of which is required under the PCT and its Regulations;

(d) information on the question of whether the requirements provided for in Art.22 or Art.39 (copy, translation and fee to designated/elected offices) have been complied with in respect of the international applications designating or electing the office concerned, if, and to the extent that, such an office furnishes such information to the International Bureau; and

(e) any other useful information, provided that access to such information is not prohibited under the PCT or its Regulations.

## Definitions/Interpretations 3–007

Unless expressly stated otherwise, the following definitions apply: Art.2

**Agent**: an agent appointed under r.90.1, unless the contrary clearly follows from the wording of the nature of the provision, or the context in which the word is used. r.2

**Applicant**: includes the agent or other representative of the applicant, except where the contrary clearly follows from the wording or the nature of the provision, or the context in which the word is used, such as, in particular, where the provision refers to the residence or nationality of the applicant. r.2

**Application**: an international or national application for the protection of an invention including patents, inventors' certificates, utility certificates, utility models, patents or certificates of addition, inventors' certificates of addition and utility certificates of addition. Art.2

**Assembly**: the Assembly of the Union. Art.2

**Common Representative**: an applicant appointed as, or considered to be, the common representative under r.90.2. r.2

**Contracting States**: states party to the PCT. Art.1

**Designated Office**: the national office of or acting for a state designated by the applicant under Chapter I of the PCT. Art.2

**Designated States**: those Contracting States in which protection for the invention is required on the basis of the international application and which are designated in the request. Art.4

**Director General**: the Director General of the Organisation and, as long as the United International Bureaux for the Protection of Intellectual Property (BIRPI) subsists, the Director of the BIRPI. Art.2

**Elected Office**: the national office of or acting for a State elected by the applicant under Chapter II of the PCT. Art.2

**International Application**: an application filed under the PCT. Art.2

**International Bureau**: the International Bureau of the Organisation and, as long as it subsists, the United International Bureaux for the Protection of Intellectual Property (BIRPI). Art.2

| | |
|---|---|
| Art.2 | **National Application**: an application for a national or a regional patent other than an application under the PCT. |
| Art.2 | **National Law**: the national law of a Contracting State or, where a regional application or a regional patent is involved, to the treaty providing for the filing of regional applications or the granting of regional patents. |
| Art.2 | **National Office**: the government authority of a Contracting State entrusted with the granting of patents or any intergovernmental authority which several states have entrusted with the task of granting regional patents, provided that at least one of those states is a Contracting State and provided that the said states have authorised that authority to assume the obligations and exercise the powers which the PCT and its Regulations provide for in respect of national offices. |
| Art.2 | **National Patent**: a patent granted by a national authority. |
| Art.2 | **Organisation**: the World Intellectual Property Organisation |
| Art.2 | **Patent**: a national or regional patent for an invention, an inventors' certificate, a utility certificate, a utility model, a patent or certificate of addition, an inventors' certificate of addition or a utility certificate of addition. |
| Art.2 | **Priority Date**: The priority date is: (a) where the international application contains a priority claim under Art.8, the filing date of the application whose priority is so claimed; (b) where the international application contains several priority claims under Art.8, the filing date of the earliest application whose priority is so claimed; or (c) where the international application does not contain any priority claim under Art.8, the international filing date of such an application. |
| Art.2 | **Receiving Office**: the national office or intergovernmental organisation with which the international application has been filed. |
| Art.2 | **Regional Application**: an application for a regional patent. |
| Art.2 | **Regional Patent**: a patent granted by a national or an intergovernmental authority having the power to grant patents effective in more than one state. |
| r.2 | **Signature**: if the national law applied by the Receiving Office or the competent International Searching or Preliminary Examining Authority requires the use of a seal instead of a signature, the word for the purposes of that office or Authority, means seal. |
| r.1 | **Treaty**: the Patent Co-operation Treaty (PCT). |
| Art.2 | **Union**: the International Patent Cooperation Union. |

## 2. Filing an international patent application

**3–008** **Who is entitled to file an international patent application?**

| | |
|---|---|
| Art.9(1) | Any resident or national of a PCT Contracting State may file an international application. |
| Art.9(2) | In addition, the Assembly may decide to extend this right to residents and nationals of non-PCT countries party to the Paris Convention. |
| Art.9(3)/r.18.1 | Questions of residency and nationality are decided by the Receiving Office under the national law of the appropriate Contracting State but in any case: (a) possession of a real and effective industrial or commercial establishment in a Contracting State is |

considered to be residence there; and (b) a legal entity constituted according to the national law of a Contracting State is considered a national of that state.

Where the International Bureau is the Receiving Office it asks (in the circumstances specified in the Administrative Instructions) the national office of, or acting for, the Contracting State concerned to decide any question of residency or nationality and informs the applicant that it is doing so. The applicant has the right to submit arguments to the national office directly and the national office must decide the question promptly. r.18.1(c)

Different applicants may be indicated for different states in respect of the same application. (NB. Not for different kinds of protection in respect of the same State—see Applicant's Guide, Vol.1, para.62.) r.4.5(d)

See s.203. Different applicants may be indicated for different States within the designation of a regional patent but where the same State has been indicated for both a national and regional patent, the applicants for each must be the same. AdminInst

If there are two or more applicants at least one of them must be entitled to file an international application. r.18.3

The International Bureau periodically publishes information on the various national laws in respect of who is qualified to file a national application (*e.g.* the inventor, his successor in title, the owner of the invention) accompanied by a warning that the effect of the international application in any designated state may depend on whether the person designated as applicant for that state is qualified, under the law of that state, to file a national application. r.18.4

In particular, the international application may be rejected in the US national phase if the applicant is not the inventor. Art.27(3)

### Where may an international patent application be filed? 3–009

An international patent application must be filed at a competent Receiving Office who will check and process it according to the PCT. Art.10

The competent Receiving Offices are: r.19.1(a)(b)

(a) the International Bureau, in all cases;

(b) a national office of, or acting for, the Contracting State of which the applicant is resident or a national;

(c) the national office of another state or an intergovernmental organisation where a relevant agreement has been implemented between the state of which the applicant is a national or resident and the other state. Even so, the national office of the former state is considered the competent office for the purposes of Art.15(5) (whether national law permits the carrying out of an international-type search on a national application).

The delegating state under (c) must promptly inform the International Bureau of such an agreement which will then be promptly published in the Gazette. r.19.3

Where residents or nationals of a country party to the Paris Convention but not the PCT are allowed to file international applications under Art.9(2), the Assembly appoints the national office or intergovernmental organisation (with its consent) which will act as Receiving Office in respect of that country. r.19.1(c)

Where there are two or more applicants, the application must be filed at the national office of, or acting for, a Contracting State of which at least one of the applicants is a r.19.2

national or resident or at the International Bureau (as long as one of the applicants is a resident or national of a Contracting State).

Art.27(8)

Nothing in the PCT or its Regulations limits the freedom of each Contracting State to apply measures deemed necessary for the preservation of its national security or to limit, for the protection of the general economic interests of that state, the right of its own residents or nationals to file international applications.

**3–010**     **Procedure when the application is filed in the wrong place**

r.19.4

When the application is filed with a national office but:

(a) that office is not competent to act as a Receiving Office under r.19.1 (applicant must be a resident or national) or r.19.2 (one of joint applicants must be a resident or national), or

(b) the application is in a language not accepted by the national office under r.12.1 but accepted by the International Bureau under that Rule (see below), or

(c) the national office, International Bureau and applicant all agree for whatever reason,

the application is considered to have been received by the national office on behalf of the International Bureau under r.19.1(a)(iii), and is promptly transmitted to the International Bureau unless prescriptions concerning national security apply. A fee equal to the transmittal fee charged under r.14 may be levied by the national office for such transmittal. The application is considered to have been received by the International Bureau on the date that it was received by the national office except that the date of receipt for the purposes of r.14.1(c), r.15.4(a)–(c) and r.16.1(f) (deadlines for paying the transmittal fee, international filing fee and search fee) is the actual date of receipt by the International Bureau.

**3–011**     **The Receiving Office can apply national law relating to representation**

Art.27(7)

Any Receiving Office may apply national law in so far as it relates to any requirement that the applicant be represented by an agent having the right to represent applicants before that Office.

Where the EPO is Receiving Office, Art.133 and Art.134 EPC determine the requirements for representation. Due to the restrictions on who can use the EPO as Receiving Office (see below) representation will rarely be obligatory.

**3–012**     **Those entitled to use the EPO as a Receiving Office**

*Art.151*

The EPO may act as a Receiving Office if:

(a) the applicant is a resident or national of an EPC Contracting State in respect of which the PCT has entered into force; or

(b) the applicant is a resident or national of a state which is not an EPC Contracting State but which is a PCT Contracting State and has concluded an agreement with the European Patent Organisation whereby the EPO acts as a Receiving Office instead of the national office of that state; or

(c) the applicant comes within the terms of an agreement between the European Patent Organisation and the International Bureau which has the prior approval of the Administrative Council.

## Filing an international application with the EPO 3–013

See Vol.1, Annex C. The EPO can, subject to certain national security requirements, act as a receiving office for nationals and residents of any EPC Contracting State.  AppGuide

An international application for which the EPO is to act as a Receiving Office must be filed directly at the EPO. Nevertheless, the national security requirements allowed by Art.75(2) EPC continue to apply and hence such applications can be filed via the national offices.  **Art.152(1)**

Where an international application for which the EPO is to act as a Receiving Office is filed via the patent office of an EPC Contracting State, that state must take all necessary measures to ensure that the international application is transmitted to the EPO in time for the EPO to comply with its obligations for transmitting the application under the PCT.  **Art.152(2)**

This means that the application should reach the EPO not later than two weeks before the end of the 13th month after the filing date/priority date.  r.104(3)

See E/IX/2.  Guidelines

## Manner of filing the application

### *The use of paper* 3–014

All Receiving Offices must permit the filing of international applications on paper.  r.89*bis*.1(a)

Any office or intergovernmental organisation may provide that, where an international application is filed on paper, a copy thereof in electronic form, in accordance with the Administrative Instructions, may be furnished by the applicant.  r.89*ter*

### *The use of telegraph, teleprinter, or facsimile* 3–015

A document making up the international application may be transmitted, if feasible, by telegraph, teleprinter, facsimile or other like means of communication resulting in the filing of a printed or written document but no national office or intergovernmental organisation is obliged to receive a document submitted in this way unless it has notified the International Bureau to the effect that it will and such information has been published in the Gazette.  r.92.4(a)(h)

Where such means are used to transmit the application and part or all of it is not received or is illegible on receipt, the application is treated as not received to the extent that it is not received or illegible. The relevant national office or intergovernmental organisation will promptly inform the applicant accordingly.  r.92.4(c)

Where such means are used to transmit the application, any national office or intergovernmental organisation may require that the original and an accompanying letter identifying the earlier transmission is forwarded within 14 days of such transmission, provided that such a requirement has been notified to the International Bureau and published in the Gazette. Where the original is not so forwarded, the relevant office or organisation may, depending on the kind of document involved, and having regard to r.11 (physical requirements) and r.26.3 (checking of physical requirements): (i) waive the requirement; or (ii) invite the applicant to forward the original within a reasonable time limit fixed in the invitation; or (iii) where the document transmitted contains defects or shows that the original contains defects warranting an invitation to correct, issue such an invitation instead or in addition to (i) or (ii).  r.92.4(d)–(e)

If the forwarding of an original is not required as specified in r.92.4(d)), but the relevant office or organisation nevertheless considers it necessary to receive the original, it may invite the applicant to forward the original in accordance with r.92.4(e) above.  r.92.4(f)

| | |
|---|---|
| r.92.4(g) | Where the applicant fails to comply with an invitation under r.92.4(e), the application will be considered to be withdrawn and the Receiving Office will so declare. |
| r.92.4(b) | A signature appearing on a document transmitted by facsimile is recognised for the purposes of the PCT and its Regulations as a proper signature. |
| [2005] O.J. 41 | The EPO will accept filings by fax but not by telegraph or teleprinter anymore. Confirmation is still required, in contrast to the procedure for European applications where it is no longer routinely required. |

### 3–016 *Filing in electronic form*

| | |
|---|---|
| r.89*bis*.1(a) | International applications may be filed in electronic form or by electronic means (in accordance with the Administrative Instructions). |
| r.89*bis*.1(b)(c) | The PCT Regulations apply equally to applications filed electronically, subject to any special provisions of the Administrative Instructions which set out the requirements for the filing and processing of applications filed wholly or partly in electronic form. |
| r.89*bis*.1(d)(e) | No national office or intergovernmental organisation is required to receive international applications filed in electronic form or by electronic means unless it has notified the International Bureau that it is prepared to do so according to the provisions of the Administrative Provisions. Such notification is published by the International Bureau in the Gazette. Having issued such a notification, a Receiving Office may not refuse to process international applications filed in electronic form or by electronic means which comply with the requirements of the Administrative Instructions. |
| AdminInst | See Part 7 and Annex F. |
| AnReg | See under *r.24(1)*. The EPO does permit such electronic filing ([2002] O.J. 543). |

## 3. REQUIREMENTS RELATING TO THE APPLICATION AS FILED

### 3–017 **Requirements relating to the request**

| | |
|---|---|
| Art.3(2) | An international application must contain a request. |

### 3–018 **Use of a specified form**

| | |
|---|---|
| r.3.1/r.3.4 | The request must be made on a printed form or presented as a computer print-out. Particulars are given in the Administrative Instructions (see s.102(h)). |
| r.3.2 | Copies of the printed form are furnished free of charge by the Receiving Offices and the International Bureau. |

### 3–019 **Petition**

| | |
|---|---|
| Art.4(1)(i) | The request must contain a petition asking that the application be processed according to the PCT (see also r.4.1(a)(i)). |
| r.4.2 | The petition is preferably worded as "The undersigned requests that the present international application be processed according to the PCT." |

### 3–020 **Title**

| | |
|---|---|
| Art.4(1)(iv) | The request must contain the title of the invention (see also r.4.1(a)(ii)). |
| r.4.3 | The title should be short (preferably 2–7 words when in English or translated into English) and precise. |

## Details of the applicant

3–021

The request must contain the name of and other prescribed data concerning the applicant (see also r.4.1(a)(iii)).

Art.4(1)(iii)

Apart from the name, the request must indicate the address, nationality and residence of the applicant or applicants, the nationality and residence being indicated by the name of the appropriate state. Names and addresses must be indicated in accordance with r.4.4 (see below). There may be different applicants in respect of different designated states. Any number or other indication under which the applicant is registered with the Receiving Office may be indicated.

r.4.5(a)–(e)

## Details of the inventor

3–022

The request must contain the name of and other prescribed data concerning the inventor, when the law of at least one designated state requires this information to be disclosed on filing. Otherwise, this information can either be supplied in the request or communicated to designated offices separately. See also r.4.1(a)(iv).

Art.4(1)(v)

The consequences of not supplying inventor details in the request or later on are determined according to the national law of each designated state.

Art.4(4)

The request may contain indications concerning the inventor even where the national law of none of the designated states requires the name of the inventor to be furnished on filing.

r.4.1(c)

Apart from the name, the address of the inventor or inventors should be indicated. Alternatively a statement that the applicant is the inventor may be included. Due to differences in national law, different inventors may be indicated for different States. Names and addresses must be indicated in accordance with r.4.4 (see below).

r.4.6(a)–(c)

## Details of any agent

3–023

The request must contain the name of and other prescribed data concerning any appointed agent (see also r.4.1(a)(iii)).

Art.4(1)(iii)

Apart from the name, the request must indicate an address of any appointed agent. The name and address must be indicated in accordance with r.4.4 (see below). Any number or other indication under which the agent is registered with the Receiving Office may be indicated.

r.4.7

## Details of any common representative

3–024

Where a common representative is appointed, the request must so indicate.

r.4.8

## Address for correspondence

3–025

Whilst, in general, only one address may be indicated for each applicant, inventor and agent, where no agent is appointed the applicant or common representative may indicate a further address for correspondence.

r.4.4(d)

# PCT

## REQUEST

The undersigned requests that the present international application be processed according to the Patent Cooperation Treaty.

---

**For receiving Office use only**

International Application No.

International Filing Date

Name of receiving Office and "PCT International Application"

Applicant's or agent's file reference *(if desired) (12 characters maximum)*

---

| Box No. I | TITLE OF INVENTION |
|---|---|

| Box No. II | APPLICANT | ☐ This person is also inventor |
|---|---|---|

Name and address: *(Family name followed by given name; for a legal entity, full official designation. The address must include postal code and name of country. The country of the address indicated in this Box is the applicant's State (that is, country) of residence if no State of residence is indicated below.)*

Telephone No.

Facsimile No.

Teleprinter No.

Applicant's registration No. with the Office

State *(that is, country)* of nationality:

State *(that is, country)* of residence:

This person is applicant for the purposes of:
☐ all designated States
☐ all designated States except the United States of America
☐ the United States of America only
☐ the States indicated in the Supplemental Box

| Box No. III | FURTHER APPLICANT(S) AND/OR (FURTHER) INVENTOR(S) |
|---|---|

Name and address: *(Family name followed by given name; for a legal entity, full official designation. The address must include postal code and name of country. The country of the address indicated in this Box is the applicant's State (that is, country) of residence if no State of residence is indicated below.)*

This person is:
☐ applicant only
☐ applicant and inventor
☐ inventor only *(If this check-box is marked, do not fill in below.)*

Applicant's registration No. with the Office

State *(that is, country)* of nationality:

State *(that is, country)* of residence:

This person is applicant for the purposes of:
☐ all designated States
☐ all designated States except the United States of America
☐ the United States of America only
☐ the States indicated in the Supplemental Box

☐ Further applicants and/or (further) inventors are indicated on a continuation sheet.

| Box No. IV | AGENT OR COMMON REPRESENTATIVE; OR ADDRESS FOR CORRESPONDENCE |
|---|---|

The person identified below is hereby/has been appointed to act on behalf of the applicant(s) before the competent International Authorities as:   ☐ agent   ☐ common representative

Name and address: *(Family name followed by given name; for a legal entity, full official designation. The address must include postal code and name of country.)*

Telephone No.

Facsimile No.

Teleprinter No.

Agent's registration No. with the Office

☐ **Address for correspondence:** Mark this check-box where no agent or common representative is/has been appointed and the space above is used instead to indicate a special address to which correspondence should be sent.

Form PCT/RO/101 (first sheet) (April 2006)   *See Notes to the request form*

*3. Requirements Relating to the Application as Filed* 537

Sheet No. . . . . . . .

| Continuation of Box No. III    FURTHER APPLICANT(S) AND/OR (FURTHER) INVENTOR(S) |
|---|
| *If none of the following sub-boxes is used, this sheet should not be included in the request.* |

Name and address: *(Family name followed by given name; for a legal entity, full official designation. The address must include postal code and name of country. The country of the address indicated in this Box is the applicant's State (that is, country) of residence if no State of residence is indicated below.)*

This person is:
☐ applicant only
☐ applicant and inventor
☐ inventor only *(If this check-box is marked, do not fill in below.)*

Applicant's registration No. with the Office

State *(that is, country)* of nationality:    State *(that is, country)* of residence:

This person is applicant for the purposes of:  ☐ all designated States   ☐ all designated States except the United States of America   ☐ the United States of America only   ☐ the States indicated in the Supplemental Box

Name and address: *(Family name followed by given name; for a legal entity, full official designation. The address must include postal code and name of country. The country of the address indicated in this Box is the applicant's State (that is, country) of residence if no State of residence is indicated below.)*

This person is:
☐ applicant only
☐ applicant and inventor
☐ inventor only *(If this check-box is marked, do not fill in below.)*

Applicant's registration No. with the Office

State *(that is, country)* of nationality:    State *(that is, country)* of residence:

This person is applicant for the purposes of:  ☐ all designated States   ☐ all designated States except the United States of America   ☐ the United States of America only   ☐ the States indicated in the Supplemental Box

Name and address: *(Family name followed by given name; for a legal entity, full official designation. The address must include postal code and name of country. The country of the address indicated in this Box is the applicant's State (that is, country) of residence if no State of residence is indicated below.)*

This person is:
☐ applicant only
☐ applicant and inventor
☐ inventor only *(If this check-box is marked, do not fill in below.)*

Applicant's registration No. with the Office

State *(that is, country)* of nationality:    State *(that is, country)* of residence:

This person is applicant for the purposes of:  ☐ all designated States   ☐ all designated States except the United States of America   ☐ the United States of America only   ☐ the States indicated in the Supplemental Box

Name and address: *(Family name followed by given name; for a legal entity, full official designation. The address must include postal code and name of country. The country of the address indicated in this Box is the applicant's State (that is, country) of residence if no State of residence is indicated below.)*

This person is:
☐ applicant only
☐ applicant and inventor
☐ inventor only *(If this check-box is marked, do not fill in below.)*

Applicant's registration No. with the Office

State *(that is, country)* of nationality:    State *(that is, country)* of residence:

This person is applicant for the purposes of:  ☐ all designated States   ☐ all designated States except the United States of America   ☐ the United States of America only   ☐ the States indicated in the Supplemental Box

☐ Further applicants and/or (further) inventors are indicated on another continuation sheet.

Form PCT/RO/101 (continuation sheet) (April 2006)    *See Notes to the request form*

Sheet No. . . . . . . .

| **Supplemental Box** | *If the Supplemental Box is not used, this sheet should not be included in the request.* |

1. *If, in any of the Boxes, except Boxes Nos. VIII(i) to (v) for which a special continuation box is provided, **the space is insufficient** to furnish all the information: in such case, write "Continuation of Box No...." (indicate the number of the Box) and furnish the information in the same manner as required according to the captions of the Box in which the space was insufficient, in particular:*

    (i) **if more than two persons are to be indicated as applicants and/or inventors** *and no "continuation sheet" is available: in such case, write "Continuation of Box No. III" and indicate for each additional person the same type of information as required in Box No. III. The country of the address indicated in this Box is the applicant's State (that is, country) of residence if no State of residence is indicated below;*

    (ii) *if, in Box No. II or in any of the sub-boxes of Box No. III, the indication **"the States indicated in the Supplemental Box"** is checked: in such case, write "Continuation of Box No. II" or "Continuation of Box No. III" or "Continuation of Boxes No. II and No. III" (as the case may be), indicate the name of the applicant(s) involved and, next to (each) such name, the State(s) (and/or, where applicable, ARIPO, Eurasian, European or OAPI patent) for the purposes of which the named person is applicant;*

    (iii) *if, in Box No. II or in any of the sub-boxes of Box No. III, **the inventor or the inventor/applicant is not inventor for the purposes of all designated States or for the purposes of the United States of America**: in such case, write "Continuation of Box No. II" or "Continuation of Box No. III" or "Continuation of Boxes No. II and No. III" (as the case may be), indicate the name of the inventor(s) and, next to (each) such name, the State(s) (and/or, where applicable, ARIPO, Eurasian, European or OAPI patent) for the purposes of which the named person is inventor;*

    (iv) *if, in addition to the agent(s) indicated in Box No. IV, there are **further agents**: in such case, write "Continuation of Box No. IV" and indicate for each further agent the same type of information as required in Box No. IV;*

    (v) *if, in Box No. VI, there are **more than three earlier applications whose priority is claimed**: in such case, write "Continuation of Box No. VI" and indicate for each additional earlier application the same type of information as required in Box No. VI.*

2. *If the applicant intends to make an indication of the wish that the international application be treated, in certain designated States, as an application for a patent of addition, certificate of addition, inventor's certificate of addition or utility certificate of addition: in such a case, write the name or two-letter code of each designated State concerned and the indication "**patent of addition**," "**certificate of addition**," "**inventor's certificate of addition**" or "**utility certificate of addition**," the number of the parent application or parent patent or other parent grant and the date of grant of the parent patent or other parent grant or the date of filing of the parent application (Rules 4.11(a)(iii) and 49bis.1(a) or (b)).*

3. *If the applicant intends to make an indication of the wish that the international application be treated, in the United States of America, as a continuation or continuation-in-part of an earlier application: in such a case, write "United States of America" or "US" and the indication "**continuation**" or "**continuation-in-part**" and the number and the filing date of the parent application (Rules 4.11(a)(iv) and 49bis.1(d)).*

Form PCT/RO/101 (supplemental sheet) (April 2006)  *See Notes to the request form*

## Designations

3–026

The request must contain the designation of those Contracting States in which protection is desired, either as a national patent or a regional patent.

Art.4(1)(ii)

The filing of a request is now taken to constitute the designation of all Contracting States for which the PCT is in force on the filing date, in respect of every kind of protection available in those states (Art.43 and 44) and in respect of both a national and regional patent where a choice is available (Art.45). The request may, however, specifically exclude the designation of certain states in which the filing of an international application claiming priority from a national application in that country has the effect of the automatic withdrawal of that national application. Such states must have informed the International Bureau accordingly by January 5, 2006. These states are Germany, the Republic of Korea, the Russian Federation and Japan. NB. This provision, which dates from 1.1.2004, was amended slightly as of 1.4.2006. The main change was the addition of Japan as a designation which may be disclaimed.

r.4.9

Note that designations can still be withdrawn during the international phase.

R90bis.2(a)

Any Regional Patent Treaty which gives to all persons entitled to file international applications (under Art.9) the right to file applications under such a treaty may provide that international applications designating a state party to both that Regional Patent Treaty and the PCT may be filed as applications for such patents.

Art.45(1)

The national law of said designated state may provide that the designation of that state has the effect of an indication of the wish to obtain a regional patent under the Regional Patent Treaty.

Art.45(2)

The PCT allows national law to specify that designation of that State will have the effect of the designation of a regional patent (e.g. Belgium, Cyprus, France, Greece, Ireland, Italy, Monaco, the Netherlands and (since December 1, 2002) Slovenia provide that their designation via the PCT indicates the wish to obtain a European Patent). Conversely, the PCT allows that where a regional patent treaty specifies that the applicant cannot limit his application to certain states then designation of one of those states for a regional patent will be treated as designation of all the states to the treaty.

Art.4(1)(ii)

An international application may designate a state in which a prior application whose priority it claims was filed (see under priority claim below).

Art.8

## Designation of the EPO

3–027

The EPO will act as a designated office for those EPC Contracting States in respect of which the PCT has entered into force and which are designated in the international application if the applicant informs the Receiving Office in the international application that that he wishes to obtain a European patent for those states (now automatic).

*Art.153(1)*

Further, the EPO will act as a designated office for those EPC Contracting States in respect of which the PCT has entered into force and which are designated in the international application if the national law of such a state provides that the designation of that state has the effect of an application for a European patent (currently Belgium, Cyprus, France, Greece, Ireland, Italy, Monaco, the Netherlands and Slovenia).

*Art.153(1)*

Extension states must be separately designated for a national patent (now automatic).

The EPO is designated as long as this is apparent from the Request, regardless of whether the designation is noted in the application as published.

J26/87

Article 26 PCT gives a purported designated office the authority to consider if its designation can be added or not (under r.88 EPC). However, in accordance with decisions

J8/01

|        |                                                                                                                                                                                                      |
|--------|------------------------------------------------------------------------------------------------------------------------------------------------------------------------------------------------------|
|        | relating to regular European patent applications, the mistake must be corrected early enough for the public to be warned on international publication.                                               |
| 3–028  | ***Kind of protection sought***                                                                                                                                                                      |
| Art.4(3) | The designation of a State means its designation in respect of obtaining a patent (the Art.2(ii) definition does not apply here) unless the applicant asks for any other kind of protection.        |
| r.4.9  | However, filing the request now amounts to the designation of all states in respect of all kinds of protection (see above).                                                                          |
| 3–029  | ***Priority claim***                                                                                                                                                                                 |
| Art.8  | The request may contain a declaration claiming the priority of an earlier application or applications (see also r.4.1(b)(i)).                                                                        |
| r.4.10 | The request must state the date on which the earlier application was filed (within 12 months preceding the international filing date), its number and the Convention country or World Trade Organisation Country (for national applications), regional authority (for regional applications) or Receiving Office (for international applications) in/with which it was filed. When claiming the priority of an international or regional application, one or more countries party to the Paris Convention for which the application was filed may be indicated. In the case of a regional application where at least one of the Contracting States is neither a member of the Paris Convention or the World Trade Organisation, at least one Contracting State which is a member of the Paris Convention or the World Trade Organisation must be indicated. The definition of "national patent" given in Art.2(vi) does not apply for the purpose of r.4.10. |
| r.26*bis*.1 | Under the PCT, claims to priority may also be made after filing the request—see below.                                                                                                          |
| 3–030  | ***Choice of international searching authority***                                                                                                                                                    |
| r.4.14*bis* | The applicant must indicate his choice of International Searching Authority if two or more are competent (see also r.4.1(b)(iv)).                                                               |
| AppGuide | See Vol.I, Annex C. When the EPO acts as Receiving Office, the EPO is the only competent International Searching Authority.                                                                        |
| 3–031  | ***Reference to an earlier search***                                                                                                                                                                 |
| r.4.11 | A reference to (a) an earlier international or international-type search performed on the application (Art.15(5)) or (b) a non-international or non-international-type search carried out by the International Searching Authority may be indicated if the applicant wishes the International Searching Authority to base the international search report wholly or partly on such a search. The reference must identify (a) the application or translation on which the search was carried out (country, date, number) or (b) the date and number of the request for the search. See also r.4.1(b)(ii). |
| 3–032  | ***Standardised declarations***                                                                                                                                                                      |
| r.4.17 | One or more declarations may be included in the request for the purposes of the national law applicable to one or more designated states (see also r.4.1(c)(iii)). The relevant wording is prescribed by the Administrative Instructions (see ss.211 to 215). These declarations are: |
| r.4.17(i) | (a) a declaration as to the identity of the inventor as referred to in r.51*bis*.1(a)(i);                                                                                                         |
| r.4.17(ii) | (b) a declaration as to the applicant's entitlement, as at the international filing date, to apply for and be granted a patent as referred to in r.51*bis*.1(a)(ii);                             |

(c) a declaration as to the applicant's entitlement, as at the international filing date, to claim the priority of the earlier application as referred to in r.51*bis*.1(a)(iii);  
    r.4.17(iii)

(d) a declaration of inventorship (only for the purposes of a US designation) as referred to in r.51*bis*.1(a)(iv) and signed as indicated in the Administrative Instructions; and  
    r.4.17(iv)

(e) a declaration as to non-prejudicial disclosures or exceptions to lack of novelty as referred to in r.51*bis*.1(a)(v).  
    r.4.17(v)

The applicant may correct or add any of these declarations up until 16 months from the priority date by writing to the International Bureau. Any such addition or correction received late but before the technical preparations for publication are complete will be considered as received in time. If any addition or correction is received late the International Bureau will notify the applicant and proceed as provided in the Administrative Instructions.  
    r.26*ter*

Sheet No. .......

### Box No. V  DESIGNATIONS

The filing of this request **constitutes under Rule 4.9(a), the designation** of all Contracting States bound by the PCT on the international filing date, for the grant of every kind of protection available and, where applicable, for the grant of both regional and national patents. However,

☐ DE Germany **is not designated** for any kind of national protection
☐ JP Japan **is not designated** for any kind of national protection
☐ KR Republic of Korea **is not designated** for any kind of national protection
☐ RU Russian Federation **is not designated** for any kind of national protection

*(The check-boxes above may only be used to exclude (irrevocably) the designations concerned if, at the time of filing, the international application contains in Box No. VI a priority claim to an earlier national application filed in the particular State concerned, in order to avoid the ceasing of the effect, under the national law, of this earlier national application. See the Notes to Box No. V as to the consequences of such national law provisions in these States).*

### Box No. VI  PRIORITY CLAIM

The priority of the following earlier application(s) is hereby claimed:

| Filing date of earlier application *(day/month/year)* | Number of earlier application | Where earlier application is: | | |
|---|---|---|---|---|
| | | national application: country or Member of WTO | regional application:* regional Office | international application: receiving Office |
| item (1) | | | | |
| item (2) | | | | |
| item (3) | | | | |

☐ Further priority claims are indicated in the Supplemental Box.

The receiving Office is requested to prepare and transmit to the International Bureau a certified copy of the earlier application(s) *(only if the earlier application was filed with the Office which for the purposes of this international application is the receiving Office)* identified above as:

☐ all items   ☐ item (1)   ☐ item (2)   ☐ item (3)   ☐ other, see Supplemental Box

\* Where the earlier application is an ARIPO application, indicate at least one country party to the Paris Convention for the Protection of Industrial Property or one Member of the World Trade Organization for which that earlier application was filed (Rule 4.10(b)(ii)):
.................................................................................................................................................................

### Box No. VII  INTERNATIONAL SEARCHING AUTHORITY

**Choice of International Searching Authority (ISA)** *(if two or more International Searching Authorities are competent to carry out the international search, indicate the Authority chosen; the two-letter code may be used)*:

ISA / ..........................................................................................................................

**Request to use results of earlier search; reference to that search** *(if an earlier search has been carried out by or requested from the International Searching Authority)*:

Date *(day/month/year)*       Number       Country *(or regional Office)*

### Box No. VIII  DECLARATIONS

The following **declarations** are contained in Boxes Nos. VIII (i) to (v) *(mark the applicable check-boxes below and indicate in the right column the number of each type of declaration)*:     Number of declarations

☐ Box No. VIII (i)      Declaration as to the identity of the inventor      :

☐ Box No. VIII (ii)     Declaration as to the applicant's entitlement, as at the international filing date, to apply for and be granted a patent      :

☐ Box No. VIII (iii)    Declaration as to the applicant's entitlement, as at the international filing date, to claim the priority of the earlier application      :

☐ Box No. VIII (iv)     Declaration of inventorship (only for the purposes of the designation of the United States of America)      :

☐ Box No. VIII (v)      Declaration as to non-prejudicial disclosures or exceptions to lack of novelty      :

Form PCT/RO/101 (second sheet) (April 2006)                    *See Notes to the request form*

Sheet No. . . . . . . .

**Box No. VIII (i)   DECLARATION: IDENTITY OF THE INVENTOR**

*The declaration must conform to the standardized wording provided for in Section 211; see Notes to Boxes Nos. VIII, VIII (i) to (v) (in general) and the specific Notes to Box No.VIII (i). If this Box is not used, this sheet should not be included in the request.*

Declaration as to the identity of the inventor (Rules 4.17(i) and 51*bis*.1(a)(i)):

☐ This declaration is continued on the following sheet, "Continuation of Box No. VIII (i)".

Form PCT/RO/101 (declaration sheet (i)) (April 2006) *See Notes to the request form*

Sheet No. . . . . . . .

**Box No. VIII (ii)   DECLARATION: ENTITLEMENT TO APPLY FOR AND BE GRANTED A PATENT**
*The declaration must conform to the standardized wording provided for in Section 212; see Notes to Boxes Nos. VIII, VIII (i) to (v) (in general) and the specific Notes to Box No.VIII (ii). If this Box is not used, this sheet should not be included in the request.*

Declaration as to the applicant's entitlement, as at the international filing date, to apply for and be granted a patent (Rules 4.17(ii) and 51*bis*.1(a)(ii)), in a case where the declaration under Rule 4.17(iv) is not appropriate:

☐ This declaration is continued on the following sheet, "Continuation of Box No. VIII (ii)".

Form PCT/RO/101 (declaration sheet (ii)) (April 2006)                                    *See Notes to the request form*

Sheet No. .......

**Box No. VIII (iii)  DECLARATION: ENTITLEMENT TO CLAIM PRIORITY**

*The declaration must conform to the standardized wording provided for in Section 213; see Notes to Boxes Nos. VIII, VIII (i) to (v) (in general) and the specific Notes to Box No. VIII (iii). If this Box is not used, this sheet should not be included in the request.*

Declaration as to the applicant's entitlement, as at the international filing date, to claim the priority of the earlier application specified below, where the applicant is not the applicant who filed the earlier application or where the applicant's name has changed since the filing of the earlier application (Rules 4.17(iii) and 51*bis*.1(a)(iii)):

☐ This declaration is continued on the following sheet, "Continuation of Box No. VIII (iii)".

Form PCT/RO/101 (declaration sheet (iii)) (April 2006) *See Notes to the request form*

Sheet No. .......

**Box No. VIII (iv) DECLARATION: INVENTORSHIP (only for the purposes of the designation of the United States of America)**
*The declaration must conform to the following standardized wording provided for in Section 214; see Notes to Boxes Nos. VIII, VIII (i) to (v) (in general) and the specific Notes to Box No. VIII (iv). If this Box is not used, this sheet should not be included in the request.*

**Declaration of inventorship (Rules 4.17(iv) and 51*bis*.1(a)(iv))
for the purposes of the designation of the United States of America:**

I hereby declare that I believe I am the original, first and sole (if only one inventor is listed below) or joint (if more than one inventor is listed below) inventor of the subject matter which is claimed and for which a patent is sought.

This declaration is directed to the international application of which it forms a part (if filing declaration with application).

This declaration is directed to international application No. PCT/............................ (if furnishing declaration pursuant to Rule 26*ter*).

I hereby declare that my residence, mailing address, and citizenship are as stated next to my name.

I hereby state that I have reviewed and understand the contents of the above-identified international application, including the claims of said application. I have identified in the request of said application, in compliance with PCT Rule 4.10, any claim to foreign priority, and I have identified below, under the heading "Prior Applications," by application number, country or Member of the World Trade Organization, day, month and year of filing, any application for a patent or inventor's certificate filed in a country other than the United States of America, including any PCT international application designating at least one country other than the United States of America, having a filing date before that of the application on which foreign priority is claimed.

Prior Applications: . . . . . . . . . . . . . . . . . . . . . . . . . . . . . . . . . . . . . . . . . . . . . . . . . . . . . . . . . . . . . . . . . . . . . . . . . . . . . . . . . . . . . . . . . . . . .

. . . . . . . . . . . . . . . . . . . . . . . . . . . . . . . . . . . . . . . . . . . . . . . . . . . . . . . . . . . . . . . . . . . . . . . . . . . . . . . . . . . . . . . . . . . . . . . . . . . . . . . . . . .

I hereby acknowledge the duty to disclose information that is known by me to be material to patentability as defined by 37 C.F.R. § 1.56, including for continuation-in-part applications, material information which became available between the filing date of the prior application and the PCT international filing date of the continuation-in-part application.

I hereby declare that all statements made herein of my own knowledge are true and that all statements made on information and belief are believed to be true; and further that these statements were made with the knowledge that willful false statements and the like so made are punishable by fine or imprisonment, or both, under Section 1001 of Title 18 of the United States Code and that such willful false statements may jeopardize the validity of the application or any patent issued thereon.

**Name:** . . . . . . . . . . . . . . . . . . . . . . . . . . . . . . . . . . . . . . . . . . . . . . . . . . . . . . . . . . . . . . . . . . . . . . . . . . . . . . . . . . . . . . . . . . . . . . . . . . . . . . .

**Residence:** . . . . . . . . . . . . . . . . . . . . . . . . . . . . . . . . . . . . . . . . . . . . . . . . . . . . . . . . . . . . . . . . . . . . . . . . . . . . . . . . . . . . . . . . . . . . . . . . . .
(city and either US state, if applicable, or country)

Mailing Address: . . . . . . . . . . . . . . . . . . . . . . . . . . . . . . . . . . . . . . . . . . . . . . . . . . . . . . . . . . . . . . . . . . . . . . . . . . . . . . . . . . . . . . . . . . . . . .

. . . . . . . . . . . . . . . . . . . . . . . . . . . . . . . . . . . . . . . . . . . . . . . . . . . . . . . . . . . . . . . . . . . . . . . . . . . . . . . . . . . . . . . . . . .

Citizenship: . . . . . . . . . . . . . . . . . . . . . . . . . . . . . . . . . . . . . . . . . . . . . . . . . . . . . . . . . . . . . . . . . . . . . . . . . . . . . . . . . . . . . . . . . . . . . . . . . . .

Inventor's Signature: . . . . . . . . . . . . . . . . . . . . . . . . . . . . . . . . . . .    Date: . . . . . . . . . . . . . . . . . . . . . . . . . . . . . . . . . . . . . .
(The signature must be that of the inventor, not that of the agent)


**Name:** . . . . . . . . . . . . . . . . . . . . . . . . . . . . . . . . . . . . . . . . . . . . . . . . . . . . . . . . . . . . . . . . . . . . . . . . . . . . . . . . . . . . . . . . . . . . . . . . . . . . . . .

**Residence:** . . . . . . . . . . . . . . . . . . . . . . . . . . . . . . . . . . . . . . . . . . . . . . . . . . . . . . . . . . . . . . . . . . . . . . . . . . . . . . . . . . . . . . . . . . . . . . . . . .
(city and either US state, if applicable, or country)

Mailing Address: . . . . . . . . . . . . . . . . . . . . . . . . . . . . . . . . . . . . . . . . . . . . . . . . . . . . . . . . . . . . . . . . . . . . . . . . . . . . . . . . . . . . . . . . . . . . . .

. . . . . . . . . . . . . . . . . . . . . . . . . . . . . . . . . . . . . . . . . . . . . . . . . . . . . . . . . . . . . . . . . . . . . . . . . . . . . . . . . . . . . . . . . . .

Citizenship: . . . . . . . . . . . . . . . . . . . . . . . . . . . . . . . . . . . . . . . . . . . . . . . . . . . . . . . . . . . . . . . . . . . . . . . . . . . . . . . . . . . . . . . . . . . . . . . . . . .

Inventor's Signature: . . . . . . . . . . . . . . . . . . . . . . . . . . . . . . . . . . .    Date: . . . . . . . . . . . . . . . . . . . . . . . . . . . . . . . . . . . . . .
(The signature must be that of the inventor, not that of the agent)

☐   This declaration is continued on the following sheet, "Continuation of Box No. VIII (iv)".

Form PCT/RO/101 (declaration sheet (iv)) (April 2006)                                         *See Notes to the request form*

Sheet No. . . . . . . .

**Box No. VIII (v)   DECLARATION: NON-PREJUDICIAL DISCLOSURES OR EXCEPTIONS TO LACK OF NOVELTY**
*The declaration must conform to the standardized wording provided for in Section 215; see Notes to Boxes Nos. VIII, VIII (i) to (v) (in general) and the specific Notes to Box No. VIII (v). If this Box is not used, this sheet should not be included in the request.*

Declaration as to non-prejudicial disclosures or exceptions to lack of novelty (Rules 4.17(v) and 51*bis*.1(a)(v)):

☐ This declaration is continued on the following sheet, "Continuation of Box No. VIII (v)".

Form PCT/RO/101 (declaration sheet (v)) (April 2006)                                                    *See Notes to the request form*

Sheet No. .......

**Continuation of Box No. VIII (i) to (v)    DECLARATION**

*If **the space is insufficient** in any of Boxes Nos. VIII (i) to (v) to furnish all the information, including in the case where **more than two inventors are to be named** in Box No. VIII (iv), in such case, write "Continuation of Box No. VIII ..." (indicate the item number of the Box) and furnish the information in the same manner as required for the purposes of the Box in which the space was insufficient. If additional space is needed in respect of two or more declarations, a separate continuation box must be used for each such declaration. If this Box is not used, this sheet should not be included in the request.*

Form PCT/RO/101 (continuation sheet for declaration) (April 2006)   *See Notes to the request form*

## Check list

3–033

The request must contain a list indicating:

r.3.3

(i) the number of sheets comprising: (a) the request; (b) the description (separately indicating the number of sheets of any sequence listing part of the description); (c) the claims; (d) the drawings; (e) the abstract; and (f) the international application as a whole;

(ii) that the application is accompanied, where applicable, by: (a) a power of attorney, (*i.e.* a document appointing an agent or a common representative); (b) a copy of a general power of attorney; (c) a priority document; (d) a sequence listing in electronic form; (e) a document relating to the payment of fees; or (f) any other document (to be specified in the checklist); and

(iii) the number of the figure of the drawings which the applicant suggests should accompany the abstract on publication (in exceptional cases, more than one may be nominated).

If the applicant does not complete the list, it will be completed by the Receiving Office except for item (iii) above.

## Signature of the applicant

3–034

The request must be signed.

r.4.1(d)

The signature must be that of the applicant or, if there is more than one, all of them, except in the case where the international application designates a state whose national law requires the inventor to file and one of the applicants for that state who is a inventor refuses to sign or could not be found or reached after diligent effort, in which case the request need not be signed by that applicant as long as at least one applicant signs and a statement is furnished explaining the circumstances.

r.4.15

In respect of some Offices, a seal is required rather than a signature (*e.g.* Korea). See Applicant's Guide, Vol.I, para.110.

r.2.3

Once properly appointed, an agent can sign the request on the applicant's behalf.

r.90.3

A signature appearing on a document transmitted by facsimile is recognised for the purposes of the PCT and its Regulations as a proper signature.

r.92.4(b)

Note that in the case of multiple applicants, the Receiving office will not object if the request is signed by at least one of them, despite the requirements of R4.15.

R.26.2.bis(a)

Sheet No. . . . . . . .

**Box No. IX    CHECK LIST; LANGUAGE OF FILING**

| This international application **contains**: | This international application is **accompanied by** the following item(s) *(mark the applicable check-boxes below and indicate in right column the number of each item)*: | Number of items |
|---|---|---|

(a) **on paper,** the following number of sheets:

    request (including declaration sheets) :

    description (excluding sequence listing and/or tables related thereto) :

    claims :

    abstract :

    drawings :

    **Sub-total number of sheets** :   0

    sequence listing :

    tables related thereto :

    *(for both, actual number of sheets if filed on paper, whether or not also filed in electronic form; see (c) below)*

    **Total number of sheets** :   0

(b) ☐ **only in electronic form** (Section 801(a)(i))
    (i) ☐ sequence listing
    (ii) ☐ tables related thereto

(c) ☐ **also in electronic form** (Section 801(a)(ii))
    (i) ☐ sequence listing
    (ii) ☐ tables related thereto

**Type and number of carriers** (diskette, CD-ROM, CD-R or other) on which are contained the
    ☐ sequence listing: . . . . . . . . . . . . . . . .
    ☐ tables related thereto: . . . . . . . . . . . .
*(additional copies to be indicated under items 9(ii) and/or 10(ii), in right column)*

1. ☐ fee calculation sheet :
2. ☐ original separate power of attorney :
3. ☐ original general power of attorney :
4. ☐ copy of general power of attorney; reference number, if any: . . . . . . . . . . . . . . . . . . . . . . . . . . . . . . . . . . . . . . . . :
5. ☐ statement explaining lack of signature :
6. ☐ priority document(s) identified in Box No. VI as item(s): . . . . . . . . . . . . . . . . . . . . . . . . . . . . . . . . . . . . . :
7. ☐ translation of international application into *(language)*: . . . . . . . . . . . . . . . . . . . . . . . . . . . . . . . . . . :
8. ☐ separate indications concerning deposited microorganism or other biological material :
9. ☐ sequence listing in electronic form *(indicate type and number of carriers)*
    (i) ☐ copy submitted for the purposes of international search under Rule 13*ter* only (and not as part of the international application) :
    (ii) ☐ *(only where check-box (b)(i) or (c)(i) is marked in left column)* additional copies including, where applicable, the copy for the purposes of international search under Rule 13*ter* :
    (iii) ☐ together with relevant statement as to the identity of the copy or copies with the sequence listing mentioned in left column :
10. ☐ tables in electronic form related to sequence listing *(indicate type and number of carriers)*
    (i) ☐ copy submitted for the purposes of international search under Section 802(b-*quater*) only (and not as part of the international application) :
    (ii) ☐ *(only where check-box (b)(ii) or (c)(ii) is marked in left column)* additional copies including, where applicable, the copy for the purposes of international search under Section 802(b-*quater*) :
    (iii) ☐ together with relevant statement as to the identity of the copy or copies with the tables mentioned in left column :
11. ☐ other *(specify)*: . . . . . . . . . . . . . . . . . . . . . . . . . . . . . . . . . . . . . . . . . . . . :

**Figure of the drawings** which should accompany the abstract:

**Language of filing** of the international application:

**Box No. X    SIGNATURE OF APPLICANT, AGENT OR COMMON REPRESENTATIVE**
*Next to each signature, indicate the name of the person signing and the capacity in which the person signs (if such capacity is not obvious from reading the request).*

───────────── For receiving Office use only ─────────────

1. Date of actual receipt of the purported international application:

2. Drawings:
    ☐ received:

3. Corrected date of actual receipt due to later but timely received papers or drawings completing the purported international application:

4. Date of timely receipt of the required corrections under PCT Article 11(2):

    ☐ not received:

5. International Searching Authority (if two or more are competent):    ISA /

6. ☐ Transmittal of search copy delayed until search fee is paid

───────────── For International Bureau use only ─────────────

Date of receipt of the record copy by the International Bureau:

Form PCT/RO/101 (last sheet) (April 2006)        *See Notes to the request form*

## *Reference to a parent application or patent* 3–035

The request may contain a reference to a parent application or parent patent. r.4.1(b)(iii)

If the applicant intends to make an indication under r.49*bis*.1(a) or (b) of the wish that the international application be treated, in any designated state, as an application for a patent of addition, certificate of addition, inventor's certificate of addition or utility certificate of addition or the applicant intends to make an indication under r.49*bis*.1(d) of the wish that the international application be treated, in any designated state, as an application for a continuation or a continuation-in-part of an earlier application, the request must so indicate and must, as the case may be, identify the relevant parent application or parent patent or other parent grant. r.4.11(a)

The inclusion in the request of such an indication under r.4.11 will have no effect on the operation of r.4.9 (filing the request automatically designates all states for all kinds of protection). r.4.11(b)

## *No further content of the request is allowed* 3–036

The request may only contain those matters specified in rr.4.1 to 4.17 and any other matter specified by the Administrative Instructions. Any additional matter will be deleted by the Receiving Office *ex officio*. Any additional matter specified in the Administrative Instructions is purely optional. r.4.18

## *Requirements for providing names and addresses* 3–037

The names of natural persons must be indicated by the person's family name (first) and given names (last). The names of legal entities must be indicated by their full, official designations. Addresses must be detailed enough to satisfy prompt postal delivery, indicating relevant administrative units up to and including the house number, if any (failure to indicate a house number will only have negative consequences in designated states whose national law so provides). It is recommended that other means of communication (phone, facsimile, teleprinter) are also indicated. Only one address may be indicated for each applicant/inventor/agent except that where no agent has been appointed an additional address for notifications may be indicated. r.4.4

Where any name or address is written in characters other than those of the Latin alphabet the same must be indicated in characters of the Latin alphabet either through transliteration or translation into English. The name of any country written in characters other than those of the Latin alphabet must also be indicated in English. r.4.16

## Requirements relating to the description 3–038

An international application must contain a description. Art.3(2)

## *Need for a sufficient disclosure* 3–039

The description must disclose the invention in a sufficiently clear and complete manner for the invention to be carried out by a person skilled in the art. Art.5

## *Content of the description* 3–040

The description must: r.5.1(a)

   (a) state the title as it appears in the request;
   (b) specify the technical field to which the invention relates;

(c) indicate the background art which, as far as the applicant knows, is useful for the understanding, searching and examination of the invention and preferably cite documents reflecting such art;

(d) disclose the invention, as claimed, in such a way that the technical problem (even if not expressly stated as such) and its solution can be understood and state the advantageous effects, if any, of the invention with reference to the background art;

(e) briefly described the figures in the drawings, if any;

(f) in respect of any designated states that so require, set forth at least the best mode contemplated by the applicant for carrying out the invention claimed in terms of examples, where appropriate, and with reference to the drawings; and

(g) indicate explicitly, when it is not obvious from the description or nature of the invention, the way in which the invention is capable of exploitation in industry and the way in which it can be made and used, or, if it can only be used, the way in which it can be used. "Industry" is as defined in the Paris Convention.

| | |
|---|---|
| 3–041 | ***Order of presentation of the content of the description*** |
| r.5.1(b)(c) | The order and manner of presentation described in r.5.1 above should be followed unless, due to the nature of the invention, a different order or manner would facilitate understanding or lead to a more economical presentation and each of (b) to (g) above should preferably be preceded by an appropriate heading as suggested in the Administrative Instructions. |
| AdminInst | See s.204. The headings are "Technical Field", "Background Art", "Disclosure of Invention", "Brief Description of Drawings", "Best Mode for Carrying Out the Invention", "Industrial Applicability", "Sequence Listing' and "Sequence Listing Free Text". |
| 3–042 | **Requirements relating to the claims** |
| Art.3(2) | An international application must contain one or more claims. |
| 3–043 | ***Requirement for clarity, conciseness and support*** |
| Art.6 | The claims must be clear and concise and fully supported by the description. |
| 3–044 | ***Claims to define matter the applicant seeks to protect*** |
| Art.6/r.6.3 | The claims must define the matter for which protection is sought. Such definition must be in terms of the technical features of the invention. |
| 3–045 | ***Situations in which two-part form is required*** |
| r.6.3 | Wherever appropriate a claim should contain: |

(i) a statement indicating those technical features of the invention which are necessary for the definition of the claimed subject matter but which, in combination, are part of the prior art; and

(ii) a characterising part (preceded by the words "characterised in that" "characterised by" "wherein the improvement compromises" or other such phrase) stating concisely the technical features which, in combination with the features stated in (i), it is desired to protect;

except that in countries where the national law does not require this manner of claiming, failure to use it has no effect in that state.

## Number and type of claims allowed 3–046

The number of claims must be reasonable in consideration of the nature of the invention claimed.  r.6.1

Subject to the requirement for unity of invention, a reasonable number of dependent claims, claiming specific forms of the invention claimed in an independent claim, are allowed, even where the features of such a dependent claim could be considered as constituting an invention in themselves.  r.13.4

Any dependent claim (i.e. a claim which includes all the features of one or more other claim(s)) should refer to the other claim or claims, if possible at the beginning, and then state the additional feature claimed.  r.6.4(a)

A multiple dependent claim (i.e. one referring to more than one other claim) must do so in the alternative and must not serve as a basis for any other multiple dependent claim.  r.6.4(a)

Where the national law of a national office acting as an International Searching Authority stipulates that multiple dependent claims must be drafted as indicated above, failure to comply may result in an indication under Art.17(2)(b) (no search report established in respect of these claims) but will have no effect in a designated state which allows the actual manner of claiming used.  r.6.4(a)

Any dependent claim will be construed as including all the limitations contained in the claim to which it refers or, if the claim is a multiple dependent claim, all the limitations contained in the particular claim in relation to which it is considered.  r.6.4(b)

All dependent claims referring back to a single previous claim or several previous claims must be grouped together to the extent and in the most practicable way possible.  r.6.4(c)

## Numbering of the claims 3–047

The claims must be numbered consecutively in arabic numerals. The Administrative Instructions indicate how claims should be numbered in the case of amendment.  r.6.1

See s.205. Claims do not have to be renumbered where one is deleted but, if they are, they must be renumbered consecutively.  AdminInst

## Omnibus claims generally not allowed 3–048

Except where absolutely necessary, the claims may not rely in respect of technical features of the invention, on references to the description or drawings such as "as described in part . . . of the description" or "as illustrated in figure . . . of the drawings".  r.6.2(a)

## References in claims to reference signs in figures 3–049

Where the international application contains drawings, the technical features mentioned in the claims should preferably be followed by the reference signs relating to such features (preferably placed between parentheses) unless this would not particularly facilitate quicker understanding of the claim.  r.6.2(b)

## Manner of claiming in respect of an application for a utility model 3–050

Any designated state in which the grant of a utility model is sought on the basis of an international application may substitute for rr.6.1–6.4 (relating to the claims) the provisions of its national law concerning utility models once national processing of the application has begun. The applicant is allowed at least two months from the expiration of the Art.22 time limit (normally 30 months from the priority date) to adapt his application to the requirements of these provisions of national law.  r.6.5

| | |
|---|---|
| **3–051** | ***Unity of invention*** |
| Art.3(4)(iii) | An international application must comply with the prescribed requirement of unity of invention. |
| r.13.1 | This means that the international application must relate to one invention only or to a group of inventions so linked as to form a single general inventive concept. |
| r.13.2 | Such a general inventive concept is taken to unite a group of inventions claimed in the same application when there is a technical relationship among them involving one or more of the same or corresponding special technical features, i.e. those technical features that define a contribution which each of the claimed inventions, considered as a whole, makes over the prior art. |
| r.13.3 | This will be determined in the same way whether the inventions are claimed in separate claims or as alternatives within a single claim. |
| AdminInst | See s.207. The determination of unity by an International Searching or Preliminary Examining Authority must be made in line with the instructions in Annex B of the Administrative Instructions. |
| r.13.5 | Any state in which the grant of a utility model is sought on the basis of an international application may, instead of the above, apply the provisions of its national law concerning utility models once the processing of the application has started in that state, provided that the applicant is allowed at least two months from the expiry of the time limit applicable under Art.22 (normally 30 months from the priority date) to adapt his application to those provisions. |
| **3–052** | **Requirements relating to the abstract** |
| Art.3(2) | An international application must contain an abstract. |
| Art.3(3) | The abstract merely serves as a source of technical information and cannot be used to interpret the scope of protection or for any other purpose. |
| r.8.3 | The abstract must be drafted so that it can efficiently serve the researcher as a scanning tool for the purposes of searching in the particular art and formulating an opinion as to whether the international application itself needs to be consulted. |
| r.8.1(a) | The abstract must contain a summary of the disclosure as contained in the description, the claims and any drawings, indicating the technical field to which the invention pertains and allowing a clear understanding of the technical problem, the gist of the solution of that problem through the invention and the principle use or uses of the invention. The abstract should also, where applicable, contain the chemical formula which, among all the formulae contained in the international application, best characterises the invention. |
| r.8.1(b)–(d) | The abstract must be as concise as possible (preferably 50 to 150 words in English or when translated into English) and avoid statements as to the alleged merits or value of the claimed invention or on its speculative use. Each main technical feature mentioned in the abstract and illustrated by a drawing in the international application should be followed by a reference sign, placed between parentheses. |
| r.8.2 | If the applicant fails to include in the request the number of the figure or figures of the drawings which he suggests should accompany the abstract on publication (r.3.3(a)(iii)—should be in checklist part of Request) or if the International Searching Authority finds a different figure or different figures would be more appropriate, the International Bureau will publish the abstract accompanied by the choice of figure indicated by the International Searching Authority. If the International Searching Authority finds that |

none of the figures are useful for the understanding of the abstract it will notify the International Bureau accordingly and no figure will be included on publication (even if the applicant has suggested one or more).

## Requirements relating to the drawings 3–053

An international application must, where required, contain one or more drawings. Art.3(2)

One or more drawings must be provided (a) where necessary for the understanding of the invention or (b) where they are not necessary but the invention admits of illustration by drawings and the applicant wishes to include them (on filing) or a designated office requires them (within a time limit). Art.7

This time limit under (b) must be reasonable under the circumstances of the case and in any case not shorter than two months from the date of the written invitation to provide drawings. r.7.2

Flow sheets and diagrams are considered to be drawings. r.7.1

This rule sets out the detailed physical requirements for the presentation of drawings (see also Applicant's Guide, Vol.I, paras 146–175). r.11.13

## Requirements relating to a priority claim 3–054

### *Relevance of the Paris Convention*

The conditions for and effect of any priority claim follow Art.4 of the Stockholm Act of the Paris Convention. Art.8

### *Who may make a claim to priority?* 3–055

Any person who has duly filed a certain kind of application, or his successor in title, enjoys a right of priority. PCA4(A1)

### *Time limit for making a claim to priority* 3–056

The priority period in respect of a patent is 12 months. PCA4(C1)

The period starts from the filing date of the first application and does not include the day of filing. PCA4(C2)

The priority year is extended where the last day in any relevant office is a closed day until the next day when that office is open for business. PCA4(C3)

### *The whole content of the previous application can support a priority claim* 3–057

Priority may not be refused on the ground that certain elements of the invention for which priority is claimed do not appear among the claims formulated in the application in the country of origin, provided that the application documents as a whole specifically disclosed such elements. PCA4(H)

### *What kind of application may be used as a basis for claiming priority?* 3–058

Priority may be claimed from an application for a patent, or for the registration of a utility model. PCA4(A1)

Applications for inventors' certificates also give rise to a right of priority. PCA4(I1)

| | |
|---|---|
| Art.8/Art.2 | The international application may claim the priority of an earlier application or applications, "application" in this context being an international or national application for the protection of an invention including patents, inventors' certificates, utility certificates, utility models, patents or certificates of addition, inventors' certificates of addition and utility certificates of addition. |
| PCA4(A2) | Any filing that is equivalent to a regular national filing under the domestic legislation of any country of the Union or under bilateral or multilateral treaties concluded between countries of the Union is recognised as giving rise to the right of priority. |
| PCA4(A3) | By regular national filing is meant any filing that is adequate to establish the date on which the application was filed in the country concerned, whatever may be the subsequent fate of the application. |
| r.4.10 | Under the PCT, the earlier application must have been filed in or for any country party to the Paris Convention for the Protection of Industrial Property or in or for any Member of the World Trade Organisation that is not party to the Paris Convention. This version of r.4.10 applies to international applications filed on or after January 1, 2000. Before that time, only priority rights in respect of Paris Convention countries were recognised. The EPO has filed reservations and continues to operate under the old law—see below. |
| PCA4(C4) | A subsequent application concerning the same subject as a previous first application within the meaning of PCA4(C2) filed in the same country of the Union, will be considered as the first application, of which the filing date will be the starting point of the period of priority, if, at the time of filing the subsequent application, the said previous application has been withdrawn, abandoned or refused, without having been laid open to public inspection and without leaving any rights outstanding, and if it has not yet served as a basis for claiming a right of priority. The previous application may not thereafter serve as a basis for claiming a right of priority. |

**3–059** *Priority claims originating in World Trade Organisation countries do not apply in respect of the EPO*

| | |
|---|---|
| r.4.10(d) | If on September 29, 1999 r.4.10(a) and (b) as amended with effect from January 1, 2000 are not compatible with the national law applied by a designated office, those paragraphs as in force until December 31, 1999 will continue to apply after that date in respect of that designated office for as long as the said paragraphs as amended continue not to be compatible with that law, provided that the said office informed the International Bureau accordingly by October 31, 1999. The information received is promptly published by the International Bureau in the Gazette. |
| | The EPO is the only State in respect of which such reservations still apply. Paragraphs (a) and (b) of old r.4.10 therefore still apply in respect of the EPO as a designated office and a priority claim originating in a non-Paris Convention country is not recognised. |
| G2/02 | The Enlarged Board has confirmed that priority rights originating in a non-Paris Convention WTO country are not recognised under the EPC. |

**3–060** *Procedure for claiming priority*

| | |
|---|---|
| PCA4(D1) | Any person desiring to take advantage of the priority of a previous filing is required to make a declaration indicating the date of such filing and the country in which it was made. Each country determines the latest date on which such declaration must be made. |
| PCA4(D5) | Any person who avails himself of the priority of a previous application will be required to specify the number of that application. |

### 3. Requirements Relating to the Application as Filed 557

The declaration must be made in the request (but see below; later declarations are also possible). Art.8

The request must state the date on which the earlier application was filed (within 12 months preceding the international filing date), its number and the Convention country or World Trade Organisation Country (for national applications), regional authority (for regional applications) or Receiving Office (for international applications) in/with which it was filed. When claiming the priority of an international or regional application, one or more countries party to the Paris Convention for which the application was filed may be indicated. In the case of a regional application where at least one of the Contracting States is neither a member of the Paris Convention or the World Trade Organisation, at least one Contracting State which is a member of the Paris Convention or World Trade Organisation must be indicated. The definition of "national patent" given in Art.2(vi) does not apply for the purpose of r.4.10. r.4.10

The countries of the Union may require any person making a declaration of priority to produce a copy of the application previously filed. The copy, certified as correct by the authority which received it, does not require any authentication, and may in any case be filed, without fee, any time within three months of the filing of the subsequent application. PCA4(D3)

A copy of the earlier application, certified by the authority with which it was filed (the priority document) must be submitted to the International Bureau or the Receiving Office no later than 16 months from the priority date (it will be taken to have arrived on the last day of that period if received by the International Bureau before the date of publication) unless: r.17.1(a)(b)

(a) it was filed with the application itself; or

(b) the priority document is to be issued by the Receiving Office in which case the applicant may request that the Receiving Office (who may levy a fee) transmit it to the International Bureau directly as long as the request is made no later than 16 months from the priority date.

See under RRF. The cost for the EPO to provide a certified copy of the priority document is 35 euros ([2006] O.J. 255). AnReg

Such a request for the Receiving Office to transmit a copy of the priority document to the International Bureau under r.17 may be made on filing the application in the request. r.4.1(c)(ii)

Where the priority document is, in accordance with the Administrative Instructions, available to the Receiving Office or to the International Bureau from a digital library, the applicant may, instead of submitting the priority document: (i) request the Receiving Office to obtain the priority document from such a digital library and transmit it to the International Bureau; or (ii) request the International Bureau to obtain the priority document from such digital library. Such a request may not be made later than 16 months after the priority date and may be subjected by the Receiving Office or the International Bureau to the payment of a fee. r.17.1(b–bis)

Where no priority document is submitted, as outlined above, any designated state may, in principle, disregard the priority claim, but it must first give the applicant a further chance to submit the priority document within a reasonable time limit. In any case, it may not disregard the priority claim if the priority document was filed with it in its capacity as a national office or if the priority document is, in accordance with the Administrative Instructions, available to it from a digital library. r.17.1(c)(d)

A translation of the priority document may also be required by any country of the Union. PCA4(D3)

### 3–061 *Allowability of multiple priority claims*

PCA4(F)     No country of the Union may refuse a priority or a patent application on the ground that the applicant claims multiple priorities, even if they originate in different countries.

### 3–062 *Effect of the claim to priority in the international phase*

Art.2     For the purposes of the PCT a priority date means: (a) where the international application contains a priority claim under Art.8, the filing date of the application whose priority is so claimed; (b) where the international application contains several priority claims under Art.8, the filing date of the earliest application whose priority is so claimed; or (c) where the international application does not contain any priority claim under Art.8, the international filing date of such an application.

### 3–063 *Addition or correction of a priority claim after filing the request*

r.26*bis*.1(a)(b)     A priority claim may be corrected or added if the applicant submits a notice to the Receiving Office or the International Bureau within the later of (a) four months from the international filing date or (b) the earlier of 16 months from the priority date and 16 months from the corrected/added priority date if this is different. The correction may include the addition of any indication referred to in r.4.10 (date, number, filing country/authority/Receiving Office). Such notice, if received after the applicant has made a request for early publication (Art.21(2)(b)) will be considered not submitted unless the request for early publication is withdrawn before the technical preparations for publication are complete.

r.26*bis*.1(c)     Where a priority date is changed, any outstanding time limit that has not yet expired is recomputed from the new date.

### 3–064 *Effect of designating a state in which the priority application was filed*

Art.8     The international application may designate a state in which a priority application was filed. In such a case, or where the priority of an international application only designating one state is claimed, the national law of such a state governs the conditions for and the effect of the priority claim.

## General and physical requirements of the application

### 3–065 *Prohibited matter*

r.9.1/9.3     The international application must not contain:

      (i) expressions or drawings contrary to morality;

      (ii) expressions or drawings contrary to public order;

      (iii) "disparaging statements", i.e. statements disparaging the products or processes of those other than the applicant, or to the validity of such a person's application(s) or patent(s) (mere comparisons with the prior art, however, not being considered disparaging *per se*); or

      (iv) statements or other matter obviously irrelevant or unnecessary.

r.9.2     If lack of compliance is noted by the Receiving Office or the International Searching Authority they may suggest to the applicant that he voluntarily corrects the application. The lack of compliance is notified to the International Bureau and the Receiving Office/International Searching Authority as appropriate.

Art.21(6)     The International Bureau may omit offending material on publication (see section on international publication).

## 3. Requirements Relating to the Application as Filed

### Number of copies to be filed — 3–066

The application and documents referred to in the checklist (r.3.3 (a)(ii)) should normally be filed in one copy. However, the Receiving Office may demand they be filed in two or three copies (except for the receipt for fees paid or the check for the payment of fees). In the case that multiple copies are filed, the Receiving Office must check their identity. See r.21 for the consequences of not submitting enough copies. — r.11.1

Where the EPO is Receiving Office, the international application, including the documents referred to in the r.3.3(a)(ii) PCT checklist except the receipt for fees paid and the cheque for payment of fees, must be filed in three copies, unless the President of the EPO decides otherwise. — *r.104(1)*

If insufficient copies are filed the EPO will prepare the missing copies at the applicant's expense. — *r.104(2)*

See Vol.I, Annex C. Only one copy is required by the EPO ([2006] O.J. 439). — AppGuide

### Terminology and signs — 3–067

Requirements relating to terminology and signs are listed. — r.10

### Physical requirements — 3–068

An international application must comply with the prescribed physical requirements. — Art.3(4)(ii)

Detailed physical requirements are laid down. — r.11.2–11.13

See s.207 for further details of the order of presentation of parts of the application and rules for numbering these parts. — AdminInst

## Language requirements of the application

### Acceptable languages of filing — 3–069

The international application must be in a prescribed language. — Art.3(4)(i)

The international application may be filed in any language that is accepted by the Receiving Office with the proviso that: — r.12.1

(i) the request must be in a language selected from Arabic, Chinese, English, French, German, Japanese, Russian or Spanish (i.e. a language of publication—r.48.3); and

(ii) any text in a sequence listing in the description must be in line with the Administrative Instructions (r.5.2(a)).

The EPO accepts applications in English, French or German. — *r.104(1)*

### Languages the Receiving Office must accept — 3–070

Each Receiving Office must accept at least one language selected from Arabic, Chinese, English, French, German, Japanese, Russian or Spanish (i.e. a language of publication) that is also accepted by at least one of the International Searching Authorities competent for searching international applications filed with that office. — r.12.1(b)

### Circumstances in which the applicant must provide a translation for international search — 3–071

Where the language in which the international application is filed is not accepted by the International Searching Authority that is to carry out the international search, the — r.12.3(a)(b) applicant must, within one month of the date of receipt of the application by the Receiving Office, provide the Receiving Office with a translation of the application (except the request and any sequence listing part of the description) into a language of publication which is accepted by the Searching Authority and, unless the filing language was a language of publication, accepted by the Receiving Office.

r.12.3(c)(i)(ii)  Where such a translation has not been supplied before the Receiving Office sends the applicant notification of the application number and filing date under r.20.5(c), the office will (preferably with that notification) invite the applicant to (i) furnish the translation within the one month deadline and, (ii) where the one month deadline has expired and no translation has been received, to furnish it within one month of the invitation or two months from the date of receipt of the application by the Receiving Office (whichever is later) along with a late furnishing fee (if the Receiving Offices so chooses).

r.12.3(c)(ii)

r.12.3(e)  The late furnishing fee is for the benefit of the Receiving Office and is 25 per cent of the international filing fee, not taking into account any fee for each sheet in excess of 30.

r.12.3(d)  Where such an invitation is ignored by the applicant and the translation is not furnished within the time limit set under r.12.3(c)(ii), or the late furnishing fee, where required, is not paid within that time limit, the application will be considered to be withdrawn and the Receiving Office will so declare. However, any translation and/or fee received by the Receiving Office before such a declaration is made and before the expiry of 15 months from the priority date is considered to have been received before the expiry of the time limit.

AppGuide  See Vol.I, Annex D. For the EPO as International Searching Authority, the application must be in English, French or German (or Dutch if the Receiving Office was the Belgian or Netherlands office). Otherwise, a translation into English, French or German is required.

**3–072**  ***Circumstances in which the applicant must provide a translation for international publication***

r.12.4(a)  Where the language in which the international application is filed is not a language of publication (i.e. Arabic, Chinese, English, French, German, Japanese, Russian or Spanish) and no translation is required for international search under r.12.3(a), the applicant must provide the Receiving Office with a translation of the application into any of the languages of publication accepted by the Receiving Office for this purpose. The translation must be provided within 14 months from the priority date.

r.12.4(b)  This requirement does not, however, apply to the request or any sequence listing part of the description.

r.12.4(c)  Where no translation is provided within the time limit, the Receiving Office will invite the applicant to file such a translation and, at the discretion of the Receiving Office, pay a late furnishing fee within 16 months from the priority date. However, any translation received before the invitation is sent is considered received within the normal time limit.

r.12.4(e)  The late furnishing fee is for the benefit of the Receiving Office and is 25 per cent of the international filing fee, not taking into account any fee for each sheet in excess of 30.

r.12.4(d)  Where no translation is submitted or, where applicable, the late furnishing fee is not submitted within the r.12.4(c) time limit, the application will be considered withdrawn and the Receiving Office will so declare. However, any translation or payment received before the Receiving Office so declares, and before 17 months from the priority date, is considered received within the 16-month period.

### *Procedure where the request is not in a language of publication* — 3–073

Where the request is not in a language of publication the Receiving Office will invite the applicant to file a translation. Rules 3 (form of request), 26.1(a) (timing of invitation to correct), 26.2 (time limit for correction), 26.5 and 29.1 (procedure when time limit missed) apply to such a translation *mutatis mutandis*.

r.26.3ter(c)

### *Procedure where language of filing is not accepted by the Receiving Office* — 3–074

In this circumstance, the application is deemed to have been received by the relevant office on behalf of the International Bureau (which accepts applications in any language). The office concerned will transmit the application to the International Bureau and may charge a fee equivalent to the transmittal fee for the service. The date of filing with the inappropriate office counts as the filing date except that the actual date of receipt by the International Bureau counts as the filing date for the purposes of r.14.1(c) (one-month period for paying the transmittal fee), r.15.4 (time limit for paying the international filing fee) and r.16.1(f) (time limit for paying the search fee).

r.19.4(a)(ii)

### **Fees** — 3–075

An international application is subject to the payment of fees.

Art.3(4)(iv)

### *Transmittal fee* — 3–076

Any Receiving Office may charge the applicant a transmittal fee for receiving and transmitting the international application and other associated tasks. The amount is fixed by the Receiving Office.

r.14.1(a)(b)

The transmittal fee is due within one month of the date of receipt of the application by the Receiving Office (except where the application is forwarded to the International Bureau—see r.19.4(c)). The amount payable is the amount applicable on the date of receipt of the application by the Receiving Office.

r.14.1(c)

### *Transmittal fee where the EPO is the Receiving Office* — 3–077

Where the EPO is acting as the Receiving Office for an international application, a transmittal fee is due within one month of receipt of the application.

**Art.152(3)**

The fee is 105 euros.

RRF2(18)

### *International filing fee (as from January 1, 2004)* — 3–078

An international filing fee must be paid to the Receiving Office for the benefit of the International Bureau. The amount is specified in the Schedule of Fees (currently 1,400 Swiss francs plus 15 Swiss francs for each sheet of the application in excess of 30). The Receiving Office decides which currency the fee is to be paid in and the amount in any currency other than Swiss francs is established by the Director General in consultation with the Receiving Office. Such amounts are published in the Gazette and may change due to exchange rate fluctuations or where the amount in Swiss francs changes.

r.15.1/15.2

The international filing fee is due within one month of the date of receipt of the application by the Receiving Office (except where the application is forwarded to the International Bureau—see r.19.4(c)). The amount payable is the amount applicable on the date of receipt of the application by the Receiving Office.

r.15.4

The international fee is refunded if either:

r.15.6

(i) the determination under Art.11(1) (whether to accord a filing date) is negative;

(ii) the application is withdrawn or considered so before transmittal of the record copy to the International Bureau; or

(iii) the international application is not treated as such due to prescriptions concerning national security.

## International filing fee (before January 1, 2004)

3–079

r.15.4

The old version of r.15.4 applies to applications received before January 1, 2004, even if allocated a filing date on or after January 1, 2004. Under the previous system the international filing fee consisted of a basic fee and designation fees. The basic fee had to be paid within one month of the date of receipt of the international application, the amount due being the amount applicable on that date of receipt. The designation fees had to be paid before the later of: (a) one year from the priority date; and (b) one month from the date of receipt of the application. The amount due was the amount applicable on the date of receipt if filed within one month of that date or the date of payment when filed after one month from the date of receipt.

## Search fee

3–080

r.16.1(a)(b)

A search fee, collected by the Receiving Office, may be charged by the International Searching Authority for its own benefit for carrying out the international search and its other duties under the PCT.

RRF2(2)

The fee is 1615 euros where the EPO is International Searching Authority.

r.16.1(f)

The search fee must be paid within one month from the date of receipt of the international application by the Receiving Office (except where the application is forwarded to the International Bureau—see r.19.4(c)) and the amount payable is the amount due on that date of receipt.

r.16.1(b)–(e)

The Receiving Office decides which currency the fee is to be paid in and the amount in any currency other than a currency accepted by the International Searching Authority is established by the Director General in consultation with the Receiving Office. Such amounts are published in the Gazette and may change due to exchange rate fluctuations or where the amount set by the International Searching Authority changes. Where the amount the International Searching Authority gets is less than or more than the amount it sets, the balance is paid by or received by the International Bureau.

r.16.2

The search fee is refunded to the applicant by the Receiving Office if:

(a) the determination under Art.11(1) (according a filing date to the application) is negative;

(b) before transmittal of the application to the Searching Authority, the application is withdrawn or considered to be withdrawn; or

(c) the application is not treated as such due to prescriptions concerning national security.

r.16.3

The search fee is partly refunded to the applicant by the International Searching Authority if the international application claims the priority of an earlier international application which has been the subject of an international search by the same Searching Authority and the later report could be wholly or partly based on the earlier report. The refund is provided to the extent specified and under the conditions provided for in the agreement under Art.16(3)(b) (between the International Searching Authority and the International Bureau, approved by the Assembly).

r.41.1

See also under the chapter on international search for circumstances where the search fee is partly refunded if the search can be based on the results of a previous search — in the EPO the amount of reduction is specified in [2006] O.J. 252.

See under *Art.157(3)*. Where the EPO is International Searching Authority, the fee is reduced by 75 per cent for applicants from certain poor states (see [2000] O.J. 446). See also Applicant's Guide, Vol.I, para.202.

*AnReg*

## *Extension of time limits for paying fees*

**3–081**

With respect to the transmittal fee, the international filing fee and the search fee, if, on the due date, they are not paid or underpaid, the Receiving Office will invite the applicant to correct the deficiency and, at the option of the Receiving Office, pay a late payment fee, within one month of the invitation. However, if payment is received before the invitation is sent, it will be considered to have been received before the expiry of the appropriate time limit.

r.16*bis*.1(a)(d)

The amount of the late payment fee is (a) 50 per cent of the unpaid fees or (b) the transmittal fee, whichever is higher, but is capped at 50 per cent of the international filing fee specified in item 1 of the Schedule of fees, not taking into account the fee for any sheet in excess of 30.

r.16*bis*.2

See under *Art.151*. The EPO late payment fee is 50 per cent of the unpaid fees as specified in r.16*bis*.2 PCT ([1992] O.J. 383).

AnReg

Where such an invitation is not complied with the Receiving Office will make a declaration under Art.14(3) (application considered withdrawn) and proceed as provided for in r.29, though if payment is received before the Art.14(3) declaration is made it will be considered to have been received before the end of the one month deadline.

r.16*bis*.1(c)(e)

## Requirements relating to biotechnological inventions

### *Sequence listings*

**3–082**

Where one or more amino acid and/or nucleotide sequences are disclosed, the description must contain a sequence listing complying with the Administrative Instructions and presented as a separate part of the description. If the sequence listing contains any free text, that free text must also appear in the main part of the description in the language thereof.

r.5.2

Any sequence listing not contained in the international application as filed does not (subject to Art.34) form part of the application.

r.13*ter*.1(f)

For procedure where an International Searching or Preliminary Examining Authority or a designated office finds that the sequence listing is not supplied or is supplied in the wrong form see under the appropriate chapter below.

r.13*ter*

See paras 118–119E of the Applicant's Guide, Vol.I for further details.

### *Deposit of biological material*

**3–083**

Any reference to a deposit of biological material must be made in accordance with r.13*bis* and, if so made, will be taken to satisfy the requirements of the national law of each designated state.

r.13*bis*.2

Failure to include a reference to a deposit in an application or failure to include any indication under r.13*bis*.3(a) has no effect in a state which does not require such a reference or indication.

r.13*bis*.3(b)

## 4. PROCEDURE OF THE RECEIVING OFFICE

**3–084** **Marking and dating of the sheets of the application**

r.20.1 — Upon receipt of papers purporting to be an international application, the Receiving Office will indelibly mark the request of each copy with the actual date of receipt and each sheet of each copy with the international application number (as specified in the Administrative Instructions).

r.20.2(a) — Where sheets pertaining to the same application are received on different days, the Receiving Office will correct the date shown on the request (leaving the earlier date(s) legible) to indicate the day on which papers completing the application were received, provided that:

(a) where no invitation to correct the documents as filed under Art.11(2)(a) has been issued, the said papers are received within 30 days from the date on which sheets were first received;

(b) where an invitation to correct the documents as filed under Art.11(2)(a) has been issued, the said papers are received within the time limit set for reply under r.20.6;

(c) where drawings are missing (Art.14(2)), they are received within 30 days from the date on which the incomplete papers were filed; and

(d) the absence of the abstract does not in itself require a redating of the request.

r.20.2(b) — The later sheets are marked with the date on which they were received.

**3–085** **Examination as to whether a filing date can be accorded**

*Requirements for a filing date*

Art.11(1)/r.20.4 — The Receiving Office will determine whether a filing date can be accorded. This is the date on which the international application is received by the Receiving Office if, at that date:

(i) the applicant apparently has the right to file an international application with the Receiving Office (Art.9);

(ii) the description (excepting any sequence listing) and the claim(s) are in a language accepted by the Receiving Office under r.12(1)(a) (and the other parts of the application are also in such a language if the national law operated by the Receiving Office so prescribes—see r.20.4(d), applies to the US only); and

(iii) it contains at least:

    (a) an indication that it is intended to be an international application;
    (b) the designation of at least one Contracting State;
    (c) the applicant's name (such that his identity can be established, regardless of misspellings, incomplete or abbreviated names and incompletely indicated given names);
    (d) a description; and
    (e) one or more claims.

r.19.4(a) — In fact, however, the fact that the applicant lacks the right to file with the Receiving Office or the language of the application is not accepted by the Receiving Office is not fatal to the award of a filing date—see sections above under Receiving Office (r.19.4(a)(i)) and languages (r.19.4(a)(ii)) respectively.

AppGuide — See Vol. I, para.240 for common defects that do not prejudice the award of a filing date (*e.g.* lack of title or abstract, failure to comply with physical requirements, etc.).

## *Procedure where a filing date can be accorded*     3–086

Where a filing date can be accorded, the Receiving Office will stamp the request with the name of the Receiving Office and the words "PCT International Application" or "Demande internationale PCT". If the official language of the Receiving Office is neither English nor French, one of the above phrases may be accompanied by a translation of it into that official language.    r.20.5(a)

The copy that the stamped request belongs to is the record copy.    r.20.5(b)

The record copy is considered to be the true copy of the international application.    Art.12(2)

The Receiving Office will promptly notify the applicant of the international application number and the filing date and send a copy of this notification to the International Bureau at the same time (unless it has sent or is sending at the same time the record copy under r.22.1 (a)).    r.20.5(c)

## *Procedure where a filing date cannot be accorded*     3–087

For the procedure where the applicant lacks the right to file with the Receiving Office or the language of the application is not accepted by the Receiving Office, see the sections above under Receiving Office (r.19.4(a)(i)) and languages (r.19.4(a)(ii)) respectively.    r.19.4(a)

Where a filing date cannot be accorded the applicant is invited to file any necessary correction.    Art.11(2)(a)

A reasonable time limit is set of not less than ten days and not more than a month from the date of the invitation. The Receiving Office specifies the deficiency under Art.11(2) and may alert the applicant to the fact that the time limit set expires after the expiration of one year from the priority date if this is so.    r.20.6

If the applicant complies with the invitation, the Receiving Office will accord as the date of filing the date on which the corrections were received.    Art.11(2)(b)

If the Receiving Office discovers, on the basis of the reply or otherwise, that it has erred in issuing an invitation to correct, it will proceed as in r.20.5 (i.e. as if it had made a positive determination) and accord a filing date to the application.    r.20.8

When corrected sheets are received in response to the invitation to correct, the date on the request is corrected (whilst leaving the earlier date legible) to the date on which the last correction is received.    r.20.3

If no reply is received within the time limit set or if the corrections received are inadequate then the Receiving Office will:    r.20.7

(a) promptly notify the applicant that his application is not and will not be treated as an international application and explain why;

(b) notify the International Bureau that the number it has marked on the papers will not be used as an international application number;

(c) keep the papers purporting to be the international application and any correspondence as provided for by r.93.1; and

(d) send a copy of those papers to the International Bureau where, pursuant to a request by the applicant under Art.25(1) (review by designated offices), the International Bureau needs and specially asks for such a copy.

An incorrect filing date can be corrected by a designated office where the mistake was on the part of the Receiving Office and filing dates can be corrected under similar circumstances according to national law.    r.82ter

| | |
|---|---|
| **3-088** | ***Supply to the applicant of certified copies of the application as filed*** |
| r.20.9 | On request and the payment of a fee, the Receiving Office must supply the applicant with certified copies of the international application as filed and any corrections made thereto. |

**Copying and transmittal of the international application by the Receiving Office**

| | |
|---|---|
| **3-089** | ***National security provisions*** |
| Art.27(8)/r.22.1 | National security restrictions are allowed under the PCT and may prevent the Receiving Office from transmitting the application. |
| **3-090** | ***Number of copies of the application required—responsibility for their provision*** |
| Art.12(1) | Three copies of the international application are necessary, a home copy, a record copy and a search copy. |
| r.11.1 | Only one copy of the international application must be filed by the applicant unless the Receiving Office prescribes the filing of two or three copies. |
| r.21.1(a)(b) | Where the Receiving Office requires the filing of only one copy, this copy becomes the record copy (see.r.20.5(b)) and the Receiving Office is responsible for preparing the other two copies. In the case where the Receiving Office requires the filing of two copies, the Receiving Office is responsible for preparing the home copy. |
| r.21.1(c) | Where less than the prescribed number of copies are filed by the applicant, the Receiving Office must still prepare the other copies but may charge the applicant a fee for doing so. |
| AppGuide | See Vol.I, Annex C. When the EPO acts as the Receiving Office, three copies of the international application must be provided by the applicant. |
| **3-091** | ***Retention of the home copy by the Receiving Office*** |
| Art.12(1) | The home copy is kept by the Receiving Office. |
| **3-092** | ***Transmittal by the Receiving Office of the record copy to the International Bureau*** |
| Art.12(1) | The record copy is transmitted by the Receiving Office to the International Bureau. |
| r.22.1(a) | Where a filing date has been accorded (Art.11(1)), the record copy is sent immediately by the Receiving Office to the International Bureau unless any national security provisions prevent such transmission. It must be sent in time to reach the International Bureau by the expiration of the 13th month from the priority date (five days must be allowed if transmitted by mail). |
| Art.12(2) | The record copy is considered the true copy of the international application. |
| **3-093** | ***An international application is considered withdrawn if the International Bureau does not receive the record copy in time*** |
| r.22.1(b) | When the International Bureau has received a notification under r.20.5(c) (that an application number and filing date have been accorded to a new international application) |

but is not in possession of the record copy by 13 months from the priority date, it reminds the Receiving Office to transmit it promptly.

When the International Bureau has received a notification under r.20.5(c) but is not in possession of the record copy by 14 months from the priority date it notifies the applicant and Receiving Office accordingly.

r.22.1(c)

If the record copy is not received by the International Bureau within three months of the notification sent to the applicant and Receiving Office under r.22.1(c), the international applications is considered withdrawn.

Art.12(3)/r.22.3

After expiration of 14 months from the priority date the applicant may request the Receiving Office to certify a copy of the application as being identical to the application as filed (free of charge) and transmit it himself to the International Bureau. The request may only be refused if

r.22.1(d)

   (i) the copy is not identical to the application as filed; or

   (ii) national security provisions apply; or

   (iii) the Receiving Office has already transmitted the record copy and the International Bureau has acknowledged receipt to the office.

In these circumstances, the certified copy will be considered by the International Bureau to be the record copy unless or until it receives the genuine record copy.

If, by the expiration of the time limit under Art.22 (usually 30 months) the applicant has discharged his duties under that Article (*i.e.* entered the national or regional phase) but the designated office has not been informed by the International Bureau that it has received the record copy, the designated office informs the International Bureau who promptly informs the applicant and the Receiving Office unless it is in possession of the record copy or it has already notified them at the 14 month stage under r.22.1(c). This rule also applies to national phase entry under Chapter II by virtue of r.76.5.

r.22.1(g)

If the record copy is not received by the International Bureau within three months of the notification sent to the applicant and Receiving Office under r.22.1(g), the international applications is considered withdrawn.

Art.12(3)/r.22.3

If the record copy is received by the International Bureau after the expiration of the time limit under r.22.3 (usually three months from notification at the 14 months stage) and the application is considered withdrawn under Art.12(3) it notifies the applicant, Receiving Office and International Searching Authority accordingly.

r.24.2(c)

The applicant can, within a prescribed two month time limit (r.51.1), get the International Bureau to forward copies of any document in the file to any designated office and, within the same time limit, enter the national phase in such a state, requesting review of the decision under Art.12(3) that the application is considered withdrawn.

Art.25

### *Procedure where the International Bureau receives the record copy in time —notification of receipt*

3–094

On receiving the record copy, the International Bureau promptly notifies the applicant, the Receiving Office and the International Searching Authority (unless it has declared it does not wish to be informed) of the fact and the date of the receipt, identifying the number of the application, the international filing date, the name of the applicant and the filing date of any priority document. The notification sent to the applicant also includes a list of designated states and, in the case of regional patent offices, the states designated for such a regional patent.

r.24.2

| | |
|---|---|
| 3–095 | ***Transmittal by the Receiving Office of a translation of the international application to the International Bureau*** |
| r.22.1(h) | Where the international application is to be published in the language of a translation provided for under r.12.3 (for the purposes of international search) or r.12.4 (filing language not a language of publication), that translation must be transmitted by the Receiving Office to the International Bureau together with the record copy or, if the record copy has already been transmitted, promptly after receipt of the translation. |
| 3–096 | ***Transmittal by the Receiving Office of the search copy to the International Searching Authority*** |
| Art.12(1) | The search copy is transmitted by the Receiving Office to the International Search Authority. |
| r.23.1(a) | If no translation is required under r.12.3(a) (for international search), and the search fee has been paid, the Receiving Office will transmit the search copy to the International Searching Authority at the latest on the same day that the record copy is transmitted to the International Bureau. Where the search fee has not been paid, it will be transmitted promptly after the payment of that fee. |
| r.23.1(b) | Where a translation is provided under r.12.3(a) (for international search), and the search fee has been paid, a copy of the translation and the request, together considered as the search copy, are transmitted to the International Searching Authority by the Receiving Office. Where the search fee has not been paid, they are transmitted promptly after the payment of that fee. |
| r.23.1(c) | Any sequence listing in electronic form submitted to the Receiving Office is forwarded by the Receiving Office to the International Searching Authority. |
| 3–097 | ***Procedure of the International Searching Authority on receipt of the search copy*** |
| r.25 | The International Searching Authority promptly notifies the International Bureau, the applicant and the Receiving Office (unless it is itself the Receiving Office) of the fact and the date of receipt of the search copy. |

**Examination of formal requirements**

| | |
|---|---|
| 3–098 | ***Was the decision to award a filing date correct?*** |
| Art.14(4)/r.30 | If the Receiving Office finds within four months of the international filing date that, despite the award of an international filing date, the requirements of Art.11(1)(i)–(iii) were not complied with at that date, the application will be considered withdrawn and the Receiving Office will so declare. |
| r.29.4 | However, before the Receiving Office makes such a declaration under Art.14(4) it must first notify the applicant of its intention and the reasons therefor. The applicant has one month in which to submit arguments as to why the declaration should not be made. |
| Art.25 | If the application is considered withdrawn, the applicant can, within a prescribed two month time limit (r.51.1), get the International Bureau to forward copies of any document in the file to any designated office and, within the same time limit, enter the national phase in such a state, requesting review of the decision. |
| 3–099 | ***Was the application signed properly?*** |
| Art.14(1)(a)(i) | The Receiving Office will check whether the application is signed as provided for in the Regulations (see r.4.15). |

Where there is more than one applicant, it is sufficient for the purposes of this check that it is signed by one of them. r.26.2*bis*(a)

Where there is a defect, see below for the procedure to be followed. Art.14(1)(b)

### *Are the correct indications concerning the applicant present?*     3–100

The Receiving Office will check whether the prescribed indications concerning the applicant are contained in the application (see r.4.4 and r.4.5). Art.14(1)(a)(ii)

Where there is more than one applicant, it is sufficient for the purposes of this check that indications required under r.4.5(a)(ii) (address) and (iii) (nationality and residence) are supplied in respect of one applicant who is entitled under r.19.1 to file an international application with the Receiving Office. r.26.2*bis*(b)

Where there is a defect, see below for the procedure to be followed. Art.14(1)(b)

### *Does the application contain a title?*     3–101

The Receiving Office will check whether the application contains a title (see r.4.1(a)(ii)). Art.14(1)(a)(iii)

Where there is a defect, see below for the procedure to be followed. Art.14(1)(b)

### *Does the application contain an abstract?*

The Receiving Office will check whether the application contains an abstract (see Art.3(2) and r.8). Art.14(1)(a)(iv)

Where there is a defect, see below for the procedure to be followed. Art.14(1)(b)

### *Are certain of the physical requirements met?*     3–102

The Receiving Office will check whether the application meets the prescribed physical requirements, but only in certain respects as described below. Art.14(1)(a)(v)

Where the application is filed in a language of publication, the Receiving Office will check: r.26.3(a)

(a) that the requirements of r.11 (physical requirements) have been met to the extent that compliance is necessary for the purpose of reasonably uniform international publication; and

(b) that any translation filed under r.12.3 (for international search) complies with r.11 to the extent that compliance is necessary for the purpose of satisfactory reproduction.

Where the application is filed in a language which is not a language of publication, the Receiving Office will check: r.26.3(b)

(a) that the requirements of r.11 (physical requirements) have been met to the extent that compliance is necessary for the purpose of satisfactory reproduction; and

(b) that any translation filed under r.12.3 (for international search) or 12.4 (for publication) and the drawings comply with r.11 to the extent that compliance is necessary for the purposes of uniform international publication.

Where there is a defect, see below for the procedure to be followed. Art.14(1)(b)

| | |
|---|---|
| **3–104** | ***Invitation to correct defects where formal requirements of Art.14(1)(a) are not met*** |
| Art.14(1)(b) | If the Receiving Office finds any of the defects listed in Art.14(1)(a) it will invite the applicant to correct the application within the prescribed time limit. |
| r.26.1 | Such an invitation to correct must be issued by the Receiving Office as soon as possible and preferably within one month of receiving the international application. Where the invitation concerns a missing title or abstract the Receiving Office will notify the International Searching Authority accordingly. |
| r.26.2 | The prescribed time limit for correcting the application is fixed by the Receiving Office but must be reasonable under the circumstances and in any case may not be less than one month. In can be extended at the discretion of the Receiving Office at any time before a decision is taken. |
| r.12.2(c) | Any correction of a defect in the application submitted by the applicant under r.26 must be in the language in which the application is filed. Any correction of a defect in the translation of the application furnished under r.12.3 (for international search) or in a translation of the request furnished under r.26.3*ter*(c), must be in the language of the translation. |
| r.26.3bis | The Receiving Office is not required to issue an invitation to correct under Art.14(1)(b) where the defect relates to physical requirements prescribed by r.11 and the application meets the minimum physical requirements specified in r.26.3. |
| Art.14(1)(b) | If the applicant does not correct the application within the time limit set, the application will be considered withdrawn and the Receiving Office will so declare. |
| r.26.5 | The Receiving Office decides whether any correction is submitted in due time and whether it is sufficient to avoid the application being considered withdrawn. However, no application should be considered withdrawn because the physical requirements (r.11) are not met to any extent other than to ensure reasonably uniform international publication. |
| Art.25 | If the application is considered withdrawn, the applicant can, within a prescribed two month time limit (r.51.1), get the International Bureau to forward copies of any document in the file to any designated office and, within the same time limit, enter the national phase in such a state, requesting review of the decision under Art.14(1)(b) that the application is considered withdrawn. |
| **3–105** | ***Format of any correction offered to the Receiving Office*** |
| r.26.4 | The corrections may be set out in a letter if they can be transferred to the record copy without affecting its clarity and direct reproducibility; otherwise the applicant must submit replacement sheets and a letter drawing attention to where the changes have been made. |
| **3–106** | ***Are any drawings missing?*** |
| Art.14(2) | If the international application refers to drawings which are missing, the Receiving Office will notify the applicant, giving him a chance to supply them within the prescribed time limit. If the drawings are supplied in time the international filing date will be the date of receipt of the drawings. Otherwise, references to the drawings in the application will be considered non-existent. |
| r.20.2(a)(iii) | Missing drawings must be received within 30 days of the other papers being received in order for the filing date to be changed. |
| r.26.6(b) | The date of notification by the Receiving Office does not affect the time limit fixed by r.20.2(a)(iii). |
| r.26.6(a) | Where the application refers to drawings that are not included, the Receiving Office indicates this in the application. |

## 4. Procedure of the Receivng Office

### *Are the abstract, request and text matter of the drawings in the correct language?*

3–107

Where the abstract or any text matter of the drawings is filed in a language which is different from the language of the description and the claims, the Receiving Office will invite the applicant to furnish a translation of these sections into the language in which the application is to be published, unless:

r.26.3ter(a)

(a) a translation of the application is required under r.12.3(a) (for international search); or

(b) the alternative language used is the language in which the application is to be published.

The following rules apply *mutandis mutatis*: r.26.1(a) (issue of invitation to correct to be timely), r.26.2 (time limit for reply reasonable), r.26.3 (requirement for compliance with physical requirements is limited), r.26.3*bis* (only some objections to physical requirements possible), r.26.5 (Receiving Office to decide whether time limit complied with and whether application to be considered withdrawn) and r.29.1 (actions of the Receiving Office if the application is considered withdrawn).

r.26.3ter(a)

Where the request does not comply with r.12.1(c) (must be in a language of publication which is accepted by the Receiving Office) the Receiving Office will invite the applicant to supply a translation that does.

r.26.3ter(c)

The following rules apply *mutandis mutatis*: r.3 (regulations governing the form of the request), r.26.1(a) (issue of invitation to correct to be timely), r.26.2 (time limit for reply reasonable), r.26.5 (Receiving Office to decide whether time limit complied with and whether application to be considered withdrawn) and r.29.1 (actions of the Receiving Office if the application is considered withdrawn).

r.26.3ter(c)

If on October 1, 1997, either of the above two paragraphs 26.3*ter*(a) and (c) is not compatible with the law applied by any Receiving Office, it will not apply to that office for as long as it is incompatible provided the office informed the International Bureau by December 31, 1997. Such information is promptly published in the Gazette. In such an office the filing date will be the date of receipt of the translation. Only the US has filed such reservations.

r.26.3ter(b)(d)

### *Have the necessary fees been paid?*

3–108

If any prescribed fees have not been paid (Art.3(4)(iv) and Art.4(2)) the international application will be considered withdrawn and the Receiving Office will so declare.

Art.14(3)

The relevant prescribed fees under Art.3(4)(iv) are the transmittal fee (r.14), the international filing fee (r.15.1), the search fee (r.16) and, where required, the late payment fee (r.15.1). The designation fees provided for by Art.4(2) are now part of the international filing fee.

r.27

If the application is considered withdrawn, the applicant can, within a prescribed two-month time limit (r.51.1), get the International Bureau to forward copies of any document in the file to any designated office and, within the same time limit, enter the national phase in such a state, requesting review of the decision under Art.14(3) that the application is considered withdrawn.

Art.25

### *Has any priority claim been made correctly?*

3–109

Where the Receiving Office or the International Bureau find that the priority claim does not comply with the requirements of r.4.10 or indications supplied are inconsistent with indications in the priority document itself, the applicant will be invited to correct the priority claim. If, in response to such an invitation, the applicant does not submit a priority claim complying with r.4.10 within the time limit for adding/

r.26bis.2

correcting a priority claim (r.26*bis*.1(a)) the priority claim will be deemed never to have been made for the purposes of the PCT and the Receiving Office or International Bureau will so declare and inform the applicant, unless the correction concerns a missing indication of the earlier application number or concerns a discrepancy between an indication in the claim and the corresponding indication in the priority document. When such a declaration has been made the International Bureau, when requested by the applicant prior to the completion of the technical preparations for international publication (and subject to the payment of a fee as fixed in the Administrative Instructions), will publish, together with the application, information concerning the priority claim which was considered not to have been made. A copy of any such request will be included in the communication under Art.20 (of the application and search report to designated offices) where the international application is not published by virtue of Art.64(3) (only states waiving international publication have been designated).

AdminInst    See s.113. The fee is 50 Swiss francs plus 12 Swiss francs for each page in excess of one.

## 3–110  Is any declaration under r.4.17 correctly made?

r.26ter.2    If the Receiving Office or International Bureau finds that one of the r.4.17 declarations is not worded properly or the declaration of inventorship referred to in r.4.17(iv) is not signed properly it will invite the applicant to correct the deficiency within 16 months from the priority date. Where a correction is received late, the International Bureau will notify the applicant and proceed as set out in the Administrative Instructions.

## 3–111  Requirements relating to the submission of a translation

See above in the section on language requirements of the application.

## 3–112  The role of the International Bureau and International Searching Authority in identifying defects

r.28    If the International Bureau is of the opinion that the application contains a defect mentioned in Art.14(1)(a)(i) (not signed), Art.14(1)(a)(ii) (absence of information concerning the applicant) or Art.14(1)(a)(v) (non-compliance with physical requirements) it will inform the Receiving Office who will, unless in disagreement with the International Bureau, proceed under Art.14(1)(b) and r.26 (invitation to correct).

r.29.3    If the International Bureau or the Searching Authority considers that the Receiving Office should make a declaration under Art.14(4) (application considered withdrawn due to defects found at a later stage which mean a filing date should not have been accorded) it will call the relevant facts to the attention of the Receiving Office.

## 3–113  Procedure when the Receiving Office declares that the application is considered withdrawn

r.29    If the Receiving Office declares that an international application is considered withdrawn because:

(a) the applicant failed to correct certain defects (Art.14(1)(b) and r.26.5);

(b) the applicant failed to pay prescribed fees under r.27.1(a) (Art.14(3)(a));

(c) there is a later finding of non-compliance with Art.11(1)(i)–(iii) (Art.14(4));

(d) the applicant failed to furnish a required translation for search or the late-furnishing fee (r.12.3(d)); or

(e) the applicant failed to furnish the original of a document (r.92.4 (g)(i));

the following consequences will ensue:

(i) the Receiving Office will transmit the record copy (unless already transmitted) and any corrections offered by the applicant to the International Bureau (which is not be required to notify the applicant of receipt);

(ii) the Receiving Office will promptly notify the applicant and the International Bureau of the declaration and the International Bureau will subsequently notify all the designated offices which have already been notified of their designation; and

(iii) the Receiving Office will not transmit the search copy under r.23 or, if it has already done so, will inform the International Searching Authority of the declaration.

In these circumstances, the applicant can, within a prescribed two-month time limit (r.51.1), get the International Bureau to forward copies of any documents in the file to any designated office and, within the same time limit, enter the national phase in such a state, requesting review of the decision. Art.25

## 5. DRAWING UP THE INTERNATIONAL SEARCH REPORT

### Authorities competent to carry out international search

#### *What is an International Searching Authority?* 3–114

The international search is carried out by an International Searching Authority which is a national office or intergovernmental organisation set up to locate prior art. Art.16(1)

#### *Requirements that must be met by an International Searching Authority* 3–115

Any prospective International Searching Authority must satisfy certain minimum requirements in order to be appointed and to remain appointed. Art.16(3)(c)

It must have access to the minimum documentation listed in r.34 in searchable form and at least 100 full-time employees technically qualified to carry out searches in the required technical fields and having the language facilities to understand at least those languages in which the minimum documentation is written or translated. It must also be appointed as an International Preliminary Examining Authority. r.36

#### *Appointment of International Searching Authorities* 3–116

International Searching Authorities are appointed by the Assembly. Such appointment is conditional on the consent of the national office or intergovernmental organisation concerned and the conclusion of an agreement with the International Bureau, specifying rights and obligations, which is approved by the Assembly. Art.16(3)(a)(b)

See under *Art.150* for details of the EPO agreement with the International Bureau ([2001] O.J. 601). AnReg

Each appointment is for a fixed (and extendable) period. Art.16(3)(d)

Before deciding to appoint a new Authority, extend an appointment or allow an appointment to lapse, the Assembly must hear the relevant office or organisation and seek advice from the Committee for Technical Cooperation (see Art.56). Art.16(3)(e)

#### *Receiving Offices specify the competent International Searching Authority or Authorities* 3–117

In the case where more than one International Searching Authority has been appointed by the International Bureau, each Receiving Office must state which International Searching Authority or Authorities are competent to search applications filed with it. Art.16(2)

The International Bureau publishes this information. In the case where more than one Searching Authority is competent, the Receiving Office may leave the choice of which r.35.1/35.2

one to select with the applicant or may declare that one or more of them are competent for specific types of applications. In any event, where more than one Searching Authority is competent for a particular application, the applicant is allowed to choose which one to use.

r.35.3 When the International Bureau acts as the Receiving Office, any International Searching Authority is competent if it would have been competent had the application been filed with a Receiving Office itself competent under r.19.1(a)(i) and (ii), (b) or (c) or r.19.2(i) (rules specifying which Receiving Offices are competent for a particular national or resident). The applicant can choose where two or more are competent. The provisions r.35.1 and r.35.2 do not apply to the International Bureau as Receiving Office.

AppGuide See Vol. I, Annex C. When the EPO acts as Receiving Office, the EPO is the only competent International Searching Authority.

AnReg Apart from the Contracting States to the EPC (see Protocol on Centralisation), some non-European states have also given the EPO competence as an International Searching Authority. Applicants from Japan ([1985] O.J. 331 and [1990] O.J. 443), the US ([1987] O.J. 266 and [1990] O.J. 443) and Poland ([1991] O.J. 124), for instance, can choose between their national patent office and the EPO as International Searching Authority.

**3–118** ***Limitations set by the EPO on its competence as International Searching Authority***

*Art.154(1)* The EPO may act as International Searching Authority for an applicant who is a resident or national of an EPC Contracting State in respect of which the PCT has entered into force, subject to the conclusion of an agreement between the European Patent Organisation and the International Bureau.

*Art.154(2)* The EPO may also act as International Searching Authority for any other applicants in accordance with an agreement between the European Patent Organisation and the International Bureau, subject to the prior approval of the Administrative Council.

AnReg See under *Art.150* for details of the agreement. The EPO has, in principle, agreed to act as International Searching Authority for applications filed with any Receiving Office that specifies it for this purpose, subject to the imposition of restrictions if its workload becomes too great ([2001] O.J. 601). The agreement was modified in 2002 ([2002] O.J. 52), with effect from November 1, 2001, to restrict the EPO's competence in respect of an applicant who is a US national or resident and has filed an application relating to biotechnology or a business method. This competence has since been restored in respect of biotechnological inventions ([2003] O.J. 633) for applications filed after January 1, 2004 ([2003] O.J. 633), but remains excluded until at least 2007 for business methods ([2005] O.J. 149).

**The nature of an international search**

**3–119** ***The purpose of an international search***

*Art.15(1)(2)(4)* An international search is conducted on every international application in order to discover relevant prior art. The International Searching Authority must attempt to discover as much prior art as possible, consulting at least the minimum documentation specified in the Regulations.

**3–120** ***Basis of the international search***

*Art.15(3)* An international search is made on the basis of the claims, with due regard to the description and drawings (if any).

r.33.3 There is a particular emphasis on the inventive concept towards which the claims are directed. In so far as possible an international search should cover the entire subject matter to which the claims are directed or to which they might reasonably be expected to be directed after they have been amended.

## *Definition of relevant prior art* 3–121

Relevant prior art (within the meaning of Art.15(2)) consists of everything which has been made available to the public, prior to the international filing date, anywhere in the world, by means of written disclosure (including drawings and other illustrations) and which is capable of being of assistance in determining whether the claimed invention is new and non-obvious. r.33.1(a)

When a written disclosure (made available to the public on the same day as or later than the international filing date) refers to an oral disclosure, use, exhibition or other means whereby the contents of the written disclosure were made available to the public on a date before the filing date, that fact and the earlier date are separately mentioned in the search report. r.33.1(b)

Any application or patent published on the same day or later than the international application having an earlier filing/priority date which would constitute relevant prior art had it been published before the international filing date is also mentioned in the search report. r.33.1(c)

## *Fields to be covered* 3–122

The international search must cover all technical fields that may contain material pertinent to the invention, including arts analogous to the art in which the invention is classifiable (analogy being judged by what appears to be the necessary essential function or use of the invention as well as functions expressly indicated in the application). r.33.2(a)–(c)

The international search should embrace all subject matter that is generally recognised as equivalent to the subject matter of the claimed invention for all or certain of its features. r.33.2(d)

## *Minimum documentation* 3–123

This rule specifies the minimum documentation that must be consulted when drawing up the international search report. r.34

## The nature of an international-type search 3–124

If allowable under national law of a Contracting State, and subject to the conditions of that law, an applicant who files an application with the national office of (or acting for) such a state may request that an international-type search be conducted on that application. With the same provisos, any national office may decide to subject a national application to such a search. Art.15(5)(a)(b)

Where the national office of one state is acting as the competent Receiving Office for nationals and residents of another state, the law of the latter state is relevant for the purposes of Art.15(5). r.19.1

Such an international-type search is carried out by a competent International Searching Authority (according to Art.16), if necessary on a translation of the national application prepared by the applicant in a language prescribed for international applications which is acceptable to the International Searching Authority chosen. The national application (and translation when required) must be presented in the form prescribed for international applications. Art.15(5)(c)

See under *Art.150*. The EPO will carry out an international type search on a national patent application filed in an EPC Contracting State if the law of that State so allows ([1999] O.J. 300). AnReg

**Procedure for conducting the search**

### 3–125 *General aspects*

Art.17(1)     Procedure before the International Searching Authority is governed by the PCT, its Regulations and the appropriate agreement between the International Searching Authority and the International Bureau.

### 3–126 *Check that title and abstract are present and appropriate*

r.37.1/r.38.1     If the international application does not contain a title (Art.14(1)(a)(iii)) or an abstract (Art.14(1)(a)(iv)) and the Receiving Office has notified the International Searching Authority that it has invited the applicant to correct such a defect, the Searching Authority will proceed with its search unless, and until, it receives notification that the application has been withdrawn.

r.37.2/r.38.2     If there is no title or there is no abstract and the International Searching Authority has not received such notification, or if the title does not comply with r.4.3 [short and precise] or the abstract does not comply with r.8, the International Searching Authority will establish a title or abstract (as appropriate) for itself in the language in which the application is to be published or, if a translation was transmitted by the Receiving Office under r.23.1(b) (translation for the purposes of international search) and the International Searching Authority so wishes, in the language of that translation.

r.38.2(b)     The applicant may within one month of the date of mailing of the international search report, submit comments on any abstract established by the International Searching Authority. Any subsequent amendment by the International Searching Authority is notified by the International Searching Authority to the International Bureau.

r.8.2     The best Figure to accompany the abstract is also chosen.

### 3–127 *Check whether sequence listings have been provided properly*

r.13*ter*.1(a)     Where an application discloses a nucleotide and/or amino acid sequence the International Searching Authority may invite the applicant to furnish a sequence listing in electronic form complying with the Administrative Instructions unless such a listing is already available to it. A late furnishing fee may be charged.

r.13*ter*.1(b)     Where at least part of the international application is filed on paper and the International Searching Authority finds that the description does not comply with r.5.2(a), it may invite the applicant to furnish a sequence listing in paper form complying with the standard provided for in the Administrative Instructions unless such a listing is already available to it, whether or not an invitation under r.13*ter*.1(a) is made. A late furnishing fee may be charged.

r.13*ter*.1(c)     The late furnishing fee under r.13*ter*.1(a) or r.13*ter*.1(b) is fixed by the International Searching Authority but my not exceed 25 per cent of the international filing fee (excluding the fee for each sheet in excess of 30). Furthermore, a fee may be demanded in respect of r.13*ter*.1(a) or r.13*ter*.1(b) but not both.

r.13*ter*.1(d)     If the required listing under r.13*ter*.1(a) or r.13*ter*.1(b) is not furnished, or a required late furnishing fee paid, the search only has to be carried out to the extent it is meaningfully possible without the sequence listing.

[2005] O.J. 225     The EPO now charges a late furnishing fee of 200 euros when it makes such an invitation.

r.13*ter*.1(e)     Any sequence listing submitted under r.13*ter*.1(a) or r.13*ter*.1(b) or otherwise and not contained in the application as filed is not part of the applications as filed except that amendment pursuant to Art.34(2)(b) is allowed.

Where the International Searching Authority finds that the description does not comply with r.5.2(b), it invites the applicant to submit the required correction, to which r.25.4 applies *mutatis mutandis*. The correction is submitted by the International Searching Authority to the receiving office and to the International Bureau.

r.13*ter*.1(f)

## *Determination as to whether a search is possible*

3–128

If the International Searching Authority considers either:

Art.17(2)/r.39

(a) that the international application concerns subject matter which it is not required to search, that is:

    (i) scientific and mathematical theories,
    (ii) plant or animal varieties or essentially biological processes for the production of plants and animals, other than microbiological processes or the products thereof,
    (iii) schemes, rules or methods of doing business, performing purely mental acts or playing games,
    (iv) methods of treatment of the human or animal body by surgery or therapy, as well as diagnostic methods,
    (v) mere presentations of information, or
    (vi) computer programs (to the extent that the Authority is not equipped to search prior art concerning such programs)

and it decides therefore not to search it; or

(b) that the description, claims or drawings fail to comply with the prescribed requirements (see Art.5 to Art.7) to such an extent that a meaningful search cannot be carried out;

the International Searching Authority will notify the applicant and the International Bureau that no international search report will be established.

This may apply to the whole application or one or more claims only.

Art.17(2)(b)

See under *Art.150* for Art.4 of the agreement between the International Bureau and the International Bureau ([2001] O.J. 601). Before the EPO, those matters listed by r.39 and also excluded under the EPC will not be searched ([1998] O.J. 92).

AnReg

## *Check for unity of invention*

3–129

See s.207. The determination of unity by the International Searching Authority must be made in line with the instructions in Annex B of the Administrative Instructions.

AdminInst

If the International Searching Authority considers the claims lack unity (see under requirements of the claims above), the applicant will be invited to pay additional fees.

Art.17(3)(a)

The fees must be paid within one month of the invitation.

r.40.1

The invitation will specify the reasons why the application lacks unity and the amount to be paid. The amount is determined by the International Searching Authority and is payable direct to that Authority. The invitation must also invite the payment of a protest fee, where one is due (see below) within one month of the date of the invitation and indicate the amount to be paid.

r.40.1/r.40.2

The applicant may pay the additional fees under protest *i.e.* accompanied by a statement explaining why the application complies with the requirement of unity or why the fees are excessive. The protest will be examined by a review body of the Searching Authority or of any competent higher authority, which may include but may not be limited to the person responsible for the decision under protest. To the extent that the protest is found justified, the total or partial reimbursement of the additional fees will be ordered. If the applicant so requests, the text of the protest and subsequent decision

r.40.2(c)(d)

| | will be notified to the designated offices together with the search report. The applicant must submit any translation thereof with the furnishing of any translation of the international application required under Art.22. |
|---|---|
| r.40.2(e) | The examination of such a protest may be made conditional by the International Searching Authority on the payment of a protest fee. Where the applicant has not furnished the protest fee within the one-month time limit of r.40.1(iii) the protest will be considered not to have been made and the International Searching Authority will so declare. The protest fee will be refunded if examination of the protest reveals that it was entirely justified. |
| Art.17(3)(a) | The International Searching Authority will establish the International Search Report on those parts of the application which relate to the invention first mentioned in the claims (the main invention) and, in the case where additional fees have been paid within the prescribed time limit, on those parts of the application which relate to inventions for which fees have been paid. |
| Art.17(3)(b) | Where additional fees are not paid, there are potential consequences in the national phase—see the section on national phase aspects below. |

**3–130**    ***Lack of unity where the EPO is the International Searching Authority***

| | |
|---|---|
| r.105(1) | An additional fee, equal to the search fee, is payable in respect of each additional invention. |
| RRF2(2) | The fee is 1,615 euros. |
| r.105(3) | Without prejudice to r.40.2(e) PCT, where an additional fee has been paid under protest, the EPO will review whether the request for the additional fee was justified. If it finds the request unjustified, it will refund the additional fee. If, however, it finds the request justified, it will inform the applicant and invite him to pay the protest fee. If the protest fee is paid in due time, the protest will be referred to a board of appeal for a decision. |
| [2005] O.J. 226 | Until the implementation of EPC2000, the EPO will continue to review the decision to request additional fees prior to demanding a protest fee (as was previously dictated by the PCT). A protest fee will be demanded within one month of notification of the result of the review. If the review is entirely in favour pf the applicant, the additional fees are refunded. If the review confirms the previous position, the protest fee is requested. If the review is partly in favour of the application, appropriate fees are refunded and the protest is referred to the Board of Appeal if the protest fee has already been paid; otherwise the protest fee is requested. If the Board of Appeal finds the protest fully justified, all additional fees and the protest fee are refunded; if only partly justified, only the relevant additional fees are refunded. |
| RRF2(21) | The protest fee is 1,065 euros. |
| AnReg | See under *Art.154*. The review panel usually consists of the search examiner, the head of his directorate and another examiner skilled in the determination of unity (see [1992] O.J. 547 for the full protest procedure). |
| **Art.154(3)** | In the EPO, a Board of Appeal is responsible for examining any protest made by an applicant against an additional fee charged by EPO under Art.17(3)(a) PCT. |
| G1/89 | Headnote: "The agreement between the EPO and WIPO dated October 7, 1987, including the obligation under its Art.2 for the EPO to be guided by the PCT guidelines for international search, is binding on the EPO when acting as an International Searching Authority and upon the Boards of Appeal of the EPO when deciding on protests against the charging of additional search fees under the provisions of Art.17(3)(a) PCT. Consequently, as foreseen in these guidelines, an international application may, under Art.17(3)(a) PCT, be considered not to comply with the requirement of unity of inven- |

tion, not only *a priori* but also *a posteriori, i.e.* after taking prior art into consideration. However, such consideration has only the procedural effect of initiating the special procedure laid down in Art.17 and r.40 PCT and is, therefore, not a "substantive examination" in the normal sense of the term.

Headnote: "The EPO in its function as an International Searching Authority may, pursuant to Art.17(3)(a) PCT, request a further search fee where the international application is considered to lack unity *a posteriori*." G2/89

Extra fees can't be refunded if the statement of grounds supporting the protest is submitted late. W4/87

The mere fact that a process can be used to make other products does not imply a lack of unity between product and process claims. W11/99

See CLBA, pp.575–582. CLBA

### *Use of a previous search as the basis for the international search*      3–131

If reference is made in the request (r.4.11) to an international-type search (or any other search), asking for the international search to be based thereon, the International Searching Authority must, as far as possible, use that search in establishing the international search report and must refund the search fee to the extent and under the conditions provided for in the agreement under Art.16(3)(b) (between the International Bureau and the International Searching Authority) or in a communication addressed to the International Bureau and published in the Gazette (e.g. it might be possible for the EPO to base a search entirely or partly on a search report prepared by the EPO on an application whose priority is claimed). r.41

See under Art.150 for the agreement between the EPO and the International Bureau ([2006], O.J. 252). The amount refunded depends on whether full or partial use is made of the previous report, what kind of search it is (e.g. European or International) and whether it is accompanied by a report on patentability or not. AnReg

### The international search report, the written opinion and the international preliminary report on patentability

#### *Time limit for establishing the search report*      3–132

The search report (or the declaration under Art.17(2)(a)—inability to establish a search report) must be established within a prescribed time limit, which is the later of three months from the receipt of the search copy by the International Searching Authority or nine months from the priority date. Art.18(1)/r.42

#### *Form of the search report*      3–133

The search report must be established in the prescribed form. Art.18(1)

It must indicate the name of the International Searching Authority, the international application number, the name of the applicant and the international filing date. r.43.1

It must be dated and also indicate the date on which the international search report was actually completed and the filing date of any earlier application whose priority is claimed (or the earliest in the case where there is more than one). r.43.2

It must contain the classification of the subject matter, at least according to the International Patent Classification (as determined by the International Searching Authority). r.43.3

It must be in the language in which the international application is to be published or, if a translation into a different language was transmitted under r.23.1(b) (for the r.43.4

| | purpose of international search) and the International Searching Authority so wishes, in the language of the translation (this applies to Art17(2)(a) declarations as well). When a search report or declaration is not in English, it must be translated into English by the International Bureau—see below, r.45. |
|---|---|
| r.43.5 | It must cite the documents considered to be relevant in the form regulated by the Administrative Instructions and specially indicate citations of particular relevance. Citations which are not relevant to all the claims should be cited in relation to the claim or claims to which they are relevant. Where only certain passages of a document are relevant, or particularly relevant, they should be identified (*e.g.* by page and line numbers). |
| AdminInst | See s.505. The indication "X" is used where a document prejudices the novelty or inventive step of a claim on its own and "Y" where it prejudices the novelty or inventive step of a claim in combination with another document, the combination being obvious to the skilled person. See s.507 for the meaning of other indications used. |
| r.43.6 | It must list the classification identification of the fields searched. The International Searching Authority must publish the name of the classification used if it is other than the International Patent Classification. If any relevant document is a patent, inventor's certificate, utility certificate, utility model, patent or certificate of addition, utility certificate of addition, or published application relating to any of these (definitions in Art.2(ii) do not apply here) which relates to a state, period or language outside the scope of the minimum documentation (see r.34), the search report must, where practicable, identify the kinds of document, states, periods and languages to which it is extended. If an electronic database was used for any part of the search, the search report may indicate its name and, where considered useful to others and practicable, the search terms used. |
| r.43.7 | It must, where appropriate, indicate the fact that the applicant has paid additional fees in response to a unity objection. Where only part of the application has been searched (see Art.17(3)(a)), the search report must indicate that part. |
| r.43.8 | It must indicate the name of the responsible officer who drew up the report. |
| r.43.9 | It must not contain any matter other than that specified in rr.33.1(b) (written account of an oral disclosure or prior use), 33.1(c) (intervening publication), 43.1, 43.2, 43.3, 43.5, 43.6, 43.7, 43.8, 44.2 (approval of the title and abstract) and Art.17(2)(b) (claims not searchable) and any matter specified by the Administrative Instructions. No expressions of opinion, reasoning, arguments or explanations may be included, by permission of the Administrative Instructions or otherwise. |
| r.43.10 | It must conform to the physical requirements indicated in the Administrative Instructions. |
| r.44.2 | It must state that the title and abstract as submitted by the applicant are approved or be accompanied by the text of the title and/or abstract as established by the International Searching Authority (see r.37 and r.38 above). |

## 3–134    *Written opinion of the International Searching Authority*

| | |
|---|---|
| r.43*bis*.1(a) | The International Searching Authority will, for all applications filed on or after January 1, 2004, and subject to r.69.1(b-*bis*) (search and preliminary examination to start at the same time) at the same time that it establishes the search report, establish a written opinion as to whether the claimed invention appears to be novel, to involve an inventive step and to be industrially applicable and whether the international application complies with the requirements of the PCT and its Regulations in so far as checked. The written opinion may be accompanied by other observations provided for in the Regulations. |
| r.69.1(b-*bis*) | However, where the International Searching and Preliminary Examining Authorities are the same, and the International Searching Authority wants to start international preliminary examination at the same time as carrying out the international search and the conditions set out in Art.34(2)(c)(i)–(iii) are met (the invention is novel, inventive and industrially applicable, the application complies with the provisions of the PCT |

and Regulations checked and no supplementary observations are to be made) no written opinion according to r.43*bis*.1 is necessary.

When establishing the written opinion Art.33(2)–(6), Art.35(2) and Art.35(3) and rr.43.4, 64, 65, 66.1(e), 66.7, 67, 70.2(b) and (d), 70.3, 70.4(ii), 70.5(a), 70.6 to 70.10, 70.12, 70.14 and 70.15(a) apply *mutatis mutandis* (these articles and rules establish the procedure for carrying out international preliminary examination). r.43*bis*.1(b)

The written opinion must contain a notification informing the applicant that, if a demand for international preliminary examination is made, the written opinion will, under r.66.1*bis*(a), but subject to r.66.1*bis*(b), be considered to be a written opinion of the International Preliminary Examining Authority for the purposes of r.66.2(a), in which case the applicant is invited to submit to that Authority, before the expiration of the r.54*bis*.1(a) time limit (time limit for making a demand), a written reply together, where appropriate, with amendments. r.43*bis*.1(c)

The written opinion of the International Searching Authority is considered to be a written opinion of the International Preliminary Examining Authority unless, where the two Authorities are different, the International Preliminary Examining Authority notifies the International Bureau otherwise, in respect of one or more International Searching Authorities. The EPO have filed reservations. r.66.1*bis*(a)(b)

### *Transmittal of the search report and written opinion to the applicant and the International Bureau*   3–135

The search report and written opinion (or the declaration that some or all the claims were unsearched under Art.17(2)(a)) must be submitted immediately, and on the same day, to both the applicant and the International Bureau. Art.18(2)/r.44.1

If the PCT application proceeds to publication, the search report will be published with that application, or will be published separately if the application has already been published. The written opinion will not, however be published in this way. It will subsequently become available to the public, typically after 30 months from priority along with any observations which the applicant has made on the opinion.

Although not expressly provided for in the regulations, the applicant can submit to the International Bureau comments on the written opinion produced by the International Search Authority. Any such comments will subsequently be sent with the IPRP, by the International Bureau, to the designated offices.

### *Preparation by the International Bureau of an international preliminary report on patentability (IPRP) and transmission to the applicant*   3–136

Unless an international preliminary examination report has been or is to be established, *i.e.* unless a demand has been filed, the International Bureau will issue a report on behalf of the International Searching Authority having the same contents as the written opinion established under r.43*bis*.1. The report will be called "international preliminary report on patentability" and will contain an indication that it is issued under r.44*bis* by the International Bureau on behalf of the International Searching Authority. A copy will promptly be transmitted to the applicant by the International Bureau. r.44*bis*.1

### *Translation of the search report by the International Bureau*   3–137

The international search report (or the declaration that some or all the claims were unsearched under Art.17(2)(a)) is translated by the International Bureau into English when in another language. Art.18(3)/r.45

### *Translation of the written opinion or preliminary report on patentability by the International Bureau and communication of the report and its translation to designated offices*   3–138

Where an international preliminary report on patentability has been issued by the International Bureau under r.44*bis*.1, the International Bureau will communicate it to r.44*bis*.2

each designated office in accordance with r.93*bis*.1 (on request and at the requested time) but not before the expiration of 30 months from the priority date. However, a copy of the written opinion of the International Searching Authority may be communicated earlier at the request of the applicant or a designated office where the applicant has requested early national processing under Art.23(2). If the applicant has submitted comments on the written opinion to the International Bureau, those comments will also be sent to each designated office.

r.44*bis*.3(a)

Any designated state may, where an international preliminary report on patentability has been issued by the International Bureau under r.44*bis*.1 in a language other than the official language, or one of the official languages, of its national office, require a translation of the report into English. Any such requirement must be notified to the International Bureau, and will be promptly published in the Gazette.

r.44*bis*.3(b)(c)

Such a translation is prepared by or under the responsibility of the International Bureau and will be transmitted to the applicant and any interested designated office at the same time.

r.44*bis*.3(d)

In the case referred to in r.44*bis*.2(b) (supply of a copy of the written opinion of the International Searching Authority on early national processing), the written opinion will, upon request of the designated office concerned, be translated by or under the responsibility of the International Bureau into English. Such a translation will be transmitted within two months of the request, simultaneously to the interested designated office and to the applicant.

r.44*bis*.4

The applicant may make written observations as to the correctness of the translations referred to in r.44*bis*.3(b) and (d) and must send a copy of such observations to each of the interested designated offices and to the International Bureau.

r.62*bis*

The International Bureau will also translate the written opinion of the International Searching Authority into English when requested to do so by the International Preliminary Examining Authority. Copies of the translation will be sent to the applicant and the relevant Authority at the same time and within two months of the receipt of the request. The applicant may make written observations on the correctness of the translation and must send a copy of such observations to the International Bureau and International Preliminary Examining Authority.

3–139      *Requests by a Receiving Office or the applicant for copies of cited documents*

Art.20(3)/r.44

The International Searching Authority will supply copies of documents cited in an international search report when so requested by a designated office or the applicant at any time during seven years from the international filing date of the corresponding application. A fee for preparing and mailing the copies may be requested, the amount of which is fixed in the agreement under Art.16(3)(b) between the International Searching Authority and the International Bureau. The Searching Authority may use an agency to perform this function if it wishes.

## 6. AMENDMENT OF THE APPLICATION UNDER ARTICLE 19

3–140      **Amendment of claims before the International Bureau**

Art.19(1)   *When can the applicant amend the claims?*

r.46.1

Having received the international search report, the applicant is entitled to one chance to amend the claims before the International Bureau within a prescribed time limit.

The prescribed time limit is the later of:

(a) 16 months from the priority date; and

(b) two months from the date of transmittal of the international search report to the International Bureau and the applicant by the International Searching Authority;

provided that if the amendment is received before the technical preparations for international publication have been completed it will be considered to have been received on the last day of the time limit.

### *Where should any amendments be filed?* 3–141

Any such amendment should be filed directly with the International Bureau.     r.46.2

### *Language of any amendments* 3–142

In general, any amendment of the international application must be in the language in which the international application was filed.     r.12.2

However, if the language of publication is different from the language of filing any Art.19 amendment must be in the language of publication.     r.46.3

### *Form of any amendments* 3–143

Replacement sheets for every altered sheet of the claims must be submitted by the applicant. The letter accompanying the replacement sheets must indicate whether any pages have been cancelled entirely and draw attention to the differences between the replaced sheets and the replacement sheets.     r.46.5

### *Statement accompanying the amendments* 3–144

The applicant may also file a brief statement explaining the amendments and their possible impact on the description and drawings, identified as such by a heading, preferably "Statement under Article 19(1)". The statement must be in the language of publication and should not exceed 500 words in English or if translated into English. It must not contain any disparaging comments on the international search report or the relevance of the citations given therein. Reference to a citation, relevant to a given claim and contained in the international search report, may be made only in connection with an amendment of that claim.     Art.19(1)/r.46.4

The statement will be published if in the correct form.     r.48.2(a)(vi)

### *Prohibition on added subject matter* 3–145

Any amendments may not go beyond the disclosure of the international application as filed but such a transgression will have no consequences in designated states that allow such added subject matter.     Art.19(2)(3)

### Notification of amendments to the International Preliminary Examining Authority when a demand has been filed 3–146

When the International Bureau receives a copy of the demand from the International Preliminary Examining Authority, it will promptly transmit a copy of any amendments filed under Art.19 and any statement filed under Art.19 explaining such amendments to the International Preliminary Examining Authority, unless International Preliminary Examining Authority has indicated that it has already received such a copy.     r.62.1

If a demand has already been submitted when the applicant files amendments under Art.19, the applicant should preferably file simultaneously with the International Preliminary Examining Authority a copy of such amendments and a copy of any accompanying statement under Art.19. In any case, the International Bureau will promptly transmit a copy of such amendments and any accompanying statement to the International Preliminary Examining Authority.     r.62.2

## 7. PUBLICATION OF THE APPLICATION AND THE SEARCH REPORT

**3–147**     **Responsibility for international publication**

Art.21(1)     The International Bureau is responsible for the publication of international applications.

**3–148**     **Timing of international publication**

Art.21(2)(a)(b)     The International Bureau normally publishes international publications promptly after the expiration of 18 months from the priority date. However, it may be published earlier at the request of the applicant. Publication takes place once a week, usually on a Thursday.

r.48.4(b)     Where the applicant has made a request for early publication under Art.21(2)(b) or Art.64(3)(c)(i), the International Bureau will proceed to publication promptly after it has received the request and any extra fee due concerning the search report under r.48.4(a) (special publication fee where the search report is not yet available).

r.90*bis*.3(d)(e)     Where the withdrawal of a priority claim changes the priority date, time limits starting on the priority date which have not already expired may be recalculated from the new priority date with the proviso that the International Bureau may nevertheless publish the application 18 months from original priority under Art.21(2)(a) if the withdrawal is received by the International Bureau after the technical preparations for publication are complete. See also r.26*bis*.1(c).

**3–149**     **Circumstances where no publication takes place**

Art.64(3)     Any state may declare that it does not require international publication and where the application contains only the designation of such states, no publication will occur at 18 months unless the applicant requests it or the national office of one of these states has published a national application or patent based on the international publication. In the second case, the national office concerned must notify the International Bureau of the publication promptly after it has taken place (r.48.5). This provision relates only to the US.

Art.21(5)     No publication takes place if the international application is withdrawn or considered withdrawn before the technical preparations for publication have been completed (see r.90*bis* for withdrawal procedure).

AppGuide     Such preparations are normally complete 15 days prior to the date of publication (Applicant's Guide, Vol.I, para.305).

### Language and form of the Publication

**3–150**     *Where the language of filing is used*

r.48.3(a)     If the international application is filed a language of publication (Arabic, Chinese, English, French, German, Japanese, Russian or Spanish) it will be published in that language.

**3–151**     *Where the language of a translation is used*

r.48.3(b)     If the international application was not filed in a language of publication but a translation into a language of publication has been furnished under r.12.3 (for international search) or r.12.4 (for publication) then the application will be published in the language of that translation.

## 7. Publication of the Application and the Search Report

*Translation of parts if the pamphlet into English where English is not the language of publication*  3–152

If the international application is published in a language other than English, then the following documents will also be published in an English translation prepared by the International Bureau:  r.48.3(c)

(a) the international search report, to the extent that it is published under r.48.2(a)(v), or the Art.17(2)(a) declaration;

(b) the title of the invention; and

(c) the abstract and any text matter pertaining to the figure(s) accompanying the abstract.

*Form of the publication*  3–153

The form of international publication is laid down in the Regulations.  Art.21(4)

The form in which and the means by which international applications are published are governed by the Administrative Instructions.  r.48.1

As of April 1, 2006, international publication takes place solely in electronic form. Published applications can be downloaded free from the internet. The applicant is only provided with a paper copy of the publication if one is specifically requested.  AdminInst 406(b)

### Contents of the publication  3–154

The pamphlet prepared for international publication must contain the following elements.  r.48.2

*A standardised front page*  3–155

The standardised front page must include:  r.48.2(b)(d)(e)

(a) data from the request sheet and other data prescribed by the Administrative Instructions (See s.406).

(b) a figure, where the application contains drawings (unless r.8.2(b) applies—International Searching authority considers none of the drawings suitable). The figure is chosen according to r.8.2 (the International Searching Authority having the final say) and may be reduced.

(c) the abstract. If the abstract is both in English and another language, the English version will appear first. If the abstract (or translation thereof under r.48.3 (c)) is too long, it may be continued on the back of the front page.

(d) an indication that the request contains one of the special declarations referred to in r.4.17 received before the appropriate time limit (r.26*ter*.1).

Where the search report could not be established (Art.17(2)(a)), this will be conspicuously noted on the front page and the abstract and any figure may be omitted.  r.48.2(c)

Where a designation is withdrawn, that designation will not be included in the international publication if the notice of withdrawal reaches the International Bureau (from the applicant or via the Receiving Office or International Preliminary Examining Authority) before the technical preparations for publication have been completed.  r.90*bis*.2(e)

There are no consequences for the applicant if the International Bureau does not publish a designation that was validly made.  J26/87

| | |
|---|---|
| 3–156 | *The description* |
| 3–157 | *The claims* |
| r.48.2(f) | If the claims have been amended under Art.19, the publication will contain the full text of the claims as filed and as amended. Any statement under Art.19(1) will also be published unless the International Bureau finds that it does not comply with r.46.4. The date of receipt of the amended claims will also be indicated. See also r.48.1(a)(vi) below. |
| r.48.2(h) | If, when the technical preparations for international publication are complete, the time limit for amending the claims under Art.19 has not expired, the front page will say so and indicate that, should the claims be amended, the full text on the amended claims will be published later along with a revised front page. Any A19(1) statement will also be published unless the International Bureau finds it does not comply with R46.4. |
| 3–158 | *Any drawings* |
| 3–159 | *The international search report* |
| r.48.2(a)(v) | The international search report or Art.17(2)(a) declaration (that no search report could be established) will be published, except those parts that would be a duplication of the standardised front page. |
| r.48.2(g) | If, however, when the technical preparations for international publication are complete, the search report is not ready (e.g. because the applicant has asked for early publication under Art.21(2)(b) or publication under Art.64(3)(c)(i)) the front page will explain that this is the case and the search report will be separately published when available together with a revised front page. |
| 3–159A | *Any statement filed under A19(1)* |
| R48.2(a)(vi) | The publication contains any statement filed under A19(1) (explaining amendments made) unless the International Bureau finds that the statement does not comply with R46.4. |
| 3–160 | *Any request for rectification* |
| r.48.2(a)(vii) | Any request for rectification referred to in the third sentence of r.91.1(f) will be published (where authorisation of a request for correction of an obvious error has been refused). |
| 3–161 | *Indications relating to biological material* |
| r.48.2(a)(viii) | The relevant data from any indications in relation to deposited biological material furnished under r.13*bis* will be published separately from the description, together with an indication of the date on which the International Bureau received such indications. |
| 3–162 | *Information concerning a priority claim* |
| r.48.2(a)(ix) | Any information concerning a priority claim considered not to have been made under r.26*bis*.2(b) (invitation to correct defects not satisfied) will be published if such publication has been requested under r.26*bis*.2(c) (by the applicant). |
| 3–163 | *Declaration relating to non-prejudicial disclosures* |
| r.48.2(a)(x) | Any declaration referred to in r.4.17(v) (as to non-prejudicial disclosures or exceptions to lack of novelty) and any correction of such a declaration under r.26*ter*.1 received in time will be published. |
| 3–164 | **Matter excluded from the publication** |
| Art.21(6) | If, in the opinion of the International Bureau, the international application contains expressions or drawings which are contrary to morality or public order, or disparaging |

statements, it may omit them on publication, indicating the place and the number of words or drawings omitted. Individual copies of the omitted passages will be provided on request. See above under "Regulations governing the content of the application" for the definition of disparaging statements (r.9.1(iii)) and the duties of other offices to inform the International Bureau when they are discovered.

### Notice of publication in the Gazette 3–165

Certain information, specified in the Administrative Instructions, taken from the front of the pamphlet, is published in the Gazette (see Annex D of the Administrative Instructions). r.86.1(a)(i)

### Publication of a notice that the application is considered withdrawn where withdrawal is received too late to stop publication 3–166

If a notification under r.29.1(a)(ii), that the Receiving Office considers the international application to be withdrawn, reaches the International Bureau too late to prevent international publication of the application, the International Bureau will promptly publish a notice in the Gazette reproducing the essence of such a notification. r.48.6(a)

If the application, the designation of a state or a priority claim is withdrawn by the applicant under r.90*bis* after the technical preparations for publication have been completed, notice of the withdrawal will be published in the Gazette. r.48.6(c)

## 8. COMMUNICATIONS TO NATIONAL/REGIONAL OFFICES AND ENTRY INTO THE NATIONAL PHASE

### Communication of the application under Art.20 to designated states by the International Bureau

#### *In what circumstances does the communication occur?* 3–167

The communication occurs to all designated offices unless a particular designated office waives the requirement in full or in part. Art.20(1)(a)

Designated and elected offices now have to specifically request that the communication take place. r.93*bis*.1

#### *Normal timing of the communication and procedure where early national processing has been requested* 3–168

The Art.20 communication is effected by the International Bureau in accordance with r.93*bis*.1. It may not, subject to r.47.4, be effected before international publication. Any Art.19 amendments submitted too late for the communication must be separately communicated. r.47.1(a)(b)

Designated and elected offices that specifically request that the communication takes place specify the timing of the communication. r.93*bis*.1

The Art.20 communication can be made earlier than publication where the applicant has requested that a designated office proceed to examination earlier than the end of the international phase (Art.23(2)) and the applicant or the designated office so requests. r.47.4

The Art.20 communication may also be made earlier where the applicant has requested that an elected office (under Chapter II) proceed to examination earlier than the end of the international phase (Art.40(2)) and the applicant or the elected office so requests. r.61.2(d)

588  *Complete Guide to Passing the EQE*

r.76.1  Rule 47.1 applies whether national phase entry is under Chapter I or Chapter II.

**3–169**  *Content of the communication*

Art.20  The communication includes:

(a) the international application;

(b) the search report (including any indication that some or all of the claims have not been searched under Art.17);

(c) any prescribed translations of the search report or the Art.17 indication (see r.45.1 for possible translation into English);

(d) any Art.19 amendments, either by including the claims as filed and as amended or the claims as filed and an indication of the amendments; and

(e) any statement under Art.19(1) accompanying Art.19 amendments.

**3–170**  *Responsibility for making copies*

r.47.2  The International Bureau is responsible for preparing the necessary copies for the communication. Further details are provided in the Administrative Instructions.

**3–171**  *Language of the communication*

r.47.3  The international application is communicated in the language in which it is published but, where the language of publication is different from the language of filing, the International Bureau will furnish, on request by a designated state, a copy of the application in the language of filing.

**3–172**  *Notification of the Art.20 communication to the applicant*

r.47.1(c)  The International Bureau sends a notice to the applicant, promptly after the expiration of 28 months from the priority date, indicating which designated offices have asked to receive the Art.20 communication (pursuant to r.93*bis*.1), the date of the communication to those offices and those offices which have not asked to receive the Art.20 communication.

However, such a notice must be sent promptly after the expiration of 19 months from the priority date in respect of any designated office which has an outstanding reservation relating to the Art.22(1) time limit (currently Luxembourg, Sweden, Switzerland, Uganda and United Republic of Tanzania).

**3–173**  *Designated offices must accept the r.47.1(c) notification as evidence that the Art.20 communication has occurred or is not necessary*

r.47.1(c-*bis*)  The notice sent to the applicant under r.47.1 must be accepted by the designated offices as conclusive evidence that the Art.20 communication has duly taken place on the date specified in the notice (in the case of designated offices that have requested the Art.20 communication) or that the Art.20 communication is not required (in the case of designated states that have not requested the Art.20 communication).

**Other information that is communicated to designated states by the International Bureau on request**

**3–174**  *Fact and date of receipt of the record copy and priority document*

r.47.1(a-*bis*)  If requested to do so by a designated state under r.93*bis*.1, the International Bureau will notify a designated office of the fact and date of receipt of (i) the record copy and (ii) any priority document.

## Transmission of the application to a designated office other than the Art.20 communication

3–175

If asked by a designated office, the International Bureau will transmit to it a copy of: (a) all; (b) some kinds of; or (c) individual international applications before the Art.20 communication and as soon as possible after one year from the priority date. Requests for all or some kinds of applications must be renewed annually before November 30 of the previous year.

Art.13(1)/r.31.1

The applicant may himself, or by asking the International Bureau so to do, transmit a copy of his international application to any designated office at any time but the International Bureau will not do this in respect of any national office that has notified it that it does not wish to receive copies in this way. For its services in this regard, the International Bureau may charge the applicant a fee.

Art.13(2)/r.31.1

The preparation of copies required for any transmission under Art.13 and r.31.1 is the responsibility of the International Bureau.

r.31.2

## National and Regional phase entry under Art.22

### Overview

3–176

In order to continue the prosecution of an international application in designated states, the applicant must enter the national/regional phase by carrying out certain acts within a deadline. Such acts may include the provision of a copy of the application, the provision of a translation of the application, the payment of a fee and the provision of indications relating to the inventor.

Art.22

### Timing of national phase entry under Art.22

3–177

The relevant acts must be carried out no later than 30 months from the priority date or, where national law so allows, a later date, regardless of whether the international searching authority has declared that no international search report will be established under Art.17(2)(a) or not.

Art.22(1)(3)

The time limit used to be 20 months but changed to 30 months as of April 1, 2002. However, if on October 3, 2001 this change was incompatible with the law of any designated office, it will not apply to that office for as long as such incompatibility exists provided that the office notified the International Bureau of the incompatibility by January 31, 2002. Such a notification is published in the Gazette. Where a notification is subsequently withdrawn by a designated office by notification sent to the International Bureau, such notification is also be published and the change enters into force two months after the date of such publication or on an earlier or later date indicated in the notice.

As of July 2006, the new time limit did not apply to Luxembourg, Sweden, Switzerland, Uganda and United Republic of Tanzania. This reservation applies only for national applications and not to regional phase applications. The operative time limit for regional phase entry for all these states is 31 months. So, a European application designating Switzerland, Finland, Sweden and Luxembourg, can still validly enter the regional phase at 31 months.

Where the Art.22 time limit is missed, designated offices must, upon request of the applicant, reinstate the rights of the applicant if it finds that any delay in meeting that time limit was unintentional or, at the option of the designated office, that the failure to meet the time limit occurred in spite of due care required by the circumstances having been taken. See below under time limits and procedural safeguards—some states have filed reservations.

r.49.6(a)

| | |
|---|---|
| r.26*bis*.1(c) | Where a priority date is changed, any outstanding time limit that has not yet expired is recomputed from the new date. |

## 3–178     *Specification of a later time limit than 30 months by a designated office*

| | |
|---|---|
| Art.22(3)/r.50.1 | Any national law may specify an Art.22 time limit later than 30 months. If so, the state must notify the International Bureau of the later time limit and the fact will be promptly published by the International Bureau in the Gazette. Where a previously fixed time limit is shortened it will become effective in relation to applications filed after three months from the date of publication of the notification. Where a previously fixed time limit is lengthened it will become effective in relation to applications pending at the time of or filed after the date of publication of the notification or at a later date if the Contracting State so stipulates. |
| | Most countries, including Germany, Japan, the USA and Canada have specified 30 months from the priority date as the relevant time limit under Art.22. Others, however, such as the UK, the EPO and Australia have specified a later time limit of 31 months. |

## 3–179     *Supply of a copy of the international application*

| | |
|---|---|
| Art.22(1) | The applicant must supply to each designated office a copy of the international application within the Art.22(1) time limit, unless the Art.20 communication has already taken place or the designated office has informed the International Bureau under r.49.1(a-*bis*) that such supply is in any case not necessary (in which case the International Bureau will publish such information promptly in the Gazette). |
| r.47.1(e) | Where any designated office has not, before the expiration of 28 months from the priority date, requested the International Bureau to effect the Art.20 communication, the Contracting State for which that office acts as designated office is considered to have notified the International Bureau under r.49.1(a-*bis*), that it does not require furnishing, under Art.22, by the applicant of a copy of the international application. |
| | However, the relevant time is 19 months from the priority date in respect of any designated office which has an outstanding reservation relating to the Art.22(1) time limit (Luxembourg, Sweden, Switzerland, Uganda, United Republic of Tanzania and Zambia as of July 2005). |
| r.49.3 | For these purposes, any Art.19(1) statement (re. amendments) and any r.13*bis*.4 indication (*re* biological material) are considered part of the international application. |
| r.47.1(c-*bis*) | The notice sent to the applicant under r.47.1 must be accepted by the designated offices as conclusive evidence that the Art.20 communication has duly taken place (see above). |
| AnReg | See under *Art.158(2)*. The EPO has indicated pursuant to r.49.1(a-*bis*) that it does not require a copy of the application. |

## 3–180     *Supply of a translation of the international application*

| | |
|---|---|
| Art.22(1) | The applicant must supply to each designated office, where necessary, a translation of the international application within the Art.22(1) time limit. |
| r.49.1(a) | The languages from which and into which the translation must occur must be notified by each designated office to the International Bureau and are promptly published in the Gazette. |
| r.49.2 | The language into which translation is required must be an official language of the designated office. Where several official languages exist: (i) the designated office may not |

require translation where the application is already in one of them and (ii) the applicant may choose any of them for the translation unless one particular official language is prescribed for use by foreigners by that office.

For these purposes, any Art.19(1) statement (*re* amendments) and any r.13*bis*.4 indication (*re* biological material) are considered part of the international application.

r.49.3

A translation under Art.22 must contain:

r.49.5(a)

(a) the description (except text matter contained in a sequence listing part of the description, if such a sequence listing part of the description complies with r.12.1(d) (as prescribed by the Administrative Instructions) and the description complies with r.5.2(b) (free text in language of the description));

(b) the claims;

(c) any text matter of the drawings, furnished either in the form of a drawing executed anew or a copy of the drawing with the translation pasted on the original text matter (the expression "Fig." does not require translation); and

(d) the abstract.

In addition, if required by any designated office (such requirements will be published by the International Bureau in the Gazette) the translation must:

(e) contain the request. In this case, the designated office must furnish to the applicant, free of charge, copies of the request form in the language of translation, the use of which is optional. The translated form may not ask for any additional information and must have the same form and contents (see r.3 and r.4);

(f) contain both claims as filed and as amended if amendment under Art.19 has taken place;

(g) be accompanied by a copy of the drawings.

No designated office may require that the translation of the international application comply with any physical requirements other than those prescribed for the application as filed.

r.49.5(a)

Where a title has been established by the International Searching Authority under r.37.2 (no title in application or title not complying with r.4.3), the translation must contain the title as established by that Authority (see r.49.5(l) for circumstances where this does not apply due to conflict with national law notified to the International Bureau by December 31, 1991—only the US).

r.49.5(j)

r.49.5(k)

National law may require that the translation submitted by the applicant is verified or certified—see below under national phase aspects.

r.51*bis*.1(d)

## *Payment of the national fee*

3–181

The applicant must pay any necessary national fee within the Art.22(1) time limit, the amount of which, if required, will be notified by each designated office to the International Bureau under r.49.1 and promptly published in the Gazette.

Art.22(1)

## *Supply of indications concerning the inventor*

3–182

The applicant must supply to each designated office any indications concerning the inventor, within the Art.22(1) time limit, where national law allows such indications to be provided later than the filing date and they were not included in the request.

Art.22(1)

### 3–183    *Consequences of certain defects in the translation*

r.49.5(h)    Where the translation of the abstract or any indication under r.13*bis*.4 (to deposited biological material) is not furnished and the designated office deems it to be necessary, it will invite the applicant to correct this defect within a reasonable time limit fixed in the invitation.

r.49.5(c)    If there is no translation of a statement regarding amendments made under Art.19(1), any designated office may disregard such a statement.

r.49.5(c-*bis*)    Where the claims have been amended under Art.19, and a designated office requires translations of the claims both as filed and amended and a translation of only one of these is provided, such a designated office may disregard the untranslated claims or invite the applicant to provide a translation thereof within a reasonable time limit that it sets in the invitation. Where the terms of such an invitation are not met the designated office may either disregard the untranslated claims or consider the application withdrawn. See r.49.5(l) for circumstances where this provision does not apply due to conflict with national law notified to the International Bureau by December 31, 1991 — Brazil and the US.

r.49.5(e)    When a copy of the drawings is required and is not furnished within the Art.22 time limit, the designated office will invite the applicant to correct this defect within a reasonable time limit fixed in the invitation.

r.49.5(g)    When a copy of the drawings or drawings executed anew does not conform to r.11, the designated office may invite the applicant to correct this defect within a reasonable time limit fixed in the invitation.

### 3–184    *Use of a national form*

r.49.4    The use of a national form may not be made mandatory for the Art.22 procedure.

### 3–185    *Where requirements regarding the translation or fee change*

r.49.1(c)    Any changes in these details must be notified by the relevant Contracting State to the International Bureau who will promptly publish the new details in the Gazette. If the change involves translation into a language not previously required the change will only apply to international applications filed later than two months from the date of publication in the Gazette. In other cases, the Contracting State determines the effective date.

### 3–186    *Maintenance of the Art.11(3) effect by a designated office in spite of the applicant not supplying a copy of the international application in time*

r.49.1(a-*ter*)    Any designated Contracting State which maintains pursuant to Art.24(2) that the application will have the effect of a regular national filing as of the international filing date (Art.11(3)), even if a copy of the international application is not furnished by the Art.22 time limit, must notify the International Bureau accordingly and the fact will be promptly published in the Gazette.

### 3–187    *Procedure where applicant has performed the Art.22 acts and the designated office has not been informed that the International Bureau has received the record copy*

r.22.1(g)    If, by the expiration of the time limit under Art.22 (usually 30 months) the applicant has discharged his duties under that Article but the designated office has not been informed by the International Bureau that it has received the record copy, the designated office will inform the International Bureau who will promptly inform the applicant and the Receiving Office unless it is in possession of the record copy or it has already notified them at the 14-month stage (see under procedure of the Receiving Office).

## *Indications as to protection sought for the purposes of national processing*     3–188

If the applicant wishes the international application to be treated, in a designated state in respect of which Art.43 applies (kinds of protection other than patent protection available), as an application not for the grant of a patent but for the grant of another kind of protection referred to in Art.43, the applicant, when performing the acts referred to in Art.22, must so indicate to the designated office and, in the case of a patent, certificate, inventor's certificate or utility certificate of addition, indicate the parent patent or other parent grant.    r.49*bis*.1(a)(c)

Where the amount of the national fee paid under Art.22 corresponds to a particular kind of protection, payment of that amount is considered to be an indication that the applicant wishes the application to be considered as an application for that kind of protection, even when no express indication to that effect is made. The designated office will inform the applicant accordingly.    r.49*bis*.1(e)

The applicant must also indicate at the same time if he wishes to obtain protection of more than one kind, as allowed by Art.44, and, if necessary, which kind of protection is sought primarily and which is sought secondarily.    r.49*bis*.1(b)

If the applicant wishes the international application to be treated, in a designated state, as an application for a continuation or a continuation-in-part of an earlier application, the applicant, when performing the acts referred to in Art.22, must so indicate to the designated office, identifying the relevant parent application.    r.49*bis*.1(d)

No designated office may require that the applicant furnish an indication referred to in r.49*bis*.1, or an indication as to whether the applicant seeks the grant of a national or regional patent, before performing the acts referred to in Art.22.    r.49*bis*.2(a)

Furthermore, the applicant may, if so permitted by national law, furnish such an indication or convert one kind of protection to another, at any later time.    r.49*bis*.2(b)

Rule 49*bis* applies whether national phase entry is under Chapter I or Chapter II.    r.76.1

## *Consequences of not performing the Art.22 acts*     3–189

The effect of an international application provided for in Art.11(3) will cease in any designated state, with the same consequences as withdrawal of any national application in that state, if the applicant fails to perform the acts referred to in Art.22 within the applicable time limit.    Art.24(1)(iii)

For the chance to reinstate rights in this situation, see under time limits and procedural safeguards below.    r.49.6

### National and regional phase entry under Art.39

### *Effect of election prior to 19 months on the application of Art.22*     3–190

If the election of a Contracting State has been effected prior to the expiration of the 19th month from the priority date Art.22 ceases to apply in respect of that state and Art.39 applies instead.    Art.39(1)(a)

Any state, though not having renounced Chapter II under Art.64(1) may declare that it is not bound by Art.39(1) (currently no reservations filed).    Art.64(2)(a)(i)

A demand filed after the expiry of 19 months from the priority date (and before the r.54*bis*(a) time limit for submitting a demand: the later of three months from the transmittal to the applicant of the ISR and the written opinion of r.43*bis*.2 or the declaration under Art.17(2)(a) or 22 months from priority) is valid but does not have the effect of delaying entry into the regional/national phase in states where the Art.22 and Art.39 time limits are different.

594     *Complete Guide to Passing the EQE*

**3–191**     *Necessary acts to enter the national phase under Art.39 and the relevant time limit*

Art.39     Under Art.39, the applicant must supply to each elected office a copy of application (unless the Art.20 communication has already occurred), any prescribed translation thereof and any necessary fee before the end of 30 months from the priority date.

Art.39(1)(b)     Any Contracting State may specify a later time limit if it wishes.

r.77     If it chooses to specify a later time limit, a Contracting State must inform the International Bureau who will promptly publish such information in the Gazette. If the time limit is lengthened, such a change applies from the date of publication to demands pending at the time or submitted later, or, if the relevant state fixes some later date, as from that later date. If such a time limit is shortened, the shortened time limit only applies to demands submitted after the period of three months from the date of such publication.

Most states now have the same time limit under Art.39 as under Art.22. For instance, Germany, Japan, the USA and Canada have specified 30 months from the priority date and the UK, the EPO and Australia have specified 31 months.

**3–192**     *Consequences of missing the Art.39 time limit*

Art.39(2)(3)     The effect under Art.11(3) (international application to have same effect as a regular national application in each designated state as of the filing date) ceases in an elected state with the same consequences as the withdrawal of a national application if the applicant fails to enter the national phase before expiry of the Art.39 time limit, unless the national office wishes to maintain this effect.

**3–193**     *Application of certain rules to national phase entry under Art.39*

r.76.5     Rule 22.1(g) (procedure where designated office has not been informed by the International Bureau of receipt of the record copy by the time the applicant enters the national phase), r.49 (details of entering the national phase—see above under Art.22 procedure), r.51*bis* (national requirements that are allowed), r.13*ter*.3 (limitation on request of sequence listing by designated office), r.47.1 (communication to designated office by the IB) and r.49*bis* (indications as to protection sought for national processing) apply to national phase entry under Art.39, except that:

(a) "designated" should be replaced with "elected", Art.22 or Art.24(2) should be replaced with Art.39(1) or Art.39(3) respectively, "international applications filed" in r.49.1(c) should be replaced with "a demand submitted" and the reference to r.47.4 in r.47.1(a) should be construed as a reference to r.61.2(d);

(b) a translation of any Art.19 amendment is only necessary where it is annexed to the international preliminary examination report.

**3–194**     *Time limit for supplying a translation of the priority document to an elected state*

r.76.4     The applicant is not required to furnish a translation of the priority document to any elected office before the expiration of the Art.39 time limit.

**Procedure before the EPO as a designated or elected office**

**3–195**     **General comments**

r.107(1)     In order to enter the EPO regional phase, whether under Chapter I or Chapter II, the applicant must file a translation (if the application was published in a language other than English, French and German), specify which documents examination is to be based on and pay various fees within 31 months from the priority date.

See [2003] O.J. 509. When the current uniform time limit came into force on January 2, 2002, applying to all applications for which, on that date, the time limit for national phase entry had not yet expired, the EPO regarded any applicant who satisfied all the requirements to enter the regional phase before 21 months to have made an express request for regional processing to start under Art.23(2) PCT. This presumption was withdrawn from October 31, 2003 and from this date regional processing does not start until 31 months from the priority date unless the applicant has made an express request under Art.23(2) or Art.40(2) PCT. *O.J.*

## *Supply of a translation* 3–196

The applicant must supply to the EPO a translation of the international application, where it is not already in an official language as specified by Art.158(2) EPC, within 31 months from the priority date. *r.107(1)(a)*

The international application must be supplied to the EPO in one of its official languages (Guidelines, E-IX 4.3), *i.e.* in English, French or German (Art.14(1) EPC). *Art.158(2)*

Where the translation is not filed in due time, the application is deemed withdrawn (see below for chance to make good the loss of rights). *r.108(1)*

## *Payment of the national basic fee* 3–197

The national fee allowed by Art.22(1) or Art.39(1) must be paid by the applicant to the EPO. *Art.158(2)*

This national fee includes a national basic fee equal to the filing fee provided for in Art.78(2) EPC. *r.106(a)*

The national basic fee, provided by r.106(a) EPC must be paid within 31 months from the priority date. *r.107(1)(c)*

Where the national basic fee is not paid in due time, the application is deemed withdrawn (see below for chance to make good the loss of rights). *r.108(1)*

No *restitutio* is available where the time limit is missed. See also G5/93. *G3/91*

Deemed withdrawal takes place at the end of the normal period, not the grace period (see below for grace period). *G4/98*

The national basic fee is 95 or 170 euros depending on whether the filing is made online or on paper, respectively. *RRF2(1)*

## *Payment of designation fees* 3–198

The national fee allowed by Art.22(1) or Art.39(1) must be paid by the applicant to the EPO *Art.158(2)*

This national fee includes the designation fees provided for in Art.79(2) EPC. *r.106(b)*

The designation fees are due within 31 months of the priority date where the Art.79(2) EPC time limit has already expired. *r.107(1)(d)*

Designation fees must be paid within six months of the date on which the European patent bulletin mentions the publication of the European search report. *Art.79(2)*

The publication of the International Search Report under Art.21 PCT takes the place of the mention of publication in the bulletin. *Art.157(1)*

Where no designation fees are paid in due time, the application is deemed withdrawn (see below for chance to make good the loss of rights). *r.108(1)*

*[Next paragraph number is 3-200]*

| | |
|---|---|
| r.108(2) | Where any particular designation fee is not paid in due time, designation of the relevant state is deemed withdrawn (see below for chance to make good the loss of rights). |
| G3/91 | No *restitutio* is available where the time limit is missed. |
| G4/98 | Deemed withdrawal takes place at the end of the normal period, not the grace period (see below for grace period). |

## 3–200    *Payment of a search fee*

| | |
|---|---|
| r.107(1)(e) | A search fee must be paid within 31 months of the priority date where a supplementary search report is necessary according to Art.157(2)(b) EPC (Guidelines E/IX/4.4 and B/III/4.3). |
| Art.157(2)(b) | The search fee, where necessary, is due within the Art.21/Art.39 PCT time limit and if it is not paid in time, the application is deemed to be withdrawn. |
| AnReg | See under *Art.157(3)*. Before July 1, 2005 no supplementary search was necessary if the international search was carried out by the EPO or the Austrian, Spanish or Swedish patent office ([1979] O.J. 4; [1979] O.J. 248; [1995] O.J. 511). However, this only now applies to applications searched in the international phase by the EPO. |
| J8/83 | Where a supplementary search is necessary, and the examination fee has already been paid, an Art.96(1) communication is sent to the applicant asking whether he wishes to proceed with examination (see CLBA 418 and Guidelines A/VII/5.3). |
| r.108(1) | Where the search fee is not paid in due time, the application is deemed withdrawn (as set out in Art.157(2)—see below for chance to make good the loss of rights). |
| G3/91 | No *restitutio* is available where the time limit is missed. See also G5/93. |
| G4/98 | Deemed withdrawal takes place at the end of the normal period, not the grace period (see below for grace period). |
| RRF2(2) | The search fee is 1000 euros, for applications filed on or after 1.7.2005 and 720 euros otherwise. |
| Art.157(3)(4) | The Administrative Council decides under what conditions the search fee is to be reduced. Such a decision may be rescinded at any time. |
| AnReg | See under *Art.157(3)*. The search fee is reduced by 190 euros if an International Searching Authority selected from Australia, China, Japan, Korea, Russia and the US carried out the international search ([2005] O.J. 548). And the application was filed on or after 1.7.2005. Before this date the reduction was 20% of the fee. |
| | By a Decision of the Administrative Council of June 10, 2005 the fee for a supplementary European search has been reduced by 845 euros for international applications for which the international search report was drawn by the patent authority of Austria, Finland, Spain or Sweden. The decision entered into force on July 1, 2005 and has effect until June 30, 2008 ([2005] O.J. 422). A potential EQE question arises from the fact that this fee reduction applies to international applications filed on or after July 1, 2005, unless the international search was drawn up by the National Board of Patents and Registration of Finland—in which case it applies to applications filed on or after April 1, 2005. |
| RRF10(1) | The search fee paid for a European or supplementary European search will be fully refunded if the European patent application is withdrawn or refused or deemed to be withdrawn at a time when the office has not yet begun to draw up the search report (amended as at July 1, 2005). |
| RRF10(2) | Where the European search report is based on an earlier search report prepared by the EPO or an application whose priority is claimed or an earlier application within the meaning of Art.76 or an original application within the meaning of r.15 the EPO will |

refund the applicant, in accordance with a decision of the president, an amount which depends on the type of the earlier search and the extent to which the EPO benefits from the earlier search report when carrying out the subsequent search (amended as at February 17, 2006 ([2006] O.J. 189).

## Payment of renewal fees 3–201

A renewal fee is due within 31 months from the priority date where such a fee in respect of the third year, provided for by Art.86(1) EPC, has fallen due earlier under r.37.1 (Guidelines, A/II/2.4). The grace period for payment under A86(2) EPC is a composite time limit running from the 31 month regional phase entry date (J1/89, LA5/93).     *r.107(1)(g)*

## Payment of the examination fee 3–202

An examination fee is due within 31 months of the priority date where the request for examination is due within the same time limit.     *r.107(1)(f)*

The request for examination (which is not deemed filed until the examination fee has been paid) is due within six months of the date on which the European patent bulletin mentions the publication of the European search report.     *Art.94(2)*

The publication of the International Search Report under Art.21 PCT takes the place of the mention of publication in the bulletin.     *Art.157(1)*

The examination fee is 1,335 euros where a supplementary search is to be performed and 1,490 euros where no such search is necessary.     *RRF2(6)*

The examination fee may be reduced where the EPO was the International Preliminary Examining Authority and it can use the International Preliminary Examination Report as the basis of examination.     *r.107(2)*

The reduction is 50 per cent (but there is no reduction where the preliminary examination fee has been refunded under RRF10d).     *Art.12(2)RRF*

## Payment of claims fees 3–203

Within the r.107(1) time limit, *i.e.* 31 months from the priority date, claims fees must be paid on the eleventh and each subsequent claim in a set of more than 10 claims.     *r.110(1)*

Any claims fees not paid may still be paid within a non-extensible grace period of one month from notification by the EPO. Where amendments are filed in this period the amount of claims fees due is re-calculated. Any excess fees are refunded.     *r.110(2)(3)*

Where claims fees are not paid in due time any claim concerned is deemed abandoned.     *r.110(4)*

## Specification of documents on which examination will be based 3–204

Within 31 months of the priority date the applicant must specify which documents the European grant procedure is to be based on.     *r.107(1)(b)*

## Request for examination 3–205

The time limit for requesting examination under Art.94(2) EPC cannot expire before the time limit prescribed by Art.22 or Art.39 PCT, as the case may be.     *Art.150(2)*

Within 31 months of the priority date the applicant must file a request for examination if the Art.94(2) EPC time limit has expired.     *r.107(1)(f)*

Such a request must be filed before the end of six months from the mention of the publication of the European search report in the Bulletin. It is not deemed filed until the examination fee is paid (see above).     *Art.94(2)*

| | |
|---|---|
| Art.157(1) | The publication of the International Search Report under Art.21 PCT takes the place of the mention of publication in the bulletin. |
| r.108(1) | Where the request for examination is not filed in due time, the application is deemed withdrawn (see below for chance to make good the loss of rights). |

## 3–206 *Certificate of exhibition*

| | |
|---|---|
| r.107(1)(h) | Where applicable, a certificate of exhibition must be filed under Art.55(2) and r.23 EPC, within 31 months from the priority date. |

## 3–207 *Chance to make good a loss of rights*

| | |
|---|---|
| r.108(3) | Where an application or the designation of a state is deemed withdrawn under r.108(1) EPC or r.108(2) EPC the EPO will communicate such a loss of rights to the applicant. |
| r.108(3) | The loss of rights will be deemed not to have occurred if the applicant completes the omitted act and pays a surcharge within two months of the notification of loss of rights by the EPO. |
| r.108(4) | If the applicant has dispensed with notification under r.108(3) in respect of one or more designation fees, they may still be validly paid within two months of the expiry of the applicable time limit along with a surcharge (added as at April 1, 2005). |
| RRF2(3c) | The surcharge is 50 per cent of the unpaid fee/fees up to a maximum of 1,820 euros, but at least 520 euros for the late filing of the translation. |
| r.108(3) | The applicant may also apply for a decision if he disagrees with the finding of the EPO as set out in r.69(2) EPC. |

## 3–208 *Submission of information concerning the inventor*

| | |
|---|---|
| r.111(1) | Where the data concerning the inventor prescribed by r.17(1) EPC (designation of the inventor, explanation of right to be granted a patent where applicant and inventor are not the same) have not been submitted by 31 months from the priority date, the EPO will invite the applicant to furnish the data within a period it sets itself (Guidelines, A/VII/3.4). |

## 3–209 *Furnishing of the file number and a copy of the priority document*

| | |
|---|---|
| r.111(2) | Where priority is claimed and the file number of the earlier application or the copy of the earlier application (as provided by Art.88(1) EPC and r.38(1)–(3) EPC) has not been supplied to the EPO before the expiry of 31 months from the priority date, the EPO will invite the applicant to furnish the number and/or copy within a period it sets itself. Rule 38(4) EPC applies, so that the copy is deemed filed where such a copy is available to the EPO and other conditions set by the President are met (see AnReg under *r.38(3)(4)*—[1999] O.J. 80 —EP applications, international applications where EPO is Receiving Office and certain Japanese applications are included). The EPO informs the applicant when it has copied documents from one file to another (see AnReg under *r.38(3)(4)*—[2000] O.J. 227). |
| Art.91(5) | If the certified copy is not supplied the right to claim priority is lost. |
| CLBA | See CLBA, p. 416 and J11/95. |

## 3–210 *Representation*

| | |
|---|---|
| Art.133(2) | Any applicant can carry out the acts necessary to enter the regional phase but from that point onwards, non-EPC resident applicants must appoint a representative who is entitled to practice before the EPO. Fees may be paid by anybody. See AnReg, legal advice 18/92; [1992] O.J. 58. If entering the regional phase after 31 months from the priority date a professional representative is necessary from the start. |

## 3–211 Summary of acts on entry into EPO regional phase

| Act | Reference | Time limit | Consequences of non-compliance | Extension/grace period? | r.69(2) Decision/appeal possible? | Further processing? | *Restitutio* possible? |
|---|---|---|---|---|---|---|---|
| Supply a translation in an EPO official language | *Art.158(2)* EPC *Art.14(1)* EPC *Art.22/Art.39* PCT | Within 31 months of the priority date (*r.107(1)(a)*) | The application is deemed to be withdrawn (*r.108(1)*) | A two-month grace period is available (*r.108(3)*) | Yes (*r.108(3)*) | No (time limit in the Regulations) | Yes (analogous to *Art.90(2)*) |
| Pay the national basic fee | *Art.158(2)* EPC *r.106(a)* EPC *Art.22/Art.39* PCT | Within 31 months of the priority date (*r.107(1)(c)*) | The application is deemed to be withdrawn (*r.108(1)*) | A two-month grace period is available (*r.108(3)*) | Yes (*r.108(3)*) | No (time limit in the Regulations) | No *Art.122(5)* G3/91 |
| Pay the designation fees if the *Art.79(2)* time limit has expired (six months from the publication of the international search report—*Art.157(1)*) | *Art.158(2)* EPC *r.106(b)* EPC | Within 31 months of the priority date (*r.107(1)(d)*) | The application is deemed to be withdrawn (*r.108(1)*) or designations for which no fee is paid are deemed to be withdrawn (*r.108(2)*) | A two-month grace period is available (*r.108(3)*) | Yes (*r.108(3)*) | No (time limit in the Regulations) | No *Art.122(5)* G3/91 |
| Pay a supplementary search fee where required | *Art.157(2)(b)* EPC | Within 31 months of the priority date (*r.107(1)(e)*) | The application is deemed to be withdrawn (*r.108(1)* and *Art.157(2)*) | A two month grace period is available (*r.108(3)*) | Yes (*r.108(3)*) | No (time limit in the Regulations) | No *Art.122(5)* G3/91 |
| Pay any renewal fee that is due in respect of the third year from the filing date | *Art.86(1)* EPC *r.37(1)* EPC | Due on the 31 month regional phase entry date (not the end of the month) (*r.107(1)(g)*) | The application is deemed to be withdrawn (*Art.86(3)*) | Can pay within six months of the due date with an additional fee (*Art.86(2)*) | Yes | No (time limit in the Regulations) | Yes |
| Request examination if the *Art.94(2)* EPC time limit has expired (six months from the publication of the international search report—*Art.157(1)*) | *Art.94(2)* | Within 31 months of the priority date (*r.107(1)(f)*) if later than the normal period | The application is deemed to be withdrawn (*r.108(1)*) | A two-month grace period is available (*r.108(3)*) | Yes (*r.108(3)*) | No (time limit in the Regulations) | No *Art.122(5)* G5/92 G6/92 |

| Act | Reference | Time limit | Consequences of non-compliance | Extension/grace period? | r.69(2) Decision/ appeal possible? | Further processing? | *Restitutio* possible? |
|---|---|---|---|---|---|---|---|
| Pay the examination fee if the *Art.94(2)* EPC time limit has expired (six months from the publication of the international search report— *Art.157(1)*) | *Art.94(2)* | Within 31 months of the priority date (*r.107(1)(f)*) if later than the normal period | Request for examination deemed not filed (*Art.94(2)*) | See above | See above | See above | See above |
| Pay any claims fee due on the 11th and any subsequent claim | *r.110(1)* | Within 31 months of the priority date (*r.110(1), r.107(1)*) | Any claim for which a fee is not paid is deemed to be abandoned (*r.110(4)*) | A one month grace period is available (*r.110(2)*) | No | No | Yes |
| Specify the documents on which the grant procedure to be based | *r.107(1)(b)* | Within 31 months of the priority date (*r.107(1)(b)*) | Examination will be based on the application as published or as amended during international preliminary examination | | | | |
| File a certificate of exhibition if necessary | *r.107(1)(h)* *Art.55(2)* *r.23* | Within 31 months of the priority date (*r.107(1)(h)*) | Novelty exemption of *Art.55(1)* will not apply (*Art.55(2)*) | None | No | No | Yes |
| Submission of information regarding the inventor | *r.111(1)* *r.17(1)* *Art.81* *Art.91(1)(f)* | If not submitted within *r.107(1)* (31-month) period then within a period set by the EPO | The application is deemed to be withdrawn (*Art.91(5)*) | Extension possible on request | Yes | Yes, for period set by EPO | Yes |
| Submission of information regarding the priority claim | *r.111(2)* *Art.88(1)* *r.38(1)–(3)* | If not submitted within *r.107(1)* (31-month) period then within a period set by the EPO | The priority claim is lost—*Art.91(3)*. | Extension possible on request | No | No (application not deemed withdrawn etc.) | Yes |

## 9. INTERNATIONAL PRELIMINARY EXAMINATION

### Which designated states does Chapter II apply to? 3–212

Any state may declare that it is not bound by the provisions of Chapter II and this has the effect that such a state is not bound by the provisions of Chapter II and the corresponding provisions of the Regulations.  Art.64(1)

At present, all Contracting States are bound by Chapter II.

### Who may apply for international preliminary examination and which states may be elected 3–213

The following people may demand international preliminary examination:  Art.31(2)/r.54

(a) any applicant who is a resident or national (as defined below) of a Contracting State bound by Chapter II and whose international application has been filed with the Receiving Office of or acting for a state bound by Chapter II (or the International Bureau—see r.54.3); and

(b) if the Assembly so decides, persons who are not residents or nationals of a State party to the PCT or bound by Chapter (II) but who are entitled to file international applications (Art.9(2)).

Where there are joint applicants, it will suffice that one of them qualifies under (a) above.  r.54.2

Applicants falling under (a) may elect any Contracting State bound by Chapter II (currently all of them) which they have previously designated whereas applicants under (b) may only elect those states bound by Chapter II that have declared they are willing to be so elected.  Art.31(4)(a)(b)

Questions of residency and nationality are decided according to r.18.1(a) and (b) by the Receiving Office under the national law of the appropriate Contracting State but in any case: (a) possession of a real and effective industrial or commercial establishment in a Contracting State is considered residence there; and (b) a legal entity constituted according to the national law of a Contracting State is considered to be a national of that state.  r.54.1(a)

The International Preliminary Examining Authority will, in circumstances specified in the Administrative Instructions, ask the Receiving Office (or, where the International Bureau is the Receiving Office, the national office of, or acting for, the state concerned) to decide any question of residency or nationality and will inform the applicant that it is doing so. The applicant will have an opportunity to submit arguments to the office concerned directly and that office will decide the question promptly.  r.54.1(b)

Where the applicant does not have the right to make a demand (or in the case of joint applicants, none of them has) the demand is considered not to have been submitted.  r.54.4

### Who may conduct the international preliminary examination— the competent Authority

#### *Receiving Offices specify the competent International Preliminary Examining Authority or Authorities* 3–214

International preliminary examination is carried out by an International Preliminary Examining Authority.  Art.32

| | |
|---|---|
| r.59.1 | Each Receiving Office specifies which International Preliminary Examining Authority or Authorities are competent in respect of applications filed with that Receiving Office by residents and nationals of the Contracting State that the Receiving Office acts for. The International Bureau publishes this information. In the case where more than one Examining Authority is competent, the Receiving Office may leave the choice of which one to select with the applicant or may declare that one or more of them are competent for specific types of applications. In any event, where more than one Examining Authority is competent for a particular application, the applicant may choose which one to use. When an application is filed with the International Bureau as Receiving Office, the above does not apply. Instead, any International Examining Authority will be competent if it would have been competent had the application been filed with a Receiving Office itself competent under r.19.1(a)(i) and (ii), r.19.1(b), r.19.1(c) or r.19.2(i) (rules specifying which Receiving Office is competent for a particular resident or national). The applicant has the choice of which one to select where two or more are competent. |
| AppGuide | See Vol. I, Annex C. When the EPO acts as Receiving Office, the EPO is the only competent International Preliminary Examining Authority. |
| AnReg | Apart from the Contracting States to the EPC (see Protocol on Centralisation), some non-European states have also given the EPO competence as an International Preliminary Examining Authority. Applicants from Japan ([1985] O.J. 331 and [1990] O.J. 443), the US ([1987] O.J. 266 and [1990] O.J. 443) and Poland ([1991] O.J. 124), for instance, can choose between their national patent office and the EPO as International Preliminary Examining Authority. |
| r.59.2 | In the case of applicants who are making a demand under Art.31(2)(b) (residents or nationals of states not bound by the PCT or Chapter II), the Assembly chooses which Authority is competent. Preference is given to the national office of such an unbound state if it is an International Preliminary Examining Authority, or, if it is not, preference is given to the Authority which it recommends. |
| Art.32(3) | The provisions of Art.16(3) (appointment of International Searching Authorities by the Assembly) applies *mutatis mutandis* in respect of International Preliminary Examining Authorities. |
| r.63 | The minimum requirements that such an Authority must comply with are: |

    (i) it must have at least 100 full-time employees with sufficient technical qualifications to carry out examinations;

    (ii) it must have at its disposal the minimum documentation referred to in r.34 for International search, properly arranged for examination purposes; and

    (iii) it must have a staff capable of examining in the required technical fields and possessing the language facilities to understand at least those languages in which the minimum documentation of (ii) above is written or translated; and

    (iv) it must be an International Searching Authority.

## 3–215 *Limitations set by the EPO on its competence as International Preliminary Examining Authority*

| | |
|---|---|
| **Art.155(1)** | The EPO may act as International Preliminary Examining Authority for applicants who are residents or nationals of an EPC Contracting State bound by Chapter II of the PCT, subject to the conclusion of an agreement between the European Patent Organisation and the International Bureau. |
| **Art.155(2)** | The EPO may also act as International Preliminary Examining Authority for any other applicant in accordance with an agreement between the European Patent Organisation and the International Bureau, subject to the prior approval of the Administrative Council. |

See under *Art.150* for details of the agreement. The EPO has, in principle, agreed to act as International Preliminary Examining Authority for applications filed with any Receiving Office that specifies it for this purpose, subject to the imposition of restrictions if its workload becomes too great ([2001] O.J. 601). The agreement was modified in 2002 ([2002] O.J. 52), with effect from November 1, 2001 to restrict the EPO's competence in respect of an applicant who is a US national or resident and has filed an application relating to biotechnology, telecommunications or a business method. This competence has since been restored in respect of biotechnological and telecommunications inventions for applications filed after January 1, 2004 ([2003] O.J. 633), but remains excluded until at least 2007 for business methods ([2005] O.J. 149).
AnReg

As a further restriction, the EPO may only be selected as International Preliminary Examining Authority if the International Searching Authority was the EPO or the Austrian, Spanish or Swedish patent office (see E/IX/1). See also Applicant's Guide, Vol. I, Annex E.
Guidelines

### How to apply for international preliminary examination—the demand

#### *How to apply* — 3–216

The applicant must demand examination, separately from the international application. The demand must contain certain particulars and be in the prescribed form and in the prescribed language.
Art.31(3)

#### *Time limit for applying* — 3–217

A demand may be made at any time prior to the later of (i) three months from the date of transmittal to the applicant of the international search report and the written opinion established under r.43*bis*.1, or of the delaration referred to in Art.17(2)(a) (no search report to be established) and (ii) 22 months from the priority date.
r.54*bis*(a)

#### *Consequences of the demand being made late* — 3–218

Any demand made late is considered as if it had not been submitted and the International Preliminary Examining Authority so declares.
r.54*bis*(b)

#### *Where to apply* — 3–219

The demand must be submitted to the competent International Preliminary Examining Authority (see Art.32).
Art.31(6)(a)

#### *Consequences of the demand being sent to the wrong place* — 3–220

Where the demand is submitted to:
r.59.3(a)(b)

   (i) a Receiving Office;

   (ii) an International searching Authority;

   (iii) an International Preliminary Examining Authority which is not competent; or

   (iv) the International Bureau;

that office, Authority or Bureau will mark the date of receipt on it and, in the case of (i) to (iii), transmit it promptly to the International Bureau or directly to the competent International Examining Authority.

The International Bureau or the office or Authority who decides to submit the demand directly will promptly either:
r.59.3(c)(d)(f)

   (a) transmit the demand to the competent International Preliminary Examining Authority, where only one is competent, and inform the applicant; or

(b) invite the applicant to indicate, by the later of 15 days from the date of the invitation or the r.54*bis*.1(a) time limit (time limit for making a demand) the International Preliminary Examining Authority that he wishes the demand to be sent to, where more than one is competent. It will carry out the wishes of the applicant in this matter unless no reply is obtained in which case the demand will be considered not to have been submitted such will be declared.

r.59.3(e)(f) Where the competent International Examining Authority receives the demand under (a) or (b), it will be considered to have been received by that Authority on the date stamped on it by the relevant organisation (i)–(iv) above.

## 3–221 *Form of the demand—use of a form*

r.53.1 The demand must be made on a printed form or a computer print out, the details of which are specified in the Administrative Instructions. Copies of the form are available free of charge from the Receiving Office and the International Preliminary Examining Authority.

## 3–222 *Content of the demand*

r.53.2 The demand must contain:

r.53.3 (a) a petition to the effect of, and preferably worded as, "Demand under Article 31 of the PCT: The undersigned requests that the international application specified below be the subject of international preliminary examination according to the PCT."

r.53.6 (b) indications concerning the international application to which the demand relates including the name and address of the applicant, the title of the invention, the international filing date (if known by the applicant) and the international application number (or where such number is not know to the applicant, the name of the Receiving Office with which the application was filed);

r.53.4 (c) indications concerning the applicant(s) for the elected states (r.4.4 and r.4.16 apply and r.4.5 applies *mutatis mutandis*);

r.53.5 (d) indications concerning the agent or common representative, if one exists (r.4.4 and r.4.16 apply and r.4.7 applies *mutatis mutandis*);

r.53.9 (e) where appropriate, a statement concerning amendments. Where amendments under Art.19 have been made, the statement must indicate whether the applicant wishes those amendments (i) to be taken into account for international preliminary examination (in which case a copy of the amendments should preferably be submitted with the demand) or (ii) to be considered as reversed by an amendment made under Art.34. Where no Art.19 amendments have been made but the time limit for making them has not expired the statement may indicate that, if the examining authority wishes to start preliminary examination and search at the same time (as per r.69.1(b)), the applicant wishes the start of preliminary examination to be postponed until the expiration of the applicable time limit (set by r.46.1) (as per r.69.1(d)). If any amendments under Art.34 are submitted with the demand, the statement must so indicate;

r.53.8 (f) the signature of the applicant or where there is more than one, the signatures of all those applicants making the demand. Where a state is elected whose law requires that national applications are filed by the inventor(s) and one of the applicants who is an inventor refuses to sign the demand or cannot be reached after diligent effort, the demand need not be signed by the applicant-inventor concerned if it is signed by at least one applicant and (i) a statement is provided explaining, to the satisfaction of the International Preliminary Examining Authority, the lack of such a signature or (ii) the applicant-inventor concerned did not sign the request but the requirements of r.4.15(b) were complied with (same situation on filing). A seal (see r.2.3) is sometimes required rather than a signature (*e.g.* Korea).

r.66.1*bis* The written opinion produced by the International Search Authority is, if a demand is filed, considered to be a written opinion from the International Preliminary

Examination Authority (although IPEAs can decide not to accept written opinions from certain ISAs). This means that if the applicant wants to influence the content of the International Preliminary Examination Report any amendments or arguments that are needed should be submitted with the demand or shortly thereafter. If no amendments or arguments are filed, no further opinion or invitation will be issued and the IPER will reproduce the contents of the written opinion. This is not clearly set out in r.66.

## *Filing the demand constitutes the election of all eligible states* 3–223

The filing of a demand (on or after January 1, 2004) constitutes the election of all Contracting States which have been designated and are bound by Chapter II of the PCT.

*r.53.7*

## *The EPO as an elected office* 3–224

The EPO will act as an elected office if the applicant has elected any of the designated states referred to in Art.153(1) EPC or Art.149(2) EPC (special agreements between EPC states) for which Chapter II of the PCT has become binding.

*Art.156*

The EPO will also act as an elected office if the applicant is not a resident or national of a PCT Contracting State (or a PCT Contracting State in respect of which Chapter II has become binding) provided that the applicant is entitled to make a demand for international preliminary examination by virtue of a decision of the PCT Assembly under Art.31(a)(b) PCT.

*Art.156*

## *Fees due* 3–225

The demand for international preliminary examination is subject to the payment of certain fees within set time limits.

*Art.31(5)*

A handling fee, paid for the benefit of the International Bureau, is collected by the International Preliminary Examining Authority to which the demand is submitted. The amount is set out in the Schedule of Fees.

*r.57.1*

In addition, each International Preliminary Examining Authority may require a preliminary examination fee, for its own benefit which is paid directly to that Authority. The amount is fixed by that Authority.

*r.58.1*

Both fees must be paid within the later of:

*r.57.3/r.58.1*

(a) one month from the date when the demand was submitted; or

(b) 22 months from the priority date;

except that where the demand is transmitted to the International Preliminary Examining Authority indirectly under r.59.3, the relevant date under (a) is one month from the date of receipt by that Authority and where, under r.69.1(b), international preliminary examination and international search are to start at the same time, that Authority will invite the applicant to pay the fees within a month of the date of the invitation.

The amount due is the amount applicable on the date of payment.

*r.57.3(d)*

Where the fees are not paid by the time limit or they are insufficient, the International Preliminary Examining Authority will invite the applicant to pay the outstanding amount (together with any late payment fee—see below) within one month of the invitation, except that if the fees are received before such an invitation is sent, they are considered to have been received on time. Where the terms of the invitation are not complied with, the demand will be considered as if it had not been submitted and the International Preliminary Examining Authority will so declare except that if payment

*r.58bis.1*

| | |
|---|---|
| r.58bis.2 | Where an invitation is submitted because fees have not been paid by the time limit or they are insufficient, the International Preliminary Examining Authority may charge a late payment fee for its own benefit (see above). The amount of such a fee is 50 per cent of the amount of unpaid fees or, if that amount is less than the handling fee, an amount equal to the handling fee, up to a maximum of twice the amount of the handling fee. |
| AnReg | See under *Art.151*. Before the EPO, the surcharge is 50 per cent of the unpaid fees ([1998] O.J. 282). |
| r.57.2 | The handling fee must be paid in the currency or one of the currencies prescribed by the International Preliminary Examining Authority and on payment to the International Bureau is freely convertible into Swiss currency. The amounts due in currencies other than Swiss currency are equivalents in round terms of the amount due in Swiss currency as fixed by the Director General and the office with which consultation takes place under r.15.2(b) in relation to that currency, or, if there is no such office, with the Authority which prescribes payment in that currency. The amount in such currency is notified to each concerned International Preliminary Examining Authority by the International Bureau and published in the Gazette. Any changes to the Schedule of Fees apply to fees in alternative currencies from the same date. Due to fluctuations in currency, the Director General will establish new amounts in the alternative currencies (according to directives from the Assembly) applicable two months after their publication in the Gazette unless the Director General and the International Preliminary Examining Authority agree an earlier date in the two-month period. |
| r.58.1 | Where the International Preliminary Examining Authority is a national office, the preliminary examination fee is payable in the currency prescribed by that office and where such Authority is an intergovernmental organisation, it is payable in the currency of the state in which the intergovernmental organisation is located or in any other currency which is freely convertible into the currency of the said state. |
| RRF2(19) | The preliminary examination fee is 1,595 euros where the EPO is International Preliminary Examining Authority. |
| AnReg | See the agreement between the EPO and the International Bureau ([2001] O.J. 601). The amount of the international preliminary examination fee is reduced by 75 per cent for certain applicants from poor countries when the EPO is International Preliminary Examining Authority ([2000] O.J. 446). |
| r.57.6 | The International Preliminary examining Authority will refund the handling fee to the applicant:<br><br>(a) if the demand is withdrawn before the demand has been sent by that Authority to the International Bureau; or<br><br>(b) if the demand is considered, under r.54.4 (applicant not having the right to make a demand) or r.54*bis*.1(b) (demand made too late), not to have been sent. |
| r.58.3 | The International Preliminary Examining Authorities inform the International Bureau of the extent, if any, to which, and the conditions, if any, under which they will refund any amount paid as a preliminary examination fee where the demand is considered as if it had not been submitted and the International Bureau promptly publishes such information. |
| AnReg | See under *Art.150* for the agreement between the EPO and the International Bureau ([2001] O.J. 601). The EPO refunds 75 per cent of the examination fee where the international application or the demand is withdrawn before examination has started and 100 per cent where the demand is deemed not to have been filed (r.58.3). |

*(First paragraph at top of page, continuation:)* is received before such an Authority so proceeds it will be considered to have been received before the expiration of the relevant time limit.

## Acceptable languages of the demand

**3–226**

Where a translation of the international application is required under r.55.2 (see below), the demand must be in the language of the translation. Otherwise, it must be in either:

r.55.1

(a) the language of the international application as filed; or

(b) the language of publication, if it is different.

## Acceptable languages of the application

**3–227**

Where neither the language of the international application as filed, nor the language of publication is accepted by the International Preliminary Examining Authority, the applicant must furnish with the demand a translation of the international application into a language which is both:

r.55.2(a)(b)

(a) accepted by that Authority; and

(b) a language of publication;

unless such a translation has already been transmitted to the International Searching Authority under r.23.1(b) and the International Preliminary Examining Authority is part of the same national office or intergovernmental organisation. In this case, unless such a translation is nevertheless transmitted, examination will be carried out on the basis of the r.23.1(b) translation.

Where a required translation is not submitted, the International Preliminary Examining Authority will invite the applicant, within a reasonable time limit (not shorter than a month), which may be extended at that Authority's discretion at any time before a decision is taken, to correct the deficiency. Where the invitation is not complied with, the demand will be considered never to have been submitted and the International Preliminary Examining Authority will so declare.

r.55.2(c)(d)

Any correction, under r.26, of a defect in a translation of the international application furnished under r.55.2(a) for preliminary examination must be in the language of the translation.

r.12.2(c)

## Acceptable languages of amendments

**3–228**

Any amendment that:

r.55.3(a)

(a) is referred to in the statement concerning amendments under r.53.9 (part of the demand) and which the applicant wishes to be taken into account for preliminary examination; or

(b) is to be taken into account under r.66.1(c) (any Art.19 amendment made before the demand was filed unless superseded or considered as reversed by an Art.34 amendment);

must be translated into the language of any translation submitted under r.55.2 if it is not already in that language.

Where a required translation of an amendment is not submitted, the International Preliminary Examining Authority will invite the applicant, within a reasonable time limit (not shorter than a month), which may be extended at that Authority's discretion at any time before a decision is taken, to correct the deficiency. Where the invitation is not complied with, the amendment willl not be taken into account for the purposes of international preliminary examination.

r.55.3(b)(c)

| | |
|---|---|
| **3–229** | ***Languages before the EPO*** |
| AppGuide | See Vol. I, Annex E. The languages accepted by the EPO for international preliminary examination are English, French and German. |
| **3–230** | **Later election of states** |
| Art.31(6)(b) | States may be elected subsequent to submission of the demand. Such election should be submitted to the International Bureau. |
| r.53.7 | This provision has been rendered obsolete since the filing of a demand now has the effect of electing all eligible states. |

### Procedure where there are defects in the demand

| | |
|---|---|
| **3–231** | ***Applicant not entitled to make a demand*** |
| r.54.4 | Where the applicant does not have the right to make a demand within the meaning of r.54.2 (or, in the case of joint applicants, none of them has) the demand is considered not to have been submitted. |
| r.61.1(b) | The applicant and International Bureau are informed of the decision. |
| **3–232** | ***Invitation by the International Preliminary Examining Authority to correct formal defects*** |
| r.60.1 | Where the demand: |
| r.53.1 | (i) has not been made on a printed form or presented as a computer print-out complying with the Administrative Instructions; |
| r.53.2(a) | (ii) does not contain a petition complying with r.53.3, indications concerning the applicant complying with r.53.4, indications concerning any agent appointed complying with r.53.5 or indications concerning the relevant international application complying with r.53.6; |
| r.53.2(b) | (iii) is not signed in the manner indicated by r.53.8; |
| r.55.1 | (iv) is not in the appropriate language; |
| | the International Preliminary Examining Authority will invite the applicant to correct the deficiency within a reasonable time limit which may not be less than one month from the date of the invitation and can be extended by that Authority at any time before a decision is taken. |
| r.60.1(a-*bis*) | However, where there are two or more applicants, it is sufficient that the indications referred to in r.4.5(a)(ii) (address) and (iii) (nationality and residence) are provided in respect of one of them who has the right according to r.54.2 to file a demand. |
| r.60.1(a-*ter*) | Furthermore, where there are two or more applicants, it is sufficient for the purposes of r.53.8, that the demand is signed by one of them. |
| r.60.1(b) | If the applicant complies with the invitation within the time limit then the corrected demand will either: |
| | (i) be considered as received on its actual filing date if the demand as submitted permitted the international application to be identified, or else |
| | (ii) be considered as received on the date when the correction was received. |

If the applicant does not comply with the invitation within the time limit then the demand will be considered as if it had never been submitted and the International Preliminary Examining Authority will so declare.

r.60.1(c)

See also above under fees for the procedure where insufficient fees are paid.

## *Procedure where a statement concerning amendments is omitted or is misleading*

3–233

Where a statement concerning amendments in the demand indicates that amendments under Art.34 are submitted, as *per* r.59.3(c), but no such amendments are, in fact, submitted, the International Preliminary Examining Authority will invite the applicant to supply the amendments within a fixed time-limit and proceed as provided by r.69.1(e) (start of examination will be delayed until the amendments are received or the time limit in the invitation is exceeded).

r.60.1(g)

Where the statement concerning amendments is omitted, the International Preliminary Examining Authority will proceed in its absence under r.69.1(a) or (b) (regarding when to start examination) and r.66.1 (which amendments are to be taken into account).

r.60.1(f)

## *Defects noticed by the International Bureau*

3–234

If the International Bureau notices a defect in the demand it will bring it to the attention of the International Preliminary Examining Authority which will proceed as if it had noticed the defect itself under r.60.1(a) to (c).

r.60.1(e)

## Procedural steps taken by the international authorities on receipt of the demand

### *Procedure of the International Preliminary Examining Authority on receipt of the demand—notification to the International Bureau and the applicant*

3–235

On receiving a demand, the International Preliminary Examining Authority will:

r.61.1(a)(b)

(i) indicate on the demand the date of receipt (or the date of receipt of a correction that leads to a later date under r.60.1(b);.

(ii) send a copy of the demand to the International Bureau and keep the original in its files or vice versa;

(iii) promptly notify the applicant of the date of receipt of the demand; and

(iv) where the demand has been considered as if it had not been submitted under r.54.4 (applicant not entitled to make a demand), r.55.2(d) (translation not furnished), r.58*bis*.1(b) (fees not paid) or r.60.1(c) (defects in the demand not corrected), notify the International Bureau and the applicant accordingly.

### *Notification to elected states of their election by the International Bureau and other related actions*

3–236

The International Bureau notifies each elected state of its election.

Art.31(7)/r.61.2

The notification will be sent together with the Art.20 communication (of the international application to designated offices), if the elections are made in time, or else promptly if they are made later. The notification will indicate:

r.61.2(b)(c)

(i) the number and filing date of the international application;

(ii) the name of the applicant;

(iii) the filing date of any application whose priority is claimed; and

(iv) the date the demand was received by the International Preliminary Examining Authority.

| r.61.3 | The International Bureau informs the applicant in writing that the notification under r.61.2 has taken place, stating which elected offices have been notified. |
|---|---|
| r.61.4 | The International Bureau publishes in the Gazette, promptly after the filing of the demand but not before international publication, the States elected and the information on the demand provided for by the Administrative Instructions. |

## 3–237 Notification of the written opinion and any Art.19 amendments to the International Preliminary Examining Authority by the International Bureau

| r.62.1 | When the International Bureau receives the demand or a copy of the demand from the International Preliminary Examining Authority, it will promptly transmit to the International Preliminary Examining Authority: |
|---|---|

(a) a copy of the written opinion established under r.43*bis*.1, unless the International Searching Authority and International Preliminary Examination Authority are the same office or organisation; and

(b) a copy of any amendments filed under Art.19 and any statement filed under Art.19 explaining such amendments (unless the International Preliminary Examining Authority has indicated that it has already received such a copy).

| r.62.2 | If a demand has already been submitted when the applicant files amendments under Art.19 with the International Bureau, the applicant should simultaneously file a copy of such amendments and a copy of any accompanying statement under Art.19 with the International Preliminary Examining Authority. In any case, the International Bureau will promptly transmit a copy of such amendments and any accompanying statement to the International Preliminary Examining Authority. |
|---|---|

**The objective of international preliminary examination**

## 3–238 Aspects of patentability examined

| Art.33(1) | The objective of the examination is not to decide whether the claimed invention is patentable in the Contracting States but to formulate a preliminary and non-binding opinion as to whether the claimed invention appears to be novel, to involve an inventive step (to be non-obvious) and to be industrially applicable, as defined by the PCT. |
|---|---|

## 3–239 Definitions of novelty, inventive step and industrial applicability

| Art.33(2) | For the purpose of international preliminary examination, "novel" means not anticipated by the prior art. |
|---|---|
| Art.33(3)/r.65 | For the purpose international preliminary examination, "involve an inventive step" means not to be obvious to a person skilled in the art having regard to the prior art and taking into account the relation of a claim to individual documents of the prior art and combinations of such documents where the combination would have been obvious to a person skilled in the art. Inventive step is to be judged at the relevant date as defined in r.64.1 (see below under the definition of prior art). |
| Art.33(4) | For the purpose of international preliminary examination, "industrially applicable" means can be made or used (in the technological sense) in any kind of industry (understood in its broadest sense as in the Paris Convention). |

## 3–240 Definition of prior art

| r.64.1 | For the purposes of Art.33(2) (novelty) and Art.33(3) (inventive step), prior art is defined as everything made available to the public anywhere in the world by means of written disclosure (including drawings and other illustrations) prior to the filing date |
|---|---|

of the international application, or where priority is validly claimed, the filing date of the priority document ("the relevant date").

The prior art does not therefore include:  r.64.2/r.64.3

(i) anything made available to the public by oral disclosure, use, exhibition or other non-written means before the relevant date (r.64.1(b)) even if the date of such non-written disclosure is indicated in a written disclosure whose date is the same as or after the relevant date; or

(ii) patents and patent applications filed earlier than, or having an priority date earlier than, the relevant date but published on or later than the relevant date.

Nevertheless, the international preliminary examination report will call attention to such non-written disclosures under (i) and patents or patent applications under (ii) as indicated in r.70.9 (kind of disclosure and dates of written and non-written forms made available to the public) and r.70.10 (filing/priority date, publication date, whether priority validly claimed).  r.64.2/r.64.3

### Documents to be taken into consideration  3–241

The examination will take into consideration all the documents cited in the international search report and any others considered to be relevant.  Art.33(6)

## Procedure before the International Preliminary Examining Authority

### When International Preliminary Examination starts and finishes  3–242

The International Preliminary Examining Authority will start international preliminary examination when the time limit under r.54*bis*.1(a) (time limit for making a demand) has expired (unless the applicant waives this requirement) and when it is in possession of: (a) the demand; (b) all fees that are due; and (c) either the international search report or the Art.17(2)(a) declaration that no search report will be established and the written opinion established under r.43*bis*.1 except that:  r.69.1(a)

(i) where the statement concerning amendments states that amendments made under Art.19 are to be taken into account (r.53.9(a)(i)) preliminary examination may not start until the International Preliminary Examining Authority has received a copy of such amendments;

(ii) where the statement concerning amendments states that preliminary examination is to be postponed (r.53.9(b)), preliminary examination may not start until the International Preliminary Examining Authority has either received a copy of any amendments made under Art.19, or the International Preliminary Examining Authority has received a notice from the applicant that no Art.19 amendments are to be made or the r.46.1 time limit has expired; and

(iii) where the statement concerning amendments states that amendments made under Art.34 are submitted with the demand and none are submitted, preliminary examination may not start until the amendments are received or the r.60.1(g) time limit has expired (time limit set in an invitation from the International Preliminary Examining Authority).

However, where the competent International Searching and Preliminary Examining Authorities are part of the same national office or intergovernmental organisation and the International Preliminary Examining Authority so wishes, international preliminary examination may start at the same time as international search, except that:  r.69.1(b)

(i) where the statement concerning amendments states that preliminary examination is to be postponed (r.53.9(b)), preliminary examination may not start until the International Preliminary Examining Authority has either received a copy of any amendments made under Art.19, or the International Preliminary Examining Authority has received a notice from the applicant that no Art.19 amendments are to be made or the r.54*bis*.1(a) time limit has expired; and

(ii) where the statement concerning amendments states that amendments made under Art.34 are submitted with the demand and none are submitted, preliminary examination may not start until the amendments are received or the r.60.1(g) time limit has expired (time limit set in an invitation from the International Preliminary Examining Authority).

r.69.2  The International Preliminary Examining Authority must finish the examination (i.e. establish the International Preliminary Examination Report) by the later of:

(a) 28 months from the priority date;

(b) six months from the r.69.1 time limit for the start of international preliminary examination; and

(c) six months from the date of receipt by the International Preliminary Examining Authority of a translation which is necessary under r.55.2.

3–243 *General provisions governing procedure*

Art.34(1)  Procedure is governed by the provisions of the PCT, its Regulations and the agreement between the International Bureau and the International Preliminary Examining Authority.

3–244 *Right of the applicant to communicate with the International Preliminary Examining Authority*

Art.34(2)(a)  The applicant has the right to communicate orally and in writing with the International Preliminary Examining Authority.

r.66.6  The International Preliminary Examining Authority may communicate informally (by telephone, personal interview or by letter) with the applicant at any time. It will decide, at its discretion, whether to grant more than one personal interview (if so requested by the applicant) or whether it wishes to reply to any informal written communication from the applicant.

3–245 *Documents on which the examination is based*

r.66.1(a)–(d)  The international preliminary examination is based on the application as filed, taking into account any amendment made under Art.19, either before or after the filing of the demand, and any amendments made under Art.34 when filing the demand or later, subject to r.66.4*bis* (no amendment needs to be taken into account if received after preparation of a written opinion or the examination report has started).

r.66.1(e)  However, any claim relating to an invention in respect of which no international search report has been established need not be the subject of international preliminary examination.

3–246 *Applicant's right to amend*

Art.34(2)(b)  The applicant has the right to amend the claims, description and drawings in the prescribed manner (in particular not going beyond the disclosure in the application as filed) and within the prescribed time limit. See r.70.2(c) for the consequences for drafting of the International Preliminary Examination Report where subject matter has been added.

r.66.1(b)  The applicant may submit amendments under Art.34 when filing the demand or at any time until the International Preliminary Examination Report is established, subject to r.66.4*bis* (they must be submitted to the International Preliminary Examining Authority and arrive before that Authority has begun to draw up a relevant opinion or report to be taken into account).

An amendment is defined as any change other than the rectification of an obvious error in the claims, description or drawings, including the cancellation of claims, omission of passages in the description and omission of certain drawings.     r.66.5

Amendments must be in the form of either:     r.66.8

(a) replacement sheets, submitted for every sheet of the application differing from that sheet as previously filed because of an amendment and an accompanying letter drawing attention to such differences and also preferably explaining the reasons for the amendments; or

(b) where passages are deleted or minor alterations/additions are made, replacement sheets that are copies of the relevant sheet of the application containing the alterations/additions, provided that the clarity and direct reproducibility of such a sheet are not adversely affected; or

(c) a letter explaining that one or more entire sheets are cancelled by an amendment and preferably also explaining the reasons for the amendment.

The amendments must comply with all the requirements of r.10 (terminology and signs) and r.11.1 to r.11.13 (physical requirements).     r.11.14

The language of any amendment and any letter furnished under r.66.8 (explaining an amendment) must be either:     r.66.9(a)(b)

(a) the language of publication of the application if it was filed in a language other than the language of publication; or

(b) if international preliminary examination has been carried out on a translation of the application under r.55.2, the language of that translation instead.

If an amendment and/or letter is submitted in a language not complying with (a) and (b) above, the Examining Authority must, if there is time, invite the applicant to furnish the amendment and/or letter in an appropriate language within a reasonable time limit. If the applicant fails to furnish a translation of an amendment, that amendment will not be taken into account. If the applicant fails to furnish a translation of a letter, the amendment need not be taken into account.     r.66.9(c)(d)

See also similar provisions for providing translations of amendments made prior to International Preliminary Examining when a translation of the application for International Preliminary Examining Authority is necessary.     r.55.3

## Situations where the International Preliminary Examining Authority is not obliged to examine part of or the whole of an application     3–247

If the International Preliminary Examining Authority considers that the subject matter of the international application relates to:     Art.34(4)(a)(i)

(i) a scientific or mathematical theory;     r.67

(ii) a plant or animal variety or an essentially biological process for the production of plants or animals, other than a microbiological process or the product of such a process;

(iii) a scheme, rule or method of doing business, performing a purely mental act or playing a game;

(iv) a method of treatment of the human or animal body by surgery or therapy, or a diagnostic method;

(v) a mere presentation of information; or

(vi) a computer program (to the extent that the Examining Authority is not equipped to carry out an international preliminary examination concerning such programs);

that Authority is not required to examine that application and will inform the applicant of its opinion and the reasons therefore (in the written opinion (r.66.2(a)(i) and in the international preliminary examination report (r.70.12(iii))).

Art.34(4)(a)(ii) If the Examining Authority considers that the description, claims or drawings are so unclear or the claims are so inadequately supported by the description that no meaningful examination can be formed on the novelty, inventive step or industrial applicability of the claimed invention then it will inform the applicant of its decision not to carry out a preliminary examination and the reasons therefore (in the written opinion (r.66.2(a)(i)) and the international preliminary examination report (r.70.12(iii))).

Art.34(4)(b) If any of these circumstances relate only to certain claims, then the remedy will likewise apply only to those claims.

r.66.1(e) Claims relating to inventions in respect of which no international search report has been established need not be the subject of international preliminary examination (the applicant being notified in the written opinion (r.66.2(a)(vi)) and the International Preliminary Examination Report (r.70.2(d))).

r.66.2 Where multiple dependent claims have been drafted in a manner incompatible with r.6.4(a), second and third sentences (they must refer to the other claims in the alternative only and not serve as the basis for any other multiply dependent claim) and the national law of a national office acting as International Preliminary Examining Authority does not so allow, that Authority will apply Art.34(4)(b) (that claim will not be examined) and notify the applicant accordingly in writing (in the written opinion (r.66.2)).

**3–248** *The written opinion of the International Preliminary Examining Authority and responses thereto*

Art.34(2)(c) The International Preliminary Examining Authority must send the applicant at least one written opinion unless it considers that:

(i) the invention satisfies the requirements of Art.33(1), i.e. is novel, involves and inventive step and is industrially applicable; and

(ii) the international application complies with the requirements of the PCT in so far as checked by the International Preliminary Examining Authority; and

(iii) no comments under Art.35(2), last sentence, are necessary (any other observations on the application provided for in the Regulations).

r.66.4 But see the section below on the use of the written opinion of the International Search Authority as the written opinion of the International Preliminary Examining Authority.

r.66.2(a) In addition, the International Preliminary examining Authority may issue one or more additional written opinions using the same rules outlined below (r.66.2 and r.66.3) and if the applicant so requests, that Authority may give him one or more additional opportunities to submit amendments or arguments.

When drawing up a first written opinion, the International Preliminary Examining Authority must notify the applicant in writing if it:

(i) considers that one of the situations referred to in Art.34(4) exists (the application relates to subject matter not requiring examination or the description/

claims/drawings are so unclear or the claims so lack support that examination is not possible);

(ii) considers that any claim describes an invention which does not appear to be novel, appears to be obvious or does not appear to be industrially applicable;

(iii) notices that there is some defect in the form or contents of the international application under the PCT and its Regulations;

(iv) considers that any amendment goes beyond the disclosure of the application as filed;

(v) wishes to accompany the international preliminary examination report with observations on the clarity of the claims, description or drawings or wishes to question whether the claims are fully supported by the description;

(vi) considers that a claim relates to an invention in respect of which no international search report has been established and has decided not to examine that claim;

(vii) considers that a nucleotide and/or amino acid sequence listing is not available to it in such a form that a meaningful examination can be carried out; or

(viii) decides not to examine certain claims which are multiply dependent in a manner different from that provided for by r.6.4(a) due to provisions of national law.

The first written opinion must state the reasons underlying the opinion of the International Preliminary Examining Authority. r.66.2(b)

In its notification, the International Preliminary Examining Authority will invite the applicant to submit a written reply (together, where appropriate, with amendments) and will fix a reasonable time limit for reply which is between one and three months from the date of notification (usually two months) and at least two months if the written opinion is submitted with the international search report. It may be extended if the applicant so requests before its expiry. But note that no such invitation is issued if the written opinion established by the International Searching Authority is considered to be the written opinion of the International Preliminary Examining Authority—see below. r.66.2(c)(d)

The applicant may respond to the written opinion. Art.34(2)(d)

The response should be submitted directly to the International Preliminary Examining Authority and may include arguments and amendments as appropriate. r.66.3

### *Use of the written opinion established by the International Searching Authority as a first written opinion of the International Preliminary Examining Authority*     **3–249**

The written opinion established by the International Searching Authority pursuant to r.43*bis*.1 will be considered to be the written opinion of the International Preliminary Examining Authority for the purposes of r.66.2(a) unless the International Preliminary Examining Authority has notified the International Bureau that it will not apply this procedure in respect of written opinions established under r.43*bis*.1 by one or more International Searching Authorities specified in the notification (such notification not applying where the International Searching Authority and International Preliminary Examining Authority are the same office or organisation). Such notification will be published by the International Bureau in the Gazette. r.66.1*bis*(a)(b)

This means that the applicant needs to make any necessary arguments and amendments in response to the already-received written opinion from the International Searching Authority, as no further opinion or invitation will be issued in respect of defects mentioned in that written opinion unless the applicant has provided a response (argument and/or amendment) to the International Preliminary Examining Authority. Any informal comments on the written opinion of the International Search Authority which the applicant submitted to the International Bureau will not be sent by the Bureau to either the International Preliminary Examining Authority or the International Searching Authority (generally the same organisation, of course). Thus, if the applicant wants such comments to be considered in the preliminary examination, the applicant must submit them to the International Preliminary Examining Authority.

r.66.1*bis*(c)(d) Where the written opinion of the International Searching Authority is not to be used as the written opinion of the International Preliminary Examining Authority, the International Preliminary Examining Authority will notify the applicant accordingly in writing and will nevertheless take into account the written opinion of the International Searching Authority when preparing its own written opinion under r.66.2(a).

## 3–250 *Situation where amendments and arguments may be ignored*

r.66.4*bis* Amendments and arguments need not be taken into account by the International Preliminary Examining Authority for the purposes of a written opinion or the international preliminary examination report if they are received after that Authority has begun to draw up that opinion or report.

## 3–251 *Procedure where the International Preliminary Examining Authority needs a copy of the priority document*

r.66.7(a)(b) If the International Preliminary Examining Authority needs a copy of the priority document, the International Bureau will furnish a copy on request. If such a document is not in one of the languages of that Authority and the priority document is necessary in order to conduct international preliminary examination, it may invite the applicant to furnish a translation in one of the said languages within two months from the date of the invitation.

r.66.7(a) If the International Bureau cannot furnish the priority document because the applicant failed to comply with r.17.1 (i.e. supply a certified copy) and the priority document was neither filed with the International Preliminary Examining Authority nor available to it from a digital library or if the applicant fails to furnish a translation within the time limit, the international preliminary examination report may be established as if the relevant priority had not been claimed.

## 3–252 *Procedure where unity is in dispute*

AdminInst See s.207. The determination of unity by the International Preliminary Examining Authority must be made in line with the instructions in Annex B of the Administrative Instructions.

Art.34(3) If the International Preliminary Examining Authority considers that the claims lack unity (see r.13) it may give the applicant the option of restricting the claims or paying an extra fee (payable directly to that Authority, which decides the amount—r.68.3(a)(b)).

r.68.1 Where the International Preliminary Examining Authority decides not to so invite the applicant it must proceed to examine the whole application (subject to Art.34(4)(b) (certain claims not examined—see above) and r.66.1(e) (unsearched claims need not be examined)) but may indicate in any written opinion and in the international preliminary examination report that it considers unity to be lacking and the reasons therefor.

r.68.2 Where the International Preliminary Examining Authority does decide to so invite the applicant, it must specify its reasons for denying unity, at least one restriction which, in its opinion, would comply with the unity requirement and the amount of the additional fees. It will set a time limit for complying with the invitation of one month from the date of the invitation.

r.68.2 It must also invite the applicant to pay, where applicable, a protest fee (see below) within one month from the date of the invitation and indicate the amount to be paid.

r.68.3(c)–(e) Any applicant may pay the additional fees under protest, i.e. accompanied by a statement explaining why the claims comply with the requirement for unity or why the fees are excessive. The protest will be examined by a review body of the Examining Authority or any competent higher authority (which may include, but not be limited to the person who made the decision under protest) which will order the total or partial reimbursement of the additional fees to the extent it finds the protest justified. If the applicant so requests, the text of the protest and the subsequent decision will be notified to the designated offices as an annex to the international preliminary examination report. Where an additional fee is paid under protest, the Examining Authority may require the applicant to pay a protest fee. Where the applicant has not within the one month time limit according to r.68.2(v), paid any required protest fee, the protest will be considered not to have been made and the examining authority will so declare. The protest fee will be refunded if examination of the protest reveals that the protest was entirely justified.

If the applicant does not comply with the invitation within the time limit set, or if the applicant restricts his claims but not sufficiently to comply with the unity requirement (r.68.4), the International Preliminary Examining Authority will establish their report on those parts of the application which relate to what appears to be the main invention, and indicate the relevant facts in that report. Art.34(3)(c)

In cases of doubt, the invention first mentioned in the claims is considered to be the main invention. r.68.5

### Lack of unity where the EPO is International Preliminary Examining Authority

**3–253**

An additional fee, equal to the international preliminary examination fee, is payable in respect of each additional invention. *r.105(2)*

In the EPO, a Board of Appeal is responsible for examining any protest made by an applicant against an additional fee charged by EPO under Art.34(3)(a) PCT. *Art.155(3)*

Without prejudice to r.68.3(e) PCT, where an additional fee has been paid under protest, the EPO will review whether the request for the additional fee was justified. If it finds the request unjustified, it will refund the additional fee. If, however, it finds the request justified, it will inform the applicant and invite him to pay the protest fee. If the protest fee is paid in due time, the protest will be referred to a Board of Appeal for a decision. See Guidelines, E-IX 5.2. *r.105(3)*

The protest fee is 1,020 euros. RRF2(21)

See para.3–130, above. The EPO continues to review the decision to demand additional fees even though not required to do so by the provisions of the PCT. [2005] O.J. 226

See under *Art.154*. The review panel usually consists of the examiner, the head of his directorate and another examiner skilled in the determination of unity (see [1992] O.J. 547 for the full protest procedure). AnReg

See E/IX/5.2. Guidelines

### Procedure where a sequence listing is absent or in the wrong format

**3–254**

Rule 13*ter*.1 (provision of sequence listing) applies to international preliminary examination in the same way it applies to international search (see para.3–127, above). r.13*ter*.1

The International Preliminary Examining Authority will use the first written opinion to inform the applicant where it considers that a sequence listing is not available in such a form that a meaningful examination can be carried out. r.66.2(a)(vii)

**The international preliminary report on patentability (IPRP) (formerly known as the international preliminary examination report (IPER))**

3–255    *Time limit for establishing the international preliminary report on patentability*

Art.35(1)

The International Preliminary Examination Report must be established within the time limit set by r.69.2. This shall be whichever of the following periods expires last:

(i) 28 months from the priority date; or

(ii) six months from the time provided under r.69.1 for the start of on international preliminary examination; or

(iii) six months from the date of receipt by the International Preliminary Examining Authority of the translation of the application furnished under r.55.2.

3–256    *Requirements as to form*

r.70.15(a)

Physical requirements relating to the prescribed form (Art.35(1)) are laid out in the Administrative Instructions.

3–257    *Language of the report (and any annexes)*

r.70.17

The report and any annex must be in the language in which the application was published or, if a translation under r.55.2 has been supplied for the purposes of international preliminary examination, in the language of that translation.

3–258    *Documents on which the report is based*

r.70.2

The report must be based on any amended claims submitted by the applicant unless the International Preliminary Examining Authority considers that the amendments go beyond the disclosure of the international application as filed, in which case such amendments may be ignored and the report will so state (indicating the relevant reasons).

3–259    *Information on the first page*

r.70.15(b)

The report bears the title "international preliminary report on patentability (Chapter II of the Patent Co-operation Treaty)" together with an indication that it is an international preliminary examination report established by the International Preliminary Examining Authority.

The report contains the following information:

r.70.3    (a) the international application number;

r.70.3    (b) the international filing date;

r.70.5    (c) the classification, either as given in the international search report if the International Preliminary Examining Authority agrees with that classification, or the classification according to the International Patent Classification which it considers correct;

r.70.3    (d) the name of the applicant;

r.70.4    (e) the date on which the demand was submitted

r.70.4    (f) the date on which the report was completed;

r.70.3    (g) the name of the International Preliminary Examining Authority; and

[r.70.12(iv)] This information is also contained in the International Preliminary Examination Report.

(h) the name of the officer of the International Preliminary Examining Authority responsible for the report.  
r.70.14

## Comments on amendments

3–260

The report will indicate whether any amendments have been made before the International Preliminary Examining Authority, whether an amendment has resulted in the cancellation of an entire sheet and whether, in establishing the report, certain amendments have been ignored since they go beyond the disclosure of the application as filed (r.70.2(c)).  
r.70.11

## Comments on priority

3–261

The report will indicate, in appropriate cases, that, pursuant to r.66.7(a) or (b), it has been established as if priority had not been claimed.  
r.70.2(b)

## Comments on the non-establishment of an opinion

3–262

If the International Preliminary Examining Authority considers that the application relates to subject matter not requiring examination or, the claims so lack clarity or support that a meaningful opinion cannot be established (Art.34(4)(a)) it will state as much in the International Preliminary Examination Report and give the reasons therefore (r.70.12(iii)). If only some of the claims are so prejudiced (Art.34(4)(b)) then such an opinion and the reasons therefor will be stated in relation to the prejudiced claims and a statement as provided for in Art.35(2) (as to novelty, inventive step and industrial applicability) will be provided for the remainder.  
Art.35(3)

Where a claim relates to an invention in respect of which no international search report has been established and has therefore not been examined, the report will so indicate.  
r.70.2(d)

The report will state, where appropriate, that a nucleotide and/or amino acid sequence listing was not available in such a form that a meaningful international preliminary examination could be carried out.  
r.70.12(iv)

## Comments on lack of unity

3–263

The report will indicate, where the International Preliminary Examining Authority has found that the claims lack unity:  
r.70.13

(i) whether the applicant has paid additional fees (Art.34(3));

(ii) whether the application/examination report has been restricted (Art.34(3));

(iii) if examination has been carried out on restricted claims (Art.34(3)(a)) or on the main invention only (Art.34(3)(c)), what parts of the application were and were not the subject of examination; and

(iv) whether the Examining Authority has chosen not to invite the applicant to restrict the claims or pay an additional fee (r.68.1).

## Statement regarding patentability under Art.35(2)

3–264

Rather than considering the patentability of the invention under national law, the report will state in relation to each claim whether the claim is novel, inventive and industrially applicable as defined in Art.33.  
Art.35(2)

The statement will employ the words "YES" and "NO" or their equivalents in the language of the report (or some appropriate sign indicated in the Administrative Instructions.  
r.70.6(a)

| | |
|---|---|
| r.70.6(b) | The determination for a particular claim will be negative if any of the three criteria are not met but if one or two of the criteria taken separately is/are satisfied that fact will be acknowledged. |
| Art.35(2) | The statement will be accompanied by a citation of the documents relied upon in coming to the conclusion reached, any necessary explanations required by the circumstances and any other observations provided by the Regulations (r.70.6(a)). |
| r.70.7 | Relevant documents should be cited, whether or not they are cited in the International Search Report, identifying relevant or especially relevant passages where possible (documents cited in said search report but not considered relevant need not be cited). The method of identifying any document is given in the Administrative Instructions. |
| r.70.8 | Whether or not any explanations under Art.35(2) should be included, and their form, will be determined according to guidelines in the Administrative Instructions (s.604) based on the following principles: |

> (i) where the statement in relation to a claim is negative, an explanation should be given;
>
> (ii) where the statement in relation to a claim is positive an explanation should be given unless the reason for citing any document is easy to imagine on consultation of that document and
>
> (iii) where the statement in relation to a claim is negative in relation to only one or two of the criteria (r.70.6(b), second sentence) an explanation should generally be given.

### 3–265 *Certain documents cited*

| | |
|---|---|
| r.70.10 | The report must mention any patent or published patent application relevant under r.64.3 (a co-pending application or patent) by indicating its date of publication, filing date and claimed priority date (if any). The report may also indicate the opinion if the Examining Authority as to whether the cited patent or application is entitled to its priority date. |
| r.70.9 | The report must mention any non-written disclosure relevant under r.64.2 by indicating its kind, the date of the non-written disclosure and the date of the subsequent written report. |

### 3–266 *Certain defects in the application*

| | |
|---|---|
| r.70.12(i) | The report will mention any defects in the form or contents of the application under r.66.2(a)(iii) that the Examining Authority believes to be present. |

### 3–267 *Certain observations on the application*

| | |
|---|---|
| r.70.12(ii) | The report may optionally include any comments under r.66.2(a)(v) regarding the clarity of the claims, description or drawings or whether the claims are adequately supported by the description. If included, such comments must be supported by reasons. |

### 3–268 *Annexes to the report*

| | |
|---|---|
| r.70.16(a) | The following replacement sheets are annexed to the examination report, unless superseded by later replacement sheets or amendments resulting in the cancellation of entire sheets under r.66.8(b): |

> (a) each replacement sheet submitted under r.66.8(a) or (b) (during international preliminary examination);
>
> (b) each replacement sheet containing amendments submitted under Art.19; and

(c) each replacement sheet containing rectifications of obvious errors authorised under r.91.1(e)(iii).

Amendments under Art.19 which have been considered as reversed by an amendment under Art.34 and letters under r.66.8 (accompanying Art.34 amendments) are not annexed.  
r.70.16(a)

However, any superseded or reversed sheet is also annexed where the International Preliminary Examining Authority considers the relevant superseding or reversing amendment to add subject matter and the International Preliminary Examination Report contains an indication provided for in r.70.2(c). In such cases, the superseded or reversed replacement sheet will be marked as provided for in the Administrative Instructions.  
r.70.16(b)

## Translation and communication of the international preliminary report on patentability and its annexes

### Transmission of international preliminary report on patentability to the International Bureau and the applicant by the International Preliminary Examining Authority
3–269

The International Preliminary Examining Authority will transmit, on the same day, a copy of the international preliminary examination report, together with its annexes, if any, to the applicant and the International Bureau.  
Art.36(1)/r.71.1

### Translation by the International Bureau of the International Preliminary Examination Report and transmission of the international preliminary report on patentability and any translation to the elected offices and the applicant
3–270

The international preliminary examination report must be translated into the prescribed languages by the International Bureau.  
Art.36(2)

Any state may require that an international preliminary examination report which is established in a language which is not the/an official language of its national office must be translated into English. Such a requirement must be notified to the International Bureau who will publish it in the Gazette.  
r.72.1

Any translation so prepared will be transmitted by the International Bureau to each elected office along with a copy of the International Preliminary Examination Report and any annexes in the original language.  
Art.36(3)(a)

All necessary copies for such transmittal under Art.36(3)(a) will be prepared by the International Bureau.  
r.73.1

The transmittal will only take place, however, if such transmittal has been specifically asked for by an elected state in accordance with r.93*bis*.1. The timing of the transmittal will be specified by each elected state in the request pursuant to r.93*bis*.1, but may not take place before the expiration of 30 months from the priority date unless the applicant makes a request for early national processing under Art.40(2). In the latter case, the International Bureau will, at the request of the applicant or the relevant elected office, send the International Preliminary Examination Report, it annexes and the translation, where required, of the International Preliminary Examination Report (Art.36(3)(a)) to that office.  
r.73.2(a)(b)

The transmittal will even take place to elected offices affected by any withdrawal of the demand or withdrawal of one or more elections by the applicant so long as the International Bureau is already in receipt of the International Preliminary Examination Report.  
r.73.2(c)

| | |
|---|---|
| r.72.2 | The International Bureau will send a copy of the translation of the International Preliminary Examination Report to the applicant at the same time as it effects the Art.36(3)(a) transmission. |
| r.72.3 | The applicant has the right to make written observations on what he believes to be errors in such a translation which he must send to the International Bureau and the interested elected office or offices. |

### 3–271 Translation and transmission of the written opinion prepared under r.43bis.1 where the international preliminary report on patentability is not available and the applicant has requested early processing in an elected office

| | |
|---|---|
| r.73.2(b)(ii) | Where the applicant has made a request for early national processing in an elected office, pursuant to Art.40(2), the applicant or elected office has requested the Art.36(3) transmission and the International Bureau is not yet in possession of the International Preliminary Examination Report, it will send a copy of the written opinion established by the International Searching Authority under r.43*bis*.1 instead. |
| r.72.2*bis* | In such circumstances, where it is necessary to transmit a copy of the written opinion of the International Searching Authority under r.73.2(b)(ii), the International Bureau must, at the request of any elected office, translate the written opinion into English and transmit such a translation to the relevant elected office within two months of the request. A copy is sent to the applicant at the same time who may make written observations as to the correctness of the translation and send copies of such observations to each interested elected office and the International Bureau. |

### 3–272 Translation of the annexes of the international preliminary report on patentability by the applicant and transmission of the translation to the elected offices

| | |
|---|---|
| Art.36(2) | Any annexes to the international preliminary examination report must be translated into the prescribed languages by the applicant. |
| r.74.1 | Where a translation of the application is required by an elected office under Art.39(1) on entry into the national phase, the applicant must translate any replacement sheets referred to in r.70.16 (*i.e.* those sheets annexed to the International Preliminary Examination Report) into the same language (unless already in that language). Where such a translation of the application is not required by an elected office, that office may nevertheless require a translation of the annexed sheets into the language of publication, where they are not already in that language. |
| Art.36(3)(b) | Such a prescribed translation must be transmitted by the applicant to the elected offices within the prescribed time limit. |
| r.74.1(a) | Where an elected office requires the translation it must be transmitted by the applicant before the end of the Art.39 time limit (usually 30 months from the priority date). |

### 3–273 Supply of documents cited in the international preliminary report on patentability to the applicant and elected offices by the International Preliminary Examining Authority

| | |
|---|---|
| Art.36(4)/r.71.2 | At the request of an elected office or the applicant, within seven years from the filing date of the relevant application, the International Preliminary Examining Authority will supply copies of any document cited in the international preliminary examination report which was not cited in the international search report. A fee may be claimed by the International Preliminary Examining Authority from the office or applicant who makes such a request covering the cost of preparing and mailing the copies, the level of which will be set in the agreement under Art.32(2) between the International Preliminary Examining Authority and the International Bureau. Such an Authority may perform these obligations through another agency responsible to it. |

# 10. National phase aspects

## The effect of an international patent application having a filing date

### Nature of the effect

3–274

Subject to Art.64(4) (see below), an application satisfying the requirements of Art.11(1) and hence accorded a filing date has the effect of a regular national application in each designated state (and is equivalent to a regular national filing within the meaning of the Paris Convention) from the filing date of the international application, which is considered the actual filing date in each Contracting State.

Art.11(3)(4)

### Circumstances in which the effect is lost

3–275

The effect of the international application provided for in Art.11(3) will cease in any designated state with the same consequences as the withdrawal of any national application in that state:

Art.24(1)

(a) if the applicant withdraws his international application or the designation of that state;

(b) if the international application is considered withdrawn by virtue of Art.12(3) (record copy not received by the International Bureau within the time limit), Art.14(1)(b) (failure to correct defects in the application within the prescribed time limit), Art.14(3)(a) (prescribed filing and designation fees not paid within the prescribed time limit) or Art.14(4) (requirements for filing date not complied with) or if the designation of that state is considered withdrawn by virtue of Art.14(3)(b) (one or more designation fees not paid), unless the finding is reversed under Art.25; or

(c) if the applicant fails to perform the acts necessary under Art.22 (to enter the national phase) within the time limit (usually 30 months).

It is nevertheless the prerogative of any designated office to maintain the effect of Art.11(3) if it wishes, even when not obliged so to do under Art.25.

Art.24(2)

### Exceptions to the effect—the prior art effect of an international application in a designated state

3–276

If a state, by virtue of its national law, provides for prior art effect of its patents as from a date before publication but does not equate for prior art purposes the priority date claimed under the Paris Convention to the actual filing date in that state, it may declare that the filing outside that state of an international application designating that state is not equated to an actual filing in that state for prior art purposes.

Art.64(4)

Any state making such a declaration will, to that extent, not be bound by Art.(11)(3) (international applications to have the same effect as a regular national application in each designated state as of the filing date). Such a state must at the same time state in writing the date from which and the conditions under which the prior art effect of any international application designating that state become effective in that state. Such a statement may be modified at any time by notification addressed to the Director General.

See under Vol.II. This provision applies only to the US. An Art.102(e) date applies in respect of an international application not published in English only from entry into the US national phase and in other cases only to the international filing date (unless a US priority is claimed).

AppGuide

### Definition of a Euro-PCT application

3–277

An international application for which the EPO acts as a designated or elected office is a European patent application.

Art.150(3)

### The effect of a published international patent application

**3–278** *Provisions of the PCT*

Art.29

The rights in terms of protection in a designated state following the international publication of an international application are the same as those which the national law of such a state provides following the compulsory national publication of unexamined national applications unless:

(a) the language of the published international application is different from the language of publication under national law in any designated state in which case the national law may provide that such protection will only start when either (i) a translation into the latter language has been published as provided for by national law or (ii) a translation into the latter language has been made available to the public by laying open for public inspection as provided by national law or (iii) a translation into the latter language has been transmitted by the applicant to the actual or prospective unauthorised user of the invention claimed in the international invention or (iv) both acts described in (i) and (iii) or both acts described in (ii) and (iii) have taken place;

(b) the national law of any designated state provides that where an international application has been published before 18 months from the priority date at the request of the applicant, such rights will only apply from the expiration of this period; or

(c) the national law of any designated state provides that such rights will only be applicable from the date on which a copy of the international application as published under Art.21 has been received in the national office of or acting for that state in which case the said office will publish the date of receipt in its Gazette as soon as possible after receiving the application.

**3–279** *Provisions of the EPC—publication of the translation*

Art.158(1)

International publication usually takes the place of European publication.

Art.158(3)

However, where international publication is not in an EPO official language, provisional protection under Art.67(1) and (2) EPC will only be effective from the date of publication of a translation in an EPO official language (and subject to Art.67(3) EPC, regarding the language requirements of individual EPC states).

### Examination by national offices

**3–280** *When national processing may begin*

Art.23

No designated office may process or examine the international application prior to the expiry of the applicable time limit under Art.22 (usually 30 months from the priority date) unless the applicant has expressly requested so.

Art.40

When the election of a Contracting State has been effected before the end of the 19th month from the priority date, Art.23 will not apply to such state and its national office will not examine or otherwise process the application prior to the expiry of the time limit under Art.39 (usually 30 months from the priority date) unless, at any time, the applicant expressly requests examination or other processing.

Art.64(2)(a)(ii)

Any state, though not having renounced Chapter II under Art.64(1), may declare that the obligation to delay national processing under Art.40 will not prevent publication, by or through its national office, of the international application or a translation thereof, it being understood that it is not exempt from the limitations provided for in Art.30 (confidential nature of international applications before international publication) and Art.38 (confidential nature of international preliminary examination). States making such a declaration are bound accordingly. Such states were Finland, Norway, Poland and Sweden as of July 2006.

### *Right to amend when entering the national phase under Chapter I*     3–281

Where, in any state, examination or processing starts without a special request, that state must give the applicant a chance to amend the claims, description and drawings of his application either:     Art.28(1)/r.52

(a) within one month of fulfilling the requirements under Art.22; or

(b) if the communication under r.47.1 (Art.20 communication by the International Bureau to designated offices) has not been effected by the expiry of the time limit under Art.22, not later than four months after such expiry date;

and no decision to grant or refuse can be taken before the time limit for amendment has expired without the express consent of the applicant.

The right to amend may also be exercised at any other time allowed by national law.     r.52.1(a)

Where under national law, examination only starts on special request, the time limit within which or the time at which amendment under Art.28 is allowed is the same as would be provided for a regular national application provided that such a time limit may not expire before and such time may not come before the expiry of the time limit applicable under (a) or (b) above.     r.52.1(b)

Any amendment must not go beyond the disclosure in the international application as filed unless the national law of the designated state allows it to and must be in accordance with the national law of the designated state in all respects not provided for in the PCT and its Regulations.     Art.28(2)(3)

Where the designated office requires a translation of the international application, the amendments must be in the language of the translation.     Art.28(4)

### *Right to amend when entering the national phase under Chapter II*     3–282

Where a Contracting State is elected prior to the expiry of the period for filing a demand specified in r.54*bis*, the applicant has the right to amend the claims, description and drawings before that elected office either:     Art.41(1)/r.78.1

(a) within one month from the fulfilment of the requirements under Art.39(1)(a) (entering national phase within 30 months, usually); or

(b) if the transmittal of the international preliminary examination report under Art.36(1) has not taken place by the end of the Art.39(1)(a) time limit, not later than four months from the expiry of that time limit.

The right may also be exercised at any other time allowed by national law.     r.78.1(a)

However, where the national law of an elected state provides that examination starts only on special request, that national law may provide that the time limit within which or time at which the applicant may amend under Art.41 is the same as that which applies to the filing of amendments in the case of examination, on special request, of national applications, provided that such a time limit may not expire prior to and such a time may not come before expiration of the applicable time limit under (a) and (b) above.     r.78.1(b)

Until such time limit has expired, no elected office may grant or refuse a patent without the express consent of the applicant.     Art.41(4)

Any amendment must not go beyond the disclosure in the international application as filed unless the national law of an elected state allows it to and must be in accordance     Art.41(2)(3) with the national law of the elected state in all respects not provided for in the PCT and its Regulations.

Art.41(4) — Where an elected office requires a translation of the international application, any amendment must be in the language of the translation.

### 3-283 Right to amend on entering the EPO regional phase

r.109 — Apart from the usual opportunities to amend provided by r.86(2)–(4) EPC, the applicant will be invited by the EPO to file amendments on entering the national phase. Such amendments must be filed within a non-extendable period of one month from notification of the invitation. The application as amended serves as the basis for any necessary supplementary search.

### 3-284 Procedure where unity has been impugned in the international phase

Art.17(3)(b) — Where the International Searching Authority has invited the applicant to pay extra fees in response to a finding of lack of unity and the additional fees have not been paid, the national law of a Contracting State may provide that where the national office of that state considers the International Searching Authority justified on the question of unity the parts of the application consequently unsearched will be considered withdrawn in that state unless a special fee is paid to that national office.

Art.34(3)(b) — Where the applicant has elected to restrict his claims in response to a lack of unity objection during international preliminary examination, the national law of an elected state may provide that those parts of the application which are not examined will, as far as that state is concerned, be considered withdrawn unless a fee is paid to the national office of that state.

Art.34(3)(c) — The national law of any elected state may provide that where its national office finds an invitation of the International Preliminary Examining Authority to restrict or pay extra fees justified, the applicant has not complied and that Authority has only examined the main invention, those parts of the application which do not relate to the main invention will, as far as that state is concerned, be considered withdrawn unless a special fee is paid to that office by the applicant.

### 3-285 Consideration of unity by the EPO

r.112 — Where the International Searching Authority considered the application to lack unity and issued a request for extra fees (Art.17(3)(a) PCT) which were not paid such that the International Search Report was only partial the EPO will consider whether the claims have unity.

r.112 — If the EPO decides that the claims lack unity it will inform the applicant that a search report can only be drawn up in respect of unsearched matter if additional search fees are paid. A time limit will be set which is not shorter than two weeks or longer than six weeks.

r.112 — The search division will draw up a search report relating to those inventions for which search fees have been paid.

r.112 — Where there was no unity objection in the international phase or where all fees were paid in response to such an objection, but the EPO considers a lack of unity to exist and a supplementary search is necessary, then one or more supplementary search fees will be due.

r.112 — Rule 46(2) EPC applies such that any fees paid are refunded where the examining division agrees with the applicant that the application did in fact have unity.

## *Requirements relating to form or contents additional to those in the PCT may not be imposed by national offices*     3–286

It is forbidden for national law to lay down requirements relating to the form and contents of international applications different from or additional to those provided for in the PCT and its Regulations.     Art.27(1)

This does not affect the operation of Art.7(2) (requirement that an applicant submit drawings that are necessary for understanding the invention).     Art.27(2)

Further, a national office may nevertheless require that the application, a translation thereof or any other document relating thereto be submitted in more than one copy.     r.51*bis*.1(c)

Where any requirement of national law that a designated office may apply under Art.27(1) and Art.27(2) or r.51*bis*.1(c) is not fulfilled before the time limit specified in Art.22 the designated office must invite the applicant to comply with that requirement within a time limit which may not be less than two months from the date of the invitation. A fee may be charged by the designated office for complying with such a national requirement in response to the invitation.     r.51*bis*.3(a)

Where r.51*bis*.3(a) is not compatible, in relation to the time limit, with national law on March 17, 2000, it will not apply, as regards the time limit, to any designated office for as long as the incompatibility lasts so long as the office informed the International Bureau of this fact by November 30, 2000. This information is published by the International Bureau in the Gazette. Currently (July 2006) applies to Hungary, Singapore, Korea and Switzerland.     r.51*bis*.3(c)

The requirements of r.51*bis* apply equally whether national phase entry is under Chapter I or Chapter II.     r.76.5

National offices, courts of designated states and other competent bodies may apply their own national law in respect of form or contents to the processing of an international application where that law is more favourable to applicants than the requirements of the PCT and its Regulations unless the applicant objects.     Art.27(4)

One of the requirements covered by Art.27(1) is unity of invention (see applicants guide, para.138).     AppGuide

## *Requirements relating to the submission of certain documents (e.g. as evidence) that may be imposed by national offices*     3–287

Any designated office may require the applicant to submit, once processing of the international application has started in that office:     Art.27(2)

when the applicant is a legal entity, the name of an officer entitled to represent such legal entity;     Art.27(2)(i)(a)

documents which are not part of the international application but constitute proof of allegations or statements made in the application including the signature of the applicant to confirm the application when the agent or representative signed the application as filed;     Art.27(2)(ii)(b)

any document relating to the identity of the inventor (but see below);     r.51*bis*.1(a)(c)

any document relating to the applicant's entitlement to apply for or be granted a patent (but see below);     r.41*bis*.1(a)(d)

any document containing any proof of the right of the applicant to claim priority where he is different from the applicant having filed the earlier priority application or where his name has changed in the meantime (but see below);     r.41*bis*.1(a)(e)

any document containing an oath or declaration by the inventor alleging his inventorship, where national law requires the applicant to be the inventor (but see below);     r.41*bis*.1(a)(f)

| | |
|---|---|
| r.41*bis*.1(a)(g) | the address, nationality and residence of the applicant, where missing; or |
| r.41*bis*.1(h) | evidence concerning non-prejudicial disclosures or exceptions to lack of novelty, such as disclosures resulting from abuse, disclosures at certain exhibitions and disclosures by the applicant during a certain period of time. |
| r.51*bis*.2(a) | However, where national law does not require applications to be filed in the name of the inventor(s), a designated office may not, unless it has reasonable doubts about the veracity of the indications or declaration concerned, require any document or evidence: |

    (i) relating to the identity of he inventor, where indications concerning the inventor and complying with r.4.6 are contained in the request or a declaration as to the identity of the inventor complying with r.4.17(i) is contained in the request or submitted directly to the designated office; or

    (ii) relating to the applicant's entitlement, at the international filing date, to apply for or be granted a patent, where a declaration as to that matter complying with r.4.17(ii) is contained in the request or submitted directly to the designated office; or

    (iii) relating to the applicant's entitlement, at the international filing date, to claim priority, where a declaration as to that matter complying with r.4.17(iii) is contained in the request or submitted directly to the designated office.

| | |
|---|---|
| r.51*bis*.2(c) | Where r.51*bis*.2(a) is not compatible, in any respect, with national law on March 17, 2000, it will not apply to any designated office for as long as the incompatibility lasts so long as the office informed the International Bureau of this fact by November 30, 2000. This information is published by the International Bureau in the Gazette. Such offices (in July 2006) were Sweden and Switzerland in respect of r.51*bis*.2(a)(i), Canada, Hungary, Sweden and Switzerland in respect of r.51*bis*.2(a)(ii) and Switzerland in respect of r.51*bis*.2(a)(iii). |
| r.51*bis*.2(b) | Furthermore, where national law does require applications to be filed in the name of the inventor(s), a designated office may not, unless it has reasonable doubts about the veracity of the indications or declaration concerned, require any document or evidence: |

    (i) relating to the identity of he inventor (other than a document containing an oath or declaration of inventorship) where indications concerning the inventor and complying with r.4.6 are contained in the request; or

    (ii) relating to the applicant's entitlement, at the international filing date, to claim priority, where a declaration as to that matter complying with r.4.17(iii) is contained in the request or submitted directly to the designated office; or

    (iii) containing an oath or declaration of inventorship, if a declaration of inventorship, complying with r.4.17(iv), is contained in the request or submitted directly to the designated office

| | |
|---|---|
| r.51*bis*.3(a) | Where any requirement of r.51*bis*.1(a)(i)–(iv) ((c) to (f) above) is not fulfilled before the time limit specified in Art.22 the designated office must invite the applicant to comply with that requirement within a time limit which may not be less than two months from the date of the invitation. A fee may be required by the designated office for complying with such a national requirement. |
| r.51*bis*.3(c) | Where r.51*bis*.3(a) is not compatible, in relation to the time limit, with national law on March 17, 2000, it will not apply, as regards the time limit, to any designated office for as long as the incompatibility lasts so long as the office informed the International Bureau of this fact by November 30, 2000. This information is published by the International Bureau in the Gazette. Such offices were Hungary, Singapore, Korea and Switzerland in July 2006. |
| r.76.5 | The requirements of r.51*bis* apply equally whether national phase entry is under Chapter I or Chapter II. |

### Requirements relating to the certification/verification of the Art.22 translation that may be imposed by national offices

3–288

National law may, in accordance with Art.27(2)(ii), require that the translation submitted by the applicant under Art.22 is:

r.51*bis*.1(d)

(a) verified by the applicant or the translator in a statement to the effect that, to the best knowledge of that person, the translation is complete and faithful; or

(b) certified by a public authority or a sworn translator (but only if the designated office doubts the accuracy of the translation).

Where any requirement of r.51*bis*.1(d) is not fulfilled before the time limit specified in Art.22 the designated office must invite the applicant to comply with that requirement within a time limit which may not be less than two months from the date of the invitation. The designated office may charge the applicant a fee for complying with the national requirement in response to the invitation.

r.51*bis*.3(a)

Where r.51*bis*.3(a) is not compatible, in relation to the time limit, with national law on March 17, 2000, it will not apply, as regards the time limit, to any designated office for as long as the incompatibility lasts so long as the office informed the International Bureau of this fact by November 30, 2000. This information is published by the International Bureau in the Gazette. Such offices were Hungary, Singapore, Korea and Switzerland in July 2006.

r.51*bis*.3(c)

The requirements of r.51*bis* apply equally whether national phase entry is under Chapter I or Chapter II.

r.76.5

### Consequences of submitting or not submitting a copy of the priority document in the international phase—how a designated office obtains a copy

3–289

If the requirements of r.17.1(a) or (b) or r.17.1(b-*bis*) (supply of copy of priority document) are not met, any designated state may disregard the claim to priority as long as it has given the applicant an opportunity to furnish the priority document within a reasonable time limit (see *r.111(2) EPC* under chapter on entry into the national phase).

r.17.1(c)

Where the requirements of r.17.1(a), r.17.1(b) or r.17.1(b-*bis*) have been met, the International Bureau, when requested by a designated office, will promptly (but not before publication) furnish a copy of the priority document to that office. The applicant may not be asked to do this himself. Where the applicant has made an Art.23(2) request to a designated office (for examination before publication of the application) the International Bureau will supply the relevant designated office with a copy of the priority document, when so requested, promptly after receiving it.

r.17.2

### Requirement to submit a translation of the priority document

3–290

The applicant may not be required to furnish a translation of the priority document to a designated office before the expiry of the Art.22 time limit (normally 30 months).

r.17.2(a)

National law may, in accordance with Art.27, require the applicant to submit a translation of the priority document with the proviso that such submission may only be required where the validity of the priority claim is relevant to patentability.

r.51*bis*.1(e)

Where this proviso is not compatible with national law on March 17, 2000, it will apply to any designated office for as long as the incompatibility lasts so long as the office informed the International Bureau of this fact by November 30, 2000. This information is published by the International Bureau in the Gazette. Such offices were the EPO, Korea, Spain and Switzerland in July 2006

r.51*bis*.1(f)

Where any requirement of r.51*bis*.1(e) is not fulfilled before the time limit specified in Art.22 the designated office must invite the applicant to comply with that requirement

r.51*bis*.3(a)

within a time limit which may not be less than two months from the date of the invitation. The designated office may charge the applicant a fee for complying with national requirements in response to the invitation.

r.51*bis*.3(c)

Where r.51*bis*.3(a) is not compatible, in relation to the time limit, with national law on March 17, 2000, it will not apply, as regards the time limit, to any designated office for as long as the incompatibility lasts so long as the office informed the International Bureau of this fact by November 30, 2000. This information is published by the International Bureau in the Gazette. Such offices are Hungary, Singapore, Korea and Switzerland as of July 2006.

r.76.5

The requirements of r.51*bis* apply equally whether national phase entry is under Chapter I or Chapter II.

## 3–291 *Substantive conditions of patentability that may be imposed by Contracting States*

Art.27(5)

Nothing in the PCT and its Regulations limits the freedom of each Contracting State to prescribe such substantive conditions of patentability as it desires. In particular, the definition of "prior art" in the PCT applies exclusively to the international procedure.

Art.27(6)

Furthermore, national law may require the submission of evidence in respect of any substantive condition of patentability.

r.51*bis*.3(b)

Where any requirement of national law that a designated office may apply under Art.27(6) is not fulfilled before the time limit specified in Art.22 the applicant must have an opportunity to comply with that requirements after the expiration of that period.

r.76.5

The requirements of r.51*bis* apply equally whether national phase entry is under Chapter I or Chapter II.

## 3–292 *Requirement by Contracting States that the inventor(s) must be the applicant(s)—procedure when not abided by*

Art.27(3)

Where the applicant is not entitled to apply for a national application because he is not an inventor, the international application may be rejected.

## 3–293 *Conditions imposed by Contracting States to protect national security and to limit the freedom of its residents and nationals to file international applications*

Art.27(8)

Nothing in the PCT or its Regulations limits the freedom of each Contracting State to apply measures deemed necessary for the preservation of its national security or to limit, for the protection of the general economic interests of that state, the right of its own residents or nationals to file international applications.

## 3–294 *Requirements relating to representation that may be imposed by contracting states*

Art.27(7)

Any designated office, once processing of the international application has started in that office, may apply national law as it relates to any requirement that:

(a) the applicant be represented by an agent having the right to represent applicants before the said office;

(b) the applicant have an address in the designated state for the purposes of receiving notifications.

r.51*bis*.1(b)

(c) the agent representing the applicant (if any) be duly appointed by the applicant.

r.51*bis*.3(b)

Where any requirement of national law that a designated office may apply under Art.27(7) is not fulfilled before the time limit specified in Art.22 the applicant must have an opportunity to comply with that requirement after the expiration of that period.

The requirements of r.51*bis* apply equally whether national phase entry was under Chapter I or Chapter II. r.76.5

### *Removal of reference signs in claims for publication* — 3–295

Reference signs in claims may be removed by a designated office for the purposes of publication by such an office. r.6.2

### *Submission of a sequence listing* — 3–296

No designated office may require the applicant to submit a sequence listing to it other than one which complies with the Administrative Instructions. r.13*ter*.3

Rule 13*ter*.3 applies whether national phase entry is under Chapter I or Chapter II. r.76.5

Where a sequence listing as prescribed by r.5.2 PCT is not available to the EPO before the expiration of 31 months from the priority date, or does not conform to the prescribed standard or has not been filed on the prescribed data carrier, the applicant will be invited to remedy the defect within a time limit set by the EPO. *r.111(3)*

### *Special provisions relating to utility models* — 3–297

Any designated state in which the grant of a utility model is sought on the basis of an international application may substitute for r.6.1–6.4 (claims) the corresponding provisions of its national law concerning utility models once national processing of the application has begun. r.6.5

Any designated state in which the grant of a utility model is sought on the basis of an international application may also substitute for r.13.1–13.4 (unity) the corresponding provision of its national law concerning utility models once national processing of the application has begun. r.13.5

The applicant must be allowed at least two months from the expiration of the Art.22 time limit (or the Art.39 time limit if the election was made before the end of 19 months from the priority date—r.78.3) to adapt the application to the requirements of these provisions of national law. r.6.5/r.13.5

### *Any requirement to supply the results of examination in other states is not allowed if an International Preliminary Examination Report has been received* — 3–298

No elected office receiving the International Preliminary Examination Report may require that the applicant provide copies of, or information regarding the content of, any papers connected with the examination of the same application in any other elected office. Art.42

## Examination by the EPO

### *The international search report takes the place of the European search report* — 3–299

The international search report under Art.18 PCT (or any declaration under Art.17(2)(a) PCT) and its publication under Art.21 PCT takes the place of the European Search Report and the mention of its publication in the European Patent Bulletin. *Art.157(1)*

| | |
|---|---|
| 3–300 | ***Need for a supplementary European search report*** |
| Art.157(2)(3) | A supplementary European search report is drawn up in respect of all international applications except those in respect of which the Administrative Council has decided it can be dispensed with. |
| Art.157(4) | Such a decision of the Administrative Council can be rescinded. |
| r.109 | The application as amended under r.109 (on invitation by the EPO) serves as the basis for any supplementary search which is necessary. |
| AnReg | See under *Art.157(3)*. Before July 1, 2005 no supplementary search was necessary if the international search was carried out by the EPO or the Austrian, Spanish or Swedish patent office ([1979] O.J. 4; [1979] O.J. 248; [1995] O.J. 511). This is no longer the case. |
| 3–301 | ***Circumstances in which international publication takes the place of European publication*** |
| Art.158(1) | Publication of an international application for which the EPO is a designated office under Art.21 PCT will usually take the place of publication of a European patent application and will be mentioned in the European Patent Bulletin. |
| Art.158(3) | However, where international publication is not in an EPO official language, the EPO will publish the application in the translation supplied under Art.158(2) EPC (for entry into the national phase). |
| 3–302 | ***Circumstances in which a published international application is comprised in the state of the art under Art.54(3) EPC*** |
| Art.158(1) | A published international application is comprised in the state of the art under Art.54(3) EPC when the conditions of Art.158(2) EPC are satisfied (entry into the national phase). |
| 3–303 | **Consequences of an incorrect translation on the scope of a patent obtained** |
| Art.46 | If, because of an incorrect translation of the international application, the scope of any patent granted on that application exceeds the scope of the international application in its original language, the competent authorities of any Contracting State concerned may retroactively limit the scope of the patent and declare it null and void to the extent that its scope has exceeded the scope of the international application in its original language. |

## 11. THE CALCULATION OF TIME LIMITS AND PROCEDURAL SAFEGUARDS

| | |
|---|---|
| 3–304 | **Expression of dates** |
| r.79 | Applicants, national offices, Receiving Offices, International Searching and Preliminary Examining Authorities and the International Bureau must, for the purposes of the PCT and its Regulations, express any date in terms of the Christian era and the Gregorian calendar, either as the sole method of expression or in addition to their preferred method. |
| 3–305 | **Computation of time limits** |
| r.80.1/2/3 | The computation of time limits starts on the day following the day on which the relevant event occurred. To calculate the expiry of that time limit: |

| ... when a period is expressed as ... | .. the period expires ... |
|---|---|
| one or more years | in the relevant subsequent year in the month having the same name and on the day having the same number as the month and day on which the event occurred (where the month has no day of that number the last day of that month will count instead). |
| one or more months | in the relevant subsequent month on the day having the same number as the day on which the event occurred (where the month has no day of that number the last day of that month will count instead). |
| a number of days | on the day on which the last day of the count has been reached. |

The applicable starting date for calculating any of the above is the date which prevails in the locality at the time when the relevant event occurred and the applicable date on which any period expires is the date which prevails in the locality in which the required document must be filed or the required fee must be paid.

r.80.4

A period expiring on a particular day expires at the moment the relevant national office or intergovernmental organisation closes for business on that day unless that office or organisation allows for a later time up to a maximum of midnight on that day.

r.80.7

### Extension of time limits where a national office or intergovernmental organisation is not open for business

3–306

If a time limit relating to the supply of a document or fee to a national office or intergovernmental organisation expires on a day:

r.80.5

(a) on which that office or organisation is closed for official business; or

(b) which is an official holiday in at least one of the localities in which such office or organisation is located and the national law applicable to the office or organisation provides that in respect of national applications the time limit would be extended; or

(c) which is an official holiday in the part of a Contracting State where such an office is located and national law provides that in respect of national applications the time limit would be extended;

the period will expire on the next subsequent day on which none of these circumstances exists.

### Extension of time limits where mail is not delivered in a relevant locality on the last day of a time limit

3–307

If a time limit relating to the supply of a document or fee to a national office or intergovernmental organisation expires on a day on which ordinary mail is not delivered in the locality in which that office or organisation is situated, the period will expire on the next subsequent day when mail is delivered.

r.80.5

### Circumstances in which a missed time limit is excused where a document is sent in good time

3–308

Where any time limit in the PCT is not met because of interruption in the mail service or unavoidable loss or delay in the mail, the time limit will be deemed to have been met in the cases and subject to the proof and other conditions prescribed in the Regulations.

Art.48(1)

If an interested party offers satisfactory evidence to a national office or intergovernmental organisation showing that he mailed that office or organisation a document or

r.82.1(a)(b)

letter five days prior to the expiration of a time limit, the mail was registered by the postal authorities (but see below) and either:

(a) he mailed it my airmail; or

(b) surface mail normally arrives within two days of mailing; or

(c) no airmail service is available

then delay in arrival will be excused or, in the case of loss, substitution with a new copy will be allowed, provided that satisfactory proof is offered that the substitution is identical with the document or letter lost.

r.82.1(c)     Any evidence of the mailing date, a substitute document or letter and evidence concerning the identity of the replacement document/letter with the lost document/letter must be offered within one month of the date on which the interested party noticed, or with due diligence should have noticed, the delay or loss and in any case no later than six months from the expiration of the time limit.

r.82.1(d)(e)     Any office or intergovernmental organisation may extend these privileges to delivery services other than postal services by informing the International Bureau, who will publish such information in the Gazette. The requirement for registered mail is replaced in these cases by a requirement that details of the mailing must be recorded by the delivery service at the time of mailing. The extension may be limited to specified delivery services or delivery services satisfying specified criteria. The office or organisation may, in fact, apply this extension even if it has not informed the International Bureau or if such limitations are not met.

The EPO will generally take into account those delivery services it accepts for the purposes of r.84a EPC.

## 3–309     Extension of time limits where there is a general interruption in mail delivery

Art.48(1)     Where any time limit in the PCT is not met because of interruption in the mail service or unavoidable loss or delay in the mail, the time limit will be deemed to have been met in the cases and subject to the proof and other conditions prescribed in the Regulations.

r.82.2(a)(b)     If any interested party offers satisfactory evidence to a national office or an intergovernmental organisation that on any of the 10 days preceding the expiry of a time limit the postal service was interrupted on account of war, revolution, civil disorder, strike, natural calamity or other reason in the locality where he resides, is staying or has his place of business, delay in arrival will be excused provided that he effected the mailing within five days after the service was resumed.

r.82.2(b)     Any such evidence must be offered within one month of the date on which the interested party noticed, or with due diligence should have noticed, the delay and in any case no later than six months from the expiration of the time limit.

**Extension of a time limit where a notification is sent later than the day marked or is received more than seven days after posting**

### 3–310     *Actual date of mailing later than date marked*

r.80.6     If any interested party proves that a document or letter emanating from a national office or intergovernmental organisation was actually mailed on a later day than the date marked on it, then a period to be calculated from the date of that document or letter will start on the actual date of mailing rather than the marked date.

## *Date of receipt of letter more than seven days after posting*                    3–311

If the applicant offers satisfactory evidence to a national office or intergovernmental organisation that a letter or document was received more than seven days after the date it bears, any period to be calculated from the date of the letter or document will be extended by the number of days later than seven that the document was received.                    r.80.6

## Chance for the applicant to escape a negative determination made in the international phase

### *Duty of the International Bureau to supply documents to designated states when the International Bureau or Receiving Office has made a negative determination*                    3–312

Where the receiving office has:                    Art.25(1)

(a) refused to accord a filing date (Art.11(1));

(b) declared that the international application is considered withdrawn (r.29.1); or

(c) declared that the designation of any given state is considered withdrawn (Art.14(3)(b)/r.27.1(b));

or where the International Bureau has:

(d) made a finding under Art.12(3) (record copy not received within the prescribed time limit prescribed by r.22.3);

the International Bureau will, when asked by the applicant within the prescribed time limit, promptly send copies of any documents in the file to any of the designated offices named (as long as, under (c), they are offices the designation of which is considered withdrawn).

The prescribed time limit is two months computed from the date of the notification sent to the applicant under r.20.7(i) (refusal to accord a filing date), r.24.2(c) (lack of receipt by the International Bureau of the record copy) or r.29.1(a)(ii) (finding by the Receiving Office that the application is considered withdrawn).                    r.51.1

Where a filing date cannot be allocated [negative determination under Art.11(1)] and the applicant requests the International Bureau to proceed as above, he must attach to his request a copy of the r.20.7(i) notice (that his application is not and will not be treated as an international application and the reasons therefor).                    r.51.2

### *Assessment by the designated office as to whether the applicant or the International Bureau/Receiving Office is at fault according to the PCT*                    3–313

Each designated office must, providing the national fee (if any) has been paid and any appropriate translation has been supplied within the prescribed time limit (same as for Art.25(1), *i.e.* two months from notification—r.51.3), decide whether any such refusal, declaration or finding was justified under the PCT and its Regulations and if it finds that the refusal, declaration or finding was due to an error or omission on behalf of the Receiving Office or the International Bureau, respectively, it will, as far as that state is concerned, treat the application as if the error or omission had not occurred.                    Art.25(2)(a)

However, when the record copy has reached the International Bureau late under Art.12(3) because of an error or omission on the part of the applicant, the provisions of Art.25.2(a) only apply where the designated office excuses the delay in meeting the time limit under national law or for any other reason (Art.48(2)).                    Art.25(2)(b)

| | |
|---|---|
| 3–314 | **Right of any designated state to maintain the effect of an international application in that state when it does not have to** |
| Art.24(2) | It is the prerogative of any designated office to maintain the effect of Art.11(3) if it wishes, even when not obliged so to do under Art.25(2). |
| 3–315 | **Competent EPO authority for making a decision under Art.25(2)(a)** |
| Art.153(2) | When the EPO acts as a designated office the examining division is competent to take any decision required by Art.25(2)(a) PCT. |
| 3–316 | **The duty of Contracting States to excuse missed time limits under provisions of national law** |
| Art.48(2) | Any state, as far as that state is concerned, must excuse, for reasons admitted under its national law, and may excuse for any other reason, any delay in meeting any time limit: |
| r.82bis.1 | (a) fixed in the PCT and its Regulations; |
| | (b) fixed by the Receiving Office, the International Searching Authority, the International Preliminary Examining Authority or the International Bureau or applicable by the Receiving Office under its national law; or |
| | (c) fixed by, or in the national law applied by, the designated or elected office, for the performance of any act by the applicant before that office. |
| r.82bis.2 | Such provisions of national law are those which provide for reinstatement of rights, restoration, *restitutio in integrum* or further processing where a time limit has been missed and any other provision providing for the extension of time limits or for excusing delays in meeting time limits. |
| AppGuide | See Vol.II, para.67. This mechanism only operates when the national or regional phase has been entered but may then be used to excuse the missing of a time limit in the international or national/regional phase. |
| 3–317 | **Opportunity to correct an application where allowed under national law** |
| Art.26 | No designated office may reject an international application on the grounds that it does not comply with the PCT and Regulations without first giving the applicant the opportunity to correct the application to the extent and according to the procedure provided by national law for the same or comparable situations in respect of national applications. |
| J8/01 | Article 26 PCT gives a purported designated office the authority to consider if its designation can be added or not (*e.g.* under r.88 EPC). However, in accordance with decisions relating to regular European patent applications, the mistake must be corrected early enough for the public to be warned on international publication. |
| 3–318 | **Rectification of errors made by the receiving office or the International Bureau concerning filing date and priority claim** |
| r.82ter | If the applicant proves to the satisfaction of any designated or elected office that either: |
| | (a) the international filing date is incorrect due to an error made by the Receiving Office, or |
| | (b) the priority claim has been erroneously considered by the Receiving Office or the International Bureau not to have been made |

and the error is such that if it was made by such an office, that office would rectify it under the national law or practice, it will rectify the error and treat the application as if it had been accorded the correct filing date or had been recognised as claiming priority. A request for rectification should be made on entering the national or regional phase.

## Reinstatement of rights after failure to enter the national phase within the time limit

3–319

Where the effect of the international application provided for in Art.11(3) ceases because the applicant fails to perform the acts referred to in Art.22 within the applicable time limit (Art.24(1)(iii)), the designated office will, upon request of the applicant, reinstate the rights of the applicant with respect to that international application if it finds that any delay in meeting that time limit was unintentional or, at the option of the designated office, that the failure to meet the time limit occurred in spite of due care required by the circumstances having been taken.

r.49.6(a)

Such a request must be submitted to the designated office and the Art.22 acts must be completed within the earlier of:

r.49.6(b)

(i) two months from the date of removal of the cause of the failure to meet the applicable time limit under Art.22; or

(ii) 12 months from the date of the expiration of the applicable time limit under Art.22;

provided that the applicant may submit the request at any later time if so permitted by the national law applicable by the designated office.

The request must state the reasons for the failure to meet the Art.22 time limit and national law may provide that a declaration or other evidence be filed in support of such reasons.

r.49.6(c)(d)

Furthermore, national law may require that a fee be paid in respect of such a request.

r.49.6(d)

A designated office may not refuse such a request without giving the applicant a chance to make observations on the intended refusal within a reasonable time limit.

r.49.6(e)

The provisions of new r.49.6 apply, in respect of designated offices that have not made a reservation under r.49.6(f) below, to applications that had not entered the national/regional phase within the applicable time limit under Art.22 or Art.39(1) on January 1, 2003.

If, on October 1, 2002, paras (a)–(e) of r.49.6 are not compatible with the national law applied by a designated office, those paragraphs will not apply in respect of that designated office for as long as they continue not to be compatible with that law, provided that the said office informed the International Bureau accordingly by January 1, 2003. The information received is promptly published by the International Bureau in the Gazette.

r.49.6(f)

Such reservations are in force (as of July 2006) in respect of Canada, China, Croatia, the EPO, Germany, New Zealand, the Philippines, Japan, Korea, Latvia, Mexico, India, Poland and the UK.

The provisions of new r.49.6 will apply, in respect of designated offices that have made a reservation under r.49.6(f), to applications that have not entered the national/regional phase on the date on which r.49.6 enters into force for that office.

## 12. CORRECTION

**3–320** **Errors that may be corrected**

r.91.1(a)(b)
Obvious errors (*i.e.* errors which are due to the fact that something other than what was obviously intended was written) in the international application or other papers submitted by the applicant may be rectified as long as the rectification is obvious in the sense that anyone would immediately realise that nothing else could have been intended than what is offered as rectification.

**3–321** **Errors that may not be corrected**

r.91.1(c)
The omission of entire elements or sheets of the application cannot be rectified under any circumstances.

**3–322** **The applicant or an international authority may initiate correction**

r.91.1(d)
The applicant may request rectification or an Authority that discovers what appears to be an obvious error may invite him so to do.

**3–323** **Procedure for correcting**

r.91.1(d)
Rule 26.4 (procedure for correcting before the Receiving Office—see above) applies *mutatis mutandis*.

**3–324** **Authorisation is required for a correction**

r.91.1(e)
The following authorisation is required:

| Kind of error | Authorisation required from | Conditions |
|---|---|---|
| In the request. | The Receiving Office. | Notification must reach the International Bureau before the expiry of 17 months from the priority date.[1,2,3] |
| In any part of the application other than the request or in any paper sent to the International Searching Authority. | The International Searching Authority. | Notification must reach the International Bureau before the expiry of 17 months from the priority date.[1,2,3] |
| In any part of the application other than the request or in any paper sent to the International Preliminary Examining Authority. | The International Preliminary Examining Authority. | Authorisation must be given before the international preliminary examination report is established. |
| In any paper, other than the international application or amendments or corrections thereto, submitted to the International Bureau. | The International Bureau. | Authorisation must be given before the expiry of 17 months from the priority date.[1,2,3] |

Notes:

r.91.1(g-*bis*)
1. If notification reaches the International Bureau or authorisation is given by that Bureau after 17 months from the priority date but before the technical preparations for international publication are complete, the authorisation is effective and rectification will be incorporated in that publication.

2. Where the applicant has requested international publication before the expiry of 18 months from the priority date, any notification must reach the International Bureau or any rectification must be authorised by that Bureau not later than the time of the completion of the technical preparations for international publication for the authorisation to be effective. r.91.1(g-*ter*)

3. Where the international application is not published by virtue of Art.64(3) (only states not requiring publication designated—applies only to the US) any notification must reach the International Bureau or any rectification must be authorised by that Bureau not later than the time of communication of the application under Art.20 for the authorisation to be effective. r.91.1(g-*quat*)

Any authority which authorises a rectification will promptly inform the applicant and the International Bureau accordingly. r.91.1(f)

Any authority which refuses a rectification will promptly inform the applicant accordingly, give the reasons therefor and, where the applicant so requests before the time relevant under r.91.1(g-*bis*), (g-*ter*) or (g-*quater*), and subject to the payment of a special fee (amount fixed in the Administrative Instructions), the International Bureau will publish the request for rectification together with the application. A copy of the request for rectification will be included in the communication under Art.20 where the international application is not published by virtue of Art.64(3) (only states not requiring publication designated—applies only to the US). r.91.1(f)

See s.113. The special fee is 50 Swiss francs plus 12 Swiss francs for each sheet in excess of one. AdminInst

## Language of the correction 3–325

Any rectification of an obvious error must be in the language in which the application is filed provided that: r.12.2(b)

(i) where a translation of the international application is required under r.12.3(a) (translation for international search), r.12.4(a) (for international publication) or r.55.2(a) (translation for preliminary examination), rectifications under r.91.1(e)(ii) and (iii) (authorised by the International Searching Authority or International Preliminary Examining Authority) must be filed in both the languages of filing and translation; and

(ii) where a translation of the request is required under r.26.3*ter*(c) (where the request is not filed in a language of publication acceptable to the Receiving Office), rectifications under r.91.1(e)(i) (authorised by the Receiving Office) need only be filed in the language of the translation.

## 13. REPRESENTATION

### Requirements relating to representation that may be imposed by the Receiving Office 3–326

Any Receiving Office may apply national law in so far as it relates to any requirement that the applicant be represented by an agent having the right to represent applicants before that Office. Art.27(7)

Where the EPO is Receiving Office, Art.133 and Art.134 EPC determine the requirements for representation. Due to the restrictions on who can use the EPO as Receiving Office (see below) representation will rarely be obligatory.

| | |
|---|---|
| 3–327 | **Requirements relating to representation that may be imposed by contracting states** |
| Art.27(7) | Any designated office, once processing of the international application has started in that office, may apply national law as it relates to any requirement that: |
| | (a) the applicant be represented by an agent having the right to represent applicants before the said office; |
| | (b) the applicant have an address in the designated state for the purposes of receiving notifications. |
| r.51*bis*.1(b) | (c) the agent representing the applicant (if any) be duly appointed by the applicant. |
| r.51*bis*.3(b) | Where any requirement of national law that a designated office may apply under Art.27(7) is not fulfilled before the time limit specified in Art.22 the applicant must have an opportunity to comply with that requirement after the expiration of that period. |
| r.76.5 | The requirements of r.51*bis* apply equally whether national phase entry was under Chapter I or Chapter II. |
| 3–328 | **Right to practice before international authorities** |
| Art.49 | Any attorney, patent agent or other person having the right to practice before the national office with which the international application was filed is entitled to practice before the International Bureau, the competent International Searching Authority and the competent International Preliminary Examining Authority in respect of that application. |
| r.83.1 | The International Bureau, the competent International Searching Authority and the competent International Preliminary Examining Authority may require proof of the right to practice before a national office referred to in Art.49. |
| r.83.1*bis* | Where the International Bureau is the Receiving Office, any person who has the right to practice before the national office of, or acting for, a Contracting State of which the applicant (or one of them if there are more than one) is a resident or national is entitled to practice in respect of the international application before the International Bureau in its capacity as Receiving Office (r.19.1(a)(iii)), before the International Bureau in any other capacity and before the competent International Searching and Preliminary Examining Authorities. |
| r.83.2 | To decide any question as to such an entitlement to practice (r.83.1*bis*), the national office or intergovernmental organisation before which the interested person is alleged to have the right to practice will inform the relevant Bureau or Authority, on request, whether such a person has such a right and such information is binding on the Bureau or Authority concerned. |

**Agents and common representatives**

| | |
|---|---|
| 3–329 | *Appointment of an agent* |
| r.90.1(a) | The applicant may appoint any person to represent him before the Receiving Office, the International Bureau, and the International Searching and Preliminary Examining Authorities if that person: |
| | (a) has the right to practice before the national office with which the international application is filed; or |
| | (b) has the right to practice in respect of the international application before the International Bureau as Receiving Office when the international application is filed with the International Bureau. |

Unless otherwise indicated in the document appointing him, such an agent may appoint one or more sub-agents to represent the applicant: r.90.1(d)

(a) before the Receiving Office, the International Bureau and the International Searching and Preliminary Examining Authorities, provided the sub-agent has the right to practice before the national office with which the international application was filed or to practice in respect of the international application before the International Bureau as Receiving Office, as the case may be; or

(b) specifically before the International Searching or Preliminary Examining Authority provided that the sub-agent has the right to practice before that relevant Authority.

The applicant may appoint an agent to specifically represent him before the International Searching or Preliminary Examining Authority where that agent has the right to practice before the national office or intergovernmental organisation acting as the relevant Authority. r.90.1(b)(c)

## Representative where there are two or more applicants    3–330

Where there are two or more applicants, they will be represented by: r.90.2

(a) a common agent appointed by the applicants under r.90.1(a); or

(b) one of the applicants appointed by the others as common representative as long as he is entitled to file an international application under Art.9; or, where neither (a) or (b) apply,

(c) the applicant first named on the request who is entitled to file an international application with the Receiving Office under r.19.1.

## Effects of acts by representatives and agents    3–331

Any act by, or in relation to, an agent, or one of the agents when there are two or more, or a common representative or a common representative's agent will have the effect of an act by or in relation to the applicant or applicants concerned, subject to r.90*bis*.5(a) (signatures necessary to effect withdrawal of the application, a designation, a priority claim, an election or a demand). r.90.3

## Manner of appointment of an agent or common representative    3–332

The appointment of an agent, common agent or common representative is effected by the applicant (or each applicant where there are two or more) signing the request, the demand or a separate power of attorney. r.90.4(a)

Subject to r.90.5 (general power of attorney), such a separate power of attorney (under r.90.4) must be submitted to the Receiving Office or the International Bureau, provided that where an agent is appointed specifically in respect of an International Searching or Preliminary Examining Authority (r.90.1(b), (c) or (d)(ii)), it should be submitted to that relevant Authority. Where a power of attorney is not signed, is missing or contains indications of the name and address of the appointed person that do not comply with r.4.4, it will be considered non-existent unless the defect is corrected. r.90.4(b)(c)

Any Receiving Office or International Searching or Preliminary Examining Authority or the International Bureau may waive the requirement that a separate power of attorney be submitted to it under r.90.4(b), in which case any defect in the power of attorney under r.90.4(c) will not cause it to be considered non-existent. However, this does not apply where the agent or common representative submits any notice of withdrawal pursuant to r.90*bis*.1 to r.90*bis*.4. Many offices, and the IB, have waived the requirement for a separate power of attorney. r.90.4(d)(e)

The EPO has waived the requirement for a separate power of attorney except (a) where the agent of record changes and the new and old agents do not belong to the same office O.J.

or are not employees of the applicant and (b) where there is any doubt as to the entitlement of the agent to act (see [2004] O.J. 305).

r.90.5(a)(b) The appointment of an agent in respect of a particular international application may also be effected by referring in the request, demand or a separate notice to an existing separate power of attorney appointing that agent to represent the applicant in relation to any international application filed by that applicant (a general power of attorney), provided that:

(a) the general power has been deposited with the Receiving Office, or, where it appoints an agent specifically before an International Searching or Preliminary Examining Authority under r.90.1(b), (c) or (d)(ii), that Authority; and

(b) a copy of the general power is attached to the request, demand or separate notice as the case may be (signed or unsigned).

r.90.5(c)(d) Any Receiving Office or International Searching or Preliminary Examining Authority may waive the requirement that a copy of a general power of attorney is attached to the request, demand or separate notice under r.90.5(a)(ii). However, this does not apply where the agent submits any notice of withdrawal pursuant to r.90*bis*.1 to r.90*bis*.4.

O.J. The EPO has waived the requirement for a copy of a general power of attorney to be submitted except (a) where the agent or record changes and the new and old agents do not belong to the same office or are not employees of the applicant and (b) where there is any doubt as to the entitlement of the agent to act (see [2004] O.J. 305).

3–333 *Manner of renunciation of an agent or common representative*

r.90.6(a) Any appointment of an agent or common representative or a sub-agent under r.90.1(d) may be revoked by those who made the appointment or their successors in title (and a revocation of the appointment of an agent will automatically revoke the appointment under r.90.1(d) of a sub-agent working under that agent).

r.90.6(b)(c) The appointment of an agent under r.90.1(a) or the appointment of a common representative will, unless otherwise indicated, have the effect of revoking any earlier appointment of an agent under r.90.1(a) or a common representative, respectively.

r.90.6(d) An agent or common representative may renounce his appointment by filing a signed notification.

r.90.6(e) Such a revocation or renunciation must be submitted to the Receiving Office or the International Bureau, provided that where an agent is appointed specifically in respect of an International Searching or Preliminary Examining Authority (r.90.1(b), (c) or (d)(ii)), it should be submitted to that relevant Authority. Where the revocation or renunciation is not signed, is missing or contains indications of the relevant name and address that do not comply with r.4.4, it will be considered non-existent unless the defect is corrected.

## 14. MISCELLANEOUS COMMON PROVISIONS

**Relationship between the PCT and the EPC**

3–334 *How the EPC and PCT are to be applied to Euro-PCT applications*

Art.150(1) The PCT is to be applied, as far as European patent applications and patents are concerned, according to the provisions of Part X of the EPC (International application pursuant to the PCT).

In proceedings before the EPO concerning an international application filed under the PCT, the provisions of the PCT will be applied, supplemented by the provisions of the EPC. In the case of conflict, the provisions of the PCT will prevail.

*Art.150(2)*

### References to the PCT in the EPC to embrace Regulations

3–335

Any reference in the EPC to the "Co-operation Treaty" includes a reference to the Regulations under the PCT.

*Art.150(4)*

### Rules relating to documents filed subsequently to the filing of the application

#### Need for papers to be accompanied by a signed letter

3–336

Any paper submitted by the applicant during the international procedure, other than the application, provided for under the PCT and its Regulations, must, if not itself a letter, be accompanied by a letter, signifying the international application to which it relates and signed by the applicant.

*r.92.1(a)*

Where such a letter is not provided, the applicant will be invited to remedy the omission within a time limit which is reasonable (between 10 days and a month from the date of the invitation, even where the time limit so fixed expires later than the time limit for supplying the paper, or the latter time limit has already expired) and fixed in the invitation. Either the omission or the paper will be disregarded depending on whether the omission is remedied within the time limit fixed.

*r.92.1(b)*

Where such a letter has not been provided but the non-compliance is overlooked, and the paper taken into account international procedure, such non-compliance will be disregarded.

*r.92.1(c)*

#### Language of letters and documents

3–337

Any letter or document submitted by the applicant to an International Searching or Preliminary Examining Authority must be in the same language as the application to which it relates except that:

*r.92.2(a)(b)*

(a) where a translation of the international application has been submitted under r.23.1(b) (for international search) or r.55.2 (for international preliminary examination), the language of such a translation must be used in the letter or document;

(b) any letter submitted to an International Searching or Preliminary Examining Authority may be in any other language provided such an Authority authorises the use of that language;

(c) the demand must be in the language specified in r.55.1; and

(d) amendments must be in the language specified in r.66.9.

Any letter from the applicant to the International Bureau and any letter or notification from the International Bureau to the applicant or any national office must be in English or French.

*r.92.2(d)(e)*

#### Form of subsequently filed documents

3–338

Rules 10 (terminology and signs) and 11.1–11.13 (physical requirements) apply to any document (for example corrected pages, amended claims, translations) submitted after the filing of the international application.

*r.11.14*

| | |
|---|---|
| **3–339** | ***The use of telegraph, teleprinter, facsimile to transmit subsequently filed documents*** |
| r.92.4(a)(h) | Notwithstanding r.11.14 (rules for documents filed later than the application) and r.92.1(a) (any paper to be accompanied by a letter), any document filed subsequent to the filing of the international application or correspondence relating thereto may be transmitted, if feasible, by telegraph, teleprinter, facsimile or other like means of communication resulting in the filing of a printed or written document provided that no national office or intergovernmental organisation is obliged to receive a document submitted in this way unless it has notified the International Bureau to the effect that it will and such information has been published in the Gazette. |
| r.92.4(c) | Where such means are used to transmit a document and part or all of the document is not received or is illegible on receipt, it will be treated as not received to the extent that it is not received or illegible. The relevant national office or intergovernmental organisation must promptly inform the applicant accordingly. |
| r.92.4(d)–(g) | Where such means are used to transmit a document, any national office or intergovernmental organisation may require: |

    (a) that the original and an accompanying letter identifying the earlier transmission be forwarded within 14 days of such transmission, provided that such a requirement has been notified to the International Bureau (specifying whether the requirement extends to all or only certain kinds of documents) and published in the Gazette. Where the original is not so forwarded, the relevant office or organisation may, depending on the kind of document involved, and having regard to r.11 (physical requirements) and r.26.3 (checking of physical requirements):

        (i) waive the requirement; or
        (ii) invite the applicant to forward the original within a reasonable time limit fixed in the invitation; or
        (iii) where the document transmitted contains defects or shows that the original contains defects warranting an invitation to correct, issue such an invitation instead or in addition to (a) or (b).

    (b) even where the forwarding of an original is not required as specified under (a), but the relevant office or organisation considers it necessary to receive the original nevertheless, that the applicant forwards the original within a reasonable time limit fixed in the invitation.

| | |
|---|---|
| r.92.4(g) | Where the applicant fails to comply with an invitation under (a)(ii) or (b), then if the document is a document subsequent to an international application, that document will be considered as not having been submitted. |
| r.92.4(b) | A signature appearing on a document transmitted by facsimile will be recognised for the purposes of the PCT and its Regulations as a proper signature. |
| [2005] O.J. 41 | Subsequent documents may be filed by fax at the EPO but not by telegraph or teleprinter. Confirmation is still necessary, in contrast with the procedure for a European application where it is no longer routinely required. |
| **3–340** | ***The use of electronic means to transmit subsequently filed documents*** |
| r.89*bis*.2 | Documents and correspondence relating to an international application may be filed and processed in electronic form or by electronic means (in accordance with the Administrative Instructions) but Receiving Offices must also permit the filing of such documents and correspondence on paper. |
| r.89*bis*.2 | The PCT Regulations apply equally to documents and correspondence filed electronically, subject to any special provisions of the Administrative Instructions which set out the requirements for the filing and processing of documents and correspondence filed wholly or partly in electronic form including, but not limited to: |

(a) acknowledgement of receipt;

(b) physical requirements;

(c) consequences of not complying with the physical requirements;

(d) signature of documents;

(e) means of authentication of documents;

(f) means of authentication of the identity of parties communicating with offices and authorities; and

(g) language-specific provisions.

No national office or intergovernmental organisation is required to receive or process documents and correspondence filed electronically unless it has notified the International Bureau that it is so prepared to do according to the provisions of the Administrative Instructions. Such notification will be published by the International Bureau in the Gazette. Having issued such notification, a Receiving Office may not refuse to process documents and correspondence filed electronically which comply with the requirements of the Administrative Instructions.  r.89*bis*.2

Transmittal of documents, notifications, communications or correspondence between one national office or intergovernmental organisation and another may, if both sender and receiver agree, be effected in electronic form or by electronic means.  r.89*bis*.3

Any office or intergovernmental organisation may provide that, where a document relating to an international application is filed on paper, a copy thereof in electronic form, in accordance with the Administrative Instructions, may be furnished by the applicant.  r.89*ter*

See Part 7 and Annex F.  AdminInst

See [2003] O.J. 609. No document subsequent to the application may be filed electronically where the EPO acts as Receiving Office, international searching or international preliminary examining authority.  O.J.

## Withdrawal of an international application, a designation, an election, a demand or a priority claim

### *Withdrawal of an international application*  3–341

An international application may be withdrawn by the applicant at any time prior to the expiration of 30 months from the priority date.  r.90*bis*.1(a)

Such withdrawal is effected by submission of a notice addressed by the applicant to any of the International Bureau, the Receiving Office or (where Art.39(1) applies) the International Preliminary Examining Authority and is effective on receipt.  r.90*bis*.1(b)

Such a withdrawal must be signed by the applicant, or all the applicants when there is more than one. A common representative under r.90.2(b) is not entitled to sign on behalf of another applicant. However, where two or more applicants have filed an international application designating a state whose national law requires that national applications be filed by the inventor(s) and where an inventor-applicant for that state could not be found or reached after diligent effort, that applicant's signature may be omitted if at least one applicant signs it and:  r.90*bis*.5

(a) a statement is furnished explaining, to the satisfaction of the Receiving Office, International Bureau or International Preliminary Examining Authority (as the case may be), the lack of the applicant's signature; or

(b) the applicant concerned did not sign the request but the requirements of r.4.15(b) were complied with.

| | |
|---|---|
| r.90.4/r.90.5 | A separate power of attorney or a copy of a general power of attorney must be submitted to the relevant authority where an agent or common representative submits a notice of withdrawal under r.90*bis*.1 to r.90*bis*.4. |
| r.90*bis*.1(c) | A withdrawal will have the effect of preventing international publication of the application if the notice of withdrawal reaches the International Bureau (from the applicant or via the Receiving Office or International Preliminary Examining Authority) before the technical preparations for publication have been completed. |
| r.90*bis*.6(b) | International processing of the application will be discontinued. |
| r.90*bis*.6(a) | Withdrawal of the application will have no effect in any designated or elected office where the processing or examination of the international application has already started under Art.23(2) or Art.40(2) (on the express request of the applicant). |

### 3–342  Withdrawal of a designation

| | |
|---|---|
| r.90*bis*.2(a) | The designation of any state may be withdrawn by the applicant at any time prior to the expiration of 30 months from the priority date. |
| r.90*bis*.2(d) | Such withdrawal is effected by submission of a notice addressed by the applicant to any of the International Bureau, the Receiving Office or (where Art.39(1) applies) the International Preliminary Examining Authority and is effective on receipt. |
| r.90*bis*.5 | The requirement for the withdrawal of a designation to be signed is identical to the requirement for a withdrawal of the application to be signed (see above). |
| r.90.4/r.90.5 | A separate power of attorney or a copy of a general power of attorney must be submitted to the relevant authority where an agent or common representative submits a notice of withdrawal under r.90*bis*.1 to r.90*bis*.4. |
| r.90*bis*.2(a) | Withdrawal of the designation of an elected state entails withdrawal of the election of that state as well under r.90*bis*.4. |
| r.90*bis*.2(c) | Withdrawal of the designation of all states is treated as withdrawal of the international application under r.90*bis*.1. |
| r.90*bis*.2(b) | Withdrawal of the designation of a state which has been designated for the purpose of obtaining a national and a regional patent will be taken to mean withdrawal only of the designation for the purpose of obtaining a national patent unless otherwise indicated. |
| r.90*bis*.2(e) | Where a designation is withdrawn, that designation will not be included in the international publication if the notice of withdrawal reaches the International Bureau (from the applicant or via the Receiving Office or International Preliminary Examining Authority) before the technical preparations for publication have been completed. |
| r.90*bis*.6(a) | Withdrawal of a designation will have no effect in any designated or elected office where the processing or examination of the international application has already started under Art.23(2) or Art.40(2) (on the express request of the applicant). |

### 3–343  Withdrawal of a priority claim

| | |
|---|---|
| r.90*bis*.3(a) | A priority claim made under Art.8(1) may be withdrawn by the applicant at any time prior to the expiration of 30 months from the priority date. |
| r.90*bis*.3(c) | Such withdrawal is effected by submission of a notice addressed by the applicant to any of the International Bureau, the Receiving Office or (where Art.39(1) applies) the International Preliminary Examining Authority and is effective on receipt. |

The requirement for the withdrawal of a priority claim to be signed is identical to the requirement for a withdrawal of the application to be signed (see above). r.90*bis*.5

A separate power of attorney or a copy of a general power of attorney must be submitted to the relevant authority where an agent or common representative submits a notice of withdrawal under r.90*bis*.1 to r.90*bis*.4. r.90.4/r.90.5

Where the international application contains more than one priority claim, one or more or all of them may be withdrawn. r.90*bis*.3(b)

Where the withdrawal of a priority claim changes the priority date, time limits starting on the priority date which have not already expired may be recalculated from the new priority date with the proviso that the International Bureau may nevertheless publish the application 18 months from original priority under Art.21(2)(a) if the withdrawal is received by the International Bureau after the technical preparations for publication are complete. r.90*bis*.3(d)(e)

Withdrawal of a priority claim has no effect in any designated or elected office where the processing or examination of the international application has already started under Art.23(2) or Art.40(2) (on the express request of the applicant). r.90*bis*.6(a)

## *Withdrawal of the demand or of elections* 3–344

The applicant may withdraw any or all elections. Art.37(1)

The demand, or any or all elections, may be withdrawn by the applicant at any time prior to the expiry of 30 months from the priority date. r.90*bis*.4(a)

The withdrawal of an election must be notified to the International Bureau. Art.37(3)(a)

Such a withdrawal is effective on receipt. r.90*bis*.4(b)

Such a withdrawal submitted to the International Preliminary Examining Authority will be date-stamped by that Authority and forwarded promptly to the International Bureau and its date of submission to the International Bureau will be considered to be the date so marked. r.90*bis*.4(c)

Such a withdrawal must be signed by the applicant, or all the applicants when there is more than one. A common representative under r.90.2(b) is not entitled to sign on behalf of another applicant. However, where two or more applicants have filed an international application designating a state whose national law requires that national applications be filed by the inventor(s) and where and inventor-applicant for that state could not be found or reached after diligent effort, that applicant's signature may be omitted if at least one applicant signs it and: r.90*bis*.5

(a) a statement is furnished explaining, to the satisfaction of the office, Bureau or Authority (as the case may be), the lack of the applicant's signature; or

(b) in the case of the withdrawal of a demand or election(s), the applicant concerned did not sign the demand but the requirements of r.53.8(b) were complied with.

A separate power of attorney or a copy of a general power of attorney must be submitted to the relevant authority where an agent or common representative submits a notice of withdrawal under r.90*bis*.1 to r.90*bis*.4. r.90.4/r.90.5

The International Bureau will notify the elected offices concerned and the International Preliminary Examining Authority. Art.37(3)(b)

If the election of all states is withdrawn then the demand will be considered withdrawn. Art.37(2)

| | |
|---|---|
| r.90bis.6(c) | Where the demand or all the elections are withdrawn, the processing of the application by the International Preliminary Examining Authority will be discontinued. |
| Art.37(4) | Withdrawal of the demand or the election of a Contracting State will, unless the national law of that state provides otherwise, be considered withdrawal of the international application, as far as that state is concerned, unless it is effected prior to the expiration of the applicable time limit under Art.22 (usually 30 months). National law may require that the applicant supply the national office with a copy of the international application, any prescribed translation and the national fee within the said time limit for this proviso to apply. |
| r.90bis.7 | Any such provision of national law must be notified by the relevant Contracting State to the International Bureau in writing and the International Bureau will publish such information in the Gazette. It has effect in respect of international applications filed more than one month after the date of such publication. |
| r.90bis.6(a) | Withdrawal of the demand or an election will have no effect in any designated or elected office where the processing or examination of the international application has already started under Art.23(2) or Art.40(2) (on the express request of the applicant). |

### 3–345 Recordal of changes concerning an applicant, inventor, agent or common representative by the International Bureau

r.92bis

On the request of the Receiving Office or the applicant, the International Bureau will record changes in the following indications appearing in the request or the demand:

(a) the person, name, residence, nationality or address of the applicant; and

(b) the person, name or address of the agent, common representative or inventor;

unless it receives such a request after the expiry of 30 months from the priority date.

### 3–346 Notification by national offices and intergovernmental organisations

r.92.3

Any document or letter sent by a national office or intergovernmental organisation and constituting an event from the date of which any time limit under the PCT and its Regulations commences must be sent by air mail except that:

(a) surface mail may be used when it normally arrives within two days of mailing; and

(b) surface mail may be used where air mail is not available.

### 3–347 Schedule of fees

r.96

The schedule of fees is annexed to, and forms an integral part of, the Regulations under the PCT. It contains the amounts of the fees due under r.15 and r.57 expressed in Swiss currency.

## 15. INFORMATION MADE AVAILABLE BY THE INTERNATIONAL AUTHORITIES AND DESIGNATED/ELECTED OFFICES

### 3–348 Confidential nature of the international application before its publication

Art.30(1)

The International Bureau and the International Searching Authorities may not allow access by any person or authority to the international application before its publication, unless requested or authorised by the applicant, except in regard to any transmittal to the competent International Searching Authority or any transmittal to a designated office under Art.13 and Art.20.

No national office or Receiving Office may allow access to the international application by third parties (except for transmittals under Art.12(1)), unless requested or authorised by the applicant, before the earlier of:   Art.30(2)(3)

(a) the date of international publication; or

(b) the date of receipt of the communication of the international application under Art.20; or

(c) the date of receipt of a copy of the international application under Art.22;

though this does not prevent any national office from informing third parties that it has been designated or from publishing this fact as long as the information conveyed is no more than (i) the identification of the Receiving Office, (ii) the name of the applicant, (iii) the international filing date, (iv) the international application number and (v) the title of the invention. A national office may also allow access by judicial authorities at an earlier date.

"Access" covers any means by which third parties may acquire cognisance, including individual communication and general publication provided that no national office may generally publish an international application or its translation before the international publication or the expiry of 20 months from the priority date, whichever is earlier.   Art.30(4)

## Confidential nature of the written opinion of the International Searching Authority and related documents

**3–349**

The International Bureau and the International Searching Authority may not, unless requested or authorised by the applicant, allow access by any person or authority before the expiration of 30 months from the priority date:   r.44*ter*.1(a)

(i) to the written opinion established under r.43*bis*.1, to any translation thereof prepared under r.44*bis*.3(d) or to any written observations on such a translation sent by the applicant under r.44*bis*.4;

(ii) if a report is issued under r.44*bis*.1, to that report, to any translation of it prepared under r.44*bis*.3(b) or to any written observations on that translation sent by the applicant under r.44*bis*.4.

If the applicant does not request international preliminary examination, so that a report is issued under r.44bis.1, the report and any comments made by the applicant on the written opinion of the International Searching Authority are made available to the public (although not formally published in the way that the search and pamphlet are).

For these purposes, "access" covers any means by which third parties may acquire cognizance, including individual communication and general publication.   r.44*ter*.1(b)

## Confidential nature of international preliminary examination

**3–350**

Neither the International Bureau or the International Preliminary Examining Authority may, unless requested or authorised by the applicant, allow access to any file of the examination by any person or authority at any time except by the elected offices once the International Preliminary Examination Report has been established.   Art.38(1)

"Access" is as defined by Art.30(4) and covers any means by which third parties may acquire cognisance, including individual communication and general publication, provided that no national office generally publishes an international application or its translation before the international publication or 20 months from the priority date, whichever is sooner.

Art.38(2)

Subject Art.38(1) (above), Art.36(1) (International Preliminary Examination Report to be transmitted to the applicant and the International Bureau), Art.36(3) (International Preliminary Examination Report, translation and annexes to be transmitted by the International Bureau to each elected office) and Art.37(3)(b) (relevant national offices notified of the withdrawal of their election) neither the International Bureau or the International Preliminary Examining Authority may, unless requested or authorised by the applicant, give information on the issuance or non-issuance of an International Preliminary Examination Report or on the withdrawal or non-withdrawal of the demand or of any election.

**Records and files—keeping them and allowing access to them**

3–351

*Obligation for international authorities to keep files*

r.93

The following records will be kept, optionally as photographic, electronic or other reproductions as long as such a reproduction allows the obligations of r.93 to be met.

| Organisation | Document | How long to be kept |
| --- | --- | --- |
| Receiving Office | Records relating to each international application or purported application, including the home copy. | At least 10 years from the filing date (or where none is accorded, the date of receipt). |
| International Bureau | The file relating to each international application (including the record copy). | At least 30 years from the date of receipt of the record copy. |
| | The basic records of the Bureau. | Indefinitely. |
| International Searching and Preliminary Examining Authorities | The file relating to each international application it receives. | At least 10 years from the filing date. |

## 15. Information Made Available by the International Authorities and Designated/Electoral Offices

### Access allowed to files (applications filed on or after July 1, 1998)

3–352

Subject to the reimbursement of the cost of the service, the following will be made available:

r.94

| Holder of document | Documents made available | Made available to | Condition |
|---|---|---|---|
| International Bureau | Any document contained in the file. | The applicant or anybody authorised by the applicant. | None |
| International Bureau | Any document contained in the file. | Any person | Not before international publication and subject to Art.38 (confidential nature of International Preliminary Examination) and r.44*ter*.1 (confidential nature of the written opinion of the International Searching Authority). |
| International Bureau | International preliminary examination report.* | Any person on behalf of an elected office.* | As above. Details of any request to be published in the Gazette.* |
| International Preliminary Examining Authority | Any document contained in the file. | The applicant, anybody authorised by the applicant or any elected office once the International Preliminary Examination Report has been established. | None |
| Elected office | Any document relating to the international application (including international preliminary examination) contained in the file. | Any third party that would be allowed access to the file of a national application under national law. | To the same extent as allowed by national law and not before international publication. |

This provision is in force from January 1, 2004 and applies to the furnishing of copies of the International Preliminary Examination Report in respect of any international application filed before, on or after that date.

See under *Art.150*. Where the EPO has acts as International Preliminary Examining Authority, the International Preliminary Examination Report has been established, and the EPO is an elected office, documents relating to international preliminary examination will be made available for third party access ([1999] O.J. 329 and [2003] O.J. 382).

AnReg

### Access allowed to files (applications filed before July 1, 1998)

3–353

At the request of the applicant or any person authorised by the applicant, the International Bureau and the International Preliminary Examining Authority will furnish, subject to reimbursement of the cost of the service, copies of any document contained in the file of the applicant's international application or purported international application.

r.94

### Availability of the priority document from the International Bureau

3–354

Copies of the priority document may not be made available to the public by the International Bureau prior to international publication. After publication, they may be made available to anybody, subject to a fee, unless, prior to publication, the application has been withdrawn or the relevant priority claim has been withdrawn or has

r.17.2(b)(c)

been considered not to have been made under r.26*bis*.2 (b) (information in the request (r.4.10) and on the priority document don't agree).

## 3–355 Availability of translations required by national offices

r.95

At the request of the International Bureau, any designated or elected office will provide it with a copy of the translation of the international application furnished by the applicant to that office and the International Bureau may furnish to any person copies of such a translation upon request and subject to the reimbursement of the cost.

## 3–356 Availability of citations in the international search report from the International Searching Authority

Art.20(3)/r.44

The International Searching Authority will supply copies of documents cited in the international search report to any designated office or the applicant when requested by such an office or the applicant at any time during seven years from the international filing date of the corresponding application. A fee for preparing and mailing the copies may be requested, the amount of which will be fixed in the agreement under Art.16(3)(b) between the International Searching Authority and the International Bureau. The Searching Authority may use an agency to perform this function if it wishes.

## 3–357 Availability of citations in the International Preliminary Examination Report from the International Preliminary Examining Authority

Art.36(4)/r.71.2

At the request of an elected office or the applicant, within seven years from the filing date of the relevant application, the International Preliminary Examining Authority will supply copies of any document cited in the international preliminary examination report which was not cited in the international search report. A fee may be claimed by the International Preliminary Examining Authority to the office or applicant who makes such a request covering the cost of preparing and mailing the copies, the level of which will be set in the agreement under Art.32(2) between the International Preliminary Examining Authority and the International Bureau. Such an Authority may perform these obligations through another agency responsible to it.

# INDEX

(*References are to paragraph numbers*)

**Abstract**
  European Patent Convention (EPC),
    contents, 2–104
    drawings, 2–104
    filing, 2–142
    length, 2–104
    purpose, 2–104
    requirement, 2–104
  Patent Co-operation Treaty (PCT), 3–052

**Additional fee.** *See* **Renewal fees**

**Administrative and legal co-operation**, 2–448

**Administrative Council**
  language, 2–366
  select committee, 2–452

**Aesthetic creations**
  European Patent Convention (EPC), 2–026

**Agriculture**
  industrial application, 2–037

**Amendment**
  European Patent Convention (EPC)
    adding subject matter, 2–316, 2–317
    after receipt of search report, 2–313
    before receipt of search report, 2–312
    errors, correction of, 2–322–2–328
    extending protection conferred by patent, amendment not, 2–319–2–320
    form, 2–315
    opposition proceedings, 2–221
    receipt of first examination report, after, 2–314
    unsearched subject matter, claims not relating to, 2–318
  Patent Co-operation Treaty (PCT)
    added subject matter, 3–145
    form, 3–143
    language, 3–142
    notification to IPEA, 3–146
    statement accompanying, 3–144
    when can applicant amend claims, 3–140
    where should amendments be filed, 3–141

**Amino acid sequences**
  application relating to, 2–130, 3–082, 3–127, 3–248, 3–262

**Animals**
  biotechnological inventions, 2–034
  examining the application, 3–247
  modifying the genetic identity of, 2–032
  non-human, 1–199
  not obliged to examine, 3–247
  not required to search, 3–128
  processes for the production of, 2–035
  second medical use, 2–049

**Animal varieties**
  European Patent Convention (EPC), 2–034

**Appeals**
  European Patent Convention (EPC),
    admissibility, 2–251
    binding effect of decision on remittal, 2–264
    content of decision, 2–265
    content of the notice of, 2–247
    decision, discretion to remit to the first instance, 2–263
    decisions which can be appealed, 2–243
    Enlarged Board of Appeal, 2–269
    examination,
      accelerated procedure, 2–262
      amendment during proceedings, 2–261
      generally, 2–251, 2–253
      impartiality of Board of Appeal, 2–259
      intervention of assumed infringer possible, 2–257
      introduction of new grounds or claims, 2–254, 2–255
      new grounds or claims, 2–254, 2–255
      procedure, 2–253
      *reformatio in peius*, 2–256
      request for revocation by proprietor, 2–260
    filing of grounds, 2–249
    form of decision, 2–265
    interlocutory revision, 2–252
    lack of unity, 3–130, 3–253
    language of notice, 2–250
    nature of proceedings, 2–242
    party to appeal, 2–245
    persons entitled to, 2–245
    reimbursement of appeal fee, 2–267
    request for information on national application, 2–266
    time limit and form of appeal, 2–246
    suspensive effect on decision appealed, 2–244
    who may appeal, 2–245
    withdrawal, 2–268, 2–379

**Appeal fees**
  additional fees, 3–130, 3–253
  reduction in, 2–250
  reimbursement, 2–252, 2–267

**Applicant**
  claims against the, 2–334
  comments by the, during the examination procedure, 2–176
  death or legal incapacity of the, 1–168, 2–307
  details of the, 2–075
  identity, 1–199, 2–134
  preserving the rights of, 1–162
  residence, 2–075

**Applicant**—cont.
  status of, 1–199, 1–207
  student as, 1–212
**Applicants**
  different, 2–196, 3–008, 3–021
  joint 1–193–1–194, 2–435, 3–010, 3–213, 3–231
  multiple, 2–060, 3–008, 3–009, 3–222, 3–232, 3–330, 3–341, 3–344
**Application**
  amendment of the, 1–093
  describing the, 1–095
  entitled persons, 2–060
  replacement, 2–083
**Application documents**
  copies, number of, 2–118
  deficiencies, 2–140, 2–141, 2–142, 2–143, 2–144, 2–146
  filed subsequently, 2–141
  physical requirements, 2–141
  signature of, 2–086
  translations of, 2–117
**Applicable law**
  European Patent Convention (EPC), 2–391
**Appointment of employees**
  European Patent Office, 2–007
**Assignment**
  European Patent Convention (EPC), 2–389
**Associations**
  representation by, 2–356
**Authentic text**
  European Patent Convention (EPC), 2–434
**Authorisations**
  filing of, 1–161, 1–188, 2–351–2–356
**Awarding of costs.** *See* **Costs**

**Basis of decisions**, 2–406
**Biotechnological inventions**
  biological material, deposit of
    Patent Co-operation Treaty (PCT), 3–083
  European Patent Convention (EPC)
    deposit of biological material, 2–131
    sequence listings, 2–130
  Patent Co-operation Treaty (PCT)
    biological material, deposit of, 3–083
    sequence listings, 3–082
  sequence listings
    European Patent Convention (EPC), 2–130
    Patent Co-operation Treaty (PCT), 3–082
**BIRPI**, 3–007
**Bulletin**
  European Patent Office, 2–447

**Chemistry**
  Paper A. *See* **Paper A (Chemistry); Paper B (Chemistry)**
**Claims**
  clarity
    European Patent Convention (EPC), 2–094
    Patent Co-operation Treaty (PCT), 3–043

**Claims**—cont.
  conciseness
    European Patent Convention (EPC), 2–094
    Patent Co-operation Treaty (PCT), 3–043
  defining matter client seeking to protect
    European Patent Convention (EPC), 2–095
    Patent Co-operation Treaty (PCT), 3–044
  European Patent Convention (EPC)
    clarity, 2–094
    conciseness, 2–094
    defining matter client seeking to protect, 2–095
    disclaimers, 2–102
    fees, 2–127, 2–128
    figures, references to signs in, 2–100
    functional features, 2–103
    number of claims allowed, 2–097
    numbering claims, 2–098
    omnibus claims, 2–099
    requirements, 2–093
    support, 2–094
    two-part form required, where, 2–096
    type of claims allowed, 2–097
    unity of invention, 2–101
  figures, references to signs in,
    European Patent Convention (EPC), 2–100
    Patent Co-operation Treaty (PCT), 3–049
  functional features under EPC, 2–103
  number of claims allowed,
    European Patent Convention (EPC), 2–097
    Patent Co-operation Treaty (PCT), 3–046
  omnibus claims,
    European Patent Convention (EPC), 2–099
    Patent Co-operation Treaty (PCT), 3–048
  Patent Co-operation Treaty (PCT)
    clarity, 3–043
    conciseness, 3–043
    defining subject matter client seeking to protect, 3–044
    figures, references to signs in, 3–049
    number of claims, 3–046
    numbering claims, 3–047
    omnibus claims, 3–048
    requirements, 3–042–3–051
    support, 3–043
    two-part form required, where, 3–045
    type of claims, 3–046
    unity of invention, 3–051
    utility model, 3–050
  requirements,
    European Patent Convention (EPC), 2–093
    Patent Co-operation Treaty (PCT), 3–042–3–051
  support
    European Patent Convention (EPC), 2–094
    Patent Co-operation Treaty (PCT), 3–043
  two-part form required, where
    European Patent Convention (EPC), 2–096
    Patent Co-operation Treaty (PCT), 3–045
  type of claims allowed
    European Patent Convention (EPC), 2–097
    Patent Co-operation Treaty (PCT), 3–046

**Claims**—*cont.*
  unity of invention,
    European Patent Convention (EPC), 2–101
    Patent Co-operation Treaty (PCT), 3–051
  utility model under PCT, 3–050
**Computer program**
  European Patent Convention (EPC), 2–030
**Conversion**
  circumstances permitting, 2–277
  fee for, 2–279
  into a national application, request for, 1–171, 2–279, 2–438
  publicity for, 2–281
  time limit for, 2–278
**Corrections**
  amendment,
    after receipt of first examination report, 2–314
    after receipt of search 2–313
      before receipt of search, 2–312
      on entering national phase, 3–317, 3–281–3–283
  applicant, identity of, 2–114
  deciding body for, 2–327
  description, 2–323
  disclaimer, introduction of, 2–317
  discretion to permit, 2–192
  designation of the EPO, 3–027
  errors in decisions, 2–328
  errors in documents, 2–322
  examples of, 2–324
  missing drawing, 2–147
  permissible amendments during opposition, 2–221
  priority claim, of, 2–114
  proceedings pending, 2–326
  refusal of, 2–191
  text not acceptable to applicant, 2–191
**Costs**
  enforcement, 2–238
  fixing of costs, 2–015, 2–235–2–239

**Date of filing**
  not accorded, 2–135, 3–086
  requirement for, 2–134
**Death or legal incapacity**, 1–168, 2–307
**Decision**
  European Patent Office
    agreed text, 2–407
    auxiliary requests, 2–407
    basis, 2–406
    correction of errors, 2–413
    finality, 2–409
    form, 2–408
    identification, 2–411
    interlocutory decisions, 2–414
    loss of rights, obtaining after, 2–410
    notification, 2–412
    opportunity to comment on grounds/ evidence, parties having, 2–406
    reasons for, 1–063, 1–091, 1–111
    signature, 2–411

**Description**
  content,
    European Patent Convention (EPC), 2–091
    Patent Co-operation Treaty (PCT), 3–040
  European Patent Convention (EPC),
    content, 2–091
    order of presentation of content, 2–092
    requirements, 2–089
    sufficient disclosure, need for, 2–090
  order of presentation of content,
    European Patent Convention (EPC), 2–092
    Patent Co-operation Treaty (PCT), 3–041
  Patent Co-operation Treaty (PCT),
    content, 3–040
    order of presentation of content, 3–041
    requirements, 3–038–3–041
    sufficient disclosure, 3–039
  requirements,
    European Patent Convention (EPC), 2–089
    Patent Co-operation Treaty (PCT), 3–038–3–041
  sufficient disclosure,
    Patent Co-operation Treaty (PCT), 3–039
    requirements, 2–089
**Designation**
  fees, 1–198, 1–211, 2–126, 2–145, 3–199
  inventor, 2–077, 2–115, 2–146, 2–329, 2–330
  joint 2–455
  of Contracting States, 2–080, 2–166, 2–279
  withdrawal of, 2–374, 2–376
**Diagnostic methods**, 2–038
**Disclaimers**
  European Patent Convention (EPC), 2–102
  Paper A (Chemistry), 1–009
  Paper B (Chemistry), 1–093
  Paper B (Electricity/Mechanics), 1–114
**Discoveries**
  European Patent Convention (EPC), 2–024
  excluded from patentability, 2–024
**Divisional application**
  European Patent Convention (EPC),
    circumstances of filing, 2–070
    fees, 2–128
    filing date, 2–136
    indication of status, 2–082
    language, 2–123
    special requirements, 2–132
    where application files, 2–062
**Documents**
  effective dates of prior art documents, 1–132, 1–140
  excluded from file inspection, 2–443
  notification, 2–396, 2–398–2–404
  late-filed or missing, 2–147, 3–209
**Drawings**
  European Patent Convention (EPC),
    abstract, in, 2–104
    late filed, 2–147
  Patent Co-operation Treaty (PCT), 3–053

**Electricity/mechanics**. *See* **Paper A (Electricity/ mechanics)**; **Paper B (Electricity/mechanics)**

**Embryos**, 2–032
**Enlarged Board of Appeal**
  decisions and opinion of, 1–158, 1–161
**EPC.** *See* **European Patent Convention (EPC)**
**Errors, correction of**
  European Patent Convention (EPC)
    allowable corrections, 2–322, 2–324
    claims, 2–323
    competent body to decide, 2–327
    decisions, 2–328
    description, corrections to, 2–323
    drawings, 2–323
    non-allowable corrections, 2–324
    non-payment of fees, 2–325
    pending proceedings, 2–326
  Patent Co-operation Treaty (PCT)
    authorization, 3–324
    errors that may be corrected, 3–320
    initiation, 3–322
    language, 3–325
    procedure, 3–323
    that may not be corrected, 3–321
**European divisional application**
  designation of Contracting States, 2–080
**European patent application**
  added matter, 1–113
  application filed via PCT, 1–139
  entitlement to file a, 2–060
  independent claims, number of, 1–090
  regular, 1–198
**European Patent Convention (EPC).** *See also*
    **European Patent Office**; **European Patent Organisation**
  abstract,
    contents, 2–104
    drawings, 2–104
    filing, 2–142
    length, 2–104
    purpose, 2–104
    requirement, 2–104
  abusive disclosure exemption, 2–051
  Administrative Council,
    language, 2–366
    select committee, 2–452
  aesthetic creations, 2–026
  aims in drafting, 2–001
  amendment,
    adding subject matter, 2–316, 2–317
    after receipt of search report, 2–313
    before receipt of search report, 2–312
    errors, correction of, 2–322–2–328
    extending protection conferred by patent, amendment not, 2–319–2–320
    form, 2–315
    opposition proceedings, 2–221
    receipt of first examination report, after, 2–314
    unsearched subject matter, claims not relating to, 2–318
  animal varieties, 2–034
  appeals, 2–242–2–269

**European Patent Convention (EPC)**—*cont.*
  appeals—*cont.*
    admissibility, 2–251
    binding effect of decision on remittal, 2–264
    content of decision, 2–265
    decision,
      discretion to remit to the first instance, 2–263
    decision which can be appealed, 2–243
    Enlarged Board of Appeal, 2–269
    examination,
      accelerated procedure, 2–262
      amendment during proceedings, 2–261
      impartiality of Board of Appeal, 2–259
      intervention of assumed infringer possible, 2–257
      introduction of new grounds or claims, 2–254, 2–255
      new grounds or claims, 2–254, 2–255
      procedure, 2–253
      *reformation in pieus*, 2–256
      request for revocation by proprietor, 2–260
    filing of grounds, 2–249
    form of decision, 2–265
    interlocutory revision, 2–252
    language of notice, 2–250
    nature of proceedings, 2–242
    party to appeal, 2–245
    reimbursement of appeal fee, 2–267
    request for information on national applications, 2–266
    suspensive effect on decision appealed, 2–244
    who may appeal, 2–245
    withdrawal, 2–379
    withdrawal of appeal, 2–268
  applicable law, 2–391
  applicant having no right to European patent,
    calculation of time limits where proceedings resumed, 2–337
    EPO division responsible, 2–341
    jurisdiction of Contracting States, 2–334
    opposition, suspension during, 2–336
    partial transfer of right by virtue of final decision, 2–340
    remedies following final decision, 2–339
    resumption of proceedings, 2–335
    suspension during examination, 2–335
    suspension, no withdrawal during, 2–338
  assignment, 2–389
  authentic text, 2–434
  biotechnical inventions
    deposit of biological material, 2–131
    sequence listings, 2–130
  claims,
    clarity, 2–094
    conciseness, 2–094
    defining matter client seeking to protect, 2–095
    disclaimers, 2–102
    figures, references to signs in, 2–100
    functional features, 2–103
    number of claims allowed, 2–097

**European Patent Convention (EPC)**—*cont.*
  claims—*cont.*
    numbering claims, 2–098
    omnibus claims, 2–099
    requirement, 2–093
    support, 2–094
    two-part form required, where, 2–096
    type of claims allowed, 2–097
    unity of invention, 2–101
  collision of European and national patents, 2–284
  computer program, 2–030
  constitution of rights, 2–388
  contracting states, 2–080
  contractual licensing, 2–390
  conversion of European patent into national patent application, 2–277–2–281
  decisions,
    basis, 2–406
  description,
    content, 2–091
    order of presentation of content, 2–092
    requirement, 2–089
    sufficient disclosure, need for, 2–090
  designation of inventor, 2–115
    withdrawal, 2–376
  disclaimers, 2–102
  discoveries, 2–024
  divisional application
    circumstances of filing, 2–070
    fees, 2–128
    filing date, 2–136
    indication of status, 2–082
    language, 2–123
    special requirements, 2–132
    where application filed, 2–062
  drawings, 2–105
    abstract, in, 2–104
    late filed, 2–147
  errors, correction of,
    allowable correction, 2–322, 2–324
    claims, 2–323
    competent body to decide, 2–327
    decisions, 2–328
    description, corrections to, 2–323
    drawings, 2–323
    non-allowable correction, 2–324
    non-payment of fees, 2–325
    pending proceedings, 2–326
  examination on filing,
    abstracts, 2–142
    content of request, 2–143
    designation fees, 2–145
    designation of inventor, 2–146
    divisional application, 2–136
    fees paid, determination whether, 2–137
    filing date cannot be accorded, procedure where, 2–135
    filing date, requirements for, 2–134
    formal requirements, examination of, 2–139
    late filed drawings, 2–147

**European Patent Convention (EPC)**—*cont.*
  examination on filing—*cont.*
    physical requirements, 2–141
    priority claims, 2–144
    procedure on receipt of new application, 2–133
    prohibited matter, 2–149
    representation, 2–140
    title of invention, 2–148
    translations filed, determination whether, 2–138
  exhibition exemption, 2–052
  expenditure for carrying out special tasks, 2–453
  extension, 2–081
  extension states, list, 2–081
  fees, 2–124
    adoption of rules, 2–456
    cheque payment, 2–463
    claims, 2–127
    currency, 2–461
    designation, 2–126
    determination whether paid, 2–137
    divisional applications, 2–128
    due dates, 2–460
    establishing what payment is for, 2–466
    filing, 2–125
    insignificant amounts, refund of, 2–469
    insufficient amount paid, 2–468
    methods of payment, 2–461–2–464
    opposition, 2–205
    payment or transfer to EPO bank account or Giro account, 2–462
    President, role of, 2–458
    publication in Journal of amounts, 2–459
    purpose of rules, 2–457
    refunds, 2–467
    renewal. *See* **Renewal fees**
    replacement applications, 2–129
    rules, 2–456–2–469
    safeguards where payment not made in time, 2–465
    search, 2–125
    who may make, 2–467
  filing application,
    additional copies of citations, 2–085
    applicants details, 2–075
    claims. *See* **Claims** *above*
    Contracting State language, 2–121
    correction of request, 2–088
    designation of inventor, 2–077
    designations, 2–080, 2–081
    divisional application,
      circumstances of filing, 2–070
      fees, 2–128
      indication of status, 2–082
      language, 2–123
      where filed, 2–062
    documents filed subsequently,
      content, 2–371
      copies, 2–373
      form, 2–371
      language, 2–370
      means of communication, 2–369

**European Patent Convention (EPC)**—*cont.*
  filing application—*cont.*
    documents filed subsequently—*cont.*
      signature, 2–372
      where to file, 2–368
    entitlement, 2–060
    examination on filing. *See* **Examination on filing** *above*
    extension of European patent, 2–081
    fees
      claims, 2–127
      designation, 2–126
      divisional applications, 2–128
      filing, 2–125
      replacement applications, 2–129
      search, 2–125
    figures of drawings to be published with abstract, 2–084
    filing date, 2–134
    form, 2–073
    language,
      contracting state, 2–121
      divisional application, 2–123
      EPO official language, 2–120
      national office, 2–122
      replacement application, 2–123
    list of documents accompanying request, 2–087
    manner of filing,
      electronic, 2–068
      fax, 2–067
      hand, 2–066
      other means, 2–069
      post, 2–066
    national office, 2–122
    number of copies to be filed, 2–118
    petition for grant, 2–074
    physical requirements, 2–119
    priority claim, 2–079
    registration of European patent, 2–081
    replacement applications, 2–083, 2–123, 2–129
    representative's details, 2–076
    request, 2–072
    requirements of application, 2–071–2–076
    restrictions under national law, 2–064
    signature, 2–086
    specified form, 2–073
    time limit for forwarding application to EPO, 2–065
    title of the invention, 2–078
    translations, 2–117, 2–121
    where filed,
      divisional application, 2–062
      regular application, 2–061
      replacement application, 2–063
  grant procedure,
    approval of text for grant, 2–188
    certificate, 2–197
    circumstance of grant, 2–187
    communication from Examining Division, 2–188

**European Patent Convention (EPC)**—*cont.*
  grant procedure—*cont.*
    consequences of not responding to R.51(4) communication, 2–189
    date grant takes effect, 2–194
    decision, 2–193
    different applicants, grant to, 2–196
    implicit approval of text, 2–190
    oral proceedings after approval, 2–192
    payment of fees, 2–190
    proposed text not acceptable to applicant, 2–191
    publication of granted patent, 2–195
    translations, filing, 2–190
    validation in designated states, 2–198
  industrial application, inventions capable of,
    definition of industrial application, 2–037
    diagnostic exclusion, 2–038–2–039
    diagnostic method practiced on the human or animal body, 2–041
    method of treatment, 2–038–2–039
    surgery, method of treatment of the human or animal body by, 2–040
    therapy, method of treatment of the human or animal body by, 2–039
  interpretation principles, 2–367
  invention,
    abusive disclosure exemption, 2–051
    aesthetic creations, 2–026
    animal varieties, 2–034
    barred from patentability, 2–032–2–035
    computer program, 2–030
    discoveries, 2–024
    earlier publications, 2–043
    essentially biological processes, 2–035
    exhibition exemption, 2–052
    first medical use, 2–048
    industrial application, capable of, 2–037–2–041
    inventive step. *See* **Inventive step**
    made available to the public,
      judging content of, 2–046
      prejudicial to novelty, 2–047
    mathematical methods, 2–025
    medical use,
      first, 2–048
      second, 2–049
    morality exemption, 2–032
    new, 2–042–2–053. *See also* **New inventions**
    patentable, 2–036
    plant varieties, 2–033
    presentation of information, 2–031
    scheme, rule or method for doing business, 2–029
    scheme, rule or method for performing a mental act, 2–027
    scheme, rule or method for playing games, 2–028
    scientific theories, 2–025
    second medical use, 2–049
    second non-medical use, 2–050
    selection inventions, novelty of, 2–053
    state of the art, 2–043
    technical subject matter, 2–023

**European Patent Convention (EPC)**—*cont.*
  invention—*cont.*
    title, 2–148
  inventor,
    designation, 2–329, 2–330
    right to be mentioned, 2–329–2–332
    right to European patent, 2–333
  joint designation, 2–455
  language,
    Administrative Council, 2–366
    authentic text, 2–357
    Bulletin, 2–365
    certification of translated documents, 2–364
    contracting state language, 2–121
    divisional application, 2–123
    EPO official language, 2–120
    exceptions,
      oral proceedings, 2–363
      written procedures, 2–362
    filing application, 2–359
    national office, 2–122
    notice of appeal, 2–250
    Official Journal, 2–365
    official language, 2–358
    opposition, 2–206
    oral proceedings, 2–363
    proceedings, 2–360
    publication of application and search report, 2–165
    publications, 2–365
    Register entries, 2–365
    replacement application, 2–123
    request for examination, 2–175
    written procedures, 2–362
  made available to the public,
    judging the content, 2–046
    meaning, 2–045
    prejudicial to novelty, 2–047
  mathematical methods, 2–025
  morality exemption, 2–032
  national phase,
    authentic text, 2–287
    collision of European and national patents, 2–284
    conversion of European patent into national patent application, 2–277–2–281
    extent of protection, 2–275
    filing date, effect of, 2–270
    granted European patent, effect of, 2–272
    national utility models and certificates, effect of, 2–286
    published application, effect of, 2–271
    renewal fees, 2–285
    revocation during opposition, effect of, 2–274
    revocation of European patent in Contracting States, 2–282, 2–283
    technical opinion, request for, 2–288
    term of patent, 2–276
    translation, filing of, 2–273
  new, 2–042–2–053. *See also* **New inventions**

**European Patent Convention (EPC)**—*cont.*
  opposition,
    acceleration of proceedings, 2–226
    admissibility, 2–208
    beyond stated extent, 2–225
    change of proprietor through entitlement proceedings, 2–217
    communication of inadmissibility to proprietor, 2–212
    continuation of opposition by EPO, 2–223
    costs,
      enforcement of decision, 2–238
      no appeal solely on, 2–239
      registry to fix amount paid, 2–236
      rules for apportionment, 2–235
    deemed not to have been filed, opposition, 2–213
    deficiencies must be corrected, 2–210, 2–211
    designated states, application to all, 2–215
    different claims for different states, 2–228
    documents to file, 2–222
    examination of opposition, 2–208–2–213
    failed opposition, 2–231
    fee, 2–205
    filing, 2–200–2–206
    formalities, 2–209
    further searches, 2–227
    generally, 2–199
    grounds, 2–204
    intervention, 2–214
    language, 2–206
    lapsed patent, 2–207, 2–224
    opponent as party, 2–216
    parties, 2–216, 2–217
    partly successful opposition, 2–232–2–234
    permissible amendments, 2–221
    prejudicing the patent, 2–220
    procedure for examination, 2–218–2–229
    revocation where no text is approved, 2–229
    successful opposition, 2–230
    surrender of patent, 2–207
    surrendered patent, 2–224
    transfer of opposition to another party, 2–241
    transfer of patent during, 2–240
    withdrawal, 2–223, 2–378
  Patent Co-operation Treaty (PCT), relationship with, 3–334, 3–335
  patentable invention, 2–036
  petition, 2–074
  plant varieties, 2–033
  preamble, 2–001
  priority claim,
    applications used as basis, 2–110
    correction of claim, 2–114
    effect of priority right, 2–113
    filing claim, 2–111
    multiple priority claims, 2–112
    Paris Convention, 2–106
    procedure, 2–111
    same invention, in respect of, 2–109
    time limit, 2–108

**European Patent Convention (EPC)**—*cont.*
   priority claim—*cont.*
      who may make claim, 2–107
   priority claims,
      examination on filing, 2–144
      withdrawal, 2–377
   procedural law, 2–436
   prohibited matter, 2–116, 2–149
   publication of application and search report,
      communication to applicant, 2–168
      contents, 2–166
      excluded matter, 2–167
      form, 2–165
      language, 2–165
      refusal of application, 2–164
      timing, 2–163
      withdrawal of application, 2–164
   registration, 2–081
   registration of grant or transfer of licence, 2–393
   registration of transfer of application, 2–392
   renewal fees. *See* **Renewal fees**
   representation,
      associations, 2–356
      authorisation,
         consequences of not filing, 2–353
         content, 2–352
         form, 2–352
         requirement to file, 2–351
         termination, 2–354
         withdrawal, 2–354
      choice, 2–342, 2–343
      person having residence or principal place of business in Contracting State, 2–342
      person not having residence or principal place of business within Contracting State, 2–343
      professional representation. *See* **Professional representation**
      several representatives appointed, 2–355
      types, 2–342–2–344
   request for substantive examination,
      consequences of not requesting, 2–172
      extension of period, 2–177
      fee, 2–171
      filed before transmittal of search report, 2–176
      grace period, 2–173
      language, 2–175
      refund of examination fee, 2–174
      requirement, 2–169
      time limit, 2–170
      withdrawal, 2–170
   *restitutio in integrum*,
      conditions necessary, 2–299
      Contracting States, grant by, 2–306
      department qualified to decide on application, 2–304
      exclusion of certain time limits, 2–301
      grounds must be filed and fee paid, 2–303
      procedure for applying, 2–302
      third party rights may be awarded, 2–305
      who can file an application, 2–300

**European Patent Convention (EPC)**—*cont.*
   revocation of European patent in Contracting States
      grounds, 2–282
      partial, 2–283
   scientific theories, 2–025
   search,
      accelerated procedure, 2–157
      basis of search, 2–152
      cannot be established, where, 2–153
      commencement of search, 2–150
      conducting, 2–150–2–157
      definitive content of abstract, 2–155
      drawing up, 2–150–2–162
      fee, 2–154
      patent classification, 2–156
      purpose, 2–151
      scope of search, 2–151
      unity, application lacking, 2–154
   search report,
      chance to amend after receipt, 2–162
      content, 2–158
      definitive content of abstract, 2–161
      extended, 2–160
      language, 2–159
      publication, 2–163–2–168
      transmittal, 2–161
   selection inventions, novelty of, 2–053
   special agreements,
      expenditure for carrying out special tasks, 2–453
      joint designation, 2–455
      property, patent as object of, 2–454
      representation before special departments, 2–451
      select committee of Administrative Council, 2–452
      special departments of EPO, 2–450
      unitary patents, 2–449
   substantive examination
      procedure,
         accelerated, 2–184
         auxiliary requests, 2–181
         consolidation of proceedings, 2–183
         double patenting, 2–182
         formal written procedure, 2–178
         further searches, 2–180
         informal communications, 2–179
         request for information, 2–185
      refusal of application, 2–186
   technical opinion, request for, 2–288
   term, 2–276
   termination of financial obligations, 2–437
   third party observations, 2–394
   time limits,
      computation of units of time used, 2–289
      duration, 2–292
      excusal of missed time limit, 2–293
      extension,
         EPO ceasing to function properly, 2–297
         EPO not open for business, 2–294
         interruption of mail delivery, 2–295
         war, revolution or similar event, 2–296
      good faith principle, 2–311

**European Patent Convention (EPC)**—*cont.*
  time limits—*cont.*
    interruption of proceedings,
      circumstances, 2–307
      department responsible, 2–310
      resumption after, 2–308
      time limits, 2–309
    legitimate expectations, protection of, 2–311
    refusal, 2–298
  transactions relating to patent, 2–393
  transfer of rights, 2–388
  translations, 2–117, 2–121, 2–138
  unitary patents, 2–449
  unity, 2–435
  unity of invention, 2–101
  withdrawal,
    appeal, 2–379
    application, 2–374
    designation, 2–376
    opposition, 2–378
    part of subject matter of application, 2–375
    patent, 2–380
    priority claim, 2–377

**European Patent Institute**, 2–348

**European Patent Office**
  administrative structure, 2–011
  appointments, 2–007
  Boards of Appeal, 2–010
    adoption of rules of procedure, 2–021
    composition, 2–017
    enlarged, 2–019
    exclusion, 2–020, 2–022
    independence, 2–020
    members, 2–007
    objection, 2–022
    Presidium, 2–018
  Bulletin, 2–447
  classification, patent, 2–156
  decision,
    agreed text, 2–407
    auxiliary requests, 2–407
    basis, 2–406
    correction of errors, 2–413
    finality, 2–409
    form, 2–408
    identification, 2–411
    interlocutory decisions, 2–414
    loss of rights, obtaining after, 2–410
    notification, 2–412
    opportunity to comment on grounds/ evidence,
      parties having, 2–406
    signature, 2–411
  departments, 2–010
  disclosure of confidential information, 2–008
  disputes with Organisation ,2–009
  evidence,
    commissioning member of Examining/
      Opposition Division to examine evidence,
      2–429
    conservation, 2–432

**European Patent Convention (EPC)**—*cont.*
  evidence—*cont.*
    costs, 2–431
    decision to take, 2–426
    experts' opinion, 2–430
    forms of available evidence, 2–424
    minutes, 2–433
    own motion, of, 2–225
    principles for evaluation, 2–425
    procedure, 2–427, 2–428
  examination of its own motion, 2–415
  Examining Divisions, 2–010, 2–014
  information,
    Bulletin, 2–447
    exchange with national authorities/courts,
      2–448
    inspection of files, 2–442–2–445
    Official Journal, 2–446
    Register of European Patents,
      content, 2–438
      language, 2–441
      no entry prior to publication, 2–439
      open to public, 2–440
  inspection of files, 2–442–2–445
  language, 2–358
  late submission of facts and evidence, 2–416
  Legal Division, 2–010, 2–016
  location, 2–005
  members, 2–017
  notification,
    central industrial property office of Contracting
      State, 2–402
    deemed, 2–398
    form, 2–396
    hand delivery, 2–399
    identification, 2–405
    irregularities, 2–403
    loss of rights, 2–404
    person to whom made, 2–397
    postal, 2–398
    public notice, 2–400
    signatures, 2–405
    subject matter, 2–395
    technical means, 2–401
  Official Journal, 2–446
  Opposition Divisions, 2–010, 2–015
  oral proceedings,
    extent of right, 2–417
    minutes, 2–423
    non-appearance by summoned party, 2–419
    preparation by parties, 2–420
    procedure, 2–422
    public, whether open to, 2–421
    summons, 2–418
  President,
    appointment, 2–007
    duties, 2–006
  Receiving Section, 2–010, 2–012
  Register of European Patents,
    contents, 2–438

**European Patent Convention (EPC)**—*cont.*
  Register of European Patents—*cont.*
    language, 2–441
    no entry prior to publication, 2–439
    open to public, register, 2–440
  Search Divisions, 2–010, 2–013
  senior employees, appointment of, 2–007
  special departments, 2–450
    representation, 2–451
  suboffices, 2–005
  Vice Presidents, 2–007
**European Patent Organisation**
  disputes with European Patent Office employees, 2–009
  formation, 2–002
  legal personality, 2–004
  organs, 2–003
  purpose, 2–004
  seat, 2–004
  structure, 2–003
  task, 2–004
**Evidence**
  European Patent Office
    commissioning member of Examining/Opposition Division to examine evidence, 2–429
    conservation, 2–432
    costs, 2–431
    decision to take, 2–426
    experts' opinion, 2–430
    forms of available evidence, 2–424
    minutes, 2–433
    principles for evaluation, 2–425
    procedure, 2–427, 2–428
**Examination by the EPO**
  own motion, of 2–225
**Examination fee**
  reduction in, 2–175
**Examination on filing**
  European Patent Convention (EPC),
    abstracts, 2–142
    content of request, 2–143
    designation fees, 2–145
    designation of inventor, 2–146
    divisional application, 2–136
    fees paid, determination whether, 2–137
    filing date cannot be accorded, 2–135
    filing date, requirements for, 2–134
    formal requirements, examination of, 2–139–2–149
    late filed drawings, 2–147
    physical requirements, 2–141
    priority claims, 2–144
    procedure on receipt of new application, 2–133
    prohibited matter, 2–149
    representation, 2–140
    title of invention, 2–148
    translations filed, determination whether, 2–138
  Patent Co-operation Treaty (PCT),
    formal requirements, 3–098–3–112

**Fees**
  European Patent Convention (EPC), 2–124
    adoption of rules, 2–456
    cheque payment, 2–463
    claims, 2–127
    currency, 2–461
    designation, 2–126
    determination whether paid, 2–137
    divisional applications, 2–128
    establishing what payment is for, 2–466
    filing, 2–125
    insignificant amounts, refund of, 2–469
    insufficient amount paid, 2–468
    methods of payment, 2–461–2–464
    opposition, 2–205
    payment or transfer to EPO bank account or Giro account, 2–462
    President, role of, 2–458
    publication in Journal of amounts, 2–459
    purpose of rules, 2–457
    refunds, 2–467
    renewal. *See* **Renewal fees**
    replacement applications, 2–129
    rules, 2–456–2–469
    safeguards where payment not made in time, 2–465
    search, 2–125
    who may make, 2–467
  Patent Co-operation Treaty (PCT), 3–075
    basic fee, 3–198
    claims, 3–203
    designation, 3–199
    examination, 3–202
    extension of time for payment, 3–081
    filing, 3–078, 3–079
    renewal, 3–201
    search, 3–080, 3–200
    transmittal, 3–076, 3–077
**Filing application**
  additional copies of citations under EPC, 2–085
  address for correspondence under PCT, 3–025
  agent's details under PCT, 3–023
  applicant's details
    European Patent Convention (PCT), 2–075
    Patent Co-operation Treaty (PCT), 3–021
  claims. *See* **Claims**
  common representatives under PCT, 3–024
  correction of request under EPC, 2–088
  declaration under PCT, 3–032
  designations,
    European Patent Convention (EPC), 2–077, 2–080, 2–081
    Patent Co-operation Treaty (PCT), 3–026
  earlier search under PCT, 3–031
  electronically, 2–068
  entitlement,
    European Patent Convention (EPC), 2–060
    Patent Co-operation Treaty (PCT), 3–008
  European Patent Convention (EPC),
    additional copies of citations, 2–085
    applicant's details, 2–075

Filing application—*cont.*
  European Patent Convention (EPC)—*cont.*
    claims. *See* **Claims**
    Contracting State language, 2–121
    correction of request, 2–088
    designations, 2–080, 2–081
    divisional application,
      circumstances of filing, 2–070
      indication of status, 2–082
      language, 2–123
      where filed, 2–062
    entitlement, 2–060
    examination on, 2–133
    extension of European patent, 2–081
    fax, by, 2–067
    fees,
      claims, 2–127
      designation, 2–126
      divisional applications, 2–128
      filing, 2–125
      generally, 2–124
      replacement applications, 2–129
      search, 2–125
    figures of drawings to be published with abstract, 2–084
    first filing, importance of, 1–140B
    form, 2–073
    language,
      contracting state language, 2–121
      divisional application, 2–123
      EPO official language, 2–120
      national office, 2–122
      replacement application, 2–123
    list of documents accompanying request, 2–087
    manner of filing,
      electronic, 2–068
      fax, 2–067
      hand, 2–066
      other means, 2–069
      post, 2–066
    national office, 2–122
    number of copies filed,
      European Patent Convention (EPC), 2–118
      Patent Co-operation Treaty (PCT), 3–066
    petition for grant, 2–074
    physical requirements, 2–119
    post, by, 2–066
    priority claim, 2–079
    registration of European patent, 2–081
    replacement applications, 2–083, 2–123
    representative's details, 2–076
    request, 2–072
    requirements of application, 2–071–2–086
    restrictions under national law, 2–064
    signature, 2–086
    specified form, 2–073
    subsequent, 1–140C, 2–368
    time limit for forwarding application to EPO, 2–065
    title of the invention, 2–078
    translations, 2–117

Filing application—*cont.*
  European Patent Convention (EPC)—*cont.*
    where filed,
      divisional application, 2–062
      regular applications, 2–061
      replacement application, 2–063
  fees. *See* **Fees**
  figures of drawings to be published with abstract,
    European Patent Convention (EPC), 2–084
  international searching authority under PCT, 3–030
  inventor's details,
    Patent Co-operation Treaty (PCT), 3–022
  kind of protection sought under, 3–028
  language. *See* **Language**
  manner of filing,
    European Patent Convention (EPC), 2–066–2–069
    Patent Co-operation Treaty (PCT), 3–014–3–016
  Patent Co-operation Treaty (PCT),
    address for correspondence, 3–025
    agent's details, 3–023
    applicant's details, 3–021
    checklist, 3–033
    claims. *See* **Claims**
    common representatives, 3–024
    designations, 3–026
    details of applicant, 3–021
    earlier search, reference to, 3–031
    entitlement, 3–008
    EPO, designation of, 3–027
    EPO used as receiving office, 3–012
    facsimile, 3–015
    further content of request not allowed, 3–036
    international application with EPO, 3–013
    international searching authority, 3–030
    inventor's details, 3–022
    kind of protection sought, 3–028
    manner of filing, 3–014–3–016
    names and addresses, 3–037
    number of copies, 3–066
    paper, use of, 3–014
    petition, 3–019
    physical requirements, 3–068
    priority claim, 3–029
    prohibited matter, 3–065
    reference to a parent application or patent, 3–035
    representation, 3–011
    request, 3–017
    requirements of application, 3–017–3–041
    signature of applicant, 3–034
    signs, 3–067
    specified form, 3–018
    standardised declarations, 3–032
    telegraph, 3–015
    teleprinter, 3–015
    terminology, 3–067
    title, 3–020
    where filed, 3–009
    wrong place, application filed in, 3–010
  petition,
    European Patent Convention (EPC), 2–074

**Filing application**—*cont.*
  petition—*cont.*
    Patent Co-operation Treaty (PCT), 3–019
  physical requirements,
    European Patent Convention (EPC), 2–119
    Patent Co-operation Treaty (PCT), 3–068
  priority claim,
    European Patent Convention (EPC), 2–079
    Patent Co-operation Treaty (PCT), 3–029
  reference to a parent application or patent under PCT, 3–035
  request,
    European Patent Convention (EPC), 2–072
    Patent Co-operation Treaty (PCT), 3–017
  requirements of application,
    European Patent Convention (EPC), 2–071–2–076
    Patent Co-operation Treaty (PCT), 3–017–3–086
  signature of applicant,
    European Patent Convention (EPC), 2–086
    Patent Co-operation Treaty (PCT), 3–034
  specified form
    European Patent Convention (EPC), 20–73
    Patent Co-operation Treaty (PCT), 30–18
  standardised declarations under PCT, 3–032
  title,
    European Patent Convention (EPC), 3–078
  where filed,
    European Patent Convention (EPC),
      divisional application, 2–062
      regular applications, 2–061
      replacement application, 2–063
    Patent Co-operation Treaty (PCT), 3–009
  writing, in, 2–066

**First medical use**
  new inventions, 2–048

**Games**, 2–028

**Gazette**
  International Patent Cooperation Union, 3–006

**Germ line of human beings**, 2–032

**Grant procedure**
  European Patent Convention (EPC),
    amendments after, 2–192
    approval of text for grant, 2–188
    certificate, 2–197
    circumstance of grant, 2–187
    communication from Examining Division, 2–188
    consequences of not responding to R.51(4) communication, 2–189
    date grant takes effect, 2–194
    decision, 2–193
    different applicants, grant to, 2–196
    generally, 2–187
    implicit approval of text, 2–190
    oral proceedings after, 2–192
    payment of fees, 2–190
    proposed text not acceptable to applicant, 2–191
    publication of granted patent, 2–195
    translations, filing, 2–190
    validation in designated states, 2–198

**Human body**, 2–024, 2–032

**Inadmissible extension**, 2–319

**Industrial application, inventions capable of**,
  definition of industrial application, 2–037
  diagnostic exclusion, 2–038
  diagnostic method practiced on the human or animal body, 2–041
  method of treatment, 2–038
  surgery, method of treatment of the human or animal body by, 2–040
  therapy, method of treatment of human or animal body by, 2–039

**Inspection of files**
  European Patent Office, 2–442–2–445

**International Patent Cooperation Union**. *See also* **Patent Co-operation Treaty (PCT)**
  Assembly, 3–002
  establishment, 3–001
  Gazette, 3–006
  International Bureau, 3–003
  parts,
    Assembly, 3–002
    International Bureau, 3–003
  purpose, 3–001

**Interruption of proceedings**,
  circumstances, 2–307
  department responsible, 2–310
  EP Office, record of, 2–438
  resumption after, 2–308
  termination of financial obligations, 2–437
  time limits, 2–309

**Invention**
  European Patent Convention (EPC),
    abusive disclosure exemption, 2–051
    aesthetic creations, 2–026
    animal varieties, 2–034
    barred from patentability, 2–032–2–035
    computer program, 2–030
    discoveries, 2–024
    earlier publications, 2–043
    essentially biological processes, 2–035
    exhibition exemption, 2–052
    first medical use, 2–048
    industrial application, capable of, 2–037–2–041
    inventive step. *See* **Inventive step**
    made available to the public,
      judging content of, 2–046
      prejudicial to novelty, 2–047
    mathematical methods, 2–025
    medical use, 2–048, 2–049
    morality exemption, 2–032
    new, 2–042–2–052. *See also* **New inventions**
    patentable invention, 2–036
    plant varieties, 2–033
    presentation of information, 2–031
    scheme, rule or method for doing business, 2–029
    scheme, rule or method for performing a mental act, 2–027
    scheme, rule or method for playing games, 2–028

**Invention**—*cont.*
European Patent Convention (EPC)—*cont.*
scientific theories, 2–025
second medical use, 2–049
selection inventions, novelty of, 2–053
state of the art, 2–043
technical subject matter, 2–023
title, 2–148
industrial application. *See* **Industrial application, inventions capable of**
inventive step. *See* **Inventive step**
medical use,
first, 2–048
second, 2–049
new, 2–042–2–052. *See also* **New inventions**
second medical use, 2–049
second non-medical use, 2–050
state of the art,
earlier publications, 2–043
European patent applications, 2–044

**Inventive step**
common general knowledge, 2–056
definition, 2–054
further indicators, 2–059
obvious, considerations when asking whether, 2–057
problem-solution approach, 2–055
skilled man, 2–056
unexpected advantage, 2–058

**Inventor**
European Patent Convention (EPC),
certificate, 2–110
designation, 2–329, 2–330
right to be mentioned, 2–329–2–332
right to European patent, 2–333

**Japan**
patent law, 1–199

**Language**
Administrative Council, 2–366
European Patent Convention (EPC),
Administrative Council, 2–366
authentic text, 2–357
Bulletin, 2–365
certification of translated documents, 2–364
contracting state language, 2–121
divisional application, 2–123
EPO official language, 2–120
exceptions, 2–361
oral proceedings, 2–363
filing application, 2–359
national office, 2–122
notice of appeal, 2–250
Official Journal, 2–365
official language, 2–358
opposition, 2–206
oral proceedings, 2–363
proceedings, 2–360
publication of application and search report, 2–165

**Language**—*cont.*
European Patent Convention (EPC)—*cont.*
publications, 2–365
Register entries, 2–365
replacement application, 2–123
request for examination, 2–175
written procedures, 2–362
European Patent Office, 2–358
Patent Co-operation Treaty (PCT),
acceptable language, 3–069
must accept, languages Receiving Office must accept, 3–070
not accepted by Receiving Office, language, 3–074
publication, request not in language of, 3–073
translation, 3–071, 3–072
Register of European Patents, 2–441

**Made available to the public**
judging content, 2–046
meaning, 2–045
prejudicial to novelty, 2–047

**Mathematical methods**
European Patent Convention (EPC), 2–025

**New inventions,**
abusive disclosure exemption, 2–051
earlier European patent applications, state of the art includes, 2–044
earlier publications, state of the art includes, 2–043
exhibition exemption, 2–052
first medical use, 2–048
made available to the public, 2–045
judging content, 2–046
prejudicial to novelty, 2–047
medical use
first, 2–048
second, 2–049
novelty, 2–042
second medical use, 2–049
second non-medical use, 2–050
selection inventions, novelty of, 2–053
state of the art
earlier European patent applications, 2–044
earlier publications, 2–043

**Novelty**
definition, 2–042
state of the art,
earlier European patent applications, 2–044
earlier publications, 2–043

**Official Journal**
European Patent Office, 2–446

**Opposition**
*See also* **Paper C**
European Patent Convention (EPC), 2–199–2–241
change of proprietor through entitlement proceedings, 2–217
costs,
enforcement of decisions, 2–238
no appeal solely on costs, 2–239

**Opposition**—*cont.*
  European Patent Convention (EPC)—*cont.*
    costs—*cont.*
      registry to fix amount to be paid, 2–236
      review of costs fixed by registry, 2–237
      rules for apportionment, 2–235
    designated states, application to, 2–215
    failed opposition, 2–231
    fee, 2–205
    filing,
      content of notice, 2–203
      fee, 2–205
      grounds, 2–204
      language of notice, 2–206
      lapsed patent, 2–207
      surrender of patent, 2–224, 2–229
      time limit, 2–200
      where to file opposition, 2–201
      who may file, 2–202
    generally, 2–199
    grounds, 2–204
    intervention, 2–214
    language, 2–206
    lapsed patent, 2–207
    opponent as party, 2–216
    parties, 2–216, 2–217
    partly successful opposition,
      filing of claim translation, 2–233
      new patent certificate where patent amended, 2–234
      notification of text which proposing to maintain, 2–232
      printing fee, 2–233
      publication of new specification, 2–234
    procedure for examination, 2–218–2–229
    successful opposition, 2–230
    surrender of patent, 2–207
    transfer of opposition to another party, 2–241
    transfer of patent during, 2–240
    withdrawal, 2–223
  examination of opposition,
    acceleration of proceedings, 2–226
    admissibility, 2–208
    beyond stated extent, 2–225
    communication of inadmissibility to proprietor, 2–212
    continuation of opposition by EPO, 2–223
    deemed not to have been filed, opposition, 2–213
    deficiencies must be corrected, 2–210, 2–211
    different claims for different states, 2–228
    documents to file, 2–222
    formalities, 2–209
    further searches, 2–227
    lapsed patent, 2–224
    permissible amendments, 2–221
    prejudicing the patent, 2–220
    revocation where no text is approved, 2–229
    surrendered patent, 2–224
    withdrawal, 2–223

**Oral proceedings**
  European Patent Office
    extent of right, 2–417
    minutes, 2–423
    preparation by parties, 2–420
    procedure, 2–422
    public, whether open to, 2–421
    summons, 2–418

**Paper A (Chemistry)**
  annotating paper, 1–002, 1–035, 1–050
  case law
    disclaimers, 1–009
    disclosure of prior art, 1–008
    purity, novelty by, 1–011
    selection inventions, 1–010
  checking answer, 1–007
  claim language, 1–025, 1–056
  claim order, 1–045
  claim types,
    apparatus for applying compound/composition, 1–022
    article incorporated or when treated with compound/composition, 1–021
    combination claims, 1–023
    composition claims, 1–014, 1–015
    intermediate claims, 1–020
    introduction, 1–001
    method of using claims, 1–016, 1–017
    omnibus claims, 1–024
    process claims, 1–018, 1–019
    product claims, 1–012, 1–013
    use claims, 1–016, 1–017
  claiming the invention, 1–004, 1–037–1–047, 1–052–1–057
  combination claims, 1–023, 1–043
  composition claims, 1–014, 1–015, 1–040
  compound claims, 1–039
  cut and paste technique, 1–001
  dependent claims, 1–046, 1–055
  drafting claims,
    content, 1–026
    form, 1–026
    further examples, 1–034
    language, 1–025, 1–056
    unity between a process claim and a use claim, 1–033
    unity between a product claim and a process claim, 1–031
    unity between a product claim and a use claim, 1–032
    unity between two independent process claims, 1–029
    unity between two independent product claims, 1–028
    unity between two independent use claims, 1–030
    unity of invention, 1–027, 1–044
  drafting introduction, 1–005, 1–048, 1–057
  duration of paper, 1–001
  guide to preparing and passing, 1–001

**Paper A (Chemistry)**—*cont.*
  identification of subject matter, 1–002
  intermediate claims, 1–020, 1–042
  marks, 1–001
  necessary steps to make invention as described patentable, 1–003
  notes to examiner, 1–006, 1–049
  novel subject matter, establishing, 1–036
  omnibus claims, 1–024
  partial worked example, 1–050–1–057
  patentable subject matter, establishing, 1–003
  process claims, 1–018, 1–019
  product claims, 1–012, 1–013
  scheme of paper, 1–001
  tackling paper, 1–002
  understanding paper, 1–002
  worked example, 1–029–1–043
**Paper A (Electricity/Mechanics)**
  annotating paper, 1–045
  checking answer, 1–064
  claim languge, 1–065
  claiming invention, 1–061, 1–071, 1–079, 1–084
  dependent claims, 1–073
  drafting claims
    content, 1–066
    form, 1–066
    language, 1–065
    unity of invention, 1–067
  drafting introduction, 1–062, 1–068, 1–075, 1–085
  duration, 1–058
  general comments, 1–058
  identifying invention, 1–078
  language of claim, 1–065
  marks, 1–058
  nature of client's business, 1–061
  notes to the examiner, 1–063, 1–076
  partial worked examples, 1–077–1–085
  patentable subject matter, establishing, 1–060
  summary of priorart, 1–082
  tackling paper, 1–059–1–064
  understanding paper, 1–059, 1–069, 1–077, 1–081
  unity of invention, 1–067, 1–072
  worked example, 1–069–1–076
**Paper B (Chemistry)**
  amended claim set, drafting, 1–089, 1–097
  amendment, notes on,
    added matter, 1–093
    disclaimers, 1–093
    unsearched subject matter, 1–094
  annotating paper, 1–087, 1–095, 1–099
  checking answer, 1–092
  claiming invention, 1–101–1–105
  dependent claims, 1–105
  duration, 1–086
  general comments, 1–086
  marks, 1–086
  method/use claims, 1–103
  notes to the examiner, 1–091
  partial worked example, 1–099–1–105

**Paper B (Chemistry)**—*cont.*
  patentable subject matter, establishing, 1–088, 1–096, 1–100
  process claims, 1–104
  product claims, 1–102
  response to Art.96(2) communication, 1–090, 1–098
  tackling paper, 1–087–1–092
  understanding paper, 1–087, 1–095, 1–099
  unity of invention, 1–101
  use claims, 1–101, 1–103
  worked example, 1–073–1–076
**Paper B (Electricity/Mechanics)**
  amended claims set, drafting, 1–109, 1–118, 1–121
  amendment, notes on
    added matter, 1–113
    disclaimers, 1–114
    unsearched subject matter not having unity, not relating to, 1–115
  annotating paper, 1–078
  checking answer, 1–112
  duration, 1–106
  general comments, 1–106
  marks, 1–106
  notes to the examiner, 1–111
  patentable subject matter, establishing, 1–108, 1–117, 1–120
  responding to Art.96(2) communication, 1–110, 1–119, 1–122
  tackling the paper, 1–107–1–112
  understanding paper, 1–107, 1–116, 1–119A
  worked examples, 1–116–1–122
**Paper C**
  added matter, issues of, 1–128
  analysis,
    clients letter, 1–126, 1–138, 1–155
  assessing relevance of prior art, 1–133, 1–157
  client's letter, working with, 1–130
  determining effective dates of prior art documents, 1–132, 1–140
  duration, 1–123
  formulating attack strategy, 1–134, 1–151
  fundamental tasks, 1–124
  general comments, 1–123
  identifying claim variants and effective dates, 1–131, 1–139, 1–156
  legal issues, 1–129
  letter to client, 1–137
  marks, 1–123
  materials taken into, 123
  organising the paper, 1–125, 1–154
  overview, 1–123
  a priorart, 1–132–1–133, 1–140–1–150
  priority, issues of, 1–127
  statement of the grounds, 1–136, 1–153, 1–158
  tackling the paper, 1–125–1–137
  worked examples, 1–138–1–158
  writing notice of opposition, 1–135, 1–152
**Paper D1**
  common errors, 1–188

**Paper D1**—*cont.*
  fees,
    appeal, 1–185
    claims, 1–179
    designation, 1–180
    examination, 1–181
    filing, 1–182
    further proceeding, 1–186
    grant, 1–182
    introduction, 1–177
    opposition, 1–184
    renewal, 1–183
    restitution, 1–187
    search, 1–178
  finding the answer, 1–160
  general comments, 1–158A
  marks, 1–113
  preservation of apparently lost rights
    appeal, filing, 1–170
    conversion, 1–171
    extension of time limit, 1–164, 1–174
    fee not paid on time, excusing, 1–172
    further processing, 1–166
    good faith principle, 1–169
    grade period, availability of, 1–165, 1–175
    international phase, 1–174–1–176
    interruption of proceedings, 1–168
    introduction, 1–114
    late arrival of documents at EPO, 1–173
    notification sent to correct address, whether, 1–163
    restitution, 1–167
  tackling the paper, 1–159–1–161
  time, use of, 1–159
  worked example, 1–189
  writing the answer, 1–161

**Paper D2**
  analysing paper, 1–192–1–196, 1–206–1–207, 1–216
  answering paper, 1–197, 1–208–1–214, 1–217–1–122
  general comments, 1–190
  Japanese patent law, 1–199
  notes on claiming priority,
    examples of questions relating to priority rights, 1–204
    illustrative examples, 1–203
    importance of the 'first filing' under European Patent Convention, 1–201
    limited circumstances in which priority may be claimed from second or subsequent filing, 1–202
    relevance of Paris Convention to European and Euro-PCT applications, 1–200
  tackling the paper,
    analysing the paper, 1–192–1–196
    answering the paper, 1–197
    application filed for invention, 1–193
    national rights obtainable, 1–195–1–196
    timeline, preparation of, 1–191
  timelines for applications, 1–198, 1–205, 1–215
  US patent law, 1–199
  worked examples, 1–205–1–222

**Paris Convention.** *See* **Priority claims**
**Patent Co-operation Treaty (PCT)**
  abstract, 3–052
  administrative instructions, 3–005
  agent,
    definition, 3–007
  amendment,
    added subject matter, 3–145
    form, 3–143
    language, 3–142
    notification to IPEA, 3–146
    statement accompanying, 3–144
    when can applicant amend claims, 3–140
    where should amendments be filed, 3–141
  applicant,
    definition, 3–007
    signature, 3–034
  application,
    definition, 3–007
  biotechnological inventions,
    biological material, deposit of, 3–083
    sequence listings, 3–082
  claims,
    clarity, 3–043
    conciseness, 3–043
    defining matter client seeking to protect, 3–044
    figures, references to signs in, 3–049
    number of claims, 3–046
    numbering claims, 3–047
    omnibus claims, 3–048
    requirements, 3–042–3–051
    support, 3–043
    two-part form required, where, 3–045
    type of claims, 3–046
    unity of invention, 3–051
    utility model, 3–050
  common representative,
    definition, 3–007
  communications to national/regional offices,
    applications under Art.20, 3–168–3–173
    designated office other than under Art.20 communication, 3–176
    International Bureau on request, communication to designated states by, 3–167–3–176
    national phase entry under Art.22, 3–177–3–190
    national phase entry under Art.39, 3–191–3–195
  Contracting States, definition of, 3–007
  declaration that application withdrawn, 3–113
  definitions, 3–007
  description,
    content, 3–040, 3–041
    order of presentation of content, 3–041
    requirements, 3–038–3–041
    sufficient disclosure, 3–039
  designated office,
    definition, 3–007
  designated states,
    definition, 3–007
  Director General, 3–007
  drawings, 3–053

**Patent Co-operation Treaty (PCT)**—*cont.*
  elected office, 3–007
  EPO, procedure before,
    certificate of exhibition, 3–206
    chance to make good loss of rights, 3–207
    designation fees, 3–199
    examination fee, 3–202
    furnishing of file number, 3–209
    generally, 3–196
    national basic fee, 3–198
    renewal fees, 3–201
    representation, 3–210
    request for examination, 3–205
    search fees, 3–200
    specification of documents, 3–204
    submission of information concerning inventor, 3–208
    translation, 3–197
  errors, correction of,
    authorisation, 3–324
    errors that may be corrected, 3–320
    errors that may not be corrected, 3–321
    initiation, 3–322
    language, 3–325
    procedure, 3–323
  establishment of a union, 3–001
  European Patent Convention, relationship with, 3–334, 3–335
  examination by EPO,
    incorrect translation, 3–303
    international publication taking place of European publication, when, 3–301
    international search report, 3–299
    supplementary European search report, 3–300
  formal requirements, 3–098–3–113
  fees,
    basic fee, 3–198
    claims, 3–203
    designation, 3–199
    examination, 3–202
    extension of time for payment, 3–081
    filing, 3–078, 3–079
    generally, 3–075
    renewal, 3–201
    search, 3–080, 3–200
    transmittal, 3–076, 3–077
  filing application
    agent's details, 3–023
    checklist, 3–033
    claims. *See* **Claims**
    common representatives, 3–024
    designations, 3–026
    details of applicant, 3–021
    earlier search, reference to, 3–031
    entitlement, 3–008
    EPO, designation of, 3–027
    EPO used as receiving office, 3–012
    facsimile, 3–015
    further content of request not allowed, 3–036
    international application with EPO, 3–013

**Patent Co-operation Treaty (PCT)**—*cont.*
  filing application—*cont.*
    international searching authority, 3–030
    kind of protection sought, 3–028
    manner of filing,
      electronic form, 3–016
      facsimile, 3–015
      paper, use of, 3–014
      telegraph, 3–015
      teleprinter, use of, 3–015
    names and addresses, 3–037
    number of copies, 3–066
    paper, use of, 3–014
    petition, 3–019
    physical requirements, 3–068
    priority claim, 3–029
    prohibited matter, 3–065
    representation, 3–011
    request, 3–017
    requirements of application, 3–017–3–064
    signature of applicant, 3–034
    signs, 3–067
    specified form, 3–018
    standardised declarations, 3–032
    telegraph, 3–015
    teleprinter, 3–015
    terminology, 3–067
    title, 3–020
    where filed, 3–009
    wrong place, application filed in, 3–010
  Gazette, 3–006
    publication in, 3–166
  information,
    availability of priority document, 3–354
    citations, 3–356, 3–357
    confidential,
      examination, 3–350
      international preliminary examination, 3–350
      pre-publication application, 3–348
      written opinion, 3–349
    records and files, 3–351–3–353
    translations, 3–355
  international application,
    definition, 3–007
  International Patent Cooperation Union. *See* **International Patent Cooperation Union**
  international preliminary examination,
    defects in demand, 3–231–3–234
    demand, 3–216–3–237
    designated states to which Chap.II applies, 3–212
    how to apply, 3–216–3–237
    later election of states, 3–230
    objective, 3–238–3–241
    procedural steps on receipt of demand, 3–235–3–237
    procedure before IPEA, 3–242–3–254
    who may apply, 3–213
    who may conduct, 3–214–3–215

**Patent Co-operation Treaty (PCT)**—*cont.*
  International Preliminary Examining Authority,
    amendment, 3–246
    commencement, 3–242
    communications with, 3–244
    copy of priority document, 3–251
    documents, 3–245
    ending, 3–242
    general provisions, 3–243
    ignoring amendments and arguments, 3–250
    lack of unity, 3–252, 3–253
    procedure before, 3–242–3–254
    response to written opinion, 3–248
    sequence listing absent or in wrong format, 3–254
    situations where no obligation to examine, 3–247
    unity disputed, 3–252
    written opinion, 3–248, 3–249
  international preliminary report on patentability (IPRP),
    amendments, 3–260
    annexes, 3–268
    citation of documents, 3–265
    defective applications, 3–266
    documents upon which based, 3–258
    first page, information on, 3–259
    form, 3–256
    generally, 3–136
    lack of unity, 3–263
    language, 3–257
    non-establishment of opinion, 3–262
    observations on application, 3–267
    patentability, 3–264
    priority, 3–261
    time limit, 3–255
    translation, 3–269–3–272
  International Searching Authority
    appointment, 3–116
    competent authorities, 3–117
    limitations set by EPO on own competence, 3–118
    meaning, 3–114
    requirements, 3–115
  language,
    acceptable language, 3–069
    languages Receiving Office must accept, 3–070
    not accepted by Receiving Office, language, 3–074
    publication, request not in language of, 3–073
    translation required, 3–071
  national application,
    definition, 3–007
  national law, 3–007
  national office,
    definition, 3–007
  national patent, 3–007
  national phase,
    additional requirements as to form or contents, 3–286
    amendment, 3–281–3–283
    certification/valuation of Art.22 translation, 3–288
    commencement of national processing, 3–280
    consideration of unity by EPO, 3–285

**Patent Co-operation Treaty (PCT)**—*cont.*
  national phase—*cont.*
    effect of published international patent application, 3–278–3–279
    examination by national offices, 3–280–3–303
    international patent applications having filing date, effect of, 3–274–3–277
    inventor must be applicant requirement, 3–292
    national security, 3–293
    priority document, 3–289
    removal of reference signs in claims for publication, 3–295
    representation, 3–294
    requirement to supply results of examination, 3–298
    submission of a sequence listing, 3–296
    submission of certain documents, 3–287
    substantive conditions of patentability, 3–291
    translation of priority document, 3–290
    unity impugned, where, 3–284
    utility models, 3–297
  petition, 3–019
  priority claim,
    addition of claim after filing, 3–063
    applications used as basis, 3–058
    basis, 3–058
    correction of claim, 3–063
    designation of state, 3–064
    filing application, 3–029
    international phase, 3–062
    multiple priority claims, 3–061
    previous application, 3–057
    procedure, 3–060
    relevance of Paris Convention, 3–054
    time limit, 3–056
    who may make claim, 3–055
    WTO countries, 3–059
  priority date, 3–007
  prohibited matter, 3–065
  publication of application
    biological material indications, 3–161
    circumstances where no publication takes place, 3–149
    claims, 3–157
    contents, 3–154–3–163
    excluded matter, 3–164
    form, 3–153
    Gazette, notice in, 3–165
    international search report, 3–159
    language, 3–150–3–152
    non-prejudicial disclosures, 3–163
    priority claims, 3–162
    rectification requests, 3–160
    responsibility, 3–147
    standardised front page, 3–155
    timing, 3–148
    translation, 3–152
    withdrawn applications, 3–166
  receiving office
    copying international application, 3–089–3–091

**Patent Co-operation Treaty (PCT)**—*cont.*
   receiving office—*cont.*
      dating sheets of application, 3–084
      declaration that application withdrawn, 3–113
      examination whether filing date can be accorded, 3–085–3–088
      home copy retained, 3–091
      International Searching Authority procedure, 3–097
      marking sheets of application, 3–084
      national security, 3–009
      notification of receipt of record copy, 3–094
      number of copies required, 3–090
      procedure, 3–084–3–113
      procedure where filing date can be accorded, 3–086
      procedure where filing date cannot be accorded, 3–087
      requirements for a filing date, 3–085
      search copy, transmittal of, 3–096
      supply to applicant of certified copies, 3–088
      translation, transmittal of, 3–095
      transmittal of record copy, 3–092
      withdrawal if IB does not receive record copy, 3–093
   record of changes, 3–345
   regional application, 3–007
   regional patent, 3–007
   regulations, 3–004
   relevant prior art, 3–121
   representation,
      acts by representatives or agents, 3–331
      agents, 3–329–3–333
      appointment of agent, 3–329
      common representatives, 3–329–3–333
      Contracting State, requirements imposed by, 3–327
      manner of appointment, 3–332
      Receiving Office, requirements imposed by, 3–326
      renunciation of agent or common representative, 3–333
      right to practice, 3–328
      two or more applicants, where, 3–330
   search,
      basis, 3–120
      competent authorities, 3–114–3–118
      copies of cited documents, requests for, 3–139
      fields to be covered, 3–122
      international preliminary report on patentability (IPRP), 3–136
      International Searching Authority, 3–114–3–118
      minimum documentation, 3–123
      nature, 3–119–3–123
      nature of international-type search, 3–124
      procedure, 3–125–3–131
      purpose, 3–119
      relevant prior art, 3–121
      report,
         drawing up, 3–114–3–139
         form of, 3–133
         time limit for establishing, 3–132
         translations, 3–137, 3–138

**Patent Co-operation Treaty (PCT)**—*cont.*
   search—*cont.*
      report—*cont.*
         transmittal, 3–135
         written opinion of International Searching Authority, 3–134
   signature, 3–007, 3–034
   subsequently filed documents,
      electronic means, 3–340
      facsimile, 3–339
      form of, 3–338
      language of letters and documents, 3–337
      papers to be accompanied by signed letter, 3–335
      telegraph, 3–339
      teleprinter, 3–339
      transmission, 3–339
   time limits,
      computation, 3–305
      correction of application where allowed under national law, 3–316
      duty to excuse missed time limits in national law, 3–316
      escaping negative determination in international phase, 3–312–3–315
      excusal of missed time limit, 3–308
      expression of dates, 3–304
      extensions,
         interruption in mail delivery, 3–309
         mail not delivered in relevant locality, 3–307
         national office or organisation not open for business, 3–306
         notification sent later than day marked or received more than seven days after posting, 3–310, 3–311
      mail delivery, interruption in, 3–309
      rectification of errors, 3–318
   title, 3–020
   translation for search, 3–071
   United International Bureaux for the Protection of Intellectual Property (BIRPI), 3–007
   utility models, 3–297
   withdrawal,
      demand, 3–344
      designation, 3–342
      elections, 3–344
      international application, 3–341
      priority claim, 3–343
**PCT.** *See* **Patent Co-operation Treaty (PCT)**
**Petition**
   European Patent Convention (EPC), 2–074
   Patent Co-operation Treaty (PCT), 3–019
**Plant varieties**
   European Patent Convention (EPC), 2–033
**Post**
   interruption in delivery of, 2–295, 3–309
      EPO not open for business, 2–294
      not delivered in relevant locality, 3–307
      national office, application to, 3–306
      notification sent later than day marked, 3–310
      war, revolution or similar event, 2–296

**Priority claim**
  applications used as basis,
    European Patent Convention (EPC), 2–110
    Patent Co-operation Treaty (PCT), 3–058
  correction of claim,
    European Patent Convention (EPC), 2–114
  date of claims, 1–136, 1–153
  designation of state under PCT, 3–064
  European Patent Convention (EPC),
    applications used as basis, 2–110
    correction of claim, 2–114
    effect of priority right, 2–113
    examination on filing, 2–144
    filing claim, 2–111
    invention, in respect of same, 2–109
    issues of, 1–127
    multiple priority claims, 2–112
    Paris Convention, 2–106
    procedure, 2–111
    right of, 1–201, 1–204
    same invention, in respect of, 2–109
    second or subsequent filing, 1–202
    time limit, 2–108
    who may make claim, 2–107
    withdrawal, 2–377
    workings of, 1–203
  filing application,
    European Patent Convention (EPC), 2–079
    Patent Co-operation Treaty (PCT), 3–029
  international phase,
    Patent Co-operation Treaty (PCT), 3–062
  multiple priority claims,
    European Patent Convention (EPC), 2–112
    Patent Co-operation Treaty (PCT), 3–061
  Patent Co-operation Treaty (PCT),
    addition of claim after filing, 3–063
    applications used as basis, 3–058
    basis, 3–058
    correction of claim, 3–063
    designation of state in which priority
        application filed, 3–064
    filing application, 3–029
    international phase, 3–062
    multiple priority claims, 3–061
    previous application, 3–057
    procedure, 3–060
    relevance of Paris Convention, 3–054
    time limit, 3–056
    who may make claim, 3–055
    WTO countries, 3–059
  procedure,
    European Patent Convention (EPC),
      2–111
    Patent Co-operation Treaty (PCT), 3–060
  time limit,
    European Patent Convention (EPC), 2–108
    Patent Co-operation Treaty (PCT), 3–056
  who may make claim,
    European Patent Convention (EPC), 2–107
    Patent Co-operation Treaty (PCT), 3–055

**Procedural law of contracting states**
  European Patent Convention (EPC), 2–436
**Professional representation**
  deleting representative from list, 2–349
  European Patent Institute, 2–348
  European qualifying exam, 2–347
  procedure for being entered on list, 2–346
  re-entry following deletion, 2–350
  right to set up in business, 2–345
  who can act as, 2–345
**Prohibited matter**
  European Patent Convention (EPC), 2–116

**Register of European Patents**
  contents, 2–438
  language, 2–441
  no entry prior to publication, 2–439
  open to public, 2–440
**Renewal fees**
  additional fees, 2–384
  divisional applications, 2–385
  due date, 2–382
  grace period for late payment, 2–383
  late payment, 2–383
  non-payment, 2–384
  period for payment, 2–382
  refund, 2–387
  replacement applications, 2–386
  years in respect of which due, 2–381
**Representation**
  European Patent Convention (EPC),
    authorisation,
      consequences of not filing, 2–353
      content, 2–352
      form, 2–352
      requirement to file, 2–351
      termination, 2–354
      withdrawal, 2–354
    choice, 2–342, 2–343
    common, parties acting in, 2–344
    person having residence or principal place of
      business in Contracting State, 2–342
    person not having residence or principal place
      of business within Contracting State, 2–343
    professional representation. *See* **Professional
      representation**
    several representatives appointed, 2–355
    special departments, 2–451
    types, 2–342–2–344
  Patent Co-operation Treaty (PCT),
    acts by representatives or agents, 3–331
    agents, 3–329–3–333
    appointment of agent, 3–329
    common representatives, 3–329–3–333
    Contracting State, requirements imposed by, 3–327
    manner of appointment, 3–332
    Receiving Office, requirements imposed by, 3–326
    renunciation of agent or common representative,
      3–333
    right to practice, 3–328

**Representation**—*cont.*
　Patent Co-operation Treaty (PCT)—*cont.*
　　two or more applicants, where, 3–330
**Request**
　European Patent Convention (EPC), 2–072
　Patent Co-operation Treaty (PCT), 3–017
*Restitutio in integrum*
　conditions necessary for, 2–299
　filing for, 2–300
　grant, by Contracting States, 2–306
　procedure for applying for, 2–302
　time limits, exclusion of, 2–301

**Scientific theories**
　European Patent Convention (EPC), 2–025
**Search**
　European Patent Convention (EPC),
　　accelerated procedure, 2–157
　　basis of search, 2–152
　　cannot be established, where, 2–153
　　commencement of search, 2–150
　　conducting, 2–150–2–157
　　definitive content of abstract, 2–155
　　drawing up, 2–150–2–162
　　fee, 2–154
　　patent classification, 2–156
　　purpose of search, 2–151
　　report,
　　　chance to amend after receipt, 2–162
　　　content, 2–158
　　　definitive content of abstract, 2–161
　　　extended, 2–160
　　　language, 2–159
　　　publication, 2–163–2–168
　　　transmittal, 2–161
　　scope of search, 2–151
　　search,
　　　language, 2–159
　　unity, application lacking, 2–154
　Patent Co-operation Treaty (PCT),
　　basis, 3–120
　　competent authorities, 3–114–3–118
　　fields to be covered, 3–122
　　international preliminary report on patentability
　　　(IPRP), 3–136
　　International Searching Authority, 3–114–3–118
　　minimum documentation, 3–123
　　nature, 3–119–3–123
　　nature of international-type search, 3–124
　　procedure, 3–125–3–131
　　purpose, 3–119
　　relevant prior art, 3–121
　　report,
　　　drawing up, 3–114–3–139
　　　form, 3–133
　　　time limit, 3–132
　　　translations, 3–137, 3–138
　　　transmittal, 3–135
　　　written opinion of International Searching
　　　　Authority, 3–134

**Signature of applicant**
　filing application,
　　European Patent Convention (EPC), 2–086
　　Patent Co-operation Treaty (PCT), 3–034
**State of the art**
　earlier European patent applications, 2–044
　earlier publications, 2–043
**Substantive examination**
　European Patent Convention (EPC),
　　refusal of application,
　　procedure,
　　　accelerated procedure, 2–184
　　　auxiliary requests, 2–181
　　　consolidation of proceedings, 2–183
　　　double patenting, 2–182
　　　formal written procedure, 2–178
　　　further searches, 2–180
　　　informal communications by telephone or
　　　　interview, 2–179
　　　request for information concerning national patent
　　　　applications, 2–185–2–186
　　request,
　　　consequences of not requesting, 2–172
　　　extension of period, 2–177
　　　fee, 2–171
　　　filed before transmittal of search report, 2–176
　　　generally, 2–169
　　　grace period, 2–173
　　　language, 2–175
　　　refund of examination fee, 2–174
　　　time limit, 2–170
　　　withdrawal, 2–170
**Surgery, method of treatment of the human or animal
　body by**, 2–040

**Therapy, method of treatment of the human or animal
　body by**, 2–039
**Time limits**
　European Patent Convention (EPC),
　　amendment, before receipt of search report,
　　　2–312
　　computation,
　　　day on which computation starts, 2–290
　　　expiry of time limits, 2–291
　　　units of time used, 2–289
　　duration, 2–292
　　excusal of missed time limit, 2–293
　　extension,
　　　EPO ceasing to function properly, 2–297
　　　EPO not open for business, 2–294
　　　interruption in mail delivery in Contracting
　　　　State, 2–295
　　　war, revolution or similar event, 2–296
　　good faith principle, 2–311
　　interruption of proceedings,
　　　circumstances, 2–307
　　　department responsible, 2–310
　　　resumption of proceedings, 2–308
　　　time limits on resumption, 2–309
　　legitimate expectations, protection of, 2–311

**Time limits**—*cont.*
  European Patent Convention (EPC)—*cont.*
    refusal,
      *restitutio in integrum*, 2–299–2–306
      conditions necessary, 2–299
      Contracting States, grant by, 2–306
      department qualified to decide on application, 2–304
      exclusion of certain time limits,
        generally, 2–301
        grounds must be filed and fee paid, 2–303
        procedure for applying, 2–302
        third party rights may be awarded, 2–305
  Patent Co-operation Treaty (PCT),
    computation, 3–305
    correction of application where allowed under national law, 3–317
    escaping negative determination in international phase, 3–312
    excusal of missed time limit, 3–308
    expression of dates, 3–304
    extensions,
      interruption in mail delivery, 3–309
      mail not delivered in relevant locality, 3–307
      national office or organisation not open for business, 3–306
      notification sent later than day marked, 3–310
    mail delivery, interruption in, 3–309
    rectification of errors, 3–318

**Title**
  European Patent Convention (EPC), 2–078
  Patent Co-operation Treaty (PCT), 3–020

**Translations**
  European Patent Convention (EPC), 2–117
    determination whether filed, 2–138

**Translations**—*cont.*
  Patent Co-operation Treaty (PCT), 3–071, 3–072

**Unitary patents**
  European Patent Convention (EPC), 2–449

**United International Bureaux for the Protection of Intellectual Property (BIRPI)**, 3–007

**United States**
  patent law, 1–199

**Unity of a European Patent**
  European Patent Convention (EPC), 2–435

**Unity of invention**
  European Patent Convention (EPC), 2–101
  Patent Co-operation Treaty (PCT), 3–051, 3–252, 3–253

**Utility models,**
  Patent Co-operation Treaty (PCT), 3–297

**Withdrawal**
  European Patent Convention (EPC),
    appeal, 2–268
    application, 2–374
    designation, 2–376
    opposition, 2–223
    part of subject matter of application, 2–375
    patent, 2–380
    priority claim, 2–377
  Patent Co-operation Treaty (PCT),
    demand, 3–344
    designation, 3–342
    elections, 3–344
    international application, 3–341
    priority claim, 3–343

**World Intellectual Property Organisation**, 3–007